DATE DUE

			PRINTED IN U.S.A.

Contemporary
U.S. Foreign Policy

Public Policy Formation

These reference books deal with the development of U.S. policy in various "single-issue" areas. Most policy areas are to be represented by three types of sourcebooks: (1) Institutional Profiles of Leading Organizations, (2) Collections of Documents and Policy Proposals, and (3) Bibliographies.

Public Interest Law Groups: Institutional Profiles
Karen O'Connor and Lee Epstein

U.S. National Security Policy and Strategy: Documents and Policy Proposals
Sam C. Sarkesian with Robert A. Vitas

U.S. National Security Policy Groups: Institutional Profiles
Cynthia Watson

U.S. Agricultural Groups: Institutional Profiles
William P. Browne and Allan J. Cigler, editors

Military and Strategic Policy: An Annotated Bibliography
Benjamin R. Beede, compiler

U.S. Energy and Environmental Interest Groups: Institutional Profiles
Lettie McSpadden Wenner

CONTEMPORARY U.S. FOREIGN POLICY

Documents and Commentary

Edited by
ELMER PLISCHKE

GREENWOOD PRESS
New York • Westport, Connecticut • London

Library of Congress Cataloging-in-Publication Data

Contemporary U.S. foreign policy : documents and commentary /
    [compiled and edited by] Elmer Plischke.
        p.   cm.
    Includes bibliographical references and index.
    ISBN 0-313-26032-X (alk. paper)
        1. United States—Foreign relations—1945–   2. United States—
    Foreign relations administration.   I. Plischke, Elmer.
    II. Title: Contemporary US foreign policy.   III. Title: Contemporary
    United States foreign policy.
    JX1405.C66   1991
    327.73—dc20   90-43385

British Library Cataloguing in Publication Data is available.

Library of Congress Catalog Card Number: 90-43385
ISBN: 0-313-26032-X

First published in 1991

Greenwood Press, 88 Post Road West, Westport, CT 06881
An imprint of Greenwood Publishing Group, Inc.

Printed in the United States of America

The paper used in this book complies with the
Permanent Paper Standard issued by the National
Information Standards Organization (Z39.48-1984).

10 9 8 7 6 5 4 3 2 1

Copyright Acknowledgments

Grateful acknowledgment is given for permission to quote from
the following sources:

Selections from *U.S. Foreign Relations: A Guide to Information
Sources* by Elmer Plischke. Copyright © 1980 by Elmer Plischke.
Reprinted by permission of Gale Research, Inc.
    Henry Kissinger, "Continuity and Change in American Foreign
Policy," *For the Record, Selected Statements, 1977-1980* (1981):
87-91.
    Richard Nixon, *The Real War* (New York: Warner Books, 1980),
pp. 267-69.
    John W. Bowling, "How We Do Our Thing: Policy Formation,"
Foreign Service Journal (January 1970), reprinted in *U.S. Army War
College: Readings* (Carlisle, Pennsylvania: U.S. Army War College,
1972), pp. 1-5.
    Herbert Hoover, "Address, August 10, 1962," *Vital Speeches of
the Day*, vol. 28 (September 1, 1962), pp. 702-704.

*to those who labor in the vineyard
often without appreciation or understanding*

Contents

PART V. BASIC FUNCTIONAL POLICIES

PART VI. SPECIALIZED FUNCTIONAL POLICIES

PART VII. COLLECTIVE COOPERATION

PART VIII. REGIONAL POLICIES AND ISSUES

Table of Documents

PART II. CONDUCT OF FOREIGN RELATIONS

PART IV. CRISIS DIPLOMACY

PART VII. COLLECTIVE COOPERATION

PART VIII. REGIONAL POLICIES AND ISSUES

Preface

Documentation on American foreign policy and relations is readily available in massive quantities and a broad variety of published official documents and other materials. Policy statements and commentary are embodied in thousands of addresses and other public papers, and their practical applications are prescribed in legislative enactments, executive orders, and administrative regulations; in congressional committee hearings and reports; in diplomatic exchanges; in press accounts and official releases; and in such engagements as international declarations and understandings, resolutions of international conferences and organizations, treaties and agreements, and other negotiated arrangements.

Contrary to general perception and the allegations of critics, since its inception the government of the United States has pursued a liberal revelation and publication policy for its foreign relations documentation. The inventory of regularized and ad hoc documents on the goals and essence of foreign policy, diplomatic intercourse, and the conduct of foreign affairs is impressive if not staggering. The opening and public availability of American diplomatic archival papers, though not always immediate, has been generous, and the texts of all treaties and most important executive agreements have been systematically published throughout our history.

It is not surprising that not all foreign policy information and documents become available immediately and automatically. The problems pertaining to revelation and publication are diplomatically sensitive, complex, and often unappreciated or misunderstood. The crucial issues center upon the question: What needs to be, or should be, made public or released--by whom, when, in what forum and format, and in how much detail? Whatever materializes is bound to necessitate compromise between the interests of the public, led by the media's insistence on the "right to know," and those who bear responsibility for the management of foreign affairs on behalf of the people.

To understand the intricacies of the revelation process, it is essential to appreciate interrelated sets of differentiating factors. As noted in the Prologue, these embrace comparisons between "information" and "documentation" as well as between preliminary input and eventuating output or end products and distinctions among methods of placing them into the public domain. The latter include such matters as availability, formal release, and actual publication; fundamental stages in the conduct of foreign relations--differentiating foreign policy making, policy objectives, the substance of policies, and the manner of implementing policy; levels of intragovernmental and international involvement and depth of penetration; and categories of security classification, other forms of confidentiality, and the need for, and manner of, obtaining permission from foreign governments to publicize their confidential positions, mutual discussions, and resulting documents.

Three major developments compound the matter of documents production, public availability, and publication. On the one hand, since World War II, the quantity of states with which the President and Department of State deal has nearly tripled. Second, the number of international conferences and international agencies in which the United States participates has proliferated substantially. Equally significant, the variety of subjects, issues, experiences, challenges, and crises with which the government is diplomatically concerned has mushroomed.

These changes resulted in the expansion of foreign affairs documentary resources, reaching massive quantities. As a consequence, to illustrate, in the preparation of this anthology, it was necessary to peruse such official sources as more than 60 volumes of published presidential papers (each averaging more than 1,000 pages); compilations of legislation, including dozens of volumes of the *Statutes at Large* and the *U.S. Code;* collections of bilateral and multilateral treaties and agreements (consisting of at least 125 volumes of the Bevans and the *U.S. Treaties* series, each containing some 1,200 pages); and more than two dozen volumes of basic/current documents on foreign policy (averaging 1,400 pages per volume). They aggregate well over a quarter-million pages of printed documentation. To these must be added the many volumes of the *Foreign Relations* series, the *Department of State Bulletin,* digests of United States practice in international law, and many others.

Preparing a manageable anthology from such voluminous documentation requires prudent selection and excerpting of material. The method employed to identify and choose documents involved three procedures: securing key documents, such as basic legislative enactments, international accords and understandings, policy addresses, and commentaries; surveying general documentary collections to locate salient and representative records pertaining to particular subjects or developments; and preparing a chronology of important events and then searching for documents pertaining to them. This necessitated examining tens of thousands of pages, reducing these to approximately 8,000 photocopied pages, and then extracting from them the specific items to be incorporated. The objective of this process is to provide comprehensive coverage by excerpting critical or illustrative segments pertaining to a wide range of topics rather than merely producing a limited compilation of noteworthy documents presented in their entirety, including their obsolescent and tertiary segments of passing significance.

In some cases this refinement process resulted in series of documents that evidence alternative approaches, perceptions, and emphases concerning American national interests, goals, objectives, policies, and pragmatic actions. In others, attention is paid to the sequence of, and reaction to, particular developments and events, as in the chapters on presidential doctrines and international crises in which the United States was a primary participant. In dealing with others, the purpose is to supply broad-scale treatment of selected pragmatic subjects, notably peaceful settlement, various forms of international assistance, and United States alliance, antiterrorism, maritime, outer-space, and similar policy concerns. Many consist of cumulations of interrelated documents that concern treatment of a variety of issues and specific American policies, illustrated by those that deal with aspects of the conduct of foreign relations and such functional issues as the maintenance of peace, the promotion of self-determination and human rights, the enhancement and management of trade and commerce, the fabrication of international law, East-West and North-South relations as well as those devoted to major geographic areas, and United States participation in the United Nations and inter-American systems.

In summary, the end product constitutes a collection of selected documents and commentary that encompass a broad range of topics, some depth of treatment, and considerable illustrative or representative selections. The contents of the volume are arranged topically, with major segments devoted to foreign policy making and the management of foreign affairs, crisis diplomacy, general foreign policy principles and presidential doctrines, basic and specialized functional foreign policies, and regional issues. Chapters consist of topically or chronologically arranged subsections. Primary emphasis is on substantive themes, although some attention is paid to procedural matters. Internal cross-referencing links related subjects and documents, and citations provide sources and some guidance to additional materials.

As might be expected, the categories of documents range from policy pronouncements of government leaders to legislative enactments and international compacts, from presidential doctrines and messages to Congress to diplomatic exchanges, and from international declarations and resolutions to legal analyses and press accounts and releases. Some are simply declaratory, informational, or explanatory in nature or deal with the mediation of differences and conflicts, whereas others contribute to the creation of national and international law, binding undertakings, and similar commitments. A few charts are provided to depict phases of the policy-making process and the structure of major international organizations in which the United States participates, and for reference guidance, several documents consist of listings of such matters as human rights declarations and conventions, multilateral contractual arrangements concerning the seas and maritime affairs, summit meetings of the President with the leaders of the Soviet Union and the People's Republic of China, the membership of the United Nations and the Organization of American States, and the specialized agencies of the United Nations and the inter-American system.

Aside from realizing how much official documentation on United States foreign policy and relations is systematically published in readily available form, and how well informed one may become if one utilizes these resources, the production of this anthology suggests a number of tangible conclusions. A great many policy statements are more concerned with national interests, goals, and objectives than with plans of action to pursue and achieve them. Often these statements are addressed to the American people as well as to foreign nations and their governments. American foreign policy interests are universal and extend substantively to a constantly proliferating gamut of topics and geographically to the four corners of the globe, to the high seas and territorial waters, to the airspace that surrounds it, and even to the outer reaches of interplanetary and interstellar space.

Often policy is reactive to developments, specific events, and the policies and practices of other governments, resulting in interlaced continuums of actions and reactions. Many policy themes, such as the maintenance of peace and international stability, and the promotion of self-determination, free trade, interdependence and international commitment and responsibility, freedom of the seas, human rights, partnership, and international cooperation, are frequently reiterated. Much policy is concretized in hundreds of legislative enactments and thousands of international declarations, resolutions, and bilateral and multilateral treaties and agreements. Finally, the totality of American foreign policy is complex, astatic, overwhelming, and virtually uncomprehendable, so that even policy makers and other experts either deal with it in broad or general terms or focus on some specific and manageable aspect. As a consequence, any depiction, whether graphic or documentary, must be selective.

Major Sources
and Citations

This volume constitutes a selected anthology of official, primary, published documentation on United States foreign policy and the conduct of foreign affairs. It consists primarily of statements of goals, objectives, policies, and developments issued by the President and other leaders or embodied in congressional resolutions and enactments; international commitments and other arrangements contained in international declarations, treaties, and agreements; and a few graphic representations and listings.

The following denote the principal documentary collections and other materials that concern American diplomacy and foreign relations including, where pertinent, the abbreviated citations employed in this compilation. Except as noted, all citations are published by the Government Printing Office. For additional guidance to official resources, see the "bibliographical guides" provided in the last section of this listing.

PRESIDENT

CODE OF FEDERAL REGULATIONS (1938--). Irregular. Contains the texts of presidential proclamations, executive orders, administrative regulations, and similar documents of legal significance.

FEDERAL REGISTER (1936--). Published daily, except holidays; with annual cumulations, and periodic indexes. Contains materials similar to those in the *Code of Federal Regulations*.

PUBLIC PAPERS OF THE PRESIDENTS OF THE UNITED STATES (1957--). Began with the papers of Harry Truman for 1945, and published in one or more volumes annually for each President. Contains presidential messages, statements, addresses, joint statements with foreign leaders, press conferences, and others. Appendixes list presidential proclamations, executive orders, and White House releases. The law governing this compilation also authorizes the issuance of volumes for earlier Presidents. Cited as *Papers of Presidents*, with name of President and year.

U.S. FOREIGN POLICY FOR THE 1970's: A REPORT TO THE CONGRESS BY RICHARD NIXON, PRESIDENT OF THE UNITED STATES (1970-1973). Four annual volumes, dealing with years 1969-1972. Each volume carries a subtitle and constitutes a descriptive account of American foreign relations for the year, generally arranged in parts concerned with selected important themes and usually including a section on analysis of the machinery and process of policy making. Cited as *U.S. Foreign Policy for the 1970's,* with subtitle.

WEEKLY COMPILATION OF PRESIDENTIAL DOCUMENTS (published by the National Archives and Records Service, General Services Administration, 1965--). Issued weekly. Contains similar materials to those appearing in the *Public Papers of the Presidents of the United States.* Cited as *Weekly Compilation of Presidential Documents.*

WHITE HOUSE, "PRESS RELEASES." Issued by the White House, irregular. No official titles, but generally the heading indicates that it is released by the White House and gives date of issue. These provide the texts of addresses, statements, communications, proclamations, and the like, issued by the President or his press secretary. Often they contain background information not available in other publications. Practice varies, but several hundred may be issued in a single year.

CONGRESS

CONGRESSIONAL RECORD (1873--). Issued daily while Congress is in session. Biweekly compilation, and also issued in bound volumes for each session of each Congress (per year). Contains a record of the debates and the public proceedings of the House of Representatives and the Senate. Legislative history of bills and resolutions, with an index, is included in the bound congressional session volumes.

LEGISLATION ON FOREIGN RELATIONS THROUGH ---- (1957--). Originally titled LEGISLATION ON FOREIGN RELATIONS--WITH EXPLANATORY NOTES (1957). Annual, published in two or more volumes. One or more volumes contain the texts of legislation, executive orders, and related documents and one volume contains treaties, agreements, UN resolutions, and related materials, revised as necessary.

PUBLIC LAWS--Slip laws (18--? to date). Each law is published separately. Irregular. Cited as *P.L.*

REQUIRED REPORTS TO CONGRESS IN THE FOREIGN AFFAIRS FIELD. Periodic, early 1970's to date. Previously entitled REPORTING REQUIREMENTS IN LEGISLATION ON FOREIGN RELATIONS (1970). Prepared by the Foreign Affairs Division of the Library of Congress for the House of Representatives and Senate committees on foreign relations. By legal stipulation, Congress requires the executive and administrative agencies to file various periodic and special reports, which are generally published either by such agencies or by congressional committees. Congress has established more than one hundred such requirements.   Illustrations include regularized reports on United States participation in the United Nations, contributions to international organizations, foreign assistance, aeronautic and space developments and policy, arms control and disarmament, and the Peace Corps.

UNITED STATES CODE (1926--). Irregular. This provides an organized compilation of general and permanent laws of the United States in force at the time of publication of the periodically updated version. It is organized topically by "Titles," the following of which are of special concern to foreign affairs: Armed Forces, Commerce and Trade, Customs Duties, Foreign Relations and Intercourse, Territories and Insular Possessions, and War and National Defense. Cited as *U.S. Code.*

UNITED STATES STATUTES AT LARGE (1875--). Annual. Contains the texts of public laws, government reorganization plans, constitutional amendments, private laws, concurrent resolutions, and proclamations. Through 1951, volumes were published in parts, a portion of part 2 or part 3 devoted to treaties and international agreements. Since 1950 the texts of treaties and agreements are published separately on an annual basis (see UNITED STATES TREATIES AND OTHER INTERNATIONAL AGREEMENTS below). Cited as *Statutes at Large.*

Also relevant are many House of Representatives, Senate, and joint documents, hearings, and reports.

DEPARTMENT OF STATE

Basic Sources for Diplomatic and Current Foreign Policy Documents

FOREIGN RELATIONS OF THE UNITED STATES (1862--). Originally titled PAPERS RELATING TO FOREIGN AFFAIRS, but changed to FOREIGN RELATIONS OF THE UNITED STATES: DIPLOMATIC PAPERS in 1932, and to its current title following World War II. This series--the most long-lived, comprehensive compilation of foreign affairs records-- contains the texts of diplomatic communications, exchanges of notes, position papers, and other official documents relating to foreign policy, diplomacy, and negotiations. Materials are generally arranged by country, grouped by geographic areas, and selected functional fields arranged separately in recent years, including national security affairs, foreign economic policy, and relations with the United Nations. Cited as *Foreign Relations.*

POSTWAR FOREIGN POLICY PREPARATION, 1939-1945 (1950). Prepared by Harley A. Notter, et al. A narrative and documentary record of the structure and conduct of the preparation of United States post-World War II foreign policy compiled for President Truman and the Department of State. Analysis is arranged chronologically in five parts, and sixty-four documents are provided in the appendix.

A DECADE OF AMERICAN FOREIGN POLICY: BASIC DOCUMENTS, 1941-49 (1950). Prepared by the Department of State. Issued as Senate Document no. 123, 81st Cong., 1st sess. A compilation of more than 300 basic documents, including policy statements, addresses, treaties and agreements, statutes, constitutive acts of international organizations, communiques, and the like. Contains largely policy end product documents.

AMERICAN FOREIGN POLICY: BASIC DOCUMENTS, 1950-1955 (1957). Two volumes. Provides approximately 3,250 pages of documentation. Continues the practice begun in A DECADE OF AMERICAN FOREIGN POLICY. Serves as an interim compilation prior to the publication of the more comprehensive *Foreign Relations* series. Contains largely end product documents. Commenced a series identified in the following entry.

AMERICAN FOREIGN POLICY: CURRENT DOCUMENTS, 1956-- (1959--). Annual compilations, continuing the two-volume anthology cited in the preceding entry. Intended to provide ready access to basic end product documentation at an early date. This series ended with the volume for 1967, but was subsequently revived.

DEPARTMENT OF STATE BULLETIN (1939-1989). Issued monthly; originally published weekly. Contains articles by public officials, addresses by the President, secretary of state, and other officials, news items, current information on treaties and agreements, important press releases, and similar materials. Discontinued in 1989.

TREATIES AND AGREEMENTS

UNITED STATES TREATY SERIES, 1908-1946. Irregular. Treaties numbered serially beginning with number 489; these numbers constitute the treaty file numbers in Department of State archives. Prior to 1929, the series included both treaties and agreements; after 1929, it embodied only treaties submitted to the Senate for approval. Each treaty text is published separately in pamphlet form. Cited as *TS*.

EXECUTIVE AGREEMENT SERIES 1929-1946. Irregular. Executive agreements numbered serially from 1 to 506. Format and content similar to the U.S. TREATY SERIES. Cited as *EAS* or as *AS*.

TREATIES AND OTHER INTERNATIONAL ACTS SERIES, 1945--. Irregular. Combines and supersedes the TREATY SERIES and the EXECUTIVE AGREEMENT SERIES, cited above. Treaties and agreements are numbered serially, commencing with number 1501. Each text is published separately in pamphlet form, giving the text in the languages of the original instrument and the dates of signature, ratification, proclamation, and implementation. Cited as *TIAS*.

TREATIES AND OTHER INTERNATIONAL AGREEMENTS OF THE UNITED STATES OF AMERICA, 1776-1949 (1968-1976). Thirteen volumes. Compiled and edited by Charles I. Bevans. Cumulative compilation of treaties and agreements, which, together with the following entry, constitutes a complete collection of United States treaties and agreements throughout its independent history. Volumes 1 to 4 contain multilateral treaties and agreements, arranged chronologically by date of signature. Bilateral treaties and agreements, beginning with Volume 5, are grouped alphabetically by name of the country with whom they were concluded, and chronologically thereunder by date of signature. Cited as Bevans, *Treaties and Other International Agreements.*

UNITED STATES TREATIES AND OTHER INTERNATIONAL AGREEMENTS, 1950-. Annual, with one or more Parts for each year, and published biennially since the mid-1970's. A continuing series consisting of several volumes and parts for each calendar year or biennium. Instruments are numbered and arranged in the order in which they are published in the TREATIES AND OTHER INTERNATIONAL ACTS SERIES, cited above, beginning with the number 2010. Treatment is similar to that described in the preceding entry. Prior to the publication of this compilation, treaties and agreements were printed in the UNITED STATES STATUTES AT LARGE. Cited as *U.S. Treaties* or *UST*.

TREATIES IN FORCE: A LIST OF TREATIES AND OTHER INTERNATIONAL AGREEMENTS OF THE UNITED STATES IN FORCE ON JANUARY 1, ---- (1956--)'. Annual. Earlier issues of a similar nature were published in 1932 and 1941. Arranged in two parts, followed by an appendix. Part 1 lists bilateral treaties and other agreements arranged alphabetically by country or other political entity, and thereunder by functional subject headings, and chronologically thereunder. Part 2 lists multilateral treaties, arranged by subject headings, together with a list of states which are parties to each such treaty and agreement.

The texts of all treaties and agreements registered by the United States and other countries with the United Nations are published in the UNITED NATIONS TREATY SERIES, cited as *UNTS*.

INTERNATIONAL LAW

DIGEST OF INTERNATIONAL LAW (1963-1973). Fifteen volumes. Edited by Marjorie M. Whiteman. Covers the period after World War II. Provides extracts from diplomatic communications, Department of State instructions and rulings, treaties and agreements, a variety of archival materials, and similar materials, as well as editor's notes and comments. Emphasizes legal aspects of diplomatic and foreign relations topics. General index in Volume 15. This continues earlier compilations: John Bassett Moore, ed., A DIGEST OF INTERNATIONAL LAW (1906), 8 volumes; and Green H. Hackworth, ed., DIGEST OF INTERNATIONAL LAW (1940-1944), 8 volumes. For subsequent materials, see next entry.

DIGEST OF UNITED STATES PRACTICE IN INTERNATIONAL LAW, 1973--. Annual. Compiled by the Office of the Legal Adviser of the Department of State. Updates the earlier DIGESTS, and consists of materials selected on the basis of importance in the development of United States foreign policy and law, its role in confirming international legal precedents, or for purposes of noting the record of the American position on significant areas of foreign affairs and international law.

INTERNATIONAL CONFERENCES AND ORGANIZATIONS

INTERNATIONAL ORGANIZATIONS IN WHICH THE UNITED STATES PARTICIPATES (1950). Provides descriptive analysis concerning some sixty-five international organizations, grouped functionally. Contains discussion on their origin and development, membership, functions, structure, finances, and current status. Two appendixes are provided: one lists international organizations in which the United States participated but which were terminated or superseded, or which became inactive after 1945. The second is a chart indicating the membership of states in the components of the United Nations and its specialized agencies. For earlier version, see INTERNATIONAL AGENCIES IN WHICH THE UNITED STATES PARTICIPATES (1946).

PARTICIPATION OF THE UNITED STATES IN INTERNATIONAL CONFERENCES, 1947-1962. Annual. Conferences and sessions of agencies of international organizations are grouped in major functional categories, giving such information as composition of the American delegation, principal officers, participation by other countries, and a summary of action taken.

REVIEW OF THE UNITED NATIONS CHARTER: A COLLECTION OF DOCUMENTS. Senate Document no. 87, 83d Cong., 2d sess. (1954). Consists of 186 documents concerning the United Nations, grouped into segments concerned with background, action by Congress, and selected problem areas, such as national sovereignty and the United Nations, treaties and domestic law, membership and representation, development of the General Assembly, voting in the Security Council, collective security, and financing.

UNITED STATES CONTRIBUTIONS TO INTERNATIONAL ORGANIZATIONS, 1953-. Annual. Contains a descriptive analysis of the contributions of the United States to individual international organizations, with commentary on budgetary and financial deliberations and action, supplemented with summary tables.

U.S. PARTICIPATION IN THE UN: REPORT BY THE PRESIDENT TO THE CONGRESS FOR THE YEAR ---- (1945--). Annual. Originally titled THE UNITED STATES AND THE UNITED NATIONS. Describes the work of the United Nations throughout the year and the policy position of the United States in its various organs, specialized agencies, and subsidiary administrative units. Appendixes include description of the units of the United Nations, brief statement on U.S. representation missions, and, in earlier reports, a selected list of United Nations documents and publications. Cited as *U.S. Participation in the UN.*

OTHER OFFICIAL SOURCES

COMMISSION ON THE ORGANIZATION OF THE GOVERNMENT FOR THE CONDUCT OF FOREIGN POLICY, JUNE 1975. (1976). Consists of a report and seven volumes of appendixes, labeled Appendix A through X, each dealing with a separate functional subject, such as Foreign Policy for the Future, Multilateral Diplomacy, Use of Information, Policy Planning, Foreign Economic Policy, Congress and Executive Relations, Intelligence Functions, Ethical Considerations in Foreign Policy, and the like.

DIPLOMACY FOR THE 70's: A PROGRAM OF MANAGEMENT REFORM FOR THE DEPARTMENT OF STATE (1970). Consists of a summary report and individual task force reports dealing with career management policies, performance and promotion in the diplomatic service, personnel requirements and resources, training, prerequisites, recruitment, stimulation of creativity, openness in the foreign affairs community, management evaluation system and tools, the roles and functions of United States diplomatic missions, and related matters. An appendix is devoted to management strategy--a program for the 1970's.

DOCUMENTS ON GERMANY, 1944-1985. Published jointly by the Senate Foreign Relations Committee and the Department of State. This is the fourth edition of this compilation, which first appeared in 1959. Provides 1421 pages of documents, arranged chronologically, on American policy and action on the German and Berlin questions. Cited as *Documents on Germany.*

FOREIGN POLICY CHOICES FOR THE 70s AND 80s (1976). 94th Cong., 1st and 2d sess., two volumes. This is a survey, involving thirteen hearings conducted by the Senate Foreign Relations Committee, in connection with the American bicentennial, to probe the long-range foreign policy goals of the United States.

PRINCIPAL OFFICERS OF THE DEPARTMENT OF STATE AND UNITED STATES CHIEFS OF MISSION, 1778-1988 (1988). Contains lists of secretaries of state and other high-ranking officers of the Department of State, ambassadors at large (1949-1988), career ambassadors (1956-1988), chiefs of mission to specific countries (arranged alphabetically by country), and chiefs of mission to international organizations. Individuals are listed chronologically. Also contains an index to persons, giving their assignments to these positions, arranged chronologically, and noting Foreign Service careerists. Earlier versions were published in 1973 and 1982 under the title UNITED STATES CHIEFS OF MISSION.

REALISM, STRENGTH, NEGOTIATION: KEY FOREIGN POLICY STATEMENTS OF THE REAGAN ADMINISTRATION (1984). Contains an introduction and twenty-nine major addresses by the President, Vice President, and Secretary of State during the first Reagan administration. Cited as *Realism, Strength, Negotiation.*

UNITED STATES FOREIGN POLICY, 1969-1972: A REPORT OF THE SECRETARY OF STATE (1971-1973). Three annual volumes. These contain narrative accounts of developments, with separate sections devoted to functional and areal affairs, the management of foreign relations, and a chronology of events. Annexes provide the texts of selected documents and lists of current treaties and agreements, as well as the principal officers of the Department of State and related agencies.

UNITED STATES FOREIGN POLICY: COMPILATION OF STUDIES (1961). Provides 1473 pages of documentary materials, consisting of an introductory statement, fourteen studies prepared by different unofficial agencies and institutions, and a letter to retired Foreign Service Officers with their commentary. Segments deal with the formulation and administration of foreign policy and studies on major geographic areas, basic policy aims, ideology, and operational matters.

Also of interest is a series of Department of State "in-house studies." Some of these are security classified or are otherwise limited to internal governmental use. Since World War II, the Office of the Historian (formerly the Historical Office) of the Department of State has produced hundreds of these studies and reports of two basic types: fundamental and substantial "research projects" and less comprehensive, shorter "research memoranda." These are produced in response to specific needs and official requests from the White House, Congress, senior departmental officers, or other government agencies.

UNOFFICIAL SOURCES

DOCUMENTS ON AMERICAN FOREIGN RELATIONS 1939-1970. Annual. Various compilers. Published by the World Peace Foundation, 1939-1951, and the Council on Foreign Relations beginning with 1952. Arrangement varies, but volumes generally include sections and subsections devoted to aspects of the conduct of foreign relations and to specific geographic areas. Provides such documents as official statements, reports, releases, addresses, legislation, diplomatic communications, treaties and agreements, and similar instruments.

HISTORIC DOCUMENTS OF ---- (1972--). Annual, published by Congressional Quarterly. Anthology of basic documents with commentary on a broad range of topics including foreign relations. Cited as *Historic Documents*.

U.S. FOREIGN POLICY DOCUMENTS (Brunswick, Ohio: King's Court Communications, 1978). Four volumes. Edited by Nicholas A. Berry. Collection of official documents, principally of the executive branch of the government, including addresses, policy statements, memoranda, and treaties and agreements. Covers an extensive span of American foreign relations grouped in four periods--1620-1876, 1877-1932, 1933-1963, and 1963-1977.

VITAL SPEECHES OF THE DAY (New York: City News Publishing Co., 1934--). Published semimonthly, with annual index. Contains addresses by government and other leaders, covering a variety of subjects, including foreign affairs.

Additional information concerning current documentation may be found in the AMERICAN JOURNAL OF INTERNATIONAL LAW, published quarterly, which provides the texts of official materials on international law and current foreign affairs developments; and FOREIGN AFFAIRS, issued five times per year, which contains sections on selected source materials and annual chronologies.

BIBLIOGRAPHICAL GUIDES

Additional, more comprehensive guidance to official sources and documentation is available in such publications as:

GOVERNMENT PUBLICATIONS: A GUIDE TO BIBLIOGRAPHIC TOOLS (Washington: Library of Congress, 4th ed., 1975). Compiled by Vladimir M. Palic.

MONTHLY CATALOGUE OF UNITED STATES GOVERNMENT PUBLICATIONS (1895--). Issued monthly, listing the voluminous documentation of the United States government.

AMERICAN FOREIGN RELATIONS: A BIBLIOGRAPHY OF OFFICIAL SOURCES (College Park, Maryland: Bureau of Governmental Research, University of Maryland, 1955; reprinted New York: Johnson Reprint Corp., 1966). Compiled by Elmer Plischke.

U.S. FOREIGN RELATIONS: A GUIDE TO INFORMATION SOURCES (Detroit: Gale Research Co., 1980). Compiled by Elmer Plischke. Chapters 21 and 22 (pp. 503-609) deal with official sources and resources.

Acronyms

AID	Agency for International Development
ANZUS	Australia, New Zealand, and United States (defense arrangement)
BENELUX	Belgium, the Netherlands, and Luxembourg (customs union)
CENTO	Central Treaty Organization
CIA	Central Intelligence Agency
CIEC	Conference on International Economic Cooperation
CSCE	Conference on Security and Cooperation in Europe
EAS	Executive Agreement Series (U.S.)
EC	European Community
ECA	Economic Cooperation Administration
ECOSOC	Economic and Social Council (in UN and OAS)
ECSC	European Coal and Steel Community
EDC	European Defense Community
EDF	European Development Fund
EEC	European Economic Community
EFTA	European Free Trade Association
EO	Executive Order
EPU	European Payments Union
ERP	European Recovery Program
EURATOM	European Atomic Energy Community
FAO	Food and Agriculture Organization
FBI	Federal Bureau of Investigation
FEA	Foreign Economic Administration
FOA	Foreign Operations Administration
FRG	Federal Republic of Germany
GATT	General Agreement on Tariffs and Trade
GDR	German Democratic Republic
GNP	Gross National Product

I A E A	International Atomic Energy Agency
I A P G	Inter-Agency Arctic Policy Group
I B / I B R D	International Bank for Reconstruction and Development
I C A	International Cooperation Administration
I C A O	International Civil Aviation Organization
I C J	International Court of Justice
I D A	International Development Association
I D C A	International Development Cooperation Agency
I F C	International Finance Corporation
I G Y	International Geophysical Year
I L O	International Labor Organization
I M F	International Monetary Fund
I M O	International Maritime Organization (formerly IMCO)
I N F	Intermediate-Range Nuclear Force (Treaty)
I R B M	Intermediate-range ballistic missile
I R O	International Refugee Organization
I T O	International Trade Organization
I T U	International Telecommunication Union
J C S	Joint Chiefs of Staff
L D C	Less Developed Country
M A A G	Military Assistance Advisory Group
M D A P	Mutual Defense Assistance Program
M E T O	Middle East Treaty Organization
M F L	Multinational Force Lebanon
M N F	Multinational Force
M R B M	Medium-range ballistic missile
M S A	Mutual Security Agency
M S P	Mutual Security Program
N A S A	National Aeronautics and Space Administration
N A T O	North Atlantic Treaty Organization
N I E O	New International Economic Order
N S C	National Security Council
O A S	Organization of American States
O A U	Organization of African Unity
O C B	Operations Coordinating Board
O E C D	Organization for Economic Cooperation and Development
O E C S	Organization of Eastern Caribbean States
O E E C	Organization for European Economic Cooperation
O P E C	Organization of Petroleum Exporting Countries
O T C	Organization for Trade Cooperation
P L	Public Law
P L O	Palestine Liberation Organization

S D I	Strategic Defense Initiative
SEATO	South-East Asia Treaty Organization
STS	Space Transportation System
SUNFED	Special U.N. Fund for Economic Development
TCA	Technical Cooperation Administration
TIAS	Treaties and Other International Acts Series (U.S.)
TS	Treaty Series (U.S.)
UN	United Nations
UNCDF	U.N. Capital Development Fund
UNCLOS	U.N. Conference on the Law of the Sea
UNCTAD	U.N. Conference on Trade and Development
UNDP	U.N. Development Program
UN-EPTA	U.N. Expanded Program of Technical Assistance
UNESCO	U.N. Educational, Scientific and Cultural Organization
UNICEF	U.N. International Children's Emergency Fund
UNIDO	U.N. Industrial Development Organization
UNITAR	U.N. Institute for Training and Research
UNRRA	U.N. Relief and Rehabilitation Administration
UNTS	U.N. Treaty Series
UPU	Universal Postal Union
USC	U.S. Code
USIA	United States Information Agency
USTS	United States Treaties Series
WEU	Western European Union
WFP	World Food Program
WHO	World Health Organization
WIPO	World Intellectual Property Organization
WMO	World Meteorological Organization

This list does not include standard abbreviations or those that are under-standable from the context.

Contemporary
U.S. Foreign Policy

Prologue: Foreign Relations Documentation— An Analysis

The "new diplomacy" of the twentieth century consists of several components. Aside from such concepts as "total," "multilateral," "summit," and "ministerial" diplomacy, it also involves several elements that relate to the role of the people. These embrace "open diplomacy," "democratic diplomacy," "public" or "popular diplomacy," and "consensus diplomacy," which are interrelated and are subject to widespread analysis and controversy. Fundamental is the question: How and to what extent can, or should, the American people influence or determine the nature of foreign policy and the conduct of foreign relations?

In the aftermath of World War I, Elihu Root, former Secretary of State and Nobel Peace Prize winner, contended that the people in a democracy, who are theoretically responsible, have an obligation to become knowledgeable respecting the control of foreign affairs. After World War II President Truman endorsed the principle that in our democratic system foreign policy decisions ultimately flow from our democratic process and denote the collective judgment of the people. Many others reiterate and support these propositions and argue that vigorous and supportive public opinion constitutes an added weapon in our diplomatic arsenal, that to engender dependable opinion the public must be informed, and that for the people to be informed, if not knowledgeable, government information and records must be available to them.

SECRECY VS. OPENNESS

Despite widespread public debate, and contrary to popular belief and the allegations of an insatiable press and certain elements of the academic world, the government of the United States pursues a liberal revelation and publication policy for its foreign relations documentation, a practice begun early in the nineteenth century. The inventory of regularized and ad hoc official publications

* Revised and augmented version from *U. S. Foreign Relations: A Guide to Information Sources*, Chapter 21, by Elmer Plischke. Copyright (c) 1980 by Elmer Plischke. Reprinted by permission of Gale Research, Inc.

on the conduct of foreign relations, together with those on the essence of foreign policy, is impressive, and the opening of American diplomatic archival documentation, though not immediate, has been systematized and comprehensive.

Since the establishment of the American republic, a great debate has raged over government secrecy in general and, more precisely, the issue of confidentiality in its foreign affairs.   This has flowed, in part, from an abiding popular suspicion of both governance and governors, from the role of the public and the information media in the American political process, from the very nature of the democratic system, and from twentieth-century emphasis on "openness." This dispute has been waged in waves, cresting in the twentieth century at the time of World War I and Woodrow Wilson's plea for "open covenants . . . openly arrived at," following World War II in connection with the Yalta agreements, the proposals to amend the President's treaty-making authority in the 1950's, the Freedom of Information Act deliberations in the 1960's, and subsequently in relation to presidential war-making powers, executive privilege, intelligence operations, and the publication of the "Pentagon Papers" and similar journalistic revelations.

This debate on confidentiality in foreign relations has proliferated to distinguish "open covenants" from "openly arrived at" and policy making from policy implementation. It has engendered spirited dialogue with respect to the security classification system for information and documents, established policy vs. contingency planning, and confidentiality of information vs. confidentiality of relations. It also raises issues concerning the proprieties of the "injunction to secrecy," executive privilege, the immune sources of the press and other media, news management, planned and uncontrolled leaks and "leakeries," and government public relations, press conferences, official releases, and "backgrounders." It all boils down to the fundamental issue of the public's "right to know"--what and when--as against the public's "need to know"--why.   The basic problem is epitomized by the appellation "secret diplomacy," which automatically evokes an unfavorable perception and a negative response, and which therefore has been called "quiet diplomacy" by Dag Hammarskjöld, secretary general of the United Nations, and others.

The matter of confidentiality requires a rational as well as rationalized compromise between the extremes of complete secrecy and immediate, wholesale revelation. Central is the alignment of the public interest, from the point of view of the individual member of the polity (the right and need to know), with the collective national concern, from the perspective of the aggregate community (its right or need to determine the nature and degree of revelation). Resolution of this juxtaposition of the interests of individuals within the community as against those of the community comprised of those individuals must, at best, accommodate both, must entail realistic compromise, and is not likely to satisfy fully the extreme of either.   In 1972, modifying the documentary classification system of the United States, President Nixon declared: "Clearly, the two principles of an informed public and of confidentiality within the Government are irreconcilable in their purest forms, and a balance must be struck between them" (White House Release, March 8, 1972).

To understand the intricacies of this problem, several interrelated sets of differentiating factors must be considered. These include distinguishing among:

(1) information and documentation, (2) various basic methods of placing them in the public domain (including documentary availability, release, and publication), (3) fundamental components of the foreign relations process (including the separable elements of policy making, policy objectives and substance, and policy implementation), (4) levels of international and intragovernmental penetration, and (5) categories of security classification.

INFORMATION AND DOCUMENTATION--RELEASE AND PUBLICATION

The concepts "information" and "documentation" need to be clearly differentiated. The former is the more general and inclusive. It is essentially equatable with knowledge, usually communicable, and embraces, not only written and printed documentation, but oral information as well as pictorial, graphic, film and filmstrip, audiotape, and other forms of material that convey verifiable perceptions, depictions, facts, proof, or evidence. The term "documents" is more restrictive, connoting the nonoral forms of these materials. Often, information is publicly available, though not in its documentary form, and sometimes it is released even before it is reduced to documentary form.

In considering methods whereby information and documentary materials enter the public domain, including distinctions among "availability," "release," "dissemination," and "publication" of knowledge and documents, a number of concepts need to be understood. Some are fairly obvious, others are more subtle, and still others tend to be imprecise and confusing. The terms "records" and "papers" are often used interchangeably with "documents," although the concept "records" is broader in scope than the other two and, together with "materials," is used as the most generic expression. In essence, "records" encompass books, papers, maps, photographs, charts, and other documentary materials or copies thereof, regardless of physical form and characteristics. Technically, "nontextual" may be differentiated from "textual" records on the basis of content and format. "Papers" and "documents" are distinguished in that they are generally in written (or, in some cases graphic or pictorial) form, as differentiated from oral documentation, and, although a "document," in its broadest sense, may be any written or graphic instrument that conveys information or proof, the term is often applied to the final version of an official "paper." "Archives," on the other hand, are all those records that are deliberately set aside, usually for long-term preservation.

The titles of certain categories of diplomatic records and documents, by way of comparison, are fairly precise, such as the various types of instruments employed in diplomacy, including the "aide mémoire," "circular note," "communique," "declaration," "final act," "note verbale," "procés verbal," "protocol," and "ultimatum." The same may be said of such documentation forms as the "letter," "despatch," "memorandum," "note," "report," "airgram," and "telegram." This also is the case with formal diplomatic credentials, including the "exequatur," "full power," and "letter of credence." The meaning of "drafts" (including the distinction between the "initial," "original," or "preliminary" as against the "final" draft), distinguishable from "final copies" of papers or documents and of "working papers" involved in producing "end-product" documents in their ultimate, official version, is also readily comprehensible.

It is more difficult, however, to differentiate precisely the meaning of "publication" and "publishing" as applied to government documents and records. "To publish," by definition, means "to make public" or "to divulge," and, while this is normally assumed to apply to the issuance of printed or processed materials, in reality it may also denote the revealing of information in oral as well as written form. "Publication" pertains to the act of publishing but traditionally is reserved for the issuance to the public of material in written or graphic rather than oral form. The dissemination of information in an oral fashion is characterized rather by the words "announcement," "divulgement," and "revelation," whereas the terms "dissemination," "issuance," and "release" may refer to both oral and written information and documentation. When made available or disseminated, such information and documents are said to be "in the public domain." Written publications, as distinct from oral information, may be "printed" or "processed" (i.e., mimeographed, photocopied, faxed, or otherwise reproduced), whereas "original" (inceptive or primigenial) documents usually are handwritten, typewritten, word processed, teletyped, or in the form of telegrams.

A final, important distinction to be noted is that documents and information may be "publicly available" even though they are neither published nor overtly issued publicly in some other form. Such documents and information may be said to be "available," but the initiative to acquire or extract them is up to the user, and they are potentially in the public domain, even if unused.

The delineation between "published," "disseminated," and "available" documents and information, therefore, may occasion some confusion, and caution must be exercised in evaluating degrees of confidentiality and openness respecting them. That which is explicitly published or disseminated is clearly made public, while that which is available but unused is neither secret nor overtly in the public domain. By comparison, the distinction between "open" and "closed" documentation and between "classified" and "unclassified" materials--both of which sets of differentiations are discussed later--is fairly precise, at least so far as general categories are concerned. At this point, suffice it to say that both published and unpublished records, as well as both documents and information, may be either classified or unclassified.

In short, appreciation of distinctions among these concepts and practices is essential to adjudging the problem of secrecy vs. openness as it relates to the use of foreign relations information and records. It must be realized that, so far as official sources and resources are concerned, a great deal more information is available than is reduced to documentary form, that considerably more documentation is publicly available than has been published by the government, and that far more has been published, disseminated in some other fashion, or produced in a refined manner primarily for internal use than is reproduced in printed or processed versions. On the other hand, substantial documentation and information are obtainable in some organized or collated form, even though unpublished, to supplement the basic raw records of the President, Congress, the Department of State, and other government agencies.

FOREIGN RELATIONS POLICY MAKING, SUBSTANCE, AND IMPLEMENTATION

To cope with the problem of the availability of foreign relations resources, it also is imperative to understand that, while much of the information
and documentation that flow from official sources are intended to be made public
when perfected, it may be that what goes into perfecting them is not everybody's
business--at least not immediately. The consummated needs to be clearly
distinguished from the pending. On the one hand, there is the determined goal or
objective, the reasoned conclusion, the decided policy, or the completed action.
These need to be differentiated from the initiatives and proposals raised and
discarded, the diplomatic methods, plans, strategies, and tactics pursued to gain
ends, and the functioning of policy formulation and negotiatory procedures, as
well as intraagency and intergovernmental deliberation and bargaining while in
progress to achieve the diplomatic end products desired. Such differentiations
apply to both the processes of policy making respecting important and sensitive
foreign relations matters and to the forging of end products in the field.

Policy making internally and negotiation externally, by their very
nature, involve advocacies, consideration and determination of options, the
exercise of choice, and the fixing of priorities. To be fruitful, these normally
entail adjustment, accommodation, bargaining, compromise, and concession.
Distinctions respecting information and documentation--so far as confidentiality and revelation are concerned--clearly need to be drawn in their application to the three primary components of foreign relations: policy making,
policy essence, and policy implementation.

Delving deeper, additional discrimination must be made between policy
making centrally and in the field, between policy which is substantive and that
which is procedural, and between policy implementation at the national capitol
and through diplomatic agents or missions abroad. Discretion must be exercised
in applying qualities of confidentiality and revelation to each of these subaspects
of the diplomatic process. The amount of openness is greater with respect to
some, and constraint may be far more necessary for others. They can scarcely
be regarded as equals under the generic designations "diplomacy" or "foreign
affairs."

Generally, end-product foreign policy is made public relatively early in
the United States, especially if it is self-executing and may be enunciated
unilaterally. On the other hand, if it requires negotiation with other governments, sometimes basic policy but more often supportive subpolicy, which may
be modified by international bargaining and compromise, together with
diplomatic strategies, tactics, and the process of deliberation, tends to be
withheld pending its consummation and outcome.

Governments, like other human institutions, usually are least willing to
divulge information and documents at an early date respecting the details of
their internal policy-making process or their bargaining during negotiations.
At the same time, since World War II, it is often these very elements of foreign
relations, rather than the substance of policy or the results of negotiation, that
appear to be challenged on grounds of government secretiveness or the
unavailability of information and documentation. The issue tends to become
whether the right to know exceeds the realm of policy essence and negotiated con-

sequences, and it extends to the detailed processes of policy formulation and implementation and to whether these should be publicized even before decisions are made or actions are taken.

PRELIMINARY VS. END PRODUCT DOCUMENTATION

Another consideration central to the concerns of the user of foreign relations information and documentation is the distinction between diplomatic end products and those that are initiatory, preliminary, or otherwise contributory to the eventuating decision, policy, action, or document. In terms of elementary logic, this is a relatively simple proposition, while, on examination, because of the varying, interrelated degrees of "end-productness" at differing stages of the process, it frequently becomes surprisingly intricate.

For example, a treaty draft proposal originating in a component of the Department of State, while propositional and initiatory with respect to that which follows, may actually be an end product of the deliberation that precedes it. Within the department, it then becomes the basis for intraagency consideration at upper levels of the administrative hierarchy, and in this consideration it loses its earlier character as an end product. Discussion, refinement, and modification may remold it into a departmental end product, which then becomes initiatory in interdepartmental negotiation, producing a still later end-product version. As consideration moves up to the White House level, including, possibly, National Security Council or cabinet deliberation, it undergoes another stage of transition from draft to end product, eventually taking on the character of the resultant United States draft treaty.

Within the international forum, however, the American proposal reverts to proposal status. At the same time, other governments may engage in similar deliberations, producing their own national draft documents. An intermediate stage may involve the interchange by governments of formal or informal comments on individual national proposals, sometimes resulting in modifications and the preparation of new, more highly refined national versions, which become the end products of this phase of the evolution. These treaty drafts (and some may have become joint propositions) may then be dealt with collectively in differing ways.

If the objective is a multipartite treaty, for purposes of illustration, negotiations could be direct and bilateral (which tends to be exceptional) or they may be simultaneous and multilateral (as is the common practice for such a treaty), and procedures for the two processes would vary. In the case of the multipartite convention negotiated at a multilateral conference, the various national drafts may all be regarded as initiatory proposals, or one of them may be made the basic negotiating version with the others viewed as proposals for modifying the working draft. The conference may fragment the composite into segments, each of which is negotiated into end product form by a separate committee. These partial end products would need to be integrated by a coordinating facility, producing its amalgamated, multipartite end product. The latter, finally, becomes the proposal considered (and possibly amended) in plenary session, the resulting version of which eventually becomes the conference end product--and the ultimate end product of the entire process, providing no textual changes are produced by interpretations, reservations, and amendments during national government review and ratification.

Even in this generalized illustration (and a good deal of diplomacy is far more intricate and may range over a span of years rather than weeks or months), it is possible to identify at least seven major stages of "end-productness," and to argue for the automatic publication of foreign relations end products raises serious questions of delineation among the respective stages in such a process and of the probable effects of premature release or publication at each stage on the likelihood of gaining the objective sought. Discretion needs to be exercised, and determinations must safeguard the viability and success of the venture. In general, however, the closer the end product is to the conclusion of the proceeding and the effectuation of its implementation, the more likely is its public divulgence, providing this violates neither the security of the United States nor the confidence of other governments.

At some half-dozen points in this illustration, the end product of one phase of consideration becomes the draft basis of the next. Often, ideas, suggestions, comments, reactions to comments, and alternatives may be proposed, adopted, and negotiated, modifying that which was previously deemed to constitute an end product. The contributing materials and documents and information concerning them, leading to the final end product, may therefore be massive--illustrated by the thirteen volumes of selected and published documentation (nearly twelve thousand pages) on the Paris Peace Conference following World War I and the mass of papers pertaining to the negotiation of treaties dealing with the law of the seas since World War II--and much of the material may be inconsequential, ineffective, unproductive, or even trivial. Some of the documentation may not materially influence the process, and some may raise alternatives that are never forcefully advocated or conscientiously considered. A key issue involved in appraising the interrelation of such a mass of documentation, so far as depth of documentary and information penetration is concerned, centers on the realistic determination of a cutoff line below which materials--even those of a preliminary end-product nature during the preparatory and negotiatory stages--may not be automatically put into the public domain at an early date.

Assuming that not all documentation is expected to be systematically published, or even to be made publicly available immediately, discretion respecting selection must be exercised. This determination must bridge four sets of factors, namely, recency, the degree of "end-productness" of the documentation, the level of penetration into the foreign relations process (including policy making, document devisement, intragovernmental and international discussion, and negotiation), and the relationship of revelation to the needs of both public knowledge and national expediency. Decision on the drawing of a rational dividing line within the parameters of these demands and needs is far from simple. Furthermore, it must take into account the relations of the United States with other governments, which are likely to be sensitive to, if not critical of, the revelation by the United States of their policies, roles, and concessions without their consent, and it must protect pending negotiations that may be compromised or otherwise disaffected by premature disclosure of too great a depth.

Moreover, the definitive compilation and total immediate informational and documentary revelation may not really be indispensable to the establishment of essential truth. The true account, or a system of published documentation that enables its user to project an accurate chronicle of the verities, may be more vital than early definitive revelation, and it may be singularly preferable to complete secrecy. The prime difficulty is to define reasonable, workable, and acceptable criteria for fixing the demarcation line that satisfies the needs, not only of scholarly researchers, the press, and the public, but of the government, yet avoids implications of unessential secretiveness and appellations of incredibility. A secondary difficulty is the establishment of a general acceptance of the fact that neither the information media (given their biases and special interests), nor the scholars (given theirs), nor the public at large (given its), is necessarily better qualified than the government to fix such delineations in the interests of both the people and the polity. In short, in this regard the best system is bound to be imperfect, and the resolution of the problem is essentially one of prescribing operational principles as liberally as is reasonable and implementing them in as generous as well as realistic a fashion as possible.

CLASSIFICATION OF INFORMATION AND DOCUMENTATION

Additionally, it is necessary to understand the practice and problem of security "classification" and other methods of designating the treatment of information and documents, that directly affect the availability of foreign relations resources. In essence, a document is classified--and thereby restricted to use only by those who are authorized access to it--because of the information it contains. Not all information incorporated in a document may in and of itself be classified, but it becomes classified by virtue of embodiment within an instrument that contains some classified content. Different portions of the information included in a single document may warrant varying degrees or levels of classification, and in the past, the document as a whole has usually been ascribed the classification of the most highly classified information it contains.

Sometimes, however, a document is classified, not particularly because of the information contained therein, but simply because it reflects the intention at the time of withholding from the public domain the very existence of the document. Ventures in policy initiation prior to determination, policy formulation during the decision-making process, and diplomatic negotiation prior to reaching international understanding and agreement, together with the information and documents relating to them, are usually regarded by governments as being privileged and currently unavailable.

Confidential information and documentation are normally sought to be safeguarded by what is broadly termed "security classification." More precisely, in the United States they are reserved or vouchsafed by executive order when they require protection in the interest of "national security." In 1954, the attorney general advised the Department of State that defense classifications may be interpreted "to include the safeguarding of information and material" developed in the course of the conduct of foreign affairs "whenever it appears that the effect of the unauthorized disclosure of such information or material upon international relations or upon policies being pursued through diplomatic channels could result in serious damage to the Nation" (Department of State, *Foreign Affairs Manual*, vol. 5, 1969, sec. 911.2). This extended the applicability of classification considerably beyond strictly defined security or defense considerations, and it was confirmed by Executive Orders 11652 in 1972, 12065 in 1978, and 12356 in 1982. The Freedom of Information Act of 1966, discussed later, also recognized the necessity for the government to withhold from the public certain categories of information and records, including, but not restricted to, those whose disclosure would result in a "clearly unwarranted invasion of personal privacy" or would "violate a privileged relationship."

To systematize current practice concerning the classification of information and records for national security reasons, on March 8, 1972, President Nixon issued Executive Order 11652, establishing new rules for both classification and declassification of government documents. Based on a fourteen-month review, this was designed "to lift the veil of secrecy which now enshrouds" too many official papers and to reduce abuses of withholding information and documents from the public. This executive order established tighter rules for classification, reduced classifying authority, provided procedures and time limits for downgrading and declassification, specified sanctions for overclassification, and created a method for monitoring the new system. For President Nixon's comments, see Document 61. Subsequently, these rules were revised and superseded by Executive Order 12065, issued by President Carter on June 28, 1978, and by Executive Order 12356, promulgated by President Reagan on April 2, 1982. (See *Papers of Presidents: Nixon*, 1972, 401-6; *Carter*, 1978, I, 1194-1208; and *Reagan*, 1982, I, 411-21.)

As stipulated in these directives, the three primary security classification categories, in descending order, are designated "top secret," "secret," and "confidential," which the Executive Order 12356 of 1982 defined as follows:

"Top Secret" shall be applied to information, the unauthorized disclosure of which reasonably could be expected to cause exceptionally grave damage to the national security.

"Secret" shall be applied to information, the unauthorized disclosure of which reasonably could be expected to cause serious damage to the national security.

"Confidential" shall be applied to information, the unauthorized disclosure of which reasonably could be expected to cause damage to the national security.

These categories were essentially the same in the executive orders for 1972 and 1978.

Other materials are nonclassified, but they are not formally designated "unclassified" except in certain specific cases. Some years ago, the lowest-ranking classification category, designated "restricted", was eliminated, but the appellation "limited official use" was created to identify nonclassified information that required physical protection comparable to that given confidential material in order to safeguard it from unauthorized access. This administrative control designation, as it was called, was applied by the Department of State to information received through privileged sources; specific references to the contents of diplomatic pouches; certain personnel, medical, investigative, commercial, and financial records; and other similar material. Another such administrative designation--"official use only"--applied where operational principles warranted more expeditious transmission, wider distribution, and less secure storage. Under the 1978 and 1982 executive orders, such designations may no longer be employed to identify classified information.

However, additional systems of designation have been designed to limit access and distribution, to assign attention priorities, and for other reasons. For example, the characterization "eyes only" restricts distribution of documents, regardless of security classification, to a specially delimited group of officials. Priority designations for purposes of decision and action have also been employed by the Department of State. In ascending order of urgency, they are "routine," "priority," "immediate," and "flash." Such designations as "limited distribution," "special handling," and "NIACT" (for night action, requiring immediate action, day or night) have also been utilized, and at the highest levels, documents are sometimes denominated "personal" and "private."

Admittedly unique, the World War II communications between President Roosevelt, Prime Minister Churchill, and Premier Stalin bore some interesting designations. Because of their content, it may be presumed that utmost security precautions were maintained in their preparation, transmission, and custody. Most of them were marked "personal" and either "secret" or "top secret," a good many were labeled "urgent" or "priority," and occasionally they were regarded as being "private." One message of Prime Minister Churchill to Premier Stalin in 1945 even carried the distinction of being denominated "personal, most secret, and quite private."

Information, and a document based thereon, that is "in confidence," needs to be distinguished from that which is "confidential" or otherwise restricted for security reasons under the established classification system. Information that is held to be in confidence need not necessarily involve security or defense constraints but simply evidences that a particular matter or document is not to be publicized at the moment or that, while the information is not intended to be withheld, its source is not to be revealed or that it is otherwise deemed to be "privileged." This is especially important in the field of diplomacy, because much documentation involves foreign governments to which the American security classification and the release and publication systems do not apply, and which are entitled to expect their trust and confidence to be maintained. This imbues such diplomatic documents with a unique quality, which is recognized in the executive orders.

A number of difficulties flow from the nature and operation of the classification system. Fundamental is the practice of employing a single set of designations founded largely on national security requirements for classification purposes rather than separate sets of firm and well-structured designations for this and other purposes, including the "in confidence," "limited official use," raw intelligence documentation, and other categories. Inasmuch as the objectives, the intentions, and the degree of willingness to frame and attribute the information and the documents containing it vary, control of, and flow into, the public domain might best be managed and liberalized by separate sets of designations and procedures.   In other words, the lowering or declassification of foreign relations materials (which were highly classified initially to prevent undermining the government's international negotiating posture rather than to protect the physical security of the nation) might be facilitated if they bore a different set of classification designations.   For example, a treaty draft might be classified, not because revelation would threaten U.S. security, but merely to maintain its confidentiality during the bargaining process.   A special classification designation for such documents might render reclassification and declassification easier if the system were not related to national security considerations.

A second problem is the devisement of methods for distinguishing levels of classification or other confidentiality distinctions for segments of information and documents in order to avoid overrestricting those portions to which the higher levels of classification need not apply.   Overclassification results from an attitude of resolving doubt in favor of classification at the highest requisite or justifiable level (i.e., "when in doubt--classify"), from the practice of classifying an entire document in accordance with the most highly classified information within it even though much of the content could be unclassified and in some cases may already be in the public domain, and from the disposition to classify a complete package of documents, an extensive compilation, or a comprehensive account in accordance with its most highly classified component. The 1978 executive order introduced the principle of identifying those portions of documents that are classified.

To induce greater restraint in classification practices, a number of additional reforms were introduced in the executive orders of the 1970's and 1980's.   For example, to reduce the amount of material that may be classified, the number of executive departments and agencies authorized to employ classification designations and the number of individual officials within these agencies who are empowered to classify documents and information were circumscribed.   The burden of proof was reversed, requiring that each official be held personally accountable for the propriety of the classifications, authorizing administrative sanctions against such officials for repeated abuses, and empowering the National Security Council to provide overall policy direction for the program and a special administrative agency to monitor the implementation of the rules.

Much overclassification also has resulted from the condition that, while particular information and documents may be properly classified initially, in the course of time--and in certain cases this may actually be very short--the need for maintaining the original classification, or to continue any clas-sification at all, may cease to exist.   Resolution of this problem requires either an automatic system of reclassification-declassification, by which designations are arbitrarily reduced or eliminated entirely on a fixed time schedule, or a system of wholesale, periodic review and reclassification-declassification in accordance with explicit guidelines.   A third possibility is a system of initial double classification under which the classifier ascribes two designations, the first of which has a time limit affixed, following which the document automatically permutes to a lower classification or becomes unclassified. Although such methods appear to be reasonable and manageable, and while each has its exponents, each also is fraught with difficulties and disadvantages.

All of these procedures have been used by the United States for its foreign relations documentation. Double or multiple classification and selective declassification are implied, so that documents and materials may be downgraded or declassified in advance or by overt reclassification by the agency applying the original classification. In addition, a wholesale and automatic schedule of downgrading and declassification is prescribed. Under the arrangement of the 1972 executive order, "confidential" material became automatically declassified at the end of six years; "secret" documents were required to be automatically downgraded to "confidential" at the end of the second full calendar year and declassified in eight years; and "top secret" information and material were required to be downgraded to "secret" in two years, to "confidential" in the fourth year, and to be declassified at the end of ten years. The 1978 executive order further liberalized the process, providing that each classified document would be ascribed a date for its automatic declassification that could not exceed six years, although it could be downgraded or declassified at an earlier date. The 1982 executive order generalized rules concerning duration, declassification, and downgrading as well as procedures for mandatory review for declassification, but it reconfirmed earlier executive orders respecting automatic review and action. It is noteworthy, however, that certain categories of information and documentation are exempted from this arrangement, such as materials furnished by, or requiring confidentiality with, foreign governments and international organizations and those specifically protected by U.S. statute.

A final classification problem results simply from the fact that the government itself is responsible for classification and declassification. In the past, it has tended to pursue a conservative, protective, and reluctant attitude toward maximal classification. Presumably, the changes instituted in the 1970's and 1980's were intended to overcome this difficulty, to reduce classification both quantitatively and qualitatively, and to establish a systematic method of declassification. Essential caveats, such as exemptions to the automatic declassification schedule, however, leave considerable room for continued classification. An ultimate safeguard exists in the requirement for automatic review of information and documentation, with declassification at the end of twenty years, noted later, and in the application of this principle beyond the Department of State to other executive agencies, thereby rendering it universally applicable for U.S. government documentation.

FREEDOM OF INFORMATION ACT

Paralleling the liberalizing executive orders of the 1970's and 1980's, the Freedom of Information Act, which became effective in 1967, provided a special mechanism for rendering individual documents publicly available pursuant to specific request. This enactment requires that the documents sought be easily identifiable and that the Department of State or other responsible agency might deny the request if the documents remain classified or fall into certain exempted categories. The act was not intended to produce the release of large batches of documents, but it does enable the researcher to obtain copies of particular, readily identifiable documents at nominal cost. When a classified document is requested under the Freedom of Information Act, its classification status is reviewed to determine whether the request can be accommodated. Individual documents, which may not be published by the Department of State, may thus be made available to the researcher long before departmental files are opened to public use or are transferred to the National Archives.

Under this law, as amended in 1974, The Department of State and other agencies are required to publicize descriptions of their organization and to make available for public inspection and copying statements of policy, administrative staff manuals and instructions, specific requested documents, and other papers. Exceptions include classified information and materials; interagency and intraagency memorandums or letters that by law would not be available to parties in litigation; personnel, medical, and other records that constitute an invasion of privacy; and information specifically exempted from disclosure by statute, such as tax returns and patent applications. (See P.L. 89-554, 80 *Statutes at Large* 383, and P.L. 93-502, 88 *Statutes at Large* 1501, in 5 *U.S. Code,* 1982, section 552. For commentary on the attorney general's guidelines issued in May, 1981--replacing those issued in 1977--which permitted each federal agency to develop its own release arrangements, see *Historic Documents,* 1981, pp. 393-400.)

DOCUMENTATION INVOLVING FOREIGN GOVERNMENTS

So far as foreign relations are concerned, a final distinction must be drawn between information and documents that flow from and directly concern only the United States as compared with those that implicate a foreign government--as initiator, sender, recipient, commentator, or negotiating party. In keeping with historical practice, the Department of State cannot, on its own authority and without violating the mutuality of confidence and undermining its international reliability and credibility, reveal or publish information or documents that directly involve foreign powers. Sometimes, while it may be anxious to publish and may actually compile and prepare resulting materials for the press, the Department of State must stand by awaiting acquiescence from abroad, and securing such "clearance" may be delicate and time consuming.

A unilateral policy statement, a telegram from the Department of State to the head of an American diplomatic mission abroad, a national treaty draft, a report to Washington from a field mission, and the like are publishable without foreign approval. On the other hand, unpublished incoming messages from the foreign ministries of other countries, memoranda of discussions or negotiations with foreign emissaries, exchanges of views and documentary comments thereon, inquiries to the United States and foreign responses to American queries, and similar documentation involving other countries, according to the rules of the game, may be published by the United States only with the consent of the specific foreign governments concerned.

Even though the Department of State has published and currently publishes such documentation more systematically, in greater overall depth, and more expeditiously than other powers, care is exercised not to violate this arrangement. In part, this accounts for the delay of some of its publication. It is axiomatic that a government that rapidly publishes diplomatic documentation involving another country without clearance either has no such understood gentlemen's agreement with the other country (that, in fact, it is an adversary, if not an enemy) or, more probably, it publishes not so much to inform its own public as to gain international propaganda advantage.

AVAILABILITY OF UNPUBLISHED FOREIGN RELATIONS INFORMATION AND DOCUMENTATION

Unpublished foreign relations information and documentation are basically of two types: information and materials that are available, though unpublished, and those that are classified or otherwise unavailable. The mass of Department of State records and documents are located in the department and in the National Archives and their depositories, and they fall into two basic groupings, the "open" and the "closed" categories.

Under an earlier traditional "thirty-year rule," the documents remained under Department of State control for thirty years and generally were then transferred to the National Archives, where they became available to the public. Foreign relations records physically located in the Department of State and American missions abroad were closed to en masse access by nonofficial users in advance of the publication of the official diplomatic documentation of the United States, titled *Foreign Relations of the United States,* which is discussed in the next section. The beginning date of the closed period was advanced automatically as the annual *Foreign Relations* volumes were released.

These practices were changed under the 1978 twenty-year rule and the Freedom of Information Act. Except for records involving foreign governments --the availability of which remain under the earlier thirty-year rule-- availability of documentation now is less related to the publication of *Foreign Relations* and the transfer of records to the National Archives. Such transfers still tend to be made at about thirty years and involve blocs of documentation. The preponderance of such foreign relations documentation held by the National Archives is publicly available. However, much of that in the Department of State is also obtainable under Freedom of Information Act procedures, but because of physical access problems, it is not readily accessible to massive public usage.

Under the Freedom of Information Act, copies of identifiable, unclassified foreign relations records, even within the twenty-year "closed" period, may be obtained by the outsider (although the requester may not personally go through the files). This must be done in accordance with a fixed request and search procedure and at the requester's cost in keeping with a prescribed schedule of fees for search, true copy certification, and reproduction. Consequently, substantial quantities of materials are available during this "closed" period, and the executive orders of 1978 and 1982 specifically authorize the granting of conditional access even to certain classified information for historical research purposes.

At times, special releases of documentation may hasten this process. For example, on January 21, 1972, the Department of State announced the en bloc declassification and opening of its foreign relations records for the years 1942 to 1945, through the World War II period. Inasmuch as the British government took similar action for its records, the department also opened most of its files of formerly classified papers of British origin for those years.

In short, established American procedure provides an automatic method for opening the mass of U.S. foreign relations documentary materials to public scrutiny and usage. By comparison with other governments, this is one of the most liberal and systematized arrangements. According to a 1976 report of the Department of State, of approximately 120 countries surveyed, the diplomatic records of more than half were found to be largely inaccessible. Some twenty specifically prohibited public access or made no provision for the availability of their records, and nearly thirty governments stipulated no established policy regarding the matter, which means that their documents could be assumed not to be public. It is possible, however, that under appropriate circumstances, bona fide researchers might obtain access for limited purposes under specified restrictions, and then most likely only with respect to nonsensitive matters. An additional twenty-two governments had no fixed policy on the matter other than to stipulate that the foreign ministry, the national archives, or some other agency could authorize specific individuals to use particular documents on a limited basis.

The largest single category consisted of those forty-seven governments that fixed particular dates for the opening of their records. Two forms of this arrangement were employed, namely, that by which documents were opened automatically at the end of a prescribed number of years, and that which fixed a specific date as the dividing point, with records subsequent to these dates not being available. Sixteen governments used the basic fifty-year period for the opening of their diplomatic archives, which appeared to be the most common but declining practice for automatic opening of foreign relations archives. Nine governments used the thirty-year arrangement. Aside from the United States, which commenced this practice in the 1920's, these included Great Britain, which changed from fifty to thirty years in 1968, and Australia, Ghana, Guyana, India, Israel, Peru, and Tanzania. Others varied from one hundred years (the Vatican) to twenty-five and even as low as twenty years. Only a small number of governments used the fixed cutoff date arrangement. For example, the records of Portugal were open to inspection prior to 1851, Spain used the year 1900, Luxembourg used 1914, Thailand used 1932, and several states employed dates relating to World War II, including Germany and Japan, whose records were generally closed after 1945. (See Office of the Historian, Department of State, *Public Availability of Diplomatic Archives,* 1976.)

Analysis of comparative governmental practices also reveals that important distinctions are made, not only between classified and unclassified documents, but as to whether the researcher is a national or a foreigner, whether bona fide research is involved or simply general availability to the public, and among open, restricted, and closed periods. Availability normally is freer when the documents are under the control of the national archives of a country than when they are in the foreign ministry.

An earlier report of the Department of State (*Public Availability of Diplomatic Archives in the United States and Certain Foreign Countries,* 1961), surveyed the practices of seventy-five foreign governments with respect to the systematic serial publication of their diplomatic papers. It reveals that at the time no country other than the United States had a comparable ongoing, long-range, and comprehensive publication program for its foreign relations documentation. As a matter of fact, two-thirds had no publication system or plans whatsoever. Some governments undertook the publication on a regularized basis of only their treaties, agreements, laws, and ordinances. A few issued selected diplomatic papers in annual foreign ministry reports or periodical bulletins of various types, a half-dozen had published extensive collections for limited earlier periods or for specific situations, such as World War I, and some governments contributed to the "rainbow books"--usually referred to as "white papers" despite the color of their jackets.

FOREIGN RELATIONS OF THE UNITED STATES SERIES

To summarize U.S. practice, foreign relations documentation generally is declassified and made publicly available in twenty years or less. In addition, as documents are published in the *Foreign Relations* series, not only are they declassified and entered into the public domain on a regularized basis, but the bulk raw materials from which they are taken become available as they are transferred to the National Archives.

Nevertheless, a few types of documents remain unpublished, whether they bear security classification or not. The preface to the *Foreign Relations* volumes indicates that certain categories of materials may be omitted in order to avoid publication of matters that would tend to impede current diplomatic negotiations or other official business, to condense the record and avoid repetition of unnecessary details, to preserve the confidence reposed in the Department of State by individuals and foreign governments, to avoid giving needless offense to other nationalities or individuals, and to eliminate personal opinions presented in dispatches and not acted upon by the Department of State (except that, in connection with major decisions, it is intended, where possible, to show the alternatives presented to the department before decisions are made).

In preparing the volumes of *Foreign Relations* for publication, the Department of State refers to appropriate policy officers of the department and to other government agencies those papers that require policy clearance--which means declassification if necessary--and it refers to individual foreign governments requests for permission to print as part of the diplomatic documentation those previously unpublished documents that were initiated by such governments. Similarly, foreign relations records originated by a foreign government or another agency of the United States government, and not yet published or opened to access by that government or agency, are not made publicly available by the Department of State without the consent of the government or agency concerned.

Serious difficulties are encountered in obtaining such consent to publication, and the Department of State has been plagued by delays in gaining requisite clearances. Moreover, in the post-World War II period, greater clearance difficulty is encountered with respect to special types of records, such as those involving intelligence matters, the National Security Council, and crisis diplomacy. Whereas refined intelligence reports may, in the course of time, be made available or published, it is unlikely that the bulk of raw intelligence materials, which may reveal precise intelligence sources, agents, or methods, will flow freely into the public domain. These were explicitly reserved by the executive order of 1972, and the 1978 directive broadened this to provide that information concerning "intelligence activities, sources or methods" could remain classified if it "continues to meet the classification requirements . . . despite the passage of time."

Special problems characterize the documents of the National Security Council. By their very nature, they may be deemed to require more protracted confidentiality because of the matters to which they pertain, because many are preliminary to decision making, and because many relate to contingency considerations which never materialize so that they address probabilities or possibilities, often inchoate, the revelation of which may be deemed detrimental to United States interests and diplomacy. Assurance of early publication might very well inhibit the very documentation of such considerations. In addition, records of the National Security Council introduce a unique problem in that, technically, clearance is required both of the individual officials or agencies represented in its deliberations and of the council, as a collective interdepartmental agency. This is tantamount to requiring multiple clearance, and at any given moment the current National Security Council is likely to be reluctant to authorize publication or access to its highly classified documentation.

This special problem within the broader issue of the availability and publication of foreign relations materials needs to be faced, and a formula needs to be generated for releasing this important category of documentation. It is clear, however, that its resolution lies beyond the authority simply of the Department of State. Recognizing this, President Nixon instructed, not only the National Security Council, but the Central Intelligence Agency and the Defense Department, to cooperate in expediting the publication by the Department of State of the *Foreign Relations* series on a twenty-year cycle, and the declassification rules of the 1970's and 1980's may help to ameliorate this problem. As a consequence, many of these volumes contain selected National Security Council documents and reports on its sessions, as well as national intelligence estimates.

Certain categories of documents may remain unavailable indefinitely, beyond the commencement of the open period. Examples include specific types of personnel and medical records, which are withheld because they contain private or personal information which, if disclosed, would amount to an invasion of the privacy of the persons concerned, and investigative records, because they are compiled for the enforcement of law or in preparation of government litigation and adjudicative proceedings. These remain unavailable to the public even if transferred to the National Archives.

In the past, telegrams and cryptographic information were given special protection by government regulations, but this was changed in 1978. After World War II, under Executive Order 10501 of 1953, classified telegrams were not to be referred to, paraphrased, downgraded, declassified, or disseminated, except in accordance with prescribed controls issued by the head of the originating government agency. Furthermore, classified telegrams transmitted over cryptographic systems were required to be handled in accordance with the regulations of the transmitting agency. Executive Order 11652 of 1972 continued to exempt cryptographic information and materials from the revised classification system. This arrangement created an exceptional problem, because these restrictions were patently designed to protect the system of communications rather than the information they contained. As a result, while the information itself could be unclassified or eventually declassified, the nature of the original documentary form in which it was contained could prevent its entering the public domain unless it was converted into some other documentary or oral form or unless security ceased to be essential to its telegraphic or cryptographic form. This exemption was omitted in the 1978 and 1982 executive orders.

The foreign relations documentation that remains unavailable and unpublished in the long run is quantitatively small but qualitatively may range from the important to the unimportant for purposes of projecting or determining the essential truth. Restrictions flow from obvious necessity, such as specific covert intelligence sources or clearance by foreign governments of their communications, to problems of interpreting the rules, such as determining which revelation would impede current negotiations, would give needless offense to other nations, would constitute an invasion of personal privacy, or would violate trust reposed in the United States by a foreign government. Nevertheless, the bulk of foreign relations documents enter the public domain eventually--automatically after twenty years or, in the case of documents involving foreign governments, after thirty years. They may become accessible earlier, as they are automatically or systematically declassified, are published in *Foreign Relations* and other periodic and ad hoc publications, or made available on a limited basis for bona fide research in other ways, or if they are final end products or otherwise unclassified, they may become public at a still earlier date.

The specific aspects of the problem of revelation that appear to have been most seriously questioned--aside from the application of the security classification system--were the fixed-time rule and the delay in publishing the *Foreign Relations* volumes. Proposals to modify the traditional thirty-year rule have been freely made, ranging from contentions that all confidentiality should be eliminated, to those which propose advancing the opening date on the basis of historical events, to those continuing the automatic aspect but shortening the number of years to twenty (as in the 1978 executive order), fifteen, or even eight (to cover a presidential administration of two terms). Serious consideration needs to be given to both the criteria and the rationale on which any availability or publication program is based, and such determination would need to be founded on a careful analysis and appreciation of all factors and interests involved. The changes instituted in the 1970's and 1980's reflect a determined effort to liberalize documentary availability.

Additional advantage to the researcher would be gained from advancing the publication schedule of the *Foreign Relations* series. Such publication essentially constitutes a planned process of surveying massive documentary resources and putting extensive portions of them into the public domain on a systematic and liberal basis, while simultaneously placing the residuum of the documentary resources from which they are extracted generally into the available though unpublished category. In principle, the fundamental difficulties with this publication venture are fourfold: the growing mass of documentary materials to be examined, the quantity of documents to be published in the series, the depth to which they penetrate, and the time lag between publication and the date to which they pertain. In practice, the problem is one of funds, personnel to handle the assignment, the cost of publication, and the problem of expediting clearance.

The mass of documentation of the Department of State has increased substantially by comparison with earlier times. In 1980, to illustrate, the total quantity of departmental official resources amounted to approximately 275,000 cubic feet of documentation. Of this immense reservoir, nearly 125,000 cubic feet of records were found in the Department of State, including its central files and its operational and staff bureaus and offices, together with the overseas diplomatic and consular missions and posts. Because they were not archivally refined, duplication existed. State Department records, it has been estimated, increase by an average of from 5 to 10 percent each year. It is a simple matter of arithmetic to conclude, therefore, that some 2,000 to 3,000 cubic feet of such unrefined documentation need to be surveyed per year in order to produce the annual contribution to the *Foreign Relations* series.

Initially, commencing in the 1860's, one or two volumes of *Foreign Relations* per year sufficed for the important documentation concerning all countries and issues. Beginning with 1932, five or more volumes were needed for each year, and for the years since World War II, this increased to from eight to eleven volumes per year. A few years ago, the Department of State concluded that it would be called upon to produce a published, high-quality collection of ten volumes per year, each averaging one thousand pages--or one hundred volumes consisting of one hundred thousand pages per decade. Subsequently, this goal was reduced to some six to nine volumes per year, and, more recently, because of increasing costs, it has been suggested that this quota be reduced still further. Beginning with the volumes for the 1950's, volumes cover three-year periods rather than single years, with some 15 to 25 volumes for each three-year period.

On the matter of the depth of penetration, it need only be added that the deeper the penetration, particularly in the policy-making function (as distinct from end-product policy and policy implementation), together with the closer to currency, the more difficult it is to obtain requisite publication clearances-- inside the department, from other United States agencies, and from foreign governments. On the other hand, the shallower the penetration, the less complete will inclusion be. Compromise between this factor of depth of penetration and currency of publication, therefore, is essential, and the potential user can scarcely have it both ways. The choice is between the earlier, less inclusive compilation, or one which, while more definitive, is also more delayed.

When *Foreign Relations* was first published, each volume was issued shortly after the year to which it pertained. The lag was only a year or two, but this gradually eroded, to a fifteen-year delay by the end of World War I, to twenty years by 1960, and, by the early 1970's, it exceeded twenty-five years, and the prospects of preventing this delayed production schedule from slipping even more appeared murky. In 1962, the Secretary of State officially set the publication time lapse at twenty years, except in exceptional circumstances, but this schedule was not maintained, in part because of the size of the documentary resources and the clearance problem, but also because of budgetary and personnel restrictions. In March 1972, President Nixon issued directives to the Secretary of State and the heads of other relevant agencies to cooperate in returning to the twenty-year standard, but this also proved to be optimistic (see *Papers of Presidents: Nixon,* 1972, pp. 406-8). For President Nixon's comments, see Document 62.

Success in achieving and maintaining this rate of production would depend upon an enlightened attitude respecting the role and value of the published *Foreign Relations* series, adequate staffing for the task, and accommodation for the exigencies of depth of penetration and clearance. A supplementary way of helping to reduce the degree of confidentiality would be to extend the publication of ad hoc studies and special documentary compilations, including selected case studies of both crisis situations and a broad spectrum of other functional and areal matters, such as more reports on important international conferences, reports on participation in international organizations (in addition to the United Nations), analyses of the diplomatic function, and various occasional studies and other materials.

To summarize, despite existing shortcomings, the American venture offers a sophisticated, high-quality, carefully managed, sagacious, increasingly liberalized, and relatively inexpensive system of diplomatic information and documentary revelation and publication. It has been well tested over the years --since the eighteenth century for legislation and treaties, since World War II for presidential papers, and for more than a century and a quarter in the case of the *Foreign Relations* series--and has produced a library of convenient, basic diplomatic sources and resources. Problems of classification, fixing delineations for depth of penetration into the national policy-making process and for the degree of "end-productness" of documentation to be released into the public domain, and compromise between the relatively comprehensive as against the less definitive though earlier special compilations and studies are not insuperable, and pragmatic solutions can be found. This would go a long way to bridge the gap between the essential truth now and the definitive truth later and to satisfy both the legitimate needs of the government and the information and resource requirements of the citizenry.

1

Introduction

In any event he [the policy maker] knows that an idea is not a policy and that the transformation of an idea into a policy is frequently an exhausting and frustrating process. He is aware of the difference between a conclusion and a decision . . . the policy officer must move from conclusion to decision and must be prepared to live with the results. . . . the white heat of responsibility is upon him and he cannot escape it, however strenuously he tries.

Dean Rusk
Address, February 20, 1961

Throughout the world today America is respected. This is partly because we have entered a new era of initiative in American foreign policy, and the world's leaders and its people have seen the results. But it is also because the world has come to know America. It knows we are a nation of peaceful intentions, of honorable purposes, true to our commitments. We are respected because . . . we have met the responsibilities of a great and free nation. We have not retreated from the world. We have not betrayed our allies. We have not fallen into the foolish illusion that we could somehow build a wall around America, here to enjoy our comforts, oblivious to the cries or threats of others. We have maintained our strength.

Richard Nixon
Radio address, White House, November 4, 1972

Major developments in world affairs since World War II required significant changes in American foreign relations. The United States emerged as a super-power, renounced its former isolationism, assumed responsibility as a world leader, and promoted international cooperation and integration--globally in creating the United Nations system and regionally in formalizing and expanding the inter-American system and launching the Atlantic Union. It also led in promoting interdependence and widespread multilateralism. And, beginning in the 1940's, the United States participated in escalating the status of diplomacy to the ministerial and summit levels, so that presidential personal communications (both written and telephonic), presidential visits and tours abroad, summit visits to this country, and summit conferences and meetings--as well as those of the Secretary of State with other foreign ministers--have become traditional.

Other major postwar changes that affect American foreign policy include the proliferation of relations--of participants, the subjects of concern, negotiations, and resulting legislation, treaties, and agreements. Decolonization, commencing with the granting of independence to the Philippines in 1946, resulted in tripling the size of the community of nations, requiring the devisement of policy for dealing with more than 100 new states, especially in Africa, Asia and the Pacific, and the Caribbean.

The subjects of policy concern also expanded geometrically in quantity and scope. Whereas previously the primary areas of policy development were devoted to such matters as national security, boundaries, recognition, diplomatic and consular representation, navigation and shipping, customs, and the devisement of international law governing maritime jurisdiction, war, neutrality, and the pacific settlement of disputes, together with extradition and the international transmission of mails, during the postwar decades the scope of these topics was extended to virtually every subject in which the United States and other nations have any conceivable interest.

These now range from the refinement of the law of the sea and the continental shelf, space exploration and jurisdiction, and biological, chemical, and nuclear weapons and missiles to the conservation of polar bears, seals, and whales; from alliances and collective defense commitments to the protection of endangered species and cultural artifacts; from the international management of pollution, the environment, narcotic drugs, aerial hijacking, and international terrorism to a variety of specific commodity and double taxation arrangements; from postal, telecommunications, and customs affairs to those concerned with automotive traffic, hydrography, and even epizootics; and from the establishment of international organizations that deal with agriculture, civil aviation, education, health, labor, loans and currency exchange, maritime, meteorological, national defense, and other matters to the treatment of tourism, refugees, and weights and measures. Adding to these the Marshall Plan and the European Recovery Program; economic, military, technical, and humanitarian assistance; information offices and the Peace Corps; denuclearization, arms control and reduction, and the settlement of international crises, the list of policy concerns is virtually endless.

Another factor that affected foreign relations during the second half of the twentieth century is the Cold War, pitting the United States against the Soviet Union--the Free World against the Communist bloc--resulting in East-West conflict, a series of confrontations, the devisement of the containment policy, bilateral and multilateral defense pacts, and eventually attempts to generate detente and rapprochement. Moreover, as a result of the emergence of many new states, coupled with their desire to remain uninvolved in the East-West conflict and to extend their collective power in the international arena in order to promote their development and to achieve a "new international economic order" and a global redistribution of economic wealth, new problems in Third

World or North-South relations confronted the United States.

Finally, as United States participation in world affairs proliferated, the disparity between domestic and foreign policy diminished. Whereas previously policies, laws, and agencies dealt with either internal or external affairs, many of these distinctions evanesced. Consequently, the making and implementation of foreign policy now involves, not only the President, Congress, and the Department of State, but the Defense, Treasury, and most other departments, the intelligence community, and the foreign assistance, information, and other agencies, some of which are represented abroad by their own attaches and agents. This proliferation generated serious problems of policy coordination and control within and among these agencies both in Washington and abroad.

Turning to the future, as the United States approaches the twenty-first century, the international environment is likely to be influenced by recurring and new challenges and opportunities. The most obvious include: the creation of a few additional states and the eruption of new crises, as well as the emergence of democracy in Eastern Europe and elsewhere, globalization of the world economy, increased emphasis on the extension of human rights, exploration and utilization of the deep seas and outer space, amplification of the endeavor to reduce pollution and improve the environment, intensification of technological developments and modernization of peoples and their governments, advancement of global communications facilities, utilization of multilateral diplomatic forums, resort to international cooperative processes and the development of international law, and reliance upon ministerial and summit diplomacy.

Moreover, during the 1990's, if the superpowers overcome their security psychosis and Communist expansion diminishes, East-West relations will improve, confrontation will be superseded by more cooperative negotiation, conventional military establishments in Europe will be reduced to purely defensive forces, and progress will be made in reducing nuclear arsenals.

FOREIGN POLICY COMPLEX

To comprehend the complexity of American foreign relations, it is necessary to appreciate the nature and functioning of "foreign policy." It must be distinguished from such broader concepts as "foreign affairs," "international politics," and the "foreign policy process." The latter consists of three elements --the making of foreign policy, the policy made, and the execution of policy. Two of these components--the formulation and implementation of policy--are often combined as the "conduct of foreign affairs," which, together with "diplomacy," need to be differentiated conceptualistically from the essence of policy.

Foreign policy also is closely related to, but distinguishable from, other primary factors in the foreign relations cosmography. Aside from values and ideals, these embrace national interests, vital interests, fundamental goals, and concrete implementable objectives. Ideals, generally regarded as models of perfection or excellence or as ultimate aims, may be articulated as general national goals, or they may be more amorphous and unachievable and therefore may not be operationalizable as concrete policy objectives and may be unrealistic. Interests are usually defined as standards, criteria, determinants, or concerns, and goals and objectives are the ends sought by the nation. Policies, on the other hand, constitute the "courses of action" or the means to achieve the country's goals and objectives in accordance with its interests. These fundamental constituents, as well as national influence, power and capability, and the devisement of national strategies, essential to implement policies, are defined and illustrated with documentation in Chapters 2 and 3. For a comprehensive analysis of the conceptualization of these components, see Elmer Plischke, *Foreign Relations: Analysis of Its Anatomy* (Westport, Connecticut: Greenwood Press, 1988).

Certain characteristics and special features of foreign policy also need to be understood. Much that is posed or regarded as foreign policy--by statesmen, other practitioners, and publicists--really represents the prescription of aspirations, the defining of ideals and values, and the promulgation of interests, goals, and objectives. Often they are framed as human and national hopes, desires, ambitions, aims, or expectations. These are largely ends sought, whereas the policies consist of operationalized positions, principles, plans, and programs.

It will be noted that, in practice, a great many "policy documents" are essentially declarations of ends sought. Only when these are transmuted into concrete means of achievement, such as the specification of actionable legislation, treaties, declarations, directives, orders, or instructions, do they embody or reflect policy. For example, many of the documents included in this volume that deal with such matters as peace, national security, or human rights articulate American goals and objectives. However, only when they are embodied in specific truces, peace treaties, peaceful settlement commitments (that provide for mediation, conciliation, arbitration, or adjudication), alliances and collective defense pacts, and human rights declarations and conventions, do they formally evidence genuine foreign policies.

Some policies, frequently and extensively reiterated, are elevated to the status of fundamental policy principles, precepts, and rules--sometimes referred to as the tenets or pillars of policy. These may be exemplified by self-preservation, self-determination, freedom of the seas, free trade, international stability, and collective cooperation. In other cases, documents present guidelines to, fundamentals or essentials of, or prerequisites or requisites for policy.

A distinction is drawn between foreign policy that is initiatory and that which is reactive. As it may be contended that cause may produce an effect, which then becomes the cause for subsequent effect, resulting in a viable progression, so does a policy action that evokes a reaction, which then becomes an action that produces another reaction, and so on. Thus, if our government institutes a policy and other countries react by generating compensating or countervailing policies of their own, the United States may view these responses as actions to which it needs to react, launching the next stage of actions and reactions, which produce a continuous sequence of policies and interactions, and which often result in the incremental development of policy, or a policy continuum.

Critics of American foreign affairs tend to address themselves to a particular reactive stance in the sequence and fail to appreciate the preceding steps in the succession or to envision the totality of the policy complex applicable to all functional subjects, all nations, and all circumstances. Nevertheless, there are times when ideals and goals are promulgated without concretizing objectives and formulating policies until policy makers are pressured to do so by developments that mandate action. President Nixon may have had this in mind when, in a press conference held in Guam in 1969, he observed: "One of the weaknesses in American foreign policy is that too often we react rather precipitately to events as they occur" and "fail to have the perspective of the long-range view which is essential for a policy that will be viable."

Additional distinctions among types of policy are based on differing criteria. As noted in Chapter 3, in terms of longevity or durability, foreign policies may be categorized as long-range (or strategic), intermediate-range, and short-range (or tactical). On the other hand, on the basis of importance, the policy complex, in descending order, consists of vital or primary, secondary, subsidiary, and tertiary levels of policies, with those at each stratum supported by those at lesser levels. Normally, the long-range, strategic policies are more general, more basic, and more constant, and the short-range, tactical, and tertiary are more precise and mutable.

Other distinctions in policy analysis compare verbal or declaratory with actualized, substantive or functional (which evidence content, essence, or sub-stantiality) with procedural (which deal with how and when actions are to be taken), traditional with special or exceptional, standard with crisis-oriented, and unilateral with bilateral and multilateral policies. Furthermore, positive or affirmative policy (to do something) also must be distinguished from negative policy (not to do anything). But care must be exercised by the policy maker and the analyst to differentiate between doing nothing as a result of dereliction and abstaining from action as a result of deliberate decision.

Another feature of the conduct of foreign affairs, which the policy maker must calculate into his equation, but which is frequently overlooked by the critic and the public, is its cost. The use of means, it has been said, requires the commitment of resources, such as capital, equipment, time, personnel, status, credibility, respect, and other factors. The cost aspects of foreign policy are those despite which the course of action is taken, whereas the benefit aspects are those because of which it is undertaken. The policy maker's task is to blend them in determining an acceptable and viable balance. As Charles Burton Marshall sees it, the limits of foreign policy are determined, not alone by our inherent finiteness or our extrinsic capability, but also by the degree of our steadfastness in shouldering the burdens. That, rather than the righteous-ness of unexecuted wishes, he concludes, is the true test of a great nation.

Aside from costs, there are other recognizable limitations on the formulation and implementation of foreign policy. Policy makers acknowledge that they are far from completely free agents. Such limits derive from both external and internal causes. The principal external constraints flow from the very nature of the society of nations consisting of some 160 sovereign equals, each with its own interests, objectives, and policies; the unique processes whereby governments deal with one another, including the craft of diplomacy and the manner of international conferencing; the rules of law and commitments embodied in treaties and agreements; the growing number of universal and regional institutionalized forums, such as the United Nations, with their own legal restrictions, purposes, and procedures; and the global, regional, and more immediate power relationships of the United States with other powers.

The internal delimiting factors may be grouped as ideological (traditions, ideals, and perspectives), constitutional (the legal decision determinants), the institutional (the decision-making mechanism), and the sociopolitical (the decision influencers). The last two elements embrace the organizational fabric and system of governance of the American polity, the extragovernmental pluralistic structure of American society consisting of political parties, vested interest and action groups, and the instrumentalities of the mass media. These and other external and internal restraining elements not only impinge upon the freedom of action of policy makers but affect the quality and practicability of their options.

The foreign policy complex of the United States, like that of other major and highly involved powers, contains some actual or apparent amount of schizophrenia--some antithetical or seemingly divergent objectives and policies. This is most conspicuous in the realm of tactical and supportive or tertiary policies, which are intended to remain fluid and subject to variation and change. For example, the United States may establish extensive foreign assistance programs but over time may vary them in form and intent. Thus, it may grant foreign aid of one type to a given country that it denies to another, or it may supply assistance to a particular government one year but not the next, or it may provide one kind of support but not another.

Juxtapositional dichotomies also occur in the areas of more fundamental policies, however, and it is here that the achievability of one may be seriously impeded by the pursuance of another. To illustrate, the United States supports the preservation of peace, but will resort to hostilities when confronted with aggression in violation of treaty commitments, as in the case of the North Korean attack upon South Korea, when assistance is requested by other countries, as in the cases of Vietnam and Grenada, and when American lives are in jeopardy, as in the cases of Panama and Nicaragua. So far as fundamental goals are concerned, the preservation of independence, national security, and territorial integrity are likely to be given priority over the maintenance of peace and international stability and the promotion of human welfare (including economic well-being).

Also indicative of policy complexity and contributing to confusion, the relationship of ends and means varies with respect to the nature of the particular policy issue. From the perspective of operational methodology--in terms of increasing significance or criticality--the policy maker and analyst may distinguish four types of policy. Some issues arise in ordinary day-to-day activities and problems, both substantive and procedural. Many policies of this nature fall into the tertiary and tactical categories. The next level of issues evokes anticipatory, long-range policies, in the planning of which policy makers enjoy lead time to refine both objectives and methods of implementation. Another sphere involves contingency planning, either advance planning for probable contingencies or designing of preferred policies to attain concrete objectives that support America's purposes, accompanied by rationalized alternatives should the primary choices prove to be undesirable, unachievable, or hazardous.

The remaining level of policy issues pertains to crisis management and resolution, in which lead time is limited, and for which crisis mitigation may become the principal immediate objective. The essence and pertinence of both the policy objectives and the policies initiated to achieve them, and their correlation with national goals in keeping with national interests, therefore, vary considerably and complicate the policy maker's agenda.

Such complexities and other factors may produce official and popular confusion. In the American experience, the dichotomous relationship of values and ideals, on the one hand, and the realities of practical developments and reactions, on the other hand, often result in a lack of consensus on what United States policy is or should be. Conventional wisdom affirms that, to be effective in the long run, in democracies foreign policies require the support of the people. The public normally supports basic American values, ideals, and general policy tenets. Often the people are confused, however, respecting priorities among interests, goals, objectives, and policies.

Moreover, in recent decades the media and the public often have sought to pass judgment on issues before policy is framed, on discussions with foreign governments while they are being planned or are in progress, and on treaties while they are being negotiated. This has produced "great debates," political and sometimes partisan confrontation, public demonstrations, and a general spirit of adversariness, which weakens, and sometimes undermines, consensus in dealing with international affairs.

Commenting on presidential leadership, Henry Kissinger has said that what the nation expects of a President is that he define clearly what the national purpose is, what the policies are, and then defend these against the inevitable criticisms that a pluralistic society tends to generate. He also has cautioned that the statesman's duty is to bridge the gap between the nation's experience and his vision, stressing that if he gets too far ahead of the people, he may lose his mandate, but if he confines himself to the conventional, he may lose control over events. One of the difficulties in the American system is that each new administration--especially when the incoming President represents a political change in the White House and seeks to promote his revisionist leadership-- tends to dissociate itself from important policy positions of its predecessor. Consequently, over time, the United States appears to speak with a changing voice, so that other nations may regard it as irresponsible or unreliable in world political, economic, and military affairs.

Addressing themselves to the role of public opinion and consensus, some question the effects of overemphasis on popular endorsement. Columnist Walter Lippmann reasoned that people cannot be expected "to transcend their particular, localized, and self-regarding opinions," and he concluded that their opinions and interests should be taken for what they are and for no more because they are not, as such, "propositions in the public interest." Ambassador George Kennan has questioned whether the government should be "beholden" to short-term trends of public opinion that involve "emotionalism and subjectivity" and therefore render it "a poor and inadequate guide for national action."

In making and evaluating foreign policy, it is judicious if not essential to appraise it in relation to commitment, cost, and consequences, rather than merely in terms of desire or expectation. Care must be taken to avoid frozen positions, cross-purposes, and overlap. Attention also needs to be paid to priorities--long-term merit, practicability, risks, expediency, and national credibility and prestige. Advance assessment must be made concerning achievability of objectives in the sense that certain policies can be consummated by some precise action whereupon they no longer constitute compelling needs or aspirations. Examples include the establishment of diplomatic representation, the satisfactory resolution of a boundary issue, the formation of an alliance, or the negotiation of a treaty. Others that relate to such fundamental goals as the preservation of national security, the maintenance of peace, and the promotion of the welfare of the United States and its nationals remain ongoing and are rarely fully achievable.

Foreign relations success is difficult to assess and usually is colored by subjective predisposition. In 1976 the Department of State reported, in a pamphlet entitled *United States Foreign Policy,* that no nation can choose the timing of its fate, that the tides of history take no account of the fatigue of the helmsman, and that posterity will regard, not the difficulty of the challenge, but only the adequacy of the response. Based on years of personal experience, Henry Kissinger warned that each foreign relations success only buys an admission ticket to a more difficult problem.

In any case, the decision maker should be concerned with formulating good policy--the best that can be achieved under existing circumstances, not simply the best that can be imagined. Often he must decide without having all the information later available to the historian. He must deal with the real world, settle for the possible and the practicable rather than the utopian ideal, and be satisfied with compromise. And he must realize that he is responsible for the consequences--for the disadvantages and risk of failure as well as the benefits.

Finally, in view of the intricacy of the interrelations of the spectrum of policy components, it is difficult to extrapolate a cohesive mental or graphic depiction of the totality of American objectives and courses of action to achieve them, because these vary from time to time, topic to topic, and country to country, and because one would be required to take account of the history, traditions, political structure, geographic considerations, and commercial, political, and many other interests of the United States, to say nothing of the persuasions and ambitions of its political leaders and the exigencies of the moment. It would take volumes to achieve this for the United States, and much of their content would necessitate revision before this monumental task could be completed. Perhaps the best that can be hoped for is a partial representation--for a single policy or, more likely, for some specific action or supporting subpolicy relating to some particular situation or event.

CORPUS OF AMERICAN FOREIGN POLICY

A review of American foreign relations documents reveals contemporary concern with a plethora of substantive themes and concepts. The most general and most frequently addressed relate to the fundamental goals of achieving or preserving self-determination, national security and territorial integrity, peace, and the enhancement of human welfare, which are referred to in Chapter 2. Since the days of early statesmen, such as George Washington and Thomas Jefferson, who propounded the pragmatic precept of unity of the country for "the common good," political leaders have been concerned with the viability of "the American experiment" and the fundamental foreign policy of the nation.

Augmenting these are such propositions as: the right of peoples to guarantee their national survival and to govern themselves, shape their own institutions, exercise freedom of choice, and design and preserve a way of life; government by the consent of the governed, democracy, constitutionalism, majority rule, and political pluralism; freedom from attack, external interference and physical intervention, or domination; international stability and equilibrium; peaceful and evolutionary change, the pacific settlement of disputes, and the amicable resolution of crises; and the promotion of human rights, equality, human dignity, nondiscrimination, and mutual respect; as well as guarantees of justice, due process, the rule of law, and the blessings of liberty. Speaking of the formulation of policy, in 1961 Dean Rusk reported that such central themes of American foreign policy are more or less constant and that they derive from the kind of people we are and from the shape of the world situation.

In addition, the United States acknowledges the reality of interdependence and espouses international cooperation and confederal integration, partnership with friendly nations, collective defense and the balance of power, freedom of the seas and superjacent airspace and outer space, open diplomacy (of policy, treaties, and other diplomatic end products, but not of the policy-making process or negotiations while they are underway), and, in the economic area, free trade, open market economic relations, and the most-favored-nation principle.

More specifically, if one examines American policy statements, declarations, diplomatic exchanges, legislation, and treaties and agreements, the profusion of functional subjects of contemporary American foreign affairs is overwhelming. Aside from those enumerated earlier, they encompass a host of more precise matters. To illustrate, in recent decades these have embraced embargoes, sanctions, and the blocking of foreign assets, revision of our documents classification system, the removal of Cuban forces from Africa, the Berlin Wall, jurisdiction over Jerusalem and East Timor, the Panama Canal, diplomatic representation to the Vatican, space satellites, the polar sector principle, the continental shelf, the new international economic order, Third World neutralism, double taxation, South Africa's *apartheid,* the Washington-Moscow hot line, and many others.

In short, the foreign policy concerns of the United States extend to every matter in which it has any acknowledged interest, to relations with some 160 nations and dozens of global, regional, and bipartite international organizations, and geographically to the four corners of the globe ranging from pole to pole, as well as to the depths of the seas, to the airspace that surrounds the earth, and to the distant reaches of outer space.

The documents provided in this anthology consist of several types of materials. These are gleaned from thousands of policy pronouncements, messages, statements, and reports; scores of legislative enactments, treaties, and agreements; and dozens of multipartite resolutions, declarations, and determinations. In terms of topics treated, they encompass selected factors in executive-legislative relations (such as the War Powers Act, the nature and function of the treaty- and agreement-making and termination processes, and restraints on the intelligence aspect of decision making); general statements of ideals, goals, objectives, and policies (including presidential doctrines); particular areas of purpose and policy reduced to legislative prescriptions (exemplified by the Freedom of Information and the Taiwan Relations Acts) and to treaties and agreements (such as those establishing the North Atlantic and other alliances; those pertaining to the law of the sea and outer space, the Antarctic, international terrorism and skyjacking, trade and commerce, foreign assistance, and the pacific settlement of disputes; and the Helsinki Conference Final Act).

Concentrating on contemporary American foreign policy, this volume focuses on the post-World War II era, particularly since 1960. For purposes of convenience and usage, the structure of its content is topical rather than chronological, with chapters grouped to deal with: foreign policy making; the conduct of foreign relations; general foreign policies and presidential doctrines; more than fifteen cases of crisis diplomacy involving the United States as a primary participant; a series of basic functional policy areas embracing peace, freedom, self-determination, human rights, and international trade and commerce; a separate series of more specialized functional policies concerned with alliances and ententes, international terrorism, the seas and maritime affairs, outer space, East-West and North-South relations, and foreign assistance; collective cooperation in the United Nations and inter-American systems; and selected policies and issues pertaining to six primary geographic areas, including the polar regions.

PART I

FOREIGN POLICY MAKING

2

Foreign Relations Determinants

In today's world, it is vital to match the pursuit of ideals with the responsible use of force and of power. The United States is a source of both--ideals and power. Our ideals have inspired the world for more than two centuries; and for three generations, since World War II, our power has helped other nations to realize their own ideals.

The determination and strength of purpose of the American people are crucial for stability in a turbulent world. If we stand together in maintaining a steady course, America can protect its principles and interest and also be a force for peace.

Jimmy Carter
Address, Georgia Institute of Technology, February 20, 1979

Foreign relations consists of a complex, interrelated network of components. This chapter, devoted to its principal determinants, consists of four segments that pertain to the formulation and execution of foreign policy. These embrace: national and vital interests; national purposes, goals, and concrete policy objectives, which constitute the package of ends sought; national power and capability to maintain those interests, achieve the nation's aims, and effectuate its policies; and planning to integrate these components in the process of formulating foreign policies and designing national strategies.

As concepts--distinguishing them from their particularization and prag-matization--these components are definable as:

1. NATIONAL INTERESTS are the fundamental determinants, intrinsic needs, operational criteria, or ultimate standards in accordance with which the United States frames its national purposes and goals, prescribes its concrete policy objectives, and formulates its foreign policies, strategies, and diplomatic tactics. Such interests, or concerns, may vary in constancy, importance, and intensity, and they serve as critical guideposts for decision makers throughout the foreign relations process.

2.   VITAL INTERESTS are those national interests that are indispensable and intrinsically nonnegotiable, which the United States will not willingly or voluntarily bargain away and will preserve at any cost, including resort to force if necessary.

3.   NATIONAL PURPOSES are the basic, pervading, and motivating missions of the United States, which ought to be identifiable to, and comprehended by, the body politic and which imbue the government and people with a willingness to sacrifice for their fulfillment.

4.   FUNDAMENTAL NATIONAL GOALS are those primary aims that are deemed to be most essential to maintaining and enhancing American ideals, values, character, traditions, and status and to promoting United States interests as a national entity. They embrace the achievement of national independence and identity, the maintenance of national security and territorial integrity, the extension of human welfare, the strengthening of national honor and prestige, and the preservation of peace, order, and tranquility. Other national goals are subsidiary to, and supportive of, these general goals.

5.   FOREIGN POLICY OBJECTIVES are the concrete and actionable aims that are established in pursuance of national interests and in support of national purposes and goals, for the attainment of which foreign policies are formulated and implemented. Foreign policies are discussed in the next chapter.

6.   NATIONAL POWER is the sum total of the abilities or capacities of the United States--persuasive and coercive, peaceful and forceful, actual and potential--to preserve interests, achieve purposes, goals, and objectives, and institute policies and strategies. Comprised of an aggregate of qualities, elements, and factors--or capabilities--it constitutes an indispensable means of influencing other nations and forestalling them from impinging upon the United States to its disadvantage.

7.   FOREIGN RELATIONS STRATEGY is a plan of action to promote United States interests and ideals in the pursuit of its purposes, goals, and objectives by means of substantive and procedural foreign policies for the implementation of which the United States commits its political, economic, diplomatic, military, psychological, and moral resources.

Despite widespread consensus on these definitions, much confusion exists concerning their interpretation and appplication, both in theory and in practice. To illustrate, at times statesmen and scholars use the term "national interest" as synonymous with "national concerns," which is understandable, or as aims or ends sought, which fails to differentiate them as fundamental and enduring criteria, standards, or principles and therefore leads to misunderstanding.

The expressions "national purposes," "national goals," and "policy objectives" are variants of ends sought, often generalized as aims or aspirations. The concept "national purpose," as a permeative mission of the nation, is frequently confused with the use of "purposes" as a generic denotation of aims, thereby encompassing either a fundamental national drive or any goal or operationalized policy objective. In practice, the term "national goals" is often employed synonymously with purposes and objectives. Technically, the nation's goals vary from those that are quintessential and ongoing, as listed earlier, to lesser, often secondary or supportive goals. When such a goal is action-oriented and concretized, on the other hand, it may be identified as a specific policy objective.

"National power" and "capability," frequently perceived as identical and used interchangeably, denote the ability or capacity of the United States to sustain its interests, attain its goals and objectives, and implement its policies and strategies. Such ability signifies national "strength" (which is usually preferred in public pronouncements); it is founded, not only on military might or the ability to coerce, but more frequently is based on political, economic, psychological, moral, and diplomatic factors.

If the terms "power" and "capability" are to be distinguished, aside from viewing capabilities simply as components of power, some regard them as potentialities mobilizable to produce the nation's power. Others, relating them to national action, conceive of power as connoting the essence of the capacity to influence, persuade, or coerce, whether the nation does so or not, and therefore as existing independently of the decision to act, while capability is the actual capacity to perform pragmatically with respect to existing conditions and specific circumstances. In statecraft, although the word "power" is employed in considerations of "power politics" and "balance of power," there is reluctance in the United States to emphasize or even to use the term without linking it with national responsibility. In any case, the expressions "capability" and "strength" are usually preferred in the arena of foreign relations and diplomacy.

"Foreign relations strategy" is a distinct form of policy doctrine (distinguished from military strategy), which integrates the nation's ideals, interests, purposes, goals, objectives, policies, and capabilities into a structured plan of action. This may apply to a particular functional matter, series of events, group of countries, or geographic region. If it is global, broad-scale, and/or encompassing, it may be called "**the** national strategy" or "**grand strategy.**"

Adding to existing confusion, depending on perception or intent, such basic foreign relations concepts as national security, peace, and human rights may be viewed variously as national interests, goals, concrete objectives, foreign policies, and in some cases, national strategies. For example, unless peace, as a goal, is not projected concretely as specific action-oriented policies with operationalized objectives (such as peaceful settlement of disputes, arms reduction or elimination, balance of power, partnership, or international integration), it remains fundamentally an abstract goal and fails to enter the arena of effective diplomatic practice. Often foreign relations pronouncements epitomize such theoretical if not visionary goals or ideals, not tangible and explicit foreign policies.

Rather than explicating the nature or interpretation of these concepts, most documents in this chapter focus largely on applying them pragmatically to United States ideals, principles, criteria, aims, power, and strategy. They represent a variety of perceptions and applications. And they need to be related especially to those documents contained in Chapter 3 (on policy making) and 7 (on presidential doctrines). For additional statements on American aims, also see Chapters 6 (on general policy themes) and 15 to 17 (on basic functional policies).

NATIONAL INTERESTS

1   CONCEPTIONS OF "NATIONAL INTEREST"

Perhaps in the abstract sense there is an objective category which can be called the "national interest." Human affairs, however, are not conducted in the abstract, and as one moves from the theoretical to the operational, objectivity diminishes and sentiment rises; ideas give way to ideology, principle to personality, reason to rationalization. As formulated by men of power, the national interest is a subjective and even capricious potpourri, with ingredients of strategic advantage, economic aspiration, national pride, group emotion, and the personal vanity of the leaders themselves. This is not to suggest that the concept of "national interest" is false but that it is elusive and far from self-evident, and when statesmen invoke it, they raise more questions than they answer.

There have been in recent American usage at least three separate conceptions of national interest; the ideological, exemplified by the anti-Communist crusade of the cold war; the geopolitical, which treats international relations as an endless struggle for power as an end in itself; and the legal-institutional, an approach which holds that international affairs, like domestic affairs, must be brought under the regulation of law, an approach which gave rise under American leadership to the League of Nations Covenant and the United Nations Charter. Depending upon which approach you embrace, or deplore, your conception of the national interest will differ from, or conflict with, that of others. My own preference--bias if you like--is toward the legal-institutional. . . .

J. William Fulbright, address, U.S. Senate, October 9, 1973, 93d Congress, 1st Session; *Congressional Record* 119 (October 9, 1973), No. 150.

2   NATIONAL INTEREST--ESSENCE AND APPLICATION

It may seem obvious to say that our foreign policy is designed to serve our national interests. But let us not forget that the foreign policies of governments have sometimes been designed to serve purposes other than national interests--for example: the whim or ambition of a prince, the defense or propagation of a particular ideology, the special interests or sentiments of an influential minority, inflamed emotions, national honor. . . .

But the foreign policy of a government chosen by the people obviously should be designed to serve their interests, and these become the national interest. And as a rule, our Presidents, beginning with

Washington, have sought to justify their foreign policies primarily in terms of national interest. But they and others have defined the national interest in many different ways. At times the term was narrowly construed, at times broadly. And doubtless, even from a relatively detached viewpoint, the national interest required different policies and actions at different times.

Let us explore briefly where our national interest lies in the world of today. Probably none would dispute that our national interest requires, above all, the survival of our people and way of life. Our first objective is to "secure the Blessings of Liberty to ourselves and our Posterity."

We must defend our security. But we must try to defend it without a major war if possible. . . .

Dean Rusk, "The National Interest," address, commencement, Smith College, June 7, 1964; 50 *Department of State Bulletin* (June 22, 1964): 956. Rusk then lists the following as United States national interests: the decisive repulse of aggression, the peaceful settlement of disputes, a spirit of rectitude and living up to commitments, holding others to honor their commitments, a strategy of peace, the control and limitation of armaments, strengthening the peacekeeping facilities of the United Nations and other international organizations, peaceful change, economic and social well-being of other peoples, and building a stable world community.

3   FUNCTIONAL INTERESTS

In my remarks today, I will discuss eight central American interests for the coming years. Each is broad in its own terms. But I do not believe that any of these interests can be narrowed, much less disregarded, without doing damage to the others.

Our most basic interest, and first priority, is the physical security of our nation--the safety of our people. This requires strong defense forces and strong alliances.

It also requires that we and our allies firmly and carefully manage a second area of concern: East-West relations.

A third interest--controlling the growth and spread of nuclear and other weapons--enhances our collective security and international stability.

Fourth, we must confront the global energy crisis and strengthen the international economy, for doing so is central to our well-being as a people and our strength as a nation.

A fifth interest, peace in troubled areas of the world, reduces potential threats of wider war and removes opportunities for our rivals to extend their influence.

Our diplomacy in troubled regions and our ability to pursue our global economic goals are strengthened by pursuing a sixth interest: broadening our ties to other nations--with China, for example, and throughout the Third World.

The advancement of human rights is more than an ideal. It, too, is an interest. Peaceful gains for freedom are also steps toward stability abroad and greater security for America.

And finally, we cannot disregard our interest in addressing environmental and other longer term global trends that can imperil our future.

Pursuit of each of these interests helps shape the kind of world we want to see. Each is important--as a part of this broader conception and because failure in one area can lead to failure in another. . . .

Our course in the world must be defined by a mix of interests, sensibly balanced, meeting always the central imperative of national security for our country and our people. No simple slogan or single priority can answer in advance the dilemmas of the coming decade.

Nor can we define our security interests in ways that exclude any region. To do so could leave beyond the lines of our interest nations of genuine importance to our well-being or tempt others to believe that we were ceding to them new spheres of influence. . . .

Cyrus Vance, statement, Senate Foreign Relations Committee, March 27, 1980; *American Foreign Policy: Basic Documents,* 1977-1980, pp. 61-62.

4   WORLD INTERESTS

Here at the United Nations, there are many matters of major and immediate global concern on which nations even when they are competitors have a mutual interest in working together as part of the community of nations.

In approaching these matters each of us represented here, in our national interest as leaders and in our self-interest as human beings, must take into consideration a broader element: "The World Interest."

It is in the world interest to avoid drifting into a widening division between have and have-not nations. . . .

It is in the world interest for the United States and the United Nations, all nations, not to be paralyzed in its most important function, that of keeping the peace. . . .

It is in the world interest that we cooperate, all of us, in preserving and restoring our natural environment. . . .

It is in the world interest for the resources of the sea to be used for the benefit of all--and not to become a source of international conflict, pollution, and unbridled commercial rivalry. . . .

It is in the world interest to ensure that the quantity of life does not impair the quality of life. . . .

It is in the world interest that the narcotics traffic be curbed. . . .

It is in the world interest to put a decisive end to sky piracy and the kidnaping and murder of diplomats. . . .

Finally, it is in the world interest to ensure that the human rights of prisoners of war are not violated. . . .

The United States came to its present position of world power without either seeking the power or wanting the responsibility. We shall meet that responsibility as well as we can.

Richard Nixon, address, twenty-fifth anniversary session of United Nations General Assembly, October 23, 1970; *Papers of Presidents: Nixon*, 1970, pp. 929-30.

5   NATIONAL INTERESTS AND THE FOREIGN RELATIONS PROCESS

The enormous proliferation of the overseas interests and activities of domestic agencies has not been a smooth and carefully planned process. The interests which have sprung up have been, and remain, incredibly numerous and diverse, frequently parochial, often overlapping, occasionally conflicting. Unless they can be forged into a coherent and unified national policy, there is danger that our voice abroad will be discordant and our programs at cross purposes. To prevent this, the President must be able to rely on a staff arm capable of taking the lead in directing and coordinating both the formulation and execution of foreign policy.

*   *   *

The U.S. interest in foreign affairs has been defined as "the life, liberty and pursuit of happiness of Americans." We accept this definition as one which succinctly makes the point that our governmental activities abroad cannot be justified in vague terms but must relate directly to the interests of Americans, public and private. If we are to accept responsibility for shaping the roles and functions of diplomatic missions we have an obligation to get away from the practice of adding one "useful" function after another. We should adopt methods and means of tailoring our missions staff to conform to the functions essential to our interests and implementing policy--and nothing more.

The general U.S. national interest is hard to define, but specific interests can be identified. They are wide ranging, as can be expected from a pluralistic society. They extend from retention of base facilities essential to our physical security, through increased opportunities for trade, to diplomatic representation whose only purpose seems to be to assure a newly developing country that the U.S. respects its sovereignty and independence.

It is difficult to list the U.S. interests in a specific country, especially in any order of priority. To do the task effectively, systematic means must be found to define interests, and then identify specific U.S. interests in a country or area. The assessment process has certain steps which follow logically: (1) determining the challenges to U.S. interest; (2) acquiring information most relevant to policy formulation; (3) formulating policies or, alternatively, objectives designed to advance interests or respond to the challenges; (4) creating programs to achieve these objectives; (5) allocating resources; (6) continually evaluating objectives and the effectiveness of programs designed to achieve them.

Analyzing the problem through such a systematic approach has the advantage of giving Washington means to evaluate the effectiveness of programs and the need for functions and staff. It also permits evaluation of [diplomatic] missions in their role as implementers of those programs. Ideally, it would be able to adjust easily to either changed U.S. interests or different conditions in the foreign country.

Department of State, *Diplomacy for the 70's,* pp. 3-4, 449-50.

6   NATIONAL INTEREST AS ANALYTICAL TOOL--A "NON-OPERATIONAL GOAL"

The concept of "national interest" continues to be important to foreign policy-makers despite its limitations as a theoretical and scientific concept. They have used the concept in two different ways: first, as a criterion to assess what is at stake in any given situation and to evaluate what course of action is "best"; second, as a justification for decisions taken. Particularly with respect to the latter use of "national interest" there is reason to be uneasy and dissatisfied.

Admittedly, the task of justifying decisions has become increasingly important with the rise of public opinion and the remarkable changes in communications technology in the last century. Foreign policy is now conducted in a much more open environment than used to be the case, and the public's demand for an "instant history" of what is taking place and why a particular decision was made has created unusual pressures on leaders to explain and justify all of their important decisions and actions. It is not surprising that, under these circumstances, the "national interest" tends to become a somewhat shopworn part of the political rhetoric of every Administration and at times a psychological crutch for leaders who become locked into disastrous policies.

Many thoughtful observers of foreign policy would readily agree that the "national interest" concept does indeed lend itself much more readily to being used as political rhetoric for legitimizing decisions and actions than as an exact, well-defined criterion for enabling policy officials to determine what those policies should be. But it is possible to be too cynical about this. For it is by no means the case that "national interest" has been without value to conscientious policy-makers who were determined to set reasonable objectives, to judge carefully what was at stake in particular situations, and to act prudently in any given situation.

The surpassing need for a superordinate criterion such as the "national interest" is evident. Foreign policy issues typically engage a multiplicity of values and interests which are often difficult to harmonize. Not only is much at stake, but the various values imbedded in the policy problem often pull the decision in different directions. In addition, uncertainty clouds the decision-maker's judgment as to the benefits to be expected and the likely costs/risks of each of the options he has under consideration.

Under these circumstances it is understandable that the decision-maker should attempt to apply the criterion of "national interest" in an effort to cut through the problem of value-complexity and to cope with the uncertainties affecting choice among alternative policies. A conscientious effort to consider the over-all national interest can indeed help to alleviate the psychological malaise an executive experiences in making difficult decisions of this kind. He can justify the ensuing decision both to himself and to others as one based on careful consideration of "the national interest.". . .

Alexander L. George and Robert Keohane, "The Concept of National Interests: Uses and Limitations," *Commission on the Organization of the Government for the Conduct of Foreign Policy,* June 1975, vol. 2, Appendix D, pp. 64-65.

NATIONAL PURPOSES, GOALS, AND OBJECTIVES

7   AMERICA'S "CENTRAL" PURPOSE

. . . Now the central purpose of our foreign policy is the security of the United States--in a familiar phrase in the preamble of our Constitution, to "secure the Blessings of Liberty to ourselves and our Posterity." Our foreign policy also reflects our basic convictions, the enduring values to which we a people are dedicated: a belief in human dignity--not just a phrase; in government with the consent of the governed, the most powerful and revolutionary political idea in the world today; in freedom of worship and other freedoms for all in the brotherhood of man. Both our national security and our basic convictions compel us to work for a peaceful and orderly world and impel us to help our fellow man to achieve a more decent life.

Dean Rusk, "The Central Purpose of United States Foreign Policy," address, Catholic War Veterans Convention, Washington, August 5, 1967; 57 *Department of State Bulletin* (August 28, 1967): 251. For Rusk's explication of the Blessings of Liberty also see Document 101.

8   AMERICA'S "TRUE" PURPOSES

At this crucial moment in history, what precisely do we Americans seek? In other words, what is our national purpose?

Some will answer that our national purpose is self-evident: to preserve the American way of life. But in today's tightly interrelated world, is this answer still adequate? . . .

Others may suggest that America's national purpose should be expressed in broader terms. "Is it not our true objective," they may ask, "to capture the minds of men and, through economic aid and skilled diplomacy, to bring them into line behind American leadership? . . .

What then are America's true purposes, and how can we present them to the world in understandable terms?

Although the obstacles to the kind of world which we seek are formidable, our goals, at least, are clear.

Since the beginning of time, men of all races and creeds have worked slowly and tortuously to establish certain universal values. In one form or another these values have provided the dynamic core of every major civilization. They are reflected in the world's great religions, each of which in its own way expresses the Golden Rule.

Chester Bowles, "It is Time to Reaffirm Our National Purpose," address, Adult Education Conference of the U.S.A., Washington, November 5, 1961; *Department of State Bulletin,* November 27, 1961, reprint, pp. 5-6.

9   NATIONAL PURPOSES AND IDEALS

For 200 years America has been confident of its purposes, secure in its strength, and certain of its growing prosperity. . . .

George Kennan, the first Director of the State Department's Policy Planning Staff, put the need concisely:

> If we are to regard ourselves as a grown-up nation--and anything else will henceforth be mortally dangerous--then we must, as the Biblical phrase goes, put away childish things; and among these childish things the first to go . . . should be self-idealization and the search for absolutes in world affairs: for absolute security, absolute amity, absolute harmony. . . .

Finally, how do we reconcile the pragmatic pursuit of peace with the promotion of our ideals? Concerned Americans have wondered whether we can be true to our values while dealing realistically with adversaries, friends, and the nonaligned.

Secretary Kissinger described the tension between our goals in a speech he made a year ago:

> In a community of sovereign states, the quest for peace involves a paradox: The attempt to impose absolute justice by one side will be seen as absolute injustice by all others; the quest for total security for some turns into total insecurity for the remainder. Stability depends on the relative satisfaction and therefore also the relative dissatisfaction of the various states. The pursuit of peace must therefore begin with the pragmatic concept of coexistence. . . .
> We must, of course, avoid becoming obsessed with stability. An excessively pragmatic policy will be empty of vision and humanity. It will lack not only direction, but also roots and heart. . . . America cannot be true to itself without moral purpose. This country has always had a sense of mission. Americans have always held the view that America stood for something above and beyond its material achievements. A purely pragmatic policy provides no criteria

for other nations to assess our performance and no standards to which the American people can rally.

So, our foreign policy must reflect our national ideals. Otherwise it cannot be sustained in a democracy. But for the first time in history man can destroy mankind. In this nuclear age the pursuit of peace is itself a profound moral concern. In this nuclear age the loss of peace could mean the loss of all values and ideals.

Winston Lord, *America's Purposes in an Ambiguous Age,* address, Commonwealth Club, San Francisco, October 11, 1974 (Washington: Government Printing Office for Department of State, 1974), pp. 1-3, 8-9.

1 0   NATIONAL PURPOSES AND THE PEOPLE

United States foreign policy must never be made by an elite establishment nor bent to the fears of a frustrated few. It must reflect the real purposes of the American people when they follow their very finest instincts.

Gerald Ford, remarks, Portland World Affairs Council, May 22, 1976; *Papers of Presidents: Ford,* 1976-1977, II, 1647.

*   *   *

A world of increasing complexity demands much of the American people and their government. We must recognize both practical goals and practical limits on our capacity.

Under our system of government, the only source of a strong, steady, and durable national purpose lies within the people. We are seeking to restore their confidence in America's international objectives. My greatest hope is that the path we are taking can help create among Americans a new national unity and purpose in our foreign policy--a policy no longer haunted by the past, but committed freshly to the opportunities of the future.

United States Foreign Policy, 1969-1970: A Report of the Secretary of State (Washington: Government Printing Office, 1971), pp. II-III.

1 1   NATIONAL PURPOSES AND POPULAR CONSENSUS

This is a great and powerful nation, with more power than the mind of man can conceive, with enormous wealth, with great scientific and technical capacity, with great human resources. It makes a difference, therefore, in what happens in the world, as to what our purposes are. And I would suggest to you that this great nation of ours is moved by very simple purposes: to do our part in building a reliable peace, to entertain no special ambitions of our own, to covet no one's territory, to refrain from taking away from anyone else anything that is theirs, to live and let live, to build toward a regime of law--the law which does not restrict but which liberates by making it possible to predict what the other fellow is going to do--and to cooperate across national frontiers to get on with the common, ordinary, daily tasks of men and women in our own country and right around the globe. Our purpose is to do our best to create a chance for simple human dignity.

Now, these are purposes which you recognize in your own homes and in your own communities. They are the purposes which our people share with ordinary people in all parts of the earth, and they are purposes which are compelling when great public policies and policy decisions are being made. . . .

Dean Rusk, "American Purposes and the Pursuit of Human Dignity," address, American Legion National Convention, Boston, August 29, 1967; 57 *Department of State Bulletin* (September 18, 1967): 348.

1 2   REVITALIZING AMERICA'S NATIONAL PURPOSES

Above all, I want to complete the foundations for a world at peace--so that the next generation can be the first in this century to live without war and without the fear of war.

Beyond this, I want Americans--all Americans--to see more clearly and to feel more deeply what it is that makes this Nation of ours unique in history, unique in the world, a nation in which the soul and spirit are free, in which each person is respected, in which the individual human being, each precious, each different, can dare to dream and can live his dreams.

I want progress toward a better life for all Americans--not only in terms of better schools, greater abundance, a cleaner environment, better homes, more attractive communities, but also in a spiritual sense, in terms of greater satisfaction, more kindness in our relations with each other, more fulfillment.

I want each American--all Americans--to find a new zest in the pursuit of excellence, in striving to do their best and to be their best, in learning the supreme satisfaction of setting a seemingly impossible goal, and meeting or surpassing that goal, of finding in themselves that extra reserve of energy or talent or creativity that they had not known was there.

These are goals of a free people, in a free nation, a nation that lives not by handout, not by dependence on others or in hostage to the whims of others, but proud and independent--a nation of individuals with self-respect and with the right and capacity to make their own choices, to chart their own lives.

That is why I want us to turn away from a demeaning, demoralizing dependence on someone else to make our decisions and to guide the course of our lives.

That is why I want us to turn toward a renaissance of the individual spirit, toward a new vitality of those governments closest to the people, toward a new pride of place for the family and the community, toward a new sense of responsibility in all that we do, responsibility for ourselves and to ourselves, for our communities and to our communities, knowing that each of us, in every act of his daily life, determines what kind of community and what kind of a country we all will live in.

If, together, we can restore this spirit, then 4 years from now America can enter its third century buoyant and vital and young, with all the purpose that marked its beginning two centuries ago.

Richard Nixon, address to the nation entitled "Look to the Future," November 2, 1972; *Papers of Presidents: Nixon*, 1972, pp. 1084-85. In 1960 the editors of *Life* magazine and *The New York Times* published a series of articles constituting what they called "an urgent debate" on the nature of, and the need for, a genuine national purpose in the United States. This symposium, edited by John K. Jessup, contains essays by Walter Lippmann, Archibald MacLeish, Adlai Stevenson, John Gardner, Albert Wohlstetter, James Reston, Clinton Rossiter, and then presidential candidates John Kennedy and Richard Nixon. These were republished under the title *The National Purpose*, edited by Jessup (New York: Holt, Rinehart, and Winston, 1960). The following year *American Principles and Issues: The National Purpose*, edited by Oscar Handlin (New York: Holt, Rinehart, and Winston) broadened this analysis, and in 1963 Leonard G. Benson published one of the most comprehensive treatises on the subject entitled *National Purpose: Ideology and Ambivalence in America* (Washington: Public Affairs Press).

*   *   *

With the help of my predecessor, we have come through a very difficult period in our Nation's history. But for almost 10 years, we have not had a sense of a common national interest. We have lost faith in joint efforts and mutual sacrifices. Because of the divisions in our country many of us cannot remember a time when we really felt united.

But I remember another difficult time in our Nation's history when we felt a different spirit. During World War II we faced a terrible crisis --but the challenge of fighting Nazism drew us together.

Those of us old enough to remember know that they were dark and frightening times--but many of our memories are of people ready to help each other for the common good.

I believe that we are ready for that same spirit again--to plan ahead, to work together, and to use common sense. Not because of war, but because we realize that we must act together to solve our problems, and because we are ready to trust one another.

Jimmy Carter, initial "Report to the American People," February 2, 1977; *Papers of Presidents: Carter*, 1977, pp. 76-77.

1 3   FOUR PRIMARY GOALS

But the heritage of the Second World War--the supremacy of two superstates, the unregulated growth of nuclear arsenals, the divisions of the cold war--is giving way to new forces, circumstances, and aspirations. Our policy is being adapted to such realities. It seeks to anticipate the agenda of tomorrow even while it deals with the necessities of today.

In pursuing it we are intent on keeping before us the goals of:

--peace, a fair one, one that will last, one we can live with in confidence;

--the achievement of self-determination and democratic government, not as a way of remaking the world in our own image, nor as a barrier to productive relations with conflicting social systems, but because we believe that political power should rest on the consent of the governed;

--economic well-being for ourselves and others, for its own sake and because we can never be secure and content if much of the world is struggling to survive;

--security, finally, because the other objectives have no meaning unless they can be pursued with national survival firmly assured.

United States Foreign Policy, 1969-1970: A Report of the Secretary of State (Washington: Government Printing Office, 1971), p. I. For earlier versions of basic goals, see *Department of State, Five Goals of U.S. Foreign Policy* (Washington: Government Printing Office, 1962), pp. 5-6, and Department of State, six American goals, in *How Foreign Policy is Made* (Washington: Government Printing Office, 1965), p. 20.

1 4   MAJOR GOALS IN PURSUANCE OF NATIONAL INTERESTS

To serve the interests of every American, our foreign policy has three major goals.

The first and prime concern is and will remain the security of our country. Security is based on our national will, and security is based on the strength of our armed forces. We have the will, and militarily we are very strong. . . .

Every American has a stake in our second major goal--a world at peace. In a nuclear age, each of us is threatened when peace is not secured everywhere. We are trying to promote harmony in those parts of the world where major differences exist among other nations and threaten international peace. . . .

Our third major foreign policy goal is one that touches the life of every American citizen every day--world economic growth and stability.

Jimmy Carter, address on State of the Union, January 19, 1978; *Papers of Presidents: Carter,* 1978, I, pp. 95-96, and *American Foreign Policy: Basic Documents,* 1977-1980, p. 19.

1 5   NATIONAL SECURITY--BASIC GOAL AND FOUR OBJECTIVES

Our goals are simple but profound: security, honor, and peace. Those
are the victories we seek for ourselves, for our children, and for our
children's children. These victories can be won but not by nostalgic nor
wishful thinking and not by bravado. They cannot be won by a futile effort
either to run the world or to run away from the world. Both of these are
dangerous myths that cannot be the foundation for any responsible national policy.

America requires the authority and the strength--and the moral
force--to protect ourselves, to provide for the defense of our friends, and
to promote the values of human dignity and well-being that have made our
own nation strong at home and respected abroad. To this end, our national
security policy has four specific objectives;

First, to prevent war, through the assurance of our nation's
strength and our nation's will--in this we will not fail;

Second, to share with our friends and allies the protection of
industrial democracies of Europe and Asia--In this we will not fail;

Third, to safeguard and to strengthen our vital links to the nations
and the resources of the Middle East--in this we will not fail; and

Fourth, to defend America's vital interests if they are threatened
anywhere in the world--and in this we will not fail.

Jimmy Carter, "Our Goals Are Simple But Profound," address, Annual Convention of the American Legion, Boston, August 21, 1980; *Papers of Presidents:
Carter,* 1980-1981, II, 1551, and *American Foreign Policy: Basic Documents,*
1977-1980, p. 73.

1 6   WORLD PEACE--THE FIRST IMPERATIVE

The first imperative of our time is world peace, . . .

The goal of the foreign policy of the United States is, and must be, a
lasting peace in which free societies can thrive, the kind of world order
sketched out in the preamble and article 1 of the United Nations Charter:
a world of independent nations, each free to choose its own institutions but
cooperating with each other to prevent aggression, to preserve peace, and
to promote their mutual interests; a world in which all nations and people
can make economic and social and human progress; a world which increasingly respects the rule of law; a world which also encourages, in the
words of the charter, "respect for human rights and for fundamental freedoms for all without distinction as to race, sex, language, or religion.". . .
In other words, we should like to have a chance to build upon the most
elementary commitments of our nation and to lend a hand to those abroad
who are trying to build a decent world of that type.

Dean Rusk, "The Central Purpose of United States Foreign Policy," address,
Catholic War Veterans Convention, August 5, 1967; 51 *Department of State*

Bulletin   (August 28, 1967):   252, 255.

1 7   PEACEFUL WORLD--BASIC GOAL AND FIVE OBJECTIVES

In political terms, we seek a peaceful world of independent nations, each free to choose its own institutions so long as it does not threaten the freedom of others and all free to cooperate in their common interests and in the welfare of mankind.   That is the kind of world described in the Charter of the United Nations.   And that is the kind of world to which we committed ourselves in those days when we had been purified by the sacrifices of a terrible war and we were thinking long and hard about the purposes of man.

In working toward our goals we have five basic policies.   First--and indispensably--we seek to protect the free world against aggression. . . .

While we, with our allies, seek to check aggression, we are also building the strength of the free world.

We seek to enlarge and improve our partnerships with the other economically advanced nations of the free world--with Western Europe, Canada, Japan, Australia, New Zealand, and others.   Our partnerships with these nations embrace defense. They also embrace political problems and trade and economics. . . .

A third major element in our policy is assistance to the less developed nations in advancing economically, socially, and politically. We have welcomed with open arms the nearly 50 nations which have emerged in Asia and Africa since the Second World War.   National independence does not automatically lead to economic progress. . . .

A fourth element in our policy is to improve and strengthen the organizations and institutions which enable the nations of the world to work together more effectively.   Some of these are regional, some are specialized.   Others are of broader scope.   And above them all stands the United Nations. . . .

On every working day throughout the year the United States attends some 15 or 20 conferences somewhere in the world on some subject. There are those who would be skeptical or cynical about this activity. But this is where the work of the world is going on, to build for peace. . . .

I turn now to a fifth element in our foreign policy. While we seek to protect and build the free world, we search earnestly and untiringly for areas of common interest with our adversaries--and especially for measures to reduce the danger of a great war. . . .

There can be no full and lasting detente between the chief Communist states and the free world without settlement of critical and dangerous political issues. . . .

Dean Rusk, "History Tells Us That Men Will be Free, and That Is Our Commitment," address, St. Paul, Minn.; *American Foreign Policy: Current Documents,* 1963, pp. 38-41.   These five objectives were propounded earlier by Secretary Rusk, which he designated "Security Through Strength," "Progress Through

Partnership," "Revolution of Freedom," "Community Under Law," and "Peace Through Perseverance"; see transcript of television program, September 24, 1962, in 47 *Department of State Bulletin* (October 15, 1962): 548.

NATIONAL POWER, RESPONSIBILITY, AND COMMITMENTS

1 8   POWER AND RESPONSIBILITY

As for the United States, I can state here today without qualification: We have not turned away from the world.

We know that with power goes responsibility.

We are neither boastful of our power, nor apologetic about it. We recognize that it exists, and that, as well as conferring certain advantages, it also imposes upon us certain obligations.

As the world changes, the pattern of those obligations and responsibilities changes

At the end of World War II, the United States for the first time in history assumed the major responsibility for world peace.

We were left in 1945 as the one nation with sufficient strength to contain the new threats of aggression, and with sufficient wealth to help the injured nations back to their feet. . . .

The next step was toward independence, as new nations were born and old nations revived.

Now we are maturing together into a new pattern of interdependence.

Richard Nixon, address, General Assembly of the United Nations, September 18, 1969; *Papers of Presidents: Nixon,* 1969, p. 725.

1 9   BURDENS OF RESPONSIBILITY AND LIMITATIONS OF POWER

We know all about our errors in 1919. They were, simply, to re- peat the policies of the last century: high moral tone and noninvolvement. President Wilson attempted through the League of Nations to bring our Idealism down to earth in the first sketch of a functioning world society based on law, on self-determination, on the organized institutions of peace. But this dive into reality was too much for us. We retreated to an old isolation and continued to mistake exhortation for power.

Could we have repeated this error in 1945? Perhaps. But in fact we were presented with the opposite temptation. What a heyday of con- quest we could have had--alone with the atom bomb, alone with a healthy economy in a shattered world, alone with our energy unleashed and un- broken by the ordeal of war.

But we are not conquerors. We are perhaps the most unwilling great power in history. And certainly no great power has been plunged so suddenly from the temptations of lofty noninvolvement to the opposite temptations of almost total power.

Yet we did not lose our idealism. We set up the United Nations on the basis of equality and self-determination, and have helped mightily to make it work ever since. We have pressed for decolonization. We offered to internationalize atomic energy. We gave Europe the Marshall Plan. . . . We preached the ideal of unity and federation to Europe. All this was very far from a selfish exercise of our power.

But of course it was power. The United States was dominant.   The Western alliance was guided by us. The United Nations majorities voted with us. The economic assistance was all from us. The Communists were largely contained by us.

It is a great record of magnanimous and responsible leadership. But I suspect we became used to the idea that, although all nations are equal, we were somehow a little more equal than anyone else. And, of course, for any nation, this sense of leadership is very heady stuff! I have myself said of flattery that "it is fine provided you don't inhale." The same is true of leadership. It's fine--and we did inhale.

Today, however, we face entirely new conditions.   Preponderant power is a thing of the past. . . .

So we face a new situation, less manageable and less appealing. What do we do about it? . . .

The old isolationism was always too naive about power and about the pretensions of power. We must not make that mistake again.

But equally we must not make the opposite mistake and put too much faith in power. We have among us advocates of much stronger action. . . .

If total isolationism is no answer, total interventionism is no answer either. In fact the clear, quick, definable, measurable answers are all ruled out. In this new twilight of power there is no quick path to a convenient light switch.

What then can we do? What are the options? I want to suggest that the extremes are not exhaustive. In between--less exciting perhaps, less nationally satisfying, but safer and more humane--are other routes and methods which recognize the limits of our power, allow for our tradition- al idealism, take account of the world's ideological struggle, and include no fantasies of either total withdrawal or total control.   But they are all paths which demand a high degree of genuine partnership, of genuine cooperation. As such they will often seem more arduous and more tedious than the old pursuits--for it is easier to command than to persuade. . . .

In short, what I believe we should seek in this new age of more limited power but still unlimited challenge is not so much new policies but a new emphasis, a new tone. We should be readier to listen than to instruct--with that curiosity which is the beginning of wisdom.   It will take a greater effort of imagination for us to see the world through others' eyes, to judge our policies as they impinge on others' interests.

For what we attempt today is to extend to the whole society of man the techniques, the methods, the habits--if you will, the courtesies-- upon which our own sense of citizenship is based. In our free society we ask that citizens participate as equals. We accept their views and interests as significant. We struggle for unforced consensus. We tolerate conflict and accept dissent. But we believe that because each citizen knows he is valued and has his chance for comment and influence, his final loyalty to the social order will be more deeply rooted and secure.

As heirs to the tradition of free government, what else can we do? Our founders had the audacity to proclaim their ideals "self-evident" for all mankind. We can hardly be less bold when "all mankind" is no longer an abstraction but a political fact. . . .

Adlai Stevenson, address, Harvard Alumni Association, June 17, 1965; *American Foreign Policy: Current Documents*, 1965, pp. 28-32.

2 0   POWER AND COMMITMENT

Today . . . we find ourselves in a position unique in world history. Over the centuries a number of nations have exercised world power, and many have accepted at least some of the responsibilities that go with power. But never before in human history has a nation undertaken to play a role of world responsibility except in defense and support of a world empire. Our actions have not been motivated by pure altruism; rather we have recognized that world responsibility and American security are inseparably related. But, nevertheless, what America has done is an achievement of which the American people can be justly proud.

Those who advocate a progressive withdrawal of American power have, it seems to me, never made clear where or how a withdrawal, once begun, could end without great damage to freedom. They have never acknowledged the fact that in today's interdependent world no action by a global power can ever be taken in isolation. . . .

Our power cannot and should not be exercised in the same fashion and to the same degree in every trouble spot throughout the world. We must measure and weigh the nature and extent of each involvement. But it is hardly useful to call for the wholesale withdrawal of American commitments without a careful examination of the consequences in each case. . . .

Admittedly the assumption of world responsibilities is difficult, even for a global power. . . . What is required is not unlimited resources but the will to use such resources as are available. . . .

And so, while it would be comforting to think that our postwar tasks around the world were largely over--that we could now withdraw our attention from the far corners of the globe with the satisfying feeling of a job well done--that our massive responsibilities could all be shifted to other shoulders--this is simply not the case. For, like it or not, we live in a world that will almost certainly remain for a long time to come turbulent, difficult, frustrating, and complex.

George W. Ball, "The United States and Western Europe Within the Framework of World Responsibilities," address, National Foreign Policy Conference, Washington, March 16, 1965; *American Foreign Policy: Current Documents*, 1965, pp. 432-33.

2 1   POWER AND DIPLOMACY

Over 20 years ago, President John Kennedy pledged that the United States would "pay any price, bear any burden, meet any hardship, support any friend, oppose any foe, in order to assure the survival and the success of liberty." We know now that the scope of that commitment is too broad--though the self-confidence and courage in those words were typically American and most admirable. More recently, another administration took the view that our fear of communism was "inordinate" and that there were very complicated social, economic, religious, and other factors at work in the world that we had little ability to affect. This, in my view, is a counsel of helplessness that substantially underestimates the United States and its ability to influence events.

Somewhere between these two poles lies the natural and sensible scope of American foreign policy. We know that we are not omnipotent and that we must set priorities. We cannot pay any price or bear any burden. We must discriminate; we must be prudent and careful; we must respond in ways appropriate to the challenge and engage our power only when very important strategic stakes are involved. Not every situation can be salvaged by American exertion even when important values or interests are at stake.

At the same time, we know from history that courage and vision and determination can change reality. We can affect events, and we all know it. The American people expect this of their leaders. And the future of the free world depends on it.

Americans, being a moral people, want their foreign policy to reflect the values we espouse as a nation. But Americans, being a practical people, also want their foreign policy to be effective. If we truly care about our values, we must be prepared to defend them and advance them. Thus we as a nation are perpetually asking ourselves how to reconcile our morality and our practical sense, how to pursue noble goals in a complex and imperfect world, how to relate our strength to our purposes--in sum, how to relate power and diplomacy. . . .

. . . Noble aspirations are not self-fulfilling. Our aim must always be to shape events and not be the victim of events. In this fast-moving and turbulent world, to sit in a reactive posture is to risk being overwhelmed or to allow others, who may not wish us well, to decide the world's future.
. . .

This is a way of saying that our forefathers understood quite well that power and diplomacy always go together. It is even clearer today that a world of peace and security will not come about without exertion or without facing up to some tough choices. Certainly power must always be guided by purpose, but the hard reality is that diplomacy not backed by strength is ineffectual. . . .

The lesson is that power and diplomacy are not alternatives. They must go together, or we will accomplish very little in this world. . . .

If we are to protect our interests, values, and allies, we must be engaged. And our power must be engaged. . . .

The United States faces a time of challenge ahead as great as any in recent memory. We have a diplomacy that has moved toward peace through negotiation. We have rebuilt our strength so that we can defend our interests and dissuade others from violence. We have allies whom we value and respect. Our need is to recognize both our challenge and our potential.

Americans are not a timid people. A foreign policy worthy of America must not be a policy of isolationism or guilt but a commitment to active engagement. We can be proud of this country, of what it stands for, and what it has accomplished. Our morality should be a source of courage when we make hard decisions, not a set of excuses for self-paralysis. . . .

We will use our power and our diplomatic skill in the service of peace and of our ideals. We have our work cut out for us. But we will not shrink from our responsibility.

George Shultz, "Power and Diplomacy in the 1980s," address, Trilateral Commission, Washington, April 3, 1984; Department of State, *Realism, Strength, Negotiation*, pp. 7-10. For President Kennedy's quote, see leading quotation, Chapter 16. In this address, p. 7, Secretary Shultz reiterated President Kennedy's allusion to the American eagle depicted clutching arrows and the olive branch, quoted in Chapter 6, Document 99.

2 2   POWER AND PARTNERSHIP

And so our task has been to use our margin of influence to encourage abroad what we have always set as our target at home; namely, the effective organization of diffuse centers of power and authority.

Again, I would underline, this kind of world cannot be created by the United States acting alone; but we remain, whether we like it or not, the critical margin; in Europe, in Latin America, in Asia, in Africa, and, I believe also, in the end, in the Middle East. And we shall remain the critical margin in the years ahead if the world is going to make its way through the great transition toward the goal of stable peace.

We cannot abdicate our responsibilities as the greatest industrial power in the world. We cannot abdicate our responsibilities as one of the two great nuclear powers in the world. And we cannot--in our interest or in the common interest--opt out of our treaty responsibilities; for if we create vacuums . . . they are not likely to remain empty. But what we can do, and are doing, is to use our influence and power to help organize the world community in ways which distribute the burdens more evenly and give to others a sense that they, too, are shaping the destiny of man.

The nation-state, whatever its size and resources, cannot solve the vast problems now before us or foreseeable in the future. Nor is this any longer a bipolar world, despite the continued disproportionate concentration of nuclear power in the United States and the Soviet Union. The dynamics of the first postwar generation have yielded a world area of diverse nations determined . . . to take a hand in their own destiny. We shall achieve arrangements of authentic partnership based on mutual respect and acknowledgement of interdependence, or we shall not move successfully through the great transition.

Despite the debates and anxieties at home about our world role, I deeply believe our nation will continue to play its proper role--as the decisive margin--in such partnerships.   And it is in a world of partnership and fair shares that we shall find the right answer to the limits and responsibilities of American power.

Walt W. Rostow, "Limits and Responsibilities of American Power," address, Student Conference on National Affairs, Texas A and M University, December 4, 1968; 60 *Department of State Bulletin* (January 6, 1969): 7.

NATIONAL PLANNING AND STRATEGY

2 3   PLANNING AND FOREIGN RELATIONS

The planner does not face a choice between long-run and short-term interests. . . .

The critical question is whether a particular decision, taken at any moment of time, does or does not move one toward the long-run goal that is sought.

It is, of course, basic that a planner should consider and speculate about the longrun forces at work on the world scene and about long-run U.S. objectives and specific goals. But a planner who wishes to bring about a certain result at some future period of time must concern himself not merely with goals but also with how to get from here to there. This means he must understand fully the operational environment in which a new concept must take hold if it is to be successful. . . .

As in active warfare, it is important in foreign policy to have lucid long-run objectives defined with sufficient precision to serve as touchstones for operational decisions. One needs a doctrine in foreign policy as in war. Winston Churchill once said: "Those who are possessed of a definite body of doctrine and of deeply rooted convictions upon it will be in a much better position to deal with the shifts and surprises of daily affairs than those who are merely taking short views, and indulging their natural impulses as they are evoked by what they read from day to day." But doctrine is not enough: one must work constantly, as I say, on how to get from here to there.

Thus foreign policy planning, as we define it, is the art of thinking in ways that lead you to begin to do something now which will make the nation's position on the world scene better in the future.

There is a second definition of planning which I respect. . . . It appears in Eugene Black's book on *The Diplomacy of Economic Development*: "Between the idealists, who are more interested in imposing solutions than in illuminating choices, and the cynics who distrust planning in all its interpretations, lies, I think, a rational definition of the concept which should be nourished. Planning, simply defined, should be the place where the political leader is faced with an awareness of the consequences of his decisions before he makes them instead of afterwards. Taking the definition one step further, it should be the means by which the lines of communication are kept open between those who make decisions, those who illuminate them, and those who carry them out. . . ."

Most of our errors in foreign policy have stemmed from a failure to take fully into account a factor which may not have seemed of critical importance in the immediate operational setting, but which emerged as of critical importance as events unfolded. The normal and understandable tendency to concentrate on the immediate and palpable requires constant correction; and it is part of a planner's duty firmly--even boldly--to insist on the relevance of the less obvious.

Walt W. Rostow, "The Planning of Foreign Policy," address, School of Advanced International Studies, Johns Hopkins University, Washington; Department of State, *Newsletter* (June 1964): 3. On American planning, also see Lincoln P. Bloomfield, "Parameters of Planning" and "Limitations on Planning," *Commission on the Organization of the Government for the Conduct of Foreign Policy, June 1975,* vol. 2, Appendix F, pp. 215-18.

2 4   DIMENSIONS OF AMERICAN NATIONAL STRATEGY

In the light . . . of what we confront in the world around us, our strategy has five dimensions.

First, we are strengthening the bonds of association among the more industrialized nations, which lie mainly in the northern portion of the free world: Western Europe, Canada, and Japan. . . .

The second dimension of our strategy concerns our posture toward the revolution of modernization going forward in Latin America, Africa, Asia, and the Middle East.

The building of this new north-south tie is the third major dimension of our strategy on the world scene. It goes forward in the Alliance for Progress, in our relations with the new African nations, in the meetings of the Development Assistance Committee of the OECD in Paris, in the consortium arrangements of the International Bank for Reconstruction and Development, in the transformed relations of the British Commonwealth and the French Community, in the enlarging contribution of Germany, Japan, and other nations to economic development. And above all, it goes forward in the minds of citizens in both the north and the south who are gradually coming to perceive that, however painful the memories of the colonial past may be, major and abiding areas of common interest are emerging between nations at different stages of the growth process which are authentically committed to the goals of national independence and human freedom.

The fourth dimension of our strategy is military. There is much for us to build within the free world, but we must protect what we are building or there will be no freedom.

The fifth element in our strategy concerns our posture toward the nations now under Communist rule. We have made it clear that we do not intend to initiate nuclear war to destroy the Communist world. The question then arises: Are we content merely to fend off Communist intrusion, military and subversive? What are our hopes and our prospects with respect to the Communist world? Are we reconciled to a planet that shall, at best, be forever split?

We are engaged in an historic test of strength--not merely of military strength but of our capacity to understand and to deal with the forces at work in the world about us. The ultimate question at issue is whether this small planet is to be organized on the principles of the Communist bloc or on the principles of voluntary cooperation among independent nation-states dedicated to human freedom. If we succeed in defending the present frontiers of freedom, the outcome of that test of strength will be determined by slow-moving forces of history. It will be determined by whether the elements in the world environment . . . are more successfully gripped and organized by ourselves and our friends than by the Communists. . . .

Finally, the Communist bloc itself is now in the midst of a slow-moving but great historical crisis. This crisis takes the form of the deep dispute between Moscow and Peiping, a dispute which has engaged in one way or another Communist parties throughout the world. What lies behind this dispute, among other factors, is the rise of nationalism as a living and growing force within the Communist bloc. It is a force within Russia itself, and it is a growing force as well in other regions where Communist regimes are in power. Despite the interest of Communists in maintaining their cohesion against the West, the slow fragmentation of the Communist bloc and the diffusion of power within it goes forward.

We expect no quick or cheap benefits from this process. In the short run it may present problems to us, . . . But fundamentally the assertion of nationalism and national interests within the Communist bloc should tend to produce a more livable world. The diffusion of power, we know, is the basis for human liberty within societies, and on the world scene it is the basis for independent nations.

Walt W. Rostow, "American Strategy on the World Scene," address, Conference on International Affairs, Purdue University, March 15, 1962; 46 *Department of State Bulletin* (April 16, 1962): 625-31. On strategy also see Rostow, address, Institute of American Studies, Barcelona, Spain, October 6, 1964; *American Foreign Policy: Current Documents,* 1964, pp. 41-48.

3

Policy Making

Decision making is not a science but an art. It requires, not calculation, but judgment. There is no unit of measure which can weigh the substantial consequences of a decision against the political consequences, or judge the precise portions of public opinion and congressional pressure, or balance domestic against foreign, short-range against long-range, or private against public considerations.

Theodore C. Sorensen
Decision-Making in the White House, 1963

The fifth layer in the foreign relations hierarchy--after national interests, vital interests, national purposes, national goals, and concrete operationalized objectives--consists of United States foreign policies. Although the concept "foreign policy" is variously interpreted and applied in both practice and analysis, it is widely regarded as a means to achieve the nation's ends. Policies are action-oriented and they are the product, not the essence, of the policy process. They apply to the gamut of relations of the United States with the rest of the world and, as an aggregate, they constitute a program for future action. Reducing such qualities to the most critical and material, the concept may be defined as:

> Foreign policies are future courses of action for dealing with other nations, decided upon by United States policy makers exercising judgment and choice among alternative possibilities, and are designed in keeping with the nation's interests and in pursuit of its purposes, fundamental goals, and concrete objectives.

Although considerations of foreign policies frequently concentrate upon individual functional topics--such as economic, security, or human rights policies--or upon specific regions or countries, conditions, or events, often they are regarded as an agglomerate of components, an interrelated totality, or a "policy complex." The constituents are generally delineated as verbal (or declaratory) versus actualized (which involves explicit practical implementation); positive (to do something) versus negative (not to do anything); unilateral (to act independently) versus multilateral (through cooperation with other nations); and substantive (which evidences content, essence, or sub-stantiality--that which is to be done) versus procedural (which focuses on how or when it is to be done).

The most material distinctions among policy components--to both the statesman and the commentator--pertain to the corpus of foreign policies on the basis of duration and importance. In terms of durability, foreign policies may be categorized as long-range or strategic (which are long-lived though not necessarily immutable), intermediate-range (which tend toward constancy but may differ for geographic areas or other particular groups of states but may eventually evolve into strategic policies), and the panoply of short-range, tactical policies (which are intended to refine and support the more permanent and are subject to change from time to time, place to place, and situation to situation).

Based on importance, the components of the policy complex may be viewed, in descending order, as consisting of primary, secondary, subsidiary, and tertiary policies, with those at each level supported by those at lesser levels. Relating them to the matter of durability, normally the primary, secondary, and subsidiary tend to be either strategic or intermediate, whereas the tertiary are likely to be tactical (Document 25).

Aside from the difficulty of extrapolating the intricate totality, or even a major segment, of American foreign policy in terms of longevity and impor-tance, and despite the merits of systematic policy making, it must be realized that there are limits, both internal and external, within which policies can be formulated and implemented. In other words, foreign policy makers, at all levels, including the President and the Secretary of State, are far from com-pletely free agents.

Inasmuch as this volume is devoted in its entirety to the broad spectrum of American foreign policies, containing chapters dealing with distinct strategic policies and doctrines, specific crises and other developments, a variety of functional policies, and individual countries and geographic areas, this chapter is restricted to considerations of the general nature of policy (Documents 26-27), selected aspects of policy making (Documents 28-34), and commentary on the decision-making process (Documents 35-39). Extensive analytical literature has been produced in recent decades to survey and analyze these topics, to which guidance may be found in Elmer Plischke, *U.S. Foreign Relations: A Guide to Information Sources* (Detroit: Gale Research Co., 1980), especially Chapters 14 (on decision making) and 16 (section on policy formulation).

The materials provided in this chapter need to be related, not only to the foreign relations determinants discussed in Chapter 2 but also to such matters as policy preconditions and requirements, traditional principles, and related topics dealt with in Chapter 6 (Documents 85-94).

ESSENCE OF FOREIGN POLICY

25   FOREIGN POLICY COMPLEX

(_Durability_)   (_Importance_)

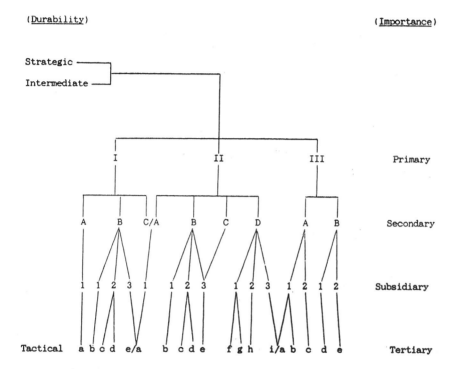

Elmer Plischke, *Foreign Relations: Analysis of Its Anatomy* (Westport, Conn.: Greenwood, 1988), p. 136.

26   POLICY PRIORITIES

I pointed out--when one of the questioners said, "What is the most important decision that you have to make? What is the greatest problem that you have to confront?"--I pointed out what is the fact: And that is that it is difficult to try to select priorities among the many problems that confront this Nation at home and abroad, but I do know that there are certain decisions in foreign policy that only the President of the United States can make. It is here that he must devote that extra effort if there is any extra effort he can devote to it because if he makes a mistake in this area, it is a mistake that no one else is going to be able to correct.

Richard Nixon, remarks to key personnel of Department of State, January 29, 1969; *Papers of Presidents: Nixon,* 1969, p. 28.

2 7   NATURE AND LIMITS OF FOREIGN POLICY

I shall define the foreign policy of the United States as the courses of action undertaken by authority of the United States in pursuit of national objectives beyond the span of jurisdiction of the United States.

That is a lot of big words. Let me put the idea another way. Our foreign policy unfolds in the things done by the U.S. Government to influence forces and situations abroad.

The meaning of the phrase "things done" should not be construed too narrowly. In this field, utterance is a form of action, and pronouncements may be deeds, especially when they convey meaning about intended or possible actions rather than merely expressing abstractions and moralizations. . . .

The two elements in my definition to be stressed are these: Foreign policy is generated in actions. The things acted upon in foreign policy are things lying beyond the direct control of this country. . . .

I was thinking of foreign policy as relating to means and ends and to the gap between them.

Ends are concepts. Means are facts. Making foreign policy consists of meshing concepts and facts in the field of action. . . .

. . . The real work comes not in deciding where you want to go--that is the easiest part of it--but in figuring out how to get there.

One could no more describe a nation's foreign policy in terms solely of objectives than one could write a man's biography in terms of his New Year's resolutions.

Foreign policy consists of what a nation does in the world--not what it yearns for or aspires to. The sphere of doing, as distinguished from the sphere of desire and aspiration, is governed by limits. Adam Smith pointed out that economic behavior derives from imbalance between means and ends and the circumstance that ends therefore tend to conflict. The same is true in foreign policy.

Let me illustrate that in terms of present problems.

To begin, let me identify the fundamental purpose enlightening our conduct as that of preserving a world situation and enabling our constitutional values to survive.

That we must keep in mind when speaking of national interest as the basis of our foreign policy. To me the phrase "national interest" does not mean a set of aims arrived at without regard to values. I cannot think of our foreign policy except in relation to the character of the Nation and its political institutions.

That has a bearing on the choice of means in the conduct of foreign policy. An accountable government cannot lead a double life. It is foreclosed from using such means as would destroy the very values it would save.

The main purpose enlightening our foreign policy holds true in all stages of our national life. It will continue as long as our country continues in the tradition we know. It is objectified in different ways as the world situation changes. . . .

What requires judgment and timing in the highest degree, along with the fortitude that can defer hopes without surrendering them, is the job of threading a course through such contradictions as these and striving as best one can to find choices of action consistent with all of the aims concurrently. . . .

Charles B. Marshall, "The Nature of Foreign Policy," 26 *Department of State Bulletin* (March 17, 1952): 415-20.

POLICY MAKING

2 8   PRESIDENTIAL FOREIGN POLICY ADVISORY SYSTEM

The Secretary of State is my principal foreign policy adviser. As such, he is responsible for the formulation of foreign policy and for the execution of approved policy.

I have assigned to the Secretary of State authority and responsibility, to the extent permitted by law, for the overall direction, coordination, and supervision of the interdepartmental activities incident to foreign policy formulation, and the activities of executive departments and agencies of the United States overseas. Such activities do not include those of United States military forces operating in the field under the command of a United States area military commander, and such other military activities as I elect, as Commander in Chief, to conduct exclusively through military or other channels. Activities that are internal to the execution and administration of the approved programs of a single department or agency and which are not of such nature as to affect significantly the overall U.S. overseas program in a country or region are not considered to be activities covered within the meaning of this directive. . . .

The Secretary of Defense is my principal defense policy adviser. As such, he is responsible for the formulation of general defense policy, policy related to all matters of direct and primary concern to the Department of Defense, and for the execution of approved policy. The Joint Chiefs of Staff are the principal military advisers to me, the Secretary of Defense, and the NSC.

I have assigned to the Secretary of Defense authority and responsibility, to the extent permitted by law, for the overall direction, coordination, and supervision of the interdepartmental activities incident to defense policy formulation. . . .

The Director of Central Intelligence is my principal adviser on intelligence matters. As such, he is responsible for the formulation of intelligence activities, policy, and proposals, as set forth in relevant Executive orders. I have assigned to the Director of Central Intelligence authority and responsibility, to the extent permitted by law and Executive order, for the overall direction, coordination, and supervision of the interdepartmental activities incident to intelligence matters.

The Director of Central Intelligence is responsible for the preparation of those papers addressing matters affecting the intelligence activities, policy, and proposals of the United States for consideration by the NSC. . . .

Ronald Reagan, statement on National Security Council system, January 12, 1982; *Papers of Presidents: Reagan,* I, 19. Also see presidential directive for American Ambassadors in Chapter 4, Document 56; and see documents on the intelligence system in Chapter 5, Documents 66-70.

2 9   ANATOMY OF FOREIGN POLICY MAKING

. . . I wish . . . to talk about a professional concern which you and we in government share: the anatomy of foreign policy decisions. The word is "decision" and not "opinion" or "judgment." I put upon your agenda an examination of the difference between conclusions unencumbered by official responsibility and those with which you and the Nation as a whole must live. . . .

What questions should a foreign policy officer ask himself before he takes off on a policy? How does he avoid the fatal flaw which comes from overlooking a factor which proves to be decisive in the flow of events? Let me emphasize that I am not now talking about bureaucratic procedure . . . but about the thought processes of those who are involved in a decision. . . .

General George C. Marshall used to admonish his colleagues, "Gentlemen, don't fight the problem, solve it." Steadily the policy officer works his way through the alternative answers--testing, rejecting, or revising them. In most matters he will find none which is completely satisfactory. He does not live in Utopia but in a real world filled with human frailty--including his own. He cannot find logical and consistent answers for situations filled with contradictions. He is the first to know that his answer is subject to criticism from one flank or the other. But he cannot avoid an answer. For inaction is itself a policy decision.

He knows that he must recommend who ought to do what, when, and how. He is aware that the United States has not been chosen to solve all the world's problems, that we do not drum up business for ourselves which others can handle without us. But he is also aware that our attitude makes a difference and that we seldom enjoy a free ride on any major problem. . . .

He knows that miracles are rare and few problems will be completely and permanently solved overnight. He is engaged in a process over time, and his proposals must be related to that process and to the entire texture of our foreign relations. . . .

In commenting briefly upon the structure of foreign policy decisions, I have not had time to go into the detail which the subject deserves. Perhaps I have given you the impression that it is always a time-consuming process. But the pace of events does not always afford time, and the process may have to be telescoped into a few hours--and, on rare occasions, perhaps even into a few minutes. . . .

Dean Rusk, "The Anatomy of Foreign Policy Decisions," address, American Political Science Association, Washington, September 7, 1965; 53 *Department of State Bulletin* (September 27, 1965): 502-9.

3 0 STEPS IN POLICY-MAKING PROCESS

1. Perceiving the decision-making need, as related to the problem, the crisis, the challenge, or the opportunity, respecting the matters on which objectives, policy positions, strategies, and methods of procedure require determination. This initial and sometimes most difficult task is to define the question or issue itself and, when accurately identified and framed, sometimes it evokes automatic response, and the very way in which the problem is posed may help to shape the decision.

2. Designing the assumptions (where essential) and fixing the scope and parameters of the consideration. This is so vital that a major difference in assumptions may completely alter the decision determination.

3. Ascertaining, ordering, and evaluating relevent facts and information concerning the problem under consideration. The degree of thoroughness and accuracy of fact-gathering and evaluation may influence or even predetermine certain phases of decision-making. In short, the validity of those decisions that convert observations or perceptions into facts is crucial to the process.

4. Perceiving and analyzing rationally conceived alternative national interests, goals, and primary and secondary, long-range and immediate, objectives to be served by policy formulation.

5. Assessing the desirability and practicality of operational objectives, and deciding on the preferred option(s) or establishing priorities among them.

6. Identifying and evaluating rationally conceived alternative substantive policy solutions--both primary and subsidiary.

7. Weighing the desirability, feasibility, practicability, and possible consequences and costs of each substantive policy and sub-policy alternative, assessing the advantages and disadvantages of each, and deciding on the preferred option(s) or ascribing priorities to them.

8. Defining and scrutinizing alternatives respecting foreign relations methods and procedures, agents, and forums which may be employed, and timing relevant to the pursuance of substantive policy.

9.   Contemplating the desirability, feasibility, practicality, and likely consequences respecting each alternative diplomatic method, procedure, agent, forum, and time sequence, and deciding on the preferred option(s) or determining priorities among them, paying particular attention to the possible employment, simultaneously or sequentially, of multiple techniques and forums.

10.   Analyzing alternatives respecting the form and timing of policy enunciation--both substantive and procedural.

11.   Deciding on the manner of policy enunciation and communication-- who, how (both forum and format), and when.

12.   Allocating organizational and functional responsibility for policy application and implementation.

13.   Reviewing and assessing the effectiveness of both the policy and the fashion in which it is instituted and perceived, and determining whether the consequences are acceptable or reconsideration is required or desirable.

Elmer Plischke, *Foreign Relations: Analysis of Its Anatomy* (Westport, Conn.: Greenwood, 1988), p. 257. For alternative lists of policy-making steps, see Dean Rusk's "checklist" of seven items, "Anatomy of Foreign Policy Decisions," 53 *Department of State Bulletin* (September 27, 1965): 503-8, and Theodore Sorensen's list of eight steps, in *Decision-Making in the White House* (New York: Columbia University Press, 1963), pp. 18-19.

3 1   GUIDELINES FOR POLICY OFFICERS

. . . The policy officer lives with his antennae alerted for the questions which fall within his range of responsibility.

His first thought is about the question itself: Is there a question here for American foreign policy, and, if so, what is it? For he knows that the first and sometimes most difficult job is to know what the question is--that when it is accurately identified it sometimes answers itself, and that the way in which it is posed frequently shapes the answer.

Chewing it over with his colleagues and in his own mind, he reaches a tentative identification of the question--tentative because it may change as he explores it further and because, if no tolerable answer can be found, it may have to be changed into one which can be answered.

Meanwhile he has been thinking about the facts surrounding the problem, facts which he knows can never be complete, and the general background, much of which has already been lost to history. He is appreciative of the expert help available to him and draws these resources into play, taking care to examine at least some of the raw material which underlies their frequently policy-oriented conclusions. He knows that he must give the expert his place, but he knows that he must also keep him in it.

He is already beginning to box the compass of alternative lines of action, including doing nothing. He knows that he is thinking about action in relation to a future which can be perceived but dimly through a merciful fog. But he takes his bearings from the great guidelines of policy, well-established precedents, the commitments of the United States under international charters and treaties, basic statutes, and well-understood notions of the American people about how we are to conduct ourselves. . . .

He will not be surprised to find that general principles produce conflicting results in the factual situation with which he is confronted. He must think about which of these principles must take precedence. He will know that general policy papers written months before may not fit his problem because of crucial changes in circumstance. He is aware that every moderately important problem merges imperceptibly into every other problem. He must deal with the question of how to manage a part when it cannot be handled without relation to the whole--when the whole is too large to grasp.

He must think of others who have a stake in the question and in its answer. Who should be consulted among his colleagues in the Department [of State] or other departments and agencies of the Government? Which American ambassadors could provide helpful advice? Are private interests sufficiently involved to be consulted? What is the probable attitude of other governments, including those less directly involved? How and at what stage and in what sequence are other governments to be consulted?

If action is indicated, what kind of action is relevant to the problem? The selection of the wrong tools can mean waste, at best, and at worst an unwanted inflammation of the problem itself. Can the President or the Secretary [of State] act under existing authority, or will new legislation and new money be required? Should the action be unilateral or multilateral? Is the matter one for the United Nations or some other international body? For, if so, the path leads through a complex process of parliamentary diplomacy which adds still another dimension to the problem.

What type of action can hope to win public support, first in this country and then abroad? For the policy officer will know that action can almost never be secret and that in general the effectiveness of policy will be conditioned by the readiness of the country to sustain it. He is interested in public opinion for two reasons: first, because it is important in itself, and, second, because he knows that the American public cares about a decent respect for the opinions of mankind. And, given probable public attitudes--about which reasonably good estimates can be made--what action is called for to insure necessary support? . . .

The problem in the policy officer's mind thus begins to take shape as a galaxy of utterly complicated factors--political, military, economic, financial, legal, legislative, procedural, administrative--to be sorted out and handled within a political system which moves by consent in relation to an external environment which cannot be under control.

And the policy officer has the hounds of time snapping at his heels. He knows that there is a time to act and a time to wait. But which is it in this instance? Today is not yesterday and tomorrow will be something else, and his problem is changing while he and his colleagues are working on it. He may labor prodigiously to produce an answer to a question which no longer exists.

In any event he knows that an idea is not a policy and that the transformation of an idea into a policy is frequently an exhausting and frustrating process. He is aware of the difference between a conclusion and a decision. The professor, the commentator, the lecturer may indulge in conclusions, may defer them until all the evidence is in, may change them when facts so compel. But the policy officer must move from conclusion to decision and must be prepared to live with the results, for he does not have a chance to do it again. If he waits, he has already made a decision, sometimes the right one, but the white heat of responsibility is upon him and he cannot escape it, however strenuously he tries.

There is one type of study which I have not seen, which I hope we can do something about in the months ahead. The pilot of a jet aircraft has a check list of many dozen questions which he must answer satisfactorily before he takes off his plane on a flight. Would it not be interesting and revealing if we had a check list of questions which we should answer systematically before we take off on a policy? . . .

Dean Rusk, "The Formulation of Foreign Policy," remarks, policy-making officers of Department of State, February 20, 1961; *American Foreign Policy: Current Documents,* 1961, pp. 22-28.

3 2   MORALITY AND EXPEDIENCY IN FOREIGN POLICY MAKING

. . . America cannot be true to itself without moral purpose. This country has always had a sense of mission. Americans have always held the view that America stood for something above and beyond its material achievements. A purely pragmatic policy provides no criteria for other nations to assess our performance and no standards to which the American people can rally.

But when policy becomes excessively moralistic it may turn quixotic or dangerous. A presumed monopoly on truth obstructs negotiation and accommodation. Good results may be given up in the quest for ever-elusive ideal solutions. Policy may fall prey to ineffectual posturing or adventuristic crusades.

There must be understanding, as well, of the crucial importance of timing. Opportunities cannot be hoarded; once past, they are usually irretrievable. New relationships in a fluid transitional period . . . are delicate and vulnerable; they must be nurtured if they are to thrive. We cannot pull up young shoots periodically to see whether the roots are still there or whether there is some marginally better location for them.

The policymaker often must settle for the gradual, much as he might prefer the immediate. He must be concerned with the best that can be achieved, not just the best that can be imagined. He has to act in a fog of incomplete knowledge without the information that will be available later to the analyst. He knows--or should know--that he is responsible for the consequences of disaster as well as for the benefits of success. He may have to qualify some goals not because they would be undesirable if reached, but because the risks of failure outweigh potential gains.

The policymaker must understand that the critic is obliged to stress imperfections in order to challenge assumptions or goad actions. But equally the critic should understand the complexity and inherent ambiguity of the policymaker's choices.

Department of State, United States Foreign Policy (Washington: Government Printing Office, 1975), p. 4.

3 3   LINKAGE OF FOREIGN POLICY ISSUES

. . . Foreign policy issues are interrelated--"linked"--as never before. A consistent, coherent, and moral foreign policy must be grounded in an understanding of the world in which we pursue our goals.

The concept of linkage--the suggestion that we should design and manage our policy with a clear understanding of how changes in one part of the international system affect other parts--was first put forth in 1969 in the context of US--Soviet affairs. We proceeded from the premise that to separate issues into distinct compartments would encourage the Soviet leaders to believe that they could reap the benefits of cooperation in one area, using it as a safety valve, while striving for unilateral advantages elsewhere. We considered this a formula for disaster.

So strong is the pragmatic tradition of American political thought that linkage was widely debated as if it were an idiosyncrasy of a particular group of policymakers who chose this approach by an act of will.

But linkage comes in two forms: first, when policymakers relate two separate objectives in negotiation, using one as pressure on the other; second by virtue of reality, because in an interdependent world the actions of a major power are inevitably interrelated and have consequences beyond the issue or region immediately concerned.

Of these two concepts of linkage, the latter is by far the more important. It says, in effect, that significant changes of policy or behavior in one region or on one issue inevitably affect other and wider concerns. . . .

Perception of linkage is, in short, synonymous with an overall strategic view. We ignore it only at our peril. It is inherent in the real world. The interrelationship of our interests, across issues and boundaries, exists regardless of the accidents of time or personality; it is not a matter of decision or will but of reality. And it cannot be ended by an act of policy. If we are to have a permanent conception of American foreign policy there must be an appreciation of the fact that merits of individual actions can be judged only on a wider canvas. . . .

Linkage is not a natural concept for Americans, who have traditionally perceived foreign policy as an episodic enterprise. Our bureaucratic organization, divided into regional and functional bureaus, and indeed our academic tradition of specialization compound this tendency to compartmentalization. And American pragmatism produces a penchant for examining issues separately: to deal with issues individually, as if they existed as abstractions, without the patience, timing, or sense of political complexity which are so often vital to their achievement; to display our morality in the proclamation of objectives rather than in a commitment to the operational consequences of our actions in an inherently ambiguous environment.

Henry Kissinger, "Continuity and Change in American Foreign Policy," Salomon Lecture, New York University, September 19, 1977; Henry Kissinger, *For the Record: Selected Statements, 1977-1980* (Boston: Little, Brown, 1981), pp. 87-91. Reprinted by permission of Henry A. Kissinger.

3 4   LINKAGE PRINCIPLE--NEGOTIATING WITH THE SOVIET UNION

There is one cardinal rule for the conduct of international relations: Don't give anything to your adversary unless you get something in return.

It was during the transition period between my election in 1968 and my first inauguration in 1969 that Henry Kissinger and I developed what is now widely called the concept of linkage. We determined that those things the Soviets wanted . . . would not be gained by them without a quid pro quo. . . . In diplomacy, as in other walks of life, you can only get something you want if you can give your opponent something he wants. Unilateral concessions on our part--to prove our "goodwill"--are stupid and dangerous. As Henry Kissinger puts it, "As a general rule the Soviet Union does not pay for services that have already been rendered."

We "linked" our goals to theirs, and though it took two years for the Kremlin to accept this policy in the SALT I negotiations, it finally did.

Linkage remains a viable strategy. . . .

There are no hard and fast boundaries that separate one form of Soviet imperialism from another. They are linked by a common thread that leads to the Kremlin. The Soviets know this, and if compelled by the leadership in the United States to accept linkage, they will do so. They have done so in the past. They will do so again.

They will not accept linkage, however, out of an unselfish concern for preserving peace in the world. If we do not demand it, we will not get it. . . .   Linkage is a just concept. If pursued vigorously and from a position of sufficient strength, it will   produce fair results. . . .

Trade and arms control must be linked with the settlement of political differences if the danger of war is to be reduced. Only if we use linkage in this way will we be attacking the root causes of war.

Richard Nixon, *The Real War* (New York: Warner Books, 1980), pp. 267-69. Reprinted by permission of the publisher.

*   *   *

The President, therefore, decided that the United States should work to create a set of circumstances which would offer the Soviet leaders an opportunity to move away from confrontation through carefully prepared negotiations. From the first, we rejected the notion that what was lacking was a cordial climate for conducting negotiations.

Past experience has amply shown that much-heralded changes in atmosphere, but not buttressed by concrete progress, will revert to previous patterns at the first subsequent clash of interests.

We have, instead, sought to move forward across a broad range of issues so that progress in one area would add momentum to the progress of other areas.

We hoped that the Soviet Union would acquire a stake in a wide spectrum of negotiations and that it would become convinced that its interests would be best served if the entire process unfolded. We have sought, in short, to create a vested interest in mutual restraint.

At the same time, we were acutely conscious of the contradictory tendencies at work in Soviet policy. Some factors--such as the fear of nuclear war, the emerging consumer economy, and the increased pressures of a technological, administrative society--have encouraged the Soviet leaders to seek a more stable relationship with the United States. Other factors--such as ideology, bureaucratic inertia, and the catalytic effect of turmoil in peripheral areas--have prompted pressures for tactical gains.

The President has met each of these manifestations on its own terms, demonstrating receptivity to constructive Soviet initiatives and firmness in the face of provocations or adventurism. He has kept open a private channel through which the two sides could communicate candidly and settle matters rapidly The President was convinced that agreements dealing with questions of armaments in isolation do not, in fact, produce lasting inhibitions on military competition because they contribute little to the kind of stability that makes crises less likely. In recent months, major progress was achieved in moving toward a broadly based accommodation of interests with the U.S.S.R., in which an arms limitation agreement could be a central element.

This approach was called linkage, not by the administration, and became the object of considerable debate in 1969. Now, three years later, the SALT agreement does not stand alone, isolated and incongruous in the relationship of hostility, vulnerable at any moment to the shock of some sudden crisis. It stands, rather, linked organically to a chain of agreements and to a broad understanding about international conduct appropriate to the dangers of the nuclear age.

Henry Kissinger, briefing of members of Congress, June 15, 1972; 07 *Department of State Bulletin* (July 10, 1972): 42. Also see brief comments of President Reagan on linking nuclear weapons negotiations with the Soviet government, February 24, 1981; *Papers of Presidents: Reagan,* 1981, p. 153. For United States-Soviet relations, also see Chapter 22.

DECISION MAKING

President Eisenhower observed that "Every single day there are new and tough decisions that have to be made within a foreign policy" (press conference, October 15, 1958; *Papers of Presidents: Eisenhower,* 1958, p. 741). A few years later Secretary of State Dean Rusk pointed out the vast difference "between a conclusion and a decision," noting that analysts and critics may arrive at conclusions, often with hindsight, whereas the policy maker must move from conclusion to decision and must live with it (see Document 31). Considering the function of decision making in the context of events, referred to in Chapter 1, President Nixon concluded: "I think that one of the weaknesses in American foreign policy is that too often we react rather precipitately to events as they occur. We fail to have the perspective of the long-range view which is essential for a policy that will be viable" (Guam press conference, July 25, 1969; see Document 118).

Decision making in foreign relations applies, not only to the formulation of foreign policies, but to other factors in the policy-making process. To summarize, it may be defined as:

Decision-making is an intellectual process whereby human beings --usually the political leaders--define, analyze, assess, and determine the interests, aims, policies, procedures, capabilities, and strategies of the United States, in coping with developments and problems in its relations with other countries. In doing so, decision makers consider alternatives and, by deliberate choice, or acts of will, they decide on preferred options for application or implementation that are intended to result in optimum benefits at minimum risk and disadvantage.

Discussing the political, bureaucratic, and intellectual/psychological aspects of exercising judgment and choice, analysts who have contributed substantially in recent decades to the study of foreign relations decision making, as both a theory and a process, include: Graham T. Allison, *Essence of Decision: Explaining the Cuban Missile Crisis* (Boston: Little Brown, 1971); John W. Bowling (see Document 38); Joseph Frankel, *The Making of Foreign Policy: An Analysis of Decision Making* (New York: Oxford University Press, 1963); Alexander L. George, "The Case for Multiple Advocacy in Making Foreign Policy," 66 *American Political Science Review* (September 1972): 751-95; John P. Lovell, *Foreign Policy in Perspective: Strategy, Adaptation, Decision-Making* (New York: Holt, Rinehart, and Winston, 1970); Elmer Plischke, *Foreign Relations Decisionmaking: Options Analysis* (Beirut, Lebanon: Catholic Press for Institute of Middle Eastern and North African Affairs, 1973), and *Foreign Relations: Analysis of Its Anatomy* (Westport, Conn.: Greenwood, 1988), Chapter 9; and Richard C. Snyder et al., eds., *Foreign Policy Decision Making: An Approach to the Study of International Politics* (New York: Free Press, 1962).

3 5   TASKS OF DECISION-MAKING PROCESS

    . . . there is substantial agreement that a policy-making process should accomplish the following tasks:

    (1) Ensure that sufficient information about the situation at hand is obtained and that it is analyzed adequately so that it provides policy makers with an incisive and valid diagnosis of the problem;

    (2) Facilitate consideration of all the major values and interests affected by the policy issue at hand. Thus, the initial objectives and goals established to guide development and appraisal of options should be examined to determine whether they express adequately the values and interests imbedded in the problem and, if necessary, objectives and goals should be reformulated;

    (3) Assure search for a relatively wide range of options and a reasonably thorough evaluation of the expected consequences of each. The possible costs and risks of an option as well as its expected or hoped for benefits should be carefully assessed; uncertainties affecting these calculations should be identified, analyzed, and taken into account before determining the preferred course of action;

    (4) Provide for careful consideration of the problems that may arise in implementing the options under consideration; such evaluations should be taken into account in weighing the attractiveness of the options under consideration; and

    (5) Maintain receptivity to indications that current policies are not working out well, and an ability to learn from experience.

Alexander L. George, "Towards a More Soundly Based Foreign Policy," *Commission on the Organization of the Government for the Conduct of Foreign Policy, June 1975,* vol. 2, Appendix D, p. 10.

3 6   DECISION MAKING--JUDGMENT AND CHOICE

    Certain essential elements of judgment are required by a decision-maker to reach a sound decision for preserving and advancing U.S. interests abroad. Sometimes these decisions involve resolution of a narrow, short-term issue. At other times they have broader implications; in the latter case, such decisions are often referred to as "policy decisions" and the decisionmaker is often referred to as a "policymaker." These elements of judgment include:
- -   U.S. interests involved.
- -   The differing degrees of importance the U.S. normally attaches to each of the interests involved.
- -   The other country's, or group of countries', interests involved.
- -   The differing degree of importance the other country, or group of countries, attaches to each of its interests involved.
- -   Existing U.S. policies that are pertinent.
- -   Other major pertinent considerations such as the current political/

military/economic situations both at home and in the country, or group of countries, affected, which challenge or offer opportunities for the advancement, or preservation, of U.S. interests.

- - Costs in terms of time, people, money, influence and goods.

Pervading all stages of decisionmaking and decision implementation is a requirement that the principal officers have quick access to information attuned to their activities with respect to current issues. They should also be aware of issues and developments not requiring their decisions at a given time or at their level of the hierarchy. Officers require an awareness, in depth and perspective, of significant international trends and situations which are of potential concern or are part of the ever-changing framework of relevant events within which all their actions take place. They also require conceptual as well as topical information to facilitate their linking disparate situations into broader patterns. It is likewise important that their sources of information be widely diverse and cover official and unofficial, written and oral, general, and particular sources.

Department of State, *Diplomacy for the 70's* (Washington: Government Printing Office, 1970), pp. 545-46. For analysis of six psychological aids to enable the decision maker to cope with the intellectual problem of deciding, see Alexander L. George, "Psychological Aspects of Decision-Making," *Commission on the Organization of the Government for the Conduct of Foreign Policy, June 1975*, vol. 2, Appendix D, pp. 25-29.

37   PRESIDENT AND NATIONAL SECURITY COUNCIL SYSTEM--POLICY PRIORITIES

Systematic Planning: American foreign policy must not be merely the result of a series of piecemeal tactical decisions forced by the pressures of events. If our policy is to embody a coherent vision of the world and a rational conception of America's interests, our specific actions must be the products of rational and deliberate choice. We need a system which forces consideration of problems before they become emergencies, which enables us to make our basic determinations of purpose before being pressed by events, and to mesh policies. . . .

Full Range of Options: I do not believe that Presidential leadership consists merely in ratifying a consensus reached among departments and agencies. The President bears the Constitutional responsibility of making the judgments and decisions that form our policy.

The new NSC system is designed to make certain that clear policy choices reach the top, so that the various positions can be fully debated in the meeting of the Council. Differences of view are identified and defended, rather than muted or buried. I refuse to be confronted with a bureaucratic consensus that leaves me no options but acceptance or rejection, and that gives me no way of knowing what alternatives exist. . . .

Conclusions

There is no textbook prescription for organizing the machinery of policymaking, and no procedural formula for making wise decisions. The policies of this Administration will be judged on their results, not on how methodically they were made.

The NSC system is meant to help us address the fundamental issues, clarify our basic purposes, examine all alternatives, and plan intelligent actions. It is meant to promote the thoroughness and deliberation which are essential for an effective American foreign policy. It gives us the means to bring to bear the best foresight and insight of which the nation is capable.

Richard Nixon, *U.S. Foreign Policy for the 1970's: A New Strategy for Peace* (1970), pp. 19, 22-23.

3 8   DEPARTMENT OF STATE DECISION-MAKING PROCESS

What is the Department's self-image in terms of policy formulation? . . .

According to the formal image, policy formulation moves on channels similar to the pattern of water drainage in a river valley, with small streams uniting to form larger streams in a complicated and constantly changing network culminating in the mouth of the river where it flows into the sea. The river mouth is the President as foreign policy decision-maker, the mouth of the largest and most central of the rivers flowing into the final delta is the Secretary of State as the principal adviser to the President--perhaps the swamps of the delta itself can be compared to the NSC machinery! . . . Policy is made in two ways--by decisions as to how existing policy directives should be executed, made at decreasing levels of importance as one moves away from the river mouth and up among the rivulets, and by recommendations coming flowing from the rivulets to the river mouth, and being modified by rejection, acceptance, or amalgamation in the intermediate decision points. . . .

The formal image of the State Department's process of policy formulation, through many-leveled recommendations and decisions, is that of a glorified military staff system. Each man, to the best of his ability, is expected to put into those decisions and recommendations which are within his range his own best judgment as to the way in which the President himself would make the decision if the President sat in the same spot with the same information available to him. Each man assumes that his own immediate superior does the same. This system is an admirable system of decision-making, understanding the core of policy formulation to be decisions--decisions as to execution within a directive from a higher level or decisions as to the content of direct and indirect recommendations for new policies or for changes in existing policies. This system has worked well in many organizations, but it has its faults as well as its advantages. There is no reason to attempt here to argue its relative merits as against other forms of decision-making. It is important only to note the function of the ideal military staff officer and to agree that the Department's formal image of itself requires that its officer personnel conduct themselves as ideal military staff officers in their roles as formal and informal contributors to the making of policy decisions. . . .

The Supreme Court does not use a staff at all in making its decisions --the use of military-type staff by an American judicial decision-making body in other than very specialized functions would fly in the face of the basic assumption of the system, which is that a judge can best arrive at the truth by comparing the carefully prepared recommendations of special interests with each other and with rules laid down by higher authority. In comparing these and other systems and combinations of systems, it can be noted in passing that an adversary-judge decision-making system sets itself lower targets, in terms of load and efficiency and is less dependent than is the military staff system on the ability of large numbers of men to separate the general interest from their special interests.

The policy formulation process of the State Department (and possibly that of other institutions involved in the process) actually has little resemblance in practice to the formal image of a military staff system. It is in fact much more like the process employed so well by the Supreme Court: skilled experts are employed to collect information and arguments for particular decisions maximizing the benefits accruing to different special interests or a coalition of such interests. The special interest in each case uses the best professional talent it can find to present to the judge the reasons why he should decide in favor of its own special interest. The judge realizes that the advocate . . . is working for the best interests of his client; the judge accepts, nay, welcomes this fact; and the judge utilizes it to make what he believes to be a good decision, probably a better decision than he could have made with a military staff instead of an adversary proceeding. . . .

If the advocacy and judgment of conflicting geographical interests is the warp of a Foreign Service officer's work, its woof is the advocacy of operational programs in a constant unspoken dogfight with each other and with domestic programs for allocations of time, interest, and money. This advocacy of operational programs consists, as does the geographical interest pattern, of mini-advocacies within macro-advocacies within mega-advocacies. Much more clearly than does the geographical warp, this operational woof applies to all, or almost all, elements in the foreign policy and national security complex. Often an officer, in State [Department] or in some other agency, finds himself in a position where he is engaged in a geographical and an operational advocacy at the same time. . . .

The formal image is not necessarily "right," and the actual system is not necessarily "wrong." Each system of decision-making has its own advantages and disadvantages. The judge-advocate system is admirable for (a) reducing personality and personal idiosyncrasy to a minimum, (b) reducing to a minimum the possibility of favoritism and corruption, (c) insuring that top decision-makers at or near the Presidential level have all the possible arguments for most alternatives brought before them, and (d) avoiding gyrations of policy and operations--this quality can be compared to a very slow steering ratio in a vehicle in that one has to work hard and consciously at the wheel to effect anything other than the most minor change of course. It also has its disadvantages as against a classic military staff model. For instance, it is slow to adjust to changes in the environment; it is very hard for the system to examine its own errors and learn from them; it does not have the potential for effectiveness that the military staff system has--like free enterprise, it relies on the statistical averages in a number of decisions, any one of which could be wrong; decisions tend to be compromises between different viewpoints, even if these conflicting viewpoints are essentially incompatible, and the overall result is often mushy. It is difficult to imagine this kind of decision-making system making a series of catastrophically bad decisions, even though it is equally difficult to imagine it doing anything like unifying Germany in the Bismarckian era, or bringing France back into the Concert of Europe in Talleyrand's time. . . .

An understanding of the real nature of the system is obviously widespread in the Department and in other foreign affairs agencies; after all, the system works and works fairly well. But the same people who understand it pretend not to understand it, and pretend it is something it is not. . . .

John W. Bowling, "How We Do Our Thing: Policy Formulation," *Foreign Service Journal* (January 1970), reprinted in *U.S. Army War College: Readings* (Carlisle, Pennsylvania: U.S. Army War College, 1972), pp. 1-5. Reprinted by permission of the *Foreign Service Journal.* For a brief statement on the Secretary of State's policy-making role, see Department of State, *How Foreign Policy Is Made* (Washington: Bureau of Public Affairs, Department of State, 1965), especially pp. 10-14.

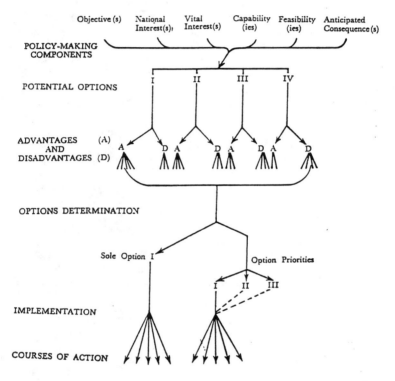

Elmer Plischke, *Foreign Relations: Analysis of Its Anatomy* (Westport, Conn.: Greenwood, 1988), p. 275.

PART II

CONDUCT OF FOREIGN RELATIONS

4

Management of
Foreign Relations

While Mr. Truman's remark, "The President makes foreign policy,"
is not the whole story, it serves very well if one wishes to deal with
the matter in five words.

*   *   *

The President, with the aid of his Secretary of State and the support
of Congress, supplies the leadership in our foreign relations.

Dean Rusk
"The President," *Foreign Affairs,* April 1960

This chapter is concerned with two major features of the conduct of American
foreign relations--the doctrine of separation of powers as applied to the
relations of the President and Congress, and several aspects of the management
of diplomatic representation. Related matters, such as policy making, war
powers, crisis handling, alliances, and collective cooperation, are treated in
other chapters.

SEPARATION OF POWERS--THE PRESIDENT AND CONGRESS

"Separation of powers" is one of the fundamental but unique principles of
the American governmental system. Executive, legislative, and judicial functions, authority, and responsibility are constitutionally vested in separate and
independent organs of the government, and are subject to a comprehensive
system of checks and balances. Although the Constitution stipulates certain
general and specific foreign relations powers, it contains no special "dis-
tributing clause," nor does it ascribe prescriptive authority for either foreign
policy making or implementation.

Volumes have been written on the nature of governmental powers distribution, the intent of the Founding Fathers and the Framers of the Constitution,
historical development and practice, constraining checks and balances,
executive-legislative conflicts, litigation and court decisions, and the need for
cooperation between the branches of the government. In time, to render this

skeletal constitutional system viable and enduring, it has been augmented by a host of statutes, congressional resolutions, executive orders, judicial opinions and determinations, and incrementally established "extra-constitutional" practices. Overall these have expanded and rendered the original stipulations of the Constitution workable.

The resultant process, however, has produced a number of serious areas of conflict between the President and Congress. Aside from their treaty and war-making powers, executive confidentiality, and overseas intelligence operations--dealt with in Chapter 5--these include such issues as foreign relations paramountcy and the distinction between foreign policy making and implementation (Documents 40 and 41), nonpartisanship in foreign affairs (Document 42), the undertaking of national commitments abroad (Document 43), and the "legislative veto" (Document 44). For illustrative specific congressional enactments involving executive-legislative relations pertaining to foreign affairs, see Documents 75 (on submitting treaties and agreements to Congress), 78 (Senate Treaty Powers Resolution), 80 (War Powers Resolution), and 497 (Taiwan Relations Act).

4 0   CONSTITUTIONAL FRAMEWORK FOR EXECUTIVE AND LEGISLATIVE RESPONSIBILITY

The Constitution does not speak of "foreign policy," nor of making or implementing foreign policy. It is not apparent that the Framers thought in those terms. They did assign particular powers and responsibilities relating to intercourse with other nations to different branches of the federal government, and they foreclosed foreign intercourse to the states. Looking at the Constitution through our own lenses, we are free to characterize the constitutional distribution as a "system" for formulating and implementing foreign policy, but we should not be surprised if what we see in the Constitution does not conform nicely to contemporary notions.

In particular, the Constitution does not reflect, or lend itself to, sharp distinctions between "formulating" and "implementing" foreign policy. Pursuant to the constitutional allocations of power and responsibility, some foreign policy is made by Congress, some by the President, and some by the President-and-Senate. Both the President and Congress also implement foreign policy. (To some extent, even, the courts and the states also formulate as well as implement foreign policy.) Foreign policy is also inherently made in the course and by the manner of implementing it.

The provisions in the Constitution which explicitly allocate authority and responsibility in foreign affairs are few. Essentially, Congress is given power to regulate commerce with foreign nations, and to decide for war or peace. (While Congress has the power also to define piracy and offenses against the law of nations, its exercise has not loomed large in our national history.) The President has the power to make treaties and to appoint ambassadors, each with the advice and consent of the Senate; he also receives ambassadors.

There are other enumerated powers, of general applicability, which have important uses for foreign affairs. Congress has the power to tax and spend for the common defense and for the general welfare. It can raise and support an army and a navy. It can establish and regulate executive offices. It can legislate, and appropriate funds, as is necessary and proper to carry out its various powers and those of the other branches of government. The President's authority to appoint officers (with advice and consent of the Senate, or alone upon authorization from Congress), his responsibility to see that the laws are faithfully executed, and his command of the armed forces, are as relevant for foreign as for domestic affairs.

The enumerated powers were obviously important to the Founding Fathers; they are important today and, contrary to common impression, they remain essentially unchanged and raise few legal issues. The uncertainties and the sources of controversy about the constitutional blueprint lie in what the Constitution does not say. For the enumerated powers relating to foreign affairs, even as supplemented by the powers of general applicability, seem spare, sparse, leaving much unsaid. The power to make treaties is allocated to the President-and-Senate, but who has authority to terminate treaties? Congress has the power to declare war, but who can make peace? More importantly, who formulates that foreign policy which is neither a regulation of commerce nor a declaration of war, and is not embodied in a treaty? Indeed, who formulates general principles of policy of which commerce, and war-or-peace, and treaties may be particular expressions? Finally, who controls, supervises, regulates the conduct of our relations with other nations? . . .

. . . Whatever the reason for constitutional inarticulation, no one has doubted that the United States has the missing powers cited and all other powers possessed by other sovereign nations, and that these powers are in the federal government. What has been uncertain is which branch has the constitutional authority to act for the United States.

There is a basis for arguing that the Constitutional Fathers intended the President to be the agent and executor of congressional policy in foreign as in domestic affairs. Some have suggested, alternatively . . . that the unarticulated foreign relations powers of the United States should be divided "naturally," with those inherently "executive" allocated to the President and those "legislative" in character, to Congress. But is formulating national foreign policy, other than that contained or reflected in statutes, "legislative" or "executive"? Alexander Hamilton early launched the argument that when the Constitution vested in the President "the Executive Power" (not only, as for Congress, the powers "herein granted") it included much more than the responsibility of executing congressional policy; it gave him also a different, independent authority known to the Framers, by way of Montesquieu and Locke, as "executive power," that is, full powers in foreign relations, except as the Constitution expressly provided otherwise. . . .

While constitutional exegesis has not been irrelevant, argument and authority are available for at least two possible principles of distribution of authority, and interpretation has not determined the shape of the constitutional "system"--not, in particular, the respective authority of President and Congress. What has shaped the system primarily have been the character and needs of foreign relations, responding to the respective constitutional and political power of Presidents and Congresses in our system generally and the respective influence of particular Presidents and Congresses at several times in our history.

. . . But domestic legislation apart, power to act where the Constitution is silent began to flow to the President from the beginning. For Hamilton this was what the Constitution intended; intended or not, it was perhaps the inevitable consequence of other constitutional dispositions. . . .

. . . From the beginning the President represented the United States to the world. He was the sole organ of communication with other governments and had exclusive control of the channels and processes of communication, usually discreet, often secret. The President had charge of daily relations with other nations. Continuous intercourse generated innumerable issues, and someone had to formulate United States policy about them.

The President began to make that policy. Small decisions in daily intercourse inevitably were made "on the spot" by those engaged in the process. Even as to larger issues, the President was always in session; Congress was not, and could be specially convened only with difficulty, especially in our early days. The President had the facts, and the advice of expert subordinates. He could act quickly, decisively; only he could act when Congress was not in session and decision was urgent. . . . He, or his cabinet, or his ambassadors, made a myriad of smaller decisions-- "formulated national policy"--in conducting relations with other countries every day. . . .

As the President established sole control of the conduct of daily foreign relations and achieved policy-making authority in foreign affairs, other presidential functions also assumed a policy-making character. The power to appoint ambassadors (with the consent of the Senate) and the task of receiving foreign ambassadors became authority to recognize (or not recognize) states and governments, and to begin, terminate, or resume relations with them. The power to appoint other officers with the consent of the Senate (or alone, by legislative authorization), and the early practice of appointing special agents for ad hoc assignments without Senate consent, also acquired policy-making purpose and overtones. The President's task of faithfully executing the laws and his responsibility of defending United States interests around the world became authority to use the armed forces under his command, short of war, for these purposes and for implementing treaties, laws, and other national policies (including presidential foreign policy).

Congress contributed to the early and continuing growth of presidential power in foreign affairs, although perhaps it could not have prevented it. Congress early recognized and confirmed the President's control of daily foreign intercourse. It did not organize itself, and equip itself with expertise, so as to acquire a dominant authority in foreign relations, or even a continuous, informed participation. Any constitutional power it might have had to do so soon atrophied. It never even developed a way to follow closely what the President was doing. Nor did it often bestir itself to disown or to dissociate itself from what the President had done, to condemn him for doing it, or even to question his authority to do it. When issues of authority arose, they became enmeshed in partisan dispute. The President's party in Congress generally defended his authority; the opposition's strictures became, or appeared, partisan rather than principled, institutional, constitutional. Even as regards international agreements, as to which the Senate had an explicit constitutional role, the Senate could not complain about executive agreements it did not know of; it did not complain of many it knew of; occasional complaints did not challenge or affect the President's asserted power in principle.

Congressmen sometimes grumbled or even "reserved their positions," but usually acquiesced; rarely did Congress resist formally. Often, informal consultations with congressional leaders before the President declared, or acted on, national policy disarmed congressmen who might have been disposed to constitutional battle and thus helped confirm presidential authority to act without formal congressional participation. Congress further conceded an extended presidential primacy when early it began to delegate to him huge grants of power with only general lines of guidance thus effectively leaving to the Executive the formulation of policy as well as large discretion in carrying it out.

In a word, Congress allowed itself to become removed from the process of conducting foreign relations and formulating foreign policy, appearing only late when formal action was constitutionally required and in an independent, almost adversary posture towards the Executive. By then it often did not feel free to refuse to consummate policies which the President had developed for the United States, thus effectively confirming his authority to make them.

In time, the issue became not whether the President had authority to act but what the limits on his authority were; not whether the President could act when Congress was silent, but whether he could act even contrary to the expressed wishes of Congress--whether Congress could direct, control, or supersede his decisions, whether Congress was constitutionally free not to implement his policies.

Emphasis on the President's power to formulate foreign policy, with its roots in his control of foreign relations, should not depreciate the part which Congress continues to have in the formulation of foreign policy. Congress formulates major foreign policy by legislation regulating commerce with foreign nations or authorizing international trade agreements. The Foreign Commerce Power has grown enormously on the wings of the Interstate Commerce Power so that Congress now has nearly-unlimited power to regulate anything that is, is in, or affects, either interstate or foreign commerce. Congress, and Congress alone, also has the power to make the national policy to go to war or to stay at peace; it has determined United States neutrality in the wars of others. The War Powers of Congress include the power to legislate and spend as necessary to wage war successfully; to prepare for, deter, or defend against war; and to deal with the consequences of war. Under the "general welfare" clause, Congress can decide where, for what, how much, and on what conditions to spend, as in foreign aid. There are implications for foreign policy when Congress establishes and regulates the Foreign Service and the bureaucracies of various departments and agencies dealing with foreign affairs. The innumerable uses of the "necessary and proper" clause include many that "formulate foreign policy." Since foreign policy and foreign relations require money, which only Congress can appropriate, Congress has some voice in all foreign policy through the appropriations process, although Congress would probably not be constitutionally justified in refusing to support policies which are within the President's power to make. Congress' unenumerated power to legislate on all matters relating to "nationhood" and foreign affairs may reach far beyond regulation of immigration, nationality, and diplomacy. It includes, apparently, the power to join the President in making international agreements by resolution of both houses of Congress as an alternative to the treaty process. . . .

The implementation of policy is, in constitutional terms, more easily described. The President--through the State Department, the Foreign Service, and some other departments and agencies--implements all foreign policy whether made by the President, the President-and-Senate, or the Congress. Congress implements foreign policy by enacting necessary and proper legislation, and by appropriating funds. . . .

Our system for formulating and implementing foreign policy, then, is inherently and purposefully less "effective" than it might be if foreign policy were made and implemented under a single constitutional authority, say, the President. To some, the need for Senate consent to a treaty or to a presidential appointment makes our system less "effective." To some, including John Quincy Adams, lodging the power to declare war in Congress is an "absurdity." Some may decry especially the system, as we now have it, in which Congress retains authority over commerce, spending, and war-or-peace but the President formulates foreign policy generally. Indeed, one must recognize that the "ineffectiveness" produced by such separation is responsible in substantial measure for modifications or circumventions--for the growth and acceptance of presidential agents, presidential agreements, presidential "war" or hostilities-short-of-war. . . .

Louis Henkin, "A More Effective System for Foreign Relations: The Constitutional Framework," *Commission on the Organization of the Government for the Conduct of Foreign Policy, June 1975,* vol. 5, Appendix L, pp. 9-15. Also see responses and commentary of Gerhard Casper, Thomas Ehrlich, Eugene V. Rostow, and Arthur Schlesinger, Jr., pp. 22-43. Also see Chapter 5 for additional documentation on executive-legislative relations, including treaty-making and war powers, Documents 71-84.

4 1   CONSTRAINING FOREIGN RELATIONS POWERS

There is no great mystery in the inclination of executives to override legislatures whenever they can get away with it. The real puzzle is the frequency with which legislative bodies acquiesce tamely in the loss of their own authority. All over the world constitutional government is in decline. . . .

The genius of the American Constitution is that it does not compel us to rely on the conscience and principles of our Presidents to protect us from dictatorship. Through the separation of powers and the federal system, our Constitution provided countervailing institutions with countervailing powers to protect us against the danger of executive usurpation. If our Presidents are men of conscience and principle, that is all to the good, but it is not something you can count on. Under our Constitution we do not have to rely on such good fortune for the protection of our liberties--as long as the countervailing institutions, which is to say, Congress, the courts and the state governments, exercise their countervailing powers. The contingency that the Founding Fathers could not have foreseen--and could not have done anything about if they had--was that one or more of the other institutions of government would cease to exercise and cease to defend their own authority against executive incursions.

That, however, is exactly what Congress let happen in the field of foreign relations. . . .

The cause of the constitutional imbalance, by and large, has been crisis. Perspective is easily lost in time of crisis; you do what you think you have to do to meet a threat or an imagined threat or seize an opportunity--with little regard for procedure or precedent. Ends give way to means, law is subordinated to policy, in an atmosphere or urgency, real or contrived. . . .

These occurrences have one common attribute: the subordination of constitutional process to political expediency in an atmosphere of urgency and seeming danger, resulting in each case in an expansion of Presidential power at the expense of Congress. The fact that Roosevelt and Truman were substantially correct in their assessment of the national interest in no way diminishes the banefulness of the precedents they set. Roosevelt's deviousness in a worthy cause made it much easier for Presidents Johnson and Nixon to practice the same kind of deviousness in a mistaken cause.

Only if one subscribes to the cult of the "strong" Presidency which mesmerized American political science in the fifties and early sixties can one look with complacency on the growth of Presidential dictatorship in foreign affairs. . . . it was possible to forget the wisdom of the Founding Fathers, who had taught us to mistrust power, to check it and balance it, and never to yield up the means of thwarting it. Now, after bitter experience, we are having to learn all over again what those pre-Freudian students of human nature who framed the American Constitution understood well: that no single man or institution can ever be counted upon as a reliable or predictable repository of wisdom and benevolence; that the possession of great power can impair a man's judgment and cloud his perception of reality; and that our only protection against the misuse of power is the institutionalized interaction of a diversity of politically independent opinions. In this constitutional frame of reference, a good executive is not one who strengthens his own office by exercising his powers to the legal utmost and beyond, but one who, by respecting the limits of his own authority, contributes to the vitality of the constitutional system as a whole. . . .

J. William Fulbright, "Congress and Foreign Policy," *Commission on the Organization of the Government for the Conduct of Foreign Policy, June 1975*, vol. 5, Appendix L, pp. 58-59.

4 2   NONPARTISANSHIP IN FOREIGN AFFAIRS

. . . we need nonpartisanship in foreign affairs today more than we have ever needed it in the history of this America. We need more, not less credibility and continuity; we need more, not less confidence in the honest motives and high patriotic concerns of one another.

That is not to say that I wish the Congress would keep out of foreign affairs, and that I want to run everything beyond the water's edge in my own way without legislative interference. Under the Constitution, the Congress has a fundamental responsibility in the shaping of all broad matters of public policy, both foreign and domestic. . . . But while the Congress together with the President makes foreign policy, only the Executive can execute it. . . .

Now, clearly the Constitution contemplates a political partnership beyond the water's edge, and it clearly does not contemplate the day-to-day conduct of foreign policy any more than the day-to-day conduct of military operations by many, many different voices in the deliberative legislative branch. . . .

In this very difficult time, the American people expect responsible conduct from individual Members of Congress and from Congress as a whole, as well as from the President. . . .

The issue is not the goals of foreign policy; the executive and legislative branches share the same hope for America. What is at issue is the process of executing our foreign policy, not its objectives. But as men of good will, we must solve the problem of our respective roles. It would be a national tragedy if conflict between the Congress and the Chief Executive jeopardized the achievements of the 1970's and prevented further progress toward our common goals.

. . . I doubt that restrictive amendments are an adequate tool for shaping the conduct of foreign policy. An attitude frozen in a statute, however noble, cannot shape events. In a world of 150 nations and fast-moving change, diplomacy is a process, not execution of a rigid blueprint. . . .

Gerald Ford, remarks, February 13, 1975, *Papers of Presidents: Ford,* 1975, I, 251-54. Also see President Ford's comments, question and answer press conference, February 20, 1976, *Papers of Presidents: Ford,* 1976-1977, I, 402-3. Because of the difficulties in executive-legislative relations following the Vietnam War, the Watergate affair, and the enactment of the War Powers Resolution and restraints on overseas intelligence operations, President Ford was especially sensitive on the matter of presidential-congressional coopera- tion, which was evidenced in a number of his addresses and other policy state- ments.

4 3   SENATE NATIONAL COMMITMENTS RESOLUTION, 1969

Whereas accurate definition of the term "national commitment" in recent years has become obscured: Now, therefore, be it

Resolved, That (1) a national commitment for the purpose of this resolution means the use of the Armed Forces of the United States on for- eign territory, or a promise to assist a foreign country, government, or people by the use of the Armed Forces or financial resources of the United States, either immediately or upon the happening of certain events, and (2) it is the sense of the Senate that a national commitment by the United States results only from affirmative action taken by the executive and legislative branches of the United States Government by means of a treaty, statute, or concurrent resolution of both Houses of Congress specifically providing for such commitment.

Senate Resolution 85, 91st Congress, June 25, 1969; Senate Committee on Foreign Relations and House Committee on Foreign Affairs, *Legislation on For- eign Relations Through 1978,* Joint Committee Print (Washington: Government Printing Office, 1979), II, 443.

*   *   *

The National Commitments Resolution, . . . which was adopted by the Senate on June 25, 1969, by a vote of 70 to 16, affirmed the sense of the Senate. . . .

The resolution employed the term "commitment" in two distinct meanings: "commitment" in the sense of assigning, employing or involv- ing American military forces abroad; and "commitment" in the sense of contracting or obligating the United States to specified arrangements with foreign countries by means of treaties or executive agreements.   In neither sense did the National Commitments Resolution have immediate tangible results.

The War Powers Act of 1973 was designed to remedy that difficulty with respect to "commitments" in the first sense, that is, the commitment of American forces to hostilities abroad.   The Act has not yet been put to the test, and one hopes that it will not soon be tested.   As adopted in November 1973 over the President's veto, however, the War Powers Act (P.L. 93-148) appears to be a strong and potentially effective legislative restraint on executive warmaking, . . .

While acting decisively on the war powers, Congress has done little to assert its responsibilities over "commitments" in the second sense, having to do with treaties and executive agreements. The Case Act of 1972 (P.L. 92-403) requiring the Secretary of State to submit all executive agreements to Congress for its information--but not for its approval or disapproval--is useful as far as it goes, but that is not very far. It is perhaps noteworthy that the Nixon Administration at first opposed this very limited measure which asserts no Congressional authority at all but only Congress's right to be informed. In due course the Administration dropped its opposition, in grudging recognition, it would seem, of the point made by the principal witness for the bill before the Foreign Relations Committee, that "this proposed measure is so limited in its scope, so inherently reasonable, so obviously needed, so mild and gentle in its demands, and so entirely unexceptionable that it should receive the unanimous approval of the Congress."

J. William Fulbright, "Congress and Foreign Policy," *Commission on the Organization of the Government for the Conduct of Foreign Policy, June 1975*, vol. 5, Appendix L, p. 60. The War Powers Act, the treaty-making authority, and the Case Act are treated in Chapter 5, Documents 71-84.

4 4   "LEGISLATIVE VETO" IN FOREIGN RELATIONS

The Supreme Court has now decided, in INS v. Chadha and two related cases, that the legislative veto is unconstitutional. The Department of State and this Committee both recognize that the Court's historic decision affects a considerable body of legislation in the field of foreign affairs and national security. My principal theme here today is that our two branches of government have a common interest in devising cooperative ways to fulfill our shared responsibilities. We owe the American people a constructive response to the issues we now face. . . .

In The Federalist No. 47, James Madison referred to the separation of powers as "this essential precaution in favor of liberty." The genius of our constitutional system is that a structure of dispersed powers and checks and balances, designed to limit government power and preserve our freedom, has also been able to produce coherent and effective national policy. This success is a tribute to the Founding Fathers who built the structure; it is also a tribute to the generations of leaders and statesmen since them who have put the nation's well-being first and foremost as they played their constitutional roles in the various branches of government. . . .

"Legislative veto" is a term describing a variety of statutory devices that were meant to give the Congress legal control over actions of executive departments and agencies by means other than the enactment of laws. Legislative veto provisions have been included in statutes for more than 50 years. The procedure was first passed into law in the Act of June 30, 1932, which authorized President Hoover to reorganize the structure of the Federal Government subject to congressional review. The device was added to various statutes during World War II, when the Congress delegated greater authority to the President in the area of foreign affairs and national security, subject to the legislative veto procedure. Enactment of the procedure became frequent again in the 1960's and 1970's, as Congress sought to strengthen its oversight over the expanding practice of rulemaking by administrative agencies. Adoption of the legislative veto procedure reached its zenith in the early 1970's, in connection with some major controversies in the area of foreign affairs and national security.

Some of these statutes provide for congressional disapproval of proposed administrative regulations. Some involve review of decisions of individual cases . . . or review of other executive actions under authority granted by statute. Other legislation, such as the War Powers Resolution, involves the allocation of broad constitutional powers.

The legislative vetoes in all these statutes fall into two general categories. First, there are those in which the full Congress, or one House or one committee, is purportedly given a right to "veto" an administrative action. A typical statute of this kind requires the President to report an action or rule to both Houses of Congress. The executive action may not be made or take effect until after a fixed period (60 days, for example). If Congress does not act during the period, the executive action can take effect, but if the Congress disapproves (or one House or committee, as the statute may provide), it does not take effect. Second, there are statutory schemes by which an administrative action purportedly becomes valid only when approved by Congress. The typical statute of this kind requires the President to report a proposed action and then provides for affirmative approval by one or two Houses of the Congress. Most legislative vetoes, like the one in *Chadha,* fall within the first category. . . .

The legislative veto has long been controversial, ever since Woodrow Wilson first vetoed a bill incorporating a legislative veto in 1920.

Since then, most administrations have considered the device unconstitutional, while the Congress has tended to favor it as another useful check on executive authority. This specific controversy is now decided. Yet paradoxically, the *practice* of executive-legislative relations is unlikely to undergo any radical change in the wake of *Chadha,* for several reasons.

For one thing, *Chadha* does not affect other statutory procedures by which the Congress is informed of or involved in actions by the executive branch. Specifically, the Court's decision does not affect statutory requirements for notifications, certifications, findings or reports to Congress, consultations with Congress, or waiting periods which give Congress an opportunity to act before executive actions take effect. In the foreign affairs field, moreover, the executive branch and the Congress have generally reconciled or disposed of controversies and differences without resort to the process of legislative veto. Therefore, we see no reason why the Court's decision need cause a fundamental change in our relationship. . . .

Perhaps the key legal question raised by *Chadha* is that of "severability." The problem is an intriguing one: Since the legislative veto provision of a statute is unconstitutional, is any of the rest of the law tainted by that defect?

The Supreme Court has given us a basis for answering that question. The general principle is that the provision containing the legislative veto will be found to be severable, and the remainder of the statute will continue unaffected, unless it is evident that the Congress would not have enacted the remainder of the law without the legislative veto. That test establishes a strong presumption in favor of severability. . . .

There are more than a dozen statutes in the foreign affairs and national security area that are affected by the *Chadha* decision. I would say that four statutes or groups of statutes are of particular importance. These are arms export controls, the War Powers Resolution, nuclear nonproliferation controls, and trade controls related to emigration. . . .

. . . The War Powers Resolution contains four major operative parts. The first of these is a consultation requirement. . . .

The second operative part is a reporting requirement. . . .

The third operative part . . . requires the President to withdraw U.S. troops not later than 60 days after a report of actual or imminent involvement in hostilities unless the Congress has affirmatively authorized their continued presence.

The fourth operative part is a legislative veto. . . . the President must withdraw U.S. troops introduced into hostilities even before the end of 60 days if the Congress so directs by concurrent resolution.

The first and second provisions of the War Powers Resolution, on consultation and reporting, are in our view unaffected by the *Chadha* decision. We do not intend to change our practice with respect to consultation and reporting.

The fourth provision, which asserted a right of Congress by concurrent resolution to order the President to remove troops engaged in hostilities, is clearly unconstitutional under the Supreme Court's holding in *Chadha*. It must be said, however, that this holding is unlikely to have a significant impact on the way national security policy is conducted. In the decade since the enactment of the War Powers Resolution, no U.S. forces have been committed to long-term hostilities. It is doubtful that Presidents have refrained from such commitments simply because of the legislative veto in the War Powers Resolution; it is equally doubtful that Presidents will now feel freer of restraints because of *Chadha*. The lesson of recent history is that a President cannot sustain a major military involvement without congressional and public support.

The legislative veto provision of the War Powers Resolution is severable from the others, in our view, according to the Supreme Court's test and guidelines. The resolution itself includes a severability clause, and the other operative portions of the resolution need not be affected by the dropping of the veto provision.

The third operative part of the resolution, requiring positive congressional authorization after 60 days, does not fall within the scope of *Chadha.* Its constitutionality is neither affirmed, denied, nor even considered in the *Chadha* decision. As you know, the executive branch has traditionally had questions about this requirement of congressional authorization for Presidential disposition of our armed forces, both in light of the President's Commander-in-Chief power and on practical grounds. Congress, of course, has had a different view. I do not believe that any purpose would be served by debating these questions here, in the abstract. . . . I want to reaffirm the administration's strong commitment to the principles of consultation and reporting, confident that in a spirit of cooperation the Executive and the Congress can meet future challenges together in the national interest. . . .

The spirit with which we expect to work with Congress in the future, in all statutory fields, is illustrated by another example. We are required by the Case-Zablocki Act to report executive agreements to the Congress, and we do so regularly. That procedure notifies the Congress of agreements already signed. There is also a procedure for enabling this Committee and the House Foreign Affairs Committee to consult with us as to the form of significant international agreements *prior* to their conclusion. This practice was arranged between the Department of State and the Chairman of the two Committees in 1978. It is not required by law, but makes good sense. We will maintain it.

As I have emphasized, little of practical significance need in fact change as a result of the Supreme Court decision. The Department of State is committed to continue working closely with the members and committees of Congress and to take their concerns into account in reaching decisions on issues of policy. If anything, I believe *Chadha* will make the departments and agencies of the executive branch more, not less, conscious that they are accountable for their actions.

There are many basic questions about these separation of powers which the Supreme Court will probably never settle. In that realm our constitutional law is determined, in a sense, as in Britain--by constitutional practice, by political realities, by the fundamental good sense and public conscience of the American people and their representatives. This is how we have always settled these questions, and this is how we, the Executive and the Congress, must approach these problems in the aftermath of *Chadha.*

Our Constitution has proved to be a wise and enduring blueprint for free government. In this period of our history, our Nation faces challenges that the drafters of that document could not have imagined. The Federal Government has the duty to conduct this Nation's foreign policy and ensure its security in a nuclear age, in an era of instantaneous communications, in a complex modern world in which international politics has become truly global. America's responsibility as a world leader imposes on us a special obligation of coherence, vision, and constancy in the conduct of our foreign relations. For this there must be unity in our national government. The President and the Congress must work in harmony, or our people will not have the effective, strong, and purposeful foreign policy which they expect and deserve.

Kenneth W. Dam, Deputy Secretary of State, statement, Senate Foreign Relations Committee, July 28, 1983, *American Foreign Policy: Current Documents*, 1983, pp. 25-30. For commentary on the War Powers Act, and the Case Act, see Chapter 5, Documents 75, 80-84.

DIPLOMATIC RELATIONS AND REPRESENTATION

This segment deals with three major aspects of the conduct of diplomatic relations--recognition, diplomatic representation, and American diplomats and their missions. Although the Constitution fails to specify this, normally, by virtue of his authority to send and receive diplomatic emissaries, the President exercises the function of recognizing both new states and governments. Documents 45 and 46 present general United States recognition policy, American criteria for recognition, and a stipulation distinguishing between recognition and approval of a foreign government.

Documents 47 to 51 provide selected illustrations of United States practice with respect to terminating diplomatic and consular relations (Cuba, 1961), closing of an American embassy without terminating diplomatic relations (Uganda, 1973), United States policy to normalize diplomatic relations in the 1970's, launching such relations with a new state (East Germany, 1974), and commencing formal relations with the Holy See/Vatican (1984).

So far as the last of these is concerned, the President commissioned charges d'affaires to the Papal States from 1848 to 1867. On February 2, 1867, Congress enacted a law which prohibited the appropriation of funds for the support of an American mission to the Papal States. Pursuant to an act of Congress passed in 1931, President Roosevelt sent a charge to the Holy See from December 1941 to July 1944. In addition, during World War II he appointed Myron C. Taylor, with the rank of Ambassador, as his special diplomatic envoy and personal surrogate to the Vatican. This appointment continued until 1950, despite active opposition by an organization of "Protestants and Other Americans United for the Separation of Church and State" founded in 1948, which sought to terminate United States representation to the Vatican. It was not until November 22, 1983, that Congress repealed the law of 1867 (P.L. 98-164, Sec. 134), and in 1984, by an exchange of diplomatic notes, United States relations were regularized with the Holy See and William A. Wilson was appointed as the American Ambassador.

The final portion, consisting of Documents 52 to 56, focusing on American diplomatic missions, contains illustrative materials on the integration, roles, and streamlining of overseas establishments (Documents 52 to 54) and the nature and status of American ambassadors (Documents 55 and 56). For a complete listing, with tabular data, of all ranking Department of State officers and United States diplomats who functioned as chiefs of mission, see Department of State, *Principal Officers of the Department of State and United States Chiefs of Mission, 1778-1988* (Washington: Government Printing Office, 1988).

For comprehensive multilateral conventions--the first such treaties-- on diplomatic and consular officers and relations, negotiated and signed in 1961 and 1963, see the Vienna Convention on Diplomatic Relations, TIAS 7502; 23 *U.S. Treaties* 3227-3373; and the Vienna Convention on Consular Relations, TIAS 6820; 21 *U.S. Treaties* 77-374. These treaties deal with the titles, classification, and ranks, and with agrement, reception, inviolability, precedence, and privileges and immunities of diplomats, as well as comparable matters for consular officers, and with their functions, staffs, families, premises, communications, and related matters. The Convention on Diplomatic Relations was supplemented with an Optional Protocol Concerning the Compulsory Settlement of Disputes--see 23 *U.S. Treaties* 3374-3434.

4 5   RECOGNITION CRITERIA AND PRACTICE

Under our constitutional system, recognition and the establishment of diplomatic relations are Presidential prerogatives. Establishing and maintaining diplomatic relations with governments, however, is not a unilateral process: both states must agree that it serves their national interests.

The United States maintains relations with other governments because it helps us achieve our basic foreign policy objectives: By communicating directly with governments on a full range of issues--by stating our views and listening to theirs--we can help avoid misunderstandings and affect the decisions and actions of other governments. This is particularly true in crises, when good communication is essential.

Criteria for Recognition

Diplomatic recognition of governments is a comparatively recent practice in the history of international relations. Traditionally some European governments used nonrecognition of revolutionary change to protect monarchies and to emphasize the unique legitimacy of dynastic heirs and their governments. France ignored this tradition by recognizing the United States during our Revolutionary War. Later, when the revolutionary French Government took power in 1792, Thomas Jefferson, our first Secretary of State, instructed the U.S. envoy in Paris to deal with it because it had been "formed by the will of the nation substantially declared."

Throughout most of the 19th century, the United States recognized stable governments without thereby attempting to confer approval. U.S. recognition policy grew more complex as various Administrations applied differing criteria for recognition and expressed differently the reasons for their decisions. For example, Secretary of State William Seward (1861-69) added as a criterion the government's ability to honor its international obligations; President Rutherford Hayes (1877-81) required a demonstration of popular support for the new government; and President Woodrow Wilson (1913-21) favored using recognition to spread democracy around the world by demanding free elections.

Other criteria have been applied since then. These include the degree of foreign involvement in the government as well as the government's political orientation, attitude toward foreign investment, and treatment of

U.S. citizens, corporations, and government representatives.

One result of such complex recognition criteria was to create the impression among other nations that the United States approved of those governments it recognized and disapproved of those from which it withheld recognition. This appearance of approval, in turn, affected our decisions in ways that have not always advanced U.S. interests. In recent years, U.S. practice has been to deemphasize and avoid the use of recognition in cases of changes of governments and to concern ourselves with the question of whether we wish to have diplomatic relations with the new governments.

The Administration's policy is that establishment of relations does not involve approval or disapproval but merely demonstrates a willingness on our part to conduct our affairs with other governments directly. In today's interdependent world, effective contacts with other governments are of ever-increasing importance.

U.S. policy statement based on Department of State publication in its GIST series, August 1977; *Digest of United States Practice in International Law,* 1977, pp. 19-20.

4 6 RECOGNITION AND DIPLOMATIC REPRESENTATION NOT IMPLY APPROVAL OF FOREIGN GOVERNMENT

The Congress finds that the conduct of diplomatic relations with a foreign government has as its principal purpose the discussion and negotiation with that government of outstanding issues and, like the recognition of a foreign government, does not in itself imply approval of that government or of the political-economic system it represents.

Foreign Relations Authorization Act, Fiscal Year 1979 (P.L. 95-426; 92 Statutes at Large 963), approved by President Carter, October 7, 1978, in *Digest of United States Practice in International Law,* 1978, p. 64.

4 7 TERMINATION OF DIPLOMATIC AND CONSULAR RELATIONS WITH CUBA, 1 9 6 1

Between one and two o'clock this morning, the Government of Cuba delivered to the United States Charge d'Affaires ad interim of the United States Embassy in Habana a note stating that the Government of Cuba had decided to limit the personnel of our Embassy and Consulate in Habana to eleven persons. Forty-eight hours was granted for the departure of our entire staff with the exception of eleven. This unusual action on the part of the Castro Government can have no other purpose than to render impossible the conduct of normal diplomatic relations with that Government.

Accordingly, I have instructed the Secretary of State to deliver a note to the Charge d'Affaires ad interim of Cuba in Washington which . . .

states that the Government of the United States is hereby formally terminating diplomatic and consular relations with the Government of Cuba. Copies of both notes are being made available to the press.

This calculated action on the part of the Castro Government is only the latest of a long series of harassments, baseless accusations, and vilification. There is a limit to what the United States in self-respect can endure. That limit has now been reached. . . .

Dwight D. Eisenhower, statement, January 3, 1961; *Papers of Presidents: Eisenhower,* 1960, p. 891.

*   *   *

I have the honor to refer to a note dated January 2, 1961, from the Government of Cuba to the Charge d'Affaires of the United States Embassy in Habana stating that the Government of Cuba has decided that personnel of the Embassy and Consulate of the United States in the City of Habana, regardless of nationality, shall not exceed eleven persons.

This unwarranted action by the Government of Cuba places crippling limitations on the ability of the United States Mission to carry on its normal diplomatic and consular functions. It would consequently appear that it is designed to achieve an effective termination of diplomatic and consular relations between the Government of Cuba and the Government of the United States. Accordingly, the Government of the United States hereby formally notifies the Government of Cuba of the termination of such relations. . . .

The Government of Cuba is requested to withdraw from the United States as soon as possible all Cuban nationals employed in the Cuban Embassy in Washington and in all Cuban Consular establishments in the United States.

The Government of the United States is requesting the Government of Switzerland to assume diplomatic and consular representation in Cuba on behalf of the Government of the United States.

Diplomatic note of Secretary of State Christian Herter to Cuban Government, January 3, 1961; *American Foreign Policy: Current Documents,* 1960, pp. 251-52. Texts of exchange of notes also given in 44 *Department of State Bulletin* (January 23, 1961): 103-4. On January 4, the White House announced that this action had no effect on the status of the United States naval station at Guantanamo. For related documents on United States relations with Cuba, see Chapters 11 (on Bay of Pigs and Missile Crises) and 26 (the exclusion of Cuba from the inter-American system and the application of sanctions against Cuba)--Documents 449 and 459.

4 8   CLOSING OF UNITED STATES EMBASSY IN UGANDA, 1973

Upon instructions from the Government of the United States, the Embassy wishes to inform the Government of Uganda that all diplomatic and consular representatives of the United States are being withdrawn from Uganda.

This decision by the Government of the United States results from actions of the Government of Uganda contrary to its international obligations which have created intolerable conditions for the conduct of diplomatic relations in Uganda. These have included, inter alia, official threats against the safety and dignity of diplomatic representatives of the Government of the United States in Uganda, unfounded accusations by high Ugandan officials, and the precipitous and unjustified expulsion from Uganda of American personnel responsible for the protection of the Embassy and its personnel.

The Embassy will, without delay, inform the Ministry of Foreign Affairs regarding the United States Government's intention to request another power to assume the protection of its interests and property in Uganda. . . .

The Government of the United States does not intend to request the Government of Uganda to take reciprocal action with regard to its diplomatic and consular representatives in the United States and accordingly does not intend by its action to initiate a severance of diplomatic relations between the two governments.

The Government of the United States regrets the circumstances requiring that its representatives in Uganda be withdrawn and looks forward to the time when they may safely return. The Government of the United States hopes that it can continue to work with the Government of Uganda on issues of common concern through the protecting power in Kampala and the Ugandan Embassy in Washington.

Diplomatic note to Government of Uganda, November 8, 1973; *Digest of United States Practice in International Law,* 1973, pp. 11-12. Although the American mission was closed, this action did not constitute a break in diplomatic relations.

4 9   NORMALIZING UNITED STATES DIPLOMATIC RELATIONS

. . . We don't want to be in a position that once a country is not friendly to us, and once they are completely within the influence of the Soviet Union they should forever be in that status.

And as I've already indicated, . . . I want to move as best I can to re-establish normal friendly relationships with those countries.

In some instances, the obstacles are quite severe, as in the case of Cuba and perhaps Vietnam. But I think this is what our Government ought to do. And I would like to have a situation when I go out of office that all the nations in the world have diplomatic relationships with us.

We now have 14 who don't, and I've been pursuing this aggressively.

. . .

Jimmy Carter, statement, press conference, June 13, 1977; *Digest of United States Practice in International Law,* 1977, pp. 17-18.

*   *   *

[The 14 countries with which the United States did not (at the time) have such diplomatic relations were Albania, Angola, Cambodia, the People's Republic of China, the Comoros Islands, the People's Republic of the Congo, Cuba, Equatorial Guinea, Iraq, North Korea, Mongolia, Southern Rhodesia, Vietnam, and the People's Democratic Republic of Yemen, as well as the Holy See/ Vatican.]

*   *   *

We live . . . in an interdependent world. And in one way or another we find our fate and our futures tied increasingly to those of other peoples. If we cannot communicate easily with them, we cannot effectively promote our own interests or build new bonds of common interest.

This brings me to my central point: We believe that diplomatic relations help us to discharge our basic duty to protect the interests of our government and our citizens. By keeping open a channel of communication with other countries, we best serve our long-range objective of encouraging the growth of democratic institutions. . . .

We maintain diplomatic relations with many governments of which we do not necessarily approve. The reality is that, in this day and age, coups and other unscheduled changes of government are not exceptional developments. Withholding diplomatic relations from these regimes after they have obtained effective control penalizes us. It means we forsake much of the chance to influence the attitudes and conduct of a new regime. Without relations we forfeit opportunities to transmit our values and communicate our policies. Isolation may well bring out the worst in the new government.

For the same reasons, we eschew withdrawal of diplomatic relations except in rare instances--for example the outbreak of war or events which make it physically impossible to maintain a diplomatic presence in another capital.

If we continue to withhold diplomatic relations, this hesitancy invites confusion and can become the center of a touchy political issue. Eventual establishment of diplomatic relations then comes wrongly to be considered as a form of approval. . . .

Indeed, efforts to restore relations once broken often encounter special difficulties. Inevitably, constituencies in both countries develop an emotional investment in the absence of relations. Financial claims and counter-claims pile up, and there is a backlog of issues which might have been resolved if normal relations had existed. Faced with this legacy of problems, the process of restoring relations must be approached with great care and deliberation. . . .

In sum, we believe normal diplomatic relations are an asset to promote other objectives, an asset we cannot deny ourselves without incurring substantial cost. As Churchill put it: "When relations are most difficult, that is the time diplomacy is most needed."

There is no certainty that two nations will be able to resolve their disputes by talking about them. But without effective communications, without some form of dialogue, the odds are high that there will be no progress at all.

Warren Christopher, address, Occidental College, June 11, 1977, concerning normalization of diplomatic relations with other governments; *Digest of United States Practice in International Law,* 1977, pp. 18-19.

50   COMMENCEMENT OF DIPLOMATIC RELATIONS--EAST GERMANY, 1974

On September 4, 1974, the United States and the German Democratic Republic (G.D.R.) agreed to establish diplomatic relations and to exchange ambassadors. A joint U.S.-G.D.R. communique issued on September 4, after negotiations in Washington during the period July 15-26, 1974, stated, inter alia, the agreement of the two governments to "establish diplomatic relations as of today in accordance with the Vienna Convention on Diplomatic Relations of April 18, 1961, and to base the conduct of these relations on the Charter of the United Nations." The communique noted the intention of the two governments to exchange diplomatic representatives with the rank of Ambassador Extraordinary and Plenipotentiary.

Digest of United States Practice in International Law, 1974, p. 11. Also see documents on the German question in Chapter 8, especially Document 146.

51   COMMENCEMENT OF DIPLOMATIC RELATIONS WITH THE HOLY SEE (VATICAN), 1984

Myron C. Taylor was appointed as the President's Personal Representative at the Vatican on December 31, 1939; his resignation became effective on January 18, 1950. . . .

On October 20, 1951, the President appointed Gen. Mark W. Clark to be the first U.S. Ambassador to Vatican City. According to reports in the press the White House reaffirmed the power of the President to establish diplomatic relations with the Vatican without consulting Congress but announced that the President would request congressional approval of the nomination.

After widespread controversy on the appointment and protests from numerous Protestant groups, General Clark withdrew as the nominee on January 13, 1952. A U.S. Ambassador to Vatican City was not appointed during the Truman administration.

Note appended to President Truman's press conference, January 19, 1950; *Papers of Presidents: Truman,* 1950, p. 116. For commentary on the international status of, and diplomatic relations with, the Holy See, see Marjorie

Whiteman, *Digest of International Law*, I, 587-93, and II, 1200-2.

*   *   *

Q. Mr. President, in view of the increased contact between the Vatican and the Iron Curtain countries, do you feel it would be fruitful at this time to consider setting up some regular channel of communication between the United States and the Vatican?

THE PRESIDENT. No. It seems to me that the present methods of communication, which are the obvious ones and have been in effect . . . for a great many years--any time anyone wants to get in communication, it's possible to get messages to the Vatican. The Embassy in Rome, I am sure, would be available. It doesn't seem to me that there is any need for changing procedures.

John Kennedy, press conference question and answer session, July 17, 1963; *Papers of Presidents: Kennedy*, 1963, p. 567.

*   *   *

The United States of America and the Holy See, in the desire to further promote the existing mutual friendly relations, have decided by common agreement to establish diplomatic relations between them at the level of embassy on the part of the United States of America and nunciature on the part of the Holy See, as of today, Jan. 10, 1984.

*   *   *

The Holy See and the United States of America, in the desire to further promote the existing mutual friendly relations, have decided by common agreement to establish diplomatic relations between them on the level of embassy on the part of the United States of America and of nunciature on the part of the Holy See, as of today [Jan. 10, 1984].

*   *   *

The President today announced his intention to nominate William A. Wilson to be Ambassador to the Holy See.

Mr. Wilson has been serving since February of 1981 as the President's Personal Representative to the Holy See.

*   *   *

Q. How do you respond to protests from the American Jewish Congress and other religious groups that this is a violation of the separation of church and state?

A. Well, it isn't.

Q. Why isn't it?

A. It's not a violation of church and state because for a long time, we recognized the Holy See as having an international personality distinct from the Roman Catholic Church. This relationship will be with the Holy See. The Holy See is distinct from the Catholic Church.

*   *   *

To us, Your Holiness, the Holy See and your pastorate represent one of humanity's greatest moral and spiritual forces. And your visit is particularly significant, coming as it does soon after the reestablishment of relations between the Holy See and the United States. For over a century we maintained warm and fruitful, but informal relations. Now we have exchanged Ambassadors, and we hope to build on this new relationship to our mutual benefit and to the benefit of peace-loving people everywhere.

Exchange of diplomatic notes, January 10, 1984; White House statement, January 10, 1984, in *Papers of Presidents: Reagan,* 1984, I, 22; Department of State press briefing, January 10, 1984, in *American Foreign Policy: Current Documents,* 1984, p. 464; and Ronald Reagan, remarks at welcoming ceremony for Pope John Paul II, Fairbanks, Alaska, May 2, 1984, in *Papers of Presidents: Reagan,* 1984, I, 619. For commentary, including official and public reaction, see "U.S.-Vatican Diplomatic Relations," January 10, 1984, *Historic Documents,* 1984, pp. 19-22.

5 2   INTEGRATING PROLIFERATION OF OVERSEAS MISSIONS

For the United States, the day of traditional diplomacy came to an end with our reentry into the world arena in World War II. The war and its aftermath led to American involvement in a wide range of new activities abroad. More recently, the rapid growth of technology has not only made further additions to the agenda of diplomacy but has changed the very character of the diplomatic profession.

With the enormous growth of U.S. interests and activities abroad, foreign relations were no longer the virtual monopoly of the Department of State and the issues of foreign policy were no longer exclusively diplomatic problems in the old and narrow sense. Foreign relations now covered a range of interests and activities emanating from and stretching across the whole broad spectrum of departments and offices making up the executive branch of the government. Dynamic new foreign affairs agencies such as those for foreign aid, information and intelligence activities were created. Older agencies as diverse as the Department of Agriculture and the Treasury Department became deeply involved in activities abroad. Today, to cite but a few examples, we have critically important programs for promoting our commercial exports, for concessional sales of agricultural commodities, for narcotics control, for military and development aid, for the inspection of aircraft and the licensing of airline routes, for cooperation in the peaceful applications of atomic energy, for scientific and technological exchange, for coordinating international monetary policy, and for communicating directly with people of other countries through the media of press, radio, and television.

The enormous proliferation of the overseas interests and activities of domestic agencies has not been a smooth and carefully planned process. The interests which have sprung up have been, and remain, incredibly numerous and diverse, frequently parochial, often overlapping, occasionally conflicting. Unless they can be forged into a coherent and unified national policy, there is danger that our voice abroad will be discordant and our programs at cross purposes. To prevent this, the President must be able to rely on a staff arm capable of taking the lead in directing and coordinating both the formulation and execution of foreign policy.

Department of State, *Diplomacy for the 70's*, pp. 3-4.

5 3   ROLES OF DIPLOMATIC MISSIONS

. . . the first step is to compare the roles embassies and ambassadors have traditionally been asked to perform--as opposed to the means of performing them--with the requirements of today's diplomacy. For in spite of technical developments, much of what embassies have done in the past remains relevant.

To enumerate:

--An American ambassador, whether he is in London, Tokyo, or Ouagadougou, is there first of all as the personal representative of the President of the United States. As such, until worldwide diplomatic agreement or custom concludes there is no need for countries to be represented in their neighbors' lands, we, with our worldwide interests, are going to have to continue having embassies, with accredited ambassadors, in all but the most trivial countries. . . .

--Overseas missions have always served, in addition to what we might call the traditional representative functions, as listening posts or information-gathering spots to provide our government with factual and up-to-date information about what is going on in a particular country. In our shrinking, interdependent world, the U.S. cannot afford to ignore or cut itself off from even an apparently insignificant country, for as we have found, . . . insignificant countries are seldom so by choice and make the best of passing opportunities to become significant. For us as a "superpower", the necessity of knowing what's going on in a particular country is correspondingly greater than it has been for us in the past or than it is for other countries.

--The increase in U.S. business and trade abroad, most obviously as a result of multinational activities, has also meant that a U.S. embassy or consulate's responsibility to oversee the interests of U.S. citizens abroad has become more important than it was.

--Finally, the embassy, and specifically the American ambassador, has traditionally been assigned the function of carrying out negotiations, discussions, or other daily business with the countries to which they are accredited--in other words, of implementing our foreign policy. It is this last function that transportation and communication advances have most significantly (and some would say deleteriously) affected. Whereas the lack of such facilities in the "good old days" left the ambassador to a large extent on his own in reacting to activities of the host country or negotiating particular arrangements with them, in today's world, the ambassador is often nothing more than a well-paid and appropriately-dressed messenger. And sometimes, when Washington thinks the messages are too important, a high-ranking emissary is sent to deal directly with the host government, . . .

. . . it is clear that tasks remain for overseas missions to perform that cannot be handled effectively, or at all, any other way. Thus while some contend our missions should be redesigned so as to have fewer ambassadors, or regional ambassadors, or roving ambassadors, or that ambassadors be called managers, and embassies, offices, there are convincing arguments that show we will need roughly the same number of missions abroad in the coming decade as we have now, that they must be staffed with Americans, and that someone must be running them.

T. McAdams Deford, "Posts and Missions," *Commission on the Organization of the Government for the Conduct of Foreign Policy, June 1975,* vol. 6, Appendix Q, pp. 348-49.

5 4   STREAMLINING DIPLOMATIC MISSIONS

It is obvious that the mission of the future must be related to the world in which it will operate. That world is rapidly changing, and as problems in foreign relations become more complex, so do the solutions.

Since World War II, increasing complexities in foreign affairs have been dealt with by adding new agencies to the foreign affairs community and by expanding the responsibilities of existing ones. We have done little to clear away the deadwood of the past and until 2 years ago the bureaucracy abroad had continued to grow, in part through a constant addition of other agency representations.

Increased staff has been the answer of the past but the point has already been reached where further increase becomes counterproductive. To the foreigner the mission often appears as a threatened intrusion into internal affairs of another country if only because of its manpower, buildings, and tendency to reach out into every facet of local life, both for information and for influence. To the Ambassador it often seems uncontrollable as he cannot successfully coordinate it and provide the positive contribution to policy and problem-solving that Washington expects of him. . . .

Constant staff increase can only compound existing problems and will not enable an Ambassador to deal with the real problems. . . . These will be, it must be constantly stressed, more multilateral and multinational in nature than ever before. In 1964 Senator Jackson said: "On many fronts our government is seeking to accomplish its goals through regional programs and international agencies but it has not yet taken adequate steps to relate the American country mission and program to multilateral efforts." . . .

It is our strong belief that cobwebs of tradition and the inertia of bureaucracy which control operations in Washington have led to a situation where microcosms of that bureaucracy are recreated at capitals throughout the world; microcosms that often have little relevance to the true interests of the United States in the country or to the complex technical and evolving nature of international relationships.   While it will essentially be through the restructuring of the Washington system that we will be able to reshape our overseas missions . . . we can and should take steps now to make them leaner and more efficient.

Department of State, *Diplomacy for the 70's*, p. 451.

5 5   THE CONTEMPORARY AMERICAN AMBASSADOR

With respect to representation, it used to be that an Ambassador represented his sovereign at the court of the other sovereign.   Now things are different.   An Ambassador still has the tedious round of official parties and entertainment.   He must still participate in the pomp and ceremony of official life.   But he must also hold the hands of newsmen, open doors for businessmen, and attend to visiting Congressmen.   Besides, today's Ambassador is expected to get away from the capital and to acquire first-hand knowledge of the country's political, social and economic life.   What the people are saying is often more important than the gossip of high society, and his business suits and even more informal attire may wear out sooner than his white tie and tails. . . .

An Ambassador is the personal representative of our Chief of State and Government to the Chief of State to whom he is accredited. . . .

A Chief of Mission customarily works in the framework of the State Department, he reports to the Department, his salary and administrative support come from the Department.   The source of his instructions is normally the Secretary of State, acting for the President, or, in appropriate cases, an Assistant Secretary of State, acting for the Secretary.   This is as it should be.

But, in practice, an Ambassador needs status as the President's man. Present and former Ambassadors emphasized . . . that a chief asset an Ambassador can bring to his job is the reputation for having the special confidence and trust of the President.   When an Ambassador overseas negotiates, or speaks in private or in public, his audience needs to feel that he has the confidence and speaks with the authority of the President of the United States. . . .

The modern Ambassador plies his diplomatic trade with less autonomy than in earlier days.   But he is still the spearhead of American influence abroad.   A President and a Secretary of State, in setting and maintaining our national course, are heavily dependent upon him for advice and help.   And no quantity of messages and visitors from Washington can take the place of an Ambassador's personal judgment and effectiveness in the field situation. . . .

It is obvious that an Ambassador's first job is to carry out his instructions.   The problem is to find a balance between the extremes of overinstruction, on the one hand, and freewheeling, on the other. . . .

Basic policy decisions will continue to be made in Washington--for obvious reasons. Yet it is up to the Ambassador to make clear to Washington what he believes is needed in his country of assignment, and what he thinks is likely to work. The advice of our Ambassadors should be significant in shaping policy, and could be more important than it has been in the past.

Committee on Government Operations, Subcommittees on National Security Staffing and Operations, U.S. Senate, *Administration of National Security: The American Ambassador,* 88th Congress, 2d session, Committee Print, 1964, pp. 3-7.

*   *   *

. . . the Ambassador is the key to the proper functioning of a diplomatic mission. In the end it is his views and recommendations which are sought and it is largely through him that the U.S. Government deals with the foreign country. We can only reecho the words of Senator Jackson when he said in 1964: "There's no substitute for the broadly experienced Ambassador who exercises leadership of American government activities in his area, who makes a positive contribution to policy plans and operations, and who has reserves of judgment, nerve, and know-how to call upon in a pinch." . . .

Whether or not an Ambassador should have the ability to use his people as he deems best has been repeatedly argued. The argument usually takes the form of an Ambassador trying to obtain enough flexibility to allow him to deal with urgent tasks while, across the seas, government agencies resist the diversion of "their" people from what they consider proper tasks in accord with carefully spelled out job descriptions. A demanding Ambassador can often succeed at the price of somewhat strained relations with the Washington agency. Others, perhaps unfortunately, find the bureaucratic battle not worth the effort and make do with perhaps less-qualified personnel over whom their authority is more direct.

We will suggest some management reforms to give an Ambassador better control over the activities of the mission and to insure an improved, more rapid response to Washington's needs. Essentially, these changes are problem-oriented and designed to give the mission the flexibility it needs to solve problems. Traditional compartmentalization may have to be sacrificed in some cases. We do not think, however, that precise guidelines can be laid out that are applicable to all posts. The workload of the Ambassador will be increased if he is asked to design his post to increase efficiency, but we consider that this is indeed part of his role. Our suggestions are, therefore, calculated to give him choices.

Department of State, *Diplomacy for the 70's,* p. 452.

*   *   *

THE BASIC PRINCIPLE

As is attested by his commission and letters of credence, the Ambassador is the direct representative of the President, as Chief of State and Head of Government of the United States, to the Chief of State (and Head of Government) of the country of his residence. He is thus the President's counterpart, responsible for the full panoply of interests and activities of the United States within his area of jurisdiction. This status has not only been traditionally recognized and accepted, but was wisely reflected in the Rogers Act of 1924 and the Foreign Service Act of 1946, which established not a foreign service of the Department of State but *The Foreign Service of the United States.* This is not to say that every Foreign Service Officer can expect to rise to the rank of Ambassador or that qualified persons from outside the Government should be excluded from appointment as Chiefs of Mission, but it does mean that every Foreign Service Officer is expected to consider himself as being in the service of the nation as a whole and to prepare and conduct himself accordingly.

The implementation of the concept presented no problem, other than occasional skirmishes with the Departments of Commerce and Agriculture, so long as the activity of American Missions abroad was largely limited to the traditional functions of representation, negotiation, reporting, assistance to citizens and promotion of trade.

However, with the emergence of the United States as a "superpower" on the world scene during and after World War II, new instruments of foreign policy were developed and new agencies were established to operate them, both at home and overseas--propaganda, intelligence, cultural relations, military and economic aid, and disarmament. At the same time, the explosion of American interests on a global scale soon impinged on the functions of practically all Departments and agencies of the Federal Government as the boundary between foreign and domestic policies became blurred, and these organizations began to seek representation of what they considered to be their legitimate (if specialized) interests abroad.

Washington: I leave aside the consequent and repeated efforts to bring under control of the President and the Secretary of State the formulation and conduct of the nation's foreign policy in the capital, other than to express my conviction that agencies dealing exclusively and overtly with foreign policy operations should be integrated into and administered uniformly by the Department of State, and that the foreign activities of other agencies should be closely coordinated by State. But whatever bureaucratic structures, pressures and conflicts may be tolerated in Washington, the United States Government must speak with one voice and act as one person--the person of the President as represented by the Ambassador--in foreign lands.

Overseas: With the mushrooming of separate overseas services after World War II, confusion arose abroad as well as at home. Here, too, efforts were made to restore order by a series of Presidential pronouncements, executive orders and letters affirming the primacy of the Ambassador over all elements (except military theater commands) and by the administrative introduction of the "country team" concept. These were perhaps useful devices for the times. However, they fell short of a clearcut confirmation of the authority of the Ambassador commensurate with his responsibilities as established by law and long-standing practice. They also deviated from the basic principle by implicitly, or in some cases explicitly, treating the Ambassador as the representative, not of the President, but of the Department of State (the senior Department) and thus tended to transfer some interagency conflicts from Washington to the field. . . .

The basic concept was succintly set forth by Ambassador Graham Martin in his article "Organizational Imperatives" in the *Annals* of the American Academy of Political and Social Science (November, 1968):

The ambassador, as the personal representative of the President of the United States, must assume responsibility, in the President's name, for everything that the United States government does in the country to which he is accredited. To discharge that responsibility effectively, he must also assume command in the President's name, of all activities of all United States personnel in the country. No ambassador worthy of being given such authority in the first place is likely to abuse it. If he does, the remedy is not to overrule him constantly, but to dismiss him.

IMPLEMENTATION OF THE PRINCIPLE

The extent to which our overseas missions can be expected to operate efficiently and effectively depends primarily on two factors.

1. The attitudes and method of operation of the President and the Secretary of State;

2. The quality of our Ambassadors and their supporting personnel.

Washington Aspects

Identification with the President: The President's "special trust and confidence" in his Ambassadors must be more than the words on their commissions. It is essential to the Ambassador's status and performance that he know the President, and that he be known in the country of his residence to have a personal relationship with him (as well as, of course, with the Secretary of State). With the proliferation of Missions to the emergent nations (in excolonial areas previously not even warranting a Consulate) and to multilateral organizations. . . . some problems arise which cannot be solved by the traditional personally autographed photograph. The President should see and should want to see individually his Ambassadors. . . .

Informing the Ambassador: The Ambassador must be kept informed of all Government decisions and activities affecting the relationship between the United States and the country to which he is accredited. . . .

Overseas Aspects

Department Support: The Ambassador must have strong rear echelon support in the State Department. His back-up at home should be raised from its present level and strengthened to provide a sort of duplicate of the mission abroad, able to maintain liaison and get action from all interested agencies in Washington, and to provide quick replies to the Ambassador's communications. . . .

Communications: The Ambassador will normally use the State Department channels of communications. He must, however, have access to and authority over channels of communications from the Embassy operated by Defense and CIA. He must be kept regularly informed of all important substantive matters reported through these channels and be provided, at his request, with all reports or other communications sent through them.

Contacts: The Ambassador must control access by all members of his Embassy to officials of the government to which he is accredited. No element of the Embassy can be authorized to establish or maintain official contacts without the Ambassador's knowledge and approval. THis is not to say that contacts should be restricted to or handled by the Ambassador himself. On the contrary, a good Ambassador will delegate responsibility broadly . . . and not only authorize but actively encourage the development of working and social relationships at all levels and by all elements of the Embassy. . . .

A Unified Mission: An effective Ambassador will encourage all elements of the Mission to consider their specialized activities as contributing to the accomplishment of the overall objectives of the United States in the country of their assignment.   Indeed, with a proper understanding of the common mission of all elements useful intramural cooperation in exchange of information and other forms of mutual aid can be developed, enhancing the overall performance of the Mission. . . .

Foy D. Kohler, "The Role of the Ambassador," in *Commission on the Organization of the Government for the Conduct of Foreign Policy, June 1975,* vol. 6, Appendix Q, pp. 319-24. Also see J. Robert Schaetzel, "Is the Ambassador an Endangered Species, or Merely Obsolete?" pp. 325-33.

56   AMERICAN AMBASSADORS' FUNCTIONS AND AUTHORITY

Please accept my personal best wishes for success in your mission. As my personal representative, you will share with me and with the Secretary of State the responsibility for the conduct of our relations with _____.

I want to state clearly that, as Chief of the United States Diplomatic Mission to _____, and my representative, you have the strongest mandate possible. As P.L. 93-475 [the State Department Authorization Act for Fiscal Year 1975] states, you have "full responsibility for the direction, coordination, and supervision of all United States Government officers and employees" in your country of accreditation. This authority includes all United States Government programs and activities in that country. The only exceptions to this rule are personnel under the Chief of a United States Mission accredited to an international organization, personnel detailed to duty with international organizations, and, as stated in P.L. 93-475, "personnel under the command of a United States area military commander." I expect you to provide positive direction, assuring that all United States Government activities under the authority of your Mission reflect and support current United States policy, are effectively coordinated, and are economically administered.

I expect the highest standards of professional and personal conduct by the personnel from all agencies assigned to our missions abroad. As my personal representative you have the authority and my full support in taking actions required to assure that these standards are maintained. All United States Government personnel in your country of assignment should be made aware of your authority and responsibilities. It is their duty to keep you thoroughly and currently informed about all their activities so you can effectively direct, coordinate and supervise United States programs and operations under your jurisdiction and recommend missionwide policies to Washington. . . .

I have notified all heads of departments and agencies of the Government concerning the authority and responsibilities of the Chiefs of American Diplomatic Missions, and I have asked them to inform their personnel in the field accordingly.

You have my personal confidence as you undertake your mission. I am sure that you will represent our country with the skill, dedication and goodwill which your post demands.

Jimmy Carter, letter sent to United States Ambassadors, October 25, 1977; *Digest of United States Practice in International Law,* 1977, pp. 244-46. Since World War II, beginning with Harry Truman, most Presidents have either issued executive orders or sent personal letters to American ambassadors prescribing their coordination, oversight, and direction functions, their authority, and their responsibility for American foreign relations abroad; for the text of these documents, see Elmer Plischke, *Modern Diplomacy: The Art and the Artisans* (Washington: American Enterprise Institute, 1979), pp. 427-34. For the Secretary of State's foreign relations functions, see Document 28.

5

Problems in the Conduct of Foreign Relations

Can't we [the President and Congress] consult and act rather than pontificate and poke? I refuse to believe that we have passed the point of no return in discarding our tradition of nonpartisanship in foreign policy. Further, I refuse to believe that it will become easier to negotiate with foreign adversaries and allies than with the Congress of the United States.

Gerald Ford
Address, February 13, 1975

This chapter deals with four major problems in the conduct of American foreign affairs. Each of them involves some aspect of relations between the executive and legislative branches of the government under our system of separation of powers and checks and balances, which was introduced in the first section of Chapter 4.

The first portion of this chapter, concerning secrecy and openness, also touches on the relations of the government and the people. It and the second segment, which deals with intelligence operations, raise the perennial issue of drawing a viable dividing line between secrecy and openness in a democratic system. The last two sections, on treaty making and war powers, illustrate recent constitutional as well as political conflicts in executive-legislative relations, primarily emphasizing congressional action to restrain the authority and practices of the President and his executive agencies. Despite the arrangements devised to cope with this contestation, the conflict over the interpretation and application of the Constitution and laws is unlikely to be resolved to the full satisfaction of either the President or Congress.

SECRECY AND OPENNESS

In 1918, as the first of his Fourteen Points, Woodrow Wilson propounded "open covenants of peace, openly arrived at" and that diplomacy "shall proceed always frankly and in the public view." However, once he became personally involved in negotiations at the Paris Peace Conference, he modified his view, acknowledging the need for confidentiality during the diplomatic process. Epitomizing the contemporary goal of qualified openness, in 1954 Dwight Eisenhower declared: "it is obvious that much of the diplomatic work, particularly those efforts that . . . are preparatory toward the reaching of agreements, be conducted in confidence."

While the goal of openness in foreign affairs has been traditional in American practice, there are limits to which it can be carried--in theory and in practice--without disaffecting United States national interests. Both the nature of the dividing line between secrecy and openness and the authority for prescribing it, are complex and troublesome issues in the relations of the executive and legislative branches and in those of the government vis-a-vis the people. These issues have been debated throughout our history and are not likely to be fully resolved.

The general allegation that "the public has a right to know" raises serious questions of the need and desire to be informed respecting who, what, in how much detail, when, how and in what form, and for what purpose? It is absurd to assume that the people have a right to know "everything"--now, or that they might even have an interest in becoming fully knowledgeable, to say nothing of the average person's capacity for "knowing everything." Full, immediate dis- closure not being either reasonable, rational, or practical, there must be some line of demarcation, and someone needs to possess authority to delineate it.

"Openness"--or secrecy--is a complicated issue and a relative matter in democratic governance. The basic questions this dichotomy raises include: Does the public--led by the media--have a right to know equally the details of policy making, of the policy made, and of the actions taken to implement that policy? The record of the American government in publicizing substantive foreign policy is scarcely subject to serious criticism. The issues, therefore, are how much information concerning the making of foreign policy (including deliberations and negotiations within the executive branch and between it and Congress) should be made public before policy is decided upon, and how much information should be made available while it is being implemented by negoti- ations with foreign governments before such negotiations are consummated? During these stages public debate may impede rather than promote the inter- ests, goals, and objectives of the United States.

The third aspect of the problem is the matter of "confidentiality," which consists of two features--classification of information and documents for na- tional security reasons or to protect personal privacy, and maintaining the credibility of mutual confidence in foreign affairs. The first of these is handled by the government through a variety of laws and executive orders to define authority, rights, restrictions, and procedures to provide a realistic classifi- cation and declassification system and to guarantee reasonable freedom of information to those who are interested.

The second feature, frequently overlooked, which is even more sensitive, pertains to the matter of maintaining mutual confidence--among members of the executive and legislative branches of the government, between the President and his advisers, and between United States officials and foreign leaders and emissaries or between American diplomats and foreign officials--even when no security classification is involved. If such confidence is violated, the credibility of those concerned may be compromised and they may cease to trust one another. In other words, there are many reasons for not putting certain information or documents into the public domain, at least not immediately or in detail. If the public is informed too early, so will those with whom the United States needs to deal, including adversaries. Because discretion is required, even among friends and allies, lines need to be drawn, and where they are drawn may advance or contravene our national policies and welfare.

The documents presented in this section are of two types: those that focus on the general principle of openness as an ideal in the American system (Documents 57-59) and those that deal with recent developments in reforming the availability of information and documents, including the Freedom of Information Act (Document 60), revision of the documents classification arrangement (Document 61), expediting the systematic publication of American diplomatic records (in the *Foreign Relations of the United States* series, Document 62, and the Department of State's program for enlightening the public, Document 63). For an illustration of an open summit exchange of diplomatic notes during the Cuban missile crisis in 1962, see Documents 184-188.

On the matter of relations between the executive and Congress relating to openness, see the commentary, for example, of McGeorge Bundy, "Towards an Open Foreign Policy," Richard A. Frank, "Public Participation in the Foreign Policy Process," and Stanley N. Futterman, "Foreign Policy Information" (*Commission on the Organization of the Government for the Conduct of Foreign Policy, June 1975,* vol. 1, Appendix A, pp. 32-39, and vol. 5, Appendix L, pp. 66-77). For a general statement on openness and the reform of Department of State management, see *United States Foreign Policy, 1972: A Report of the Secretary of State,* pp. 249-52. For commentary on the nature of "executive privilege"--an extra-constitutional practice that originated with President Washington and has been debated in executive-legislative relations since the eighteenth century--see the summary statement of Rita A. Hauser, "Executive Privilege in the Conduct of Foreign Policy," *Commission on the Organization of the Government for the Conduct of Foreign Policy, June 1975,* vol. 5, Appendix L, pp. 78-79; also see *Historic Documents,* 1973, pp. 337-42.

5 7   THE VOICE OF THE PEOPLE

In a representative democracy, all public policy decisions are subject to review and in a sense are ultimately made by the people. Foreign policy is no exception. Secretary of State Henry Kissinger has stated his belief that "any foreign policy of the United States that is not based on public support, and above all on congressional support, will not have a firm foundation."

American foreign policy at its best represents the consensus of the nation, arrived at by a continuing process of debate in which the Government, political parties, private organizations and interest groups of all kinds, and individual citizens interact. At times a large number of people may disagree with specific foreign policy decisions, but under our system this can be only a temporary condition. In the long run, the government must either convince the people of the wisdom of the course it is pursuing or it must change that course.

The people express their views most directly every four years in the election of a President, and every two years in congressional elections. Between elections, there is a substantial and continuing public contribution to the making of foreign policy. Hundreds of well-informed and qualified private citizens serve on commissions and advisory boards for various international programs such as military and economic aid. Others are consulted by the Government in their specific fields of expertise or are named to represent this country at some of the 800 international conferences the United States attends each year.

Moreover, the American people make their views felt on foreign policy in a variety of other ways. When they feel strongly enough about an issue, they organize and mobilize thousands to support specific legislation and policies. . . . And as individuals, Americans write in great numbers to the President, Members of Congress, and the Secretary of State. The decisionmaker must weigh these often times conflicting interests, positions, and pressures of various groups and then fashion a policy based on the long-term interests of the entire country.

The mass media provide important channels both for the expression of public opinion and for informing the public on foreign policy issues. More than 600 newspaper, radio, and television correspondents are accredited to the State Department; hundreds more cover the White House and Congress. The widespread dissemination of news and opinions by the mass media keeps the foreign policy process in the steady glare of public scrutiny.

"The Voice of the People," Department of State, *Foreign Policy and the Department of State* (Washington: Government Printing Office, 1976), p. 4.

5 8   OPENNESS IN FOREIGN AFFAIRS

Openness is essentially a state of mind. It means open channels of communication both within the governmental structure and among diverse elements of American society. It is the opposite of parochial insularity and in today's highly technological world it is the opposite of the narrowness and particularism of the traditional professional elite. The goal of openness is to produce a foreign affairs system and individuals within it who, by virtue of their profound understanding of our own nation, its strengths and shortcomings, its values and aspirations, will serve the President and represent the interests of the United States with increased insight and effectiveness. . . .

. . . Traditionally, diplomacy has not been known for qualities of openness. In fact, open diplomacy has been thought by many to be an impossibly idealistic goal. Why, then, should we be particularly concerned today with openness in the foreign affairs community?

First, the fact that we are an open, democratic society must be reflected in our diplomacy. Recent trends, particularly in the United States, have reinforced the natural, healthy American penchant for questioning the judgments of authority.

Second, discourse between nations in its traditional diplomatic form has changed and will change drastically in the future. Openness to new skills, ideas and attitudes, here and abroad, will become not the desirable thing it is today but a necessity.

Third, as technological advances result in new transnational ties among peoples, foreign relations and diplomacy will more and more take multilateral forms. These by definition will rely less on private communication and the arcane practices of the past and more on the formation of worldwide communities of interest.

Fourth, in an era of preoccupation with internal problems, the interconnection of domestic and foreign priorities can be better tested by full knowledge and discussion of our objectives in each area.

Fifth, the complexities of problems and choices in foreign affairs are so great that the political leadership must be assured open access to all relevant facts and options. The risks and costs of our mistakes are as susceptible to exponential growth as are the opportunities for achieving great progress in the efficient application of limited resources through modern management techniques.

Sixth, a credible foreign policy requires an informed supportive public opinion even more today than in the past. Assumptions and conclusions must be widely debated and understood.

Thus, this state of mind--openness--is an essential ingredient in the foreign affairs process and must be imbedded in the structure of our foreign affairs institutions.

Department of State, *Diplomacy for the 70's,* pp. 377-79.

5 9   PUBLIC PARTICIPATION IN THE FOREIGN AFFAIRS PROCESS

What of foreign policy? Is the country better served by exempting from citizen involvement decision making concerning matters with an international dimension? Are foreign relations necessarily vested with such different ingredients that they should or must be conducted by bureaucratic experts secretly, perhaps even without significant Congressional input? And, if some aspects of foreign affairs do lend themselves to a greater public role, which aspects are these and what suitable form should the involvement take? . . .

The foreign policy process can be divided into a number of different categories, and the kind of participation that is most suitable may depend on the sort of action involved. For example, it could be argued that the nature of public participation should be different for legislative foreign policy making than for that of the Executive. Within the latter area, action pursuant to delegated authority may call for mechanisms unlike those used when the President's constitutional authority is being exercised. (One very practical difference is that Congress could direct that the Executive permit public participation when implementing delegated authority; if Congress attempted to do so in connection with the President's exercise of his inherent, exclusive powers, a constitutional conflict would, no doubt, ensue.) Actions can be categorized by subject matter; the role of the public may be quite different if the subject is an economic or social matter as opposed to being military or purely political. Such a division ultimately breaks down if the Executive, as has been its wont, claims that virtually all foreign affairs matters are "political" or "diplomatic" and thus sacrosanct. Lastly, subjects can be analyzed and divided functionally according to their specific and uniquely foreign affairs needs, for example into those which require secrecy or speed and those which do not. . . .

Richard A. Frank, "Public Participation in the Foreign Policy Process," *Commission on the Organization of the Government for the Conduct of Foreign Policy, June 1975,* vol. 5, Appendix L, pp. 66, 68.

Addressing himself to public comprehension of foreign affairs, President Carter has observed: "The complexity of interrelated and sometimes disturbing events and circumstances requires that we in America increase the degree of public understanding of our foreign policy and public support of it." See his address, World Affairs Council, Philadelphia, May 9, 1980; *American Foreign Policy: Basic Documents,* 1977-1980, p. 63.

6 0   FREEDOM OF INFORMATION ACT, 1967

552. Public information; agency rules, opinions, orders, records, and proceedings
- (a) Each agency shall make available to the public information as follows:
- (1) Each agency shall separately state and currently publish in the Federal Register for the guidance of the public--
- (A) descriptions of its central and field organization and the established places at which, the employees (and in the case of a uniformed service, the members) from whom, and the methods whereby, the public may obtain information, make submittals or requests, or obtain decisions;
- (B) statements of the general course and method by which its functions are channeled and determined, including the nature and requirements of all formal and informal procedures available;
- (C) rules of procedure, descriptions of forms available or the places at which forms may be obtained, and instructions as to the scope and contents of all papers, reports, or examinations;
- (D) substantive rules of general applicability adopted as authorized by law, and statements of general policy or interpretations of general applicability formulated and adopted by the agency; and

(E) each amendment, revision, or repeal of the foregoing.

Except to the extent that a person has actual and timely notice of the terms thereof, a person may not in any manner be required to resort to, or be adversely affected by, a matter required to be published in the Federal Register and not so published. For the purpose of this paragraph, matter reasonably available to the class of persons affected thereby is deemed published in the Federal Register when incorporated by reference therein with the approval of the Director of the Federal Register.

(2) Each agency, in accordance with published rules, shall make available for public inspection and copying--

(A) final opinions, including concurring and dissenting opinions, as well as orders, made in the adjudication of cases;

(B) those statements of policy and interpretations which have been adopted by the agency and are not published in the Federal Register; and

(C) administrative staff manuals and instructions to staff that affect a member of the public;

unless the materials are promptly published and copies offered for sale. To the extent required to prevent a clearly unwarranted invasion of personal privacy, an agency may delete identifying details when it makes available or publishes an opinion, statement of policy, interpretation, or staff manual or instruction. However, in each case the justification for the deletion shall be explained fully in writing. Each agency shall also maintain and make available for public inspection and copying current indexes providing identifying information for the public as to any matter issued, adopted, or promulgated after July 4, 1967, and required by this paragraph to be made available or published. Each agency shall promptly publish, quarterly or more frequently, and distribute (by sale or otherwise) copies of each index or supplements thereto unless it determines by order published in the Federal Register that the publication would be unnecessary and impracticable, in which case the agency shall nonetheless provide copies of such index on request at a cost not to exceed the direct cost of duplication. A final order, opinion, statement of policy, interpretation, or staff manual or instruction that affects a member of the public may be relied on, used, or cited as precedent by an agency against a party other than an agency only if--

(i) it has been indexed and either made available or published as provided by this paragraph; or

(i i) the party has actual and timely notice of the terms thereof.

(3) Except with respect to the records made available under paragraphs (1) and (2) of this subsection, each agency, upon any request for records which (A) reasonably describes such records and (B) is made in accordance with published rules stating the time, place, fees (if any), and procedures to be followed, shall make the records promptly available to any person.

(4) (A) In order to carry out the provisions of this section, each agency shall promulgate regulations, pursuant to notice and receipt of public comment, specifying a uniform schedule of fees applicable to all

constituent units of such agency. Such fees shall be limited to reasonable standard charges for document search and duplication and provide for recovery of only the direct costs of such search and duplication. Documents shall be furnished without charge or at a reduced charge where the agency determines what waiver or reduction of the fee is in the public interest because furnishing the information can be considered as primarily benefiting the general public.
. . .

[Subsections (B) to (G) provide for court adjudication of complaints against agencies for the withholding of documents.]

(5) Each agency having more than one member shall maintain and make available for public inspection a record of the final votes of each member in every agency proceeding.

(6) (A) Each agency, upon any request for records made under paragraph (1), (2), or (3) of this subsection, shall--

    (i) determine within ten days (excepting Saturdays, Sundays, and legal public holidays) after the receipt of any such request whether to comply with such request and shall immediately notify the person making such request of such determination and the reasons therefor, and of the right of such person to appeal to the head of the agency any adverse determination; and

    (ii) make a determination with respect to any appeal within twenty days (excepting Saturdays, Sundays, and legal public holidays) after the receipt of such appeal. If on appeal the denial of the request for records is in whole or in part upheld, the agency shall notify the person making such request of the provisions for judicial review of that determination under paragraph (4) of this subsection.

(B) In unusual circumstances as specified in this subparagraph, the time limits prescribed in either clause (i) or clause (ii) of subparagraph (A) may be extended by written notice to the person making such request setting forth the reasons for such extension and the date on which a determination is expected to be dispatched. No such notice shall specify a date that would result in an extension for more than ten working days. As used in this subparagraph, "unusual circumstances" means, but only to the extent reasonably necessary to the proper processing of the particular request--

    (i) the need to search for and collect the requested records from field facilities or other establishments that are separate from the office processing the request;

    (ii) the need to search for, collect, and appropriately examine a voluminous amount of separate and distinct records which are demanded in a single request; or

    (iii) the need for consultation, which shall be conducted with all practicable speed, with another agency having a substantial interest in the determination of the request or among two or more components of the agency having substantial subject-matter interest therein.

(C) Any person making a request to any agency for records under paragraph (1), (2), or (3) of this subsection shall be deemed to have exhausted his administrative remedies with respect to such request if the agency fails to comply with the applicable time limit provisions of this paragraph. If the Government can show exceptional circumstances exist and that the agency is exercising due diligence in responding to the request, the court may retain jurisdiction and allow the agency additional time to complete its review of the records. Upon any determination by an agency to comply with a request for records, the records shall be made promptly available to such person making such request. Any notification of denial of any request for records under this subsection shall set forth the names and titles or positions of each person responsible for the denial of such request.

(b) This section does not apply to matters that are--

   (1) (A) specifically authorized under criteria established by an Executive order to be kept secret in the interest of national defense or foreign policy and (B) are in fact properly classified pursuant to such Executive order;

   (2) related solely to the internal personnel rules and practices of an agency;

   (3) specifically exempted from disclosure by statute (other than section 552b of this title), provided that such statute (A) requires that the matters be withheld from the public in such a manner as to leave no discretion on the issue, or (B) establishes particular criteria for withholding or refers to particular types of matters to be withheld;

   (4) trade secrets and commercial or financial information obtained from a person and privileged or confidential;

   (5) inter-agency or intra-agency memorandums or letters which would not be available by law to a party other than an agency in litigation with the agency;

   (6) personnel and medical files and similar files the disclosure of which would constitute a clearly unwarranted invasion of personal privacy;

   (7) investigatory records compiled for law enforcement purposes, but only to the extent that the production of such records would (A) interfere with enforcement proceedings, (B) deprive a person of a right to a fair trial or an impartial adjudication, (C) constitute an unwarranted invasion of personal privacy, (D) disclose the identity of a confidential source and, in the case of a record compiled by a criminal law enforcement authority in the course of a criminal investigation, or by an agency conducting a lawful national security intelligence investigation, confidential information furnished only by the confidential source, (E) disclose investigative techniques and procedures, or (F) endanger the life or physical safety of law enforcement personnel;

(8) contained in or related to examination, operating, or condition reports prepared by, on behalf of, or for the use of an agency responsible for the regulation or supervision of financial institutions; or

(9) geological and geophysical information and data, including maps, concerning wells.

Any reasonably segregable portion of a record shall be provided to any person requesting such record after deletion of the portions which are exempt under this subsection.

(c) This section does not authorize withholding of information or limit the availability of records to the public, except as specifically stated in this section. This section is not authority to withhold information from Congress. . . .

[Sec. (d) specifies the type of reports that need to be filed with Congress.]

(e) For purposes of this section, the term "agency" as defined in section 551(1) of this title includes any executive department, military department, Government corporation, Government controlled corporation, or other establishment in the executive branch of the Government (including the Executive Office of the President), or any independent regulatory agency.

U.S. Code, Title V, Section 552, pp. 407-11, which consists of the act of 1966, as amended. The Freedom of Information Act (Moss Act) was passed July 4, 1966, effective July 4, 1967 (PL 89-487, 80 Stat. 250). This was repealed by PL 90-23 (81 Stat. 54), approved June 5, 1967 and effective July 4, 1967, to amend 5 *U.S. Code* 552 to codify the provisions of the 1966 law.

6 1   REVISION OF DOCUMENTS CLASSIFICATION SYSTEM, 1972

I have today signed an Executive order [11652] establishing a new, more progressive system for classification and declassification of Government documents relating to national security. This reform . . . represents the first major overhaul of our classification procedures since 1953.

By a separate action, I have also directed the Secretary of State to accelerate publication of the official documentary series, "Foreign Relations of the United States," so that historians and others will have more rapid access to papers created after World War II.

Both of these actions are designed to lift the veil of secrecy which now enshrouds altogether too many papers written by employees of the Federal establishment--and to do so without jeopardizing any of our legitimate defense or foreign policy interests. . . .

The new system will become effective on June 1, 1972. Among its most significant features are these:

-- The rules for classifying documents are more restrictive.

-- The number of departments and people who can originally classify information has been substantially reduced.

-- Timetables ranging from 6 to 10 years have been set for the automatic declassification of documents. Exceptions will be allowed only for such information as falls within four specifically defined categories.

-- Any document exempted from automatic declassification will be subject to mandatory review after a 10-year period.

Thus, for the first time, a private citizen is given a clear right to have national security information reviewed on the basis of specified criteria to determine if continued classification is warranted, so long as the document can be adequately identified and obtained by the Government with a reasonable amount of effort.

-- if information is still classified 30 years after origination, it will then be automatically declassified unless the head of the originating department determines in writing that its continued protection is still necessary and he sets a time for declassification.

-- Sanctions may be imposed upon those who abuse the system.

-- And a continuing monitoring process will be set up under the National Security Council and an Interagency Classification Review Committtoo, whoco Chairman is to be appointed by the President

Richard Nixon, statement, March 8, 1972; *Papers of Presidents: Nixon*, 1972, pp. 401-6. Elements of the new system are described in pp. 403-6. For text of Executive Order 11652, March 8, 1972, see 38 *Federal Register* 5209.

6 2   ACCELERATING PUBLICATION OF *FOREIGN RELATIONS OF THE UNITED STATES* SERIES

My second action today was to direct an acceleration in the publication by the Department of State of the official documentary series, "Foreign Relations of the United States." Since 1861, that series has been an invaluable resource for historians and others interested in our past. For many years each publication contained documents written only a few years before, but soon after the Second World War, when Government files were bulging with war papers, a 20-year lag developed between origination and publication. Now, however, the lag has stretched to 26 years. . . . This delay is too long, and I have directed the Secretary of State to institute immediately a program to reduce this time lag to 20 years, and to accomplish this mission within 3 years. I have also instructed the Secretary of Defense, the Director of Central Intelligence, and my Assistant for National Security Affairs to cooperate fully with this effort.

Richard Nixon, statement, March 8, 1972; *Papers of Presidents: Nixon*, 1972, p. 406. For the text of President Nixon's memorandum to the Secretary of State on this matter, see p. 407.

The *Foreign Relations of the United States* series--originally titled *Papers Relating to Foreign Affairs*, has been published regularly since 1861, except for the year 1869. Initially one volume was published each year; since 1932 there have been five or more volumes per year, and occasionally additional volumes--appendixes and supplements--have been published, dealing with a particular country, territory, event, or negotiation. These volumes contain the texts of diplomatic communications, exchanges of notes, reports, policy papers, and other official papers relating to the foreign affairs and diplomacy of the United States. This series constitutes the most comprehensive and systematized resource on the diplomacy of any country. For commentary on the series, see William M. Franklin, *The Availability of Department of State Records* (Washington: Government Printing Office, 1973), reprint from 68 *Department of State Bulletin* (January 29, 1973): 101-7; Richard W. Leopold, "The Foreign Relations Series Revisited: One Hundred Plus Ten," 59 *Journal of American History* (March 1973): 935-57; David F. Trask and William Z. Slany, "What Lies Ahead for the Foreign Relations Series?" 9 *Society for Historians of American Foreign Relations Newsletter* (March 1978): 26-29.

6 3   INFORMING THE PUBLIC--DEPARTMENT OF STATE PROGRAM

During the post-World War II era, the information disseminated by the Department of State and other agencies tended to stress international involvement, reflecting a determination to avoid a return to the disastrous isolationism of the 1930's. At the same time, cold-war pressures and national security considerations tended to tighten restraints on the availability of foreign policy information. . . .

Today we are reversing these trends. More information is being declassified and published or made available sooner; strong efforts have been made to improve our information output in tone as well as in content; and the daily dialogue between private citizens and government officials has been strengthened. . . .

This concept of openness toward the public was stressed in the Department's 1970 report, *Diplomacy for the 70's*, . . . It was reinforced on March 8, 1972, by President Nixon's Executive Order 11652, establishing a new system to minimize classification and accelerate declassification of government documents containing national security information. It was underscored further by changes on September 14 in the Freedom of Information regulations of the Department of State-- changes designed to improve our implementation of the Freedom of Information Act of 1967 by encouraging the broadest possible release of previously classified information.

In response to the President's Executive order, the State Department has substantially reduced the number of people (from 5,435 to 2,009) who are authorized to classify information. For the first time declassification will become largely automatic, on a shortened timetable ranging from 6 to 10 years, according to category (Confidential, Secret, or Top Secret). Previously, automatic declassification was to be carried out only after 12 years, but most material could be exempted from declassification for 30 years. . . .

Since the Freedom of Information Act took effect on July 4, 1967, the great bulk of public requests for declassification have been approved in whole or in part by the Department. More than 13,000 pages of documentation have been released through the special Freedom of Information procedures. (A great deal more, of course, has been released on the Department's own initiative, through normal declassification processes.) All bureaus of the State Department are working together to see that this record and the attitudes it reflects are maintained and improved.

It must be kept in mind, nonetheless, that no matter how well the Department performs in this area, there will always be a gap between what the public would like to know and what the nature of the diplomatic process and the requirements of national security will permit the government to reveal.

United States Foreign Policy, 1972: A Report of the Secretary of State, pp. 186-88.

INFORMATION AND INTELLIGENCE

For the formulation of foreign policy and making foreign relations decisions, the importance of adequate and reliable information cannot be over-emphasized. Information has been called the taproot of sound policy in that foreign affairs decisions and the foreign policy that results are not likely to be more efficacious or meritorious than the validity and completeness of the information on which they are founded. During the process of refining such information it is essential to differentiate between assumptions or perceptions and facts--or between "hard facts" and "speculation or estimates," and some of the most crucial judgments require deciding when a perception is indeed a fact.

Governments, therefore, establish intelligence systems to provide them with an essential and systematized supply of information. The principal elements of such intelligence operations include the gathering of information (the acquisition and verification of data), analysis (the ordering and interpreting of such data), and communication of the results in usable form to appropriate officials and agencies in the foreign relations structure.

The traditional American intelligence community has consisted of all those agencies that possess information needs. Aside from the Department of State and the defense establishment, the network of units range from the Department of Justice (including the Federal Bureau of Investigation, the Immigration and Naturalization Service, and the Drug Enforcement Administration), the Treasury Department (dealing with customs, internal revenue, and counterfeiting, as well as the Secret Service), and the postal system (concerned with the illegal use of the mails) to the Department of Agriculture (responsible for foreign agricultural marketing and inspection), the Department of Transportation (the Coast Guard), and many others.

Following World War II, when the Office of Strategic Services was disestablished, the Central Intelligence Agency (CIA) was created by the National Security Act of 1947 as amended, to serve as an "independent agency" (not a part of any of the regular government departments), but responsible to the President and the National Security Council (NSC), to coordinate and consolidate intelligence activities for purposes of national security.

Among the many problems that emerged concerning intelligence operations are: distinguishing intelligence gathering and analysis from policy making, preserving the confidentiality of the system and its agents, differentiating information services from engagement in foreign operations, maintaining essential controls over covert activities, protecting the privacy of individuals from improper intelligence scrutiny, and providing flexible executive management with cooperative legislative oversight. The last of these has engendered continuing conflict over the purpose, administration, and functioning of the intelligence system and the nature of congressional monitoring and restraint.

The documents contained in this section fall into three broad categories: the need for information (Document 64); the character, role, and limits of intelligence (Documents 65-67); and intelligence reform fomented by congressional demands in the 1970s. Concerning the latter, for example, see the Rockefeller Commission Report and the Colby Report on the CIA (*Historic Documents,* 1975, pp. 401-36 and 523-28; the House of Representatives Intelligence Committee report and the Senate Select Intelligence Committee Report (*Historic Documents,* 1976, pp. 115-24 and 235-85); and the Supreme Court decision on the secrecy of Central Intelligence Agency sources (*Historic Documents,* 1986, pp. 333-44). Presidents Ford, Carter, and Reagan issued executive orders instituting major reforms in the operations of the intelligence system (Documents 68-70).

6 4   NEED FOR EFFECTIVE INTELLIGENCE SERVICE

In a world where information is power, a vital element of our national security lies in our intelligence services. They are essential to our Nation's security in peace as in war. Americans can be grateful for the important but largely unsung contributions and achievements of the intelligence services of this Nation.

It is entirely proper that this system be subject to Congressional review. But a sensationalized public debate over legitimate intelligence activities is a disservice to this Nation and a threat to our intelligence system. It ties our hands while our potential enemies operate with secrecy, with skill, and with vast resources. Any investigation must be conducted with maximum discretion and dispatch to avoid crippling a vital national institution.

The Central Intelligence Agency has been of maximum importance to Presidents before me. The Central Intelligence Agency has been of maximum importance to me. . . . I think it would be catastrophic for the Congress or anyone else to destroy the usefulness by dismantling, in effect, our intelligence systems upon which we rest so heavily.

Now, as Congress oversees intelligence activities, it must, of course, organize itself to do so in a responsible way. It has been traditional for the Executive to consult with the Congress through specially protected procedures that safeguard essential secrets. But recently, some of those procedures have altered in a way that makes the protection of vital information very, very difficult. I will say to the leaders of the Congress . . . that I will work with them to devise procedures which will meet the needs of the Congress for review of intelligence agency activities and the needs of the Nation for an effective intelligence service.

Gerald Ford, foreign policy address to Congress, April 10, 1975; *Papers of Presidents: Ford,* 1975, p. 471; also see *Historic Documents,* 1975, pp. 236-37. Also see Document 68.

6 5   NATURE OF INTELLIGENCE

It is a truism that "Intelligence is the first line of national defense," but few people ever think through its implications. Most citizens are vaguely aware that foreign policy decisions are made by the President with the advice of his Secretary of State based in theory on the best information available to experts throughout the government. The same applies to the Secretary of Defense and the U.S. military forces of which the President is also, of course, the Commander-in-Chief. The collection and evaluation of the information on which these decisions are based is one of the primary functions of Intelligence. It is essentially research and analysis utilizing both open and classified materials. But, in foreign and military affairs, strategic decisions should take into account not only past and present "facts bearing on the situation," but also careful estimates of the capabilities and intentions of other major powers. The production of such national estimates is a second major function of intelligence.

Paul W. Blackstock, "Intelligence, Covert Operations, and Foreign Policy," *Commission on the Organization of the Government for the Conduct of Foreign Policy, June 1975,* vol. 7, Appendix U, p. 95.

6 6   INTELLIGENCE AND POLICY MAKING

Intelligence collection and production have become major activities of the United States government in the past few decades. Intelligence organizations employ thousands of people and cost billions of dollars, and the finished intelligence products--current intelligence reports, basic research, national estimates, and special studies--influence important policy decisions and the allocation of many additional billions of dollars. The willingness of several Administrations to devote such extensive resources to intelligence is a clear indication that the importance of the intelligence function is recognized by top U.S. officials. . . .

Simply stated, the task of the intelligence officer is to tell the policy makers what has happened throughout the world in the recent past, what is happening currently (and why), and what the future is likely to hold. Thus he must be part historian, part journalist, and part forecaster. . . .

The second development is the knowledge explosion. The growing interdependence of nations means that a particular event may have very serious secondary and tertiary consequences which are difficult to trace out in advance. In theory the knowledge explosion--and the development of new techniques and equipment for processing and analyzing information --should be a help to the analyst, and in some ways they are. However, they often provide a flood of information which is more than an individual can digest. . . .

The producer of finished intelligence stands between the intelligence collector and the policy maker. This involves him in two rather different types of relationships and creates two different sets of issues. The first involves providing coordinated guidance to the collectors of information by setting forth requirements in a regular and systematic manner, but without letting the whole procedure become a purely mechanical process divorced from the shifting concerns of the producers. The second involves the production of intelligence that is useful as well as accurate, and involves the uneasy relationship between the reporter and the analyst on the one hand and the policy maker on the other. Success or failure in the latter centers as much if not more on the *attitudes* of the officials involved toward each other's function as on *organizational* arrangements, but the *procedures* for guiding the analyst and for the transmission of intelligence are of considerable importance in the whole process. . . .

There are two main views of the appropriate relationship between the intelligence officer and the policy maker. The traditional or classic view is that this should be an arm's-length relationship, so that the dangers of the intelligence officer's judgment being swayed by the views of the policy maker are kept to a minimum. This view stresses that intelligence should tell the policy maker what he needs to know rather than what he wants to hear. The other view agrees that the intelligence officer must be rigorously honest and independent in his relationship with the policy maker, but stresses that if the former is to tell the latter what he "needs to know" he must have considerable knowledge of the specific concerns of the policy maker. Otherwise, intelligence analysis becomes an isolated intellectual effort carried out in a vacuum--the pursuit of knowledge for its own sake--rather than a carefully focused input to the policy maker's thinking and decision-making process. . . .

*   *   *

Intelligence has four separate but related functions it must perform if it is to play its proper role in the foreign policy decision-making process. Its first and most obvious task is that of following events abroad and reporting on important developments so as to alert policy makers to impending opportunities and problems. A second task is estimating future developments in other parts of the world so as to reduce the uncertainties and risks facing the policy maker. A third function also involves estimating, but in the particular context of requests by policy makers for appraisals of likely foreign reactions to alternative U.S. policies currently under consideration. The fourth involves monitoring conditions that could affect U.S. policies adopted or operations underway. Verification of compliance or noncompliance by foreign governments of agreements, such as

those on arms control, is an important example of this type of activity.
. . .

If the intelligence officer is to fulfill his essential functions, he must perform four separate tasks. The first is providing guidance for the collection process, so that information is collected on the subjects that the analyst must deal with in his reports to the policy maker. The second is to keep attuned to the concerns of the policy maker so that the analyst can produce intelligence that is relevant to forthcoming policy decisions. The third is to produce high-quality, objective, and relevant intelligence reports and appraisals, something as simple to state as it is difficult to do. The fourth task is to convey his reports and estimates in a persuasive manner, which is essential if the intelligence produced is to have the impact it warrants.

The policy maker also must perform several related tasks if the relationship is to be successful. First, he must provide guidance to intelligence officers on the types of intelligence needed lest the intelligence officer be forced to operate in the dark--both as to his own production and in his guidance of the collectors. Estimating likely developments abroad is difficult enough without having to guess at the needs of one's own government. A second and closely related task is to keep intelligence officers informed not only of policies under consideration but of actions and operations of the U.S. government. Intelligence officers can hardly be expected to interpret the actions of foreign governments successfully if they are unaware of U.S. actions, promises, or threats that may be influencing the decisions of other states. Third, the policy maker must convey his evaluations of the intelligence he receives so that the intelligence officer knows whether or not what he has produced is meeting the needs of the policy maker. There are obvious limitations on the ability of busy men to perform these tasks in a regular and systematic manner, but, if extensive resources are to be devoted to intelligence, they are too important to be ignored.

William J. Barnds, "Intelligence Functions" and "Intelligence and Policymaking in an Institutional Context," *Commission on the Organization of the Government for the Conduct of Foreign Policy, June 1975,* vol. 7, Appendix U, pp. 13-15, 29-30.

67   LIMITS ON INTELLIGENCE FUNCTION

The next issue centers on the question of the distinction between the knowable and the unknowable. Perhaps the central problem here, to be understood by intelligence producers as well as users, is the need for clearer consensus about what can be empirically known and about what can only be estimated or speculated about. Furthermore it needs to be better understood that, even if one could know "all the relevant facts" prior to a decision, this would not necessarily eliminate the need for hard choices. There may be a tendency of intelligence professionals to overrate their estimating capacities.   And there probably is a tendency for intelligence users to act as their own intelligence men. . . .

It is important to keep in mind what Admiral Roscoe Hillenkoetter, an early Director of Central Intelligence, once described as the main limitation of intelligence:

Its job requires the systematic and critical examination of intel-ligence information, the synthesis of that information and the determination of the probable significance of evaluated intelligence. [But] to predict the intentions of the enemy, you would need a crystal ball.

Finally it should be recognized that there is the constant danger that policy makers will want to use intelligence staff and intelligence professionals for their own policy preference or even partisan ends. The system should be organized so that the dangers of distance from policy makers, creating a tendency to irrelevance, are weighed against the dangerous use of intelligence for partisan political ends. There may be a fine point between too much policy guidance and too little.

In general, I have a negative reaction to the abolition of the Office of National Estimates. While the creation of National Intelligence Officers may solve the problem of gap between producer and user, it is likely to be ultimately at a cost in objectivity. Knowledge is power, and power tends to be used by "men of power" for their own ends.

Harry Howe Ransom, "The Limits of Intelligence," *Commission on the Organization of the Government for the Conduct of Foreign Policy, June 1975,* vol. 7, Appendix U, pp. 50-51.

6 8   REFORMING THE INTELLIGENCE SYSTEM--FORD, 1976

By virtue of the authority vested in me . . . I have today issued an Executive Order [11905] pertaining to the organization and control of the United States foreign intelligence community.   This order establishes clear lines of accountability for the Nation's foreign intelligence agencies. It sets forth strict guidelines to control the activities of these agencies and specifies as well those activities in which they shall not engage.

In carrying out my Constitutional responsibilities to manage and conduct foreign policy and provide for the Nation's defense, I believe it essential to have the best possible intelligence about the capabilities, intentions and activities of governments and other entities and individuals abroad. To this end, the foreign intelligence agencies of the United States play a vital role in collecting and analyzing information related to the national defense and foreign policy.

It is equally as important that the methods these agencies employ to collect such information for the legitimate needs of the government conform to the standards set out in the Constitution to preserve and respect the privacy and civil liberties of American citizens.

The Executive Order I have issued today will insure a proper balancing of these interests. It establishes government-wide direction for the foreign intelligence agencies and places responsibility and accountability on individuals, not institutions.

I believe it will eliminate abuses and questionable activities on the part of the foreign intelligence agencies while at the same time permitting them to get on with their vital work of gathering and assessing information. It is also my hope that these steps will help to restore public confidence in these agencies and encourage our citizens to appreciate the valuable contribution they make to our national security.

Beyond the steps I have taken in the Executive Order, I also believe there is a clear need for some specific legislative actions. I am today submitting to the Congress of the United States proposals which will go far toward enhancing the protection of true intelligence secrets as well as regularizing procedures for intelligence collection in the United States.

My first proposal deals with the protection of intelligence sources and methods. . . .

Therefore, I am proposing legislation to impose criminal and civil sanctions on those who are authorized access to intelligence secrets and who willfully and wrongfully reveal this information. This legislation is not an "Official Secrets Act," since it would affect only those who improperly disclose secrets, not those to whom secrets are disclosed. Moreover, this legislation could not be used to cover up abuses and improprieties.
. . .

It is essential, however, that the irresponsible and dangerous exposure of our Nation's intelligence secrets be stopped. The American people have long accepted the principles of confidentiality and secrecy in many dealings--such as with doctors, lawyers and the clergy. It makes absolutely no sense to deny this same protection to our intelligence secrets. Openness is a hallmark of our democratic society, but the American people have never believed that it was necessary to reveal the secret war plans of the Department of Defense. . . .

Second, I support proposals that would clarify and set statutory limits, where necessary, on the activities of the foreign intelligence agencies. . . .

Third, I will neet with the appropriate leaders of Congress to try to develop sound legislation to deal with a critical problem involving personal privacy. . . .

I will also seek Congressional support for sound legislation to expand judicial supervision of mail openings. The law now permits the opening of United States mail, under proper judicial safeguards, in the conduct of criminal investigations. We need authority to open mail under the limitations and safeguards that now apply in order to obtain vitally needed foreign intelligence information. . . .

Fourth, I would like to share my views regarding appropriate Congressional oversight of the foreign intelligence agencies. It is clearly the business of the Congress to organize itself to deal with these matters. Certain principles, however, should be recognized by both the Executive and Legislative Branches if this oversight is to be effective. . . .

Congress should seek to centralize the responsibility for oversight of the foreign intelligence community. The more committees and sub-committees dealing with highly sensitive secrets, the greater the risks of disclosure. I recommend that Congress establish a Joint Foreign Intelligence Oversight Committee. Consolidating Congressional oversight in one committee will facilitate the efforts of the Administration to keep the Congress fully informed of foreign intelligence activities.

It is essential that both the House and the Senate establish firm rules to insure that foreign intelligence secrets will not be improperly disclosed. There must be established a clear process to safeguard these secrets and effective measures to deal with unauthorized disclosures.

Finally, successful and effective Congressional oversight of the foreign intelligence agencies depends on mutual trust between the Congress and Executive. Each branch must recognize and respect the rights and prerogatives of the other if anything is to be achieved.

Gerald Ford, Special Message to Congress to Reform the United States Foreign Intelligence Community, February 18, 1976; *Papers of Presidents: Ford,* 1976-1977, I, 362-66.

6 9   REFORMING THE INTELLIGENCE SYSTEM--CARTER, 1978

I have issued today an Executive order [12036] concerning the organization and control of United States foreign intelligence activities. It is the product of the most extensive and highest level review ever conducted through the National Security Council system of our Nation's foreign intelligence activities and of an unprecedented dialog with the congressional oversight committees.

The new order, which builds on the experience under President Ford's Executive Order 11905, is intended to provide a foundation for the drafting of statutory charters, and I intend to work closely with congressional leaders to enact such legislation. Until then, however, the new order will:

-- ensure that foreign intelligence and counterintelligence activities are conducted in full compliance with the laws of the United States and are consistent with broader national security policies;

-- establish effective oversight of the direction, management, and conduct of the foreign intelligence activities of the Federal Government;

-- clarify the authority and responsibilities of the Director of Central Intelligence (DCI) and the departments and agencies that have foreign intelligence and counterintelligence responsibilities.

The most important features of the new Executive order are as follows:

1. The National Security Council . . . will, short of the President, provide the highest level review of and guidance for the policies and practices of the Intelligence Community. . . .

2. The authorities and responsibilities of all departments, agencies, and senior officials engaged in foreign intelligence and counterintelligence activities are being made public. Those implementing directives which must remain classified for security reasons will be made available to the appropriate congressional oversight committees. . . .

3. Our intelligence agencies have a critical role to play in collecting and analyzing information important to our national security interests and, on occasion, acting in direct support of major foreign policy objectives. It is equally important, however, that the methods employed by these agencies meet constitutional standards protecting the privacy and civil liberties of U.S. persons and are in full compliance with the law.

To accomplish this objective a major section of the Executive order is devoted entirely to setting forth detailed restrictions on intelligence collection, covert activities in support of foreign policy objectives, experimentation, contracting, assistance to law enforcement authorities, personnel assigned to other agencies, indirect participation in prohibited activities, dissemination and storage of information, and a prohibition on assassinations. . . .

4. As an added protection against abuses and to help ensure effective performance, the intelligence oversight process is strengthened.

-- The Intelligence Oversight Board is retained, and its responsibilities for review of foreign intelligence activities that may be illegal or improper is extended to the counterintelligence area, and it is given new authority to conduct investigations.

-- The DCI and senior officers of the Intelligence Community are instructed to report to the congressional intelligence committees in a complete and prompt manner.

Jimmy Carter, statement concerning Executive Order 12036, January 24, 1978; *Papers of Presidents: Carter,* 1978, I, 214-16. For President Carter's remarks on signing the Executive Order, see pp. 189-94, and for the text of the Executive Order, see pp. 194-214.

7 0   REFORMING THE INTELLIGENCE SYSTEM--REAGAN, 1981

Today I an issuing two Executive orders, one to govern the activities of our intelligence agencies and one to reestablish the Intelligence Oversight Board, which works to ensure that our intelligence activities are lawful. These orders are designed to provide America's intelligence community with clearer, more positive guidance and to remove the aura of suspicion and mistrust that can hobble our nation's intelligence efforts.

. . . The American people are well aware that the security of their country--and in an age of terrorism, their personal safety as well--is tied to the strength and efficiency of our intelligence-gathering organizations.

These orders have been carefully drafted--in consultation with the intelligence committees of both Houses of the Congress--to maintain the legal protection of all American citizens. They also give our intelligence professionals clear guidelines within which to do their difficult and essential job. Contrary to a distorted image that emerged during the last decade, there is no inherent conflict between the intelligence community and the rights of our citizens. Indeed, the purpose of the intelligence community is the protection of our people. . . .

Most Americans realize that intelligence is a good and necessary profession to which high caliber men and women dedicate their lives. We respect them for their honorable and often perilous service to our nation and the cause of freedom. For all our technological advances, the gathering of information and its analysis depend finally on human judgment; and good judgment depends on the experience, integrity, and professionalism of those who serve us in the intelligence community. . . .

These orders charge our intelligence agencies to be vigorous, innovative, and responsible in the collection of accurate and timely information--information essential for the conduct of our foreign policy and crucial to our national safety. The country needs this service and is willing to allocate the resources necessary to do the job right.

It is not enough, of course, simply to collect information. Thoughtful analysis is vital to sound decisionmaking. The goal of our intelligence analysts can be nothing short of the truth, even when that truth is unpleasant or unpopular. I have asked for honest, objective analysis, and I shall expect nothing less. When there is disagreement, as there often is, on the difficult questions of our time, I expect those honest differences of view to be fully expressed.

These orders stipulate that special attention be given to detecting and countering the espionage and other threats that are directed by hostile intelligence services against us at home and abroad. These hostile services respect none of the liberties and rights of privacy that these orders protect. Certainly the same can be said of international terrorists, who present another important area of concern and responsibility for our intelligence professionals.

I want to stress that the primary job of the CIA is to conduct intelligence activities overseas and to deal with certain foreign persons who come into this country. The FBI takes primary responsibility for security activities within the United States, directed against hostile foreigners and those Americans who seek to do damage to our national security.

These orders do not alter this basic division of labor; they reaffirm it. They also encourage the fullest possible cooperation among the CIA, the FBI, and other agencies of the intelligence community as they seek to deal with fundamental challenges to our national security--challenges that respect neither national boundaries nor citizenship. . . .

Ronald Reagan, statement on intelligence activities, December 4, 1981; *Papers of Presidents: Reagan*, 1981, pp. 1126-27. For text of Executive Order 12333, December 4, 1981, see pp. 1128-39, and for text of Executive Order 12334 on the Intelligence Oversight Board, see pp. 1139-40. For background, commentary, and excerpts of Executive Order 12333, see *Historic Documents,*

1981, pp. 861-68, and for commentary on the Supreme Court on secrecy of CIA sources, and excerpts of its decision, April 16, 1985, see *Historic Documents,* 1985, pp. 333-44.

TREATY MAKING

Treaty making has produced one of the more troublesome continuous debates in executive-legislative relations as they apply to foreign affairs. From the international perspective, such matters as negotiating procedures, the form of the end product, signature, ratification, reservations, proclamation, publication, interpretation, legal effect and duration, change in the circumstances detrimental to treaty viability, and suspension or termination have evoked considerable discussion and attempts to codify treaty law and procedure. It was not until 1969, however, following nearly two decades of deliberation by the United Nations International Law Commission to produce a draft treaty, that the multipartite Vienna Convention on the Law of Treaties was signed, which came into force in 1980. See U.N. Doc. A/CONF. 39/27, May 23, 1969; and for text see Yearbook of the United Nations, 1969, pp. 734-43, and 63 *American Journal of International Law* (October 1969): 875-903. This convention--consisting of 83 articles dealing with the conclusion and entry into force, ratification, observance and interpretation, termination and suspension, depositories and registration of treaties--was not ratified by the United States. For American analysis of, and objections to, the convention, see *Digest of United States Practice in International Law,* 1974, pp. 195-99.

In international parlance, bilateral and multilateral "treaties" and "agreements" are generic expressions, often used synonymously for all international engagements. Other terms, usually denoting specific types, include: "act" (formal statement of proceedings and commitments of a law creating nature embodied in a single document signed at the close of an international conference); "convention" (usually of a general law-creating nature, concluded at a multipartite international conference); modus vivendi (a temporary agreement between two states providing a workable compromise); "pact" (an especially solemn and important agreement, often concerned with peacekeeping); procès-verbal (an agreed formal record of the proceedings of an international conference); and protocol (less formal and important than a basic treaty, and generally used to supplement, amend, elucidate, or qualify a treaty). These differ from a "declaration" which establishes future mutual policy, or international law as mutually understood, without the procedure or binding effect of a treaty. Those treaties and agreements that serve as the constitutive acts of international organizations may also bear such titles as "articles of agreement," "charter," "constitution," "covenant," or "statute."

So far as the United States is concerned, irrespective of the titles used internationally, the principal legal differentiation is between the terms "treaty" and "agreement." The Constitution stipulates that the President has power "to make treaties," by and with "the advice and consent of the Senate," provided that "two thirds of the Senators present consent" therein (Art. II, Sec. 2). In addition, the President engages the United States in what are called "executive agreements." They are not subject to the formal restraints required for treaties but, nevertheless, become the "law of the land." Most of these executive agreements are either based on prior legislative authorization or are approved by subsequent congressional action, often consisting of implementing legislation, approved by ordinary majority vote of both houses of Congress.

Throughout our history, executive-legislative differences--both legal and political, and sometimes partisan--have arisen respecting the distinction between treaties and agreements, the determination as to who decides the delineation of agreements, the role played by the Senate in amending treaty texts or appending reservations and interpretations, and the action of the President to establish policy or to honor commitments as commander in chief or diplomat in chief without legislative approval.

One such confrontation peaked during the early 1950's when Senator John W. Bricker proposed a constitutional amendment which provided that a treaty should become effective as internal law only through legislation that would be valid in the absence of a treaty, and that Congress be empowered to regulate executive agreements. A modified version of the "Bricker amendment" was defeated in the Senate in 1954, when it fell one vote short of receiving the required two-thirds majority.

Parallelling this development, another aspect of this post-World War II confrontation focussed more directly on the President's authority to exercise agreement-making authority respecting the broadening of American responsibilities as a major world power, thereby circumventing the two-thirds Senate treaty approval requirement or, in some cases, obviating congressional approval on policy commitments that do not require implementing legislation. The documents that follow illustrate various contemporary aspects of these executive-legislative relations. Aside from background commentary (Document 71), they emphasize the nature of presidential treaty-making powers (Document 72), official distinctions in the nature and functions of treaties and executive agreements (Documents 73-74 and 76), legislatively mandated requirements to transmit their texts to Congress (Document 75), and to publish them (Document 77), and congressional challenge of presidential authority to make treaties and agreements (Document 78), or to terminate a treaty without legislative concurrence (Document 79).

7 1   CONSTITUTIONAL ASPECTS OF TREATY MAKING

Largely as a result of the controversy over the war in Vietnam, considerable attention and debate have centered on the constitutional aspects of foreign affairs, especially the Constitution's allocation of power and responsibility in the conduct of foreign affairs among the President, the House of Representatives, and the Senate. An important component of the debate has involved issues concerning the division of authority in the international agreement-making process among the President and the two Houses of Congress. A number of recent developments have put these issues into sharp focus and deserve discussion and analysis. The purpose of this Article is to consider these developments, as well as the issues they have raised, in light of the Constitution and requirements for an effective foreign policy. . . .

. . . Specifically, it may be helpful to distinguish between use of the term "treaty" in international law and practice and its use under the United States Constitution. According to the recently concluded Vienna Convention on the Law of Treaties, a treaty "means an international agreement concluded between states in written form and governed by international law, whether embodied in a single instrument or in two or more related instruments and whatever its particular designation." In international practice agreements are given various designations, such as treaties, conventions, acts, general acts, protocols, agreements, modi vivendi, etc. But the juridical effect of a treaty is not dependent upon the name given to the agreement.

Under United States constitutional law and practice a treaty has a more restricted meaning. That is, the term "treaty" is applied only to international agreements, however denominated, that become binding upon the United States through ratification by the President with the advice and consent of the Senate through a two-thirds vote of that body. As to the classification of international agreements other than treaties, there has been much confusion in terminology, and the situation is presently in flux. Traditionally, the term "executive agreement," which is not employed in international practice, has been used for domestic purposes to describe all international agreements that become binding upon the United States in ways other than by the ratification of the President with the advice and consent of the Senate. Executive agreements in turn have been classified into several categories. These include (1) so-called presidential agreements, i.e., self-executing agreements made in accordance with the President's independent constitutional powers and not dependent upon subsequent congressional legislation for implementation; (2) non-self-executing agreements made subject to implementating legislation by Congress; (3) agreements made pursuant to or in accordance with existing legislation or a treaty; and (4) agreements made subject to subsequent congressional approval by majority vote of both houses of Congress.

It has been said that it is confusing and misleading to apply the term "executive agreement" to all these categories of international agreements, because the term implies that only presidential power is involved when in fact the power of the President and of Congress may be brought to bear. In order to obviate this confusion, it has been suggested that international agreements other than treaties be classified into two broad categories-- presidential agreements and congressional-executive agreements. Under this classification presidential agreements include only those international agreements made solely on the basis of the constitutional authority of the President; congressional-executive agreements cover all international agreements entered into under the combined powers of the President and of Congress. . . .

As is well known, international agreements other than treaties, however classified, have been used by the United States with increasing frequency in place of the treaty. For example, in 1930, 25 treaties and only nine international agreements other than treaties were concluded. As of January 1, 1972, the total number of treaties and other international agreements in force for the United States was 5,306, consisting of 947 treaties and 4,359 international agreements other than treaties. According to the Department of State, most of these international agreements other than treaties--approximately 97 percent of them--fall into the congressional-executive agreement category, while only two to three percent are classified as executive agreements. It is these two to three percent, however, that have been the object of the sharpest criticism on the ground that they violate constitutional law and policy. . . .

John F. Murphy, "Treaties and International Agreements Other Than Treaties," *Commission on the Organization of the Government for the Conduct of Foreign Policy, June 1975,* vol. 5, Appendix L, pp. 99-101. For additional analysis, including background on executive-legislative relations, military base agreements, and related issues, see pp. 101-15.

7 2   PRESIDENT'S AUTHORITY TO MAKE TREATIES AND AGREEMENTS

The United States Constitution suggests a narrower definition of the term "treaty." Article II, Section 2, Clause 2, in delineating the powers of the President, states that:

He shall have Power, by and with the Advice and Consent of the Senate, to make Treaties, provided two thirds of the Senators present concur. . . .

Although this clause might suggest that the President cannot enter into agreements with other nations without the advice and consent of the Senate, the actual evolution of the relationship between the Executive and Legislative Branches, together with a recognition of the President's powers in managing the foreign relations of the United States, have led to a recognition of the use of agreements between governments without the advice or consent of the Senate. . . . It is presently beyond dispute that the President may enter into such agreements, known as executive agreements, and that such agreements are binding upon the United States. . . .

. . . [Louis] Henkin notes that the constitutional basis of such agreements is unclear, but goes on to state:

Neither Congresses nor Presidents nor courts have been troubled by these conceptual difficulties and differences. Whatever their theoretical merits, it is now widely accepted that the Congressional-Executive agreement is a complete alternative to a treaty: the President can seek approval of any agreement by joint resolution of both houses of Congress instead of two-thirds of the Senate only. Like a treaty, such an agreement is the law of the land, superseding inconsistent state laws as well as inconsistent provisions in earlier treaties, in other international agreements or acts of Congress.

Digest of United States Practice in International Law, 1979, p. 773.   For comprehensive commentary on executive agreements, see pp. 771-80.

7 3   TRADITIONAL DEFINITION OF "TREATIES" AND "AGREEMENTS"

In the United States the term "treaty" is normally used to indicate an international agreement that is to be or has been brought into force with respect to the United States by and with the advice and consent of the Senate in conformity with Article II of the Constitution of the United States.   By the terms of Clause 2 of Section 2 of that Article,   the President ". . . shall have Power, by and with the Advice and Consent of the Senate, to make Treaties, provided two thirds of the Senators present concur. . .".   An international agreement that is brought into force with respect to the United States in any other manner is usually referred to as an "executive agreement."

*   *   *

The Foreign Affairs Manual of the Department of State provides that the "executive agreement form is used only for agreements which fall into one or more of the following categories:
"a. Agreements which are made pursuant to or in accordance with existing legislation or a treaty;
"b. Agreements which are made subject to congressional approval or implementation; or
"c. Agreements which are made under and in accordance with the President's constitutional power."

*   *   *

The Department of State wrote in 1964:
1. The basic distinction between executive agreements which can be concluded by the President under his constitutional authority and those which require Congressional consent or approval lies in whether the subject matter and its treatment fall wholly within the authority of the President as Commander-in-Chief of the armed forces and Chief Executive in the conduct of foreign relations, or whether they fall partly within the powers delegated to Congress by the Constitution.   The vast majority of executive agreements are in fact made pursuant to legislation enacted by Congress.   Of course, all international agreements involve the exercise of some measure of the President's constitutional authority, since the Executive is the exclusive organ of the Government for the conduct of foreign relations.   However, the number made solely on the basis of his constitutional authority is relatively small.   An examination of executive agreements made during a representative 11-year period shows that less than 3 percent were made solely on the basis of the President's constitutional authority.

While the number of these agreements is quite small, some are very important, such as the agreements for military armistice or surrender in World War II, the liberation of prisoners of war and civilians, the termination of the Berlin Blockade, and arrangements on the status of United States forces abroad. Some, while appearing routine in nature are also important in the conduct of foreign relations, such as agreements for the settling of certain claims, provisional arrangements concerning international organizations, and the like.

Whiteman, *Digest of International Law,* XIV, 1 and 195-96. For generic definitions of the Vienna Convention on the Law of Treaties (1969) and of the International Law Commission, see p. 2.

7 4   PROCEDURE FOR DISTINGUISHING TREATIES AND AGREEMENTS

721   Exercises of the International Agreement Power
721.1 Determination of Type of Agreement
The following considerations will be taken into account along with other relevant factors in determining whether an international agreement shall be dealt with by the United States as a treaty to be brought into force with the advice and consent of the Senate, or as an agreement to be brought into force on some other constitutional basis.
721.2 Constitutional Requirements
There are two procedures under the Constitution through which the United States becomes a party to international agreements. Those procedures and the constitutional parameters of each are:
a. Treaties
International agreements (regardless of their title, designation, or form) whose entry into force with respect to the United States takes place only after the Senate has given its advice and consent are "treaties." The President, with the advice and consent of two-thirds of the Senators present, may enter into an international agreement on any subject genuinely of concern in foreign relations, so long as the agreement does not contravene the United States Constitution; and
b. International Agreements Other Than Treaties
International agreements brought into force with respect to the United States on a constitutional basis other than with the advice and consent of the Senate are "international agreements other than treaties." (The term "executive agreement" is appropriately reserved for agreements made solely on the basis of the constitutional authority of the President.) There are three constitutional bases for international agreements other than treaties as set forth below. An international agreement may be concluded pursuant to one or more of these constitutional bases:
(1) Agreements Pursuant to Treaty
The President may conclude an international agreement pursuant to a treaty brought into force with the advice and consent of the Senate,

whose provisions constitute authorization for the agreement by the Executive without subsequent action by the Congress;

(2) Agreements Pursuant to Legislation

The President may conclude an international agreement on the basis of existing legislation or subject to legislation to be enacted by the Congress; and

(3) Agreements, Pursuant to the Constitutional Authority of the President

The President may conclude an international agreement on any subject within his constitutional authority so long as the agreement is not inconsistent with legislation enacted by the Congress in the exercise of its constitutional authority. The constitutional authority for the President to conclude international agreements include:

(a) The President's authority as Chief Executive to represent the nation in foreign affairs;

(b) The President's authority to receive ambassadors and other public ministers;

(c) The President's authority as "Commander-in-Chief"; and

(d) The President's authority to "take care that the laws be faithfully executed."

721.3   Considerations for Selecting Among Constitutionally Authorized Procedures

In determining a question as to the procedure which should be followed for any particular international agreement, due consideration is given to the following factors along with those in section 721.2:

a. The extent to which the agreement involves commitments or risks affecting the nation as a whole;

b. Whether the agreement is intended to affect State laws;

c. Whether the agreement can be given effect without the enactment of subsequent legislation by the Congress;

d. Past United States practice with respect to similar agreements;

e. The preference of the Congress with respect to a particular type of agreement;

f. The degree of formality desired for an agreement;

g. The proposed duration of the agreement, the need for prompt conclusion of an agreement, and the desirability of concluding a routine or short-term agreement; and

h. The general international practice with respect to similar agreements.

In determining whether any international agreement should be brought into force as a treaty or as an international agreement other than a treaty, the utmost care is to be exercised to avoid any invasion or compromise of the constitutional powers of the Senate, the Congress as a whole, or the President.

Department of State Circular 175, October 25, 1974; Senate Committee on Foreign Relations and House Committee on Foreign Affairs, *Legislation on Foreign Relations Through 1977,* Joint Committee Print (Washington:

Government Printing Office, 1978), III, 90-91. For description of purpose, negotiation and signature procedure, guidelines for concluding international agreements, consultation with Congress on agreement types, transmittal to Congress and publication of treaty and agreement texts, and related matters, see pp. 89-103. Also see Document 76.

75 TRANSMISSION OF TEXTS OF INTERNATIONAL AGREEMENTS TO CONGRESS --CASE ACT, 1972

The Secretary of State shall transmit to the Congress the text of any international agreement, other than a treaty, to which the United States is a party as soon as practicable after such agreement has entered into force with respect to the United States but in no event later than sixty days thereafter. However, any such agreement the immediate public disclosure of which would, in the opinion of the President, be prejudicial to the national security of the United States shall not be so transmitted to the Congress but shall be transmitted to the Committee on Foreign Relations of the Senate and the Committee on Foreign Affairs of the House of Representatives under an appropriate injunction of secrecy to be removed only upon due notice from the President.

Public Law 92-403, August 22, 1972; *U.S. Statutes at Large*, 1972, vol. 86, p. 619.

*   *   *

. . . neither the form in which an agreement is expressed nor the fact that an agreement is of a subordinate or implementing character in itself removes the agreement from the requirements of the Case Act or of the law regarding the publication of international agreements (1 U.S.C. 112a). The determination whether an instrument or a series of instruments constitutes an international agreement that is required to be transmitted to the Congress and to be published is based upon the substance of that agreement, not upon its form or its character as a principal agreement or as a subordinate or implementing agreement.

As the subject matter of our international agreements is, in general, as broad as the scope of our foreign relations, it is not practicable to enumerate every type of agreement which the Department of State should receive from the other executive departments and agencies. However, it seems clear that texts should be transmitted to the Department of State of [all subordinate and implementing agreements involving substantial amounts of U.S. funds or other tangible assistance] and of any agreements of political significance, any that involve a substantial grant of funds, any involving loans by the United States or credits payable to the United States, any that constitute a commitment of funds that extends beyond a fiscal year or would be a basis for requesting new appropriations, and any that involve continuing or substantial cooperation in the conduct of a particular program or activity, such as scientific, technical, or other cooperation, including the exchange or receipt of information and its treatment.   In general, the instruments transmitted to the Congress pursuant to the Case Act, and those published (other than those classified under E.O. 11652), should reflect the full extent of obligations undertaken by the United States and of rights to which it is entitled pursuant to instruments executed on its behalf.

The fact that an agency reports fully on its activities to a given Committee or Committees of Congress, including a discussion of agreements it has entered into, does not exempt the agreements concluded by such agency from transmission to the Congress by the Department of State under the Case Act.

Department of State letter to all executive departments and agencies, implementing the Case Act, September 6, 1973; *Digest of United States Practice in International Law*, 1973, pp. 187-88.

7 6   MEANING OF THE TERM "EXECUTIVE AGREEMENT" UNDER THE CASE ACT

The expression "executive agreement" is understood by the Department of State to include any international agreement brought into force with respect to the United States without the advice and consent of the Senate under the provisions of clause 2 of Section 2, Article II of the Constitution of the United States. The words "all international agreements other than treaties to which the United States is a party" in the act of September 23, 1950 (Par. 2, 64 Stat. 980; 1 U.S.C. 112a) and the words "any international agreement, other than a treaty, to which the United States is a party" in the Case Act (86 Stat. 619; 1 U.S.C. 112b) are considered as including all international agreements covered by the expression "executive agreement."

Accordingly, the Department of State considers the Case Act as covering "all international agreements other than treaties" specified in the act of September 23, 1950 and required by that act to be published in the new compilation entitled "Treaties and Other International Agreements of the United States" (UST), plus comparable agreements that are classified in the interest of national security and not published in that compilation. . . .

To list specifically all the kinds of international agreements that will be submitted under the Case Act would require a tabulation of every kind of agreement published in "United States Treaties and Other International Agreements," plus the kinds of classified agreements that are being concluded. Any such list could only be considered as giving examples and not as all inclusive. The specific listing could not, for example, include international agreements of an entirely new kind that are concluded to meet circumstances that cannot be envisaged at the present time. The Department considers that the Case Act is intended to include every international agreement, other than a treaty, brought into force with respect to the United States after August 22, 1972, regardless of its form, name or designation, or subject matter.

Digest of United States Practice in International Law, 1973, pp. 185-86.

7 7   SYSTEMATIC PUBLICATION OF U.S. TREATIES AND AGREEMENTS

The Secretary of State shall cause to be compiled, edited, indexed, and published, beginning as of January 1, 1950, a compilation entitled "United States Treaties and Other International Agreements," which shall contain all treaties to which the United States is a party that have been proclaimed during each calendar year, and all international agreements other than treaties to which the United States is a party that have been signed, proclaimed, or with reference to which any other final formality has been executed, during each calendar year. The said United States Treaties and Other International Agreements shall be legal evidence of the treaties, international agreements other than treaties, and proclamations by the President of such treaties and agreements, therein contained, in all the courts of the United States, the several States, and the Territories and insular possession of the United States.

Act of September 23, 1950 (in 64 Stat. 980 and 1 U.S. Code 112a); *Digest of United States Practice in International Law*, 1973, p. 186. The United States has a liberal record of publication of its treaties and many of its agreements. In 1908 the Department of State commenced the systematic publication of the *United States Treaty Series* (USTS). Each treaty text, in the languages in which it was signed, was published separately in pamphlet form, numbered serially. Prior to 1929, this series also included executive agreements. In 1929 the latter began to be published in a separate *Executive Agreement Series,* also in serially numbered pamphlet form. At the end of World War II, commencing in 1945, these two series were combined and superseded by the *Treaties and Other International Acts Series* (TIAS). United States treaties and agreements have also been published in cumulative volumes, including the U.S.T. volumes, as described in the statement on "Major Sources and Citations."

7 8   DRAFT SENATE "TREATY POWERS RESOLUTION," 1978

Sec. 502. (a) This section may be cited as the "Treaty Powers Resolution."
(b) This section--
(1) is enacted as an exercise of the rulemaking power of the Senate and as such is deemed to be a part of the rules of the Senate;
(2) supersedes other rules of the Senate only to the extent that it is inconsistent therewith;
(3) shall be deemed to be a resolution of the Senate and shall take effect upon the date of passage of this bill by the Senate; and
(4) may not be construed as derogating from the constitutional right of the Senate to change its rules at any time, in the same manner and to the same extent as any other rule of the Senate.

(c) It is the purpose of this Resolution to fulfill the intent of the Framers of the Constitution and to ensure, through use of the rule-making and legislative power of the Senate, that no international agreement which in the judgment of the Senate should be submitted as a treaty will be implemented by the Senate without its prior advice and consent to ratification of that agreement.

(d) The Senate finds that--

(1) article II, section 2, clause 2 of the Constitution empowers the President "by and with the advice and consent of the Senate to make treaties, provided two-thirds of the Senators present concur";

(2) the requirement for Senate advice and consent to treaties has in recent years been circumvented by the use of "executive agreements";

(3) the Senate may refuse to consider legislative measures to authorize or appropriate funds to implement those international agreements which, in its opinion, constitute treaties and to which the Senate has not given its advice and consent to ratification; and

(4) article I, section 5, clause 2 of the Constitution grants to the Senate plenary power to "determine the rules of its proceedings."

(e) It is the sense of the Senate that, in determining whether a particular international agreement should be submitted as a treaty, the President should, prior to and during the negotiation of such agreement, seek the advice of the Committee on Foreign Relations.

(f) (1) Where the Senate, by resolution, expresses its sense that any international agreement hereafter entered into which has not been submitted to the Senate for its advice and consent to ratification as a treaty, should be so submitted, it shall not thereafter be in order to consider any bill or joint resolution or any amendment thereto, or any report of a committee of conference, which authorizes or provides budget authority (including budget authority for salaries and administrative expenses) to implement such international agreement.

(2) Any such resolution shall be privileged in the same manner and to the same extent as a concurrent resolution of the type described in section 5 (c) of the War Powers Resolution is privileged under section 7 (a) and (b) of that law.

(3) No point of order may be made pursuant to a resolution adopted under paragraph (1) of this subsection--

(A) after such date as the Senate has given its advice and consent to ratification of such agreement as a treaty;

(B) in the event such resolution is adopted later than sixty days after the transmittal of such agreement under section 112b of title 1, United States Code; or

(C) with respect to any international agreement which has been expressly authorized by statute or treaty which takes effect prior to the date on which such agreement takes effect.

Senate Resolution 3076 (1978), not approved; *Digest of United States Practice in International Law,* 1978, pp. 781-99, with text of the draft Treaty Powers Resolution, pp. 788-89. On September 8, 1978, in Senate Resolution 536, section 2, it was specified that in determining whether a particular agreement should be submitted to the Senate as a treaty, the President "should have the timely advice of the Committee on Foreign Relations" through agreed procedures established with the Secretary of State; see p. 799. For War Powers Resolution, see next section of this chapter.

79   TREATY TERMINATION--MUTUAL DEFENSE TREATY, U.S. AND REPUBLIC OF CHINA, 1979

Following transfer by the United States of formal diplomatic recognition as the sole Government of China from the Republic of China (Taiwan) to the People's Republic of China, effective January 1, 1979, and notification of termination of the 1954 Mutual Defense Treaty between the United States and the Republic of China, effective also on January 1, 1979, legislative proposals were introduced in the Congress to provide a statutory framework for continuing relationships between the people of the United States and the people on Taiwan on an unofficial basis. The proposals ultimately resulted in adoption of the Taiwan Relations Act (Public Law 96-8, approved April 10, 1979, 93 Stat. 14, 22 U.S.C. 3301-3316).

Digest of United States Practice in International Law, 1979, p. 751. For documents on the recognition and normalization of relations with the People's Republic of China, see Chapter 28. For Mutual Defense Treaty with the Republic of China, see Document 313.

*   *   *

RESOLUTION CONCERNING THE TERMINATION OF TREATIES

Resolved, That it is the sense of the Senate that treaties or treaty provisions to which the United States is a party should not be terminated or suspended by the President without the concurrence of the Congress except where--

(1) the treaty provisions in question have been superseded by a subsequent, inconsistent statute or treaty; or

(2) material breach, changed circumstances, or other factors recognized by international law, or provisions of the treaty itself, give rise to a right of termination or suspension on the part of the United States;

but in no event where such termination or suspension would--

(A) result in the imminent involvement of United States Armed Forces in hostilities or otherwise seriously and directly endanger the security of the United States; or

(B) be inconsistent with the provisions of--

(i) a condition set forth in the resolution of ratification to a particular treaty; or

      (ii) a joint resolution; specifying a procedure for the termination or suspension of such treaty.

Proposed Senate Resolution 15 (March 8, 1979), not approved by the Senate. In March 1979, Senator Harry F. Byrd introduced a proposal that it was the sense of the Senate that its "approval is required to terminate any mutual defense treaty" between the United States and another nation. This was withdrawn and a broadened substitute resolution was introduced to provide guidelines for presidential action not confined to mutual defense treaties, the text of which is provided in this document. See *Digest of United States Practice in International Law,* 1979, pp. 751-52. For additional commentary, see pp. 753-71.

*   *   *

While treaty termination may be, and sometimes has been, undertaken by the President following Congressional or Senate action, such action is not legally necessary; and numerous authorities recognize the President's power to terminate treaties acting alone. Presidents have exercised that power on several occasions.

Herbert J. Hansell, Legal Adviser, Department of State, in a memorandum to the Secretary of State, December 16, 1978, specified that the President could give notice to terminate the treaty with the Republic of China without congressional or Senate action. *Digest of United States Practice in International Law,* 1978, p. 735. For additional commentary, including examples of previous presidential treaty terminations and a history of treaty termination by the United States since 1798, see pp. 735-65. On December 13, 1979, the Supreme Court, by a 6 to 3 decision, authorized President Carter to terminate this mutual defense treaty without the approval of Congress, vacating a judgment of a Court of Appeals, and remanding the case (Barry Goldwater et al v. James Earl Carter) to the District Court and ordering the case to be dismissed; see *Historic Documents,* 1979, pp. 917-38.

WAR POWERS

As with treaty making and other aspects of the conduct of foreign affairs, war-making entails both international and national components. From the international perspective, the development and application of the "laws of war," the "laws of neutrality," treaties and agreements governing peacekeeping, the peaceful settlement of disputes, and mutual defense commitments, and other rules and practices are crucial. From the internal perspective, authority for warmaking has engendered serious conflict between the President and Congress concerning the separation of powers and governmental cooperation. This conflict has intensified since World War II.

The Constitution confers upon Congress the power "to declare"--not "to make"--war, leaving the President some degree of flexibility in the use of military forces. Technically, the United States can enter upon a formal state of war with another nation only by means of a congressional "declaration of war." In practice, however, Congress has lost much of its discretion for two reasons.

Historically, Congress has normally not been inclined to pass, or even to consider, a resolution declaring the existence of a state of war except on the initiative of the President, which he usually requests in a formal "war message."

The second reason is that, since the Paris Peace Pact (the Kellogg-Briand Anti-War Treaty, 1928), hostilities or "acts of war" are frequently engaged in without a formal "state of war." For the United States, the significant fact is that, as commander in chief, the President may constitutionally order the performance of such hostile acts even though Congress does not declare war. One significant consequence of a declaration of war, internationally and internally, is that the laws of war and neutrality come into play as soon as war is formally declared.

Following the Korean and Vietnam wars, which were undeclared, and the consummation of a network of alliance and mutual defense commitments (see Chapter 18), serious conflict arose in executive-legislative relations concerning the President's authority to employ American armed forces abroad in hostile and other actions short of a formally declared war. Congress sought to establish constraints on the President, whereas the President insisted on maintaining the credibility of his authority as commander in chief in implementing foreign policy and engaging in diplomatic negotiations.

Illustrating this conflict, the documents provided in this section consist of the War Powers Act (1973) (Document 80), President Nixon's veto which was overridden (Document 81), and analysis of the nature and effect of the act (Documents 82-84). For illustrations of, and commentary on, the interpretation of presidential authority and application of the War Powers Act in specific circumstances, see the chapters on crises involving the *Pueblo* and the *Mayaguez* (Chapter 13, Documents 218-226), the attempted rescue mission of the American hostages held by Iran (Chapter 14, Document 230), the Grenada and Lebanon crises (Chapter 12, Document 206, and Chapter 14, Documents 235 and 240), and the air strike on Libya (Chapter 14, Document 244). For examples of earlier practice, prior to the enactment of the War Powers Resolution, see congressional action during the Gulf of Tonkin crisis (Chapter 7, Document 116), the Formosa Strait crisis (Chapter 10, Documents 159-160), the Vietnam War (Chapter 10, Document 166), and the Cuban missile crisis (Chapter 11, Document 180).

80   WAR POWERS RESOLUTION, 1973

Short Title
SECTION 1. This joint resolution may be cited as the "War Powers Resolution."

Purposes And Policy
SEC. 2. (a) It is the purpose of this joint resolution to fulfill the intent of the framers of the Constitution of the United States and insure that the collective judgment of both the Congress and the President will apply to the introduction of United States Armed Forces into hostilities, or into situations where imminent involvement in hostilities is clearly

indicated by the circumstances, and to the continued use of such forces in hostilities or in such situations.

(b) Under article I, section 8, of the Constitution, it is specifically provided that the Congress shall have the power to make all laws necessary and proper for carrying into execution, not only its own powers but also all other powers vested by the Constitution in the Government of the United States, or in any department or officer thereof.

(c) The constitutional powers of the President as Commander-in-Chief to introduce United States Armed Forces into hostilities, or into situations where imminent involvement in hostilities is clearly indicated by the circumstances, are exercised only pursuant to (1) a declaration of war, (2) specific statutory authorization, or (3) a national emergency created by attack upon the United States, its territories or possessions, or its armed forces.

Consultation

SEC. 3. The President in every possible instance shall consult with Congress before introducing United States Armed Forces into hostilities or into situations where imminent involvement in hostilities is clearly indicated by the circumstances, and after every such introduction shall consult regularly with the Congress until United States Armed Forces are no longer engaged in hostilities or have been removed from such situations.

Reporting

SEC. 4. (a) In the absence of a declaration of war, in any case in which United States Armed Forces are introduced--

(1) into hostilities or into situations where imminent involvement in hostilities is clearly indicated by the circumstances;

(2) into the territory, airspace or waters of a foreign nation, while equipped for combat, except for deployments which relate solely to supply, replacement, repair, or training of such forces; or

(3) in numbers which substantially enlarge United States Armed Forces equipped for combat already located in a foreign nation;

the President shall submit within 48 hours to the Speaker of the House of Representatives and to the President pro tempore of the Senate a report, in writing, setting forth--

(A) the circumstances necessitating the introduction of United States Armed Forces;

(B) the constitutional and legislative authority under which such introduction took place; and

(C) the estimated scope and duration of the hostilities or involvement.

(b) The President shall provide such other information as the Congress may request in the fulfillment of its constitutional responsibilities with respect to committing the Nation to war and to the use of United States Armed Forces abroad.

(c) Whenever United States Armed Forces are introduced into hostilities or into any situation described in subsection (a) of this section, the President shall, so long as such armed forces continue to be engaged in such hostilities or situation, report to the Congress periodically on the status of such hostilities or situation as well as on the scope and duration of such hostilities or situation, but in no event shall he report to the Congress less often than once every six months.

Congressional Action

SEC. 5. (a) Each report submitted pursuant to section 4(a)(1) shall be transmitted to the Speaker of the House of Representatives and to the President pro tempore of the Senate on the same calendar day. Each report so transmitted shall be referred to the Committee on Foreign Affairs of the House of Representatives and to the Committee on Foreign Relations of the Senate for appropriate action. If, when the report is transmitted, the Congress has adjourned sine die or has adjourned for any period in excess of three calendar days, the Speaker of the House of Representatives and the President pro tempore of the Senate, if they deem it advisable (or if petitioned by at least 30 percent of the membership of their respective Houses) shall jointly request the President to convene Congress in order that it may consider the report and take appropriate action pursuant to this section.

(b) Within sixty calendar days after a report is submitted or is required to be submitted pursuant to section 4(a)(1), whichever is earlier, the President shall terminate any use of United States Armed Forces with respect to which such report was submitted (or required to be submitted), unless the Congress (1) has declared war or has enacted a specific authorization for such use of United States Armed Forces, (2) has extended by law such sixty-day period, or (3) is physically unable to meet as a result of an armed attack upon the United States. Such sixty-day period shall be extended for not more than an additional thirty days if the President determines and certifies to the Congress in writing that unavoidable military necessity respecting the safety of United States Armed Forces requires the continued use of such armed forces in the course of bringing about a prompt removal of such forces.

(c) Notwithstanding subsection (b), at any time that United States Armed Forces are engaged in hostilities outside the territory of the United States, its possessions and territories without a declaration of war or specific statutory authorization, such forces shall be removed by the President if the Congress so directs by concurrent resolution. . . .

Interpretation of Joint Resolution

SEC. 8. (a) Authority to introduce United States Armed Forces into hostilities or into situations wherein involvement in hostilities is clearly indicated by the circumstances shall not be inferred--

(1) from any provision of law (whether or not in effect before the date of the enactment of this joint resolution), including any provision contained in any appropriation Act, unless such provision specifically authorizes the introduction of United States Armed

Forces into hostilities or into such situations and states that it is intended to constitute specific statutory authorization within the meaning of this joint resolution; or

(2) from any treaty heretofore or hereafter ratified unless such treaty is implemented by legislation specifically authorizing the introduction of United States Armed Forces into hostilities or into such situations and stating that it is intended to constitute specific statutory authorization within the meaning of this joint resolution.

(b) Nothing in this joint resolution shall be construed to require any further specific statutory authorization to permit members of United States Armed Forces to participate jointly with members of the armed forces of one or more foreign countries in the headquarters operations of high-level military commands which were established prior to the date of enactment of this joint resolution and pursuant to the United Nations Charter or any treaty ratified by the United States prior to such date.

(c) For purposes of this joint resolution, the term "introduction of United States Armed Forces" includes the assignment of members of such armed forces to command, coordinate, participate in the movement of, or accompany the regular or irregular military forces of any foreign country or government when such military forces are engaged, or there exists an imminent threat that such forces will become engaged, in hostilities.

(d) Nothing in this joint resolution--

(1) is intended to alter the constitutional authority of the Congress or of the President, or the provisions of existing treaties; or

(2) shall be construed as granting any authority to the President with respect to the introduction of United States Armed Forces into hostilities or into situations wherein involvement in hostilities is clearly indicated by the circumstances which authority he would not have had in the absence of this joint resolution.

Separability Clause

SEC. 9. If any provision of this joint resolution or the application thereof to any person or circumstance is held invalid, the remainder of the joint resolution and the application of such provision to any other person or circumstance shall not be affected thereby.

Public Law 93-148, November 7, 1973; *U.S. Statutes at Large,* 1973, vol. 87, pp. 555-60. Sections 6 and 7, which are omitted, deal with congressional procedure. The text is also provided in Senate Committee on Foreign Relations and House Committee on Foreign Affairs, *Legislation on Foreign Relations Through 1978,* Joint Committee Print, March 1979 (Washington: Government Printing Office, 1979), II, 421-25; and for summary statement, see *Digest of United States Practice in International Law,* 1973, pp. 551-63. The War Powers Resolution was passed by Congress in July, vetoed in October, and passed over the President's veto in November. For examples of presidential reports to Congress under the War Powers Resolution, see Documents 206, 223, 225, 235, 240, 242, and 244.

8 1   NIXON'S VETO OF WAR POWERS RESOLUTION, 1973

I hereby return without my approval House Joint Resolution 542--the War Powers Resolution. While I am in accord with the desire of the Congress to assert its proper role in the conduct of our foreign affairs the restrictions which this resolution would impose upon the authority of the President are both unconstitutional and dangerous to the best interests of our Nation.

The proper roles of the Congress and the Executive in the conduct of foreign affairs have been debated since the founding of our country. Only recently, however, has there been a serious challenge to the wisdom of the Founding Fathers in choosing not to draw a precise and detailed line of demarcation between the foreign policy powers of the two branches.

The Founding Fathers understood the impossibility of foreseeing every contingency that might arise in this complex area. They acknowledged the need for flexibility in responding to changing circumstances. They recognized that foreign policy decisions must be made through close cooperation between the two branches and not through rigidly codified procedures.

These principles remain as valid today as they were when our Constitution was written. Yet House Joint Resolution 542 would violate those principles by defining the President's powers in ways which would strictly limit his constitutional authority.

Clearly Unconstitutional

House Joint Resolution 542 would attempt to take away, by a mere legislative act, authorities which the President has properly exercised under the Constitution for almost 200 years. One of its provisions would automatically cut off certain authorities after sixty days unless the Congress extended them. Another would allow the Congress to eliminate certain authorities merely by the passage of a concurrent resolution--an action which does not normally have the force of law, since it denies the President his constitutional role in approving legislation.

I believe that both these provisions are unconstitutional. The only way in which the constitutional powers of a branch of the Government can be altered is by amending the Constitution--and any attempt to make such alterations by legislation alone is clearly without force.

Undermining Our Foreign Policy

While I firmly believe that a veto of House Joint Resolution 542 is warranted solely on constitutional grounds, I am also deeply disturbed by the practical consequences of this resolution. For it would seriously undermine this Nation's ability to act decisively and convincingly in times of international crisis. As a result, the confidence of our allies in our ability to assist then could be diminished and the respect of our adversaries for our deterrent posture could decline. A permanent and substantial element of unpredictability would be injected into the world's assessment of American behavior, further increasing the likelihood of miscalculation and war. . . .

While all the specific consequences of House Joint Resolution 542 cannot yet be predicted, it is clear that it would undercut the ability of the United States to act as an effective influence for peace. For example, the provision automatically cutting off certain authorities after 60 days unless they are extended by the Congress could work to prolong or intensify a crisis. Until the Congress suspended the deadline, there would be at least a chance of United States withdrawal and an adversary would be tempted therefore to postpone serious negotiations until the 60 days were up. Only after the Congress acted would there be a strong incentive for an adversary to negotiate. In addition, the very existence of a deadline could lead to an escalation of hostilities in order to achieve certain objectives before the 60 days expired . . . .

Finally, since the bill is somewhat vague as to when the 60 day rule would apply, it could lead to extreme confusion and dangerous disagreements concerning the prerogatives of the two branches, seriously damaging our ability to respond to international crises.

Failure To Require Positive
Congressional Action

I am particularly disturbed by the fact that certain of the President's constitutional powers as Commander in Chief of the Armed Forces would terminate automatically under this resolution 60 days after they were invoked. No overt Congressional action would be required to cut off these powers--they would disappear automatically unless the Congress extended them. In effect, the Congress is here attempting to increase its policy-making role through a provision which requires it to take absolutely no action at all.

In my view, the proper way for the Congress to make known its will on such foreign policy questions is through a positive action, with full debate on the merits of the issue and with each member taking the responsibility of casting a yes or no vote after considering those merits. . . . It would give every future Congress the ability to handcuff every future President merely by doing nothing and sitting still. In my view, one cannot become a responsible partner unless one is prepared to take responsible action.

Richard Nixon, Veto Message to Congress, October 24, 1973; *Papers of Presidents: Nixon,* 1973, pp. 893-95.

8 2   WAR POWERS--EXECUTIVE-LEGISLATIVE RELATIONS

The issue before us involves the constitutional authority to commit forces to armed combat and related questions. These questions have been the subject of considerable debate and scholarly attention. Unfortunately, they are often approached polemically, with one side arguing the President's constitutional authority as Commander in Chief and the other side asserting Congress' constitutional power to declare war--the implication being that these powers are somehow incompatible. The contrary is true. The framers of the Constitution intended that there be a proper balance between the roles of the President and Congress in decisions to use force in the conduct of foreign policy. . . .

First, let me stress that cooperation between the executive and legislative branches is the heart of the political process as conceived by the framers of the Constitution. In the absence of such cooperation, no legislation which seeks to define constitutional powers more rigidly can be effective. Conversely, given such cooperation, such legislation is unnecessary. Obviously there is need for, and great value in, congressional participation in the formulation of foreign policy and in decisions regarding the use of force. But at the same time there is a clear need in terms of national survival for preserving the constitutional power of the President to act in emergency situations. . . .

Let me turn, then, first to the historical background, beginning with the Constitution. Article I, section 8, of the Constitution grants Congress a number of specific powers relevant to our discussion, including the power "to . . . provide for the common Defence . . .; To declare War . . .; To raise and support Armies . . .; To provide and maintain a Navy; To make Rules for the Government and Regulation of the land and naval Forces . . . ." The Senate, in particular, is given certain foreign relations powers, to advise and consent to treaties and to the appointment of ambassadors and other officials. Congress has the power to make all laws which are necessary and proper for carrying out powers vested by the Constitution in the Federal Government. In addition, Congress has the sole authority to appropriate funds--a vital power in the war powers and foreign relations area.

The powers of the President which are relevant to this inquiry are found in article II. The President is vested with the executive power of the Government, he is named Commander in Chief of the Army and Navy and is required to "take Care that the Laws be faithfully executed." From these powers and the power to make treaties and to appoint and receive ambassadors is derived the President's constitutional authority to conduct the foreign relations of the United States.

The framers of the Constitution were not writing in a historical or political vacuum. Experience during the colonial period and under the Articles of Confederation has shown the need to strengthen the Central Government. The problem was to create a strong Federal system and yet prevent tyranny. . . .

The division of the war powers between the legislative and executive branches is illustrative of the general constitutional framework of shared powers and checks and balances. By this division, the framers changed prior United States practice under the Articles of Confederation, where the "sole and exclusive right and power of determining on peace and war" had been vested in the Legislature. They wished to take advantage of executive speed, efficiency, secrecy, and relative isolation from "public passions." At the same time, they wished to avoid the dangers to democratic government exemplified by the unchecked British monarch, who, as Hamilton noted, had supreme authority not only to command the military and naval forces but also to declare war and to raise and regulate fleets and armies. Mindful of the hardships which war can impose on the citizens of a country and fearful of vesting too much power in any individual, the framers intended that decisions regarding the initiation of hostilities be made not by the President alone, nor by the House or Senate alone, but by the entire Congress and the President together. Yet it is also clear that the framers intended to leave the President certain indispensable emergency powers.

The grant to Congress of the power to declare war was debated briefly at the Constitutional Convention, and that well-known debate reveals the essential intention of the framers. The Committee of Detail submitted to the general Convention a draft article which gave the Congress the power "to make war." Pursuant to a motion by Madison and Gerry, this was amended to the power "to declare war." This change in wording was not intended to detract from Congress' role in decisions to engage the country in war. Rather, it was a recognition of the need to preserve in the President an emergency power--as Madison explained it --"to repel sudden attacks" and also to avoid the confusion of "making" war with "conducting" war, which is the prerogative of the President.". . .

As we turn from an examination of history to an analysis of the modern context in which the President and Congress operate, I am impressed by the fundamental changes in the factual setting in which the war powers must be exercised. And indeed, it is this very change in setting which has raised difficult constitutional issues that cannot be answered by reference to history alone.

The primary factors underlying this transformation are rather evident and need only be summarized. They include, first, the emergence of the United States as a world power. . . .

The second factor which characterizes the modern context is the development of technology, especially in the field of nuclear weaponry. The fear of nuclear war and the importance of deterrence have engendered a sense of need to be able to take prompt, decisive Executive action. On the other hand, the fact that even a minor skirmish could lead to a confrontation of the major powers and raise the specter of nuclear war serves to emphasize the desirability of appropriate congressional participation in decisions which risk involving the United States in hostilities.

Third, the institutional capacities of the Presidency have facilitated the broad use of Presidential powers. The heightened pace, complexity, and hazards of contemporary events often require rapid and clear decisions. The Nation must be able to act flexibly and, in certain cases, without prior publicity. The institutional advantages of the Presidency, which are especially important in the area of foreign affairs, were pointed out in The Federalist: the unity of office, its capacity for secrecy and dispatch, and its superior sources of information.

Unlike the Presidency, the institutional characteristics of Congress have not lent themselves as well to the requirements of speed and secrecy in times of recurrent crises and rapid change. The composition of Congress with its numerous members and their diverse constituencies, the resultant complexity of the decisionmaking process, and Congress' constitutional tasks of debate, discussion, and authorization inevitably make it a more deliberative, public, and diffuse body.

Yet, in order to balance this picture, we must also note the inherent limitations of the Presidency. There are few significant matters which can be accomplished by Presidential order alone. The essence of Presidential power is the ability to enlist public support for national policy, and in this the President needs the cooperation of Congress. Virtually every Presidential program requires implementing legislation and funding. . . .

Of course, the electorate is the ultimate restraint upon the President and Congress in the exercise of the war powers. As President Nixon said in his "state of the world" message: "our experience in the 1960's has underlined the fact that we should not do more abroad than domestic opinion can sustain." The President and Congress must be sensitive to the people's willingness to suffer the potential physical, economic, and political costs of military actions. The Nation's ability to sustain long-term military action depends on the ability of the President and Congress to convince the people of the wisdom of their policies. . . .

. . . The most difficult question is still before us: What should we seek for the future--what is the proper balance between the Congress and the President?

It seems to me that we must start from the recognition that the exercise of the war powers under the Constitution is essentially a political process. It requires cooperation and mutual trust between the President and Congress and wise judgment on the part of both if the Nation's interests are to be well served. . . .

. . . We both want to avoid involving the Nation in wars, but if hostilities are forced upon us, we want to make certain that United States involvement is quickly and effectively undertaken and is fully in accordance with our constitutional processes. So the difference is not in our objectives but in how to achieve those objectives.

I am opposed to the legislation before you as a way to achieve these objectives because (1) it attempts to fix in detail, and to freeze, the allocation of the war power between the President and Congress--a step which the framers in their wisdom quite deliberately decided against-- and (2) it attempts in a number of respects to narrow the power given the President by the Constitution.

Regarding the first point, these bills reflect an approach which is not consistent with our constitutional tradition. The framers of the Constitution invested the executive and legislative branches with war powers appropriate to their respective roles and capabilities, without attempting to specify precisely who would do what in what circumstances and in what time period or how far one branch could go without the other. This was left to the political process, which is characteristic of the constitutional system of separation of powers. Our constitutional system is founded on an assumption of cooperation rather than conflict, and this is vitally necessary in matters of war and peace. The effective operation of that system requires that both branches work together from a common perspective rather than seeking to forge shackles based on the assumption of divergent perspectives.

As for the second aspect, although the bills recognize to a significant extent the President's full range of constitutional authority, they do tend to limit the President in some questionable ways. . . .

Some of the bills would also seek to restrict the President's authority to deploy forces abroad short of hostilities. This raises a serious constitutional issue of interference with the President's authority under the Constitution as Commander in Chief. Moreover, requiring prior congressional authorization for deployment of forces can deprive the President of a valuable instrument of diplomacy which is used most often to calm a crisis rather than inflame it. . . .

There is another consideration. To circumscribe Presidential ability to act in emergency situations--or even to appear to weaken it--would run the grave risk of miscalculation by a potential enemy regarding the ability of the United States to act in a crisis. This might embolden such a nation to provoke crises or take other actions which undermine international peace and security.

I do not believe we have sufficient foresight to provide wisely for all contingencies that may arise in the future. I am sure the Founding Fathers acted on that premise, and we should be most reluctant to reverse that judgment. Moreover, I firmly believe that Congress' ability to exercise its constitutional powers does not depend on restricting in advance the necessary flexibility which the Constitution has given the President. . . .

My own view is that the constitutional framework of shared war powers is wise and serves the interests of the Nation well in the modern world. The recognition of necessity for cooperation between the President and Congress in this area and for the participation of both in decisionmaking could not be clearer than it is today. What is required is the judicious and constructive exercise by each branch of its constitutional powers rather than seeking to draw arbitrary lines between them.

William P. Rogers, "Congress, the President, and the War Powers," statement, Senate Foreign Relations Committee, May 14, 1971, prior to enactment of War Powers Resolution; Department of State, *United States Foreign Policy, 1971: A Report of the Secretary of State,* pp. 503-15. For selected list of previous presidential use of the armed forces without congressional approval, see pp. 505-10.

8 3   RESTRAINT ON PRESIDENTIAL WAR POWERS

. . . The last 15 years left a legacy of contention between the executive and legislative branches and a web of restrictions on executive action embedded permanently in our laws. At the same time, the diffusion of power within the Congress means that a President has a hard time when he wants to negotiate with the Congress, because congressional leaders have lost their dominance of the process and often cannot produce a consensus or sometimes even a decision.

The net result . . . is an enormous problem for American foreign policy--a loss of coherence and recurring uncertainty in the minds of friend and foe about the aims and constancy of the United States.

Particularly in the war powers field, where direct use of our power is at issue, the stakes are high. Yet the war powers resolution sets arbitrary 60-day deadlines that practically invite an adversary to wait us out. Our Commander in Chief is locked in battle at home at the same time he is trying to act effectively abroad. Under the resolution, even inaction by the Congress can force the President to remove American forces from an area of challenge, which, as former President Ford has put it, undermines the President even when the Congress can't get up the courage to take a position. Such constraints on timely action may only invite greater challenges down the road. . . . As the distinguished Majority Leader, Senator Howard Baker, said on the floor of the Senate 4 weeks ago:

[W]e cannot continue to begin each military involvement abroad with a prolonged, tedious and divisive negotiation between the executive and the legislative branches of Government. The world and its many challenges to our interests simply do not allow us that luxury.

I do not propose changes in our constitutional system. But some legislative changes may be called for. And I propose, at a minimum, that all of us, in both Congress and the executive branch, exercise our prerogatives with a due regard to the national need for an effective foreign policy. Congress has the right, indeed the duty, to debate and criticize, to authorize and appropriate funds and share in setting the broad lines of policy. But micromanagement by a committee of 535 independent-minded individuals is a grossly inefficient and ineffective way to run any important enterprise. The fact is that depriving the President of flexibility weakens our country. Yet a host of restrictions on the President's ability to act are now built into our laws and our procedures. Surely there is a better way for the President and the Congress to exercise their prerogatives without hobbling this country in the face of assaults on free-world interests abroad. Surely there can be accountability without paralysis. The sad truth is that many of our difficulties over the last 15 years have been self-imposed.

The issue is fundamental. If the purpose of our power is to prevent war, or injustice, then ideally we want to discourage such occurrences rather than have to use our power in a physical sense. But this can happen only if there is assurance that our power would be used if necessary.

A reputation for reliability becomes, then, a major asset--giving friends a sense of security and adversaries a sense of caution. A reputation for living up to our commitments can, in fact, make it less likely that pledges of support will have to be carried out. Crisis management is most successful when a favorable outcome is attained without firing a shot. Credibility is an intangible, but it is no less real. The same is true of a loss of credibility. A failure to support a friend always involves a price. Credibility, once lost, has to be reearned.

George Shultz, address, Trilateral Commission, April 3, 1984; *American Foreign Policy: Current Documents*, 1984, pp. 5-6.

8 4   WAR POWERS AND NON-AUTOMATICITY OF MILITARY COMMITMENTS OF COLLECTIVE DEFENSE ARRANGEMENTS

This memorandum discusses the extent of the United States' commitment under mutual security treaties by addressing the question, "Does any treaty to which the United States is a party authorize the President to introduce the Armed Forces into hostilities or require the United States to do so, automatically, if another party to any such treaty is attacked?"

The two issues posed are actually one; if a treaty requires the United States to introduce its armed forces into hostilities upon the happening of certain events and thus precludes a decision by the United States not to do so, then it is fair to construe that treaty as authorizing the President to introduce the Armed Forces into hostilities. Conversely, if a treaty allows the United States to decide in each situation whether to introduce its Armed Forces into hostilities, it is not necessary to construe it as conferring upon the President the authority to introduce the armed forces into hostilities.

The memorandum concludes that the answer to the question posed is no, for two reasons: (A) the wording of the treaties and their legislative histories make clear that they were not intended to be so construed; and (B) such a construction would be constitutionally dubious.

A. Text and Intent of the Treaties. An analysis of the texts of the United States mutual security treaties indicates no intent to bind parties to introduce their armed forces into hostilities. Indeed, each treaty explicitly recognizes that a decision to do so must be made by each party as specific situations arise. Each of the treaties provides that it will be carried out by the United States in accordance with its "constitutional processes" or it contains other language to make clear that the United States commitment is a qualified one--that the distribution of power within the United States Government is precisely what it would be in the absence of the treaty, and that the United States reserves the right to determine for itself what military action, if any, is appropriate.

In short, each treaty contains an international requirement with a domestic escape clause; each requires that under certain circumstances the parties will consult with one another, but none requires that the parties act in any predetermined way. The legislative histories of the treaties bear out this analysis, and it has been the consistent position of legal authorities and of the executive branch.

B. Constitutionality. Because the Constitution vests the power to declare war in the Congress rather than the Senate, a strong argument can be made from its text that approval for United States entry into war must involve the House of Representatives and therefore cannot be accomplished by treaty. . . . However, a review of the statements and actions of the Framers suggests a specific intent to include the House in the decision to go to war. Moreover, it is doubtful whether the authority to make that decision could constitutionally be delegated to the President, whether by treaty or by law. Serious constitutional questions would thus be raised by any treaty purporting to place the United States automatically at war; those problems can be avoided only by construing the treaties as not doing so.

Conclusion

United States mutual security treaties represent affirmations of a general intent to render assistance in good faith to another party if that party is attacked. However, no treaty to which the United States is a party authorizes the President to introduce the Armed Forces into hostilities or requires the United States to do so, automatically, if another party is attacked. Any treaty purporting to do so would be constitutionally dubious and should be construed as not doing so.

Michael J. Glennon, Legal Counsel of Senate Foreign Relations Committee, memorandum to the committee on non-automaticity of military commitment of mutual defense treaties, July 11, 1977; *Digest of United States Practice in International Law*, 1977, pp. 970-71. For additional commentary on the War Powers Resolution, see pp. 968-80. For the texts of collective defense arrangements, see Chapter 18.

PART III

GENERAL FOREIGN POLICIES AND DOCTRINES

6

General Policy Statements and Themes

It is quite true that the central themes of American foreign policy are more or less constant. They derive from the kind of people we are in this country and from the shape of the world situation.

Dean Rusk
"The Formulation of Foreign Policy," 1961

Foreign policies, as indicated in Chapter 3, are courses of action designed to maintain national interests and achieve the nation's purposes, goals, and concrete objectives. They vary in importance and longevity, and may be expressed in swooping policy statements or be more precise in terms of intent, applicability, and duration. At times their articulation degenerates into cliches or slogans, and frequently they are confused with national ideals or aims. In devising them, attention needs to be paid not only to costs and benefits but also to risks and consequences. Usually they are directly related to domestic or internal policies and affairs.

Diplomatic history reveals that over the years the United States has evolved a dozen or more basic and durable foreign policies. Some of these are in keeping with American traditions, such as preserving national security, peace, and human freedom, and promoting self-determination, arms limitation, free trade, and most-favored-nation treatment. A number of long-term policies, several of which have been superseded, have had geographic orientation, including the twin policies of isolationism and neutrality applied to European affairs, the Monroe Doctrine and inter-Americanism to the Western Hemisphere, and the Open Door and preservation of territorial integrity to the Far East. More recent policies of similar fundamentality embrace widespread cooperation in organized global and regional institutions and, since World War II, formal alliances and informal ententes, collective defense arrangements, and containment of Communist expansion and hegemonism.

On a few occasions American leaders have propounded anthologies of such policies, customarily expressed as war aims or aspirations for peaceful settlement and relations. These are exemplified in the twentieth century by Woodrow Wilson's Fourteen Points (1918), Franklin Roosevelt's eight-paragraph Atlantic Charter (1941), and Harry Truman's less well-known but equally historic twelve points, incorporated into his Navy Day Address (1946). All three stressed United States support of self-determination of peoples (given the greatest emphasis), arms reduction, free and nondiscriminatory trade (expressed as equal access to the trade and raw materials of the world), and international cooperation in a global association of nations to provide collective security and maintain the peace.

To these Wilson added "open covenants . . . openly arrived at" (his first point), Roosevelt appended two of his Four Freedoms (freedom from want and from fear), and Truman incorporated Western Hemisphere inter-Americanism and all of Roosevelt's Four Freedoms. Except for Wilson's prescription of open diplomacy, these policy precepts have been reiterated, refined, or amplified in dozens of subsequent policy proposals and actions.

Also of historic significance are such memorable policy pronouncements as Washington's Farewell Address (1796), Monroe's message to Congress (containing the Monroe Doctrine, 1823), the war messages of Wilson (1917) and Roosevelt (1941), Truman's appeal to Congress for aid to Greece and Turkey (Truman Doctrine, 1947), George Marshall's speech at Harvard University (Marshall Plan, 1947), Kennedy's Strategy for Peace Plan (1963), Nixon's press remarks at Guam (Nixon Doctrine, 1969), and others. They produced major changes in the direction of American foreign policy.

Contemporary documentary resources provide a profusion of general foreign policy statements by American political leaders. They are embodied in a variety of inaugural addresses and periodic messages and reports to Congress, legislative proposals, studies, reports, and enactments, treaties and agreements, public addresses, oral and written political commentaries, and press statements and interviews. For example, in addition to dealing with a score of domestic problems, a single state of the union message may deal with an equal number of foreign relations developments, policies, and programs.

Most foreign policy statements apply to particular functional matters (treated in Chapters 15-24), international cooperation in the United Nations and inter-American systems (Chapters 25-26), or geographically oriented issues (Chapters 27-32). Some pertain to problems in the conduct of foreign relations (Chapters 4-5) and specific crises involving the United States (Chapters 8-14), and a few are elevated to the stature of national policy doctrines (Chapter 7).

This chapter presents a sampling of general policy pronouncements. They fall into three categories: commentary about policy, including preconditions, requirements, guidelines, and the pertinence of negotiation and public consensus; prevailing policy themes; and considerations respecting national security policy.

All political leaders espouse policies intended to preserve or enhance national identity, security, liberty, peace, human welfare, and international cooperation. These are universally regarded as heading the list of American foreign relations goals. Often they are coupled with dissemination of American traditions, values, and ideals abroad. Other themes run the gamut from self-determination, independence, and democratization to arms reduction, international trade, rapprochement and detente with adversaries, and international involvement, commitment, and responsibility. Still others embrace the promotion of national honor, equality, and justice and such specific matters as healing existing international wounds, and even the right of legation (the right to maintain diplomatic relations).

It will be noted that, despite the manner in which they are posed, the more they are articulated as broad-scale and amorphous precepts or standards, the more they constitute purposes or goals rather than concrete courses of action to achieve actionable objectives. Only when they are concretized and priorities are prescribed as to how to pursue and implement them, do they take on the character of genuine foreign policies.

ABOUT FOREIGN POLICY AND RELATIONS

8 5   TOUCHSTONE OF WORLD POLICY

The world has changed many times since General Washington counseled his new and weak country to "observe good faith and justice toward all nations." Great empires have risen and dissolved. Great heroes have made their entrances and have left the stage. And America has slowly, often reluctantly, grown to be a great power and a leading member of world society.

So we seek today, as we did in Washington's time, to protect the life of our nation, to preserve the liberty of our citizens, and to pursue the happiness of our people. This is the touchstone of our world policy.

Thus we seek to add no territory to our dominion, no satellites to our orbit, no slavish followers to our policies. The most impressive witness to this restraint is that for a century our own frontiers have stood quiet and stood unarmed. But we have also learned . . . that our own freedom depends on the freedom of others, that our own protection requires that we help protect others, that we draw increased strength from the strength of others. . . .

The principles of this foreign policy have been shaped in battle, have been tested in danger, have been sustained in achievement. They have endured . . . because they reflect the realities of our world and they reflect the aims of our country. . . .

Lyndon Johnson, address, Associated Press, New York, April 20, 1964; *American Foreign Policy: Current Documents*, 1964, p. 26.

8 6   PURPOSES AND POLICIES

. . . There is no shortcut. We have no alternative but to deal with the world as it is and to address ourselves to the problems that actually confront us.

The challenge of our perilous environment can only be met by positive, realistic policies. We cannot escape the world; we must face it boldly, and with confidence in our basic strength.

This strength is not confined to military power, essential though we know it to be. It is rooted deep in the moral faith on which our country was based. It is expressed in what may be called our national purpose.

We Americans want peace, freedom, justice, prosperity, and well-being for ourselves and for all other people. We want to assure freedom of choice to all nations and societies.

No people is our enemy, although some peoples are controlled by governments which may be antagonistic to the United States. . . . Our ultimate aim is not only to preserve and strengthen our way of life here at home but to help all other peoples attain a way of life that is a natural reflection of their history and culture. For freedom in today's world is indivisible.

To achieve these purposes we must simultaneously pursue a variety of policies aimed at a variety of specific results.

Chester Bowles, address, Kansas City, October 26, 1961; *American Foreign Policy, Current Documents,* 1961, p. 51.

8 7   POLICY PRECONDITIONS

There are two obvious preconditions for an effective American foreign policy: a strong national economy and a strong national defense. . . .

The response of our democracy to economic challenges will determine whether we will be able to manage the challenge of other global responsibilities. . . . If we cannot meet these international economic problems successfully, then our ability to meet military and political and diplomatic challenges will be doubtful indeed.

Jimmy Carter, address, World Affairs Council, Philadelphia, May 9, 1980; *American Foreign Policy: Basic Documents,* 1977-1980, p. 63.

8 8   SIX POLICY REQUIREMENTS

Our fresh purposes demanded new methods of planning and a more rigorous and systematic process of policymaking. We required a system which would summon and gather the best ideas, the best analyses and the best information available to the government and the nation.

Efficient procedure does not insure wisdom in the substance of policy. But given the complexity of contemporary choices, adequate procedures are an indispensable component of the act of judgment. I have long believed that the most pressing issues are not necessarily the most fundamental ones; we know that an effective American policy requires clarity of purpose for the future as well as a procedure for dealing with the present. We do not want to exhaust ourselves managing crises; our basic goal is to shape the future. . . .

--Our policy must be **creative**: foreign policy must mean more than reacting to emergencies; we must fashion a new and positive vision of a peaceful world, and design new policies to achieve it.

--Our policymaking must be **systematic**: our actions must be the products of thorough analysis, forward planning, and deliberate decision. We must master problems before they master us.

--We must know the **facts**: intelligent discussions . . . and wise decisions require the most reliable information available. Disputes in the government have been caused too often by an incomplete awareness or understanding of the facts.

--We must know the **alternatives**: we must know what our real options are and not simply what compromise has found bureaucratic acceptance. Every view and every alternative must have a fair hearing. Presidential leadership is not the same as ratifying bureaucratic consensus.

--We must be prepared if **crises** occur: we must anticipate crises where possible. If they cannot be prevented, we must plan for dealing with them. All the elements of emergency action, political as well as military, must be related to each other.

--Finally, we must have effective **implementation**: it does little good to plan intelligently and imaginatively if our decisions are not well carried out.

Richard Nixon, *U.S. Foreign Policy for the 1970's: A New Strategy for Peace* (1970), pp. 17-18.

89   POLICY GUIDELINES

For our part, we shall achieve that peace only with patience and perseverance and courage--the patience and perseverance necessary to work with allies of diverse interests but common goals, the courage necessary over a long period of time to overcome an adversary skilled in the arts of harassment and obstruction.

There is no way to maintain the frontiers of freedom without cost and commitment and risk. There is no swift and easy path to peace in our generation. No man who witnessed the tragedies of the last war, no man who can imagine the unimaginable possibilities of the next war, can advocate war out of irritability or frustration or impatience.

But let no nation confuse our perseverance and patience with fear of war or unwillingness to meet our responsibilities. We cannot save ourselves by abandoning those who are associated with us, or rejecting our responsibilities.

In the end, the only way to maintain the peace is to be prepared in the final extreme to fight for our country--and to mean it.

As a nation, we have little capacity for deception. We can convince friend and foe alike that we are in earnest about the defense of freedom only if we are in earnest--and I can assure the world that we are.

John Kennedy, remarks, Veteran's Day, Arlington National Cemetery, November 11, 1961; *Papers of Presidents: Kennedy,* 1961, pp. 713-14.

9 0 TRADITIONAL PRINCIPLES AND REALITIES

Domestic political tides ebb and flow, but foreign policy is a continuous stream. Its course is affected by changes in elective officials, but it is mainly formed from our geography, our ancestral ties, our natural resources and economic needs, and above all, the common principles and beliefs on which our Nation was founded 200 years ago. . . .

American foreign policy has been shaped not only by the realities of an imperfect world order and by events that we cannot control, but also by certain truths we believe--inalienable rights such as freedom and justice, self-determination, and the duty of the strong towards the weak, and the prosperous towards the poor. As we have matured and grown more mighty, we have learned some hard lessons in world affairs--that we cannot force freedom on the unwilling, that we cannot police every distant corner or fill every empty bowl.

We have made mistakes. We have been disillusioned. But we have never wholly abandoned Jefferson's decent respect for the opinions of mankind or Lincoln's faith that right does make might or Eisenhower's that freedom today is indivisible. Thus, our foreign policy today is a mixture of the principles that unite us and make us the hope of freedom for others, and the practical counsel of George Washington that the best way to preserve peace is to be prepared for war. Peace through strength is neither a new policy nor a bad one. . . .

United States foreign policy must never be made by an elite establishment nor bent to the fears of a frustrated few. It must reflect the real purposes of the American people when they follow their very finest instincts.

Gerald Ford, remarks, press conference, May 22, 1976; *Papers of Presidents: Ford,* 1976, pp. 1645, 1647.

9 1 TOTAL DIPLOMACY

We are also coming to realize that foreign operations in today's world call for a total diplomacy that reflects all of the dynamic phases of our own American society--from our industrial capacity and military defense to our educational system and our dedication to the rights of the human individual.

American ambassadors can no longer be content with wining and dining, reporting, analyzing, and cautiously predicting. They must act as administrators and coordinators, responsible for the effective operation of all U.S. Government activities in the countries of their assignment.

Growing out of these factors is a new understanding in every nation and in every corner of every nation of the overriding importance of people--what they think, what they fear, what they seek. . . .

Not even the best equipped, American-trained troops can success-fully defend their own country unless their fellow citizens feel that they have something meaningful of their own for which they are prepared to give their lives. This is a decisive new factor in world affairs and there-fore a basic new element of power.

Chester Bowles, address, National Press Club, March 23, 1962; *American Foreign Policy: Current Documents,* 1962, p. 990.

9 2   OVERSIMPLIFICATION, SLOGANS, MYTHS

What we try to avoid is to reduce great policy matters to empty or misleading slogans or pat phrases. We do so because we must forever concern ourselves with the underlying realities of policy, in the real world in which we live and in the light of real responsibilities, real threats, real opportunities, and the prospects for building a real environment in the world in which our institutions of freedom can flourish. It is inevitable, however, that public debate, which is crucial to the vitality of our democracy, produces oversimplification. And some of this conceals rather than illuminates the truth.

I am referring not only to the most notorious use of inverted and distorted language of our present time--the corruption by Communism of such notions as "peace," "democracy," "aggression," "liberation." I have in mind also the sometimes well-meaning but confused men in our own society who hamper the conduct of our foreign policy by propagating myths and fallacies which divert us from the real job at hand. I have in mind especially the various groups of pessimistic sloganeers who apparently believe that the Communists are as invincible as they claim to be, who concede to them victories which they have not won, who doubt the intelligence and dedication of our own people and appear to distrust the ability of our principles and ideals to prevail in open competition.

Dean Rusk, remarks, Advertising Council, Washington, March 6, 1962; *American Foreign Policy: Current Documents,* 1962, p. 15.

9 3   FOREIGN AND DOMESTIC POLICY

The overriding rule which I want to affirm today is this: that our foreign policy must always be an extension of this nation's domestic policy. . . .

The great creative periods of American foreign policy have been the great periods of our domestic achievement. Abraham Lincoln, Woodrow Wilson, and Franklin D. Roosevelt, to mention but three, projected their image of concern and accomplishment to the entire world.   I would mistrust any expert on foreign affairs, however deeply he might be informed, if he confessed ignorance of the politics of the United States of America.

The reason for this is quite simple. Politics are the means by which men give their collective voice to their hopes and aspirations. Can we suppose that these are so very different for Americans than for the people of the other lands from which our parents came? Certainly not. Nor will we long have the confidence and respect of other people if we hold what is necessary for Americans is too good for other people.

The rule, to repeat, is that a sound foreign policy is in the main a longer reach of what we do and what we seek here at home. . . .

Lyndon Johnson, address, University of Denver, August 26, 1966; *American Foreign Policy: Current Documents,* 1966, p. 27.

9 4   NOTHING TO FEAR FROM NEGOTIATIONS

Let us never negotiate out of fear.
But let us never fear to negotiate.
*   *   *

But as long as we know what comprises our vital interests and our long-range goals, we have nothing to fear from negotiations at the appropriate time and nothing to gain by refusing to play a part in them. . . .

If vital interests under duress can be preserved by peaceful means, negotiations will find that out. If our adversary will accept nothing less than a concession of our rights, negotiations will find that out. And if negotiations are to take place, this nation cannot abdicate to its adversaries the task of choosing the forum and the framework and the time.

For there are carefully defined limits within which any serious negotiations must take place. . . .

No one should be under the illusion that negotiations for the sake of negotiations always advance the cause of peace. If for lack of preparation they break up in bitterness, the prospects of peace have been endangered. If they are made a forum for propaganda or a cover for aggression, the processes of peace have been abused.

But it is a test of our national maturity to accept the fact that negotiations are not a contest spelling victory or defeat. They may succeed; they may fail. They are likely to be successful only if both sides reach an agreement which both regard as preferable to the status quo--an agreement in which each side can consider its own situation to be improved. And this is most difficult to obtain.

John Kennedy, Inaugural Adress, January 20, 1961, and address, University of Washington, Seattle, November 16, 1961; *Papers of Presidents: Kennedy,* 1961, pp. 2 and 727.

PREVAILING POLICY THEMES

9 5   EISENHOWER'S EFFORT TO PRESERVE SECURITY AND FREEDOM

In these years of ever-present danger what has been the US effort to preserve security and freedom and to channel into constructive directions, as best we can, these surging forces which are rolling over our world?

The United States has sought to strengthen collective security, deter the use of force, create international status in new areas of activity, progress toward safeguarded arms control, promote negotiation of out- standing international disputes, increase the role of the United Nations and make of the interdependence of a shrunken world a force for peace rather than a breeding ground for war. . . .

In conclusion, President Eisenhower's foreign policy has rested on two simple propositions: Peace, liberty, and well-being for the United States. This depends in good part on the peace, liberty, and well-being of other nations.

Christian Herter, summary statement submitted to President Eisenhower, January 6, 1961; *American Foreign Policy: Current Documents,* 1960, pp. 13, 23.

9 6   PEACE, FREEDOM, AND DIGNITY

. . . the American people seek to act as a force for peace in the world and to further the cause of human freedom and dignity. Indeed, an appreciation for the unalienable rights of every human being is the very concept that gave birth to this nation. Few have understood better than our nation's Founding Fathers that claims of human dignity transcend the claims of any government, and that this transcendent right itself has a transcendent source. Our Declaration of Independence four times acknowl- edges our country's dependence on a Supreme Being, and its principal author and one of our greatest Presidents, Thomas Jefferson, put it simply: "The God who gave us life, gave us liberty at the same time."

Ronald Reagan, remarks, welcoming Pope John Paul II, May 2, 1984; *Papers of Presidents: Reagan,* 1984, p. 619.

9 7   PEACE, FREEDOM, AND COOPERATION--PRINCIPLE AND POWER

Peace--a peace that preserves freedom--remains America's first goal. In the coming years as a mighty nation, we will continue to pursue peace. But to be strong abroad we must be strong at home. And in order to be strong, we must continue to face up to the difficult issues that confront us as a nation today.

*   *   *

Our world is one of conflicting hopes, ideologies, and powers. It's a revolutionary world which requires confident, stable, and powerful American leadership--and that's what it is getting and that's what it will continue to get--to shift the trend of history away from the specter of fragmentation and toward the promise of genuinely global cooperation and peace. So, we must strive in our foreign policy to blend commitment to high ideals with a sober calculation of our own national interests.

Unchanging American ideals are relevant to this troubling area of foreign policy and to this troubled era in which we live. Our society has always stood for political freedom. We have always fought for social justice, and we have always recognized the necessity for pluralism. Those values of ours have a real meaning, not just in the past, 200 years ago or 20 years ago, but now, in a world that is no longer dominated by colonial empires and that demands a more equitable distribution of political and economic power.

But in this age of revolutionary change, the opportunities for violence and for conflict have also grown. American power must be strong enough to deal with that danger and to promote our ideals and to defend our national interests. That's why the foreign policy which we've shaped . . . must be based simultaneously on the primacy of certain basic moral principles--principles founded on the enhancement of human rights-- and on the preservation of an American military strength that is second to none. This fusion of principle and power is the only way to ensure global stability and peace while we accommodate to the inevitable and necessary reality of global change and progress.

Jimmy Carter, State of the Union Adress, January 23, 1980, and address, World Affairs Council, Philadelphia, May 9, 1980; *American Foreign Policy: Basic Documents*, 1977-1980, pp. 57, 63. When inaugurated, President Carter not only delivered the customary inaugural address, but also issued an "inaugural statement to the world," January 20, 1977; *Papers of Presidents: Carter*, 1977, I, 4-5.

9 8   SECURITY, HONOR, PEACE, AND STABILITY

Our goals are simple but profound: security, honor, and peace. Those are the victories we seek for ourselves, for our children, and for our children's children. These victories can be won but not by nostalgic nor wishful thinking and not by bravado. They cannot be won by a futile effort either to run the world or to run away from the world. Both of these are dangerous myths that cannot be the foundation for any responsible national policy.

America requires the authority and the strength--and the moral force--to protect ourselves, to provide for the defense of our friends, and to promote the values of human dignity and well-being that have made our own nation strong at home and respected abroad. . . .

All of these objectives require America's great military strength. But arms alone cannot provide the security within which our values and our interests can flourish. Our foreign policy must be directed toward greater international stability, without which there is no real prospect for a lasting peace. Thus, our strength in arms--very important--must be matched by creative, responsible, and courageous diplomacy.

Edmund Muskie, address, Los Angeles, October 7, 1980; *American Foreign Policy: Basic Documents*, 1977-1980, p. 73.

99   AMERICAN EAGLE FACES THE OLIVE BRANCH: PREPAREDNESS AND PEACE

For the American eagle on the Presidential seal holds in his talons both the olive branch of peace and the arrows of military might. On the ceiling in the Presidential office, constructed many years ago, that eagle is facing the arrows of war on its left. But on the newer carpet on the floor, reflecting a change initiated by President Roosevelt and implemented by President Truman immediately after the war, that eagle is now facing the olive branch of peace. And it is in that spirit--the spirit of both preparedness and peace--that this nation is stronger than ever before--strengthened by both the increased power of our defenses and our increased efforts for peace, strengthened by both our resolve to resist coercion and our constant search for solutions. And it is in this spirit that I assure you that the American eagle still faces toward the olive branch of peace.

John Kennedy, address, University of Maine, October 19, 1963; *American Foreign Policy: Current Documents*, 1963, p. 33. This notion of the American eagle depicted as clutching arrows and the olive branch is repeated by Secretary of State George Shultz; see Chapter 2, note to Document 21.

100   WORLD WITHOUT WAR--TEN COURSES

. . . Our ultimate goal is a world without war, a world made safe for diversity, in which all men, goods, and ideas can freely move across every border and every boundary. We must advance toward this goal . . . in at least 10 different ways, not as partisans but as patriots.

First, we must maintain . . . that margin of military safety and superiority obtained through . . . years of steadily increasing both the quality and the quantity of our strategic, our   conventional, and our antiguerrilla forces. . . .

Second, we must take new steps--and we shall make new proposals . . . toward the control and the eventual abolition of arms. Even in the absence of agreement we must not stockpile arms beyond our needs or seek an excess of military power that could be provocative as well as wasteful.

Third, we must make increased use of our food as an instrument of peace, making it available by sale, trade, loan, or donation to hungry people in all nations which tell us of their needs and accept proper conditions of distribution.

Fourth, we must assure our preeminence in the peaceful exploration of outer space . . . in cooperation with other powers if possible, alone if necessary.

Fifth, we must expand world trade. . . .

Sixth, we must continue . . . our recent progress toward balancing our international accounts. . . .

Seventh, we must become better neighbors with the free states of the Americas, working with the councils of the OAS [Organization of American States] . . . and with all the men and women of this hemisphere who really believe in liberty and justice for all.

Eighth, we must strengthen the ability of free nations everywhere to develop their independence and raise their standard of living--and thereby frustrate those who prey on poverty and chaos. . . .

Ninth, we must strengthen our Atlantic and Pacific partnerships, maintain our alliances, and make the United Nations a more effective instrument for national independence and international order.

Tenth, and finally, we must develop with our allies new means of bridging the gap between the East and the West, facing danger boldly wherever danger exists, but being equally bold in our search for new agreements which can enlarge the hopes of all while violating the interests of none.

In short, I would say . . . that we must be constantly prepared for the worst and constantly acting for the best. We must be strong enough to win any war, and we must be wise enough to prevent one. We shall neither act as aggressors nor tolerate acts of aggression. We intend to bury no one, and we do not intend to be buried.

Lyndon Johnson, Annual Message on State of the Union, January 8, 1964; *American Foreign Policy: Current Documents*, 1964, pp. 1-2.

1 0 1   BLESSINGS OF LIBERTY

Our foreign policy derives from the kind of people we are and from the international environment in which we live. It is relatively simple, relatively long term, and nonpartisan. . . .

Our supreme aspiration is "to secure the Blessings of Liberty to ourselves and Our Posterity." This means that the beginning of our foreign policy is the kind of society we build here at home. Our example casts its shadow around the globe. Our words about freedom and justice would ring hollow if we were not making it apparent that we were trying to make our own society a gleaming example of what free men can accomplish under the processes of consent. . . .

A central problem of our nation, therefore, must be to pursue an organized peace--a lasting peace, a world in which disputes are settled by peaceful means, a world free of the threat of thermonuclear catastrophe, in which each nation lives under institutions of its own choice but in which all nations and peoples cooperate to promote their mutual welfare.

This does not mean that we are the world's policeman. It does not mean we aspire to a Pax Americana. We do not participate in most of the crises which arise in different parts of the world. We use our diplomatic resources and our membership in such bodies as the United Nations to try to lay the hand of restraint upon high tempers and excessive violence and to help find ways and means to bring about a peaceful settlement of the many disputes that appear upon the world's agenda. . . .

We must try with all of our intelligence and skill to turn downward the arms race. It is not easy when there are those who will not accept simple requirements of inspection to give assurance that agreements will be carried out. It will not be easy so long as there are major unresolved questions. . . . It will not be easy when there are powerful countries who are committed to what they consider a world revolution--fundamentally in opposition to the kind of world envisaged in the United Nations Charter. But we must continue to try. . . .

Even before vast resources might be freed through disarmament, we must take a responsible share in the process of economic and social development among those nations who are just beginning to enter the age of science and technology. We cannot sustain our own prosperity in a poverty-stricken world. Nor can we allow ourselves to be indifferent to misery and disease which burden so vast a proportion of the world's population. . . .

Nor do we forget that the United States is a trading nation. The promotion of trade is a major object of our diplomacy--and has been since the time of Benjamin Franklin. We have an important role in creating a vigorous system of international trade and monetary arrangements which are adequate to the needs of an expanding world economy.

In our relations with present or potential adversaries we must be resolute when firmness is required. On the other hand, we should make it clear that we are prepared to meet everyone else more than halfway in building a durable peace. Despite the presence of tension and violence, we should try to resolve every outstanding question and extend the hand of cooperation where there is any response from the other side.

We need not be under illusions about the word detente, but we must work toward a genuine reduction of tensions. . . .

Dean Rusk, address, U.S. Chamber of Commerce, May 1, 1967; *American Foreign Policy: Current Documents,* 1967, pp. 12-13. The expression "blessings of liberty" appears in the preface to the Constitution of the United States. Rusk also refers to it in Document 2 as our primary objective, and in Document 7 as America's central purpose.

1 0 2   INVOLVEMENT, RESPONSIBILITY, AND GREATNESS

The underlying questions are really these: What is America's role in the world?   What are the responsibilities of a great nation toward protecting freedom beyond its shores?   Can we ever be left in peace if we do not actively assume the burden of keeping the peace? . . .

Imagine for a moment, if you will, what would happen to this world if America were to become a dropout in assuming the responsibility for defending peace and freedom in the world. As every world leader knows, and as even the most outspoken critics of America would admit, the rest of the world would live in terror. . . .

We must rule out unilateral disarmament, because in the real world it wouldn't work. If we pursue arms control as an end in itself, we will not achieve our end.   The adversaries in the world are not in conflict because they are armed. They are armed because they are in conflict, and have not yet learned peaceful ways to resolve their conflicting national interests. . . .

There is no advancement for Americans at home in a retreat from the problems of the world. I say that America has a vital national interest in world stability, and no other nation can uphold that interest for us.

We stand at a crossroad in our history. We shall reaffirm our destiny for greatness or we shall choose instead to withdraw into ourselves. The choice will affect far more than our foreign policy; it will determine the quality of our lives.

A nation needs many qualities, but it needs faith and confidence above all. Skeptics do not build societies; the idealists are the builders. Only societies that believe in themselves can rise to their challenges. Let us not, then, pose a false choice between meeting our responsibilities abroad and meeting the needs of our people at home. We shall meet both or we shall meet neither. . . .

We will know then that every man achieves his own greatness by reaching out beyond himself, and so it is with nations. When a nation believes in itself . . . that nation can perform miracles. Only when a nation means something to itself can it mean something to others.

Richard Nixon, address, Air Force Academy, June 4, 1969; *Papers of Presidents: Nixon,* 1969, pp. 433-34.

103 AMERICAN PLEDGES

On behalf of the American people, I renew these basic pledges to you today:
--We are committed to a pursuit of a more peaceful, stable, and cooperative world. While we are determined never to be bested in a test of strength, we will devote our strength to what is best. And in the nuclear era, there is no rational alternative to accords of mutual restraint between the United States and the Soviet Union, two nations which have the power to destroy mankind.
--We will bolster our partnerships with traditional friends in Europe, Asia, and Latin America to meet new challenges in a rapidly changing world. The maintenance of such relationships underpins rather than undercuts the search for peace.
--We will seek out, we will expand our relations with old adversaries.
. . .
--We will strive to heal old wounds. . . . Peace cannot be imposed from without, but we will do whatever is within our capacity to help achieve it.
--We rededicate ourselves to the search for justice, equality, and freedom. . . . Behavior appropriate to an era of dependence must give way to the new responsibilities of an era of interdependence.

No single nation, no single group of nations, no single organization can meet all of the challenges before the community of nations. We must act in concert. Progress toward a better world must come through cooperative efforts across the whole range of bilateral and multilateral relations.

Gerald Ford, address, United Nations, September 18, 1974; *Papers of Presidents: Ford,* 1974, pp. 157-58.

NATIONAL SURVIVAL, SECURITY, AND STRENGTH

104 STRENGTH FOR SURVIVAL

. . . we must find a way to insure the survival of civilization in this nuclear age. That, to me, is the greatest single requirement on the world's statesmen today. And from this, in turn, there follow two basic rules for all of our policies . . . America must be strong, but America must be temperate and America must be just.

Lyndon Johnson, remarks, Department of State, December 5, 1963; *American Foreign Policy: Current Documents,* 1963, p. 519. He also cautioned that national strength must be tempered by national restraint, November 27, 1963; *Papers of Presidents: Johnson,* 1963, II, 8.

1 0 5   STRENGTH AND PEACE

Since George Washington first enjoined the American people to recognize a connection between the maintenance of adequate military strength and the maintenance of the peace, our history has underlined that the danger of war is greatest when potential enemies are in doubt about the capacity of nations to defend their vital interests, about their will to defend them, or about how they define those vital interests. All three of those conditions for a peaceful resolution of differences are heightened in a world where the use of nuclear weapons may quickly come into play once conflict begins at any level.

Dean Rusk, address, American Historical Association, Washington, December 30, 1961; *American Foreign Policy: Current Documents,* 1961, p. 58. The combination of strength and peace appears in many foreign policy documents.

1 0 6   TWO REQUIREMENTS FOR SECURITY: BALANCE OF POWER AND STRENGTH TO SHAPE THE WORLD

First, the United States must maintain a military balance of power. Our defense forces must remain unsurpassed. Our strategic deterrent must be unquestionable. Our conventional forces must be strong enough and flexible enough to meet the full range of military threats we may face. As a global power, we must maintain the global military balance. Our strength is important to our own safety, to a strong foreign policy free from coercion, to the confidence of allies and friends, and to the future of reciprocal arms control and other negotiations. . . .

The second central point is this: that our military strength, while an essential condition for an effective foreign policy, is not in itself a sufficient condition. We must nurture and draw upon our other strengths as well--our alliances and other international ties, our economic resources, our ability to deal with diversity, and our ideals. By drawing fully on these strengths, we can help shape world events now in ways that reduce the likelihood of using military force later. A global American foreign policy can succeed only if it has both these dimensions. . . .

It is just as illusory, and just as dangerous, to believe that there can be a fortress America or that the world will follow our lead solely because of our military strength. America's future depends not only on our grow-ing military power, it also requires the continued pursuit of energy security and arms control, of human rights and economic development abroad.

Cyrus Vance, statement, Senate Foreign Relations Committee, March 27, 1980; *American Foreign Policy: Basic Documents,* 1977-1980, p. 61.

1 0 7   SECURITY, STRENGTH, ARMS, AND PEACE

But my first concern, and the first concern of every President who has ever lived in this house, is and must be the security of our Nation. This security rests on many kinds of strength, on arms and also on arms control, on military power and on economic vitality and the quality of life of our own people, on modern weapons, and also on reliable energy sup- plies. The well-being of our friends and our allies is also of great impor- tance to us. Our security is tied to human rights and to social justice which prevails among the people who live on Earth and to the institutions of international force and peace and order which we ourselves have helped to build.

We all hope and work and pray that we will see a world in which the weapons of war are no longer necessary, but now we must deal with the hard facts, with the world as it is. In the dangerous and uncertain world of today, the keystone of our national security is still military strength, strength that is clearly recognized by Americans, by our allies, and by any potential adversary.

*   *   *

Down through the generations, the purposes of our Armed Forces have always been the same, no matter what generation it was: to defend our security when it's threatened and, through demonstrated strength, to reduce the chances that we will have to fight again. These words of John Kennedy will still guide our actions, and I quote him: "The purpose of our arms is peace, not war--to make certain that they will never have to be used." That purpose is unchanged. But the world has been changing and our responses as a nation must change with it.

*   *   *

But the path of the future must be charted in peace. We must continue to build a new and a firm foundation for a stable world community.

We are building that new foundation from a position of national strength--the strength of our own defenses, the strength of our friend- ships with other nations, and of our oldest American ideals.

Jimmy Carter, addresses, Business Council, Washington, December 12, 1979; Wake Forest University, March 17, 1978; and State of the Union, January 23, 1979; *American Foreign Policy: Basic Documents*, 1977-1980, pp. 20-21, 24, 49-50.

1 0 8   NEGOTIATING FROM STRENGTH

. . . But I do say this: I do not want to see an American President in the future, in the event of any crisis, have his diplomatic credibility be so impaired because the United States was in a second-class or inferior position. We saw what it meant to the Soviets when they were second. I don't want that position to be the United States in the event of a future diplomatic crisis.

*   *   *

In foreign affairs, we have pursued a policy of peace through strength. That policy has been successful, so successful that tonight we can say that America is at peace with every nation on Earth, and we will keep it that way in the future.

We will keep it that way by keeping our defenses strong. As long as I am President, America's defenses will be strong and ready without equal in the world in which we live. Our strength makes it possible for us to negotiate with other great powers of the world from a position that commands their respect and invites their cooperation.

Richard Nixon, remarks, news conference, April 18, 1969, and Gerald Ford, remarks, news conference, February 19, 1976; *Papers of Presidents: Nixon,* 1969, p. 303, and *Papers of Presidents: Ford,* 1976-1977, pp. 372-73.

7

Presidential Doctrines

The concept of foreign relations "doctrines" is distinctive in that it may be applied largely as a general aspiration or goal, and it may be concretized as specific objectives and implementable policies and programs of action. It may therefore be distinguished from both the concepts "policy" and "strategy." Normally such doctrines--not usually so designated by their initiators, but subsequently labeled by historians, publicists, and the media--were relatively rare in American history prior to the 1940's, and usually pertain to particular geographic areas.

Except for such illustrations as the "Doctrine of the Two Spheres" and the "Stimson Doctrine," they are historically associated with individual Presidents. Originating prior to American independence, but indigenous to United States foreign affairs for more than a century, the "Doctrine of the Two Spheres" provided that the wars of European powers would not extend to their overseas colonies and, conversely, that conflicts between their colonies would not spread to Europe. Founded on the belief that the United States could have a destiny separate from that of Europe, this doctrine was expanded into the principle of non-involvement in the political interrelations of the nations of Europe and their non-involvement in the affairs of independent nations in the Americas, and thus eventually into United States isolationism and the Monroe Doctrine.

The "Stimson Doctrine," identified with Secretary of State Henry L. Stimson but sometimes also referred to as the "Hoover-Stimson Doctrine," was more limited in scope and duration. Promulgated in 1932, in response to the Japanese conquest of Manchuria, it specified that the United States would not recognize the validity of political and jurisdictional changes perpetrated in violation of international obligations and preexisting treaty obligations, including the Pact of Paris (see Document 255).

The first, and historically most significant, presidential doctrine, was enunciated by President James Monroe in 1823; all others have been promulgated since World War II, when the United States, as a major world power, became involved in global affairs. The Monroe Doctrine, embodied in a presidential message to Congress, December 2, 1823, constituted a quid pro quo --by which the United States promised not to become enmeshed in wars between the European powers over matters pertaining to themselves, in return for which the United States, while prepared to recognize the status of existing European colonies and dependencies in the Western Hemisphere, would consider attempts by European powers "to extend their system" to any portion of the Americas "as dangerous to our peace and safety" and would regard their "interposition" to oppress independent American countries or to control "their destiny" as "the manifestation of an unfriendly disposition toward the United States" (Document 109).

This doctrine set forth an interesting but important combination of foreign relations precepts.   To summarize, in its relations with Europe respecting the affairs of the Western Hemisphere, the United States committed itself to "non-involvement" (in Europe's politics and wars)--known as isolationism--and "non-interference" (with European colonies in the Americas) in return for Europe's commitment to "non-colonization," "non-extension of non-indigenous systems" of governance, and "non-intervention" in this hemisphere.   These principles were addressed to Russia's territorial expansion in northwest North America, the possible actions of the Holy Alliance to retrieve Europe's lost colonies in Latin America, and the imposition of monarchical government in the newly independent republics of Central and South America.

Virtually sacrosanct in American diplomacy, the Monroe Doctrine has frequently been reiterated and refined, and sometimes reinterpreted, and it has endured for nearly a century and three-quarters.   Despite the fact that it was superseded by multilateral hemisphere commitment in the Rio Pact (1947) and its predecessors (see Document 304) and the Charter of the Organization of American States (1948, see Chapter 26), it continues to permeate United States expressions of policy and practice.   For reaffirmation in 1962, see Document 110.

After World War II, beginning with Harry Truman, it became common practice--some call it "doctrine mania"--to credit Presidents with indi- vidualized foreign policy doctrines.   Thus, chronologically, in 1947 the "Truman Doctrine" established the policy of providing United States support for the "free peoples" of Greece and Turkey to resist "terrorist activities" and "subjugation by armed minorities" or outside Communist forces.   He had already established a precedent for this by the stand he took during the Azerbaijan Crisis in 1946, obliging Soviet military forces to leave Iranian territory in accordance with its wartime commitments.   In a presidential message, March 12, 1947, he requested Congress to provide what turned out to be the largest American bilateral aid program in the nation's peacetime history and the first in which United States military personnel were to be stationed in Europe (Documents 111-112).   This action presaged the formulation of the containment policy and the negotiation of the North Atlantic Treaty (see Document 306) to halt post-World War II Soviet expansion in Europe.

As a vital American national interest and in support of world peace the "Eisenhower Doctrine" was enunciated in 1957 to preserve the "territorial integrity and political independence" of Middle East nations by means of United States economic and military cooperation and assistance. Propounded by the President in January 1957, also in a message to Congress, it solicited congressional authorization for the President to undertake cooperative arrangements for such assistance (Document 113). Congress passed a joint resolution to implement the doctrine in March (Document 114). It empowered the President to create programs of assistance for those Middle East nations that desired it, to maintain Western rights in the region, and to thwart "armed aggression from any country controlled by international communism." President Eisenhower also commissioned James P. Richards, formerly chairman of the House Foreign Affairs Committee, as his personal emissary to explain and promote the doctrine in the Middle East.

President Johnson bears the distinction of having two doctrines ascribed to him--a rarity in American foreign affairs. These grew out of two unrelated crises--one in East Asia during the Vietnam War, in 1964, and the second at the time of the Dominican Crisis the following year. When North Vietnamese gunboats attacked U.S. destroyers--the *Maddox* and the *C. Turner Joy*--in international waters in the Gulf of Tonkin, in August 1964 (for background, see Chapter 13), the President sent a message to Congress requesting it to enact a resolution authorizing him to take "all necessary action to protect our Armed Forces," to assist nations "covered by the SEATO [Southeast Asia Collective Defense Treaty Organization] treaty," and to preserve "the independence of the nations" in Southeast Asia. Congress passed the Gulf of Tonkin Resolution on August 10, granting the President such authority (Documents 115-116). Subsequent actions pursuant to this resolution brought the President into heated conflict with Congress over the expansion of the Vietnam War, and the resolution was rescinded in 1970.

When a military coup in the Dominican Republic erupted into a bloody civil war in 1965, President Johnson, in keeping with his second doctrine, dispatched United States troops to protect American lives and prevent Communists from taking over the Dominican government. In a series of public statements he justified intervention as essential to protect United States citizens; to preserve genuine self-determination in keeping with the will of the Dominican people, the "liberty" of the Caribbean republic, and the "principles and values" of Western Hemisphere nations; to prevent "the establishment of another Communist government in the Western Hemisphere" in keeping with the inter-American declaration of 1962 that branded the dicta of Communism to be "incompatible with the principles of the inter-American system;" to re-establish "liberty, justice, dignity, and a better life for all" in the beleaguered country; and to restore peace and democracy in the hemisphere (Document 117). For additional commentary on the Dominican crisis, see Chapter 12.

The "Nixon Doctrine," which also grew out of developments during the Vietnam War, focused initially on Indo-China but was later broadened to review and redesign the global commitments of the United States. Originally broached in President Nixon's comments during an informal meeting with the press at Guam in July 1969 (Document 118), it was elucidated and augmented in a series of addresses and annual reports to Congress (Documents 119-121). Aside from endorsing "Vietnamization" during the Indo-China War, it encompassed such concepts as United States involvement abroad, the fulfillment of existing international commitments, partnership, and the promotion and expectation of extensive self-help by other nations. Its main thrust was that allies and other nations should assume greater burdens, commitments, and responsibilities for their own security, development, and progress--to "make their destiny truly their own." This doctrine proved to be unique in several respects--the title "doctrine" was appropriated and popularized by President Nixon, it was generalized to apply to reassessment of American commitments throughout the world, and, in this sense, it extended beyond Southeast Asia and survived beyond the Vietnam War and the Nixon administration.

In 1975, in an address delivered in Honolulu, President Ford launched what he called "a new Pacific Doctrine." In it he stressed the shift of the American "center of political power" to the Pacific Basin, our "vital stake" in Asia, and our responsibility for maintaining a leading role "in lessening tensions, preventing hostilities, and preserving peace" in the area. The premises on which he founded this doctrine include the essentiality of United States strength to maintain "any stable balance of power in the Pacific" and "stability and security in Southeast Asia," the development of "partnership" with Japan and the "normalization of relations" with the People's Republic of China, and the preservation of peace by resolving "outstanding political conflicts" and establishing a "structure of economic cooperation" that benefits "all the peoples in the region." Reflecting the stance of both Presidents Johnson and Nixon respecting the importance of the Pacific Basin to the United States, much of this proposition was not new, but President Ford himself dignified it as an American doctrine (Document 122).

As a consequence of the Iranian Hostage Crisis (see Chapter 14), the outbreak of the Iran-Iraq War (see Chapter 30), and Soviet military inter-vention in Afghanistan (December 1979), President Carter proclaimed a succinct policy principle for the Persian Gulf in what came to be called the "Carter Doctrine." In his State of the Union address, January 23, 1980, he warned the Soviet Union and the world that an attempt "by any outside force to gain control of the Persian Gulf region" would be regarded "as an assault on the vital interests of the United States" and would be "repelled by any means necessary, including military force" (Document 123). This dictum was repeated by him on subsequent occasions (Document 124) and was implemented by him and subsequently by President Reagan during the Iran-Iraq War.

In the 1980's, launched in a news interview on March 3, 1981, and ex-plicated in a series of public addresses, President Reagan propounded his anti-Communist policies for the Caribbean and Central America. In combination, labeled the "Reagan Doctrine," these principles, intended to halt Communist-engendered attempts--by the Soviet Union, Cuba, and their allies--to export their philosophy of world revolution and their totalitarian political system via intervening surrogate agents and guerillas, as well as terrorism and covert political and military forces, and to undermine national security, democracy and representative institutions, pluralism, economic development, and freedom and human rights in the Caribbean and Central America. President Reagan contended that these Communist actions violated United States national interests, our strategic posture in the Western Hemisphere, peace and security, and the principles on which the United States and the Organization of American States were founded. He sought congressional legislation to provide both economic and military assistance to achieve his purposes, attempted to negotiate a constraining settlement in Central America, and undertook forceful action in Grenada (see Chapter 12) and in Nicaragua by supporting "freedom fighters" to achieve security and democratic objectives in the area. Because, in part, of the "Vietnam syndrome"--fearing direct and prolonged United States military involvement in Central America--Congress grudgingly provided only limited and sporadic legislative support for his requests to effectuate his doctrine.

Surprisingly, certain other major American policy pronouncements--concerning such traditional goals and policies as self-determination, liberty and human rights, free trade, the Open Door, freedom of the seas, and arms limitation, as well as Manifest Destiny, containment, collective cooperation, dollar diplomacy, and others (referred to in Chapter 6 and elsewhere) have not been elevated to the status of presidential doctrines.

Viewing these doctrines as a package, certain similarities and differences are readily apparent. On the one hand, they are usually posed as involving the national interests if not the vital interests of the United States; establishing, reiterating, or refining American commitments abroad; emanating from developments that are regarded as critical; reflecting active United States foreign involvement; requiring United States economic and/or military assistance; supporting the principles of freedom, self-determination, and democracy; and, since World War II, thwarting Communism and Communist-sponsored insurgency, intervention, and hegemonism (which even applied to the post-World War II application of the Monroe Doctrine).

Each presidential doctrine, when initiated, focused on a particular geographic area--the Western Hemisphere (Monroe, Johnson, and Reagan), Europe (Truman), the Middle East (Eisenhower and Carter), and Asia and the Pacific (Johnson, Nixon, and Ford). Whereas a few also acquired broader geographic connotations (such as the Truman Doctrine and containment), the Nixon Doctrine was unique in that it rapidly transmuted into a change in attitude respecting global commitments and partnership. Except for Ford's "New Pacific Doctrine," none was originally enunciated formally as a presidential doctrine, but had this appellation applied by others.

Finally, these doctrines bear several discernible common characteristics. They usually are cast and justified as transcendental precepts or virtual "articles of faith." Second, their purposes characteristically reflect traditional American political values--self-determination, democracy, the will of the people, freedom, and human rights. Third, they are perceived by their initiators and supporters as voicing reasonable and significant international benefits, not only to the United States but also to other nations on whose behalf they are propounded. Often these benefits are posed in terms of common fundamental goals--independence, national security, peace, and human welfare and progress. Fourth, to some they denote implications of ideology, as evidenced by the degree to which the Monroe Doctrine distinguished between the American and European "systems," and post-World War II doctrines (except perhaps for those espoused by Nixon and Ford) apposed the United States and the Communist countries. Fifth, they reiterate, specify, generate, or at least imply legal principles--appealing to the United States law-oriented disposition and extolling "the rule of law."

On the other hand, aside from their areal applicability, significant differences among them are also discernable. So far as articulation is concerned, some are capsulated in a single initial presidential statement (such as the Monroe, Truman, Eisenhower, Johnson [Tonkin Gulf], and Ford Doctrines); others are promulgated and then reiterated (Carter); and still others need to be gleaned from a variety of statements (Johnson--Dominican Crisis, Nixon, and Reagan). Certain presidential doctrines set forth relatively concise propositions (such as Truman, Eisenhower, Johnson [Tonkin Gulf], and Carter), while others are more complex (Monroe, Johnson [Dominican Crisis], Nixon, Ford, and Reagan). Whereas all of them constitute presidential prescriptions for executive purpose, policy, and action, many of them require legislative implementation (Truman, Eisenhower, Johnson [Tonkin Gulf], and Reagan) and/or are confirmed by negotiation or reinterpretation of treaties and agreements (Monroe, Truman, Eisenhower, Johnson, Nixon, Ford, and Reagan), or they involve action by international agencies such as the United Nations and the Organization of American States. Another significant difference is their longevity and duration. Except for the Monroe Doctrine, and in some respects the Nixon Doctrine, they generally tend to be temporary if not short-lived, although most have some potentiality for durability.

For a comprehensive analysis of presidential doctrines, see Cecil V. Crabb, Jr., *The Doctrines of American Foreign Policy: Their Meaning, Role, and Future* (Baton Rouge: Louisiana State University Press, 1982).

MONROE DOCTRINE, 1823

> . . . we could not view any interposition for the purpose of oppressing them [independent Latin American countries], or controlling in any other manner their destiny, by any European power in any other light than as the manifestation of an unfriendly disposition toward the United States.
>
> James Monroe, 1823

109 MONROE DOCTRINE, 1823

In the wars of the European powers in matters relating to themselves we have never taken any part, nor does it comport with our policy so to do. It is only when our rights are invaded or seriously menaced that we resent injuries or make preparation for our defense. With the movements in this hemisphere we are of necessity more immediately connected, and by causes which must be obvious to all enlightened and impartial observers. The political system of the allied powers is essentially different in this respect from that of America. This difference proceeds from that which exists in their respective Governments; and to the defense of our own, which has been achieved by the loss of so much blood and treasure, and matured by the wisdom of their most enlightened citizens, and under which we have enjoyed unexampled felicity, this whole nation is devoted.

We owe it, therefore, to candor and to the amicable relations existing between the United States and those powers to declare that we should consider any attempt on their part to extend their system to any portion of this hemisphere as dangerous to our peace and safety. With the existing colonies or dependencies of any European power we have not interfered and shall not interfere. But with the Governments who have declared their independence and maintained it, and whose independence we have, on great consideration and on just principles, acknowledged, we could not view any interposition for the purpose of oppressing them, or controlling in any other manner their destiny, by any European power in any other light than as the manifestation of an unfriendly disposition toward the United States.

James Monroe, Message to Congress, December 2, 1823; James D. Richardson, ed., *A Compilation of the Messages and Papers of the Presidents, 1789-1908* (Washington: Government Printing Office, 1909), II, 218. Also see congressional resolution to deter aggression in the Western Hemisphere, 1962--Document 180--at the time of the Cuban missile crisis, and Document 263, Article 2, par. c, and Document 312, section on "Monroe Doctrine" formula.

1 1 0   REAFFIRMATION OF MONROE DOCTRINE, 1962

The Monroe Doctrine means what it has meant since President Monroe and John Quincy Adams enunciated it, and that is that we would oppose a foreign power extending its power to the Western Hemisphere. And that's why we oppose what is being--what's happening in Cuba today. That's why we have cut off our trade. That's why we worked in the OAS and in other ways to isolate the Communist menace in Cuba. That's why we'll continue to give a good deal of our effort and attention to it.

John Kennedy, response to question at news conference concerning relations with Cuba, August 29, 1962; *American Foreign Policy: Current Documents,* 1962, p. 368.

TRUMAN DOCTRINE, 1947

I believe that it must be the policy of the United States to support free peoples who are resisting attempted subjugation by armed minorities or by outside pressures.

Harry Truman, 1947

1 1 1   TRUMAN DOCTRINE, 1947

The United States has received from the Greek Government an urgent appeal for financial and economic assistance. . . .

I do not believe that the American people and the Congress wish to turn a deaf ear to the appeal of the Greek Government. . . .

The very existence of the Greek state is today threatened by the terrorist activities of several thousand armed men, led by Communists, who defy the government's authority at a number of points, particularly along the northern boundaries. . . .

Greece must have assistance if it is to become a self-supporting and self-respecting democracy.

The United States must supply this assistance. . . .

The future of Turkey as an independent and economically sound state is clearly no less important to the freedom-loving peoples of the world than the future of Greece. The circumstances in which Turkey finds itself today are considerably different from those of Greece. Turkey has been spared the disasters that have beset Greece. And during the war, the United States and Great Britain furnished Turkey with material aid.

Nevertheless, Turkey now needs our support. . . .

As in the case of Greece, if Turkey is to have the assistance it needs, the United States must supply it . . . .

One of the primary objectives of the foreign policy of the United States is the creation of conditions in which we and other nations will be able to work out a way of life free from coercion. . . .

At the present moment in world history nearly every nation must choose between alternative ways of life. The choice is too often not a free one.

One way of life is based upon the will of the majority, and is distinguished by free institutions, representative government, free elections, guarantees of individual liberty, freedom of speech and religion, and freedom from political oppression.

The second way of life is based upon the will of a minority forcibly imposed upon the majority. It relies upon terror and oppression, a controlled press and radio, fixed elections, and the suppression of personal freedoms.

I believe that it must be the policy of the United States to support free peoples who are resisting attempted subjugation by armed minorities or by outside pressures.

I believe that we must assist free peoples to work out their own destinies in their own way.

I believe that our help should be primarily through economic and financial aid which is essential to economic stability and orderly political processes.

The world is not static, and the *status quo* is not sacred. But we cannot allow changes in the status quo in violation of the Charter of the United Nations by such methods as coercion, or by such subterfuges as political infiltration. In helping free and independent nations to maintain their freedom, the United States will be giving effect to the principles of the Charter of the United Nations.

It is necessary only to glance at a map to realize that the survival and integrity of the Greek nation are of grave importance in a much wider situation. If Greece should fall under the control of an armed minority, the effect upon its neighbor, Turkey, would be immediate and serious. Confusion and disorder might well spread throughout the entire Middle East.

Moreover, the disappearance of Greece as an independent state would have a profound effect upon those countries in Europe whose peoples are struggling against great difficulties to maintain their freedoms and their independence while they repair the damages of war.

It would be an unspeakable tragedy if these countries, which have struggled so long against overwhelming odds, should lose that victory for which they sacrificed so much. Collapse of free institutions and loss of independence would be disastrous not only for them but for the world. Discouragement and possibly failure would quickly be the lot of neighboring peoples striving to maintain their freedom and independence.
. . .

The free peoples of the world look to us for support in maintaining their freedoms.

If we falter in our leadership, we may endanger the peace of the world--and we shall surely endanger the welfare of this Nation.

Harry Truman, Special Message to Congress on Greece and Turkey, March 12, 1947; *Papers of Presidents: Truman,* 1947, pp. 176-80, and *A Decade of American Foreign Policy: Basic Documents,* 1941-49, pp. 1253-57.

1 1 2 ACT TO PROVIDE ASSISTANCE TO GREECE AND TURKEY, 1947

Whereas the Governments of Greece and Turkey have sought from the Government of the United States immediate financial and other assistance which is necessary for the maintenance of their national integrity and their survival as free nations; and

Whereas the national integrity and survival of these nations are of importance to the security of the United States and of all freedom-loving peoples and depend upon the receipt at this time of assistance;
. . .

Be it enacted by the Senate and House of Representatives of the United States of America in Congress assembled, That . . . the President may from time to time when he deems it in the interest of the United States furnish assistance to Greece and Turkey, upon request of their governments, and upon terms and conditions determined by him--

(1) by rendering financial aid in the form of loans, credits, grants, or otherwise, to those countries;

(2) by detailing to assist those countries any persons in the employ of the Government of the United States . . . Provided, however, That no civilian personnel shall be assigned to Greece or Turkey to administer the purposes of this Act until such personnel have been investigated by the Federal Bureau of Investigation;

(3) by detailing a limited number of members of the military

services of the United States to assist those countries, in an advisory capacity only; . . .

(4) by providing for (A) the transfer to, and the procurement for by manufacture or otherwise and the transfer to, those countries of any articles, services, and information, and (B) the instruction and training of personnel of those countries; and

(5) by incurring and defraying necessary expenses, including administrative expenses and expenses for compensation of personnel, in connection with the carrying out of the provisions of this Act.

Public Law 75, 80th Congress, 1st session; *A Decade of American Foreign Policy: Basic Documents*, 1941-49, pp. 1257-61. For Truman's statement on signing bill endorsing Truman Doctrine, May 22, 1947, see *Papers of Presidents: Truman,* 1947, pp. 254-55. On the same day the President issued Executive Order 9857 prescribing regulations to carry out the act; 3 *Code of Federal Regulations,* 1943-1948, p. 646. For texts of agreements with Greece and Turkey to implement the Truman Doctrine, see *A Decade of American Foreign Policy: Basic Documents,* 1941-49, pp. 1261-67, and for the Greek-Turkish Assistance Act of 1948, Public Law 472, 80th Congress, 2d session, see p. 1267.

EISENHOWER DOCTRINE, 1957

We have shown, so that none can doubt, our dedication to the principle that force shall not be used internationally for any aggressive purpose and that the integrity and independence of the nations of the Middle East should be inviolate . . . nations of the Middle East are aware of the danger that stems from International Communism and welcome closer cooperation with the United States to realize for themselves United Nations goals of independence, economic well-being and spiritual growth.

Dwight Eisenhower, 1957

113 EISENHOWER DOCTRINE, 1957

The Middle East has abruptly reached a new and critical stage in its long and important history. In past decades many of the countries in that area were not fully self-governing. Other nations exercised considerable authority in the area and the security of the region was largely built around their power. But since the First World War there has been a steady evolution toward self-government and independence. This development the United States has welcomed and has encouraged. Our country supports without reservation the full sovereignty and independence of each and every nation of the Middle East.

The evolution to independence has in the main been a peaceful process. But the area has been often troubled. Persistent cross-currents of distrust and fear with raids back and forth across national boundaries have brought about a high degree of instability in much of the Mid East. . . . All this instability has been heightened and, at times, manipulated by International Communism. . . .

The reason for Russia's interest in the Middle East is solely that of power politics. Considering her announced purpose of Communizing the world, it is easy to understand her hope of dominating the Middle East.

This region has always been the crossroads of the continents of the Eastern Hemisphere. The Suez Canal enables the nations of Asia and Europe to carry on the commerce that is essential if these countries are to maintain well-rounded and prosperous economies. The Middle East provides a gateway between Eurasia and Africa.

It contains about two thirds of the presently known oil deposits of the world and it normally supplies the petroleum needs of many nations of Europe, Asia and Africa. . . .

These things stress the immense importance of the Middle East. If the nations of that area should lose their independence, if they were dominated by alien forces hostile to freedom, that would be both a tragedy for the area and for many other free nations whose economic life would be subject to near strangulation. . . .

International Communism . . . seeks to mask its purposes of domination by expressions of good will and by superficially attractive offers of political, economic and military aid. But any free nation, which is the subject of Soviet enticement, ought, in elementary wisdom, to look behind the mask. . . .

Thus, we have these simple and indisputable facts:

1. The Middle East, which has always been coveted by Russia, would today be prized more than ever by International Communism.

2. The Soviet rulers continue to show that they do not scruple to use any means to gain their ends.

3. The free nations of the Mid East need, and for the most part want, added strength to assure their continued independence. . . .

Under all the circumstances I have laid before you, a greater responsibility now devolves upon the United States. We have shown, so that none can doubt, our dedication to the principle that force shall not be used internationally for any aggressive purpose and that the integrity and independence of the nations of the Middle East should be inviolate. . . .

If the Middle East is to continue its geographic role of uniting rather than separating East and West; if its vast economic resources are to serve the well-being of the peoples there, as well as that of others; and if its cultures and religions and their shrines are to be preserved for the uplifting of the spirits of the peoples, then the United States must make more evident its willingness to support the independence of the freedom-loving nations of the area. . . .

. . . It is now essential that the United States should manifest through joint action of the President and the Congress our determination to assist those nations of the Mid East area, which desire that assistance.

The action which I propose would have the following features.

It would, first of all, authorize the United States to cooperate with and assist any nation or group of nations in the general area of the Middle East in the development of economic strength dedicated to the maintenance of national independence.

It would, in the second place, authorize the Executive to undertake in the same region programs of military assistance and cooperation with any nation or group of nations which desires such aid.

It would, in the third place, authorize such assistance and cooperation to include the employment of the armed forces of the United States to secure and protect the territorial integrity and political independence of such nations, requesting such aid, against overt armed aggression from any nation controlled by International Communism. . . .

The present proposal would, in the fourth place, authorize the President to employ, for economic and defensive military purposes, sums available under the Mutual Security Act of 1954, as amended, without regard to existing limitations. . . .

The proposed legislation is primarily designed to deal with the possibility of Communist aggression, direct and indirect. There is imperative need that any lack of power in the area should be made good, not by external or alien force, but by the increased vigor and security of the independent nations of the area.

Experience shows that indirect aggression rarely if ever succeeds where there is reasonable security against direct aggression; where the government disposes of loyal security forces, and where economic conditions are such as not to make Communism seem an attractive alternative. The program I suggest deals with all three aspects of this matter and thus with the problem of indirect aggression.

It is my hope and belief that if our purpose be proclaimed, as proposed by the requested legislation, that very fact will serve to halt any contemplated aggression. We shall have heartened the patriots who are dedicated to the independence of their nations. They will not feel that they stand alone, under the menace of great power. . . .

In the situation now existing, the greatest risk, as is often the case, is that ambitious despots may miscalculate. If power-hungry Communists should either falsely or correctly estimate that the Middle East is inadequately defended, they might be tempted to use open measures of armed attack. If so, that would start a chain of circumstances which would almost surely involve the United States in military action. I am convinced that the best insurance against this dangerous contingency is to make clear now our readiness to cooperate fully and freely with our friends of the Middle East in ways consonant with the purposes and principles of the United Nations.

Dwight Eisenhower, Special Message to Congress on Situation in the Middle East, January 5, 1957; *Papers of Presidents: Eisenhower*, 1957, pp. 6-16. Also see *American Foreign Policy: Current Documents*, 1957, pp. 783-91.

114 MIDDLE EAST RESOLUTION, 1957

That the President be and hereby is authorized to cooperate with and assist any nation or group of nations in the general area of the Middle East desiring such assistance in the development of economic strength dedicated to the maintenance of national independence.

Sec. 2. The President is authorized to undertake, in the general area of the Middle East, military assistance programs with any nation or group of nations of that area desiring such assistance. Furthermore, the United States regards as vital to the national interest and world peace the preservation of the independence and integrity of the nations of the Middle East. To this end, if the President determines the necessity thereof, the United States is prepared to use armed forces to assist any such nation or group of such nations requesting assistance against armed aggression from any country controlled by international communism; Provided, That such employment shall be consonant with the treaty obligations of the United States and with the Constitution of the United States.

Joint Resolution, Public Law 7, 85th Congress, approved by President on March 9, 1957; *American Foreign Policy: Current Documents,* 1957, pp. 829-31. For earlier version, see pp. 791-92, and for full treatment of the Middle East issue, see pp. 761-1014. For Eisenhower statement on signing Middle East Resolution, March 9, 1957, see *Papers of Presidents: Eisenhower,* 1957, pp. 187-88. For the White House announcement concerning the appointment of James P. Richards as the President's personal emissary to implement the Eisenhower Doctrine, January 7, 1957, see *American Foreign Policy: Current Documents,* 1957, p. 792. For additional documents on the Richards' mission, see pp. 831-71.

JOHNSON DOCTRINE--SOUTHEAST ASIA, 1964

Congress approves and supports the determination of the President . . . to take all necessary measures to repel any armed attack against the forces of the United States and to prevent further aggression . . . the United States is, therefore, prepared . . . to take all necessary steps, including the use of armed force, to assist any member or protocol state of the Southeast Asia Collective Defense Treaty requesting assistance in defense of its freedom.

Tonkin Gulf Resolution, 1964

115 JOHNSON DOCTRINE--SOUTHEAST ASIA, 1964

As I have repeatedly made clear, the United States intends no rashness, and seeks no wider war. We must make it clear to all that the United States is united in its determination to bring about the end of Communist subversion and aggression in the area. . . .

I recommend a resolution expressing the support of the Congress for all necessary action to protect our Armed Forces and to assist nations covered by the SEATO Treaty. At the same time, I assure the Congress that we shall continue readily to explore any avenues of political solution that will effectively guarantee the removal of Communist subversion and the preservation of the independence of the nations of the area.

The resolution could well be based upon similar resolutions enacted by the Congress in the past--to meet the threat to Formosa in 1955, to meet the threat to the Middle East in 1957, and to meet the threat in Cuba in 1962. It could state in the simplest terms the resolve and support of the Congress for action to deal appropriately with attacks against our Armed Forces and to defend freedom and preserve peace in southeast Asia in accordance with the obligations of the United States under the Southeast Asia Treaty. I urge the Congress to enact such a resolution promptly and thus to give convincing evidence to the aggressive Communist nations, and to the world as a whole, that our policy in southeast Asia will be carried forward--and that the peace and security of the area will be preserved.

Lyndon Johnson, recommendation for a congressional resolution to protect American armed forces in Southeast Asia, message to Congress, August 5, 1964; *Papers of Presidents: Johnson,* 1963-1964, II, 930-32; and *American Foreign Policy: Current Documents,* 1964, pp. 984-85.   For additional documents and commentary, see pp. 979-1002, and *Papers of Presidents: Johnson,* 1963-1964, II, 926-30, 1098-99; 1965, I, 575; 1966, I, 221-22; and 1967, II, 793-95. For background and documentation on the attacks on American ships in the Gulf of Tonkin, 1964, see Chapter 13, Documents 211-214.

116 CONGRESSIONAL RESOLUTION TO PROTECT AMERICAN ARMED FORCES IN SOUTHEAST ASIA --TONKIN GULF RESOLUTION, 1964

Whereas naval units of the Communist regime in Vietnam, in violation of the principles of the Charter of the United Nations and of international law, have deliberately and repeatedly attacked United States naval vessels lawfully present in international waters, and have thereby created a serious threat to international peace; and

Whereas these attacks are part of a deliberate and systematic campaign of aggression that the Communist regime in North Vietnam has been waging against its neighbors and the nations joined with them in the collective defense of their freedom; . . .

Resolved by the Senate and House of Representatives of the United States of America in Congress assembled, That the Congress approves and supports the determination of the President, as Commander in Chief, to take all necessary measures to repel any armed attack against the forces of the United States and to prevent further aggression.

Sec. 2. The United States regards as vital to its national interest and to world peace the maintenance of international peace and security in southeast Asia. Consonant with the Constitution of the United States and the Charter of the United Nations and in accordance with its obligations under the Southeast Asia Collective Defense Treaty, the United States is, therefore, prepared, as the President determines, to take all necessary steps, including the use of armed force, to assist any member or protocol state of the Southeast Asia Collective Defense Treaty requesting assistance in defense of its freedom.

Congressional resolution, August 10, 1964; Public Law 88-408; *American Foreign Policy: Current Documents,* 1964, pp. 991-92. This resolution was passed by a vote of 416 to 0 in the House and 88 to 2 in the Senate. For Johnson statement on signing Tonkin Gulf Resolution, August 10, 1964, see *Papers of Presidents: Johnson,* 1963-1964, II, 946-47. For commentary on the relation of this resolution and the Southeast Asia Collective Defense Treaty, see Whiteman, *Digest of International Law,* XII, 108-20. In 1967 the Undersecretary of State termed this resolution the functional equivalent of a declaration of war, and the Senate rescinded it in 1970. For President Nixon's explanation of his authority to continue the war in Southeast Asia, see *Papers of Presidents: Nixon,* 1970, pp 546-47.

JOHNSON DOCTRINE--DOMINICAN CRISIS, 1965

The American nations cannot, must not, and will not permit the establishment of another Communist government in the Western Hemisphere.

Lyndon Johnson, 1965

117 JOHNSON DOCTRINE--DOMINICAN CRISIS, 1965

There are times in the affairs of nations when great principles are tested in an ordeal of conflict and danger. This is such a time for the American nations.

At stake are the lives of thousands, the liberty of a nation, and the principles and the values of all the American Republics. . . .

The cable reported that Dominican law enforcement and military officials had informed our embassy that the situation was completely out of control and that the police and the Government could no longer give any guarantee concerning the safety of Americans or of any foreign nationals. . . .

In this situation hesitation and vacillation could mean death for many of our people, as well as many of the citizens of other lands.

I thought that we could not and we did not hesitate. Our forces, American forces, were ordered in immediately to protect American lives. They have done that. . . .

I want you to know that it is not a light or an easy matter to send our American boys to another country, but I do not think that the American people expect their President to hesitate or to vacillate in the face of danger just because the decision is hard when life is in peril.

Meanwhile, the revolutionary movement took a tragic turn. Communist leaders, many of them trained in Cuba, seeing a chance to increase disorder, to gain a foothold, joined the revolution. They took increasing control. And what began as a popular democratic revolution, committed to democracy and social justice, very shortly moved and was taken over and really seized and placed into the hands of a band of Communist conspirators. . . .

The American nations cannot, must not, and will not permit the establishment of another Communist government in the Western Hemisphere. This was the unanimous view of all the American nations when, in January 1962, they declared, and I quote: "The principles of communism are incompatible with the principles of the inter-American system."

This is what our beloved President John F. Kennedy meant when, less than a week before his death, he told us: "We in this hemisphere must also use every resource at our command to prevent the establishment of another Cuba in this hemisphere."

This is and this will be the common action and the common purpose of the democratic forces of the hemisphere. For the danger is also a common danger, and the principles are common principles. . . .

We know that many who are now in revolt do not seek a Communist tyranny. We think it is tragic indeed that their high motives have been misused by a small band of conspirators who receive their directions from abroad.

To those who fight only for liberty and justice and progress I want to join with the Organization of American States in saying, in appealing to you tonight, to lay down your arms, and to assure you there is nothing to fear. The road is open for you to share in building a Dominican democracy and we in America are ready and anxious and willing to help you. Your courage and your dedication are qualities which your country and all the hemisphere need for the future. Your are needed to help shape that future. And neither we nor any other nation in this hemisphere can or should take it upon itself to ever interfere with the affairs of your country or any other country.

. . . Our goal is a simple one. We are there to save the lives of our citizens and to save the lives of all people. Our goal, in keeping with the great principles of the inter-American system, is to help prevent another Communist state in this hemisphere. And we would like to do this without bloodshed or without large-scale fighting. . . .

We hope to see a government freely chosen by the will of all the people.

We hope to see a government dedicated to social justice for every single citizen.

We hope to see a government working, every hour of every day, to feeding the hungry, to educating the ignorant, to healing the sick--a government whose only concern is the progress and the elevation and the welfare of all the people. . . .

. . . I want you to know and I want the world to know that as long as I am President of this country, we are going to defend ourselves. We will defend our soldiers against attackers. We will honor our treaties. We will keep our commitments. We will defend our Nation against all those who seek to destroy not only the United States but every free country of this hemisphere. We do not want to bury anyone as I have said so many times before. But we do not intend to be buried.

Lyndon Johnson, radio and television report to the American people on the situation in the Dominican Republic, May 2, 1965; *Papers of Presidents: Johnson,* 1965, pp. 469-74. For earlier statements, see pp. 461-62, 465-67. Also see *American Foreign Policy: Current Documents,* 1965, pp. 955-1010.

*   *   *

Just as these lessons of the past 4 weeks are clear, so are the basic principles which have guided the purpose of the United States of America.

We seek no territory. We do not seek to impose our will on anyone. We intend to work for the self-determination of the peoples of the Americas within the framework of freedom.

In times past large nations have used their power to impose their will on smaller nations. Today we have placed our forces at the disposition of the nations of this hemisphere to assure the peoples of those nations the right to exercise their own will in freedom.

In accordance with the resolution of the eighth meeting of the ministers at Punta del Este, we will join with the other OAS nations in opposing a Communist takeover in this hemisphere. . . .

We want for the peoples of this hemisphere only what they want for themselves --liberty, justice, dignity, a better life for all. . . .

Lyndon Johnson, address, commencement exercises, Baylor University, May 28, 1965; *American Foreign Policy: Current Documents,* 1965, pp. 987-90.

*   *   *

. . . participation in the inter-American system, to be meaningful, must take into account the modern-day reality that an attempt by a conspiratorial group, inspired from the outside, to seize control by force can be an assault upon the independence and integrity of a state. The rights and obligations of all members of the OAS must be seen in the light of this reality.

Adlai Stevenson, United States Representative to the United Nations, statement in Security Council, May 5, 1905; *American Foreign Policy. Current Documents,* 1965, p. 972. For additional documents and commentary, see pp. 955-1010. On the Dominican crisis, also see Chapter 12, Documents 198-202, especially Document 199.

NIXON DOCTRINE, 1969

> . . . I believe that the time has come when the United States, in our relations with all of our Asian friends, be quite emphatic on two points: One, that we will keep our treaty commitments; . . . two, that as far as the problems of internal security are concerned, as far as the problems of military defense, except for the threat of a major power involving nuclear weapons, that the United States is going to encourage and has a right to expect that this problem will be increasingly handled by, and the responsibility for it taken by, the Asian nations themselves.
>
> Richard Nixon, 1969

118 NIXON DOCTRINE--INFORMAL REMARKS, GUAM, 1969

The United States is going to be facing, we hope before too long . . . a major decision: What will be its role in Asia and in the Pacific after the end of the War in Vietnam? We will be facing that decision, but also the Asian nations will be wondering about what that decision is. . . .

This is a decision that will have to be made, of course, as the war comes to an end. But the time to develop the thinking which will go into that decision is now. I think that one of the weaknesses in American foreign policy is that too often we react rather precipitately to events as they occur. We fail to have the perspective and the long-range view which is essential for a policy that will be viable.

As I see it, even though the war in Vietnam has been . . . a terribly frustrating one, and, as a result of that frustration, even though there would be a tendency for many Americans to say, "After we are through with that, let's not become involved in Asia," I am convinced that the way to avoid becoming involved in another war in Asia is for the United States to continue to play a significant role.

I think the way that we could become involved would be to attempt withdrawal, because, whether we like it or not, geography makes us a Pacific power. . . .

So, as we consider our past history, the United States involvement in war so often has been tied to our Pacific policy, or our lack of a Pacific policy, as the case might be.

As we look at Asia today, we see that the major world power which adopts a very aggressive attitude and a belligerent attitude in its foreign policy, Communist China, of course, is in Asia, and we find that the two minor world powers . . . that most greatly threaten the peace of the world, that adopt the most belligerent foreign policy, are in Asia, North Korea and, of course, North Vietnam. . . .

So, what I am trying to suggest is this: As we look at Asia, it poses, in my view, over the long haul . . . the greatest threat to the peace of the world, and, for that reason the United States should continue to play a significant role. It also poses . . . the greatest hope for progress in the world. . . . And for these reasons, I think we need policies that will see that we play a part and a part that is appropriate to the conditions that we will find. . . .

. . . the answer to that question [United States military relations in Asia] is not an easy one--not easy because we will be greatly tempted when that question is put to us to indicate that if any nation desires the assistance of the United States militarily in order to meet an internal or external threat, we will provide it.

However, I believe that the time has come when the United States, in our relations with all of our Asian friends, be quite emphatic on two points: One, that we will keep our treaty commitments; . . . but, two, that as far as the problems of internal security are concerned, as far as the problems of military defense, except for the threat of a major power involving nuclear weapons, that the United States is going to encourage and has a right to expect that this problem will be increasingly handled by, and the responsibility for it taken by, the Asian nations themselves. . . .

. . . It will not be easy. But if the United States just continues down the road of responding to requests for assistance, of assuming the primary responsibility for defending these countries when they have internal problems or external problems, they are never going to take care of themselves.

Richard Nixon, informal remarks to media, Guam, en route on Asian summit tour, July 25, 1969; *Papers of Presidents: Nixon*, 1969, pp. 544-56.

119 NIXON DOCTRINE--PARTNERSHIP, COMMITMENTS, RESPONSIBILITY

Perception of the growing imbalance between the scope of America's role and the potential of America's partners thus prompted the Nixon Doctrine. It is the key to understanding what we have done during the past two years, why we have done it, and where we are going.

The Doctrine seeks to reflect these realities:
-- that a major American role remains indispensable.
-- that other nations can and should assume greater responsibilities, for their sake as well as ours.
-- that the change in the strategic relationship calls for new doctrines.
-- that the emerging polycentrism of the Communist world presents different challenges and new opportunities.

The tangible expression of the new partnership is in greater material contributions by other countries. But we must first consider its primary purpose--to help make a peace that belongs to all.

For this venture we will look to others for a greater share in the definition of policy as well as in bearing the costs of programs. This psychological reorientation is more fundamental than the material redistribution; when countries feel responsible for the formulation of plans they are more apt to furnish the assets needed to make them work. . . .

The Nixon Doctrine, then, should not be thought of primarily as the sharing of burdens or the lightening of our load. It has a more positive meaning for other nations and for ourselves.

In effect we are encouraging countries to participate fully in the creation of plans and the designing of programs. They must define the nature of their own security and determine the path of their own progress. For only in this manner will they think of their fate as truly their own.
. . .

It was in this context that at Guam in the summer of 1969, and in my November 3, 1969, address to the Nation, I laid out the elements of new partnership.

"First, **the United States will keep all of its treaty commitments.**" We will respect the commitments we inherited--both because of their intrinsic merit, and because of the impact of sudden shifts on regional or world stability. To desert those who have come to depend on us would cause disruption and invite aggression. It is in everyone's interest, however, including those with whom we have ties, to view undertakings as a dynamic process. . . .

In contemplating new commitments we will apply rigorous yardsticks. What precisely is our national concern? What precisely is the threat? What would be the efficacy of our involvement? We do not rule out new commitments, but we will relate them to our interest. . . .

"Second, **we shall provide a shield if a nuclear power threatens the freedom of a nation allied with us or of a nation whose survival we consider vital to our security.**" Nuclear power is the element of security that our friends either cannot provide or could provide only with great and disruptive efforts. Hence, we bear special obligations toward non-nuclear countries. . . .

Third, **in cases involving other types of aggression we shall furnish military and economic assistance when requested in accordance with our treaty commitments. But we shall look to the nation directly threatened to assume the primary responsibility of providing the manpower for its defense.**" No President can guarantee that future conflicts will never involve American personnel--but in some theaters the threshold of involvement will be raised and in some instances involvement will be much more unlikely. This principle, first applied to security matters, applies as well to economic development. Our economic assistance will continue to be substantial. But we will expect countries receiving it to mobilize themselves and their resources; we will look to other developed nations to play their full role in furnishing help. . . .

We will continue to provide elements of military strength and economic resources appropriate to our size and our interests. But it is no longer natural or possible in this age to argue that security or development around the globe is primarily America's concern. The defense and progress of other countries must be first their responsibility and second, a regional responsibility. Without the foundations of self-help and regional help, American help will not succeed. The United States can and will participate, where our interests dictate, but as **a** weight--not **the** weight--in the scale.

Richard Nixon, *U.S. Foreign Policy for the 1970's: Building for Peace* (1971), pp. 10-21. For additional commentary, see Department of State, *United States Foreign Policy, 1971: A Report of the Secretary of State* (1972), pp. 50-52, and Richard Nixon, U.S. *Foreign Policy for the 1970's: The Emerging Structure of Peace* (1972), pp. 3-4, on "The Philosophy of a New American Foreign Policy," and pp. 86-88 on "Meeting the Requirements of Security" in the Far East.

120 NIXON DOCTRINE--SHARED RESPONSIBILITY, MATERIAL AND PSYCHOLOGICAL

To these ends, we developed the Nixon Doctrine of shared responsibilities. This Doctrine was central to our approach to major allies in the Atlantic and Pacific. But it also shaped our attitude toward those in Latin America, Asia, and Africa with whom we were working in formal alliances or friendship.

Our primary purpose was to invoke greater efforts by others--not so much to lighten our burdens as to increase their commitment to a new and peaceful structure. This would mean that increasingly they would man their own defenses and furnish more of the funds for their security and economic development. The corollary would be the reduction of the American share of defense or financial contributions.

More fundamental than this material redistribution, however, was a psychological reorientation. Nations had habitually relied on us for political leadership. Much time and energy went into influencing decisions in Washington. Our objective now was to encourage them to play a greater role in formulating plans and programs. For when others design their security and their development, they make their destiny truly their own. And when plans are their plans, they are more motivated to make them realities.

The lowering of our profile was not an end in itself. Other countries needed to do more, but they could not do so without a concerned America. Their role had to be increased, but this would prove empty unless we did what we must. We could not go from overinvolvement to neglect. A changing world needed the continuity of America's strength.

Thus we made clear that the Nixon Doctrine represented a new definition of American leadership, not abandonment of that leadership.

Richard Nixon, *U.S. Foreign Policy for the 1970's: Shaping A Durable Peace* (1973), pp. 9-10.

121 NIXON DOCTRINE--BASIC PRECEPTS

The Nixon Doctrine sets out these three precepts:
"The United States will keep all its treaty commitments.

"We shall provide a shield if a nuclear power threatens the freedom of a nation allied with us or of a nation whose survival we consider vital to our security and the security of the region as a whole.

"In cases involving other types of aggression we shall furnish military and economic assistance when requested and as appropriate. But we shall look to the nation directly threatened to assume the primary responsibility of providing the manpower for its defense."

This policy is in no sense a rationale for our withdrawal from Asia; it is a way for us to establish a better and more realistic basis of continuing our Asian role. We will remain a Pacific power, but we intend that our presence will be more in keeping with the changing situation in the area and that our diplomacy consequently will be more flexible.

United States Foreign Policy, 1969-1970: A Report of the Secretary of State (1971), pp. 36-37.

FORD DOCTRINE, 1975

The center of political power in the United States has shifted westward. Our Pacific interests and concerns have increased. We have exchanged the freedom of action of an isolationist state for the responsibilities of a great global power.

Gerald Ford, 1975

122 FORD--NEW PACIFIC DOCTRINE, 1975

America, a nation of the Pacific Basin, has a very vital stake in Asia and a responsibility to take a leading part in lessening tensions, preventing hostilities, and preserving peace. World stability and our own security depend upon our Asian commitments. . . .

The security concerns of great world powers intersect in Asia. The United States, the Soviet Union, China, and Japan are all Pacific powers. Western Europe has historic and economic ties with Asia. Equilibrium in the Pacific is absolutely essential to the United States and to the other countries in the Pacific.

The first premise of a new Pacific Doctrine is that American strength is basic to any stable balance of power in the Pacific. We must reach beyond our concern for security. But without security, there can be neither peace nor progress. The preservation of the sovereignty and the independence of our Asian friends and allies remain a paramount objective of American policy. . . .

The second basic premise of a new Pacific Doctrine is that partnership with Japan is a pillar of our strategy. . . .

The third premise of a new Pacific Doctrine is the normalization of relations with the People's Republic of China, the strengthening of our new ties with this great nation representing nearly one-quarter of mankind. . . .

A fourth principle of our Pacific policy is our continuing stake in stability and security in Southeast Asia . . . .

A fifth tenet of our new Pacific policy is our belief that peace in Asia depends upon a resolution of outstanding political conflicts. . . .

The sixth point of our new policy in the Pacific is that peace in Asia requires a structure of economic cooperation reflecting the aspiration of all the peoples in the region. . . .

There is one common theme which was expressed to me by the leaders of every Asian country that I visited. They all advocate the continuity of steady and responsible American leadership. They seek self-reliance in their own future and in their own relations with us. . . .

I emphasized to every leader I met that the United States is a Pacific nation. I pledged, as President, I will continue America's active concern for Asia and our presence in the Asian-Pacific region.

Asia is entering a new era. We can contribute to a new structure of stability founded on a balance among the major powers, strong ties to our allies in the region, an easing of tension between adversaries, the self-reliance and regional solidarity of smaller nations, and expanding economic ties and cultural exchanges. . . .

If we can remain steadfast, historians will look back and view the 1970's as the beginning of a period of peaceful cooperation and progress, a time of growing community for all the nations touched by this great ocean.

Gerald Ford, address, University of Hawaii, Honolulu, on return from Pacific summit tour, December 7, 1975; *Papers of Presidents: Ford,* 1975, II, 1950-55. This reconfirmed the views of Presidents Johnson and Nixon concerning America's interest and role in the Far East and Pacific.

CARTER DOCTRINE, 1980

An attempt by any outside force to gain control of the Persian Gulf region will be regarded as an assault on the vital interests of the United States of America, and such an assault will be repelled by any means necessary, including military force.

Jimmy Carter, 1980

123 CARTER DOCTRINE, 1980

In response to the abhorrent act in Iran, our nation has never been aroused and unified so greatly in peacetime. Our position is clear. The United States will not yield to blackmail. We continue to pursue these specific goals:

First, to protect the present and long-range interests of the United

States;

Secondly, to preserve the lives of the American hostages and to secure as quickly as possible their safe release;

If possible, to avoid bloodshed which might further endanger the lives of our fellow citizens;

To enlist the help of other nations in condemning this act of violence which is shocking and violates the moral and the legal standards of a civilized world;

To convince and to persuade the Iranian leaders that the real danger to their nation lies in the north in the Soviet Union and from the Soviet troops now in Afghanistan and that the unwarranted Iranian quarrel with the United States hampers their response to this far greater danger to them.

If the American hostages are harmed, a severe price will be paid. We will never rest until every one of the American hostages is released. But now we face a broader and more fundamental challenge in this region because of the recent military action of the Soviet Union. Now, as during the last three and one-half decades, the relationship between our country --the United States of America--and the Soviet Union is the most critical factor in determining whether the world will live in peace or be engulfed in global conflict.

Since the end of the Second World War, America has led other nations in meeting the challenge of mounting Soviet power. This has not been a simple or a static relationship. Between us there has been cooperation, there has been competition, and at times there has been confrontation. . . .

In all these actions, we have maintained two commitments: to be ready to meet any challenge by Soviet military power and to develop ways to resolve disputes and to keep the peace. . . .

We superpowers will also have the responsibility to exercise restraint in the use of our great military force. The integrity and the independence of weaker nations must not be threatened. They must know that in our presence they are secure. But now the Soviet Union has taken a radical and an aggressive new step. It's using its great military power against a relatively defenseless nation. The implications of the Soviet invasion of Afghanistan could pose the most serious threat to the peace since the Second World War.

The vast majority of nations on Earth have condemned this latest Soviet attempt to extend its colonial domination of others and have demanded the immediate withdrawal of Soviet troops. The Moslem world is especially and justifiably outraged by this aggression against an Islamic people. No action of a world power has ever been so quickly and so overwhelmingly condemned.

But verbal condemnation is not enough. The Soviet Union must pay a concrete price for their aggression. While this invasion continues, we and the other nations of the world cannot conduct business as usual with the Soviet Union. . . .

Meeting this challenge will take national will, diplomatic and political wisdom, economic sacrifice, and, of course, military capability. We must call on the best that is in us to preserve the security of this crucial region.

Let our position be absolutely clear: An attempt by any outside force to gain control of the Persian Gulf region will be regarded as an assault on the vital interests of the United States of America, and such an assault will be repelled by any means necessary, including military force. . . .

Jimmy Carter, State of the Union Address, January 23, 1980; *American Foreign Policy: Basic Documents*, 1977-1980, pp. 53-57.

124   REITERATION OF CARTER DOCTRINE

And finally, I've served clear notice, in my State of the Union message, and I would like to quote the words: "An attempt by any outside force to gain control of the Persian Gulf region will be regarded as an assault on the vital interests of the United States of America, and such an assault will be repelled by any means necessary, including military force.". . .

It's important that everyone understand that every action I have taken is peaceful and is designed to preserve peace. Because we seek peace, we have pursued and will pursue every opportunity to ease tensions. Because we seek peace, we have been cautious and restrained. Because we seek peace, we must leave no room for doubt among our allies and no room for miscalculation among our potential adversaries. . . .

We are capable today of responding to a threat to peace in almost any part of the world. Our naval task force now in the Persian Gulf region testifies to our mobility and our strength. . . .

Jimmy Carter, address, Annual Conference of American Legion, Washington, February 19, 1980; *American Foreign Policy: Basic Documents*, 1977-1980, pp. 57-60.

*   *   *

. . . The West must defend its strategic interests wherever they are threatened. . . .

In recent years it's become increasingly evident that the well-being of those vital regions and our own country depend on the peace, stability, and independence of the Middle East and the Persian Gulf area. Yet both the Soviet invasion of Afghanistan and the pervasive and progressive political disintegration of Iran put the security of that region in grave jeopardy.

I want to reemphasize what I said in my State of the Union Address on January 23d, and I quote:

"Let our position be absolutely clear: An attempt by any outside force to gain control of the Persian Gulf region will be regarded as an assault on the vital interests of the United States of America, and such an assault will be repelled by any means necessary, including military force."

Jimmy Carter, address, World Affairs Council, Philadelphia, May 9, 1980; *American Foreign Policy: Basic Documents,* 1977-1980, pp. 62-67. Also see his address to American Legion Convention, Boston, August 21, 1980, p. 76. For commentary on the relation of the Carter Doctrine and the War Powers Resolution (Document 80), provided by the Legal Adviser of the Department of State, see *Digest of United States Practice in International Law,* 1980, pp. 1046-55.

REAGAN DOCTRINE, 1982

I believe free and peaceful development of our hemisphere requires us to help governments confronted with aggression from outside their borders to defend themselves. . . . we will do whatever is prudent and necessary to ensure the peace and security of the Caribbean area.

Ronald Reagan, 1982

125 REAGAN DOCTRINE--CARIBBEAN BASIN INITIATIVE, 1982

. . . The dark future is foreshadowed by the poverty and repression of Castro's Cuba, the tightening grip of the totalitarian left in Grenada and Nicaragua, and the expansion of Soviet-backed, Cuban-managed support for violent revolution in Central America.

The record is clear. Nowhere in its whole sordid history have the promises of communism been redeemed. Everywhere it has exploited and aggravated temporary economic suffering to seize power and then to institutionalize economic deprivation and suppress human rights . . . .

Our economic and social program cannot work if our neighbors cannot pursue their own economic and political future in peace, but must divert their resources, instead, to fight imported terrorism and armed attack. Economic progress cannot be made while guerillas systematically burn, bomb, and destroy . . . with the deliberate intention of worsening economic and social problems in hopes of radicalizing already suffering people.

Our Caribbean neighbors' peaceful attempts to develop are feared by the foes of freedom, because their success will make the radical message a hollow one. Cuba and its Soviet backers know this. Since 1978 Havana has trained, armed, and directed extremists in guerilla warfare and economic sabotage as part of a campaign to exploit troubles in Central America and the Caribbean. Their goal is to establish Cuban-style, Marxist-Leninist dictatorships. . . .

For almost 2 years, Nicaragua has served as a platform for covert military action. Through Nicaragua, arms are being smuggled to guerillas in El Salvador and Guatemala. . . . Very simply, guerillas, armed and supported by and through Cuba, are attempting to impose a Marxist-Leninist dictatorship on the people of El Salvador as part of a larger imperialistic plan. If we do not act promptly and decisively in defense of freedom, new Cubas will arise from the ruins of today's conflicts . . . .

I believe free and peaceful development of our hemisphere requires us to help governments confronted with aggression from outside their borders to defend themselves. . . . Since 1947 the Rio Treaty has established reciprocal defense responsibilities linked to our common democratic ideals.   Meeting these responsibilities is all the more important when an outside power supports terrorism and insurgency to destroy any possibility of freedom and democracy. Let our friends and our adversaries understand that we will do whatever is prudent and necessary to ensure the peace and security of the Caribbean area.

In the face of outside threats, security for the countries of the Caribbean and Central American area is not an end in itself, but a means to an end. It is a means toward building representative and responsive institutions, toward strengthening pluralism and free private institutions-- churches, free trade unions, and an independent press. It is a means to nurturing the basic human rights freedom's foes would stamp out. In the Caribbean we above all seek to protect those values and principles that shape the proud heritage of this hemisphere.

Ronald Reagan, remarks on Caribbean Basin Initiative, to Permanent Council of the Organization of American States, February 24, 1982; *Papers of Presidents: Reagan*, 1982, I, 213-14. For earlier statement of President Reagan's views, see interview with Walter Cronkite, March 3, 1981; *Papers of Presidents: Reagan*, 1981, pp. 191-96. Also see Document 565.

126 REAGAN DOCTRINE--STATEMENTS TO CONGRESS, 1983 AND 1986

Meanwhile, the Government of El Salvador, making every effort to guarantee democracy, free labor unions, freedom of religion, and a free press, is under attack by guerrillas dedicated to the same philosophy that prevails in Nicaragua, Cuba, and, yes, the Soviet Union. Violence has been Nicaragua's most important export to the world. It is the ultimate in hypocrisy for the unelected Nicaraguan Government to charge that we seek their overthrow when they're doing everything they can to bring down the elected Government of El Salvador. . . .

But let us be clear as to the American attitude toward the Government of Nicaragua. We do not seek its overthrow. Our interest is to ensure that it does not infect its neighbors through the export of subversion or violence. Our purpose, in conformity with American and international law, is to prevent the flow of arms to El Salvador, Honduras, Guatemala, and Costa Rica. . . .

Are democracies required to remain passive while threats to their security and prosperity accumulate? Must we just accept the destabilization of an entire region from the Panama Canal to Mexico on our southern border? Must we sit by, while independent nations of this hemisphere are integrated into the most aggressive empire the modern world has seen? Must we wait while Central Americans are driven from their homes. . . .

We will pursue four basic goals in Central America. First, in response to decades of inequity and indifference, we will support democracy, reform and human freedom. This means using our assistance, our powers of persuasion and our legitimate leverage to bolster humane democratic systems where they already exist and to help countries on their way to that goal complete the process as quickly as human institutions can be changed. . . .

Second, in response to the challenge of world recession and, in the case of El Salvador, to the unrelenting campaign of economic sabotage by the guerillas, we will support economic development. . . .

And, third, in response to the military challenge from Cuba and Nicaragua--to their deliberate use of force to spread tyranny--we will support the security of the region's threatened nations. We do not view security assistance as an end in itself, but as a shield for democratization, economic development, and diplomacy. . . .

And, fourth, we will support dialogue and negotiations--both among the countries of the region and within each country. . . . The United States will work toward a political solution in Central America which will serve the interests of the democratic process.

Ronald Reagan, address, Joint Session of Congress, April 17, 1983; *American Foreign Policy: Current Documents*, 1983, pp. 1314-20. For Defense Department views on the security issue, see pp. 1306-8, and for the President's radio address to the nation on Central America, see *Papers of Presidents: Reagan*, 1983, II, 1156-57.

*   *   *

Since the beginning of my first Administration, there has been no foreign policy issue more directly affecting United States national interests than the conflict in Central America, for this conflict challenges not only our strategic position but the very principles upon which this Nation is founded. . . .

Few now question that the rulers of Nicaragua are deeply committed communists, determined to consolidate their totalitarian communist state. Their long, documented record of brutal repression leaves no room for doubt. Nor can there be any dispute that they seek to export their ideology through terrorism and subversion to neighboring countries. Their neighbors' success in offering democracy as a viable alternative for the people of Central America is a major threat to the system they advocate. . . .

The cause of the United States in Nicaragua, as in the rest of Central America, is the cause of freedom and ultimately, our own national security.

The Soviet Union and its satellites understand the great stakes in

Nicaragua. . . .

If the enemies of democracy thousands of miles away understand the strategic importance of Nicaragua, understand that Nicaragua offers the possibility of destabilizing all Central America, of sending a tidal wave of refugees streaming toward our southern border, and of tying down the United States and weakening our ability to meet our commitments overseas, then we Americans must understand that Nicaragua is a foreign policy question of supreme importance which goes to the heart of our country's freedom and future.

Ronald Reagan, message to Congress respecting assistance for Nicaraguan "democratic resistance," February 25, 1986; *Papers of Presidents: Reagan,* 1986, I, 253-59. For report of Henry Kissinger, chairman of the National Bipartisan Commission on Central America, Senate Foreign Relations Committee, February 7, 1984, see *American Foreign Policy: Current Documents,* 1984, pp. 1008-13.

127 REAGAN DOCTRINE--ADDRESS TO THE NATION, 1986

. . . Central America is vital to our own national security, and the Soviet Union knows it. The Soviets take the long view, but their strategy is clear: to dominate the strategic sealanes and vital chokepoints around the world. . . .

The Soviet Union already uses Cuba as an air and submarine base in the Caribbean. It hopes to turn Nicaragua into the first Soviet base on the mainland of North America. . . .

Eventually, we Americans have to stop arguing among ourselves. We will have to confront the reality of a Soviet military beachhead inside our defense perimeters. . . .

Some ask: What are the goals of our policy toward Nicaragua? They are the goals the Nicaraguan people set for themselves in 1979: democracy, a free economy, and national self-determination. . . .

. . . can we responsibly ignore the long-term danger to American interests posed by a Communist Nicaragua, backed by the Soviet Union, and dedicated--in the words of its own leaders--to a "revolution without borders"? My friends, the only way to bring true peace and security to Central America is to bring democracy to Nicaragua. And the only way to get the Sandinistas to negotiate seriously about democracy is to give them no other alternative. . . .

The question before the House is not only about the freedom of Nicaragua and the security of the United States but who we are as a people. President Kennedy wrote on the day of his death that history had called this generation of Americans to be "watchmen on the walls of world freedom."

Ronald Reagan, Address to the Nation on United States Assistance for the Nicaraguan Democratic Resistance, June 24, 1986; *Papers of Presidents: Reagan,* 1986, I, 833-38.

PART IV
CRISIS DIPLOMACY

8

Berlin Crises
and German Question

Any lasting relaxation of tension in Europe must include progress in resolving the issues related to the division of Germany.

The German national question is basically one for the German people . . . . The reshaping of German relations with the East inevitably affects the interests of all European states, as well as the relationship between the U.S. and the Soviet Union.

Richard Nixon
U.S. Foreign Policy for the 1970's: Building for Peace (1971)

When Germany was defeated in 1945 the victorious allies divided the country into four "zones" of occupation and Berlin into four "sectors," administered by the United States, France, and the United Kingdom in the Western components and the Soviet Union in the Eastern zone. In 1949 the Western segments were united to form the Federal Republic of Germany (FRG) and the Eastern portion became the German Democratic Republic (GDR)--in effect resulting in two Germanies. This constituted one of the major factors in the division of Europe, the lowering of the Iron Curtain, the East-West conflict, and the Cold War. In the meantime, Berlin, which lies more than 100 miles within East Germany, administered as an entity under quadripartite agreements subscribed to in the mid-1940's by the four occupying powers, was bifurcated into West and East Berlin and, beginning in the late 1940's, the Soviet and East German governments sought to drive the Western powers out of the city.

The status and development of both Germany and Berlin raised a complex of thorny problems. The major issues regarding Germany embrace its division into two national states, antithetical proposals for reunification, and the acceptance by the Western and Eastern powers of two Germanies; their rearmament and the affiliation of West Germany with the North Atlantic Treaty Organization and East Germany with the Warsaw Pact and, therefore, the crucial military balance of power in Central Europe; integration of the two Germanies into the Western and Eastern economic systems; the negotiation of a postwar peace treaty with Germany (or separately with either or both of the Germanies); and East-West trade and other forms of cooperation between the two Germanies and with other countries.

Berlin--because of its location, the quadripartite agreements for its administration dating back to the mid-1940's, and the East German decision to make the city its national capital--has posed a series of vexatious difficulties in East-West relations. The principal issues include division of the city into two segments and the question of reunification and treatment as a single entity; the West German constitutional stipulation that Greater Berlin constitutes one of the component Laender (states) in the federal union (which the Western occupying powers refused to recognize) vs. East Germany's designation of Berlin as its national capital; Western powers access to West Berlin through East German territory; trade, travel, and other interrelations between the two segments of the metropolis and between West Germany and Berlin; the Soviet proposal to convert West Berlin into a neutralized "free city"; and, crucial in United States-Soviet relations, the residual quadripartite rights and responsibilities for allied administration of Berlin as a whole.

This chapter highlights some of the circumstances that pertain to both the German and Berlin questions. Most serious East-West crises over Germany centered on Berlin. The documents provided are grouped in three chronological periods--negotiations and crises from World War II to 1970, the devisement of the "resolution arrangements" during the early 1970's, and selected subsequent actions.

Specifically, the first group embraces general commentary and documents concerning (1) the crisis of 1948, including the Berlin blockade and airlift (Documents 128-130), (2) the crisis of 1958 (Documents 131-133), and (3) the crisis of 1961 (Documents 134-135), including the Kennedy-Khrushchev Summit Meeting at Vienna and the construction of the Berlin Wall (Documents 136-139).

The second group of materials consists of the results of several years of negotiations commencing late in the 1960's, which produced a network of agreements and other actions concerning both Germany and Berlin that were consummated in the early 1970's. The resulting "settlement," though not the preference of any major party, perhaps constituted the best that could be achieved under the circumstances and at a cost beyond which none of them was willing to commit itself. Although entailing scores of documents, they are epitomized by two key quadripartite arrangements, supplemented by a variety of bilateral agreements that, in effect, recognized the continuing division of both Germany and Berlin and concretized the quadripartite status of Berlin (Documents 140-145).

The final group of documents--concerned with subsequent developments--deals with such matters as the establishment of diplomatic relations between the United States and the German Democratic Republic (1974) (Document 146), and continuing United States policy in support of, and guaranteeing the free status and security of West Berlin, and condemnation of the existence of the Berlin Wall. Reiterating United States concern over the "tragic division of Berlin" and the preservation of a free West Berlin, beginning in the 1960s American Presidents have sought to encourage its government and inhabitants with such expressions as: "Ich bin ein Berliner" (Kennedy), "all the people of the world are truly Berliners" (Nixon), "Was immer sei, Berlin bleibt frei"

(Carter), and "Berlin bleibt doch Berlin" and "Ich hab noch ein koffer in Berlin" (Reagan). The Wall came to be regarded as a symbol of political depravity. Recent leaders have branded it "ugly," "cruel," "brutal," "hated," and an "iron curtain" that produced a "tragic division" of Berlin, as well as "an affront to the human spirit" and a "vivid demonstration of the failures of the Communist system," and have declared that it must be destroyed (Document 147).

Such actions were supplemented, in 1975, by the Final Act of the Helsinki Conference on Security and Cooperation in Europe (CSCE) to stabilize European affairs. It specifies continental acceptance of the existing status quo concerning the two Germanies and Berlin (as well as that of other countries, and territorial changes effected during and after World War II). The final act, signed on August 1 by the United States, Canada, and 33 European countries and principalities, including both Germanies, consummated agreement on such matters as sovereign equality, inviolability of existing frontiers, territorial integrity of states, peaceful settlement of disputes, respect for human rights and fundamental freedoms, nonintervention in internal affairs, equal rights and self-determination of peoples, and fulfillment in good faith of obligations under international law. For its text, see Document 517.

Commencing with the easing of Western relations with the Soviet Union, the reforms undertaken in the Warsaw bloc nations, leadership changes, and the democratizing of Communist political and economic systems in the late 1980's and commencement of the 1990's, the Iron Curtain began to erode, East Germans demonstrated for freedom, the German Wall was severed, East Germany instituted political and social changes, and the possibility of German reunification gained widespread attention and credence. For the American reaction to the dismantling of the Wall in November 1989 and its position on the German reunification process, see Documents 148-149. Also see related commentary on changing East-West relations in Chapter 22.

Aside from the detailed materials on post-World War II Germany and Berlin contained in the *Foreign Relations of the United States* series and various monographs and other official publications, the Department of State has produced a comprehensive compilation entitled *Documents on Germany*. First published to cover the period 1945-1959, it has thrice been revised and updated, and the fourth edition, encompassing the period 1944-1985, provides more than 1,420 pages of documents and commentary. This compilation is herein cited simply as *Documents on Germany*. For an earlier anthology of documents on the occupation of Germany, see Department of State, *Germany, 1947-1949: The Story in Documents* (Washington: Government Printing Office, 1950).

DEVELOPMENTS AND CRISES, 1945-1970

128 BERLIN CRISES, 1945-1970

. . . Over the years the Soviet Union and East German authorities have challenged the position of the three Western Powers in Berlin, have interfered with free circulation within the city, and have hindered travel between the city and the outside world. This has not prevented the Western sectors from enjoying democratic government and increasing prosperity. Communist pressures have, however, inconvenienced Berlin's residents and those visiting and trading with the city and threatened the city's freedom and viability. International tension over Berlin problems has at times reached critical dimensions. . . .

The London Protocol, signed by the United States, Great Britain, and the Soviet Union on September 12, 1944, and amended on July 26, 1945, to permit participation by France, established Berlin as a special occupation area, distinct from the zones into which the rest of Germany was to be divided. The forces of each of the Four Powers would occupy a separate sector in Berlin and a Kommandatura, composed of the four Commandants, would administer the area jointly on the basis of unanimous decisions, under the general direction of the Allied Control Council, the supreme governing authority for Germany. . . .

In July 1946 the Kommandatura approved a temporary constitution for Berlin which specified that the legislative city assembly would be subordinate to the Kommandatura. Under the provisions of the constitution, city elections were held in October 1946 and the Communist-dominated Socialist Unity Party (SED) was decisively defeated. The Soviets subsequently used their position in the Kommandatura to block many measures of the new city government. On June 16, 1948, the Soviet Commandant walked out of the Kommandatura, following similar action by the Soviet representative in the Allied Control Council. This ended quadripartite administration of Berlin as a whole.

The London Protocol did not contain specific provisions for Western access to Berlin on the principle that the Western right to occupy Berlin carried with it the right of access. Such rights were specifically confirmed in the letters to Marshal Stalin from President Truman and Prime Minister Churchill dated respectively June 14 and 15, 1945, proposing movement of their national garrisons into Berlin with provisions for free road, rail, and air access to the city, and in Stalin's reply to President Truman dated June 16, 1945, assuring him that "all necessary measures will be taken. . . ." Specific arrangements were then discussed at a conference on July 29, 1945, among the American, British, and Soviet commanders in Germany, and an oral agreement was reached for Western road, rail, and air access. . . . In addition, a variety of working arrangements were established by consistent practice over the years.

During the first half of 1948 the Soviets gradually stepped up interference with traffic to Berlin. Finally, they stopped all traffic by road on June 18, 1948, and all traffic by rail on June 24, 1948, leaving only air access open to Berlin. The blockade lasted 11 months, during which time the allied powers supplied West Berlin by a massive airlift of food, fuel, and vital goods. Faced with its obvious failure to force the Western Powers to withdraw, the Soviets, in an agreement with the three powers reached in New York on May 4, 1949, and supplemented in Paris on June 20, 1949, restored access to the status existing before the blockade began. This status included the free movement of German civilian persons and goods between Berlin and the Western zones.

Since then Soviet and East German authorities have continued sporadically to hamper Berlin access. Surface traffic has been blocked and subjected to arbitrary controls and searches. Both military and civilian aircraft have been harassed in the air corridors to Berlin. . . .

Following the end of the blockade the Western sectors of Berlin experienced a notable economic revival which has continued until today. This was made possible by the security provided by the three Western Powers and the North Atlantic Alliance, and by the close economic and social ties between the Western sectors and the Federal Republic. Within the city, however, the division between the Soviet sector and the Western sectors became ever sharper. The central organs of the East German regime were established in the Soviet sector, and the East German constitution of October 1949 proclaimed Berlin the capital of the German Democratic Republic, an act to which the three Western Powers, but not the Soviet Union, took strong exception. In the Federal Republic, Article 23 of the Basic Law [constitution] provided that Berlin was a Federal "Land." The three Western Powers suspended this Article on the ground that Berlin continued under the control of the Four Powers and was not an integral part of either East or West German territory. The Western Powers, however, welcomed the development of economic, financial, legal, and cultural ties between the Western sectors and the Federal Republic in order to insure the viability of the city and to provide an environment in which a free and democratic society could flourish. Federal parliamentary bodies met frequently in Berlin. A substantial number of Federal offices were established there, providing jobs and a sense of security for Berlin's residents. . . . During the late fifties and sixties, however, Federal activities in the city came under growing challenge from the Soviet Union and the East German authorities.

The position of the Western Powers in Berlin had also again been challenged by the Soviet Union. In November 1958 Khrushchev asserted that the Western Powers had violated the Potsdam Agreement and had thereby rendered the London Protocol null and void and had forfeited their occupation rights in Berlin. Khrushchev demanded that the Western Powers leave Berlin and that West Berlin be made a demilitarized and free city. The Western Powers maintained that the quadripartite rights to occupy Berlin by right of conquest prevailed and that the Soviet Union could not unilaterally relieve itself of quadripartite responsibilities.

The Western Powers also denied that they had violated the Potsdam Agreement. They affirmed that the status of the Potsdam Agreement was in any event irrelevant to the continued validity of the London Protocol since the London Protocol predated the Potsdam Agreement by six months and neither agreement, by its terms or by implication, was made dependent for its continued validity upon the status of the other.

A conference of the four foreign ministers took place in Geneva in the summer of 1959 but ended in a deadlock since the Soviet Union was unwilling to assure the continuation of Western rights in Berlin following the termination of any interim settlement. This was the last quadripartite meeting on Berlin prior to the negotiations of 1970 and 1971.

Throughout the summer and early fall of 1961 the Berlin problem assumed the proportions of a major international crisis. The Western powers repeatedly affirmed their determination not to be driven out of Berlin. They defined the four essentials which would have to underlie any Berlin settlement as, (1) the right of the Berliners to be free, (2) to live in a viable community, (3) the right of the Western allies to be in Berlin, and (4) the right of free access to the city. On August 13, 1961, East German authorities erected a barrier physically cutting off East Berlin from the rest of the city. This subsequently developed into a continuous wall which prevented circulation between the two parts of the city. A similar barrier was placed around the small inhabited exclave of the Western sectors called Steinstuecken, which was located within East German territory and had over the years been subject to frequent East German harassment.

By the end of the sixties the Western sectors of Berlin were prosperous and their residents lived in freedom. They could not, however, travel to East Berlin except for urgent family reasons. Travel to the surrounding German Democratic Republic (GDR) was totally forbidden. The ties between the Western sectors and the Federal Republic were close but under challenge through sporadic harassment of access and through Communist refusal to accept any form of representation of the Western sectors abroad by the Federal Republic. Countering this, the determination of the Western Powers to maintain their position in the city had been clearly established and was no longer under Soviet attack.

United States Foreign Policy, 1971: A Report of the Secretary of State, pp. 39-43. For additional commentary and early documents on the German and Berlin issues, 1944-1947, see *Documents on Germany,* pp. 1-139 (including the London Protocol of 1944 as amended in 1945, pp. 1-3, 44-48, and the Potsdam Conference agreements of 1945, pp. 54-65, especially pp. 56-57). For documentation on the Berlin crises and the Berlin Wall, 1948-1961, see *Documents on Germany,* pp. 140-804, on the Geneva Foreign Ministers Meeting (1959), see pp. 624-83, and on the Eisenhower and Kennedy Summit Meetings with Khrushchev in 1959 and 1961, see pp. 521-36, 729-36, 745-46, and 760-65.

129 UNITED STATES OBJECTION TO BERLIN BLOCKADE, 1948

The United States Government wishes to call to the attention of the Soviet Government the extremely serious international situation which has been brought about by the actions of the Soviet Government in imposing restrictive measures on transport which amount now to a blockade against the sectors in Berlin occupied by the United States, United Kingdom and France. The United States Government regards these measures of blockade as a clear violation of existing agreements concerning the administration of Berlin by the four occupying powers.

The rights of the United States as a joint occupying power in Berlin derive from the total defeat and unconditional surrender of Germany. The international agreements undertaken in connection therewith by the Governments of the United States, United Kingdom, France and the Soviet Union defined the zones in Germany and the sectors in Berlin which are occupied by these powers. They established the quadripartite control of Berlin on a basis of friendly cooperation which the Government of the United States earnestly desires to continue to pursue.

These agreements implied the right of free access to Berlin. This right has long been confirmed by usage. It was directly specified in a message sent by President Truman to Premier Stalin on June 14, 1945, which agreed to the withdrawal of United States forces to the zonal boundaries, provided satisfactory arrangements could be entered into between the military commanders, which would give access by rail, road and air to United States forces in Berlin. Premier Stalin replied on June 16 suggesting a change in date but no other alteration in the plan proposed by the President. Premier Stalin then gave assurances that all necessary measures would be taken in accordance with the plan. . . .

It clearly results from these undertakings that Berlin is not a part of the Soviet zone, but is an international zone of occupation. Commitments entered into in good faith . . . as well as practices sanctioned by usage, guarantee the United States together with other powers, free access to Berlin for the purpose of fulfilling its responsibilities as an occupying power. . . .

In order that there should be no misunderstanding whatsoever on this point, the United States Government categorically asserts that it is in occupation of its sector in Berlin with free access thereto as a matter of established right deriving from the defeat and surrender of Germany and confirmed by formal agreements among the principal Allies. It further declares that it will not be induced by threats, pressures or other actions to abandon these rights. It is hoped that the Soviet Government entertains no doubts whatsoever on this point.

Note from United States to Soviet government, regarding the lifting of the Berlin Blockade, July 6, 1948; *Documents on Germany,* pp. 156-58. For a chronological account of developments, March 30-July 3, 1948, see Department of State statement, pp. 152-56. The blockade went into effect in June and the United States responded immediately with the Berlin Airlift-- called "Operation Vittles." The United States took the issue to the United Nations, see pp. 175-84, 192, and for comprehensive documentation on the blockade, see *Foreign Relations,* 1948, II, 886-1225, especially pp. 909-10, 950-53, 960-63, 990-91.

130 ARRANGEMENTS FOR LIFTING BERLIN BLOCKADE, 1949

The Governments of France, the Union of Soviet Socialist Republics, the United Kingdom, and the United States have reached the following agreement:

1. All the restrictions imposed since March 1, 1948 by the Government of the Union of Soviet Socialist Republics on communications, transportation, and trade between Berlin and the Western zones of Germany and between the Eastern zone and the Western zones will be removed on May 12, 1949.

2. All the restrictions imposed since March 1, 1948 by the Governments of France, the United Kingdom, and the United States, or any one of them, on communication, transportation, and trade between Berlin and the Eastern zone and between the Western and Eastern zones of Germany will also be removed on May 12, 1949.

Four-Power Communique, issued in New York, May 4, 1949, effective May 12; *Documents on Germany,* p. 221. The four occupying governments also agreed to convene the Council of Foreign Ministers to consider the German and Berlin questions; for its communique, see pp. 269-70.

1 3 1   SOVIET ARGUMENT TO CHANGE STATUS OF BERLIN, 1958

Actually, of all the Allied agreements on Germany, only one is being carried out today. It is the agreement on the so-called quadripartite status of Berlin. On the basis of that status, the Three Western Powers are ruling the roost in West Berlin, turning it into a kind of state within a state and using it as a center from which to pursue subversive activity against the GDR, the Soviet Union, and the other parties of the Warsaw Treaty. The United States, Great Britain, and France are freely communicating with West Berlin through lines of communication passing through the territory and the airspace of the German Democratic Republic, which they do not even want to recognize.

The governments of the Three Powers are seeking to keep in force the long-since obsolete part of the wartime agreements that governed the occupation of Germany and entitled them in the past to stay in Berlin. At the same time . . . the Western Powers have grossly violated the Four-Power agreements, including the Potsdam Agreement, which is the most concentrated expression of the obligations of the Powers with respect to Germany. . . . In other words the Three Powers are demanding, for their own sake, the preservation of the occupation privileges based on those Four-Power agreements, which they themselves have violated. . . .

At one time, the agreement on the Four-Power status of Berlin was an agreement providing for equal rights of the Four-Powers, which was concluded for peaceful democratic purposes, which purposes later became known as the Potsdam principles. At that time, this agreement met the requirements of the day and was in accordance with the interests of all its signatories. . . . Now that the Western Powers have begun to arm West Germany and turn it into an instrument of their policy directed against the Soviet Union, the very essence of this erstwhile Allied agreement on Berlin has disappeared. . . .

An obviously absurd situation has thus arisen, in which the Soviet Union seems to be supporting and maintaining favorable conditions for the Western Powers in their activities against the Soviet Union and its Allies under the Warsaw Treaty.

It is obvious that the Soviet Union, just as the other parties to the Warsaw Treaty, cannot tolerate such a situation any longer. . . .

In view of all these considerations, the Soviet Government on its part would consider it possible to solve the West Berlin question at the present time by the conversion of West Berlin into an independent political unit--a free city, without any state, including both existing German states, interfering in its life. Specifically, it might be possible to agree that the territory of the free city be demilitarized and that no armed forces be contained therein. The free city, West Berlin, could have its own government and run its own economic, administrative, and other affairs.

Note from Soviet government to United States, November 27, 1958; *Documents on Germany*, pp. 552-59

132   UNITED STATES POSITION ON MAINTAINING STATUS OF BERLIN, 1958

The agreements made by the Four Powers cannot be considered obsolete because the Soviet Union has already obtained the full advantage therefrom and now wishes to deprive the other parties of their compensating advantages. These agreements are binding upon all of the signatories so long as they have not been replaced by others following free negotiations.

Insofar as the Potsdam Agreement is concerned, the status of Berlin does not depend upon that agreement. Moreover, it is the Soviet Union that bears responsibility for the fact that the Potsdam Agreement could not be implemented. . . .

The United States Government cannot prevent the Soviet Government from announcing the termination of its own authority in the quadripartite regime in the sector which it occupies in the city of Berlin. On the other hand, the Government of the United States will not and does not, in any way, accept a unilateral denunciation of the accords of 1944 and 1945; nor is it prepared to relieve the Soviet Union from the obligations which it assumed in June 1949. Such action on the part of the Soviet Government would have no legal basis, since the agreements can only be terminated by mutual consent. The Government of the United States will continue to hold the Soviet Government directly responsible for the discharge of its obligations undertaken with respect to Berlin under existing agreements. . . .

The continued protection of the freedom of more than two million people of West Berlin is a right and responsibility solemnly accepted by the Three Western Powers. Thus the United States cannot consider any proposal which would have the effect of jeopardizing the freedom and security of these people. The rights of the Three Powers to remain in

Berlin with unhindered communications by surface and air between that city and the Federal Republic of Germany are under existing conditions essential to the discharge of that right and responsibility. Hence the proposal for a so-called "free city" for West Berlin as put forward by the Soviet Union, is unacceptable.

Note from United States to Soviet government, December 31, 1958; *Documents on Germany,* pp. 573-76. Similar notes were sent to France, the United Kingdom, and West Germany. Also see Department of State, *The Soviet Note on Berlin: An Analysis,* Department of State publication 6757 (1958).

133 FOUR-POWER AGREEMENT TO NEGOTIATE CONCERNING GERMAN AND BERLIN QUESTIONS, 1959

The Conference of Foreign Ministers met in Geneva from May 11 to June 20 and from July 13 to August 5, 1959.

The Conference considered questions relating to Germany, including a peace treaty with Germany and the question of Berlin.

The positions of the participants in the Conference were set out on these questions.

A frank and comprehensive discussion took place on the Berlin question.

The positions of both sides on certain points became closer.

The discussions which have taken place will be useful for the further negotiations which are necessary in order to reach an agreement.

Furthermore the Conference provided the opportunity for useful exchanges of views on other questions of mutual interest.

The Foreign Ministers have agreed to report the results of the Conference to their respective governments.

The date and place for the resumption of the work of the Conference will be settled through diplomatic channels.

Four-power communique issued at close of Foreign Ministers Meeting, Geneva, August 5, 1959; *Documents on Germany,* p. 683. For additional documents on the Geneva meeting, see pp. 624-683. Nikita Khrushchev prescribed a time limit for the resolution of the Berlin issue, which President Eisenhower regarded as an ultimatum; at the Camp David bilateral Summit Meeting in September 1959, Khrushchev agreed to rescind the time limit, which returned the issue to the status quo ante and therefore negotiable; for documentation, see pp. 684-86.

134 SOVIET PROPOSAL FOR "PEACE TREATY" WITH GERMANY AND "FREE CITY" STATUS FOR WEST BERLIN, 1961

3. Proceeding from a realistic evaluation of the situation, the Soviet Government stands for the immediate conclusion of a peace treaty with Germany. . . . The time has already passed for allowing the situation in

Germany to remain unchanged. All the conditions for the conclusion of a peace treaty matured a long time ago and this treaty must be concluded. The point is who will conclude it and when, and whether this will entail unnecessary costs. . . .

5. The conclusion of a German peace treaty would also solve the problem of normalizing the situation in West Berlin. Deprived of a stable international status, West Berlin at present is a place where the Bonn revanchist circles continually maintain extreme tension and organize all kinds of provocations very dangerous to the cause of peace. We are duty-bound to prevent a development where intensification of West German militarism could lead to irreparable consequences due to the unsettled situation in West Berlin.

At present, the Soviet Government does not see a better way to solve the West Berlin problem than by transforming it into a demilitarized free city. The implementation of the proposal to turn West Berlin into a free city, with the interests of all parties duly taken into consideration, would normalize the situation in West Berlin. The occupation regime now being maintained has already outlived itself and has lost all connection with the purposes for which it was established, as well as with the Allied agreements concerning Germany that established the basis for its existence. The occupation rights will naturally be terminated upon the conclusion of a German peace treaty, whether it is signed with both German States or only with the German Democratic Republic, within whose territory West Berlin is located.

The position of the Soviet Government is that the free city of West Berlin should have unobstructed contacts with the outside world and that its internal regulations should be determined by the freely expressed will of its population. The United States as well as other countries would naturally have every possibility to maintain and develop their relations with the free city. In short, West Berlin, as the Soviet Government sees it, should be strictly neutral. Of course, the use of Berlin as a base for provocative activities, hostile to the U.S.S.R., the G.D.R. or any other State, cannot be permitted in the future, nor can Berlin be allowed to remain a dangerous hotbed of tension and international conflicts.

The U.S.S.R. proposes that the most reliable guarantees be established against interference in the affairs of the free city on the part of any State. Token troop contingents of the United States, the United Kingdom, France and the U.S.S.R. could be stationed in West Berlin as quarantors of the free city. The U.S.S.R. would have no objections, either, to the stationing in West Berlin, for the same purpose, of military contingents from neutral States under the aegis of the U.N. The status of free city could be duly registered by the United Nations and consolidated by the authority of that international organization. The Soviet side is prepared to discuss any other measures that would guarantee the freedom and independence of West Berlin as a free demilitarized city.

All this considered, the settlement of the West Berlin problem should naturally take into account the necessity of respecting and strictly observing the sovereign rights of the German Democratic Republic, which, as is well known, has declared its readiness to adhere to such an agreement and respect it.

Aide-memoire from Soviet government to the United States, handed by Chairman Nikita Khrushchev to President Kennedy at Vienna Summit Meeting, June 4, 1961; *Documents on Germany*, pp. 729-32.   Also see earlier aide-memoire from Soviet Government to Federal Republic of Germany, February 17, 1961, pp. 723-27.

1 3 5   UNITED STATES RESPONSE TO SOVIET THREAT TO WEST BERLIN, 1961

Our most somber talks were on the subject of Germany and Berlin. I made it clear to Mr. Khrushchev that the security of Western Europe and therefore our own security are deeply involved in our presence and our access rights to West Berlin, that those rights are based on law and not on sufferance, and that we are determined to maintain those rights at any risk and thus meet our obligation to the people of West Berlin and their right to choose their own future. . . . A binding German peace treaty is a matter for all who were at war with Germany, and we and our allies cannot abandon our obligations to the people of West Berlin.

John Kennedy, report to the nation delivered by radio and television, following his summit meeting with Chairman Khrushchev at Vienna, June 6, 1961; *Documents on Germany*, pp. 732-33.

*   *   *

. . . It is of the greatest importance that the American people understand the basic issues involved and the threats to the peace and security both of Europe and of ourselves posed by the Soviet announcement that they intend to change unilaterally the existing arrangements for Berlin. . . .

In November 1958 the Soviets began a new campaign to force the Allied Powers out of Berlin, a process which led up to the abortive summit conference in Paris in May of last year. Now they have revived that drive. They call upon us to sign what they call a "peace treaty" with the regime they have created in Eastern Germany. If we refuse, they say they themselves will sign such a "treaty." The obvious purpose here is not to have peace but to make permanent the partition of Germany. The Soviets also say that their unilateral action in signing a "peace treaty" with East Germany would bring to an end Allied rights to be in West Berlin and to have free access to the city. It is clear that such unilateral action cannot affect these rights, which stem from the surrender of Nazi Germany. Such action would simply be a repudiation by the Soviets of multilateral commitments to which they solemnly subscribed, and have repeatedly reaffirmed, about the exercise of the rights of the principal powers associated in World War II. . . .

No one can fail to appreciate the gravity of this threat. . . . It involves the peace and security of the people of West Berlin. It involves the direct responsibilities and commitments of the United States, the United Kingdom and France. It involves the peace and security of the Western World.

John Kennedy, statement, news conference, June 28, 1961; *Documents on Germany*, pp. 745-46.

        *   *   *

In consultation and full agreement with its British and French allies, and with the benefit of the views of the Federal Republic of Germany, and after consultation with the other member governments of the North Atlantic Treaty Organization, the United States on Monday delivered through its Embassy in Moscow its reply to the aide memoire on Germany and Berlin received from the Soviet Government on June 4. . . .

The real intent of the June 4 aide-memoire is that East Berlin, a part of a city under Four Power status, would be formally absorbed into the so-called "German Democratic Republic" while West Berlin, even though called a "free city," would lose the protection presently provided by the Western Powers and become subject to the will of a totalitarian regime. . . .

A city does not become free merely by calling it a "free city." For a city or a people to be free requires that they be given the opportunity, without economic, political, or police pressure, to make their own choice and to live their own lives. The people of West Berlin today have their freedom. It is the objective of our policy that they shall continue to have it.

John Kennedy, statement, read at news conference, July 19, 1961; *Documents on Germany*, pp. 760-62.

136 EAST GERMAN RESTRICTIONS ON TRAVEL BETWEEN EAST AND WEST BERLIN, 1961

To put an end to the hostile activities of the revanchist and militarist forces of Western Germany and West Berlin, such control is to be introduced on the borders of the German Democratic Republic, including the border with the Western sectors of Greater Berlin, which is usually introduced along the borders of every sovereign state.

Reliable safeguards and effective control must be insured on the West Berlin borders in order to block the way to the subversive activities.

The citizens of the German Democratic Republic may cross these borders only with special permission.

Until West Berlin is turned into a demilitarized neutral free city, the citizens of the capital of the German Democratic Republic will have to have a special permit for crossing the border to West Berlin.

The West Berlin civilians may visit the capital of the German Democratic Republic (Democratic Berlin) on presenting West Berlin identity cards.

Revanchist politicians and agents of West German militarism are not permitted to enter the territory of the G.D.R. capital (Democratic Berlin).

As regards visits to Democratic Berlin by the citizens of the West German Federal Republic, former decisions on control remain valid.

These decisions do not affect the visits of the citizens of other states to the capital of the German Democratic Republic.

Decree, German Democratic Republic, August 13, 1961; *Documents on Germany,* pp. 775-76.

137 UNITED STATES REACTION TO TRAVEL RESTRICTIONS IN BERLIN, 1961

The authorities in East Berlin and East Germany have taken severe measures to deny to their own people access to West Berlin. These measures have doubtless been prompted by the increased flow of refugees in recent weeks. The refugees are not responding to persuasion or propaganda from the West but to the failures of communism in East Germany. These failures have created great pressures upon communist leaders who, in turn, are trying to solve their own problems by the dangerous course of threats against the freedom and safety of West Berlin. The resulting tension has itself stimulated flights from the East.

Having denied the collective right of self determination to the peoples of East Germany, communist authorities are now denying the right of individuals to elect a world of free choice rather than a world of coercion. The pretense that communism desires only peaceful competition is exposed; the refugees, more than half of whom are less than 25 years of age, have "voted with their feet" on whether communism is the wave of the future.

Available information indicates that measures taken thus far are aimed at residents of East Berlin and East Germany and not at the allied position in West Berlin or access thereto. However, limitation on travel within Berlin is a violation of the four-power status of Berlin and a flagrant violation of the right of free circulation throughout the city. . . .

Dean Rusk, statement, August 13, 1961; *Documents on Germany,* p. 776.

138 UNITED STATES PROTEST TO SOVIET GOVERNMENT CONCERNING BERLIN WALL, 1961

On August 13, East German authorities put into effect several measures regulating movement at the boundary of the western sectors and the Soviet sector of the city of Berlin. These measures have the effect of limiting to a degree approaching complete prohibition, passage from the Soviet sector to the western sectors of the city. These measures were accompanied by the closing of the sector boundary by a sizable deployment of police forces and by military detachments brought into Berlin for this purpose.

All this is a flagrant and particularly serious, violation of the quadripartite status of Berlin.   Freedom of movement with respect to Berlin was reaffirmed by the quadripartite agreement of New York of May 4, 1949, and by the decision taken at Paris on June 20, 1949, by the Council of the Ministers of Foreign Affairs of the Four Powers. The United States Government has never accepted that limitations can be imposed on freedom of movement within Berlin. The boundary between the Soviet sector and the western sectors of Berlin is not a state frontier. The United States Government considers that the measures which the East German authorities have taken are illegal. It reiterates that it does not accept the pretension that the Soviet sector of Berlin forms a part of the so-called "German Democratic Republic" and that Berlin is situated on its territory. Such a pretension is in itself a violation of the solemnly pledged word of the U.S.S.R. in the Agreement on the Zones of Occupation in Germany and the administration of Greater Berlin. Moreover, the United States Government cannot admit the right of- the East German authorities to authorize their armed forces to enter the Soviet sector of Berlin.

The United States Government solemnly protests against the measures referred to above, for which it holds the Soviet Government responsible. The United States Government expects the Soviet Government to put an end to these illegal measures. This unilateral infringement of the quadripartite status of Berlin can only increase existing tension and dangers.

United States note to Soviet government for violation of quadripartite status of Berlin, August 17, 1961; *Documents on Germany*, pp. 777-78.

139   UNITED STATES CONDEMNATION OF "IRON CURTAIN" DIVIDING BERLIN, 1961

Divided, you have never been dismayed. Threatened, you have never faltered. Challenged, you have never weakened. Today, in a new crisis, your courage brings hope to all who cherish freedom and is a massive and majestic barrier to the ambitions of tyrants.

As the personal representative of President Kennedy and the American people, I have come here to salute your courage, to honor your faith in freedom, and to assure you that your friends will never forget their obligations to you. Standing together and working together, you shall prevail. This city will continue to be the fortress of the free because it is the home of the brave   . . . .

In this threatened city we can never forget the suffering and the heroism of the people in East Berlin who have now been forced into a bondage that mocks the essential rights of free men and women. They are the victims of tyranny, but their protests have rung round the world and have shamed the cruel dictatorship before the indignant judgment of mankind. An "iron curtain" now divides this city, but it cannot hide the misery and brutality imposed by these harsh and illegal decrees.

They have divided Berlin, but they have united us even more strongly and we will be separated neither by Communist tricks nor Communist threats. That is the pledge I bring to you from America.

Vice President Lyndon Johnson, statement on arrival in West Berlin, August 19, 1961; *Documents on Germany,* pp. 781-82. For subsequent statements by American leaders concerning United States support of free Berlin and condemnation of the Berlin Wall, see Document 147.

"RESOLUTION ARRANGEMENTS," EARLY 1970's

140 NEGOTIATING SETTLEMENTS, 1970-1972

The objective of the complex negotiations which took place during 1970 and 1971 was to reduce the causes of tension, while preserving the status of the city and the rights and responsibilities of the Four Powers for Berlin and Germany as a whole. The resultant agreement . . . constitutes the most comprehensive and important understanding reached on Berlin since the immediate post World War II period. . . .

The Berlin negotiations of 1970 and 1971, unlike earlier Four Power discussions on Berlin, were not in response to an immediate crisis. As early as the NATO ministerial conferences in June and November of 1968 there was discussion of a possible new Western initiative with the Soviets in connection with Berlin. In February 1969, President Nixon visited Berlin and called for a new effort to find ways of reducing the tensions of the past. Two months later, the NATO ministers in a communique following their April meeting endorsed "concrete measures aimed at improving the situation in Berlin, safeguarding free access to the city, and removing restrictions which affect traffic and communications between the two parts of Germany." Subsequently, with the encouragement of the Federal Republic, the United States, the United Kingdom, and France agreed to sound out Moscow concerning improvements in the Berlin situation.

Meanwhile in a speech on July 10, 1969, Soviet Foreign Minister Gromyko offered to "exchange views as to how complications concerning West Berlin can be prevented now and in the future." On August 6 and 7 the three powers made oral statements in Moscow which referred to the Soviet Foreign Minister's remarks and expressed their desire to see the situation in Berlin improved. After further exchanges, the Soviets on February 10, 1970, accepted the Western proposal for talks in Berlin and suggested that they be held at the Ambassadorial level in the building formerly occupied by the Allied Control Council. While confirming their readiness to discuss improvement of the situation in "West Berlin" and the elimination of frictions in the region, they said that the first topic of discussion should be the exclusion of "activities incompatible with the international situation of West Berlin." They stated further that GDR interests must be taken into account in the settlement of access issues. The first Ambassadorial meeting took place on March 26, 1970, in the Control Council building in the American sector of Berlin. There followed almost a year and a half of difficult and complicated negotiations in a long series of meetings finally ending in the signature of the Quadripartite Agreement--the first phase of the overall Berlin Agreement--on September 3, 1971. This landmark was followed by inner German negotiations, which lasted until December 20, 1971.

The preparation and conduct of negotiations concerning Berlin involved unique and complicated factors. Since basic responsibility for Berlin lies with the Four Powers, any agreement on Berlin must in the first instance be reached by them. At the same time, German authorities had an essential role to play in working out procedural details for the implementation of improvements agreed upon by the Four Powers. Moreover, the positions put forward and the decisions taken by the Four Powers were of vital interest to German authorities in Bonn and in both East and West Berlin.

Throughout the negotiations, there was close coordination between the three Western Powers and both the Federal Republic and the West Berlin Government (the Senat). A phased approach to negotiations provided for an initial quadripartite agreement followed by supplementary agreements and understandings between German authorities which would be encompassed, and brought into effect, by a Final Quadripartite Protocol. . . .

. . . throughout the negotiations initial positions were formulated on the Western side in capitals, but developed and coordinated by the Western representatives meeting almost without interruption in Bonn. The wording of texts tabled by the Western side was for the most part drafted in Bonn. Having participated directly in this process in Bonn, the three Western Ambassadors were able in the Berlin meetings to function as a team in dealing with their Soviet colleague.

When the stage of inner German negotiations was reached a similar procedure was followed in reverse. Initial positions were developed by the Federal Republic and the Berlin Senat on the basis of the provisions of the Quadripartite Agreement. They were then coordinated with the Western Powers in meetings both in Bonn and in Berlin in preparation for sessions with the East German negotiators. The text of the Quadripartite Agreement was concurred in by the Federal Government before it was signed by the three Western Powers, and the texts of the agreements and arrangements negotiated by the Federal Government and the Senat with East German authorities were approved by the three Western Powers before they were signed by German representatives.

United States Foreign Policy, 1971: A Report of the Secretary of State, pp. 39, 43-45.

141 PRELIMINARY QUADRIPARTITE AGREEMENT ON BERLIN, 1971

Part I
General Provisions

1. The four Governments will strive to promote the elimination of tension and the prevention of complications in the relevant area.

2. The four Governments, taking into account their obligations under the Charter of the United Nations, agree that there shall be no use or threat of force in the area and that disputes shall be settled solely by peaceful means.

3. The four Governments will mutually respect their individual and joint rights and responsibilities, which remain unchanged.

4. The four Governments agree that, irrespective of the differences in legal views, the situation which has developed in the area, and as it is defined in this Agreement as well as in the other agreements referred to in this Agreement, shall not be changed unilaterally.

Part II
Provisions Relating to the Western Sectors of Berlin

A. The Government of the Union of Soviet Socialist Republics declares that transit traffic by road, rail and waterways through the territory of the German Democratic Republic of civilian persons and goods between the Western Sectors of Berlin and the Federal Republic of Germany will be unimpeded; that such traffic will be facilitated so as to take place in the most simple and expeditious manner, and that it will receive preferential treatment.

Detailed arrangement concerning this civilian traffic, as set forth in Annex I, will be agreed by the competent German authorities.

B. The Governments of the French Republic, the United Kingdom and the United States of America declare that the ties between the Western Sectors of Berlin and the Federal Republic of Germany will be maintained and developed, taking into account that these Sectors continue not to be a constituent part of the Federal Republic of Germany and not to be governed by it. . . .

C. The Government of the Union of Soviet Socialist Republics declares that communications between the Western Sectors of Berlin and areas bordering on these Sectors and those areas of the German Democratic Republic which do not border on these Sectors will be improved. Permanent residents of the Western Sectors of Berlin will be able to travel to and visit such areas for compassionate, family, religious, cultural or commercial reasons, or as tourists, under conditions comparable to those applying to other persons entering these areas. . . .

D. Representation abroad of the interests of the Western Sectors of Berlin and consular activities of the Union of Soviet Socialist Republics in the Western Sectors of Berlin can be exercised as set forth in Annex IV.

Signed at Berlin, September 3, 1971; *Documents on Germany,* pp. 1135-37, with annexes, pp. 1137-43, including communications from the three Western governments to the Soviet government, pp. 1139, 1140-41.

142 UNITED STATES STATEMENT ON SIGNING QUADRIPARTITE AGREEMENT OF 1971

The Western objective was to bring about practical improvements in and around the city without altering the status of Berlin or diminishing our rights and responsibilities there. That objective has been achieved. Among other things--according to the agreement--traffic between Berlin and West Germany by persons and goods on road, rail, and waterways will move unimpeded, West Berliners will be able again to visit East Berlin and East Germany, and ties between the Western sectors of Berlin and the Federal Republic will be maintained and developed.

To be meaningful this first step must be followed by a successful round of inner-German talks. This second step need not be long delayed, given good faith on the part of all the parties.

The third step, the signing of a four-power protocol, will bring the entire Berlin understanding into effect.

William P. Rogers, Secretary of State, September 3, 1971; *Documents on Germany*, pp 1149-50.

143 FINAL QUADRIPARTITE PROTOCOL ON BERLIN, 1972

1. The four Governments, by virtue of this Protocol, bring into force the Quadripartite Agreement, which, like this Protocol, does not affect quadripartite agreements or decisions previously concluded or reached.

2. The four Governments proceed on the basis that the following agreements and arrangements concluded between the competent German authorities (list of agreements and arrangements) shall enter into force simultaneously with the Quadripartite Agreement.

3. The Quadripartite Agreement and the consequent agreements and arrangements of the competent German authorities referred to in this Protocol settle important issues examined in the course of the negotiations and shall remain in force together.

4. In the event of a difficulty in the application of the Quadripartite Agreement or any of the above-mentioned agreements or arrangements which any of the four Governments consider serious, or in the event of non-implementation of any part thereof, that Government will have the right to draw the attention of the other three Governments to the provisions of the Quadripartite Agreement and this Protocol and to conduct the requisite quadripartite consultations in order to ensure the observance of the commitments undertaken and to bring the situation into conformity with the Quadripartite Agreement and this Protocol.

Signed at Berlin, June 3, 1972; *Documents on Germany*, pp. 1204-6. For the agreements and arrangements referred to in paragraph 2, see pp. 1167-68, 1169-79, 1191-1200 for the West and East German governments, and pp.

1182-85 for the West Berlin and East German governments. For Secretary of State Rogers' statement at the signing of the Final Quadripartite Protocol, see pp. 1206-7.

1 4 4   ESSENCE OF THE BERLIN AGREEMENT, 1972

Major substantive provisions of the Berlin Agreement may be summarized as follows:

Status of Berlin. The Agreement does not in any way change the legal status of Berlin or the rights and responsibilities of the Four Powers, which extend to the whole of the city. . . .

Access. In the Quadripartite Agreement the Soviet Union declares "that transit traffic by road, rail, and waterways through the territory of the German Democratic Republic of civilian persons and goods between the Western sectors of Berlin and the Federal Republic of Germany will be unimpeded; that such traffic will be facilitated so as to take place in the most simple and expeditious manner; and that it will receive preferential treatment.". . .

The Relationship Between the Western Sectors and the Federal Republic. The Quadripartite Agreement confirms that the Western sectors are not a constituent part of the Federal Republic and will not be governed by it. This is in accordance with the position taken by the three Western Powers at the time the Federal Republic was established. Within this framework, the ties between the Western sectors and the Federal Republic will be maintained and developed. . . .

Reflecting the continuation of the close ties between the Western sectors and the Federal Republic, the three powers have long relied on the Federal Republic to represent the Western sectors abroad and this practice has been uniformly accepted in non-Communist countries. In the Quadripartite Agreement the Soviet Union for the first time acknowledged the legitimacy of this practice, including the holding of international meetings in Berlin sponsored jointly by the Senat and the Federal Republic, and the inclusion of Berlin residents in teams and delegations of the Federal Republic. Where appropriate Berlin has been included in treaties concluded by the Federal Republic through a Berlin Clause. The Soviet Union also acknowledged that residents of the Western sectors could travel on Federal passports.

United States Foreign Policy, 1971: A Report of the Secretary of State, pp. 45-47. Also, see *United States Foreign Policy, 1972: A Report of the Secretary of State*, pp. 295-98.

1 4 5   UNITED STATES ASSESSMENT OF "SETTLEMENTS ARRANGEMENTS"

We see the Four-Power Agreement on Berlin of 1971 as the end of a perennial crisis that on at least three occasions brought the world to the brink of doom.

The agreements between the Federal Republic of Germany and the states of Eastern Europe and the related intra-German accords enable Central Europe and the world to breathe easier.

Gerald Ford, address, Helsinki Conference on Security and Cooperation in Europe, August 1, 1975; *Papers of Presidents: Ford,* 1975, II, 1076. For the text of the Helsinki Final Act, see *Documents on Germany,* pp. 1285-96, especially pp. 1287-90, and Chapter 29, Document 517.

SUBSEQUENT DEVELOPMENTS

146 ESTABLISHMENT OF DIPLOMATIC RELATIONS BETWEEN THE UNITED STATES AND THE GERMAN DEMOCRATIC REPUBLIC, 1974

The Governments of the United States of America and the German Democratic Republic, having conducted negotiations in a cordial atmosphere in Washington July 15-26, 1974, have agreed to establish diplomatic relations as of today in accordance with the Vienna Convention on Diplomatic Relations of April 18, 1961 and to base the conduct of these relations on the Charter of the United Nations. The two Governments will exchange diplomatic representatives with the rank of Ambassador Extraordinary and Plenipotentiary.

The two delegations also exchanged views on the future development of relations between the two States. It was agreed that, pending the entry into force of a comprehensive consular agreement, their consular relations will be based in general on customary international law on consular relations. They also agreed to negotiate in the near future the settlement of claims and other financial matters outstanding between them.

Joint communique, United States and East Germany, September 4, 1974; *Documents on Germany,* p. 1273; also see pp. 1273-76. For documentation on such additional actions as the admission of West and East Germany into the United Nations, see pp. 1212, 1234-56; the establishment by West Germany of diplomatic relations with Czechoslovakia, Bulgaria, Hungary, and East Germany, see pp. 1260-62, 1264-66; the "recognition" by the United States of East Germany, see pp. 1273-76; and the consummation of treaties by West Germany with East Germany (December 21, 1972), see pp. 1215-30, and by East Germany with the Soviet Union (October 7, 1975), see pp. 1297-1301. These represented elements of normalizing and stabilizing relations in Europe. Also see Document 50.

147 UNITED STATES POSITION ON BERLIN, ITS WALL, AND FREEDOM

Freedom has many difficulties and democracy is not perfect, but we have never had to put a wall up to keep our people in, to prevent them from leaving us. . . . While the wall is the most obvious and vivid demonstration of the failures of the Communist system, for all the world to see, we take no satisfaction in it . . . an offense not only against history, but an offense against humanity. . . .

All free men, wherever they may live, are citizens of Berlin, and, therefore, as a free man, I take pride in the words "Ich bin ein Berliner."

John Kennedy, remarks, upon signing "Golden Book" in West Berlin, June 26, 1963; *Documents on Germany,* pp. 849-50.

*   *   *

Berlin may look lonely on the map. But it is a vital part of the world that believes in the capacity of man to govern himself with responsibility and to shape his destiny in dignity. . . .

. . . Sometimes you must feel that you are very much alone. But always remember we are with you and always remember that people who are free and who want to be free around the world are with you. In the sense that the people of Berlin stand for freedom and peace, all the people of the world are truly Berliners.

Richard Nixon, remarks, West Berlin, February 27, 1969, *Documents on Germany,* pp. 1032-34. Addressing the West Berlin House of Representatives, May 21, 1975, Henry Kissinger declared, "Berlin will continue to be a symbol of freedom. We shall stand with you, and we are confident that history will record Berlin not merely as a great city but as a great principle in the story of man's struggle for freedom"; see pp. 1278-81.

*   *   *

The Bible says a city that is set on a hill cannot be hidden. What has been true of my own land for 3 1/2 centuries is equally true here in Berlin. As a city of human freedom, human hope, and human rights, Berlin is a light to the whole world; a city on a hill--it cannot be hidden; the eyes of all people are upon you. Was immer sei, Berlin bleibt frei. (No matter what happens, Berlin will stay free).

Jimmy Carter, remarks, wreathing ceremony at the Airlift Memorial in Berlin, July 15, 1978; *Documents on Germany,* pp. 1314-16.

*   *   *

You are a constant inspiration for us all--for our hopes and ideals, and for the human qualities of courage, endurance, and faith that are the one secret weapon of the West no totalitarian regime can ever match. As long as Berlin exists, there can be no doubt about the hope for democracy.

Yes, the hated wall still stands. But taller and stronger than that bleak barrier dividing East from West, free from oppressed, stands the character of the Berliners themselves. You have endured in your splendid city on the Spree, and my return visit has convinced me, in the words of the beloved old song that "Berlin bleibt doch Berlin"--Berlin is still Berlin.

Ronald Reagan, remarks to the people of Berlin, June 11, 1982; *Documents on Germany*, pp. 1352-56. Also see Department of State, statement on the twentieth anniversary of "the ugly East German Wall," issued as press release, August 12, 1981, pp. 1337-38; statement of President Reagan on twentieth anniversary of the wall, August 13, 1981, pp. 1338-39; address by Secretary of State Alexander Haig, Berlin Press Association, September 13, 1981, in which he called Berlin "one of the cornerstones of American engagement in Europe" and "an island of liberty," pp. 1342-43; President Reagan, remarks concerning the defense of West Berlin, White House interview, June 1, 1982, p. 1344; statement on the importance of Berlin, Washington, May 23, 1984, pp. 1375-77; and his message to the people of Berlin, January 1, 1985, pp. 1383-84. Also see President Reagan's statement on the twenty-fifth anniversary of the Berlin Wall, August 13, 1986, in *Papers of Presidents: Reagan*, 1986, II, 1090-91.

*   *   *

Nowhere is the division between East and West seen more clearly than in Berlin. There the brutal wall cuts neighbor from neighbor, brother from brother. And that wall stands as a monument to the failure of communism. It must come down.

Now, glasnost may be a Russian word, but "openness" is a Western concept. West Berlin has always enjoyed the openness of a free city, and our proposal would make all Berlin a center of commerce between East and West, a place of cooperation, not a point of confrontation. . . .

This, then, is my second proposal: Bring *glasnost* to East Berlin.

George Bush, address on East-West relations, Mainz, June 1, 1989; 25 *Weekly Compilation of Presidential Documents* (June 5, 1989): 814.

1 4 8 BEGINNING OF DENOUEMENT--OPENING THE WALL

. . . I've just been briefed by the Secretary of State and my national security adviser on the latest news coming out of Germany. . . . I welcome the decision by the East German leadership to open the borders to those wishing to emigrate or travel. And this, if it's implemented fully, certainly conforms with the Helsinki Final Act, which the GDR [German Democratic Republic] signed. And if the GDR goes forward now, this wall built in '61 will have very little relevance.

*   *   *

. . . I was moved . . . by the pictures of Berliners from East and West, standing atop the Wall with chisels and hammers, celebrating the opening of the most vivid symbol of the Iron Curtain. And then today . . . I read a report where 18 new border crossings would be made in the Wall in the near future. . . . Twenty-eight years after the desperate days of 1961, when tanks faced off at Check Point Charlie and that terrible barrier was built--now the East German Government has responded to the wishes of its people.

*   *   *

. . . Uplifted by the hope that Europe will one day be whole and free, last week we watched in awe as Berliners danced atop the Berlin Wall. And we watched as a deep wound, a wound that has scarred the heart of Europe for 28 years, began to heal. And we saw it in the joyful faces of families reunited, in the smiles and laughter and tears of people greeting freedom like a long-lost friend, and in the wonder of children getting their first taste of freedom.

Last summer, I remember predicting that the Wall would come down. I expected it during my lifetime; I hoped for it during these next 3 years. But you know, quite apart from predictions, change has a way of sweeping through like a fast-moving train. And no one and no government should stand in its way.

*   *   *

. . . But now the world has a new image, reflecting a new reality: that of Germans, East and West, pulling each other to the top of the Wall, a human bridge between nations; entire peoples all across Eastern Europe bravely taking to the streets, demanding liberty, talking democracy. This is not the end of the book of history, but it is a joyful end to one of history's saddest chapters. . . .

. . . For 40 years, we have not wavered in our commitment to freedom. . . .

For so many of these 40 years, the test of Western resolve, the contest between the free and the unfree, has been symbolized by an island of hope behind the Iron Curtain: Berlin. In the 1940's, West Berlin remained free because Harry Truman said: Hands off. In the 1950's, Ike backed America's words with muscle. In the 1960's, West Berliners took heart, when John F. Kennedy said: "I am a Berliner." In the 1970's, Presidents Nixon, Ford, and Carter stood with Berlin by standing with NATO. And in the 1980's, Ronald Reagan went to Berlin to say: "Tear down this wall." Now we are at the threshold of the 1990's. And as we begin the new decade, I am reaching out to President Gorbachev, asking him to work with me to bring down the last barriers to a new world of freedom. Let us move beyond containment and once and for all end Cold War.

George Bush, press conference, November 9, and statements, National Association of Realtors (Dallas, Texas), ceremony at White House, and Thanksgiving address to the nation, November 10-22, 1989; 25 *Weekly Compilation of Presidential Documents* (November 13-27, 1989), pp. 1712, 1716, 1757, 1820.

149   AMERICAN POLICY CONCERNING GERMAN REUNIFICATION PROCESS

On the question of German reunification, let me simply say that I think that our position on that should essentially embrace four principles. . . . First of all, that self-determination must be pursued without prejudice as to its outcome; that is, we really shouldn't endorse or exclude any particular vision of unity. Unity can mean a lot of things. It can mean a single federal state; it can mean a confederation; or it could mean something else.

If there is unification--the second principle, I think--if there is unification, it should occur in the context of Germany's continued alignment with NATO [North Atlantic Treaty Organization] and an increasingly integrated European Community; that is, there should be no trade of neutralism for unity, and there should be no dilution of the Federal Republic of Germany's liberal democratic character.

Third principle: In the interests of general European stability, I think I would prefer to see moves toward unification be peaceful, gradual, and part of a step-by-step process.

And lastly, with respect to the question of borders . . . I think we should reiterate our support for the principles of the Helsinki Final Act, recognizing the inviolability where I said, "We are of the view that we should seize the opportunity where we can and where it is to the mutual advantage of the United States and Soviet Union, seize the opportunity to engage." That would include political engagement. It would include military and arms control engagement. And it would certainly include economic engagement.

*   *   *

Let me just read the four points that represent the U.S. position on reunification. Self-determination must be pursued without prejudice to its outcome, and we should not at this time endorse any particular vision. Secondly, unification should occur in the context of Germany's continued commitment to NATO and an increasingly integrated European Community, and with due regard for the legal role and responsibilities of the allied powers. Third, in the interest of general European stability, moves toward unification must be peaceful, gradual, and part of a step-by-step basis. And lastly, on the question of borders, we should reiterate our support for the principles of the Helsinki Final Act.

So, I am not trying to accelerate that process. I don't think our allies are. . . . And so, I think it's better to let things move on their own and without the United States certainly setting some kind of deadline.

James A. Baker III, statement, Briefing Room, White House, November 29, 1989, and George Bush, comments, news conference, Brussels, December 4, 1989; 25 *Weekly Compilation of Presidential Documents* (December 4 and 11, 1989): 1842-43, 1892. For additional presidential commentary on reunification, see pp. 1827, 1877-78, 1888, 1934-35. Also see Chapter 22, on changing East-West relations, Documents 378-380.

The process of German reunification was complex, said from the outset to require "two plus four" negotiations--initially by the two Germanys, subject to parallel negotiations by the four original post-World War II occupying powers (the United States, Britain, France, and the Soviet Union) to protect their rights and interests, including long-range security interests in Europe, and perhaps eventually necessitating a mutually acceptable peace treaty.

* * * * * * * * * * * * * * * * *

Late in 1989 East Germany liberalized travel and emigration to West Germany, East German leaders were ousted from office, the Wall was opened and eventually dismantled, and the heads of the two Germanys met in Dresden to plan for reunification.

1990 ushered in a new era for Germany and East-West relations in Europe. Plans were developed and a schedule was devised for the unification of Germany and Berlin. The primary issues on this agenda included eliminating the Wall and other vestiges of division; formulating processes for economic, political, and social unification and reform; extending the federal Constitution (*Grundgesetz*), reviving the East German *Laender* (states) for admission into the federal union, and restructuring governmental institutions and political parties; deciding on the permanent capital of the united Germany; and determining the applicability of existing West and East German legislation and treaties.

To summarize developments, in May 1990, the two Germanys signed a treaty providing for economic union and a single currency (which went into effect on July 1), and the following month they passed a joint resolution guaranteeing Poland's western boundary. In August the East German parliament agreed to amalgamation by acceding to the jurisdiction of the Federal Republic under its *Grundgesetz*, and the two Germanys signed a political unification treaty which specified the terms of consolidation, named Berlin as the capital of the unified country, and provided for an all-German parliamentary election. This treaty was implemented on October 3, the general election was scheduled for December, and East Germany ceased to exist.

These were essentially German problems, requiring German negotiations and decisions. Other matters involved the interests of the United States and other powers, such as terminating the vestiges of post-World War II occupation rights; aligning the two (West and East Germany) plus four (France, the Soviet Union, the United Kingdom, and the United States) negotiation processes; formulating a World War II peace settlement with the united Germany; deciding on Germany's status in the North Atlantic Alliance, the European Economic Community, and other international organizations; reconfirming post-World War II German boundary changes (especially that with Poland); establishing restraints on unified Germany's conventional military forces (through the CSCE --Conference on Security and Cooperation in Europe) and maintaining prohibitions on German nuclear, biological, and chemical weapons (as embodied in Western European Union commitments); and reorienting the North Atlantic Treaty Organization into a broader-focussed alliance and defining its relations with the Warsaw Pact powers.

The Western European Union--an alliance of seven countries, which the United States supports although it is not a member--was created by the Brussels Pact of 1948, as amended by four protocols, signed October 23, 1954. Protocol III prohibits the Federal Republic of Germany from manufacturing in its territory any nuclear, biological, or chemical weapons. For the texts of the Brussels Treaty, the protocols, and commentary, including Senate consideration of them and other security and military affairs involving Germany, see *American Foreign Policy: Current Documents*, 1950-1955, I, 619-21, 633-34, 968-91, with Protocol III at pp. 979-84.

9

U-2 Incident and Aborted Paris Summit Conference, 1960

Considered in the light of the end purpose of espionage activities, which may be summarized as the acquisition of information which the state, against which the activities are directed, wishes to conceal from the knowledge of one or more foreign powers, there would appear to be no fundamental distinction between the various means which might be employed in securing such information.

Department of State
Response to Inquiry, 1960

The long-awaited second East-West four-power summit conference, scheduled to convene on May 16, 1960, in Paris, collapsed on May 17, even before it was formally begun--because Soviet Premier Nikita Khrushchev refused to meet with the three Western leaders unless President Eisenhower apologized personally for authorizing espionage flights over Soviet territory. The tortuous route to the summit and amelioration of the Cold War, begun at the Geneva four-power summit in July 1955, followed by Khrushchev's visit to the United States in September 1959, was to be capped by the Paris summit conference and Eisenhower's trip to Moscow scheduled for June 1960--during his last year as President.

The simple facts are that an unarmed U-2 high-altitude aircraft, piloted by Francis Gary Powers, engaged in photographic and electronic reconnaissance for the Central Intelligence Agency and flying from Turkey, via Pakistan, over the Soviet Union, to Norway, was shot down on May 1, 1960, by a rocket near Sverdlovsk, approximately 1,250 miles within Soviet territory. The United States had employed such overflights successfully for four years.

The incident was made the central subject of more than fifteen key Soviet and American statements and diplomatic exchanges between May 1 and 15. They reflect several developmental phases: the first was confined to the fallacious United States explanation of the flight; the second concerned Soviet revelations of the downing of the U-2 and capture of the pilot, and American rationalization of its actions; the third centered on President Eisenhower's personal assumption of responsibility for United States intelligence activities, including overflights; and the final phase involved Khrushchev's demands concerning such intelligence activities presented to the President at Paris, Eisenhower's rejection of Khrushchev's "ultimatum," and the scuttling of the summit conference as well as the withdrawal of the invitation for the President to visit the Soviet Union. Virtually the entire interchange constituted a public dialogue rather than an attempt to resolve the issue by "quiet diplomacy."

It takes little effort to catalogue the parade of blunders committed in handling this crisis. President Eisenhower found himself in the untenable position of having a series of United States explications proven to be falsehoods, of having the American government plead guilty before the bar of world opinion not only to spying but also to authorizing this particular unsuccessful U-2 mission, of reaping the consequences of the President's assumption of personal responsibility for the reconnaissance flights, and of seeing the summit conference aborted and the invitation for his trip to the Soviet Union summarily canceled.

The documents selected for this chapter include a comprehensive list of the major documents concerning both the U-2 incident and the collapse of the Paris conference (with sources) (Document 150); a chronology and discussion of day-by-day events from May 1 to 16 (Document 151); Khrushchev's preconditions for convening the summit conference (Document 152); Eisenhower's rejection of the Soviet "ultimatum" (Document 153); the tripartite Western powers communique concerning the collapse of the conference (Document 154); Khrushchev's post-summit condemnation of American reconnaissance overflights (Document 155); Eisenhower's post-summit address to the nation (Document 156); and the Senate Foreign Relations Committee's assessment of the misadventure (Document 157).

150 MAJOR DOCUMENTS--U-2 INCIDENT AND PARIS SUMMIT CONFERENCE, MAY 1960*

PRIOR TO SUMMIT CONFERENCE, MAY 1-15

National Aeronautics and Space Administration, statement on "apparent" downing of U-2 (on May 1), May 3--42 *Department of State Bulletin* (May 23, 1960): 817.

Khrushchev, address, preliminary report on United States aerial reconnaissance over Soviet Union, Supreme Soviet of U.S.S.R., May 5-- *Current Documents:* 409-12; *Senate Hearings:* 175-77.

Defense Department, news release on missing U-2, May 5--*Senate Hearings:* 178.

* *Current Documents* refers to *American Foreign Policy: Current Documents,* 1960, and *Senate Hearings* refers to Senate Committee on Foreign Relations, *Events Incident to the Summit Conference: Hearings,* May 27, June 1, 2, 1960 (Washington: Government Printing Office, 1960).

Department of State, news briefing, statement regarding alleged shooting down of U-2 over Soviet Union, May 5--*Current Documents:* 412-13; *Senate Hearings:* 178-79.

National Aeronautics and Space Administration, news release concerning upper atmosphere research, May 5--*Current Documents:* 413-14; *Senate Hearings:* 180-81.

U.S. note to Soviet Government requesting results of U.S.S.R. investigation of U-2 and fate of American pilot, May 6--*Senate Hearings:* 181.

Khrushchev, address on U-2 mission and fate of American pilot, Supreme Soviet of U.S.S.R., May 7--*Current Documents:* 415-17; *Senate Hearings:* 181-87.

Department of State, statement regarding United States program of U-2 flights for four years, May 7--*Current Documents:* 417-18; *Senate Hearings:* 187.

Khrushchev, speech warning nations with bases used by United States planes, May 9--*Senate Hearings:* 188-93.

Christian A. Herter, statement defending need for United States intelligence operations, May 9--*Current Documents:* 418-20; *Senate Hearings.* 193-94.

U.S. note to Soviet Government requesting permission to interview pilot of U-2, May 10--42 *Department of State Bulletin* (May 30, 1960):   852.

Soviet note to United States Government, condemning United States for "poisoning" relations before summit conference, May 10--42 *Department of State Bulletin* (May 30, 1960):   852-54; *Senate Hearings:* 195-98.

Eisenhower, statement, news conference, on need for intelligence operations, May 11--*Current Documents:* 423-25; *Senate Hearings:* 198-203.

Khrushchev, comments, informal news conference, on effect of U-2 incident on Paris summit conference, May 11--*Current Documents:* 420-23; *Senate Hearings:* 203-11.

U.S. note to Soviet Government, explaining that U-2 mission not intended to prejudice Paris summit conference, May 12--*Current Documents:* 425; *Senate Hearings:* 211-12.

George V. Allen, Director of U.S. Information Agency, statement, "ABC's College News Conference," May 15--*Senate Hearings:* 212-20.

PARIS SUMMIT CONFERENCE, MAY 16-17

Khrushchev, statement, at preliminary summit session, on Soviet conditions for holding summit conference, May 16--*Current Documents:* 426-28; *Senate Hearings:* 220-24.

Eisenhower, statement, at preliminary summit session, on suspension of aerial surveillance of Soviet Union, May 16--*Current Documents:* 428-29.

Eisenhower, statement, issued following preliminary summit session, rejecting Khrushchev "ultimatum," May 16--*Current Documents:* 429-30; *Senate Hearings:* 225-26.

James C. Hagerty, Andrew H. Berding, and Charles E. Bohlen, combined news briefing, May 16--*Senate Hearings:* 226-35.

James C. Hagerty, statement on conditions for United States participation in formal opening of summit conference, May 17--*Current Documents:* 430-31.

Tripartite Communique (United States, France, and United Kingdom) regarding aborting of Paris summit conference, May 17--*Current Documents:* 431; *Senate Hearings:* 235.

IMMEDIATE POST-SUMMIT CONFERENCE PERIOD, MAY 18-25

Khrushchev, prepared statement on U-2 and Paris summit conference, at news conference, May 18--*Senate Hearings:* 235-47.

Soviet memorandum, cabled to United Nations Security Council, condemning United States for "aggressive acts," May 19--*Current Documents:* 432.

North Atlantic Council, communique, endorsing Western Powers Tripartite Communique, May 19--*Current Documents:* 432; *Senate Hearings:* 247.

Eisenhower, remarks, on arrival at Andrews Field, May 20--*Senate Hearings:* 247-49.

Khrushchev, address, Soviet policy in view of collapse of Paris summit conference, delivered in East Berlin, May 20--*Current Documents:* 433-34.

Henry Cabot Lodge, statement, United Nations Security Council, May 23-- 42 *Department of State Bulletin* (June 13, 1960): 955-57. For additional documentation on United Nations Security Council consideration of Soviet complaint against the United States, and Security Council Resolution, see pp. 955-61.

Eisenhower, address to the nation on collapse of Paris summit conference and portent of the future, May 25--*Current Documents:* 434-41; *Senate Hearings:* 249-55.

ASSESSMENT AND COMMENTARY

Chalmers M. Roberts (Washington Post)--*Senate Hearings:* 163.

Christian A. Herter, May 27--*Senate Hearings:* 3-16.

Department of State, responses to questions raised by Senator Frank J. Lausche, at Senate Foreign Relations Committee hearings, May 22 and June 1-2--*Senate Hearings:* 255-60.

Senate Committee on Foreign Relations, *Events Relating to the Summit Conference: Report,* June 28, 1960, 86th Congress, 2d session, Report No. 1761 (Washington: Government Printing Office, 1960).

For a comprehensive compilation of more than 90 documents presaging the U-2 crisis and Paris summit conference, see Department of State, *Background of Heads of Government Conference--1960: Principal Documents, 1955-1959* (Washington: Government Printing Office, 1960). Also see *Current Documents,* 1960, pp. 409-77.

151 CHRONOLOGY OF EVENTS, MAY 1 TO 16, 1960

May 1--The U-2 flight of pilot Francis G. Powers took place on this date because of a clear weather forecast. That forecast also indicated that such good weather probably would not be repeated for some weeks; that is, until after the Summit Conference, then 2 weeks off . . . .

The day of Powers' flight, there was a second U-2 flight from Turkey. This was a meteorological flight outside the Soviet Union, the kind of flight the National Aeronautics and Space Administration unwittingly thought all U-2's were making. NASA was, of course, the "cover" for the clandestine flights over the Soviet Union. . . .

CIA officials contend that there was to be a cutoff of U-2 flights before the Summit, that the question was how much time constituted a margin of safety. Nevertheless, the Powers mission was permitted to take place two weeks before the Summit. In his speech on Wednesday the President implied he fully approved of that. . . .

There is no evidence, however, that the President was aware beforehand of this particular flight or that either the State Department or the CIA thought his specific approval necessary. He had delegated authority for the flights, once having approved the entire U-2 scheme following Soviet rejection of his "open skies" plan at the 1955 Geneva Summit conference.

May 1-4--During this period the CIA and the State Department knew that Powers was missing; they hoped he had crashed and that pilot and plane had left no tell-tale evidence. The initial confusion over the missing plane, as to whether it was Powers or the legitimate meteorological flight in Turkey the same day, was soon cleared up. There is no evidence that the Administration laid out any plan of how to handle the possible disclosures later made by Khrushchev. . . .

On May 3 it was announced from Istanbul, Turkey that a single-engine Air Force plane was missing near Lake Van, not far from the Soviet border. It was described as a high attitude research plane belonging to NASA. . . .

This was the standard sort of "cover" story for the missing U-2, issued in the hopes that it would suffice. It was not known here whether Powers' U-2 went down or why. . . .

May 5--Khrushchev announced to the Supreme Soviet in Moscow the bare details of the U-2 flight, deliberately (he said later) withholding information which would have let Washington know that Powers was alive and that much of his equipment had been captured intact. He set a trap into which the Eisenhower Administration fell.

In his Wednesday speech, Mr. Eisenhower contended that the "covering statement," as he called it, was imperative "to protect the pilot, his mission, and our intelligence processes at a time when the true facts were still undetermined.". . .

. . . It was on May 5 and 6 that the administration allowed itself to be entangled in a series of lies about the U-2.

When newsmen went to Press Secretary Hagerty for comment on Khrushchev's speech, Hagerty was careful to say only that the President did not know of the news story about the speech. . . .

State Department spokesman Lincoln White, . . . said that "it may be" that the plane Khrushchev referred to was the missing so-called NASA aircraft. It was also announced that the President had ordered an immediate inquiry into Khrushchev's accusation.

This semi-lie was aggravated by NASA's press chief, Walter T. Bonney. Unaware that NASA was being used as a "cover" for the spy flights, Bonney said at a press conference that the plane was on a wholly peaceful mission. . . . The Administration's story thus was that a peaceful flight outside Soviet borders might have by accident transgressed the Soviet-Turkish border.

There is no evidence that the President, . . . or anyone else in authority in the Administration, took charge of the whole affair and told NASA to say nothing.

May 6--In Moscow it was claimed the U-2 was shot down by a rocket on Khrushchev's personal order, but other details still were withheld. . . .

The State Department said it was asking the "full facts" in Moscow. White declared that "there was absolutely no--n-o--. . . deliberate attempt to violate the Soviet airspace." The lie thus was compounded. . . .

May 7--Khrushchev, in a second Moscow speech on the U-2, disclosed the pilot was alive and talking and that much of his equipment had been captured intact. . . .

American officials, who received the speech in the morning, Washington time, knew Khrushchev was using information that was genuine and that some of it could have come only from Powers himself.

Khrushchev quoted Hagerty as saying that "the President, in his opinion, knew nothing about the incident involving the American plane. I fully admit (said Khrushchev) that the President did not know that a plane was sent beyond the Soviet frontier and did not return."

The Khrushchev speech resulted in a series of all-day conferences. . . .

Out of this came a unanimous decision to tell the truth--but not all the truth. The dinner-hour State Department statement said that the flight referred to by Khrushchev "was probably undertaken by an unarmed civilian U-2 plane. . . ."

The flight was justified on the grounds of the need "to obtain information now concealed behind the Iron Curtain" to lessen the dangers of a surprise attack on the free world in general and the United States in particular.

On the critical issue of who was responsible for the flight, however, the statement lied. It said that "as a result of the inquiry ordered by the President it has been established that insofar as the authorities in Washington are concerned there was no authorization for any such flight as described by Mr. Khrushchev."

In making this statement, chiefly the decision of Secretary [of State Christian] Herter, those involved were guided by a number of considerations. They felt that Khrushchev had the evidence and therefore an admission was essential despite the earlier lies. But they were trapped in a dilemma on the issue of responsibility. They decided it was best to avoid admitting any responsibility by President Eisenhower even at the cost of accepting the resultant impression that Washington's control was so lax that American pilots around the world could go off on their own on a mission that might provoke a war.

During the State Department deliberations Allen Dulles made it clear that he, as head of CIA, was prepared to take full responsibility for the flight, that if the Administration wanted to pin the blame on him to avoid blaming the President, he would agree. But this idea was not accepted as being practical in view of Khrushchev's disclosures.

Herter read the draft statement on the phone to the President in Gettysburg. He approved it without changing a word.

In part, at least, Herter's decision to tell the lie that no one in Washington authorized the flight also was based in the slim hope that somehow Khrushchev would accept it. The Secretary and his aides had noted Khrushchev's acceptance of what he had taken as Hagerty's disclaimer of any Eisenhower responsibility.

May 8--. . . The same day Khrushchev sent notes to Britain and France about the forthcoming summit conference. In them he complained about the U-2 but gave no indication it would be used to wreck the conference as was to be the case.

By now Hagerty was alarmed at the implications of the admission statement, implications that the President did not know what was going on. He was insistent to Herter that this should somehow be eliminated. . . .

May 9--After another State Department conference, Herter put out a statement in his name saying that "penetration" by the U-2's of the Soviet Union had been going on for four years, that this had been done by presidential orders "since the beginning of his Administration" in order to gather intelligence. But Herter added that "specific missions of these unarmed civilian aircraft have not been subject to presidential authorization." This, at last, appeared to be the truth.

This was the statement which left the implication that such U-2 flights would be continued over the Soviet Union. But there is reason to believe that none of those involved at State Department was conscious of any such implication when they drafted the statement. They took the view, shared by the CIA, that the U-2 setup now was "a blown agent" to be discarded, that other intelligence gathering methods would continue, however.

Nonetheless the implication was there and neither State nor the White House did anything to correct it until the President himself told Khrushchev in Paris a full week later that "these flights were suspended after the recent incident and are not to be resumed."

The President said Wednesday he wanted no public announcement until he met Khrushchev in Paris. American officials also claimed the flight suspension was ordered the previous Thursday, May 12, which is at cross-purposes with the claim that no implication of further flights was contained in Herter's May 9 statement. . . .

May 10--The Soviet news agency, Tass, described Herter's statement as "a frank attempt to legalize and justify violation of the state frontiers of other nations for espionage purposes." A Soviet note to the United States avoided blaming President Eisenhower personally but, in referring to the May 7 statement by State, said it did "not correspond to reality." It charged that the U-2 flights "are carried on with the sanction of the Government of the United States of America."

May 11--At an exhibition in Moscow of the U-2 wreckage and equipment, Khrushchev said Herter's May 9 statement made him doubt "Our earlier conclusion" that the President himself did not know of the flights. He said he doubted the President would be welcome in Russia during his scheduled June visit there.

When asked whether the U-2 incident would come up at the Summit Conference, Khrushchev replied: "It is already the subject of worldwide discussion. Therefore I believe there is no need to put it on the discussion schedule at the Summit Conference."

The same day at his press conference here President Eisenhower took full responsibility for the U-2 flights, said nothing to counter the implication that they would continue, remarked that "no one wants another Pearl Harbor."

May 12-14--During this period Khrushchev went to Paris a day early, arriving on Saturday, May 14. Herter arrived on May 13 but there was no United States-Soviet contact. On the 13th the Soviet Union sent protest notes to Norway, Pakistan and Turkey warning against further use of their territory for such missions as those of the U-2 which Khrushchev had claimed took off from Pakistan with the expectation of landing in Norway.

On the 12th the United States sent a note to Moscow which said the United States had "fully stated its position" about the U-2 incident in the May 9 Herter statement.

By now President Eisenhower's responsibility for the U-2 flights, if not for the specific Powers mission, had been firmly established on the public record.

May 15--The President arrived in Paris just before Khrushchev's call on French President de Gaulle. The President considered two possible moves in this final day before the Summit Conference was to open: To ask for a bilateral meeting with Khrushchev and to announce publicly that no more flights would be made.

But the President decided against either step. He did so chiefly on the basis of de Gaulle's report of the hard stand taken by Khrushchev in their talk that morning. His aides told him they deduced from Khrushchev's words with de Gaulle that the Soviet leader had come to Paris bound by a prior Moscow decision by the ruling Presidium, that he therefore could not be swayed by either suggested Eisenhower move. . . .

May 16--At the only Paris confrontation between President Eisenhower and Khrushchev, the Soviet leader said the United States had "torpedoed" the conference. He demanded that the President apologize for the flights, call off further flights and punish those responsible for Powers' mission. These were the same demands of which he had informed de Gaulle the day before. He charged the President with making "treachery" the basis of his policy toward the Soviet Union.

To this the President responded by terming Khrushchev's demands an "ultimatum" which "would never be acceptable to the United States." He also told Khrushchev that U-2 flights had been suspended and would not be resumed. The two men parted in anger. The Summit had collapsed before it had begun.

Chalmers M. Roberts, in Senate Committee on Foreign Relations, *Events Incident to the Summit Conference: Hearings,* May 27, June 1, 2, 1960 (Washington: Government Printing Office, 1960), pp. 163-68.

152 KHRUSHCHEV STATEMENT AT PARIS SUMMIT CONFERENCE--CONDITIONS FOR MEETING WITH PRESIDENT EISENHOWER, MAY 16

Now, at a time when the leaders of the Governments of the four powers are arriving in Paris to take part in the conference, the question arises of how is it possible productively to negotiate and examine the questions confronting the conference when the United States Government and the President himself have not only failed to condemn this provocative act--the intrusion of the American military aircraft into the Soviet Union--but, on the contrary, have declared that such actions will continue to be state policy of the U.S.A. with regard to the Soviet Union. . . .

It is clear that the declaration of such a policy, which can be pursued only when states are in a state of war, dooms the summit conference to complete failure in advance. . . .

From all this it follows that for the success of the conference it is necessary that the Governments of all the powers represented at it pursue an overt and honest policy and solemnly declare that they will not undertake any actions against one another which amount to violation of the state sovereignty of the powers.

This means that if the United States Government is really ready to cooperate with the Governments of the other powers in the interests of maintaining peace and strengthening confidence between states it must, firstly, condemn the inadmissible provocative actions of the United States Air Force with regard to the Soviet Union and, secondly, refrain from continuing such actions and such a policy against the U.S.S.R. in the future.

It goes without saying that in this case the United States Government cannot fail to call to strict account those who are directly guilty of the deliberate violation by American aircraft of the state borders of the U.S.S.R.

Until this is done by the United States Government, the Soviet Government sees no possibility for productive negotiations with the United States Government at the summit conference. . . .

It stands to reason that if the United States Government were to declare that in the future the United States will not violate the state borders of the U.S.S.R. with its aircraft, that it deplores the provocative actions undertaken in the past and will punish those directly guilty of such actions, which would assure the Soviet Union equal conditions with other powers, I, as head of the Soviet Government, would be ready to participate in the conference and exert all efforts to contribute to its success.

American Foreign Policy: Current Documents, 1960, pp. 426-28; *Senate Hearings,* pp.   220-24.

153 EISENHOWER STATEMENT AT PARIS SUMMIT CONFERENCE--REJECTION OF SOVIET ULTIMATUM, MAY 16

In my statement of May 11 and in the statement of Secretary Herter of May 9 the position of the United States was made clear with respect to the distasteful necessity of espionage activities in a world where nations distrust each other's intentions. We pointed out that these activities had no aggressive intent but rather were to assure the safety of the United States and the free world against surprise attack by a power which boasts of its ability to devastate the United States and other countries by missiles armed with atomic warheads. . . .

There is in the Soviet statement an evident misapprehension on one key point. It alleges that the United States has, through official statements, threatened continued overflights. The importance of this alleged threat was emphasized and repeated by Mr. Khrushchev. The United States has made no such threat. . . .

In point of fact, these flights were suspended after the recent incident and are not to be resumed. Accordingly, this cannot be the issue.

I have come to Paris to seek agreements with the Soviet Union which would eliminate the necessity for all forms of espionage, including overflights. I see no reason to use this incident to disrupt the conference. . . .

We of the United States are here to consider in good faith the important problems before this Conference. We are prepared either to carry this point no further, or to undertake bilateral conversations between the United States and the U.S.S.R. while the main Conference proceeds.

My words were seconded and supported by my Western colleagues, who also urged Mr. Khrushchev to pursue the path of reason and common sense, and to forget propaganda. Such an attitude would have permitted the Conference to proceed. Mr. Khrushchev was left in no doubt by me that his ultimatum would never be acceptable to the United States.

Mr. Khrushchev brushed aside all arguments of reason, and not only insisted upon this ultimatum, but also that he was going to publish his statement in full at the time of his own choosing. It was thus made apparent that he was determined to wreck the Paris Conference.

In fact, the only conclusion that can be drawn from his behavior this morning was that he came all the way from Moscow to Paris with the sole intention of sabotaging this meeting on which so much of the hopes of the world have rested.

American Foreign Policy: Current Documents, 1960, pp. 429-30; *Senate Hearings,* pp. 225-26. For Eisenhower's statement of May 11, see *Current Documents,* pp. 423-25, and for Secretary Herter's statement of May 9, see pp. 418-20.

154 TRIPARTITE WESTERN POWERS COMMUNIQUE, PARIS SUMMIT CONFERENCE, MAY 17

The President of the United States, the President of the French Republic and the Prime Minister of the United Kingdom take note of the fact that because of the attitude adopted by the Chairman of the Council of Ministers of the Soviet Union it has not been possible to begin, at the Summit Conference, the examination of the problems which it had been agreed would be discussed between the four Chiefs of State or Government.

They regret that these discussions, so important for world peace, could not take place. For their part, they remain unshaken in their conviction that all outstanding international questions should be settled not by the use or threat of force but by peaceful means through negotiation. They themselves remain ready to take part in such negotiations at any suitable time in the future.

American Foreign Policy: Current Documents, 1960, p. 431; *Senate Hearings,* p. 235.

155 KHRUSHCHEV CONDEMNATION OF AMERICAN OVERFLIGHTS--NEWS CONFERENCE, MAY 18

. . . I have in view the aggressive flights of American warplanes over the Soviet Union, undertaken on the eve of the summit conference, and the public declaration of the United States Government that such flights are its official policy.

Now attempts are being made to lay the blame on us for the alleged refusal of the Soviet Union to take part in the meeting and for making some sort of ultimatums to the United States.

But we have declared and we declare that we are ready to take part in the conference if the United States Government makes up publicly for the insult inflicted upon our country by its aggressive action. However, we are still not sure that the espionage flights, which are undertaken by the United States, will not be repeated.

Nikita Khrushchev, news conference, Paris, May 18; Senate Hearings, pp. 235-36.

156 EISENHOWER RADIO AND TELEVISION ADDRESS TO NATION ON COLLAPSE OF THE SUMMIT CONFERENCE, MAY 25

Moreover, as President, charged by the Constitution with the conduct of America's foreign relations, and as Commander in Chief, charged with the direction of the operations and activities of our Armed Forces and their supporting services, I take full responsibility for approving all the various programs undertaken by our government to secure and evaluate military intelligence.

It was in the prosecution of one of these intelligence programs that the widely publicized U-2 incident occurred.

Aerial photography has been one of many methods we have used to keep ourselves and the free world abreast of major Soviet military developments. The usefulness of this work has been well established through four years of effort. The Soviets were well aware of it. Chairman Khrushchev has stated that he became aware of these flights several years ago. . . .

Now, two questions have been raised about this particular flight; first, as to its timing, considering the imminence of the Summit meeting; second, our initial statements when we learned the flight had failed.

As to the timing, the question was really whether to halt the program and thus forego the gathering of important information that was essential and that was likely to be unavailable at a later date. The decision was that the program should not be halted.

The plain truth is this: when a nation needs intelligence activity, there is no time when vigilance can be relaxed. . . .

Next, as to our government's initial statement about the flight, this was issued to protect the pilot, his mission, and our intelligence processes, at a time when the true facts were still undetermined.

Our first information about the failure of this mission did not disclose whether the pilot was still alive, was trying to escape, was avoiding interrogation, or whether both plane and pilot had been destroyed. Protection of our intelligence system and the pilot, and concealment of the plane's mission, seemed imperative. It must be remembered that over a long period, these flights had given us information of the greatest importance to the Nation's security. In fact, their success has been nothing short of remarkable.

For these reasons, what is known in intelligence circles as a "covering statement" was issued. It was issued on assumptions that were later proved incorrect. Consequently, when later the status of the pilot was definitely established, and there was no further possibility of avoiding exposure of the project, the factual details were set forth.

I then made two facts clear to the public: first, our program of aerial reconnaissance had been undertaken with my approval; second, this government is compelled to keep abreast, by one means or another, of military activities of the Soviets, just as their government has for years engaged in espionage activities in our country and throughout the world. Our necessity to proceed with such activities was also asserted by our Secretary of State who, however, had been careful--as was I--not to say that these particular flights would be continued.

In fact, before leaving Washington, I had directed that these U-2 flights be stopped.   Clearly their usefulness was impaired.   Moreover, continuing this particular activity in these new circumstances could not but complicate the relations of certain of our allies with the Soviets. And, of course, new techniques, other than aircraft, are constantly being developed.

Now I wanted no public announcement of this decision until I could personally disclose it at the Summit meeting in conjunction with certain proposals I had prepared for the conference.

At my first Paris meeting with Mr. Khrushchev, and before his tirade was made public, I informed him of this discontinuance and the character of the constructive proposals I planned to make. These contemplated the establishment of a system of aerial surveillance operated by the United Nations.

The day before the first scheduled meeting, Mr. Khrushchev had advised President de Gaulle and Prime Minister Macmillan that he would make certain demands upon the United States as a precondition for beginning a Summit conference.

Although the United States was the only power against which he expressed his displeasure, he did not communicate this information to me. I was, of course, informed by our allies.

At the four power meeting on Monday morning, he demanded of the United States four things: First, condemnation of U-2 flights as a method of espionage; second, assurance that they would not be continued; third, a public apology on behalf of the United States; and fourth, punishment of all those who had any responsibility respecting this particular mission.

I replied by advising the Soviet leader that I had, during the previous week, stopped these flights and that they would not be resumed. I offered also to discuss the matter with him in personal meetings, while the regular business of the Summit might proceed. Obviously, I would not respond to his extreme demands. He knew, of course, by holding to those demands the Soviet Union was scuttling the Summit Conference.

In torpedoing the conference, Mr. Khrushchev claimed that he acted as the result of his own high moral indignation over alleged American acts of aggression. As I said earlier, he had known of these flights for a long time. It is apparent that the Soviets had decided even before the Soviet delegation left Moscow that my trip to the Soviet Union should be canceled and that nothing constructive from their viewpoint would come out of the Summit Conference. . . .

On our side, at Paris, we demonstrated once again America's willingness, and that of her allies, always to go to the extra mile in behalf of peace. Once again, Soviet intransigence reminded us all of the unpredictability of despotic rule, and the need for those who work for freedom to stand together in determination and in strength.

American Foreign Policy: Current Documents, 1960, pp. 434-41; *Senate Hearings*, pp. 249-55.

157 ASSESSMENT OF U-2 INCIDENT AND COLLAPSE OF PARIS SUMMIT CONFERENCE

Let it be said at the outset that the gathering of intelligence with respect to foreign activities potentially inimical to our security and that of the free world is fully justified by precedent as well as by vital necessity. Since time immemorial, nations have found it necessary to engage in such activities of both the overt and covert variety. . . . What the [Senate] committee is concerned with respecting the U-2 program is not the propriety, desirability, or necessity of such operations, but the lessons, if any, which can be drawn from the failure of the May 1 flight and related events.

On the basis of classified testimony which cannot be discussed, the committee has no reason to believe that technical preparations for the flight were faulty or that the pilot was unreliable in any respect. . . .

There remains the question of the wisdom of sending the flight at all. The committee was told that the flight was after information of well above average importance, but it was not told what this information was. The committee cannot, therefore, come to any conclusion as to whether the importance of the information sought justified the risks which were taken.

The U-2 overflights had a record of almost 4 years of unbroken success. The Soviet Union had been aware of these overflights during this time and had been unable to do anything about them. Against this background, there would seem to be no reason to assume that the May 1 flight would be any different from any of its predecessors.

In approving the flight, little, if any, consideration was given to the proximity of May 1 to the date of the summit conference. An argument was made to the committee that if diplomatic considerations were taken into account, there would always be some reason for canceling or postponing a flight. . . . The question here is whether the information sought by the May 1 flight was of sufficient importance to justify the hazards to which the summit conference would be subjected by failure of the flight. . . .

In view of the combination of circumstances surrounding the loss of the U-2 on May 1, the next question which arises concerns the reaction of the U.S. Government. The first conclusion on this point is that the cover story, which had been designed in advance to meet such a contingency, was inadequate for the circumstances which in fact existed. The cover story which was used in regard to the U-2 for the period May 1 to 7 might have served its purpose if the plane had come down under different circumstances. Until May 7, it was not known in Washington where the U-2 had come down. . . .

At any rate, the cover story was quite obviously outflanked on May 7, and the responsible officials felt that it was then necessary to discuss the matter in greater detail. It was admitted that the U-2 was on a reconnaissance mission, but it was denied that the mission had been authorized from Washington.

In Khrushchev's early statements about the plane, he had implied doubt that President Eisenhower knew about the operation. The May 7 statement of the State Department seemed to confirm this doubt. However, on May 9 Secretary Herter said the program of flights--though not specific flights as such--had been authorized by the President. The substance of this statement was repeated by the President himself May 11.

The course which the President took is unprecedented in intelligence operations, so far as the committee knows or the record discloses. It is known that Allen Dulles was prepared to accept the full responsibility himself, which is the traditional procedure under the circumstances.

The committee feels that perhaps too much emphasis may have been placed on justification of the flights. If justification was to be made, it would have been enough simply to say we were seeking intelligence vital to our own security.

It seems clear that the situation was complicated by the unnecessarily elaborate NASA statement of May 5 and the categorical statements of the State Department Press Officer on May 5 and 6.

In regard to this whole period of May 1 to 9, the record is full of references to coordination among the various agencies of the government --and yet at crucial points, the coordination broke down, . . . Further, there are few, if any, references in the record to direction, and this seems to the committee to be what was most lacking in this period. There were many interagency meetings to coordinate activities, but there was apparently no one official or agency to direct activities. If this direction is not to come from the White House, then it ought to be made clear, by the White House, that it is to come from the State Department. . . .

Given the situation which existed by the time the President arrived in Paris, it is difficult to see what course of action he could have reasonably followed other than the one he took.

The crucial questions in regard to the events in Paris are whether the U-2 incident was the reason or the excuse for Khrushchev's behavior and whether his behavior would have been significantly different if the U-2 incident had been handled differently.

In the view of Secretary Herter, the U-2 incident was a contributing factor to Khrushchev's attitude toward the summit. The Secretary also said that prior to May 1 there had been no indications that Khrushchev intended to wreck the summit. Without doubt, the U-2 was a contributing factor to the breakup of the summit conference, so far as the

Soviet Government was concerned. The other factors which the Secretary mentioned as contributing to the Soviet attitude in Paris all existed prior to May 1. It can be accepted that they did play a part in Soviet policy formation, and still be reasonably concluded that they would not, in and of themselves, have led to the precipitate and violent action taken by the Soviet Government in Paris. The U-2 incident therefore was the immediate excuse seized upon for not proceeding with the conference.

Senate Committee on Foreign Relations, *Events Relating to the Summit Conference: Report*, June 28, 1960, 86th Congress, 2d Session, Report No. 1761 (Washington: Government Printing Office, 1960), pp. 22-26.

10

Formosa Strait Crisis and Vietnam War

Wo aro noithor "warmongorc" nor "appoacorc," noithor "hard" nor "soft." We are Americans determined to defend the frontiers of freedom by an honorable peace if peace is possible but by arms if arms are used against us.

John Kennedy
Address, University of Washington, November 16, 1961

This chapter deals with two major crises in United States relations with Communist forces in the Far East--the Formosa crisis, 1954-1955 and 1958, in which the United States countered the attacks of the People's Republic of China on Quemoy and Matsu Islands in the Formosa Strait, and the Vietnam War. These events need to be related to such matters as the War Powers Resolution (Chapter 5), the Johnson and Nixon Doctrines (Chapter 7), the Gulf of Tonkin Resolution (Chapter 7, Documents 115-116, and Chapter 13, Documents 211-214), the Southeast Asia Collective Defense Treaty (Chapter 18, Document 308), the Cold War (Chapter 22), and relations with the People's Republic of China (Chapter 28).

FORMOSA STRAIT CRISIS, 1954-1955 AND 1958

In 1949 Communist forces overran mainland China and in September established the People's Republic of China. In December the Nationalist forces of Chiang Kai-shek retreated to Formosa (Taiwan) and continued as the Republic of China. Communist China's relations with the United States were envenomed following the Korean War, and to implement its containment policy in eastern Asia, the United States signed mutual defense treaties with both Korea (1953) and Nationalist China (1954) (see Documents 312-313). Both the Communist and Nationalist governments viewed mainland China and Formosa as constituting a single nation. Aggressive Communist actions, consisting of bombardment and other military measures, were launched against the offshore islands--Quemoy and Matsu--in the Formosa Strait, as a prelude to forceful reannexation of Formosa. These attacks began in 1949 and peaked in 1954-1955 and 1958, producing a menacing crisis with the United States.

The documents contained in this section include a general background statement concerning these attacks (Document 158), President Eisenhower's request for, and the enactment of, a congressional resolution in 1955 empowering the President to use American armed forces to defend Formosa (Documents 159-160), and a description of developments and United States policy to counter Communist China's aggression and apply the Formosa Resolution in 1958 (Documents 161-162). In the 1970's, as relations with the People's Republic were normalized (see Documents 492-495), the Mutual Security Treaty with the Republic of China was terminated (see Chapter 5, Document 79, and Chapter 18, bilateral Far East alliances, commentary).

158 FORMOSA ISSUE--BACKGROUND

Close to the mainland of China, in the vicinity of the city of Amoy and about 5 miles away, is the Quemoy group of islands. . . . About 120 miles up the mainland coast and in the vicinity of Foochow and about 10 miles off the coast is the Matsu group of islands. Both these groups are in the control of the Republic of China. I shall hereafter speak of them as the offshore islands. . . .

Since the middle of the 17th century and up to 1895 Formosa was a part of the Chinese Empire. In 1895 under the Treaty of Shimonoseki China ceded Formosa to Japan. In the Cairo conference in November 1943 the United States, United Kingdom, and China declared it was their "purpose" that Manchuria, Formosa, and the Pescadores "shall be restored to the Republic of China." Thereafter in August 1945 in the Potsdam conference the United States, United Kingdom, and China declared that "the terms of the Cairo Declaration shall be carried out." This Potsdam declaration was subsequently adhered to by the U.S.S.R. On September 2, 1945, the Japanese Government, in the instrument of surrender, accepted the provisions of the declaration. . . . Since September 1945 the United States and the other Allied Powers have accepted the exercise of Chinese authority over the island. . . .

In the meantime, since the end of the war in 1945, the Chinese Communists had been engaged in open hostilities with the Republic of China. On October 1, 1949, they proclaimed the establishment of the People's Republic of China. . . . The Chinese Communists made their first attempt to capture Quemoy in late 1949 and were repulsed with heavy losses by the Chinese Government on October 27. The Chinese Government had been transferring its offices to Taipei, Formosa, and early in December 1949 Taipei became the provisional capital of the Republic of China.

On January 5, 1950, President Truman, in a public statement regarding Formosa, declared that the United States had no predatory designs on Formosa or on any other Chinese territory, did not seek any special privileges therein, and would not pursue a course which would lead to involvement in the civil conflict in China. However, when the Communists attacked the Republic of Korea on June 25, 1950, President Truman issued a public statement noting that the Communists had made clear their intent to use armed invasion and war for purposes of conquest and that defied the Security Council of the United Nations. He thereupon ordered the Seventh Fleet "to prevent any attacks on Formosa" and as a corollary called upon the Chinese Government to cease all operations against the mainland. In addition he stated that "The determination of the future status of Formosa must await the restoration of security in the Pacific, a peace settlement with Japan, or consideration by the United Nations.". . .

In July of 1954, at the time when the Geneva Accords were being negotiated to end hostilities in Indochina, the Chinese Communist regime launched a massive propaganda campaign for the "liberation of Taiwan." On September 3 the Chinese Communists began a heavy bombardment of the island of Quemoy, and military attacks spread to coastal islands including the Tachen Islands to the north. Against this background the United States-Republic of China Mutual Defense Treaty was signed on December 2, 1954. The territorial coverage of the treaty in respect of China was limited to Formosa. The treaty was accompanied by an exchange of notes of December 10 by which the United States and the Republic of China undertook not to use force from the Formosa area or the offshore islands except by joint agreement or in self-defense. It might be pointed out that these defensive arrangements merely formalized and did not in any way extend the United States undertaking for the defense of Formosa going back to June 1950.

Assistant Legal Advisor, Department of State, address, Federal Bar Association, Washington, November 20, 1958; *American Foreign Policy: Current Documents,* 1958, pp. 1189-91. For President Truman's policy to defend Formosa, June 27, 1950, see *Papers of Presidents: Truman,* 1950, pp. 769-70.

159 PRESIDENT EISENHOWER'S REQUEST FOR CONGRESSIONAL RESOLUTION AUTHORIZING USE OF AMERICAN ARMED FORCES

The most important objective of our nation's foreign policy is to safeguard the security of the United States by establishing and preserving a just and honorable peace. In the Western Pacific, a situation is developing in the Formosa Straits, that seriously imperils the peace and our security.

Since the end of Japanese hostilities in 1945, Formosa and the Pescadores have been in the friendly hands of our loyal ally, the Republic of China. We have recognized that it was important that these islands should remain in friendly hands. In unfriendly hands, Formosa and the Pescadores would seriously dislocate the existing, even if unstable, balance of moral, economic and military forces upon which the peace of the Pacific depends. . . .

Meanwhile Communist China has pursued a series of provocative political and military actions, establishing a pattern of aggressive purpose. That purpose, they proclaim, is the conquest of Formosa.

In September 1954 the Chinese Communists opened up heavy artillery fire upon Quemoy island, one of the natural approaches to Formosa, which had for several years been under the uncontested control of the Republic of China. Then came air attacks of mounting intensity against other free China islands. . . .

The Chinese Communists themselves assert that these attacks are a prelude to the conquest of Formosa. For example, after the fall of Ichiang, the Peiping Radio said that it showed a "determined will to fight for the liberation of Taiwan (Formosa). Our people will use all their strength to fulfill that task.". . .

Meanwhile, the situation has become sufficiently critical to impel me, without awaiting action by the United Nations, to ask the Congress to participate now, by specific resolution, in measures designed to improve the prospects for peace. These measures would contemplate the use of the armed forces of the United States if necessary to assure the security of Formosa and the Pescadores. . . .

I do not suggest that the United States enlarge its defensive obligations beyond Formosa and the Pescadores. . . . But unhappily, the danger of armed attack directed against that area compels us to take into account closely related localities and actions which, under current conditions, might determine the failure or the success of such an attack. The authority that may be accorded by the Congress would be used only in situations which are recognizable as parts of, or definite preliminaries to, an attack against the main positions of Formosa and the Pescadores.

Authority for some of the actions which might be required would be inherent in the authority of the Commander-in-Chief. Until Congress can act I would not hesitate, so far as my Constitutional powers extend, to take whatever emergency action might be forced upon us in order to protect the rights and security of the United States.

However, a suitable Congressional resolution would clearly and publicly establish the authority of the President as Commander-in-Chief to employ the armed forces of this nation promptly and effectively for the purposes indicated if in his judgment it became necessary. It would make clear the unified and serious intentions of our Government, our Congress and our people. Thus it will reduce the possibility that the Chinese Communists, misjudging our firm purpose and national unity, might be disposed to challenge the position of the United States, and precipitate a major crisis which even they would neither anticipate nor desire.

Dwight Eisenhower, Special Message to Congress, January 24, 1955; *Papers of Presidents: Eisenhower*, 1955, pp. 207-11.

1 6 0   FORMOSA RESOLUTION, 1955

Resolved . . . That the President of the United States be and he hereby is authorized to employ the Armed Forces of the United States as he deems necessary for the specific purpose of securing and protecting Formosa and the Pescadores against armed attack, this authority to include the securing and protection of such related positions and territories of that area now in friendly hands and the taking of such other measures as he judges to be required or appropriate in assuring the defense of Formosa and the Pescadores.

This resolution shall expire when the President shall determine that the peace and security of the area is reasonably assured by international conditions created by action of the United Nations or otherwise, and shall so report to the Congress.

Joint Resolution of Congress, 159, 84th Congress, 1st Session, authorizing employment of American armed forces to protect Formosa (Taiwan), January 29, 1955; *American Foreign Policy: Basic Documents,* 1950-1955, pp. 2486-87. This antedated the War Powers Resolution (1973), see Document 80.

1 6 1   SITUATION IN FORMOSA STRAIT, 1958

. . . The President has authorized me to make the following statement.

1. Neither Taiwan (Formosa) nor the islands of Quemoy and Matsu have ever been under the authority of the Chinese Communists. Since the end of the Second World War, a period of over 13 years, they have continuously been under the authority of Free China, that is, the Republic of China.

2. The United States is bound by treaty to help to defend Taiwan (Formosa) from armed attack and the President is authorized by Joint Resolution of the Congress to employ the armed forces of the United States for the securing and protecting of related positions such as Quemoy and Matsu.

3. Any attempt on the part of the Chinese Communists now to seize these positions or any of them would be a crude violation of the principles upon which world order is based, namely, that no country should use armed force to seize new territory.

4. The Chinese Communists have, for about 2 weeks, been subjecting Quemoy to heavy artillery bombardment and, by artillery fire and use of small naval craft, they have been harassing the regular supply of the civilian and military population of the Quemoys, which totals some 125 thousand persons. The official Peiping radio repeatedly announces the purpose of these military operations to be to take by armed force Taiwan (Formosa), as well as Quemoy and Matsu. In virtually every Peiping broadcast Taiwan (Formosa) and the offshore islands are linked as the objective of what is called the "Chinese People's Liberation Army."

5. Despite, however, what the Chinese Communists say, and so far have done, it is not yet certain that their purpose is in fact to make an all-out effort to conquer by force Taiwan (Formosa) and the offshore islands. Neither is it apparent that such efforts as are being made, or may be made, cannot be contained by the courageous, and purely defensive, efforts of the forces of the Republic of China, with such substantial logistical support as the United States is providing.

6. The Joint Resolution of Congress, above referred to, includes a finding to the effect that "the secure possession by friendly governments of the Western Pacific Island chain, of which Formosa is a part, is essential to the vital interests of the United States and all friendly nations in and bordering upon the Pacific Ocean." It further authorizes the President to employ the Armed Forces of the United States for the protection not only of Formosa but for "the securing and protection of such related positions and territories of that area now in friendly hands and the taking of such other measures as he judges to be required or appropriate in insuring the defense of Formosa." In view of the situation outlined in the preceding paragraph, the President has not yet made any finding under that Resolution that the employment of the Armed Forces of the United States is required or appropriate in insuring the defense of Formosa. The President would not, however, hesitate to make such a finding if he judged that the circumstances made this necessary to accomplish the purposes of the Joint Resolution. . . . Military dispositions have been made by the United States so that a Presidential determination, if made, would be followed by action both timely and effective. . . .

John Foster Dulles, authorized statement following review with President Eisenhower, September 4, 1958; *Papers of Presidents: Eisenhower,* 1958, pp. 687-89.

162 OPPOSING AGGRESSION TO PRESERVE UNITED STATES INTERESTS AND PEACE

So the world is again faced with the problem of armed aggression. Powerful dictatorships are attacking an exposed, but free, area.

What should we do?

Shall we take the position that, submitting to threat, it is better to surrender pieces of free territory in the hope that this will satisfy the appetite of the aggressor and we shall have peace? . . .

Let us suppose that the Chinese Communists conquer Quemoy. Would that be the end of the story? . . . History teaches that when powerful despots can gain something through aggression, they try, by the same methods, to gain more and more and more.

Also, we have more to guide us than the teachings of history. We have the statements, the boastings, of the Chinese Communists them-selves. They frankly say that their present military effort is part of a program to conquer Formosa.

It is as certain as can be that the shooting which the Chinese Communists started on August 23rd had as its purpose not just the taking of the island of Quemoy. It is part of what is indeed an ambitious plan of armed conquest.

This plan would liquidate all of the free world positions in the Western Pacific area and bring them under captive governments which would be hostile to the United States and the free world. Thus the Chinese and Russian Communists would come to dominate at least the Western half of the now friendly Pacific Ocean.

So, aggression by ruthless despots again imposes a clear danger to the United States and to the free world. . . .

If the Chinese Communists have decided to risk a war, it is not because Quemoy itself is so valuable to them. They have been getting along without Quemoy ever since they seized the China mainland nine years ago.

If they have now decided to risk a war, it can only be because they, and their Soviet allies, have decided to find out whether threatening war is a policy from which they can make big gains. . . .

I do not believe that the United States can be either lured or frightened into appeasement. I believe that in taking the position of opposing aggression by force, I am taking the only position which is consistent with the vital interests of the United States, and, indeed with the peace of the world. . . .

There is not going to be any appeasement.

I believe that there is not going to be any war.

But there must be sober realization by the American people that our legitimate purposes are again being tested by those who threaten peace and freedom everywhere.

Dwight Eisenhower, radio and television report to the American people, September 11, 1958; *Papers of Presidents: Eisenhower,* 1958, pp. 695-700. The President also described the attacks on Quemoy and Matsu. Also see President Eisenhower's letter to Senator Theodore Francis Green, October 5, 1958, pp. 723-25, in which the President responds to four issues raised by Senator Green, including his interpretation of the Formosa Resolution and his views on popular support of the use of armed force. In 1962 President Kennedy reaffirmed the American commitment on the Formosa Strait issue; see *Papers of Presidents: Kennedy,* 1962, pp. 509-10, 512.

VIETNAM WAR

This "unwanted" war, inherited by the United States from France--which President Nixon inherited from President Johnson, who inherited it from President Kennedy, who, in turn, inherited it from President Eisenhower--was an "undeclared" war that raged for more than three decades and turned out to be the longest war in American history. The United States became incrementally and increasingly involved economically and militarily, eventually the will to win on the battlefield failed to maintain popular support, and hostilities were formally terminated for the United States by a cease-fire agreement in 1973 that was expected to end the war but which, violated by North Vietnam, ultimately gave it the victory it failed to achieve militarily.

By way of background, Vietnam, part of the French protectorate of Indochina established in the 1880's, was occupied by the Japanese during World War II, and continued in a state of war until 1976. Following the Japanese surrender in 1945, Communist Viet Minh guerillas, under the leadership of Ho Chi Minh, waged war against the French for eight years and defeated them at Diem Bien Phu in 1954. At the multipartite Geneva Conference of 1954, an armistice was concluded and Vietnam was divided along the 17th parallel, with the northern territory established as the Democratic Republic of Vietnam and the southern segment becoming the Republic of Vietnam. The Geneva accords also provided for reunification following free elections to be held in 1956-- which never materialized. For a comprehensive compendium of diplomatic documents and commentary on the Geneva Conference, see *Foreign Relations of the United States, 1952-1954:   XIII, Indochina* (2 Parts, 1982) and *XVI, Geneva Conference* (1981). The latter includes draft proposals and the texts of the Geneva Accords, with annexes.

The Vietnam War (or Second Indochina War) began in 1957 when Communist-led rebels (Vietcong) mounted attacks against the government of the Republic of Vietnam. In the meantime, American involvement commenced in the mid-1950's, during the Eisenhower administration, with annually increasing financial assistance, a small military advisory group (MAAG), and, most important, pledges to preserve South Vietnam's freedom and independence. Incrementally, the United States became embroiled in a major war which intensified during the Kennedy, Johnson, and Nixon administrations. The United States frequently reiterated and expanded its commitments to assist South Vietnam, extended its containment policy to Asia, augmented its economic and military assistance programs, and increased its military contribution, converting it from a passive into an active role and expanding American military forces from 16,000 (1963) to more than half a million during the Johnson administration.

The documents selected for this section are restricted largely to four categories: expressions of United States commitment, general purposes, negotiations to end the hostilities and produce a political settlement, and the agreement signed to end the war. So far as primary American goals and objectives are concerned, these ranged from economic and military aid to providing training missions, major war, and military victory; from halting Communist aggression and the use of force to preserving the territorial integrity and independence of South Vietnam; and from Vietnamization and the Nixon Doctrine to United States military and diplomatic withdrawal with honor and winning the war by winning the peace. American documents contain hundreds of expressions of its objectives, including such matters as preserving South Vietnam's freedom, self-determination, and national integrity; maintaining South Vietnam's national security, stability, and law and order; averting foreign territorial aggrandizement; reestablishing peace through negotiated settlement; and providing an opportunity for South Vietnam to shape its own future. These are overlayed by insistence on preserving United States national interests and security in the Far East and the moral determination to fulfill American commitments to free peoples throughout the world.

Specifically, the documents that follow deal with: early American commitments to support South Vietnam (Documents 163-164); subsequent reiteration of commitments (Document 165); the congressional resolution that empowered the President to employ American forces to repel armed attack, prevent further aggression in Vietnam, and assist allies under the Southeast Asia Collective Defense Treaty (Document 166) (for the Manila Pact, see Document 308); a statement on the legality of United States participation in the defense of South Vietnam (Document 167); selected statements concerning the primary goals and objectives of the United States (Document 168); attempts to negotiate an acceptable settlement (Document 169); expressions of the desire to end the war permanently and with justice and honor (Document 170); a summary description of negotiations producing the final peace settlement (Document 171); the cease-fire agreement of 1973 (Document 172); and a brief post-mortem on achieving America's primary goal (Document 173). Scores of additional documents deal with United States commitments, purposes, negotiations, and the final settlement. For subsequent developments, see the brief commentary appended to Document 172.

Of related importance are the Johnson Doctrine and the Tonkin Gulf Resolution of 1954 (see Documents 115-116, 211-214) and the Nixon Doctrine (see Documents 118-121). For more comprehensive documentation, in addition to the relevant volumes of the *Foreign Relations of the United States,* see such compilations as *American Foreign Relations: Basic Documents,* 1950-1955 (pp. 750-87), the annual *Current Documents* volumes, the *Papers of Presidents* (Eisenhower to Nixon), and Department of Defense, *United States-Vietnam Relations, 1945-1967,* 12 vols. (1971). For the final cease-fire and peace settlement, also see *Digest of United States Practice in International Law,* 1973, pp. 177-78, 188-89, 471-84, and *Historic Documents,* 1973, pp. 115-67, 331-36, 447-51.

163 AGREEMENT TO COOPERATE WITH SOUTH VIETNAM, 1957

. . . President Eisenhower assured President Ngo Dinh Diem of the willingness of the United States to continue to offer effective assistance within the constitutional processes of the United States to meet these objectives.

President Eisenhower and President Ngo Dinh Diem looked forward to an end of the unhappy division of the Vietnamese people and confirmed the determination of the two Governments to work together to seek suitable means to bring about the peaceful unification of Vietnam in freedom in accordance with the purposes and principles of the United Nations Charter. . . .

. . . President Eisenhower and President Ngo Dinh Diem expressed concern over continuing Communist subversion capabilities in this area and elsewhere. In particular, they agreed that the continued military buildup of the Chinese Communists, their refusal to renounce the use of force, and their unwillingness to subscribe to standards of conduct of civilized nations constitute a continuing threat to the safety of all free nations in Asia. To counter this threat, President Ngo Dinh Diem indicated his strong desire and his efforts to seek closer cooperation with the free countries of Asia.

Noting that the Republic of Viet-Nam is covered by Article IV of the Southeast Asia Collective Defense Treaty, President Eisenhower and President Ngo Dinh Diem agreed that aggression or subversion threatening the political independence of the Republic of Viet-Nam would be considered as endangering peace and stability. . . . Finally, President Eisenhower and President Ngo Dinh Diem expressed the desire and determination of the two Governments to cooperate closely together for freedom and independence in the world.

Dwight Eisenhower, joint statement with President of Vietnam, May 11, 1957; *American Foreign Policy: Current Documents,* 1957, pp. 1215-16. For documentation on initial American foreign aid to South Vietnam, see communique on United States-French conversations, September 29, 1954, in *American Foreign Policy: Basic Documents,* 1950-1955, pp. 2400-1, and Department of State statement on direct aid, p. 2403.

1 6 4   UNITED STATES NATIONAL INTERESTS DEMAND SUPPORT OF VIETNAM'S FREEDOM

Unassisted, Viet-Nam cannot at this time produce and support the military formations essential to it or, equally important, the morale-- the hope, the confidence, the pride--necessary to meet the dual threat of aggression from without and subversion within its borders.

Still another fact! Strategically south Viet-Nam's capture by the Communists would bring their power several hundred miles into a hitherto free region. The remaining countries in Southeast Asia would be menaced by a great flanking movement. . . . The loss of south Viet-Nam would set in motion a crumbling process that could, as it progressed, have grave consequences for us and for freedom. . . .

We reach the inescapable conclusion that our own national interests demand some help from us in sustaining in Viet-Nam the morale, the economic progress, and the military strength necessary to its continued existence in freedom.

Dwight Eisenhower, address, Gettysburg College, Gettysburg, Pennsylvania, April 4, 1959; *American Foreign Policy: Current Documents,* 1959, p. 1256.

1 6 5   UNITED STATES COMMITMENTS TO THE REPUBLIC OF VIETNAM

. . . We have been deeply disturbed by the assault on your country. Our indignation has mounted as the deliberate savagery of the Communist program of assassination, kidnapping and wanton violence became clear.
. . .

At that time, the United States, although not a party to the [Geneva] Accords, declared that it "would view any renewal of the aggression in violation of the agreements with grave concern and as seriously threatening international peace and security." We continue to maintain that view.

In accordance with that declaration, and in response to your request, we are prepared to help the Republic of Viet-Nam to protect its people and to preserve its independence.

John Kennedy, message to the President of the Republic of Vietnam, December 15, 1961; *American Foreign Policy: Current Documents*, 1961, pp. 1056-57.

*   *   *

As you know, the United States for more than a decade has been assisting the government, the people of Viet-Nam, to maintain their independence. Way back in December 23, 1950, we signed a military assistance agreement with France and with Indochina, which at that time included Viet-Nam, Laos, and Cambodia. We also signed in December of 1951 an agreement directly with Viet-Nam.

Now, in 1954, the Geneva agreements were signed, and, while we did not sign those agreements, nevertheless, Under Secretary [of State] Bedell Smith stated that he would view any renewal of the aggression in Viet-Nam in violation of the aforesaid agreements with grave concern and as seriously threatening international peace and security. And, at the time that the SEATO Pact was signed in 1954, September 8, though Viet-Nam was not a signatory, it was a protocol state, and therefore this pact, . . . under article 4 stated that the United States recognized that aggression by means of armed attack against Viet-Nam would threaten our own peace and security. So, since that time, the United States has been assisting the Government of Viet-Nam to maintain its independence. . . .

As you know, during the last two years that war has increased. . . . The attack on the government by the Communist forces, with assistance from the north, became of greater and greater concern to the Government of Viet-Nam and the Government of the United States. . . . The President of Viet-Nam asked us for additional assistance. We issued, as you remember, a white paper which detailed the support which the Viet Minh in the north were giving to this Communist insurgent movement, and we have increased our assistance there. And we are supplying logistic assistance, transportation assistance, training, and we have a number of Americans who are taking part in that effort. . . .

. . . So that there's a long history of our effort to prevent Viet-Nam from falling under control of the Communists. That is what we are now attempting to do, and as the war has increased in scope, our assistance has increased as a result of the requests of the government [of Viet-Nam].

John Kennedy, remarks, news conference, February 14, 1962; *American Foreign Policy: Current Documents*, 1962, pp. 1099-1100.

*   *   *

We are there because we have a promise to keep. Since 1954 every American President has offered support to the people of South Viet-Nam. We have helped to build, and we have helped to defend. Thus, over many years, we have made a national pledge to help South Viet-Nam defend its independence.

And I intend to keep that promise.

To dishonor that pledge, to abandon this small and brave nation to its enemies, and to the terror that must follow, would be an unforgivable wrong.

We are also there to strengthen world order. Around the globe, from Berlin to Thailand, are people whose well-being rests in part on the belief that they can count on us if they are attacked. To leave Viet-Nam to its fate would shake the confidence of all these people in the value of an American commitment and in the value of America's word. The result would be increased unrest and instability, and even wider war.

We are also there because there are great stakes in the balance. Let no one think for a moment that retreat from Viet-Nam would bring an end to conflict. The battle would be renewed in one country and then another. The central lesson of our time is that the appetite of aggression is never satisfied. To withdraw from the battlefield means only to prepare for the next.

Lyndon Johnson, address, Johns Hopkins University, April 7, 1965; *American Foreign Policy: Current Documents*, 1965, pp. 848-49.

*   *   *

Against that background, let me discuss first, what we have rejected, and second, what we are prepared to accept.

We have ruled out attempting to impose a purely military solution on the battlefield.

We have also ruled out either a one-sided withdrawal from Vietnam, or the acceptance in Paris of terms that would amount to a disguised American defeat.

When we assumed the burden of helping defend South Vietnam, millions of South Vietnamese men, women, and children placed their trust in us. To abandon them now would risk a massacre that would shock and dismay everyone in the world who values human life.

Abandoning the South Vietnamese people, however, would jeopardize more than lives in South Vietnam. It would threaten our long-term hopes for peace in the world. A great nation cannot renege on its pledges. A great nation must be worthy of trust. . . .

In determining what choices would be acceptable, we have to understand our essential objective in Vietnam: What we want is very little, but very fundamental. We seek the opportunity for the South Vietnamese people to determine their own political future without outside interference.

Richard Nixon, Address to the Nation, May 14, 1969; *Papers of Presidents: Nixon,* 1969, p. 370. Also see his seven principles to achieve this objective, p. 371.

166 CONGRESSIONAL RESOLUTION EMPOWERING THE PRESIDENT TO USE AMERICAN FORCES IN SOUTHEAST ASIA, 1964

Resolved . . . That the Congress approves and supports the determination of the President, as Commander in Chief, to take all necessary measures to repel any armed attack against the forces of the United States and to prevent further aggression.

Sec. 2. The United States regards as vital to its national interest and to world peace the maintenance of international peace and security in southeast Asia. Consonant with the Constitution of the United States and the Charter of the United Nations and in accordance with its obligations under the Southeast Asia Collective Defense Treaty, the United States is, therefore, prepared, as the President determines, to take all necessary steps, including the use of armed force, to assist any member or protocol state of the Southeast Asia Collective Defense Treaty requesting assistance in defense of its freedom.

Sec. 3.   This resolution shall expire when the President shall determine that the peace and security of the area is reasonably assured by international conditions created by action of the United Nations or otherwise, except that it may be terminated earlier by concurrent resolution of the Congress.

Congress, Joint Resolution to Promote the Maintenance of International Peace and Security in Southeast Asia, Public Law 88-408; *American Foreign Policy: Current Documents,* 1964, pp. 991-92. For President Johnson's remarks on signing this resolution, see *Papers of Presidents: Johnson,* 1963-1964, II, 946-47. Also see War Powers Resolution (Document 80) and Tonkin Gulf Resolution (Document 116).

167   LEGALITY OF UNITED STATES PARTICIPATION IN DEFENSE OF SOUTH VIETNAM

South Viet-Nam is being subjected to armed attack by Communist North Viet-Nam, through the infiltration of armed personnel, military equipment, and regular combat units. International law recognizes the right of individual and collective self-defense against armed attack. South Viet-Nam, and the United States upon the request of South Viet-Nam, are engaged in such collective defense of the South. Their actions are in conformity with international law and with the Charter of the United Nations. The fact that South Viet-Nam has been precluded by Soviet veto from becoming a member of the United Nations and the fact that South Viet-Nam is a zone of a temporarily divided state in no way diminish the right of collective defense of South Viet-Nam.

The United States has commitments to assist South Viet-Nam in defending itself against Communist aggression from the North. The United States gave undertakings to this effect at the conclusion of the Geneva conference in 1954. Later that year the United States undertook an international obligation in the SEATO treaty to defend South Viet-Nam against Communist armed aggression. And during the past decade the United States has given additional assurances to the South Vietnamese Government.

The Geneva accords of 1954 provided for a cease-fire and re-groupment of contending forces, a division of Viet-Nam into two zones, and a prohibition on the use of either zone for the resumption of hostilities or to "further an aggressive policy." From the beginning, North Viet-Nam violated the Geneva accords through a systematic effort to gain control of South Viet-Nam by force. In the light of these progressive North Vietnamese violations, the introduction into South Viet-Nam beginning in late 1961 of substantial United States military equipment and personnel, to assist in the defense of the South, was fully justified; substantial breach of an international agreement by one side permits the other side to suspend performance of corresponding obligations under the agreement. South Viet-Nam was justified in refusing to implement the provisions of the Geneva accords calling for reunification through free elections throughout Viet-Nam since the Communist regime in North Viet-Nam created conditions in the North that made free elections entirely impossible.

The President of the United States has full authority to commit United States forces in the collective defense of South Viet-Nam. This authority stems from the constitutional powers of the President. However, it is not necessary to rely on the Constitution alone as the source of the President's authority, since the SEATO treaty--advised and consented to by the Senate and forming part of the law of the land--sets forth a United States commitment to defend South Viet-Nam against armed attack, and since the Congress--in the joint resolution of August 10, 1964, and in authorization and appropriations acts for support of the U.S. military effort in Viet-Nam--has given its approval and support to the President's actions. United States actions in Viet-Nam, taken by the President and approved by the Congress, do not require any declaration of war, as shown by a long line of precedents for the use of United States armed forces abroad in the absence of any congressional declaration of war.

Legal Adviser, Department of State, memorandum submitted to Senate Foreign Relations Committee, March 8, 1966; *American Foreign Policy: Current Documents,* 1966, pp. 794-95. Also see commentary on "para-war" and other legal matters in Marjorie M. Whiteman, *Digest of International Law,* X, 23-27, 37-38. On the matter of Congress declaring war, see comments of President Johnson, news conference, August 18, 1967, in *American Foreign Policy: Current Documents,* 1967, pp. 959-61.

168   UNITED STATES PRIMARY GOALS AND OBJECTIVES IN VIETNAM

Your letter underlines what our own information has convincingly shown--that the campaign of force and terror now being waged against your people and your Government is supported and directed from the out- side by the authorities at Hanoi. They have thus violated the provisions of the Geneva Accords designed to ensure peace in Viet-Nam and to which they bound themselves in 1954. . . .

The United States, like the Republic of Viet-Nam, remains devoted to the cause of peace and our primary purpose is to help your people main- tain their independence.

John Kennedy, message to the President of the Republic of Vietnam, December 15, 1961; *Papers of Presidents: Kennedy,* 1961, p. 801. Also see Document 173, in which President Nixon, following the signing of the peace settlement in 1973, claimed that our primary goal was to prevent the imposition by force of a Communist government in South Vietnam.

*   *   *

. . . What helps to win the war, we support; what interferes with the war effort, we oppose. I have already made it clear that any action by either government which may handicap the winning of war is inconsistent with our policy or our objectives. . . .

But we have a very simple policy in that area, . . . we want the war to be won, the Communists to be contained, and the Americans to go home. That is our policy. . . . But we are not there to see a war lost, and we will follow the policy which I have indicated today of advancing those causes and issues which help win the war.

John Kennedy, comment, news conference, September 12, 1963; *Papers of Presidents: Kennedy,* 1963, p. 673. Note emphasis on winning the Vietnam War.

*   *   *

1. The security of South Viet-Nam is a major interest of the United States as of other free nations. We will adhere to our policy of working with the people and Government of South Viet-Nam to deny this country to communism and to suppress the externally stimulated and supported in- surgency of the Viet Cong as promptly as possible. Effective performance in this undertaking is the central objective of our policy in South Viet- Nam. . . .

5. It remains the policy of the United States, in South Viet-Nam as in other parts of the world, to support the efforts of the people of that country to defeat aggression and to build a peaceful and free society.

White House statement, October 2, 1963; *Papers of Presidents: Kennedy,* 1963, pp. 759-60.

*   *   *

Why should three Presidents and the elected representatives of our people have chosen to defend this Asian nation more than 10,000 miles from American shores?

We cherish freedom--yes.   We cherish self-determination for all people--yes.   We abhor the political murder of any state by another, and the bodily murder of any people by gangsters of whatever ideology.   And for 27 years--since the days of lend-lease--we have sought to strengthen free people against domination by aggressive foreign powers.

But the key to all that we have done is really our own security.   At times of crisis--before asking Americans to fight and die to resist aggression in a foreign land--every American President has finally had to answer this question:

Is the aggression a threat--not only to the immediate victim--but to the United States of America and to the peace and security of the entire world of which we in America are a very vital part? . . .

Those who tell us now that we should abandon our commitment-- that securing South Vietnam from armed domination is not worth the price we are paying--must also answer this question.   And the test they must meet is this: What would be the consequences of letting aggression against South Vietnam succeed?

Lyndon Johnson, address, National Legislative Conference, San Antonio, Texas, September 29, 1967; *Papers of Presidents: Johnson*, 1967, II, 876-77. This was a major address on the United States in Vietnam. In it President Johnson quotes Presidents Eisenhower and Kennedy as well as foreign leaders concerning the strategic importance of Vietnam, the significance to the world of the American commitment, internal South Vietnamese politics and developments, the desire for peace, and attempts to promote negotiations for a settlement.

*   *   *

Our presence in Vietnam is in keeping with a foreign policy which has guided this Nation for more than 20 years.   Four Presidents, 11 Congresses, and the most thoughtful men of our generation have endorsed that policy from the ground up.

For two decades, we have made it clear that we will use American strength to block aggression when our security is threatened, and when-- as in Vietnam--the victims of aggression ask for our help and are prepared to struggle for their own independence and for their own freedom. . . .

Our purpose is not to breed violence, but to build peace.

Lyndon Johnson, remarks, Foreign Policy Conference for Business Executives, Washington, December 4, 1967; *Papers of Presidents: Johnson*, 1967, p. 1095.

*   *   *

But the heart of our involvement in South Vietnam--under three different Presidents, three separate administrations--has always been America's own security.

And the larger purpose of our involvement has always been to help the nations of Southeast Asia become independent and stand alone, self-sustaining, as members of a great world community--at peace with themselves, and at peace with all others.

Lyndon Johnson, Address to the Nation on steps to limit the war in Vietnam, March 31, 1968; *Papers of Presidents: Johnson,* 1968, p. 474. He also summarized his attempts to negotiate a settlement, pp. 469-70 and 473. In this address he also announced his decision not to seek reelection to the presidency.

169 ATTEMPTS TO NEGOTIATE A LASTING SETTLEMENT

Many nations are deeply desirous of an end to this conflict as quickly as possible. Few are specific as to the manner in which this end can be brought about or the shape it is likely to take. . . .

Negotiations at this time, moreover, if they do come about, and if they are accompanied by a cease-fire and standfast, would serve to stabilize a situation in which the majority of the population remains under nominal government control but in which dominance of the countryside rests largely in the hands of the Vietcong. What might eventually materialize through negotiations from this situation cannot be foreseen at this time with any degree of certainty.

That is not . . . a very satisfactory prospect. What needs also to be borne in mind, however, is that the visible alternative at this time and under present terms of reference is the indefinite expansion and intensification of the war which will require the continuous introduction of additional U.S. forces. The end of that course cannot be foreseen, either, and there are no grounds for optimism that the end is likely to be reached within the confines of South Vietnam or within the very near future.

In short, such choices as may be open are not simple choices. They are difficult and painful choices and they are beset with many imponderables. The situation, as it now appears, offers only the very slim prospect of a just settlement by negotiations or the alternative prospect of a continuance of the conflict in the direction of a general war on the Asian mainland.

Mike Mansfield, Senate Majority Leader, report to Chairman of Senate Foreign Relations Committee, January 3, 1966; *American Foreign Policy: Current Documents,* 1966, p. 740. For earlier commentary on United States willingness to negotiate with adversaries, see President Kennedy's address, University of Washington, November 16, 1961; *Papers of Presidents: Kennedy,* 1961, pp. 724-28.

*   *   *

We are very agreeable and rather anxious to meet, as I have said over the past months, anywhere, any time that Hanoi is willing to come to a conference table. . . .

We will be glad to meet anyone more than halfway, insofar as talking instead of fighting is concerned. . . .

We will be very glad to do more than our part in meeting Hanoi halfway in any possible cease-fire, or truce, or peace conference negotiations. . . .

You just can't have a one-sided peace conference, or a one-sided cessation of hostilities, or ask our own boys not to defend themselves, or to tie their hands behind them, unless the other side is willing to reciprocate.

Lyndon Johnson, comment, news conference, December 31, 1966; *American Foreign Policy: Current Documents*, 1966, p. 893. President Johnson frequently proclaimed that he would go anywhere, any time in the cause of peace.

*   *   *

There is no need to delay the talks that could bring an end to this long and this bloody war.

Tonight, I renew the offer I made last August--to stop the bombardment of North Vietnam. We ask that talks begin promptly, that they be serious talks on the substance of peace. We assume that during those talks Hanoi will not take advantage of our restraint.

We are prepared to move immediately toward peace through negotiations. . . .

Now, as in the past, the United States is ready to send its representatives to any forum, at any time, to discuss the means of bringing this ugly war to an end. . . .

I call upon President Ho Chi Minh to respond positively, and favorably, to this new step toward peace.

But if peace does not come now through negotiations, it will come when Hanoi understands that our common resolve is unshakable, and our common strength is invincible.

Lyndon Johnson, Address to the Nation, March 31, 1968; *Papers of Presidents: Johnson,* 1968, I, 469-70.

*   *   *

First, I propose that all armed forces throughout Indochina cease firing their weapons and remain in the positions they now hold. This would be a "cease-fire-in-place." It would not in itself be an end to the conflict, but it would accomplish one goal all of us have been working toward: an end to the killing. . . .

This cease-fire proposal is put forth without preconditions. The general principles that should apply are these:

A cease-fire must be effectively supervised by international observers, as well as by the parties themselves. Without effective supervision a cease-fire runs the constant risk of breaking down. . . .

A cease-fire should not be the means by which either side builds up its strength by an increase in outside combat forces in any of the nations of Indochina.

And a cease-fire should cause all kinds of warfare to stop. This covers the full range of actions that have typified this war, including bombing and acts of terror.

A cease-fire should encompass not only the fighting in Vietnam but in all of Indochina. Conflicts in this region are closely related. The United States has never sought to widen the war. What we do seek is to widen the peace.

Finally, a cease-fire should be part of a general move to end the war in Indochina. . . .

A second point of the new initiative for peace is this:

I propose an Indochina Peace Conference. At the Paris talks today, we are talking about Vietnam. But North Vietnamese troops are not only infiltrating, crossing borders, and establishing bases in South Vietnam-- they are carrying on their aggression in Laos and Cambodia as well.

An international conference is needed to deal with the conflict in all three states of Indochina. The war in Indochina has been proved to be of one piece; it cannot be cured by treating only one of its areas of outbreak. . . .

The third part of our peace initiative has to do with the United States forces in South Vietnam. . . .

We are ready now to negotiate an agreed timetable for complete withdrawals as part of an overall settlement. We are prepared to withdraw all our forces as part of a settlement based on the principles I spelled out previously and the proposals I am making tonight.

Fourth, I ask the other side to join us in a search for a political settlement that truly meets the aspirations of all South Vietnamese.

Three principles govern our approach:

-- We seek a political solution that reflects the will of the South Vietnamese people.

-- A fair political solution should reflect the existing relationship of political forces in South Vietnam.

-- And we will abide by the outcome of the political process agreed upon. . . .

Finally, I propose the immediate and unconditional release of all prisoners of war held by both sides. . . .

I propose that all prisoners of war, without exception, without condition, be released now to return to the place of their choice.

Richard Nixon, negotiation proposals in Address to the Nation on new initiative for peace, October 7, 1970; *Papers of Presidents: Nixon,* 1970, pp. 825-27. Also see his earlier commentary in his Address to the Nation, November 3, 1969; *Papers of Presidents: Nixon,* 1969, p. 903, in which he discusses the situation in Vietnam when he was inaugurated, his peace proposals, and the need to break the deadlock with the North Vietnamese in the Paris negotiations.

*   *   *

Here is what over 3 years of public and private negotiations with Hanoi has come down to: The United States, with the full concurrence of our South Vietnamese allies, has offered the maximum of what any

President of the United States could offer.

We have offered a deescalation of the fighting. We have offered a cease-fire with a deadline for withdrawal of all American forces. We have offered new elections which would be internationally supervised with the Communists participating both in the supervisory body and in the elections themselves.

President [Nguyen Van] Thieu has offered to resign one month before the elections. We have offered an exchange of prisoners of war in a ratio of 10 North Vietnamese prisoners for every one American prisoner that they release. And North Vietnam has met each of these offers with insolence and insult. They have flatly and arrogantly refused to negotiate an end to the war and bring peace. Their answer to every peace offer we have made has been to escalate the war. . . .

We now have a clear, hard choice among three courses of action: Immediate withdrawal of all American forces, continued attempts at negotiation, or decisive military action to end the war. . . .

The second course of action is to keep on trying to negotiate a settlement. Now this is the course we have preferred from the beginning and we shall continue to pursue it. We want to negotiate, but we have made every reasonable offer and tried every possible path for ending this war at the conference table.

The problem is . . . it takes two to negotiate and now, as throughout the past 4 years, the North Vietnamese arrogantly refuse to negotiate anything but an imposition, an ultimatum that the United States impose a Communist regime on 17 million people in South Vietnam who do not want a Communist government.

It is plain then that what appears to be a choice among three courses of action for the United States is really no choice at all.

Richard Nixon, Address to the Nation, May 8, 1972; *Papers of Presidents: Nixon,* 1972, pp. 583-84.

170   ENDING THE WAR--PERMANENTLY AND WITH JUSTICE AND HONOR

. . . I know that some believe that I should have ended the war immediately after the inauguration by simply ordering our forces home from Vietnam.

This would have been the easy thing to do. It might have been a popular thing to do. But I would have betrayed my solemn responsibility as President of the United States if I had done so.

I want to end this war. The American people want to end this war. The people of South Vietnam want to end this war. But we want to end it permanently so that the younger brothers of our soldiers in Vietnam will not have to fight in the future in another Vietnam someplace else in the world.

Richard Nixon, Address to the Nation, May 14, 1969; *Papers of Presidents: Nixon,* 1969, p. 369. On occasion President Nixon also referred to achieving a "stable" peace "that lasts."   Note comparison with President Kennedy's emphasis on winning the war; see Document 168, section 2.

*   *   *

A political settlement is the heart of the matter. That is what the fighting in Indochina has been about over the past 30 years. . . .

Let me briefly review for you the principles that govern our view of a just political settlement.

First, our overriding objective is a political solution that reflects the will of the South Vietnamese people and allows them to determine their future without outside interference. . . .

Second, a fair political solution should reflect the existing relationship of political forces within South Vietnam. We recognize the complexity of shaping machinery that would fairly apportion political power in South Vietnam. We are flexible; we have offered nothing on a take-it-or-leave-it basis.

And third, we will abide by the outcome of the political process agreed upon. President Thieu and I have repeatedly stated our willingness to accept the free decision of the South Vietnamese people. But we will not agree to the arrogant demand that the elected leaders of the Government of Vietnam be overthrown before real negotiations begin.

Richard Nixon, Address to the Nation, April 20, 1970; *Papers of Presidents: Nixon,* 1970, p. 375. President Nixon also referred to a "just peace" in other statements; for example, see his Address to the Nation, November 3, 1969, in *Papers of Presidents: Nixon,* 1969, p. 905. Note emphasis on a political settlement.

*   *   *

We are not trying to conquer North Vietnam or any other country in this world. We want no territory. We seek no bases. We have offered the most generous peace terms--peace with honor for both sides--with South Vietnam and North Vietnam each respecting the other's independence.

But we will not be defeated, and we will never surrender our friends to Communist aggression.

Richard Nixon, Address to the Nation, April 26, 1972; *Papers of Presidents: Nixon,* 1972, p. 553. In the later stages of negotiating a settlement, President Nixon preferred referring to peace "with honor."

171 CONSUMMATING THE PEACE SETTLEMENT, 1973

The Agreement which was signed in Paris on January 27, 1973, culminated four years of intensive negotiating effort. Throughout this process, our fundamental attitude was as I described it on November 2,

1972:

> "We are going to sign the agreement when the agreement is right, not one day before. And when the agreement is right, we are going to sign without one day's delay.". . .

Our preference was always to solve military questions alone. The best way to ensure that the South Vietnamese could determine their own political future was to leave political questions to them. We believed that we should not negotiate a political settlement for South Vietnam. . . .

Until the final stage the North Vietnamese and their allies insisted on a settlement that would effectively guarantee that the future of South Vietnam would be Communist. Public speculation and commentary to the contrary, they never agreed to separate military from political issues until the end of 1972. And when, in light of this position, we presented comprehensive proposals, including political elements, they never wavered from their basic goals.

However they packaged their proposals, the fundamental provisions were a fixed date for our total and unconditional withdrawal; the removal of the leadership of the Government of South Vietnam; and the installation of Communist rule disguised as a so-called coalition government.

This basic philosophic clash, not the failure to find precise formulas, delayed a settlement for four years. So long as the Communists insisted on their basic demands, we were faced at the conference table with one overriding issue. I addressed this question in last year's Report:

> "Will we collude with our enemies to overturn our friends?
> Will we impose a future on the Vietnamese people that the other side has been unable to gain militarily or politically?
> This we shall never do." . . .

In the end we emerged with a settlement that met our basic principles and gave the South Vietnamese people a chance to determine their own future. . . .

On October 8, 1972, the North Vietnamese presented a new plan in Paris accepting the basic principles of our position. It was the essential breakthrough toward a negotiated settlement. For the first time, Hanoi agreed, in effect, to separate military questions from the principal political issues. They spelled out specific solutions to the former while the latter were to follow later and were left basically up to the South Vietnamese. . . .

On January 23, 1973, Dr. [Henry] Kissinger returned to Paris for a final meeting. On that date the United States and North Vietnam, with the concurrence of their allies, initialled the agreement. . . .

In Paris, on January 27, 1973 . . . Secretary of State [William P.] Rogers signed the agreement for the United States.

This Agreement met the essential conditions that we had laid down on January 27, and on May 8, 1972; a ceasefire, return of all prisoners, the withdrawal of American forces, and the political future of the South Vietnamese to be determined by the people themselves. The major elements were:

-- An internationally-supervised ceasefire throughout Vietnam, effective at 7:00 p.m., Eastern Standard Time, Saturday, January 27, 1973.
-- The release within 60 days of all captured Americans held throughout Indochina, and the fullest possible accounting for those missing in action.
-- The parallel withdrawal of all United States and allied forces and military personnel from South Vietnam.
-- A ban on infiltration of personnel into South Vietnam.
-- A ban on the introduction of war material into South Vietnam except one-for-one replacement of military equipment worn out, damaged, destroyed, or used up after the ceasefire.
-- The reduction and demobilization of both sides' forces in South Vietnam.
-- The withdrawal of all foreign troops from Laos and Cambodia.
-- A ban on the use of Laotian or Cambodian base areas to encroach on the sovereignty and security of South Vietnam.
-- The determination of the political future of South Vietnam by the South Vietnamese themselves.
-- Formation of a non-governmental National Council of National Reconciliation and Concord operating by unanimity, to organize elections as agreed by the parties and to promote conciliation between the parties and implementation of the Agreement.
-- Respect for the Demilitarized Zone dividing South and North Vietnam.
   The eventual reunification of North and South Vietnam through peaceful means, step by step, through direct negotiations.
-- Respect for the independence, sovereignty, unity, territorial integrity, and neutrality of Laos and Cambodia.
-- In accordance with traditional United States policy, U.S. participation in postwar reconstruction efforts throughout Indochina.
-- An International Commission of Control and Supervision (ICCS) composed of Canada, Hungary, Indonesia, and Poland to control and supervise the elections and various military provisions of the Agreement.
-- Joint Military Commissions of the parties to implement appropriate provisions of the Agreement.
-- An International Conference within thirty days to guarantee the Agreement and the ending of the war.

Richard Nixon, U.S. *Foreign Policy for the 1970's: Shaping a Durable Peace* (1973), pp. 48-60. For additional details concerning negotiations, 1969-1972, see pp. 49-51, and for final stages of negotiations, see pp. 55-57. For his annual summary accounts of United States objectives, policies, and role in the Vietnam War, also see his annual reports for 1970, pp. 62-76; 1971, pp. 58-81; 1972, pp. 110-29; and 1973, pp. 42-67.

172 AGREEMENT ENDING THE VIETNAM WAR, 1973

With a view to ending the war and restoring peace in Viet-Nam on the basis of respect for the Vietnamese people's fundamental national rights and the South Vietnamese people's right to self-determination, and to contributing to the consolidation of peace in Asia and the world,

Have agreed on the following provisions and undertake to respect and to implement them:

Article 1

The United States and all other countries respect the independence, sovereignty, unity, and territorial integrity of Viet-Nam as recognized by the 1954 Geneva Agreements on Viet-Nam.

Article 2

A cease-fire shall be observed throughout South Viet-Nam as of 2400 hours G.M.T., on January 27, 1973. . . .

The complete cessation of hostilities mentioned in this Article shall be durable and without limit of time. . . .

Article 3

The parties undertake to maintain the cease-fire and to ensure a lasting and stable peace.

As soon as the cease-fire goes into effect:

(a) The United States forces and those of the other foreign countries allied with the United States and the Republic of Viet-Nam shall remain in-place pending the implementation of the plan of troop withdrawal. . . .

(c) The regular forces of all services and arms and the ir-regular forces of the parties in South Viet-Nam shall stop all offensive activities against each other and shall strictly abide by the following stipulations:

-- All acts of force on the ground, in the air, and on the sea shall be prohibited;

-- All hostile acts, terrorism and reprisals by both sides will be banned.

Agreement Ending the War and Restoring Peace in Viet-Nam, signed by the United States, the Republic of Vietnam, the Democratic Republic of Vietnam, and the (Communist) Provisional Revolutionary Government of South Vietnam on January 27, 1973, 23 articles.   TIAS 7542; 24 *U.S. Treaties* 1-23. Simultaneously the United States signed a separate bilateral Agreement with North Vietnam, 23 articles, pp. 115-32. Together with their foreign language texts, with protocols, see pp. 1-224. In addition, see the twelve-government Act of the International Conference on Vietnam, signed March 2, 1973, 9 articles--TIAS 7568, 24 *U.S. Treaties* 485-521, and the Joint Communique respecting implementation of these agreements, signed June 13, 1973--TIAS 7674, 24 *U.S. Treaties* 1675-1719.

By these agreements the United States was committed to withdraw its military forces from Vietnam and the last American troops departed in March 1973. North Vietnam's forces were not required to withdraw, so that fighting between them and South Vietnam's forces continued, Saigon fell in the spring of 1975, and the unified Socialist Republic of Vietnam was proclaimed in July 1976. For commentary, see *Historic Documents*, 1975, pp. 259-99, 301-7. In the meantime, Congress refused to continue United States aid to South Vietnam, and in July 1973 it passed the War Powers Resolution--see Documents 80-84.

173 GENERAL POST-MORTEM--NIXON, 1973

We did not go to South Vietnam, and our men did not go there, for the purpose of conquering North Vietnam. Our men did not go to South Vietnam for the purpose of getting bases in South Vietnam or acquiring territory or domination over that part of the world. They went for a very high purpose, and that purpose can never be taken away from them or this country. It was, very simply, to prevent the imposition by force of a Communist government on the 17 million people of South Vietnam. That was our goal, and we achieved that goal, and we can be proud that we stuck it out until we did reach that goal.

Richard Nixon, remarks, joint session of South Carolina General Assembly, February 20, 1973; *Papers of Presidents: Nixon*, 1973, p. 109. For additional commentary, also see *Historic Documents,*1973, pp. 269-76.

11

Cuban Crises

If at any time the Communist buildup in Cuba were to endanger or interfere with our security in any way, including our base at Guantanamo, our passage to the Panama Canal, our missile and space activities at Cape Canaveral, or the lives of American citizens in this country, or if Cuba should ever attempt to export its aggressive purposes by force or the threat of force against any nation in this hemisphere, or become an offensive military base of significant capacity for the Soviet Union, then this country will do whatever must be done to protect its own security and that of its allies.

John Kennedy
Statement, news conference, September 13, 1962

Relations with Cuba following the ascendancy of Fidel Castro in 1959 brought into juxtaposition such traditional United States policies as the Monroe Doctrine, self-determination, and nonintervention by extra- and intrahemispheric forces and manifested aspects of several interdependent themes of United States diplomacy. These embrace Manifest Destiny, democratization and the sanctity of human rights, hemispheric leadership, and post-World War II cooperation, consultation in the event of external threats, national and areal security, and collective defense against foreign aggrandizement.

Following the Spanish-American War, Spain was ejected from the Caribbean and the United States achieved paramountcy in the area, constructed the Panama Canal, and established a protectorate over Cuba, with a naval base at Guantanamo. After 1945 multilateral nonintervention was superseded by collective solidarity and defense (under the aegis of the Inter-American system and the United Nations), which functioned until the penetration of international Communism after the accession of Castro.

This confronted the United States with the dilemma of intervention in the internal affairs of a neighboring sovereign nation or the establishment of Communism in the hemisphere and its export of revolution and subversion to other American republics, or of nonintervention by the United States in Cuba while intervening elsewhere to prevent Cuba's export of Communist power and influence, especially in the Caribbean and Central America.

The most critical problems in United States-Cuban affairs--focused upon in this chapter--include the Bay of Pigs abortive invasion by Cuban refugees supported by the United States in 1961 and the Cuban missile crisis the following year. Other developments that disturbed bilateral relations involve Castro's complaint about United States reconnaissance overflights in the 1960's (see, for example, *American Foreign Policy: Current Documents*, 1962, pp. 320-21); Cuba's severing of the water supply to the United States base at Guantanamo in 1964 (see *American Foreign Policy: Current Documents*, 1964, pp. 311, 313-14); and the flurry over the "Soviet brigade" in Cuba in 1979 (see *American Foreign Policy: Basic Documents*, 1977-1980, pp. 1342-52).

Other issues, of a continuing nature, include conflict over fishing rights, the flight and sanctuary of Cuban refugees, Cuba's export of arms and subversion, the Cuban-Soviet political impact on the Western Hemisphere, and the diplomatic, economic, travel, and other sanctions applied by the United States against the Castro regime. In the 1980's the United States also challenged Cuba's intervention in Southern Africa and Grenada, and its military support of the Sandinista regime in Nicaragua and subversive forces in other Central American nations.

With the leadership and support of the United States, the Organization of American States took a number of concrete actions to restrain the extension of international Communism to the Western Hemisphere--to condemn this process; maintain hemispheric solidarity (see Document 458); exclude Cuba from the inter-American system (see Document 449); apply collective sanctions against Cuba for its conduct (see Document 459); and condemn Cuban human rights violations (see Document 462).

This chapter needs to be related to the documents provided in others, especially Chapters 7 (the Monroe, Johnson, and Reagan Doctrines), 12 (Grenada Crisis), 18 (Rio Pact), 26 (Inter-American System), and 31 (Western Hemisphere).

BAY OF PIGS INVASION, 1961

The United States welcomed the overthrow of the Cuban dictator, Fulgencio Batista, in 1959. Following the accession to power of Fidel Castro, he rapidly embarked on policies that alienated the United States and Latin American countries--confiscation of foreign property without compensation; intervention in, and subversion of, other Latin American countries (such as Haiti, Dominican Republic, Nicaragua, and Panama); and the development of close relations with the Soviet Union and proclamation of a Communist government.

Relations with the United States were strained, diplomatic relations were severed, and thousands of Cuban refugees fled to neighboring countries and the United States. Those in Florida organized an invasion of Cuba, intent on overthrowing the Castro regime. They were supported, financed, and armed by the United States. Castro charged that the United States planned to invade Cuba, which was denied by the Kennedy administration.

On April 15, 1961--three months after Kennedy was inaugurated--airplanes stationed in Florida bombed the Cuban mainland, and on the morning of the 17th some 1,200 Cuban refugee forces, from Florida and Guatemala, launched their invasion, which failed; within a few days most of the invading forces were either captured or killed. President Kennedy permitted United States vessels to convoy the invaders but canceled plans for United States air cover.

Supported by the Soviet Union, Cuba brought charges in the United Nations, alleging that this constituted United States aggression. The Kennedy administration invoked the support of the inter-American system, which took stringent action to isolate Cuba and apply sanctions against the Castro government.

The documents provided in this section are devoted primarily to explain United States policy toward Castro, the Cuban refugees, their attempted invasion, the Soviet Union, and Western Hemisphere security (Documents 174-179). For a comprehensive list and compilation of more than 50 documents on United States-Cuban relations in 1961, including 20 documents during the crucial month of April, see *American Foreign Policy: Current Documents,* 1961, pp. xviii-xxii, 278-326. On the severance of United States diplomatic relations with Cuba, see Document 47.

174 BAY OF PIGS LANDING--ANNOUNCEMENT

The Cuban Revolutionary Council announces a successful landing of military supplies and equipment in the Cochinos Bay area.

Overcoming some armed resistance by Castro supporters, substantial amounts of food and ammunition reached elements of internal resistance forces engaged in active combat.

Cuban Revolutionary Council, bulletin, New York City, April 17, 1961; *American Foreign Policy: Current Documents,* 1961, p. 292.

175 UNITED STATES POLICY RESPECTING CUBA--STATEMENTS IN UNITED NATIONS

. . . I should like to make several points quite clear. . . .

First, as the President of the United States said a few days ago, there will not be under any conditions--and I repeat, any conditions--any intervention in Cuba by the United States armed forces.

Secondly, the United States will do everything it possibly can to make sure that no Americans participate in any actions against Cuba.

Thirdly, regarding the events which have reportedly occurred this morning and yesterday, the United States will consider, in accordance with its usual practices, the request for political asylum. This principle has long been enshrined as one of the fundamental principles of the Americas and, indeed, of the world. Those who believe in freedom and seek asylum from tyranny and oppression will always receive sympathetic understanding and consideration by the American people and the United States Government.

Fourthly, regarding the two aircraft which landed in Florida today, they were piloted by Cuban Air Force pilots. These pilots and certain other crew members have apparently defected from Castro's tyranny. No United States personnel participated. No United States Government airplanes of any kind participated. . . .

Adlai Stevenson, statement, United Nations General Assembly Committee, April 15, 1961; *American Foreign Policy: Current Documents,* 1961, pp. 290-92.

* * *

We sympathize with the desire of the people of Cuba--including those in exile who do not stop being Cubans merely because they could no longer stand to live in today's Cuba--we sympathize with their desire to seek Cuban independence and freedom. We hope that the Cuban people will succeed in doing what Castro's revolution never really tried to do: that is, to bring democratic processes to Cuba.

. . . I wish to make clear also that we would be opposed to the use of our territory for mounting an offensive against any foreign government. . . .

Let me make it clear that we do not regard the Cuban problem as a problem between Cuba and the United States. The challenge is not to the United States but to the hemisphere and its duly constituted body, the Organization of American States. The Castro regime has betrayed the Cuban revolution. . . .

Our only hope is that the Cuban tragedy may awaken the people and governments of the Americas to a profound resolve--a resolve to concert every resource and energy to advance the cause of economic growth and social progress throughout the hemisphere, but to do so under conditions of human freedom and political democracy. This cause represents the real revolution of the Americas.

Adlai Stevenson, statement, United Nations General Assembly Committee, April 17, 1961; *American Foreign Policy: Current Documents,* 1961, pp. 293-94.

* * *

Let me be absolutely clear: that the present events are the uprising of the Cuban people against an oppressive regime which has never given them the opportunity in peace and by democratic process to approve or to reject the domestic and foreign policies which it has followed.

For our part, our attitude is clear. Many Americans looked with sympathy. . . . on the cause espoused by Dr. Castro when he came to power. They look with the same sympathy on the men who today seek to bring freedom and justice to Cuba--not for foreign monopolies, not for the economic or political interests of the United States or any foreign power, but for Cuba and for the Cuban people.

It is hostility of Cubans, not Americans, that Dr. Castro has to fear. It is not our obligation to protect him from the consequences of his treason to the revolution, to the hopes of the Cuban people, and to the democratic aspirations of the hemisphere.

The United States sincerely hopes that any difficulties which we or other American countries may have with Cuba will be settled peacefully. We have committed no aggression against Cuba. We have no aggressive purposes against Cuba. We intend no military intervention in Cuba. We seek to see a restoration of the friendly relations which once prevailed between Cuba and the United States.

Adlai Stevenson, statement, United Nations General Assembly Committee, April 18, 1961; *American Foreign Policy: Current Documents*, 1961, p. 298. For commentary of United States Attorney General on United States neutrality respecting the Bay of Pigs invasion, see Whiteman, *Digest of International Law*, V, 275-76.

176   CUBAN ISSUE--CASTRO VERSUS THE CUBAN PEOPLE

The issue in Cuba is not between Cuba and the United States but between the Castro dictatorship and the Cuban people. This is not the first time that dictators have attempted to blame their troubles with their own people on foreigners. Nor is it the first time that refugees from tyranny have attempted to join their own countrymen to challenge a dictatorial regime. . . .

There is no secret about the sympathy of the American people for those who wish to be free, whether in distant parts of the world or in our own neighborhood. We are not indifferent to intrusion into this hemisphere by the Communist conspiracy which, as recently as December 1960, declared its intentions to destroy free institutions in all parts of the world. We shall work together with other governments of this hemisphere to meet efforts by this conspiracy to extend its penetration. The present struggle in Cuba, however, is a struggle by Cubans for their own freedom. There is not and will not be any intervention there by United States forces. The President has made this clear as well as our determination to do all we possibly can to insure that Americans do not participate in these actions in Cuba.

Dean Rusk, statement at news conference, April 17, 1961; *American Foreign Policy: Current Documents*, 1961, pp. 292-93. Also see earlier, similar comment by President Kennedy, news conference, April 12, 1961; *Papers of Presidents: Kennedy*, 1961, pp. 258-59.

177   UNITED STATES COMMITMENT TO OPPOSE MILITARY INTERVENTION IN WESTERN HEMISPHERE

You are under a serious misapprehension in regard to events in Cuba. For months there has been evident and growing resistance to the Castro dictatorship. More than 100,000 refugees have recently fled from Cuba into neighboring countries. Their urgent hope is naturally to assist their fellow Cubans in their struggle for freedom. Many of these refugees fought alongside Dr. Castro against the Batista dictatorship; among them are prominent leaders of his own original movement and government.

These are unmistakable signs that Cubans find intolerable the denial of democratic liberties and the subversion of the 26th of July Movement by an alien-dominated regime. It cannot be surprising that, as resistance within Cuba grows, refugees have been using whatever means are available to return and support their countrymen in the continuing struggle for freedom. Where people are denied the right of choice, recourse to such struggle is the only means of achieving their liberties.

I have previously stated, and I repeat now, that the United States intends no military intervention in Cuba. In the event of any military intervention by outside force we will immediately honor our obligations under the inter-American system to protect this hemisphere against external aggression. While refraining from military intervention in Cuba, the people of the United States do not conceal their admiration for Cuban patriots who wish to see a democratic system in an independent Cuba. The United States government can take no action to stifle the spirit of liberty.

John Kennedy, message to Chairman Khrushchev, April 18, 1961; *Papers of Presidents: Kennedy,* 1961, pp. 286-87; and *American Foreign Policy: Current Documents,* 1961, pp. 296-97.

178   UNITED STATES SECURITY COMMITMENT IN WESTERN HEMISPHERE

On that unhappy island, as in so many other areas of the contest for freedom, the news has grown worse instead of better. I have emphasized before that this was a struggle of Cuban patriots against a Cuban dictator. While we could not be expected to hide our sympathies, we made it repeatedly clear that the armed forces of this country would not intervene in any way.

Any unilateral American intervention, in the absence of an external attack upon ourselves or an ally, would have been contrary to our traditions and to our international obligations. But let the record show that our restraint is not inexhaustible. Should it ever appear that the inter-American doctrine of noninterference merely conceals or excuses a policy of nonaction--if the nations of this hemisphere should fail to meet their commitments against outside Communist penetration--then I want it clearly understood that this Government will not hesitate in meeting its primary obligations, which are to the security of our Nation. . . .

Meanwhile we will not accept Mr. Castro's attempts to blame this Nation for the hatred with which his onetime supporters now regard his repression. But there are from this sobering episode useful lessons for all to learn. Some may be still obscure and await further information. Some are clear today.

First, it is clear that the forces of communism are not to be underestimated, in Cuba or anywhere else in the world. The advantages of a police state--its use of mass terror and arrests to prevent the spread of free dissent--cannot be overlooked by those who expect the fall of every fanatic tyrant. If the self-discipline of the free cannot match the iron discipline of the mailed fist--in economic, political, scientific, and all the other kinds of struggles as well as the military--then the peril to freedom will continue to rise.

Secondly, it is clear that this Nation, in concert with all the free nations of this hemisphere, must take an even closer and more realistic look at the menace of external Communist intervention and domination in Cuba. The American people are not complacement about Iron Curtain tanks and planes less than 90 miles from our shores. But a nation of Cuba's size is less a threat to our survival than it is a base for subverting the survival of other free nations throughout the hemisphere. . . .

The evidence is clear--and the hour is late. We and our Latin friends will have to face the fact that we cannot postpone any longer the real issue of the survival of freedom in this hemisphere itself. On that issue, unlike perhaps some others, there can be no middle ground. . . .

Third, and finally, it is clearer than ever that we face a relentless struggle in every corner of the globe that goes far beyond the clash of armies or even nuclear armaments. . . .

Power is the hallmark of this offensive--power and discipline and deceit. The legitimate discontent of yearning peoples is exploited. The legitimate trappings of self-determination are employed. But once in power, all talk of discontent is repressed--all self-determination disappears--and the promise of a revolution of hope is betrayed, as in Cuba, into a reign of terror. . . .

John Kennedy, address, American Society of Newspaper Editors, Washington, April 20, 1961; *Papers of Presidents: Kennedy,* 1961, pp. 304-6; and *American Foreign Policy: Current Documents,* 1961, pp. 299-302.

179 NEED FOR REASSESSMENT OF UNITED STATES POLICY REGARDING CUBA

I don't think it would be possible to generalize the reaction on it. But the thing to do now, it seems to me--in the face of this setback which this group suffered there, and which we suffered--the thing to do now is to draw a deep breath and look over the situation very carefully and consider a wide range of problems invoked and possible actions which ought to be taken; and, most of all, to stay on the main road of hemispheric development and hemispheric solidarity.   That is the object of the exercise at present.   And, of course, that will be somewhat complicated by the special issue involved in the Cuban question.   But a great deal of the Cuban question arises because it is a hemispheric question and the hemisphere is the great concern.   And we must turn our attention to the unity and solidarity and strengthening of the hemisphere.

Dean Rusk, response to question at news conference, May 4, 1961; *American Foreign Policy: Current Documents*, 1961, p. 307-8.

CUBAN MISSILE CRISIS, 1962

In December 1961, Fidel Castro openly boasted that he and his regime were dedicated to Marxism-Leninism.   Soviet shipments of arms to Cuba, begun late the previous year, accelerated after the Bay of Pigs incident, and Soviet military advisers appeared in Cuba early in 1962.   Reacting to this attempt by the Soviet Union to establish a military base in Cuba, on September 4 President Kennedy warned the Castro government that the United States was determined to take whatever steps were necessary to prevent the installation of Soviet "offensive weapons" in Cuba, and on September 13 he announced that the United States would do whatever was necessary to protect its security and that of other American republics (see *American Foreign Policy: Current Documents,* 1962, pp. 369-70 and 373-75).

The crisis that ensued in October 1962 consisted of three phases: the United States response to the Soviet military challenge, negotiating a solution with the Soviet Union, and implementing that solution.   During the first phase, to summarize, the United States mobilized its forces, decided on action to be taken (of the half-dozen options considered, President Kennedy decided on a "quarantine" or partial blockade), and instituted a means of interdicting the shipment of offensive Soviet weapons to Cuba.   When convinced that the Soviet government was establishing missile sites with nuclear capability in Cuba, in a dramatic television address Kennedy informed the world of this threat and outlined the seven steps the United States was taking to deal with it, including the naval blockade or quarantine (Documents 180-183).

During the second, crucial phase, October 27-28, by means of five summit exchanges between Nikita Khrushchev and President Kennedy--which, except for the first Khrushchev message, were immediately made public--an accommodation was negotiated.   On the 27th the Soviet leader sought to trade the removal of Soviet missiles from Cuba for the removal of American missiles from Turkey; this was rejected by the United States.   The following day Khrushchev acceded to Kennedy's demand and agreed to remove the Soviet missiles (subject to inspection by the United Nations) in return for a promise by the United States not to invade Cuba (Documents 184-188).   In the ensuing phase the offensive weapons were removed and returned to the Soviet Union, and the missile sites were disassembled (Documents 189-190).

Thus, while the "eyeball-to-eyeball" confrontation (as characterized by Secretary of State Dean Rusk) was ameliorated, it must be noted that Khrushchev was unable to persuade Castro to permit United Nations verification of the removal of the offensive Soviet weapons from Cuba; that the agreement between Khrushchev and Kennedy was reached at the highest level, by the unique process of public personal exchanges of summit communications; and that the inter-American system acted in concert, not to intervene in Cuba's internal political affairs, but to estop a foreign threat to hemispheric security. Furthermore, the resolution of the crisis did not terminate Communism in Cuba or its subversion elsewhere in the Americas. Finally, it should be added that, because of the inadequacy of the traditional diplomatic communications process during a perilous confrontation, the United States and Soviet governments rapidly agreed to create the Washington-Moscow hot line (see Document 372).

180 CONGRESSIONAL RESOLUTION TO DETER AGGRESSION AND SUBVERSION IN THE WESTERN HEMISPHERE, 1962

Whereas President James Monroe, announcing the Monroe Doctrine in 1823, declared that the United States would consider any attempt on the part of European powers "to extend their system to any portion of this hemisphere as dangerous to our peace and safety"; and

Whereas in the Rio Treaty of 1947 the parties agreed that "an armed attack by any State against an American State shall be considered as an attack against all the American States, and consequently, each one of the said contracting parties undertakes to assist in meeting the attack in the exercise of the inherent right of individual or collective self-defense recognized by article 51 of the Charter of the United Nations"; and

Whereas the Foreign Ministers of the Organization of American States at Punta del Este in January 1962 declared: "The present Government of Cuba has identified itself with the principles of Marxist-Leninist ideology, has established a political, economic, and social system based on that doctrine, and accepts military assistance from extra-continental Communist powers, including even the threat of military intervention in America on the part of the Soviet Union"; and

Whereas the international Communist movement has increasingly extended into Cuba its political, economic, and military sphere of influence; Now, therefore, be it

Resolved by the Senate and House of Representatives of the United States of America in Congress assembled, That the United States is determined

—

(a) to prevent by whatever means may be necessary, including the use of arms, the Marxist-Leninist regime in Cuba from extending, by force or the threat of force, its aggressive or subversive activities to any part of this hemisphere;

(b) to prevent in Cuba the creation or use of an externally supported military capability endangering the security of the United States; and

(c) to work with the Organization of American States and with freedom-loving Cubans to support the aspirations of the Cuban people for self-determination.

Public Law 87-733, October 3, 1962; *American Foreign Policy: Current Documents*, 1962, pp. 389-90. Also see Congressional Resolution authorizing the President to mobilize United States forces, Public Law 87-736, October 3, 1962; *American Foreign Policy: Current Documents*, 1962, p. 390. Previously, as noted, President Kennedy warned the Castro government that the United States was determined to take whatever steps were necessary to prevent the installation of offensive weapons in Cuba, and that the United States would do whatever was necessary to preserve its security and that of the Western Hemisphere; see *American Foreign Policy: Current Documents*, 1962, pp. 369-70 and 373-75. For Monroe Doctrine and Rio Pact, see Documents 109 and 304, and for Final Act of Punta del Este meeting, January 31, 1962, see *American Foreign Policy: Current Documents*, 1962, pp. 320-31, especially p. 326.

181 UNITED STATES RESPONSE TO SOVIET OFFENSIVE ARMS BUILDUP IN CUBA

This Government, as promised, has maintained the closest surveillance of the Soviet military buildup on the island of Cuba. Within the past week, unmistakable evidence has established the fact that a series of offensive missile sites is now in preparation on that imprisoned island. The purpose of these bases can be none other than to provide a nuclear strike capability against the Western Hemisphere.

Upon receiving the first preliminary hard information of this nature last Tuesday morning at 9 a.m., I directed that our surveillance be stepped up. And having now confirmed and completed our evaluation of the evidence and our decision on a course of action, this Government feels obliged to report this new crisis to you in fullest detail.

The characteristics of these new missile sites indicate two distinct types of installations. Several of them include medium range ballistic missiles, capable of carrying a nuclear warhead for a distance of more than 1,000 nautical miles. Each of these missiles, in short, is capable of striking Washington, D.C., the Panama Canal, Cape Canaveral, Mexico City, or any other city in the southeastern part of the United States, in Central America, or in the Caribbean area.

Additional sites not yet completed appear to be designed for intermediate range ballistic missiles--capable of traveling more than twice as far--and thus capable of striking most of the major cities in the Western Hemisphere, ranging as far north as Hudson Bay, Canada, and as far south as Lima, Peru. In addition, jet bombers, capable of carrying nuclear weapons, are now being uncrated and assembled in Cuba, while the necessary air bases are being prepared.

This urgent transformation of Cuba into an important strategic base --by the presence of these large, long-range, and clearly offensive weapons of sudden mass destruction--constitutes an explicit threat to the peace and security of all the Americas, in flagrant and deliberate defiance of the Rio Pact of 1947, the traditions of this Nation and hemisphere, the joint resolution of the 87th Congress, the Charter of the United Nations, and my own public warnings to the Soviets on September 4 and 13. This action also contradicts the repeated assurances of Soviet spokesmen, both publicly and privately delivered, that the arms buildup in Cuba would retain its original defensive character, and that the Soviet Union had no need or desire to station strategic missiles on the territory of any other nation. . . .

. . . Our unswerving objective, therefore, must be to prevent the use of these missiles against this or any other country, and to secure their withdrawal or elimination from the Western Hemisphere. . . .

Acting, therefore, in the defense of our own security and of the entire Western Hemisphere, and under the authority entrusted to me by the Constitution as endorsed by the resolution of the Congress, I have directed that the following *initial* steps be taken immediately:

First: To halt this offensive buildup, a strict quarantine on all offensive military equipment under shipment to Cuba is being initiated. All ships of any kind bound for Cuba from whatever nation or port will, if found to contain cargoes of offensive weapons, be turned back. This quarantine will be extended, if needed, to other types of cargo and carriers. . . .

Second: I have directed the continued and increased close surveillance of Cuba and its military buildup. The foreign ministers of the OAS, in their communique of October 6, rejected secrecy on such matters in this hemisphere. Should these offensive military preparations continue, thus increasing the threat to the hemisphere, further action will be justified. I have directed the Armed Forces to prepare for any eventualities; and I trust that in the interest of both the Cuban people and the Soviet technicians at the sites, the hazards to all concerned of continuing this threat will be recognized.

Third: It shall be the policy of this Nation to regard any nuclear missile launched from Cuba against any nation in the Western Hemisphere as an attack by the Soviet Union on the United States, requiring a full retaliatory response upon the Soviet Union.

Fourth: As a necessary military precaution, I have reinforced our base at Guantanamo, evacuated today the dependents of our personnel there, and ordered additional military units to be on a standby alert basis.

Fifth: We are calling tonight for an immediate meeting of the Organ of Consultation under the Organization of American States, to consider this threat to hemispheric security and to invoke articles 6 and 8 of the Rio Treaty in support of all necessary action. . . .

Sixth: Under the Charter of the United Nations, we are asking tonight that an emergency meeting of the Security Council be convoked without delay to take action against this latest Soviet threat to world peace. Our resolution will call for the prompt dismantling and withdrawal of all offensive weapons in Cuba, under the supervision of U.N. observers, before the quarantine can be lifted.

Seventh and finally: I call upon Chairman Khrushchev to halt and eliminate this clandestine, reckless, and provocative threat to world peace and to stable relations between our two nations. I call upon him further to abandon this course of world domination, and to join in an historic effort to end the perilous arms race and to transform the history of man. He has an opportunity now to move the world back from the abyss of destruction--by returning to his government's own words that it had no need to station missiles outside its own territory, and withdrawing these weapons from Cuba--by refraining from any action which will widen or deepen the present crisis--and then by participating in a search for peaceful and permanent solutions. . . .

Our goal is not the victory of might, but the vindication of right--not peace at the expense of freedom, but both peace and freedom, here in this hemisphere, and, we hope, around the world.

John Kennedy, radio and television report to the nation, October 22, 1962; *Papers of Presidents: Kennedy,* 1962, pp. 806-9; and *American Foreign Policy: Current Documents,* 1962, pp. 399-404. For Kennedy's warnings of September 4 and 13, see pp. 369-70 and 373-75.

182   INTERDICTING DELIVERY OF OFFENSIVE WEAPONS TO CUBA

Whereas the Organ of Consultation of the American Republics meeting in Washington on October 23, 1962, recommended that the Member States, in accordance with Articles 6 and 8 of the Inter-American Treaty of Reciprocal Assistance, take all measures, individually and collectively, including the use of armed force, which they may deem necessary to ensure that the Government of Cuba cannot continue to receive from the Sino-Soviet powers military material and related supplies which may threaten the peace and security of the Continent and to prevent the missiles in Cuba with offensive capability from ever becoming an active threat to the peace and security of the Continent:

Now, therefore, I, John F. Kennedy, President of the United States of America, acting under and by virtue of the authority conferred upon me by the Constitution and statutes of the United States, in accordance with the aforementioned resolutions of the United States Congress and of the Organ of Consultation of the American Republics, and to defend the security of the United States, do hereby proclaim that the forces under my command are ordered, beginning at 2:00 p.m. Greenwich time October 24, 1962, to interdict, subject to the instructions herein contained, the delivery of offensive weapons and associated material to Cuba.

Proclamation 3504, October 23, 1962; *Papers of Presidents: Kennedy,* 1962, pp. 809-10, and *American Foreign Policy: Current Documents,* 1962, pp. 410-

12. The quarantine went into effect at 10:00 a.m. local time on October 24. For Department of State announcement respecting United States procedures for clearing vessels destined for Cuban ports with cargoes containing no offensive weapons or associated material, October 27, 1962, see *American Foreign Policy: Current Documents,* 1962, pp. 442-43. For an address entitled "The Legal Case for U.S. Action on Cuba" by the Legal Adviser of the Department of State, November 3, 1962, see Whiteman, *Digest of International Law,* X, 16-18; for commentary on collective defense and the Cuban missile crisis, see vol. V, 1051-57, and on the general relation of the American quarantine and armed conflict, see vol. X, 8-20.

183 CONTINUING DEVELOPMENT OF BALLISTIC MISSILE SITES IN CUBA

The development of ballistic missile sites in Cuba continues at a rapid pace. Through the process of continued surveillance directed by the President, additional evidence has been acquired which clearly reflects that as of Thursday, October 25, definite buildup in these offensive missile sites continued to be made. The activity at these sites apparently is directed at achieving a full operational capability as soon as possible. . . .

In summary, there is no evidence to date indicating that there is any intention to dismantle or discontinue work on these missile sites. On the contrary the Soviets are rapidly continuing their construction of missile support and launch facilities, and serious attempts are under way to camouflage their efforts.

White House, statement, October 26, 1962; *Papers of Presidents: Kennedy,* 1962, p. 812; and *American Foreign Policy: Current Documents,* 1962, pp. 437-38. The United States was highly concerned with getting the Soviet government to cease its program before the missiles were made operational.

184 UNITED STATES PRECONDITIONS FOR SETTLING CUBAN MISSILE CRISIS

Several inconsistent and conflicting proposals have been made by the U.S.S.R. within the last 24 hours, including the one just made public in Moscow. The proposal broadcast this morning involves the security of nations outside the Western Hemisphere. But it is the Western Hemisphere countries and they alone that are subject to the threat that has produced the current crisis--the action of the Soviet Government in secretly introducing offensive weapons into Cuba. Work on these offensive weapons is still proceeding at a rapid pace. The first imperative must be to deal with this immediate threat, under which no sensible negotiations can proceed.

It is therefore the position of the United States that as an urgent preliminary to consideration of any proposals work on the Cuban bases must stop; offensive weapons must be rendered inoperable; and further shipment of offensive weapons to Cuba must cease--all under effective international verification.

White House, statement, October 27, 1962; *Papers of Presidents: Kennedy,* 1962, p. 813; and *American Foreign Policy: Current Documents,* 1962, pp. 440-41.

185 KHRUSHCHEV PROPOSAL TO REMOVE OFFENSIVE WEAPONS FROM CUBA IN RETURN FOR UNITED STATES REMOVAL OF "ANALOGOUS WEAPONS" FROM TURKEY

. . . I make this proposal: We agree to remove those weapons from Cuba which you regard as offensive weapons. We agree to do this and to state this commitment in the United Nations. Your representatives will make a statement to the effect that the United State, on its part, bearing in mind the anxiety and concern of the Soviet state, will evacuate its analogous weapons from Turkey. Let us reach an understanding on what time you and we need to put this into effect.

After this representatives of the U.N. Security Council could control on-the-spot the fulfillment of these commitments. Of course, it is necessary that the Governments of Cuba and Turkey would allow these representatives to come to their countries and check fulfillment of this commitment, which each side undertakes. Apparently, it would be better if these representatives enjoyed the trust of the Security Council and ours --the United States and the Soviet Union--as well as of Turkey and Cuba. I think that it will not be difficult to find such people who enjoy the trust and respect of all interested sides.

We, having assumed this commitment in order to give satisfaction and hope to the peoples of Cuba and Turkey and to increase their confidence in their security, will make a statement in the Security Council to the effect that the Soviet Government gives a solemn pledge to respect the integrity of the frontiers and the sovereignty of Turkey, not to intervene in its domestic affairs, not to invade Turkey, not to make available its territory as a place d'armes for such invasion, and also will restrain those who would think of launching an aggression against Turkey either from Soviet territory or from the territory of other states bordering on Turkey.

The U.S. Government will make the same statement in the Security Council with regard to Cuba. It will declare that the United States will respect the integrity of the frontiers of Cuba, its sovereignty, undertakes not to intervene in its domestic affairs, not to invade and not to make its territory available as place d'armes for the invasion of Cuba, and also will restrain those who would think of launching an aggression against Cuba either from U.S. territory or from the territory of other states bordering on Cuba.

Of course, for this we would have to reach agreement with you and to arrange for some deadline. Let us agree to give some time, but not to delay, two or three weeks, not more than a month.

Second summit letter from Khrushchev to Kennedy, October 27, 1962; *American Foreign Policy: Current Documents*, 1962, pp. 439-40. The first letter from Khrushchev, of the same date, was not published.

186 KENNEDY RESPONSE TO KHRUSHCHEV MESSAGE

I have read your letter of October 26th with great care and welcomed the statement of your desire to seek a prompt solution to the problem. The first thing that needs to be done, however, is for work to cease on offensive missile bases in Cuba and for all weapons systems in Cuba capable of offensive use to be rendered inoperable, under effective United Nations arrangements.

Assuming this is done promptly, I have given my representatives in New York instructions that will permit them to work out this weekend-- in cooperation with the Acting Secretary General and your representative --an arrangement for a permanent solution to the Cuban problem along tho linoo ouggcoted in your letter of October 26th. As I read your letter, the key elements of your proposals--which seem generally acceptable as I understand them--are as follows:

1) You would agree to remove these weapons systems from Cuba under appropriate United Nations observation and supervision; and undertake, with suitable safeguards, to halt the further introduction of such weapons systems into Cuba.

2) We, on our part, would agree--upon the establishment of adequate arrangements through the United Nations to ensure the carrying out and continuation of these commitments--(a) to remove promptly the quarantine measures now in effect and (b) to give assurances against an invasion of Cuba. I am confident that other nations of the Western Hemisphere would be prepared to do likewise.

If you will give your representative similar instructions, there is no reason why we should not be able to complete these arrangements and announce them to the world within a couple of days. The effect of such a settlement on easing world tensions would enable us to work toward a more general arrangement regarding "other armaments", as proposed in your second letter which you made public. . . .

But the first ingredient, let me emphasize, is the cessation of work on missile sites in Cuba and measures to render such weapons inoperable, under effective international guarantees. The continuation of this threat, or a prolonging of this discussion concerning Cuba by linking these problems to the broader questions of European and world security, would surely lead to an intensification of the Cuban crisis and a grave risk to the peace of the world.

John Kennedy, letter to Khrushchev, October 27, 1962; *Papers of Presidents: Kennedy*, 1962, pp. 813-14; and *American Foreign Policy: Current Documents*, 1962, pp. 441-42. Khrushchev's letter of October 26 was not published. Note that President Kennedy did not accept the mutual tradeoff of missiles in Turkey and Cuba.

187 KHRUSHCHEV AGREEMENT TO REMOVE OFFENSIVE WEAPONS FROM CUBA

In order to eliminate as rapidly as possible the conflict which endangers the cause of peace, to give an assurance to all people who crave peace, and to reassure the American people, who, I am certain, also want peace, as do the people of the Soviet Union, the Soviet Government, in addition to earlier instructions on the discontinuation of further work on weapons constructions sites, has given a new order to dismantle the arms which you described as offensive, and to crate and return them to the Soviet Union. . . .

I regard with respect and trust the statement you made in your message of 27 October 1962 that there would be no attack, no invasion of Cuba, and not only on the part of the United States, but also on the part of other nations of the Western Hemisphere, as you said in your same message. Then the motives which induced us to render assistance of such a kind to Cuba disappear.

It is for this reason that we instructed our officers--these means as I had already informed you earlier are in the hands of the Soviet officers-- to take appropriate measures to discontinue construction of the afore-mentioned facilities, to dismantle them, and to return them to the Soviet Union. As I had informed you in the letter of 27 October, we are prepared to reach agreement to enable U.N. representatives to verify the dis-mantling of these means. Thus in view of the assurances you have given and our instructions on dismantling, there is every condition for eliminating the present conflict.

Third letter from Khrushchev to Kennedy, October 28, 1962; *American Foreign Policy: Current Documents,* 1962, pp. 443-44.

188 KENNEDY RESPONSE TO KHRUSHCHEV MESSAGE ON REMOVAL OF OF-FENSIVE WEAPONS

I am replying at once to your broadcast message of October twenty-eight, even though the official text has not yet reached me, because of the great importance I attach to moving forward promptly to the settlement of the Cuban crisis. I think that you and I, with our heavy responsibilities for the maintenance of peace, were aware that developments were ap-proaching a point where events could have become unmanageable. So I welcome this message and consider it an important contribution to peace.

. . . I consider my letter to you of October twenty-seventh and your reply of today as firm undertakings on the part of both our governments which should be promptly carried out. I hope that the necessary measures can at once be taken through the United Nations, as your message says, so that the United States in turn will be able to remove the quarantine measures now in effect.

John Kennedy, letter to Khrushchev, October 28, 1962; *Papers of Presidents: Kennedy,* 1962, pp. 814-15; and *American Foreign Policy: Current Documents,* 1962, pp. 445-46.   Also see Kennedy statement welcoming Khrushchev's "statesmanlike decision," October 28, 1962, pp. 444-45.

189 CONFIRMATION OF REMOVAL OF OFFENSIVE MISSILES FROM CUBA

The U.S. Government has confirmed through aerial reconnaissance that medium-range ballistic missile and intermediate-range ballistic missile equipment is being removed from Cuba. . . .

As a result of aerial reconnaissance, the U.S. has photographs which indicate that all known MRBM and IRBM missile bases in Cuba have been dismantled.

Later photographs indicate the movement of significant items of equipment from the missile sites to port areas. Still later photographs give evidence that a substantial number of missile transporters have been loaded on to the main decks of certain Soviet cargo vessels and that several of these vessels have already departed Cuban ports.

Photographs and visual inspection from U.S. Naval vessels should provide further confirmation that the actual missiles (normally carried in missile transporters that have been photographed on board these vessels) have left Cuba.

Department of Defense, statement, November 8, 1962; *American Foreign Policy: Current Documents,* 1962, p. 458.   Also see Kennedy radio and television remarks, November 2, 1962, pp. 451-52.

190 REPORTS ON REMOVAL OF OFFENSIVE WEAPONS FROM AND LIFTING OF QUARANTINE OF CUBA

I have today been informed by Chairman Khrushchev that all of the IL-28 bombers now in Cuba will be withdrawn in 30 days. He also agrees that these planes can be observed and counted as they leave. Inasmuch as this goes a long way towards reducing the danger which faced this hemisphere 4 weeks ago, I have this afternoon instructed the Secretary of Defense to lift our naval quarantine.

In view of this action, I want to take this opportunity to bring the American people up to date on the Cuban crisis and to review the progress made thus far in fulfilling the understandings between Soviet Chairman Khrushchev and myself as set forth in our letters of October 27 and 28. Chairman Khrushchev, it will be recalled, agreed to remove from Cuba all weapons systems capable of offensive use, to halt the further introduction of such weapons into Cuba, and to permit appropriate United Nations observation and supervision to insure the carrying out and continuation of these commitments. We on our part agreed that once these adequate arrangements for verification had been established we would remove our naval quarantine and give assurance against an invasion of Cuba.

The evidence to date indicates that all known offensive missile sites in Cuba have been dismantled. The missiles and their associated equipment have been loaded on Soviet ships. And our inspection at sea of these departing ships has confirmed that the number of missiles reported by the Soviet Union as having been brought into Cuba, which closely corresponded to our own information, has now been removed. In addition, the Soviet Government has stated that all nuclear weapons have been withdrawn from Cuba and no offensive weapons will be reintroduced. . . .

I repeat, we would like nothing better than adequate international arrangements for the task of inspection and verification in Cuba, and we are prepared to continue our efforts to achieve such arrangements. Until that is done, difficult problems remain. As for our part, if all offensive weapons systems are removed from Cuba and kept out of the hemisphere in the future, under adequate verification and safeguards, and if Cuba is not used for the export of aggressive Communist purposes, there will be peace in the Caribbean. And as I said in September, "we shall neither initiate nor permit aggression in this hemisphere."

We will not, of course, abandon the political, economic, and other efforts of this hemisphere to halt subversion from Cuba nor our purpose and hope that the Cuban people shall some day be truly free. But these policies are very different from any intent to launch a military invasion of the island.

In short, the record of recent weeks shows real progress and we are hopeful that further progress can be made. The completion of the commitment on both sides and the achievement of a peaceful solution to the Cuban crisis might well open the door to the solution of other outstanding problems.

John Kennedy, statement, news conference, November 20, 1962; *Papers of Presidents: Kennedy,* 1962, pp. 83;-31, and *American Foreign Policy: Current Documents,* 1962, pp. 461-63. For termination of United States quarantine measures against Cuba, see Proclamation 3507, November 21, 1962, in *American Foreign Policy: Current Documents,* 1962, p. 463; and for subsequent statements by President Kennedy concerning the missile crisis, December 14, 16, and 29, 1962, see pp. 469-73. For the report of the Secretary of Defense on the removal of the missiles, February 6, 1963, see *American Foreign Policy: Current Documents,* 1963, pp. 249-50.

12

Crises in
Central America
and Caribbean

In the commitment to freedom and independence, the peoples of this hemisphere are one. In this profound sense, we are all Americans. Our principles are rooted in self-government and nonintervention. We believe in the rule of law. We know that a nation cannot be liberated by depriving its people of liberty. We know that a state cannot be free when its independence is subordinated to a foreign power.

Ronald Reagan
Caribbean Basin Initiative Address, 1982

I believe our government has a responsibility to go to the aid of its citizens, if their right to life and liberty is threatened.

Ronald Reagan
Televised address, White House, October 27, 1983

Since World War II dozens of major and minor crises have occurred in the Caribbean and Central America. Political violence (of both the left and the right), coups and other types of armed revolt and guerilla action, civil war, military dictatorships, and Communist revolutions have been frequent, often explosive, and usually debilitating. While most crises affect interrelations with other nations, including the United States, and many evoke consideration and action by the Organization of American States and other components of the inter-American system, this chapter--paralleled by Chapters 11 (which deals with the Bay of Pigs and Cuban Missile Crises) and 31 (which touches on United States relations with Nicaragua in the 1980's)--concentrates on those in which the United States has been directly involved as a primary participant.

The most important are the Panamanian Crisis of 1964, the Dominican Crisis of 1965, the Grenada invasion or "rescue mission" of 1983, and the Panamanian Crisis of 1989. In each of these the United States employed military forces, all of them involved consideration by the Organization of American States and the United Nations, in two of them--the Dominican

Republic and Grenada--the United States acted to counter the alleged threat of external Communist intrigue, and two of them--Panama (1964) and the Dominican Republic--illustrate the use of pacific settlement processes.

Other chapters that relate to these and the Cuban crises include Chapters 7 (on the Monroe, Johnson, and Reagan Doctrines), 18 (on the inter-American multilateral and bilateral alliances and collective defense arrangements), 26 (on the functioning of the inter-American system), and 31 (on the Western Hemisphere, especially the documents on human rights, the new Panama Canal Treaties of 1977, the Caribbean Basin Initiative, and the struggle to promote and preserve democracy in Central America).

PANAMANIAN CRISIS, 1964

United States-Panamanian relations concerning the Panama Canal and the Canal Zone, and the rights and responsibilities of the two countries under the Canal Treaty of 1903 (see T.S. 431, in 10 Bevans, *Treaties and Other International Agreements,* 663-72, were under discussion for several decades (for major revisions of 1936, see T.S. 945, in 10 Bevans, *Treaties and Other International Agreements*, 742-77, and of 1955, see TIAS 3297, in 6 *U.S. Treaties,* 2273-2367).

Violence erupted in January 1964, when a dispute by high school students over the flying of the United States and Panamanian flags within the Canal Zone touched off wild demonstrations that degenerated into bloody riots, resulting in the death of some twenty-five persons (including several United States soldiers), injury to scores of others, considerable property damage, and the evacuation of the American embassy. The Panamanian government broke off diplomatic relations with Washington and charged the United States with aggression.

President Johnson telephoned Panamanian President Roberto Chiari, seeking to end the violence and restore peace. He also sent Thomas C. Mann of the Department of State, heading a five-person delegation, to negotiate and report, later named Edwin M. Martin, newly appointed Ambassador to Argentina, to continue on-the-spot deliberations, and eventually commissioned Robert A. Anderson, former Secretary of the Treasury, to discuss consideration of possible changes under the Canal Treaty of 1903. All of these emissaries served as the President's personal surrogates to negotiate at the highest levels. Throughout these proceedings the President's objectives were initially to restore peace and then to discuss "all problems" in our relations with Panama, including arrangements respecting the Canal Zone, and to revive our "special relation" with that country, but without "preconditions" for the restoration of peaceful relations, "precommitments" to rewrite the 1903 Canal Treaty, or yielding to Panama's charges of United States aggression (Documents 191-195).

In the meantime the crisis was considered by the United Nations (see *American Foreign Policy: Current Documents,* 1964, pp. 346-50) and the Organization of American States (see *American Foreign Policy: Current Documents,* 1964, pp. 350-53, 355-62, 365-66). It was not until April 3 that a

Joint United States-Panamanian Declaration to resolve the crisis was agreed upon (Document 196).

After peace was restored, in December President Johnson presented his plan for an alternative isthmian sea-level canal and the negotiation of a revised treaty respecting the existing Panama Canal (Document 197). New canal treaties with Panama were not signed until 1977 (see Chapter 31, Documents 560-563). For a compilation of twenty-nine documents concerning the crisis of 1964, see *American Foreign Policy: Current Documents,* 1964, pp. 345-72.

191 UNITED STATES WILLINGNESS TO DISCUSS ALL PROBLEMS IN RELATIONS WITH PANAMA

The United States Government is ready and willing to discuss all problems affecting the relationship between the United States and Panama. It was our understanding that the Government of Panama was also willing to undertake these discussions. Our position is unchanged. We feel in this time of difficulty between the two countries that it is time for the highest exercise of responsibility by all those involved.

White House, statement read to news correspondents, January 16, 1964; *American Foreign Policy: Current Documents,* 1964, p. 353. For earlier White House statements, January 10 and 14, see pp. 345, 352, and for reiteration, March 21, 1964, see pp. 364-65.

192 NO UNITED STATES PRECONDITIONS FOR RESUMPTION OF PEACEFUL DISCUSSIONS WITH PANAMA

I want to take this opportunity to restate our position on Panama and the Canal Zone. No purpose is served by rehashing either recent or ancient events. There have been excesses and errors on the part of both Americans and Panamanians. Earlier this month actions of imprudent students from both countries played into the hands of agitators seeking to divide us. What followed was a needless and tragic loss of life on both sides.

Our own forces were confronted with sniper fire and mob attack. Their role was one of resisting aggression and not committing it. At all times they remained inside the Canal Zone, and they took only those defensive actions required to maintain law and order and to protect lives and property within the canal itself. Our obligation to safeguard the canal against riots and vandals and sabotage and other interference rests on the precepts of international law, the requirements of international commerce, and the needs of free-world security.

These obligations cannot be abandoned. But the security of the Panama Canal is not inconsistent with the interests of the Republic of Panama. Both of these objectives can and should be assured by the actions and the agreement of Panama and the United States. This Government has long recognized that our operation of the canal across Panama poses special problems for both countries. It is necessary, therefore, that our relations be given constant attention. . . .

We have set no preconditions to the resumption of peaceful discussions. We are bound by no preconceptions of what they will produce. And we hope that Panama can take the same approach. In the meantime, we expect neither country to either foster or yield to any kind of pressure with respect to such discussions. We are prepared, 30 days after relations are restored, to sit in conference with Panamanian officials to seek concrete solutions to all problems dividing our countries. Each Government will be free to raise any issue and to take any position. And our Government will consider all practical solutions to practical problems that are offered in good faith.

Certainly solutions can be found which are compatible with the dignity and the security of both countries as well as the needs of world commerce. And certainly Panama and the United States can remain, as they should remain, good friends and good neighbors.

Lyndon Johnson, statement read at news conference, January 23, 1964; *American Foreign Policy: Current Documents*, 1964, pp. 353-54.

193 REJECTION OF PANAMANIAN CHARGE OF UNITED STATES "AGGRESSION"

The Government of the United States regrets that the Government of Panama has chosen to break off not only diplomatic relations and direct talks but discussions which were going on through the Inter-American Peace Committee, and to take instead the course of bringing this matter before the Council to level charges of aggression against the United States.

Both the U.S. Government and our people were profoundly saddened by the unfortunate events which transpired in Panama on January 9, 1964, and on the days immediately following. These events, which have left a tragic balance of dead and wounded on both sides, cannot in any way be considered to have served the best interests of either the United States or Panama but rather have redounded to the sole benefit of those who seek the breakdown of the inter-American system, of those who would sow the seeds of discord among the sister Republics of the New World, of those who seek to reap the bitter harvest that would result from internecine strife in the Americas.

Ellsworth Bunker, United States representative, statement, in Council of Organization of American States, January 31, 1964; *American Foreign Policy: Current Documents*, 1964, pp. 355-58. Also see Adlai Stevenson, statement, United Nations Security Council, January 10, 1964, pp. 347-50.

194 NO UNITED STATES PRECOMMITMENTS FOR REWRITING PANAMA CANAL TREATIES

I would hope that we could reach an agreement [with Panama] as early as possible. As soon as I learned that the Panamanians had marched on our zone and we had a disturbance there, and some of our soldiers had been killed, some of the students had raised the flag and this disturbance had resulted, I immediately called the President of Panama on the telephone and said to him in that first exchange, "I want to do everything I can to work this problem out peacefully and quickly. Therefore our people will meet with your people any time, anywhere, to discuss anything that will result in bringing peace and stopping violence.". . .

So we are not refusing to discuss and evolve a program that will be fair and just to all concerned. But we are not going to make any pre-commitments, before we sit down, on what we are going to do in the way of rewriting new treaties with a nation that we do not have diplomatic relations with. Once those relations are restored, we will be glad, as I said the first day, and as we have repeated every day since, to discuss anything, any time, anywhere, and do what is just and what is fair and what is right. Just because Panama happens to be a small nation . . . is no reason why we shouldn't try in every way to be equitable and fair and just. We are going to insist on that. But we are going to be equally insistent on no preconditions.

Lyndon Johnson, reply to question at news conference, February 29, 1964; *American Foreign Policy; Current Documents.* 1964, p. 363.

195 NEED TO REVIVE SPECIAL UNITED STATES RELATIONSHIP WITH PANAMA

The present inability to resolve our differences with Panama is a source of deep regret.

Our two countries are not linked by only a single agreement or a single interest. We are bound together in an inter-American system whose objective is, in the words of the [OAS] charter, ". . . through their mutual understanding and respect for the sovereignty of each one, to provide for the betterment of all. . . ."

Under the many treaties and declarations which form the fabric of that system, we have long been allies in the struggle to strengthen democracy and enhance the welfare of our people. . . .

We have also had a special relationship with Panama, for they have shared with us the benefits, the burdens and trust of maintaining the Panama Canal as a lifeline of defense and a keystone of hemispheric prosperity. All free nations are grateful for the effort they have given to this task.

As circumstances change, as history shapes new attitudes and expectations, we have reviewed periodically this special relationship.

We are well aware that the claims of the Government of Panama, and of the majority of the Panamanian people, do not spring from malice or hatred of America. They are based on a deeply felt sense of the honest and fair needs of Panama. It is, therefore, our obligation as allies and partners to review these claims and to meet them, when meeting them is both just and possible.

We are ready to do this.

We are prepared to review every issue which now divides us, and every problem which the Panama Government wishes to raise.

We are prepared to do this at any time and at any place.

Lyndon Johnson, statement read at news conference, March 21, 1964; *American Foreign Policy: Current Documents,* 1964, pp. 364-65.

196 JOINT UNITED STATES-PANAMANIAN DECLARATION TO RESOLVE CRISIS

In accordance with the friendly declarations of the Presidents of the United States of America and of the Republic of Panama of the 21st and 24th of March, 1964 . . . which are in agreement in a sincere desire to resolve favorably all the differences between the two countries;

Meeting under the Chairmanship of the President of the Council and recognizing the important cooperation offered by the Organization of American States through the Inter-American Peace Committee and the Delegation of the General Committee of the Organ of Consultation, the Representatives of both governments have agreed:

1. To re-establish diplomatic relations.

2. To designate without delay Special Ambassadors with sufficient powers to seek the prompt elimination of the causes of conflict between the two countries, without limitations or preconditions of any kind.

3. That therefore, the Ambassadors designated will begin immediately the necessary procedures with the objective of reaching a just and fair agreement which would be subject to the constitutional processes of each country.

Announcement by chairman of General Committee of Council of Organization of American States, April 3, 1964; *American Foreign Policy: Current Documents,* 1964, pp. 365-66.

197 UNITED STATES DECISION TO PLAN NEW ISTHMIAN SEA-LEVEL CANAL AND NEGOTIATE NEW TREATY ON EXISTING PANAMA CANAL

This Government has completed an intensive review of policy toward the present and the future of the Panama Canal. On the basis of this review I have reached two decisions.

First, I have decided that the United States should press forward with Panama and other interested governments in plans and preparations for a sea-level canal in this area.

Second, I have decided to propose to the Government of Panama the negotiation of an entirely new treaty on the existing Panama Canal. . . .

These two steps, I think, are needed now--needed for the protection and the promotion of peaceful trade--for the welfare of the hemisphere-- in the true interests of the United States--and in fairness and justice to all. . . .

The Panama Canal, with its limiting locks and channels, will soon be inadequate to the needs of our world commerce. Already more than 300 ships built or building are too big to go through with full loads. Many of them--like our own modern aircraft carriers--cannot even go through at all.

So I think it is time to plan in earnest for a sea-level canal. Such a canal will be more modern, more economical, and will be far easier to defend. It will be free of complex, costly, vulnerable locks and seaways. It will serve the future as the Panama Canal we know has served the past and the present. . . .

Today we have informed the Government of Panama that we are ready to negotiate a new treaty. In such a treaty we must retain the rights which are necessary for the effective operation and the protection of the canal and the administration of the areas that are necessary for these purposes. Such a treaty would replace the treaty of 1903 and its amendments. It should recognize the sovereignty of Panama. It should provide for its own termination when a sea-level canal comes into operation. It should provide for effective discharge of our common responsibilities for hemi- spheric defense. Until a new agreement is reached, of course, the present treaties will remain in effect

Lyndon Johnson, televised address, December 18, 1964; *American Foreign Policy: Current Documents,* 1964, pp. 370-72. New Panama Canal Treaties, replacing that of 1903, as amended, were signed in 1977--see Chapter 31, Documents 560-563.

DOMINICAN CRISIS, 1965

On April 24, 1965, the Dominican Republic erupted into the gravest crisis in the Western Hemisphere since the Cuban Missile Crisis of 1962. What started as a routine military coup rapidly produced a battle between two armed political groups--that which supported Juan Bosch and that which opposed him. The initial revolt was followed by a mass uprising that de- generated into a bloody civil war, in which public order and safety were subverted and some 2,000 Dominicans were killed.

The United States Ambassador, W. Tapley Bennet, who sought to mediate among the competing political forces, reported that the country was ap- proaching anarchy and local authorities could not guarantee the safety of American lives, and he appealed for United States intervention. President Johnson ordered 400 Marines into Santo Domingo on April 28 to protect American citizens and to evacuate them and other foreign nationals. During the next few weeks the United States force grew to approximately 25,000 Marines and paratroops, who were later joined by small contingents from Brazil, Paraguay, and several Central American republics--which constituted an Organization of American States Peace Force, the first such multipartite inter-American collective defense garrison.

At the outset the United States insisted that its action was taken solely to protect American lives. On May 2, however, in a telecast to the nation, President Johnson declared that the American nations must not and will not "permit the establishment of another Communist government in the Western Hemisphere." He charged that foreign Communist forces were threatening to take over the Dominican revolution. Thus, while the United States intervention began as a relief mission, the President's primary purposes, while claiming to remain neutral in the internal political conflict, was to protect the security of this country and its Western Hemisphere neighbors, restore Dominican democracy, and prevent Communism, with external direction and support, from gaining ascendency in another Caribbean nation.

Initially President Johnson sought to resolve the outbreak through the mediation of the American ambassador in Santo Domingo. His next diplomatic initiative was to send special presidential emissaries for this purpose, including John Bartlow Martin, former ambassador to Santo Domingo, who reported that the revolution appeared to have come under Communist domination, and subsequently a four-member negotiating team headed by McGeorge Bundy, the President's special assistant, to seek to induce the leading factions to agree upon a moderate interim coalition government. Ultimately the United States persuaded the Organization of American States to establish a three-member inter-American Peace Commission, including veteran Ambassador Ellsworth Bunker, which negotiated a modus vivendi and "Act of Reconciliation" that was accepted by the contesting parties late in August. Although United States troop withdrawal began in mid-1965, this task was not completed until the following year, after the Dominican election in June.

The first document contained in this section presents a brief chronology of events during the early days of the crisis (Document 198). President Johnson's major policy address, delivered May 2, in which he introduced the Communist threat as justification for the large-scale intervention of United States forces and which constituted the basis of the Johnson Doctrine for the Western Hemisphere, is provided in Chapter 7, Document 117. The remaining documents focus on the President's denial of the Dominican allegation of United States "aggression" and assessments of the Dominican venture (Documents 200-202). For a comprehensive compilation of thirty-eight documents on this crisis, see *American Foreign Policy: Current Documents,* 1965, pp. 955-1010, which includes consideration of the crisis by the Organization of American States (pp. 957-68, 973-87, 992-1001) and the United Nations Security Council (pp. 977-80, 982-87, 996-97).

198 EVENTS CREATING CRISIS IN DOMINICAN REPUBLIC, APRIL 1965

On April 24, 1965, dissident civilian and military elements, among them followers of ex-President Juan Bosch's Democratic Revolutionary Party (PRD), rebelled against the "Triumvirate" government headed by Donald Reid Cabral. They succeeded in taking over some key installations in the city of Santo Domingo, including radio broadcasting facilities over which they urged the populace to join the revolt, and began to distribute indiscriminately to civilians large quantities of arms taken from captured government arsenals. When the regular Armed Forces failed to come to the support of President Reid, he was forced to step down on April 25 after the rebels had seized the National Palace.

During the afternoon of April 25, officers of the regular and insurrectionary forces, and leaders of the PRD and other elements met to discuss the formation of a provisional government. The representatives of the regular Armed Forces favored the establishment of a military junta and the holding of early elections. The insurrectionary leaders wanted the formation of an interim government under PRD leader Jose Rafael Molina Urena, pending the expected early return and reinstatement of former President Bosch who had been ousted from office in September 1963.

The regular military forces, strongly opposed to Bosch's return, demanded the immediate designation of a military junta to prepare for national elections in September 1965. They accompanied their demand with an ultimatum that the regular forces would attack unless their terms were met. The rebel forces disregarded the ultimatum and hostilities began late on the afternoon of April 25.

During April 25-28, the tempo of the fighting increased. Efforts by the American Embassy, the Papal Nuncio, and others to arrange a cease-fire failed. Violence and lawlessness in Santo Domingo steadily mounted to the point where civil authority disappeared. The lives of U.S. citizens and other foreign nationals were seriously threatened. Under these conditions, the American Embassy began the evacuation of American citizens on April 27.

The following day, in the face of a further deterioration of the situation, notification by Dominican military authorities that they could no longer guarantee the safety of Americans, and the growing danger of interference with the evacuation effort, Ambassador Bennett . . . recommended the immediate landing of U.S. Marines. Pursuant to orders from the President, the Marines began landing at approximately 7 p.m., Washington time.

Two rival "governments" eventually emerged in the Dominican Republic during the first weeks of the civil war--the pro-Bosch (rebel) "Constitutional Government,". . . and the "Government of National Reconstruction," a civilian-military junta. . . .

White House summary; *American Foreign Policy: Current Documents,* 1965, p. 955.

199 UNITED STATES POLICY IN DOMINICAN CRISIS--JOHNSON DOCTRINE

Lyndon Johnson, radio and television report to the American people, May 2, 1965; see Chapter 7, Document 117. For initial response to the crisis, see Lyndon Johnson, statements, April 28 and 30, 1965; *American Foreign Policy: Current Documents,* 1965, pp. 555-57.

200 UNITED STATES NOT "AGGRESSOR" IN DOMINICAN REPUBLIC

. . . We are not the aggressor in the Dominican Republic. Forces came in there and overthrew that government and became alined with evil persons who had been trained in overthrowing governments and in seizing governments and establishing Communist control, and we have resisted that control and we have sought to protect our citizens against what would have taken place.

. . . With reports of that kind, no President can stand by. So we resisted their aggression to the extent that (a) we protected our own people and (b) we hope that we have exposed what leadership attempted to seize that little land.

Lyndon Johnson, statement, White House session with members of congressional committees, May 4, 1965; *American Foreign Policy: Current Documents,* 1965, pp. 968-70.

201 ASSESSMENT OF DOMINICAN VENTURE--SEARCH FOR A DURABLE PEACE

. . . The tragedy of the past 4 weeks in the Dominican Republic renews our common resolution to accept common responsibility in dealing with common dangers.

In that unfortunate nation, 4 weeks ago, the legacy of dictatorship exploded in fury and anarchy. Hundreds of Dominicans died, leaving thousands of widows and orphans of war. Nineteen of our own American boys lost their lives. The capital city . . . was split asunder. Blood and hate drowned ideals. And for days freedom itself stood on the edge of disaster.

In those early terrible hours, we did what we had to do. . . .

Since then, working with the Organization of American States . . . the forces of democracy have acted. The results are clear.

More than 6,500 men and women and children from 46 different countries have been evacuated. Not a single life was lost.

A cease-fire was achieved, bringing an end to the threat of wholesale bloodshed.

An international zone of refuge was opened as a haven for all men of peace, and a safe corridor 17 miles long was established by American men.

More than 8 million pounds of food have been distributed to the Dominican people.

A well-trained, disciplined band of Communists was prevented from destroying the hopes of Dominican democracy.

Political avenues were opened to help the Dominican people find a Dominican solution to their problems.

Today those achievements are guaranteed--guaranteed by the troops of five nations representing this hemisphere. . . .

For the first time in history the Organization of American States has created and sent to the soil of an American nation an international peacekeeping military force.

That may be the greatest achievement of all. . . .

First, the Dominican people--and the people of their sister Republics--do not want government by extremists of either the left or right. That is clear. They want to be ruled neither by an old conspiracy of reaction and tyranny nor by a new conspiracy of Communist violence.

Second, they want--as we do--an end to slaughter in the streets and to brutality in the barrios.

Third, they want--as we do--food and work and quiet in the night

Fourth, they want--as we do--a constitutional government that will represent them all--and work for all their hopes.

Fifth, the Dominican people know they need the help of sympathetic neighbors in healing their wounds and in negotiating their divisions--but what they want ultimately is the chance to shape their own course.

Those are the hopes of the Dominican people. But they are our hopes, too. And they are shared by responsible people in every nation of this hemisphere. . . .

We believe the New World may most widely approach this task guided by new realities.

The first reality is that old concepts and old labels are largely obsolete. In today's world, with the enemies of freedom talking about "wars of national liberation," the old distinction between "civil war" and "international war" has already lost much of its meaning.

Second is the reality that when forces of freedom move slowly--whether on political, economic, or military fronts--the forces of slavery and subversion move rapidly, and they move decisively.

Third, we know that when a Communist group seeks to exploit misery, the entire free American system is put in deadly danger. We also know that these dangers can be found today in many of our lands. There is no trouble anywhere these evil forces will not try to turn to their advantage. We can expect more efforts at triumph by terror and conquest through chaos.

Fourth, we have learned in the Dominican Republic that we can act decisively and together.

Fifth, it is clear that we need new international machinery geared to meet the fast-moving events. When hours can decide the fate of generations the moment of decision must become the moment of action.

Just as these lessons of the past 4 weeks are clear, so are the basic principles which have guided the purpose of the United States of America.

We seek no territory. We do not seek to impose our will on anyone. We intend to work for the self-determination of the peoples of the Americas within the framework of freedom.

In times past large nations have used their power to impose their will on smaller nations. Today we have placed our forces at the disposition of the nations of this hemisphere to assure the peoples of those nations the right to exercise their own will in freedom.

In accordance with the resolution of the eighth meeting of the ministers at Punta del Este, we will join with the other OAS nations in opposing a Communist takeover in this hemisphere.

And in accordance with the Charter of Punta del Este, we will join with other OAS nations in pressing for change among those who would maintain a feudal system--a feudal system that denies social justice and economic progress to the ordinary people of this hemisphere.

We want for the peoples of this hemisphere only what they want for themselves--liberty, justice, dignity, a better life for all.

Lyndon Johnson, Commencement Address, Baylor University, May 28, 1965; *American Foreign Policy: Current Documents*, 1965, pp. 987-90. For resolutions passed by the Organization of American States and United Nations, see pp. 959-60, 974-75, 977-82, 993, 999-1000.

202   ASSESSMENT OF DOMINICAN VENTURE--LEGAL ISSUES

If we start from this point, it is not difficult to identify two distinct areas of confusion:

The first confusion comes from those who say, however obliquely, that it is necessary unilaterally to intervene--"support" is the word most often used--in favor of political parties of the non-Communist left. . . .

But this thesis overlooks the fact that countries want to solve their internal political problems in their own way. Latin Americans do not want a paternalistic United States deciding which particular political faction should rule their countries. . . .

This explains why, in the case of the Dominican Republic, we refrained during the first days of violence from "supporting" the outgoing government or "supporting" either of the factions contending for power. It explains why we and others thought it best to work for a cease-fire and to encourage the rival Dominican factions to meet together and agree on a Dominican solution to a Dominican problem. It explains why, to use a phrase of international law, we offered our good offices rather than attempting to preside over a meeting for the purpose of proposing political solutions with a "made in USA" label on them.

The second area of confusion concerns the response which an American state, or the Organization of American States as a whole, can make to intervention. When, in other words, a Communist state has intervened in the internal affairs of an American state by training, directing, financing and organizing indigenous Communist elements to take control of the government of an American state by force and violence, should other American states be powerless to lend assistance? Are Communists free to intervene while democratic states are powerless to frustrate that intervention?

This is not so much a question of intervention as it is of whether weak and fragile states should be helped to maintain their independence when they are under attack by subversive   elements responding to direction from abroad. . . .

A number of juridical questions deserve consideration--not in an atmosphere of crisis, demanding an immediate decision, but in an atmosphere of calmness and objectivity.   As illustrative of the kind of questions that ought to be considered, I pose these two:

What distinctions ought to be made, on the one hand, between subversive activities which do not constitute an immediate danger to an American state and, on the other, those which, because of their intensity and external direction, do constitute a danger to the peace and security of the country and the hemisphere?

Second, assuming that, as I have suggested, certain subversive activities do constitute a threat to the peace and security of the hemisphere, what response is permitted within the framework of the inter-American system?

I do not offer precise answers to these questions at this time. I only wish to say that the problem of Communist subversion in the hemisphere is a real one. It should not be brushed aside on a false assumption that American states are prohibited by inter-American law from dealing with it.

Thomas C. Mann, Under Secretary of State, address, Inter-American Press Association, San Diego, October 12, 1965; *American Foreign Policy: Current Documents,* 1965, pp. 1002-9. He also discusses the factual background, developments, and the nature of the major decisions that had to be made during the crisis.

GRENADA INVASION, 1983

Grenada, a small Caribbean island, only twice the size of our national capital, gained independence from the United Kingdom in 1974. Five years later it came under the leadership of Maurice Bishop, a Marxist with close ties to Cuba and the Soviet Union. On October 12, 1983, Bishop was deposed and arrested by military extremists, and a week later he was rescued, recaptured, and executed together with several of his cabinet members. At the time of the coup there were approximately 1,000 Americans in Grenada, some 800 of whom were students at St. George's University of Medicine.

President Reagan feared another hostage crisis like that in Iran in 1979-1980, and he decided to prevent Grenada from becoming another Communist military base in the Caribbean. As early as March 23, in an address to the nation, he divulged the construction by Cubans of a 10,000-foot airport runway, which could accommodate Soviet and Cuban warplanes.

Requested by the Organization of Eastern Caribbean States (OECS) on October 23 to participate in a joint effort to restore order in Grenada (Document 203), President Reagan two days later announced the landing of a rescue mission of some 2,000 United States and Caribbean troops on the island (Document 204). During the next few days American forces were increased to nearly 6,000. On October 27, in a major address to the nation on Communist attempts to export terrorism and undermine democracy, President Reagan described developments and explained his initial decisions (Document 205).

The joint inter-American forces rapidly took over control, armed conflict ended by November 2, the Cubans were shipped home early that month, and on December 8 the President reported that all United States Marines and Rangers were withdrawn and that residual forces merely provided local security and technical services (Document 206). Document 207 sets forth the legal authority for this military mission. For additional documentation, see *American Foreign Policy: Current Documents,* 1983, pp. 59, 1392-1426; and for background, see "Reagan Address on Grenada Invasion," *Historic Documents, 1983,* pp. 847-53.

203 REQUEST FOR UNITED STATES SUPPORT FOR COLLECTIVE DEFENSE IN GRENADA

The authority of the Organization of Eastern Caribbean States (OECS) met at Bridgetown, Barbados on Friday 21st October 1983, to consider and evaluate the situation in Grenada arising out of the overthrow of the Government led by Prime Minister Maurice Bishop and the subsequent killing of the Prime Minister together with some of his colleagues and a number of other citizens.

The authority is aware that the overthrow of the Bishop administration took place with the knowledge and connivance of forces unfriendly to the OECS, leading to the establishment of the present military regime.

The meeting took note of the current anarchic conditions, the serious violations of human rights and bloodshed that have occurred and the consequent unprecedented threat to the peace and security of the region created by the vacuum of authority in Grenada.

The authority was deeply concerned that military forces and supplies are likely to be shortly introduced to consolidate the position of the regime and that the country can be used as a staging post for acts of aggression against its members.

The authority further noted that the capability of the Grenada armed forces is already at a level of sophistication and size far beyond the internal needs of that country. Furthermore the member states of the OECS have no means of defence against such forces. . . .

Under the authority of Article 8 of the Treaty establishing the Organization of Eastern Caribbean States, the authority proposes therefore to take action for collective defence and the preservation of peace and security against external aggression by requesting assistance from friendly countries to provide transport, logistics support and additional military personnel to assist the efforts of the OECS to stabilize this most grave situation within the Eastern Caribbean.

The authority of the OECS wishes to establish a peace keeping force with the assistance of friendly neighbouring states to restore on Grenada conditions of tranquility and order so as to prevent further loss of life and abuses of human rights pending the restoration of constitutional government.

Letter from Chairman of the Organization of Eastern Caribbean States (OECS) to the United States, October 23, 1983; *American Foreign Policy: Current Documents,* 1983, pp. 1397-98.

204 RESPONSE OF UNITED STATES FOR PARTICIPATION IN INVASION OF GRENADA

On Sunday, October 23d, the United States received an urgent, formal request from the five member nations of the Organization of Eastern Caribbean States to assist in a joint effort to restore order and democracy on the island of Grenada. We acceded to the request to become part of a multinational effort with contingents from Antigua, Barbados, Dominica, Jamaica, St. Lucia, St. Vincent and the United States. . . .

Early this morning, forces from six Caribbean democracies and the United States began a landing or landings on the island of Grenada in the eastern Caribbean.

We have taken this decisive action for three reasons. First, and of overriding importance, to protect innocent lives, including up to 1,000 Americans whose personal safety is, of course, my paramount concern. Second, to forestall further chaos. And third, to assist in the restoration of conditions of law and order and of governmental institutions to the island of Grenada, where a brutal group of leftist thugs violently seized power, killing the Prime Minister, three Cabinet members, two labor leaders and other civilians, including children.

Let there be no misunderstanding, this collective action has been forced on us by events that have no precedent in the eastern Caribbean and no place in any civilized society. . . .

From the start we have consciously sought to calm fears. We were determined not to make an already bad situation worse and increase the risks our citizens faced. But when I received reports that a large number of our citizens were seeking to escape the island, thereby exposing themselves to great danger, and after receiving a formal request for help, a unanimous request from our neighboring states, I concluded the United States had no choice but to act strongly and decisively.

Ronald Reagan, statement, press conference, October 25, 1983; *American Foreign Policy: Current Documents,* 1983, pp. 1398-99. Also see remarks of

Secretary of State George Shultz, press conference, October 25, 1983, pp. 1401-7.

205   EXPLANATION OF UNITED STATES ACTION IN GRENADA

In 1979 trouble came to Grenada.   Maurice Bishop, a protege of Fidel Castro, staged a military coup and overthrew the government which had been elected under the Constitution left to the people by the British. He sought the help of Cuba in building an airport, which he claimed was for tourist trade, but which looked suspiciously suitable for military aircraft, including Soviet-built long-range bombers. . . .

Last weekend, I was awakened in the early morning hours and told that six members of the Organization of Eastern Caribbean States, joined by Jamaica and Barbados, had sent an urgent request that we join them in a military operation to restore order and democracy to Grenada.

They were proposing this action under the terms of a treaty, a mutual assistance pact that existed among them.   These small, peaceful nations needed our help.   Three of them don't have armies at all, and the others have very limited forces.   The legitimacy of their request, plus my own concern for our citizens, dictated my decision. . . .

We knew we had little time and that complete secrecy was vital to ensure both the safety of the young men who would undertake this mission, and the Americans they were about to rescue. . . . We had to assume that several hundred Cubans working on the airport could be military reserves.   As it turned out, the number was much larger and they were a military force. Six hundred of them have been taken prisoner, and we have discovered a complete base with weapons and communications equipment which makes it clear a Cuban occupation of the island had been planned.

Ronald Reagan, radio and television address on involvement of the United States in Lebanon and Grenada, October 27, 1983; *American Foreign Policy: Current Documents,* 1983, pp. 1410-12.   Also see his comment, press conference, November 3, 1983, pp. 1419-20.

206   PRESIDENT REAGAN'S REPORT TO CONGRESS ON INVASION OF GRENADA

In accordance with my desire that you be kept informed concerning the situation in Grenada, about which I reported to you on October 25, I am providing this further report on the presence of United States Armed Forces in Grenada.

Since then, the circumstances which occasioned the introduction of United States Armed Forces into Grenada have substantially changed.   On November 2, the armed conflict in Grenada came to an end, and our task now, together with neighboring countries, is to assist the Grenadians in their effort to restore and revitalize their political institutions in a stable security environment.

Although it is still not possible to predict the precise duration of the temporary presence of United States Armed Forces in Grenada, our forces are continuing to work closely with other components of the collective security force in assisting the Grenadian authorities in the maintenance of conditions of law and order and the restoration of functioning governmental institutions to the island of Grenada.

All elements of the U.S. Marines and U.S. Army Rangers have now been withdrawn from Grenada; at this time, less than 2,700 U.S. Armed Forces personnel remain on the island. U.S. Armed Forces will continue to withdraw from the island as a part of a process whereby a peacekeeping force, composed of units contributed by friendly countries, takes over these responsibilities. I anticipate that this will be accomplished in the near future and that any members of the U.S. Armed Forces remaining in Grenada thereafter will have normal peacetime assignments, such as training, local security and the furnishing of technical services.

Ronald Reagan, letter to Speaker of the House of Representatives, December 8, 1983; *American Foreign Policy: Current Documents,* 1983, pp. 1425-26. This was the President's second report under the War Powers Act. For his earlier report at the time of the invasion, October 25, 1983, see pp. 1407-8.

207 LEGAL BASIS FOR UNITED STATES ACTION IN GRENADA

U.S. actions have been based on three legal grounds.

First, as these events were taking place, we were informed, on October 24, by Prime Minister Adams of Barbados that Grenada's Governor General, Sir Paul Scoon, had used a confidential channel to transmit an appeal to the OECS and other regional states to restore order on the island. The Governor General has since confirmed this appeal. We were unable to make this request public until the Governor General's safety had been assured, but it was an important element--legally as well as politically--in our respective decisions to help Grenada. The legal authorities of the Governor General were the sole remaining source of governmental legitimacy on the island in the wake of the tragic events I have described. We and the OECS countries accorded his appeal exceptional moral and legal weight. The invitation of lawful governmental authority constitutes a recognized basis under international law for foreign states to provide requested assistance.

Second, the OECS determined to take action under the 1981 treaty establishing that organization. That treaty contains a number of provisions--in articles 3, 4, and 8--which deal with local as well as external threats to peace and security. Both the OAS [Organization of American States] Charter, in articles 22 and 28, and the UN Charter, in article 52, recognize the competence of regional security bodies in ensuring regional peace and stability. Article 22 of the OAS Charter, in particular, makes clear that action pursuant to a special security treaty in force does not constitute intervention or use of force otherwise prohibited by articles

18 or 20 of that charter. In taking lawful collective action, the OECS countries were entitled to call upon friendly states for appropriate assistance, and it was lawful for the United States, Jamaica, and Barbados to respond to this request.

Third, U.S. action to secure and evacuate endangered U.S. citizens on the island was undertaken in accordance with well-established principles of international law regarding the protection of one's nationals. That the circumstances warranted this action has been amply documented by the returning students themselves. There is absolutely no requirement of international law that compelled the United States to await further deterioration of the situation that would have jeopardized a successful operation. Nor was the United States required to await actual violence against U.S. citizens before rescuing them from the anarchic and threatening conditions the students themselves have described.

. . . Let me say that the distinctions are clear. The United States participated in a genuine collective effort--the record makes clear the initiative of the Caribbean countries in proposing and defending this action. This action was based on an existing regional treaty and at the express invitation of the Governor General of Grenada. Our concern for the safety of our citizens was genuine. The factual circumstances on Grenada were exceptional and unprecedented in the Caribbean region--a collapse of law, order, and governmental institutions. Our objectives are precise and limited--to evacuate foreign nationals and to cooperate in the restoration of order. Our objectives do not involve the imposition on the Grenadians of any particular form of government. Grenadians are free to determine their institutions for themselves. Finally, our troops have already begun to leave; we will complete our withdrawal as soon as other forces are ready to take over from us.

Kenneth W. Dam, Deputy Secretary of State, address, Associated Press Managing Editors' Conference, Louisville, November 4, 1983; *American Foreign Policy: Current Documents*, 1983, pp. 1420-23. This address also describes developments, discusses external Communist penetration into Grenada, and addresses the lessons learned from the venture, pp. 1423-25.

PANAMANIAN CRISIS, 1989

When in February 1988 General Manuel Noriega, Panamanian dictator, was indicted in the United States for helping and protecting international drug traffickers, laundering drug profits through Panamanian banks, and allegedly receiving a multimillion-dollar payoff from drug cartels, the United States brought pressure to remove him from power and try him for his crimes. Under Panamanian law, he was not extraditable. In May 1989, despite Noriega-managed irregularities at the polls, the opposition won an overwhelming victory, which the Noriega regime annulled. The United States regarded the new Noriega government as illegitimate, refused to recognize its leaders, severed diplomatic relations, intensified economic sanctions begun in 1988, sent

American reinforcements to the Canal Zone, and joined the Organization of American States in condemning the Panamanian leaders and calling for the transfer of power and return to legitimacy.

The new Panamanian government was installed in September 1989, the following month a military coup against Noriega's leadership was aborted, and in December he declared his government to be at war with the United States. He publicly threatened the lives of United States citizens, and several Americans were shot, arrested, or beaten.

Faced not only with the violation of political and human rights in Panama but with threats to Americans and the Panama Canal, President Bush ordered a military incursion to oust the Noriega regime, to see the duly elected officials installed, and to capture Noriega. Initially he took refuge in the Papal nunciature, but eventually he surrendered to American officials and was brought to the United States for trial. The American constabulary forces assisted the new, elected government to restore order and to organize its own administration and security establishment, and then returned to the United States.

Tho following documents specify the attitude of the United States government toward the Noriega regime and the reasons for instituting sanctions against it, the President's address to the nation explaining the American military action, and his directive to apprehend Noriega and others under American indictment and turn them over for trial in the United States (Documents 208-210).

208   UNITED STATES ATTITUDE TOWARD NORIEGA REGIME AND REASONS FOR SANCTIONS

On September 1, 1989, I announced that, as a consequence of General Noriega's actions to prevent the candidates chosen by the Panamanian people to take office, Panama was as of that date without any legitimate government, and the United States would not recognize any government installed by Noriega. Our Ambassador will not return, and we will not have any diplomatic contact with the Noriega regime. The United States will continue to take other steps, including the tightening of measures to deprive the illegal regime of funds that belong to the Panamanian people, in support of self-determination and democracy, and to counter the threat posed by General Noriega's support for drug trafficking and other forms of subversion. . . .

The objective of Administration policy remains support for a return to civilian constitutional rule and the development of an apolitical military establishment in Panama. In furtherance of our policy, the Administration has imposed economic sanctions against the Noriega regime. Our judgment remains that the root cause of the current crisis is the fact that the Panamanian people have lost confidence in a political system widely perceived as corrupt, repressive, and inept. A genuine Panamanian resolution of the political crisis is necessary to restore confidence in the Panamanian economy, a precondition to the return of economic stability and growth in Panama. Accordingly, our efforts have been directed at supporting Panamanian efforts to resolve the underlying political crisis as rapidly as possible.

George Bush, Message to Congress Reporting on Economic Sanctions Against Panama, October 19, 1989; 25 *Weekly Compilation of Presidential Documents* (October 23, 1989): 1576-77. Most of this message details the application of these sanctions. For earlier comments on Noriega and United States relations with Panama, see pp. 685-86, 706-74, 1497.

209 ANNOUNCEMENT CONCERNING UNITED STATES MILITARY ACTION IN PANAMA

For nearly 2 years, the United States, nations of Latin America and the Caribbean have worked together to resolve the crisis in Panama. The goals of the United States have been to safeguard the lives of Americans, to defend democracy in Panama, to combat drug trafficking, and to protect the integrity of the Panama Canal treaty. Many attempts have been made to resolve this crisis through diplomacy and negotiations. All were rejected by the dictator of Panama, General Manuel Noriega, an indicted drug trafficker.

Last Friday, Noriega declared his military dictatorship to be in a state of war with the United States and publicly threatened the lives of Americans in Panama. The very next day, forces under his command shot and killed an unarmed American serviceman; wounded another; arrested and brutally beat a third American serviceman; and then brutally interrogated his wife, threatening her with sexual abuse. That was enough.

General Noriega's reckless threats and attacks upon Americans in Panama created an imminent danger to the 35,000 American citizens in Panama. As President, I have no higher obligation than to safeguard the lives of American citizens. And that is why I directed our Armed Forces to protect the lives of American citizens in Panama and to bring General Noriega to justice in the United States. . . .

At this moment, U.S. Forces, including forces deployed from the United States last night, are engaged in action in Panama. The United States intends to withdraw the forces newly deployed to Panama as quickly as possible. . . .

The brave Panamanians elected by the people of Panama in the elections last May, President Guillermo Endara and Vice Presidents Calderon and Ford, have assumed the rightful leadership of their country. You remember those horrible pictures of newly elected Vice President Ford, covered head to toe with blood, beaten mercilessly by so-called "dignity battalions." Well, the United States today recognizes the democratically elected government of President Endara. I will send our Ambassador back to Panama immediately.

Key military objectives have been achieved. Most organized resistance has been eliminated. But the operation is not over yet. General

Noriega is in hiding.   And nevertheless, yesterday a dictator ruled Panama, and today constitutionally elected leaders govern.

I have today directed the Secretary of the Treasury and the Secretary of State to lift the economic sanctions with respect to the democratically elected government of Panama and, in cooperation with that government, to take steps to effect an orderly unblocking of Panamanian Government assets in the United States.   I'm fully committed to implement the Panamal Canal treaties and turn over the Canal to Panama in the year 2000.   The actions we have taken and the cooperation of a new, democratic government in Panama will permit us to honor these commitments. . . .

I am committed to strengthening our relationship with the democratic nations in this hemisphere.   I will continue to seek solutions to the problems of this region through dialog and multilateral diplomacy. I took this action only after reaching the conclusion that every other avenue was closed and the lives of American citizens were in grave danger. I hope that the people of Panama will put this dark chapter of dictatorship behind them and move forward together as citizens of a democratic Panama with this government that they themselves have elected.

The United States is eager to work with the Panamanian people in partnership and friendship to rebuild their economy.   The Panamanian people want democracy, peace, and the chance for a better life in dignity and freedom.   The people of the United States seek only to support them in pursuit of these noble goals.

George Bush, Address to the Nation, December 20, 1989; 25 *Weekly Compilation of Presidential Documents* (December 25, 1989): 1974-76.   Also see statement of Press Secretary, White House, December 20, 1989, describing the process for arriving at the determination to resort to military action and monitoring its progress, pp. 1975-76.

210 PRESIDENT'S MEMORANDUM DIRECTING THE APPREHENSION OF GENERAL MANUEL NORIEGA

In the course of carrying out the military operation in Panama which I have directed, I hereby direct and authorize the units and members of the Armed Forces of the United States to apprehend General Manuel Noriega and any other persons in Panama currently under indictment in the United States for drug-related offenses.   I further direct that any persons apprehended pursuant to this directive are to be turned over to civil law enforcement officials of the United States as soon as practicable.   I also authorize and direct members of the Armed Forces of the United States to detain and arrest any persons apprehended pursuant to this directive if, in their judgment, such action is necessary.

George Bush, memorandum to Secretary of Defense, December 20, 1989; 25 *Weekly Compilation of Presidential Documents* (December 25, 1989):   1976. For subsequent comments, press conference, January 5, 1990, see volume 26, pp. 15-19.

13

Attacks on
American Ships

Aggression--deliberate, willful, and systematic aggression--has unmasked its face to the entire world. The world remembers--the world must never forget--that aggression unchallenged Is aggression unleashed.

Lyndon Johnson
Remarks, Syracuse University, August 5, 1964

During periods of hostilities and the Cold War a number of incidents occurred involving attacks upon and seizure of American ships. In earlier history, the depredations of the Barbary pirates, the British Impressment of American seaman, the sinking of the *Maine,* the torpedoing of the *Lusitania* and other ships by German submarines, and the Japanese attack at Pearl Harbor produced major United States policy reaction.

This chapter focuses on four of the more critical post-World War II incidents--the attacks on American naval vessels (the *Maddox* and others) in the South China Sea during the Vietnam War and on the *Liberty* during the Arab-Israeli Six-Day War, and the seizure of the *Pueblo* off the coast of Korea in 1968 and the *Mayaguez* in the Gulf of Siam in 1975.

All of these aggressive actions, except the *Mayaguez,* were directed against American naval vessels and all, except the *Liberty,* occurred in the Far East and were produced by incidents perpetrated by the forces of Communist countries. Two crisis situations grew out of outright attacks and two out of the seizure of American ships and their crews. In two incidents the crisis was short-lived (the *Liberty* and the *Mayaguez*) and in two cases the United States responded with forceful action (the *Maddox* and the *Mayaguez*). Only the Tonkin Gulf crisis, involving attacks on several United States destroyers, resulted in a major foreign policy development (for the Tonkin Gulf Resolution, see Chapter 7, Document 116).

Such threatening situations raise questions of the President's authority as commander in chief to protect American lives and interests, of his need for congressional enactments, such as supporting authorization resolutions, and of the effects of constraining legislation including the War Powers Resolution, which is discussed in Chapter 5.

ATTACKS ON UNITED STATES SHIPS IN THE GULF OF TONKIN, 1964

On August 2, 1964, North Vietnam gunboats attacked an American destroyer--the U.S.S. *Maddox*--and two days later they attacked the *Maddox* and the U.S.S. *C. Turner Joy* in international waters in the Gulf of Tonkin (South China Sea). President Johnson immediately ordered retaliation by both naval vessels and aircraft against North Vietnam gunboats and "certain supporting facilities." Several attacking vessels were sunk, and aerial sorties hit North Vietnam gunboat and oil storage bases. The United States publicly protested the attacks and brought a formal complaint against North Vietnam in the United Nations Security Council. A third attack on two American destroyers--the U.S.S. *Edwards* and *Morton*--was made on September 18, and again the navy opened fire upon North Vietnam gunboats.

In the meantime, to empower him to take forceful action against such attacks upon American armed forces and to assist our Southeast Asia Treaty allies during the Vietnam War, on August 5--launching the Johnson Doctrine-- the President requested Congress to enact a broad-scale authorizing resolution, and five days later Congress passed the Gulf of Tonkin Resolution (see Documents 115 and 116).

The documents contained in this section consist of reports on the North Vietnam attacks and on United States retaliation (Documents 211-214). For President Johnson's commentary on these attacks and the Gulf of Tonkin Resolution as compared with a formal United States declaration of war, see his subsequent press conference statements in *Papers of Presidents: Johnson, 1963-1964*, II, 937, 965-66, 1098-99; 1965, I, 448-49; 1966, I, 221-22; and 1967, pp. 793-95.

211   REPORT ON NORTH VIETNAM ATTACKS ON *MADDOX* AND *C. TURNER JOY*

The initial attack on the destroyer *Maddox,* on August 2, was repeated today by a number of hostile vessels attacking two U.S. destroyers with torpedoes. The destroyers and supporting aircraft acted at once on the orders I gave after the initial act of aggression. We believe at least two of the attacking boats were sunk. There were no U.S. losses.

The performance of commanders and crews in this engagement is in the highest tradition of the United States Navy. But repeated acts of violence against the Armed Forces of the United States must be met not only with alert defense but with positive reply. That reply is being given as I speak to you tonight. Air action is now in execution against gunboats and certain supporting facilities in North Viet-Nam which have been used in these hostile operations.

In the larger sense this new act of aggression, aimed directly at our own forces, again brings home to all of us in the United States the importance of the struggle for peace and security in Southeast Asia. . . .

It is a solemn responsibility to have to order even limited military action by forces whose overall strength is as vast and as awesome as those of the United States of America, but it is my considered conviction, shared throughout your Government, that firmness in the right is indispensable today for peace. That firmness will always be measured. Its mission is peace.

Lyndon Johnson, Address to the Nation, August 4, 1964; *American Foreign Policy: Current Documents,* 1964, pp. 980-81.

2 1 2   UNITED STATES PROTEST CONCERNING "UNPROVOKED ATTACK"

The United States Government takes an extremely serious view of the unprovoked attack made by Communist North Vietnamese torpedo boats on an American naval vessel, the U.S.S. *Maddox,* operating on the high seas, in the Gulf of Tonkin, on August 2. United States ships have traditionally operated freely on the high seas, in accordance with the rights guaranteed by international law to vessels of all nations. They will continue to do so and will take whatever measures are appropriate for their defense. The United States Government expects that the authorities of the regime in North Viet-Nam will be under no misapprehension as to the grave consequences which would inevitably result from any further unprovoked offensive military action against United States forces.

Department of State, message, August 3, 1964, read to correspondents on August 4; *American Foreign Policy: Current Documents,* 1964, pp. 979-80.

2 1 3   PRESIDENT'S INSTRUCTIONS TO RETALIATE FOR ATTACK

I have instructed the Navy:

1. to continue the patrols in the Gulf of Tonkin off the coast of North Viet-Nam,

2. to double the force by adding an additional destroyer to the one already on patrol,

3. to provide a combat air patrol over the destroyers, and

4. to issue orders to the commanders of the combat aircraft and the two destroyers [U.S.S. *Maddox* and U.S.S. *C. Turner Joy*],

    (a) to attack any force which attacks them in international waters and

    (b) to attack with the objective not only of driving off the force but of destroying it.

Lyndon Johnson, statement, read to correspondents, August 3, 1964; *American Foreign Policy: Current Documents,* 1964, p. 980. For additional documents and commentary, see pp. 982-91.

214   THIRD NORTH VIETNAM ATTACK ON AMERICAN DESTROYERS

Yesterday we received reports from the Commander-in-Chief of the Pacific Fleet that a nighttime incident was occurring in international waters in the Gulf of Tonkin.

CINCPAC [Commander-in-Chief of the Pacific Fleet] reports that two United States destroyers on a routine patrol 42 miles from land in the Gulf of Tonkin were menaced by four unidentified vessels which, because of their dispositions, courses, and speed, indicated hostile intent.

The destroyers, after changing course to minimize danger to themselves and after the unidentified vessels continued to close, fired warning rounds. In spite of these warning rounds, the unidentified vessels continued to close. The destroyers then properly opened fire and the approaching craft disappeared without closing sufficiently to open fire on the destroyers.

The destroyers are continuing their patrols in the international waters in the Gulf of Tonkin and United States air and sea forces remain prepared to respond immediately to any attack.

Robert McNamara, statement, to news correspondents, September 19, 1964; *American Foreign Policy: Current Documents*, 1964, pp. 999-1000.

ATTACK ON THE *LIBERTY*, 1967

The *Liberty* incident is strange for several reasons. Without warning, the U.S.S. *Liberty*--a Navy communications and intelligence ship, cruising in international waters off the Sinai coast during the Arab-Israeli Six-Day War--was attacked on June 8, 1967, by the aircraft and torpedo boats of Israel--a "friendly power." At the outset there was uncertainty as to which country was responsible, and confusion persists as to the reasons for the attack. To clarify our reaction, President Johnson immediately sent a hot line message to the Soviet government, advising Chairman Alexsei Kosygin that American carrier aircraft were dispatched solely to investigate and clarify the situation, not to become involved in the Six-Day War, and the Soviet leader indicated that he was relaying this information to Mideast Arab governments.

On June 10 Israel's ambassador in Washington submitted a formal apology to the Secretary of State, calling the attack a "tragic accident," to which the United States responded that the ship was clearly identified and flew the American flag and that Israeli aircraft had flown over the ship for some time before the attack and therefore had ample opportunity to verify its identity. Although Israel admitted responsibility, apologized, and promised and eventually made compensation to bereaved families and the injured and paid a share of the cost of the damage to the ship, the motives for the attack have not been satisfactorily explained. Both the Israeli and American governments downplayed the incident.

The second peculiarity is that, despite Israeli Defense Forces official investigations, the mystery as to whether the *Liberty* attack was intentional or inadvertent remains. The Israeli fact-finding report, while admitting error, asserted that the attack was not deliberate and was undertaken without malice.

The third surprising feature is that, although the incident was regarded as sufficiently serious to cause President Johnson to communicate with Moscow via the hot line, virtually no significant documents on the matter were published by the United States government in the usual official compilations, as illustrated by Documents 215-217. Moreover, by comparison with other attacks on American ships, President Johnson only referred to the *Liberty* once in his press conferences when, on June 13, in a noncommittal response to a question, he told the assemblage, "I think you know about as much about it as we do." As a result, information and analysis need to be gleaned from secondary sources, such as media reports and, subsequently, memoirs and biographies, and other unofficial historical accounts. For additional commentary on the Six-Day War, see Chapter 30, section on Arab-Israeli Wars.

215 STATEMENTS CONCERNING ATTACK ON THE *LIBERTY*

The fighting has already brought the suffering and pain that comes with all such conflict. These losses have included the lives of Americans engaged in the work of peaceful communication on the high seas. On this matter we have found it necessary to make a prompt and firm protest to the Israel Government which, to its credit, had already acknowledged its responsibility and had apologized. This tragic episode will underline for all Americans the correctness of our own urgent concern that the fighting should stop at once.

Lyndon Johnson, letter to Senator Mike Mansfield, referring to the attack on the *Liberty,* June 8, 1967; *American Foreign Policy: Current Documents,* 1967, p. 517.

*   *   *

Now, reference has been made to the attack on our ship *Liberty.* I stated in this Council, in the strongest terms, the protest of our Government against that attack, and we have renewed that protest in the strongest terms to the Israeli authorities. We regard that attack to be an unjustified attack. And I have welcomed expressions made by some, but not by all, of the members of the Council expressing regret about the lives we have lost in this conflict, just as I have expressed regret about the lives of all other personnel lost in this conflict, including the lives of the combatants themselves.

Arthur Goldberg, statement, United Nations Security Council, discussing the Middle East war, June 13, 1967; *American Foreign Policy: Current Documents,* 1967, p. 529.

2 1 6   PRESIDENT'S COMMENT ON USE OF WASHINGTON-MOSCOW HOT LINE

I think it is always helpful when you can convey your thought orally or in writing to a person whom you want to communicate with. . . . I did not see, except for the time involved, a great deal of difference between this [hot line] and the other communications that save time.

You send a message just like you send a cable. There is no voice involved. The "hot line" was something dramatic, I guess. We just write out our message, giving our views, and say, "Here is how we feel about it." They come back with the same message. You take it and read it as you would any other message.

Lyndon Johnson, comment, news conference, June 13, 1967; *Papers of Presidents: Johnson,* 1967, I, 615. For commentary on the use of the hot line during the Six-Day War, see Lyndon Johnson, *The Vantage Point* (New York: Holt, Rinehart, and Winston, 1971), pp. 287, 298-99, 301-3, 484. On the establishment of the Washington-Moscow hot line, see Document 372.

2 1 7   ISRAEL PAYS COMPENSATION FOR ATTACK ON *LIBERTY*

On April 28, the United States Government received $3,566,457 from the Government of Israel in settlement of certain claims arising out of the attack on the U.S.S. *Liberty* on June 8, 1967. The amount received represents payment in full of the following United States claims:

A. 164 claims totaling $3,452,275 on behalf of the members of the crew of the U.S.S. *Liberty* who were injured in the attack;

B. A claim for $92,437 for expenses incurred by the United States Government in providing medical treatment to the injured men;

C. A claim for $21,745 for expenses incurred by the United States Government in reimbursing members of the crew of the U.S.S. *Liberty* for personal property damaged or destroyed in the attack. . . .

On May 31, 1968, the Government of Israel paid in full claims totaling $3,323,500 on behalf of the families of the 34 men killed in the attack.

The only unsettled claim arising out of the attack on the U.S.S. *Liberty* is the claim for damage to the ship, which remains under discussion.

Department of State press release, May 13, 1969; 60 *Department of State Bulletin* (June 2, 1969):   473.

SEIZURE OF THE *PUEBLO,* 1968

On January 23, 1968, North Korean patrol boats surrounded and seized the U.S.S. *Pueblo,* an American intelligence-gathering ship, in international waters in the Sea of Japan, and forced it into the North Korean port of Wonsan. The United States protested this action as a violation of conventional international law of the sea and the common practice of nations, and demanded the immediate release of the ship and its crew of eighty-three. When North Korea refused, President Johnson ordered the mobilization of approximately 15,000 air and naval reservists, sent additional forces to South Korea, and stationed the U.S.S. *Enterprise* off the coast of Wonsan.

The United States also took its case, which the President called a "wanton and aggressive act," to the United Nations Security Council and to the Military Armistice Commission at Panmunjom, and sought by indirect diplomatic means --through what Dean Rusk called "channels that are available to us," including attempts to establish contact with North Korea through the International Red Cross and the Soviet and other governments--to persuade the world community to pressure North Korean leaders to return the ship and its crew. This case illustrates the difficulty of dealing with an adversary power with which Washington lacks normal diplomatic channels and of taking effective action, diplomatic and military, when the lives of American hostages are at stake and viable American options are therefore limited.

Despite the measures taken, the North Koreans held the *Pueblo* and its crew and did not release the latter until December, and then only after the United States signed an apology--which it repudiated in advance, but which North Korea sought and employed for propaganda purposes. The *Pueblo* was confiscated. The documents contained in this section constitute reports of the President, the White House, and the Departments of State and Defense on the North Korean seizure, attempts to get North Korea to return the Americans, and the welcoming of the crew members when they were finally released (Documents 218-222).

2 1 8   CRISIS WITH NORTH KOREA OVER SEIZURE OF THE *PUEBLO*

This week the North Koreans committed yet another wanton and aggressive act by seizing an American ship and its crew in international waters. Clearly, this cannot be accepted.

We are doing two things: First, we are very shortly today taking the question before the Security Council of the United Nations. The best result would be for the whole world community to persuade North Korea to return our ship and our men, and to stop the dangerous course of aggression against South Korea.

We have been making other diplomatic efforts as well. We shall continue to use every means available to find a prompt and a peaceful solution to the problem.

Second, we have taken and we are taking certain precautionary measures to make sure that our military forces are prepared for any contingency that might arise in this area. . . .

I hope that the North Koreans will recognize the gravity of the situation which they have created. I am confident that the American people will exhibit in this crisis, as they have in other crises, the determination and unity which are necessary to see it through.

Lyndon Johnson, Address to the Nation, January 26, 1968; *Papers of Presidents: Johnson*, 1968-1969, I, 77. Also in 58 *Department of State Bulletin* (February 12, 1968): 189.

219 INITIAL REPORTS ON SEIZURE OF THE *PUEBLO*

The U.S.S. *Pueblo*, a Navy intelligence collection auxiliary ship, was surrounded by North Korean patrol boats and boarded by an armed party in international waters in the Sea of Japan shortly before midnight e.s.t. last night [January 22].

The United States Government acted immediately to establish contact with North Korea through the Soviet Union.

When the *Pueblo* was boarded, its reported position was approximately 25 miles from the mainland of North Korea.

The ship reported the boarding took place at 127 degrees, 54.3 minutes east longitude; 39 degrees, 25 minutes north latitude. The time was 11:45 p.m. e.s.t.

The ship's complement consists of 83, including six officers and 75 enlisted men and two civilians.

At approximately 10 p.m. e.s.t., a North Korean patrol boat approached the *Pueblo*. Using international signals, it requested the *Pueblo's* nationality. The *Pueblo* identified herself as a U.S. ship. Continuing to use flag signals, the patrol boat said: "Heave to or I will open fire on you." The *Pueblo* replied: "I am in international waters." The patrol boat circled the *Pueblo*.

Approximately 1 hour later, three additional patrol craft appeared. One of them ordered: "Follow in my wake; I have a pilot aboard." The four ships closed in on the *Pueblo*, taking different positions on her bow, beam, and quarter. Two MIG aircraft were also sighted by the *Pueblo* circling off the starboard bow.

One of the patrol craft began backing toward the bow of the *Pueblo*, with fenders rigged. An armed boarding party was standing on the bow.

The *Pueblo* radioed at 11:45 p.m. that she was being boarded by North Koreans.

At 12:10 a.m. e.s.t. today [January 23] the *Pueblo* reported that she had been requested to follow the North Korean ships into Wonsan and that she had not used any weapons.

The final message from the *Pueblo* was sent at 12:32 a.m. It reported that it had come to "all stop" and that it was "going off the air."

Defense Department, statement, press release, January 23, 1968; 58 *Department of State Bulletin* (February 12, 1968): 189-90.

*   *   *

You've all seen or had the statement by the Department of Defense this morning about the boarding in international waters of a U.S. naval vessel by North Koreans. I'm authorized to state that the United States

Government views this action by North Korea with utmost gravity. We have asked the Soviet Union to convey to the North Koreans our urgent request for the immediate release of the vessel and crew.

The matter will also be raised directly with the North Koreans in a meeting of the Military Armistice Commission. We will, of course, use any other channels which might be helpful.

I wish to reemphasize the seriousness with which we view this flagrant North Korean action against the United States naval vessel on the high seas.

*   *   *

At the meeting of the Military Armistice Commission in Panmunjom, the reaction of the North Korean side was cynical, denunciatory of the United States, and a distortion of the facts in the case.

Department of State, statements, January 23 and 24, 1968; 58 *Department of State Bulletin* (February 12, 1968): 190. For additional commentary, see pp. 189-200.

*   *   *

The President this afternoon, after intensive consultations with his senior advisers, instructed Ambassador Goldberg [U.S. Representative to the United Nations Arthur J. Goldberg] to request an urgent meeting of the Security Council of the United Nations to consider the grave situation which has arisen in Korea by reason of North Korean aggressive actions against the Republic of Korea and the illegal and wanton seizure of a United States vessel and crew in international waters.

This action by the President reflects his earnest desire to settle this matter promptly and, if at all possible, by diplomatic means.

White House, statement, read to news correspondents, January 25, 1968; 58 *Department of State Bulletin* (February 12, 1968): 192.

220 SUBSEQUENT REPORTS ON THE *PUEBLO* CRISIS

Let me point out something that is quite important here. Warships on the high seas--according to the 1958 conventions on the law of the sea --warships on the high seas have complete immunity from the jurisdiction of any state other than the flag state.

Now, let's assume just for a moment what is obviously not true from the testimony from all sides, including the North Korean side, that this ship was picked up in territorial waters, or in waters claimed by North Korea to be territorial waters. Even there, under the convention of the law of the sea, 1958, article 23, it makes it quite clear that if any warship comes into territorial waters, the coastal state can require it to leave. It does not obtain a right to seize it.

Now, in 1965 and in 1966 there were three incidents in which a Soviet war vessel came into American territorial waters within our 3-mile limit. We didn't seize those vessels; we simply required them to depart. That is the civilized practice among nations in dealing with such questions, because warships have a sovereign immunity attached to them, you see. So under no theory of the case can the action taken by North Korea be justified.

Dean Rusk, comment, "Meet the Press," February 4, 1968; 58 *Department of State Bulletin* (February 26, 1968): 265. For the text of the Convention on the High Seas, April 29, 1958, not signed by North Korea, see TIAS 5200; 13 *U.S. Treaties* 2312-21. For this convention also see Document 344.

*   *   *

Then, on January 23, North Korea seized the *Pueblo* in international waters. This may or may not have been part of the North Korean program for trying to intimidate the South Koreans, disrupt their progress, and divert South Korean and American armed forces from South Viet-Nam.

The *Pueblo* is an intelligence-gathering ship, one of a number of such vessels which we and the Soviet Union and others have long had on the high seas. The Soviet Union has had such ships operating along both our east and our west coasts, off Guam, and near our naval task forces in the Mediterranean, the Western Pacific, and elsewhere.

In a genuinely peaceful and open world these operations would not be needed. In the world of today they are essential. They are especially important to us because our adversaries have closed societies. They don't publish the sort of facts that the Communists know about our military disposition simply from reading newspapers and department and committee reports.

There is not a scrap of evidence to indicate that the *Pueblo* was at any time inside the 12-mile limit which North Korea claims as territorial waters. It was under strict orders to stay outside the 12-mile limit. It was outside that limit when it was intercepted and seized. We know that not only from our own data but from intercepted North Korean messages.

The most essential fact is that, under accepted international law, North Korea had no right to seize the *Pueblo* either on the high seas or in territorial waters. The convention on the law of the sea, adopted in 1958, makes it entirely clear that, if any warship comes inside territorial waters, the coastal state can require it to leave but does not have the right to seize it. At least three times in recent years Soviet war vessels have come inside our territorial limit of only three miles. We didn't seize them; we simply required them to depart.

So this North Korean action was a very grave violation of the law and practice of nations.

The President's first concern has been to recover the crew and the ship. And he has hoped to avoid a renewal of major warfare in Korea. So, while taking various precautionary measures, he has been seeking to obtain the return of the crew and ship by peaceful means.

We asked the International Red Cross to intercede on behalf of the crew, and it agreed to do so.

We have asked many other nations to cooperate with our efforts to recover the crew and ship by peaceful means.

At our suggestion, an emergency session of the United Nations Security Council was convened.

Then the North Koreans said the matter was not within the jurisdiction of the United Nations but should be discussed through the Military Armistice Commission at Panmunjom. We have been meeting with them there, so far with very little result. They have given us the names of the one member of the crew who was killed and of three who were injured-- that is all.

There are 50,000 American troops in the Republic of Korea. The President has taken steps to strengthen our forces in the area, without diminishing our forces in South Viet-Nam.

North Korea will make a grave error if it interprets our restraint as a lack of determination or deludes itself into thinking that the American commitment to defend the Republic of Korea has weakened in the slightest.

Dean Rusk, address, "Our Concern for Peace in East Asia," National Association of Secondary School Principals, February 10, 1968; 58 *Department of State Bulletin* (March 4, 1968): 301-2. For additional commentary, see pp. 307-8, and Secretary Rusk's response to questions, interview with college editors, February 2, 1968, pp. 352-53.

221 RELEASE OF THE CREW OF THE *PUEBLO*

I am deeply gratified that after a long 11 months of totally unjustified detention by the North Koreans, the crew of the U.S.S. *Pueblo* have been freed. They should be reunited with their families in time for Christmas and I am happy for them that their time of ordeal ends on a note of joy. . . .

The negotiations at Panmunjom were cruelly drawn out and I am grateful for the understanding which the *Pueblo* families showed through the long and painful period during which their Government has sought to free the crew.

Lyndon Johnson, statement on release of eighty-two surviving crew members and one deceased member, December 22, 1968; *Papers of Presidents: Johnson,* 1968-1969, II, 1210. Also in 60 *Department of State Bulletin* (January 6, 1969): 1-2.

*   *   *

The crew of the U.S.S. *Pueblo* was freed today at Panmunjom. They will immediately be given medical examinations and returned to the United States. Their families will meet them in San Diego.

The agreement to free the men involved the acceptance by both sides of the following procedure. General Woodward, our negotiator, signed a document prepared by the North Koreans. He made a formal statement for the record just before signing. The text of his statement had earlier been transmitted to the North Koreans and they had accepted our requirement that this statement be coupled with the signature of their document. Our statement read:

> The position of the United States Government with regard to the *Pueblo,* as consistently expressed in the negotiations at Panmunjom and in public, has been that the ship was not engaged in illegal activity, that there is no convincing evidence that the ship at any time intruded into the territorial waters claimed by North Korea, and that we could not apologize for actions which we did not believe took place. The document which I am going to sign was prepared by the North Koreans and is at variance with the above position, but my signature will not and cannot alter the facts. I will sign the document to free the crew and only to free the crew.

General Woodward then signed the North Korean document and received the custody of the crew.

As he said, General Woodward placed his name on the false North Korean document for one reason only: to obtain the freedom of the crew who were illegally seized and have been illegally held as hostages by the North Koreans for almost exactly 11 months. He made clear that this signature did not imply the acceptance by the United States of the numerous false statements in that document. Indeed, the prior acceptance by the North Koreans of the statement which General Woodward read into the record just before signing shows clearly their recognition of our position that the facts of the case call for neither an admission of guilt nor for an apology.

Department of State, statement, December 22, 1969; 60 *Department of State Bulletin* (January 6, 1969): 1. Also see statement of Secretary of State Dean Rusk, December 22, 1969, p. 2.

2 2 2   UNITED STATES "APOLOGY"--CONDITION FOR RELEASE OF *PUEBLO* CREW

To the Government of the Democratic People's Republic of Korea,

The Government of the United States of America,

Acknowledging the validity of the confessions of the crew of the USS *Pueblo* and of the documents of evidence produced by the Representative of the Government of the Democratic People's Republic of Korea to the effect that the ship, which was seized by the self-defense measures of the naval vessels of the Korean People's Army in the territorial waters of the Democratic People's Republic of Korea on January 23, 1968, had illegally intruded into the territorial waters of the Democratic People's Republic of Korea,

Shoulders full responsibility and solemnly apologizes for the grave acts of espionage committed by the U.S. ship against the Democratic People's Republic of Korea after having intruded into the territorial waters of the Democratic People's Republic of Korea,

And gives firm assurance that no U.S. ships will intrude again in the future into the territorial waters of the Democratic People's Republic of Korea.

Meanwhile, the Government of the United States of America earnestly requests the Government of the Democratic People's Republic of Korea to deal leniently with the former crew members of the USS *Pueblo* confiscated by the Democratic People's Republic of Korea side, taking into consideration the fact that these crew members have confessed honestly to their crimes and petitioned the Government of the Democratic People's Republic of Korea for leniency.

Simultaneously with the signing of this document, the undersigned acknowledges receipt of 82 former crew members of the *Pueblo* and one corpse.

On behalf of the Government of the United States of America
GILBERT H. WOODWARD, Major General, USA

North Korean document, signed under duress by General Gilbert Woodward, United States negotiator at Panmunjom, to free the *Pueblo* crew members; 60 *Department of State Bulletin* (January 6, 1969): 2-3.

SEIZURE OF THE *MAYAGUEZ,* 1975

Seven years after North Korea captured the *Pueblo,* two years after the Vietnam War truce was signed, and shortly after the Khmer Rouge forces toppled the Cambodian coalition government, on May 12, 1975, Cambodian forces seized a United States merchant ship--the S.S. *Mayaguez*--which was en route from Hong Kong to Thailand. Manned by an American citizen crew of thirty-nine, the *Mayaguez* was fired upon, boarded, and seized in international waters by Cambodian patrol boats, and it was forced to proceed to Koh Tang Island. The reasons for this attack are unclear, it being alleged both that it was undertaken by a local army unit without the knowledge or approval of the Phnom Penh government and that it was designed to forestall American spying and subversion in the area.

The United States reaction differed markedly from that at the time of the *Pueblo* seizure. President Ford ordered American naval forces to conduct reconnaissance and then to mobilize in order to prevent movement of the ship into a mainland port and removal of the crew to the mainland, and also to interdict any movement between the ship or the island and the mainland, while seeking to prevent the loss of life or injury to the American captives. Three Cambodian patrol boats were destroyed during the encounter and four others were damaged and immobilized.

The objective of the United States was to rescue both the crew and the *Mayaguez.* Demands for release were levied, both publicly and privately, without success. Consequently, Air, Navy, and Marine forces were employed in an integrated rescue mission. Fifteen Americans were killed and others died in a helicopter crash. On May 14 both the ship and the crew were retrieved. According to President Ford, these military measures were undertaken under his "constitutional Executive power and his authority as Commander-in-Chief," supplemented by a Senate resolution (approved May 14), authorizing military action in implementation of the War Powers Resolution (Documents 223-226). For additional commentary, see *Historic Documents,* 1975, pp. 311-18.

223 PRESIDENT'S REPORT TO CONGRESS ON THE *MAYAGUEZ* CRISIS

On 12 May 1975, I was advised that the S.S. *Mayaguez,* a merchant vessel of United States registry en route from Hong Kong to Thailand with a U.S. citizen crew, was fired upon, stopped, boarded, and seized by Cambodian naval patrol boats of the Armed Forces of Cambodia in international waters in the vicinity of Poulo Wai Island. The seized vessel was then forced to proceed to Koh Tang Island where it was required to anchor. This hostile act was in clear violation of international law.

In view of this illegal and dangerous act, I ordered, as you have been previously advised, United States military forces to conduct the necessary reconnaissance and to be ready to respond if diplomatic efforts to secure the return of the vessel and its personnel were not successful. Two United States reconnaissance aircraft in the course of locating the *Mayaguez* sustained minimal damage from small firearms. Appropriate demands for the return of the *Mayaguez* and its crew were made, both publicly and privately, without success.

In accordance with my desire that the Congress be informed on this matter and taking note of Section 4(a) (1) of the War Powers Resolution, I wish to report to you that at about 6:20 a.m., 13 May, pursuant to my instructions to prevent the movement of the *Mayaguez* into a mainland port, U.S. aircraft fired warning shots across the bow of the ship and gave visual signals to small craft approaching the ship. Subsequently, in order to stabilize the situation and in an attempt to preclude removal of the American crew of the *Mayaguez* to the mainland, where their rescue would be more difficult, I directed the United States Armed Forces to isolate the island and interdict any movement between the ship or the island and the mainland, and to prevent movement of the ship itself, while still taking all possible care to prevent loss of life or injury to the U.S. captives. During the evening of 13 May, a Cambodian patrol boat attempting to leave the island disregarded aircraft warnings and was sunk. Thereafter, two other Cambodian patrol craft were destroyed and four others were damaged and immobilized. One boat, suspected of having some U.S. captives aboard, succeeded in reaching Kompong Som after efforts to turn it around without injury to the passengers failed.

Our continued objective in this operation was the rescue of the captured American crew along with the retaking of the ship *Mayaguez.* For that purpose, I ordered late this afternoon [May 14] an assault by United States Marines on the island of Koh Tang to search out and rescue such Americans as might still be held there, and I ordered retaking of the *Mayaguez* by other Marines boarding from the destroyer escort *Holt.* In addition to continued fighter and gunship coverage of the Koh Tang area, these Marine activities were supported by tactical aircraft from the *Coral Sea,* striking the military airfield at Ream and other military targets in the area of Kompong Som in order to prevent reinforcement or support from the mainland of the Cambodian forces detaining the American vessel and crew.

At approximately 9:00 p.m. EDT on 14 May, *Mayaguez* was retaken by United States forces. At approximately 11:30 p.m., the entire crew of the *Mayaguez* was taken aboard the *Wilson.* U.S. forces have begun the process of disengagement and withdrawal.

This operation was ordered and conducted pursuant to the President's constitutional Executive power and his authority as Commander-in-Chief of the United States Armed Forces.

Gerald Ford, letter to the Speaker of the House of Representatives and the President Pro Tempore of the Senate, reporting on United States actions in the recovery of the *Mayaguez,* May 15, 1975; *Papers of Presidents: Ford,* 1975, I, 669-70. This constitutes President Ford's report under the War Powers Resolution.

224 SENATE RESOLUTION SUPPORTING THE PRESIDENT IN THE *MAYAGUEZ* CRISIS

[The Senate Foreign Relations] Committee condemns an act of armed aggression on an unarmed United States merchant vessel in the course of innocent passage on an established trade route.

The President has engaged in diplomatic means to secure its release, and we support that.

Third, we support the President in the exercise of his constitutional powers within the framework of the War Powers Resolution to secure the release of the ship and its men.

We urge the Cambodian Government to release the ship and the men forthwith.

Resolution of Senate Foreign Relations Committee, approved unanimously May 14, 1975; *Digest of United States Practice in International Law,* 1975, p. 881.

225 PRESIDENT'S REPORT FOLLOWING RECOVERY OF THE *MAYAGUEZ*

At my direction, United States forces tonight boarded the American merchant ship SS *Mayaguez* and landed at the Island of Koh Tang for the purpose of rescuing the crew and the ship, which had been illegally seized by Cambodian forces. They also conducted supporting strikes against nearby military installations.

I have now received information that the vessel has been recovered intact and the entire crew has been rescued. The forces that have successfully accomplished this mission are still under hostile fire, but are preparing to disengage.

I wish to express my deep appreciation and that of the entire Nation to the units and the men who participated in these operations for their valor and for their sacrifice.

Gerald Ford, remarks, broadcast live from White House, May 15, 1975; *Papers of Presidents: Ford,* 1975, p. 668.

226   COMMENTARY ON APPLICATION OF THE WAR POWERS RESOLUTION

Although there appears to be almost universal agreement that the Nation has the right and duty to use reasonable force to safeguard citizens and nationals abroad, opinions vary as to whether the President is constitutionally authorized to undertake such an initiative. . . . However one views the matter, that is, either as an exercise of constitutional power or a statutorily delegated power, the *Mayaguez* episode stands as evidence that that and similar rescue efforts are not out of the question. In the aftermath of the *Mayaguez* affair, Senator Eagleton proposed various amendments to the War Powers Resolution, including one which would declare that the President has the right to rescue endangered citizens even in the absence of congressional authorization. S. 1790, 94th Cong., 1st Sess. Obviously, passage of such an amendment would resolve the existing uncertain situation.

Legal memorandum of American Law Division, Congressional Research Service, August 4, 1976, inserted in the *Congressional Record* of September 29, 1976; *Digest of United States Practice in International Law,* 1976, pp. 741-43. For additional commentary on the President's authority to undertake rescue operations of brief duration involving limited force, see *Digest of United States Practice in International Law,* 1980, pp. 1049-52. For President Ford's views pertaining to the War Powers Resolution restraints on the President, see *Papers of Presidents: Ford,* 1975, I, 706-7. For War Powers Resolution, see Document 80.

14

Middle East Crises

... there is no security, no safety, in the appeasement of evil. It must be the core of Western policy that there be no sanctuary for terror.

Ronald Reagan
Address to the Nation, 1986

Post-World War II involvement of the United States in the Middle East--as exponent of self-determination, as peacemaker in Arab-Israeli relations, as a major oil importer and protector of Western oil interests, and as leader of the Western powers in preserving their strategic interests--has implicated this country in many of its diplomatic disputes and conflicts. Dozens of crises, beginning with that in Azerbaijan in 1946 and including such events as the Arab-Israeli wars, affected American goals, policies, interests, and strategy.

This chapter focuses on three of the most important crises that involved the United States as a principal participant, in each of which Middle East terrorism was a major issue, and in each of which the President reported to Congress in compliance with the War Powers Resolution. In other respects they differ markedly. For example, in the hostage crisis with Iran, a small contingent of United States military forces was employed on an ill-fated rescue mission; in Lebanon American diplomats and peacekeeping Marines were attacked by terrorist bombings; and in the air strike on Libya, United States aircraft were employed to attack military and terrorist targets in one of the most active and defiant centers of international terrorism.

This chapter needs to be related to Chapters 7 (the Eisenhower and Carter Doctrines), 13 (the attack on the U.S.S. *Liberty*), 19 (international terrorism), and 30 (on the Middle East).

IRANIAN SEIZURE OF AMERICAN HOSTAGES, 1979-1981

Although the United States maintained friendly relations with Iran, led by Shah Mohammad Reza Pahlavi, for many years, supported Iran's modernization, and regarded Iran as virtually a Middle East ally, internal opposition to the Shah's rule flamed during the 1970's, and on January 16, 1979, he fled the country, abdicating his throne after a thirty-seven-year reign. Mass violence broke out in Iran in 1978, intensified the following year, and virtually produced anarchy by mid-1980. Eventually an Islamic fundamentalist government emerged under the Ayatollah Ruholla Khomeini, whose autocratic regime held the United States responsible for Iran's Westernization.

When the Carter administration decided to permit the deposed Shah to come to the United States for major medical treatment in October 1979, a band of militants overran and seized the United States embassy in Tehran on November 4, took more than sixty Americans as hostages, and held fifty-two of them as prisoners for nearly fifteen months. This action was a blatant violation of the Vienna Convention on Diplomatic Relations (1961)--cited in Chapter 4 --of which Iran was a signatory.

Wavering between diplomatic compromise and punitive action, President Carter employed a variety of measures to persuade or pressure Iran to release the American hostages. These included appointing special presidential envoys to negotiate with Iranian authorities, encouraging foreign leaders to support the United States and attempt to mediate to free the hostages, applying economic and other sanctions against Iran, breaking off diplomatic relations, and even launching a military rescue mission. Only when the hostage detention reached a point of diminishing returns, Iran found itself internationally isolated and embroiled in a war with Iraq, and the International Court of Justice ruled that the Iranian government must release the hostages, return the embassy to the United States, and pay reparations was the Khomeini regime willing to negotiate a settlement.

This crisis consisted of five phases: the seizure of the embassy and taking American diplomatic staff members as hostages, and initial United States reaction (Documents 227-228), the levying of American sanctions against Iran (Document 229), the aborted United States rescue mission (Document 230), bargaining on the conditions for the release of the hostages (Documents 231-232), and the negotiation of an agreement to release the hostages (Document 233) and their return to the United States. For a compilation of forty-eight documents concerning United States relations with Iran, 1979-1980, see *American Foreign Policy: Basic Documents,* 1977-1980, pp. 728-86. For commentary on three major aspects of the crisis, see "American Hostages in Iran, November 4-December 31, 1979," "Iran Rescue Attempt, April 25 and August 23, 1980," and "Iranian Release of U.S. Hostages, January 20, 1981," in *Historic Documents,* 1979, pp. 867-93; 1980, pp. 351-85; and 1981, pp. 145-62.

227 UNITED STATES GENERAL POLICY TOWARD IRAN

The U.S. policy toward Iran has been based on three consistent principles as events there have evolved over recent months.

First, we have repeatedly made it clear that decisions affecting the future of Iran and the relationship between the Iranian people and their government are decisions which must be made in Iran by Iranians. . . .

Second, the U.S. Government has worked within the institutional framework of Iran, under its Constitution, with the duly established authorities of Iran as specified in the Iranian Constitution. . . .

Third, we have supported Iranian independence. We have taken the position that no outside power should exploit instability in Iran or any other country for its own advantage. The overriding American objective for Iran is simply that it should have the freedom to work out its own future free from such interference. . . .

Within the general context of those principles, we have pursued the following objectives: First, we hope to see an end to the bloodshed so that the people of Iran can return to normal life. . . .

Second, we want to maintain a close and friendly relationship with an independent, stable and secure Iran. We believe the interests of Iran and of the United States are closely intertwined and we seek an environment of mutual respect and positive cooperation. . . .

Third, we seek a stable and prosperous Iran which can play its rightful role in the region and in the international community. . . .

We believe that these objectives serve not only the interests of our own country but also the interests of the Iranian people. We believe they offer a practical basis for cooperation.

Assistant Secretary of State for Near Eastern and South Asian Affairs, statement, House Foreign Affairs Committee, January 17, 1979; *American Foreign Policy: Basic Documents,* 1977-1980, pp. 730-31. For earlier statements, see pp. 725-27.

228 REPORT ON TAKING OF UNITED STATES HOSTAGES IN IRAN

The seizure of more than 60 Americans in our Embassy in Tehran has provoked strong feelings here at home. There is outrage. There is frustration. And there is deep anger.

There is also pride in the courage of those who are in danger and sympathy for them and for their families. But the most important concern for all Americans at this moment is safety of our fellow citizens held in Tehran.

The President shares these feelings. He is pursuing every possible avenue in a situation that is extremely volatile and difficult. His efforts involve many countries and individuals. Many of these efforts must of necessity be conducted without publicity, and all require the calmest possible atmosphere.

The President knows that no matter how deeply we may feel, none of us would want to do anything that would worsen the danger in which our fellow Americans have been placed.

. . . The President expects every American to refrain from any action that might increase the danger to the American hostages in Tehran.

White House statement, to reporters, November 9, 1979; *Papers of Presidents: Carter,* 1979, II, 2102-3. The United States embassy was seized and Americans were taken hostage on November 4; also see pp. 2105, 2167-74, 2194-95. For statement of Secretary of State Vance concerning diplomatic efforts to obtain release of Americans held in Iran, November 8, 1979, see *American Foreign Policy: Basic Documents,* 1977-1980, p. 737.

229   UNITED STATES SANCTIONS APPLIED AGAINST IRAN

Ever since Iranian terrorists imprisoned American Embassy personnel in Tehran early in November, these 50 men and women--their safety, their health, and their future--have been our central concern. We've made every effort to obtain their release on honorable, peaceful, and humanitarian terms, but the Iranians have refused to release them or even to improve the inhumane conditions under which these Americans are being held captive.

The events of the last few days have revealed a new and significant dimension in this matter. The militants controlling the Embassy have stated they are willing to turn the hostages over to the Government of Iran, but the Government has refused to take custody of the American hostages. This lays bare the full responsibility of the Ayatollah Khomeini and the Revolutionary Council for the continued illegal and outrageous holding of the innocent hostages. . . .

It must be made clear that the failure to release the hostages will involve increasingly heavy costs to Iran and to its interests. I have today ordered the following steps.

First, the United States of America is breaking diplomatic relations with the Government of Iran. The Secretary of State has informed the Government of Iran that its Embassy and consulates in the United States are to be closed immediately. . . .

Second, the Secretary of the Treasury will put into effect official sanctions prohibiting exports from the United States to Iran, in accordance with the sanctions approved by 10 members of the United Nations Security Council on January 13 in the resolution which was vetoed by the Soviet Union. . . .

Third, the Secretary of the Treasury will make a formal inventory of the assets of the Iranian Government, which were frozen by my previous order, and also will make a census or an inventory of the outstanding claims of American citizens and corporations against the Government of Iran. This accounting of claims will aid in designing a program against Iran for the hostages, for the hostage families, and other U.S. claimants. . . .

Fourth, the Secretary of Treasury [State] and the Attorney General will invalidate all visas issued to Iranian citizens for future entry into the United States, effective today. . . .

Jimmy Carter, statement to reporters, April 7, 1980; *American Foreign Policy: Basic Documents,* 1977-1980, pp. 758-59. For earlier statements concerning sanctions, November 1979 and January 1980, see pp. 737-40, 752-56.

230 ABORTED ATTEMPT TO RESCUE AMERICAN HOSTAGES IN IRAN

Late yesterday, I cancelled a carefully planned operation which was underway in Iran to position our rescue team for later withdrawal of American hostages, who have been held captive there since November 4. Equipment failure in the rescue helicopters made it necessary to end the mission.

As our team was withdrawing, after my order to do so, two of our American aircraft collided on the ground following a refueling operation in a remote desert location in Iran. . . .

There was no fighting; there was no combat. But to my deep regret, eight of the crewmen of the two aircraft which collided were killed, and several other Americans were hurt in the accident. Our people were immediately airlifted from Iran. Those who were injured have gotten medical treatment, and all of them are expected to recover.

No knowledge of this operation by any Iranian officials or authorities was evident to us until several hours after all Americans were withdrawn from Iran.

Our rescue team knew and I knew that the operation was certain to be difficult and it was certain to be dangerous. We were all convinced that if and when the rescue operation had been commenced that it had an excellent chance of success. . . .

The mission on which they were embarked was a humanitarian mission. It was not directed against Iran; it was not directed against the people of Iran. It was not undertaken with any feeling of hostility toward Iran or its people. It has caused no Iranian casualties. . . .

This rescue attempt had to await my judgment that the Iranian authorities could not or would not resolve this crisis on their own initiative. With the steady unraveling of authority in Iran and the mounting dangers that were posed to the safety of the hostages themselves and the growing realization that their early release was highly unlikely, I made a decision to commence the rescue operations plans. . . .

It was my decision to attempt the rescue operation. It was my decision to cancel it when problems developed in the placement of our rescue team for a future rescue operation. The responsibility is fully my own.

Jimmy Carter, Address to the Nation, April 25, 1980; *American Foreign Policy: Basic Documents*, 1977-1980, I, 764-65. For President Carter's report to Congress under the War Powers Resolution, see pp. 777-79.

231 IRAN'S CONDITIONS FOR RELEASE OF AMERICAN HOSTAGES

1. Since, in the past, the American Government has always interfered in various ways in Iran's political and military affairs, she should make a pledge and a promise that from now on she will in no way interfere, either directly or indirectly, politically or militarily, in the affairs of the Islamic Republic of Iran.

2. Unfreeze all of our assets and to put all these assets and all the assets and capital of Iran which are in America or which are in organizations belonging to America and to American subjects in other countries at the disposal of Iran in such a way that the Government of the Islamic Republic of Iran can use them in any manner it wishes. And that the decree of the American President dated 14 November 1979 and subsequent decrees concerning the blocking of Iranian assets will be declared null and void. . . .

3. Abrogation and cancellation of all economic and financial decisions and measures against the Islamic Republic of Iran and implementation of all the necessary administrative and legal measures with regard to cancellation and abrogation of all claims by the U.S. Government and U.S. companies and institutions against Iran in any form and for any reason. Implementation by the American Government of all necessary administrative and legal measures with regard to not raising any form of new legal or criminal or financial measures by official and unofficial and legal persons. . . .

4. Return of the assets of the cursed Shah, while officially recognizing the measures taken by Iran and their effectiveness in asserting its sovereignty in confiscating the assets of the cursed Shah and his close relatives, whose assets, according to Iranian laws belong to the Iranian nation. . . .

According to this recommendation, the Islamic Republic Government will release all 52 U.S. criminals in return for the fulfillment of these conditions by the U.S. Government. However, should some of these conditions require more time, then when all conditions are accepted by the U.S. Government, with the fulfillment of each condition a number of criminals will be released at the discretion of the Islamic Government.

Report of Iranian Special Commission to the Islamic Consultative Assembly, November 2, 1980; *American Foreign Policy: Basic Documents,* 1977-1980, pp. 774-75.

232 UNITED STATES REPLY TO IRAN'S CONDITIONS FOR RELEASE OF HOSTAGES

The Government of the United States has received and has carefully reviewed the Resolution adopted on November 2, 1980, by the Islamic Consultative Assembly of Iran.

The United States accepts in principle the Resolution as the basis for ending the crisis, and hereby proposes the following series of

Presidential orders and declarations in response to the Resolution. Each of the Presidential orders and declarations is to be made public and become effective upon safe departure from Iran of the 52 hostages. . . .

The United States believes that this response to the decision of the Iranian Majlis represents the completion of the penultimate stage in resolving the hostage issue. The final step, which the United States believes should be taken in the next several days, would be to arrange, through the good offices of the Government of Algeria, release of all hostages concurrent with the United States taking all the specific steps noted above.

To implement this final step, the United States will deposit with the Government of Algeria copies of the Presidential declarations and orders noted above, to be effective upon the safe departure of all the hostages from Iran. When their safe departure is confirmed by the Government of Algeria, the Government of the United States will publicly release the Presidential orders and declarations.

Message from United States to government of Iran, November 11, 1980; *American Foreign Policy: Basic Documents, 1977-1980*, pp. 777-78. See document for detailed plans. Also see supplementary United States message, December 3, 1980, pp. 778-80, and Iranian message, December 19, 1980, pp. 781-85.

233 ANNOUNCEMENT CONCERNING AGREEMENT TO RELEASE AMERICAN HOSTAGES

We have now reached an agreement with Iran which will result, I believe, in the freedom of our American hostages. The last documents have now been signed in Algiers, following the signing of the documents in Iran which will result in this agreement. We still have a few documents to sign before the money is actually transferred and the hostages are released.

The essence of the agreement is that following the release of our hostages, then we will unfreeze and transfer to the Iranians a major part of the assets which were frozen by me when the Iranians seized our Embassy compound and took our hostages. We have also reached complete agreement on the arbitration procedures between ourselves and Iran with the help of the Algerians which will resolve the claims that exist between residents of our Nation and Iran and vice-versa.

. . . All the preparations have been completed pending the final documents being signed.

Jimmy Carter, remarks to White House reporters, January 19, 1981; *Papers of Presidents: Carter*, 1980-1981, III, 3019. The "agreement," so far as the United States is concerned--signed and issued on January 19, 1981--consists of two "Statements of Adherence" and ten Executive Orders concerning the establishment of escrow accounts for transfer of funds to Iran, directions for the transfer of impounded Iranian assets including Iranian governmental assets and those held by non-banking institutions, revocation of prohibitions against transactions involving Iran, restrictions on transfer of property of the former Shah, release of the American hostages, and non-prosecution of claims of the hostages and for Iranian actions against the American embassy and elsewhere-- see pp. 3026-40. Also see President Carter's message to Congress explaining this agreement, pp. 3040-43. These actions were taken on President Carter's last day in office, and the hostages were released in Tehran at 12:25 (EST), in the early minutes of the Reagan presidency on January 20, and returned to the United States five days later. For President Reagan's remarks on welcoming the hostages in a White House ceremony on January 27, see *Papers of Presidents: Reagan*, 1981, pp. 41-44; also see pp. 17-24, 31, 39.

LEBANON CRISIS AND BOMBING OF AMERICAN MARINES IN BEIRUT, 1983

Lebanon, once a peaceful and prospering country, became embroiled in a conflict of Moslems vs. Christians and Israelis vs. Arabs and the Palestine Liberation Organization (PLO), and in internecine violence among a host of religious, political, and social factions. For years Lebanon suffered from foreign interventions, pitched battles, guerilla action, and rampant terrorism. In June 1982 Israeli troops invaded the country to crush the PLO, whose forces evacuated Beirut under the surveillance of foreign constabulary troops. In September President-elect Bashir Gemayel was killed in a bombing, and Palestinian refugee camps in west Beirut were surrounded by Israeli troops, who permitted Lebanese militia to enter the camps and massacre hundreds of civilians (for commentary, see *Historic Documents*, 1982, pp. 781-95). Lebanon's new President, Amin Gemayel, was unable to achieve a national consensus or to rid the country of Israeli and Syrian occupying forces.

In addition to attempting to mediate to achieve a cease-fire and political stability (Document 234) in September 1982 the United States was joined by France and Italy, and later also the United Kingdom, in establishing a "Multinational Force Lebanon" (MFL)--a constabulary cadre to assist the Lebanese government in reestablishing its sovereign authority (Document 235).

In 1983 the United States became a prime target of Moslem terrorists in Lebanon. On April 18 they bombed and destroyed the American embassy in Beirut, killing sixteen Americans and wounding more than 100 (Document 236). Six months later, on October 23, terrorists car-bombed the American MFL Marine compound at the Beirut airport, destroying the facility and killing some 241 military personnel, and simultaneously the French MFL facility was also bombed. The documents pertaining to this atrocity include a brief description of the bombing (Document 237), denunciation of the attack (Document 238), and the decision in 1984 to remove American Marines from the Multinational Force, and President Reagan's report to Congress concerning this determination (Documents 239-240).

For a compilation of more than 125 documents on United States relations with Lebanon in 1983 and 1984, see *American Foreign Policy: Current Documents*, 1983, pp. 732-812, and 1984, pp. 732-811. For commentary, see "Reports on Terror Bombing of U.S. Marines in Beirut, December 19 and 28, 1983," in *Historic Documents*, 1983, pp. 933-66.

234   UNITED STATES OBJECTIVES IN LEBANON

One, the withdrawal of all foreign forces--Israeli, Syrian, PLO, Iranian, you name them. All armed elements remaining in Lebanon must be subject to the control of the Central Government, and this includes the militia forces in the south.

Second, arrangements to secure the security of Israel's northern border; third, the restoration and reenforcement of a stable Central Government in Lebanon, the extension of Lebanese sovereignty throughout its territory, and the unity of that territory.

Then, of course, subsumed under all of these are arrangements to assure the security of all of the residents of Lebanon, including the Palestinians. . . .

We continue to see an important role for the 6,000 [United Nations constabulary] UNIFIL troops currently in Lebanon. There is also a need for the Multinational Force. The objectives of this force would be to facilitate the withdrawal process and to assist the Lebanese Central Government in reestablishing its control throughout Lebanon.

Department of State, press briefing, March 15, 1983; *American Foreign Policy: Current Documents,* 1983, pp. 746-47. For additional statements on American objectives, see pp. 738-40, 742-44. Also see Documents 238-240.

235   UNITED STATES PARTICIPATION IN "MULTINATIONAL FORCE LEBANON" (MFI)

I am pleased to sign into law today S.J. Res. 159, the Multinational Force in Lebanon Resolution. This Resolution provides important support for the United States presence and policies in Lebanon, and facilitates the pursuit of United States interests in that region on the bipartisan basis that has been the traditional hallmark of American foreign policy. In my view, the participation and support of the Congress are exceedingly important on matters of such fundamental importance to our national security interests, particularly where United States Armed Forces have been deployed in support of our policy objectives abroad. . . .

The text of this Resolution states a number of congressional findings, determinations, and assertions on certain matters. It is, of course, entirely appropriate for Congress to express its views on these subjects in this manner. However, I do not necessarily join in or agree with some of these expressions. For example, with regard to the congressional determination that the requirements of section 4(a)(1) of the War Powers Resolution became operative on August 29, 1983, I would note that the initiation of isolated or infrequent acts of violence against United States Armed Forces does not necessarily constitute actual or imminent involvement in hostilities, even if casualties to those forces result. I think it reasonable to recognize the inherent risk and imprudence of setting any precise formula for making such determinations.

. . . I therefore sign this Resolution in full support of its policies, but with reservations about some of the specific congressional expressions.

There have been historic differences between the legislative and executive branches of government with respect to the wisdom and constitutionality of section 5(b) of the War Powers Resolution. That section purports to require termination of the use of United States Armed Forces in actual hostilities or situations in which imminent involvement in hostilities is clearly indicated by the circumstances unless Congress, within 60 days, enacts a specific authorization for that use or otherwise extends the 60-day period. In light of these historic differences, I would like to emphasize my view that the imposition of such arbitrary and inflexible deadlines creates unwise limitations on presidential authority to deploy United States Forces in the interests of United States national security.
. . .

I believe it is, therefore, important for me to state, in signing this Resolution, that I do not and cannot cede any of the authority vested in me under the constitution as President and as Commander-in-Chief of United States Armed Forces. Nor should my signing be viewed as any acknowledgment that the President's constitutional authority can be impermissibly infringed by statute, that congressional authorization would be required if and when the period specified in section 5(b) of the War Powers Resolution might be deemed to have been triggered and the period had expired, or that section 6 of the Multinational Force in Lebanon Resolution may be interpreted to revise the President's constitutional authority to deploy United States Armed Forces.

Ronald Reagan, statement with reservations, on signing Congressional Resolution, October 12, 1983; *American Foreign Policy: Current Documents,* 1983, pp. 784-85. For the "Congressional Multinational Force in Lebanon Resolution," Public Law 98-119, October 12, 1983, in implementation of the War Powers Resolution, see pp. 785-87. For Department of State report, December 12, 1983, on the MFL, see pp. 805-8, and for President Reagan's reports to Congress, see *Papers of Presidents: Reagan,* 1983, II, 1384, 1389.

236 TERRORIST ATTACK ON AMERICAN EMBASSY IN BEIRUT

My fellow Americans, in a few hours I'll undertake one of the saddest journeys of my Presidency. I'll be going to Andrews Air Force Base to meet one of our Air Force Planes bringing home 16 Americans who died this week in the terrorist attack on the United States Embassy in Beirut.
. . .

We don't know yet who bears responsibility for this terrible deed. What we do know is that the terrorists who planned and carried out this cynical and cowardly attack have failed in their purpose. They mistakenly believe that if they're cruel enough and violent enough, they will weaken American resolve and deter us from our effort to help build a lasting and secure peace in the Middle East. If they think that, they don't know too much about America. As a free people, we've never allowed intimidation to stop us from doing what we know to be right. . . .

More than ever we're committed to giving the people of Lebanon the chance they deserve to lead normal lives, free from violence and free from the presence of all unwarranted foreign forces on their soil. And we remain committed to the Lebanese Government's recovery of full sovereignty throughout all its territory.

Ronald Reagan, Address to the Nation, April 23, 1983; *American Foreign Policy: Current Documents*, 1983, pp. 750-51. The bombing occurred on April 18, 1983. Also see presidential proclamation and White House statement, April 20, 1983; *Papers of Presidents: Reagan*, 1983, I, 563-64.

237 DESCRIPTION OF TERRORIST BOMBING OF MARINE HEADQUARTERS IN BEIRUT

This past Sunday, at 22 minutes after 6, Beirut time, with dawn just breaking, a truck, looking like a lot of other vehicles in the city, approached the airport on a busy, main road. . . . At the wheel was a young man on a suicide mission. The truck carried some 2,000 pounds of explosives. But there was no way our Marine guards could know this. Their first warning that something was wrong came when the truck crashed through a series of barriers, including a chain-link fence and barbed wire entanglements. The guards opened fire; but it was too late. The truck smashed through the doors of the headquarters building in which our Marines were sleeping and instantly exploded. The four-story concrete building collapsed in a pile of rubble.

More than 200 of the sleeping men were killed in that one hideous, insane attack. Many others suffered injury and are hospitalized here or in Europe.

Ronald Reagan, Address to the Nation, October 27, 1983; *American Foreign Policy: Current Documents*, 1983, p. 795. The attack took place on October 23.

238 DENUNCIATION OF TERRORIST BOMBING OF UNITED STATES MARINE HEAD-QUARTERS

Yesterday's acts of terrorism in Beirut which killed so many young American and French servicemen were a horrifying reminder of the type of enemy that we face in many critical areas of the world today--vicious, cowardly, and ruthless. Words can never convey the depth of compassion that we feel for those brave men and for their loved ones.

Many Americans are wondering why we must keep our forces in Lebanon. The reason they must stay there until the situation is under control is quite clear. We have vital interests in Lebanon and our actions in Lebanon are in the cause of world peace. With our allies England,

France, and Italy we're part of a multinational peacekeeping force seeking a withdrawal of all foreign forces from Lebanon and from the Beirut area while the new Lebanese Government undertakes to restore sovereignty throughout that country. . . .

Peace in Lebanon is key to the region's stability now and in the future. To the extent that the prospect for future stability is heavily influenced by the presence of our forces, it is central to our credibility on a global scale. We must not allow international criminals and thugs such as these to undermine the peace in Lebanon. . . . If Lebanon ends up under the tyranny of forces hostile to the West, not only will our strategic position in the Eastern Mediterranean be threatened but also the stability of the entire Middle East including the vast resource areas of the Arabian Peninsula. . . .

Every effort will be made to find the criminals responsible for this act of terrorism so this despicable act will not go unpunished.

Ronald Reagan, statement, October 24, 1983; *American Foreign Policy: Current Documents*, 1983, p. 791. Also see President Reagan's address on "United States Responsibilities in Lebanon," October 27, 1983, pp. 794-98.

239 UNITED STATES OBJECTIVES IN TERMINATING "MULTINATIONAL FORCE LEBANON"

It has been a time of fast-moving events in the Middle East, and I wanted to say a few words about where we are and what our objectives are.

In Lebanon we face a new situation, brought about by military pressures against the legitimate government. This Syrian-sponsored violence against the government has presented us with difficult choices, in view of the legislative and other constraints under which our forces are operating. We are nonetheless proceeding:

To provide materiel support to the Lebanese Armed Forces as circumstances permit;

To respond to those who attack or threaten the safety of our personnel; and

To redeploy our Marine detachment onto ships.

The longer term problems of Lebanon, of course, can only be solved by political means. The United States is working to help end the fighting and advance a political solution.

George Shultz, statement, February 15, 1984; *American Foreign Policy: Current Documents*, 1984, pp. 578-79.

240 TERMINATION OF UNITED STATES ROLE IN "MULTINATIONAL FORCE LEBANON"

Since the date of my last report to you on the participation of United States Armed Forces in the Multinational Force (MNF) in Lebanon, I have decided that the U.S. will terminate its participation in the MNF. In accordance with my desire that Congress be kept informed on these matters, and consistent with Section 4 of the Multinational Force in Lebanon Resolution, I am hereby providing a final report on our participation in the MNF.

U.S. foreign policy interests in Lebanon have not changed, and remain as stated in my last report to Congress on February 13. The U.S. is committed to the goals of the restoration of a sovereign, independent and united Lebanon, the withdrawal of all foreign forces, and the security of Israel's northern border. However, the continuation of our participation in the MNF is no longer a necessary or appropriate means of achieving those goals. We have discussed our decision with the Government of Lebanon and the other MNF participants, and the other MNF countries have made similar decisions.

The U.S. military personnel who made up the U.S. MNF contingent were earlier redeployed to U.S. ships offshore. Likewise, the MNF personnel of other national contingents have either already departed Lebanon or are in the process of departing. . . .

During the overall course of our participation in the MNF, U.S. forces suffered a total of 264 killed (of which 4 non-MNF personnel were killed in the April 1983 bombing of the U.S. Embassy), and 137 wounded in action. (Three of these were wounded in the period since my last report to Congress on February 13). The estimated cost of U.S. participation in the MNF for FY 1984 was a total of $14.6 million for the U.S. Marine Corps deployment, $44.9 million for U.S. Navy support, and $243,000 for U.S. Army support.

Ronald Reagan, letter to Congress, March 30, 1984; *American Foreign Policy: Current Documents*, 1984, pp. 587-88. For President Reagan's earlier letter to Congress concerning this decision, see p. 578.

SANCTIONS AGAINST AND AIR STRIKE ON LIBYA, 1986

Libya, under Muammar al-Qadhafi who rose to power in 1969, assumed a leading role in plotting and supporting terrorists in their depredations on Western nations and Israel. In the 1970's there was mounting evidence that Qadhafi was aiding a variety of guerilla and dissident groups, including the Palestine Liberation Organization (PLO), volatile political factions in neighboring countries--Morocco, Tunisia, and Chad, and the Irish Republican Army. He developed personal connections with certain international terrorist groups responsible for hijackings and attacks on airports (such as those at Rome and Vienna in December 1985) and commercial aircraft.

United States relations with Libya deteriorated during the 1970's and reached an impasse by the mid-1980's. In May 1981 the United States ordered the Libyan embassy in Washington closed, and three months later, during United States naval maneuvers in international waters in the Gulf of Sidra, off Libya's coast, American fighters shot down two attacking Libyan planes. In December the White House appealed to Americans working in Libya to depart immediately and charged that Libya planned to send "hit teams" to the United States to assassinate President Reagan and other high officials (see *Papers of Presidents: Reagan,* 1981, pp. 1124, 1144, 1164-67).

Following the terrorist bombings in Rome and Vienna, in January 1986 the government imposed wholesale sanctions against Libya (Document 241). Within three months, in another Gulf of Sidra incident, American aircraft, which were attacked by surface-to-air missiles, destroyed Libya's missile-guiding radars and damaged two of its patrol boats (Document 242). Finally, when on April 2 an American TWA plane was bombed, allegedly in retaliation for the Gulf of Sidra action, and three days later a West Berlin discotheque, frequented by Americans, was bombed, killing two persons and injuring more than two hundred (including sixty Americans), the United States launched a substantial retaliatory air and naval strike against Libya on April 14. American planes were targeted on three military and terrorist bases near Tripoli, Libya's capital, and on two facilities in northeastern Libya (Documents 243-245, containing President Reagan's reports to the nation and the Congress). Four of the targets were damaged substantially, but the raid failed to spark a major upswell against Qadhafi. For commentary on the air strike, see *Historic Documents,* 1986, pp. 347-54.

241 UNITED STATES SANCTIONS AGAINST LIBYA

. . . I hereby report that I have exercised my statutory authority to declare a national emergency and to:
-- prohibit purchases and imports from and exports to Libya;
-- ban U.S.-Libya maritime and aviation relations;
-- ban trade in services relating to projects in Libya;
-- ban credits or loans or the transfer of anything of value to Libya or its nationals, except their property held prior to the effective date of this order or transactions allowed by regulations providing for normal activities by Libyans lawfully in the United States; and
-- prohibit transactions relating to travel by Americans to or in Libya, other than for commercial activities permitted until February 1, 1986, or those necessary for prompt departure from Libya or for journalistic travel. . . .

I have authorized these steps in response to the emergency situation created by international terrorism, in this instance the actions and policies of the Government of Libya. Its use and support of terrorism against the United States, other countries, and innocent persons violate international law and minimum standards of human behavior. These Libyan actions and policies constitute a threat to the security of the United

States as well as the international community. Our Nation's security in-cludes the security of its citizens and their right freely to go about their lives at home and abroad. Libyan use of and support for terrorism also constitute a threat to the vital foreign policy interests of the United States and of all other states dedicated to international peace and security.

Since Libya was officially designated under U.S. law in 1979 as a country that has repeatedly supported acts of international terrorism, the United States has taken a number of steps in response to hostile Libyan policies and actions. We have denied licenses for exports that may contribute to Libya's military potential or enhancing its ability to support acts of international terrorism. . . . On the import side, we have banned Libyan petroleum and, since November 1985, Libyan refined petroleum products. We have stopped Libyans from coming to the United States for aviation maintenance, flight operations or nuclear related studies. We have taken measures to limit the expansion of Libyan UN Mission facilities. We have also repeatedly called upon corporations to withdraw American citizens from Libya, for their safety, and we have re-stricted the use of U.S. passports for travel there. All these measures have not deterred Libya from its use and support of terrorism.

Ronald Reagan, letter to Congress on national emergency with respect to Libya, January 7, 1986; *Papers of Presidents: Reagan,* 1986, I, 15-16. Also see Executive Orders January 7 and 8, 1986, prohibiting trade and other activities involving Libya and blocking Libyan assets, pp. 14-15, 32-33. For earlier economic sanctions against Libya, for example, see *Papers of Presidents: Carter,* 1979, II, 2291-92, 2294-95.

242   REPORT ON GULF OF SIDRA INCIDENT

On March 23, United States forces in the Eastern Mediterranean began a peaceful exercise as part of a global Freedom of Navigation program by which the United States preserves its rights to use international waters and air space. This exercise is being conducted entirely in and over areas of the high seas, in accordance with international law and following aviation safety notification procedures.

On March 24, our forces were attacked by Libya. In response, U.S. forces took limited measures of self-defense necessary to protect themselves from continued attack. In accordance with my desire that the Congress be informed on this matter, I am providing this report on the actions taken by United States Armed Forces during this incident. . . .

U.S. forces will continue with their current exercises. We will not be deterred by Libyan attacks or threats from exercising our rights on and over the high seas under international law. If Libyan attacks do not cease, we will continue to take the measures necessary in the exercise of our right of self-defense to protect our forces.

The deployment of these United States Armed Forces and the measures taken by them in self-defense during this incident were undertaken pursuant to my authority under the Constitution, including my authority as Commander-in-Chief of U.S. Armed Forces.

Ronald Reagan, letter to Congress, March 26, 1986; *Papers of Presidents: Reagan,* 1986, I, 406-7. Also see White House statements to reporters, March 24, 1986, p. 394; March 25, p. 395; and March 26, pp. 401-2. For commentary on earlier Gulf of Sidra incident, see *Papers of Presidents: Reagan,* 1981, pp. 722, 729.

243 UNITED STATES AIR STRIKE ON LIBYA

At 7 o'clock this evening eastern time air and naval forces of the United States launched a series of strikes against the headquarters, terrorist facilities, and military assets that support Mu'ammar Qadhafi's subversive activities.   The attacks were concentrated and carefully targeted to minimize casualties among the Libyan people with whom we have no quarrel. From initial reports, our forces have succeeded in their mission. . . .

Colonel Qadhafi is not only an enemy of the United States. His record of subversion and aggression against the neighboring States in Africa is well documented and well known. He has ordered the murder of fellow Libyans in countless countries. He has sanctioned acts of terror in Africa, Europe, and the Middle East, as well as the Western Hemisphere. Today we have done what we had to do. If necessary, we shall do it again. . . . I'm sure that today most Libyans are ashamed and disgusted that this man has made their country a synonym for barbarism around the world. . . .

Long before I came into this office, Colonel Qadhafi had engaged in acts of international terror, acts that put him outside the company of civilized men. For years, however, he suffered no economic or political or military sanction; and the atrocities mounted in number, as did the innocent dead and wounded. And for us to ignore by inaction the slaughter of American civilians and American soldiers, whether in nightclubs or airline terminals, is simply not in the American tradition.   When our citizens are abused or attacked anywhere in the world on the direct orders of a hostile regime, we will respond. . . .   Self-defense is not only our right, it is our duty. It is the purpose behind the mission undertaken tonight, a mission fully consistent with Article 51 of the United Nations Charter.

We believe that this preemptive action against his terrorist installations will not only diminish Colonel Qadhafi's capacity to export terror, it will provide him with incentives and reasons to alter his criminal behavior. . . .

We Americans are slow to anger. We always seek peaceful avenues before resorting to the use of force--and we did.   We tried quiet diplomacy, public condemnation, economic sanctions, and demonstrations of military force.   None succeeded.   Despite our repeated warnings, Qadhafi continued his reckless policy of intimidation, his relentless pursuit of terror.

Ronald Reagan, Address to the Nation, April 14, 1986; *Papers of Presidents: Reagan,* 1986, I, 468-69. Also see White House statements to reporters, April 14, 1986, p. 468, and April 15, 1986, pp. 470-71, and President Reagan's remarks at White House meeting with members of the American Business Conference, April 15, 1986, pp. 472-73.

244 REPORT TO CONGRESS RESPECTING AIR STRIKE ON LIBYA

Commencing at about 7:00 p.m. (EST) on April 14, air and naval forces of the United States conducted simultaneous bombing strikes on headquarters, terrorist facilities and military installations that support Libyan subversive activities. These strikes were completed by approximately 7:30 p.m. (EST). . . .

These strikes were conducted in the exercise of our right of self-defense under Article 51 of the United Nations Charter. This necessary and appropriate action was a preemptive strike, directed against the Libyan terrorist infrastructure and designed to deter acts of terrorism by Libya, . . .

Should Libyan-sponsored terrorist attacks against United States citizens not cease, we will take appropriate measures necessary to protect United States citizens in the exercise of our right of self-defense.

In accordance with my desire that Congress be informed on this matter, and consistent with the War Powers Resolution, I am providing this report on the employment of the United States Armed Forces. These self-defense measures were undertaken pursuant to my authority under the Constitution, including my authority as Commander In Chief of United States Armed Forces.

Ronald Reagan, letter to Congress, in keeping with the War Powers Resolution, April 16, 1986; *Papers of Presidents: Reagan,* 1986, I, 478. Also see earlier letters to Congress, January 7 and March 26, 1986, pp. 15-16, 406-7.

245 PRESIDENT REAGAN'S ATTITUDE TOWARD LIBYAN TERRORISM

There can be no question about direct Libyan involvement in a number of recent, heinous terrorist acts which injured and killed Americans, such as the bombing of a disco in West Berlin. These indiscriminate attacks and those planned by Libya must be dealt with firmly to prevent even more indiscriminate attacks on innocent people. It is my duty to take action to protect the lives of Americans Military operations on April 14 were specifically aimed at installations of direct relevance to Libyan terrorism in an effort to preempt further acts of this kind. Our action underscored to Qadhafi that his actions will not go unpunished and cost-free. This was a principal goal, and it was achieved.

We did what we had to do. We tried peaceful options such as economic and diplomatic sanctions before resorting to force, but Qadhafi did not grasp the seriousness of our determination to bring a stop to terrorism. . . . I hope that this action will have been enough to convince Qadhafi to change his policies. If not, I will not hesitate to act again.

Ronald Reagan, written response to Japanese news organizations, May 2, 1986; *Papers of Presidents: Reagan,* 1986, I, 546-47.

PART V

BASIC FUNCTIONAL POLICIES

15

Peace and Amity

We know that we want only peace. We want peaceful relations with
those nations in the world that will be friendly with us. . . . The
United States is committed to using every peaceful means to bring
about the effectuation of its policies.

Dwight Eisenhower
News conference, March 21, 1956

American statesmen speak avidly and frequently of peace. In his farewell
address, President Johnson declared that "The quest for a durable peace . . . has
absorbed every administration since the end of World War II" (January 14,
1968, in *Papers of Presidents: Johnson,* 1968, II, 1268), and a few years
later President Nixon told a Birmingham, Alabama, audience: "Every President
in this century, and I suppose every President long before this century, has
spoken in terms of peace, not only for America but for the world" (May 25,
1971, see Document 248).

Frequently American leaders have emphasized that peace is a permeating
aspiration of foreign policy. To illustrate, President Eisenhower proclaimed:
"We are for peace--peace first, last, and always" (quoted by President Ford,
see Document 252) and "we shall continue to give expression to our people's
deep-seated desire to live at peace with all nations" (see Document 246). In
the same vein, President Carter pronounced that "Peace--a peace that
preserves freedom--remains America's first goal" (see Document 97), and
distinguishing between purpose and policy, President Reagan insisted that
"peace is an objective, not a policy" (see Document 249).

Focusing on the nature of peace, President Nixon declared that "Peace
must be far more than the absence of war" (see Document 251) and, discussing
his strategy for peace, President Kennedy maintained that the United States
aspires to "genuine peace, the kind of peace that makes life on earth worth
living, the kind that enables men and nations to grow and to hope and to build a
better life for their children--not merely peace for Americans but peace for
all men and women, not merely peace in our time but peace for all time" (see
Document 253).

Simple as it may appear, "peace" is a complex concept that bears many connotations. One of the noblest of universal ideals, as both a permeative though elusive goal and a practical matter of national action, it denotes not only the absence of war and other forms of force, violence, or hostilities, but also volitional undertakings to maintain it and, when disturbed or threatened, to regain it.

"Peace" may be perceived both as a theoretical abstraction--a state of mind--and a concrete and practical condition. In terms of the principal components of the foreign relations process, it may be simultaneously regarded as a national interest (a standard or ideal), a fundamental goal (a basic end to be sought), an operational objective (a concrete action-oriented end), a foreign policy or series of policies (the means to achieve such ends), and sometimes, even a national doctrine or strategy. In each of these guises, it is differentiable from the others.

Pragmatically, it represents both the nation's objectives and policies (or courses of action to achieve them). Aware of the need to project peaceful relations beyond the realm of visionary abstraction, at Chicago in 1937 Franklin Roosevelt observed: "There must be positive endeavors to preserve peace." As indicated in Chapter 3, only when pragmatized does an aspiration enter the arena of public policy. In doing so, attention may focus on modes of maintaining peace--or "peacekeeping," on resolving differences and crises--or "peaceful settlement," or on terminating war or other types of forceful action--or "peacemaking." Each of these represents an important, though differing, phase of peace policy.

When employed in public statements, "peace" is frequently espoused as a national desire--an ideal--or, if concretized in operationalizable form, as a specific objective. In other words, to constitute a national policy, peace needs to be reduced--or elevated--to the status of some implementable methods of preserving or restoring amicable relations.

The documents contained in this chapter consist of selected statements that emphasize peace as an aspiration, its requisites, and its correlation with other basic American goals and a sampling of the extensive network of treaties to outlaw war and provide for the pacific settlement of disputes. Other chapters deal with additional aspects of peaceful foreign affairs, such as peace as a general policy theme (Chapter 6, Documents 95-103) and specific principles, programs, and experiences that exemplify peace policies, including crisis management to maintain or restore amity (Chapters 8-14), the correlation of amity and friendship with commerce (Chapter 17), alliance arrangements to preserve peace and stability (Chapter 18), international terrorism as a threat to peace (Chapter 19), and international cooperation in the United Nations and the Organization of American States as agencies for collective peacekeeping and peaceful settlement of disputes (Chapters 25 and 26, especially Documents 419-420, 444, 446).

PEACE AS FOREIGN RELATIONS THEME

At a news conference in 1954 President Eisenhower acknowledged that the word "peaceful" has many meanings. Declarations of support for "peace" permeate hundreds of American foreign policy statements and project dozens of practical applications. Often peace is paired with other basic goals, such as national security, international tranquility and stability, liberty, and national welfare. More precisely, it has been correlated with amity and friendship, national honor and dignity, integrity and credibility, trust, freedom and human rights, the rule of law, justice and fairness, strength and preparedness, alliance arrangements or noninvolvement and appeasement, defense strategy and balance of power, arms reduction and coexistence, and especially negotiation and the pacific settlement of disputes.

The documents included in this section, largely general in scope, illustrate aspirations rather than concrete policies or programs, discuss various aspects and qualities of peace, and relate it to several other policy goals.

246   DESIRE FOR PEACE

. . . We shall continue to give expression to our people's deep-seated desire to live at peace with all nations. . . .

In the quest for peace, we have sought to resolve specific international disputes. . . .

We have suggested other means for reducing tensions. . . .

Nor do we despair of eventual success. No human problem is insoluble. In the earnest belief that these basic purposes conform to the will of the Highest of All Rulers, the United States will continue to pursue them. In this paramount cause of this century, this Nation must have the help of all its citizens. It must have their understanding, their determination, their readiness to sacrifice--and, above all, the strength and daring of their faith.

Dwight Eisenhower, address, Des Moines, Iowa, August 30, 1954; *Papers of Presidents: Eisenhower,* 1954, p. 786.

247   PARAMOUNT IMPERATIVE IS SEARCH FOR PEACE

The paramount imperative of our time is the search for world peace --genuine peace in which all men can live in dignity without fear of their neighbors. President Johnson has called the search for world peace "the assignment of the century." It is an assignment which springs from the deepest yearnings of our people and is dictated by the grim realities of modern weapons. It is one to which your Federal Government gives the highest priority.

Our goal is the sort of world community sketched in the preamble and articles 1 and 2 of the United Nations Charter--a world of independent nations, each with the institutions of its own choice but cooperating with one another to promote the mutual interests of their citizens, a world free of aggression, a world which moves toward the rule of law, a world in which human rights are secure, a world of better life for all of mankind.

That goal may seem distant. But it is a working guide to our foreign policy. Indeed, we dare not regard it as merely a dream. For unless it is actually achieved, the outlook for Homo sapiens is dark indeed.

Dean Rusk, "The Paramount Imperative of Our Time is the Search for World Peace," address, Johns Hopkins University, Baltimore, October 16, 1965; *American Foreign Policy: Current Documents*, 1965, p. 38.

248   PEACE AS TRADITIONAL AMERICAN GOAL

. . . every President in this century, and I suppose every President long before this century, has spoken in terms of peace, not only for America but for the world.

Woodrow Wilson, I think, honestly felt that the war that he was involved in, World War I, would be a war that would end wars.

Franklin D. Roosevelt felt very strongly that World War II, particularly with the United Nations following it, could be the war that, as far as major powers were concerned, that would be the last great war.

And certainly my predecessors, President Eisenhower, President Truman, President Kennedy, President Johnson, were all dedicated to that proposition, as I am.

Richard Nixon, remarks, Birmingham, Alabama, May 25, 1971; *Papers of Presidents: Nixon*, 1971, pp. 667-68. Also see Chapter 6, Documents 85-103.

249   PEACE IS AN OBJECTIVE, NOT A POLICY

Peace is a beautiful word, but it is also freely used, and sometimes even abused. As I've said before, peace is an objective, not a policy. Those who fail to understand this do so at their peril. Neville Chamberlain thought of peace as a vague policy in the thirties, and the result brought us closer to World War II. Today's so-called "peace movement"--for all its modern hype and theatrics--makes the same old mistake. They would wage peace by weakening the free. And that just doesn't make sense. My heart is with those who march for peace. I'd be at the head of the parade if I thought it would really serve the cause of peace. But the members of the real peace movement, the real peacekeepers and peacemakers, are people who understand that peace must be built on strength. . . .

Another issue of critical importance to all Americans--and one I view as the centerpiece of American foreign policy--concerns our responsibility as peacemaker.

We can't build a safe world with honorable intentions and good will alone. Achieving the fundamental goals our Nation seeks in world affairs--peace, human rights, economic progress, national independence, and international stability--means supporting our friends and defending our interests. Our commitment as peacemaker is focused on these goals.

Ronald Reagan, "Building Peace Through Strength," address, American Legion, Seattle, August 23, 1983; *American Foreign Policy: Current Documents,* 1983, p. 101.

250 REQUISITES FOR PEACE

Today the hope of free men remains stubborn and brave, but it is sternly disciplined by experience. It shuns not only all crude counsel of despair but also the self-deceit of easy illusion. It weighs the chance for peace with sure, clear knowledge of what happened to the vain hope of 1945. . . .

The way chosen by the United States was plainly marked by a few clear precepts, which govern its conduct in world affairs.

First: No people on earth can be held, as a people, to be an enemy, for all humanity shares the common hunger for peace and fellowship and justice.

Second. No nation's security and well-being can be lastingly achieved in isolation but only in effective cooperation with fellow-nations.

Third: Any nation's right to a form of government and an economic system of its own choosing is *inalienable.*

Fourth: Any nation's attempt to dictate to other nations their form of government is *indefensible.*

And fifth: A nation's hope of lasting peace cannot be firmly based upon any race in armaments but rather upon just relations and honest understanding with all other nations.

In the light of these principles the citizens of the United States defined the way they proposed to follow, through the aftermath of war, toward true peace.

Dwight Eisenhower, address, "The Chance for Peace," American Society of Newspaper Editors, April 16, 1953; *Papers of Presidents: Eisenhower,* 1953, pp. 179-80. For the entire address, see pp. 179-88.

*   *   *

For the future, the quest for peace, I believe, requires:

-- that we maintain the liberal trade policies that have helped us become the leading nation in world trade,
-- that we strengthen the international monetary system as an instrument of world prosperity, and
-- that we seek areas of agreement with the Soviet Union where the interests of both nations and the interests of world peace are properly served.

Lyndon Johnson, Farewell Address, Message on State of the Union, January 14, 1969; *Papers of Presidents: Johnson,* 1968, II, 1268.

2 5 1 GUIDELINES FOR PEACE

I have often reflected on the meaning of "peace," and have reached one certain conclusion: Peace must be far more than the absence of war. Peace must provide a durable structure of international relationships which inhibits or removes the causes of war. Building a lasting peace requires a foreign policy guided by three basic principles:

-- Peace requires **partnership**. Its obligations, like its benefits, must be shared. This concept of partnership guides our relations with all friendly nations.

-- Peace requires **strength**. So long as there are those who would threaten our vital interests and those of our allies with military force, we must be strong. American weakness could tempt would-be aggressors to make dangerous miscalculations. At the same time, our own strength is important only in relation to the strength of others. We--like others--must place high priority on enhancing our security through cooperative arms control.

-- Peace requires a **willingness to negotiate**. All nations--and we are no exception--have important national interests to protect. But the most fundamental interest of all nations lies in building the structure of peace. In partnership with our allies, secure in our own strength, we will seek those areas in which we can agree among ourselves and with others to accommodate conflicts and overcome rivalries. We are working toward the day when **all** nations will have a stake in peace, and will therefore be partners in its maintenance.

Within such a structure, international disputes can be settled and clashes contained. The insecurity of nations, out of which so much conflict arises, will be eased, and the habits of moderation and compromise will be nurtured. Most important, a durable peace will give full opportunity to the powerful forces driving toward economic change and social justice.

Richard Nixon, *U.S. Foreign Policy for the 1970's: A New Strategy for Peace* (1970), pp. 4-5.

2 5 2 FOUR BASIC MEANS OF PRESERVING PEACE

MY SUBJECT today is peace. When President Eisenhower was asked 20 years ago about the goals of his foreign policy, he said, "We are for peace-- peace first, last, and always." Today, that remains the central purpose of American foreign policy.

Throughout my time as President, I have shaped our foreign policy according to four basic principles:

First, we have sought to maintain America's unquestioned military strength. . . .

Second, we have tried to maintain and strengthen our friendship with our allies. . . .

Third, working from a position of strength, we have sought to reduce tensions in the world and to avert the threat of nuclear holocaust. . . .

Finally, we have tried to act as leader and peacemaker. . . .

The peace that exists today is directly related to our hard work, our strength, and our skillful diplomacy. I am very proud of what we have accomplished.

Gerald Ford, "Radio Address on Peace," October 28, 1976; *Papers of Presidents: Ford,* 1976-1977, III, 2762.   At the Helsinki Conference (see Documents 515-519) President Ford proclaimed: "Peace is not a piece of paper"; *Papers of Presidents: Ford,* 1975, II, 1075.

253 TOWARD A STRATEGY OF PEACE

I have, therefore, chosen this time and this place to discuss a topic on which ignorance too often abounds and the truth is too rarely perceived --yet it is the most important topic on earth: world peace.

What kind of peace do I mean? What kind of peace do we seek? Not a *Pax Americana* enforced on the world by American weapons of war. Not the peace of the grave or the security of the slave. I am talking about genuine peace, the kind of peace that makes life on earth worth living, the kind that enables men and nations to grow and to hope and to build a better life for their children--not merely peace for Americans but peace for all men and women, not merely peace in our time but peace for all time. . . .

I speak of peace . . . as the necessary rational end of rational men. I realize that the pursuit of peace is not as dramatic as the pursuit of war and frequently the words of the pursuer fall on deaf ears. But we have no more urgent task. . . .

First: Let us examine our attitude toward peace itself. Too many of us think it is impossible. Too many think it unreal. But that is a dangerous, defeatist belief. It leads to the conclusion that war is inevitable, that mankind is doomed, that we are gripped by forces we cannot control.

We need not accept that view. Our problems are manmade; therefore they can be solved by man. And man can be as big as he wants. No problem of human destiny is beyond human beings. Man's reason and spirit have often solved the seemingly unsolvable, and we believe they can do it again.

I am not referring to the absolute, infinite concept of universal peace and good will of which some fantasies and fanatics dream. . . .

. . . Genuine peace must be the product of many nations, the sum of many acts. It must be dynamic, not static, changing to meet the challenge of each new generation. For peace is a process, a way of solving problems.

With such a peace there will still be quarrels and conflicting interests, as there are within families and nations. World peace, like community peace, does not require that each man love his neighbor; it requires only that they live together in mutual tolerance, submitting their disputes to a just and peaceful settlement. And history teaches us that enmities between nations, as between individuals, do not last forever. However fixed our likes and dislikes may seem, the tide of time and events will often bring surprising changes in the relations between nations and neighbors.

So let us persevere. Peace need not be impracticable, and war need not be Inevitable. By defining our goal more clearly, by making it seem more manageable and less remote, we can help all peoples to see it, to draw hope from it, and to move irresistibly toward it. . . .

The United States, as the world knows, will never start a war. We do not want a war. We do not now expect a war. This generation of Americans has already had enough--more than enough--of war and hate and oppression. We shall be prepared if others wish it. We shall be alert to try to stop it. But we shall also do our part to build a world of peace where the weak are safe and the strong are just. We are not helpless before that task or hopeless of its success. Confident and unafraid, we labor on--not toward a strategy of annihilation but toward a strategy of peace.

John Kennedy, "Toward a Strategy of Peace," address, American University, Washington, June 10, 1963; *American Foreign Policy: Current Documents,* 1963, pp. 23-25, 29.

254   PEACE THROUGH STRENGTH AND DEMOCRACY

I speak today as both a citizen of the United States and of the world. I come with the heartful wishes of my people for peace, bearing honest proposals, and looking for genuine progress. . . .

The record of history is clear: citizens of the United States resort to force reluctantly and only when they must.   Our foreign policy, as President Eisenhower once said, ". . . is not difficult to state. We are for peace, first, last and always, for very simple reasons. We know that it is only in a peaceful atmosphere, a peace with justice, one in which we can be confident, that America can prosper as we have known prosperity in the past.". . .

America has no territorial ambitions, we occupy no countries, and we have built no walls to lock our people in. Our commitment to self-determination, freedom, and peace is the very soul of America.   That commitment is as strong today as it ever was.

The United States has fought four wars in my lifetime. In each we struggled to defend freedom and democracy. We were never the aggressors. America's strength and, yes, her military power have been a force for peace, not conquest; for democracy, not despotism; for freedom, not tyranny.

Ronald Reagan, address, United Nations General Assembly Special Session on Disarmament, June 17, 1982; Department of State, *Realism,   Strength, Negotiation* (Washington: Government Printing Office, 1984), p. 30.

*   *   *

If history teaches us anything, it is that a strong defense is the prerequisite to a lasting peace, the only credible deterrent against aggression. . . .

We Americans maintain our military strength with the fervent hope that it will never be used, and with the conviction that this is, indeed, the best way to preserve the peace. We maintain our defensive strength in concert with our allies and friends, whose freedom and independence is vital to our own security. . . . Thus, it is fitting that Americans from all walks of life and many citizens of our fellow democracies are working to strengthen democratic institutions throughout the world . . . . Democracy is the way to a more peaceful world. The ultimate goal of Peace Through Strength Week is a world where the people of each nation are free to determine their own destiny and where no state threatens its neighbors.

Ronald Reagan, statement, National Peace Through Strength Week, September 22, 1984; *Papers of Presidents: Reagan,* 1984, II, 1353.

*   *   *

Isn't it time for us to reaffirm an undeniable truth that America remains the greatest force for peace anywhere in the world today. For all the stress and strain of recent ordeals, the United States is still a young nation, a nation that draws renewed strength not only from its material abundance and economic might, but from free ideals that are as vibrant today as they were more than two centuries ago when that small but gallant band wo call our Founding Fathers pledged their lives, their fortunes, and their sacred honor to win freedom and independence.

Ronald Reagan, "Progress in the Quest for Peace and Freedom," address, American Legion, Washington, February 22, 1983; *American Foreign Policy: Current Documents,* 1983, p. 8. Also see Reagan, "Peace and National Security," March 23, 1983, pp. 37-43; and "Building Peace Through Strength," address, American Legion Convention, Seattle, August 23, 1983, in *American Foreign Policy: Current Documents,* 1983, pp. 98-103. Also see Documents 104-108.

TREATY STRUCTURE FOR PEACEKEEPING AND PACIFIC SETTLEMENT

Historically the United States has an active record in promoting the preservation of peace by means of negotiating peacekeeping and pacific settlement arrangements, involving multipartite and bipartite treaties and agreements as well as ad hoc arrangements. Seeking to ameliorate crises, prevent hostilities, and settle differences amicably by regularizing conflict resolution through preestablished commitments, the United States has subscribed to a network of treaties to outlaw war and participate in a variety of peaceful settlement processes. Most of these were consummated between the end of the nineteenth century and World War I, and during the late 1920's through the

1930's. They have subsequently been supplemented by the United Nations and the Organization of American States systems and the International Court of Justice.

Aside from the use of direct negotiations--traditionally the preferred mode of resolving differences among nations--the established methods of pacific settlement include good offices and mediation, commissions of inquiry, conciliation, arbitration, and adjudication. "Good offices" constitutes the interposition of a third party, simply through suggestion or advice, to induce the opposing nations to reconcile their disputes by direct negotiations or submittal to some other form of peaceful compromise. "Mediation" is similar except that the third party plays a more salutary role as conciliator, but not as arbiter or judge. In implementing this method the mediator may meet individually with representatives of the disputing governments, which may require shuttle diplomacy, or meet simultaneously with them. The United States has frequently played this third-party role.

"Commissions of inquiry" are third-party groups, agreed to by the disputants, primarily to investigate and report on the facts, without making concrete recommendations--which affords a "cooling-off" period. "Conciliation" is similar in that arrangements for this process are often agreed to in advance to be available when a conflict occurs, but the conciliator or commission is authorized to tender recommendations, based on equity and mutual compromise, to which the disputants need to subsequently agree.

Legally and institutionally more formal are arbitration and adjudication. "Arbitration" is the arrangement whereby nations agree in advance to submit their differences to an arbitral agent or agency--whether a single individual, an arbitral commission, or a "court"--to decide the issue either by compromise or on the basis of principles of law or equity, and the parties acknowledge in advance that they will be bound by the arbitral award. "Adjudication," the most sophisticated proceeding, involves an international court, to which contesting nations submit disputes for judicial determination by decisions based strictly on law and equity, not compromise. This process is epitomized by the World Court, established as a primary organ of the League of Nations and subsequently of the United Nations.

The United States has promoted, established, and participated in all these forms of settlement. To summarize, aside from its leading role in creating the League, the United Nations, and the Organization of American States, the United States was a party to approximately seventy arbitrations during the nineteenth century (exceeded only by Great Britain); became a charter member of, and submitted the pioneer case to, the Permanent Court of Arbitration (the "Hague Tribunal"); signed the Treaty for the Renunciation of War (1928) and the Inter-American Anti-War Treaty (called the Saavedra-Lamas Pact, 1933), which renounced war as an instrument for settling international disputes; negotiated bilateral arbitration treaties with twelve countries in 1908 and 1909 (some of which were replaced by later arrangements); concluded more than twenty bilateral "cooling-off" pacts under the leadership of Secretary of State William Jennings Bryan in 1914; negotiated twenty bilateral conciliation treaties and more than two dozen arbitration treaties in the late 1920's and early 1930's under the leadership of Secretary of State Frank B. Kellogg; and during the 1930's consummated a series of multilateral inter-American treaties designed to prevent conflict, preserve peace, and facilitate pacific settlement. In addition, other treaties--such as the Rio Pact (Document 304), the North Atlantic Treaty (Document 306), and others--denounce resort to war and the use of force, and espouse peaceful settlement.

Most of these regularized peacekeeping agreements are still in effect. To illustrate, so far as multilateral arrangements are concerned--in addition to the United Nations and the Organization of American States, which provide both mediation and conciliation services, and the International Court of Justice, which serves as the contemporary global adjudication agency--in the 1980's the United States remained a party to the Hague Convention for Pacific Settlement of Disputes (1907), the Pact of Paris (1928) and the Lamas Pact (1933), the Convention on the Recognition and Enforcement of Foreign Arbitration Awards (1958), and some ten inter-American treaties that deal with the maintenance and reestablishment of peace (1936), the prevention of controversies (1936), and pacific settlement by means of commissions of inquiry (1923), good offices and mediation (1936), conciliation (1929), and arbitration (1929).

In addition, the United States is committed to twenty-five Bryan "cooling-off" pacts, and to more than thirty Kellogg arbitration treaties and twenty conciliation pacts with thirty-two countries. Combined, these bilateral treaties encompassed a majority of the independent countries at the commencement of World War II, and most of the rest were served by the Hague Convention and multilateral inter-American treaties. The post-World War II newly independent nations are party to the peaceful settlement process provided by the United Nations and, in some cases, by regional international organizations including the Organization of American States.

Another type of bilateral peacekeeping treaty, which the United States has used extensively throughout its history, correlates peaceful relations and international commerce. Beginning with the "Treaty of Amity and Commerce" with France signed in February 1778, the United States launched the practice of negotiating dozens of these treaties. They commit the signatories to preserve "a firm, inviolable and universal peace, and a true friendship," or "perpetual amity," or "bonds of peace and friendship," and provided for mutual arrangements for commerce as well as navigation and consular rights. Some of these have been amended or superseded, whereas others, negotiated as early as 1794 (the Jay Treaty with Great Britain) and the 1820's (Brazil) and 1830's (Chile, Ecuador, and Venezuela), are still in effect. These treaties of peace, amity, friendship, and commerce are discussed more fully in Chapter 17, including Document 293.

Thus, although most contemporary peacekeeping and pacific settlement is handled by direct negotiations among the parties, ad hoc third-party mediation, conciliation within the United Nations and regional systems, and adjudication by the International Court of Justice, the United States nevertheless remains bound by an extensive network of both multilateral and bilateral treaty commitments that mandate pacific settlement of disputes. The documents contained in this section illustrate various types of these residual arrangements. In addition to the chapters on the United Nations and the Organization of American States

(Chapters 25 and 26), for commentary on the handling of recent crises, see Chapters 8-14, and on United States policy developments related to specific regional issues, see Chapters 27-32. For a complete listing of bilateral and multilateral treaties, see *Treaties in Force.*

255 TREATY FOR RENUNCIATION OF WAR--PACT OF PARIS, 1928

ARTICLE I
The High Contracting Parties solemnly declare in the names of their respective peoples that they condemn recourse to war for the solution of international controversies, and renounce it as an instrument of national policy in their relations with one another.

ARTICLE II
The High Contracting Parties agree that the settlement or solution of all disputes or conflicts of whatever origin they may be, which may arise among them, shall never be sought except by pacific means.

Also called the Kellogg-Briand Peace Pact. 2 Bevans, *Treaties and Other International Agreements,* 732-35. Originally signed on August 27, 1928; in the 1980's some sixty-five countries were bound by the pact, including all of the major powers. For listings of states bound by this and the following treaties (Documents 256 to 263), see the contemporary issues of *Treaties in Force.*

256 ANTI-WAR TREATY OF NONAGGRESSION AND CONCILIATION, 1933

ARTICLE I
The high contracting parties solemnly declare that they condemn wars of aggression in their mutual relations or in those with other states, and that the settlement of disputes or controversies of any kind that may arise among them shall be effected only by the pacific means which have the sanction of international law.

ARTICLE II
They declare that as between the high contracting parties territorial questions must not be settled by violence, and that they will not recognize any territorial arrangement which is not obtained by pacific means, nor the validity of the occupation or acquisition of territories that may be brought about by force of arms.

ARTICLE III
In case of noncompliance, by any state engaged in a dispute, with the obligations contained in the foregoing articles, the contracting states undertake to make every effort for the maintenance of peace. To that end they will adopt in their character as neutrals a common and solidary attitude; they will exercise the political, juridical, or economic means authorized by international law; they will bring the influence of public opinion to bear, but will in no case resort to intervention, either dip-

lomatic or armed; subject to the attitude that may be incumbent on them by virtue of other collective treaties to which such states are signatories.

ARTICLE IV

The high contracting parties obligate themselves to submit to the conciliation procedure established by this treaty the disputes specially mentioned and any others that may arise in their reciprocal relations, without further limitations than those enumerated in the following article, in all controversies which it has not been possible to settle by diplomatic means within a reasonable period of time.

Also called the Lamas Pact. Articles 5-14 provide for conciliation of disputes. 3 Bevans, *Treaties and Other International Agreements,* 135-40. Originally signed by six Latin American governments on October 10, 1933; it was open to adherence by "all nations." In the 1980's the United States and twenty-four Latin American and European countries were bound by the treaty.

25 / HAGUE CONVENTION--PACIFIC SETTLEMENT OF INTERNATIONAL DISPUTES, 1907

Part 1. The Maintenance of General Peace
Article 1

With a view to obviating as far as possible recourse to force in the relations between states, the Contracting Powers agree to use their best efforts to insure the pacific settlement of international differences.

Part II. Good Offices and Mediation
Article 2

In case of serious disagreement or dispute, before an appeal to arms, the Contracting Powers agree to have recourse, as far as circumstances allow, to the good offices or mediation of one or more friendly powers. . . . [Articles 3-8 provide for good offices and mediation procedures.]

Part III. International Commissions of Inquiry
Article 9

In disputes of an international nature involving neither honor nor vital interests, and arising from a difference of opinion on points of fact, the Contracting Powers deem it expedient and desirable that the parties who have not been able to come to an agreement by means of diplomacy should, as far as circumstances allow, institute an international commission of inquiry, to facilitate a solution of these disputes by elucidating the facts by means of an impartial and conscientious investigation. . . . [Articles 10-36 provide for the organization and functions of commissions of inquiry.]

Part IV.   International Arbitration
Chapter I. The system of arbitration
Article 37

International arbitration has for its object the settlement of disputes between states by judges of their own choice and on the basis of respect for laws.

Recourse to arbitration implies an engagement to submit in good faith to the award.

Article 38

In questions of a legal nature, and especially in the interpretation or application of international conventions, arbitration is recognized by the Contracting Powers as the most effective and, at the same time, the most equitable means of settling disputes which diplomacy has failed to settle.

Consequently, it would be desirable that, in disputes about the above-mentioned questions, the Contracting Powers should, if the case arose, have recourse to arbitration, in so far as circumstances permit.

Article 39

The arbitration convention is concluded for disputes already existing and for disputes which may arise in the future.

It may embrace any dispute or only disputes of a certain category.

Article 40

Independently of general or private treaties expressly stipulating recourse to arbitration as obligatory on the Contracting Powers, the said powers reserve to themselves the right of concluding new agreements, general or particular, with a view to extending compulsory arbitration to all cases which they may consider it possible to submit to it.

Chapter II. The Permanent Court of Arbitration
Article 41

With the object of facilitating an immediate recourse to arbitration for international differences, which it has not been possible to settle by diplomacy, the Contracting Powers undertake to maintain the Permanent Court of Arbitration, as established by the First Peace Conference [of 1899], accessible at all times, and operating, unless otherwise stipulated by the parties, in accordance with the rules of procedure inserted in the present convention. . . . [Articles 42-90 provide for the structure, functions, procedures, and competence of the Court.]

Signed October 18, 1907; 97 articles. 1 Bevans, *Treaties and Other International Agreements,* 577-606. Originally signed by the United States and forty other governments; in the 1980's seventy-four countries were bound by the treaty. It provides for the obviating of recourse to force in the relations of nations and lays down rules for good offices and mediation, commissions of inquiry, and international arbitration of disputes, and it established the Permanent Court of Arbitration at the Hague. It superseded the Hague Convention of 1899; see 1 Bevans, *Treaties and Other International Agreements,* 230-46, signed on July 29, 1899, by twenty-six governments.

258 TREATY ON THE AVOIDANCE OR PREVENTION OF CONFLICTS BETWEEN AMERICAN STATES--GONDRA TREATY, 1923

The Governments represented at the Fifth International Conference of American States, desiring to strengthen progressively the principles of justice and of mutual respect which inspire the policy observed by them in their reciprocal relations, and to quicken in their peoples sentiments of concord and of loyal friendship which may contribute toward the consolidation of such relations,

Confirm their most sincere desire to maintain an immutable peace, not only between themselves but also with all the other nations of the earth; . . .

Article I

All controversies which for any cause whatsoever may arise between two or more of the High Contracting Parties and which it has been impossible to settle through diplomatic channels, or to submit to arbitration in accordance with existing treaties, shall be submitted for investigation and report to a Commission to be established in the manner provided for in Article IV. The High Contracting Parties undertake, in case of disputes, not to begin mobilization or concentration of troops on the frontier of the other Party, nor to engage in any hostile acts or preparations for hostilities, from the time steps are taken to convene the Commission until the said Commission has rendered its report or until the expiration of the time provided for in Article VII.

This provision shall not abrogate nor limit the obligations contained in treaties of arbitration in force between two or more of the High Contracting Parties, nor the obligations arising out of them.

It is understood that in disputes arising between Nations which have no general treaties of arbitration, the investigation shall not take place in questions affecting constitutional provisions, nor in questions already settled by the other treaties.

Article II

The controversies referred to in Article I shall be submitted to the Commission of Inquiry whenever it has been impossible to settle them through diplomatic negotiations or procedure or by submission to arbitration, or in cases in which the circumstances of fact render all negotiation impossible and there is imminent danger of an armed conflict between the Parties. Any one of the Governments directly interested in the investigation of the facts giving rise to the controversy may apply for the convocation of the Commission of Inquiry and to this end it shall be necessary only to communicate officially this decision to the other Party and to one of the Permanent Commissions established by Article III.

Signed May 3, 1923; 2 Bevans, *Treaties and Other International Agreements*, 413-19. Originally signed by the United States and fifteen Latin American governments. It provides for pacific settlement of disputes by commissions of inquiry, located in Washington and Montevideo. Articles 3-7 provide for the composition and procedure of these commissions.

259 INTER-AMERICAN CONVENTION FOR THE MAINTENANCE, PRESERVATION, AND REESTABLISHMENT OF PEACE, 1936

Article I. In the event that the peace of the American Republics is menaced, and in order to coordinate efforts to prevent war, any of the Governments of the American Republics signatory to the Treaty of Paris of 1928 or to the Treaty of Non-Aggression and Conciliation of 1933, or to both, whether or not a member of other peace organizations, shall consult with the other Governments of the American Republics, which, in such event, shall consult together for the purpose of finding and adopting methods of peaceful cooperation.

Article II. In the event of war, or a virtual state of war between American States, the Governments of the American Republics represented at this Conference shall undertake without delay the necessary mutual consultations, in order to exchange views and to seek, within the obligations resulting from the pacts above mentioned and from the standards of international morality, a method of peaceful collaboration; and, in the event of an international war outside America which might menace the peace of the American Republics, such consultation shall also take place to determine the proper time and manner in which the signatory states, if they so desire, may eventually cooperate in some action tending to preserve the peace of the American Continent.

Article III. It is agreed that any question regarding the interpretation of the present Convention, which it has not been possible to settle through diplomatic channels, shall be submitted to the procedure of conciliation provided by existing agreements, or to arbitration or to judicial settlement.

Signed on December 23, 1936; 5 articles. 3 Bevans, *Treaties and Other International Agreements,* 338-42. Originally signed by the United States and nineteen Latin American governments; in the 1980's the United States and fifteen other countries remain bound by the treaty. It provides for consultation in the event of the threat or the outbreak of war between American states or if the American Republics are menaced from abroad.

260 INTER-AMERICAN TREATY ON THE PREVENTION OF CONTROVERSIES, 1936

Art. 1. The High Contracting Parties bind themselves to establish permanent bilateral mixed commissions composed of representatives of the signatory governments which shall in fact be constituted, at the request of any of them, and such party shall give notice of such request to the other signatory governments. . . .

Art. 2. The duty of the aforementioned commissions shall be to study, with the primary object of eliminating them, as far as possible, the causes of future difficulties or controversies; and to propose additional or detailed lawful measures which it might be convenient to take in order to promote, as far as possible, the due and regular application of treaties in force between the respective parties, and also to promote the development of increasingly good relations in all ways between the two countries dealt with in each case.

Art. 3. After each meeting of any of the said preventive Commissions a minute shall be drawn and signed by its members setting out the considerations and decisions thereof and such minute shall be transmitted to the governments represented in the commissions.

Signed December 23, 1936; 7 articles. 3 Bevans, *Treaties and Other International Agreements*, 357-61. Originally signed by eight Latin American governments; in the 1980's the United States and thirteen other countries were bound by the treaty, which remains in effect indefinitely. It provides for the establishment of "preventive" commissions to avert future controversies. Also see Document 446.

261 TREATY FOR THE ADVANCEMENT OF PEACE--COMMISSION OF INQUIRY, U.S. AND GREAT BRITAIN, 1914

Article I

The High Contracting Parties agree that all disputes between them, of every nature whatsoever, other than disputes the settlement of which is provided for and in fact achieved under existing agreements between the High Contracting Parties, shall, when diplomatic methods of adjustment have failed, be referred for investigation and report to a permanent International Commission, to be constituted in the manner prescribed in the next succeeding article; and they agree not to declare war or begin hostilities during such investigation and before the report is submitted.

Article II

The International Commission shall be composed of five members, to be appointed as follows: One member shall be chosen from each country, by the Government thereof; one member shall be chosen by each Government from some third country; the fifth member shall be chosen by common agreement between the two Governments, it being understood that he shall not be a citizen of either country. . . .

The International Commission shall be appointed within six months after the exchange of the ratifications of this treaty; and vacancies shall be filled according to the manner of the original appointment.

Article III

In case the High Contracting Parties shall have failed to adjust a dispute by diplomatic methods, they shall at once refer it to the International Commission for investigation and report. The International Commission may, however, spontaneously by unanimous agreement offer its services to that effect, and in such case it shall notify both Governments and request their cooperation in the investigation. . . .

The High Contracting Parties agree to furnish the Permanent International Commission with all the means and facilities required for its investigation and report.

The report of the International Commission shall be completed within one year after the date on which it shall declare its investigation to have begun unless the High Contracting Parties shall limit or extend the time by mutual agreement. . . .

The High Contracting Parties reserve the right to act independently on the subject matter of the dispute after the report of the Commission shall have been submitted.

Signed September 15, 1914; 5 articles. Also known as Bryan "Cooling-Off" Pact. 12 Bevans, *Treaties and Other International Agreements*, 370-72, with supplementary exchange of notes, pp. 373-74. Similar treaties, implementing the Hague Convention of 1907, were signed with more than twenty other countries.

262   CONCILIATION TREATY--U.S. AND GERMANY, 1928

Article I

Any disputes arising between the Government of the United States of America and the Government of Germany, of whatever nature they may be, shall, when ordinary diplomatic proceedings have failed and the High Contracting Parties do not have recourse to adjudication by a competent tribunal, be submitted for investigation and report to a permanent International Commission constituted in the manner prescribed in the next succeeding Article; the High Contracting Parties agree not to declare war or begin hostilities during such investigation and before the report is submitted.

Article II

The International Commission shall be composed of five members, to be appointed as follows: One member shall be chosen from each country, by the Government thereof; one member shall be chosen by each Government from some third country; the fifth member shall be chosen by common agreement between the two Governments, it being understood that he shall not be a citizen of either country. . . .

The International Commission shall be appointed within six months after the exchange of ratifications of this treaty; and vacancies shall be filled according to the manner of the original appointment.

Article III

In case the High Contracting Parties shall have failed to adjust a dispute by diplomatic methods, and they do not have a recourse to adjudication by a competent tribunal, they shall at once refer it to the International Commission for investigation and report. The International Commission may, however, spontaneously by unanimous agreement offer its services to that effect, and in such case it shall notify both Governments and request their cooperation in the investigation. . . .

The report of the Commission shall be completed within one year after the date on which it shall declare its investigation to have begun, unless the High Contracting Parties shall shorten or extend the time by mutual agreement. . . .

The High Contracting Parties reserve the right to act independently on the subject matter of the dispute after the report of the Commission shall have been submitted.

Signed May 5, 1928; 4 articles. Also known as Kellogg Conciliation Pact. 8 Bevans, *Treaties and Other International Agreements*, 194-96, still in effect with the Federal Republic of Germany. Similar treaties were signed with approximately twenty other countries. These are virtually identical with the Bryan "Cooling-Off" Pacts for the Advancement of Peace. In the 1980's such Bryan and Kellogg pacts were in effect between the United States and forty other countries.

263 ARBITRATION TREATY--U. S. AND BELGIUM, 1929

Article I

All differences relating to international matters in which the High Contracting Parties are concerned by virtue of a claim of right made by one against the other under treaty or otherwise, which it has not been possible to adjust by diplomacy, which have not been adjusted as a result of reference to an appropriate commission of conciliation, and which are justiciable in their nature by reason of being susceptible of decision by the application of the principles of law or equity; shall be submitted to the Permanent Court of Arbitration established at The Hague by the Convention of October 18, 1907, or to some other competent tribunal, as shall be decided in each case by special agreement, which special agreement shall provide for the organization of such tribunal if necessary, define its powers, state the question or questions at issue, and settle the terms of reference.

The special agreement in each case shall be made on the part of the United States of America by the President of the United States of America by and with the advice and consent of the Senate thereof, and on the part of Belgium in accordance with the constitutional laws of Belgium.

Article II

The provisions of this treaty shall not be invoked in respect of any dispute the subject matter of which

(a) is within the domestic jurisdiction of either of the High Contracting Parties,

(b) involves the interests of third Parties,

(c) depends upon or involves the maintenance of the traditional attitude of the United States concerning American questions, commonly described as the Monroe Doctrine,

(d) depends upon or involves the observance of the obligations of Belgium in accordance with the Covenant of the League of Nations.

Signed March 20, 1929; 3 articles. Also known as Kellogg Arbitration Treaty. 5 Bevans, *Treaties and Other International Agreements*, 547-48. Similar treaties were signed with more than two dozen other countries. These supplemented some twelve earlier similar arbitration treaties signed in 1908-1909, several of which are still in force. For the text of the treaty with Peru, signed in 1908, see 10 Bevans, 1081-82.

16

Freedom, Self-Determination, and Human Rights

And yet the same revolutionary beliefs for which our forebears fought are still at issue around the globe--the belief that the rights of man come not from the generosity of the state but from the hand of God. . . .

Let every nation know, whether it wishes us well or ill, that we shall pay any price, bear any burden, meet any hardship, support any friend, oppose any foe to assure the survival and the success of liberty.

John Kennedy
Inaugural Address, January 20, 1961

This chapter is concerned with the nature and application of the principles "liberty," "freedom," and "rights" in the conduct of American foreign affairs. Perspective is one of the primary criteria for differentiating among them, in that distinctions may focus on international, national, and human individual relationships. Thus, they may apply to United States goals, objectives, and policies respecting the status and developments of foreign nations and peoples, the internal affairs of other countries as well as the United States, and the interrelations of individuals within nations.

Often these concepts are used interchangeably. In one sense, historically, "liberty" has been equated with "freedom" and, in American thinking, traditionally they are both related, internationally and internally, to self-determination and independence. These, in turn, are cast as the "right" of peoples to be free of foreign domination and hegemony and to choose their own form of government.

On the other hand, the concepts "freedom" and "rights," also employed synonymously, denote the protections, rights, and privileges of individuals vis-a-vis both their system of government and one another, as exemplified by our Bill of Rights. While indigenous to American ideals and philosophy, based on natural law and universal human values, since World War II they also have been epitomized as "human rights"--civil, political, economic, social, and cultural--in American foreign affairs.

This chapter consists of two sections. The first is devoted to implementing these principles as they apply to the doctrine of self-determination and the achievement of independence. The second is concerned with these concepts as they pertain to the enhancement of human rights throughout the world. It must be realized that the United States is limited in its capacity to institute or even to propagate them in other nations. The primary techniques devised to promulgate them are setting an example to demonstrate their merit, issuing pronouncements extolling and supporting them in order to persuade other nations to accept and effectuate them pragmatically, and negotiating multilateral policy resolutions and declarations and, to bind other governments to concrete commitments, a substantial number of global and regional treaties and agreements.

SELF-DETERMINATION AND INDEPENDENCE

Self-determination--the right of nations or peoples to determine for themselves the way in which they are to be governed, and whether they shall be self-governed or associated with another power--has permeated American ideals and policies since colonial times. Imbedded in the Declaration of Independence, specified in the preamble of the Constitution ("We the people of the United States, in order to . . . secure the blessings of liberty to ourselves and our posterity, do ordain and establish this Constitution for the United States of America"), and characterized by such policy pronouncements as the Monroe Doctrine, self-determination has become a fundamental and traditional principle of American foreign affairs.

But it was not until the twentieth century that it was promoted externally on a large scale. This is evidenced, in part, by the major role it plays in three historic presidential collective policy statements--Wilson's Fourteen Points, Roosevelt's Atlantic Charter, and Truman's Fundamentals of Foreign Policy proclaimed in his Navy Day Address in 1945. Wilson devoted nine of his fourteen points to the subject, Roosevelt the first three of his eight precepts, and Truman the first six of his twelve fundamentals. Implementing this policy, immediately after World War II, based on the Tydings-McDuffie Act (1934), the United States granted independence to the Philippine Islands in 1946. This set the precedent for the extensive march to independence of more than one hundred new states--nearly tripling the size of the community of nations.

Self-determination encompasses several related precepts, such as liberty and independence, popular choice of a nation's form of governance, the doctrine of the consent of the governed, the preservation of national integrity, non-intervention in the internal affairs of nations, and during the post-World War II era, decolonization. Special machinery has been developed to implement them, including the United Nations Trusteeship Council and Decolonization Committee and the Inter-American Committee on Dependent Territories in the Western Hemisphere.

So far as the application of self-determination to United States dependent territories is concerned, aside from the Philippines, action has been taken to accord Puerto Rico commonwealth status in 1952, and to establish self-governing systems in American Samoa, Guam, and the Virgin Islands. And all four have nonvoting delegates in the House of Representatives. The status of the Trust Territory of the Pacific (the Caroline, Marianna, and Marshall Islands) is discussed in Chapter 28.

To illustrate American dedication to the cause of self-determination, the following documents embrace high-level general policy statements (Documents 264-266), bilateral and multilateral commitments to the principle (Documents 267-271), and its application to United States relations with its dependent territories (Documents 272-273).

264   PREPARATION FOR SELF-DETERMINATION AND INDEPENDENCE

There rests upon the independent nations a responsibility in relation to dependent peoples who aspire to liberty. It should be the duty of nations having political ties with such peoples, of mandatories, of trustees, or of other agencies, as the case may be, to help the aspiring peoples to develop materially and educationally, to prepare themselves for the duties and responsibilities of self-government, and to attain liberty

Cordell Hull, press statement concerning the Philippine Islands, March 21, 1944; 10 Department of State Bulletin (March 25, 1944): 275-76; and Whiteman, Digest of International Law, V, 60.

265   ATTITUDE TOWARD COLONIALISM

. . . there is in Asia and Africa the so-called problem of colonialism. Now there the United States plays a somewhat independent role. You have this very great problem of the shift from colonialism to independence which is in process and which will be going on, perhaps, for another 50 years, and there I believe the role of the United States is to try to see that that process moves forward in a constructive evolutionary way and does not either come to a halt or take a violent revolutionary turn which would be destructive of very much good. I suspect that the United States will find that its role, not only today but in the coming years, will be to try to aid that process, without identifying itself 100 percent either with the so-called colonial powers or with the powers which are primarily and uniquely concerned with the problem of getting their independence as rapidly as possible. I think we have a special role to play and that perhaps makes it impractical for us, as I say, in every respect to identify our policies with those of other countries on whichever side of that problem they find their interest.

John Foster Dulles, news conference, October 2, 1956; 35 Department of State Bulletin (October 15, 1956): 577; and Whiteman, Digest of International Law, V, 59.

266 FREEDOM OF CHOICE INDISPENSABLE TO SELF-DETERMINATION

The right of self-determination and independence cannot be limited to one particular area of the world but must be universal. We view self-determination as a continual process whereby peoples may decide, in light of existing conditions, the manner in which they seek to exercise this right. Independence is only one of the several alternatives from which peoples may choose. In some cases, through mutual consent, a decision may be taken by a group to establish relationships with existing states, for example, through voluntary incorporation in another state or a special relationship such as commonwealth status.

Freedom of choice is indispensable to the exercise of the right of self-determination. For this freedom of choice to be meaningful, there must be corresponding freedom of thought, conscience, expression, movement and association. Self-determination entails legitimate, lively dissent and testing at the ballot box with frequent regularity.

U.S. Representative to the United Nations, statement, U.N. General Assembly, November 23, 1972; *Digest of United States Practice in International Law,* 1974, p. 48.

267 UNITED NATIONS CHARTER, 1945

Article 1 (Purposes)
2. To develop friendly relations among nations based on respect for the principle of equal rights and self-determination of peoples, and to take other appropriate measures to strengthen universal peace; . . .

Article 55
With a view to the creation of conditions of stability and well-being which are necessary for peaceful and friendly relations among nations based on respect for the principle of equal rights and self-determination of peoples, the United Nations shall promote:

a. higher standards of living, full employment, and conditions of economic and social progress and development;

b. solutions of international economic, social, health, and related problems; and international cultural and educational cooperation; and

c. universal respect for, and observance of, human rights and fundamental freedoms for all without distinction as to race, sex, language, or religion.

Article 73
Members of the United Nations which have or assume responsibilities for the administration of territories whose peoples have not yet attained a full measure of self-government recognize the principle that the interests of the inhabitants of these territories are paramount, and accept as a sacred trust the obligation to promote to the utmost, within the system of international peace and security established by the present

Charter, the well-being of the inhabitants of these territories, and, to this end:

> a. to ensure, with due respect for the culture of the peoples concerned, their political, economic, social, and educational advancement, their just treatment, and their protection against abuses;
>
> b. to develop self-government, to take due account of the political aspirations of the peoples, and to assist them in the progressive development of their free political institutions, according to the particular circumstances of each territory and its peoples and their varying stages of advancement; . . . .

United Nations Charter, 3 Bevans, *Treaties and Other International Agreements*, 1153-79; Articles 1 (par. 2), 55, 73.

268 INTER-AMERICAN RESOLUTION RESPECTING COLONIALISM IN THE AMERICAS, 1948

That it is a just aspiration of the American Republics that colonialism and the occupation of American territories by extra-continental countries should be brought to an end; . . .

Resolution 33, Ninth International Conference of American States, 1948; Whiteman, *Digest of International Law*, V, 83.

269 DECLARATION OF WASHINGTON--U.S. AND UNITED KINGDOM, 1956

1. Because of our belief that the state should exist for the benefit of the individual and not the individual for the benefit of the state, we uphold the basic right of peoples to governments of their own choice.

2. These beliefs of ours are far more than theory or doctrine. They have been translated into the actual conduct of our policy both domestic and foreign. We are parties to the Atlantic Charter, the United Nations Charter, the Potomac Charter and the Pacific Charter. In them we have, with other friends, dedicated ourselves to the goal of self-government and independence of all countries whose people desire and are capable of sustaining an independent existence. During the past ten and more years 600 million men and women in nearly a score of lands have, with our support and assistance, attained nationhood. Many millions more are being helped surely and steadily toward self-government. Thus, the reality and effectiveness of what we have done is a proof of our sincerity.

Joint Declaration, President Dwight Eisenhower and Prime Minister Anthony Eden, February 1, 1956; 34 *Department of State Bulletin* (February 13, 1956): 231; and Whiteman, *Digest of International Law*, V, 46.

270 UNITED NATIONS DECLARATION ON THE GRANTING OF INDEPENDENCE TO COLONIAL COUNTRIES AND PEOPLES, 1960

Recognizing the passionate yearning for freedom in all dependent peoples and the decisive role of such peoples in the attainment of their independence, . . .

Recognizing that the peoples of the world ardently desire the end of colonialism in all its manifestations, . . .

Convinced that all peoples have an inalienable right to complete freedom, the exercise of their sovereignty and the integrity of their national territory,

Solemnly proclaims the necessity of bringing to a speedy and unconditional end colonialism in all its forms and manifestations;

And to this end

Declares that:

1. The subjection of peoples to alien subjugation, domination and exploitation constitutes a denial of fundamental human rights, is contrary to the Charter of the United Nations and is an impediment to the promotion of world peace and co-operation.

2. All peoples have the right to self-determination; by virtue of that right they freely determine their political status and freely pursue their economic, social and cultural development. . . .

5. Immediate steps shall be taken, in Trust and Non-Self-Governing Territories or all other territories which have not yet attained independence, to transfer all powers to the peoples of those territories, without any conditions or reservations, in accordance with their freely expressed will and desire, without any distinctions as to race, creed or colour, in order to enable them to enjoy complete independence and freedom.

U.N. General Assembly resolution, December 14, 1960; Whiteman, *Digest of International Law*, V, 78-80.

271 INTERNATIONAL COVENANTS ON HUMAN RIGHTS, 1966

Article 1

1. All peoples have the right of self-determination. By virtue of that right they freely determine their political status and freely pursue their economic, social and cultural development.

2. All peoples may, for their own ends, freely dispose of their natural wealth and resources without prejudice to any obligations arising out of international economic co-operation, based upon the principle of mutual benefit, and international law. In no case may a people be deprived of its own means of subsistence.

3. The States Parties to the present Covenant, including those having responsibility for the administration of Non-Self-Governing and Trust Territories, shall promote the realization of the right of self-determina-

tion, and shall respect that right, in conformity with the provisions of the Charter of the United Nations.

Identical stipulations in the International Covenant on Civil and Political Rights and the International Covenant on Economic, Social and Cultural Rights, December 16, 1966; for text of these covenants, see *American Foreign Policy: Current Documents*, 1966, pp. 101-24.

272 UNITED STATES POSITION ON DEPENDENT TERRITORIES

. . . we [the United States of America] would hold no people against its will. We are prepared to take the necessary measures to consult any or all of the approximately 100,000 people whose destinies are still associated with ours any time they request it. The people of Puerto Rico are fully self-governing, as the General Assembly [G.A. Res. 748 (VIII), November 27, 1953] has found after careful examination, enjoy the status of American citizens, and are free to request a change of status at any time. The remaining territories for which the United States exercises sovereignty are in the process of becoming self-governing.

The United States' position is that "the subjection of peoples to alien subjugation, domination and exploitation constitutes a denial of fundamental human rights, is contrary to the Charter of the United Nations and is an impediment to the promotion of world peace and co-operation.". . .

The Charter [of the United Nations] declares in effect that on every nation in possession of foreign territories, there rests the responsibility to assist the peoples of these areas in the progressive development of their free political institutions so that ultimately they can validly choose for themselves their permanent political status.

Adlai Stevenson, U.S. Representative to the United Nations, letter to President of U.N. General Assembly, November 25, 1961; Whiteman, *Digest of International Law*, V, 82-83.

273 SELF-DETERMINATION IN PUERTO RICO

On March 3, 1952, the people of Puerto Rico attained self-government by freely and fully participating in a referendum. They voted in that referendum to establish a Commonwealth of Puerto Rico freely associated with the United States and they adopted the Constitution for that Commonwealth.

In 1953 the eighth session of the General Assembly of the United Nations recognized Puerto Rico's attainment of self-government by adopting Resolution 748 (VIII). Operative paragraph 5 of that resolution
"Recognizes that, in the framework of their Constitution and of the compact agreed upon with the United States of America, the people of the Commonwealth of Puerto Rico have been invested with attributes of political sovereignty which clearly identify the status

of self-government attained by the Puerto Rican people as that of an autonomous political entity;" . . .

My delegation would also like to bring to the attention of the Assembly the following facts. In general elections in 1956, 1960, 1964, 1968 and 1972, as well as in a 1967 referendum on status, the people of Puerto Rico freely chose to retain their relationship with the United States. On six separate occasions they have reaffirmed their original decision. . . . The future of Puerto Rico will continue to be shaped by the will of the majority of the Puerto Rican people as expressed in regularly scheduled elections in which all shades of political opinion are free to participate.

It is the people of Puerto Rico who, through universal adult suffrage, have decided what their status and their form of government should be.

U.S. Representative to the United Nations, statement, U.N. General Assembly, December 14, 1974; *Digest of United States Practice in International Law,* 1974, pp. 51-52.

*   *   *

United States policy on Puerto Rico is based on complete acceptance of the right of the people of Puerto Rico to self-determination. The people of Puerto Rico exercised this right in approving Commonwealth status and their own Constitution in 1952. They reaffirmed that choice in a status referendum in 1967, in which 60.41 percent voted for Commonwealth status, 38.98 percent voted for statehood and 0.60 percent voted for independence. . . .

The United States has often made clear that the question of the status of Puerto Rico is an internal affair of the people of Puerto Rico and the United States. President Carter has stated that he will support whatever status the people of Puerto Rico wish, but that the initiative for any change should come from them. In view of the self-governing status of Puerto Rico, and the fact that the nature of its relationship with the United States is based on the free expression of the will of the Puerto Rican people, the U.S. Government regards discussion of Puerto Rico's status in international forums, particularly in forums which deal with colonial issues, as inappropriate.

U.S. Representative to the United Nations, letter to U.N. Committee on Decolonization, May 16, 1977; *Digest of United States Practice in International Law,* 1977, pp. 58-59.

*   *   *

Today marks Puerto Rico's 80th year under the American flag, and the 26th anniversary of the founding of the Commonwealth of Puerto Rico, a form of government freely and democratically adopted by the people of Puerto Rico. Since 1898 and as American citizens since 1917, you have made a rich contribution to the life of the United States while preserving your own unique culture and traditions within the broader community.

As you commemorate this anniversary, I would like to emphasize that the United States remains fully committed to the principle of self-determination for the people of Puerto Rico. President Eisenhower made that commitment in 1953, and this has been the position of all U.S. administrations since that time. We continue to regard it as the fundamental principle in deciding Puerto Rico's future.

My administration will respect the wishes of the people of Puerto Rico and your right to self-determination. Whatever decision the people of Puerto Rico may wish to take--statehood, independence, Commonwealth status, or mutually agreed modifications in that status--it will be yours, reached in accordance with your own traditions, democratically and peacefully.

Jimmy Carter, statement addressed to the people of Puerto Rico on twenty-sixth anniversary of the proclamation of the Constitution of the Commonwealth of Puerto Rico, July 1978; *Digest of United States Practice in International Law*, 1078, pp. 171 72.

HUMAN FREEDOMS AND RIGHTS

In addition to promoting certain political rights as central to the doctrine of self-determination, after World War II the United States assumed leadership in seeking to advance and guarantee individual human rights throughout the world. Never before in history has so much attention been paid to human rights as a global problem. This movement consists of three components: motivating peoples and their governments to appreciate and cope with the issue, defining those human rights that warrant political recognition and advancement, and securing them by national and international action--globally through the United Nations system and regionally through the Organization of American States and other arrangements, such as the Helsinki accords (see Documents 515-519).

Aside from espousing human rights as a major global goal, the United States pressed for and participated in formalizing policy and commitments. As a consequence, dozens of human rights resolutions, declarations, and treaties and conventions have been negotiated since World War II.

These actions fall into the following categories: multilateral organizational charters (see Document 267); basic instruments--such as the Universal Declaration of Human Rights (1948), the International Covenants on Civil and Political Rights (1966) and Economic, Social, and Cultural Rights (1966) see Document 271, and the American Convention on Human Rights (1969) (Document 460); and, more specifically, conventions dealing with the prevention of discrimination, association, cultural development, information, labor relations, marriage and childhood, nationality and statelessness, refugees, slavery and similar practices, social development, treatment of persons subject to detention and imprisonment, and war crimes and crimes against humanity. Some of the more specific categories range from the right to life to prohibitions on genocide, racial and religious discrimination, torture, and the right to emigrate. International terrorism is treated separately in Chapter 19.

It has been said that, despite the many policies and commitments embodied in these international resolutions, declarations, and treaties, implementation lags considerably behind agreed goals and international law. The United States has been reluctant to ratify some of these conventions, because they are covered by earlier resolutions and declarations, which suffice if properly implemented, certain other governments refuse to be bound by them, or authority over particular human rights impinge upon states' rights under our constitutional division of powers, and because the United States has better or more expedient laws and historic practices respecting many individual rights, has serious reservations concerning particular stipulations, votes against them or withholds its signature, is awaiting ratification by specific other governments, or views the commitments as creating complex and vexatious adjudicatory problems. For commentary on some of the American objections and reservations to human rights covenants and agreements, see *Digest of United States Practice in International Law,* 1979, pp. 481-500.

The documents provided in this section include general policy statements concerning human rights (Documents 274-277), an interpretation of the meaning of "human rights" (Document 278), guidelines for human rights policy (Document 279), a basic inter-American commitment (Document 280), commentary on problems of implementing human rights policy internationally (Document 281), and a list of major human rights resolutions, declarations, and conventions (Document 282). For additional general policy statements, also see Chapter 6, Documents 95-97 and 101, and for inter-American developments, also see Documents 460-463, 554, and 556.

274   FOUR FREEDOMS, 1941

In the future days, which we seek to make secure, we look forward to a world founded upon four essential human freedoms.

The first is freedom of speech and expression--everywhere in the world.

The second is freedom of every person to worship God in his way--everywhere in the world.

The third is freedom from want--which, translated into world terms, means economic understandings which will secure to every nation a healthy peacetime life for its inhabitants--everywhere in the world.

The fourth is freedom from fear--which, translated into world terms, means a world-wide reduction of armaments to such a point and in such a thorough fashion that no nation will be in a position to commit an act of physical aggression against any neighbor--anywhere in the world.

Franklin Roosevelt, Message to Congress, January 6, 1941; *A Decade of American Foreign Policy: Basic Documents,* 1941-49, p. 1.

275 BLESSINGS OF FREEDOM AND SELF-GOVERNMENT

 . . . we must preach, demonstrate, and tirelessly sell the vitality and value of freedom in the world. Nothing is more dangerous to our cause than to expect America's message to be heard if we don't bother to tell it.

We must reaffirm to the oppressed masses of the earth the great truth that the God who gave life to humanity, at the same time gave the right of liberty to man. And in our own interest we must apply both our intelligence and the necessary material means to assist other peoples to realize for themselves the blessing of freedom and of self-government.

Dwight Eisenhower, address, American Legion Convention, August 30, 1954; *Papers of Presidents: Eisenhower,* 1954, p. 780.

276 MANKIND MUST BE FREE

 . . . Americans truly and personally identify with human rights as few nations in history ever have.

We were born as a nation on a declaration of political rights which also stated universal and timeless ideals that we believe apply to all men, in all places, at all times--life, liberty, and happiness. . . .

Our greatest Presidents are remembered best for their successes in human rights, whether it was freeing an enslaved minority from bondage, or whether it was guaranteeing the self-determination of a small and a defenseless nation.

Twenty years ago, President Harry Truman told the Congress at a very troubled time in our history: "We in the United States are working in company with other nations who share our desire for enduring world peace and who believe with us that, above all else, men must be free."

Indeed, men must be free above all else--free to be protected equally by the law, free to choose a career or a job or a neighborhood or a way of life or a religion, free to hold and have their property protected.

Men must be free from violence or the threat of violence, free from dictatorial or arbitrary government. And men also must be free of fear-- fear of hunger, disease, secret police, ignorance, poverty, bigotry.

Lyndon Johnson, remarks, final meeting of President's Commission for the Observance of Human Rights Year, December 4, 1968; *Papers of Presidents: Johnson,* 1968-1969, II, 1162-63. Also see Dean Rusk, "The First Purpose of Our Foreign Policy . . . Is to Defend Freedom," address, Barnard College, January 22, 1964; *American Foreign Policy: Current Documents,* 1964, pp. 9-16.

277 SOUL OF AMERICAN FOREIGN POLICY

The effectiveness of our human rights policy is now an established fact. It has contributed to an atmosphere of change--sometimes disturbing--but which has encouraged progress in many ways and in many places. . . .

. . . human rights are not peripheral to the foreign policy of the United States. Our human rights policy is not a decoration. It is not something we've adopted to polish up our image abroad or to put a fresh coat of moral paint on the discredited policies of the past.

Our pursuit of human rights is part of a broad effort to use our great power and our tremendous influence in the service of creating a better world--a world in which human beings can live in peace, in freedom, and with their basic needs adequately met. Human rights is the soul of our foreign policy. And I say this with assurance, because human rights is the soul of our sense of nationhood.

Jimmy Carter, address, group of human and civil rights leaders, White House, December 6, 1978; *American Foreign Policy: Basic Documents,* 1977-1980, p. 428. President Carter also proclaimed that our support for human rights in other countries "is in our national interest" as well as "part of our own national character," January 23, 1980, in *American Foreign Policy: Basic Documents,* 1977-1980, pp. 56-57; and that the United States must always stand for human rights; see his Farewell Address to the Nation, January 14, 1981, pp. 86-88.

278 MEANING OF "HUMAN RIGHTS"

Let me define what we mean by "human rights."

First, there is the right to be free from governmental violation of the integrity of the person. Such violations include torture; cruel, inhuman, or degrading treatment or punishment; and arbitrary arrest or imprisonment. And they include denial of fair public trial, and invasion of the home.

Second, there is the right to the fulfillment of such vital needs as food, shelter, health care, and education. We recognize that the fulfillment of this right will depend, in part, upon the stage of a nation's economic development. But we also know that this right can be violated by a Government's action or inaction--for example, through corrupt official processes which divert resources to an elite at the expense of the needy, or through indifference to the plight of the poor.

Third, there is the right to enjoy civil and political liberties-- freedom of thought, of religion, of assembly; freedom of speech; freedom of the press; freedom of movement both within and outside one's own country; freedom to take part in government.

Our policy is to promote all these rights. They are all recognized in the Universal Declaration of Human Rights, a basic document which the United States helped fashion and which the United Nations approved in 1948. There may be disagreement on the priorities these rights deserve, but I believe that, with work, all of these rights can become complementary and mutually reinforcing. . . .

Since 1945 international practice has confirmed that a nation's obligaticns to respect human rights is a matter of concern in international law. . . .

In pursuing a human rights policy, we must always keep in mind the limits of our power and of our wisdom. A sure formula for defeat of our goals would be a rigid, hubristic attempt to impose our values on others. A doctrinaire plan of action would be as damaging as indifference.

We must be realistic. Our country can only achieve our objectives if we shape what we do to the case at hand . . . .

Cyrus Vance, address, University of Georgia Law School, April 30, 1977; *American Foreign Policy: Basic Documents,* 1977-1980, pp. 409-10.

279 GUIDELINES OF HUMAN RIGHTS POLICY

--Human rights are a legitimate international concern and have been so defined in international agreements for more than a generation.

--The United States will speak up for human rights in appropriate international forums and in exchanges with other governments.

--We will be mindful of the limits of our reach; we will be conscious of the differences between public postures that satisfy our self-esteem and policies that bring positive results.

--We will not lose sight of either the requirements of global security or what we stand for as a nation. . . .

. . . We do not and will not condone repressive practices. This is not only dictated by our values but is also a reflection of the reality that regimes which lack legitimacy or moral authority are inherently vulnerable. There will therefore be limits to the degree to which such regimes can be congenial partners. We have used, and we will use, our influence against repressive practices. Our traditions and our interests demand it.

But truth compels also a recognition of our limits. The question is whether we promote human rights more effectively by counsel and friendly relations where this serves our interest, or by confrontational propaganda and discriminatory legislation. And we must also assess the domestic performance of foreign governments in relation to their history and to the threats they face. We must have some understanding for the dilemmas of countries adjoining powerful, hostile, and irreconcilable totalitarian regimes.

Henry Kissinger, address, Minneapolis, July 15, 1975; *Digest of United States Practice in International Law,* 1975, pp. 180-81. For President Reagan's commitment to act against blatant affronts to human rights, see *American Foreign Policy: Current Documents,* 1983, pp. 330-31.

2 8 0   INTER-AMERICAN CONVENTION AND COMMISSION ON HUMAN RIGHTS

The American States proclaim the fundamental rights of the individual without distinction as to race, nationality, creed or sex.

*   *   *

There shall be an Inter-American Commission on Human Rights, whose principal function shall be to promote the observance and protection of human rights and to serve as a consultative organ of the Organization [OAS] in these matters.

An Inter-American convention on human rights shall determine the structure, competence, and procedure of this Commission, as well as those of other organs responsible for these matters.

Organization of American States, Charter, Article 3, paragraph j and Article 112. Also see Chapters VII on Economic Standards, VIII on Social Standards, and IX on Educational, Scientific, and Cultural Standards. For inter-American Fundamental Rights and Duties of States, see Document 445; for American Convention on Human Rights, see Document 460; also see Chapter 26, Documents 461-463.

2 8 1   PROBLEMS OF IMPLEMENTING HUMAN RIGHTS POLICY

How to embody the fundamental principles of democratic societies-- human rights--in foreign policy has become an especially pressing question for the United States. . . .

Human rights is at the core of American foreign policy because it is central to America's conception of itself. This nation did not "develop." It was created in order to make real a specific political vision. It follows that "human rights" is not something added on to our foreign policy, but its ultimate purpose: the preservation and promotion of liberty in the world. . . .

Our human rights policy has two goals. First, we seek to improve human rights practices in numerous countries--to eliminate torture or brutality, to secure religious freedom, to promote free elections, and the like. A foreign policy indifferent to these issues would not appeal to the idealism of Americans, would be amoral, and would lack public support. Moreover, these are pragmatic, not utopian, actions for the United States. Our most stable, reliable allies are democracies. . . .

As to the question of tactics, the . . . test is effectiveness. With friendly countries, we prefer to use diplomacy, not public pronounce- ments. We seek not to isolate them for their injustices and thereby render ourselves ineffective, but to use our influence to effect desirable change. Our aim is to achieve results, not to make self-satisfying but ineffective gestures.

But the second goal of our human rights policy sometimes can conflict with this search for effectiveness; we seek also a public association of the United States with the cause of liberty. This is an eminently practical goal: our ability to win international cooperation and defeat anti-American propaganda will be harmed if we seem indifferent to the fate of liberty. Friendly governments are often susceptible to quiet diplomacy, and we therefore use it rather than public denunciations. But if we never appear seriously concerned about human rights in friendly countries, our policy will seem one-sided and cynical. . . . So a human rights policy does inescapably mean trouble--for example, from friendly governments if the United States Government places pressure upon them, or from the American people if their government appears not to be doing so. Yet a human rights policy embodies our deepest convictions about political life, and our interests: the defense and expansion of liberty.

Department of State report, February 1983; *American Foreign Policy: Current Documents,* 1983, pp. 321-24. For commentary on Department of State memorandum on human rights, October 27, 1981, see *Historic Documents,* 1981, pp. 779-85.

*   *   *

In my view U.S. human rights policy has two specific goals: to improve human rights conditions in a large number of places around the world, so as to benefit the people who live in those places; and to make clear the continuing commitment of the United States to the cause of liberty throughout the world. These goals are, of course, not inconsistent; indeed, they are inseparable. Yet, in practice, formulating a policy which achieves both is extraordinarily difficult. . . .

With respect to complexity, I refer to the great difficulty in determining what U.S. Government actions will in fact help achieve human rights in a large number of specific cases. In a sense, the easiest aspect of this problem is the choice between public pressure and quiet diplomacy. . . .

I think our general views on this are by now clear. We believe that where there are good relations between a foreign government and the U.S. Government, and our influence is considerable, we should use it first through diplomatic channels. Among the advantages of this route are the careful control over it we can exercise; the fact that issues of American arrogance or neocolonialism, or a foreign government's sensitivity to public pressure and to its own sovereignty, are minimized; and the fact that we avoid adding inadvertently to any campaign aimed at delegitimizing or destabilizing the government in question. . . .

We must learn to deal with the frustration that flows from partial success in our efforts to improve respect for basic human rights Limited success is frustrating in human rights, as it is not elsewhere. In other areas of foreign policy, any advance is a gain. In human rights, partial success is always shadowed by the fact that any remaining human rights violation is still unconditionally repugnant. . . .

Through the historic encounter of America with human rights problems, there have been two traditions of response to this frustration. The first tradition has been the dominant one because it accords with

American ways of doing things in other areas. When Americans are concerned about righting a moral wrong, we are traditionally willing to work and to sacrifice to achieve our ideals. We generally commit ourselves to effective action on behalf of our principles. We are willing to make the intellectual effort to understand a complicated reality when we want to change it. We are willing to commit resources. We are willing to give of our own labor and efforts. And, when it is a question of diminishing suffering and injustice, we stick to an effort in spite of complications and difficulties. . . .

There has been another, less influential, American tradition of response to frustration in the face of a complex moral task. In the 1840's and 1850's, this tradition was represented by the attitude of some extreme abolitionists in the face of the entrenched evil of slavery. . . . This tradition saw that one way to avoid being implicated in a moral evil is to place yourself in a position where you cannot do anything about it.

I do not disparage these specific instruments of human rights policy. They have an important place as part of an integrated policy, . . . But if abstention and withdrawal become the whole of our human rights policy, that policy will be both ineffective and unworthy of us. . . .

Human rights policy is, inevitably, a difficult mixing of the highest idealism, with practical politics. It isn't easy, to practice or indeed even to explain. Yet the marriage of ideals and politics is an old American practice--as old as the country itself. We are committed to this effort, as the President has made clear time after time. Human rights policy has always been, and remains, a central element of American foreign policy.

Elliott Abrams, Assistant Secretary of State for Human Rights and Humanitarian Affairs, address, East-West Round Table, New York, April 19, 1983; *American Foreign Policy: Current Documents,* 1983, pp. 326-29.

*   *   *

There are several different ways of approaching human rights issues, and some are better than others. One thing should be clear. Human rights policy should not be a formula for escapism or a set of excuses for evading problems. Human rights policy cannot mean simply dissociating or distancing ourselves from regimes whose practices we find deficient. Too much of what passes for human rights policy has taken the form of shunning those we find do not live up to internationally accepted standards. But this to me is a "cop-out"; it seems more concerned with making us feel better than with having an impact on the situation we deplore. It is really a form of isolationism. If some liberals advocate cutting off relationships with right-wing regimes--and some conservatives seek to cut off dealings with left-wing regimes--we could be left with practically no foreign policy at all. This is not my idea of how to advance the cause of human rights. . . .

The techniques of exerting our influence are well known. We try, without letup, to sensitize other governments to human rights concerns. Every year we put on the public record a large volume of country reports examining the practices of other countries in thorough and candid detail--the rights of citizens to be free from violations of the integrity of the person and the rights of citizens to enjoy basic civil and political liberties. . . .

Wherever feasible, we try to ameliorate abuses through the kind of frank diplomatic exchanges often referred to as "quiet diplomacy." But where our positive influence is minimal, or where other approaches are unavailing, we may have no choice but to use other, more concrete kinds of leverage with regimes whose practices we cannot accept.

We may deny economic and military assistance, withhold diplomatic support, vote against multilateral loans, refuse licenses for crime control equipment, or take other punitive steps. Where appropriate, we resort to public pressures and public statements denouncing such actions. . . .

Multilateral organizations are another instrument of our human rights policy. . . . We regret that some multilateral organizations have distorted the purposes they were designed to serve--such as UNESCO [UN Educational, Scientific, and Cultural Organization], which has not been living up to its responsibility to defend freedom of speech, intellectual freedom, and human rights in general.

Friendly governments are often more amenable to traditional diplomacy than to open challenge, and we therefore prefer persuasion over public denunciations. But if we were never seriously concerned about human rights abuses in friendly countries, our policy would be one-sided and cynical. . . .

Clearly, there are limits to our ability to remake the world. In the end, sovereign governments will make their own decisions, despite external pressure. Where a system of government is built on repression, human rights will inevitably be subordinated to the perceived requirements of political survival. The sheer diversity and complexity of other nations' internal situations, and the problem of coping with them in a dangerous world, are additional limits. How we use our influence and how we reconcile political and moral interests are questions that call not for dogmatic conclusions but for painstaking, sober analysis--and no little humility. . . .

The cause of human rights is at the core of American foreign policy because it is central to America's conception of itself. These values are hardly an American invention, but America has perhaps been unique in its commitment to base its foreign policy on the pursuit of such ideals. It should be an everlasting source of pride to Americans that we have used our vast power to such noble ends. If we have sometimes fallen short, that is not a reason to flagellate ourselves but to remind ourselves of how much there remains to do.

This is what America has always represented to other nations and other peoples. But if we abandoned the effort, we would not only be letting others down, we would be letting ourselves down.

George Shultz, address, Creve Coeur Club, Peoria, Illinois, February 22, 1984; Department of State, *Realism, Strength, Negotiation* (Washington: Government Printing Office, 1984), pp. 87-90.

2 8 2   MAJOR HUMAN RIGHTS DECLARATIONS AND CONVENTIONS

FREEDOM, INDEPENDENCE, AND RIGHTS OF STATES

Convention on the Rights and Duties of States in the Event of Civil Strife, Inter-American, February 20, 1928--TS 814; 2 Bevans, *Treaties and Other International Agreements* 694-97.

Convention on the Rights and Duties of States, Inter-American, December 29, 1933--TS 881; 3 Bevans, *Treaties and Other International Agreements* 145-51.

Declaration on the Granting of Independence to Colonial Countries and Peoples, December 14, 1960--*American Foreign Policy: Current Documents,* 1960, pp. 110-11.

HUMAN RIGHTS

Global

Agreement for the Suppression of the White Slave Traffic, May 18, 1904 --TS 496; 1 Bevans, *Treaties and Other International Agreements* 424-29.   Protocol, May 18, 1904--TS 2332; 2 *U.S. Treaties* 1997-2002.

Convention to Suppress the Slave Trade and Slavery, September 25, 1926--TS 718; 2 Bevans, *Treaties and Other International Agreements* 607-16.   Protocol, December 7, 1953--TIAS 3532; 7 *U.S. Treaties* 479-82.   Supplementary Convention on the Abolition of Slavery, September 7, 1956--TIAS 6418; 18 *U.S. Treaties* 3201-8.

Convention Concerning Freedom of Association and Protection of the Right to Organize, July 9, 1948--68 UNTS 17.

Convention on the Prevention and Punishment of the Crime of Genocide, December 9, 1948--*A Decade of American Foreign Policy, 1941-49,* pp. 966-69; 78 UNTS 277.

Universal Declaration of Human Rights, December 10, 1948--*A Decade of American Foreign Policy, 1941-49,* pp. 1156-59.

Convention Concerning Equal Remuneration for Men and Women Workers for Work of Equal Value, June 29, 1951--165 UNTS 303.

Convention on the Status of Refugees, July 28, 1951--189 UNTS 137. Protocol, January 31, 1967--TIAS 6577; 19 *U.S. Treaties* 6223-29.

Convention on the International Right of Correction, March 31, 1953-- 435 UNTS 191; and Whiteman, *Digest of International Law,* XIII, 919-23.

Convention on the Political Rights of Women, March 31, 1953--TIAS 8289; 27 *U.S. Treaties* 1909-12.

Convention Relating to the Status of Stateless Persons, September 28,

1954--360 UNTS 117.

Convention on Nationality of Married Women, February 2, 1957--309 UNTS 65.

Convention Concerning the Abolition of Forced Labor, June 25, 1957-- 320 UNTS 291.

Convention Concerning Discrimination in Respect of Employment and Occupation, June 25, 1958--362 UNTS 31.

Convention Against Discrimination in Education, December 15, 1960-- 429 UNTS 93.

Convention on the Reduction of Statelessness, August 30, 1961-- Whiteman, *Digest of International Law,* VIII, 91-96.

Convention on Consent, Minimum Age, and Registration of Marriages, December 10, 1962--521 UNTS 231.

International Convention on Elimination of All Forms of Racial Discrimination, 1965--*American Foreign Policy: Current Documents,* 1965, pp. 160-69. Also earlier Declaration on Elimination of All Forms of Racial Discrimination, November 20, 1963--*American Foreign Policy: Current Documents,* 1963, pp. 152-56.

Agreement on Importation of Educational, Scientific, and Cultural Materials, November 2, 1966--TIAS 6129; 17 *U.S. Treaties* 1835- 49; and *American Foreign Policy: Current Documents,* 1966, pp. 195-99.

International Covenant on Civil and Political Rights, December 16, 1966 --*American Foreign Policy: Current Documents,* 1966, pp. 110- 24.

International Covenant on Economic, Social, and Cultural Rights, December 16, 1966--*American Foreign Policy: Current Documents,* 1966, pp. 104-10.

Convention on the Elimination of All Forms of Religious Intolerance, 1967. Also Declaration on the Elimination of Intolerance and Discrimination Based on Religion or Belief, 1981. Also earlier United Nations General Assembly resolution on Racial Prejudice and Religious Intolerance, December 7, 1962--*American Foreign Policy: Current Documents,* 1962, pp. 180-81.

Convention on Freedom of Information, December 18, 1967--Whiteman, *Digest of International Law,* XIII, 909-13. Also earlier United Nations resolution on Freedom of Information, 1948, and draft Declaration on Freedom of Information, 1960, in Whiteman, *Digest of International Law,* XIII, 908-9 and 917-19.

Convention on the Non-applicability of Statutory Limitations to War Crimes and Crimes Against Humanity, November 26, 1968. Also Principles of International Cooperation in the Detection, Arrest, Extradition, and Punishment of Persons Guilty of War Crimes and Crimes Against Humanity, December 3, 1973. Commentary in Whiteman, *Digest of International Law,* XI, 1021-25; *U.S. Participation in UN,* 1968, pp. 130-31, and 1974, pp. 146-47; 63 *American Journal of International Law* (1969): 578, and vol. 71 (1977): 510.

Convention on the Suppression and Punishment of the Crime of Apartheid, November 30, 1973--UN Doc. A/9233/Add. 1, November 19, 1973, with commentary in *Digest of United States Practice in International Law,* 1973, pp. 128-32.

Convention Against the Taking of Hostages, December 17, 1979--*Digest of United States Practice in International Law,* 1979, pp. 539-42.

Convention on the Elimination of Discrimination Against Women, December 18, 1979 --*Digest of United States Practice in International Law,* 1979, pp. 550-59. Also earlier Declaration on the Elimination of Discrimination Against Women, November 7, 1967--*American Foreign Policy: Current Documents,* 1967, pp. 113-15.

Convention Against Torture, December 10, 1984--22 *United Nations Monthly Chronicle* (No. 1, 1985): 48-53. Also earlier Declaration on Torture, December 9, 1975--*Digest of United States Practice in International Law,* 1975, pp. 217-18.

Regional

American Declaration on the Rights and Duties of Man, 1948--Resolution XXX of Ninth Inter-American Conference, in Department of State, *Ninth International Conference of American States, Bogota, Colombia, March 30-May 2, 1948* (Washington: Government Printing Office, 1948), pp. 260-66; also Whiteman, *Digest of International Law,* V, 230-34.

Convention on Granting Political Rights to Women, Inter-American, May 2, 1948--TIAS 8365; 27 *U.S. Treaties* 3301-9.

Convention for the Protection of Human Rights and Fundamental Freedoms, Europe, January 4, 1950--213 UNTS 222. Protocol, March 20, 1952--213 UNTS 262.

American Convention on Human Rights (Pact of San Jose, Costa Rica), November 22, 1969--O.A.S. Treaty Series, No. 36; 65 *American Journal of International Law* (1971): 679-702. Also see Document 460.

Declaration on Principles Guiding Relations Between Participating States, "Respect for Human Rights and Fundamental Freedoms," and "Human Contacts," Europe, Helsinki Conference Final Act, August 1, 1975--*Digest of United States Practice in International Law,* 1975, pp. 7-13 and 190-93; and 73 *Department of State Bulletin* (September 1, 1975): 323-50.

ADDITIONAL DECLARATIONS

Standard Minimum Rules for the Treatment of Prisoners, 1957 and 1977.

Declaration on the Rights of the Child, 1959.

Declaration on Promotion Among Youth of Ideals of Peace and Understanding, 1965.

Declaration of Principles of International Cultural Cooperation, 1966.

Declaration on Territorial Asylum, 1967.

Declaration on Social Progress and Development, 1969.

Declaration on Eradication of Hunger and Malnutrition, 1974.

Declaration on Protection of Women and Children in Emergency and Armed Conflict, 1974.

Declaration on the Protection of All Persons from Being Subjected to Torture and Other Cruel, Inhuman, or Degrading Treatment or Punishment, 1975.

These are multilateral declarations and conventions. Aspects of human rights guarantees also appear in stipulations embodied in other multilateral and bilateral treaties and agreements. International commitments of this nature are clearly a twentieth-century development, the preponderant majority of which were consummated since World War II. Also see Documents 329-333.

17

Trade and Commerce

Peace has an economic dimension. In a world of independent states and interdependent economies, failure to collaborate is costly--in political as well as economic terms. Economic barriers block more than the free flow of goods and capital across national borders; they obstruct a more open world in which ideas and people, as well as goods and machinery, move among nations with maximum freedom.

Richard Nixon
U.S. Foreign Policy for the 1970's:
A New Strategy for Peace (1970)

According to Lyndon Johnson, at the outset of our history George Washington declared that the United States had only one option: "Whether to be respectable and prosperous or contemptible and miserable as a nation" (*American Foreign Policy: Current Documents,* 1965, p. 27). Contemporary foreign economic policy consists of two principal components--international trade and foreign aid (foreign assistance is dealt with in Chapter 24). Historically this country has promoted international trade and commerce with both fervor and spirit.

After gaining independence, the United States endeavored to penetrate and eventually eliminate the closed trading system and doctrine of mercantilism of the European powers--in order to trade not only with them but also with their dependencies, and with other nations, including the Latin American countries as they gained independence. This objective led rapidly to the development of the concept of "free trade," which came to permeate United States international commercial policy for more than two centuries. Concomitant policies of deliberate trade expansion, open market economies, the negotiation of bilateral and eventually also multilateral trade agreements, and support of the most-favored-nation treatment principle were devised to implement the general goal of free trade.

So far as the American government is concerned, the Constitution accords Congress authority to "regulate commerce with foreign nations" (Art. 1, Sec. 8, Clause 3). By judicial interpretation this has been held to include the gamut of international commercial intercourse, which applies to both the subjects of commerce as well as the persons engaged in it, and to the means, agencies, and instrumentalities that manage it. Being a foreign relations enterprise, from the very outset the Executive has promoted international trade via the treaty process, initially formal treaties and subsequently also executive agreements based largely on prior authorizing legislation. In recent decades, therefore, American commerce is governed by an extensive network of legislative enactments and international treaties and agreements.

During the past two centuries commercial affairs have proliferated in two directions--expanding territorially from trade with a handful of nations late in the eighteenth century to more than 160 countries, and functionally from a few exports and imports to a profusion of commodities and a host of techniques and technological developments. To illustrate the latter, in addition to the general principles of free trade and open markets (and elimination of protectionism), American legislation and international agreements have come to embrace such matters as not only imports, exports, navigation rights, and tariffs to maximize American trade opportunities, but also nondiscrimination and various forms of the most-favored-nation principle, reciprocity, structured customs proce- dures and inspections, maritime shipping and overland and aerial transporta- tion, embargoes and economic sanctions, balance of payments and currency exchange, countervailing duties and nontariff trade barriers, free zones and economic unions, patents and trademark protection, machinery for the settle- ment of disputes, and in time of war, the commercial and navigation rights and duties of neutrals.

This chapter is devoted primarily to highlighting recent general policy statements and post-World War II trade legislation and international agree- ments that govern bilateral and multilateral commercial relations.

GENERAL TRADE POLICY

The dominant themes stressed in recent trade policy statements include: international economic interdependence, economic growth through free mar- kets, promotion of freer world trade, reduction of trade barriers and elim- ination of trade restrictions, elimination of commercial unfairness, relation of healthy trade practices to the enhancement of peace and human welfare, and the tailoring of these objectives to produce a "new international economic order." Most of these are touched on in Documents 283-286.

Scores of additional statements, many in considerable detail, are to be found in presidential messages and reports to Congress, addresses of other leaders, congressional hearings, reports, and enactments, and international treaties and agreements. For related policy, see also Documents 557 and 558 (Alliance for Progress), 565 (Caribbean Basin Initiative), and those contained in Chapters 22 to 24, concerned with East-West relations, North-South rela- tions, and foreign assistance.

283 TRADE IS TWO-WAY STREET

. . . If we glance back a few decades, we find the interdependence of the world economy had even then reached a point where unilateral actions on a grand scale were self-defeating. Thus, an effort by this country to isolate itself from the world economy through the Smoot-Hawley tariff [1930] led to offsetting actions by others, resulting in a spiral of trade restrictions whose invidious effects are only now--37 years later--on the verge of being eliminated as a major force in world affairs.

The name of one of my distinguished predecessors, Cordell Hull, immediately comes to mind when one reviews the recent tariff history of this country and our championship of the cause of lowering barriers to trade. I in no way minimize his tremendous contribution if I observe he has had lots of company. Democratic and Republican administrations alike --from Roosevelt to Lyndon Johnson--and the Congress, too, have con- sistently supported the broad thrust of the same foreign trade policy. . . .

The reasons for this consistency are not, I believe, very difficult to find. First, there is the fact that a policy of trade restrictionism had been tried and found to be a failure. Secondly, the extraordinary growth of science and technology gives an entirely different dimension to the old, respected, and sound theory of comparative advantage. . . . For, in the familiar phrase, "Trade is a two-way street." I don't apologize for using that cliche, because it expresses a basic truth--a reality which is vital in maintaining the prosperity of this country and the entire fabric of international cooperation we have constructed so carefully over the years.

Dean Rusk, "Trade Restrictions...Would Tear at the Fabric of International Co- operation and Economic Development," statement, Senate Finance Committee, October 18, 1967; *American Foreign Policy: Current Documents,* 1967, p. 1116.

284 FREE MARKET APPROACH TO TRADE

The basic goal of all economic policy is to provide an environment which is conducive to economic growth and development. . . .

A vivid historical testimonial to the effectiveness of the free- market approach is the remarkable performance of the Western economic system in the first two post-war decades. Domestically, most of the major industrial economies were rebuilt along free-market lines. Internationally, the major factor underlying the ensuing growth perfor- mance was a dramatic expansion in world trade and capital flows--an expansion made possible only by the open trade and payments systems that was put into place after the war.

Donald Regan, Secretary of the Treasury, address, "The Foundations of U.S. International Economic Policy," September 13, 1983; *American Foreign Policy: Current Documents,* 1983, p. 178.

285   MODERNIZING POLICY FOR FREER WORLD TRADE

For the past 35 years, the United States has steadfastly pursued a policy of freer world trade. As a nation, we have recognized that competition cannot stop at the ocean's edge. We have determined that American trade policies must advance the national interest--which means they must respond to the whole of our interests, and not be a device to favor the narrow interest. . . .

As we look at the changing patterns of world trade, three factors stand out that require us to continue modernizing our own trade policies:

First, world economic interdependence has become a fact. Reductions in tariffs and in transportation costs have internationalized the world economy. . . .

Second, we must recognize that a number of foreign countries now compete fully with the United States in world markets.

We have always welcomed such competition. It promotes the economic development of the entire world to the mutual benefit of all, including our own consumers. It provides an additional stimulus to our own industry, agriculture and labor force. At the same time, however, it requires us to insist on fair competition among all countries.

Third, the traditional surplus in the U.S. balance of trade has disappeared. . . .

The disappearance of the surplus has suggested to some that we should abandon our traditional approach toward freer trade. I reject this argument not only because I believe in the principle of freer trade, but also for a very simple and pragmatic reason: any reduction in our imports produced by U.S. restrictions not accepted by our trading partners would invite foreign reaction against our own exports--all quite legally. Reduced imports would thus be offset by reduced exports, and both sides would lose. . . .

In fact, the need to restore our trade surplus heightens the need for further movement toward freer trade. It requires us to persuade other nations to lower barriers which deny us fair access to their markets.

Richard Nixon, Special Message to Congress on U.S. Trade Policy, November 18, 1969; *Papers of Presidents: Nixon,* 1969, p. 940.

286   TRADE EXPANSION THROUGH FREER MARKETS

As the leader of the West and as a country that has become great and rich because of economic freedom, America must be an unrelenting advocate of free trade. As some nations are tempted to turn to protectionism, our strategy cannot be to follow them, but to lead the way toward freer trade.

Ronald Reagan, State of the Union Address, January 25, 1983; *Papers of Presidents: Reagan,* 1983, I, 108.

*   *   *

Our forefathers didn't shed their blood to create this Union so that we could become a victim nation. We're not sons and daughters of second-rate stock. We have no mission of mediocrity. We were born to carry liberty's banner and build the very meaning of progress, and our opportunities have never been greater. We can improve the well-being of our people, and we can enhance the forces for democracy, freedom, peace, and human fulfillment around the world, if we stand up for principles of trade expansion through freer markets and greater competition among nations. . . .

Our administration has a positive plan to meet the trade challenge on three key points. First, lay a firm foundation for non-inflationary growth based on enduring economic principles of fiscal and monetary discipline, competition, incentives, thrift and reward. Second, enhance the ability of U.S. producers and industries to compete on a fair and equal basis in the international marketplace; work with our trading partners to resolve outstanding problems of market access, and to chart new directions for free and fair trade in the products of the future. Third, take the lead in assisting international financial and trade institutions to strengthen world growth and bolster the forces of freedom and democracy. Taken together, these actions give the United States a positive framework for leading our producers and trading partners toward more open markets, greater freedom and human progress. . . .

The United States will carry the banner for free trade and a responsible financial system. These were the great principles at Bretton Woods, New Hampshire, in 1944, and they remain the core of U.S. policy. We will do so well aware of the changes that have occurred in the international trade and monetary system.

In trade, for example, we have practically eliminated the barriers which industrial countries maintain at the border on manufactured products. Today, tariffs among these countries average less than 5 per cent. Our problems arise instead from non-tariff barriers which often reflect basic differences in domestic economic policies and structures among countries. These barriers are tougher to remove. We are determined to reduce government intervention as far as possible, and where that is unrealistic, to insist on limits to such intervention.

In trade with developing countries, on the other hand, tariffs and quotas still play a significant role. Here, the task is to find a way to integrate the developing countries into the liberal trading orders of lower tariffs and dismantled quotas. They must come to experience the full benefits and responsibilities of the system that has produced unprecedented prosperity among the industrial countries. . . .

Ronald Reagan, address, Commonwealth Club, San Francisco, March 4, 1983; *American Foreign Policy: Current Documents,* 1983, pp. 183-88.

TRADE LEGISLATION AND TREATY COMPLEX

To implement American trade objectives over the years Congress passed scores of acts to deal with exports, imports, shipping, the most-favored-nation principle, and related subjects, including authorization for the President to negotiate trade treaties and agreements. These embrace, for example, major tariff acts of 1890, 1922, and 1930 (Hawley-Smoot), and the Reciprocal Trade Agreements Act of 1934 (*U.S. Statutes at Large,* 1934, vol. 48, p. 943). The latter authorized the President to negotiate agreements lowering tariffs by as much as 50 percent on the basis of reciprocity and so changed the pattern of commercial policy from protectionism by means of tariff walls to reciprocal agreements to expand and liberalize international commerce. This act was extended periodically for three decades, with additional reductions in tariff rates.

During World War II Congress also passed the Lend-Lease Act (*U.S. Statutes at Large,* 1941, vol. 55, p. 31), to authorize the President to negotiate bilateral agreements to establish the United States as the "Arsenal for Democracy" by supplying the anti-Axis states with equipment to defeat Germany and Japan. Later, in 1962, Congress enacted the Trade Expansion Act (*U.S. Statutes at Large,* 1962, vol. 76, p. 872), billed as a wholly new trade instrument, which augmented the President's authority to broaden trade and tariff policy and enabled him to reduce tariff rates up to 50 percent of the 1962 levels, again on a reciprocal basis and, over a period of years, to eliminate tariffs altogether on certain categories of imports. In 1974, Congress passed a new Trade Act, to further liberalize American commerce and emphasize foreign economic development (*U.S. Statutes at Large,* 1975, vol. 88, p. 1978), and five years later Congress passed a revised Trade Agreements Act (*U.S. Statutes at Large,* 1979, vol. 93, p. 144) to implement the enactment of 1974.

Empowered by such legislation, the President negotiated an array of bilateral and multilateral trade treaties and agreements. They may be grouped in three general categories--treaties of peace, amity, friendship, and commerce (alluded to in Chapter 15); reciprocal trade agreements; and a host of treaties and agreements concerned with various aspects of commercial relations. The latter consist of those that govern "commerce," "navigation," "commercial reciprocity," and "most-favored-nation treatment." These are supplemented with more specialized arrangements that pertain to such matters as agricultural and other commodities, consular affairs, customs, financial affairs, fisheries, maritime issues, navigation, patents, shipping, smuggling, taxation, trade-marks, and special World War II lend-lease agreements. For background commentary on United States trade after World War II, see Whiteman, *Digest of International Law,* XIV, 589-879.

Beginning with the Treaty of Amity and Commerce with France in 1778, the United States launched the two-century practice of negotiating such basic treaties. Declaring the establishment of "friendly relations," they are devoted to promoting favorable and reciprocal trade. Bearing varying titles, they create a commitment to pursue peace, amity, and friendship, as well as specifications concerning commerce, trade, navigation, and, consular affairs.

By the end of the eighteenth century the United States signed similar treaties with the Netherlands (1782), Sweden (1783), Morocco (1789), Great Britain (Jay Treaty, 1794), Spain and Algiers (1795), Tripoli (1796), and Tunis (1797). During the next half-century, such treaties were negotiated with twenty additional countries--eight in Europe, eight in Latin America, China, Muscat, the Ottoman Empire, and Thailand. This practice continued into the post-World War II era, consisting largely of successor or revised treaties (as with Japan and West Germany) and, in a few cases, with new states (such as Israel, Korea, Pakistan, Togo, and Tuvalu). By the 1980's the United States was a party to these treaties with approximately fifty countries (for listing, see *Treaties in Force*). They have been supplemented with bilateral consular affairs conventions, especially in the case of some of the newer countries.

In the earlier treaties of this type, the signatories committed themselves to maintain peace and friendship. Alternatively, they simply declared their intent "to make firm" or "to strengthen the bonds of" peace, amity, and friendship. In any case, the thrust of these treaties was to foster amicable trade relations. To this end, from the outset they stipulated, often in substantial detail, agreement respecting imports, duties and other charges, free ports, navigation and shipping rights, the personal rights of commercial agents and consular officials, and the "most-favored-nation principle." Some of the earlier treaties also addressed the issues of neutral rights in time of war and the treatment of privateering.

The second category, intended to achieve the mutual reduction of tariffs, consists of a series of reciprocal trade agreements authorized by the Reciprocal Trade Agreements Act of 1934. By 1945 more than thirty-five such treaties were signed with twenty-six countries, and a dozen were added in the immediate post-World War II period. Most of these reciprocal trade agreements have since been superseded by the General Agreement on Tariffs and Trade and other arrangements, although a few, such as those with El Salvador, Honduras, and Paraguay, remained in effect into the 1980's. For general commentary on the Roosevelt-Hull trade agreements program, see Whiteman, *Digest of International Law*, XIV, 589-617.

The third category embraces an impressive network of hundreds of contemporary bilateral treaties and agreements. To summarize, in the 1980's--in addition to more than fifty Lend-Lease Agreements (including arrangements for their termination) with twenty-one World War II allies and other friendly powers--the United States was committed to more than 1,100 bilateral commercial treaties and agreements. The largest numbers deal with agricultural commodities (more than 400), finance (more than 130), taxation (approximately 120, of which nearly 50 seek to eliminate double taxation), and trade (approximately 165, of which many pertain to specific commodities). Some 25 are designated general commercial agreements, 20 are consular conventions, 55 pertain to maritime matters, 20 concern navigation rights, and 20 govern shipping practices. The rest apply specifically to customs arrangements, patents and trademarks, and smuggling.

These are paralleled by a good many multipartite treaties, agreements, and protocols. The General Agreement on Tariffs and Trade (GATT), signed in

1947, serves as the centerpiece of contemporary global trade relations. It contains provisions respecting most-favored-nation treatment and nondiscrimination, schedules of trade concessions, freedom of transit, commodity dumping, taxation and regulation of products, countervailing duties, balance of payments and financial exchange practices, subsidies, and similar matters. The total package comprises the original agreement, containing thirty-four articles, and some eighty amendments, declarations, and protocols. For the text of GATT, see TIAS 1700; 4 Bevans, *Treaties and Other International Agreements* 639-88; and for amendments and protocols, see listing in *Treaties in Force.*

Other multipartite treaties and agreements, numbering approximately forty, are concerned with commodity, consular, customs, and maritime and shipping matters, and also with the conservation of resources and the protection of patents and trademarks. In addition, bridging the promotional, regulatory, and financial aspects of international trade, this survey must include the constitutive acts of at least eight global international organizations--the International Bank, the International Monetary Fund, the International Finance Corporation, and the regional development banks--and half a dozen development funds. The potential capstone of this arrangement--the International Trade Organization--failed to be established because its charter, signed in 1948, failed to achieve ratification.

Furthermore, to facilitate United States leadership in developing and managing commercial affairs, in 1963 the President created the office of Special Representative for Trade Negotiations (Executive Order 11075, confirmed by the Trade Act of 1974). Also, beginning in 1974 the President has participated personally in annual summit meetings of the leaders of the seven Western industrialized nations to discuss world trade and financial problems, and in 1982 the world's trading nations met to accelerate the struggle to eliminate protectionism.

In summary, the United States is a party to more than 1,300 bilateral and multilateral treaties and agreements that promote and regulate its international trade relations. These embrace some that were signed as early as the eighteenth century and a great many others that contain bipartite commitments with virtually all independent countries, as well as the General Agreement on Tariffs and Trade, the global and regional financial institutions, and other multipartite arrangements, which, collectively, affect the panoply of American commerce throughout the world.

This section provides selected samplings primarily to illustrate some key legislative stipulations concerning the purposes of, and presidential authority to negotiate, trade and commercial agreements (Documents 287-288), and the creation of the office of the Special Representative for Trade Negotiations (Document 289); the meaning and application of the "most-favored-nation" principle (Documents 290-292); the historic marriage of peace and amity with commerce and navigation in early trade treaties (Document 293); more recent trade, consular, and double-taxation treaties and agreements (Documents 294-296); the objectives and most-favored-nation treatment stipulations of the General Agreement on Tariffs and Trade (Document 297); and commentary concerning the "Kennedy" and "Tokyo" Rounds of negotiations (1960's and 1970's) to improve the GATT Agreement (Documents 298-299).

In 1985 it was agreed to hold a "Uruguay" Round, but it took several years to negotiate acceptable guidelines to govern deliberations.

287 PURPOSES AND AUTHORITY UNDER TRADE ACT, 1974

Sec. 2. Statement of Purposes.

The purposes of this Act are, through trade agreements affording mutual benefits--

(1) to foster the economic growth of and full employment in the United States and to strengthen economic relations between the United States and foreign countries through open and nondiscriminatory world trade;

(2) to harmonize, reduce, and eliminate barriers to trade on a basis which assures substantially equivalent competitive opportunities for the commerce of the United States;

(3) to establish fairness and equity in international trading relations, including reform of the General Agreement on Tariffs and Trade;

(4) to provide adequate procedures to safeguard American industry and labor against unfair or injurious import competition, and to assist industries, firms, workers, and communities to adjust to changes in international trade flows;

(5) to open up market opportunities for United States commerce in nonmarket economies; and

(6) to provide fair and reasonable access to products of less developed countries in the United States market. . . .

Sec. 101. Basic Authority for Trade Agreements.

(a) Whenever the President determines that any existing duties or other import restrictions of any foreign country or the United States are unduly burdening and restricting the foreign trade of the United States and that the purposes of this Act will be promoted thereby, the President--

(1) during the 5-year period beginning on the date of the enactment of this Act, may enter into trade agreements with foreign countries or instrumentalities thereof; and

(2) may proclaim such modification or continuance of any existing duty, such continuance of existing duty-free or excise treatment, or such additional duties, as he determines to be required or appropriate to carry out any such trade agreement . . . .

Sec. 103. Overall Negotiating Objective.

The overall United States negotiating objective under sections 101 and 102 shall be to obtain more open and equitable market access and the harmonization, reduction, or elimination of devices which distort trade or commerce. To the maximum extent feasible, the harmonization, reduction, or elimination of agricultural trade barriers and distortions shall be undertaken in conjunction with the harmonization, reduction, or elimination of industrial trade barriers and distortions. . . .

Sec. 105.   Bilateral Trade Agreements.

If the President determines that bilateral trade agreements will more effectively promote the economic growth of, and full employment in, the United States, then, in such cases, a negotiating objective under section 101 and 102 shall be to enter into bilateral trade agreements. Each such trade agreement shall provide for mutually advantageous economic benefits. . . .

Trade Act of 1974, as amended, Secs. 2, 101, 103, 105; Senate Committee on Foreign Relations and House Committee on Foreign Affairs, *Legislation on Foreign Relations Through 1978*, Joint Committee Print (Washington: Government Printing Office, 1979), II, 3-4, 6, and 7. For the full text of the act, see pp. 3-81, and for specification concerning reciprocal nondiscriminatory treatment, see sec. 126, p. 15. For full text of legislation on "Customs Duties," see *U.S. Code*, Title 19, pars. 2101-2487.

288   FOREIGN TRADE AGREEMENTS--PRESIDENTIAL AUTHORITY

1351.   Foreign trade agreements
(a)   Authority of President; modification and decrease of duties; altering import restrictions

(1) For the purpose of expanding foreign markets for the products of the United States (as a means of assisting in establishing and maintaining a better relationship among various branches of American agriculture, industry, mining, and commerce) by regulating the admission of foreign goods into the United States in accordance with the characteristics and needs of various branches of American production so that foreign markets will be made available to those branches of American production which require and are capable of developing such outlets by affording corresponding market opportunities for foreign products in the United States, the President, whenever he finds as a fact that any existing duties or other import restrictions of the United States or any foreign country are unduly burdening and restricting the foreign trade of the United States and that the purpose above declared will be promoted by the means hereinafter specified, is authorized from time to time--

(A) To enter into foreign trade agreements with foreign governments or instrumentalities thereof: Provided, That the enactment of the Trade Agreements Extension Act of 1955 shall not be construed to determine or indicate the approval or disapproval by the Congress of the executive agreement known as the General Agreement on Tariffs and Trade.

(B) To proclaim such modifications of existing duties and other import restrictions, or such additional import restrictions, or such continuance, and for such minimum periods, of existing customs or excise treatment of any article covered by foreign trade agreements, as are required or appropriate to carry out any foreign trade agreement that the President has entered into hereunder.

U.S. Code, Title 19, par. 1351 (a).

289 SPECIAL REPRESENTATIVE FOR TRADE NEGOTIATIONS

(a) Establishment within Executive Office of the President

There is established within the Executive Office of the President the Office of the Special Representative for Trade Negotiations. . . .

(c) Duties of Special Representative and Deputy Special Representatives for Trade Negotiations

(1) The Special Representative for Trade Negotiations shall--

(A) be the chief representative of the United States for each trade negotiation. . . ;

(B) report directly to the President and the Congress, and be responsible to the President and the Congress for the administration of trade agreements programs. . . ;

(C) advise the President and Congress with respect to non-tariff barriers to international trade, international commodity agreements and other matters which are related to the trade agreements programs;

(D) be responsible for making reports to Congress. . . ;

(E) be chairman of the interagency trade organization established pursuant to section 242(a) of the Trade Expansion Act of 1962. . . ;

(F) be responsible for such other functions as the President may direct

U.S. Code, Title 19, 2171.

290 MOST-FAVORED-NATION PRINCIPLE--INTERPRETATION

The answer is, of course, that the most-favored-nation clause does not pretend to insure that a country's policy will be wholly nondiscriminatory or even equitable. It has a much more modest and attainable objective which is simply that any given product of a particular foreign country will not be placed at a competitive disadvantage as compared with the like product of any third country. . . . [John Maynard Keynes]

A most-favored-nation clause is a provision, generally inserted in a commercial agreement between two states, which obligates the contracting parties to extend all concessions or favors made by each in the past, or which might be made in the future, to the articles, or instruments of commerce of any other state in such a way that their mutual trade will never be on a less favorable basis than is enjoyed by that state whose commercial relations with each is on the most favorable basis. The fundamental point is equality based upon the treatment received by any third country. . . .

Department of State memorandum, August 1, 1941; Whiteman, *Digest of International Law*, XIV, 749; for extended commentary, see pp. 748-82, which comments on consular relations, application under different economic systems, bilateral and multilateral agreements, exceptions, and related topics.

291 CONDITIONAL AND UNCONDITIONAL MOST-FAVORED-NATION TREATMENT IN MULTILATERAL TREATIES

The conditional most-favored-nation clause would extend to the other party to the clause the benefits accorded to a third country in return for reciprocal benefits only if such other party should extend like benefits in return. Consequently, it creates little or no problem in relation to benefits under multilateral conventions pursuant to which each party extends the provisions thereof to each other party on a reciprocal basis. However, broad questions of law and policy have been raised by the simultaneous development of unconditional most-favored-nation treatment to be accorded immediately and without condition and of broadly based multilateral economic agreements.

Whiteman, *Digest of International Law*, XIV, 764.

292 PRESIDENTIAL AUTHORITY TO APPLY MOST-FAVORED-NATION TREAT-MENT IN BILATERAL COMMERCIAL AGREEMENTS

(a)   Presidential authority
Subject to the provisions of subsections (b) and (c) of this section, the President may authorize the entry into force of bilateral commercial agreements providing nondiscriminatory treatment to the products of countries heretofore denied such treatment whenever he determines that such agreements with such countries will promote the purposes of this chapter and are in the national interest. . . .
(c)   Congressional action
An agreement referred to in subsection (a) of this section, and a proclamation referred to in section 2434 (a) of this title implementing such agreement, shall take effect only if (1) approved by the Congress by the adoption of a concurrent resolution referred to in section 2191 of this title, or (2) in the case of an agreement entered into before January 3, 1975, and a proclamation implementing such agreement, a resolution of disapproval referred to in section 2192 of this title is not adopted during the 90-day period specified by section 2437(c)(2) of this title.

U.S. Code, Title 19, par. 2435.   Subparagraph (b) specifies the terms of bilateral agreements.

2 9 3   TREATIES OF AMITY, FRIENDSHIP, COMMERCE, AND NAVIGATION

Article 1st

There shall be a firm, inviolable and universal Peace, and a true and sincere Friendship between the most Christian King, his Heirs and Successors, and the United States of America; and the Subjects of the most Christian King and of the said States; . . .

Article 2nd

The most Christian King, and the United States engage mutually not to grant any particular Favour to other Nations in respect of Commerce and Navigation, which shall not immediately become common to the other Party, who shall enjoy the same Favour, freely, if the Concession was freely made, or on allowing the same Compensation, if the Concession was Conditional.

Treaty of Amity and Commerce, United States and France, February 6, 1778; 33 articles.   *Treaty Series 83*; 7 Bevans, *Treaties and Other International Agreements* 764. For the full treaty, see pp. 763-66. It was superseded by a new treaty in 1784, which Congress declared abrogated in 1798.

*   *   *

Article 1

There shall be a firm, inviolable and universal Peace, and a true and sincere Friendship between His Britannick Majesty, His Heirs and Successors, and the United States of America; . . .

Treaty of Amity, Commerce, and Navigation, Jay Treaty, United States and Great Britain, November 19, 1794; 28 articles.   *Treaty series* 105; 12 Bevans, *Treaties and Other International Agreements* 14. For the full treaty, see pp. 13-33, which remains in effect, but was superseded by the Treaty of Washington in 1871.

*   *   *

The United States of America and the Republic of Korea, desirous of strengthening the bonds of peace and friendship traditionally existing between them and of encouraging closer economic and cultural relations between their peoples, and being cognizant of the contributions which may be made toward these ends by arrangements encouraging mutually beneficial investments, promoting mutually advantageous commercial intercourse and otherwise establishing mutual rights and privileges, have resolved to conclude a Treaty of Friendship, Commerce and Navigation, based in general upon the principles of national and of most-favored-nation treatment unconditionally accorded. . . .

Article I

Each Party shall at all times accord equitable treatment to the persons, property, enterprises and other interests of nationals and companies of the other Party.

Treaty of Friendship, Commerce, and Navigation, United States and Republic of Korea, November 28, 1956; 25 articles. TIAS 3947; 8 *U.S. Treaties* 2219. For the full treaty, see pp. 2217-81.

*   *   *

. . . desirous of strengthening the bonds of peace and friendship traditionally existing between their two countries and of encouraging closer economic and cultural relations between the two peoples, and being cognizant of the contributions which may be made toward these ends by arrangements specifying mutually accorded rights and privileges and promoting mutually advantageous commercial intercourse and investments,

have resolved to conclude a Treaty of Friendship, Establishment and Navigation, . . .

Article I

Each Contracting Party shall at all times accord equitable treatment and effective protection to the persons, property, enterprises, rights and interests of nationals and companies of the other Party.

Treaty of Friendship, Establishment, and Navigation, United States and Luxembourg, February 23, 1962; 19 articles. TIAS 5306; 14 *U.S. Treaties* 252-53. For the full treaty, see pp. 251-64.

294 AGREEMENT ON TRADE RELATIONS--U.S. AND ROMANIA, 1975

Article I
Most Favored Nation Treatment

1. Both Parties reaffirm the importance of their participation in the General Agreement on Tariffs and Trade and the importance of the provisions and principles of the General Agreement on Tariffs and Trade for their respective economic policies. . . .

2. . . . the Parties agree to grant each other's products most-favored-nation treatment immediately and unconditionally with respect to customs duties and charges of any kind imposed on or in connection with importation or exportation, and with respect to the method of levying such duties and charges, and with respect to all rules and formalities in connection with importation and exportation, and as otherwise provided in the General Agreement on Tariffs and Trade, provided that to the extent that this or any other provision of the General Agreement on Tariffs and Trade is inconsistent with any subsequent provision of this Agreement, the latter shall apply. . . .

Article II
Expansion of Trade

1. The Parties shall take appropriate measures, in accordance with applicable laws and regulations, to encourage and facilitate the exchange of goods and services between the two countries on the basis of mutual advantage in accordance with the provisions of this Agreement. . . .

Signed April 2, 1975; 12 articles.   TIAS 8159; 26 *U.S. Treaties* 2305-16. Other articles provide for business facilitation, financial arrangements, navigation, settlement of disputes by arbitration, duration, and entry into force.

295 CONVENTION ON CONSULAR RELATIONS--U.S. AND PHILIPPINE REPUBLIC, 1947

Article I

1. The Government of each High Contracting Party shall, in respect of any consular officer duly commissioned by it to exercise consular functions in the territories of the other High Contracting Party, give written notice to the Government of such other High Contracting Party of the appointment of such consular officer and shall request that recognition be accorded to such consular officer. The Government of each High Contracting Party shall furnish free of charge the necessary exequatur of any consular officer of the other High Contracting Party who presents a regular commission signed by the Chief Executive of the appointing country and under its great seal, and shall issue to a subordinate or substitute consular officer who is duly appointed by an accepted superior consular officer or by any other competent officer of his Government, such documents as according to the laws of the respective High Contracting Parties shall be requisite for the exercise by the appointee of the consular function; provided in either case that the person applying for an exequatur or other document is found acceptable.

2. Consular officers of each High Contracting Party shall, after entering upon their duties, enjoy reciprocally in the territories of the other High Contracting Party rights, privileges, exemptions and immunities no less favorable in any respect than the rights, privileges, exemptions and immunities which are enjoyed by consular officers of the same grade of any third country and in conformity with modern international usage. As official agents, such officers shall be entitled to the high consideration of all officials, national, state, provincial or municipal, with whom they have official intercourse in the territories of the High Contracting Party which receives them. It is understood that the term "consular officers", as used in the present Convention, includes consuls general, consuls and vice consuls who are not honorary.

Signed March 14, 1947; 16 articles. TIAS 1741; 11 Bevans, *Treaties and Other International Agreements* 74-83. Deals with defining the rights, functions, privileges, exemptions, and immunities of consular officials, as well as appointment, reception, and recognition of officers and the nature of consular offices and establishments.

296   CONVENTION ON DOUBLE TAXATION--U.S. AND POLAND, 1974

Article 5
General Rules of Taxation

(1) A resident of one of the Contracting States may be taxed by the other Contracting State on any income from sources within that other Contracting State and only on such income, subject to any limitations set forth in this Convention. . . .

Article 20
Relief From Double Taxation

Double taxation of income shall be avoided in the following manner:

(1) In accordance with the provisions and subject to the limitations of the law of Poland (as it may be amended from time to time without changing the general principles hereof), Poland shall allow to a resident of Poland as a credit against the Polish tax the appropriate amount of taxes paid to the United States.

(2) In accordance with the provisions and subject to the limitations of the law of the United States (as it may be amended from time to time without changing the general principles hereof), the United States shall allow to a citizen or resident of the United States as a credit against the United States tax the appropriate amount of taxes paid to Poland. . . .

Signed October 8, 1974; 26 articles. TIAS 8486; 28 *U.S. Treaties* 891-958. Deals with general rules of taxation, income from real property, earned income, business profits, shipping and transport, dividends, interest, royalties, capital gains, nondiscrimination, and related matters. The United States is committed to similar treaties with dozens of other countries.

297   GENERAL AGREEMENT ON TARIFFS AND TRADE (GATT), 1947

Recognizing that their relations in the field of trade and economic endeavour should be conducted with a view to raising standards of living, ensuring full employment and a large and steadily growing volume of real income and effective demand, developing the full use of the resources of the world and expanding the production and exchange of goods;

Being desirous of contributing to these objectives by entering into reciprocal and mutually advantageous arrangements directed to the substantial reduction of tariffs and other barriers to trade and to the elimination of discriminatory treatment in international commerce; . . .

Article I
General Most-Favoured-Nation Treatment

1. With respect to customs duties and charges of any kind imposed on or in connection with importation or exportation or imposed on the international transfer of payments for imports or exports, and with respect to the method of levying such duties and charges, and with respect to all rules and formalities in connection with importation and exportation, and with respect to all matters referred to in paragraphs 1

and 2 of Article III, any advantage, favour, privilege or immunity granted by any contracting party to any product originating in or destined for any other country shall be accorded immediately and unconditionally to the like product originating in or destined for the territories of all other contracting parties.

Signed October 30, 1947; 34 articles. TIAS 1700; 4 Bevans, *Treaties and Other International Agreements* 639-88. Originally the agreement was signed by 23 governments; in the 1980's there were 90 contracting nations and the agreement applied de facto to some 30 additional countries. For the Geneva protocol, with annexes, June 14, 1967, see TIAS 6425; 19 *U.S. Treaties* 1227-2619, and for June 30, 1979, see TIAS 9629; 31 *U.S. Treaties* 1015-1980.

298 MULTILATERAL TRADE NEGOTIATIONS--KENNEDY ROUND, 1964-1967

. . . An established body of principles, agreed to by virtually all major trading nations, under the General Agreement on Tariffs and Trade (GATT), has enabled us to systematically reduce and eliminate a wide range of tariff and other trade barriers. The average of all dutiable U.S. imports has been lowered from a high of 59.1 percent in 1932 to 26.4 percent in 1946, and to less than 12 percent today. The reduction in the duty levels of other countries has been hardly less spectacular. And the Kennedy Round negotiations in Geneva are aimed at further reductions based on a general rule of a 50-percent across-the-board cut in existing duties. . . .

Trade, as might be expected, has increased hand in hand with the lowering of these barriers. . . .

Looking back over the past three decades we can be justly proud of our achievements in expanding international trade to benefit all nations. Looking ahead to the next three decades, we are faced with new and equally challenging problems to surmount. We are now at the crossroads. The negotiations and decisions in coming months will set the precedent and spirit for our future course. . . .

We may speak with pride of our past achievements, but we dare not risk being complacent about the future. As in all fields of human endeavor, having the right goals is not sufficient. Our goals must be pursued with vigor, wisdom, and the courage to act in the national interest. . . .

. . . As tariffs are progressively reduced, the restrictive effect of other nontariff barriers becomes more evident. As trade in industrial products continues to expand, the lag in trade liberalization for agricultural products is made more apparent. As the economies of industrial countries are drawn into closer harmony, the need for creating a durable and progressive trading relationship with the less developed countries becomes more urgent.

W. Michael Blumenthal, Deputy Representative for Trade Negotiations, address, National Council of American Importers, New York, September 16, 1965; *American Foreign Policy: Current Documents,* 1965, pp. 1092-93, 1097.

*   *   *

. . . international trade can continue to be the world's biggest growth industry. We must continue to provide leadership in international trade policy to realize its vast potentialities and share fully in its benefits.

The results of the trade negotiations are of unprecedented scale. . . .

In approaching the trade negotiations, two fundamental standards governed our actions.

First, we sought--and achieved--reciprocity in trade concessions. Our consumers will benefit by lower import costs. Our export industries will benefit by greater market opportunities abroad.

Second, we sought to safeguard domestic industries that were especially vulnerable to import competition. We accomplished this through procedures worked out in accordance with guidelines wisely established by Congress in the Trade Expansion Act. . . .

The Geneva Conference set a solid record of achievement, unmatched in world trade history for its constructive and beneficial results.   The results represent a monument not only to our late President who gave the negotiations his name, but also to another great American,   the late Governor Christian A. Herter, whose inspiration and leadership guided us through the difficult first three years of negotiations.

Lyndon Johnson, Message to Congress, November 27, 1967; *American Foreign Policy: Current Documents,* 1967, p. 1134.

299 MULTILATERAL TRADE NEGOTIATIONS--TOKYO ROUND, 1979

I am today transmitting to the Congress, pursuant to Section 102 of the Trade Act of 1974, the texts of the trade agreements negotiated in the Tokyo Round of the Multilateral Trade Negotiations and entered into in Geneva on April 12, 1979. . . .

These agreements bring to a successful conclusion the most ambitious and comprehensive effort undertaken by the international community since World War II to revise the rules of international trade and to achieve a fairer, more open, world trading system. They come at a time when intense pressures around the world threaten to disrupt the international trading system.

Representatives of ninety-nine nations worked for five years to reduce or remove thousands of specific barriers to trade--including both tariff and nontariff barriers--and to develop new rules which will govern the international trading system in the coming decades.

Since World War II, a period of remarkable trade expansion, our experience teaches us that international trade brings strength and growth to economies throughout the world. It serves the cause of peace by enriching the lives of people everywhere.

By responding to the needs of today's rapidly changing world economy, these agreements ensure that growing prosperity and growing interdependence through increased trade will continue to benefit all nations.

World trade has expanded more than six-fold since completion of the Kennedy Round of trade negotiations in 1967, and now exceeds $1.3 trillion annually. . . .

Economic interdependence will continue to increase in the future-- and so will our opportunities.

Approval and implementation by the Congress of the Tokyo Round Agreements will be the first important step toward realizing those opportunities by building a solid foundation for continued strong growth of trade. . . .

The most important achievement of the Tokyo Round is a series of codes of conduct regulating nontariff barriers to trade. . . .

Jimmy Carter, Message to Congress, June 19, 1979; *Papers of Presidents: Carter,* 1979, I, 1092-93.   For additional commentary on Tokyo Round, as related to the Trade Agreements Act of 1979, see *Historic Documents,* 1979, pp. 637-44.

PART VI

SPECIALIZED FUNCTIONAL POLICIES

18

Alliances and Ententes

Every alliance involves burdens and obligations, but these are far less than the risks and sacrifices that would result if peace-loving nations were divided and neglectful of their common security.

Ronald Reagan
Address, United Nations, September 24, 1984

The alliance policy of the United States is largely a mid-twentieth century phenomenon, initiated for defense purposes during World War II and developed during the Cold War. Employing the term "alliance" in the political sense as an agreement of two or more states to act together for specific purposes to support one another in preserving their mutual security and/or to advance their joint interests and objectives--the United States eschewed such commitments for a century and three-quarters. The only exception, the Franco-American Alliance of 1778 committed the "good offices," "counsels," and "forces" of the two countries in a "defensive alliance" to guarantee each other's territory "forever" (see 7 Bevans, *Treaties and Other International Agreements,* pp. 777-80). This was the only alliance that bound the United States in perpetuity without a denunciation clause.

However, when war broke out between France and Great Britain in 1793, President Washington proclaimed America's neutrality and the following year Congress passed its first Neutrality Act. In his Farewell Address (1796) Washington cautioned the young Republic to avoid "political connections" with European powers, two years later Congress legislated the termination of the alliance with France, and in his first Inaugural Address (1801) Jefferson warned against further involvement in "entangling alliances." This combination of developments helped to launch the twin policies of isolationism and neutrality respecting European politics and wars which, technically, continued until the end of World War II.

In the meantime, when the United States affiliated with the "allies" as an "associated power" during World War I to defeat the Central Powers, it participated in an informal entente, which in its political connotation constitutes an understanding (not a formal treaty) between states to pursue a common course of action. Between World Wars I and II the United States returned to its policies of isolation and neutrality. But when World War II broke out, although President Roosevelt proclaimed American neutrality, eventually the United States negotiated a series of defense arrangements to protect the Western Hemisphere. Several of these continued beyond the end of the war, and some are still in effect (Documents 300-303). After the attack at Pearl Harbor, the United States joined the anti-Axis powers as one of the leaders of the wartime "United Nations."

In addition, in August 1941, the American government led in the framing of the Atlantic Charter (see introductory commentary in Chapter 6), which specified the war aims of the anti-Axis nations and projected "the establishment of a wider and permanent system of general security" based on the principle of collective security that presaged the creation of the United Nations organization. Following Pearl Harbor, in the United Nations Declaration (January 1, 1942) the United States undertook an obligation with its wartime associates to employ "its full resources, military or economic" against their enemies and, negatively, "not to make a separate armistice or peace" with them. Although these wartime arrangements created significant temporary commitments, they fell short of constituting genuine alliances.

Founded on its wartime experience and its emergent role as a leading world power, the United States sparked and joined the United Nations and the Organization of American States (see Chapters 25 and 26). As East-West relations deteriorated, the United Nations failed to provide guarantees of collective security, and the containment policy superseded isolationism, the American government proceeded to establish a network of major and minor multipartite and bipartite alliances. In a period of less than a decade the United States became committed to more than thirty-five states in multipartite as well as to some additional half-dozen bipartite alliances.

The core of this defense system consists of the Rio Pact (1947), the North Atlantic Treaty (1949), the ANZUS Treaty (1951), the Manila Pact (1954); four bilateral mutual security treaties with the Philippines, Japan, the Republic of Korea, and Nationalist China (1951-1954); and residual World War II special arrangements with the United Kingdom, Canada, Mexico, and Brazil. As new members were added to the North Atlantic Alliance and the United States "affiliated" with the Baghdad Pact powers, this network encompassed some fifty countries. These spanned the Northern Hemisphere eastward from Alaska to Japan and Korea, and latitudinally extended from Greenland and Iceland in the north to Argentina, Australia, Chile, and New Zealand in the south.

Major alliances were embodied in nine formal treaties. The remainder of the defense system was contained in a variety of executive agreements, exchanges of notes, protocols to treaties, and in one unique case, a resolution of an international agency. Supplementing these basic documents, hundreds of successor, special, and subsidiary arrangements were negotiated to deal with such functional matters as mutual security, mutual defense assistance, and military assistance--in implementation of authorizing legislation; weapons and equipment development, production, purchase, and disposition; the establishment and use of bases and other defense facilities; training and advisory (MAAG) missions; logistical support; communications equipment and facilitation; status of forces in foreign lands; and a host of related matters including research cooperation, the treatment and security of military information, and privileges and immunities of military personnel stationed abroad.

All told, over the years this aggregate package of alliance treaties and agreements, together with their supporting instruments and the arrangements to provide American defense support to those countries which are not acknowledged as allies, has mushroomed to exceed six hundred individual documents. For lists of these as well as amendatory and supplementary agreements, see the annual issues of *Treaties in Force*.

The materials presented in this chapter consist of two types. The first four sections provide basic documents pertaining to the creation, commitment, machinery, duration, and revision, termination, or supercession of alliance arrangements (Documents 300-316). The successor and supplementary agreements with Iceland, Turkey, and Spain (Documents 314-316), which number more than thirty instruments, are merely illustrative of the scores of bilateral agreements consummated since the early 1950's. Other countries with which the United States negotiated substantial quantities of such documentation include Canada, West Germany, Japan, the Philippines, and the United Kingdom. The final section of this chapter presents selected commentary on the purposes, value, and durability of alliances, and United States responsibility under them (Documents 317-322). For commentary on the effect of the War Powers Resolution (1973) on the automaticity of military commitments under collective defense pacts, see Document 84, and for the United States-Panamanian treaty commitment concerning the protection and defense of the Panama Canal, 1977, see Document 561, Article IV.

WORLD WAR II DEFENSE ARRANGEMENTS

To augment its defense posture during World War II the United States negotiated three sets of cooperative agreements with Great Britain and Western Hemisphere nations. The first was the Bases-Destroyers Agreement with the United Kingdom in 1940, which accorded the United States long-term naval and air base rights in eight territories in the Atlantic and Caribbean areas (Document 300). The second embraced bilateral agreements with Canada, Brazil, and Mexico to establish joint defense agencies for continuing consultation purposes (Documents 301-302). The third, embodied in an inter-American resolution, provided for the creation of the Inter-American Defense Board (Document 303). All of these continued into the postwar period, although eventually the Joint Commissions with Brazil and Mexico were disestablished.

300   DESTROYERS-BASES AGREEMENT, U.S.-UNITED KINGDOM, 1940

"I have the honour under instructions from His Majesty's Principal Secretary of State for Foreign Affairs to inform you that in view of the friendly and sympathetic interest of His Majesty's Government in the United Kingdom in the national security of the United States and their desire to strengthen the ability of the United States to cooperate effectively with the other nations of the Americas in the defence of the Western Hemisphere, His Majesty's Government will secure the grant to the Government of the United States, freely and without consideration, of the lease for immediate establishment and use of naval and air bases and facilities for entrance thereto and the operation and protection thereof, on the Avalon Peninsula and on the southern coast of Newfoundland, and on the east coast and on the Great Bay of Bermuda.

"Furthermore, in view of the above and in view of the desire of the United States to acquire additional air and naval bases in the Caribbean and in British Guiana, and without endeavouring to place a monetary or commercial value upon the many tangible and intangible rights and properties involved, His Majesty's Government will make available to the United States for immediate establishment and use naval and air bases and facilities for entrance thereto and the operation and protection thereof, on the eastern side of the Bahamas, the southern coast of Jamaica, the western coast of St. Lucia, the west coast of Trinidad in the Gulf of Paria, in the island of Antigua and in British Guiana within fifty miles of Georgetown, in exchange for naval and military equipment and material which the United States Government will transfer to His Majesty's Government.

"All the bases and facilities referred to in the preceding paragraphs will be leased to the United States for a period of ninety-nine years, free from all rent and charges other than such compensation to be mutually agreed on to be paid by the United States in order to compensate the owners of private property for loss by expropriation or damage arising out of the establishment of the bases and facilities in question.

"His Majesty's Government, in the leases to be agreed upon, will grant to the United States for the period of the leases all the rights, power, and authority within the bases leased, and within the limits of the territorial waters and air spaces adjacent to or in the vicinity of such bases, necessary to provide access to and defence of such bases, and appropriate provisions for their control. . . .

"The exact location and bounds of the aforesaid bases, the necessary seaward, coast and anti-aircraft defences, the location of sufficient military garrisons, stores and other necessary auxiliary facilities shall be determined by common agreement. . . ."

I am directed by the President to reply to your note as follows:

The Government of the United States appreciates the declarations and the generous action of His Majesty's Government as contained in your communication which are destined to enhance the national security of the United States and greatly to strengthen its ability to cooperate effectively with the other nations of the Americas in the defense of the Western Hemisphere. It therefore gladly accepts the proposals. . . .

In consideration of the declarations above quoted, the Government of the United States will immediately transfer to His Majesty's Government fifty United States Navy destroyers generally referred to as the twelve hundred-ton type. . . .

Cordell Hull

Exchange of notes, September 2, 1940; 12 Bevans, *Treaties and Other International Agreements,* pp. 551-54. Separate successor agreements were signed with most of the Caribbean countries after they became independent, and the Bases-Destroyers Agreement remains in effect.

301 PERMANENT JOINT BOARD ON DEFENSE, U.S. AND CANADA, 1940

The Prime Minister and the President have discussed the mutual problems of defense in relation to the safety of Canada and the United States.

It has been agreed that a Permanent Joint Board on Defense shall be set up at once by the two countries.

This Permanent Joint Board on Defense shall commence immediate studies relating to sea, land, and air problems including personnel and materiel.

It will consider in the broad sense the defense of the north half of the Western Hemisphere. . . .

Joint Statement, Ogdensburg, N.Y., August 18, 1940, in 6 Bevans, *Treaties and Other International Agreements,* p. 189.

*   *   *

Announcement was made in Ottawa and Washington on February 12 [1947] of the results of discussions which have taken place in the Permanent Joint Board on Defense on the extent to which the wartime cooperation between the armed forces of the United States and Canada should be maintained in this post-war period. In the interest of efficiency and economy, each Government has decided that its national defense establishment shall, to the extent authorized by law, continue to collaborate for peacetime joint security purposes. The collaboration will necessarily by limited and will be based on the following principles:

1. Interchange of selected individuals so as to increase the familiarity of each country's defense establishment with that of the other country.

2. General cooperation and exchange of observers in connection with exercises and with the development and tests of material of common interest.

3. Encouragement of common designs and standards in arms, equipment, organization, methods of training, and new developments. As certain United Kingdom standards have long been in use in Canada, no radical change is contemplated or practicable and the application of this principle will be gradual.

4. Mutual and reciprocal availability of military, naval, and air facilities in each country; this principle to be applied as may be agreed in specific instances. Reciprocally each country will continue to provide with a minimum of formality for the transit through its territory and its territorial waters of military aircraft and public vessels of the other country.

5. As an underlying principle all cooperative arrangements will be without impairment of the control of either country over all activities in its territory. . . .

Announcement, Washington and Ottawa, February 12, 1947, in 6 Bevans, *Treaties and Other International Agreements*, pp. 430-31.

*   *   *

I have the honour to refer to recent discussions between representatives of our two Governments concerning the establishment of a Canada-United States Ministerial Committee which would consider periodically important matters affecting the joint defence of our two countries. . . .

It was agreed that the importance and complexity of these interdependent defence relationships made it essential to supplement existing channels for consultation and to provide for a periodic review at the Ministerial level of problems which might be expected to arise. It was envisaged that the periodic review would include not only military questions but also the political and economic aspects of joint defence problems.

. . . the Committee's function shall be:

1) To consult periodically on any matters affecting the joint defence of Canada and the United States;

2) In particular, to exchange information and views at the Ministerial level on problems that may arise, with a view to strengthening further the close and intimate cooperation between the two Governments on joint defence matters;

3) To report to the respective Governments on such discussions in order that consideration may be given to measures deemed appropriate and necessary to improve defence cooperation. . . .

Sidney Smith
Secretary of State for External Affairs

*   *   *

I have the honor to refer to your Note . . . concerning the establishment of a Canada-United States Ministerial Committee which would consider periodically important matters affecting the joint defense of our two countries.

My Government concurs in the proposals contained in your note and agrees that this exchange of notes will constitute an agreement between our two Governments effective this date and to remain in force until such time as either Government shall have given notice in writing of its desire to terminate the agreement.

Livingston T. Merchant
U.S. Ambassador

Exchange of notes, August 29 and September 2, 1958, TIAS 4098; 9 *U.S. Treaties* 1159-61.

302 JOINT MILITARY AND DEFENSE COMMISSIONS, U.S.-BRAZIL, 1941 and 1955

To govern the activities of the Brazilian-American Joint Group of Staff Officers.

I. Preliminaries:

The creation of this Group results from the terms established in the Bases of the Agreement for Cooperation between the United States and Brazil, of October 29, 1940, and from the understanding expressed in the exchange of correspondence on the subject between the Chief of the General Staff of the Brazilian Army and the Chief of the United States Military Mission. Among other points it should consider in its plans the following stipulations:

1. Promise of Brazil to assist with all its forces and with the means at its disposal, the common defense of the American continent;

2. Promise of Brazil to construct air and naval bases and to authorize their use for the other Pan-American countries;

3. Promise of Brazil to organize the defense of its coast and of the islands along its seacoast, as well as the ways and means of communication of the country.

4. Promise of the United States to employ its armed forces to assist Brazil in defense against attacks by armed forces of non-American states.

5. Promise of the United States to assist Brazil in the procurement of the armament and of all the material means which it needs for the purposes in question, as well as the furnishing of technicians which Brazil declares it needs.

II. Organization:

1. The Joint Group will be constituted by General Staff officers of the two countries, six from Brazil and five from the United States, and will be presided over by the Chief of Staff of the Army of the Country in which it is assembled, or by an officer in his place, recommended by the Minister of War and designated by the President of the Republic. . . .

*   *   *

(1) The joint Brazil-United States Military Commission (JBUSMC), originally established in Rio de Janeiro during World War II by the two Governments as a means of assisting each other in achieving their common goal of mutual security, will continue to function as the principal agency in the United States of Brazil for facilitating military cooperation between the two countries.

(2) The Joint Brazil-United States Defense Commission (JBUSDC), originally established in Washington, D.C., during World War II by the two Governments as a means of assisting each other in achieving their common goal of mutual security, will continue to function as the principal agency in the United States of America for facilitating military cooperation between the two countries. . . .

(4) Arrangements governing the composition, functions, and procedures of the two commissions may be entered into from time to time,

as necessary, by the appropriate military authorities of the two Governments.

(5) This Agreement shall remain in effect until one year from the date of notice by either Government of its intention to terminate the Agreement. . . .

Terms of Agreement, in diplomatic note, July 25, 1941, *Foreign Relations, 1941*, VI, 506-8; and exchange of notes, August 1, 1955, in 6 *U.S. Treaties*, 4103-6. For background for 1941 agreement, see *Foreign Relations*, 1939, V, 349; 1941, VI, 490-514; 1942, V, 632-74. The Joint Commission with Brazil was disestablished in 1978. A similar agreement for a Joint U.S.-Mexican Commission was negotiated in 1940; see *Foreign Relations*, 1940, V, 143-45.

303   INTER-AMERICAN DEFENSE BOARD, 1942

1. In accordance with the action taken at the Conference for the Maintenance of Peace [1936] and in conformity with the Declaration of Lima [1938], a system of coordination exists between the American Republics which fortunately responds to the spirit of sincere collaboration animating the peoples of our Continent; and

2. This system, the results of which have heretofore been satisfactory, is, from every point of view, the most effective means on the part of the Western Hemisphere for meeting the present grave emergency in a coordinated and solidary manner,

The Third meeting of the Ministers of Foreign Affairs of the American Republics

Recommends:

The immediate meeting in Washington of a commission composed of military and naval technicians appointed by each of the Governments to study and to recommend to them the measures necessary for the defense of the Continent.

Resolution 39, Third Inter-American Meeting of Ministers of Foreign Affairs, Rio de Janeiro, January 28, 1942, in 3 Bevans, *Treaties and Other International Agreements*, p. 699.

*   *   *

CREATION OF A PERMANENT MILITARY AGENCY (1945)

Whereas:

The American Republics constitute a special entity due to their geographic conditions, the similarity of their institutions, and the international obligations contracted at various inter-American conferences;

The Republics of this Continent have declared their solidarity to the extent that any threat or attack against one of them constitutes a threat or an attack against all;

The existence of a permanent military agency for the study and solution of problems affecting the Western Hemisphere is indispensable;

The Inter-American Defense Board has proved to be a valuable agency for the exchange of views, the study of problems and the formulation of recommendations relating to the defense of the Hemisphere, and for the promotion of close collaboration on the part of the military, naval and air forces of the American Republics,

The Inter-American Conference on Problems of War and Peace

Recommends:

1. That the Governments consider the creation, at the earliest possible time, of a permanent agency formed by the representatives of each of the General Staffs of the American Republics, for the purpose of proposing to the said Governments measures for a closer military collaboration among all the Governments and for the defense of the Western Hemisphere.

2. That the Inter-American Defense Board continue as an agency of inter-American defense until the permanent body provided for in this recommendation is established.

Resolution 4, Inter-American Conference on Problems of War and Peace, Mexico City, March 6, 1945, in Pan American Union, *Inter-American Conference on War and Peace, Mexico City, February 21-March 8, 1945* (Washington: Pan American Union, 1945), p. 26. Also see President Truman's special message to Congress, May 6, 1946, *Papers of Presidents: Truman,* 1946, pp. 233-35, and his special message to Congress, May 26, 1947, on the Inter-American Military Cooperation Act, *Papers of Presidents,* 1947, pp. 255-57.

*   *   *

INTER-AMERICAN DEFENSE BOARD (1948)

Whereas:

An Advisory Defense Committee has been created to advise the organ of consultation on problems of military collaboration arising from the application of existing treaties on the subject of collective defense;

It is desirable for the American States to be in a position to ask the Inter-American Defense Board for information on measures aimed at the collective security of the American Continent,

The Ninth International Conference of American States

Resolves:

1. The Inter-American Defense Board shall continue to act as the organ of preparation for collective self-defense against aggression until the American Governments decide by a two thirds majority to consider its labor terminated.

2. The Board shall draw up its own regulations as to organization and activities in order to carry out, in addition to the advisory functions within its competence, any similar functions ascribed to it by the Committee established in Article 44 of the Charter of the Organization of American States.

3. The Secretariat of the Inter-American Defense Board shall serve as Secretariat of the Committee to which the foregoing paragraph refers.

Resolution 34, Ninth International Conference of American States, Bogota, 1948, in Department of State, *Ninth International Conference of American States, Bogota, Colombia, March 30-May 2, 1948* (Washington: Government Printing Office, 1948), p. 270.

MULTILATERAL ALLIANCES

During the Cold War the United States became a party to the Rio Pact, the North Atlantic Treaty, the ANZUS Treaty, and the Manila Pact, and affiliated informally with the Baghdad Pact powers.

The first of these alliances, formally known as the Inter-American Treaty of Reciprocal Assistance, was signed in 1947, under the aegis of the "Good Neighbor" policy and Pan-Americanism (Document 304). This was presaged by a series of steps seeking to multilateralize the Monroe Doctrine, which included the Declaration of Principles of Inter-American Solidarity and Cooperation (Buenos Aires, 1936), the Declaration of Lima, which proclaimed the concept of "continental solidarity" (1938), the Declaration of Reciprocal Assistance and Cooperation for the Defense of the Americas (Havana, 1940), the Convention on the Provisional Administration of European Colonies and Possessions in the Americas (Havana, 1940), the Declaration of Continental Solidarity (Washington, 1942), and the Act of Chapultepec which specified that an attack on one American state shall be considered as "an act of aggression against all" signatories (Mexico City, 1945). Although some of them were temporary declarations of mutual purpose and commitment, incrementally they paved the way for establishing the Organization of American States (see Chapter 26) and formalizing the American continental alliance in the Rio Pact. For texts, see *Peace and War: United States Foreign Policy,* 1931-1941, pp. 352-53, 439-40, 562-63; *A Decade of American Foreign Policy: Basic Documents, 1941-49,* pp. 412-21; and 3 Bevans, *Treaties and Other International Agreements,* pp. 300-301, 534-35, 1024-27.

Once the precedent had been established for the Western Hemisphere, the Cold War reached a critical state, and the United Nations faltered in guaranteeing collective security, the Senate passed the Vandenberg Resolution in 1948 (Document 305) and the United States joined Canada and the free European powers in signing the North Atlantic Treaty the following year (Document 306). After the outbreak of the Korean War, in the early 1950's new alliances were formed to extend the containment policy and American defense arrangements in the Far East. These consisted of the tripartite Security Treaty creating ANZUS (Australia, New Zealand, and the United States) in 1951 (Document 307) and the Southeast Asia Collective Defense Treaty or the Manila Pact three years later (Document 308), supplemented with a series of bilateral treaties with four Asian powers (see next section).

The United Kingdom, Pakistan, and three Mideast countries signed a similar alliance--the Baghdad Pact--in 1955 and established the Middle East

Treaty Organization (METO), subsequently renamed the Central Treaty Organization (CENTO). Although the United States never became a full-fledged member, it affiliated informally with CENTO, maintained an observership capacity at its meetings, participated in its deliberations, and thus linked its alliance ring from the Atlantic to Southeast Asia (Document 309).

These treaties uniformly stipulate that their signatories will maintain their collective capacity to resist armed attack, regard an attack on one as an attack on all, and consult respecting action to be taken. In addition to a number of protocolary articles, the treaties also define the area covered, provide for a council for mutual consultation, relate commitments and actions to United Nations Charter obligations, and specify agreement on subsequent accessions, duration, and ratification and termination procedures. Signatories agree that they will resolve their differences by peaceful means and that these arrangements are intended to implement the United Nations Charter. The treaties vary in length and detail. Whereas the Rio Pact consists of twenty-six articles, the North Atlantic Treaty contains only fourteen, and the others are even shorter. The crucial articles are those that define the nature and extent of American commitments.

304 INTER-AMERICAN TREATY OF RECIPROCAL ASSISTANCE (RIO PACT), 1947

Article 1

The High Contracting Parties formally condemn war and undertake in their international relations not to resort to the threat or the use of force in any manner inconsistent with the provisions of the Charter of the United Nations or of this Treaty.

Article 2

As a consequence of the principle set forth in the preceding Article, the High Contracting Parties undertake to submit every controversy which may arise between them to methods of peaceful settlement and to endeavor to settle any such controversy among themselves by means of the procedures in force in the Inter-American System before referring it to the General Assembly or the Security Council of the United Nations.

Article 3

1. The High Contracting Parties agree that an armed attack by any State against an American State shall be considered as an attack against all the American States and, consequently, each one of the said Contracting Parties undertake to assist in meeting the attack in the exercise of the inherent right of individual or collective self-defense recognized by Article 51 of the Charter of the United Nations.

2. On the request of the State or States directly attacked and until the decision of the Organ of Consultation of the Inter-American System, each one of the Contracting Parties may determine the immediate measures which it may individually take in fulfillment of the obligation contained in the preceding paragraph and in accordance with the principle of

continental solidarity. The Organ of Consultation shall meet without delay for the purpose of examining those measures and agreeing upon the measures of a collective character that should be taken.

3. The provisions of this Article shall be applied in case of any armed attack which takes place within the region described in Article 4 or within the territory of an American State. When the attack takes place outside of the said areas, the provisions of Article 6 shall be applied.

4. Measures of self-defense provided for under this Article may be taken until the Security Council of the United Nations has taken the measures necessary to maintain international peace and security. . . .

Article 6

If the inviolability or the integrity of the territory or the sovereignty or political independence of any American State should be affected by an agression which is not an armed attack or by an extra-continental or intra-continental conflict, or by any other fact or situation that might endanger the peace of America, the Organ of Consultation shall meet immediately in order to agree on the measures which must be taken in case of aggression to assist the victim of the aggression or, in any case, the measures which should be taken for the common defense and for the maintenance of the peace and security of the Continent.

Article 7

In the case of a conflict between two or more American States, without prejudice to the right of self-defense in conformity with Article 51 of the Charter of the United Nations, the High Contracting Parties, meeting in consultation shall call upon the contending States to suspend hostilities and restore matters to the statu[s] quo ante bellum, and shall take in addition all other necessary measures to reestablish or maintain inter-American peace and security and for the solution of the conflict by peaceful means. The rejection of the pacifying action will be considered in the determination of the aggressor and in the application of the measures which the consultative meeting may agree upon.

Article 8

For the purposes of this Treaty, the measures on which the Organ of Consultation may agree will comprise one or more of the following: recall of chiefs of diplomatic missions; breaking of diplomatic relations; breaking of consular relations; partial or complete interruption of economic relations or of rail, sea, air, postal, telegraphic, telephonic, and radiotelephonic or radiotelegraphic communications; and use of armed force. . . .

Article 9

In addition to other acts which the Organ of Consultation may characterize as aggression, the following shall be considered as such:

a. Unprovoked armed attack by a State against the territory, the people, or the land, sea or air forces of another State;

b. Invasion, by the armed forces of a State, of the territory of an American State, through the trespassing of boundaries demarcated in accordance with a treaty, judicial decision, or arbitral awards, or, in the absence of frontiers thus demarcated, invasion affecting a region which is under the effective jurisdiction of another State. . . .

Article 20

Decisions which require the application of the measures specified in Article 8 shall be binding upon all the Signatory States which have ratified this Treaty, with the sole exception that no State shall be required to use armed force without its consent. . . .

Article 25

This Treaty shall remain in force indefinitely, but may be denounced by any High Contracting Party by a notification in writing to the Pan American Union, which shall inform all the other High Contracting Parties of each notification of denunciation received. After the expiration of two years from the date of the receipt by the Pan American Union of a notification of denunciation by any High Contracting Party, the present Treaty shall cease to be in force with respect to such State, but shall remain in full force and effect with respect to all the other High Contracting Parties. . . .

Signed September 2, 1947; 26 articles. Article 4 prescribes the area of application, as depicted in the accompanying map. Articles 11 to 24 deal largely with inter-American machinery, matters of procedure and voting processes, and protocolary stipulations. TIAS 1838; 4 Bevans, *Treaties and Other International Agreements,* pp. 559-66; and *American Foreign Policy: Basic Documents,* 1950-1955, I, 789-96.

*   *   *

AREA OF APPLICABILITY OF RIO PACT, 1947

The New York Times

—————— The region defined by Article 4 of the Inter-American Treaty of Reciprocal Assistance, signed at Rio de Janeiro on September 2, 1947

A Decade of American Foreign Policy, 1941-49, p. 427; also *American Foreign Policy: Basic Documents*, 1950-1955, I, 806. Note that applicability extends from pole to pole; also see Chapter 32, especially Document 568.

*   *   *

PROTOCOL OF AMENDMENT, RIO PACT, 1975

The signing of the Protocol of San Jose was a major development for the Inter-American System and a reaffirmation of the importance of our own relationship with the countries of Latin America. The Amendments, taken as a whole, do not alter the Rio Treaty's fundamental thrust; rather, they are for the most part constructive changes which will make the Treaty more flexible and politically viable in the years ahead. . . .

The most significant changes embodied in the Protocol in the Rio Treaty are (1) a provision for lifting sanctions by majority vote rather than the two-thirds vote required for all other decisions under the Treaty; (2) specific provision for non-binding recommendations and for conciliatory and peace-making steps as well as for binding measures; (3) a narrowing of the geographic area in which the "attack against one, attack against all" applies, eliminating Greenland and some high seas areas, and limiting its applicability to attacks against other states parties (instead of all "American states"); (4) the incorporation of a more complete definition of aggression than appeared in the original treaty, following the lines of the definition approved in 1974 by the General Assembly of the United Nations; and (5) the addition of an article providing that "collective economic security" shall be guaranteed by a special treaty (a provision to which the United States submitted a reservation at the time of signature). While the inclusion of an article on collective economic security represents an unfortunate detraction from the Protocol's balance and good sense, on the whole, the amendments improve this basic instrument of inter-American security and peace-keeping. . . .

Gerald Ford, Message to Senate, November 29, 1975. *Papers of Presidents: Ford,* 1975, II, 1920-21. For commentary on this amendatory process, see *Digest of United States Practice in International Law,* 1975, pp. 791-97, with text of Protocol of Amendment, pp. 793-97, and 1977, pp. 915-16.

305 VANDENBERG RESOLUTION, 1948

Whereas peace with justice and the defense of human rights and fundamental freedoms require international cooperation through more effective use of the United Nations: Therefore be it

Resolved, That the Senate reaffirm the policy of the United States to achieve international peace and security through the United Nations so that armed force shall not be used except in the common interest, and that the President be advised of the sense of the Senate that this Government, by constitutional process, should particularly pursue the following objectives within the United Nations Charter: . . .

(2) Progressive development of regional and other collective arrangements for individual and collective self-defense in accordance with the purposes, principles, and provisions of the Charter.

(3) Association of the United States, by constitutional process, with such regional and other collective arrangements as are based on continuous and effective self-help and mutual aid, and as affect its national security.

(4) Contributing to the maintenance of peace by making clear its determination to exercise the right of individual or collective self-defense under article 51 should any armed attack occur affecting its national securitv. . . .

Senate Resolution, June 11, 1948; *A Decade of American Foreign Policy: Basic Documents,* 1941-49, p. 197.

306   NORTH ATLANTIC TREATY (NATO), 1949

Article 1

The Parties undertake, as set forth in the Charter of the United Nations, to settle any international disputes in which they may be involved by peaceful means in such a manner that international peace and security, and justice, are not endangered, and to refrain in their international relations from the threat or use of force in any manner inconsistent with the purposes of the United Nations. . . .

Article 3

In order more effectively to achieve the objectives of this Treaty, the Parties, separately and jointly, by means of continuous and effective self-help and mutual aid, will maintain and develop their individual and collective capacity to resist armed attack.

Article 4

The Parties will consult together whenever, in the opinion of any of them, the territorial integrity, political independence or security of any of the Parties is threatened.

Article 5

The Parties agree that an armed attack against one or more of them in Europe or North America shall be considered an attack against them all; and consequently they agree that, if such an armed attack occurs, each of them, in exercise of the right of individual or collective self-defense recognized by Article 51 of the Charter of the United Nations, will assist the Party or Parties so attacked by taking forthwith, individually and in concert with the other Parties, such action as it deems necessary, including the use of armed force, to restore and maintain the security of the North Atlantic area. . . .

Article 6

For the purpose of Article 5 an armed attack on one or more of the Parties is deemed to include an armed attack on the territory of any of the Parties in Europe or North America, on the Algerian departments of France, on the occupation forces of any Party in Europe, on the islands under the jurisdiction of any Party in the North Atlantic area north of the Tropic of Cancer or on the vessels or aircraft in this area of any of the Parties . . . .

Article 8

Each Party declares that none of the international engagements now in force between it and any other of the Parties or any third state is in conflict with the provisions of this Treaty, and undertakes not to enter into any international engagement in conflict with this Treaty.

Article 9

The Parties hereby establish a council, on which each of them shall be represented, to consider matters concerning the implementation of this Treaty. The council shall be so organized as to be able to meet promptly at any time. The council shall set up such subsidiary bodies as may be necessary; in particular it shall establish immediately a defense committee which shall recommend measures for the implementation of Articles 3 and 5. . . .

Article 12

After the Treaty has been in force for ten years, or at any time thereafter, the Parties shall, if any of them so requests, consult together for the purpose of reviewing the Treaty, having regard for the factors then affecting peace and security in the North Atlantic area, including the development of universal as well as regional arrangements under the Charter of the United Nations for the maintenance of international peace and security.

Article 13

After the Treaty has been in force for twenty years, any Party may cease to be a party one year after its notice of denunciation has been given to the Government of the United States of America, which will inform the Governments of the other Parties of the deposit of each notice of denunciation. . . .

Signed April 4, 1949; 14 articles.   Originally there were twelve signatories; currently there are 15.   TIAS 1964; Bevans, *Treaties and Other International Agreements*, 828-31; and *American Foreign Policy: Basic Documents*, 1950-1955, pp. 812-15. For list of supplementary agreements and protocols, see *Treaties in Force*.   In 1966 France withdrew from NATO but continued as a signatory of the North Atlantic Treaty; for commentary, see *American Foreign Policy: Current Documents*, 1966, pp. 316-79, especially pp. 316-50.

*   *   *

DECLARATION ON ATLANTIC RELATIONS, 1974

1. The members of the North Atlantic Alliance declare that the Treaty signed 25 years ago to protect their freedom and independence has confirmed their common destiny.   Under the shield of the Treaty, the Allies have maintained their security, permitting them to preserve the values which are the heritage of their civilization and enabling Western Europe to rebuild from its ruins and lay the foundations of its unity.

2. The members of the Alliance reaffirm their conviction that the North Atlantic Treaty provides the indispensable basis for their security,

thus making possible the pursuit of detente. . . .

3. The members of the Alliance reaffirm that their common defense is one and indivisible. An attack on one or more of them in the area of application of the Treaty shall be considered an attack against them all. The common aim is to prevent any atempt by a foreign power to threaten the independence or integrity of a member of the Alliance. Such an attempt would not only put in jeopardy the security of all members of the Alliance but also threaten the foundations of world peace.

4. At the same time they realize that the circumstances affecting their common defense have profoundly changed in the last ten years: the strategic relationship between the United States and the Soviet Union has reached a point of near equilibrium. Consequently, although all the countries of the Alliance remain vulnerable to attack, the nature of the danger to which they are exposed has changed. The Alliance's problem in the defense of Europe has thus assumed a different and more distinct character.

5. However, the essential elements in the situation which gave rise to the Treaty have not changed. While the Commitment of all the Allies to the common defense reduces the risk of external aggression, the contribution to the security of the entire Aliance provided by the nuclear forces of the United States based in the United States as well as in Europe and by the presence of North American forces in Europe remains indispensable.

6. Nevertheless, the Alliance must pay careful attention to the dangers to which it is exposed in the European region, and must adopt all measures necessary to avert them. The European members . . . undertake to make the necessary contribution to maintain the common defense at a level capable of deterring and if necessary repelling all actions directed against the independence and territorial integrity of the members of the Alliance.

7. The United States, for its part, reaffirms its determination not to accept any situation which would expose its Allies to external political or military pressure likely to deprive them of their freedom, and states its resolve, together with its Allies, to maintain forces in Europe at the level required to sustain the credibility of the strategy of deterrence and to maintain the capacity to defend the North Atlantic area should deterrence fail.

8. In this connection the member states of the Alliance affirm that as the ultimate purpose of any defense policy is to deny to a potential adversary the objectives he seeks to attain through an armed conflict, all necessary forces would be used for this purpose. Therefore, while reaffirming that a major aim of their policies is to seek agreements that will reduce the risk of war, they also state that such agreements will not limit their freedom to use all forces at their disposal for the common defense in case of attack. Indeed, they are convinced that their determination to do so continues to be the best assurance that war in all its forms will be prevented.

9. All members of the Alliance agree that the continued presence of Canadian and substantial U.S. forces in Europe plays an irreplaceable role in the defense of North America as well as of Europe. Similarly the substantial forces of the European Allies serve to defend Europe and North America as well. . . .

10. The members of the Alliance consider that the will to combine their efforts to ensure their common defense obliges them to maintain and improve the efficiency of their forces and that each should undertake, according to the role that it has asumed in the structure of the Alliance, its proper share of the burden of maintaining the security of all. Conversely, they take the view that in the course of current or future negotiations nothing must be accepted which could diminish this security.

11. The Allies are convinced that the fulfillment of their common aims requires the maintenance of close consultation, cooperation and mutual trust, thus fostering the conditions necessary for defense and favorable for detente, which are complementary. In the spirit of the friendship, equality and solidarity which characterize their relationships, they are firmly resolved to keep each other fully informed and to strengthen the practice of frank and timely consultations by all means which may be appropriate on matters relating to their common interests as members of the Alliance, bearing in mind that these interests can be affected by events in other areas of the world. They wish also to ensure that their essential security relationship is supported by harmonious political and economic relations. In particular they will work to remove sources of conflict between their economic policies and to encourage economic cooperation with one another.

12. They recall that they have proclaimed their dedication to the principles of democracy, respect for human rights, justice and social progress, which are the fruits of their shared spiritual heritage and they declare their intention to develop and deepen the application of these principles in their countries. . . .

Adopted by North Atlantic Council June 19, 1974; 14 articles. See *Digest of United States Practice in International Law,* 1974, pp. 685-88. This Declaration commemorated the 25th anniversary of the North Atlantic Treaty. This grew out of a proposal of Secretary of State Henry Kissinger at a meeting of NATO Foreign Ministers, April 23, 1973; see *Historic Documents,* 1973, pp. 487-98. For additional commentary, see *Historic Documents,* 1974, pp. 529-33. For the Declaration on the 40th anniversary issued by the Brussels summit session, May 30, 1989, see 25 *Weekly Compilation of Presidential Documents* (June 5, 1989): 786-91. As 1990 ushered in a new era in East-West relations, attention was devoted to reorienting NATO and its relations with the Warsaw Pact powers.

3 0 7 SECURITY TREATY--AUSTRALIA, NEW ZEALAND, AND UNITED STATES (ANZUS), 1951

Article II

In order more effectively to achieve the objective of this Treaty the Parties separately and jointly by means of continuous and effective self-help and mutual aid will maintain and develop their individual and collective capacity to resist armed attack.

Article III

The Parties will consult together whenever in the opinion of any of them the territorial integrity, political independence or security of any of the Parties is threatened in the Pacific.

Article IV

Each Party recognizes that an armed attack in the Pacific Area on any of the Parties would be dangerous to its own peace and safety and declares that it would act to meet the common danger in accordance with its constitutional processes. . . .

Article V

For the purpose of Article IV, an armed attack on any of the Parties is deemed to include an armed attack on the metropolitan territory of any of the Parties, or on the island territories under its jurisdiction in the Pacific or on its armed forces, public vessels or aircraft in the Pacific. . . .

Article VII

The Parties hereby establish a Council, consisting of their Foreign Ministers or their Deputies, to consider matters concerning the implementation of this Treaty. The Council should be so organized as to be able to meet at any time.

Article VIII

Pending the development of a more comprehensive system of regional security in the Pacific Area and the development by the United Nations of more effective means to maintain international peace and security, the Council, established by Article VII, is authorized to maintain a consultative relationship with States, Regional Organizations, Associations of States or other authorities in the Pacific Area in a position to further the purposes of this Treaty and to contribute to the security of that Area.

Article X

This Treaty shall remain in force indefinitely. Any Party may cease to be a member of the Council established by Article VII one year after notice has been given to the Government of Australia, which will inform the Governments of the other Parties of the deposit of such notice. . . .

Signed September 1, 1951; 11 articles. TIAS 2493; 3 *U.S. Treaties* 3420-25; and *American Foreign Policy: Basic Documents,* 1950-1955, pp. 878-80.

*   *   *

NEW ZEALAND'S CHANGED STATUS, 1985

On February 4 of this year, New Zealand rejected an American request for a visit by the U.S.S. *Buchanan,* a conventionally powered destroyer that was to participate in an ANZUS . . . naval exercise. The Government of New Zealand rejected the request because the United States would neither confirm nor deny the presence of nuclear weapons aboard the ship.

New Zealand's decision followed months of quiet consultations between our two countries, in which we explored an amicable solution. We pointed out that port access for our ships in accordance with our worldwide policy of neither confirming nor denying the presence of nuclear weapons aboard ships was an essential element of the ANZUS security relationship. The implication of New Zealand's decision was that no American ship that could not be identified as unambiguously non-nuclear-armed could ever call in that nation again. Without access to ports, we could not fulfill our treaty obligations either in peacetime or in a crisis.

Our policy of neither confirming nor denying the presence of nuclear weapons aboard our naval vessels is essential: it prevents adversaries from identifying our most capable ships, thereby enhancing targeting difficulties and reinforcing deterrence.

We did not challenge New Zealand's right to choose its own policy. . . . No other ally, however, refuses to permit port visits on the basis of our "neither confirm nor deny" policy as New Zealand has. And if New Zealand's objective was to enhance Pacific security and reduce the nuclear danger, it has acted against its own interests: by adding a new element of risk and uncertainty, New Zealand has weakened regional stability, one of the most important links in the efforts to prevent nuclear war. . . .

When New Zealand decided to reject the *Buchanan,* it also decided, in effect, that the basic operational elements of the ANZUS treaty would not apply to it. In a sense, New Zealand walked off the job--the job of working with each other to defend our common security. . . .

Our differences with New Zealand are specific and immediate; yet they raise the most basic questions about alliances and about alliance responsibilities in the modern world: What is the purpose of our alliances? What qualities are unique to an alliance of democracies? How do we manage our alliances in a new era in furtherance of our common purpose? . . .

And something else that was true years ago is also true today: it is not enough for allies to agree that when war starts they will come to each other's aid. Words and agreements alone will not deter war. Allies must work together to ensure that we have the capability to fight and win such a war--and that our adversaries know it. That is the real deterrent.

George Shultz, "On Alliance Responsibility," address, East-West Center, Honolulu, July 17, 1985, in 85 *Department of State Bulletin* (September 1985): 33.

*   *   *

Some would say that New Zealand should not have to bear the risks or face the moral responsibilities imposed by modern weapons; but it is not New Zealanders who bear the brunt of deterrence in the nuclear age. Americans are certainly no less concerned about the danger of nuclear war or the moral issues of defending freedom. We did not seek to be hostage to world peace, but we have accepted the role. But it is we who bear the major risks and burdens of maintaining a nuclear balance upon which all the free countries of the world depend.

We do not ask New Zealanders to shoulder the burden of maintaining a nuclear balance. We are not pronuclear; we are pro-ANZUS. But without access to ports and the surface ship deployments that access supports, we cannot maintain the naval presence in the Pacific that helps to deter war and preserve the peace. And we can't go around advertising which of those ships has nuclear weapons on board, or when they do and when they don't. For an ally to insist on that kind of disclosure as a condition for port access is just not responsible.

With words New Zealand assures us that it remains committed to ANZUS; but by its deeds New Zealand has effectively curtailed its operational role in ANZUS. A military alliance has little meaning without military cooperation. New Zealand can't have it both ways. . . .

Paul D. Wolfowitz, address, Honolulu, February 2, 1985, in 85 *Department of State Bulletin* (April 1985): 38. For additional commentary, see 84 *Department of State Bulletin* (September 1984): 60-63; and 86 *Department of State Bulletin* (September 1986): 36-37; and (October 1986): 44-48.

3 0 8   SOUTHEAST ASIA COLLECTIVE DEFENSE TREATY (MANILA PACT, SEATO), 1954

Article II

In order more effectively to achieve the objectives of this Treaty, the Parties, separately and jointly, by means of continuous and effective self-help and mutual aid will maintain and develop their individual and collective capacity to resist armed attack and to prevent and counter subversive activities directed from without against their territorial integrity and political stability.

Article III

The Parties undertake to strengthen their free institutions and to cooperate with one another in the further development of economic measures, including technical assistance, designed both to promote economic progress and social well-being and to further the individual and collective efforts of governments toward these ends.

Article IV

1. Each Party recognizes that aggression by means of armed attack in the treaty area against any of the Parties or against any State or

territory which the Parties by unanimous agreement may hereafter designate, would endanger its own peace and safety, and agrees that it will in that event act to meet the common danger in accordance with its constitutional processes. . . .

2. If, in the opinion of any of the Parties, the inviolability or the integrity of the territory or the sovereignty or political independence of any Party in the treaty area or of any other State or territory to which the provisions of paragraph 1 of this Article from time to time apply is threatened in any way other than by armed attack or is affected or threatened by any fact or situation which might endanger the peace of the area, the Parties shall consult immediately in order to agree on the measures which should be taken for the common defense.

3. It is understood that no action on the territory of any State designated by unanimous agreement under paragraph 1 of this Article or on any territory so designated shall be taken except at the invitation or with the consent of the government concerned.

Article V

The Parties hereby establish a Council, on which each of them shall be represented, to consider matters concerning the implementation of this Treaty. The Council shall provide for consultation with regard to military and any other planning as the situation obtaining in the treaty area may from time to time require. The Council shall be so organized as to be able to meet at any time. . . .

Article VII

Any other State in a position to further the objectives of this Treaty and to contribute to the security of the area may, by unanimous agreement of the Parties, be invited to accede to this Treaty. . . .

Article VIII

As used in this Treaty, the "treaty area" is the general area of Southeast Asia, including also the entire territories of the Asian Parties, and the general area of the Southwest Pacific not including the Pacific area north of 21 degrees 30 minutes north latitude. The Parties may, by unanimous agreement, amend this Article to include within the treaty area the territory of any State acceding to this Treaty in accordance with Article VII or otherwise to change the treaty area. . . .

Article X

This Treaty shall remain in force indefinitely, but any Party may cease to be a Party one year after its notice of denunciation has been given to the Government of the Republic of the Philippines, which shall inform the Governments of the other Parties of the deposit of each notice of denunciation.

*   *   *

UNDERSTANDING OF THE UNITED STATES OF AMERICA

The United States of America in executing the present Treaty does so with the understanding that its recognition of the effect of aggression and armed attack and its agreement with reference thereto in Article IV, paragraph 1, apply only to communist aggression but affirms that in the event of other aggression or armed attack it will consult under the provisions of Article IV, paragraph 2.

Signed September 8, 1954; 11 articles. TIAS 3170; 6 *U.S. Treaties* 81-89; and *American Foreign Policy: Basic Documents,* 1950-1955, pp. 912-15, with Protocol, p. 916. Also see the Pacific Charter, signed at the same time, which promoted self-determination and economic, social, and cultural cooperation; *American Foreign Policy: Basic Documents,* 1950-1955, pp. 916-17. After the Vietnam War, by decision of the SEATO Council, September 24, 1975, the SEATO organization ceased to exist as of June 30, 1977, but the Collective Defense Treaty remains in force; for commentary, see *Digest of United States Practice in International Law,* 1975, p. 789.

309 PACT OF MUTUAL COOPERATION--BAGHDAD PACT (CENTO), 1955

Article 1
Consistent with article 51 of the United Nations Charter the High Contracting Parties will co-operate for their security and defence. Such measures as they agree to take to give effect to this co-operation may form the subject of special agreements with each other.

Article 2
In order to ensure the realisation and effect application of the co-operation provided for in article 1 above, the competent authorities of the High Contracting Parties will determine the measures to be taken as soon as the present pact enters into force. These measures will become operative as soon as they have been approved by the Governments of the High Contracting Parties. . . .

Article 4
The High Contracting Parties declare that the dispositions of the present pact are not in contradiction with any of the international obligations contracted by either of them with any third State or States. They do not derogate from and cannot be interpreted as derogating from, the said international obligations. The High Contracting Parties undertake not to enter into any international obligation incompatible with the present pact.

Article 5
This pact shall be open for accession to any member of the Arab League or any other State actively concerned with the security and peace in this region and which is fully recognised by both of the High Contracting Parties. . . .

Any acceding State party to the present pact may conclude special agreements, in accordance with article 1, with one or more States parties to the present pact. The competent authority of any acceding State may determine measures in accordance with article 2. These measures will become operative as soon as they have been approved by the Governments of the parties concerned.

Article 6

A Permanent Council at ministerial level will be set up to function within the framework of the purposes of this pact when at least four Powers become parties to the pact. . . .

Article 7

This pact remains in force for a period of five years renewable for other five-year periods. Any Contracting Party may withdraw from the pact by notifying the other parties in writing of its desire to do so six months before the expiration of any of the above-mentioned periods, in which case the pact remains valid for the other parties. . . .

Signed February 24, 1955; 8 articles. *American Foreign Policy: Basic Documents,* 1950-1955, pp. 1257-59. The pact was signed by Iraq and Turkey, and later adhered to by the United Kingdom, Iran, and Pakistan. The United States did not formally join CENTO, but on invitation the United States sent observers to its sessions. Following the Iranian revolution in 1979, the pact was dissolved.

*   *   *

U.S. RELATIONSHIP WITH CENTO

. . . The United States has been, as you know, sympathetic toward the formation of the Baghdad Pact; indeed, it comes out of an idea I developed when I was in that part of the world the first year I was in office, in May 1953. Then I talked about the "northern tier" concept and that idea took hold and it resulted in the present Baghdad Pact, including the northern tier countries; namely, Pakistan, Iran, Iraq, and Turkey. On the question of its further development, the United States has no particular views. We have not urged any other countries to join the pact.

. . . I think we would consider joining the Baghdad Pact if and when it seemed in doing so it would be a contribution to the general stability of the area. We do not consider it as an isolated act.

John Foster Dulles, news conference, January 11, 1956; *American Foreign Policy: Current Documents,* 1956, p. 561.

*   *   *

The President of Pakistan, the Prime Ministers of Iraq, Turkey, and Pakistan, and the Foreign Minister of Iran in their recent meeting at Baghdad have reaffirmed their determination to further a peaceful and lasting settlement of current Middle Eastern problems. . . .

The United States has, from the inception of the Baghdad Pact, supported the pact and the principles and objectives of collective security on which it is based. Through its own bilateral arrangements with pact members in the Middle East area and its active membership in certain of the pact's committees, the United States has revealed its readiness to assist in measures to strengthen the security of those nations.

Statement released by Department of State, November 29, 1956; *American Foreign Policy: Current Documents,* 1956, p. 699.

*   *   *

1. The members of the Baghdad Pact attending the Ministerial meeting in London have re-examined their position in the light of recent events and conclude that the need which called the Pact into being is greater than ever. These members declare their determination to maintain their collective security and to resist aggression, direct or indirect.
2. Under the Pact collective security arrangements have been instituted. Joint military planning has been advanced and area economic projects have been promoted. Relationships are being established with other free world nations associated for collective security.
3. The question of whether substantive alterations should be made in the Pact and its organisation or whether the Pact will be continued in its present form is under consideration by the Governments concerned. However, the nations represented at the meeting in London reaffirmed their determination to strengthen further their united defence posture in the area.
4. Article 1 of the Pact of Mutual Co-operation signed at Baghdad on February 24, 1955 provides that the parties will co-operate for their security and defence and that such measures as they agree to take to give effect to this co-operation may form the subject of special agreements. Similarly, the United States in the interest of world peace, and pursuant to existing Congressional authorization, agrees to co-operate with the nations making this Declaration for their security and defence, and will promptly enter into agreements designed to give effect to this co-operation.

Declaration Respecting the Baghdad Pact, London, July 28, 1958. Signed by the United States, Iran, Pakistan, Turkey, and the United Kingdom. TIAS 4084; 9 *U.S. Treaties* 1077-78. For U.S. supplementary agreement with Turkey, 1959, see Document 314.

*   *   *

That matter [of possible U.S. membership in CENTO] has been considered very carefully. We have considered our relationships with other nations of the area. We have considered domestic problems. And, on balance, we have decided that we can probably be of more assistance in maintaining tranquility and helping to develop that area by remaining as an observer rather than as a full member.

Secretary of State, comment, news conference, October 6, 1959; *American Foreign Policy: Current Documents*, 1959, p. 1023.

BILATERAL FAR EAST ALLIANCES

In the early 1950's the United States negotiated bilateral alliances with the Philippines (Document 310), Japan (Document 311), the Republic of Korea (Document 312) and Nationalist China (Document 313). The treaty with Japan, signed in 1951, was superseded in 1960. That with Nationalist China was consummated after the Communists took over control on the mainland and established the People's Republic of China, and the Nationalist Government fled to Taiwan. However, it was terminated when the United States regularized diplomatic relations with the People's Republic in 1979 (Documents 79, 496-497). The treaties with the Philippine Republic and Korea remain intact.

310   MUTUAL DEFENSE TREATY, U.S. AND PHILIPPINE REPUBLIC, 1951

Desiring to declare publicly and formally their sense of unity and their common determination to defend themselves against external armed attack, so that no potential aggressor could be under the illusion that either of them stands alone in the Pacific Area,

Desiring further to strengthen their present efforts for collective defense for the preservation of peace and security pending the development of a more comprehensive system of regional security in the Pacific Area. . . .

Article I

The Parties undertake, as set forth in the Charter of the United Nations, to settle any international disputes in which they may be involved by peaceful means in such a manner that international peace and security and justice are not endangered and to refrain in their international relations from the threat or use of force in any manner inconsistent with the purposes of the United Nations.

Article II

In order more effectively to achieve the objective of this Treaty, the Parties separately and jointly by self-help and mutual aid will maintain and develop their individual and collective capacity to resist armed attack.

Article III

The Parties, through their Foreign Ministers or their deputies, will consult together from time to time regarding the implementation of this Treaty and whenever in the opinion of either of them the territorial integrity, political independence or security of either of the Parties is threatened by external armed attack in the Pacific.

Article IV

Each Party recognizes that an armed attack in the Pacific Area on either of the Parties would be dangerous to its own peace and safety and declares that it would act to meet the common dangers in accordance with its constitutional processes. . . .

Article V

For the purpose of Article IV, an armed attack on either of the Parties is deemed to include an armed attack on the metropolitan territory of either of the Parties, or on the island territories under its jurisdiction in the Pacific or on its armed forces, public vessels or aircraft in the Pacific. . . .

Article VIII

This Treaty shall remain in force indefinitely.   Either Party may terminate it one year after notice has been given to the other Party.

Signed August 30, 1951; 8 articles.   TIAS 2529; 3 *U.S. Treaties* 3947-52; and *American Foreign Policy: Basic Documents*, 1950-1955, pp. 873-75.

3 1 1   MUTUAL SECURITY TREATIES, U.S. AND JAPAN, 1951 AND 1960

MUTUAL DEFENSE, 1951

The United States of America, in the interest of peace and security, is presently willing to maintain certain of its armed forces in and about Japan, in the expectation, however, that Japan will itself increasingly assume responsibility for its own defense against direct and indirect aggression, always avoiding any armament which could be an offensive threat or serve other than to promote peace and security in accordance with the purposes and principles of the United Nations Charter.

Accordingly, the two countries have agreed as follows:

Article I

Japan grants, and the United States of America accepts, the right, upon the coming into force of the Treaty of Peace and of this Treaty, to dispose United States land, air and sea forces in and about Japan. Such forces may be utilized to contribute to the maintenance of international peace and security in the Far East and to the security of Japan against armed attack from without, including assistance given at the express request of the Japanese Government to put down large-scale internal riots and disturbances in Japan, caused through instigation or intervention by an outside power or powers.

Article II

During the exercise of the right referred to in Article I, Japan will not grant, without the prior consent of the United States of America, any bases or any rights, powers or authority whatsoever, in or relating to bases or the right of garrison or of maneuver, or transit of ground, air or naval forces to any third power.

Article III

The conditions which shall govern the disposition of armed forces of the United States of America in and about Japan shall be determined by administrative agreements between the two Governments.

Article IV

This Treaty shall expire whenever in the opinion of the Governments of the United States of America and Japan there shall have come into force such United Nations arrangements or such alternative individual or collective security dispositions as will satisfactorily provide for the maintenance by the United Nations or otherwise of international peace and security in the Japan Area.

Signed September 8, 1951; 5 articles. TIAS 2491; 3 *U.S. Treaties* 3329-40; and *American Foreign Policy: Basic Documents,* 1950-1955, pp. 885-86. For supplementary Administrative Agreement, see TIAS 2492; 3 *U.S. Treaties* 3341-3419.

*   *   *

Fourth, there should be no misunderstanding of the purpose of this Security Treaty. Its purpose is peace. In a world in which aggression and the threat of aggression are rampant, the maintenance of peace and security requires us to take affirmative steps to bulwark freedom with military strength. Weakness is an invitation to aggression, both external and internal. We are here providing for the defensive strength without which peace would be jeopardized. In building this strength, the present treaty does not create a threat of further aggression. Of importance to all Japan's neighbors in the Pacific is the principle recognized in this treaty that Japan shall avoid any armament which could be an offensive threat or serve other than to promote peace and security in accordance with the purposes and principles of the United Nations Charter.

Secretary of State, statement at signing ceremony, September 8, 1951; *American Foreign Policy: Basic Documents,* 1950-1955, p. 887.

*   *   *

MUTUAL COOPERATION AND SECURITY, 1960

Article III

The Parties, individually and in cooperation with each other, by means of continuous and effective self-help and mutual aid will maintain and develop, subject to their constitutional provisions, their capacities to resist armed attack.

Article IV

The Parties will consult together from time to time regarding the implementation of this Treaty, and, at the request of either Party, whenever the security of Japan or international peace and security in the Far East is threatened.

Article V

Each Party recognizes that an armed attack against either Party in the territories under the administration of Japan would be dangerous to its own peace and safety and declares that it would act to meet the common danger in accordance with its constitutional provisions and processes. . . .

Article VI

For the purpose of contributing to the security of Japan and the maintenance of international peace and security in the Far East, the United States of America is granted the use by its land, air and naval forces of facilities and areas in Japan.

The use of these facilities and areas as well as the status of United States armed forces in Japan shall be governed by a separate agreement, replacing the Administrative Agreement under Article III of the Security Treaty between the United States of America and Japan, signed at Tokyo on February 28, 1952 [TIAS 2492; 3 *U.S. Treaties* 3341-3419] as amended, and by such other arrangements as may be agreed upon. . . .

Article IX

The Security Treaty between the United States of America and Japan signed at the city of San Francisco on September 8, 1951 shall expire upon the entering into force of this Treaty.

Article X

This Treaty shall remain in force until in the opinion of the Governments of the United States of America and Japan there shall have come into force such United Nations arrangements as will satisfactorily provide for the maintenance of international peace and security in the Japan area.

However, after the Treaty has been in force for ten years, either Party may give notice to the other Party of its intention to terminate the Treaty, in which case the Treaty shall terminate one year after such notice has been given.

Signed January 19, 1960, 10 articles. TIAS 4509; 11 *U.S. Treaties* 1632-51.

312 MUTUAL DEFENSE TREATY, U.S. AND REPUBLIC OF KOREA, 1953

Desiring to declare publicly and formally their common determination to defend themselves against external armed attack so that no potential aggressor could be under the illusion that either of them stands alone in the Pacific area,

Desiring further to strengthen their efforts for collective defense for the preservation of peace and security pending the development of a more comprehensive and effective system of regional security in the Pacific area. . . .

Article I

The Parties undertake to settle any international disputes in which they may be involved by peaceful means in such a manner that international peace and security and justice are not endangered and to refrain in their international relations from the threat or use of force in any manner inconsistent with the Purposes of the United Nations, or obligations assumed by any Party toward the United Nations.

Article II

The Parties will consult together whenever, in the opinion of either of them, the political independence or security of either of the Parties is threatned by external armed attack. Separately and jointly, by self-help and mutual aid, the Parties will maintain and develop appropriate means to deter armed attack and will take suitable measures in consultation and agreement to implement this Treaty and to further its purposes.

Article III

Each Party recognizes that an armed attack in the Pacific area on either of the Parties in territories now under their respective administrative control, or hereafter recognized by one of the Parties as lawfully brought under the administrative control of the other, would be dangerous to its own peace and safety and declares that it would act to meet the common danger in accordance with its constitutional processes.

Article IV

The Republic of Korea grants, and the United States of America accepts, the right to dispose United States land, air and sea forces in and about the territory of the Republic of Korea as determined by mutual agreement. . . .

Article VI

This Treaty shall remain in force indefinitely. Either Party may terminate it one year after notice has been given to the other Party.

Signed October 1, 1953, 6 articles. TIAS 3097; 5 *U.S. Treaties* 2368-76; and *American Foreign Policy: Basic Documents,* 1950-1955, pp. 897-98.

* * *

UNDERSTANDING OF THE U.S.

It is the understanding of the United States that neither party is obligated, under Article III of the above treaty, to come to the aid of the other except in case of an external armed attack against such party; nor shall anything in the present Treaty be construed as requiring the United States to give assistance to Korea except in the event of an armed attack against territory which has been recognized by the United States as law fully brought under the administrative control of the Republic of Korea.

U.S. diplomatic note to Republic of Korea, January 28, 1954; *American Foreign Policy: Basic Documents,* 1950-1955, p. 898.

* * *

THE "MONROE DOCTRINE" FORMULA

The second element to be noted in the formula of article III is its replacement of the specific commitment language used in the North Atlantic Treaty, by what Secretary Dulles has called the "Monroe Doctrine" principle. Thus, each party, in article III, recognizes that the armed attack referred to therein would be dangerous to its own peace and safety. The action to be taken would then be determined in accordance with its constitutional process. By contrast, the North Atlantic Treaty formula makes an attack upon one tantamount to an attack upon all, so that such an attack, which might not take place against the United States itself, is nevertheless so regarded. Because of the constitutional issues which the approach suggests, for example, whether an attack upon another member gives the President the same inherent right to act as an attack upon United States territory, the language of President Monroe was regarded by Secretary [John Foster] Dulles as preferable when he negotiated the Philippine and Australia-New Zealand Pacts, and is reproduced in the Korean Treaty.

In short, the phraseology of article III of the Korean Pact permits the United States to take any action we deem appropriate by our constitutional processes, and gives adequate assurance of support to the other country which may be the victim of an attack. It has the additional advantage of never having been challenged throughout our history, from the constitutional standpoint, as altering the balance of power between the President and Congress.

Report by the Secretary of State to the President, December 30, 1953; *American Foreign Policy: Basic Documents,* 1950-1955, p. 907.

3 1 3 MUTUAL DEFENSE TREATY, U.S. AND REPUBLIC OF CHINA, 1954

Desiring to declare publicly and formally their sense of unity and their common determination to defend themselves against external armed attack, so that no potential aggressor could be under the illusion that either of them stands alone in the West Pacific Area, and

Desiring further to strengthen their present efforts for collective defense for the preservation of peace and security pending the development of a more comprehensive system of regional security in the West Pacific area. . . .

Article II

In order more effectively to achieve the objective of this Treaty, the Parties separately and jointly by self-help and mutual aid will maintain and develop their individual and collective capacity to resist armed attack and communist subversive activities directed from without against their territorial integrity and political stability. . . .

Article IV

The Parties, through their Foreign Ministers or their deputies, will consult together from time to time regarding the implementation of this Treaty.

Article V

Each Party recognizes that an armed attack in the West Pacific Area directed against the territories of either of the Parties would be dangerous to its own peace and safety and declares that it would act to meet the common danger in accordance with its constitutional processes. . . .

Article VI

For the purposes of Articles II and V, the terms "territorial" and "territories" shall mean in respect of the Republic of China, Taiwan and the Pescadores; and in respect of the United States of America, the island territories in the West Pacific under its jurisdiction. The provisions of Articles II and V will be applicable to such other territories as may be determined by mutual agreement.

Article VII

The Government of the Republic of China grants, and the Government of the United States of America accepts, the right to dispose such United States land, air and sea forces in and about Taiwan and the Pescadores as may be required for their defense, as determined by mutual agreement. . . .

Article X

This Treaty shall remain in force indefinitely.   Either Party may terminate it one year after notice has been given to the other Party.

Signed December 2, 1954, 10 articles.   TIAS 3178; 6 *U.S. Treaties* 433-49; and *American Foreign Policy: Basic Documents,* 1950-1955, pp. 945-47.   For supplementary exchange of notes see 6 *U.S. Treaties* 450-54.   For termination, see Document 79.

*   *   *

JOINT U.S.-CHINESE STATEMENT

The treaty will recognize the common interest of the parties in the security of Taiwan and the Pescadores and of the Western Pacific islands under the jurisdiction of the United States. It will provide for inclusion by agreement of other territories under the jurisdiction of the parties. It is directed against threats to the security of the treaty area from armed attack and provides for continuing consultation regarding any such threat or attack.

This Treaty will forge another link in the system of collective security established by the various collective defense treaties already concluded between the United States and other countries in the Pacific area. Together, these arrangements provide the essential framework for the defense by the free peoples of the Western Pacific against Communist aggression.

Like the other treaties, this treaty between the United States and the Republic of China will be defensive in character. It will reaffirm the dedication of the parties to the purposes and principles of the Charter of the United Nations.

Issued December 1, 1954; *American Foreign Policy: Basic Documents,* 1950-1955, p. 949.

SUCCESSOR AND SUPPLEMENTARY ARRANGEMENTS

To confirm its support of CENTO the United States negotiated separate bilateral defense cooperation agreements with Turkey, Iran, and Pakistan in 1959 (Document 314). That with Iran was terminated in the early 1980's and, while those with Turkey and Pakistan remained in effect, the agreement with Turkey was supplemented with special arrangements based on mutual relationship as members of NATO.

In addition, the United States established special defense arrangements with a number of other countries. For example, in the case of Iceland, which has no national military establishment, in 1951 the United States concluded an agreement that provides for American forces and material in Icelandic territory in implementation of the North Atlantic Treaty (Document 315). Before Spain joined NATO the United States acquired base rights in Spanish territory in 1970 (see bilateral agreement of August 6, 1970, TIAS 6924; 21 *U.S. Treaties* 1677-1712, especially articles 32-37), and negotiated a Treaty of Friendship and Cooperation in 1976 (Document 316). This was superseded by a Special Agreement of Friendship, Defense, and Cooperation signed in 1981.

In the case of Nationalist China, when the treaty of 1954 (see preceding section) was terminated at the end of 1979 (see Document 79), the United States nevertheless continued limited commitments to maintain "peace, security, and stability in the Western Pacific," to maintain commercial, cultural, and "other relations" with Taiwan, to consider any effort to determine the future of Nationalist China "by other than peaceful means . . . a threat to the peace and security . . . and a grave concern to the United States," and "to provide Taiwan with arms of a defensive character." This change was deemed necessary to comport with rapprochement with mainland China and recognition of its government as the sole authority in "China." (See Taiwan Relations Act, April 1979, Public Law 96-8, and President Carter's statement, April 10, 1979; *American Foreign Policy: Basic Documents,* 1977-1980, pp. 988-94. Also see Chapter 28, Documents 496-497.) For lists of special defense arrangements with other countries, see *Treaties in Force.*

314 AGREEMENT OF COOPERATION, U.S. AND TURKEY, 1959

Article I

The Government of Turkey is determined to resist aggression. In case of aggression against Turkey, the Government of the United States of

America, in accordance with the Constitution of the United States of America, will take such appropriate action, including the use of armed forces, as may be mutually agreed upon and as is envisaged in the Joint Resolution to Promote Peace and Stability in the Middle East, in order to assist the Government of Turkey at its request.

Article II

The Government of the United States of America, in accordance with the Mutual Security Act of 1954, as amended, and related laws of the United States of America, and with applicable agreements heretofore or hereafter entered into between the Government of the United States of America and the Government of Turkey, reaffirms that it will continue to furnish the Government of Turkey such military and economic assistance as may be mutually agreed upon between the Government of the United States of America and the Government of Turkey, in order to assist the Government of Turkey in the preservation of its national independence and integrity and in the effective promotion of its economic development. . . .

Article IV

The Government of the United States of America and the Government of Turkey will cooperate with the other Governments associated in the Declaration signed at London on July 28, 1958 [see above, Document 309], in order to prepare and participate in such defensive arrangements as may be mutually agreed to be desirable, subject to the other applicable provisions of this agreement. . . .

Article VI

This agreement shall enter into force upon the date of its signature and shall continue in force until one year after the receipt of either Government of written notice of the intention of the other Government to terminate the agreement.

Signed on March 5, 1959, 6 articles.   TIAS 4191; 11 *U.S. Treaties* 320-22. Identical agreements were signed simultaneously with Iran and Pakistan; see TIAS 4189 and 4190; 11 *U.S. Treaties* 314-19.   Although this agreement has remained in effect, the United States and Turkey supplemented it with additional agreements: Defense Cooperation Agreements (1969 and 1976), Cooperation on Defense and Economy (1980), and others, which reinforced the North Atlantic Treaty rather than the Baghdad Pact.   The 1980 agreement was scheduled to run for five years; for text, with three lengthy augmenting agreements plus a series of "implementing arrangements," see 32 *U.S. Treaties* 3323-88.   For a list of these successor and supplementary agreements, see *Treaties in Force;* also see commentary in *Digest of United States Practice in International Law,* 1980, pp. 240-41, 998.

315 DEFENSE AGREEMENT, U.S. AND ICELAND, 1951

Preamble

Having regard to the fact that the people of Iceland cannot themselves adequately secure their own defenses, and whereas experience has shown that a country's lack of defenses greatly endangers its security and that of its peaceful neighbors, the North Atlantic Treaty Organization has requested, because of the unsettled state of world affairs, that the United States and Iceland in view of the collective efforts of the parties to the North Atlantic Treaty to preserve peace and security in the North Atlantic Treaty area, make arrangements for the use of facilities in Iceland in defense of Iceland and thus also the North Atlantic Treaty area. In conformity with this proposal the following Agreement has been entered into.

Article I

The United States on behalf of the North Atlantic Treaty Organization and in accordance with its responsibilities under the North Atlantic Treaty will make arrangements regarding the defense of Iceland subject to the conditions set forth in this Agreement. For this purpose and in view of the defense of the North Atlantic Treaty area, Iceland will provide such facilities in Iceland as are mutually agreed to be necessary.

Article II

Iceland will make all acquisitions of land and other arrangements required to permit entry upon and use of facilities in accordance with this Agreement, and the United States shall not be obliged to compensate Iceland or any national of Iceland or other person for such entry or use.

Article III

The national composition of forces, and the conditions under which they may enter upon and make use of facilities in Iceland pursuant to this Agreement, shall be determined in agreement with Iceland.

Article IV

The number of personnel to be stationed in Iceland pursuant to this Agreement shall be subject to the approval of the Icelandic Government.

Article V

The United States in carrying out its responsibilities under this Agreement shall do so in a manner that contributes to the maximum safety of the Icelandic people, . . . Nothing in this Agreement shall be so construed as to impair the ultimate authority of Iceland with regard to Icelandic affairs. . . .

Article VII

Either Government may at any time, on notification to the other Government, request the Council of the North Atlantic Treaty Organization to review the continued necessity for the facilities and their utilization, and to make recommendations to the two Governments concerning the continuation of this Agreement. If no understanding between the two Governments is reached as a result of such request for review within a period of six months from the date of the original request, either Government may at any time thereafter give notice of its intention to terminate the Agreement, and the Agreement shall then cease to be in force twelve months from the date of such notice. . . .

Signed May 5, 1951, 8 articles.   TIAS 2266; 1 *U.S. Treaties* 1195-1201.   For annex to 1951 agreement, see TIAS 2295; 2 *U.S. Treaties* 1533-53.   For supplementary exchange of notes and memorandum of understanding, October 22, 1974, see 25 *U.S. Treaties* 3079-86.

316   TREATY OF FRIENDSHIP AND COOPERATION, U.S. AND SPAIN, 1976

Article I
The close cooperation between the two countries on all matters of common concern or interest will be maintained and developed on a basis of sovereign equality. This cooperation shall encompass economic, educational, cultural, scientific, technical, agricultural, and defense matters, as well as other matters upon which they may mutually agree.

The Governments of Spain and the United States of America will keep their cooperation in all these areas under continuous review and seek to identify and adopt all appropriate measures for carrying out this cooperation in the most effective manner possible with a view to maintaining a balance of benefits, equal and effective participation of both parties, and coordination and harmonization of their efforts with those which may be being made in other bilateral and multilateral contexts.

For these purposes, a Spanish-United States Council is established under the chairmanship of the Foreign Minister of Spain and the Secretary of State of the United States of America. The functions and organization of the Council are set forth in Supplementary Agreement Number One. The Council will meet at least semi-annually. . . .

Article V
Having recognized that their cooperation has strengthened the security of the Western World, and contributed to the maintenance of world peace, there is established a defense relationship between Spain and the United States of America. Consistent with the Declaration of Principles of July 19, 1974, they will, through this defense relationship, seek to enhance further their own security and that of the Western World. To such end, they will seek to develop the appropriate plans and coordination between their respective armed forces. This coordination will be carried out by a coordinating body as set forth in Supplementary Agreement Number Five.

To further the purposes of this Treaty, the United States of America may use specific military facilities on Spanish territory, in accordance with the provisions set forth in Supplementary Agreement Number Six. The two parties will also, for these ends, cooperate in the acquisition as well as the production of appropriate materiel for their armed forces, in accordance with the provisions of Supplementary Agreement Number Seven.

Article VI
In view of the contribution the use of the facilities mentioned in Article V makes to the defense of the West, the parties, through mutually

agreed steps, will seek on the basis of reciprocity and equality to harmonize their defense relationship with existing security arrangements in the North Atlantic area. To this end, they will, periodically, review all aspects of the matter, including the benefits flowing to those arrangements from the facilities and make such adjustments as may be mutually agreed upon. . . .

Article VIII

In order to facilitate the withdrawal of the personnel, property, equipment and materiel of the Government of the United States of America located in Spain pursuant to Article V of this Treaty and its Supplementary Agreements, a period of one year from the termination of the Treaty is provided for the completion of withdrawal which will begin immediately after such termination. During that one year period, all the rights, privileges and obligations deriving from Article V and its Supplementary Agreements shall remain in force while United States forces remain in Spain.

*   *   *

SUPPLEMENTARY AGREEMENT ON U.S.-SPANISH COUNCIL

Article I

The United States-Spanish Council will be responsible for overseeing the implementation of the Treaty of Friendship and Cooperation. It will review the cooperation under that Treaty; examine any problems which may arise as well as measures which might be taken to deal with them; consider steps to facilitate and improve United States-Spanish cooperation; and submit to the Governments such findings and recommendations as may be agreed. The Council will also be charged with carrying out the consultations provided for in Article III of Supplementary Agreement Number Six.

Article II

The Council will be chaired by the Secretary of State of the United States and the Foreign Minister of Spain, and will meet at least semiannually. Each Chairman will have a Deputy who will serve as Permanent Representative on the Council and assure its functioning in the absence of his Chairman. The Chairman of the Joint Chiefs of Staff of each party or their designated representatives will be permanent military representatives on the Council. The parties shall designate such other representatives and advisors to the Council and its subsidiary bodies as they deem appropriate, taking into account the variety of matters which may be before the Council at any particular time, and the need for adequate representation on the Council from responsible ministries and departments. . . .

Article IV

In order to establish the necessary coordination between them and to ensure greater effectiveness of the reciprocal defense support granted by each to the other, the two parties agree to establish a Joint Military Committee dependent on the Council composed of the two Chiefs of the Joint Chiefs of Staff, or their designated representatives, which shall meet semi-annually. . . .

Article V

For the purpose of obtaining the maximum effectiveness in cooperation for Western defense, the United States-Spanish Council, as one of its basic objectives, will work toward development of appropriate coordination with the North Atlantic Treaty Organization. In furtherance of this purpose, the Council will establish by mutual agreement a commission formed by members of the two contracting parties which shall propose to the Council specific measures to promote the establishment of meaningful coordination. . . .

Signed January 24, 1976, 8 articles; Supplement contains 6 articles. TIAS 8360; 27 *U.S. Treaties* 3005-43. The treaty is augmented by seven supplementary agreements, the first of which concerns the U.S.-Spanish Council. For commentary on bases in Spain, also see *Digest of United States Practice in International Law*, 1975, pp. 323-24. After Spain joined the North Atlantic Treaty Organization in the early 1980's (see TIAS 10564), a successor Agreement on Friendship, Defense, and Cooperation was signed in Madrid on July 2, 1982; see TIAS 10589. For commentary, see *American Foreign Policy: Current Documents*, 1983, pp. 593-96.

ALLIANCE POLICY--COMMENTARY

Analysis of the American alliance system is extensive, descriptive, and evaluative. The selections provided in this section illustrate the types of official commentary that emphasize a variety of themes (Documents 317-322). These touch on such matters as the purposes, defensive nature, durability, and future of alliances. They are generally regarded as an important means to achieve political, economic, and moral as well as security unity among members, provide for mutual defense, contribute to maintaining military and diplomatic solidarity and balance of power, and seek to maintain international peace, stability, and equilibrium. Several selections stress the need for and value of cooperation and the desirability of building a genuine spirit of partnership. Some contributions note the uniqueness of aligning the United States with the leading democracies and other members of the free world. Others comment on the difficulty of adapting to changing forces and conditions in international affairs, the essentiality of commitment, the costs of sustaining viable alliances, and the responsibilities they impose on member nations.

317 DEMOCRACIES AND ALLIANCES

As Dean Acheson said about the alliance, this unity "is not an improvisation. It is a statement of the facts and lessons of history."

When the Atlantic alliance was founded in 1949, the allies showed they had learned a lesson from the period before World War II--when the democracies had lacked the will to come together in the face of danger, when they had tried to evade their responsibility of maintaining their strength and permitted a dangerous imbalance of power to develop. . . .

The alliance has succeeded in preventing war.   Indeed, since its formation, the only use of military force on the Continent of Europe has been by the Soviet Union against its own "allies." But experience has also taught that the unity of the free nations is central to the achievement of any of our goals: peace, freedom, security, prosperity.

I want to say a few words now about how the democracies, learning from the "facts and lessons of history," are responding today to a new set of challenges--in the realms of political affairs, economics, and security.

The first lesson is that what the democracies have in common is of overriding importance to us and to others throughout the world.   Our common heritage gives us a common responsibility. . . .

Most alliances in history have not lasted.   The fact that the democracies have been held together by ties of political, economic, and security cooperation for more than three decades, through many profound changes in international conditions, is proof, I believe, that our unity of shared values and common purpose is something special. At the same time, the grim lesson of history should warn us that even this great coalition will not survive without conscious effort and political commit-ment.   Those statesmen who were "present at the creation" in the immediate postwar period showed enormous vision and courage. In a new era in history, it is up to all of us to summon the same vision and courage to assure that it survives and flourishes.

Therefore it is of enormous importance that our moral unity is today being so effectively translated into political unity. . . .

In the economic dimension as well, experience teaches that cooperation is essential. We now live in an interdependent world in which each country's well-being, primarily its own responsibility, is nevertheless affected powerfully by the health of the global economy, for which the industrial democracies bear a special responsibility. . . .

We cannot find security in arms alone. We are willing to negotiate differences--but we cannot do so effectively if we are weak, or if the Soviet Union believes it can achieve its objectives without any compromise.   Therefore, both these tracks--strength and diplomacy--are essential. . . .

At the same time, experience teaches that a balance of power, though necessary, is not sufficient. Our strength is a means to an end; it is the secure foundation for our effort to build a safer, more peaceful, and more hopeful world. On the basis of strength, the cohesion of our alliances, and a clear view of our own objectives, we must never be afraid to negotiate. . . .

The final lesson I want to leave you with is this: Experience teaches us that nothing is foreordained. Nations, like individuals, have choices to make. History is filled with many examples of nations and individuals that made the wrong choices; there are also many examples of foresight, wisdom, and courage.

Democracies are sometimes slow to awaken to their challenges. But once they are aroused, no force on Earth is more powerful than free peoples working together with clear purpose and determination.

George Shultz, Commencement Address, Stanford University, June 12, 1983; *American Foreign Policy: Current Documents,* 1983, pp. 14-18.

318 ALLIANCES AND SECURITY

Out of the ashes of World War II, we and our allies built a new world. We had learned from bitter experience that America's safety and world peace, America's prosperity and the world economy, were inextricably linked. In this spirit the United States promoted the economic and political recovery of Western Europe and Japan. We strengthened our defense and forged our first peacetime alliances; they have preserved the global balance of power for a generation. . . .

The allied statesmen who built the postwar international order would not recognize the international landscape we see today. The evolution that has taken place over 30 years has transformed the environment in which America lives. The world of the last quarter of the 20th century will be vastly different from that to which we have grown accustomed--but it is a world that we must help to shape.

These are the broad tasks of our foreign policy·

In an age of continuing peril and exploding technology, we must maintain and improve our national defense. . . . This process will continue. We know that peace requires an equilibrium of power--and this Government will maintain it. No nation can remain great if it leaves its safety to the mercy or the good will of others. Any realistic hope of better relations with the Communist powers--and there is such hope-- depends on a strong America which leaves other countries no realistic course except restraint and cooperation. So long as potential adversaries continue to expand and improve their forces, we will maintain a modern defense that cannot be challenged.

We will place our priority on our alliances with the great industrial democracies of the Atlantic community and Japan. In the new era, the industrial democracies have found that security involves more than common defense. We joined together out of fear; but we can stay united only if we find deeper and more positive common purposes. The moral unity of the democracies--in an era when their values are a minority in the world and buffeted by difficulties at home--is one of our greatest re- sources. A sense of solidarity in a turbulent world can help all of our peoples recover the confidence that their societies are vital, that they are the masters of their destinies, that they are not subject to blind forces be- yond their control. . . .

Henry Kissinger, "Building an Enduring Foreign Policy," address, Economic Club, Detroit, November 24, 1975; in 73 *Department of State Bulletin* (December 15, 1975):   841-43.

3 1 9   COMMON PURPOSE OF NATO COMMUNITY

Twenty-nine years ago, at an uncertain time for world peace, President Truman spoke these words on signing the North Atlantic Treaty:
"In this pact, we hope to create a shield against aggression
. . . a bulwark which will permit us to get on with the real business of government and society, the business of achieving a fuller and happier life for our citizens."
The alliance born that day in April 1949 has helped preserve our mutual security for nearly 30 years--almost a decade longer than the time between the two great wars of this century.   History records no other alliance that has successfully brought together so many different nations for so long, without the firing of a single shot in anger.
Ours is a defensive alliance.   No nation need fear aggression from us. But neither should any nation ever doubt our will to deter and defeat aggression against us.
The North Atlantic alliance is a union of peoples moved by a desire to secure a safe future for our children--in liberty and freedom.   Our alliance is unique because each of our 15 democratic nations shares a common heritage of human values, the rule of law, and faith in the courage and spirit of free men and women.
The military strength and common political purpose of the North Atlantic alliance has led us to cooperate in a thousand individual efforts, rightly conferring upon us the name of "community."   And it has given us the self-confidence and strength of will to seek improved relations with our potential adversaries.
Our alliance has never been an end in itself.   It is a way to promote stability and peace in Europe--and indeed, peace in the world at large. Our strength has made possible the pursuit of detente and agreements to limit arms, while increasing the security of the alliance.   Defense in Europe, East-West detente, and global diplomacy go hand-in-hand.
Never before has a defensive alliance devoted so much effort to negotiate limitations and reductions in armaments with its adversaries. Our record has no equal in the search for effective arms control agreements.
Finally, we face the challenge of promoting the human values and rights that are the final purpose and meaning of our alliance.   The task is not easy; the way to liberty has never been.   But our nations preeminently comprise the region of the world where freedom finds its most hospitable environment. . . .
If we continue to build on the fundamental strength of the North Atlantic alliance, I am confident that we can meet any challenge in the years ahead. In the future, as in the past, the Government and people of

the United States will remain steadfast to our commitment to peace and freedom that all of us, as allies, share together.

Jimmy Carter, address, North Atlantic Council, Washington, May 30, 1978; *American Foreign Policy: Basic Documents*, 1977-1980, pp. 478-79.

320 VALUE, DURABILITY, AND CHANGE OF ATLANTIC ALLIANCE, 1970

I believe we must build an alliance strong enough to deter those who might threaten war; close enough to provide for continuous and far-reaching consultation; trusting enough to accept a diversity of views; realistic enough to deal with the world as it is; flexible enough to explore new channels of constructive cooperation.

Address by the President
to the North Atlantic Council, April 10, 1969

*   *   *

--Genuine **partnership** must increasingly characterize our alliance. For if we cannot maintain and develop further such a relationship with our North Atlantic allies, the prospects for achieving it with our other friends and allies around the world are slim indeed. But the evolution-- past and future--of Europe and of European-American relations presents new issues. We must change the pattern of American predominance, appropriate to the postwar era, to match the new circumstances of today. . . .

--Jointly with our allies we must maintain the **strength** required to defend our common interests against external dangers, so long as those dangers exist. We have learned to integrate our forces; we now need better means of harmonizing our policies. We need a rational alliance defense posture for the longer term. . . .

--Together with our allies, we must be prepared to **negotiate**. The problems and dangers of the division of Europe persist. Our association with our friends and allies in Europe is the starting point from which we seek to resolve those problems and cope with those dangers. Our efforts to pursue genuine relaxation of tensions betwen East and West will be a test of the new trans-Atlantic partnership. . . .

Last April [1969] the North Atlantic Treaty completed its second decade and began its third. I stated on that occasion: "When NATO was founded, the mere fact of cooperation among the Western nations was of tremendous significance, both symbolically and substantively. Now the symbol is not enough; we need substance. The alliance today will be judged by the content of its cooperation, not merely by its form."

The durability of the alliance is itself a triumph, but also a challenge: It would be unreasonable to imagine that a structure and relationship developed in the late 1940's can remain the same in content and purpose in the 1970's.

The fundamentals of the relationship are not in question. The original aims of the Western Alliance are still our basic purposes: the defense of Western Europe against common challenges, and ultimately the creation of a viable and secure European order. . . .

But today, European vitality is more self-sustaining. The preponderant American influence that was a natural consequence of postwar conditions would be self-defeating today. For nations which did not share in the responsibility to make the vital decisions for their own defense and diplomacy could retain neither their self-respect nor their self-assurance.

A more balanced association and a more genuine partnership are in America's interest. As this process advances, the balance of burdens and responsibilities must gradually be adjusted, to reflect the economic and political realities of European progress. Our allies will deserve a voice in the alliance and its decisions commensurate with their growing power and contributions. . . .

Richard Nixon, *U.S. Foreign Policy for the 1970's: A New Strategy for Peace* (1970), pp. 27-32. For additional commentary, see Richard Nixon, *U.S. Foreign Policy for the 1970's: The Emerging Structure for Peace* (1972), pp. 42-45.

321 UNITED STATES PROUD OF ALLIANCE SYSTEM

. . . The starting point and cornerstone of our foreign policy is our alliance and partnership with our fellow democracies. For 35 years, the North Atlantic alliance has guaranteed the peace in Europe. In both Europe and Asia, our alliances have been the vehicle for a great reconciliation among nations that had fought bitter wars in decades and centuries past. And here in the Western Hemisphere, north and south are being lifted on the tide of freedom and are joined in a common effort to foster peaceful economic development.

We're proud of our association with all those countries that share our commitment to freedom, human rights, the rule of law, and international peace. Indeed, the bulwark of security that the democratic alliance provides is essential and remains essential to the maintenance of world peace. . . .

The people of the United States will remain faithful to their commitments. But the United States is also faithful to its alliances and friendships with scores of nations in the developed and developing worlds with differing political systems, cultures, and traditions. . . .

We're ready to be the friend of any country that is a friend to us and a friend of peace. . . .

Ronald Reagan, address, United Nations, September 24, 1984; *Papers of Presidents: Reagan*, 1984, II, 1356-57.

322 ALLIANCE RESPONSIBILITY

For our postwar alliance system is unique. Throughout history there have been many alliances; but never before has there been so enduring a partnership between so many nations committed to democracy. Today, our key alliances are democratic alliances; they are not agreements between rulers or governing elites but between peoples. The commitments made abroad must be approved and supported by our peoples through their elected representatives.

This unique quality is a continuing source of strength. Bonds among peoples who share fundamental values can survive periodic changes of leadership where other kinds of alliances might have collapsed. The democracies are united not only by strategic interest but also by moral bonds, which add a special intimacy and completeness to our cooperation. . . .

Yet alliances among peoples, as opposed to rulers, also present special problems and place greater demands on all partners.

Deterring aggression is never an easy task. But for democracies, there is a special difficulty. A democracy at peace would much rather focus on the more immediate and tangible social benefits to its people than on the potential danger that exists beyond the horizon. . . .

A democracy at peace, therefore, finds it hard to prepare for war in order to deter war. But it is a delusion to think that sacrifices can be safely deferred and that others will pick up the slack. The reality is that the collective deterrence of allies provides the umbrella of security under which nations can advance the well-being of their people.

When even one partner shirks its responsibilities, the health and unity of the entire alliance are placed in jeopardy. . . .

The first and most basic responsibility is that each of us has a share in maintaining the overall deterrent strength of the alliance. For the United States, that means restoring our own strength, in both conventional and nuclear arms. It means helping our allies, as best we can, to maintain their strength, both economically and militarily. It means consulting and planning so that collective efforts are directed effectively toward common goals. Finally, and most importantly, it means making clear, through both words and actions, that we are resolutely committed to the defense of our allies, that we have the will to act in the defense of our common ideals and our security.

Our allies, of course, have an equally grave responsibility to help maintain the deterrent strength of the alliance. They must make the necessary effort to ensure their own security--and particularly in the area of conventional defense. . . . Commitments cannot be met selectively by one nation without eroding the security of all and undermining popular support for the alliance. . . .

The shared responsibilities in a democratic alliance are broader and deeper than deterrence of a military threat. Such a partnership depends on a bond of mutual confidence and mutual support across the broad range of our relations.

Many challenges to common interests, after all, lie outside the purview of formal treaties. Yet cooperation in meeting these challenges is important not only to protect the interests of individual allies but also to bolster the mutual confidence that underpins the entire alliance system. We cannot allow the enemies of our way of life to attack each ally one by one in the hope that we will be divided and thus incapable of a coordinated response. . . .

For 35 years, our global alliance system has kept the peace and preserved our freedom in Europe and in most of Asia. For 35 years, nations and people with diverse cultures and histories, with different needs and national aspirations--and sometimes with differing views of the proper tactics for managing the many international challenges--have, nevertheless, remained committed to partnership in defense of what we hold dear. . . .

George Shultz, address, East-West Center, Honolulu, July 17, 1985; 85 *Department of State Bulletin* (September 1985): 33-36.

19

International Terrorism, Hijacking, and Skyjacking

We have learned a great deal about terrorism in recent years. . . . A pattern of terrorist violence has emerged. It is an alarming pattern, but it is something that we can identify and, therefore, a threat that we can devise concrete measures to combat. The knowledge we have accumulated about terrorism over the years can provide the basis for a coherent strategy to deal with the phenomenon, if we have the will to turn our understanding into action.

George Shultz
"Terrorism as a Phenomenon in Our Modern World," 1984

Terrorism, as ancient as the history of mankind and rampant since World War II, has accelerated since the 1960's, and has become a critical international problem. Characterized as the use or threat of violence to create fear and alarm, usually to gain political objectives, international terrorism employs a variety of vicious and increasingly more sophisticated methods. These vary from kidnaping, holding, and mistreating hostages, and from the demand for recognition, ransom, or blackmail, and retribution to assassination and murder (sometimes of innocent third parties), and from attacks on and hijacking of aircraft (air piracy) and occasionally seajacking to sabotage, arson, targeted or sometimes random bombing, and other means of creating degradation, intimidation, disruption, destruction, and subversion.

The objectives of most terrorists, who are motivated by social, religious, national, or similar causes, differ from those of ordinary criminals who generally seek money or some other form of personal gain. Most terrorist groups are small in membership and represent extremist positions. Terrorists believe that force and violence create anxiety and terror, which affords them the best or easiest way to gain publicity and support for, or submission to, their demands to further their cause. Many are idealists who view themselves as dedicated patriots or defenders of the "true faith" or of the rights of "the people."

Often their targets--political leaders, diplomats, business executives, and other prominent persons, or aircraft, public buildings, and other facilities

--are carefully selected, but sometimes they are simply chosen at random, primarily to attract media coverage and public attention.   Often terrorist organizations direct their violence against those they regard as representing foreign domination or neocolonialism. Usually they fail to achieve their long-range goals, and governments combat them by refusing to accede to their demands and by applying penalties and sanctions.

Thousands of acts of terrorism have been perpetrated worldwide since World War II, numbering as many as 600 to 1,000 or more in a single year. To mention a few, among the more widely publicized in recent years are the massacre of 11 members of the Israeli Olympic team during a gun battle in Munich (1972), the holding by Iranians of 52 American diplomats as hostages for more than a year (1979-1981), the bombing of the American embassy and the Marine barracks in Beirut killing scores of Americans, and the bombing murder of 4 members of the South Korean cabinet in Burma (1983), the Palestinian seajacking of the *Achille Lauro* in the Mediterranean (1985), the hijacking of Trans World Airlines flight 847 in which more than 150 passengers were taken hostage and an American was beaten and shot (1985), the midair bombing of (South) Korean Air Lines flight 858 by North Koreans causing the mass murder of 115 passengers and crew members (1987), and the armed attack by radical students who invaded the American Ambassador's residence in Seoul, Korea (1989).

In addition, for example, there have been attacks on American embassies in Moscow, Pakistan, and Kuwait, and South Korean students seized our information center in 1985; United States ambassadors and other diplomatic officers have been murdered in Afghanistan, Cyprus, Guatemala, Lebanon, Namibia, and elsewhere; dozens of other American officials have been kidnaped and held hostage; and many buildings have been bombed and aircraft hijacked. And in 1981 it was announced that a Libyan terrorist hit team was dispatched to this country to assassinate President Reagan and other ranking officials.

Although the United States sought to stem this mushrooming plague of terrorism by means of national legislation and multipartite declarations and treaties, it has been difficult to achieve universal commitment and action on all phases of its campaign. The following illustrate some of the principal problems encountered: distinguishing between terrorist and liberation movements; constraining terrorist disregard for life, property, and international law and treaty obligations; enlisting other governments to cooperate in exchanging intelligence both to avert terrorist crimes and to apprehend those responsible; persuading foreign governments to capture and extradite terrorists or try and punish them for their crimes; applying restraints upon those governments that support terrorist groups; and inducing other governments to join in applying collective sanctions against terrorists and the governments that support them.

Furthermore, a number of governments may become involved in dealing with the commission of a single terrorist act--such as those of the citizenship of its perpetrators, the government(s) that train and support them, those whose nationals are mistreated or whose aircraft, ships, or property are hijacked or damaged, those in which hijacked aircraft or ships take refuge or in which hostages are held, and those giving sanctuary to the terrorists.

Analysis of international terrorism needs to differentiate between hijacking and skyjacking, on the one hand, and other forms of terrorist threats and activities; between simple actions by individuals or small groups and state-sponsored and supported terrorism; between those actions that are perpetrated as retribution or those in which ransom, indemnity, release of fellow terrorists or public officials, or public recognition is demanded and those that involve assassination, bombing, and other forms of violent action for other reasons; and, most difficult, between terrorism, insurgency, and guerilla action.

The documents contained in this chapter are grouped in two categories-- United States objectives, policy themes, and other policy considerations; and national legislation, multipartite policy declarations, and antiterrorism treaties and agreements. For treatment of some specific cases, see Chapter 14 on the Iranian seizure of American hostages, bombing of the American embassy and Marine barracks in Beirut, and the application of sanctions against Libya.

POLICY THEMES

International terrorism increased after World War II, and policy concern mounted since the 1960's. During the earlier years attention focused especially on the mistreatment of diplomats, consuls, and other public officials, then expanded to include skyjacking and hostage-taking, and eventually encompassed a broad gamut of organized terrorism.

The documents selected for this section emphasize a number of general American policy considerations. These include basic policy guidelines (Document 323); the urgency of denying terrorists safe haven after they commit their crimes (Document 324); the establishment of a national antiterrorism program (Document 325); fear of the possible threat of nuclear-armed terrorists (Document 326); analysis of the nature and purposes of the terrorist menace and aspects of responding to it (Document 327); and the need for devising a strategy, not merely piecemeal tactics, for coping with the problem (Document 328).

323 UNITED STATES POLICY GUIDELINES, 1975

For Terrorism in the United States
1. The U.S. Government seeks to maintain firm, effective and consistent anti-terrorist policies at home and abroad.
2. We seek to exert leadership, by example and by diplomacy, in attempting to find collective solutions to this international problem.
3. The U.S. Government is committed to pursue legal remedies in dealing with terrorists and endeavors to influence other governments to do likewise.
4. Under principles of customary international law, the host government of a country where an act of terrorism occurs is responsible for providing protection to foreign nationals within its territory, including

securing their safe release from captors.

5. Accordingly, in an incident in the U.S. involving foreign nations, the U.S. Government undertakes negotiations to secure the release of hostages. . . .

6. The U.S. Government does not pay ransom, release prisoners or otherwise yield to blackmail by terrorist groups.

7. We establish effective communication with terrorists whose hostages are under U.S. protective responsibilities, avoiding hard and fast positions, except as noted above, while seeking to reduce, or ideally to terminate, danger to hostages.

8. The U.S. Government generally opposes but cannot prevent foreign governments, private individuals, or companies from meeting terrorists' demands, including payment of ransom.

9. The U.S. Government adheres to the principle that a terrorist should be prosecuted for criminally defined acts of terrorism within the country of commission or be extradited to a country having appropriate jurisdiction to try the offender.

10. While political motivations such as the achievement of self-determination or independence are cited by some individuals or groups to justify terrorism, the U.S. rejects terrorism in any circumstances. Political objectives should be addressed in appropriate forums rather than by resort to violence against innocent bystanders.

11. The U.S. Government seeks the reduction or elimination of the causes of terrorism at home and abroad, including legitimate grievances which might motivate potential terrorists.

For Terrorism Involving Americans Abroad

1. The U.S. Government is concerned with the security of American citizens no matter where they may be, even though primary legal responsibility for their protection rests with the country in which they are located. The U.S. Government, as employer, has an additional protective responsibility for its employees caught in terrorist situations. If terrorists seize Americans abroad, our Government reminds the host government of its primary responsibility to cope with such terrorists and to effect the safe release of the American hostages, whether they enjoy diplomatic status or otherwise. Early agreement is sought with the host government on that objective: the safe return of the hostages by whatever means may be appropriate and if possible without providing an incentive for future terrorism.

2. The U.S. Government establishes close contact with the host government and supports it with appropriate resources to help achieve that objective. We look to the host government to conduct negotiations with the terrorists but reserve the right to counsel that government on all aspects of the rescue operation. If demands are made on the U.S. Government, it will normally respond through the negotiating host government.

3. Should the matter of a monetary ransom arise, the U.S. Government would make known to the host government that, as a matter of

policy, it does not pay such money.   While we believe that other governments, companies, and individuals should follow suit, the U.S. Government has no legal means to restrain such parties if they choose to do otherwise.

4. The wishes and rights of the hostage's family or employer are borne in mind by the U.S. Government, which seeks to harmonize them with those of the host government within the context of established policy considerations.

5. During and following an incident, the U.S. Government uses every appropriate influence to induce governments to adhere to the principle of arrest or extradition of terrorists.   The full resources of our Government are used to pursue such terrorists and to see that they are brought to justice. . . .

6. The U.S. Government seeks to identify the causes of international terrorism and to remove them.   When such causes are within the domain of other governments, our influence is restrained by the principle of non-interference in the internal affairs of another country, and by other interests which the U.S. Government may be obliged to protect in those countries. . . .

7. The U.S. Government wishes to share its counterterrorism techniques with other governments.   It also seeks, for antiterrorist and other reasons, to encourage the development of societies striving for social-political-economic justice, thereby reducing legitimate grievances and the potential for terrorism.

Special Assistant to the Secretary of State and Coordinator for Combatting Terrorism, statement, Subcommittee of Senate Committee on the Judiciary, May 14, 1975; *Digest of United States Practice in International Law,* 1975, pp. 195-97.   For commentary on United States refusal to negotiate with terrorists and Secretary of State Kissinger's condemnation of terrorism, see *Digest,* 1976, pp. 155-56, and on the protection of diplomats, pp. 184-86.

324   NEED TO DENY TERRORISTS A SAFE HAVEN

Nations already have the legal obligation, recognized by unanimous resolution of the U.N. General Assembly, "to refrain from organizing, instigating, assisting, participating [or] acquiescing in" terrorist acts. Treaties have been concluded to combat hijacking, sabotage of aircraft, and attacks on diplomats.   The majority of states observe these rules; a minority do not. . . .

The United States is convinced that stronger international steps must be taken--and urgently--to deny skyjackers and terrorists a safe haven and to establish sanctions against states which aid them, harbor them, or fail to prosecute or extradite them. . . .

Terrorism, like piracy, must be seen as outside the law.   It discredits any political objective that it purports to serve and any nations which encourage it.   If all nations deny terrorists a safe haven, terrorist practices will be substantially reduced. . . .   All governments have a duty to defend civilized life by supporting such measures.

Henry Kissinger, address, annual convention, American Bar Association, August 11, 1975; *Digest of United States Practice in International Law,* 1975, pp. 197-98. Also see his comments, pp. 198-99.

325   UNITED STATES ANTITERRORISM PROGRAM, 1978

First, we have made clear to all that we will reject terrorist blackmail. We have clearly and repeatedly stated our intention to reject demands for ransom or for the release of prisoners.

Second, . . . we have strengthened airport security within the United States. . . .

Third, we have improved safety measures to protect U.S. officials and property abroad. We have provided protective armor for official vehicles and mandated security training for all personnel posted overseas. . . .

Fourth, . . . we have been working to upgrade the international standards for airport security. The primary focus of this effort is to require mandatory preflight inspection of all passengers and accompanying baggage.

Fifth, we have intensified our efforts to move other countries to ratify the Tokyo, Hague, and Montreal Conventions [see treaty texts in next section of this chapter, Documents 329-331]. . . .

Sixth, we have developed, and are improving, procedures for cooperating and exchanging information among law enforcement agencies around the world. . . .

Seventh, we have made major organizational changes within the executive branch that are designed to improve our ability to combat terrorism. . . .

Eighth, cooperation on antiterrorism has become an important part of our bilateral relations with other nations. We are urging other governments to take appropriate steps to combat terrorism and bring terrorists to justice.

Obstacles to effective cooperation among governments remain. Some governments, sympathetic to the asserted cause of particular terrorist organizations, not only provide safe haven but also arm, train, and provide cover. Others shy away from resolute action to avoid jeopardizing relations with countries that support terrorist organizations; still others prefer to avoid the apprehension or prosecution of terrorists for fear of new terrorist attacks aimed at freeing comrades. We will continue to press these governments to assume the full measure of their international responsibilities.

Cyrus Vance, testimony, Senate Governmental Affairs Committee, January 23, 1978; *Digest of United States Practice in International Law,* 1978, pp. 489-91. Secretary Vance also discussed the application of sanctions against terrorists.

326   FEAR OF ULTIMATE THREAT OF NUCLEAR ARMED TERRORISTS

> . . . one of the blights on this world is the threat and the activities of terrorists. . . .

> Ultimately, the most serious terrorist threat is if one of those radical nations, who believe in terrorism as a policy, should have atomic weapons. . . .

> This ultimate terrorist threat is the most fearsome of all, and it's part of a pattern where our country must stand firm to control terrorism of all kinds.

Jimmy Carter, remarks during presidential campaign debate, October 28, 1980; *Papers of Presidents: Carter,* 1980-1981, III, 2486-87.

327   ANALYSIS OF TERRORISM PHENOMENON, 1984

> We have learned that terrorism is, above all, a form of political violence.   It is neither random nor without purpose.   Today, we are confronted with a wide assortment of terrorist groups which, alone or in concert, orchestrate acts of violence to achieve distinctly political ends. Their stated objectives may range from separatist causes to revenge for ethnic grievances to social and political revolution. Their methods may be just as diverse: from planting homemade explosives in public places to suicide car bombings to kidnapings and political assassinations.   But the overarching goal of all terrorists is the same: they are trying to impose their will by force--a special kind of force designed to create an atmosphere of fear. The horrors they inflict are not simply a new manifestation of traditional social conflict; they are depraved opponents of civilization itself, aided by the technology of modern weaponry. The terrorists want people to feel helpless and defenseless; they want people to lose faith in their government's capacity to protect them and thereby to undermine the legitimacy of the government itself, or its policies, or both.

> The terrorists profit from the anarchy caused by their violence. They succeed when governments change their policies out of intimidation. But the terrorist can even be satisfied if a government responds to terror by clamping down on individual rights and freedoms. Governments that overreact, even in self-defense, may only undermine their own legitimacy, as they unwittingly serve the terrorists' goals.   The terrorist succeeds if a government responds to violence with repressive, polarizing behavior that alienates the government from the people.

> We must understand, however, that terrorism, wherever it takes place, is directed in an important sense against us, the democracies-- against our most basic values and often our fundamental strategic interests.   Because terrorism relies on brutal violence as its only tool, it will always be the enemy of democracy.   For democracy rejects the indiscriminate or improper use of force and relies instead on the peaceful settlement of disputes through legitimate political processes. . . .

It is not a coincidence that most acts of terrorism occur in areas of importance to the West. . . . Terrorism in this context is not just criminal activity but an unbridled form of warfare. . . .

The stakes in our war against terrorism, therefore, are high. We have already seen the horrible cost in innocent lives that terrorist violence has incurred. But perhaps even more horrible is the damage that terrorism threatens to wreak on our modern civilization. . . .

The magnitude of the threat posed by terrorism is so great that we cannot afford to confront it with half-hearted and poorly organized measures. Terrorism is a contagious disease that will inevitably spread if it goes untreated. We need a strategy to cope with terrorism in all of its varied manifestations. We need to summon the necessary resources and determination to fight it and, with international cooperation, eventually stamp it out. And we have to recognize that the burden falls on us, the democracies--no one else will cure the disease for us. . . .

And it is an unfortunate irony that the very qualities that make democracies so hateful to the terrorists--our respect for the rights and freedoms of the individual--also make us particularly vulnerable. Precisely because we maintain the most open societies, terrorists have unparalleled opportunity to strike at us. Terrorists seek to make democracies embattled and afraid, to break down democratic accountability, due process, and order; they hope we will turn toward repression or succumb to chaos.

These are the challenges we must live with. We will certainly not alter the democratic values that we so cherish in order to fight terrorism. We will have to find ways to fight back without undermining everything we stand for. . . .

The grievances that terrorists supposedly seek to redress through acts of violence may or may not be legitimate. The terrorist acts themselves, however, can never be legitimate. And legitimate causes can never justify or excuse terrorism. Terrorist means discredit their ends. . . .

. . . We must oppose terrorists no matter what banner they may fly. For terrorism in any cause is the enemy of freedom.

And we must not fall into the deadly trap of giving justification to the unacceptable acts of terrorists by acknowledging the worthy-sounding motives they may claim. . . .

While terrorism threatens many countries, the United States has a special responsibility. It is time for this country to make a broad national commitment to treat the challenge of terrorism with the sense of urgency and priority it deserves.

The essence of our response is simple to state: violence and aggression must be met by firm resistance. This principle holds true whether we are responding to full-scale military attacks or to the kinds of low-level conflicts that are more common in the modern world. . . .

But part of our problem here in the United States has been our seeming inability to understand terrorism clearly. Each successive terrorist incident has brought too much self-condemnation and dismay, accompanied by calls for a change in our policies or our principles or calls for withdrawal and retreat. We *should* be alarmed. We *should* be outraged. We *should* investigate and strive to improve. But widespread public anguish and self-condemnation only convince the terrorists that they are on the right track. It only encourages them to commit more acts of barbarism in the hope that American resolve will weaken. . . .

We have to be stronger, steadier, determined, and united in the face of the terrorist threat. We must not reward the terrorists by changing our policies or questioning our own principles or wallowing in self-flagellation or self-doubt. Instead, we should understand that terrorism is aggression and, like all aggression, must be forcefully resisted.

We must reach a consensus in this country that our responses should go beyond passive defense to consider means of active prevention, preemption, and retaliation. Our goal must be to prevent and deter future terrorist acts, and experience has taught us over the years that one of the best deterrents to terrorism is the certainty that swift and sure measures will be taken against those who engage in it. We should take steps toward carrying out such measures. There should be no moral confusion on this issue. Our aim is not to seek revenge but to put an end to violent attacks against innocent people, to make the world a safer place to live for all of us. Clearly, the democracies have a moral right, indeed a duty, to defend themselves.

A successful strategy for combating terrorism will require us to face up to some hard questions and to come up with some clear-cut answers. The questions involve our intelligence capability, the doctrine under which we would employ force, and, most important of all, our public's attitude toward this challenge. Our nation cannot summon the will to act without firm public understanding and support. . . .

The public must understand *before the fact* that there is potential for loss of life of some of our fighting men and the loss of life of some innocent people.

The public must understand *before the fact* that some will seek to cast any preemptive or retaliatory action by us in the worst light and will attempt to make our military and our policymakers--rather than the terrorists--appear to be the culprits.

The public must understand *before the fact* that occasions will come when their government must act before each and every fact is known--and the decisions cannot be tied to the opinion polls. . . .

As we fight this battle against terrorism, we must always keep in mind the values and way of life we are trying to protect. Clearly, we will not allow ourselves to descend to the level of barbarism that terrorism represents. We will not abandon our democratic traditions, our respect for individual rights, and freedom, for these are precisely what we are struggling to preserve and promote. Our values and our principles will give us the strength and the confidence to meet the great challenge posed by terrorism. If we show the courage and the will to protect our freedom and our way of life, we will prove ourselves again worthy of these blessings.

George Shultz, address, Park Avenue Synagogue, New York, October 25, 1984; *American Foreign Policy: Current Documents*, 1984, pp. 308-16. For commentary, see "George Shultz on Terrorism," *Historic Documents*, 1984, pp. 933-35. This provides one of the most comprehensive explications of the problem. For comments on CIA report on terrorism, June 15, 1981, see *Historic Documents*, 1981, pp. 461-75.

328   NEED FOR STRATEGY TO COMBAT STRATEGY OF TERRORISM

There is a temptation to see the terrorist act as simply the erratic work of a small group of fanatics. We make this mistake at great peril, for the attacks on America, her citizens, her allies, and other democratic nations in recent years do form a pattern of terrorism that has strategic implications and political goals. And only by moving our focus from the tactical to the strategic perspective, only by identifying the pattern of terror and those behind it, can we hope to put into force a strategy to deal with it. . . .

So there we have it--Iran, Libya, North Korea, Cuba, Nicaragua--continents away, tens of thousands of miles apart, but the same goals and objectives. I submit to you that the growth in terrorism in recent years results from the increasing involvement of these states in terrorism in every region of the world. This is terrorism that is part of a pattern, the work of a confederation of terrorist states. Most of the terrorists who are kidnapping and murdering American citizens and attacking American installations are being trained, financed, and directly or indirectly controlled by a core group of radical and totalitarian governments--a new, international version of "Murder, Incorporated." And all of these states are united by one, simple, criminal phenomenon--their fanatical hatred of the United States, our people, our way of life, our international stature.

And the strategic purpose behind the terrorism sponsored by these outlaw states is clear: to disorient the United States, to disrupt or alter our foreign policy, to sow discord between ourselves and our allies, to frighten friendly Third World nations working with us for peaceful settlements of regional conflicts, and finally, to remove American influence from those areas of the world where we're working to bring stable and democratic government. In short, to cause us to retreat, retrench, to become "Fortress America." Yes, their real goal is to expel America from the world.

And that is the reason these terrorist nations are arming, training, and supporting attacks against this nation. And that is why we can be clear on one point: These terrorist states are now engaged in acts of war against the government and people of the United States. And under international law, any state which is the victim of acts of war has the right to defend itself. . . .

So the American people are not--I repeat, not--going to tolerate intimidation, terror and outright acts of war against this nation and its people. And we're especially not going to tolerate these attacks from outlaw states run by the strangest collection of misfits, looney tunes and squalid criminals--since the advent of the Third Reich. . . .

Now, much needs to be done by all of us in the community of civilized nations. We must act against the criminal menace of terrorism with the full weight of the law--both domestic and international. We will act to indict, apprehend and prosecute those who commit the kind of atrocities the world has witnessed in recent weeks.

We can act together as free peoples who wish not to see our citizens kidnapped, or shot, or blown out of the skies--just as we acted together to rid the seas of piracy at the turn of the last century. And incidentally, those of you who are legal scholars will note the law's description of pirates--"hostis humanis"--"the enemies of all mankind." There can be no place on Earth left where it is safe for these monsters to rest, or train, or practice their cruel and deadly skills. We must act together, or unilaterally, if necessary, to ensure that terrorists have no sanctuary anywhere. . . .

For those countries which sponsor such acts or fail to take action against terrorist criminals, the civilized world needs to ensure that their nonfeasance and malfeasance are answered with actions that demonstrate our unified resolve that this kind of activity must cease. . . .

Ronald Reagan, address, annual convention, American Bar Association, July 8, 1985; *Papers of Presidents: Reagan*, 1985, pp. 894-900. For commentary, see "Reagan on International Terrorism," *Historic Documents*, 1985, pp. 463-77 President Reagan also discusses the escalation of worldwide terrorism and United States retaliation. Also see Robert Oakley, Director, Office for Combating Terrorism, Department of State, address, Conference on Terrorism, February 13, 1986, who discusses trends and developments, practical problems of dealing with terrorism, and the need for greater international cooperation, 86 *Department of State Bulletin* (August 1986): 9-12; and the commentaries of L. Paul Bremer and others in the issues of the *Department of State Bulletin,* 1987 and subsequently.

ENACTMENTS, DECLARATIONS, AND TREATIES

The United States pursued three general courses of action to cope with international terrorism--the enactment of national legislation, the issuance of joint policy declarations with cooperating foreign governments, and the negotiation of multipartite and bipartite treaties.

During the 1970's Congress enacted a number of landmark laws, Including an Anti-Hijacking Act (1974)--P.L. 93-366; 88 *Statutes at Large* 409-19--which specifies legal rules for the seizure of hijackers of aircraft and airport transportation security measures; and an Act to Prevent and Punish Acts of Terror Against Persons of International Significance (1976)--P.L. 94-467; 90 *Statutes at Large* 1997-2001--which provides for legal prescriptions, trial, and punishment of those who kill, or attempt to kill, foreign government leaders and diplomats, and for their protection by the United States.

On April 26, 1984, President Reagan requested Congress to pass additional legislation to deal with the prevention and punishment of hostage-taking, aircraft sabotage, rewards for revealing information concerning terrorist acts, and prohibitions against the training and support of terrorist organizations (see *Papers of Presidents: Reagan,* 1984, I, 575-77).   In the 1980's Congress passed an Act for the Prevention and Punishment of the Crime of Hostage-Taking (1984)--P.L. 98-473; 98 *Statutes at Large* 2186--which added hostage-taking to kidnaping in American criminal law; an Aircraft Sabotage Act (1984)--P.L. 98-473; 98 *Statutes at Large* 2187--an Act to Combat International Terrorism (1984)--P.L. 98-533; 98 *Statutes at Large* 2706-11--which provides rewards for information concerning terrorist acts, for strengthening the security of American missions abroad, and for the promotion of cooperation with other nations to counter terrorism; an International Security and Development Cooperation Act (1985)--P.L. 99-83; 99 *Statutes at Large* 190-283--which, in Title V, deals with terrorism and airport security, including prohibitions on assistance to, and imports from, countries that support terrorism, and with state-sponsored terrorism, foreign airport security standards, and the American air marshal program; and an Omnibus Diplomatic Security and Antiterrorism Act (1986)--P.L. 99-399; 100 *Statutes at Large* 855-901--which enhances authority and organization to improve the security of American officials and other citizens and property and to provide assistance to victims of terrorists.

Cooperating with other nations, in addition to the voting of United Nations resolutions, such as that on hijacking in 1977 (for text, see *Digest of United States Practice in International Law,* 1978, p. 492), special effort was made to create policy consensus with Allies to war against terrorism.   This is illustrated by the joint declarations of the North Atlantic Treaty Organization at its meetings in 1980, for example, and the economic summit meetings of the leaders of the Western industrial powers at Bonn (1978), Venice (1980), Ottawa (1981), London (1984), Tokyo (1986), and Toronto (1988)--for texts, see *Papers of Presidents: Carter,* 1978, II, 1308-9 and 1980-1981, II, 1171-72; and *Papers of Presidents: Reagan,* 1981, 637, 1984, I, 834, 1986, I, 557-58, and 1988 in 88 *Department of State Bulletin* (August 1988): 47-58.   Among other things, these declarations condemn hijacking, hostage-taking, and other forms of terrorism and its perpetrators and their supporting governments, pledge the Western governments to make maximum efforts to fight this scourge, promise increased collective cooperation in providing mutual exchanges of information, and specify a number of sanctions to be applied against governments that aid terrorists.

Of greater international significance in committing foreign governments to anti-terrorist action are the formal multipartite conventions that have been signed. These, negotiated through the auspices of the United Nations and presented chronologically, pertain to skyjacking and aircraft sabotage (Documents 329-331); the prevention of and punishment for crimes against diplomats and other persons of international significance (Document 332); and the taking of hostages (Document 333). In addition, the United States joined Latin American countries, through the Organization of American States, in negotiating a Convention to Prevent and Punish Acts of Terrorism Taking the

Form of Crimes Against Persons and Related Extortion That Are of International Significance, signed by the United States and half a dozen Latin American governments on February 2, 1971 (see TIAS 8413; 27 *U.S. Treaties* 3949-77). It is worthy of note that virtually all of the governments that allegedly provide training and other support for terrorists, except for Cuba, are signatories of these multipartite conventions seeking to eliminate international terrorism.

Paralleling these conventions, since 1960 the United States also negotiated a series of bilateral antiterrorism treaties and agreements. These include a Memorandum of Understanding on Hijacking of Aircraft and Vessels and Other Offenses, signed with Cuba on February 15, 1973, providing for the return of such aircraft and the hijackers for trial (see TIAS 7579; 24 *U.S. Treaties* 737-49), as well as some thirty new, amended, or supplementary extradition treaties. The latter were signed primarily with European and Latin American countries, but also with Israel, Japan, and several friendly Pacific states. Many of these treaties cover terrorists, but the difficulty with having them extradited is that they claim and may be granted political asylum in the countries of refuge.

Despite the desire of the United States to subject terrorism to rigorous national and international controls, no general treaty has been concluded that creates a universal and reliable obligation on the community of nations to capture, try or extradite, convict, and punish many terrorists. A host of acts of terrorism, consequently, still slip through the treaty network.

3.2.9 CONVENTION ON OFFENCES AND CERTAIN OTHER ACTS COMMITTED ON BOARD AIRCRAFT, 1963 (TOKYO CONVENTION)

Article 1

1. This Convention shall apply in respect of:
    a) offences against penal law;
    b) acts which, whether or not they are offences, may or do jeopardize the safety of the aircraft or of persons or property therein or which jeopardize good order and discipline on board.
2. . . . this Convention shall apply in respect of offences committed or acts done by a person on board any aircraft registered in a Contracting State, while that aircraft is in flight. . . .
3. For the purpose of this Convention, an aircraft is considered to be in flight from the moment when power is applied for the purpose of take-off until the moment when the landing run ends. . . .

Article 3

1. The State of registration of the aircraft is competent to exercise jurisdiction over offences and acts committed on board.
2. Each Contracting State shall take such measures as may be necessary to establish its jurisdiction as the State of registration over offences committed on board aircraft registered in such State. . . .

Article 4

A Contracting State which is not the State of registration may not interfere with an aircraft in flight in order to exercise its criminal jurisdiction over an offence committed on board except in the following cases:

   a) the offence has effect on the territory of such State;
   b) the offence has been committed by or against a national or permanent resident of such State;
   c) the offence is against the security of such State;
   d) the offence consists of a breach of any rules or regulations relating to the flight or manoeuvre of aircraft in force in such State;
   e) the exercise of jurisdiction is necessary to ensure the observance of any obligation of such State under a multilateral international agreement. . . .

Article 11

1. When a person on board has unlawfully committed by force or threat thereof an act of interference, seizure, or other wrongful exercise of control of an aircraft in flight or when such an act is about to be committed, Contracting States shall take all appropriate measures to restore control of the aircraft to its lawful commander or to preserve his control of the aircraft.

2. In the cases contemplated in the preceding paragraph, the Contracting State in which the aircraft lands shall permit its passengers and crew to continue their journey as soon as practicable, and shall return the aircraft and its cargo to the persons lawfully entitled to possession. . . .

Article 16

1. Offences committed on aircraft registered in a Contracting State shall be treated, for the purpose of extradition, as if they had been committed not only in the place in which they have occurred but also in the territory of the State of registration of the aircraft.

2. Without prejudice to the provisions of the preceding paragraph, nothing in this Convention shall be deemed to create an obligation to grant extradition.

Signed September 14, 1963; 26 articles. TIAS 6768; 20 *U.S. Treaties* 2942-58. This treaty also contains stipulations concerning jurisdiction, the authority of aircraft commanders, and the powers and duties of states.

330 CONVENTION ON SUPPRESSION OF UNLAWFUL SEIZURE OF AIRCRAFT (HIJACKING), 1970 (HAGUE CONVENTION)

Article 1

Any person who on board an aircraft in flight:
(a) unlawfully, by force or threat thereof, or by any other form of intimidation, seizes, or exercises control of, that aircraft, or

attempts to perform any such act, or

(b) is an accomplice of a person who performs or attempts to perform any such act

commits an offence (hereinafter referred to as "the offence").

Article 2

Each Contracting State undertakes to make the offence punishable by severe penalties.

Article 3

1. For the purposes of this Convention, an aircraft is considered to be in flight at any time from the moment when all its external doors are closed following embarkation until the moment when any such door is opened for disembarkation. In the case of a forced landing, the flight shall be deemed to continue until the competent authorities take over the responsibility for the aircraft and for persons and property on board. . . .

Article 4

1. Each Contracting State shall take such measures as may be necessary to establish its jurisdiction over the offence and any other act of violence against passengers or crew committed by the alleged offender in connection with the offence, in the following cases:

(a) when the offence is committed on board an aircraft registered in that State;

(b) when the aircraft on board which the offence is committed lands in its territory with the alleged offender still on board;

(c) when the offence is committed on board an aircraft leased without crew to a lessee who has his principal place of business or, if the lessee has no such place of business, his permanent residence, in that State.

2. Each Contracting State shall likewise take such measures as may be necessary to establish its jurisdiction over the offence in the case where the alleged offender is present in its territory and it does not extradite him. . . .

Article 7

The Contracting State in the territory of which the alleged offender is found shall, if it does not extradite him, be obliged, without exception whatsoever and whether or not the offence was committed in its territory, to submit the case to its competent authorities for the purpose of prosecution. Those authorities shall take their decision in the same manner as in the case of any ordinary offence of a serious nature under the law of that State.

Article 8

1. The offence shall be deemed to be included as an extraditable offence in any extradition treaty existing between Contracting States. Contracting States undertake to include the offence as an extraditable offence in every extradition treaty to be concluded between them. . . .

Article 9

1. When any of the acts mentioned in Article 1(a) has occurred or is about to occur, Contracting States shall take all appropriate measures to restore control of the aircraft to its lawful commander or to preserve his control of the aircraft.

2. In the cases contemplated by the preceding paragraph, any Contracting State in which the aircraft or its passengers or crew are present shall facilitate the continuation of the journey of the passengers and crew as soon as practicable, and shall without delay return the aircraft and its cargo to the persons lawfully entitled to possession.

Signed December 16, 1970; 14 articles.   TIAS 7192; 22 *U.S. Treaties* 1641-84.   This treaty also provides for the settlement of disputes concerning its interpretation.

331 CONVENTION ON THE SUPPRESSION OF UNLAWFUL ACTS AGAINST THE SAFETY OF CIVIL AVIATION (SABOTAGE), 1971 (MONTREAL CONVENTION)

Article 1

1. Any person commits an offence if he unlawfully and intentionally:

(a) performs an act of violence against a person on board an aircraft in flight if that act is likely to endanger the safety of that aircraft; or

(b) destroys an aircraft in service or causes damage to such an aircraft which renders it incapable of flight or which is likely to endanger its safety in flight; or

(c) places or causes to be placed on an aircraft in service, by any means whatsoever, a device or substance which is likely to destroy that aircraft, or to cause damage to it which renders it incapable of flight, or to cause damage to it which is likely to endanger its safety in flight; or

(d) destroys or damages air navigation facilities or interferes with their operation, if any such act is likely to endanger the safety of aircraft in flight; or

(e) communicates information which he knows to be false, thereby endangering the safety of an aircraft in flight.

2. Any person also commits an offence if he:

(a) attempts to commit any of the offences mentioned in paragraph 1 of this Article; or

(b) is an accomplice of a person who commits or attempts to commit any such offence.

Article 2

For the purposes of this Convention:

(a) an aircraft is considered to be in flight at any time from the moment when all its external doors are closed following embarkation until the moment when any such door is opened for disembarkation; in the case of a forced landing, the flight shall be deemed to continue until the competent authorities take over the responsibility for the aircraft and for persons and property on board;

(b) an aircraft is considered to be in service from the beginning of the preflight preparation of the aircraft by ground personnel or by the crew for a specific flight until twenty-four hours after any landing; the period of service shall, in any event, extend for the entire period during which the aircraft is in flight as defined in paragraph (a) of this Article.

Article 3

Each Contracting State undertakes to make the offences mentioned in Article 1 punishable by severe penalties. . . .

Article 6

1. Upon being satisfied that the circumstances so warrant, any Contracting State in the territory of which the offender or the alleged offender is present, shall take him into custody or take other measures to ensure his presence. The custody and other measures shall be as provided in the law of that State but may only be continued for such time as is necessary to enable any criminal or extradition proceedings to be instituted. . . .

Article 7

The Contracting State in the territory of which the alleged offender is found shall, if it does not extradite him, be obliged, without exception whatsoever and whether or not the offence was committed in its territory, to submit the case to its competent authorities for the purpose of prosecution. . . .

Article 8

1. The offences shall be deemed to be included as extraditable offences in any extradition treaty existing between Contracting States. Contracting States undertake to include the offences as extraditable offences in every extradition treaty to be concluded between them. . . .

Signed September 23, 1971; 16 articles. TIAS 7570; 24 *U.S. Treaties* 565-602.

332 CONVENTION ON THE PREVENTION AND PUNISHMENT OF CRIMES AGAINST INTERNATIONALLY PROTECTED PERSONS, INCLUDING DIPLOMATIC AGENTS, 1973

Article 1

For the purposes of this Convention:

1. "internationally protected person" means:

(a) a Head of State, including any member of a collegial body performing the functions of a Head of State under the constitution of the State concerned, a Head of Government or a Minister for Foreign Affairs, whenever any such person is in a foreign State, as well as members of his family who accompany him;

(b) any representative or official of a State or any official or other agent of an international organization of an intergovernmental character who, at the time when and in the place where a crime against him, his official premises, his private accommodation or his means of transport is committed, is entitled pursuant to international law to special protection from any attack on his person, freedom or dignity, as well as members of his family forming part of his household.

2. "alleged offender" means a person as to whom there is sufficient evidence to determine *prima facie* that he has committed or participated in one or more of the crimes set forth in article 2.

Article 2

1. The intentional commission of:

(a) a murder, kidnapping or other attack upon the person or liberty of an internationally protected person;

(b) a violent attack upon the official premises, the private accommodation or the means of transport of an internationally protected person likely to endanger his person or liberty;

(c) a threat to commit any such attack;

(d) an attempt to commit any such attack; and

(e) an act constituting participation as an accomplice in any such attack shall be made by each State Party a crime under its internal law.

2. Each State Party shall make these crimes punishable by appropriate penalties which take into account their grave nature.

3. Paragraphs 1 and 2 of this article in no way derogate from the obligations of States Parties under international law to take all appropriate measures to prevent other attacks on the person, freedom or dignity of an internationally protected person.

Article 3

1. Each State Party shall take such measures as may be necessary to establish its jurisdiction over the crimes set forth in article 2 in the following cases:

(a) when the crime is committed in the territory of that State or on board a ship or aircraft registered in that State;

(b) when the alleged offender is a national of that State;

(c) when the crime is committed against an internationally protected person as defined in article 1 who enjoys his status as such by virtue of functions which he exercises on behalf of that State.

2. Each State Party shall likewise take such measures as may be necessary to establish its jurisdiction over these crimes in cases where the alleged offender is present in its territory and it does not extradite him pursuant to article 8 to any of the States mentioned in paragraph 1 of this article. . . .

Article 4

States Parties shall co-operate in the prevention of the crimes set forth in article 2, particularly by:

(a) taking all practicable measures to prevent preparations in their respective territories for the commission of those crimes within or outside their territories;

(b) exchanging information and co-ordinating the taking of administrative and other measures as appropriate to prevent the commission of those crimes . . . .

Article 7

The State Party in whose territory the alleged offender is present shall, if it does not extradite him, submit, without exception whatsoever and without undue delay, the case to its competent authorities for the purpose of prosecution, through proceedings in accordance with the laws of that State.

Article 8

1. To the extent that the crimes set forth in article 2 are not listed as extraditable offenses in any extradition treaty existing between States Parties, they shall be deemed to be included as such therein. States Parties undertake to include those crimes as extraditable offences in every future extradition treaty to be concluded between them. . . .

4. Each of the crimes shall be treated, for the purpose of extradition between States Parties, as if it had been committed not only in the place in which it occurred but also in the territories of the States required to establish their jurisdiction in accordance with paragraph 1 of article 3. . . .

Signed December 28, 1973; 20 articles. TIAS 8532; 28 *U.S. Treaties* 1975-2082. This convention also provides procedures for the settlement of disputes among signatories.

333 INTERNATIONAL CONVENTION AGAINST THE TAKING OF HOSTAGES, 1979

Article 1

1. Any person who seizes or detains and threatens to kill, to injure or to continue to detain another person (hereinafter referred to as the "hostage") in order to compel a third party, namely, a State, an international intergovernmental organization, a natural or juridical person, or a group of persons, to do or abstain from doing any act as an explicit or implicit condition for the release of the hostage commits the offence of taking of hostages ("hostage taking") within the meaning of this Convention.

2. Any person who:

(a) Attempts to commit an act of hostage-taking, or

(b) Participates as an accomplice of anyone who commits or attempts to commit an act of hostage-taking likewise commits an offence for the purposes of this Convention.

Article 2

Each State Party shall make the offences set forth in article 1 punishable by appropriate penalties which take into account the grave nature of those offences.

Article 3

1. The State Party in the territory, of which the hostage is held by the offender shall take all measures it considers appropriate to ease the situation of the hostage, in particular, to secure his release and, after his release, to facilitate, when relevant, his departure.

2. If any object which the offender has obtained as a result of the taking of hostages comes into the custody of a State Party, that State Party shall return it as soon as possible to the hostage or the third party referred to in article 1, as the case may be, or to the appropriate authorities thereof.

Article 4

States Parties shall co-operate in the prevention of the offences set forth in article 1, particularly by:

(a) Taking all practicable measures to prevent preparations in their respective territories for the commission of those offences within or outside their territories, including measures to prohibit in their territories illegal activities of persons, groups and organizations that encourage, instigate, organize or engage in the perpetration of acts of taking of hostages;

(b) Exchanging information and co-ordinating the taking of administrative and other measures as appropriate to prevent the commission of those offences.

Article 5

1. Each State Party shall take such measures as may be necessary to establish its jurisdiction over any of the offences set forth in article 1 which are committed:

(a) In its territory or on board a ship or aircraft registered in that State;

(b) By any of its nationals or, if that State considers it appropriate, by those stateless persons who have their habitual residence in its territory;

(c) In order to compel that State to do or abstain from doing any act; or

(d) With respect to a hostage who is a national of that State, if that State considers it appropriate.

2. Each State Party shall likewise take such measures as may be necessary to establish its jurisdiction over the offences set forth in article 1 in cases where the alleged offender is present in its territory and it does not extradite him to any of the States mentioned in paragraph 1 of this article.

3. This Convention does not exclude any criminal jurisdiction exercised in accordance with internal law. . . .

Article 8

1. The State Party in the territory of which the alleged offender is found shall, if it does not extradite him, be obliged, without exception whatsoever and whether or not the offence was committed in its territory, to submit the case to its competent authorities for the purpose of prosecution, through proceedings in accordance with the laws of that State. . . .

Article 10

1. The offences set forth in article 1 shall be deemed to be included as extraditable offences in any extradition treaty existing between States Parties. States Parties undertake to include such offences as extraditable offences in every extradition treaty to be concluded between them. . . .

4. The offences set forth in article 1 shall be treated, for the purpose of extradition between States Parties, as if they had been committed not only in the place in which they occurred but also in the territories of the States required to establish their jurisdiction in accordance with paragraph 1 of article 5.

Signed December 21, 1979; 20 articles. *Digest of United States Practice in International Law*, 1979, pp. 538-42. Also see P.L. 98-473; 18 U.S. Code, par. 1203. For commentary, see *Digest*, 1979, pp. 535-42, and 1980, pp. 264-67; and Will D. Verwey, "The International Hostage Convention and National Liberation Movements," 75 *American Journal of International Law* (January 1981): 69-92.

20

The Seas
and Maritime Affairs

The seas are the world's oldest frontiers. As Longfellow observed,
they not only separate--but unite--mankind.

Even in the Age of Space, the sea remains our greatest
mystery. But we know that in its sunless depths, a richness is still
locked which holds vast promise for the improvement of men's lives
--in all nations.

Those ocean roads, which so often have been the path of
conquest, can now be turned to the search for enduring peace.

Lyndon Johnson
Special Message to Congress, 1968

Mankind's search for practical and acceptable rules to govern jurisdiction over,
and use of, the sea and its resources parallels the historical development of
maritime affairs. As a result, legal principles pertaining to maritime rights
and duties constitute one of the oldest branches of international law, flowing
from the customs and practices of early Egyptians, Phoenicians, Greeks, and
others. They are exemplified, for example, by the Rhodian Laws (ninth
century), Rolls of Oleron (twelfth century), and the *Consolato del Mare*
(fourteenth century).

When the United States joined the family of nations in the eighteenth
century, it became an avid exponent of the doctrine of freedom of the seas. This
was not only an expression of an American ideal. At the time it was also a
practical position for a minor naval and maritime power reacting to (1) the
doctrine of the appropriable or closed sea; illustrated by the Papal Bull (*Inter
caetera*) in 1493 which divided the Atlantic between Spain and Portugal at 100
leagues west of the Azores and Cape Verde Islands, superseded by the Treaty of
Tordesillas in the following year that moved the dividing line to 370 leagues
west of the Cape Verde Islands; (2) widespread trade and maritime restrictions
embodied in the mercantilist or closed trading system of the principal maritime
and colonial powers; (3) coping with the depradations of the Barbary pirates;
and (4) defending the maritime and trading rights of neutral states in time of
war.

Policy and law concerning the seas is an intricate subject, of concern of all riparian and, in some respects, even landlocked nations. Illustrative of its major components, in addition to the doctrine of freedom of the seas, are jurisdiction over territorial or marginal waters, as well as the continental shelf and exclusive contiguous "extraterritorial zones"; maritime boundaries respecting river mouths, seas, gulfs, and bays; jurisdiction over and overflight rights in airspace superjacent to water-covered areas; rights and control over deep seabed resource possession, extraction, and mining; navigation, shipping, and customs rights and controls; pollution; fishing and conservation of the resources of the seas; scientific research; piracy and privateering; hijacking; and national defense. Other aspects include neutral rights and duties in war-time, jurisdiction over vessels, collisions, smuggling, cable laying, and such more restricted matters as the impressment on the high seas of American seaman. For an alternative list of some thirty primary components of policy and jurisdiction, consisting of nearly one hundred subelements and a good many subsidiary constituents, see depiction in Elmer Plischke, *Foreign Relations: Analysis of Its Anatomy* (Westport: Greenwood, 1988), pp. 261-66.

Synthesizing the many topics involved in coping with the international management and legal control of the seas, Philip Allott lists approximately 175 separate items, grouped in three categories--subjects of rights and duties, legal sea areas, and legal relations; see "Power Sharing in the Law of the Sea," 77 *American Journal of International Law* (January 1983): 28-30.

The United States has played a major role in developing the contemporary law of the sea. This chapter provides documents and commentary on recent United States policy and on the post-World War II United Nations-sponsored conferences on the law of the sea and American commitments embodied in formal treaties and agreements. For related subjects, see Chapters 7 (Tonkin Gulf incident), 10 (Formosa Strait issue), 13 (attacks on American ships), 18 (alliances and ententes), 19 (international terrorism), 30 (the Suez and the Iran-Iraq Wars), 31 (Panama Canal), and 32 (polar regions).

POLICY AND DEVELOPMENTS

The United States has traditionally promoted, not only the general doctrine of freedom of the seas, but freedom from interference with navigation, transit, fishing, and utilization of marine resources--subject to sovereign control over a contiguous belt of territorial waters and, recently, international cooperation respecting the conserving of maritime resources, controlling pollution, and establishing rights and international controls over the resources of the seabed and its subsoil.

While maintaining its policy concerning freedom of the high seas, during the post-World War II years the United States took action to promote the universal adoption of multipartite treaties guaranteeing such freedom, including the rights of navigation and overflight; to regularize the status and administration of the American continental shelf and coastal fisheries; to establish international rules to govern a subjacent "economic zone"; to prohibit the emplacement of nuclear weapons on the seabed; and, despite its traditional support of the three-mile limit, to extend this to twenty miles.

The documents provided in this section are selected to illustrate both conventional policy principles and changes adopted since 1945. Arranged chronologically, they characterize policies concerned specifically with the freedom of the seas as a continuing fundamental American goal (Document 334); the unilateral extension of United States interests and jurisdiction over the continental shelf and fisheries (Document 335); explanation and defense of the United States position on basic legal and operational principles concerning the seas (Documents 336-337); proposals for some additional matters warranting negotiation and international agreement in recent decades (Documents 338-339); United States policy on the correlative rights and duties of nations, including those pertaining to the deep seabed (Documents 340-341); and the reasons for rejecting the 1982 Law of the Sea Treaty (Document 342).

Although the United States did not sign this Law of the Sea Treaty, it supports most of its principal stipulations and, in a series of actions, the government formally implemented some of them, such as those concerned with navigation and overflight, with establishing an exclusive American "economic zone" (within 200 nautical miles), and with extending the territorial sea to 12 nautical miles. For documentation and commentary on these developments, see Ronald Reagan, statement and presidential proclamation on three decisions to promote United States interests in the oceans, March 10, 1983, in *American Foreign Policy: Current Documents,* 1983, pp. 318-20; and his executive proclamation 5928, December 27, 1988, in 89 *Department of State Bulletin* (March 1989): 72. For analysis of "National Security and the Law of the Sea," see *American Foreign Policy: Current Documents,* 1977-1980, pp. 390-93.

334 FREEDOM OF THE SEAS DOCTRINE

Absolute freedom of navigation upon the seas outside territorial waters alike in peace and in war, except as the seas may be closed in whole or in part by international action or the enforcement of international covenants.

*   *   *

Seventh, such a peace should enable all men to traverse the high seas and oceans without hindrance.

*   *   *

We believe that all nations should have the freedom of the seas and equal rights to the navigation of boundary rivers and waterways and of rivers and waterways which pass through more than one country.

Respectively, stipulations by Woodrow Wilson, second of his Fourteen Points, January 8, 1918; Franklin Roosevelt, point seven of the Atlantic Charter, August 14, 1941; and Harry Truman, point seven of his Navy Day speech, October 27, 1945.

335 TRUMAN'S PROCLAMATIONS ON CONTINENTAL SHELF AND FISHERIES, 1945

The President issued two proclamations on September 28 asserting the jurisdiction of the United States over the natural resources of the continental shelf under the high seas contiguous to the coasts of the United States and its territories, and providing for the establishment of conservation zones for the protection of fisheries in certain areas of the high seas contiguous to the United States. . . .

The United States will recognize the rights of other countries to establish conservation zones off their own coasts where the interests of nationals of the United States are recognized in the same manner that we recognize the interests of the nationals of the other countries. . . .

The policy proclaimed by the President . . . is concerned solely with establishing the jurisdiction of the United States from an international standpoint. It will, however, make possible the orderly development of an underwater area 750,000 square miles in extent. Generally, submerged land which is contiguous to the continent and which is covered by no more than 100 fathoms (600 feet) of water is considered as the continental shelf. . . .

While asserting jurisdiction and control of the United States over the mineral resources of the continental shelf, the proclamation in no wise abridges the right of free and unimpeded navigation of waters of the character of high seas above the shelf, nor does it extend the present limits of the territorial waters of the United States.

White House, press release, September 28, 1945; *Foreign Relations,* 1945, II, 1528-30. For the text of the President's two proclamations and the companion executive orders to implement policy, see 10 *Federal Register* 12303-12305.

336 REPORT ON DEVELOPMENTS RESPECTING THE REGIME OF THE SEAS, 1955

The history of the law of the sea is a reflection of the changing interests of the centuries and of the influence of economics and technological developments. Most important maritime states, at one time or another, have claimed sovereignty over large areas of the seas. . . .

Such was the situation when Grotius, in 1609, published "*Mare Liberum,*" attacking on broad grounds of equity the whole principle of national dominion over the seas. Although Selden's "*Mare Clausum,*" in 1635, sought to establish that the sea was capable of appropriation and that England was sovereign in the English Sea, it did not prove to be an adequate answer to Grotius. With "*Mare Liberum*" the modern doctrine of the freedom of the seas had been born. During the early 18th century it was to become established law, and by the 19th century it was axiomatic.

Freedom of the seas as a principle of international law means that the open sea is not, and cannot be, under the sovereignty of any state. It signifies that in time of peace vessels may not be interfered with on the high seas. To this principle there are certain limited exceptions. Thus, it has long been recognized that a state may suppress piracy. It may seize a vessel flying its flag without authority. The right of hot pursuit is accepted. The enforcement, on the part of coastal states, of revenue and sanitary laws is recognized. Finally, in this modern age, the right of a state, for defense or security purposes, to take preventive measures on the high seas is in process of development.

It is the traditional policy of the United States to support the principle of freedom of the seas. Early in its history its refusal to compromise that principle was one of the causes leading to the War of 1812. The effective defense of the United States, the maintenance of its commercial shipping and air transport, and the prosperity of its fishing industry would all be prejudiced by any serious compromise of this principle.

The appropriation by any state of areas of the high seas is as unsound morally today as when Grotius wrote. In an age when technological advancement and increased population have made us indeed one world, it is more important than ever that those natural avenues of intercourse between peoples--the sea lanes and the air routes above--should remain free.

Consistent with its support of the principle of the freedom of the seas, the United States has always adhered to the 3-mile rule. From the time of Jefferson, the principle that the marginal belt extends one marine league (3 geographical or nautical miles) from the low-water mark has been supported by the State Department, by court decisions, and by treaties. . . .

The tendency of states to advance claims to territorial waters in excess of 3 miles has been particularly marked following the failure of the Codification Conference in 1930 at The Hague to agree on a convention on territorial waters. However, states still adhering to the 3-mile rule represent about 80 percent of the merchant shipping tonnage of the world and most of its naval power. . . .

On September 28, 1945, President Truman issued his proclamation on fisheries for the purpose of "improving the jurisdictional basis for conservation measures and international cooperation in this field." This declares the policy of the United States on the establishment of fishery conservation zones in the high seas contiguous to its coasts. Where such fishing activities are maintained by United States nationals alone, it regards it as proper that regulation be exercised by the United States exclusively. But where the fishing activities have been legitimately developed and maintained jointly by nationals of the United States and nationals of other states, conservation zones may be established by agreement between the United States and such other states. . . .

On September 28, 1945, the same date as his proclamation on fisheries, President Truman issued another proclamation which is also important in any consideration of this subject. This is the proclamation on the Continental Shelf.

It sets forth the view of the United States that the exercise of jurisdiction over the natural resources of the subsoil and seabed of the Continental Shelf by the contiguous nation is reasonable and just for the following reasons:

1. The effectiveness of measures to use or conserve these resources would be contingent upon cooperation and protection from the shore;

2. The Continental Shelf may be regarded as an extension of the land mass of the coastal nation and thus naturally appurtenant to it;

3. The resources under the shelf frequently form a seaward extension of a pool or deposit lying within the territorial limits; and

4. Self-protection compels a coastal nation to keep close watch over the activities off its shores which are necessary for utilization of these resources, . . .

The proclamation declares that the United States regards the natural resources of the subsoil and seabed of the Continental Shelf as appertaining to the United States and subject to its jurisdiction and control. Where the shelf extends to the shore of another state, the boundary is to be determined by the interested parties on equitable principles. Finally, the proclamation declares, "The character as high seas of the waters above the continental shelf and the right to their free and unimpeded navigation are in no way thus affected.". . .

It is submitted that the doctrine of the Continental Shelf is in no way inconsistent with the principle of the freedom of the seas. The 1945 proclamations . . . make perfectly clear that the claims of the United States in the shelf are not intended to modify in any way the freedom of the superjacent waters.

Legal Adviser, Department of State, address, International Law Association, New York, May 13, 1955; *American Foreign Policy: Basic Documents,* 1950-1955, II, 1346-56. He also discusses the history of the law of the sea, attacks on the freedom of the sea doctrine, conservation of fishery resources, and erroneous application of the continental shelf doctrine.

337 ARGUMENT FOR FREEDOM OF SEAS AND RESTRICTING TERRITORIAL WATERS, 1956

. . . In this day of improved methods of transportation and communication, which have served to bring nations ever closer together, it is vitally important that the international highways of the sea and of the superjacent air should not be brought under the domination or control of national states. Any proposals which would result in restricting the freedom of the seas would not be progress but rather a retrogression to those past eras when the high seas were under the domination of national states. We sincerely believe that the doctrine of the freedom of the seas, in its widest implications, is the principle fairest to all, large and small.

Any purported widening of the territorial sea will to that extent impinge upon the freedom of the seas. . . .

In defense of extreme claims to territorial seas, it has been stated that their objective is only the control of natural resources of such seas and that freedom of navigation will not thereby be interfered with, since under international law foreign vessels have a right of innocent passage through the territorial sea. It will be evident at once that there is quite a difference between freedom of navigation on the high seas and the right of innocent passage through the territorial sea. Once a ship leaves the high seas and enters the territorial sea of another state the exclusive jurisdiction of its own state ceases and it becomes subject to the laws and regulations of the sovereign of the territorial sea. . . .

United States representative, United Nations General Assembly Committee, statement, December 14, 1956; *American Foreign Policy: Current Documents,* 1957, pp. 270-71. For earlier statement concerning the three-mile limit, considered at the 1930 Hague Conference to codify international law, see Green H. Hackworth, *Digest of International Law,* I, 628-29, 634; also see statement of United States delegate to United Nations Conference on Law of the Sea, March 11, 1958, in *American Foreign Policy: Current Documents,* 1958, p. 257.

338 PRESIDENT JOHNSON'S PROPOSALS ON OCEAN DEPTHS AND SEABED, 1966-1968

. . . under no circumstances, we believe, must we ever allow the prospects of rich harvests and mineral wealth to create a new form of colonial competition among the maritime nations. We must be careful to avoid a race to grab and to hold the lands under the high seas. We must ensure that the deep seas and the ocean bottoms are, and remain, the legacy of all human beings.

*   *   *

This year I shall propose:
   -- That we launch, with other nations, an exploration of the ocean depths to tap its wealth, and its energy, and its abundance.

*   *   *

We must soon take up the question of arms limitations on the seabed in the light of the consideration being given by the General Assembly's Ad Hoc Committee on the Seabeds to a number of proposals for arms limitations on the seabed. Your conference should begin to define those factors vital to a workable, verifiable, and effective international agreement which would prevent the use of this new environment for the emplacement of weapons of mass destruction.

Lyndon Johnson, remarks, July 13, 1966, State of the Union Message, January 17, 1968, and message to eighteen-nation Disarmament Committee at Geneva, July 16, 1968; *Papers of Presidents: Johnson,* 1966, II, 724; and 1968, pp. 27 and 816.

339   PRESIDENT NIXON'S PROPOSAL FOR THE SEABED AND TERRITORIAL WATERS, 1970

On May 23, 1970, . . . President Nixon proposed that nations of the world adopt a major new treaty to provide for the rational and equitable use of one of the last unregulated areas of the planet--the seabeds--for the benefit of mankind. He proposed that nations renounce all claims to seabed resources beyond the point where the high seas reach a depth of 200 meters, and that they regard such resources as the common heritage of mankind.

Exploration and exploitation of seabed resources beyond 200 meters would be governed by internationally agreed rules. In an area beginning with the 200-meter depth and embracing the continental margins as precisely defined, a "trusteeship zone" would be created in which exploration and exploitation would be licensed by coastal states as trustees for the international community. Agreed international machinery would directly license such activities beyond the trusteeship zones.

In recognition of the desirability that technologically less advanced nations should benefit from such a system, the regime would provide for the collection of substantial revenues to be used for international community purposes, particularly for economic assistance to developing countries. Finally, the President proposed that permits for exploration and exploitation beyond 200 meters issued prior to the completion of the negotiations be subject to international rules to be agreed upon.

In another major departure, the President announced the intention of the United States to seek an international agreement fixing the maximum extent of the territorial sea at 12 nautical miles, assuring freedom of transit through and over international straits, and providing for defined preferential rights for coastal states regarding conservation and use of the living resources of the high seas adjacent to their coasts.

United States Foreign Policy, 1969-1970: A Report of the Secretary of State, pp. 251-53. Also see these annual reports for 1971, pp. 304-7, and 1972, pp. 131-34.   For President Nixon's declaration of May 23, see *Papers of Presidents: Nixon,* 1970, pp. 454-56.

340   UNITED STATES OCEANS POLICY--RIGHTS AND DUTIES, 1974

. . . Most delegations that have spoken have endorsed or indicated a willingness to accept, under certain conditions and as part of a package settlement, a maximum limit of 12 miles for the territorial sea and of 200 miles for an economic zone, and an international regime for the deep seabed in the area beyond national jurisdiction.

The United States has for a number of years indicated our flexibility on the limits of coastal state resources jurisdiction. . . . Accordingly, we are prepared to accept, and indeed we would welcome general agreement on a 12-mile outer limit for the territorial sea and a 200-mile outer limit for the economic zone provided it is part of an acceptable comprehensive package, including a satisfactory regime within and beyond the economic zone and provision for unimpeded transit of straits used for international navigation. . . .

Our willingness and that of many other delegations to accept a 200-mile outer limit for the economic zone depends on the concurrent negotiation and acceptance of correlative coastal state duties.

The coastal state rights we contemplate comprise fully regulatory jurisdiction over exploration and exploitation of seabed resources, non-resource drilling, fishing for coastal and anadromous species, and installations constructed for economic purposes.

The rights of other states include freedom of navigation, overflight, and other non-resource uses. . . .

Just as coastal state rights within the zone must, if we are to reach agreement, be balanced by duties, the international authority's jurisdiction over the exploitation of the deep seabed's resources--the common heritage of mankind--must be balanced by duties that protect the rights of individual states and their nationals--most critically in our view their right to nondiscriminatory access under reasonable conditions to the seabed's resources on a basis that provides for the sharing of the benefits of their exploitation with other states.

United States special representative, Law of the Sea Conference, statement, July 11, 1974; *Digest of United States Practice in International Law,* 1974, pp. 279-82. He also recommended compulsory dispute settlement.

3 4 1   UNITED STATES DEEP SEABED POLICY, 1975

Beyond the territorial sea, the offshore economic zone, and the continental margin lie the deep seabeds. They are our planet's last great unexplored frontier. For more than a century we have known that the deep seabeds hold vast deposits of manganese, nickel, cobalt, copper, and other minerals, but we did not know how to extract them. New modern technology is rapidly advancing the time when their exploration and commercial exploitation will become a reality. . . .

We believe that the Law of the Sea treaty must preserve the right of access presently enjoyed by states and their citizens under international law. Restrictions on free access will retard the development of seabed resources. Nor is it feasible, . . . to reserve to a new international seabed organization the sole right to exploit the seabeds.

Nevertheless, the United States believes strongly that law must regulate international activity in this area. The world community has an historic opportunity to manage this new wealth cooperatively and to dedicate resources from the exploitation of the deep seabeds to the development of the poorer countries. . . . The legal regime we establish for the deep seabeds can be a milestone in the legal and political development of the world community.

The United States has devoted much thought and consideration to this issue. We offer the following proposals:

-- An international organization should be created to set rules for deep seabed mining.

-- This international organization must preserve the rights of all countries and their citizens directly to exploit deep seabed resources.

-- It should also insure fair adjudication of conflicting interests and security of investment.

-- Countries and their enterprises mining deep seabed resources should pay an agreed portion of their revenues to the international organization, to be used for the benefit of developing countries.

-- The management of the organization and its voting procedures must reflect and balance the interests of the participating states. The organization should not have the power to control prices or production rates.

-- If these essential U.S. interests are guaranteed, we can agree that this organization will also have the right to conduct mining operations on behalf of the international community primarily for the benefit of developing countries.

-- The new organization should serve as a vehicle for cooperation between the technologically advanced and the developing countries. The United States is prepared to explore ways of sharing deep seabed technology with other nations.

-- A balanced commission of consumers, seabed producers, and land-based producers could monitor the possible adverse effects of deep seabed mining on the economies of those developing countries which are substantially dependent on the export of minerals also produced from the deep seabed.

Henry Kissinger, address, annual convention of American Bar Association, August 11, 1975; *Digest of United States Practice in International Law,* 1975, pp. 379-85. Also see his statement at Law of the Sea Conference, 1976, in *Digest of United States Practice in International Law,* 1976, pp. 340-43.

342 UNITED STATES REJECTION OF 1982 LAW OF THE SEA TREATY

On April 30 the [Law of the Sea] conference adopted a convention that does not satisfy the objectives sought by the United States. It was adopted by a vote of 130 in favor, with 4 against (including the United States) and 17 abstentions. Those voting "no" or abstaining appear small in number but represent countries which produce more than 60 percent of the world's gross national product and provide more than 60 percent of the contributions to the United Nations.

We have now completed a review of that convention and recognize that it contains many positive and very significant accomplishments. Those extensive parts dealing with navigation and overflight and most other provisions of the convention are consistent with United States interests and, in our view, serve well the interests of all nations. That is an important achievement and signifies the benefits of working together and effectively balancing numerous interests. . . .

Our review recognizes, however, that the deep seabed mining part of the convention does not meet United States objectives. For this reason, I am announcing today that the United States will not sign the convention as adopted by the conference, and our participation in the remaining conference process will be at the technical level and will involve only those provisions that serve United States interests.

These decisions reflect the deep conviction that the United States cannot support a deep seabed mining regime with such major problems. In our view, those problems include:

-- Provisions that would actually deter future development of deep seabed mineral resources, when such development should serve the interest of all countries.
-- A decisionmaking process that would not give the United States or others a role that fairly reflects and protects their interests.
-- Provisions that would allow amendments to enter into force for the United States without its approval. This is clearly incompatible with the United States approach to such treaties.
-- Stipulations relating to mandatory transfer of private technology and the possibility of national liberation movements sharing in benefits.
-- The absence of assured access for future qualified deep seabed miners to promote the development of these resources.

We recognize that world demand and markets currently do not justify commercial development of deep seabed mineral resources, and it is not clear when such development will be justified. When such factors become favorable, however, the deep seabed represents a potentially important source of strategic and other minerals. The aim of the United States in this regard has been to establish with other nations an order that would allow exploration and development under reasonable terms and conditions.

Ronald Reagan, statement issued by White House, July 9, 1982; *Papers of Presidents: Reagan,* 1982, pp. 911-12. Also see statement on withholding of United States funds from the Law of Sea Preparatory Commission, December 30, 1982, in *Papers of Presidents: Reagan,* 1982, II, 1652; transcript of Department of State press briefing, March 9, 1983, in *American Foreign Policy: Current Documents,* 1983, pp. 313-18; and Assistant Secretary of State, statement, September 4, 1984, in *American Foreign Policy: Current Documents,* 1984, pp. 270-76. For commentary, also see *Historic Documents,* 1982, pp. 345-61.

LAW OF THE SEA TREATIES

Whereas prior to World War II, many aspects of maritime jurisdiction and affairs were dealt with by national legislation, bilateral treaties, and customary international law, since the 1930's the United States has joined other nations in a major endeavor to codify the universal law of the sea, embodied in multilateral treaties. In 1930 the League of Nations-sponsored conference on the codification of international sea law failed to agree upon the terms of a treaty. Following World War II the United Nations convened three international conferences to codify international law--UNCLOS I (United Nations Conference on the Law of the Sea) in 1958, UNCLOS II in 1960, and UNCLOS III, which met from 1973 to 1982. The first of these produced a series of conventions, signed on April 29, 1958. The second, concerned especially with the territorial sea and the extent of marginal jurisdiction and fishery limits, failed to achieve agreement. After years of intensive negotiations, at the third conference a comprehensive Law of the Sea Treaty was finally approved in 1982 which, as noted in Document 342, the United States refused to sign.

Over the years the United States has been party to several hundred treaties and agreements concerning the seas and maritime matters. Engaged in international shipping, to advance its interests and protect its rights, at the outset it negotiated a series of bilateral treaties concerned with peace, friendship, commerce, and navigation. In the eighteenth and early nineteenth centuries, such treaties were consummated with most European and North African nations. The ten treaties with Algiers, Morocco, Muscat, Tripoli, and Tunis were also intended, in part, to end the depradations of the Barbary pirates. For discussion of these early arrangements providing for commerce and navigation, see Chapter 17, and for the text of these treaties with North African states, see 5 Bevans, *Treaties and Other International Agreements,* 32-57; 9 Bevans 1270-93; and 11 Bevans 1070-97.

Currently the United States is a party to some twenty-five multilateral conventions and more than two hundred bilateral treaties that concern the seas and maritime affairs. Approximately half deal with basic jurisdictional rights and duties, navigation, and shipping, whereas others apply to boundary waters (especially with Canada and Mexico), fisheries, smuggling, and related matters.

The documents provided in this section include a cumulative list of major multipartite conventions (Document 343); excerpts from the 1958 Conventions on the High Seas (Document 344), the Territorial Sea (Document 345), and the Continental Shelf (Document 346); and the treaty prohibiting the emplacement of nuclear and other weapons of mass destruction on the floor and in the subsoil of the sea, 1971 (Document 347). The text of the 1982 Law of the Sea Treaty, adopted by the United Nations Law of the Sea Conference on April 30, 1982, and signed by 119 delegations, may be found in UN Doc. A/CONF. 62/122, October 7, 1982, and "Law of the Sea Treaty, April 30, 1982," *Historic Documents,* 1982, pp. 347-61.

For guidance to United States legislation on maritime affairs, see *U.S. Code,* Title 33 on navigation (including par. 151 on the high seas and inland waterways demarcation lines, and Chapters 7 on piracy, 20 and 33 on pollution, 27 on ocean dumping, and 30 on collisions); and Title 43 on the continental shelf and tidelands, especially Chapter 29, pars. 1301, 1331-32. For commentary on the role of the United States in UNCLOS III, see the annual volumes of the *Digest of United States Practice in International Law.* For a statement on the significance of the United States Deep Sea Hard Minerals Resources Act of 1980, P.L. 96-283, see comments in *American Foreign Policy: Basic Documents,* 1977-1980, pp. 399-400.

343 LIST OF UNITED STATES MULTILATERAL TREATY RELATIONS--SEAS AND MARITIME AFFAIRS

Convention on Assistance and Salvage at Sea, September 23, 1910--TS 576; 1 Bevans, *Treaties and Other International Agreements* 780-90, hereafter cited as Bevans.

Convention on Bills of Lading for Carriage of Goods by Sea, August 25, 1924--TS 931; 2 Bevans 430-42.

Convention for the Prevention of Pollution of the Sea by Oil, May 12, 1954--TIAS 4900; 12 *U.S. Treaties* 2989-3027.

Agreement Regarding Financial Support of the North Atlantic Ice Patrol, January 4, 1956--TIAS 3597; 7 *U.S. Treaties* 1969-76.

Convention on the High Seas, April 29, 1958--TIAS 5200; 13 U.S. Treaties 2312-89.

Convention on the Territorial Sea and Contiguous Zone, April 29, 1958--TIAS 5639; 15 *U.S. Treaties* 1606-75.

Convention on the Continental Shelf, April 29, 1958--TIAS 5578; 15 *U.S. Treaties* 471-525.

Convention for the Safety of Life at Sea, June 17, 1960--TIAS 5780; 16 *U.S. Treaties* 185-578; also see subsequent treaty of November 1, 1974--TIAS 9700; 32 *U.S. Treaties* 47-292.

Convention for the International Council for the Exploration of the Sea, September 12, 1964--TIAS 7628; 24 *U.S. Treaties* 1080-88.

Convention on the Facilitation of International Maritime Traffic, April 9, 1965--TIAS 6251; 18 *U.S. Treaties* 410-67.

International Convention on Load Lines, April 5, 1966--TIAS 6331; 18 *U.S. Treaties* 1857-2090--which requires certification and marking of ships' load lines.

Convention on Tonnage Measurement of Ships, June 23, 1969--TIAS 10490; Executive Order 12419, in *Papers of Presidents: Reagan,* 1983, I, 656.

Convention on Intervention on High Seas in Cases of Oil Pollution Casualties, November 29, 1969--TIAS 8068; 26 *U.S. Treaties* 765-839.

Treaty on the Prohibition of the Emplacement of Nuclear Weapons and Other Weapons of Mass Destruction on the Seabed and the Ocean Floor and in the Subsoil Thereof, February 11, 1971--TIAS 7337; 23 *U.S. Treaties* 701-72.

Convention on International Regulations for Preventing Collisions at Sea, October 20, 1972--TIAS 8587; 28 *U.S. Treaties* 3459-3614.

Convention on the Prevention of Marine Pollution by Dumping Wastes and Other Matter, December 29, 1972--TIAS 8165; 26 *U.S. Treaties* 2403-85.

Convention on Conservation of Antarctic Marine Living Resources, May 20, 1980--TIAS 10240; 33 *U.S. Treaties* 3476-3558.

Agreement on Oceanographic Research, March 12, 1982--TIAS 10359.

Law of the Sea Treaty, April 30, 1982; not signed by the United States.

For additional multilateral treaties on fisheries and for the conservation of seals and whales, see *Department of State, Treaties in Force.* Also see this source for listing of related bilateral treaties to which the United States is a party.

344 CONVENTION ON THE HIGH SEAS, 1958

Article 1

The term "high seas" means all parts of the sea that are not included in the territorial sea or in the internal waters of a State.

Article 2

The high seas being open to all nations, no State may validly purport to subject any part of them to its sovereignty. Freedom of the high seas is exercised under the conditions laid down by these articles and by the other rules of international law. It comprises, *inter alia*, both for coastal and non-coastal States:

(1) Freedom of navigation;

(2) Freedom of fishing;

(3) Freedom to lay submarine cables and pipelines;

(4) Freedom to fly over the high seas.

These freedoms, and others which are recognized by the general principles of international law, shall be exercised by all States with reasonable regard to the interests of other States in their exercise of the freedom of the high seas.

Article 3

1. In order to enjoy the freedom of the seas on equal terms with coastal States, States having no sea-coast should have free access to the sea. To this end States situated between the sea and a State having no sea-coast shall by common agreement with the latter and in conformity with existing international convention accord:

(a) To the State having no sea-coast, on a basis of reciprocity, free transit through their territory; and

(b) To ships flying the flag of that State treatment equal to that accorded to their own ships, or to the ships of any other States, as regards access to seaports and the use of such ports. . . .

Article 4

Every State, whether coastal or not, has the right to sail ships under its flag on the high seas.

Article 5

1. Each State shall fix the conditions for the grant of its nationality to ships, for the registration of ships in its territory, and for the right to fly its flag. Ships have the nationality of the State whose flag they are entitled to fly. . . .

2. Each State shall issue to ships to which it has granted the right to fly its flag documents to that effect. . . .

Article 13

Every State shall adopt effective measures to prevent and punish the transport of slaves in ships authorized to fly its flag, and to prevent the unlawful use of its flag for that purpose. Any slave taking refuge on board any ship, whatever its flag, shall *ipso facto* be free.

Article 14

All States shall co-operate to the fullest possible extent in the repression of piracy on the high seas or in any other place outside the jurisdiction of any State . . . .

Article 19

On the high seas, or in any other place outside the jurisdiction of any State, every State may seize a pirate ship or aircraft, or a ship taken by piracy and under the control of pirates, and arrest the persons and seize the property on board. The courts of the State which carried out the seizure may decide upon the penalties to be imposed, and may also determine the action to be taken with regard to the ships, aircraft or property, subject to the rights of third parties acting in good faith. . . .

Article 21

A seizure on account of piracy may only by carried out by warships or military aircraft, or other ships or aircraft on government service authorized to that effect.

Article 22

1. Except where acts of interference derive from powers conferred by treaty, a warship which encounters a foreign merchant ship on the high seas is not justified in boarding her unless there is reasonable ground for suspecting:

(a) That the ship is engaged in piracy; or

(b) That the ship is engaged in the slave trade; or

(c) That, though flying a foreign flag or refusing to show its flag, the ship is, in reality, of the same nationality as the warship. . . .

Article 23

1. The hot pursuit of a foreign ship may be undertaken when the competent authorities of the coastal State have good reason to believe that the ship has violated the laws and regulations of that State. Such pursuit must be commenced when the foreign ship or one of its boats is within the internal waters or the territorial sea or the contiguous zone of the pursuing State, and may only be continued outside the territorial sea or the contiguous zone if the pursuit has not been interrupted. . . .

2. The right of hot pursuit ceases as soon as the ship pursued enters the territorial sea of its own country or of a third State. . . .

Article 24
Every State shall draw up regulations to prevent pollution of the seas by the discharge of oil from ships or pipelines or resulting from the exploitation and exploration of the seabed and its subsoil, taking account of existing treaty provisions on the subject.

Article 25
1. Every State shall take measures to prevent pollution of the seas from the dumping of radioactive waste, taking into account any standards and regulations which may be formulated by the competent international organizations. . . .

Article 26
1. All States shall be entitled to lay submarine cables and pipelines on the bed of the high seas.

2. Subject to its right to take reasonable measures for the exploration of the continental shelf and the exploitation of its natural resources, the coastal State may not impede the laying or maintenance of such cables or pipelines. . . .

Signed April 29, 1958; 37 articles. TIAS 5200; 13 *U.S. Treaties,* 2312-89. This convention constituted Annex II to the Final Act of the U.N. Conference on the Law of the Sea, 1958.

3 4 5 CONVENTION ON THE TERRITORIAL SEA AND THE CONTIGUOUS ZONE, 1958

Territorial Sea
Article 1
1. The sovereignty of a State extends, beyond its land territory and its internal waters, to a belt of sea adjacent to its coast, described as the territorial sea.

2. This sovereignty is exercised subject to the provisions of these articles and to other rules of international law.

Article 2
The sovereignty of a coastal State extends to the air space over the territorial sea as well as to its bed and subsoil.

Article 3
Except where otherwise provided in these articles, the normal baseline for measuring the breadth of the territorial sea is the low-water line along the coast as marked on largescale charts officially recognized by the coastal State.

Article 4
1. In localities where the coast line is deeply indented and cut into, or if there is a fringe of islands along the coast in its immediate vicinity, the method of straight baselines joining appropriate points may be em-

ployed in drawing the baseline from which the breadth of the territorial sea is measured.

2. The drawing of such baselines must not depart to any appreciable extent from the general direction of the coast, and the sea areas lying within the lines must be sufficiently closely linked to the land domain to be subject to the regime of internal waters. . . .

5. The system of straight baselines may not be applied by a State in such a manner as to cut off from the high seas the territorial sea of another State. . . .

Article 5

1. Waters on the landward side of the baseline of the territorial sea form part of the internal waters of the State. . . .

Article 6

The outer limit of the territorial sea is the line every point of which is at a distance from the nearest point of the baseline equal to the breadth of the territorial sea. . . .

Article 14

1. Subject to the provisions of these articles, ships of all States, whether coastal or not, shall enjoy the right of innocent passage through the territorial sea.

2. Passage means navigation through the territorial sea for the purpose either of traversing that sea without entering internal waters, or of proceeding to internal waters, or of making for the high seas from internal waters.

3. Passage includes stopping and anchoring, but only in so far as the same are incidental to ordinary navigation or are rendered necessary by force majeure or by distress.

4. Passage is innocent so long as it is not prejudicial to the peace, good order or security of the coastal State. Such passage shall take place in conformity with these articles and with other rules of international law. . . .

Article 15

1. The coastal State must not hamper innocent passage through the territorial sea. . . .

Article 16

1. The coastal State may take the necessary steps in its territorial sea to prevent passage which is not innocent. . . .

4. There shall be no suspension of the innocent passage of foreign ships through straits which are used for international navigation between one part of the high seas and another part of the high seas or the territorial sea of a foreign State. . . .

Article 18

1. No charge may be levied upon foreign ships by reason only of their passage through the territorial sea.

2. Charges may be levied upon a foreign ship passing through the territorial sea as payment only for specific services rendered to the ship.

These charges shall be levied without discrimination.

Article 19

1. The criminal jurisdiction of the coastal State should not be exercised on board a foreign ship passing through the territorial sea to arrest any person or to conduct any investigation in connection with any crime committed on board the ship during its passage, save only in the following cases:

(a) If the consequences of the crime extend to the coastal State; or

(b) If the crime is of a kind to disturb the peace of the country or the good order of the territorial sea; or

(c) If the assistance of the local authorities has been requested by the captain of the ship or by the consul of the country whose flag the ship flies; or

(d) If it is necessary for the suppression of illicit traffic in narcotic drugs. . . .

5. The coastal State may not take any steps on board a foreign ship passing through the territorial sea to arrest any person or to conduct any investigation in connection with any crime committed before the ship entered the territorial sea, if the ship, proceeding from a foreign port, is only passing through the territorial sea without entering internal waters. . . .

Contiguous Zone
Article 24

1. In a zone of the high seas contiguous to its territorial sea, the coastal State may exercise the control necessary to:

(a) Prevent infringement of its customs, fiscal, immigration or sanitary regulations within its territory or territorial sea;

(b) Punish infringement of the above regulations committed within its territory or territorial sea.

2. The contiguous zone may not extend beyond twelve miles from the baseline from which the breadth of the territorial sea is measured.

3. Where the coasts of two States are opposite or adjacent to each other, neither of the two States is entitled, failing agreement between them to the contrary, to extend its contiguous zone beyond the median line every point of which is equidistant from the nearest points on the baselines from which the breadth of the territorial seas of the two States is measured.

Signed on April 29, 1958; 32 articles.   TIAS 5639; 15 *U.S. Treaties,* 1606-76. This convention constituted Annex I to the Final Act of the U.N. Conference on the Law of the Sea, 1958.

346 CONVENTION ON THE CONTINENTAL SHELF, 1958

Article 1

For the purpose of these articles, the term "continental shelf" is used as referring (a) to the seabed and subsoil of the submarine areas adjacent to the coast but outside the area of the territorial sea, to a depth of 200 metres or, beyond that limit, to where the depth of the superjacent waters admits of the exploitation of the natural resources of the said areas; (b) to the seabed and subsoil of similar submarine areas adjacent to the coasts of islands.

Article 2

1. The coastal State exercises over the continental shelf sovereign rights for the purpose of exploring it and exploiting its natural resources.

2. The rights referred to in paragraph 1 of this article are exclusive in the sense that if the coastal State does not explore the continental shelf or exploit its natural resources, no one may undertake these activities, or make a claim to the continental shelf, without the express consent of the coastal State. . . .

4. The natural resources referred to in these articles consist of the mineral and other non-living resources of the seabed and subsoil together with living organisms belonging to sedentary species, that is to say, organisms which, at the harvestable stage, either are immobile on or under the seabed or are unable to move except in constant physical contact with the seabed or the subsoil.

Article 3

The rights of the coastal State over the continental shelf do not affect the legal status of the superjacent waters as high sea, or that of the airspace above those waters. . . .

Article 5

1. The exploration of the continental shelf and the exploitation of its natural resources must not result in any unjustifiable interference with navigation, fishing or the conservation of the living resources of the sea, not result in any interference with fundamental oceanographic or other scientific research carried out with the intention of open publication. . . .

Article 6

1. Where the same continental shelf is adjacent to the territorities of two or more States whose coasts are opposite each other, the boundary of the continental shelf appertaining to such States shall be determined by agreement between them. In the absence of agreement, and unless another boundary line is justified by special circumstances, the boundary is the median line, every point of which is equidistant from the nearest points of the baselines from which the breadth of the territorial sea of each State is measured.

2. Where the same continental shelf is adjacent to the territories of two adjacent States, the boundary of the continental shelf shall be determined by agreement between them. In the absence of agreement, and unless another boundary line is justified by special circumstances, the boundary shall be determined by application of the principle of equidistance from the nearest points of the baselines from which the breadth of the territorial sea of each State is measured. . . .

Signed on April 29, 1958; 14 articles. TIAS 5578; 15 *U.S. Treaties,* 471-525. This convention constituted Annex IV to the Final Act of the U.N. Conference on the Law of the Sea, 1958. The convention also deals with impediments to navigation, conflicts respecting boundaries of adjacent states, and tunneling.

347 TREATY ON THE PROHIBITION OF THE EMPLACEMENT OF NUCLEAR WEAPONS AND OTHER WEAPONS OF MASS DESTRUCTION ON THE SEABED AND THE OCEAN FLOOR AND IN THE SUBSOIL THEREOF, 1971

Article I

1. The States Parties to this Treaty undertake not to emplant or emplace on the seabed and the ocean floor and in the subsoil thereof beyond the outer limit of a seabed zone, as defined in article II, any nuclear weapons or any other types of weapons of mass destruction as well as structures, launching installations or any other facilities specifically designed for storing, testing or using such weapons.

2. The undertakings of paragraph 1 of this article shall also apply to the seabed zone referred to in the same paragraph, except that within such seabed zone, they shall not apply either to the coastal State or to the seabed beneath its territorial waters.

3. The States Parties to this Treaty undertake not to assist, encourage or induce any State to carry out activities referred to in paragraph 1 of this article and not to participate in any other way in such actions.

Article II

For the purpose of this Treaty, the outer limit of the seabed zone referred to in article I shall be coterminous with the twelve-mile outer limit of the zone referred to in part II of the Convention on the Territorial Sea and the Contiguous Zone [see Document 345] and shall be measured in accordance with the provisions . . . of that Convention and in accordance with international law.

Article III

1. In order to promote the objectives of and insure compliance with the provisions of this Treaty, each State Party to the Treaty shall have the right to verify through observation the activities of other States Parties to the Treaty on the seabed and the ocean floor and in the subsoil thereof beyond the zone referred to in article I, provided that observation does not interfere with such activities.

2. If after such observation reasonable doubts remain concerning the fulfillment of the obligations assumed under the Treaty, the State Party having such doubts and the State Party that is responsible for the activities giving rise to the doubts shall consult with a view to removing the doubts. If the doubts persist, the State Party having such doubts shall notify the other States Parties, and the Parties concerned shall cooperate on such further procedures for verification as may be agreed, including

appropriate inspection of objects, structures, installations or other facilities that reasonably may be expected to be of a kind described in article I. The Parties in the region of the activities, including any coastal State, and any other Party so requesting, shall be entitled to participate in such consultation and cooperation. After completion of the further procedures for verification, an appropriate report shall be circulated to other Parties by the Party that initiated such procedures. . . .

4. If consultation and cooperation pursuant to paragraphs 2 and 3 of this article have not removed the doubts concerning the activities and there remains a serious question concerning fulfillment of the obligations assumed under this Treaty, a State Party may, in accordance with the provisions of the Charter of the United Nations, refer the matter to the Security Council, which may take action in accordance with the Charter.

5. Verification pursuant to this article may be undertaken by any State Party using its own means, or with the full or partial assistance of any State Party, or through appropriate international procedures within the framework of the United Nations and in accordance with its Charter. . . .

Signed on February 11, 1971; 11 articles. TIAS 7337; 23 *U.S. Treaties,* 701-72. For commentary, see *United States Foreign Policy, 1971: A Report of the Secretary of State,* pp. 264-65, and "Seabed Arms Control Treaty," *Historic Documents,* 1972, pp. 167-71. Also see Treaty Banning Nuclear Weapons Tests in the Atmosphere, in Outer Space, and Under Water, 1963, in Chapter 21, Document 357.

21

Outer Space

Spaoo ic tho oloaroct oxamplo of tho noooccity for intornational scientific cooperation and the benefits that accrue from it. The world community has already determined and agreed that space is open to all and can be made the special province of none. Space is the new frontier of man, both a physical and an intellectual frontier.

Richard Nixon
U.S. Foreign Policy for the 1970's: Building for Peace

Policy, practice, and law concerning airspace and outer space are twentieth-century phenomena. As with the high seas, the United States has promoted the doctrine of freedom. So far as airspace is concerned, this freedom extends laterally to areas superjacent to the high seas and vertically to the outer limits of airspace--subject to national control by the subjacent state of those areas above its landed territory and territorial waters. Specific aerial relations with other nations, including jurisdiction and commercial and military aviation have been reduced to legal precepts embodied in a series of multipartite and bipartite treaties and agreements and in national legislation.

Since the beginning of the space age the United States has also pursued a policy of superatmospheric freedom. Problems of jurisdiction over and use of outer space as such generally parallel those related to airspace. But they are complicated by the need to also deal with the moon and other heavenly bodies.

As with the seas and airspace the development of policy and law respecting outer space is based partly on the results of practical developments and partly on the devisement of international agreement in advance of such actions. To summarize, the basic issues that have had to be faced include: the dichotomy of free outer space vs. national possession of space sectors superjacent to national territory; the distinction between the earth orbit and celestial, interplanetary, and interstellar space; jurisdiction over and use of spacecraft, satellites, space stations, and other man-made objects in space; jurisdiction over and use of the moon and other celestial bodies; jurisdiction over astronauts and other persons, equipment, and related matters in outer space; the nationality, marking, and registry of spacecraft, satellites, and stations; liability, collisions, and other accidents, as well as responsibility for "space junk"; technology, space research, and scientific data, and their international dissemination; and, most critical, fixing the dividing line between airspace and outer space.

Certain aspects of these matters have been incorporated into international treaties, but many, including the achievement of consensus on the outer limits of airspace--or the inner limits of outer space--still need to be resolved. For a listing of some seventy-five of these and other items requiring policy resolution--in addition to basic national goals, concrete objectives, benefits, costs, and processes required for international agreement, see Elmer Plischke, *Foreign Relations: Analysis of Its Anatomy* (Westport: Greenwood, 1988), pp. 267-69.

POLICY THEMES

The space age began with the development of rocketry and the launching of the first earth satellites, *Sputniks* I and II by the Soviet Union in October and November, 1957, and *Explorer* I by the United States on January 31, 1958. This sparked an active space race between the two countries. The United States established an earth satellite program in 1955 and Congress enacted the National Aeronautics and Space Act three years later (see P.L. 85-568 in 72 *Statutes at Large* 426 and *U.S. Code,* Title 42, par. 2451 ff.).

Since then the United States has been engaged in a variety of projects-- unmanned space flights and activities and manned space ventures, exploration, research, scientific experiments, terrestrial and celestial probes, space communications, and the like. So far as spacecraft and satellites are concerned, these space activities fall into five main categories: unmanned satellites (such as *Vanguard, Telstar, Syncom, Vela,* and *Pegasus*); manned space flights (such as *Mercury, Gemini,* and *Apollo,* which was used for moon landings); unmanned celestial probes (such as *Ranger, Pioneer, Mariner, Surveyor, Viking,* and *Voyager,* to explore the moon, Venus, Mars, Jupiter, Mercury, Saturn, and Uranus); space stations (*Skylab* and *Freedom*); and manned space shuttle flights.

To illustrate the purposes, policies, and programs of the United States, the following documents (Documents 348-356), presented chronologically, range from determinants, needs, and plans and from general goals and specific objectives to national commitment, action, burdens, and costs. Other themes include promoting United States leadership in meeting the space challenge, surmounting the obstacles encountered, and conquering mankind's last frontier; principles to govern the American space program; technological benefits and knowledge to enhance the welfare of all nations; and, permeating American policy, international cooperation for the benefit of all peoples. These documents characterize presidential policy development since the 1950's. For comprehensive commentary on developments, see the annual reports of the President to Congress on aeronautics and space activities. International treaty commitments concerning outer space are provided in the following section.

3 4 8 BASIC TESTS OF SPACE POLICY

Now, let's turn briefly to our satellite projects:

Confronted with the essential requirements I have indicated for defense, we must adopt a sensible formula to guide us in deciding what satellite and outer-space activity to undertake.

Certainly there should be two tests in this formula.

If the project is designed solely for scientific purposes, its size and its cost must be tailored to the scientific job it is going to do. . . .

If the project has some ultimate defense value, its urgency for this purpose is to be judged in comparison with the probable value of competing defense projects.

Dwight Eisenhower, address to American people, Oklahoma City, November 13, 1957; *Papers of Presidents: Eisenhower,* 1957, p. 812.

3 4 9 FACTORS DETERMINING SPACE POLICY

. . . These factors are:

(1) the compelling urge of man to explore the unknown; (2) the need to assure that full advantage is taken of the military potential of space; (3) the effect on national prestige of accomplishment in space science and exploration; and (4) the opportunities for scientific observation and experimentation which will add to our knowledge of the earth, the solar system, and the universe.

These factors have such a direct bearing on the future progress as well as on the security of our Nation that an imaginative and well-conceived space program must be given high priority and a sound organization provided to carry it out. Such a program and the organization which I recommend should contribute to (1) the expansion of human knowledge of outer space and the use of space technology for scientific inquiry, (2) the improvement of the usefulness and efficiency of aircraft, (3) the development of vehicles capable of carrying instruments, equipment and living organisms into space, (4) the preservation of the role of the United States as a leader in aeronautical and space science and technology, (5) the making available of discoveries of military value to agencies directly concerned with national security, (6) the promotion of cooperation with other nations in space science and technology, and (7) assuring the most effective utilization of the scientific and engineering resources of the United States and the avoidance of duplication of facilities and equipment.

I recommend that aeronautical and space science activities sponsored by the United States be conducted under the direction of a civilian agency, except for those projects primarily associated with military require-ments. . . .

Dwight Eisenhower, Special Message to Congress on Space Science and Exploration, April 2, 1958; *Papers of Presidents: Eisenhower*, 1958, pp. 269-70. On March 26 the President released his Science Advisory Committee's report on outer space; see pp. 242-43. On July 29 he signed the National Aeronautics and Space Act; see p. 573.

350   COMMITMENT TO LAND MAN ON MOON IN 1960's

. . . Now it is time to take longer strides--time for a great new American enterprise--time for this nation to take a clearly leading role in space achievement, which in many ways may hold the key to our future on earth.

I believe we possess all the resources and talents necessary. But the facts of the matter are that we have never made the national decisions or marshalled the national resources required for such leadership. We have never specified long-range goals on an urgent time schedule, or managed our resources and our time so as to insure their fulfillment. . . .

. . . Space is open to us now; and our eagerness to share its meaning is not governed by the efforts of others. We go into space because whatever mankind must undertake, free men must fully share. . . .

First, I believe that this nation should commit itself to achieving the goal, before this decade is out, of landing a man on the moon and returning him safely to the earth. No single space project in this period will be more impressive to mankind, or more important for the long-range exploration of space; and none will be so difficult or expensive to accomplish. . . .

I believe we should go to the moon. But I think every citizen of this country as well as the Members of the Congress should consider the matter carefully in making their judgment, to which we have given attention over many weeks and months, because it is a heavy burden, and there is no sense in agreeing or desiring that the United States take an affirmative position in outer space, unless we are prepared to do the work and bear the burdens to make it successful. . . .

John Kennedy, Special Message to Congress on Urgent National Needs, May 25, 1961; *Papers of Presidents: Kennedy*, 1961, pp. 403-5.

351   DEDICATION TO LEADERSHIP IN SPACE

. . . The exploration of space will go ahead, whether we join in it or not, and it is one of the great adventures of all time, and no nation which expects to be the leader of other nations can expect to stay behind in this race for space.

Those who came before us made certain that this country rode the first waves of the industrial revolutions, the first waves of modern invention, and the first wave of nuclear power, and this generation does not intend to founder in the backwash of the coming age of space. We mean to be a part of it--we mean to lead it. For the eyes of the world now look into space, to the moon and to the planets beyond, and we have vowed that we shall not see it governed by a hostile flag of conquest, but by a banner of freedom and peace. We have vowed that we shall not see space filled with weapons of mass destruction, but with instruments of knowledge and understanding.

Yet the vows of this Nation can only be fulfilled if we in this Nation are first, and, therefore, we intend to be first. In short, our leadership in science and in industry, our hopes for peace and security, our obligations to ourselves as well as others, all require us to make this effort, to solve these mysteries, to solve them for the good of all men, and to become the world's leading space-faring nation. . . .

We choose to go to the moon. We choose to go to the moon in this decade and do the other things, not because they are easy, but because they are hard, because that goal will serve to organize and measure the best of our energies and skills, because that challenge is one that we are willing to accept, one we are unwilling to postpone, and one which we intend to win. . . .

John Kennedy, address on space effort, Rice University, September 12, 1962; *Papers of Presidents: Kennedy,* 1962, pp. 668-71.

352   NEED FOR INTERNATIONAL SPACE TREATY

Just as the United States is striving to help achieve peace on earth, we want to do what we can to insure that explorations of the moon and other celestial bodies will be for peaceful purposes only. We want to be sure that our astronauts and those of other nations can freely conduct scientific investigations of the moon. We want the results of these activities to be available for all mankind.

We want to take action now to attain these goals. In my view, we need a treaty laying down rules and procedures for the exploration of celestial bodies. The essential elements of such a treaty would be as follows:

The moon and other celestial bodies should be free for exploration and use by all countries. No country should be permitted to advance a claim of sovereignty.

There should be freedom of scientific investigation, and all countries should cooperate in scientific activities relating to celestial bodies.

Studies should be made to avoid harmful contamination.

Astronauts of one country should give any necessary help to astronauts of another country.

No country should be permitted to station weapons of mass destruction on a celestial body. Weapons tests and military maneuvers should be forbidden.

I am convinced that we should do what we can--not only for our generation, but for future generations--to see to it that serious political conflicts do not arise as a result of space activities. I believe that the time is ripe for action. We should not lose time.

Lyndon Johnson, statement read by Press Secretary at press conference, San Antonio, May 7, 1966; *Papers of Presidents: Johnson,* 1966, I, 487-88. For Johnson's statements on the consummation of space treaties, see notes appended to documents in the following section of this chapter.

3 5 3   PURPOSES AND OBJECTIVES OF UNITED STATES SPACE PROGRAM, 1970

In my judgment, three general purposes should guide our space program.

One purpose is exploration. From time immemorial, man has insisted on venturing into the unknown despite his inability to predict precisely the value of any given exploration. . . . Man has come to feel that such quests are worthwhile in and of themselves--for they represent one way in which he expands his vision and expresses the human spirit. A great nation must always be an exploring nation if it wishes to remain great.

A second purpose of our space program is scientific knowledge--a greater systematic understanding about ourselves and our universe. With each of our space ventures, man's total information about nature has been dramatically expanded. . . .

A third purpose of the United States space effort is that of practical application--turning the lessons we learn in space to the early benefit of life on earth. Examples of such lessons are manifold; they range from new medical insights to new methods of communication, from better weather forecasts to new management techniques and new ways of providing energy. But these lessons will not apply themselves; we must make a concerted effort to see that the results of our space research are used to the maximum advantage of the human community.

We must see our space effort, then, not only as an adventure of today but also as an investment in tomorrow. . . .

We must realize that space activities will be a part of our lives for the rest of time. We must think of them as part of a continuing process--one which will go on day in and day out, year in and year out. . . .

With these general considerations in mind, I have concluded that our space program should work toward the following specific objectives:

1. We should continue to *explore the moon.* Future Apollo manned lunar landings will be spaced so as to maximize our scientific return from each mission, always providing, of course, for the safety of those who undertake these ventures. . . .

2. We should move ahead with bold *exploration of the planets and the universe.* In the next few years, scientific satellites of many types will be launched into earth orbit to bring us new information about the universe, the solar system, and even our own planet. During the next decade,

we will also launch unmanned spacecraft to all the planets of our solar system, including an unmanned vehicle which will be sent to land on Mars and to investigate its surface. In the late 1970's, the "Grand Tour" missions will study the mysterious outer planets of the solar system-- Jupiter, Saturn, Uranus, Neptune, and Pluto. The positions of the planets at that time will give us a unique opportunity to launch missions which can visit several of them on a single flight of over 3 billion miles. . . .

3. We should work to *reduce substantially the cost of space operations*. Our present rocket technology will provide a reliable launch capability for some time. But as we build for the longer-range future, we must devise less costly and less complicated ways of transporting payloads into space. Such a capability--designed so that it will be suitable for a wide range of scientific, defense, and commercial uses--can help us realize important economies in all aspects of our space program. . . .

4. We should seek to *extend man's capability to live and work in space*. . . .

We have much to learn about what man can and cannot do in space. . . . Flexible, long-lived space station modules could provide a multi-purpose space platform for the longer-range future and ultimately become a building block for manned interplanetary travel.

5. We should *hasten and expand the practical applications of space technology*. The development of earth resources satellites--platforms which can help in such varied tasks as surveying crops, locating mineral deposits, and measuring water resources--will enable us to assess our environment and use our resources more effectively. We should continue to pursue other applications of space-related technology in a wide variety of fields, including meteorology, communications, navigation, air traffic control, education, and national defense. . . .

6. We should *encourage greater international cooperation in space*. . . . I believe that both the adventures and the applications of space missions should be shared by all peoples. Our progress will be faster and our accomplishments will be greater if nations will join together in this effort, both in contributing the resources and in enjoying the benefits.

Richard Nixon, statement about future United States space program, March 7, 1970; *Papers of Presidents: Nixon*, 1970, pp. 250-53. On the same day the White House released the transcript of a news briefing about the space program. For general policy commentary, also see Nixon's annual reports on *U.S. Foreign Policy for the 1970s*.

354   PRESIDENT'S DIRECTIVE ON NATIONAL SPACE POLICY, 1978

As a result of this in-depth review, the President's directive establishes national policies to guide the conduct of United States activities in and related to space programs. The objectives are (1) to advance the interests of the United States through the exploration and use of space and (2) to cooperate with other nations in maintaining the freedom of space for all activities which enhance the security and welfare of mankind. The space principles set forth in this directive are:

-- The United States will pursue space activities to increase scientific knowledge, develop useful commercial and Government applications of space technology, and maintain United States leadership in space technology.

-- The United States is committed to the principles of the exploration and use of outer space by all nations for peaceful purposes and for the benefit of all mankind.

-- The United States is committed to the exploration and use of outer space in support of its national well-being.

-- The United States rejects any claims to sovereignty over outer space or over celestial bodies, or any portion thereof, and rejects any limitations on the fundamental right to acquire data from space.

-- The United States holds that the space systems of any nation are national property and have the right of passage through and operations in space without interference. Purposeful interference with space systems shall be viewed as an infringement upon sovereign rights.

-- The United States will pursue activities in space in support of its right of self-defense and thereby strengthen national security, the deterrence of attack, and arms control agreements.

-- The United States will conduct international cooperative space activities that are beneficial to the United States scientifically, politically, economically, and/or militarily.

-- The United States will develop and operate on a global basis active and passive remote sensing operations in support of national objectives.

-- The United States will maintain current responsibility and management relationships among the various space programs, and, as such, close coordination and information exchange will be maintained among the space sectors to avoid unnecessary duplication and to allow maximum cross-utilization of all capabilities.

Our civil space programs will be conducted to increase the body of scientific knowledge about the Earth and the universe; to develop and operate civil applications of space technology; to maintain United States leadership in space science, applications, and technology; and to further United States domestic and foreign policy objectives within the following guidelines:

-- The United States will encourage domestic commercial exploitation of space capabilities and systems for economic benefit and to promote the technological position of the United States; . . .

-- Advances in Earth imaging from space will be permitted under controls and when such needs are justified and assessed in relation to civil benefits, national security, and foreign policy. Controls, as appropriate, on other forms of remote Earth sensing will be established.

-- Data and results from the civil space programs will be provided the widest practical dissemination to improve the condition of human beings on Earth and to provide improved space services for the United States and other nations of the world.

-- The United States will develop, manage, and operate a fully operational Space Transportation System (STS). . . . The STS will service all authorized space users--domestic and foreign, commercial and governmental--and will provide launch priority and necessary security to national security missions while recognizing the essentially open character of the civil space program. . . .

-- Security, including dissemination of data, shall be conducted in accordance with Executive orders and applicable directives for protection of national security information. . . .

-- The Secretary of Defense will establish a program for identifying and integrating, as appropriate, civil and commercial resources into military operations during national emergencies declared by the President.

-- Survivability of space systems will be pursued commensurate with the planned need in crisis and war and the availability of other assets to perform the mission . . . .

-- The United States finds itself under increasing pressure to field an antisatellite capability of its own in response to Soviet activities in this area. By exercising mutual restraint, the United States and the Soviet Union have an opportunity at this early juncture to stop an unhealthy arms competition in space before the competition develops a momentum of its own. . . .

-- While the United States seeks verifiable, comprehensive limits on antisatellite capabilities and use, in the absence of such an agreement, the United States will vigorously pursue development of its own capabilities. The U.S. space defense program shall include an integrated attack warning, notification, verification, and contingency reaction capability which can effectively detect and react to threats to U.S. space systems.

Jimmy Carter, announcement on administration review of United States space policy, June 20, 1978; *Papers of Presidents: Carter,* 1978, I, 1135-37. Also see his comments in Message to Congress on science and technology, March 27, 1979; *Papers of Presidents: Carter,* 1979, I, 536.

355   PLAN FOR UNITED STATES SPACE POLICY IN 1980's

As a result, the President's directive reaffirms the national commitment to the exploration and use of space in support of our national well-being, and establishes the basic goals of United States space policy which are to:

-- strengthen the security of the United States;
-- maintain United States space leadership;
-- obtain economic and scientific benefits through the exploitation of space;
-- expand United States private-sector investment and involvement in civil space and space related activities;
-- promote international cooperative activities in the national interest; and

-- cooperate with other nations in maintaining the freedom of space for activities which enhance the security and welfare of mankind.

The principles underlying the conduct of the United States space program, as outlined in the directive are:

-- The United States is committed to the exploration and use of space by all nations for peaceful purposes and for the benefit of mankind. "Peaceful purposes" allow activities in pursuit of national security goals.

-- The United States rejects any claims to sovereignty by any nation over space or over celestial bodies, or any portion thereof, and rejects any limitations on the fundamental right to acquire data from space.

-- The United States considers the space systems of any nation to be national property with the right of passage through and operation in space without interference. Purposeful interference with space systems shall be viewed as an infringement upon sovereign rights.

-- The United States encourages domestic commercial exploitation of space capabilities, technology, and systems for national economic benefit. These activities must be consistent with national security concerns, treaties, and international agreements.

-- The United States will conduct international cooperative space-related activities that achieve scientific, political, economic, or national security benefits for the Nation.

-- The United States space program will be comprised of two separate, distinct and strongly interacting programs--national security and civil. Close coordination, cooperation, and information exchange will be maintained among these programs to avoid unnecessary duplication. . . .

-- The United States will pursue activities in space in support of its right of self-defense.

-- The United States will continue to study space arms control options. The United States will consider verifiable and equitable arms control measures that would ban or otherwise limit testing and deployment of specific weapons systems, should those measures be compatible with United States national security.

Ronald Reagan, fact sheet outlining United States space policy, July 4, 1982; *Papers of Presidents: Reagan,* 1982, II, 894-98. Based on ten-month review. Also discusses space transportation system, civil space program, national security space program, and policy implementation. For Vice President Bush's comments on the relation of outer space to national security, February 4, 1983, see *American Foreign Policy: Current Documents,* 1983, p. 113, and for his remarks on the nature of our mission in space, see pp. 303-5.

3 5 6   THREEFOLD STRATEGY FOR SPACE DEVELOPMENT, 1984

Our space goals will chart a path of progress toward creating a better life for all people who seek freedom, prosperity, and security.

Our approach to space has three elements. Let me discuss each of them briefly. The first is a commitment to build a permanently manned space station to be in orbit around the Earth within a decade. It will be a base for many kinds of scientific, commercial, and industrial activities and a stepping-stone for further goals. . . .

But most importantly, like every step forward, a space station will not be an end in itself but a doorway to even greater progress in the future. In this case, a space station will open up new opportunities for expanding human commerce and learning and provide a base for further exploration of that magnificent and endless frontier of space.

International cooperation, the second element of our plan, has long been a guiding principle of the United States space program. . . . Just as our friends were asked to join us in the shuttle program, our friends and allies will be invited to join with us in the space station project.

The third goal of our space strategy will be to encourage American industry to move quickly and decisively into space. Obstacles to private sector space activities will be removed, and we'll take appropriate steps to spur private enterprise in space. . . .

The peaceful use of space promises great benefits to all mankind. It opens vast new opportunities for our industry and ingenuity. The only limits we have are those of our own courage and imagination. . . .

Ronald Reagan, radio address to the nation, January 28, 1984; *American Foreign Policy: Current Documents,* 1984, pp. 261-62. Also see statement by Director of the International Affairs Division, National Aeronautics and Space Administration to House of Representatives Committee, on international cooperation and competition in outer space, July 25, 1984, pp. 265-68, and statement by Deputy Assistant Secretary for Science and Technology Affairs, Department of State, to Senate Foreign Relations Committee, on East-West cooperation in outer space, September 13, 1984, pp. 268-70.

SPACE TREATIES

The United States is active in promoting the development of international law to govern national rights and duties in outer space. In addition to participating in the deliberations and decisions of the United Nations on space affairs, the American government has become a party to a series of major multilateral conventions and a good many bilateral space treaties and agreements.

The multilateral conventions, presented chronologically in this section, deal with banning nuclear weapons tests in outer space, 1963 (Document 357); principles to regulate exploration in outer space, 1967 (Document 358); assistance in the rescue of astronauts and returning them and space objects to launching states, 1968 (Document 359); international liability for damage caused by space objects, 1972 (Document 360); and registration of objects launched into outer space, 1975 (Document 361).

In addition, dozens of supplementary agreements have been negotiated, such as the 1973 arrangement with West European governments providing for a cooperative program for space transportation and an orbital system, involving the space shuttle and mannable laboratory modules and instrument platforms (signed August 14, 1973; see TIAS 7722, in 24 *U.S. Treaties* 2049-

93). In the early 1970's President Nixon estimated that the United States had already negotiated some 250 such agreements with approximately 75 countries providing for space cooperation. For a listing of some of these multipartite and bipartite treaties and agreements, concerned with such matters as satellite launching and communications, space cooperation and joint research, and tracking stations, see *Treaties in Force*.

Another major convention--the Agreement Governing the Activities of States on the Moon and Other Celestial Bodies, commonly called the Moon Treaty --was negotiated during the 1970's and approved by the United Nations General Assembly and opened for signature in December 1979, but which the United States did not sign. For its text, see *Digest of United States Practice in International Law*, 1979, pp. 1178-84, and for commentary, see pp. 1172-78, and 1980, pp. 671-704. Although the United States agreed to the need for such a treaty and approved most of its stipulations, American opposition centered primarily on the meaning and application of the concept that celestial bodies and their resources "are the common heritage of mankind" (which some governments equate with the "common property" of mankind), the specifications concerning exploitation of resources for commercial purposes, and their control by a regime comprised of all nations on an equal basis with decisions made by majority vote (similar to the deep seabed resources regime).

357 TREATY BANNING NUCLEAR WEAPON TESTS IN THE ATMOSPHERE, IN OUTER SPACE, AND UNDER WATER--TEST BAN TREATY, 1963

Article I

1. Each of the Parties to this Treaty undertakes to prohibit, to prevent, and not to carry out any nuclear weapon test explosion, or any other nuclear explosion, at any place under its jurisdiction or control:

(a) in the atmosphere; beyond its limits, including outer space; or under water, including territorial waters or high seas; or

(b) in any other environment if such explosion causes radioactive debris to be present outside the territorial limits of the State under whose jurisdiction or control such explosion is conducted. . . .

2. Each of the Parties to this Treaty undertakes furthermore to refrain from causing, encouraging, or in any way participating in, the carrying out of any nuclear weapon test explosion, or any other nuclear explosion, anywhere which would take place in any of the environments described, or have the effect referred to, in paragraph 1 of this Article.

Signed August 5, 1963; 5 articles. TIAS 5433; 14 *U.S. Treaties* 1313-87.

358 TREATY ON PRINCIPLES GOVERNING THE ACTIVITIES OF STATES IN THE EXPLORATION AND USE OF OUTER SPACE, INCLUDING THE MOON AND OTHER CELESTIAL BODIES, 1967

Article I

The exploration and use of outer space, including the moon and other celestial bodies, shall be carried out for the benefit and in the interests of all countries, . . . and shall be the province of all mankind.

Outer space, including the moon and other celestial bodies, shall be free for exploration and use by all States without discrimination of any kind, on a basis of equality and in accordance with international law, and there shall be free access to all areas of celestial bodies.

There shall be freedom of scientific investigation in outer space, including the moon and other celestial bodies, and States shall facilitate and encourage international co-operation in such investigation.

Article II

Outer space, including the moon and other celestial bodies, is not subject to national appropriation by claim of sovereignty, by means of use or occupation, or by any other means. . . .

Article IV

States Parties to the Treaty undertake not to place in orbit around the Earth any objects carrying nuclear weapons or any other kinds of weapons of mass destruction, install such weapons on celestial bodies, or station such weapons in outer space in any other manner.

The moon and other celestial bodies shall be used by all States Parties to the Treaty exclusively for peaceful purposes. The establishment of military bases, installations and fortifications, the testing of any type of weapons and the conduct of military maneuvers on celestial bodies shall be forbidden. The use of military personnel for scientific research or for any other peaceful purposes shall not be prohibited. The use of any equipment or facility necessary for peaceful exploration of the moon and other celestial bodies shall also not be prohibited.

Article V

States Parties to the Treaty shall regard astronauts as envoys of mankind in outer space and shall render to them all possible assistance in the event of accident, distress, or emergency landing on the territory of another State Party or on the high seas. When astronauts make such a landing, they shall be safely and promptly returned to the State of registry of their space vehicle.

In carrying on activities in outer space and on celestial bodies, the astronauts of one State Party shall render all possible assistance to the astronauts of other States Parties.

States Parties to the Treaty shall immediately inform the other States Parties to the Treaty or the Secretary-General of the United Nations of any phenomena they discover in outer space, including the moon and other celestial bodies, which could constitute a danger to the life or health of astronauts.

Article VI

States Parties to the Treaty shall bear international responsibility for national activities in outer space, including the moon and other celestial bodies, whether such activities are carried on by governmental agencies or by non-governmental entities, and for assuring that national activities are carried out in conformity with the provisions set forth in the present Treaty. . . .

Article VII

Each ̄ State Party to the Treaty that launches or procures the launching of an object into outer space, including the moon and other celestial bodies, and each State Party from whose territory or facility an object is launched, is internationally liable for damage to another State Party to the Treaty or to its natural or juridical persons by such object or its component parts on the Earth, in air space or in outer space, including the moon and other celestial bodies.

Article VIII

A State Party to the Treaty on whose registry an object launched into outer space is carried shall retain jurisdiction and control over such object, and over any personnel thereof, while in outer space or on a celestial body. Ownership of objects launched into outer space, including objects landed or constructed on a celestial body, and of their component parts, is not affected by their presence in outer space or on a celestial body or by their return to the Earth. Such objects or component parts found beyond the limits of the State Party to the Treaty on whose registry they are carried shall be returned to that State Party, . . .

Article XII

All stations, installations, equipment and space vehicles on the moon and other celestial bodies shall be open to representatives of other States Parties to the Treaty on a basis of reciprocity. Such representatives shall give reasonable advance notice of a projected visit, in order that appropriate consultations may be held and that maximum precautions may be taken to assure safety and to avoid interference with normal operations in the facility to be visited.

Signed January 27, 1967; 17 articles. TIAS 6347; 18 *U.S. Treaties* 2410-98. For President Johnson's statements on this treaty of December 8, 1966, see *Papers of Presidents: Johnson,* 1966, II, 1441, and of October 10, 1967, see 1967, II, 918-20.

359 AGREEMENT ON THE RESCUE OF ASTRONAUTS, THE RETURN OF AS-
TRONAUTS, AND THE RETURN OF OBJECTS LAUNCHED INTO OUTER SPACE,
1968

Article I

Each Contracting Party which receives information or discovers
that the personnel of a spacecraft have suffered accident or are
experiencing conditions of distress or have made an emergency or
unintended landing in territory under its jurisdiction or on the high seas
or in any other place not under the jurisdiction of any State shall
immediately:

(a) Notify the launching authority or, if it cannot identify and
immediately communicate with the launching authority, immediately
make a public announcement by all appropriate means of communication
at its disposal;

(b) Notify the Secretary-General of the United Nations, who should
disseminate the information without delay by all appropriate means of
communication at his disposal.

Article 2

If, owing to accident, distress, emergency or unintended landing, the
personnel of a spacecraft land in territory under the jurisdiction of a
Contracting Party, it shall immediately take all possible steps to rescue
them and render them all necessary assistance. It shall inform the
launching authority and also the Secretary-General of the United Nations
of the steps it is taking and of their progress. If assistance by the
launching authority would help to effect a prompt rescue or would
contribute substantially to the effectiveness of search and rescue
operations, the launching authority shall co-operate with the Contracting
Party with a view to the effective conduct of search and rescue operations.
Such operations shall be subject to the direction and control of the
Contracting Party, which shall act in close and continuing consultation
with the launching authority.

Article 3

If information is received or it is discovered that the personnel of a
spacecraft have alighted on the high seas or in any other place not under
the jurisdiction of any State, those Contracting Parties which are in a
position to do so shall, if necessary, extend assistance in search and
rescue operations for such personnel to assure their speedy rescue. They
shall inform the launching authority and the Secretary-General of the
United Nations of the steps they are taking and of their progress.

Article 4

If, owing to accident, distress, emergency or unintended landing, the
personnel of a spacecraft land in territory under the jurisdiction of a
Contracting Party or have been found on the high seas or in any other
place not under the jurisdiction of any State, they shall be safely and
promptly returned to representatives of the launching authority.

Article 5

1. Each Contracting Party which receives information or discovers that a space object or its component parts has returned to Earth in territory under its jurisdiction or on the high seas or in any other place not under the jurisdiction of any State, shall notify the launching authority and the Secretary-General of the United Nations.

2. Each Contracting Party having jurisdiction over the territory on which a space object or its component parts has been discovered shall, upon the request of the launching authority and with assistance from that authority if requested, take such steps as it finds practicable to recover the object or component parts.

3. Upon request of the launching authority, objects launched into outer space or their component parts found beyond the territorial limits of the launching authority shall be returned to or held at the disposal of representatives of the launching authority, which shall, upon request, furnish identifying data prior to their return. . . .

5. Expenses incurred in fulfilling obligations to recover and return a space object or its component parts under paragraphs 2 and 3 of this article shall be borne by the launching authority.

Signed April 22, 1968; 10 articles.   TIAS 6599; 19 *U.S. Treaties* 7570-7631. For President Johnson's special message to the Senate seeking its approval, July 15, 1968, see *Papers of Presidents: Johnson,* 1968, II, 809-11.

360 CONVENTION ON INTERNATIONAL LIABILITY FOR DAMAGE CAUSED BY SPACE OBJECTS, 1972

Article II

A launching State shall be absolutely liable to pay compensation for damage caused by its space object on the surface of the earth or to aircraft in flight.

Article III

In the event of damage being caused elsewhere than on the surface of the earth to a space object of one launching State or to persons or property on board such a space object by a space object of another launching State, the latter shall be liable only if the damage is due to its fault or the fault of persons for whom it is responsible.

Article IV

1. In the event of damage being caused elsewhere than on the surface of the earth to a space object of one launching State or to persons or property on board such a space object by a space object of another launching State, and of damage thereby being caused to a third State or to its natural or juridical persons, the first two States shall be jointly and severally liable to the third State. . . .

Article V

1. Whenever two or more States jointly launch a space object, they shall be jointly and severally liable for any damage caused. . . .

Article VIII

1. A State which suffers damage, or whose natural or juridical persons suffer damage, may present to a launching State a claim for compensation for such damage. . . .

Article IX

A claim for compensation for damage shall be presented to a launching State through diplomatic channels. If a State does not maintain diplomatic relations with the launching State concerned, it may request another State to present its claim to that launching State or otherwise represent its interests under this Convention. It may also present its claim through the Secretary-General of the United Nations, provided the claimant State and the launching State are both Members of the United Nations.

Article X

1. A claim for compensation for damage may be presented to a launching State not later than one year following the date of the occurrence of the damage or the identification of the launching State which is liable. . . .

Article XII

The compensation which the launching State shall be liable to pay for damage under this Convention shall be determined in accordance with international law and the principles of justice and equity, in order to provide such reparation in respect of the damage as will restore the person, natural or juridical, State or international organization on whose behalf the claim is presented to the condition which would have existed if the damage had not occurred.

Article XIII

Unless the claimant State and the State from which compensation is due under this Convention agree on another form of compensation, the compensation shall be paid in the currency of the claimant State or, if that State so requests, in the currency of the State from which compensation is due.

Signed March 29, 1972; 28 articles. TIAS 7762; 24 *U.S. Treaties* 2389-2484. For President Johnson's statement in 1967 on United Nations endorsement of this treaty, see *Papers of Presidents: Johnson,* 1967, II, 1175-76.

361 CONVENTION ON REGISTRATION OF OBJECTS LAUNCHED INTO OUTER SPACE, 1975

Article II

1. When a space object is launched into earth orbit or beyond, the launching State shall register the space object by means of an entry in an

appropriate registry which it shall maintain. Each launching State shall inform the Secretary-General of the United Nations of the establishment of such a registry.

2. Where there are two or more launching States in respect of any such space object, they shall jointly determine which one of them shall register the object in accordance with paragraph 1 of this article, bearing in mind the provisions of Article VIII of the Treaty on principles governing the activities of States in the exploration and use of outer space, including the moon and other celestial bodies, and without prejudice to appropriate agreements concluded or to be concluded among the launching States on jurisdiction and control over the space object and over any personnel thereof.

3. The contents of each registry and the conditions under which it is maintained shall be determined by the State of registry concerned.

Article III

1. The Secretary-General of the United Nations shall maintain a Register in which the information furnished in accordance with article IV shall be recorded.

2. There shall be full and open access to the information in this Register.

Article IV

1. Each State of registry shall furnish to the Secretary-General of the United Nations, as soon as practicable, the following information concerning each space object carried on its registry;

(a) Name of launching State or States;

(b) An appropriate designator of the space object or its registration number;

(c) Date and territory or location of launch;

(d) Basic orbital parameters, including:

(i)   Nodal period,
(ii) Inclination,
(iii) Apogee,
(iv) Perigee;

(e) General function of the space object.

2. Each State of registry may, from time to time, provide the Secretary-General of the United Nations with additional information concerning a space object carried on its registry.

3. Each State of registry shall notify the Secretary-General of the United Nations, to the greatest extent feasible and as soon as practicable, of space objects concerning which it has previously transmitted information, and which have been but no longer are in earth orbit.

Signed January 14, 1975; 12 articles. TIAS 8480; 28 *U.S. Treaties* 695-790.

22

East-West Relations

> . . . we must develop with our allies new means of bridging the gap between the East and the West, facing danger boldly wherever danger exists, but being equally bold in our search for new agreements which can enlarge the hopes of all, while violating the interests of none.
>
> Lyndon Johnson
> Annual Message to Congress, January 8, 1964

Immediately after World War II the Soviet Union adopted an expansionist policy in Iran (Azerbaijan), tried to move into the Mediterranean area, consolidated its hold on Eastern Europe, and perpetrated the division of Germany and Europe into two confronting camps. The United States responded in 1947 with the Truman Doctrine, aid to Greece and Turkey, the Marshall Plan and the European Recovery Program (see Documents 111-112, 397), and the containment policy. Following the Soviet-sponsored coup in Czechoslovakia, the blockade of Berlin (see Documents 128-130), and the enactment of the Vandenberg Resolution (see Document 305), in April 1949 the United States, Canada, and ten West European powers signed the North Atlantic Treaty (see Document 306) and established the North Atlantic Treaty Organization. Also in 1949 Communists took over continental China and established the People's Republic, and the following year North Koreans invaded South Korea. In the early 1950's, therefore, the United States expanded its collective defense alliances in the Far East--including bilateral treaties with the Philippines, Japan, Korea, and Nationalist China, as well as the ANZUS and Manilla Pacts (see Chapter 18, Documents 307-308, 310-313). To complete its containment ring, it also affiliated unofficially with the Baghdad Pact for the Middle East (see Document 309).

In 1963 President Kennedy reported that there were more than a billion people "organized in the Communist movement," which represented a danger to the United States that "could turn the balance of power against us." During much of the 1960's the American government sought to maintain its security and restrain Communist expansion, as in Vietnam, while promoting detente with the Soviet bloc.   With the enunciation of the Nixon Doctrine in 1969 (see Documents 118-121) and the end of the Vietnam War (see Documents 167-172), effort was made to move from confrontation to coexistence and accommodation, including negotiation with the Soviet government and normalization of relations with the People's Republic of China (on China, see Chapter 28, Documents 492-497).   These peace-seeking objectives were encumbered, however, by such subsequent developments as the Soviet invasion of Afghanistan in 1979 and the Chinese government's forceful reaction to the demonstration in Tiananmen Square (Beijing) in 1989.

The Cold War confronted the American government with a fundamental policy dichotomy--to combat a political system that endorsed widespread "liberation" movements, the extension of Communism, the undermining of democracies, subversion, and world revolution, or to curb Communist imperialism, characterized by territorial expansion and hegemonism, or both. Often policy statements linked and confused these objectives. In the case of the Soviet Union, its expansionism and adventurism abroad, beyond the confines of legitimate national interest, produced the containment policy, bilateral and multilateral mutual defense arrangements, tension, confrontation, and crises. So far as China was concerned, following the Communist takeover in 1949, its recalcitrant and antagonistic attitude toward the United States and its policy in Korea and Southeast Asia resulted in political isolation of the People's Republic and the extension of containment and American mutual defense pacts to Asia.

Contributing to the war of nerves were such issues and developments as the division of Germany and the Berlin Wall, the buildup of Warsaw bloc and NATO conventional forces and nuclear weapons, nuclear balance and confrontation, the mistreatment of Western diplomats, a host of other concrete incidents (such as bugging of the American embassy in Moscow), and strident rhetoric. Aside from denouncing the Soviet and Chinese governments for their autocracy, territorial aggrandizement, direct and surrogate foreign exploits, efforts to thwart democratization in the Third World, and support of international terrorism, the United States decried their violation of such basic principles as international stability and balance of power, self-determination, nonintervention, pacific settlement, democratization, and human rights.   Epitomizing the most critical hazard of the Cold War, President Reagan warned repeatedly that a nuclear war "cannot be won and must never be fought."

The materials contained in this chapter present a number of major policy themes and commentary (Documents 362-371) and documents that touch on four specific matters: the development of the Washington-Moscow hot line to facilitate instant United States-Soviet communications (Document 372); American treaty relationships with Communist bloc countries, particularly the 1972 basic agreements with the Soviet and Chinese governments to improve relations (Documents 373-374); the use of summit diplomacy to ameliorate differences and facilitate coexistence (Document 375); and reform in the Soviet Union and Eastern Europe in the late 1980's and movement toward detente (Documents 376-380).

1990 ushered in the denouement of the Cold War and a new era in East-West relations in Europe. As noted at the end of Chapter 8, action was taken to unite West and East Germany and settle the Berlin question, and as indicated in

Chapter 18, Document 306 (note), attention was devoted to reorienting the North Atlantic Alliance and broadening its purposes and functions.

For treatment of related subjects, see Chapters 3 (on the linkage principle), 6 (section on national security and strength), 7 (Truman Doctrine), 8-9 and 11 (Berlin, U-2, and Cuban missile crises), 16 (human rights), 18 (alliances), 24 (foreign assistance, especially the European recovery, mutual defense assistance, and military assistance programs), 28 (normalizing relations with the People's Republic of China), and 29 (European affairs, especially the Helsinki accord).

MAJOR POLICY THEMES: COLD WAR, CONTAINMENT, DETENTE, AND RAPPROCHEMENT

362 COMMUNIST THREAT TO FREEDOM IN EUROPE

. . . the situation in the world today is not primarily the result of natural difficulties which follow a great war. It is chiefly due to the fact that one nation has not only refused to cooperate in the establishment of a just and honorable peace, but--even worse--has actively sought to prevent it. . . .

You know of the sincere and patient attempts of the democratic nations to find a secure basis for peace through negotiation and agreement. Conference after conference has been held in different parts of the world. We have tried to settle the questions arising out of the war on a basis which would permit the establishment of a just peace. You know the obstacles we have encountered. But the record stands as a monument to the good faith and integrity of the democratic nations of the world. The agreements we did obtain, imperfect though they were, could have furnished the basis for a just peace--if they had been kept.

But they were not kept.

They have been persistently ignored and violated by one nation. . . .

But that is not all. Since the close of hostilities, the Soviet Union and its agents have destroyed the independence and democratic character of a whole series of nations in Eastern and Central Europe.

It is this ruthless course of action, and the clear design to extend it to the remaining free nations of Europe, that have brought about the critical situation in Europe today. . . .

Faced with this growing menace, there have been encouraging signs that the free nations of Europe are drawing closer together for their economic well-being and for the common defense of their liberties. . . .

The Soviet Union and its satellites were invited to cooperate in the European recovery program. They rejected that invitation. More than that, they have declared their violent hostility to the program and are aggressively attempting to wreck it.

They see in it a major obstacle to their designs to subjugate the free community of Europe. They do not want the United States to help Europe.

They do not even want the 16 cooperating countries to help themselves.
. . .

The recent developments in Europe present this Nation with fundamental issues of vital importance.

I believe that we have reached a point at which the position of the United States should be made unmistakably clear. . . .

The door has never been closed, nor will it ever be closed, to the Soviet Union or to any other nation which genuinely cooperates in preserving the peace.

At the same time, we must not be confused about the central issue which confronts the world today.

The time has come when the free men and women of the world must face the threat to their liberty squarely and courageously.

The United States has a tremendous responsibility to act according to the measure of our power for good in the world. We have learned that we must earn the peace we seek just as we earned victory in the war, not by wishful thinking but by realistic effort.

Harry Truman, Special Message to Congress, March 17, 1948; *Papers of Presidents: Truman*, 1948, pp. 182-86. Also see his address at Laramie, Wyoming, May 9, 1950; *Papers of Presidents: Truman*, 1950, pp. 333-38.

363   DIVIDED WORLD--EAST VS. WEST

Nothing could make plainer why the world is in its present state-- and how that came to pass--than an understanding of the diametrically opposite principles and policies of these two great powers [the U.S. and the U.S.S.R.] in a war-ruined world.

For our part, we in this Republic were--and are--free men, heirs of the American Revolution, dedicated to the truths of our Declaration of Independence:

". . . That all men are created equal, that they are endowed by their Creator with certain unalienable rights . . . That to secure these rights, governments are instituted among men, deriving their just powers from the consent of the governed."

Our post-war objective has been in keeping with this great idea. The United States has sought to use its pre-eminent position of power to help other nations recover from the damage and dislocation of the war. We held out a helping hand to enable them to restore their national lives and to regain their positions as independent, self-supporting members of the great family of nations. This help was given without any attempt on our part to dominate or control any nation. We did not want satellites but partners.

The Soviet Union, however, took exactly the opposite course.

Its rulers saw in the weakened condition of the world not an obligation to assist in the great work of reconstruction, but an opportunity to exploit misery and suffering for the extension of their power.

Instead of help, they brought subjugation. They extinguished, blotted out, the national independence of the countries that the military operations of World War II had left within their grasp.

The difference stares at us from the map of Europe today. To the west of the line that tragically divides Europe we see nations continuing to act and live in the light of their own traditions and principles. On the other side, we see the dead uniformity of a tyrannical system imposed by the rulers of the Soviet Union. Nothing could point up more clearly what the global struggle between the free world and the communists is all about.

It is a struggle as old as recorded history; it is freedom versus tyranny.

For the dominant idea of the Soviet regime is the terrible conception that men do not have rights but live at the mercy of the state.

Inevitably this idea of theirs--and all the consequences flowing from it--collided with the efforts of free nations to build a just and peaceful world. The "cold war" between the communists and the free world is nothing more or less than the Soviet attempt to checkmate and defeat our peaceful purposes, in furtherance of their own broad objective.

We did not seek this struggle, God forbid. We did our utmost to avoid it. In World War II, we and the Russians had fought side by side, each in our turn attacked and forced to combat by the aggressors. After the war, we hoped that our wartime collaboration could be maintained, that the frightful experience of Nazi invasion, of devastation in the heart of Russia, had turned the Soviet rulers away from their old proclaimed allegiance to world revolution and communist dominion. But instead, they violated, one by one, the solemn agreements they had made with us in wartime. They sought to use the rights and privileges they had obtained in the United Nations, to frustrate its purposes and cut down its powers as an effective agent of world progress and the keeper of the world's peace. . . .

The world is divided, not through our fault or failure, but by Soviet design. They, not we, began the cold war. And because the free world saw this happen--because men know we made the effort and the Soviet rulers spurned it--the free nations have accepted leadership from our Republic, in meeting and mastering the Soviet offensive.

Harry Truman, Message to Congress, Farewell Address, January 7, 1953; *Papers of Presidents: Truman*, 1953, pp. 1118-19.

3 6 4   WESTERN FREEDOM: BASIC GUIDELINES

The prospects for peace are brightest when enlightened self-governing peoples control the policy of nations. Peoples do not want war. Rulers beyond the reach of popular control are more likely to engage in reckless adventures and to raise the grim threat of war. So the spread of freedom enhances the prospect for durable peace.

That prospect would be dimmed or destroyed should freedom be forced into steady retreat. Then the remaining free societies . . . would one day find themselves beleaguered and imperiled. We would face once again the dread prospect of paying dearly, in blood, for our own survival. . . .

The ideas of freedom are at work, even where they are officially rejected. As we know, Lenin and his successors, true to Communist doctrine, based the Soviet State on the denial of these ideas. Yet the new Soviet rulers who took over three years ago have had to reckon with the force of these ideas, both at home and abroad . . . .

In foreign affairs, the new regime has seemingly moderated the policy of violence and hostility which has caused the free nations to band together to defend their independence and liberties. For the present, at least, it relies more on political and economic means to spread its influence abroad. In the last year, it has embarked upon a campaign of lending and trade agreements directed especially toward the newly-developing countries.

It is still too early to assess in any final way whether the Soviet regime wishes to provide a real basis for stable and enduring relations.

Despite the changes so far, much of Stalin's foreign policy remains unchanged. The major international issues which have troubled the post-war world are still unsolved. More basic changes in Soviet policy will have to take place before the free nations can afford to relax their vigilance. . . .

As we take stock of our position and of the problems that lie ahead, we must chart our course by three main guide lines:

The first one is: We must maintain a collective shield against aggression to allow the free peoples to seek their valued goals in safety. . . .

Our second guide line is this: Within the free community, we must be a helpful and considerate partner in creating conditions where freedom will flourish.

Our third guide line is this: We must seek, by every peaceful means, to induce the Soviet bloc to correct existing injustices and genuinely to pursue peaceful purposes in its relations with other nations. . . .

The interests and purposes of the United States and of the free world do not conflict with the legitimate interests of the Russian nation or the aspirations of the Russian people. A Soviet government genuinely devoted to these purposes can have friendly relations with the United States and the free world for the asking. We will welcome that day.

Dwight Eisenhower, address, annual dinner of American Society of Newspaper Editors, April 21, 1956; *Papers of Presidents: Eisenhower*, 1956, pp. 414-21. Also see his radio-television report to the nation following the aborted Paris Summit Conference, May 25, 1960; *Papers of Presidents: Eisenhower*, 1960-1961, especially pp. 442-45.

3 6 5   COLD WAR AND PEACE

Truly as it was written long ago: "The wicked flee when no man pursueth." Yet it is sad to read these Soviet statements--to realize the extent of the gulf between us. But it is also a warning--a warning to the American people not to fall into the same trap as the Soviets, not to see only a distorted and desperate view of the other side, not to see conflict as inevitable, accommodation as impossible, and communication as nothing more than an exchange of threats.

No government or social system is so evil that its people must be considered as lacking in virtue. As Americans we find communism pro-foundly repugnant as a negation of personal freedom and dignity. But we can still hail the Russian people for their many achievements--in science and space, in economic and industrial growth, in culture and in acts of courage.

Among the many traits the peoples of our two countries have in common, none is stronger than our mutual abhorrence of war. Almost unique among the major world powers, we have never been at war with each other. And no nation in the history of battle ever suffered more than the Soviet Union suffered in the course of the Second World War. . . .

Today, should total war ever break out again--no matter how--our two countries would become the primary targets. It is an ironical but accurate fact that the two strongest powers are the two in the most danger of devastation. All we have built, all we have worked for, would be destroyed in the first 24 hours. And even in the cold war, which brings burdens and dangers to so many countries--including this nation's closest allies--our two countries bear the heaviest burdens. For we are both de-voting massive sums of money to weapons that could be better devoted to combating ignorance, poverty, and disease. We are both caught up in a vicious and dangerous cycle in which suspicion on one side breeds suspicion on the other and new weapons beget counterweapons.

In short, both the United States and its allies, and the Soviet Union and its allies, have a mutually deep interest in a just and genuine peace and in halting the arms race. Agreements to this end are in the interests of the Soviet Union as well as ours, and even the most hostile nations can be relied upon to accept and keep those treaty obligations, and only those treaty obligations, which are in their own interest.

So let us not be blind to our differences, but let us also direct at-tention to our common interests and to the means by which those dif-ferences can be resolved. And if we cannot end now our differences, at least we can help make the world safe for diversity. For in the final analysis our most basic common link is that we all inhabit this planet. We all breathe the same air. We all cherish our children's future. And we are all mortal.

John Kennedy, "Toward a Strategy of Peace," address, American University, June 10, 1963; *American Foreign Policy: Current Documents,* 1963, pp. 25-26. Also see comments of the Director, Intelligence and Research, Department of State, address, May 4, 1962; *American Foreign Policy: Current Documents*, 1962, pp. 660-74.

366   ATMOSPHERE VS. PURPOSE IN EAST-WEST RELATIONS

. . . It is clear there will be further disagreement between ourselves and the Soviets as well as further agreements. There will be setbacks in our nation's endeavors on behalf of freedom as well as successes. For a pause in the cold war is not a lasting peace, and a detente does not equal disarmament. The United States must continue to seek a relaxation of tensions, but we have no cause to relax our vigilance.

A year ago it would have been easy to assume that all-out war was inevitable, that any agreement with the Soviets was impossible, and that an unlimited arms race was unavoidable. Today it is equally easy for some to assume that the cold war is over, that all outstanding issues between the Soviets and ourselves can be quickly and satisfactorily settled, and that we shall now have, in the words of the psalmist, an "abundance of peace so long as the moon endureth."

The fact of the matter is, of course, that neither view is correct. We have, it is true, made some progress on a long journey. We have achieved new opportunities which we cannot afford to waste. We have concluded with the Soviets a few limited, enforcible agreements or arrangements of mutual benefit to both sides and to the world.

But a change in the atmosphere and in emphasis is not a reversal of purpose. Mr. Khrushchev himself has said that there can be no co-existence in the field of ideology. . . . The United States and the Soviet Union still have wholly different concepts of the world, its freedom, its future. We still have wholly different views on the so-called wars of liberation and the use of subversion. And so long as these basic differences continue, they cannot and should not be concealed; they set limits to the possibilities of agreement; and they will give rise to further crises, large and small, in the months and years ahead, both in the areas of direct confrontation . . . and in areas where events beyond our control could involve us both. . . .

. . . For all of these moves, and all of these elements of American policy and Allied policy toward the Soviet Union, are directed at a single, comprehensive goal--namely, convincing the Soviet leaders that it is dangerous for them to engage in direct or indirect aggression, futile for them to attempt to impose their will and their system on other unwilling people, and beneficial to them, as well as to the world, to join in the achievement of a genuine and enforcible peace.

John Kennedy, address, University of Maine, October 19, 1963; *American Foreign Policy: Current Documents*, 1963, pp. 31-32.

3 6 7   BRIDGES ACROSS THE GULF OF A DIVIDED EUROPE

We do not know when all European nations will become part of a single civilization. But, as President Eisenhower said in 1953: "This we do know: a world that begins to witness the rebirth of trust among nations can find its way to peace that is neither partial nor punitive."

We will continue to build bridges across the gulf which has divided us from Eastern Europe. They will be bridges of increased trade, of ideas, of visitors, and of humanitarian aid. We do this for four reasons:

First, to open new relationships to countries seeking increased independence yet unable to risk isolation.

Second, to open the minds of a new generation to the values and the visions of the Western civilization from which they come and to which they belong.

Third, to give freer play to the powerful forces of legitimate national pride--the strongest barrier to the ambition of any country to dominate another.

Fourth, to demonstrate that identity of interest and the prospects of progress for Eastern Europe lie in a wider relationship with the West. . . .

We are pledged to use every peaceful means to work with friends and allies so that all of Europe may be joined in a shared society of freedom.

Lyndon Johnson, remarks at dedication of George C. Marshall Research Library, Lexington, Virginia, May 23, 1964; *Papers of Presidents: Johnson,* 1963-1964, I, 709-10.

3 6 8   FORMULA FOR DEALING WITH THE COLD WAR

A second field of danger and opportunity is in our confrontation with Russia and Communist China.

There is no longer one cold war. There are many. They differ in temperature, intensity, and danger.

Our relations with the Soviet Union have come a long way since shoes were banged on desks here in New York and a summit meeting collapsed in Paris.

The test ban treaty and the "hot line" would not have been possible 10 years ago. Conditions did not permit such acts of reason.

When this is so men must work to change these conditions. This we did, from the Marshall plan to the Cuban crisis.

And men must also have the vision to seize the day of opportunity when it comes. This too we have done.

I believe we may be nearing a time for further and more lasting steps toward decreasing tensions and a diminishing arms race. I will try to take those steps--always in consultation with our friends.

I will expect respect for our courage and our convictions. I will offer understanding for the concerns and interests of others.

I will work for the growth of freedom and the survival of man.

In Asia there is a different prospect. On that strife-streaked continent an ambitious and aggressive power menaces weak and poor nations.

Here--as we have done in Europe--we must help create the conditions which can make peace possible. The task is different and more difficult. It is not less important.

We will assist against attack. We will strengthen our commitments of alliance. We will work with the nations of Asia to build the hope and self-confidence on which their independence must rest.

The final outcome will depend on the will of the Asian people. But as long as they turn to us for help we will be there. We will not permit the great civilizations of the East--almost half the people of the world--to be swallowed up in Communist conquest.

Let no one be foolhardy enough to doubt the strength of that unyielding American commitment.

Lyndon Johnson, remarks, Alfred E. Smith Memorial Foundation, New York, October 14, 1964; *American Foreign Policy: Current Documents,* 1964, pp. 50-51. Also see U.S. Ambassador to Yugoslavia, address, University of Louisville, January 5, 1965, in *American Foreign Policy: Current Documents,* 1965, pp. 528-32; and Under Secretary of State, address, Foreign Policy Association, New York, April 21, 1967, in *American Foreign Policy: Current Documents,* 1967, pp. 452-55.

369   FROM CONFRONTATION TO NEGOTIATION

Twenty years ago the United States and what was then the Communist bloc could be resigned to the mutual hostility that flowed from deep-seated differences of ideology and national purpose. Many of those differences remain today. But the changes of two decades have brought new conditions and magnified the risks of intractable hostility.

-- For us as well as our adversaries, in the nuclear age the perils of using force are simply not in reasonable proportion to most of the objectives sought in many cases. The balance of nuclear power has placed a premium on negotiation rather than confrontation.

-- We both have learned too that great powers may find their interests deeply involved in local conflict--risking confrontation--yet have precariously little influence over the direction taken by local forces.

-- The nuclear age has also posed for the United States and the Communist countries the common dangers of accidents or miscalculation. Both sides are threatened, for example, when any power seeks tactical advantage from a crisis and risks provoking a strategic response.

-- Reality has proved different from expectation for both sides. The Communist world in particular has had to learn that the spread of Communism may magnify international tensions rather than usher in a period of reconciliation as Marx taught.

Thus, in a changing world, building peace requires patient and continuing communication. Our first task in that dialogue is fundamental--to avert war. Beyond that, the United States and the Communist countries must negotiate on the issues that divide them if we are to build a durable peace. Since these issues were not caused by personal disagreements, they cannot be removed by mere atmospherics. We do not delude ourselves that a change of tone represents a change of policy. We are prepared to deal seriously, concretely and precisely with outstanding issues.

The lessons of the post-war period in negotiations with the Communist states--a record of some success, though much more of frustration--point to three clear principles. . . .

First: We will deal with the Communist countries on the basis of a precise understanding of what they are about in the world, and thus of what we can reasonably expect of them and ourselves. . . .

It will be the policy of the United States, therefore, not to employ negotiations as a forum for cold-war invective, or ideological debate. We will regard our Communist adversaries first and foremost as nations pursuing their own interests as **they** perceive these interests, just as we follow our own interests as we see them. We will judge them by their actions as we expect to be judged by our own. Specific agreements, and the structure of peace they help build, will come from a realistic accommodation of conflicting interests.

A second principle we shall observe in negotiating with the Communist countries relates to how these negotiations should be conducted--how they should be judged by peoples on both sides anxious for an easing of tensions. All too often in the past, whether at the summit or lower levels, we have come to the conference table with more attention to psychological effect than to substance. . . .

Negotiations must be, above all, the result of careful preparation and an authentic give-and-take on the issues which have given rise to them. They are served by neither bluff abroad nor bluster at home. . . .

The third essential in successful negotiations is an appreciation of the context in which issues are addressed. The central fact here is the inter-relationship of international events. We did not invent the inter-relationship; it is not a negotiating tactic. It is a fact of life. This Administration recognizes that international developments are entwined in many complex ways: political issues relate to strategic questions, political events in one area of the world may have a far-reaching effect on political developments in other parts of the globe.

These principles emphasize a realistic approach to seeking peace through negotiations.

Richard Nixon, "An Era of Negotiation," *U.S. Foreign Policy for the 1970's: A New Strategy for Peace* (1970), pp. 133-36. Also see his comments on this subject in his address to the United Nations General Assembly, September 18, 1969, in *Papers of Presidents: Nixon,* 1969, pp. 727-28, and his comparison of United States and Soviet differences affecting accommodation, in *U.S. Foreign Policy for the 1970's: The Emerging Structure of Peace* (1972), p. 18.

370   DETENTE AND SHARED INTERESTS

For decades, the central problems of our foreign policy revolved around antagonism between two coalitions, one headed by the United States and the other headed by the Soviet Union.

Our national security was often defined almost exclusively in terms of military competition with the Soviet Union. This competition is still critical, because it does involve issues which could lead to war. But however important this relationship of military balance, it cannot be our sole preoccupation to the exclusion of other world issues which also concern us both. . . .

Despite deep and continuing differences in world outlook, both of us should accept the new responsibilities imposed on us by the changing nature of international relations. . . .

Both the United States and the Soviet Union have learned that our countries and our people, in spite of great resources, are not all-powerful. We've learned that this world, no matter how technology has shrunk distances, is nevertheless too large and too varied to come under the sway of either one or two super powers. . . .

. . . I think that to understand today's Soviet-American relationship, we must place it in perspective, both historically and in terms of the overall global scene.

The whole history of Soviet-American relations teaches us that we will be misled if we base our long-range policies on the mood of the moment, whether that mood be euphoric or grim. All of us can remember times when relations seemed especially dangerous and other times when they seemed especially bright. . . .

The profound differences in what our two governments believe about freedom and power and the inner lives of human beings, those differences are likely to remain; and so are other elements of competition between the United States and the Soviet Union. That competition is real and deeply rooted in the history and the values of our respective societies. But it's also true that our two countries share many important overlapping interests. Our job . . . is to explore those shared interests and use them to enlarge the areas of cooperation between us on a basis of equality and mutual respect.

As we negotiate with the Soviet Union, we will be guided by a vision of a gentler, freer, and more bountiful world. But we will have no illusions about the nature of the world as it really is. The basis for complete mutual trust between us does not yet exist. Therefore, the agreements that we reach must be anchored on each side in enlightened self-interest--what's best for us, what's best for the Soviet Union. That's why we search for areas of agreement where our real interests and those of the Soviets coincide.

Jimmy Carter, remarks, Annual Meeting of the Southern Legislative Conference, July 21, 1977; *American Foreign Policy: Basic Documents,* 1977-1980, pp. 561-62. Also see his address on confrontation or cooperation with the Soviet Union, U.S. Naval Academy, June 7, 1978, pp. 565-69, and the statement of the Special Adviser to the Secretary of State, House Foreign Affairs Committee, October 16, 1979, pp. 570-74.

3 7 1   REFLECTIONS ON U.S.-SOVIET RELATIONS

I have come here today to suggest that this notion of trusting the power of human freedom and letting the people do the rest was not just a good basis for our economic policy; it proved a solid foundation for our foreign policy as well. That is what we have given to the people, why we have repeated what they instinctively knew but what the experts had shied away from saying in public. We spoke plainly and bluntly. We rejected . . . moral equivalency. We said freedom was better than totalitarianism. We said communism was bad. We said a future of nuclear terror was unacceptable. We said we stood for peace, but we also stood for freedom. We said we held fast to the dream of our Founding Fathers--the dream that someday every man, woman, and child would live in dignity and in freedom. And because of this, we said containment was no longer enough; that the expansion of human freedom was our goal. We spoke for democracy, and we said that we would work for the day when the people of every nation enjoyed the blessing of liberty.

At first, the experts said this kind of candor was dangerous, that it would lead to a worsening of Soviet-American relations. But far to the contrary, this candor made clear to the Soviets the resilience and strength of the West; it made them understand the lack of illusions on our part about them or their system. By reasserting values and defining once again what we as a people and a nation stood for, we were . . . making a moral and spiritual point. And in doing this, we offered hope for the future, for democracy; and we showed we had retained that gift for dreaming that marked this continent and our nation at its birth.

In all this, we were also doing something practical. We had learned long ago that the Soviets get down to serious negotiations only after they are convinced that their counterparts are determined to stand firm. We knew the least indication of weakened resolve on our part would lead the Soviets to stop the serious bargaining, stall diplomatic progress, and attempt to exploit this perceived weakness.

We were candid. We acknowledged the depth of our disagreements and their fundamental, moral import. In this way, we acknowledged that the differences which separated us and the Soviets were deeper and wider than just missile counts and number of warheads. As I have said before, we do not mistrust each other because we are armed; we are armed because we mistrust each other. . . .

That was why we resolved to address the full range of the real causes of that mistrust and raise the crucial moral and political issues directly with the Soviets. . . .

And now this approach to the Soviets--public candor about their system and ours, a full agenda that put the real differences between us on the table--has borne fruit.

Ronald Reagan, remarks, World Affairs Council of Western Massachusetts, Springfield, April 21, 1988; 88 *Department of State Bulletin* (July 1988): 1-3. Also see George Shultz, statement on U.S.-Soviet relations in the context of American foreign policy, Senate Foreign Relations Committee, June 15, 1983, in *American Foreign Policy: Current Documents,* 1983, pp. 507-14, and Ronald Reagan, address, United Nations General Assembly, September 24, 1984, in *Papers of Presidents: Reagan,* 1984, II, 1360-61.

WASHINGTON-MOSCOW HOT LINE

Although the desirability of establishing a White House-Kremlin hot line was under consideration in the late 1950's, the requirement for "instant" diplomatic exchanges at the highest level was accelerated by the Cuban missile crisis of 1962 (for summit notes during this crisis, see Documents 185-188). Shortly thereafter, despite the Cold War, negotiations were undertaken by United States and Soviet delegations to the Committee on Disarmament at Geneva. A preliminary agreement was reached in April 1963 and a formal accord was signed on June 20 (Document 372). This provided for a duplex wire telegraphic circuit, routed from Washington via London, Copenhagen, Stockholm, and Helsinki to Moscow, with a backup radio circuit via Tangier.

As communications technology improved, this arrangement was supplemented with an agreement signed in 1971, which added two circuits that employed satellite facilities, and with an amplifying agreement signed in 1984, which provided for a facsimile capability to transmit graphic materials as well as for techniques to speed up exchanges. This hot line is resorted to only on rare occasions--to avoid miscalculation, to emphasize the importance of policy and clarify sensitive developments, to moderate destabilizing actions and confrontation, and especially to prevent the precipitation of war.

372   HOT LINE AGREEMENT, U.S. AND U.S.S.R., 1963

For use in time of emergency the Government of the United States of America and the Government of the Union of Soviet Socialist Republics have agreed to establish as soon as technically feasible a direct communications link between the two Governments.

Each Government shall be responsible for the arrangements for the link on its own territory. Each Government shall take the necessary steps to ensure continuous functioning of the link and prompt delivery to its head of government of any communications received by means of the link from the head of government of the other party.

Arrangements for establishing and operating the link are set forth in the Annex which is attached hereto and forms an integral part hereof.

Memorandum of Understanding Between the United States and the Union of Soviet Socialist Republics Regarding the Establishment of a Direct Communications Link, June 20, 1963. TIAS 5362; 14 *U.S. Treaties* 825-35. Technical details are contained in its Annex (7 articles). This was supplemented by agreements to improve the hot line in 1971 (TIAS 7187; 22 *U.S. Treaties* 1598-1615) with an amendatory exchange of notes, April 29, 1975 (TIAS 8059; 26 *U.S. Treaties* 564-66) and in 1983 (*Papers of Presidents: Reagan*, 1983, I, 526, 759, and 1984, II, 1051). For an earlier agreement on the establishment of a commercial radio teletype communication channel linking the U.S. and U.S.S.R., May 24, 1946, see TIAS 1527; 11 Bevans, *Treaties and Other International Agreements* 1291-94. For reference to the use of the hot line during the *Liberty* crisis in 1967, see Document 216.

TREATIES AND AGREEMENTS

Despite the Cold War and the Iron and Bamboo Curtains, the United States and the Soviet Union, as well as the People's Republic of China, and their satellites, have negotiated more than 200 bilateral treaties and agreements since 1945. Of these, some 45 were signed by the United States with the Soviet Union, 25 with China, and approximately 140 with East European Communist satellites. These supplemented 75 pre 1945 agreements, thus totaling nearly 300. They deal with a variety of subjects, ranging from nuclear war and arms limitation to diplomatic and consular representation, and from agricultural, commercial, and environmental cooperation to pacific settlement, civil aviation, and maritime, postal, telecommunications, and other technical matters.

In addition, China, the Soviet Union, and its allies are party to the United Nations and fourteen of its specialized agencies (three of which antedate 1945), and signed a good many other multipartite treaties, such as those dealing with diplomatic relations (1961), consular relations (1963), nuclear nonproliferation (1968), rescue of astronauts (1968), aircraft hijacking (1970), aircraft sabotage (1971), terrorism (1971), biological warfare (1972), outer space, and many others. In sum, therefore, in the 1980's the Soviet and Chinese governments were parties to more than 250 bilateral and multilateral treaties to which the United States is a party. For a list of current treaties and agreements, see *Treaties in Force*.

Several agreements are particularly relevant to the general problem of East-West relations. In addition to the hot line agreements, to launch his program of rapprochement with China and detente with the Kremlin, in 1972 President Nixon negotiated special bilateral arrangements with their leaders to stabilize and improve relations (see Documents 373-374). Three years later the United States and the Soviet Union also signed the Helsinki Accord, providing for peace and stability in a divided Europe (see Chapter 29).

373 BASIC PRINCIPLES OF RELATIONS, U.S. AND PEOPLE'S REPUBLIC OF CHINA--SHANGHAI COMMUNIQUE, 1972

There are essential differences between China and the United States in their social systems and foreign policies. However, the two sides agreed that countries, regardless of their social systems, should conduct their relations on the principles of respect for the sovereignty and territorial integrity of all states, non-aggression against other states, non-interference in the internal affairs of other states, equality and mutual benefit, and peaceful coexistence. International disputes should be settled on this basis, without resorting to the use or threat of force. The United States and the People's Republic of China are prepared to apply these principles to their mutual relations.

With these principles of international relations in mind the two sides stated that:

-- progress toward the normalization of relations between China and the United States is in the interests of all countries;

-- both wish to reduce the danger of international military conflict;

-- neither should seek hegemony in the Asia-Pacific region and each is opposed to efforts by any other country or group of countries to establish such hegemony; and

-- neither is prepared to negotiate on behalf of any third party or to enter into agreements or understandings with the other directed at other states.

Both sides are of the view that it would be against the interests of the peoples of the world for any major country to collude with another against other countries, or for major countries to divide up the world into spheres of interest. . . .

The two sides agreed that it is desirable to broaden the understanding between the two peoples. To this end, they discussed specific areas in such fields as science, technology, culture, sports and journalism, in which people-to-people contacts and exchanges would be mutually beneficial. Each side undertakes to facilitate the further development of such contacts and exchanges.

Both sides view bilateral trade as another area from which mutual benefit can be derived, and agreed that economic relations based on equality and mutual benefit are in the interest of the peoples of the two countries. They agree to facilitate the progressive development of trade between their two countries.

The two sides agreed that they will stay in contact through various channels, including the sending of a senior U.S. representative to Peking from time to time for concrete consultations to further the normalization of relations between the two countries and continue to exchange views on issues of common interest.

The two sides expressed the hope that the gains achieved during this visit would open up new prospects for the relations between the two countries. They believe that the normalization of relations between the two countries is not only in the interest of the Chinese and American peoples but also contributes to the relaxation of tension in Asia and the world.

Joint communique, summit meeting, February 27, 1972; 66 *Department of State Bulletin* (March 20, 1972): 437-38. For presentation of independent U.S. and Chinese policy positions, see pp. 436-37, and for joint statement on the status of Taiwan, see pp. 437-38.

374 BASIC PRINCIPLES OF RELATIONS, U.S. AND U.S.S.R., 1972

The United States of America and the Union of Soviet Socialist Republics,
. . .

Have agreed as follows:

First. They will proceed from the common determination that in the nuclear age there is no alternative to conducting their mutual relations on the basis of peaceful coexistence. Differences in ideology and in the social systems of the USA and the USSR are not obstacles to the bilateral development of normal relations based on the principles of sovereignty, equality, non-interference in internal affairs and mutual advantage.

Second. The USA and the USSR attach major importance to preventing the development of situations capable of causing a dangerous exacerbation of their relations. Therefore, they will do their utmost to avoid military confrontations and to prevent the outbreak of nuclear war. They will always exercise restraint in their mutual relations, and will be prepared to negotiate and settle differences by peaceful means. Discussions and negotiations on outstanding issues will be conducted in a spirit of reciprocity, mutual accommodation and mutual benefit. . . .

Third. The USA and the USSR have a special responsibility, as do other countries which are permanent members of the United Nations Security Council, to do everything in their power so that conflicts or situations will not arise which would serve to increase international tensions. Accordingly, they will seek to promote conditions in which all countries will live in peace and security and will not be subject to outside interference in their internal affairs.

Fourth. The USA and the USSR intend to widen the juridical basis of their mutual relations and to exert the necessary efforts so that bilateral agreements which they have concluded and multilateral treaties and agreements to which they are jointly parties are faithfully implemented.

Fifth. The USA and the USSR reaffirm their readiness to continue the practice of exchanging views on problems of mutual interest and, when necessary, to conduct such exchanges at the highest level, including meetings between leaders of the two countries. . . .

Sixth. The Parties will continue their efforts to limit armaments on a bilateral as well as on a multilateral basis. They will continue to make special efforts to limit strategic armaments. Whenever possible, they will conclude concrete agreements aimed at achieving these purposes. . . .

Seventh. The USA and the USSR regard commercial and economic ties as an important and necessary element in the strengthening of their bilateral relations and thus will actively promote the growth of such ties.
. . .

Eighth. The two sides consider it timely and useful to develop mutual contacts and cooperation in the fields of science and technology. Where suitable, the USA and the USSR will conclude appropriate agreements dealing with concrete cooperation in these fields.

Ninth. The two sides reaffirm their intention to deepen cultural ties with one another and to encourage fuller familiarization with each other's cultural values. They will promote improved conditions for cultural exchanges and tourism.

Tenth. The USA and the USSR will seek to ensure that their ties and cooperation in all the above-mentioned fields and in any others in their mutual interest are built on a firm and long-term basis. To give a permanent character to these efforts, they will establish in all fields where this is feasible joint commissions or other joint bodies.

Eleventh. The USA and the USSR make no claim for themselves and would not recognize the claims of anyone else to any special rights or advantages in world affairs. They recognize the sovereign equality of all states.

The development of U.S.-Soviet relations is not directed against third countries and their interests.

Twelfth. The basic principles set forth in this document do not affect any obligations with respect to other countries earlier assumed by the USA and the USSR.

Agreement, May 29, 1972; *Papers of Presidents: Nixon*, 1972, pp. 633-35. Also see summit meeting joint communique, May 29, 1972, pp. 635-42.

SUMMIT CONFERENCES AND MEETINGS WITH SOVIET AND CHINESE LEADERS

Certain aspects of United States diplomacy with the leaders of the Soviet Union and the People's Republic of China are conducted at the highest levels, involving the President, the Secretary of State, and presidential special emissaries. So far as the President's personal involvement is concerned, this entails exchanges of written and telephonic communications and the use of the hot line, the commissioning of envoys as presidential personal surrogates, and summit conferences and meetings. For a list of such conclaves since World War II, see Document 375, and for concrete examples of presidential summit communications, see Chapters 8 and 11.

375 LIST OF PRESIDENTIAL SUMMIT CONFERENCES AND MEETINGS WITH SOVIET AND CHINESE LEADERS SINCE 1945

President	Date	Location	Country	Leaders
Eisenhower	July 1955	Geneva	U.S.S.R.-France-U.K.	Khrushchev
	Sept. 1959	Washington	U.S.S.R.	Khrushchev
	May 1960	Paris	U.S.S.R.-France-U.K.	Khrushchev
Kennedy	June 1961	Vienna	U.S.S.R.	Khrushchev
Johnson	June 1967	Glassboro, NJ	U.S.S.R.	Kosygin
Nixon	Feb. 1972	Beijing	China	Mao Tse-tung, Chou En-lai
	May 1972	Moscow	U.S.S.R.	Kosygin, Brezhnev
	June 1973	Washington	U.S.S.R.	Brezhnev

President	Date	Location	Country	Leaders
Ford	June 1974	Moscow	U.S.S.R.	Brezhnev
	Nov. 1974	Vladivostok	U.S.S.R.	Brezhnev
	July 1975	Helsinki	U.S.S.R.	Brezhnev
	Dec. 1975	Beijing	China	Mao Tse-tung, Deng Xiaoping
Carter	Jan. 1979	Washington	China	Deng Xiaoping
	June 1979	Vienna	U.S.S.R.	Brezhnev
Reagan	Jan. 1984	Washington	China	Zhao Ziyang
	Apr. 1984	Beijing	China	Deng Xiaoping, Zhao Ziyang
	July 1985	Washington	China	Li Xiannian
	Nov. 1985	Geneva	U.S.S.R.	Gorbachev
	Oct. 1986	Reykjavik	U.S.S.R.	Gorbachev
	Dec. 1987	Washington	U.S.S.R.	Gorbachev
	May 1988	Moscow	U.S.S.R.	Gorbachev
	Dec. 1988	Moscow	U.S.S.R.	Gorbachev
Bush	Feb. 1989	Beijing	China	Deng Xiaoping, Li Peng
	Dec. 1989	Malta	U.S.S.R.	Gorbachev
	May 1990	Washington	U.S.S.R.	Gorbachev
	Sept. 1990	Helsinki	U.S.S.R.	Gorbachev

Comprehensive lists of presidential participation in summitry are provided in Elmer Plischke, *Presidential Diplomacy: A Chronology of Summit Visits, Trips, and Meetings* (Dobbs Ferry: Oceana, 1986), with participation in summit conferences and meetings treated in Chapter 5.

REFORM IN SOVIET ORBIT AND DETENTE--THRESHOLD OF A NEW ERA

During the latter 1980's revolutionary changes were instituted in Eastern Europe and in East-West relations. When Mikhail Gorbachev achieved political leadership in the Soviet Union in 1985, and was named President three years later (so that he headed both the Communist Party and the government), he introduced the principles of *glasnost* (openness) and *perestroika* (restructuring), and he undertook--or permitted--a series of actions that portended critical economic, political, and military reforms in the Soviet Union and the Communist countries of Eastern Europe, which some referred to as a "velvet revolution."

These are illustrated in the economic sphere by transition from planned to open market economies, private investment and development, and agricultural and industrial modernization. In the political arena they included: allowing public demonstrations (which espoused the cause of freedom and reform), the remolding of political institutions, the emergence of new, and, in some cases, non-Communist leadership, movement toward political pluralism, elimination of Communist Party political monopoly, moderation of autocracy and statism, institution of democratization, and liberalization of human rights.

In military affairs, the Soviet government planned unilateral troop reductions, evidenced greater willingness to negotiate mutual and balanced reduction of military forces in Europe, signed and implemented the Intermediate Nuclear Force (INF) Treaty (1987), and accelerated negotiations for strategic nuclear weapons agreements. It also rescinded the Brezhnev Doctrine (which justified Soviet military intervention to preserve the Communist order in Eastern Europe), withdrew Soviet forces from Afghanistan, supported open borders in Eastern Europe, and even countenanced the withdrawal of East Germany from the Warsaw Pact. In addition, it refrained from intervening in plans to open the Berlin Wall, to reunify the two Germanys, and to resolve Germany's continued membership in the North Atlantic Alliance, nor did it prevent the raising of the Iron Curtain. For documentation on changes in Berlin and German reunification, see Chapter 8, Documents 148-149.

During the last years of the Reagan administration, the United States encouraged this emerging trend toward reform in the Communist countries of Eastern Europe, emphasizing such matters as constructive actions to buttress declarations of peaceful intent; temper public rhetoric; reduce confrontation; cease exporting Communist revolution and the Soviet system, foreign adventurism, and hegemonism (in Afghanistan and elsewhere); end the division of Europe--and of Germany and Berlin--and tear down the Wall; liberalize the application of human rights; implement the Helsinki process; and mitigate the Cold War. For illustrations, see Documents 376-377.

As the reform movement advanced in 1989 and into the 1990's, the Bush administration publicly promoted a return to the principles of the Atlantic Charter (referred to in Chapters 5 and 16); the development of a united and open Europe, linking East and West, thereby ending the division of Europe and applying the right of self-determination; the institution and strengthening of democracy; the freeing of political, economic, and social institutions; the healing of old wounds and generating friendlier relations; and the creation of a commonwealth of free nations, with Eastern Europe joining Western Europe-- thus heralding the threshold of a new era, a new European order, and a host of new interrelational issues and problems for the United States (Documents 378- 380). For additional commentary and documents on European unity and interdependence, United States partnership with Europe, and the Helsinki process, see Chapter 29, Documents 505-519.

376   COMMON INTERESTS AND CONSTRUCTIVE COOPERATION

Neither we nor the Soviet Union can wish away the differences between our two societies and our philosophies. But we should always remember that we do have common interests. And the foremost among them is to avoid war and reduce the level of arms. There is no rational alternative but to steer a course which I would call credible deterrence and peaceful competition; and if we do so, we might find areas in which we could engage in constructive cooperation. . . .

But if the United States and the Soviet Union are to rise to the challenges facing us and seize the opportunities for peace, we must do more to find areas of mutual interest and then build on them. I propose that our governments make a major effort to see if we can make progress in three broad problem areas.

First, we need to find ways to reduce--and eventually to eliminate-- the threat and use of force in solving international disputes. . . .

Our second task should be to find ways to reduce the vast stockpiles of armaments in the world. . . .

Our third task is to establish a better working relationship with each other, one marked by greater cooperation and understanding.

Cooperation and understanding are built on deeds, not words. Complying with agreements helps; violating them hurts. Respecting the rights of individual citizens bolsters the relationship; denying these rights harms it. Expanding contacts across borders and permitting a free interchange of information and ideas increase confidence; sealing off one's people from the rest of the world reduces it. Peaceful trade helps, while organized theft of industrial secrets certainly hurts.

Ronald Reagan, address to the nation, January 16, 1984; *American Foreign Policy: Current Documents,* 1984, pp. 407-8.

377 PORTENTS OF CHANGE IN EASTERN EUROPE AND IN EAST-WEST RELATIONS

And now the Soviets themselves may, in a limited way, be coming to understand the importance of freedom. We hear much from Moscow about a new policy of reform and openness. Some political prisoners have been released. Certain foreign news broadcasts are no longer being jammed. Some economic enterprises have been permitted to operate with greater freedom from state control. Are these the beginnings of profound changes in the Soviet state? Or are they token gestures, intended to raise false hopes in the West, or to strengthen the Soviet system without changing it? We welcome change and openness; for we believe that freedom and security go together, that the advance of human liberty can only strengthen the cause of world peace.

*   *   *

. . . we embarked in this decade on a new postwar strategy, a forward strategy of freedom, a strategy of public candor about the moral and fundamental differences between statism and democracy, but also a strategy of vigorous diplomatic engagement; a policy that rejects both the inevitability of war or the permanence of totalitarian rule, a policy based on realism that seeks not just treaties for treaties' sake but the recognition and resolution of fundamental differences with our adversaries.

. . . I believe this policy is bearing fruit. Quite possibly, we're beginning to take down the barriers of the postwar era; quite possibly, we are entering a new era in history, a time of lasting change in the Soviet Union. . . .

In all aspects of Soviet life, the talk is of progress toward democratic reform--in the economy, in political institutions, in religious, social, and artistic life. It is called *glasnost*--openness; it is *perestroika*--restructuring. Mr. Gorbachev and I discussed such things as official accountability, limitations on length of service in office, an independent judiciary, revisions of the criminal law, and lowering taxes on cooperatives; in short, giving individuals more freedom to run their own affairs, to control their own destinies.

To those of us familiar with the postwar era, all of this is cause for shaking the head in wonder. . . .

And yet, while the Moscow summit [May 1988] showed great promise and the response of the Soviet people was heartening, let me interject here a note of caution and, I hope, prudence. It has never been disputes between the free peoples and the peoples of the Soviet Union that have been at the heart of postwar tensions and conflicts. No, disputes among governments over the pursuit of statism and expansionism have been the central point in our difficulties. Now that the allies are strong and expansionism is receding around the world and in the Soviet Union, there is hope. And we look to this trend to continue. We must do all we can to assist it. And this means openly acknowledging positive change and crediting it. . . . Let us embrace honest change when it occurs. But let us also be wary; let us stay strong; and let us be confident, too.

*   *   *

In a number of addresses this year . . . I've pointed to the extra-ordinary progress made on so many fronts, that truly "peace is breaking out all over.". . .

And yet as we've also frequently pointed out, what prevented progress in the past in these areas, indeed, what was at the heart of the Cold War, was not some failure of communications or giant misunderstanding between East and West. Far to the contrary, it was understanding not misunderstanding that was the root cause. . . . the true nature of the Soviet regime, the fundamental distinction between totalitarianism and democracy, and the moral duty to resist the international threat to human rights posed by Soviet expansionism. It was these realities, not some unfortunate or avoidable misunderstanding, that caused East-West tension. And we can forget this lesson only at the greatest peril.

But fortunately, it's also here we see the most encouraging change of all. Every issue of the morning paper seems to bring with it news of questioning in the Soviet Union: questioning of state control of industry, of restrictions on human rights, and even of the ideology of world domination, of class warfare in international politics, all of which formed the greatest barriers between our two nations. This talk of democratic reform in the Soviet Union remains tentative, hardly the stuff of sure-fire prophecy. Still, to those of us used to the monolithic nature of Soviet society in the postwar era, these changes seem remarkable. . . .

We see a restiveness also in Eastern Europe, where peoples who've been denied their right of self-determination for four decades are exploring the limits of a new, seemingly more tolerant environment. . . . Throughout the region, the pressures of change--and, yes, for freedom--

are accelerating. . . .

Change, indeed, is inevitable. No one should doubt the instability of the present situation in Eastern Europe, in which an artificial economic and political system, long imposed on these peoples against their will, is more and more exposed as bankrupt and discredited. The new degree of tolerance of experimentation is welcome; but no one should doubt, either, that Moscow's handling of the growing drive for self-determination within its European empire will be a vital test for us of how deep is the transformation of Soviet foreign policy in a new era.

So, whatever the future may hold, it's safe to say: We've come a long way, and this is a portentous time. . . .

Ronald Reagan, remarks at Brandenburg Gate in West Berlin, June 12, 1987; remarks, Royal Institute of International Affairs, London, June 3, 1988; remarks, World Affairs Council, Los Angeles, October 28, 1988; in *Papers of Presidents: Reagan* 1987, I, 635, and 24 *Weekly Compilation of Presidential Documents* (June 6 and November 7, 1988): 735, 737, 1393-94. For his comments on the effect of his summit meeting with President Gorbachev in Iceland in 1986, also see *Presidential Papers: Reagan*, 1987, I, 75-77.

378 COMMENT ON CHANGES IN EASTERN EUROPE AND IN EAST-WEST RELATIONS

The Western strategy, our strategy of containment, was a means, but was never an end in itself. It was no substitute for a free and united Europe. And we did not forget the frustrated and lost hopes of 1945 nor the promise of a better world. . . .

And now, at long last, two developments have allowed us to redeem the principles of the Atlantic Charter. . . . One is the manifest failure of the classic Stalinist system; and the other is the indomitable will of the people. . . .

And now . . . the genuine opportunity exists for all of us to build a Europe which many thought was destroyed forever in the 1940's. That Europe, the Europe of our children, will be open, whole, and free. We can make it so in two ways. First, a new East-West relationship must rest on greatly reduced levels of arms. . . . The new willingness in Moscow to accept this Western framework for reductions in troops and tanks and aircraft and other categories of weapons gives us hope that the negotiations in Vienna will succeed. A good beginning has been made. Constructive proposals are being offered on both sides. We are determined to push hard for an early and successful conclusion to these talks. Second, reductions in military forces will go further and be more sustainable if they take place in parallel with political change. Excessive levels of arms, we believe, are the symptom, and not the source, of political tensions. In Europe those tensions spring from an unnatural and cruel division.

*　　*　　*

And there's Eastern Europe. Let me explain the approach that I take towards reform in Eastern Europe. We will never compromise our principles. We will always speak out for freedom. But we understand as well how vital a carefully calibrated approach is in this time of dynamic change. The Soviet Union has nothing, nothing, to fear from the reforms that are now unfolding in some of the nations of Eastern Europe. We support reform in Eastern Europe and in the Soviet Union. . . . I've said it many times--that I want to see *perestroika* succeed. I want to see the Soviet Union chart a course that brings itself into the community of nations.

And my visits these last 2 months demonstrate how closely the United States is linked to Europe. For half a century, America has been deeply involved in the future of this continent. And U.S. involvement will be a strategic fact the next century, as it has been for this one. We will play a constructive role in Eastern Europe's economic development, in the development of political pluralism, and in creating an international climate in which reform can succeed. . . .

The new world we seek is a commonwealth of free nations working in concert, a world where more and more nations enter a widening circle of freedom. . . .

And we all know what followed. Half of Europe entered that new era, and half of Europe found its path blocked, walled off by barriers of brick and barbed wire. The half of Europe that was free dug out from the rubble, recovered from the war [World War II] and laid the foundations of free government and free enterprise that brought unparalleled prosperity and a life in peace and freedom. And the other Europe, the Europe behind the wall, endured four decades of privation and hardship and persecution and fear.

And today that other Europe is changing. The great wheel is moving once more. And our time, the exciting time in which we live, is a time of new hope: the hope that all of Europe can now know the freedom. . . . Our hope is that the unnatural division of Europe will now come to an end, that the Europe behind the wall will join its neighbors to the West, prosperous and free.

*   *   *

The changes in recent months make clear that the process of reform initiated by the Eastern Europeans and supported by Mr. Gorbachev and by America and by our allies is real, offers us all much hope, and deserves our continued encouragement. We're living in fascinating times, and we will seize every opportunity to contribute to lasting peace and to extend democracy. And in doing so, I will conduct the foreign policy of this great country with the prudence that these fascinating times, times of change demand--and with the imagination. The 1980's has been the decade of American renewal. And I believe that around the world, the 1990's will inevitably be the decade of democracy.

*   *   *

Change is coming swiftly, and with this change, the dramatic vindi-cation of free Europe's economic and political institutions. The new Europe that is coming is being built--must be built--on the foundation of democratic values. But the faster the pace, the smoother our path must be. After all, this is serious business. The peace we are building must be different than the hard, joyless peace between two armed camps we've known so long. The scars of the conflict that began a half century ago still divide a continent. So, the historic task before us now is to begin the healing of this old wound. . . .

So, as we celebrate the events of Eastern Europe, remember that some walls still remain between East and West. These are the invisible walls of suspicion; the walls of doubt, misunderstanding, and mis-calculation. . . .

We will seek President Gorbachev's assurance that this process of reform in Eastern Europe will continue, and we will give him our assurance that America welcomes reform not as an adversary seeking advantage but as a people offering support. Our goal is to see this historic tide of freedom broadened, deepened, and sustained.

*   *   *

In any time of great change, it is good to have firm principles to guide our way. Our governments committed themselves again in May to seek an end to the painful division of Europe. We have never accepted this division. The people of every nation have the right to determine their own way of life in freedom.

Of course, we have all supported German reunification for four decades. And in our view, this goal of German unification should be based on the following principles.

First, self-determination must be pursued without prejudice to its outcome. We should not at this time endorse nor exclude any particular vision of unity. Second, unification should occur in the context of Germany's continued commitment to NATO and an increasingly integrated European Community, and with due regard for the legal role and responsibilities of the allied powers. Third, in the interests of general European stability, moves toward unification must be peaceful, gradual, and part of a step-by-step process. Lastly, on the question of borders, we should reiterate our support for the principles of the Helsinki Final Act.

An end to the unnatural division of Europe and of Germany must proceed in accordance with and be based upon the values that are becoming universal ideals, as all the countries of Europe become part of a commonwealth of free nations.

George Bush, remarks, National Assembly, Warsaw, Poland, July 10, 1989; remarks, Leiden, Netherlands, July 17, 1989; remarks, National Association of Realtors, Dallas, Texas, November 10, 1989; Thanksgiving address to the nation, November 22, 1989; and statement, North Atlantic Treaty Organization Headquarters, Brussels, December 4, 1989; in 25 *Weekly Compilation of Presidential Documents* (July to December, 1989):   1070, 1118-19, 1716,

1821, 1888. For additional comments indicating that relations have changed for the better, that events evidence progress for a Europe that is whole and free, and that the dream of the NATO powers is becoming a reality, see pp. 1850, 1885, 1920. Also see Chapter 8, Documents 148-149.

3 7 9   *PERESTROIKA* AND AMERICAN FOREIGN POLICY

What explains this mixed record? Some analysts, invoking past disappointments, argue that the Soviets are engaged in a mere "peredyshka" --a breathing space until Leninism is strong enough to do battle once more with capitalism. Others, invoking future hope, argue that the new thinkers are so consumed by domestic concerns that old thinking still holds sway over certain aspects of foreign policy.

But to me, it reveals something else.

I find a certain parallel between the course of Soviet domestic perestroika and new thinking in Soviet foreign policy. Domestically, as Gorbachev has sought to turn theory into practice, his program has altered and evolved. And just as the Soviets have come face to face with domestic dilemmas that must now be resolved if progress is to be made, so they will come face to face with the need for further change in their foreign policy.

Domestically, we can have but small direct impact on how the Soviets resolve their dilemmas. But in foreign and defense policy, through a prudent search for points of mutual advantage, we can more readily shape and alter the calculus so that the Soviets face up to the contradictions between the new thinking and old habits. In arms control, the Kremlin has made some politically difficult choices and in some areas selected the path of mutual progress. Now, we must also shape the Soviet calculus so that Moscow chooses the path of progress in regional conflicts.

In the course of our search for mutual advantage, we must not succumb to a false optimism that perestroika in Soviet foreign policy has gone far enough and that we can rely on the new thinking to take account of our interests.

It would be an equally great blunder to ignore the possibility that perestroika might go much further and to retreat instead into a suspicious stance of disengagement that would never put perestroika's promise to the test.

Either approach would sacrifice the great opportunity before us.

Thus, our mission must be to press the search for mutual advantage. Where we find Soviet agreement, we'll both be better off. Where we meet Soviet resistance, we'll know that we have to redouble our efforts so that Moscow practices, not just preaches, the new thinking. By acting realistically to engage Moscow in the search for mutual interests, we can seize the opportunities inherent in Gorbachev's revolution. By standing pat, we would gain nothing and lose this chance to revolutionize East-West relations.

James A. Baker III, address, "Points of Mutual Advantage: *Perestroika* and American Foreign Policy," 89 *Department of State Bulletin* (December 1989): 12; for entire address, see pp. 10-14.

380 THRESHOLD OF A NEW ERA--TIME FOR HOPE

This year the people of the East made fundamental choices about their destiny, and governments there began to honor the citizen's right to choose. What these changes amount to is nothing less than a peaceful revolution. And the task before us, therefore, is to consolidate the fruits of this peaceful revolution and provide for architecture for continued peaceful change, to end the division of Europe and Germany, to make Europe whole and free.

Great choices are being made. Greater opportunities beckon. . . .

Although this is a time of great hope . . . we must not blur the distinction between promising expectations and present realities. . . . The U.S. will remain a European power, and that means that the United States will stay engaged in the future of Europe and in our common defense.

Many of the values that should guide Europe's future are described in the Final Act of the [Helsinki] Conference on Security and Cooperation in Europe. These values encompass the freedom of people to choose their destiny under a rule of law with rulers who are democratically accountable. I think we can look to the CSCE to play a greater role in the future of Europe. The 35 nations of the CSCE bridge both the division of Europe and the Atlantic Ocean. It's a structure that should be able to contribute much to the future architecture of Europe. . . .

We stand on the threshold of a new era. And we know that we are contributing to a process of history driven by the peoples determined to be free. . . .

Our transatlantic partnership can create the architecture of a new Europe and a new Atlanticism, where self-determination and individual freedom everywhere replace coercion and tyranny, where economic liberty everywhere replaces economic controls and stagnation, and where lasting peace is reinforced everywhere by common respect for the rights of man.

George Bush, comments, news conference, Brussels, December 4, 1989; 25 *Weekly Compilation of Presidential Documents* (December 11, 1989): 1891.

23

North-South Relations

> . . . let me turn to the problems of the Third World and our dealings
> with them and our stake in doing so successfully. Many of our
> citizens still see the developing countries as accessories to our
> basic interests. But over the past two decades, these countries have
> increasingly moved to the front of the stage where issues of peace
> and prosperity are played out. I believe this trend has assumed
> such proportions that I can advance two propositions.
>
> First, there will be no enduring economic prosperity for our
> country without economic growth in the Third World.
>
> Second, there will not be peace and security for our citizens
> without stability and peace in developing countries.
>
> George Shultz
> Address, Southern Center for International Studies, 1983

The concept "North-South relations" generally poses the advanced industrialized nations of the northern hemisphere against the less developed nations
(LDCs), many of which lie in the southern hemisphere. However, the nature of
categories of states since World War II is far more complex. Initially, during
the war there were approximately fifty anti-Axis allies fighting the Axis
powers and a small number of neutral countries. Later, as the Cold War
intensified and newly independent states emerged, the alignment mutated. Based
on political affiliation, this produced the Western democratic and Eastern Communist blocs with a third, increasingly sizable, group of countries, which
preferred neutralism and nonalignment, and remaining unaffiliated. Their
primary goals centered on decolonization (applied primarily against the World
War II anti-Axis imperial powers) and non-involvement in East-West disputes, conflicts, and potential warfare. So far as the East-West relationship,
based on preserving their security through massive armaments and alliances,
is concerned, the bloc of neutralist or nonaligned nations still continues, as
represented by their periodic conclaves.

However, when more than one hundred new states achieved their independence and the Cold War moderated, this neutralist aggregation, beginning in the

early 1960's--while continuing diplomatic nonalignment to preserve their independence--extended their goals to economic development and a more influential role in international decision making and in shaping the world's economic system to their advantage. Emphasis on economic affairs, such as per capita income, introduced new designations called First (Western Alliance), Second (Communist bloc), Third, and Fourth World blocs--or, using the International Bank's designations, they are designated as rich, middle income, poor, and very poor classes of nations. Often those falling into the third and fourth categories are grouped simply as the "Third World," which is essentially coterminous with the neutralists.

Subsequently "development" became the criterion for distinguishing states, resulting in apposing developed versus undeveloped, underdeveloped, or less developed, industrialized versus developing, and modernized versus modernizing states. Finally, reminiscent of earlier history in which "imperial" and "dependent" entities were differentiated, but now basing distinction on economic factors, some simply label them as "have" and "have-not" nations.

This profusion of designations produced a great deal of confusion. For example, a country may belong to both the Communist bloc and the Third World, or it may be neutralist and fall into the middle-income group, or it may adhere to either the Western or the Communist alliance and be regarded as developing or less developed. To which blocs, for example, do countries like Brazil, the two Chinas, Iceland, Israel, Mexico, Saudi Arabia, South Africa, Switzerland, and Yugoslavia belong? On which issues do bloc members agree or disagree? Which states are clearly developed, industrialized, or legally and politically neutral, and which are actively developing or modernizing? And which states bridge antipodal categories? Unless clear-cut criteria for distinction--such as formal alliance affiliation (political) or reliable per capita income (economic)--are applied, the aggregating expressions "neutralist," "Third World," "less developed," and "developing" are often misleading, and as they creep into statements of national objectives, policies, and analysis, they obfuscate both official and popular understanding.

Documentation on United States purposes and policies in dealing with Third World/ developing/less developed nations is devoted to recognizing basic needs--food, health, shelter, education, employment, human rights, and the advancement of the quality of life--and to responding with proposals to overcome hunger, disease, poverty, illiteracy, and hopelessness. Often documents stress the need for peace and stability, self-help (expressed as help for others to help themselves), and social and economic reform. In addition, in the economic sphere they deal with modernization, economic growth and stability, resource development, technical advancement, industrialization, foreign assistance (both loans and grants), international trade, and foreign capital and indebtedness. Trade, in turn, raises issues of an open world economy, exports and imports, protectionism versus trade liberalization, and most-favored-nation treatment and reciprocity versus trade preferences.

Aside from direct diplomacy, the mechanisms employed by the United States and nonaligned/Third World/developing/less developed countries include a variety of forums. One group, most obvious, encompasses such global facilities as (1) the United Nations; (2) its subsidiaries--the Economic and

Social Council (ECOSOC) and regional Economic Commissions; (3) its specialized agencies including the Food and Agriculture Organization, the International Bank and International Monetary Fund (and their subsidiaries), the United Nations Educational, Scientific and Cultural Organization, and the World Health Organization; and (4) such more specialized programs and institutions as the Special Fund for Economic Development (SUNFED), the United Nations Conference on Trade and Development (UNCTAD), the Capital Development Fund (UNCDF) and Development Program (UNDP), the Expanded Program of Technical Assistance (UN-EPTA), the Industrial Development Organization (UNIDO), the Institute for Training and Research (UNITAR), and formerly the United Nations Relief and Rehabilitation Administration (UNRRA). Also see Chapter 25 on the United Nations.

A second group embraces regional groupings represented by the inter-American system (see Chapter 26), the Organization for Economic Cooperation and Development (OECD), and regional banks and development funds. A third group consists of arrangements to provide goal and policy coordination of the nonaligned/Third World/developing blocs, including periodic conferences commencing with that convened at Belgrade in 1961, and epitomized by the "Group of 77," launched at the time of the first session of UNCTAD in 1964, which has grown to approximately 160 members, as well as other regional and issue-oriented caucusing groups, which function "unofficially" throughout the United Nations system. A fourth category is represented by the annual Western economic summit meetings, which usually consider North-South economic problems and development assistance. The final category is composed of ad hoc North-South ("rich-poor") conclaves, such as the Conference on International Economic Cooperation (CIEC), convened initially at Paris in 1976, and that at Cancun, Mexico, in 1981.

The documents contained in this chapter illustrate United States perceptions, objectives, and policies respecting three aspects of North-South relations. The first, on neutralism, concerns American interpretations of purposes and the general policy of nonalignment (Documents 381-383). The second, on United States relations with the developing world, deals with America's commitment to help, its objectives, strategy, and cooperation, assessment of responsibility, the importance of the Third World, and the relations of economic and political freedom to development (Documents 384-391). The final section focuses on the North-South dialogue and the New International Economic Order (NIEO), including the progression of the dialogue and the United States position on several features of this discourse (Documents   392-396).

This chapter needs to be related particularly to Chapters 7 (presidential doctrines), 17 (trade and commerce, especially trade legislation and treaty complex), 10 (alliances and alignments), 22 (East-West relations), 24 (foreign, especially development, assistance), and 25 (United Nations system, especially on politicizing of issues and its voting process, see Documents 434-435 and 438-439). Additional documents--concerning self-determination and independence (Documents 264-273), the Alliance for Progress (Documents 557-558), and the American Caribbean Initiative (Documents 125-127 and 565)--are also relevant. On neutralism and nonalignment respecting Africa, also see Documents 477-478.

NONALIGNMENT--NEUTRALISM

3 8 1   NEUTRALISM--BETWEEN RIGHT AND WRONG OR BETWEEN EAST AND WEST

If you are waging peace, you can't be too particular sometimes about the special attitudes that different countries take. We were a young country once, and our whole policy for the first hundred years was--or more, 150--we were neutral. . . .

Now, today there are certain nations that say they are neutral. This doesn't necessarily mean what it is so often interpreted to mean, neutral as between right and wrong or decency or indecency.

They are using the term "neutral" with respect to attachment to military alliances. And may I point out that I cannot see that that is always to the disadvantage of such a country as ours.

If a nation is truly a neutral, if it is attacked by anybody--and we are not going to attack them--public opinion of the world is outraged.

If it has announced its military association with another great power, things could happen to it, difficulties along its borders, and people would say: "Good enough for it; they asked for it."

So let us not translate this meaning of the word "neutral" as between contending military forces, even though the conflict is latent, and neutral as between right and wrong.

Dwight Eisenhower, remarks, press conference, June 6, 1956; *American Foreign Policy: Current Documents*, 1956, p. 32. For White House statement commenting on the President's remarks, see pp. 32-33. It states that "in some countries of the world there are certain ideological, geographical or other reasons making military alliances impractical" so that they may "declare themselves to be neutral" between East and West, but that the President "believes in the principle of collective security whereby nations aggregate "for each other's protection."

3 8 2   GENERAL UNITED STATES POLICY TOWARD NONALIGNED NATIONS

Second, what of the developing and nonaligned nations? . . .

They are beginning to realize that the longing for independence is the same the world over, . . . They are beginning to realize that such independence runs athwart all Communist ambitions but is in keeping with our own--and that our approach to their diverse needs is resilient and resourceful, while the Communists are still relying on ancient doctrines and dogmas.

Nevertheless it is hard for any nation to focus on an external or subversive threat to its independence when its energies are drained in daily combat with the forces of poverty and despair. . . .

I am proud of a program that has helped to arm and feed and clothe millions of people who live on the front lines of freedom.

I am especially proud that this country has put forward for the 60's a vast cooperative effort to achieve economic growth and social progress throughout the Americas--the Alliance for Progress. . . .

This story is the same in Africa, in the Middle East, and in Asia. Wherever nations are willing to help themselves, we stand ready to help them build new bulwarks of freedom. We are purchasing votes for the cold war; we have gone to the aid of imperiled nations, neutrals and allies alike. What we do ask--and all that we ask--is that our help be used to best advantage, and that their own efforts not be diverted by needless quarrels with other independent nations. . . .

But free world development will still be an uphill struggle. Government aid can only supplement the role of private investment, trade expansion, commodity stabilization, and, above all, internal self-improvement. The processes of growth are gradual--bearing fruit in a decade, not a day. Our successes will be neither quick nor dramatic. But if these programs were ever to be ended, our failures in a dozen countries would be sudden and certain.

Neither money nor technical assistance, however, can be our only weapon against poverty. In the end, the crucial effort is one of purpose, requiring the fuel of finance but also a torch of idealism.

John Kennedy, Annual Message to Congress, January 14, 1963; *Papers of Presidents: Kennedy,* 1963, pp. 16-17.

3 8 3   INDEPENDENCE--OUR GOAL FOR NONALIGNED NATIONS

As for the neutrals: Why do we suppose that there is such a fundamental difference between our allies and the neutrals? I have already noted that we were not buying satellites when we went into alliances. . . . We are interested in the independence of nations, and over the years our alliances have been formed in order that others can have our support in their own attempt to be free and independent under pressure.

The President and others before him have declared that the basic policy of this country is to work toward a world community of independent nations, free to work out their own lives as they see fit but cooperating across national frontiers on matters of common interest and joining to get mutual jobs accomplished.

From that point of view, the difference between an ally and a neutral is not fundamental and far-reaching. The independence of neutrals is also important to us. The vitality of independent neutral states is a part of that world community which we see ahead of us as we work along on these foreign policy questions.

So in our approach to these questions there is no severe shock to our ultimate goals when we pass from the problems of alliances to the problems of other states, because our basic purpose . . . is a community of independent nations cooperating in common interest for the preservation of peace and for the accomplishment of great common objectives.

We don't cater to neutrals. But we do believe that any nation and people who want to preserve their independence are on the same side in this great global struggle. Certainly it is not in our interest to push them into the arms of the Communist world by any expression of hostility toward them at a time when they are, themselves, struggling for their independence.

Dean Rusk, remarks, Advertising Council, Washington, March 6, 1962; *American Foreign Policy: Current Documents,* 1962, p. 20. Also see his comments on this subject, address, Foreign Policy Association, New York, November 20, 1962, pp. 44-45; and those of Chester Bowles, Under Secretary of State, address, Kansas City, October 26, 1961, pp. 51-52. Also see the message of President Kennedy to the Belgrade Conference of nonaligned states, reported in his news conference, August 30, 1961 in *Papers of Presidents: Kennedy,* 1961, p. 573, and of President Johnson to the Cairo Conference of nonaligned states, in *Papers of Presidents: Johnson,* 1963-1964, II, 1209. For commentary on the Havana (1979) and New Delhi (1983) Conferences, see *Historic Documents* for these years.

RELATIONS WITH DEVELOPING WORLD

3 8 4   UNITED STATES COMMITMENT TO SUPPORT DEVELOPING NATIONS

A third field of opportunity and danger is our relation to the developing world. . . .

I do not believe that our island of abundance will be finally secure in a sea of despair and unrest, or in a world where even the oppressed may one day have access to the engines of modern destruction.

Moreover, there is a great moral principle at stake. It is not right --in a world of such infinite possibilities--that children should die of hunger, that young people should live in ignorance, that men should be crippled by disease, that families should live in misery, shrouded in despair.

If we truly mean our commitment to freedom, we must help strike at the conditions which make a mockery of that hope. . . .

We have the skills and resources to improve the life of man. I do not believe we lack the imagination to find ways to shatter the barrier between man's capacity and man's needs.

Lyndon Johnson, remarks, annual dinner, Alfred E. Smith Memorial Foundation, New York, October 14, 1964; *American Foreign Policy: Current Documents,* 1964, pp. 51-52.

385 STRATEGY TO DEAL WITH UNDERDEVELOPMENT

The second dimension of our strategy concerns our posture toward the revolution of modernization going forward in Latin America, Africa, Asia, and the Middle East . . . .

What we sometimes call underdeveloped nations represent a wide spectrum with different problems marking each stage along the road to self-sustained growth. Some of these nations are well along that road; others are just beginning. And, in the end, each nation, like each individual, is, in an important sense, unique. What is common throughout these regions is that men and women are determined to bring to bear what modern science and technology can afford in order to elevate the standards of life of their peoples and to provide a firm basis for positions of national dignity and independence on the world scene.

The United States is firmly committed to support this effort. We look forward to the emergence of strong, self-confident nations which, out of their own traditions and aspirations, create their own forms of modern society. We take it as our duty--and our interest--to help maintain the integrity and the independence of this vast modernization process, in as far as our resources and our ability to influence the course of events permit.

Working increasingly in partnership with our friends in Europe and Japan, our objective is to see emerge a new relation of north-south cooperation among self-respecting, sovereign nations to supplant the old colonial ties which are gone or fast disappearing from the world scene.

Walt Rostow, Chairman of Policy Planning Council, Department of State, address, Institute of North American Studies, Barcelona, Spain, October 6, 1964; *American Foreign Policy: Current Documents*, 1964, pp. 43-44.

386 STRATEGY FOR DEALING WITH THE THIRD WORLD

I speak of our relations with the developing nations. For our ability to make progress on issues of vital importance to our nation--from the search for peace to the building of an international economy that helps meet the needs of our people--depends increasingly on our having a positive, long-term strategy toward the Third World. . . .

Our approach is based on one central reality: America's interest in close relations with the developing nations is large and growing. Our policy reflects also the reality of rapid change among and within those nations. And it is grounded in the conviction that we best serve our interests there by supporting the efforts of developing nations to advance their economic well-being and preserve their political independence. . . .

Our interest in building strong relationships with the developing world, however, goes far beyond the mutual benefits of our expanding economic ties. Our efforts to build a more peaceful and secure world will continue to compel our attention to the developing countries.

During the past three decades, armed conflict in the world has centered on problems involving developing nations. And it is a fact of modern international politics that the United States can best help resolve regional disputes in the developing world with the cooperation of the nations in the region, both directly and through the United Nations and regional organizations. We must work together with the nations which have the closest understanding of local realities. . . .

And we need to work closely with the developing world on a wide range of other challenges that we share. We share an interest in narrowing the combustible disparity between wealth and poverty. We share an interest in striking a decent balance between the burgeoning demands of more people for a better life and the immutable reality of limited resources. We share an interest in achieving a steady and more equitable rise in standards of living without destroying our planet in the process.

On these, and other long-term challenges which are truly global in scope, we can make enduring progress only through cooperative action.

Our approach toward the developing world, then, must be based not only on our genuine humanitarian concern for the harsh conditions of life faced by hundreds of millions of our fellow human beings, it must also be grounded on the inescapable proposition that peace and prosperity for ourselves, now and for the future, is directly related to the strength of our relations with the developing nations and the political and economic paths they choose to pursue.

Cyrus Vance, address, National Urban League, Chicago, July 23, 1979; *American Foreign Policy: Basic Documents,* 1977-1980, pp. 303-5. For commentary of Robert McNamara, Secretary of Defense, on development and violence among developing countries, see his address "The Problem of Security in the Contemporary World," in *American Foreign Policy: Current Documents,* 1966, pp. 14-19.

3 8 7 COOPERATION STRATEGY FOR DEVELOPMENT AND GROWTH

We understand and are sensitive to the diversity of developing countries. Each is unique in its blend of cultural, historical, economic, and political characteristics. But all aspire to build a brighter future, and they can count on our strong support. We will go to Cancun ready and willing to listen and to learn. We will also take with us sound and constructive ideas designed to help spark a cooperative strategy for global growth to benefit both the developed and developing countries. Such a strategy rests upon three solid pillars.

First, an understanding of the real meaning of development, based on our own historical experience and that of other successful countries;

Second, a demonstrated record of achievement in promoting growth and development throughout the world, both through our bilateral economic relations and through cooperation with our partners. . . .

Third, practical proposals for cooperative actions in trade, investment, energy, agriculture, and foreign assistance that can contribute to a new era of prosperity and abundance exceeding anything we may dream possible today.

We very much want a positive development dialogue, but sometimes this dialogue becomes oversimplified and unproductive. For example, some people equate development with commerce, which they unfairly characterize as simple lust for material wealth. Others mistake compassion for development and claim massive transfers of wealth somehow miraculously will produce new well-being. And still others confuse development with collectivism, seeing it as a plan to fulfill social, religious, or national goals, no matter what the cost to individuals or historical traditions.

All of these definitions miss the real essence of development. In its most fundamental sense, it has to do with the meaning, aspirations, and worth of every individual. In its ultimate form, development is human fulfillment--an ability by all men and women to realize freely their full potential to go as far as their God-given talents will take them.

Ronald Reagan, "Cooperative Strategy for Global Growth," address, World Affairs Council, Philadelphia, October 15, 1981; *Papers of Presidents: Reagan*, 1981, pp. 937-38 and Department of State, *Realism, Strength, Negotiation* (Washington: Department of State, 1984), p. 138. On the Cancun Conference also see Document 396.

388 OBJECTIVES AND RESPONSIBILITIES FOR DEVELOPMENT PROGRAMS

The most important objective of the lower income countries of Africa, Asia, and Latin America--where two-thirds of humanity live--is their economic and social progress. It is their highest priority. It is the overriding commitment of most of their governments. Thus it is a subject of central importance in our relations with them. For we cannot expect these nations to join with us in building a structure of peaceful relationships unless we cooperate with them to help solve the problems which they regard as most critical to them. Nor can we expect the changes which will inevitably come in these countries to be accomplished peacefully unless we help them do so . . . .

First of all, many lower income countries are today ready and able to assume the primary responsibility for articulating their own requirements, setting their priorities, and generating the bulk of the resources necessary for their own development. They are eager to do so; in fact, they demand the recognition of their right to do so.

Secondly, while the United States remains the largest single contributor to international development, the other industrial nations of the world together extend more assistance than we do.

Thirdly, international institutions--such as the World Bank group and regional development banks--are now capable of fusing the efforts of all countries into a true multilateral partnership for development.

The new United States assistance program will be designed to realize the full potential of this broader sharing of responsibility--with the developing countries themselves, with the other industrial nations, and with multilateral organizations. . . .

Richard Nixon, *U.S. Foreign Policy for the 1970's: Building for Peace* (1971), pp. 142-43. Also see his Message to Congress, September 15, 1970, in *United States Foreign Policy: 1969-1970: A Report of the Secretary of State* (1971), pp. 469-70; and commentary in *United States Foreign Policy, 1972: A Report of the Secretary of State* (1973), pp. 45-46. On Sharing of responsibility, also see President Nixon's Special Message to Congress, May 1, 1973; *Papers of Presidents: Nixon,* 1973, p. 334.

389 IMPORTANCE OF UNITED STATES DEVELOPMENT PROGRAM

Despite a record of significant accomplishment . . . hundreds of millions of people in the developing countries still exist in conditions of extreme hunger, poverty, and disease. Basic humanitarian considerations call on us to assist these countries in improving the lives of their people. But we also have a major economic and political interest in the growth and stability of these countries and in their active cooperation. . . .

But an increased pace of development is essential. Unless substantial progress occurs--through efforts by developed and developing nations alike--the stability of many countries and regions can be jeopardized as essential needs of people go unsatisfied.

There has been a growing tendency to question our commitment to help developing nations. Attracted to rapid solutions and under-estimating the time and effort needed to stimulate development, Americans are frustrated by the slow pace of visible progress. But, our future economic and political needs will be far better served by actively cooperating with the developing countries for our mutual benefit than by neglecting their needs. We must pursue a realistic policy of development assistance and find better ways of dealing with the trade and monetary interests of developing nations.

Richard Nixon, *U.S. Foreign Policy for the 1970's: Shaping a Durable Peace* (1973), p. 172.

390 UNITED STATES AND DEVELOPING COUNTRIES--JOINT STAKE IN THE WORLD ECONOMY

More than three-quarters of the world's population live in what we call the developing world. . . . much of the world's future is being shaped by what happens in those hundred-odd nations embracing the broad majority of humanity. . . .

. . . The evolution of the developing countries and the problems they encounter challenge much of our conventional thinking about both political and economic development. And these events and trends in the developing world affect our own lives more directly than most of us realize.

The importance of development is not only economic but also political. The challenge is not so much to our resources as to our political insight into the evolution of traditional societies in the modern age. The broader problem is not simply one of economic advance but of international order. . . .

The United States shares the hope of the world's peoples that mankind will choose the first path--toward a world of progress, freedom, and peace. This is the kind of world that Americans hope to see in the remainder of this century and in the next. We are prepared to invest our fair share of effort and resources to help bring it about. . . .

We have enough experience now to see that economic development is a complex process with many pitfalls and far-reaching implications. There used to be a naive assumption that economic advance brought political stability almost automatically. . . .

Instability may well be part of the turbulent course of political and economic development in the Third World--just as it was, indeed, through the industrial revolution in what is now the advanced Western world. Growing consciousness and social participation in a traditional society may create new claimants on both economic resources and political power faster than new and untested political structures can accommodate them. . . .

The real meaning of development, after all, is what it means for the well-being, aspirations, dignity, and achievement of each individual. The process of development is fulfilled when every man and woman in a society has the opportunity to realize his or her fullest potential. We have seen in our own history how a free people, in a free market, create prosperity by their effort and imagination. But a society develops also by the free association of individuals, working together in voluntary and productive endeavors of every kind. Government has an undeniable role-- as the accountable servant of the people; as the provider of public safety and the common defense; as the guarantor of human rights, due process of law, and equal opportunity. . . .

The peoples of these vibrant, developing countries want, first of all, a voice in determining their own destiny. Therefore, they distrust ideologies and foreign forces that prescribe totalitarian rule and are notorious failures at providing economic advance. Our own democratic system, in contrast, embodies the values of freedom and progress, which the peoples of the developing countries see as not only relevant but sympathetic to their own aspirations.

Therefore, our policies toward the developing world must include a range of means and a depth of understanding.

-- We must offer patient support for social and economic reform and for the strengthening of free political, economic, and social institutions.

-- Sometimes we must offer security assistance to help ensure that the process of democratic evolution is not disrupted or overwhelmed by armed minorities backed by external powers and alien ideologies.

-- And we must continue our proud record of leadership in international trade and financial cooperation to promote economic development and progress in the developing world.

Now just let me say some things about our joint stake in the world economy, because here, again, I think we see the transformation that I don't think people quite appreciate. The American effort is important, first of all, for the reasons I have already mentioned--in helping to shape a peaceful and secure international order for the remainder of this century and beyond. But it is also important, in the here and now, because the developing countries are already a major factor in the world's economic health. We have a significant stake in their progress. . . .

This intimate link between the developing countries' and our own prosperity is financial as well as commercial. . . .

The historic lesson here is a simple one. Today the effective functioning of the global trade and financial system depends heavily on the participation, and health, of the developing countries as well as of the industrial countries. The reality of mutual interest between the Northern and Southern Hemispheres is not at all reflected in either the doctrinaire Third World theory of debilitating dependency or the aid giver's obsolete sense of patronage. There is now a relationship of mutual responsibility. Our common task is to make this link a spur to growth in both regions, instead of an entanglement of mutual decline.

George Shultz, address, Foreign Policy Association, New York, May 26, 1983; Department of State, *Realism, Strength, Negotiation* (Washington: Department of State, 1984), pp. 146-47. Also see his comments on fundamentals for dealing with developing nations, address, Southern Center for International Studies, February 24, 1983, p. 143. On growing United States stake in developing world, see earlier statement of Edmund Muskie, January 15, 1981; *American Foreign Policy: Basic Documents*, 1977-1980, p. 89.

391   DEVELOPMENT REQUIRES ECONOMIC AND POLITICAL FREEDOM

Everyday life confirms the fundamentally human and democratic ideal that individual effort deserves economic reward. Nothing is more crushing to the spirit of working people and to the vision of development itself than the absence of reward for honest toil and legitimate risk. So let me speak plainly: We cannot have prosperity and successful development without economic freedom; nor can we preserve our personal and political freedoms without economic freedom. Governments that set out to regiment their people with the stated objective of providing security and liberty have ended up losing both. Those which put freedom as the first priority find they have also provided security and economic progress.

The United States is proud of its contributions to the goals and institutions of post-war development. You can count on us to continue to shoulder our responsibilities in the challenges that we face today. We see two of overriding importance: restoring the growth and vitality of the world economy and assuring that all countries, especially the poorest ones, participate fully in the process of growth and development. But let us remember, the most important contribution any country can make to world development is to pursue sound economic policies at home.

Ronald Reagan, remarks, annual meeting of the Board of Governors of the World Bank and the International Monetary Fund, September 29, 1981; *Papers of Presidents: Reagan,* 1981, p. 855.

NORTH-SOUTH DIALOGUE AND THE NEW INTERNATIONAL ECONOMIC ORDER

392 DEVELOPMENT OF THE NORTH-SOUTH DIALOGUE

The North-South dialogue grew out of the experience of the developing countries in the 1950s and 1960s, when they discovered that in the U.N. General Assembly they could command world attention. Unlike the Bretton Woods institutions [the International Bank (IB) and Monetary Fund (IMF)], in which voting is weighted heavily in favor of industrial countries and meetings are closed to the public, in the U.N. institutions each country has an equal vote. Developing countries are able to make their demands heard and constitute majority votes in those fora, particularly when they act in unison. They first used this power to demand an end to colonialism, but by the 1960s, as the curtain rang down on the colonial empires, developing countries increasingly turned their attention to the international economic system in the U.N. fora.

The decade of the 1970s marked an intense period of North-South dialogue. Debate turned highly confrontational in the U.N. Sixth Special Session in the spring of 1974, in which the developing countries demanded a new international economic order. A more constructive tone was set in 1975 with the Seventh Special Session of the United Nations and the launching of the Conference on International Economic Cooperation in Paris, and in the spring of 1976 with UNCTAD [U.N. Conference on Trade and Development] IV in Nairobi. In 1979 the combination of a deteriorating world economic climate and dissension among the developing countries over their priorities and over the question of energy, led the developing countries to call for an inclusive, high-level round of global negotiations, to be launched by the 11th Special Session. . . .

For the United States, the developing countries are increasingly important both economically and politically. They are major suppliers of raw materials, including, of course, oil, and our most rapidly growing export markets . . . .

Thus, it is not only out of humanitarian concern but also for hardheaded economic and security reasons that the United States should listen carefully to the concerns enunciated by the developing countries in the North-South dialogue. These demands tend to revolve around three themes--obtaining needed foreign exchange, assuring availability of technology for development, and increasing the decisionmaking power of developing countries in the economic system. . . .

In sum, the goal of the developing countries in the North-South dialogue is to restructure the international economic system--to create a new international economic order--which has as primary objectives the promotion of their development and what they consider a more equitable distribution of the world's wealth.

We understand and sympathize with the aspirations of the developing countries. However, we also have an enormous stake in the continuing smooth functioning of the international economic system. . . .

In a sense, then, the North-South dialogue involves weighing a variety of politically, economically, and socially desirable goals--development, growth, efficiency, equity, and stability--in evaluating specific policy proposals. . . .

Under Secretary of State for Economic Affairs, Department of State, statement, House Foreign Affairs Committee, May 15, 1980; *American Foreign Policy: Basic Documents,* 1977-1980, pp. 308-10. For President Carter's comment on United States participation in the North-South dialogue, see *Papers of Presidents: Carter,* 1978, p. 120.

393 NORTH-SOUTH DIALOGUE AND THE "NEW INTERNATIONAL ECONOMIC ORDER"

. . . In 1974 in Algiers the new international economic order was born with its strong demands for greater equality in economic relations between the developed and the developing countries.

The new international economic order in the form of a declaration of U.N. purposes and of the obligations of industrialized states to make sweeping changes in trade, aid, and investment policy, was brought before the sixth special session of the United Nations in 1974. The United States found itself virtually isolated as European countries expressed at least rhetorical sympathy for the thrust of this new order. That session brought home starkly to American policymakers for the first time the potential impact of these demands on our political as well as our economic relations with the developing world.

The next 2 years, then, saw the beginning of a fundamental reassessment of how the have and have-not nations would relate to each other. At the seventh special session, in September of 1975, with the memory of the fruitless confrontations the previous year still fresh in their minds, both sides began to rethink their respective positions and to search for areas of constructive dialogue and possible cooperation. One of the results was the formation, in December of that year, of the Conference on International Economic Cooperation (CIEC) with 8 members from the developed world and 19 from the developing world. While CIEC did not, over the some 18 months of its existence, succeed in finding accommodation between all of the issues where the North and South differ, it did contribute measurably to the ongoing dialogue and resulted in concrete progress on some issues such as food and agriculture and technical assistance. And while CIEC did narrow some gaps between the North and the South, many of the developing countries were unhappy with their exclusion from the limited membership of the CIEC.

As a result, CIEC was succeeded by the Committee of the Whole which includes all member states of the United Nations. This is now an important forum for discussion of economic matters relating to the North-South dialogue. The developing countries would like to give it a decisionmaking role. We continue to believe decisions on major economic issues should be made by existing organizations having responsibilities in the specific functional areas, for example, the GATT [General Agreement on Tariffs and Trade] for trade, the IMF [International Monetary Fund] for monetary affairs.

There were other elements to the dialogue. The year 1976 saw the Nairobi meeting of the U.N. Conference on Trade and Development, known as UNCTAD 4. While providing its share of confrontation, this meeting saw the United States continuing to signal its willingness to maintain a constructive dialogue regarding the demands of the developing countries. This willingness to engage in dialogue was, however, clearly separated from any affirmation of the legitimacy of all the other demands of these countries. Subsequently, at Colombo, Sri Lanka, the nonaligned nations met and found that economic issues had replaced political issues as the primo vehicles for expressing their aspirations and frustrations.

Under Secretary of State for Political Affairs, Department of State, address, Commonwealth Club and World Affairs Council, San Francisco, November 16, 1978; *American Foreign Policy: Basic Documents,* 1977-1980, pp. 299-300. Also see President Carter's address on "Creating a Just International Order," Venezuelan Congress, Caracas, March 29, 1978, pp. 295-99. In 1974 the United Nations General Assembly passed a resolution to establish a New International Economic Order.

394 NEEDS AND DEMANDS OF THE THIRD WORLD

. . . And a new bloc of nations, the Third World, emerged demanding a fairer share and a greater voice in the world economy.

It is this new bloc, comprised of the developing countries, that commands majorities in the United Nations and demands attention to its own priority--a new international economic order. It wants systemic changes in the world monetary system, greater resource transfers from the industrialized countries, better access to technology, and a greater voice in international economic decision making.

The developing countries' demands do not always make economic sense, but there is a ring of justice in their call. . . . Yet they are vitally important to the industrialized countries. The dependence of the North on the oil supplies from the South only dramatizes but does not complete the picture of how mutually dependent--indeed interdependent--we have become. And the dynamics of this interdependence also imply a condition of mutual vulnerability which begs for intensive search and drastic resolution of the outstanding differences.

Assistant Secretary of State for International Organization Affairs, address, Harvard University Modal United Nations, December 4, 1980; *American Foreign Policy: Basic Documents,* 1977-1980, p. 375.

395 UNITED STATES POSITION ON ECONOMIC OBJECTIVES OF THE THIRD WORLD

I want you to know where my country stands. In recent years I know that some have come to question the motives of my country and to believe that we, as a rich and powerful nation, can only be addressed as though we were an adversary. At this meeting, and at this moment, I want the policy of the United States to be understood.

There should be a new international economic system. In that system there must be equity; there must be growth; but above all, there must be justice. We are prepared to help build that new system.

But at the same time, we are prepared to admit that it will not be built here this week, nor will it be built without many painful adjustments, accommodations, and sacrifices by all of us present here today.

The United States will not be passive in this effort. We will not merely react. We will join with you in sharing the responsibility to lead.

As a first step, and before the business of this conference has been completed, I wish to make clear that we believe the North-South dialogue should continue. We are openminded about the appropriate forum.

The larger vision underlying CIEC is far more important than the smaller and temporary interests which sometimes divide us. It is this larger vision--the vision of a world in which common humanity and common values can override regional or national selfishness--which we must continually keep foremost in our minds.

Now let me speak about the tangible ways we can begin. . . .

Development requires capital, technology, and managerial skills on an enormous scale. They must come from many nations, in many ways. Official development assistance will remain a significant source of support and must be increased worldwide. But private capital is also vital and will continue to offer even greater resources over a wider range of activities than official aid. . . .

Let me be candid. Too many of our transfers, too much of our aid, has not been intelligently directed to the purposes and priorities which will really make a difference in people's lives. . . .

We can be counted upon to help in ways the American Congress and American people will support. That means insistence upon sound development criteria in use of money we contribute. . . .

After resource transfers, there is private investment--investment that builds in a partnership that works for developing countries and investors alike. The growth plans of the world's developing economies require a level of foreign investment well beyond the capacity of official sources alone. . . .

But private investment can be effective only if it is truly acceptable to the host country. Each nation must decide for itself the role that private investment should play in development. Private firms, in turn, will invest where they are confident of positive and predictable treatment. . . .

In addition to resource transfers and capital, trade in commodities is critical, as well as our shared interests in stability of price and supply.

When commodity markets fluctuate wildly, development planning in low-income countries is disrupted or made impossible. When commodity prices rise sharply, inflation intensifies and lasts long after these prices have turned downward--hitting rich and poor countries alike. . . . We must work together:

-- To establish agreements between producers and consumers to stabilize the prices of individual commodities, wherever the nature of the commodity and the market permit;

-- To create a common fund--that is efficient and that works--to back up commodity agreements;

-- To assure the adequacy of compensatory finance to help offset fluctuation in the export earnings of developing countries;

-- To provide enough investment to develop new supplies of primary products adequate to meet the needs of an expanding world economy; and

-- To support product improvement and diversification where specific commodities face stagnant or declining demand.

The United States will take part in all these efforts.

Cyrus Vance, address, Conference on International Economic Cooperation (CIEC), Paris, May 30, 1977; *American Foreign Policy: Basic Documents,* 1977-1980, pp. 292-94.

396   UNITED STATES POSITION ON DEVELOPMENT IN NORTH-SOUTH DIALOGUE

We recognize that each nation's approach to development should reflect its own cultural, political, and economic heritage. That is the way it should be. The great thing about our international system is that it respects diversity and promotes creativity. Certain economic factors, of course, apply across cultural and political lines. We are mutually interdependent, but, above all, we are individually responsible. . . .

History demonstrates that time and again, in place after place, economic growth and human progress make their greatest strides in countries that encourage economic freedom.

Government has an important role in helping to develop a country's economic foundation. But the critical test is whether government is genuinely working to liberate individuals by creating incentives to work, save, invest, and succeed. . . .

With sound understanding of our domestic freedom and responsibilities, we can construct effective international cooperation. Without it, no amount of international good will and action can produce prosperity.

In examining our collective experience with development, let us remember that international economic institutions have also done much to improve the world economy. Under their auspices, the benefits of international commerce have flowed increasingly to all countries. . . .

Much remains to be done to help low-income countries develop domestic markets and strengthen their exports. We recognize that. But we are just as convinced that the way to do this is not to weaken the very system that has served us so well, but to continue working together to make it better.

I am puzzled by suspicions that the U.S. might ignore the developing world. The contribution America has made to development--and will continue to make--is enormous. . . .

We are prepared to carry out the commitment in the Ottawa summit declaration to conduct a more formal dialog--bilaterally, with regional groups, in the United Nations, and in specialized international agencies. We take seriously the commitment at Ottawa "to participate in preparations for a mutually acceptable process of global negotiations in circumstances offering the prospects of meaningful progress."

It is our view that "circumstances offering the prospect of meaningful progress" are future talks based upon four essential understandings among the participants:

-- The talks should have a practical orientation toward identifying, on a case-by-case basis, specific potential for or obstacles to development which cooperative efforts may enhance or remove. We will suggest an agenda composed of trade liberalization, energy and food resource development, and improvement in the investment climate.

-- The talks should respect the competence, functions, and powers of the specialized international agencies upon which we all depend, with the understanding that the decisions reached by these agencies within respective areas of competence are final. We should not seek to create new institutions.

-- The general orientation of the talks must be toward sustaining or achieving greater levels of mutually beneficial international growth and development, taking into account domestic economic policies.

-- The talks should take place in an atmosphere of cooperative spirit, similar to that which has brought us together in Cancun, rather than one in which views become polarized and chances for agreement are needlessly sacrificed. . . .

But our main purpose in coming to Cancun is to focus on specific questions of substance, not procedural matters. In this spirit, we bring a positive program of action for development, concentrated around these principles:

-- stimulating international trade by opening up markets, both within individual countries and among countries;

-- tailoring particular development strategies to the specific needs and potential of individual countries and regions;

-- guiding our assistance toward the development of self-sustaining productive activities, particularly in food and energy;

-- improving the climate for private capital flows, particularly private investment; and

-- creating a political atmosphere in which practical solutions can move forward, rather than founder on a reef of misguided policies that restrain and interfere with the international marketplace or foster inflation.

Ronald Reagan, statement, first plenary session of summit North-South Conference on Cooperation and Development, Cancun, Mexico, October 22, 1981; *Papers of Presidents: Reagan,* 1981; pp. 980-82.   Whereas the Conference at Paris in 1976 consisted of 27 participants (8 from dovolopod and 19 from undeveloped countries), attendance at the Cancun conference was roduced to 8 and 14.   Mexico did not include Fidel Castro, to encourage President Reagan to attend.   This conference sought to establish an agenda for future global negotiations.   The reference to the Ottawa declaration is to the 1981 Western industrialized states summit conference.

24

Foreign Assistance

Our foreign policy flows from what we are as a people--our history, our culture, our values, and our beliefs. One reason this nation has a foreign aid program is that we believe we have a humanitarian and moral obligation to help alleviate poverty and promote equitable economic growth in the developing world. . . .

The answer to the question of why we have foreign aid programs also goes beyond our system of values and our concern for the less fortunate. Foreign aid is clearly in our national economic and political interest.

Cyrus Vance
Address, National Convention, League of Women Voters, 1978

The development of extensive foreign assistance programs by the United States during and following World War II raised a number of thorny questions, necessitating determinations respecting the types of aid to be provided, the amount of assistance and its relation to the national economy, and administrative structuring and responsibility. Some of the specific issues that have had to be faced include: Should American support be in the nature of loans, reimbursable grants, nonreimbursable gifts, or contributions to multilateral projects? Should this country furnish direct assistance based on bilateral arrangements, or should it be multilaterally provided through the United Nations and other global and regional organizations? How and by whom should assistance be administered, what should be our goals and objectives, what conditions should be imposed, and how do assistance programs relate to our ideals, national interests, and other aspects of our foreign policies?

During World War II economic and military assistance to the Allies and other friends was dispensed principally by two agencies. The Lend-Lease Program supplied credits to the anti-Axis powers to acquire defense materiel and supplies to wage the war, administered by the Lend-Lease Administration created in 1941. Two years later this was absorbed by the Foreign Economic Administration (FEA), designed to consolidate wartime foreign aid programs. Lend-lease operations were terminated at the end of hostilities and the Foreign

Economic Administration was disestablished in September 1945.

After the war, President Truman launched new programs to provide economic assistance for European recovery, military assistance to strengthen our alliances during the Cold War, and technical assistance to assist the developing countries. Following the promulgation of the Marshall Plan and the establishment of the European Recovery Program (Document 397), the Economic Cooperation Administration (ECA) was created by law in 1948. A year later Congress passed the Mutual Defense Assistance Act (Document 398), which was administered by the Mutual Security Agency (MSA) created in 1951, to supply funds for strengthening North Atlantic Alliance and other friendly powers, and to effectuate President Truman's "Point 4" proposal (Document 399), an Act for International Development was passed in 1950, implemented by the Technical Cooperation Administration (TCA), which, in June 1953, was transferred to the Mutual Security Agency (MSA).

In the early 1950's, due to the severity of the Cold War and the outbreak of the Korean War, American foreign assistance assumed new dimensions. Military assistance supplemented economic aid, as noted, and geographic limits were broadened, especially to include Latin America and the Far East. All major assistance programs--economic, military, and technical--were amalgamated in the Mutual Security Agency, which was converted into the Foreign Operations Administration (FOA) in August 1953. This, in turn, was superseded by the International Cooperation Administration (ICA) in June 1955 and, as emphasis shifted from "aid" to "development" under the Act for International Development, in November 1961 the International Cooperation Administration was replaced by the Agency for International Development (AID).

These programs have been supplemented by other, more specialized types of assistance, such as agricultural aid, so that currently economic, military, development, technical, and humanitarian assistance are administered by the Agency for International Development. In addition, the Peace Corps was established in 1961 to provide American technicians, primarily to developing countries, to assist in local development projects. The Alliance for Progress also was created in 1961 to furnish multipartite assistance in the Western Hemisphere, and subsequently special programs, such as President Reagan's Caribbean Initiative, were instituted to enhance assistance in the Caribbean area (see Documents 125-127, 557-558, and 565). The Alliance for Progress was terminated in 1978.

In the meantime, as programs were combined in the Mutual Security Act of 1951, legislation for early postwar programs was repealed, including laws governing assistance to European countries under the Marshall Plan, assistance to Greece and Turkey, relief to war-devastated countries, and mutual defense assistance. Beginning in 1961 foreign assistance programs were generally dealt with in omnibus "Foreign Assistance Acts" and, with the revival of emphasis on national security during the Reagan administration, after 1980 in "International Security and Development Cooperation Acts."

Currently American assistance programs continue to be administered by the Agency for International Development, which is responsible for implementing the Foreign Assistance Act of 1961 (as amended, see 22 *U.S. Code,* Chapter 32, par. 2151 ff.); the Agricultural Trade Development and Assistance

Act of 1954 (as amended, see 7 *U.S. Code,* Chapter 41, par. 1691 ff.); and the Peace Corps and the Development Assistance, Military Assistance, Food for Peace (shared with the Agriculture Department), Humanitarian Relief, International Disaster Assistance, and related programs (see 22 *U.S. Code,* Chapter 32). In October 1979, the International Development Cooperation Agency (IDCA) was created as an overarching policy coordinating institution (see 22 *U.S. Code,* par. 2381, p. 467). Except as noted, citations to the *U.S. Code* are to the 1982 edition.

As might be expected, the American foreign assistance program, developed incrementally and employed to achieve American foreign relations goals and objectives, has mutated to comport with changing circumstances and national interests. It is worldwide in scope, consists of both direct and indirect bilateral and multilateral assistance, and of both general (including economic, military, technical, and humanitarian) and more specialized aid (such as the Peace Corps), as well as of global, regional, and more limited programs. Since World War II, it is estimated, the United States has furnished some $150 to $200 billion of foreign grant assistance, running about $7 billion annually in the 1980's. Statistics vary, however, depending on how "assistance" is defined, especially that which is in the nature of loans and that contributed indirectly through multilateral agencies. Cummulated American grants and loans since 1945 exceed $300 billion.

Initially American foreign assistance was generally supplied directly on a bilateral basis. This applies, for example, to the Lend-Lease, aid to Greece and Turkey (1947, see Documents 111-112), European recovery, "Point 4," and other programs. In the course of time the United States also contributed to the expanding multilateral assistance programs of the United Nations, its specialized agencies, the Organization of American States and its subsidiary organizations, the global and regional international banks and development associations, and other regional arrangements, such as the Organization for Economic Cooperation and Development (OECD) and the Alliance for Progress, and functional undertakings, including multipartite commodity enterprises. For additional commentary on these multipartite programs, see the final section of this chapter.

The documents provided in this chapter are grouped in two segments. The first focuses on United States assistance policy goals, objectives, plans, and principles. These documents include examples of early programs (European recovery, Point 4, and mutual defense assistance) (Documents 397-399); basic contemporary congressional declarations of legislative objectives and policies for international development, military, technical, and agricultural assistance (Documents 400-403), and for the Peace Corps (Document 404); and general statements concerning the principles governing foreign assistance policy and programs (Documents 405-406). The second section consists of official statements on selected aspects of American foreign assistance policy and programs (Documents 407-413). The final section constitutes a brief survey of the extensive bilateral and multilateral treaty and agreement complex to implement American foreign assistance programs. Also see commentary on trade and commerce in Chapter 17, and on North-South relations in Chapter 23, especially documents on relations with the developing world and on the new international economic order.

ASSISTANCE PURPOSES, PLANS, AND PRINCIPLES

397   EUROPEAN RECOVERY FROM WORLD WAR II, 1947

The truth of the matter is that Europe's requirements for the next three or four years of foreign food and other essential products-- principally from America--are so much greater than her present ability to pay that she must have substantial additional help or face economic, social, and political deterioration of a very grave character.

The remedy lies in breaking the vicious circle and restoring the confidence of the European people in the economic future of their own countries and of Europe as a whole. The manufacturer and the farmer throughout wide areas must be able and willing to exchange their products for currencies the continuing value of which is not open to question.

Aside from the demoralizing effect on the world at large and the pos- sibilities of disturbances arising as a result of the desperation of the people concerned, the consequences to the economy of the United States should be apparent to all. It is logical that the United States should do whatever it is able to do to assist in the return of normal economic health in the world, without which there can be no political stability and no assured peace. Our policy is directed not against any country or doctrine but against hunger, poverty, desperation, and chaos. Its purpose should be the revival of a working economy in the world so as to permit the emergence of political and social conditions in which free institutions can exist. Such assistance, I am convinced, must not be on a piecemeal basis as various crises develop. Any assistance that this Government may render in the future should provide a cure rather than a mere palliative. Any government that is willing to assist in the task of recovery will find full cooperation, I am sure, on the part of the United States Government.

*   *   *

In the light of all these factors, an integrated program for United States aid to European recovery has been prepared for submission to the Congress.

In developing this program, certain basic considerations have been kept in mind:

First, the program is designed to make genuine recovery possible within a definite period of time, and not merely to continue relief indefinitely.

Second, the program is designed to insure that the funds and goods which we furnish will be used most effectively for European recovery.

Third, the program is designed to minimize the financial cost to the United States, but at the same time to avoid imposing on the European countries crushing financial burdens which they could not carry in the long run.

Fourth, the program is designed with due regard for conserving the physical resources of the United States and minimizing the impact on our economy of furnishing aid to Europe.

Fifth, the program is designed to be consistent with other international relationships and responsibilities of the United States.

Sixth, the administration of the program is designed to carry out wisely and efficiently this great enterprise of our foreign policy.

George Marshall, Marshall Plan, address, June 5, 1947, and Harry Truman, Message to Congress, December 19, 1947; *A Decade of American Foreign Policy: Basic Documents, 1941-49,* pp. 1269, 1289-90. Truman's six "considerations" are discussed in detail on pp. 1290-97. For complete documentation, see Marshall address, pp. 1268-70; Marshall statement, Congress, November 10, 1947, pp. 1270-77; Foreign Aid Interim Act, 1947, pp. 1278-83; Truman Message to Congress, pp. 1284-98; and Economic Cooperation Act, 1948, pp. 1299-1321.

398 MUTUAL DEFENSE ASSISTANCE PROGRAM, 1949

The Congress of the United States reaffirms the policy of the United States to achieve international peace and security through the United Nations so that armed force shall not be used except in the common interest. The Congress hereby finds that the efforts of the United States and other countries to promote peace and security in furtherance of the purposes of the Charter of the United Nations require additional measures of support based upon the principle of continuous and effective self-help and mutual aid. These measures include the furnishing of military assistance essential to enable the United States and other nations dedicated to the purposes and principles of the United Nations Charter to participate effectively in arrangements for individual and collective self-defense in support of those purposes and principles. . . .

The Congress recognizes that economic recovery is essential to international peace and security and must be given clear priority. The Congress also recognizes that the increased confidence of free peoples in their ability to resist direct or indirect aggression and to maintain internal security will advance such recovery and support political stability.

Mutual Defense Assistance Act, 1949; *A Decade of American Foreign Policy: Basic Documents, 1941-49,* pp. 1356-57. For text of the entire act, see pp. 1356-64, and for text of the North Atlantic Treaty, implemented by this act, see Document 306.

399 TRUMAN'S "POINT 4" PROPOSAL, 1949--TECHNICAL ASSISTANCE

Fourth, we must embark on a bold new program making the benefits of our scientific advances and industrial progress available for the improvement and growth of underdeveloped areas.

More than half the people of the world are living in conditions approaching misery. Their food in inadequate. They are victims of disease. Their economic life is primitive and stagnant. Their poverty is a handicap and a threat both to them and to more prosperous areas.

For the first time in history, humanity possesses the knowledge and the skill to relieve the suffering of these people.

The United States is preeminent among nations in the development of industrial and scientific techniques. The material resources which we can afford to use for the assistance of other peoples are limited. But our imponderable resources in technical knowledge are constantly growing and are inexhaustible.

I believe that we should make available to peace-loving peoples the benefits of our store of technical knowledge in order to help them realize their aspirations for a better life. And, in cooperation with other nations, we should foster capital investment in areas needing development.

Our aim should be to help the free peoples of the world, through their own efforts, to produce more food, more clothing, more materials for housing, and more mechanical power to lighten their burdens.

We invite other countries to pool their technological resources in this undertaking. Their contributions will be warmly welcomed. This should be a cooperative enterprise in which all nations work together through the United Nations and its specialized agencies wherever practicable. It must be a world-wide effort for the achievement of peace, plenty, and freedom. . . .

The old imperialism--exploitation for foreign profit--has no place in our plans. What we envisage is a program of development based on the concepts of democratic fair-dealing.

All countries, including our own, will greatly benefit from a constructive program for the better use of the world's human and natural resources. Experience shows that our commerce with other countries expands as they progress industrially and economically.

Greater production is the key to prosperity and peace. And the key to greater production is a wider and more vigorous application of modern scientific and technical knowledge.

Only by helping the least fortunate of its members to help themselves can the human family achieve the decent, satisfying life that is the right of all people.

Harry Truman, Inaugural Address, January 20, 1949; *A Decade of American Foreign Policy: Basic Documents, 1941-49*, pp. 1366-67. For Truman's Message to Congress on technical assistance, June 24, 1949, see pp. 1367-72.

4 0 0   DEVELOPMENT ASSISTANCE PROGRAM

The Congress finds that fundamental political, economic, and technological changes have resulted in the interdependence of nations. The Congress declares that the individual liberties, economic prosperity, and security of the people of the United States are best sustained and enhanced in a community of nations which respect individual civil and economic rights and freedoms and which work together to use wisely the world's limited resources in an open and equitable international economic system. Furthermore, the Congress reaffirms the traditional humanitarian ideals of the American people and renews its commitment to assist people in developing countries to eliminate hunger, poverty, illness, and ignorance.

Therefore, the Congress declares that a principal objective of the foreign policy of the United States is the encouragement and sustained support of the people of developing countries in their efforts to acquire the knowledge and resources essential to development and to build the economic, political, and social institutions which will improve the quality of their lives.

United States development cooperation policy should emphasize four principal goals:

(1) the alleviation of the worst physical manifestations of poverty among the world's poor majority;

(2) the promotion of conditions enabling developing countries to achieve self-sustaining economic growth with equitable distribution of benefits;

(3) the encouragement of development processes in which individual civil and economic rights are respected and enhanced; and

(4) the integration of the developing countries into an open and equitable international economic system.

The Congress declares that pursuit of these goals requires that development concerns be fully reflected in United States foreign policy and that United States development resources be effectively and efficiently utilized. . . .

The Congress finds that the efforts of developing countries to build and maintain the social and economic institutions necessary to achieve self-sustaining growth and to provide opportunities to improve the quality of life for their people depend primarily upon successfully marshalling their own economic and human resources. The Congress recognizes that the magnitude of these efforts exceeds the resources of developing countries and therefore accepts that there will be a long-term need for wealthy countries to contribute additional resources for development purposes. The United States should take the lead in concert with other nations to mobilize such resources from public and private sources.

Provision of development resources must be adapted to the needs and capabilities of specific developing countries. United States assistance to countries with low per capita incomes which have limited access to private external resources should primarily be provided on concessional terms. Assistance to other developing countries should generally consist of programs which facilitate their access to private capital markets, investment, and technical skills, whether directly through guarantee or reimbursable programs by the United States Government or indirectly through callable capital provided to the international financial institutions.

22 *U.S. Code*, Chapter 32, pars. 2151 and 2151-1.   For stipulations concerning the form and principles governing such assistance, see par. 2151-1-b.   For additional legislative commentary on international development, see remainder of Subchapter I of Chapter 32.

4 0 1   MILITARY ASSISTANCE PROGRAM

The Congress finds that the efforts of the United States and other friendly countries to promote peace and security continue to require measures of support based upon the principle of effective self-help and mutual aid.   It is the purpose of subchapter II of this chapter to authorize measures in the common defense against internal and external aggression, including the furnishing of military assistance, upon request, to friendly countries and international organizations. . . .

The Congress recognizes that the peace of the world and the security of the United States are endangered so long as international communism and the countries it controls continue by threat of military action, by the use of economic pressure, and by internal subversion, or other means to attempt to bring under their domination peoples now free and independent and continue to deny the rights of freedom and self-government to peoples and countries once free but now subject to such domination. . . .

. . . it is therefore the intention of the Congress to promote the peace of the world and the foreign policy, security, and general welfare of the United States by fostering an improved climate of political independence and individual liberty, improving the ability of friendly countries and international organizations to deter or, if necessary, defeat Communist or Communist-supported aggression, facilitating arrangements for individual and collective security, assisting friendly countries to maintain internal security, and creating an environment of security and stability in the developing friendly countries essential to their more rapid social, economic, and political progress. . . .

It is the sense of the Congress that in the administration . . . of this chapter priority shall be given to the needs of those countries in danger of becoming victims of active Communist or Communist-supported aggression or those countries in which the internal security is threatened by Communist-inspired or Communist-supported internal subversion.

22 *U.S. Code*, Chapter 32, par. 2301.   For additional legislative provisions concerning military assistance, see remainder of Chapter 32, Subchapter II.

4 0 2   TECHNICAL ASSISTANCE PROGRAM

The President is authorized to furnish assistance on such terms and conditions as he may determine in order to promote the economic development of less developed friendly countries and areas, with emphasis upon assisting the development of human resources through such means as programs of technical cooperation and development. In so doing, the President shall take into account (1) whether the activity gives reasonable promise of contributing to the development of educational or other institutions and programs directed toward social progress, (2) the consistency of the activity with, and its relationship to, other development activities being undertaken or planned, and its contribution to realizable long-range development objectives, (3) the economic and technical soundness of the activity to be financed, (4) the extent to which the recipient country is showing a responsiveness to the vital economic, political, and social concerns of its people, and demonstrating a clear determination to take effective self-help measures and a willingness to pay a fair share of the cost of programs under this subpart, (5) the possible adverse effects upon the United States economy, with special reference to areas of substantial labor surplus, of the assistance involved, (6) the desirability of safeguarding the international balance of payments position of the United States, (7) the degree to which the recipient country is making progress toward respect for the rule of law, freedom of expression and of the press, and recognition of the importance of individual freedom, initiative, and private enterprise, and (8) whother or not the activity to be financed will contribute to the achievement of self-sustaining growth. If the President finds that assistance proposed to be furnished under this subpart would have a substantially adverse effect upon the United States economy, or a substantial segment thereof, the assistance shall not be furnished.

22 U.S. Code (1976 edition), Chapter 32, par. 2171 (a); this was subsequently superseded by general development assistance policy.

4 0 3   INTERNATIONAL AGRICULTURAL ASSISTANCE PROGRAM

The Congress hereby declares it to be the policy of the United States to expand international trade; to develop and expand export markets for United States agricultural commodities; to use the abundant agricultural productivity of the United States to combat hunger and malnutrition and to encourage economic development in the developing countries, with particular emphasis on assistance to those countries that are determined to improve their own agricultural production; and to promote in other ways the foreign policy of the United States. In furnishing food aid under this chapter, the President shall--
(1) give priority consideration, in helping to meet urgent food needs abroad, to making available the maximum feasible volume of

food commodities (with appropriate regard to domestic price and supply situations) required by those countries most seriously affected by food shortages and by inability to meet immediate food requirements on a normal commercial basis;

(2) continue to urge all traditional and potential new donors of food, fertilizer, or the means of financing these commodities to increase their participation in efforts to address the emergency and longer term food needs of the developing world;

(3) relate United States assistance to efforts by aid-receiving countries to increase their own agricultural production, with emphasis on development of small, family farm agriculture, and improve their facilities for transportation, storage, and distribution of food commodities;

(4) give special consideration to the potential for expanding markets for America's agricultural abundance abroad in the allocation of commodities or concessional financing; and

(5) give appropriate recognition to and support of a strong and viable American farm economy in providing for the food security of consumers in the United States and throughout the world.

7 *U.S. Code,* Chapter 41, par. 1691. For additional stipulations concerning agricultural trade development and assistance, see remainder of Chapter 41.

4 0 4   PEACE CORPS PROGRAM

The Congress of the United States declares that it is the policy of the United States . . . to promote world peace and friendship through a Peace Corps, which shall make available to interested countries and areas men and women of the United States qualified for service abroad and willing to serve, under conditions of hardship if necessary, to help the peoples of such countries and areas in meeting their needs for trained manpower, particularly in meeting the basic needs of those living in the poorest areas of such countries, and to help promote a better understanding of the American people on the part of the peoples served and a better understanding of other peoples on the part of the American people.

22 *U.S. Code,* Chapter 32, par. 2501. For additional stipulations on the Peace Corps, see pars. 2501-23.

4 0 5   GUIDING PRINCIPLES FOR FOREIGN ASSISTANCE PROGRAMS

1. *Self-help*--Nations develop primarily through their own efforts. Our programs can only be supplements, not substitutes. This is the overriding principle.

2. *Multilaterlism*--Every advanced nation has a duty to contribute its share of the cost.

3. *Regionalism*--The future of many countries depends upon sound development of resources shared with their neighbors.

4. *Agriculture, health, and education*--These key sectors are the critical elements of advancement everywhere in the underdeveloped world.

5. *Balance of payments*--We cannot help others grow unless the American dollar is strong and stable.

6. *Efficient administration*--Every American citizen is entitled to know that his tax dollar is spent wisely.

Lyndon Johnson, Message to Congress, February 9, 1967; *American Foreign Policy: Current Documents*, 1967, pp. 1140-41. Also see discussion of the "four pillars" of American foreign assistance by Administrator, Agency for International Development, February 2, 1984; *American Foreign Policy: Current Documents*, 1984, p. 189.

406   FOREIGN ASSISTANCE AND UNITED STATES FOREIGN POLICY

U.S. foreign assistance is central to U.S. foreign policy . . . in three ways:

First, we must help to strengthen the defense capabilities and economies of our friends and allies. This is necessary so that they can increasingly shoulder their own responsibilities, so that we can reduce our direct involvement abroad, and so that together we can create a workable structure for world peace. . . .

Second, we must assist the lower income countries in their efforts to achieve economic and social development. Such development is the overriding objective of these countries themselves and essential to the peaceful world order which we seek. The prospects for a peaceful world will be greatly enhanced if the two-thirds of humanity who live in these countries see hope for adequate food, shelter, education and employment in peaceful progress rather than in revolution.

Third, we must be able to provide prompt and effective assistance to countries struck by natural disaster or the human consequences of political upheaval. Our humanitarian concerns for mankind require that we be prepared to help in times of acute human distress.

Richard Nixon, Special Message to Congress, April 21, 1971; *Papers of Presidents: Nixon*, 1971, pp. 564-65.

OTHER POLICY THEMES

407   NEED FOR LONG-RANGE FOREIGN ASSISTANCE

. . . I believe that the United States ought to try to help in ways which will not merely relieve on a year-to-year basis but help to transform these economies into better-integrated economies of the kind that the people aspire to.

Furthermore, if our Government can engage in some of these long-term projects, they not only will have great value in catching the imagination of the people and meeting their aspirations, but also it may make it possible to get from those countries themselves, or from other countries, or from organizations like the World Bank, a considerable amount of money. So our own money will go farther--through some kind of a matching process.

I believe that, when the nature of the problem is understood, there will be a realization that the enlightened self-interest of the United States requires that we should go forward to meet this situation in terms of projects on the assumption that we would continue to give them some support over a period of years.

John Foster Dulles, response to question at news conference, January 17, 1956; *American Foreign Policy: Current Documents,* 1956, pp. 1252-53.

408   INCREASING EMPHASIS ON SELF-HELP OF ASSISTANCE RECIPIENTS

As experience with technical cooperation has grown, there is increasing evidence that the best long-run returns follow when outside aid is concentrated on helping the less developed countries in those projects which build up and expand their own indigenous skills. This emphasis on the idea of self-help enables those countries to make greater use of their human resources so that they can better exploit their natural resources and thereby stimulate economic advancement on a progressively larger scale.

Report to Congress on Mutual Security Program, April 26, 1957; *American Foreign Policy: Current Documents,* 1956, p. 1322.

409   REVISED BASIC CONCEPTS AND PRINCIPLES FOR FOREIGN ASSISTANCE

. . . This Congress at this session must make possible a dramatic turning point in the troubled history of foreign aid to the underdeveloped world. We must say to the less-developed nations, if they are willing to undertake necessary internal reform and self-help--and to the other industrialized nations, if they are willing to undertake a much greater effort on a much broader scale--that we then intend during this coming decade of development to achieve a decisive turn-around in the fate of the less-developed world, looking toward the ultimate day when all nations can be self-reliant and when foreign aid will no longer be needed. . . .

If our foreign aid funds are to be prudently and effectively used, we need a whole new set of basic concepts and principles:

1. Unified administration and operation--a single agency in Washington and the field, equipped with a flexible set of tools, in place of

several competing and confusing aid units.

2. Country plans--a carefully thought through program tailored to meet the needs and the resource potential of each individual country, instead of a series of individual, unrelated projects. Frequently, in the past, our development goals and projects have not been undertaken as integral steps in a long-range economic development program.

3. Long-term planning and financing--the only way to make meaningful and economical commitments.

4. Special emphasis on development loans repayable in dollars-- more conducive to businesslike relations and mutual respect than sustaining grants or loans repaid in local currencies, although some instances of the latter are unavoidable.

5. Special attention to those nations most willing and able to mobilize their own resources, make necessary social and economic reforms, engage in long-range planning, and make the other efforts necessary if these are to reach the stage of self-sustaining growth.

6. Multilateral approach--a program and level of commitments designed to encourage and complement an increased effort by other industrialized nations.

7. A new agency with new personnel--drawing upon the most competent and dedicated career servants now in the field, and attracting the highest quality from every part of the Nation.

8. Separation from military assistance--our program of aid to social and economic development must be seen on its own merits, and judged in the light of its vital and distinctive contribution to our basic security needs.

John Kennedy, Message to Congress, March 22, 1961; *American Foreign Policy: Current Documents,* 1961, pp. 1260-61.

4 1 0   FOREIGN ASSISTANCE FOR BENEFIT OF THE PEOPLE

But compassion is not enough. While our wealth is great, it is not un- limited. It must be used not merely to apply bandaids to superficial wounds but to remove the causes of deeper and more dangerous disorders. That is why I do not intend for American aid to become an international dole. The Congress of the United States does not want that. The people of this country do not want that. The people who benefit from our assistance, I am sure, do not want that.

Our assistance must and will go to those nations that will most use it to bring major and far-reaching benefits to their people. It will go to those willing not only to talk about basic social change but who will act immediately on these reforms. As I discharge my responsibilities . . . I will look not simply to the fact of an agreement that points toward reform but to action already taken to bring reform to fruition.

Action, not promises, will be the standard of our assistance. Accomplishments, not apologies, are what the American people expect from their desire to help others help themselves.

Lyndon Johnson, statement on signing Foreign Assistance Appropriations Act, October 20, 1965; *American Foreign Policy: Current Documents,* 1965, pp. 1150-51.

4 1 1   FOREIGN ASSISTANCE--MORAL OBLIGATION AND WORLD STABILITY

Americans have for many years debated the issues of foreign aid largely in terms of our own national self-interest.

Certainly our efforts to help nations feed millions of their poor help avert violence and upheaval that would be dangerous to peace.

Certainly our military assistance to allies helps maintain a world in which we ourselves are more secure.

Certainly our economic aid to developing nations helps develop our own potential markets overseas.

And certainly our technical assistance puts down roots of respect and friendship for the United States in the court of world opinion.

These are all sound, practical reasons for our foreign aid programs.

But they do not do justice to our fundamental character and purpose. There is a moral quality in this Nation that will not permit us to close our eyes to the want in this world, or to remain indifferent when the freedom and security of others are in danger.

We should not be self-conscious about this. Our record of generosity and concern for our fellow men, expressed in concrete terms unparalleled in the world's history, has helped make the American experience unique. We have shown the world that a great nation must also be a good nation. We are doing what is right to do. . . .

Foreign aid cannot be viewed in isolation. That is a statement with a double meaning, each side of which is true.

If we turn inward, if we adopt an attitude of letting the under-developed nations shift for themselves, we would soon see them shift away from the values so necessary to international stability.   Moreover, we would lose the traditional concern for humanity which is so vital a part of the American spirit.

In another sense, foreign aid must be viewed as an integral part of our overall effort to achieve a world order of peace and justice.   That order combines our sense of responsibility for helping those determined to defend their freedom; our sensible understanding of the mutual benefits that flow from cooperation between nations; and our sensitivity to the desires of our fellow men to improve their lot in the world.

Richard Nixon, Special Message to Congress, May 28, 1969; *Papers of Presidents: Nixon,* 1969, pp. 411 and 416.

4 1 2   CHANGES IN DEVELOPMENT ASSISTANCE

In the years since World War II, the United States has encouraged economic development throughout the world through a variety of economic assistance programs. . . .

The future of the United States will be affected by the ability of developing nations to overcome poverty, achieve healthy growth and provide more secure lives for their people. We wish to join with other nations in combining our efforts, knowledge, and resources to help poorer countries overcome the problems of hunger, disease, and illiteracy. We are seeking important improvements in our program, some of which reflect changes in emphasis and approach:

--We will ensure that lending agencies attach adequate self-help conditions to their loans so that borrowing nations will make effective use of the funds they receive. . . .

--We will encourage other wealthy nations to contribute a greater share to the multilateral aid effort, and we will reduce our own share where it has been too high.

--In close cooperation with the Congress we have made sure that our concessional aid goes to those who need it most; we will continue this approach.

--We are now reforming the policies which have, on occasion, awarded liberal grants and loans to repressive regimes which violate human rights.

--We will root out mismanagement and inefficiency where they exist in our foreign assistance programs in order to guarantee that benefits will always be delivered to those for whom the programs were designed.

Jimmy Carter, Message to Congress, March 17, 1977; *American Foreign Policy: Basic Documents,* 1977-1980, p. 313. Also see Cyrus Vance, on basic questions relating to foreign assistance, address, National Convention, League of Women Voters, May 1, 1978; *American Foreign Policy: Basic Documents,* 1977-1980, p. 319.

4 1 3   SIGNIFICANCE OF UNITED STATES ASSISTANCE

The programs and activities for which funds are authorized and appropriated . . . are vital to important United States foreign policy and national security interests. They are the principal means by which the United States contributes to the security and economic development needs of a wide range of countries less favored than our own.

Foreign aid suffers from a lack of domestic constituency, in large part because the results of the programs are often not immediately visible and self-evident. Properly conceived and efficiently administered, however, security assistance programs, an essential complement to our defense effort, directly enhance the security of the United States.

Development assistance also contributes to this effort by supplementing the indigenous efforts of recipients to achieve economic growth and meet the basic needs of their peoples. Progress in both of these areas will contribute to regional stability and to a more peaceful world, both of which are central U.S. policy objectives. . . .

The ultimate importance to the United States of our security and development assistance programs cannot be exaggerated.

Ronald Reagan, statement, signing International Security and Foreign Assistance Acts, December 29, 1981; *Papers of Presidents: Reagan,* 1981, pp. 1202 and 1204.

INTERNATIONAL TREATIES AND AGREEMENTS

American foreign assistance programs are implemented not only by legislation but also by hundreds of bilateral and multilateral treaties and agreements, most of which are in the nature of executive agreements based on prior congressional authorization. These relate to particular categories of assistance policies.

During World War II, for example, the United States negotiated Lend-Lease and Reciprocal Aid Agreements with several dozen anti-Axis countries. After the war--in addition to providing aid to Greece and Turkey in 1947 to implement the Truman Doctrine (see Chapter 7, Documents 111-112, and for complete documentation, see *A Decade of American Foreign Policy: Basic Documents, 1941-49,* pp. 1252-67)--a series of Economic Cooperation Agreements to carry out the Marshall Plan were signed with European governments to support economic recovery; after the enactment of the Mutual Defense Assistance Act in 1949 scores of mutual defense assistance, military assistance, and military training agreements were signed in the early 1950's with North Atlantic Treaty and other allies and with additional non-Communist nations to buttress United States alliance and defense policies; and following the promulgation of the "Point 4" proposal a good many technical cooperation agreements were negotiated with developing nations. Following the enactment of the Mutual Security Act in 1951, an additional series of agreements to establish assurances to comport with American law were consummated as exchanges of notes, also primarily with NATO members and other friendly powers.

Subsequently, beginning in the 1950's a host of combined economic and technical cooperation agreements were negotiated with dozens of additional countries, and to implement the Peace Corps Act of 1961, bilateral agreements were signed with more than seventy-five countries. Specifically, those grouped as economic and technical cooperation agreements are identified as commitments providing for either economic cooperation or assistance, most of which were signed in 1948; for technical cooperation, most of which were consummated in the early 1950's; and for combined economic and technical cooperation, which were signed since 1960.

A good many additional bilateral agreements were negotiated to supply United States military training and regularize the transfer or furnishing of military equipment and services; to operationalize American defense policy, such as NATO logistical support agreements; to furnish disaster cooperation; and to deal with other matters.

In the 1980's, to summarize, the United States was party to more than 500 bilateral foreign assistance treaties and agreements. They consist of more than 50 providing for World War II lend-lease (including settlement arrangements) with some 20 countries; the two aid agreements with Greece and Turkey; more than 260 economic and technical cooperation agreements with some 120 countries; two dozen military assistance and another two dozen mutual security agreements; approximately 30 mutual security assurance agreements; two dozen military training agreements and 15 concerned with furnishing or transfer of military equipment or services; more than 75 Peace Corps agreements; and other specialized arrangements. Many of these are supplemented by amendatory protocols and ancillary and other supporting understandings. To these may be added more than 400 bilateral agricultural commodity agreements, which govern both trade and assistance, including some 30 agricultural cooperation agreements (for commentary on these and other trade agreements, see Chapter 17, section on trade legislation and treaty complex).

The United States also participates in and contributes to a substantial number of multilateral foreign assistance programs. Those of global applicability encompass the United Nations and its specialized agencies, which are responsible for a variety of support services. These include both financial and other functional organizations. The financial institutions embrace the International Bank (IB), the International Monetary Fund (IMF), and their subsidiaries--the International Finance Corporation (IFC), the International Development Association (IDA), and others. Such specialized functional agencies as the Food and Agriculture Organization (FAO), the International Atomic Energy Agency (IAEA), the International Refugee Organization (IRO), whose operations terminated in 1956, the International Labor Organization (ILO), the World Health Organization (WHO), and the United Nations Educational, Scientific and Cultural Organization (UNESCO) from which the United States withdrew at the end of 1984 (see Chapter 25, note to Document 435), provide substantial assistance and services to their members. Similarly the American government contributes to supporting the regional United Nations Economic Commissions, the Children's Fund (UNICEF), the Conference on Trade and Development (UNCTAD), and the Industrial Development Organization (UNIDO).

Of related concern, the United States is a signatory of agreements establishing the International Fund for Agricultural Development, the Food Aid Program, and the General Agreement on Tariffs and Trade (GATT), as well as those agencies that promote the production of and trade in specific commodities (including coffee, cotton, rice, rubber, sugar, and wheat, and formerly also tin and wool) and those that seek to conserve particular resources (including fisheries, seals, and whales)--all of which involve cooperation and assistance.

On the regional level this country is a member of the extensive network of organizations comprising the inter-American system (see Chapter 26), the Organization for Economic Cooperation and Development (OECD, with European and several Far Eastern countries), the South Pacific Commission, and such regional financial institutions as the African, Asian, and Inter-American Banks and the African Development Fund. In the Western Hemisphere, the United States also has initiated and participated in the Alliance for Progress, the Caribbean Initiative, and similar joint assistance measures.

Most of these programs are founded on international treaties and agreements, and additional commitments are created by United Nations and other international agency resolutions. While the details of this extensive foreign assistance complex varies from decade to decade, it represents a major and persisting aspect of American foreign relations and it evidences a continuous commitment since World War II to aid other nations in a variety of ways. Lists of bilateral and multilateral treaties and agreements to which the United States currently subscribes are provided in the annual issues of *Treaties in Force.*

PART VII

COLLECTIVE COOPERATION

25

United Nations System

In an era of growing interdependence of nations the U.N. system of organizations plays an increasingly significant role. It would be difficult to find another forum for negotiating the arrangements to control the new technologies for the common good, for meeting the needs of the poor, for facilitating the exchange of knowledge, and for setting standards of behavior in many areas of international activity. It is true that the United Nations has been repeatedly frustrated as a peacemaker, but this failure is due less to the system than to a lack of the necessary political will of the members.

United States Foreign Policy, 1972:
A Report of the Secretary of State

The United Nations is an international confederation; it is neither a world government nor a federation of national states. Within it member nations pursue their interests, promote their policies, and negotiate resolutions and agreements. Its Charter--its constitution--is an international treaty negotiated by its founders and subscribed to by its members. It possesses no law-making or taxing authority, and it has no executive to enforce its determinations. It derives its funding from its members, who are sovereign equals, regardless of their size, their endowments, or their importance.

The United States played a major role in its establishment. In the Atlantic Charter, President Franklin D. Roosevelt and Winston Churchill, meeting in their first World War II summit conference off the coast of Newfoundland, agreed on August 14, 1941, to "the establishment of a wider and permanent system of general security." This generated four years of intensive planning in the United States, bilateral negotiations and meetings with the leaders of the British, Chinese, and Soviet governments, the Dumbarton Oaks conferences and agreed proposals, and eventually the approval of the Charter in 1945.

The four sponsoring powers--the United States, Great Britain, China, and the Soviet Union--issued invitations to the San Francisco Conference to all countries that were at war with the Axis powers and had signed the United Nations Declaration of January 1, 1942. Fifty states participated in the conference and signed the Charter on June 26, 1945, a few weeks after the German capitulation and two weeks prior to the Japanese surrender. Although Poland was not present at the conference, its representatives signed the Charter in October. When established, the United Nations was essentially an anti-Axis aggregation designed to preserve the peace; only later was its membership universalized. For documents and commentary, see Department of State, *Postwar Foreign Policy Preparation, 1939-1945* (Washington: Government Printing Office, 1949); *Charter of the United Nations: Report to the President on the Results of the San Francisco Conference* (Washington: Government Printing Office, 1945); and Marjorie M. Whiteman, *Digest of International Law,* XIII, 345-902.

The Charter, consisting of 19 chapters and 111 articles, stipulates the purposes and principles of the United Nations, provides for its organization and procedures, and prescribes precepts for dealing with membership, the pacific settlement of disputes, action respecting threats to the peace and acts of aggression, regional arrangements, economic and social relations, non-self-governing territories and trusteeships, and the ratification and amending processes. Although it specifies that the International Court of Justice is the principal judicial organ of the United Nations, and that all of its members are ipso facto members of the tribunal, a separate Statute of the Court accompanies the Charter. Document 414 depicts the structure of the United Nations, including its principal organs and their subsidiary agencies and commissions. For the text of the Charter, see TS 993; 3 Bevans, *Treaties and Other International Agreements* 1153-79; and for the Court's Statute, see pp. 1179-95.

The Charter also provides for the cooperative relationship of a series of functional specialized agencies. These are independent international organizations, having their own constitutions, membership, machinery, functions, and finances. Affiliation with the United Nations is achieved by formal agreement between them. A list of these agencies is provided in Document 415. Currently sixteen such agencies contribute to the United Nations system, several of which antedate the Charter.

The remaining documents selected for this chapter are grouped in six categories. The first two are concerned with advance congressional authorization for American participation and the launching of the United Nations (Documents 416-418), and general presidential statements concerning the goals and expectations of, American commitments to, and responsibilities of members of the organization (Documents 419-423). Every President since Harry Truman has addressed the General Assembly at least once, often early in his administration (for texts, see *Papers of Presidents*), and the Secretary of State frequently heads the American delegation to regular and some special sessions of the General Assembly. (For texts of their statements, see the *Department of State Bulletin* and *American Foreign Policy: Current Documents.* The latter also contain scores of statements of American representatives to the United Nations and delegates to its organs and committees and to the specialized agencies).

The remaining four segments of this chapter deal with United Nations Charter amendment, review, and adaptation (Documents 424-427); membership in the organization (Documents 428-430); financing and United States contributions (Documents 431-432); and selected problems, criticisms, and assessments of the United Nations (Documents 433-439). For stipulations concerning self-determination, see Document 267.

For comprehensive accounts of, and documentation on, United States policy and action in, and relations with, the United Nations and its specialized agencies, see the President's annual reports, originally entitled *The United States and the United Nations,* and later retitled *U.S. Participation in the UN,* which are published by the Department of State and also as congressional documents. For individual addresses and statements concerning United States policy and actions in the United Nations system, see the *Foreign Relations of the United States* series, the *American Foreign Policy: Current Documents* series, and the issues of the *Department of State Bulletin;* and for contemporary consideration of legal aspects of United Nations problems and considerations, see the annual *Digest of United States Practice in International Law.* For United Nations documents and materials, see the *United Nations Bulletin, United Nations Chronicle, United Nations Review, Issues Before the General Assembly of the United Nations* (produced by the United Nations Association), *Yearbook of the United Nations,* the annual reports of the Secretary-General, and the official working documents and records listed in the *United Nations Documents Index.*

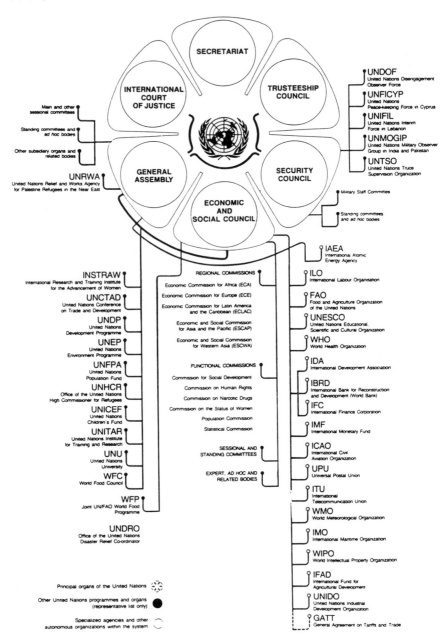

Department of Public Information, United Nations, 1990.

415   UNITED NATIONS SPECIALIZED AND AFFILIATED AGENCIES

	TITLE	ORGANIC ACT	DATE SIGNED	CITATION
FAO	Food and Agricul-ture Organization	Constitution	Oct. 16, 1945	TIAS 4803 12 UST 980-1028
IAEA	International Atomic Energy Agency	Statute	Oct. 26, 1956	TIAS 3873 8 UST 1093-1224
IB	International Bank	Articles of Agreement	Dec. 27, 1944	TIAS 1502 3 Bevans 1390-1418
ICAO	International Civil Aviation Organiza-tion	Convention	Dec. 7, 1944	TIAS 1591 3 Bevans 944-71
IDA	International Dev-elopment Associa-tion	Articles of Agreement	Jan. 26, 1960	TIAS 4607 11 UST 2284-2313
IFAD	International Fund for Agricultural Development	Agreement	June 13, 1976	TIAS 8765 28 UST 8435-78
IFC	International Finance Corpora-tion	Articles of Agreement	May 25, 1955	TIAS 3620 7 UST 2197-2228
ILO	International Labor Organization	Constitution	June 28, 1919	TS 874 2 Bevans 241-54
		Amended Constitution	Oct. 9, 1946	TIAS 1868 4 Bevans 188-230
IMO	International Mari-time Organization	Convention	Mar. 6, 1948	TIAS 4044 9 UST 621-91
IMF	International Mon-etary Fund	Articles of Agreement	Dec. 27, 1944	TIAS 1501 3 Bevans 1351-89
ITU	International Tele-communication Union	Convention	Dec. 9, 1932	TS 867 3 Bevans 65-83
		Convention	Oct. 25, 1973	TIAS 8572 28 UST 2495-2902
UNESCO	UN Educational, Scientific, and Cultural Org.	Constitution	Nov. 16, 1945	TIAS 1580 3 Bevans 1311-21
UNIDO	UN Industrial Devel-opment Organization	UN Resolutions	Dec. 20, 1965 Nov. 17, 1966	G.A. Res. 2089 G.A. Res. 2152
UPU	Universal Postal Union	Constitution	June 1, 1878	20 Stat. 734 1 Bevans 51-62
		Constitution	July 10, 1904	TIAS 5881 16 UST 1291-1615
WHO	World Health Organization	Constitution	July 22, 1946	TIAS 1808 4 Bevans 119-38
WIPO	World Intellectual Property Org.	Convention	July 14, 1967	TIAS 6932 21 UST 1749-1856
WMO	World Meteorolog-ical Organization	Convention	Oct. 11, 1947	TIAS 2050 1 UST 281

The IAEA has a working relationship without a formal treaty with the UN. In addition, the General Agreement on Tariffs and Trade (GATT) institutions have a special relationship with the UN (see Docs. 297-299 on GATT). The original constitution of the ILO was incorporated into the Versailles Treaty in 1919, and was amended in 1946. The constitution of an International Refugee Organization (IRO) was signed in December 1946 (see TIAS 1846; 4 Bevans 284-304); it was terminated in 1952. Although the Charter of an International Trade Organization (ITO) was negotiated in 1948, it was not ratified and this organization was not established (for its text, see *A Decade of American Foreign Policy: Basic Documents, 1941-49,* pp. 391-409, and for commentary, see Marjorie M. Whiteman, *Digest of International Law,* XIV, 732-35, 741-44).

LAUNCHING THE UNITED NATIONS

4 1 6   AUTHORIZING CONGRESSIONAL RESOLUTIONS, 1943

FULBRIGHT RESOLUTION, SEPTEMBER 21, 1943

That the Congress hereby expresses itself as favoring the creation of appropriate international machinery with power adequate to establish and to maintain a just and lasting peace, among the nations of the world, and as favoring participation by the United States therein through its constitutional processes.

CONNALLY RESOLUTION, NOVEMBER 5, 1943

That the United States, acting through its constitutional processes, join with free and sovereign nations in the establishment and maintenance of international authority with power to prevent aggression and to preserve the peace of the world.

That the Senate recognizes the necessity of there being established at the earliest practicable date a general international organization, based on the principle of the sovereign equality of all peace-loving states, and open to membership by all such states, large and small, for the maintenance of international peace and security.

That, pursuant to the Constitution of the United States, any treaty made to effect the purposes of this resolution, on behalf of the Government of the United States with any other nation or any association of nations, shall be made only by and with the advice and consent of the Senate of the United States, provided two-thirds of the Senators present concur.

A Decade of American Foreign Policy: Basic Documents, 1941-49, p. 54.

4 1 7   TRUMAN'S WELCOMING ADDRESS TO THE UNITED NATIONS, 1946

On behalf of the Government and the people of the United States I extend a warm and hearty welcome to the delegates who have come here from all parts of the world to represent their countries at this meeting of the General Assembly of the United Nations. . . .

For the people of my country this meeting today has a special historic significance. After the first world war the United States refused to join the League of Nations and our seat was empty at the first meeting of the League Assembly. This time the United States is not only a member; it is the host to the United Nations.

I can assure you that the Government and the people of the United States are deeply proud and grateful that the United Nations has chosen our country for its headquarters. We will extend the fullest measure of cooperation in making a home for the United Nations in this country. . . .

This meeting of the Assembly symbolizes the abandonment by the United States of a policy of isolation.

The overwhelming majority of the American people . . . support the United Nations.

They are resolved that the United States, to the full limit of its strength, shall contribute to the establishment and maintenance of a just and lasting peace among the nations of the world.

Harry Truman, address, opening session of United Nations General Assembly, October 23, 1946; *Papers of Presidents: Truman*, 1946, pp. 457-58. This address set the precedent for subsequent Presidents to address the General Assembly. For President Truman's letter of transmittal, sending his first annual report to Congress on American participation in the United Nations, see *The United States and the United Nations*, 1946, pp. iii-viii.

4 1 8 AMERICA'S PLEDGE TO THE UNITED NATIONS, 1947

We Americans must obtain a clear understanding of the role which we ourselves are called upon to play in the United Nations. We must understand the roles which others are playing or are failing to play. We must continually remind ourselves that the United Nations succeeds or fails according to the conduct of the members themselves and their willingness to act in accordance with the Charter. . . .

The limitations inherent in this great organization for the pre- servation of peace should be made clear to our citizens. We make a grave error to suppose that every international problem should be handled by the United Nations. Actually, this would neither be desirable nor practi- cable. The American Government, for example, is conducting negotiations continuously with every recognized government in the world on hundreds of subjects. Other governments are doing the same. The great majority of these matters are satisfactorily settled by mutual agreement between the parties directly concerned. Nothing would be gained and much would be lost by complicating the procedures of day-to-day negotiation by multiplying machinery where simple methods suffice.

Even in cases of international disputes the continuance of which might endanger the maintenance of peace and security--in other words, in matters of primary interest to the United Nations--the Charter enjoins the parties *first of all* to seek solution by negotiation, inquiry, mediation, conciliation, arbitration, judicial settlement, resort to regional agencies or arrangements, or other peaceful means of their own choice.   Clearly this means that parties to disputes should use such peaceful means in good faith and in a spirit of mutual accommodation. Recourse to United Nations agencies in such matters may constitute an abuse of the Charter if the purpose be merely to better a bargaining position, to obtain a larger forum for propaganda, or to create greater rather than less international friction.   Ultimately, of course, the United Nations is there and should be freely used where a basis for agreement does not exist and action or advice of the United Nations is needed for the maintenance of good relations.

Those who would understand its functions must also be aware of the part which is to be played by the specialized agencies which are now being related to the United Nations under the general coordination of the Economic and Social Council. These agencies are designed to encourage international cooperation in specific fields; they are not, in general, agencies with extensive resources of their own or with direct responsibility for the execution of policy within the United Nations, although some have important operating functions. . . .

The President and other responsible Americans have on many occasions declared that support for the United Nations is the cornerstone of our foreign policy. On this we are a united people, without party or regional differences. . . .

. . . Our faith in the United Nations has its roots in the basic moral values and spiritual aspirations of the American people. These aspirations of ours are identical with the purposes and principles of the Charter. . . .

. . . We believe that the peoples of the United Nations also have common basic purposes which provide the foundations for effective machinery for international cooperation. We should be neither surprised nor discouraged if time and great effort are required to move forward. We hope that the effort itself will produce increasing unanimity of purpose, a unanimity which will in turn make possible more effective international action.

George Marshall, address, American Association for the United Nations, September 14, 1947; *The United States and the United Nations,* 1947, pp. 253-60.   Also see his "Program for a More Effective United Nations," address, United Nations General Assembly, September 17, 1947, pp. 261-67.

UNITED STATES POLICY GOALS, COMMITMENTS, AND EXPECTATIONS

4 1 9   QUEST FOR PEACE THROUGH THE UNITED NATIONS

It is with the book of history, and not with isolated pages, that the United States will ever wish to be identified. My country wants to be constructive, not destructive. It wants agreements, not wars, among nations. It wants itself to live in freedom, and in the confidence that the people of every other nation enjoy equally the right of choosing their own way of life.

So my country's purpose is to help us move out of the dark chamber of horrors into the light, to find a way by which the minds of men, the hopes of men, the souls of men everywhere, can move forward toward peace and happiness and well being. . . .

I know that many steps will have to be taken over many months before the world can look at itself one day and truly realize that a new climate of mutually peaceful confidence is abroad in the world.

Dwight Eisenhower, address, United Nations General Assembly, December 8, 1953; *Papers of Presidents: Eisenhower,* 1953, pp. 817-18.

420 UNITED NATIONS THE ONLY TRUE ALTERNATIVE TO WAR

. . . the problem is the life of this organization. It will either grow to meet the challenges of our age, or it will be gone with the wind, without influence, without force, without respect. Were we to let it die, to enfeeble its vigor, to cripple its powers, we would condemn our future.

For in the development of this organization rests the only true alternative to war--and war appeals no longer as a rational alternative. Unconditional war can no longer lead to unconditional victory. It can no longer serve to settle disputes. It can no longer concern the great powers alone. For a nuclear disaster, spread by wind and water and fear, could well engulf the great and the small, the rich and the poor, the committed and the uncommitted alike. Mankind must put an end to war--or war will put an end to mankind. . . .

This will require new strength and new roles for the United Nations. For disarmament without checks is but a shadow--and a community without law is but a shell. Already the United Nations has become both the measure and the vehicle of man's most generous impulses. Already it has provided . . . a means of holding man's violence within bounds.

But the great question which confronted this body in 1945 is still before us: whether man's cherished hopes for progress and peace are to be destroyed by terror and disruption, whether the "foul winds of war" can be tamed in time to free the cooling winds of reason, and whether the pledges of our Charter are to be fulfilled or defied--pledges to secure peace, progress, human rights and world law.

John Kennedy, address, United Nations General Assembly, September 25, 1961; *Papers of Presidents: Kennedy,* 1961, pp. 618-19. Also see Lyndon Johnson, address, United Nations General Assembly, December 17, 1963; *Papers of Presidents: Johnson,* 1963-64, pp. 61-63.

4 2 1   SHARING RESPONSIBILITIES IN THE UNITED NATIONS

I am well aware that many nations have questions about the world role of the United States in the years ahead--about the nature and extent of our future contribution to the structure of peace. . . .

In recent years, there has been mounting criticism here in the United States of the scope and the results of our international commitments.

This trend, however, has not been confined to the United States alone. In many countries we find a tendency to withdraw from responsibilities, to leave the world's often frustrating problems to the other fellow and just to hope for the best.

As for the United States, I can state here today without qualification: We have not turned away from the world.

We know that with power goes responsibility.

We are neither boastful of our power, nor apologetic about it. We recognize that it exists, and that, as well as conferring certain advantages, it also imposes upon us certain obligations.

As the world changes, the pattern of those obligations and responsibilities changes. . . .

Now we are maturing together into a new pattern of interdependence.

It is against this background that we have been urging other nations to assume a greater share of responsibility for their own security, both individually and together with their neighbors. The great challenge now is to enlist the cooperation of many nations in preserving peace and in enriching life. This cannot be done by American edict, or by the edict of any other nation. It must reflect the concepts and the wishes of the people of those nations themselves. . . .

It would be dishonest . . . to pretend that the United States has no national interests of its own, or no special concern for its own interests.

However, our most fundamental national interest is in maintaining that structure of international stability on which peace depends, and which makes orderly progress possible.

Richard Nixon, address, United Nations General Assembly, September 18, 1969; *Papers of Presidents: Nixon,* 1969, pp. 724-25. For additional commentary, see Nixon reports, *U.S. Foreign Policy for the 1970's,* 1970, pp. 103-7; 1971, pp. 200-6; 1972, pp. 184-94; 1973, pp. 210-15.

4 2 2   UNITED STATES COMMITMENTS TO UNITED NATIONS IDEALS

We are proud that for the 32 years since its creation, the United Nations has met on American soil. And we share with you the commitments of freedom, self-government, human dignity, mutual toleration, and the peaceful resolution of disputes--which the founding principles of the United Nations . . . so well represent.

No one nation by itself can build a world which reflects all these fine values. But the United States, my own country, has a reservoir of strength--economic strength, which we are willing to share; military strength, which we hope never to use again; and the strength of ideals, which are determined fully to maintain the backbone of our own foreign policy. . . .

I see a hopeful world, a world dominated by increasing demands for basic freedoms, for fundamental rights, for higher standards of human existence. We are eager to take part in the shaping of that world. . . .

We can only improve this world if we are realistic about its complexities. The disagreements that we face are deeply rooted, and they often raise difficult philosophical as well as territorial issues. They will not be solved easily. They will not be solved quickly . . . Poverty and inequality are of such monumental scope that it will take decades of deliberate and determined effort even to improve the situation substantially.

I stress these dangers and these difficulties because I want all of us to dedicate ourselves to a prolonged and persistent effort designed first to maintain peace and to reduce the arms race; second, to build a better and a more cooperative international economic system; and third, to work with potential adversaries as well as our close friends to advance the cause of human rights.

In seeking these goals, I realize that the United States cannot solve the problems of the world. We can sometimes help others resolve their differences, but we cannot do so by imposing our own particular solutions. . . .

The search for peace and justice also means respect for human dignity. All the signatories of the U.N. Charter have pledged themselves to observe and to respect basic human rights. Thus, no member of the United Nations can claim that mistreatment of its citizens is solely its own business. Equally, no member can avoid its responsibilities to review and to speak when torture or unwarranted deprivation occurs in any part of the world.

The basic thrust of human affairs points toward a more universal demand for fundamental human rights. The United States has a historical birthright to be associated with this process. . . .

These then are our basic priorities as we work with other members to strengthen and to improve the United Nations.

First, we will strive for peace in the troubled areas of the world; second, we will aggressively seek to control the weaponry of war; third, we will promote a new system of international economic progress and cooperation; and fourth, we will be steadfast in our dedication to the dignity and well-being of people throughout the world.

I believe that this is a foreign policy that is consistent with my own Nation's historic values and commitments. And I believe that it is a foreign policy that is consonant with the ideals of the United Nations.

Jimmy Carter, address, United Nations General Assembly, March 17, 1977; *American Foreign Policy: Basic Documents,* 1977-1980, pp. 2-6.

4 2 3   KEEPING FAITH WITH THE DREAMS THAT CREATED THE UNITED NATIONS

. . . I've come today to renew my nation's commitment to peace. And I have come to discuss how we can keep faith with the dreams that created this organization. . . .

Whatever challenges the world was bound to face, the founders intended this body to stand for certain values, even if they could not be enforced, and to condemn violence, even if it could not be stopped. This body was to speak with the voice of moral authority. That was to be its greatest power.

But the awful truth is that the use of violence for political gain has become more, not less, widespread in the last decade. Events of recent weeks have presented new, unwelcomed evidence of brutal disregard for life and truth. They have offered unwanted testimony on how divided and dangerous our world is, how quick the recourse to violence. What has happened to the dreams of the U.N.'s founders? What has happened to the spirit which created the United Nations?

The answer is clear: Governments got in the way of the dreams of the people. Dreams became issues of East versus West. Hopes became political rhetoric. Progress became a search for power and domination. Somewhere the truth was lost that people don't make wars, governments do. . . .

We cannot count on the instinct for survival to protect us against war. Despite all the wasted lives and hopes that war produces, it has remained a regular, if horribly costly, means by which nations have sought to settle their disputes or advance their goals. . . .

From the beginning, our hope for the United Nations has been that it would reflect the international community at its best. The U.N. at its best can help us transcend fear and violence and can act as an enormous force for peace and prosperity. Working together, we can combat international lawlessness and promote human dignity. If the governments represented in this chamber want peace as genuinely as their peoples do, we shall find it. We can do so by reasserting the moral authority of the United Nations.

Ronald Reagan, address, United Nations General Assembly, September 26, 1983; *Papers of Presidents: Reagan,* 1983, II, 1350-53.

CHARTER REVIEW, AMENDMENT, AND ADAPTATION

Articles 108 and 109 prescribe the procedure for formal amendment of the Charter (by General Assembly action and ratification by national governments, requiring the approval of all permanent members of the Security Council) and for convening a conference of United Nations members to review the Charter (Document 424). Three amendments have been adopted, providing for four modifications: augmenting the size of the membership of the Security Council from 11 to 15 and of the Economic and Social Council from 18 to 27 and subsequently from 27 to 54 members, and for increasing the number of votes necessary to make decisions from 7 to 9 in the Security Council--see TIAS 5857 in 16 *U.S. Treaties* 1134-48 (1963); TIAS 6529 in 19 *U.S. Treaties* 5450-58 (1965); and TIAS 7739 in 24 *U.S. Treaties* 2225-38 (1971).

Charter review and modification have been under consideration on many occasions. To illustrate, in 1948 the Vandenberg Resolution, which encouraged the President to negotiate collective defense arrangements, recommended that the Charter be strengthened for dealing with the pacific settlement of disputes and that, if necessary, a conference be convened to "review the Charter at an appropriate time" (see Document 305). For commentary, see Dean Acheson, statement, Senate Foreign Relations Committee, April 27, 1949; *American Foreign Policy: Basic Documents,* 1950-1955, I, 819-20.

Under Article 109 the General Assembly was required to consider convening a Charter review conference in 1955. In preparation, the United States Senate adopted a resolution providing for a wholesale American study of proposals "to amend, revise, or otherwise modify or change the Charter." This action resulted in the production of a comprehensive report, containing 186 documents and 4 appendixes, consisting of a compilation of background documents and congressional actions and 16 functional segments. The latter dealt with the status of the United Nations, treatment of human rights, impact of treaties on domestic law, membership, representation, regulation of armaments, promotion of international law, development of the General Assembly, voting in the Security Council and the exercise of the veto power, collective security and defense, financing, non-self-governing territories, coordination of economic affairs, and the official attitudes of United Nations members toward Charter review. See *Review of the United Nations Charter: A Collection of Documents,* January 7, 1954, Senate Doc. 87, 83rd Cong., 2d sess. (Washington: Government Printing Office, 1954). The review conference was not convened, although the General Assembly passed a resolution on November 21, 1955, to hold one "at an appropriate time" (for text of the resolution, see *American Foreign Relations: Basic Documents,* 1950-1955, I, 333-34) and established a committee to study the matter and make recommendations. By the 1960's, especially because of the East-West confrontation and the proliferation of United Nations membership, wholesale Charter review and formal revision diminished as a viable option.

As a result of a number of controversial actions taken by the General Assembly in the early 1970's--including approving the establishment of an "observership" status for the Palestine Liberation Organization (PLO), adopting a Charter of Economic Rights and Duties, excluding South Africa from participating in United Nations deliberations by rejecting the credentials of the South African delegation, and passing a resolution equating Zionism with racism in order to exclude Israel from participation or to expel it from the United Nations--the matter of substantial restructuring of the United Nations to render it "more responsive to a new economic order" came under consideration. An international panel of consultants recommended reforms aimed at bypassing the conflict-ridden parliamentary processes of the General Assembly and at adjusting it to deal with demands for radical redistribution of the world's wealth. For commentary, see *Historic Documents,* 1975, pp. 325-51, and for Henry Kissinger's address on global consensus and economic development and cooperation in the United Nations, September 1, 1975, see *Historic Documents,* 1975, pp. 587-611. On Charter review in the 1970's, also see *Digest of United States Practice in International Law,* 1974, pp. 17-21; 1975, pp. 36-38; 1977, pp. 32-33; 1978, pp. 88-90.

In the meantime the role and procedures of the United Nations have been modified substantially by incremental and evolutionary changes, embodied in Charter interpretations, informal understandings, and usage, as the United Nations adapted to meet the desires and needs of its members. These include, for example, the determination not to regard an abstention of a permanent member as a negative vote in the Security Council, the creation of an "Interim Assembly" to deal with inflammatory issues between sessions of the General Assembly and the convening of special Assembly sessions, the authorizing of observer membership, the failure to establish a military staff committee (mandated to assist the Security Council in exercising its responsibility to maintain peace and security), and the adoption of the Uniting for Peace Resolution, which, in case the Security Council failed to discharge its primary obligation of dealing with threats to the peace, empowered the General Assembly to consider the matter. Other issues also have been debated, such as elimination of the Security Council veto for questions of admission to United Nations membership, weighted voting in the General Assembly (to align the voting power of nations more equitably with their responsibilities), associate membership status for minor nations, and "consensus" decision making.

In addition to the Charter provisions concerning its amendment and review (Document 424), the material selected for this section includes the Uniting for Peace Resolution of 1950 (Document 425); the American position on Charter review in the 1970's (Document 426); and commentary on weighted voting and consensus decision making (Document 427).

4 2 4   CHARTER AMENDMENT AND REVIEW PROCESS

Article 108
Amendments to the present Charter shall come into force for all Members of the United Nations when they have been adopted by a vote of two thirds of the members of the General Assembly and ratified in accordance with their respective constitutional processes by two thirds of the Members of the United Nations, including all the permanent members of the Security Council.

Article 109
1. A General Conference of the Members of the United Nations for the purpose of reviewing the present Charter may be held at a date and place to be fixed by a two-thirds vote of the members of the General Assembly and by a vote of any seven members of the Security Council. Each Member

of the United Nations shall have one vote in the conference.

2. Any alteration of the present Charter recommended by a two-thirds vote of the conference shall take effect when ratified in accordance with their respective constitutional processes by two thirds of the Members of the United Nations including all the permanent members of the Security Council.

3. If such a conference has not been held before the tenth annual session of the General Assembly following the coming into force of the present Charter, the proposal to call such a conference shall be placed on the agenda of that session of the General Assembly, and the conference shall be held if so decided by a majority vote of the members of the General Assembly and by a vote of any seven members of the Security Council.

United Nations Charter, Chapter XVIII, Articles 108-109.

425 UNITING FOR PEACE RESOLUTION, 1950

1. *Resolves* that if the Security Council, because of lack of unanimity of the permanent members, fails to exercise its primary responsibility for the maintenance of international peace and security in any case where there appears to be a threat to the peace, breach of the peace, or act of aggression, the General Assembly shall consider the matter immediately with a view to making appropriate recommendations to Members for collective measures, including in the case of a breach of the peace or act of aggression the use of armed force when necessary, to maintain or restore international peace and security. If not in session at the time, the General Assembly may meet in emergency special session within twenty-four hours of the request therefor. Such emergency special session shall be called if requested by the Security Council on the vote of any seven members, or by a majority of the Members of the United Nations.

General Assembly Resolution, item A, November 3, 1950; *American Foreign Policy: Basic Documents,* 1950-1955, I, 188. For complete text of the resolution, see pp. 187-92, and for commentary, see Marjorie M. Whiteman, *Digest of International Law,* XII, 2-3 and XIII, 563-77. The resolution also recommended that greater concordance be exercised by the Security Council in dealing with peacekeeping and established a Peace Observation Commission.

426 UNITED STATES POSITION ON CHARTER REVIEW

The Charter, as any fundamental governing document, must have the capacity to allow those who adhere to it to deal efficiently and effectively with the questions they face. Because of the broad spectrum of interests, the full range of political diversity, and the considerable discrepancy in the types of contributions which can be made by the various members of the United Nations, the Charter must truly be an extraordinary document in order to provide the basic ground rules within which we all can agree to attempt to solve our common problems.

The Charter has generally proven to be such an extraordinary document for the past twenty-nine years. For this we all owe a profound appreciation to those who developed its text during those complex and difficult negotiations in San Francisco. Neither then nor now have sensible persons believed all the Charter language was perfect and immutable for all time. We know of no significant governing document with a long life which is or could be perfect or immutable. . . .

We are surprised by the comments of some that the Charter has been unchanged since 1945. Quite apart from the several amendments which have been made to the text . . . the Charter has, by the normal process of interpretation and evolution, gone through very significant modifications as times and circumstances have changed, as new members with new views have joined the United Nations, and as we have been able through years of experience to understand better the needs of this central multinational organization. The fact that the present Charter has allowed such flexibility is clear evidence of the fundamental value and wisdom of its text. As general political needs have changed, so in many cases have our collective interpretations of Charter provisions. These changes have taken place gradually, and effectively; a constructive evolution in which all members have participated. Such an evolution is, in our view, an invaluable way in which the Charter is maintained as a living, current document--an avenue of change vastly preferable to sudden, radical shifts which, by virtue of the extreme diversity among the Member States, almost inevitably would result in loss of the fundamental consensus which is the foundation of the Charter. The loss or weakening of that consensus can only result in diminution of the effectiveness of the organization and thus the meaningfulness of any changes which some might urge. . . .

If we proceed pell-mell into a review exercise without the requisite broad agreement, we shall encourage states to harden positions, we shall widen the difference among us and reduce our own flexibility to compromise. We shall harm the chances for continued evolutionary change. A review exercise may well prove the greatest impediment to change rather than a catalyst for change.

United States representative, statement, General Assembly Committee, December 5, 1974; *Digest of United States Practice in International Law,* 1974, pp. 17-19.

* * *

With respect to Charter review, the United States in a letter of May 23, 1975, reaffirmed its basic position that "the most urgent need of the international community is for member states to strengthen their resolve to bring national policies and actions more into line with their obligations under the Charter." Describing the Charter as the principal bond creating for its members a worldwide community of nations despite the existence of widely differing views and philosophies of government, the U.S. letter warned that "any serious effort to reconsider or revise the Charter must be looked at with great care lest the basis for the sometimes fragile ties among member states be weakened." The letter further stated that the United States saw no evidence of agreement now among the United Nations membership "on even the broad objectives of overall review" and reiterated the U.S. preference for a case-by-case approach to changes in the Charter. "Only when there is a reasonable prospect for the development of necessary agreement on the specific amendment concerned," the United States asserted, "should such efforts be pursued." In conclusion the U.S. letter stated: "We believe that the United Nations overriding need at present is to function as a 'center for harmonizing the actions of nations' as stipulated by the Charter itself. We believe that the rededication to this objective and the taking of practical steps to encourage respect for both assenting and dissenting views in the decision-making process is the most important contribution that could be made to move the United Nations toward the ideal of international cooperation that the Charter was designed to attain."

U.S. Participation in the UN, 1975, pp. 91-92. For additional commentary, see *Digest of United States Practice in International Law*, 1974, pp. 17-21.

4 2 7   WEIGHTED VOTING AND CONSENSUS DECISION MAKING

There is no prospect for the adoption of a generally applicable weighted-voting system in the General Assembly. Even on a limited basis it has little likelihood of being accepted. In fact, pressure for change has been in the opposite direction: to replace weighted voting in global institutions where it now exists with decisionmaking procedures on the model of the General Assembly. The tradeoffs proposed, which involve sharp curtailment of our veto power in the Security Council, are not in U.S. interests. Nor do we believe they would serve the organization well.

Therefore, it would be better to employ our efforts toward defining voluntary but common standards to curtail the use of the veto in the Security Council and reduce the necessity of invoking it.

We are also prepared to examine the offer to very small new states of some form of associate status with the United Nations, short of full membership and voting privileges.

Consensus offers an alternative to formal voting as a way of arriving at decisions. It is increasingly used in the General Assembly and other U.N. organs. We hope that genuine consensus will become the principal method of conciliation in the continuing North/South dialogue in the United Nations. We are prepared to give substantially greater weight in our national policy to decisions so arrived at.

Digest of United States Practice in International Law, 1978, p. 152. For discussion of decision-making processes in the United Nations, including modification of the veto power in the Security Council and other alternative decision-making approaches, such as relating voting power to assessments for assistance and development programs, giving greater legal force to decisions arrived at by weighted voting, associate membership in the United Nations for microstates, and smaller forums for decision making, see pp. 153-59.

MEMBERSHIP

When the United Nations was established, as noted, its membership constituted an   anti-Axis aggregation of fifty-one nations--including new entities like India, Lebanon, and the Philippines, as well as Poland, which did not attend the San Francisco Conference but was invited to become an original signatory of the Charter. At that time only nineteen independent states and Vatican City were not members--consisting of the Axis and their occupied powers, World War II neutrals, and some half-dozen other countries. Several of these (Afghanistan, Iceland, Sweden, and Thailand) were admitted in 1946, and Yemen and three new countries (Burma, Indonesia, and Pakistan) joined by 1950. Because of the Cold War, the Soviet exercise of frequent vetoes in the Security Council, and the failure of Communist applicants to achieve requisite approval, it was not until 1955 that a bloc of sixteen, including a few newly independent nations, were admitted simultaneously, increasing membership to seventy-five.

Once the log-jam was broken, admission became routine, converting the United Nations into a universal international institution. The principal exceptions were divided countries--the two Germanys (which were not admitted until 1973), the two Vietnams (only the Socialist Republic was admitted in 1977 after the Vietnam War), and the two Koreas (which still are not members). United Nations membership increased substantially during the 1960's and 1970's, largely due to decolonization and the proliferation of nations, expanding it from 83 to 152. By 1990 it numbered 159, thus more than tripling the original membership. As indicated earlier, no major pre-World War II power and few new states have elected not to join. The United Nations, therefore, now embraces virtually the entire community of nations-- traditional and newly independent, large and small, industrialized and developing, and democratic and autocratic states.

The Charter specifies procedures for original members (simply signing and ratifying the Charter) and admitted or elected members (requiring approval of the General Assembly upon the recommendation of the Security Council). It also stipulates that for such admitted members, they must be independent "peace-loving states" which accept and are able to carry out the obligations of the Charter, and it defines processes for suspension from the rights and privileges of, and expulsion from, the United Nations. But, unlike the League of Nations Covenant and the constitutive acts of many other international organizations, it makes no provision for voluntary withdrawal from membership.

The documents provided in this section contain Charter membership stipulations (Document 428); a roster of members with the years in which they joined the United Nations (Document 429); and a statement of American policy concerning the seating of the People's Republic of China to replace the Nationalist government of China in 1971 (Document 430).

4 2 8   UNITED NATIONS MEMBERSHIP REQUIREMENTS

Article 3
The original Members of the United Nations shall be the states which, having participated in the United Nations Conference on International Organization at San Francisco, or having previously signed the Declaration by United Nations of January 1, 1942, sign the present Charter and ratify it in accordance with Article 110.

Article 4
1. Membership in the United Nations is open to all other peace-loving states which accept the obligations contained in the present Charter and, in the judgment of the Organization, are able and willing to carry out these obligations.

2. The admission of any such state to membership in the United Nations will be effected by a decision of the General Assembly upon the recommendation of the Security Council.

Article 5
A member of the United Nations against which preventive or enforcement action has been taken by the Security Council may be suspended from the exercise of the rights and privileges of membership by the General Assembly upon the recommendation of the Security Council. The exercise of these rights and privileges may be restored by the Security Council.

Article 6
A Member of the United Nations which has persistently violated the Principles contained in the present Charter may be expelled from the Organization by the General Assembly upon the recommendation of the Security Council.

United Nations Charter, Chapter II, Articles 3-6.

4 2 9   LIST OF UNITED NATIONS MEMBERS

Roster of members with years in which they joined the United Nations. Sovereign entities that are not members include Switzerland (which elected not to join), the two Koreas (which have not been approved by the Security Council), several European principalities with very small populations (Andorra, Liechtenstein, Monaco, and San Marino), Vatican City (which remains aloof from international politics and organizations), and such microstates as Nauru. On the other hand, two Soviet republics--Byelorussia and Ukraine--are original members. Vietnam was admitted in 1977, after the Vietnam War and the reunification of the two Vietnams. Although China was an original founder of the United Nations, after 1949 there were two Chinese governments and the Nationalist government was replaced in the United Nations in 1971; this was an issue of representation rather than dual membership (on this matter, also see Documents 430, 492-497).

Member	Year	Member	Year	Member	Year
Afghanistan	1946	Dominica	1978	Malaysia	1957
Albania	1955	Dominican Rep.	1945	Maldives	1965
Algeria	1962	Ecuador	1945	Mali	1960
Angola	1976	Egypt	1945	Malta	1964
Antigua and Barbuda	1981	El Salvador	1945	Mauritania	1961
Argentina	1945	Equatorial Guinea	1968	Mauritius	1968
Australia	1945	Ethiopia	1945	Mexico	1945
Austria	1955	Fiji	1970	Mongolia	1961
Bahamas	1973	Finland	1955	Morocco	1956
Bahrain	1971	France	1945	Mozambique	1975
Bangladesh	1974	Gabon	1960	Nepal	1955
Barbados	1966	Gambia	1965	Netherlands	1945
Belgium	1945	Germany, East	1973	New Zealand	1945
Belize	1981	Germany, West	1973	Nicaragua	1945
Benin (Dahomey)	1960	Ghana	1957	Niger	1960
Bhutan	1971	Greece	1945	Nigeria	1960
Bolivia	1945	Grenada	1974	Norway	1945
Botswana	1966	Guatemala	1945	Oman	1971
Brazil	1945	Guinea	1958	Pakistan	1947
Brunei	1984	Guinea-Bissau	1974	Panama	1945
Bulgaria	1955	Guyana	1966	Papua New Guinea	1975
Burkina Faso		Haiti	1945	Paraguay	1945
(Upper Volta)	1960	Honduras	1945	Peru	1945
Burma (Myanmar)	1948	Hungary	1955	Philippines	1945
Burundi	1962	Iceland	1946	Poland	1945
Byelorussia	1945	India	1945	Portugal	1955
Cambodia		Indonesia	1950	Qatar	1971
(Kampuchea)	1955	Iran	1945	Romania	1955
Cameroon	1960	Iraq	1945	Rwanda	1962
Canada	1945	Ireland	1955	Saint Christopher	
Cape Verde	1975	Israel	1949	and Nevis	1983
Central African Rep.	1960	Italy	1955	Saint Lucia	1979
Chad	1960	Jamaica	1962	Saint Vincent and	
Chile	1945	Japan	1956	the Grenadines	1980
China	1945	Jordan	1955	Samoa (Western)	1976
Colombia	1945	Kenya	1963	Sao Tome, Principe	1975
Comoros	1975	Kuwait	1963	Saudi Arabia	1945
Congo	1960	Laos	1955	Senegal	1960
Costa Rica	1945	Lebanon	1945	Seychelles	1976
Cote d'Ivoire		Lesotho	1966	Sierra Leone	1961
(Ivory Coast)	1960	Liberia	1945	Singapore	1965
Cuba	1945	Libya	1955	Solomon Islands	1978
Cyprus	1960	Luxembourg	1945	Somalia	1960
Czechoslovakia	1945	Madagascar		South Africa	1945
Denmark	1945	(Malagasy)	1960	Spain	1955
Djibouti	1977	Malawi	1964	Sri Lanka	1955

Member	Year	Member	Year	Member	Year
Sudan	1956	Tunisia	1956	Vanuatu	1981
Suriname	1975	Turkey	1945	Venezuela	1945
Swaziland	1968	Uganda	1962	Vietnam	1977
Sweden	1946	Ukraine	1945	Yemen	1947
Syria	1945	USSR	1945	Yemen, South	1967
Tanzania	1961	United Arab Emirates	1971	Yugoslavia	1945
Thailand	1946	United Kingdom	1945	Zaire	1960
Togo	1960	United States	1945	Zambia	1964
Trinidad and Tobago	1962	Uruguay	1945	Zimbabwe	1980

430 SEATING OF PEOPLE'S REPUBLIC OF CHINA, 1971

In a major policy statement, the Secretary of State announced in August that the United States would support the participation of the People's Republic of China (PRC) in the United Nations and the transfer of the Chinese seat in the Security Council to the People's Republic of China. At the same time, the Secretary said the United States would seek to preserve representation for the Government of the Republic of China.

. . . In the General Assembly Secretary William P. Rogers pointed out that for more than 20 years two governments had exercised authority over the territory and people given representation in the United Nations when China ratified the Charter in 1945. Thus, it would be realistic to accord representation--and China's Security Council seat--to the People's Republic of China, which controlled a larger number of people than any other government. At the same time it would be unrealistic-- and unjust--to expel the Republic of China, a cooperative member of the United Nations which governs a population on Taiwan greater than the populations of two-thirds of the members of the United Nations.

Despite vigorous efforts by the United States and others . . . the General Assembly voted on October 25 to seat the representatives of the People's Republic of China and to expel the representatives of the Republic of China.

In a news conference on the day following the vote, Secretary Rogers said that the decision to seat the People's Republic of China in the United Nations was consistent with U.S. policy. At the same time, he added, the United States deeply regretted the action taken by the United Nations to deprive the Republic of China of representation in that organization. He noted that this precedent, which has the effect of depriving 14 million people on Taiwan of representation in the United Nations, could have adverse effects on other members in the future. Nevertheless, the United States accepts the decision of the majority. Following the General Assembly's actions the governing bodies of several of the specialized agencies, over U.S. objections, also expelled the Republic of China while inviting the People's Republic of China to participate.

United States Foreign Policy, 1971: A Report of the Secretary of State, pp. 274-75. Also see Documents 492-497.

FINANCING AND CONTRIBUTIONS

Financing the United Nations and determining the portion and amount of American contributions have posed a continuing problem in the operation of the United Nations. The United States has been its largest contributor since its inception. As an international confederation, it does not have the power to levy taxes. Its annual operating budget assessments are distributed among the members on a percentage basis. Additional financing is gained from special or supplemental budgets, "voluntary contributions" for specific programs, floating bond issues and, to deal with unforeseen expenses, from a capital working fund created to provide temporary financial flexibility. Expenditures are used for administrative expenses, operational programs in the field, special sessions and international conferences, and constabulary forces for peacekeeping purposes. The costs of national delegations to the United Nations are borne directly by their national governments.

The most critical factors in financing the annual operating budgets are their increasing total amounts and the allocation of the American contribution. When the United Nations was established, the budget for 1946 was set at approximately $19.4 million. This was increased to some $50 million by the late 1950's, to more than $100 million by the mid-1960's, to nearly $200 million by the early 1970's, which rapidly mounted in the early 1980's to more than a billion dollars per biennium and escalated to approximately $1.8 billion for the 1988-1989 biennium.

Over the years the United States has argued that--while it is prepared to make its fair share of contribution, as other nations' economies developed following World War II and prospered and as new members were added, and because no single nation should dominate the organization's finances--the American percentage share of the budget should be reduced. Originally the United States was assessed 39.89 percent of the budget, which was gradually reduced to 33.33 percent by the mid-1950's, to 31.52 percent by 1970, and then to 25 percent by the mid-1970's. At the same time, the minimum contributors were originally assessed at .04 percent of the budget, which was gradually lowered to .01 percent by the 1980's. Some 60 percent of the members of the United Nations (which exercise 60 percent of the voting power in the General Assembly) contribute at the rate of only .03 percent or less, whereas the eight largest contributors pay approximately 70 percent of the budget.

The United Nations has been confronted with financial crises as well as delays and delinquency of national contributions. Delinquency has been endemic, for political as well as economic reasons. In the 1980's the cumulative arrears amounted to more than half a billion dollars in both the operating and peacekeeping budgets, despite the fact that Article 19 of the Charter specifies that if a member is in arrears in its contribution for two years, it loses its vote in the General Assembly. At times, some states manage to remain just short of suffering this penalty.

When certain situations developed during the 1970's and 1980's, touched on in part in the last section of this chapter (see Documents 434-439), as well as the rampant escalation in the financing of the United Nations and other international organizations, the United States waged a campaign to improve financial responsibility in financing programs and actions, to reduce the United Nations bloated bureaucracy, and to undertake other cost-saving reforms. Much of the pressure to control such financing emerged from congressional threats to unilaterally cut back and to temporarily withhold American contributions.

Documents 431-432 indicate general United States contribution policy. For comprehensive data and documentation on this subject, see such annual reports as that of the Secretary of State to Congress published as *United States Contributions to International Organizations* and *U.S. Participation in the United Nations,* and the issues of the *Department of State Bulletin.*

431 INITIAL UNITED STATES CONTRIBUTIONS TO THE UNITED NATIONS

The principal administrative and budgetary accomplishments of the General Assembly were the review and approval of budgets for the financial years 1946 and 1947 and the further development of the permanent financial system and general organization of the Secretariat.

The budgets for 1946 and 1947 were fixed at $19,390,000 and $27,740,000 respectively. . . . The Organization's working capital fund was reduced to $20,000,000 from the provisional figure of $25,000,000 established at the London session.

A scale of contributions was also set for the 1946 and 1947 budgets and the working capital fund. This scale, which is to be reviewed at the 1947 session of the General Assembly, fixes the United States contribution at 39.89 percent of the total, a reduction from the 49.89 percent originally recommended by the Committee on Contributions. It is recognized that the United States quota includes a substantial temporary assessment because of direct war damage suffered by a number of other Members. On this basis the United States share of the 1947 budget is $11,065,486 and of the 1946 budget, $7,734,671, while the United States advance to the working capital fund is $7,978,000. . . . The floor for contributions by the individual states was set at a minimum of .04 percent of the total.

Senator Vandenberg, who represented the United States on the Administrative and Budgetary Committee of the General Assembly, was instrumental in securing a downward revision of the original proposal, pointing out that it was not only statistically inadequate in certain respects, but that under its terms of reference the Committee on Contributions had not found it possible to consider the vital principle of the sovereign equality of the Members of the United Nations, which might be jeopardized if one state were to dominate the Organization's finances. A reservation by the United States was incorporated in the General Assembly resolution on contributions as follows: "Under no circumstances do we consent that under normal conditions *any one nation* should pay more than 33 1/3 percent in an organization of 'sovereign equals'." The figure of 39.89 percent for the United States contribution was accepted temporarily only on the distinct understanding, as expressed in the same reservation, "That the difference between 33 1/3 percent and 39.89 percent is voluntarily assumed by us for [1946 and] 1947 and for the

Working Capital Fund because we recognize that normal post-war economic relationships have not yet been restored and we are willing to accept this added, temporary assessment to assist the United Nations in meeting the emergency."

The United States and the United Nations, 1946, pp. 25-26.

4 3 2   UNITED STATES CONTRIBUTION POLICY

In explaining the U.S. position . . . the U.S. Representative . . . stated: "The United States and the American people are more than willing to support thrifty policies and responsible management in the United Nations and other intergovernmental organizations in which we participate. We will, however, neither condone nor excuse waste, excess, and disregard for the mounting financial burdens imposed upon the taxpayers of the world by self-serving public institutions." She went on to say that "There must be a change . . . in the attitudes and the instincts which have overtaken both the Secretariat and the Fifth Committee in the management of the United Nations and in the financing of its programs." The United States, she said, had warned repeatedly against extravagances, urged economy upon the Secretariat, and had called for prudent management and thrift in providing resources.

U.S. Participation in the UN, 1981, p. 342.

CRITIQUE AND ASSESSMENT

In 1945 Beardsley Ruml, American academic, foundation officer, and businessman, prophesied: "At the end of five years you will think the UN is the greatest vision ever realized by man. At the end of ten years you will find doubts within yourself and all through the world. At the end of fifteen years you will believe the UN cannot succeed. You will be certain that all the odds are against its ultimate life and success. It will only be when the UN is twenty years old that. . . . we will know that the UN is the only alternative to the demolition of the world." Two decades later Adlai Stevenson, United States representative, told the United Nations: "What a prescient bit of crystal-ball gazing that turned out to be!" See *American Foreign Policy: Current Documents,* 1964, pp. 16-17.

Since 1945 the United Nations has had to cope with an array of organizational and functional problems and crises. It has dealt with such general issues as peacekeeping, peacemaking, crisis management, and dispute settlement, in which at best it achieved only limited success, and it has served as a sparking agency to induce member nations to establish policy, create programs and additional agencies, convene global conferences, and develop international law and practices affecting a variety of international issues, in which it has been more successful. Those involving conferences, for example, include diplomatic and consular relations, economic development, marine and maritime affairs, population, refugees, the seas and outer space, human rights, terrorism and hijacking, energy and the environment, desertification, water resources, and many others.

Aside from these and other topics discussed earlier in this chapter, the obvious weaknesses in any global confederation exercising political and juridical as well as negotiating and recommending functions, and such specific matters as the drafting of the 1982 Law of the Sea Treaty (see Chapter 20) and the attempt to create a New International Economic Order (see Chapter 23), this section focusses on a number of critical issues in the relations of the United States with the United Nations. These embrace a proposal to parallel the United Nations with a Council of Free Nations (Document 433); criticism of the "tyranny of the majority" in United Nations decision making (Document 434); ideological confrontation and the politicizing of issues rather than dealing with them on their merits (Document 435); the questionable notion that the United Nations is a genuine parliamentary agency and its quality as a democratic forum (Document 436); the decline of American influence in its deliberations and the need for greater professionalism (Document 437); the desire to moderate bloc influence and power wielding (Dooument 430); and a summary of factors that transformed and weakened the United Nations and American influence in its deliberations (Document 439).

For additional commentary concerning strained relations between the United States and the United Nations, see the sharp statement of the American representative in the General Assembly rejecting allegations against the United States, October 6, 1975, in 73 *Department of State Bulletin* (November 3, 1975): 649-51; and Ambassador Lichtenstein's alleged statement that if nations and their delegations feel that they are not welcome or are not properly treated in the United States, then this country strongly encourages them and the United Nations to remove themselves from the United States, in *American Foreign Policy: Current Documents,* 1983, pp. 207-8.

433 PROPOSAL FOR COUNCIL OF FREE NATIONS TO SUPERSEDE UNITED NATIONS

Leaders of mankind have for centuries sought some form of organization which would assure lasting peace. The last of many efforts is the United Nations.

The time has come in our national life when we must make a new appraisal of this organization. . . .

But now we must realize that the United Nations has failed to give us even a remote hope of lasting peace. Instead, it adds to the dangers of wars which now surround us.

The disintegrating forces in the United Nations are the Communist nations in its membership.

The Communist leaders, for forty years, have repeatedly asserted that no peace can come to the world until they have overcome the free nations. One of their fundamental methods of expanding Communism over the earth is to provoke conflict, hostility and hate among other nations. One of the proofs that they have never departed from these ideas is that they have, about one hundred times, vetoed proposals in the Security

Council which would have lessened international conflict. They daily threaten free nations with war and destruction.

In sum, they have destroyed the usefulness of the United Nations to preserve peace. . . .

More unity among free nations has been urged by President Truman, President Eisenhower, and President Kennedy. In cooperation with far-seeing statesmen in other free nations, five regional treaties or pacts have been set up for mutual defense. And there are bilateral agreements among other free nations to give military support to each other in case of attack. Within these agreements are more than forty free nations who have pledged themselves to fight against aggression. . . .

The time is here when, if the free nations are to survive, they must have a new and stronger world-wide organization. For purposes of this discussion I may call it the "Council of Free Nations." It should include only those who are willing to stand up and fight for their freedom.

The foundations for this organization have already been laid by the forty nations who have taken pledges in the five regional pacts to support each other against aggression. And there are others who should join.

I do not suggest that the Council of Free Nations replace the United Nations. When the United Nations is prevented from taking action, or if it fails to act to preserve peace, then the Council of Free Nations should step in. . . .

Although the analogy of the Concert of Europe formed in 1814 is not perfect, yet, with much less unity and authority, it fended off world war for a hundred years.

Some organized Council of Free Nations is the remaining hope for peace in the world.

Herbert Hoover, address, dedication of Herbert Hoover Presidential Library, West Branch, Iowa, August 10, 1962; 28 *Vital Speeches of the Day* (September 1, 1962): 702-4. Reprinted by permission of *Vital Speeches of the Day,* City News Publishing Co.

434 MAJORITY RULE--"TYRANNY OF THE MAJORITY"

Second, a majority must take into account the proper interest of a minority if the decisions of the majority are to be accepted. We who believe in and live by majority rule must always be alert to the danger of the "tyranny of the majority." Majority rule thrives on the habits of accommodation, moderation, and consideration of the interests of others.

Gerald Ford, address, United Nations General Assembly, September 18, 1974; *Papers of Presidents: Ford,* 1974, p. 158.

*   *   *

. . . We were deeply concerned then over the growing tendency of this Organization to adopt one-sided, unrealistic resolutions that cannot be implemented. . . .

. . . Added to this, there is now a new threat--an arbitrary disregard of United Nations rules, even of its Charter. . . .

The United States Government has already made clear from this rostrum its concern over a number of Assembly decisions. . . . These decisions have dealt with some of the most important, the most controversial, and the most vexing issues of our day. . . .

The United Nations, and this Assembly in particular, can walk one of two paths. The Assembly can seek to represent the views of the numerical majority of the day, or it can try to act as a spokesman of a more general global opinion. To do the first is easy. To do the second is infinitely more difficult. But, if we look ahead, it is infinitely more useful. . . .

The General Assembly fulfills its true function when it reconciles opposing views and seeks to bridge the differences among its Member States. The most meaningful test of whether the Assembly has succeeded in this task is not whether a majority can be mobilized behind any single draft resolution, but whether those States whose cooperation is vital to implement a decision will support it in fact. A better world can only be constructed on negotiation and compromise, not on confrontation which inevitably sows the seeds of new conflicts. In the words of our Charter, the United Nations is "to be a center for harmonizing the actions of nations in the attainment of these common ends."

No observer should be misled by the coincidental similarities between the General Assembly and a legislature. A legislature passes laws. The General Assembly passes resolutions, which are in most cases advisory in nature. These resolutions are sometimes adopted by Assembly majorities which represent only a small fraction of the people of the world, its wealth, or its territory. Sometimes they brutally disregard the sensitivity of the minority.

Because the General Assembly is an advisory body on matters of world policy, the pursuit of mathematical majorities can be a particularly sterile form of international activity. Sovereign nations, and the other international organs which the Assembly advises through its resolutions, sometimes accept and sometimes reject that advice. Often they do not ask how many nations voted for a resolution, but who those nations were, what they represented, and what they advocated.

Members of the United Nations are endowed with sovereign equality. That is, they are equally entitled to their independence, to their rights under the Charter. They are not equal in size, in population, or in wealth. They have different capabilities, and, therefore, different responsibilities, as the Charter makes clear.

Similarly, because the majority can directly affect only the internal administration of this Organization, it is the United Nations itself which suffers most when a majority, in pursuit of an objective it believes overriding, forgets that responsibility must bear a reasonable relationship to capability and to authority.

Each time this Assembly adopts a resolution which it knows will not be implemented, it damages the credibility of the United Nations. Each time that this Assembly makes a decision which a significant minority of members regard as unfair or one-sided, it further erodes vital support for the United Nations among that minority. But the minority which is so offended may in fact be a practical majority, in terms of its capacity to support this Organization and implement its decisions.

Unenforceable, one-sided resolutions destroy the authority of the United Nations. Far more serious, however, they encourage disrespect for the Charter, and for the traditions of our Organization. . . .

The function of all parliaments is to provide expression to the majority will. Yet, when the rule of the majority becomes the tyranny of the majority, the minority will cease to respect or obey it, and the parliament will cease to function. Every majority must recognize that its authority does not extend beyond the point where the minority becomes so outraged that it is no longer willing to maintain the covenant which binds them. . . .

We are all aware that true compromise is difficult and time-consuming, while bloc voting is fast and easy. But real progress on contentious issues must be earned. Paper triumphs are, in the end, expensive even for the victors. The cost is borne, first of all, by the United Nations as an institution, and, in the end, by all of us. Our achievements cannot be measured in paper. . . .

I must tell you that recent decisions of this Assembly, and of other United Nations bodies, have deeply affected public opinion in my country. The American people are deeply disturbed by decisions to exclude Member States, and to restrict their participation in discussions of matters of vital concern to them. They are concerned by moves to convert humanitarian and cultural programs into tools of political reprisal. . . .

My country cannot participate effectively in the United Nations without the support of the American people, and of the American Congress. For years they have provided that support generously. But I must tell you honestly that this support is eroding--in our Congress and among our people. Some of the foremost American champions of this Organization are deeply distressed at the trend of recent events. . . .

If the United Nations ceases to work for the benefit of *all* of its members, it will become increasingly irrelevant. It will fade into the shadow world of rhetoric, abandoning its important role in the real world of negotiation and compromise.

John Scali, United States Representative to the United Nations, address, General Assembly, December 6, 1974; 72 *Department of State Bulletin* (January 27, 1975): 114-19. Also see commentary in *U.S. Participation in the UN,* 1974, pp. 125-26.

435 IDEOLOGICAL CONFRONTATION AND POLITICIZING OF ISSUES IN UNITED NATIONS

. . . Much that has transpired at the United Nations in recent years gives us pause. At the very moment when great power confrontations are waning, troubling trends have appeared in the General Assembly and some of its specialized agencies. Ideological confrontation, bloc voting, and new attempts to manipulate the Charter to achieve unilateral ends threaten to turn the United Nations into a weapon of political warfare rather than a healer of political conflict and a promoter of human welfare.

The United Nations naturally mirrors the evolution of its composition. In its first phase it reflected the ideological struggle between the West and East; during that period the United Nations generally followed the American lead. Time and again in those days there were some 50 votes in support of our position and only a handful of Communist-bloc members against.

Ten years later, when membership had grown to more than 80, our dominance in the General Assembly no longer was assured. Neither East nor West was able to prevail. In the Security Council the American position was still sustained, while the Soviet Union was required to cast veto after veto in order to protect what it considered to be its vital interests.

But with the quantum leap to the present membership of 138, the past tendencies of bloc politics have become more pronounced and more serious. The new nations, for understandable reasons, turned to the General Assembly in which they predominated in a quest for power that simply does not reside there. The Assembly cannot take compulsory legal decisions. Yet numerical majorities have insisted on their will and objectives even when in population and financial contributions they were a small proportion of the membership. In the process, a forum for accommodation has been transformed into a setting for confrontation. The moral influence which the General Assembly should exercise has been jeopardized and could be destroyed if governments particularly those who are its main financial supporters--should lose confidence in the organization because of the imposition of a mechanical and increasingly arbitrary will.

It is an irony that at the moment the United States has accepted nonalignment, and the value of diversity, those nations which originally chose this stance to preserve their sovereign independence from powerful military alliances are forming a rigid grouping of their own. The most solid bloc in the world today is, paradoxically, the alignment of the nonaligned. This divides the world into categories of North and South, developing and developed, imperial and colonial, at the very moment in history when such categories have become irrelevant and misleading.

Never before has the world been more in need of cooperative solutions. Never before have the industrialized nations been more ready to deal with the problems of development in a constructive spirit. Yet lopsided, loaded voting, biased results, and arbitrary tactics threaten to destroy these possibilities. The utility of the General Assembly both as a safety valve and as an instrument of international cooperation is being undermined. Tragically, the principal victims will be the countries who seek to extort what substantially could be theirs if they proceeded cooperatively.

An equally deplorable development is the trend in the specialized agencies to focus on political issues and thereby deflect the significant work of these agencies. UNESCO, designed for cultural matters, and the

International Labor Organization have been heavily politicized. . . .

The process is surely self-defeating. According to the rules of the General Assembly, the coerced are under no compulsion to submit. To the contrary, they are given all too many incentives simply to depart the scene, to have done with the pretense. Such incentives are ominously enhanced when the General Assembly and specialized agencies expel member nations which for one reason or another do not meet with their approval. . . .

We are determined to oppose tendencies which in our view will undermine irreparably the effectiveness of the United Nations. It is the smaller members of the organization who would lose the most. They are more in need of the United Nations than the larger powers, such as the United States, which can prosper within or outside the institution.

Ways must be found for power and responsibility in the Assembly and in the specialized agencies to be more accurately reflective of the realities of the world. The United States has been by far the largest financial supporter of the United Nations; but the support of the American people, which has been the lifeblood of the organization, will be profoundly alienated unless fair play predominates and the numerical majority respects the views of the minority. The American people are understandably tired of the inflammatory rhetoric against us, the all-or-nothing stance accompanied by demands for our sacrifice which too frequently dominate the meeting halls of the United Nations.

Henry Kissinger, address, Institute of World Affairs, Milwaukee, Wisconsin, July 14, 1975; 78 *Department of State Bulletin* (August 4, 1975): 152-54. Also see his address, special session of the General Assembly, September 1, 1975, *U.S. Participation in the UN*, 1975, pp. 363-76. The United States withdrew from the International Labor Organization in November 1977, protesting its rampant politicization, but returned in February 1980, and withdrew from UNESCO as of the end of 1984 because of its spending practices and anti-Western bias.

436 UNITED NATIONS--RECOMMENDATORY, NOT PARLIAMENTARY, INSTITUTION

I am not trying to persuade you to take the winning side in this argument. It is not clear what is the winning side. We are talking about what is the right side, the claim which every act of the General Assembly in 30 years surely attests.

Daniel Moynihan, United States Representative to the United Nations, statement, General Assembly, December 8, 1975; 74 *Department of State Bulletin* (January 19, 1976): 83.

*   *   *

None will learn with surprise that for the United States, at very least, the 30th General Assembly has been a profound, even alarming disappointment. This splendid hall has, since the opening of the Assembly, been repeatedly the scene of acts which we regard as abominations. . . .

The first lesson is the most important, which is that the General Assembly has been trying to pretend that it is a parliament, which it is not. It is a conference made up of representatives sent by sovereign governments which have agreed to *listen* to its recommendations--recommendations which are, however, in no way binding.

It is usual to use the term "recommendatory" to describe the Assembly's powers. . . . unless such recommendations have the effect of persuading, they have no effect at all. Resolutions that condemn, that accuse, that anathematize, do not bring us any nearer to agreement. They have the opposite effect. . . .

The crisis of the United Nations is not to be found in the views of the majority of its members. Rather, it resides in the essential incompatibility of the system of government which the charter assumes will rule the majority of its members and the system of government to which the majority in fact adheres.

The charter assumes that most of the members of the General Assembly will be reasonably representative governments, committed at home no less than abroad to the maintenance of representative institutions. . . .

Those who have submitted to this discipline--and obviously, at the level of individuals, this is not a variety of understanding confined to citizens of parliamentary states--will readily enough understand that the General Assembly has not attained to anything like the degree of acceptance and authority among its constituent members that warrants any transfer of genuine power of a parliamentary nature.

Now, and for the foreseeable future, it can only be a recommendatory body, a conference which adopts positions to which governments have agreed to listen. . . . But to pretend we are further than we are will serve only to set back what progress has in truth been made.

This goes to the question of legitimacy. What powers does an assembly have? How have they been conferred? How is it periodically reconfirmed that the population--be it of individuals or governments or whatever--over which such powers are exercised does indeed consent to that exercise?

This process--of definition, of conferral, of confirmation--is the essence of a representative institution. Those who understand it will readily enough understand what can and cannot be accomplished through the instrumentality of the General Assembly.

And now to the heart of the matter. Many governments--most governments--now represented in the General Assembly seem disposed to use this body as if it had powers which the General Assembly does not have, to enforce policies of a nature which the General Assembly ought not, at this stage, even to consider. . . .

. . . the reason is that most of the governments represented in the General Assembly do not themselves govern by consent. Assemblies for them, and for their peoples, are places in which decrees are announced. Where it is felt that "majorities" are needed to attest to the decree, well, such majorities are readily enough summoned.

We put the simple test. In how many of the 144 members of the United Nations is there a representative body which both has the power and periodically exercises the power of rejecting a decision of the government? Only a handful. By one competent count, there are now 28, possibly 29, functioning, representative democracies in the world, and one is not a member of the United Nations. Such governments will by instinct pay the greatest heed to winning consent, including winning consent in the General Assembly. Consent is the very essence of their being. Other governments will not pay such heed. At home they rule by decree, and it seems wholly natural to seek to emulate the same practice in the General Assembly.

. . . If only a handful of the nations represented here have representative governments today, most of them--truly!--have had such in the life of the United Nations. This is a mournful fact for those of us committed to democratic institutions. . . .

. . . But we do think it is possible for there to be a greater understanding among members at large of the nature of a representative institution and the corresponding limits of the General Assembly. We would seek this understanding not to restrict what the United Nations can accomplish but, rather, to accentuate the positive and concentrate on real possibilities rather than to squander the opportunity that does exist by the mindless pretense of legislative omnipotence.

It may be that this objective would be well served if a "parliamentary caucus" were established within the General Assembly. This would be a group of nations constituted, let us say, along the lines of the membership criteria of the Council of Europe, which would attend not so much to policy issues as to institutional ones. Its concern would be to seek to encourage those practices and approaches which enhance the effectiveness of the General Assembly and to discourage, both by example and by pronouncement, those which do not.

Daniel Moynihan, address, United Nations General Assembly, December 17, 1975; 74 *Department of State Bulletin* (February 2, 1976): 139-43. During his short tenure as United States Representative to the United Nations, Ambassador Moynihan delivered a series of blunt, often critical, statements about the United Nations late in 1975--challenging the anti-Western biases of the Third World bloc, defending the United States and other democracies against attacks by undemocratic governments, and challenging the pseudo-democratic practices of the United Nations. See, for example, his address, Annual AFL-CIO Convention, San Francisco, October 3, 1975; *Historic Documents,* 1975, pp. 645-51. Apparently President Ford and Secretary of State Kissinger encouraged him to speak out forcefully and candidly on major issues before the United Nations; for illustrations, see issues of *Department of State Bulletin,* late 1975 to spring 1976. For a Department of State response to Moynihan's criticism of undemocratic practices in the United Nations, see Assistant Secretary of State for International Organization Affairs, address, Board of Directors of the United Nations Association, New York, November 20, 1978; *American Foreign Policy: Basic Documents,* 1977-1980, pp. 357-63, especially pp. 360-61.

437 DECLINE OF UNITED STATES INFLUENCE IN UNITED NATIONS--NEED FOR
PROFESSIONALISM

. . . The analysis of voting patterns at the U.N. reveals that the decline in U.S. influence which began around 1966 or 67 continued precipitously for about 5 to 7 years at which point it reached a low level around which it has stuck ever since. . . .

There was a time when I believed that our impotence was a kind of inevitable consequence of the changed character of the membership of the United Nations. Certainly that composition changed. When the United Nations was established there were approximately fifty members and though they were not all democracies, most of the members were stable, older nation states, experienced in international affairs, democracies who had some sort of commitment to international law, and to liberal principles.

There was a degree of falsification introduced into the United Nations from the very beginning because of the presence of the Soviet Union, certain of its client states, and selected autocracies into an organization committed to the principles of freedom and democracy and self-determination. But that degree of falsification was relatively small and the facts of the United Nations were not too far from the principles enunciated in the Charter.

. . . Most of the nations that have been admitted since the U.N.'s establishment are new nations, former colonies. The big influx of the former colonies into the U.N. occurred along side the beginning of the decline of U.S. influence. . . .

These nations have had two overriding preoccupations which have dominated the U.N. agenda since then: decolonization, since they have been involved in establishing their own national independence; and economic development. Now, in principle, the United States should be the last country in the world to have problems with an organization whose agenda is dominated by decolonization and economic development. . . .

. . . Decolonization, economic development, and development assistance are utterly consistent with our national experience, our values and our practices.

Why would we have problems with an organization most of whose members are concerned with them? It is an interesting question on which I have been reflecting for months now, and I have concluded that it was not the influx of new nations that accounts for the U.S. position at the United Nations. It is not the changed composition of the United Nations that accounts for our fall from influence to impotence.

I have also examined the hypothesis that the bloc system accounts for the absence of American influence in the United Nations. Certainly it makes its contribution. . . . We are a country without a party in the United Nations and that fact, that absence of a party, certainly is relevant to our impotence in that body. But I do not think it explains the whole problem.

Yet another hypothesis with which I have attempted to explain U.S. impotence is the structure of the United Nations itself: the rules, especially the practice of applying in the General Assembly the principle of one-man-one-vote to an international assembly of terribly unequal nations. . . . Obviously, that kind of principle creates a disjunction between power and responsibility because some of the nations who have the power to influence decisions, financial decisions for instance, or the nations who have the resources to implement decisions, are not identical with those who have the power to vote to make them. . . . It is argued that only Third World countries get a good deal from the U.N. Nonetheless, I do not believe this or any other basic structural flaw accounts for our impotence.

There is, I fear, another explanation. . . . I have seen what a Western democratic nation could do inside the United Nations. The British have done it. They have made the organization function in ways that are responsive to their interests and their policy goals. . . . Why, then, haven't we been able to achieve our goals inside this organization?

My tentative conclusion is that it is due to our lack of skill in practicing international politics in multilateral arenas. It is also part and parcel of the decline of U.S. influence in the world. It is, I believe, a direct reflection of what has been a persisting U.S. ineptitude in international relations that has dogged us all our national life; an ineptitude that has persisted through centuries, through administrations headed by different parties, through different presidents, and is especially manifest in our multilateral politics. . . .

We have not been effective in defining or projecting in international arenas a conception of our national purpose. Through decades, we have not been good at politics at the United Nations. . . .

I believe that we have not understood that the same principles of politics that apply in our national life apply in multilateral international institutions as well. . . .

Another consequence of ignoring the political character of the U.N. is that we operate as though there were no difference between our relations with supporters and opponents, with no penalties for opposing our views and values, and no rewards for cooperating. We have also operated as though we had no persistent, coherent national purposes which link issue to issue. . . . Unless or until we approach the United Nations as professionals--professionals at its politics--with a clear-cut conception of our purposes and of the political arena in which we operate, knowledge of the colleagues with whom we are interacting, and of their goals and interests, then we won't ever know whether the United Nations could be made a hospitable place for the American national interest.

Jeane Kirkpatrick, American Representative to the United Nations, address, Heritage Foundation Conference, New York, June 7, 1982; 48 *Vital Speeches of the Day* (August 1, 1982): 610-12. Reprinted with permission.

438   DESIRE FOR TRUE NONALIGNMENT IN UNITED NATIONS

Arms control requires a spirit beyond narrow national interests. This spirit is a basic pillar on which the U.N. was founded. We seek a return to this spirit. A fundamental step would be a true nonalignment of the United Nations. This would signal a return to the true values of the charter, including the principle of universality. The members of the United Nations must be aligned on the side of justice rather than injustice, peace rather than aggression, human dignity rather than subjugation. Any other alignment is beneath the purpose of this great body and destructive of the harmony that it seeks. What harms the charter harms peace.

The founders of the U.N. expected that member nations would behave and vote as individuals, after they had weighed the merits of an issue--rather like a great, global town meeting. The emergence of blocs and the polarization of the U.N. undermine all that this organization initially valued.

Ronald Reagan, address, United Nations General Assembly, September 26, 1983; *Papers of Presidents: Reagan,* 1983, II, 1352.

439 IDEALISM VS. REALISM--PROBLEMS IMPEDING SUCCESS OF UNITED STATES IN UNITED NATIONS

The hardest thing for human beings to do is to set lofty goals and work hard for them while recognizing that they may never be fully realized. Yet, this is what the United Nations is really all about. In fact, most men and women of good sense *knew* 40 years ago that the United Nations was not a panacea for the world's ills. They knew that pursuing the ideals of the United Nations would be an endless task. But they were convinced that it was important to set down these ideals in concrete form, to give all nations goals to aspire toward and work for. They knew that the Charter provided a standard against which to measure the conduct of nations. If nations failed to live up to those ideals, perhaps that was to be expected in this imperfect world. But so long as the world continued to measure the behavior of nations against these high standards, progress toward a better world could be made. . . .

. . . We would all prefer that the United Nations could always play the role of peace-keeper. But we have had to accept the limitations of the real world: the international consensus which the founders hoped for has broken down.

Many factors contributed to the breakdown of the international consensus. I would like to discuss three of the most significant.

The first development has been the gradual transformation of the membership of the United Nations. Decolonization, which the United States rightly welcomed and encouraged, has brought many new nations into the United Nations, and the majority of these new members are not democratic. We hope this trend has been reversed and that the tide of freedom will continue to bring more and more nations into the family of democracies. . . .

Yet, we must recognize the fact that the swelling ranks of non-democratic nations in the United Nations have diluted the original consensus that gave meaning to the Charter. Nations that are not democratic often will not support measures in the United Nations that would call them to account for violations of freedom and human rights, even though these are precisely what the United Nations was meant to do. . . .

A second problem has been the Soviet Union. We know that the Soviet leaders never shared the original ideals that gave impetus to the United Nations. But there were hopes that the Soviet Union might evolve and play a responsible part in the postwar international system. . . . Soviet policies have continued to threaten the international order. And the Soviet Union has added steadily to the number of votes that it can count on to support its action both inside and outside the United Nations. While other countries, including the United States, have been unfairly singled out for condemnation by various UN bodies, the Soviet Union has never been named, not even for its invasion of Afghanistan.

A third problem has been the division of the United Nations into blocs, indeed, into an overlapping series of blocs . . . adding up to what Ambassador Moynihan has called the UN "party system.". . .

The reality of the General Assembly, in any case, is, as President Reagan has said, that: "the body established to serve the goals of the UN Charter is increasingly becoming, instead, a body whose members are dedicated to the goals of the majority." The contest for political influence within the United Nations, swayed by ideological fashions and manipulated by pressure tactics, has superseded the broader sense of community and the search for ways to fulfill the goals of the Charter.

. . . Politicking is a fact of life in the United Nations. Those who do not support the principles of the Charter have learned to use the "party system" to their own advantage. We have no choice but to respond in kind. *We* must use the system to defend the Charter and our own values.

This brings me to the final reason that the United Nations has not made progress toward its proclaimed goals over recent decades. . . .

For years, the United States failed to take the United Nations seriously. Disillusionment with the way the organization seemed to be evolving led us, in a sense, to withdraw. . . .

As a result of our withdrawal, we failed to take part in the "party system" that was developing inside the United Nations. While others worked hard to organize and influence voting blocs to further *their* interests and promote *their* ideologies, the United States did not make similar exertions on behalf of *our* values and *our* ideals. Indeed, we began to lose sight of the UN's importance as a place to promote the principles of freedom and democracy. . . .

When other nations wield influence in the United Nations, when they can pass resolutions with the sole intent of harming other nations, when they can shield themselves or their friends from criticism--even for flagrant violations of the Charter--they accomplish two things:

First, they build a reputation as useful and influential friends, outside as well as inside the United Nations.

Second, they make a mockery of the Charter itself. For what can the Charter mean if violations of it cannot even be denounced within the United Nations?

On the other hand, when the United States cannot protect itself or its friends from unfair attacks in the United Nations, we appear impotent, hardly a useful ally. . . .

What all this tells us is that the United States *must* play a forceful role in the United Nations to protect our interests, to promote our democratic values and our ideals, and to defend the original principles of the Charter. We cannot let our adversaries use against us, as a weapon of political warfare, our own devotion to international law and international cooperation. We should use these instruments ourselves as they were intended--as a force against aggression and against evil, and for peace and human betterment.

George Shultz, address, United Nations Association, Chamber of Commerce, and World Affairs Council, San Francisco, June 26, 1985; 85 *Department of State Bulletin* (August 1985):   19-21.

26

Inter-American System

The Organization of American States is tangible evidence of our belief that cooperative efforts among nations is essential to prevent aggression, to eliminate want, and to increase human liberty and happiness. In the achievement of these aims, the principles of mutual respect, of solidarity, and of belief in the dignity of man, upon which our inter-American system rests, are of profound importance. They express the essence of our common faith and form the basis of our common purpose.

Harry Truman
Council of Organization of American States, 1952

The spirit of inter-Americanism--originally called Pan-Americanism--was initiated early in the nineteenth century. Shortly after a dozen Latin American states gained their independence, their principal liberators dreamt of integrating them into an alliance or union, as had the British colonies that formed the United States federation in North America. At the Congress of Panama in 1826, sparked by Simon Bolivar, representatives of Colombia, Mexico, Peru, and Central America signed a Treaty of Union, League, and Perpetual Confederation. The United States was invited to attend but, because of delays while Congress debated involvement and funding of a delegation, its delegates arrived too late to participate. Subsequently the United States was excluded from a series of nineteenth-century congresses held in 1847, 1856, and 1864.

Following the Washington Conference of American States in 1889--initiated by the United States, and first in a series of such gatherings--a Commercial Bureau of the Americas was created (the predecessor of the Pan American Union) which served as a general administrative agency and clearinghouse, whose functions were progressively expanded over the years. In 1901 a Governing Board was constituted to direct the activities of the Pan American Union. From time to time it was supplemented by more technical operational hemispheric agencies--the Pan American Sanitary Bureau (1902) and the Postal Union of the Americas and Spain (1911). A Central American Court of Justice--the first genuine international tribunal--was established in 1907, but it was short-lived.

In addition to a series of Inter-American Conferences convened after 1889, other specialized organizations were created. These, dealing with non-political matters, include the Inter-American Commission of Women (1928), the Pan American Institute of Geography and History (1928), the Inter-American Institute of Agricultural Sciences (1940), the Inter-American Statistical Institute (1940), and the Inter-American Peace Commission (1940), which are merely illustrative of dozens of such undertakings. After World War II still others were added--the Inter-American Economic and Social Council (1945), the Inter-American Peace Committee (1948), the Human Rights Commission (1959), and a complex network of conciliation and arbitration machinery.

Although this hemispheric system was emerging incrementally, no regional general organization appeared to be feasible until the Axis threat energized the countries of the Western Hemisphere. Beginning with the series of Inter-American Conferences that presaged the Rio Pact (1947), which is treated in Chapter 18, primary attention focused on the security of the Americas. Special agencies were launched to cope with the wartime crisis and to cement hemispheric solidarity of purpose and action. Illustrative are the Inter-American Neutrality Committee (1939), renamed the Inter-American Juridical Committee (1942), the Inter-American Defense Board (1942, see Document 303), and the bilateral United States defense commissions with Brazil, Canada, and Mexico (see Documents 301-302). Eventually this informal inter-American system mushroomed into the most comprehensive arrangement for international integration in existence at the end of World War II.

But it was not until the Ninth International Conference of American States met at Bogota in 1948 that top priority was given to consolidating and formalizing the inter-American system. The Charter of the Organization of American States (OAS) was approved, subject to ratification by two-thirds of the American republics. It provided for periodic Inter-American Conferences (normally to meet every five years and serve as the primary deliberative or "legislative" organ); an Organ of Consultation or Foreign Ministers Meeting (to convene as necessary to consider hemispheric security and other urgent problems) with an Advisory Defense Committee under it (to furnish advice on military cooperation); a Council (superseding the former Governing Board, and possessing broad deliberative, supervisory, and coordinating functions); and several subsidiary facilities--the Inter-American Economic and Social Council, the Inter-American Cultural Council, and the Inter-American Council of Jurists. The Pan American Union continued as the administrative agency of the Organization.

To further integrate the activities of the many functionally particularized conferences and specialized organizations of the Western Hemisphere the Charter of 1948 also provided for their association with the Organization of American States. "Specialized Conferences"--previously called "technical conferences"--were interrelated with the central organs of the OAS in various respects, and independent specialized inter-American agencies were affiliated with the OAS by bilateral treaties between them, similar to the arrangement governing the relations of the United Nations and its specialized agencies. (See

OAS Charter, Chapters XX and XXI.)

The documents contained in this chapter deal primarily with the development and status of the Organization of American States, general United States policy concerning the inter-American system, and selected illustrations of the OAS in action. These documents need to be related to those provided in Chapter 7 (on presidential doctrines), Chapters 11 and 12 (on crises in Central America and the Caribbean), Chapter 18 (sections on Western Hemisphere alliance, defense, and mutual defense arrangements), and Chapter 31 (on the Western Hemisphere).

Although the Organization of American States, since 1948, has constituted the core of the inter-American system, the latter antedates it and is more comprehensive in both scope and functions. Simply put, currently the inter-American system consists of the Organization of American States, special inter-American conferences, "independent" specialized organizations, and other general and restricted agencies (Documents 440-441).

DEVELOPMENT OF INTER-AMERICAN SYSTEM

The Charter of the Organization of American States, approved at the Ninth International Conference of American States in 1948, went into de facto effect immediately although technically it was not formally operational until ratified in December 1951. Consisting of 112 articles, it established the purposes, structure, functions, and procedures of the Organization (see TIAS 2361, in 2 *U.S. Treaties* 2394-2485; and *A Decade of American Foreign Policy: Basic Documents, 1941-49*, pp. 427-46).

The Charter was amended by the Protocol of Buenos Aires in 1967, which instituted comprehensive, article-by-article changes in the structure and operation of the OAS, extending the Charter to 150 articles (and which entered into force in February 1970; see TIAS 6847, in 21 *U.S. Treaties* 607-811). As depicted in Document 440, its primary organs currently include a General Assembly (the primary policy-making organ, which superseded the Inter-American Conference); the Meeting of Consultation of Ministers of Foreign Affairs; three co-equal councils--the Permanent Council, the Inter-American Economic and Social Council, and the Inter-American Council for Education, Science, and Culture; the Inter-American Juridical Committee; the Inter-American Commission on Human Rights; and the General Secretariat, which superseded the Pan American Union. For commentary on major changes, see Document 442.

Subsequently, in 1974 the United States proposed modernizing the system to better integrate the OAS and the Rio Pact in order to cope more effectively with changing conditions (Document 443). But it was not until 1985 that a second attempt was made to amend the Charter, which was approved by the fifteenth General Assembly meeting in Cartegena in December. The principal modifications provide for expanded authorization of the OAS to engage in peace-keeping services, broadened membership admission requirements, and liberalized authority of the Secretary General to introduce for consideration matters affecting peace and security.

The sphere of activity and responsibility of the Organization of American States is comprehensive, ranging from peacekeeping and hemispheric defense (see OAS Charter, Chapters V and VI) to consideration of political questions and cooperation in cultural, economic, social, and technical affairs. Its general functions include both extracontinental and intracontinental security, resolution of American disputes, the promotion of representative democracy and human rights, economic welfare and financial assistance, industrialization and modernization, commerce, and a variety of additional matters--education, cultural cooperation, social security, urban renewal, tax reform, and many others.

During the six decades from 1889 to the creation of the OAS in 1948, nine Inter-American Conferences (originally called International Conferences of American States), four special conferences concerned with peace and security, and three Foreign Ministers Meetings were convened. Between the launching of the OAS and its modification in 1967 an additional fourteen conferences met. Thereafter the Inter-American Conference was replaced by the General Assembly, which meets annually. For a list of conferences and meetings, see Document 447. The Foreign Ministers Meetings were regularized, and occasional specialized conferences are convened to handle particularized issues, such as agriculture, child welfare, copyright, highways, public health, renewable resources, statistics, telecommunications, travel, and a variety of other matters.

Originally twenty-one nations--the United States and the twenty independent Latin American nations--were founding members of the Organization of American States. Since the Charter was revised in 1967, post-World War II newly independent states have joined, so that membership is virtually universal (Document 448). Canada prefers to maintain an observership status. While the Charter does not provide for withdrawal, suspension, or expulsion of members, in 1962 Cuba was "excluded" from participation in the OAS and other hemispheric agencies (Document 449).

INSTRUMENTS OF COOPERATION PROVIDED BY THE CHARTER

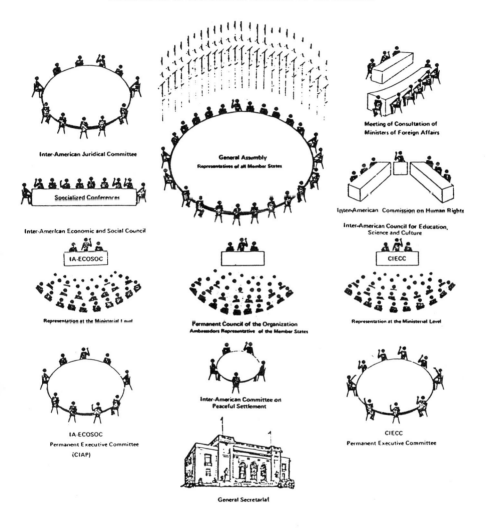

Inter-American Juridical Committee

Specialized Conferences

Inter-American Economic and Social Council

IA-ECOSOC

Representation at the Ministerial Level

IA-ECOSOC
Permanent Executive Committee
(CIAP)

General Assembly
Representatives of all Member States

Permanent Council of the Organization
Ambassadors Representative of the Member States

Inter-American Committee on
Peaceful Settlement

General Secretariat

Meeting of Consultation of
Ministers of Foreign Affairs

Inter-American Commission on Human Rights

Inter-American Council for Education,
Science and Culture

CIECC

Representation at the Ministerial Level

CIECC
Permanent Executive Committee

SPECIALIZED ORGANIZATIONS OF THE OAS

★ PAN AMERICAN INSTITUTE OF GEOGRAPHY AND HISTORY   ★ INTER-AMERICAN INSTITUTE OF AGRICULTURAL SCIENCES

★ PAN AMERICAN HEALTH ORGANIZATION   ★ INTER-AMERICAN INDIAN INSTITUTE   ★ INTER-AMERICAN CHILDREN'S INSTITUTE

★ INTER-AMERICAN COMMISSION OF WOMEN

Organization of American States, *A Handbook* (Washington: Organization of American States).

4 4 1   SPECIALIZED INTER-AMERICAN ORGANIZATIONS AND OTHER AGENCIES

Specialized Organizations

Inter-American Children's Institute (1927)
Inter-American Commission of Women (1928)
Inter-American Indian Institute (1940)
Inter-American Institute of Agricultural Sciences (1942)
Pan American Health Organization (began as Sanitary Organization, 1902)
Pan American Institute of Geography and History (1929)

Other Autonomous and Subsidiary Agencies

Inter-American Center for Public Administration (1965)
Inter-American Commission on Human Rights (1959)
Inter-American Committee on the Alliance for Progress (1963)
Inter-American Committee on Pacific Settlement (1967)--successor to Inter-American Peace Committee
Inter-American Court of Human Rights (1978)
Inter-American Defense Board (1942)
Inter-American Development Bank (1959)
Inter-American Nuclear Energy Commission (1959)
Inter-American Peace Committee (1940)
Inter-American Statistical Institute (1940)
Inter-American Telecommunication Commission (1962)

These merely illustrate the dozens of inter-American agencies established over the years, some of which have been terminated or superseded.

4 4 2   OAS CHARTER--PROTOCOL OF AMENDMENT, 1967

The signing of the protocol of Buenos Aires was a major development for the inter-American system. The amendments to be effected in the Charter of the Organization of American States by the protocol of amendment, the first such amendments since the adoption of the charter in 1948, will go far toward the necessary modernization of the structure of the Organization and the strengthening of its capacity to act effectively in the interest of hemispheric cooperation and solidarity. The amendments grant certain fuller responsibilities to some of the organs of the Organization, for instance, in the field of peaceful settlement. They establish new and specific objectives and standards for the promotion of economic, social, and cultural development.

Following in general the guidelines prepared at the Second Special Inter-American Conference at Rio de Janeiro in November 1965, and the draft amendments prepared by the OAS Special Committee which met in Panama in March 1966 and by the Inter-American Economic and Social Council which met in Washington in June 1966, the Buenos Aires Conference adopted the amendments which are embodied in the protocol of amendment.

Among the more significant changes in the amendments relating to the structure of the Organization and to the responsibilities of its organs are those concerning (1) the provision in the charter of procedures for the Organization to authorize the admission of new members; (2) the replacement of the Inter-American Conference which meets every 5 years by a General Assembly which meets annually and which assumes certain functions now performed by the OAS Council; (3) the redesignation of the OAS Council as the Permanent Council, and the granting of additional responsibilities to the Inter-American Economic and Social Council and Inter-American Council for Education, Science, and Culture--formerly the Inter-American Cultural Council--which become organs directly responsible to the General Assembly as in the Permanent Council; (4) the elimination of the Inter-American Council of Jurists and the upgrading of the Inter-American Juridical Committee; (5) the assignment to the Permanent Council of specific additional authority in the field of peaceful settlement; (6) the incorporation of the Inter American Commission on Human Rights into the OAS Charter as an organ with functions to be later determined by an inter-American convention on human rights; and (7) the election of the OAS Secretary General and Assistant Secretary General by the General Assembly for 5-year terms, rather than by the OAS Council for 10-year terms as presently provided. . . .

Lyndon Johnson, message to the Senate, June 12, 1967. *American Foreign Policy: Current Documents*, 1967, pp. 636-37. For United States proposals, also see Dean Rusk, address on need for revision and improvement, to Special Inter-American Conference, Rio de Janeiro, November 22, 1965, in *American Foreign Policy: Current Documents,* 1965, pp. 932-39.

4 4 3 MODERNIZATION OF THE ORGANIZATION OF AMERICAN STATES

A modern Inter-American System requires that the Treaty of Rio and the OAS be adjusted to new conditions. The Inter-American System is the oldest major association of nation states. It has pioneered the concept of international organization and collective security. It has been in the forefront of the development of international law. It has championed the principles of self-determination and non-intervention. It has functioned productively for more than seventy years because it has been adaptable. Today, as we contemplate past experience and future needs, we see that further modification is necessary.

First, development is impossible without security. The Rio Treaty has helped keep this Hemisphere largely free of turmoil and conflict. We should modernize it, in keeping with our times, but we should preserve its essentials. [See Document 304, Amendment, 1978.]

Second, we need to reform the OAS so that it becomes a more effective instrument for hemispheric cooperation. It is overly rigid in its structures; unnecessarily formal in its procedures, and insufficiently

broad in its membership. To remedy these weaknesses:
-- all major OAS meetings, including the General Assembly, should be made less formal;
-- the Permanent Council should be recognized as the central executive body of the OAS;
-- OAS membership should be open to all the nations who have attended the Foreign Ministers conferences; and
-- the OAS should be restructured to become a more effective instrument for our economic consultations. . . .

Henry Kissinger, address, OAS General Assembly, April 20, 1974. *Digest of United States Practice in International Law,* 1974, pp. 21-22. For text of the United States working paper on the subject, June 20, 1974, see pp. 22-25. ʼ

444   OAS PURPOSES AND PRINCIPLES

Chapter I
Nature and Purposes
Article 1

The American States establish by this Charter the international organization that they have developed to achieve an order of peace and justice, to promote their solidarity, to strengthen their collaboration, and to defend their sovereignty, their territorial integrity and their independence. Within the United Nations, the Organization of American States is a regional agency.

Article 2

The Organization of American States, in order to put into practice the principles on which it is founded and to fulfill its regional obligations under the Charter of the United Nations, proclaims the following essential purposes:

a) To strengthen the peace and security of the continent;
b) To prevent possible causes of difficulties and to ensure the pacific settlement of disputes that may arise among the Member States;
c) To provide for common action on the part of those States in the event of aggression;
d) To seek the solution of political, juridical, and economic problems that may arise among them; and
e) To promote, by cooperative action, their economic, social, and cultural development.

Chapter II
Principles
Article 3

The American States reaffirm the following principles:

a) International law is the standard of conduct of States in their reciprocal relations;

b)   International order consists essentially of respect for the personality, sovereignty, and independence of States, and the faithful fulfillment of obligations derived from treaties and other sources of international law;

c)   Good faith shall govern the relations between States;

d)   The solidarity of the American States and the high aims which are sought through it require the political organization of those States on the basis of the effective exercise of representative democracy;

e)   The American States condemn war of aggression: victory does not give rights;

f)   An act of aggression against one American State is an act of aggression against all the other American States;

g)   Controversies of an international character arising between two or more American States shall be settled by peaceful procedures;

h)   Social justice and social security are bases of lasting peace;

i)   Economic cooperation is essential to the common welfare and prosperity of the peoples of the [Hemisphere];

j)   The American States proclaim the fundamental rights of the individual without distinction as to race, nationality, creed, or sex;

k)   The spiritual unity of the [Hemisphere] is based on respect for the cultural values of the American countries and requires their close cooperation for the high purposes of civilization;

l)   The education of peoples should be directed toward justice, freedom, and peace.

OAS Charter, revised 1967, Chapters 1 and 2, articles 1-3.

4 4 5   OAS FUNDAMENTAL RIGHTS AND DUTIES OF STATES

Article 9
States are juridically equal, enjoy equal rights and equal capacity to exercise these rights, and have equal duties. The rights of each State depend not upon its power to ensure the exercise thereof, but upon the mere fact of its existence as a person under international law.

Article 10
Every American State has the duty to respect the rights enjoyed by every other State in accordance with international law.

Article 11
The fundamental rights of States may not be impaired in any manner whatsoever.

Article 12
The political existence of the State is independent of recognition by other States. Even before recognized, the State has the right to defend its

integrity and independence, to provide for its preservation and prosperity, and consequently to organize itself as it sees fit, to legislate concerning its interests, to administer its services, and to determine the jurisdiction and competence of its courts. The exercise of these rights is limited only by the exercise of the rights of other States in accordance with international law.

Article 13

Recognition implies that the State granting it accepts the personality of the new State, with all the rights and duties that international law prescribes for the two States.

Article 14

The right to each State to protect itself and to live its own life does not authorize it to commit unjust acts against another State.

Article 15

The jurisdiction of States within the limits of their national territory is exercised equally over all the inhabitants, whether nationals or aliens.

Article 16

Each State has the right to develop its cultural, political, and economic life freely and naturally. In this free development, the State shall respect the rights of the individual and the principles of universal morality.

Article 17

Respect for and the faithful observance of treaties constitute standards for the development of peaceful relations among States. International treaties and agreements should be public.

Article 18

No State or group of States has the right to intervene, directly or indirectly, for any reason whatever, in the internal or external affairs of any other State. The foregoing principle prohibits not only armed force but also any other form of interference or attempted threat against the personality of the State or against its political, economic, and cultural elements.

Article 19

No State may use or encourage the use of coercive measures of an economic or political character in order to force the sovereign will of another State and obtain from it advantages of any kind.

Article 20

The territory of a State is inviolable; it may not be the object, even temporarily, of military occupation or of other measures of force taken by another State, directly or indirectly, on any grounds whatever. No territorial acquisitions or special advantages obtained either by force or by other means of coercion shall be recognized.

Article 21

The American States bind themselves in their international relations not to have recourse to the use of force, except in the case of self-defense in accordance with existing treaties or in fulfillment thereof.

Article 22

Measures adopted for the maintenance of peace and security in accordance with existing treaties do not constitute a violation of the principles set forth in Articles 18 and 20.

OAS Charter, revised 1967, Chapter 4, articles 9-22. Also see the earlier inter-American Convention on the Rights and Duties of States, 1933, T.S. 881; 3 Bevans, *Treaties and Other International Agreements*, 145.

446 OAS--PACIFIC SETTLEMENT

Chapter V
Pacific Settlement of Disputes
Article 23

All international disputes that may arise between American States shall be submitted to the peaceful procedures set forth in this Charter, before being referred to the Security Council of the United Nations.

Article 24

The following are peaceful procedures: direct negotiation, good offices, mediation, investigation and conciliation, judicial settlement, arbitration, and those which the parties to the dispute may especially agree upon at any time.

Article 25

In the event that a dispute arises between two or more American States which, in the opinion of one of them, cannot be settled through the usual diplomatic channels, the Parties shall agree on some other peaceful procedure that will enable them to reach a solution.

Article 26

A special treaty will establish adequate procedures for the pacific settlement of disputes and will determine the appropriate means for their application, so that no dispute between American States shall fail of definitive settlement within a reasonable period.

OAS Charter, revised 1967, Chapter 5, articles 23-26.

447 MAJOR INTER-AMERICAN CONFERENCES AND MEETINGS TO 1967

Panama	First General Conference of American States	1826
Lima	Meeting of Latin American States for Unification and Alliance	1847-48
Washington	First International Conference of American States	1889-90
Mexico City	Second International Conference of American States	1901-02
Rio de Janeiro	Third International Conference of American States	1906
Buenos Aires	Fourth International Conference of American States	1910
Santiago	Fifth International Conference of American States	1923

Havana	Sixth International Conference of American States	1928
Washington	Inter-American Conference on Conciliation and Arbitration	1928-29
Montevideo	Seventh International Conference of American States	1933
Buenos Aires	Inter-American Conference for the Maintenance of Peace	1936
Lima	Eighth International Conference of American States	1938
Panama	First Inter-American Foreign Ministers Meeting	1939
Havana	Second Inter-American Foreign Ministers Meeting	1940
Rio de Janeiro	Third Inter-American Foreign Ministers Meeting	1942
Mexico City (Chapultepec Castle)	Inter-American Conference on Problems of War and Peace	1945
Rio de Janeiro	Inter-American Conference for Peace and Security (to Implement the Act of Chapultepec)	1947
Bogota	Ninth International Conference of American States	1948
Washington	Fourth Inter-American Foreign Ministers Meeting	1951
Caracas	Tenth Inter-American Conference	1954
Panama	Conference of American Presidents	1956
Santiago	Fifth Inter-American Foreign Ministers Meeting	1959
San Jose	Sixth and Seventh Inter-American Foreign Ministers Meetings	1960
Punta del Este	Eighth Inter-American Foreign Ministers Meeting	1962
Washington	Informal Inter-American Foreign Ministers Meeting	1962
Washington	Ninth Inter-American Foreign Ministers Meeting	1964
Washington	First Special Inter-American Conference	1964
Washington	Tenth Inter-American Foreign Ministers Meeting	1965
Rio de Janeiro	Second Special Inter-American Conference	1965
Buenos Aires	Third Special Inter-American Conference	1966
Buenos Aires	Eleventh Inter-American Foreign Ministers Meeting	1967
Punta del Este	Conference of American Presidents	1967

448 ORGANIZATION OF AMERICAN STATES--MEMBERSHIP

Original Members	Admitted Members
Argentina	Antigua and Barbuda
Bolivia	Bahamas
Brazil	Barbados
Chile	Dominica
Colombia	Grenada
Costa Rica	Jamaica
Cuba	St. Christopher and Nevis
Dominican Republic	St. Lucia
Ecuador	St. Vincent and Grenadines
El Salvador	Suriname
Guatemala	Trinidad and Tobago
Haiti	
Honduras	
Mexico	
Nicaragua	

Original Members
Panama
Paraguay
Peru
United States
Uruguay
Venezuela

4 4 9 EXCLUSION FROM PARTICIPATION IN INTER-AMERICAN SYSTEM--CUBA,
1962

I think that it is important for us, now that the time has come, for the Organization of American States, the governments of this hemisphere, to say formally and publicly and in unison what most of them have said privately. And that is that what has happened in Cuba is wholly incompatible with the basic commitments of this hemisphere, the basic charters of the inter-American system, and that what has happened in Cuba is incompatible with the safety and the dignity and the future of this hemisphere. And further, that the Castro solution to economic and social development is not the solution which is necessary or is possible in this hemisphere.

Dean Rusk, "What Has Happened in Cuba is Wholly Incompatible with Basic Commitments of This Hemisphere," comment on television program, January 22, 1962; *American Foreign Policy: Current Documents,* 1962, p 318.

*   *   *

. . . I suggest we must move in four major directions:

First, we must recognize that the alinement of the government of Cuba with the countries of the Sino-Soviet bloc, and its commitment to extend Communist power in this hemisphere, are incompatible with the purposes and principles of the inter-American system and that its current activities are an ever-present and common danger to the peace and security of the continent.

Second, we must now make the policy decision to exclude the Castro regime from participation in the organs and bodies of the inter-American system and to direct the Council of the Organization to determine how best to give rapid implementation to this decision. Within our own competence, since the Inter-American Defense Board was created by a meeting of consultation, we can and should now exclude the government of Cuba from membership in the Inter-American Defense Board. This step would correct at once the most obvious incongruity arising from the participation of a regime alined with the Sino-Soviet bloc in a body planning the defense of the hemisphere against the aggressive designs of international communism.

Third, we must interrupt the limited but significant flow of trade between Cuba and the rest of the hemisphere, especially the traffic in arms.

Fourth, we must set in motion a series of individual and communal acts of defense against the various forms of political and indirect aggression mounted against the hemisphere. . . .

Dean Rusk, United States proposal, statement at Eighth Meeting of Consultation of Ministers of Foreign Affairs, Punta del Este, January 25, 1962; *American Foreign Policy: Current Documents*, 1962, pp. 318-19.

*   *   *

The Eighth Meeting of Consultation of Ministers of Foreign Affairs, Serving as Organ of Consultation in Application of the Inter-American Treaty of Reciprocal Assistance,
Declares:
1. That, as a consequence of repeated acts, the present Government of Cuba has voluntarily placed itself outside the inter-American system.
2. That this situation demands unceasing vigilance on the part of the member states of the Organization of American States, which shall report to the Council any fact or situation that could endanger the peace and security of the hemisphere.
3. That the American states have a collective interest in strenthening the inter-American system and reuniting it on the basis of respect for human rights and the principles and objectives relative to the exercise of democracy set forth in the Charter of the Organization; and, therefore
Resolves:
1. That adherence by any member of the Organization of American States to Marxism-Leninism is incompatible with the inter-American system and the alignment of such a government with the communist bloc breaks the unity and solidarity of the hemisphere.
2. That the present Government of Cuba, which has officially identified itself as a Marxist-Leninist government, is incompatible with the principles and objectives of the inter-American system.
3. That this incompatibility excludes the present Government of Cuba from participation in the inter-American system.
4. That the Council of the Organization of American States and the other organs and organizations of the inter-American system adopt without delay the measures necessary to comply with this resolution.
Whereas:

The Inter-American Defense Board was established pursuant to Resolution 39 of the Third Meeting of Consultation of Foreign Ministers, held in Rio de Janeiro in 1942, recommending the immediate meeting of a commission composed of military and naval technicians appointed by each of the governments to study and to suggest to them measures necessary for the defense of the hemisphere;

The Inter-American Defense Board, on April 26, 1961, resolved that the participation of the Cuban regime in defense planning is highly prejudicial to the work of the Board and to the security of the hemisphere; and

The present Government of Cuba is identified with the aims and policies of the Sino-Soviet bloc.

The Eighth Meeting of Consultation of Ministers of Foreign Affairs, Serving as Organ of Consultation in Application of the Inter-American Treaty of Reciprocal Assistance
Resolves:

To exclude immediately the present Government of Cuba from the Inter-American Defense Board until the Council of the Organization of American States shall determine by a vote of two thirds of its members that membership of the Government of Cuba is not prejudicial to the work of the Board or to the security of the hemisphere.

"Exclusion of the Present Government of Cuba from Participation in the Inter-American System," January 31, 1961; *American Foreign Policy: Current Documents, 1962,* pp 326-28   Sanctions were also applied against Cuba, see Document 459.

GENERAL UNITED STATES POLICY

United States policy statements respecting the Western Hemisphere in general and the Organization of American States in particular are naturally interlinked. Some policy themes are generic, applied throughout the world but often with special significance in inter-American relations. These embrace the maintenance of peace and continental security, mutual and friendly cooperation, democracy and social justice, the role of the state as servant of the people, respect for life and the dignity and well-being of both nations and mankind, human rights and individual liberty, and trade and economic development.

Other themes focus specifically on the Western Hemisphere and the inter-American system. Major emphasis is given to unity and interdependence, mutual defense (also see Chapter 18), hemispheric partnership and common purpose, and pacific settlement of multipartite and bipartite disputes under a network of prearranged commitments. Somewhat unique, often at the insistence of Latin American governments, are guarantees of the sovereign equality of nations, nonintervention, noninterference, mutual respect, and the rule of law. The documents that follow merely illustrate these objectives and policies.

450 PRE-CHARTER INTER-AMERICAN SYSTEM--BASIC PRINCIPLES

Here in the Western Hemisphere we have already achieved in substantial measure what the world as a whole must achieve. Through what we call our Inter-American System, which has become steadily stronger for half a century, we have learned to work together to solve our problems by friendly cooperation and mutual respect.

We have a good-neighbor policy in common and, as a result of this sincere application of that policy, we form a good neighborhood. Our example has a salutary effect upon the whole world. The success of our cherished Inter-American System is a source of inspiration for the developing system of the United Nations, of which we are all members.

We are united by more than the common procedures and agencies of inter-American cooperation. All our peoples have a common belief which we call democracy. Democracy has a spiritual foundation because it is based upon the brotherhood of man. We believe in the dignity of the individual. We believe that the function of the state is to preserve and promote human rights and fundamental freedoms. We believe that the state exists for the benefit of man, not man for the benefit of the state. Everything else that we mean by the word democracy arises from this fundamental conviction. We believe that each individual must have as much liberty for the conduct of his life as is compatible with the rights of others. . . .

. . . Freedom and dignity of the individual can be attained only under a system of law which protects the rights of individuals, and through a government made up of freely elected representatives of the people. When we have this, we have a democratic government--one that is suited to the democratic way of life.

This is a simple, fundamental truth.

The good-neighbor policy, which guides the course of our inter-American relations, is equally simple. It is the application of democracy to international affairs. It is the application of the Golden Rule.

Harry Truman, address, Mexico City, March 3, 1947; *Papers of Presidents: Truman,* 1947, p. 165.

451   DREAM OF INTER-AMERICAN UNITY

The Organization of American States represents a great dream of those who believe that the people of this hemisphere must be bound more closely together. It seems to me it is our function and our responsibility, in our day, to make this organization alive, to make it fulfill its function, to make it meet its responsibilities, and not divert ourselves always with developing new institutions, when we have one which was nurtured in time, which has served well in the past and which can, if we give it our lasting support, serve us well in the future. . . .

Seventy-one years ago the new American nations were exploring new frontiers of international organization when they formed the International Union of the American Republics for regular consultation to solve common problems.

Today, as the Organization of American States, we constitute the oldest organization of nations now in existence.

John Kennedy, remarks, OAS Council, April 14, 1961; *Papers of Presidents: Kennedy,* 1961, pp. 276-77.

452 FOUNDATION OF INTER-AMERICAN SPIRITUAL CONVICTIONS

We here commemorate the most successfully sustained adventure in international community living that the world has seen. In spite of inescapable human errors in our long record, the Organization of American States is a model in the practice of brotherhood among nations. Our cooperation has been fruitful because all of our peoples hold certain spiritual convictions. We believe:

That all men are created equal;

That all men are endowed by their Creator with certain inalienable rights, including the right to life, liberty and the pursuit of happiness;

That government is the creation of man, to serve him; not to enslave him;

That those who demonstrate the capacity for self-government thereby win the right to self-government;

That sovereign states shall be free from foreign interference in the orderly development of their internal affairs.

Now, inspired by our faith in these convictions, our nations have developed in this hemisphere institutional relations and a rule of international law to protect the practice of that faith.

Our association began as we experienced the solemn but glorious transition from colonialism to national independence. Our association was intensified as we sought to maintain that independence against recurrent efforts of colonial powers to reassert their rule. More recently it has been perfected to protect against encroachments from the latter day depotisms abroad.

We are pledged to one another by the Inter-American Treaty of Reciprocal Assistance of 1947 to treat an armed attack by any State against an American State as an attack against all of us. We are joined in the 1954 Declaration of Solidarity for the Preservation of the Political Integrity of the American States against International Communist Intervention.

Furthermore, we are organized to assure peace among ourselves. The time is past, we earnestly believe, when any of our members would use force to resolve hemispheric disputes. Our solemn promises to each other foresee that the community will take whatever measures may be needed to preserve peace within America.

In all of these matters, our nations act as sovereign equals. Never will peace and security be sought at the price of subjecting any nation to coercion or interference in its internal affairs.

Thus, much has been done to assure the kind of national life which was the lofty vision of those early patriots who, in each of our countries, founded our Republics and foresaw the values inherent in hemispheric cooperation.

Dwight Eisenhower, address at signing of Declaration of Principles at Meeting of Presidents, Panama City, July 22, 1956; *Papers of Presidents: Eisenhower,* 1956, pp. 609-10.

4 5 3   FUNDAMENTAL INTER-AMERICAN GOALS

We've celebrated Pan American Day each year since 1931 to draw worldwide attention to the ideals of the Western Hemisphere. And let me say, after 52 years, these ideals are still worth celebrating and remembering.

This year, in addition, we celebrate the 200th anniversary of the birth of the great South American liberator Simon Bolivar. It was Bolivar's ideal of hemispheric cooperation that inspired the creation of the inter-American system. In a letter in 1824, Bolivar expressed his vision this way: "After 15 years of sacrifices devoted to the liberty of America and to obtain the system of guarantees that in peace and in war might be the shield of our new destiny, it is time now that the interests and the relations which unite the American republics have a fundamental base." Well, in the last half century, while other areas of the world have been convulsed in open strife, war between the countries of our hemisphere here have been uncommon.

The activities of the Organization of American States, moreover, reach beyond conflict resolution. They advance many fundamental goals of the nations of the Americas--justice under law, protection of human rights, and economic and social development. Democracy remains the basic bond of our nations. It is our people's permanent aspiration and, for most of them, their way of life. Two-thirds of the members of this organization govern themselves democratically. As you would agree, it is democracy that gives our people their dignity and hope for the future.

Ronald Reagan, remarks to OAS Ambassadors on Pan American Day, April 14, 1983; *Papers of Presidents: Reagan,* 1983, I, 538.

4 5 4   CONVERTING INTER-AMERICAN PURPOSES INTO REALITIES--THREEFOLD THRUST

. . . For nearly three decades the OAS has stood for mutual respect among sovereign nations, for peace, and the rule of law in this hemisphere. The OAS Charter pledges us to individual liberty and social justice. I come here now to restate our own commitment to these goals.

The challenge before us today, however, is not just to reaffirm those principles but to find ways to make them a reality. To do this, we must take account of the changes in our relationships . . . and we must candidly acknowledge the differences that exist among us. We must adapt our current policies and institutions to those changes so that we can pursue our goals more effectively. . . .

. . . a single United States policy toward Latin America and the Caribbean makes little sense. What we need is a wider and a more flexible approach, worked out in close consultation with you. Together, we will develop policies more suited to each nation's variety and potential. In this process, I will be particularly concerned that we not seek to divide the nations of Latin America one from another or to set Latin America apart from the rest of the world. Our own goal is to address problems in a way which will lead to productive solutions--globally, regionally, and bilaterally.

Our new approach will be based on three basic elements:

First of all is a high regard for the individuality and the sovereignty of each Latin American and Caribbean nation. We will not act abroad in ways that we would not tolerate at home in our own country.

Second is our respect for human rights, a respect which is also so much a part of your own tradition. Our values and yours require us to combat abuses of individual freedom, including those caused by political, social, and economic injustice. Our own concern for these values will naturally influence our relations with the countries of this hemisphere and throughout the world. You will find this country, the United States of America, eager to stand beside those nations which respect human rights and which promote democratic ideals.

Third is our desire to press forward on the great issues which affect the relations between the developed and the developing nations. Your economic problems are also global in character and cannot be dealt with solely on regional terms.

Jimmy Carter, address, OAS Permanent Council, April 14, 1977; *Papers of Presidents: Carter*, 1977, pp. 611-12.

455   INTER-AMERICAN SYSTEM AS TRAILBLAZER

Our inter-American system has always been a trail blazer in the quest for a better world. We have pioneered procedures for the peaceful settlement of disputes. There has been no armed conflict between the members of our community now for more than 30 years.

We have championed the principle of self-determination of peoples. We have acted to preserve it--collectively--when it was threatened in our hemisphere.

We have developed the modern concept of collective security. We are pursuing the goal of representative democracy. . . .

We are demonstrating that through the Alliance for Progress, by all of us working together, nations in a region can build economic democracy and Latin America recently gave the world a model for preventing the spread of nuclear weapons.

All of this could not have been achieved without the dedication of wise men--men who saw that in laboring for cooperation between all the nations of America, they would serve the interests of each nation and its people.

Lyndon Johnson, remarks, luncheon for retiring OAS officials, May 10, 1968; *Papers of Presidents: Johnson*, 1968-1969, p. 592.

456   ACHIEVEMENTS AND EXPECTATIONS

Today, this General Assembly is carrying on the tradition of adaptability to change, as we see it, in considering recommendations for reform.   Just as the inter-American system was the pathfinder in the field of international organizations, it could likewise become a pioneer in reforming the traditional way in which international organizations do business. The basic concept which holds this Organization together is that strength and progress come from cooperation rather than from conflict.

In this country, we are extremely proud of our achievements under a democratic form of government and a productive economic system. We recognize that every State has the right to adopt its own system of government and its own economic and social organization. Fortunately, we live in a hemisphere with a rich tradition of diversity.

One of our continuing tasks is to resolve issues that from time to time divide us. . . .

The world we now live in is increasingly fluid and complex, containing many new centers of power. There are new and more subtle challenges to the well-being of mankind. And the new issues reflect the major concerns of our people--economic development, growth of trade, sufficient food production, a healthy environment, and managing the growth of population. . . .

The nations of this hemisphere have individually and jointly made great progress in their efforts to promote the well-being of their peoples. Our cooperation for development requires constant redefinition and imaginative new solutions to the common problems that we face. The United States is proud of its continuing contribution to this joint effort. There is no reason we cannot conquer the last vestiges of poverty in a hemisphere which is so richly endowed.

The tradition of mutual cooperation, which is at the heart of our inter-American system, adds another dimension to the requirements of global interdependence. We must be particularly conscious of the need to avoid unnecessary damage to each other's interests. . . .

International cooperation that assures mutual respect among nations is more essential than ever, and the opportunities, particularly in this hemisphere, are without precedent.

Gerald Ford, remarks, reception for chiefs of delegation to OAS General Assembly, May 10, 1975; *Papers of Presidents: Ford,* 1975, pp. 661-62.

457   STRENGTHENING THE INTER-AMERICAN SYSTEM

Beyond our purely bilateral relations, there are important institutions and forums in which several or all of the states of the Americas are associated. And for some of these institutions, a moment of truth has arrived.

In 1822, the United States established diplomatic relations with Colombia. . . . Over the ensuing 150 years, formal and informal bonds linking the nations of the Western Hemisphere have expanded and grown strong. Gradually, machinery was developed to provide for increasing cooperation and consultation in this family of nations. It makes up what is called the inter-American system. It has been said that if this machinery had not existed, we would have been forced to invent it. But it does exist-- in the Rio Treaty; in the Inter-American Development Bank; in the Organization of American States and its associated bodies, including the Economic and Social Council, the Council for Science, Education and Culture; and in the many other groups and organizations through which we work together.

The question now facing us is not whether these organizations have served useful purposes in the past, but whether they are organized to best serve the current interests of the Americas. . . .

There has been an unfortunate tendency among some governments, in some organizations, to make forums for cooperation into arenas of confrontation. . . . There has also been a tendency to develop Latin American positions--often on a lowest-common-denominator basis--which fail to take realistic account of viewpoints strongly held by the United States. These efforts tend to provoke reactions contrary to those sought. We must recognize the dangers inherent in such an approach.

We should not deal with important questions in an emotional mood or react out of pique or frustration. The kind of mature partnership we all seek calls for calm reflection and a reasonable exchange of views. In my message to the recent OAS General Assembly, I noted: "That kind of partnership implies that there are common goals to which we aspire. It implies a trust and confidence in one another. It implies that we can attain our goals more effectively by pursuing them more cooperatively. Above all, it implies that we consider interdependence an essential ingredient in the life of our hemisphere."

Richard Nixon, *U.S. Foreign Policy for the 1970's: Shaping a Durable Peace* (1973), pp. 119-20.

ORGANIZATION OF AMERICAN STATES IN ACTION

Like the United Nations and other regional international systems, the Organization of American States operates under specified purposes and principles (Document 444). It performs such functions and services as providing forums for deliberation, debate, negotiation, and agreement; coordinating policy; initiating and administering programs; creating law and other commitments; settling disputes; and applying censure and sanctions.

Commentary and documentation consists of two types. The first, illustrated in this and other chapters, consists of inter-American declarations, resolutions, acts, and treaties and agreements. *Declarations* are general statements of mutual purpose and policy which establish intent but lack the binding effect of treaties. The inter-American system produces scores of declarations, many of which lay down principles respecting the equality of states, collective defense, self-determination, nonintervention, noninterference, representative democracy, the rule of law, peaceful settlement, respect for human rights, economic development, and the well-being of people. For examples, see Documents 282, 458, 558. Hundreds of *resolutions*--in the nature of decisions-- have been passed by inter-American conferences and meetings of the agencies of the Organization of American States. Illustrations are provided in Documents 268, 303, 449, 459.

Acts are inter-American conference stipulations of commitment short of formal treaties. These are exemplified by the Act of Havana (1940), which arranged for the administration of European colonies and other possessions in the Americas during World War II; the Act of Chapultepec (1945), which presaged the creation of the Organization of American States and the conclusion of a formal collective defense treaty (see Rio Pact, Document 304); the Act of Punta del Este (1961), which established a three-pronged approach to economic problems, consisting of aid, trade, and social reform; the Act of Washington (1964), which dealt with the admission of new members into the OAS; and the Act of Rio de Janeiro (1965), which laid the basis for the revision of the Charter in 1967.

In addition, the inter-American system generated a substantial number of more formal *treaties and agreements* during the past century. As of the 1980's the United States was a party to more than fifty such multilateral arrangements, ranging from the Rio Pact and the OAS Charter to a broad spectrum of both general and technical subjects. The latter include agriculture, status of aliens, automobile traffic, claims, consular affairs, copyright, customs, extradition, fisheries, patents, trademarks, postal affairs, radio communications, terrorism, and many other subjects. Some of these treaties and agreements antedate both the creation of the OAS and global arrangements on the same or similar subjects.

Of special note are packages that focus on alliance and hemispheric security (see Chapter 18, Documents 303-304), the settlement of disputes, and human rights. Illustrating emphasis on peaceful settlement are separate treaties concerned with the prevention of inter-American conflicts (1923), the establishment of commissions of inquiry (1923), arbitration and conciliation arrangements (1929), nonaggression and conciliation (1933), good offices and mediation (1936), and the prevention of controversies (1936).

These have been supplemented by more than a thousand bilateral treaties and agreements between the United States and individual members of the inter-American system, dozens of which deal with defense and peaceful settlement, but also with a large spectrum of other, often technical matters. For a complete list, with sources, of these multipartite and bipartite treaties and agreements, see *Treaties in Force.*

The second type of materials, illustrated in this section, embrace selected documents pertaining to specific functional matters, including the threat of Communist expansion in the Western Hemisphere (Document 458), the application of sanctions (Document 459), and the promotion of democracy and human rights (Documents 460-463). Other important examples of inter-American cooperative action relate to alliance and security (see Chapter 18), pacific settlement and crisis resolution (see Chapters 11 and 12), and creation of a unified position in time of major war. Thus, when the United States entered World War I, two-thirds of the American republics broke off diplomatic relations with the Central Powers, and more than half of these declared war; during World War II, at Rio de Janeiro in January 1942, the Foreign Ministers Meeting passed a resolution to sever diplomatic relations with the Axis powers; and at the time of the Korean War, in the Declaration of Washington (1951) the Organization of American States supported the United Nations action in the Far East (see *American Foreign Policy: Basic Documents,* 1950-1955, I, 1292-1300).

458 DECLARATION OF SOLIDARITY AGAINST INTERNATIONAL COMMUNIST INTERVENTION, 1954

Whereas:

The American republics at the Ninth International Conference of American States declared that international communism, by its antidemocratic nature and its interventionist tendency, is incompatible with the concept of American freedom, and resolved to adopt within their respective territories the measures necessary to eradicate and prevent subversive activities. . . .

The Tenth Inter-American Conference

I

Condemns:

The activities of the international communist movement as constituting intervention in American affairs;

Expresses:

The determination of the American States to take the necessary measures to protect their political independence against the intervention of international communism, acting in the interests of an alien despotism. . . .

Declares:

That the domination or control of the political institutions of any American State by the international communist movement, extending to this Hemisphere the political system of an extracontinental power, would constitute a threat to the sovereignty and political independence of the American States, endangering the peace of America, and would call for a Meeting of Consultation to consider the adoption of appropriate action in accordance with existing treaties.

II

Recommends:

That, without prejudice to such other measures as they may consider desirable, special attention be given by each of the American governments to the following steps for the purpose of counteracting the subversive activities of the international communist movement within their respective jurisdictions:

1. Measures to require disclosure of the identity, activities, and sources of funds of those who are spreading propaganda of the international communist movement or who travel in the interests of that movement, and of those who act as its agents or in its behalf; and

2. The exchange of information among governments to assist in fulfilling the purpose of the resolutions adopted by the Inter-American Conferences and Meetings of Ministers of Foreign Affairs regarding international communism.

III

This declaration of foreign policy made by the American republics in relation to dangers originating outside this Hemisphere is designed to protect and not to impair the inalienable right of each American State freely to choose its own form of government and economic system and to live its own social and cultural life.

Tenth Inter-American Conference, March 28, 1954; *American Foreign Policy: Basic Documents*, 1950-1955, I, 1300-2. Also see United States Senate resolution affirming support of the Declaration of Solidarity, June 29, 1954, in *American Foreign Policy: Basic Documents*, 1950-1955, I, p. 1302.

459   SANCTIONS AGAINST CUBA, 1964

The Ninth Meeting of Consultation of Ministers of Foreign Affairs, Serving as Organ of Consultation in Application of the Inter-American Treaty of Reciprocal Assistance,

Having seen the report on the Investigating Committee designated on December 3, 1963, by the Council of the Organization of American States, acting provisionally as Organ of Consultation, and

Considering:

That the said report established among its conclusions that "the Republic of Venezuela has been the target of a series of actions sponsored and directed by the Government of Cuba, openly intended to subvert Venezuelan institutions and to overthrow the democratic Government of Venezuela through terrorism, sabotage, assault, and guerrilla warfare," and

That the aforementioned acts, like all acts of intervention and aggression, conflict with the principles and aims of the inter-American system,

Resolves:

1. To declare that the acts verified by the Investigating Committee constitute an aggression and an intervention on the part of the Government of Cuba in the internal affairs of Venezuela, which

affects all of the member states.

2. To condemn emphatically the present Government of Cuba for its acts of aggression and of intervention against the territorial inviolability, the sovereignty, and the political independence of Venezuela.

3. To apply, in accordance with the provisions of Articles 6 and 8 of the Inter-American Treaty of Reciprocal Assistance, the following measures:

   a. That the governments of the American states not maintain diplomatic or consular relations with the Government of Cuba;

   b. That the governments of the American States suspend all their trade, whether direct or indirect, with Cuba, except in foodstuffs, medicines, and medical equipment that may be sent to Cuba for humanitarian reasons; and

   c. That the governments of the American states suspend all sea transportation between their countries and Cuba, except for such transportation as may be necesary for reasons of a humanitarian nature.

4. To authorize the Council of the Organization of American States, by an affirmative vote of two thirds of its members, to discontinue the measures adopted in the present resolution at such time as the Government of Cuba shall have ceased to constitute a danger to the peace and security of the hemisphere.

5. To warn the Government of Cuba that if it should persist in carrying out acts that possess characteristics of aggression and intervention against one or more of the member states of the Organization, the member states shall preserve their essential right as sovereign states by the use of self-defense in either individual or collective form, which could go so far as resort to armed force, until such time as the Organ of Consultation takes measures to guarantee the peace and security of the hemisphere.

6. To urge those states not members of the Organization of American States that are animated by the same ideals as the inter-American system to examine the possibility of effectively demonstrating their solidarity in achieving the purposes of this resolution. . . .

Final Act, Ninth Meeting of Consultation of Ministers of Foreign Affairs, July 26, 1964; *American Foreign Policy: Current Documents,* 1964, pp. 328-29. Also see address of Dean Rusk, Washington, February 25, 1964, in *American Foreign Policy: Current Documents,* 1964, p. 319, and Lyndon Johnson, remarks, news conference, July 30, 1964, in *Papers of Presidents: Johnson,* 1903-1904, II, 909.

For commentary of Gerald Ford, at press conference, August 28, 1974, concerning a change in United States policy respecting sanctions, see *Digest of United States Practice in International Law,* 1974, p. 601. At its meeting in San Jose, July 29, 1975, the Organ of Consultation terminated the OAS requirement of diplomatic and economic sanctions against Cuba, and allowed American governments to take individual action to terminate or continue the sanctions; see *Digest of United States Practice in International Law,* 1975, pp.

25-26, 691-93. For the suspension of United States diplomatic and consular relations with Cuba in 1961, see Document 47.

For the application of diplomatic and economic sanctions against Costa Rica, August 21, 1960, by the Organ of Consultation, for the attempted asassination of the Venezuelan President, see *American Foreign Policy: Current Documents,* 1960, pp. 260-62.

4 6 0   AMERICAN HUMAN RIGHTS CONVENTION, 1969

In 1969, when this agreement was reached in this hemisphere, the other nations came forward to commit themselves to a legally binding document which would express the aspirations that have existed among all our countries since the first governments were formed in North and South America. . . .

In 1948, another agreement was reached in our hemisphere to pursue this noble endeavor of democratic and free governments. In 1969, this covenant was signed by the other nations.

This blank place on the page has been here for a long time, and it's with a great deal of pleasure that I sign on behalf of the United States this Convention on Human Rights which will spell out in clear terms our own belief in the proper relationship between free human beings and governments chosen by them.

I believe that no one nation can shape the attitudes of the world, and that's why it's so important for us to join in with our friends and neighbors in the south to pursue as a unified group this noble commitment and endeavor.

*   *   *

Paragraph 1 of article I obliges states party to the Convention "to ensure to all persons subject to their jurisdiction the free and full exercise of those rights and freedoms [recognized in the Convention], without any discrimination for reasons of race, color, sex, language, religion, political or other opinion, national or social origin, economic status, birth, or any other social condition." Among the recognized rights are the right to life, humane treatment, personal liberty, fair trial, compensation, privacy, assembly, property, and freedom of conscience, religion, thought, and expression. To protect these rights, the Convention establishes an Inter-American Commission on Human Rights and an Inter-American Court of Human Rights.

*   *   *

. . . In essence, the [American and United Nations] treaties create an international commitment to the same basic human rights that are already guaranteed to citizens of the United States by our own laws and Constitution. U.S. ratification would not endanger any rights that we currently enjoy. On the contrary, ratification would encourage the extension of rights already enjoyed by our citizens to the citizens of other nations--

and it would allow the United States to participate in this process.

The fundamental rights enjoyed in this country are a product not only of our Founding Fathers' drafting but also of two centuries of practice and interpretation. Similarly, the rights enunciated in these treaties will be molded by the actions of the States party to them in future years. Unless the United States is a party to the treaties, we will be unable to contribute fully to this evolving international law of human rights.

Moreover, ratification of the treaties will remove a troubling complication from our diplomacy. Governments with whom we raise human rights concerns will no longer be able to blunt the force of our approaches or question the seriousness of our commitment by pointing to our failure to ratify. I have personally observed that quiet person-to-person diplomacy provides the primary, and in many instances, the best means to obtain improvements in human rights. But I have also observed personally that our effectiveness can be compromised by our own failure to ratify these treaties.

Ratification also gives the United States an additional international forum in which to pursue the advancement of human rights, and to challenge other states to meet the high standards set by this nation. We should not deny ourselves this opportunity to help shape the developing international standards for human rights, and to encourage the extension to others of the rights we have long enjoyed.

While the treaties are not subject to legally binding sanctions, they do increase the political costs attached to violations of human rights. The committees established to review compliance with the treaties provide a mechanism through which human rights practices throughout the world can be evaluated, compared and publicized. These committees will develop a sort of human rights case law--a body of precedent that can give shape and substance to the basic standards enunciated in the treaties.

It is toward this goal--the operation of the rule of law in the international human rights field--that we should strive. Ratification of these four treaties would be an important step to that end.

*   *   *

The Legal Adviser then addressed some of the criticisms that had been voiced against the treaties. He characterized as a concern common to all, the objection "that these treaties could be used to distort the constitutional legislative standards that shape our Federal and our State governments' treatment of [the] individual within the United States." He saw the specific criticisms as falling into three categories: (1) "that the human rights treaties could serve to change our laws as they are, allowing individuals in courts of law to invoke the treaty terms where inconsistent with domestic law or even with the Constitution"; (2) "that the treaties could be used to alter the jurisdictional balance between our Federal and State institutions"; and (3) "that the relationship between a government and its citizens is not a proper subject for the treatymaking process at all, but ought to be left entirely to domestic legislative processes."

This document consists of four segments: (1) President Carter's remarks on signing the American Human Rights Convention on June 1, 1977, *Papers of Presidents: Carter,* 1977, I, 1050; (2) a brief descriptive statement on the content of the Convention, *Digest of United States Practice in International Law,* 1978, p. 182; (3) Deputy Secretary of State, statement, Senate Foreign Relations Committee supporting Senate approval of this Convention as well as three United Nations human rights conventions, *Digest of United States Practice in International Law,* 1979, pp. 482-83; and (4) statement of the Legal Adviser of the Department of State to the Senate Foreign Relations Committee, specifying criticisms of these four conventions, *Digest of United States Practice in International Law,* 1979, p. 486.

President Carter submitted the American and the three United Nations conventions--the International Convention on the Elimination of All Forms of Racial Discrimination (signed September 28, 1966), the International Covenant on Civil and Political Rights (signed October 5, 1977), and the International Covenant on Economic, Social, and Cultural Rights (also signed October 5, 1977)--to the Senate for approval, February 23, 1978; see his Message to the Senate in *Papers of Presidents: Carter,* 1978, I, 395-96.

The American Convention on Human Rights was adopted at a special conference of the Organization of American States, in San Jose, Costa Rica, January 22, 1969, when it was signed by twelve Latin American states. It requires eleven ratifications to put it into effect; fourteen Latin American governments signed and ratified it by mid-1978. As noted, President Carter signed it for the United States in 1977. For its text, see 65 *American Journal of International Law* (July 1971): 679-702. It consists of 82 articles and provides for state obligations, civil and political rights, economic and social rights, and implementing machinery, including a Court of Human Rights. For additional commentary, see *Digest of United States Practice in International Law,* 1977, pp. 166-175; 1978, pp. 440-64; 1979, pp. 481-500; and 1980, pp. 243-52.

461 HUMAN RIGHTS--COMPELLING ISSUE OF OUR TIME

One of the most compelling issues of our time, and one which calls for the concerted action of all responsible peoples and nations, is the necessity to protect and extend the fundamental rights of humanity.

The precious common heritage of our Western Hemisphere is the conviction that human beings are the subjects, not the objects, of public policy; that citizens must not become mere instruments of the state. . . .

The central problem of government has always been to strike a just and effective balance between freedom and authority. When freedom degenerates into anarchy, the human personality becomes subject to arbitrary, brutal, and capricious forces. When the demand for order overrides all other considerations, man becomes a means and not an end, a tool of impersonal machinery. Clearly, some forms of human suffering are intolerable no matter what pressures nations may face or feel. Beyond that, all societies have an obligation to enable their people to fulfill their potentialities and live a life of dignity and self-respect.

. . . Human rights are the very essence of a meaningful life, and human dignity is the ultimate purpose of government. No government can ignore terrorism and survive, but it is equally true that a government that tramples on the rights of its citizens denies the purpose of its existence.

Henry Kissinger, address, OAS General Assembly, June 8, 1976, in *Digest of United States Practice in International Law*, 1976, p. 138.

4 6 2   REVULSION AGAINST HUMAN RIGHTS VIOLATIONS

. . . I have every reason to believe, based on the very favorable results of the VII General Assembly of the OAS and the other developments I have referred to since then, that human rights in this hemisphere is of growing concern to a broad range of states, leaders and peoples and that, far from standing alone, the United States is a member of a distinguished fraternity in the Americas. Defense of citizens against torture, illegal detention, summary execution or disappearance by official connivance are abominations to the most deeply held values of all the American peoples. These crimes against human rights are the target of a growing wave of revulsion that is spreading throughout the Western Hemisphere. It is not and must not be seen to be an exclusive concern of the Government of the United States.

Gale McGhee, U.S. Representative to the OAS, to subcommittee of House Committee on International Relations, September 15, 1977, in *Digest of United States Practice in International Law*, 1977, p. 185.

4 6 3   HUMAN RIGHTS AND DEMOCRATIZATION

Today no government in this hemisphere can expect silent assent from its neighbors if it tramples the rights of its own citizens. The costs of repression have increased, but so have the benefits of respecting human rights. I pray that this progress will continue, although I know from experience that progress is not always easy as we defend human rights. . . .

The cause of human rights will be all the stronger if it remains at the service of humanity, rather than at the service of ideological or partisan ends, and if it condemns both terrorism and repression. In the phrase "human rights," the "rights" are important; the "human" is very important.

As a citizen of the Americas, I'm deeply encouraged by the trend toward greater democratization. . . .

The future of our hemisphere is not to be found in authoritarianism that wears the mask of common consent, nor totalitarianism that wears the mask of justice. Instead, let us find our future in the human face of democracy, the human voice of individual liberty, and the human hand of economic development. If we build on the best of what we have begun, we can see a better time at the end of this decade.

Jimmy Carter, remarks, tenth regular session of OAS General Assembly, November 19, 1980; *American Foreign Policy: Basic Documents,* 1977-1980, p. 316.

PART VIII

REGIONAL POLICIES
AND ISSUES

27

Africa

We   share three basic commitments to the future of Africa.

We share with you a commitment to majority rule and individual human rights. In order to meet the basic needs of the people, we share with you a commitment to economic growth and to human development. We share with you a commitment to an Africa that is at peace, free from colonialism, free from racism, free from military interference by outside nations, and free from the inevitable conflicts that can come when the integrity of national boundaries are not respected.

Jimmy Carter
Address, Lagos, Nigeria, April 1, 1978

Africa, most of which was absorbed into the imperial systems of European powers, achieved independence since 1950. Only ancient Egypt and Ethiopia, and modern Liberia and South Africa, were regarded as sovereign states by the time of World War II. The United States was instrumental in assisting Liberia to establish independence as the first black African nation in 1847.

During the 1950's Libya, Morocco, Sudan, and Tunisia (in North Africa) and Ghana and Guinea (in sub-Saharan Africa) became independent countries. Since 1960 some forty additional African states joined the family of nations, so that, with fifty sovereign nations, Africa currently possesses the most numerous continental contingent--approximately one-third--in the international community and the United Nations.

This transition to independent nationhood created a need, and provided an opportunity, for major shifts in the conduct of American foreign relations. While continuing to promulgate and espouse some of its basic foreign affairs goals and ideals, in certain respects policy had to be tailored to the realities of African internal and external developments. Among the more general policy concerns are such matters as the maintenance of peace and stability (national, regional, and global); colonialism, decolonization, and neocolonialism; self-determination, orderly political development, democratization, and the creation of diplomatic missions; economic progress, modernization, and industrialization; human rights and social relations; regional and continental cooperation and integration; and foreign economic, humanitarian, and defense assistance--bilateral and multilateral.   Other major factors, relating to national security, involve issues of African neutralism and noninvolvement in East-West great power relations; foreign intervention (both by neighboring African and by extracontinental powers); and internal political crises and revolts, jurisdictional conflicts, and wars.   Concern with these and other policy issues is reflected in scores of American foreign policy considerations and documents.

Additional, more specific, areas of importance to United States relations with the countries of Africa, for example, range from population expansion, famine, and refugee problems to agricultural production, commodity agreements, economic development, foreign trade, and international financial credits; from health, education, and technical assistance (including the Peace Corps) to the development of commercial aviation and telecommunication facilities; and from specific crises and wars (involving Algeria, Angola, Chad, Congo, Eritrea, Ethiopia, Namibia, Rhodesia, and others) to American support for intra-African unification and cooperation.   Although not a formal member, the United States has supported such African regional institutions as the Organization of African Unity (OAU) and the periodic African Heads of Government Conferences, which were launched in 1961 at Belgrade (for example, see *American Foreign Policy: Current Documents,* 1961, pp. 118-24, 652-55).   And the United States has joined such agencies as the African Development Fund (November 29, 1972--see TIAS 8605; 28 *U.S. Treaties* 4547-4606) and the African Development Bank (established in 1963--see 510 UNTS 3; and Ronald Reagan, letter, U.S. acceptance of membership, February 8, 1983, in *American Foreign Policy: Current Documents,* 1983, p. 1105).

Substantial evidence of concrete American relations with African countries is characterized by the extensive network of approximately 500 treaties and agreements signed with African nations since World War II. As of the 1980's nearly 275 of these were concerned with agricultural commodities, finance and investment guarantees, economic and technical cooperation, and defense.   Some additional 125 deal with cultural, educational, health, scientific, space exploration, and other assistance and cooperation; the Peace Corps; and postal and telecommunications affairs, as well as civil aviation, extradition, peace-keeping, taxation, visas, and other subjects. (For listing, see *Treaties in Force.*)

The documents selected for this chapter are grouped in the following categories: several background statements (Documents 464-466); basic American goals, objectives, and general policy themes, arranged chronologically (Documents 467-472); colonialism, decolonization, independence, and self-determination (Documents 473-476); neutralism and nonalignment of African nations in East-West bloc relations (Documents 477-478); Communism and Soviet and Cuban intervention in Africa (Documents 479-480); and the special problem of Southern Africa and the status of South Africa (Documents 481-482).

For related subjects, see Chapters 7 (Eisenhower Doctrine), 14 (the air strike on Libya), 16 (self-determination and colonialism, especially Documents 264-267 and 270), 17 (trade and commerce), 23 (segments on nonalignment, neutralism, and relations with the developing world, especially Documents 381-391), and 24 (foreign assistance). On colonialism, also see documentation of the United Nations Decolonization Committee and the annual report on *U.S. Participation in the United Nations,* and on President Reagan's criticism of actions of the nonalignment bloc in the United Nations, see Document 438.

BACKGROUND

464   HISTORIC UNITED STATES INTERESTS IN AFRICA

What are our interests in this awakening continent?

Historically our interest in Africa dates back to the early days of our independence. In 1786 Thomas Barclay of Pennsylvania negotiated a treaty of friendship, commerce, and navigation with Morocco. In 1822 President James Monroe dispatched the U.S. Navy schooner *Alligator* to escort free American Negro colonists to the shore of West Africa. They founded what was finally proclaimed in 1847 to be the free and independent Republic of Liberia. In the east, the American consul in Zanzibar arrived on that exotic island in 1833, actually preceding the first British consul. It was under the auspices of the old New York *Herald* that the journalist Henry Morton Stanley, proceeding from Zanzibar, undertook his historic journey into Tanganyika and Nyasaland in search of Dr. Livingstone. . . . the United States was the first to recognize and send a representative to the Free States of the Congo Association, which was formed out of part of the vast Congo basin later explored by Stanley as the result of his first African expedition.

Over the years American missionary activity on the African Continent has been extensive. Beginning in the early 19th century it has grown until today more than 6,500 American missionaries representing scores of home offices, boards, and orders in this country are at work throughout Africa.

United States trade with Africa, which began in the days of the New England clipper ship, has grown to total about $1.2 billion annually and our direct investments to total more than $600 million. Sub-Saharan Africa today provides the United States with many of its most important raw materials, such as uranium, cobalt, diamonds, columbite, gold, and manganese, minerals of strategic as well as commercial importance.

From the strategic point of view also, the continent of Africa, particularly North Africa, lying as it does along NATO's southern flank is important to the defense of Europe. . . . Furthermore, the closing of the Suez Canal in 1956 demonstrated the importance of friendly African ports along the Cape of Good Hope route as an alternative for oil shipments from the Persian Gulf to the free world and for uninterrupted contact with the Middle and Far East.

In addition to these historical and strategic interests of the United States in Africa, Americans have a keen and natural popular interest in this continent to which 10 percent of our population can trace its ancestry.

Assistant Secretary of State for African Affairs, address, Chatauqua Institute, New York, August 21, 1959; *American Foreign Policy: Current Documents,* 1959, pp. 1090-91.

465 DIVERSITIES IN AFRICA

The most pertinent point I can stress is that Africa's basic ethnic, cultural, economic, and political heritage is so diverse, its geography so vast, its contact with different European, Middle Eastern, and Asian cultures so varied that most generalizations about African nationalism are subject to serious reservations.

In addition, the broad divisions of the African continent must be recognized. Among these are: (1) the difference between the Arab-Berber Mediterranean coast and the territory south of the Sahara; (2) the differences among the colonial policies and administrations of Great Britain, France, Belgium, Portugal, and Spain; and (3) the differences between colonial territories with a large white-settler population and those with a small or transient white population.

Special Assistant to Secretary of State, address, American Assembly (Columbia University), Harriman, New York, May 1, 1958; *American Foreign Policy: Current Documents,* 1958, p. 1078.

466 AFRICA'S STATUS AND POLITICAL DEVELOPMENT

A few background observations about Africa's dimension in the world scene should be noted for perspective. Africa is more than three times the size of the U.S. A look at the map will show how this huge land mass relates to the security of other continents (and vice versa)--to Europe via the Mediterranean, to Asia via the Red Sea and Indian Ocean and to our Western Hemisphere via the Atlantic. Africa's sea and air space can be friendly or hostile. In the comparatively hospitable climate that now exists, the U.S. maintains transport facilities, spacetracking stations, communications, civil and military air rights, and enjoys generally favorable relations.

Africa is also a major source of minerals and other materials vital to U.S. and other Free World economies. The Free World obtains 25 percent of its copper supplies from Africa, 72 percent of its cobalt, 77 percent of gold, 98 percent of natural diamonds, 26 percent of manganese, among other basic materials. The continent also has great reserves of petroleum, water power, iron ore, bauxite and a host of other resources. . . .

Africa has over 300 million people, most of whom have gained independence only in the last decade. . . . The emergence in Africa of so many states--some small in population and size and often inheriting boundaries that are neither logical nor economic--has far reaching implications for African development. . . .

Most people in Africa live in traditional and tribal societies relatively untouched by modern life. The average per capita GNP in Africa is about $114--a poverty level. Africans aspire to improve their lot and to make the dignity of their new independence meaningful in terms of decent living standards and economic progress. This drive for progress is a major force. When progress is slow, instability is bound to result.

The 300 million Africans and their nations have an important relationship to U.S. interests and to those of the Free World generally. I have noted the strategic position of Africa, its resources and the U.S. investment there. Also of major significance is the relationship of African events to U.S. foreign policy objectives, particularly as they relate to our efforts to help build a peaceful and prosperous world system in which nations can feel secure in their independence and cooperate with one another for the greater good. . . .

Instability in Africa in the last few years has obviously had adverse effects on development. We are all familiar with its various manifestations, both present and potential:

1) Tribal and regional differences which threaten national cohesion.

2) Arbitrary boundaries inherited from colonial times [which] are at variance with ethnic and economic considerations.

3) A tendency in some countries towards arbitrary rule and coercive measures which muffle dissent and breed discontent.

4) Non-acceptance of government by consent of the governed and of human equality in some parts of the continent.

Assistant Secretary of State for African Affairs, statement, House Foreign Affairs Committee, April 20, 1967; *American Foreign Policy: Current Documents,* 1967, pp. 234-35. Also see Richard Nixon, *U.S. Foreign Policy for the 1970's: Building for Peace* (1971), pp. 84-85.

BASIC GOALS, OBJECTIVES, AND GENERAL POLICIES

4 6 7 AMERICAN PROGRAM FOR AFRICA

The drive of self-determination and of rising human aspirations is creating a new world of independent nations in Africa, even as it is producing a new world of both ferment and of promise in all developing areas. An awakening humanity in these regions demands as never before that we make a renewed attack on poverty, illiteracy, and disease. . . .

This is, indeed, a moment for honest appraisal and historic decision.

We can strive to master these problems for narrow national advantage, or we can begin at once to undertake a period of constructive action which will subordinate selfish interest to the general well-being of the international community. The choice is truly a momentous one. . . .

These then are the five ingredients of the program I propose for Africa:

Noninterference in the African countries' internal affairs;

Help in assuring their security without wasteful and dangerous competition in armaments;

Emergency aid to the Congo;

International assistance in shaping long-term African development programs;

United Nations aid for education.

Dwight Eisenhower, address, United Nations General Assembly, September 22, 1960; *American Foreign Policy: Current Documents*, 1960, pp. 60-64.

4 6 8   FIVE PILLARS OF POLICY TOWARD AFRICA

Of the five pillars of U.S. policy toward Africa, self-determination, . . . with the several corollaries that flow from it--such as our acceptance of the African desire for nonalignment--is the first and most important.

The second main pillar of that policy is encouragement of the solution of African problems by Africans themselves and support of their institutions through which solutions can be reached, such as the Organization of African Unity and the Economic Commission for Africa.

The third is support of improved standards of living through trade and aid.

The fourth is the discouragement of arms buildups beyond the needs of internal security or legitimate self-defense.

The fifth is encouragement of other countries of the world, particularly the former European metropoles, to recognize their continuing responsibilities toward Africa.

In this statement of our African policy fundamentals, I have not mentioned opposition to, or containment of, communism. However, there is no question that the support of freedom over communism is basic to and a product of, the aforementioned tenets that guide United States policy in Africa. From time to time special measures may be needed to meet crisis situations--and they will be taken vigorously when necessary--but conditions in Africa are such that the support of true African independence and development is, in the long run, the surest guarantee that Africa will remain in the world of free choice and keep communism at arm's length.

Assistant Secretary of State for African Affairs, address, Williams College, Williamstown, Massachusetts, March 18, 1965; *American Foreign Policy:*

Current Documents, 1965, p. 629.

4 6 9   AMERICAN POLICY POSITION AND THE NEEDS OF AFRICA

Beginning in 1957, the United States sought to respond to the desires and expectations of the newly emerging African nations. Much of Africa was new to the United States. Yet ethnic ties, the work of missionaries and teachers, economic investment, and emotion and interest in our own country provided foundations for a rapid expansion of relations.

The newness of Africa presented both problems and opportunities. The problem was that Africa's new requirements arose after the time of major U.S. commitments abroad.

On the other hand, Africa was a clean slate. We had few commitments which froze us into patterns of the past. Our strategic interests were minimal. Global political rivalries did not extend significantly to Africa. We could concentrate on supplementing the established flow of resources with an interest in establishing new relationships.

In the past two years, the Administration has sought to relate our policies directly to the developing needs and opportunities of Africa.

Specifically, we have tried:

--to maintain effective diplomatic and economic relations with all nations regardless of political differences;

--to lend moral and political support to the efforts to achieve racial justice and self-determination in southern Africa while emphasizing the need for peaceful change;

--to contribute, in cooperation with other donors, to the economic development of African countries; and

--to encourage trade and investment patterns consistent with the interests of producer and consumer.

United States Foreign Policy, 1969-1970: A Report of the Secretary of State, pp. 131-32.

4 7 0   ESSENTIALS OF AMERICAN POLICY FOR AFRICA

First, the most effective policies toward Africa are affirmative policies. They should not be reactive to what other powers do, nor to crises as they arise. Daily headlines should not set our agenda for progress.

A negative, reactive American policy that seeks only to oppose Soviet or Cuban involvement in Africa would be both dangerous and futile. Our best course is to help resolve the problems which create opportunities for external intervention.

Second, our objective must be to foster a prosperous and strong Africa that is at peace with itself and at peace with the world. The long-term success of our African policy will depend more on our actual assistance to African development and our ability to help Africans resolve their disputes than on maneuvers for short-term diplomatic advantage.

Third, our policies should recognize and encourage African nationalism. Having won independence, African nations will defend it against challenges from any source. If we try to impose American solutions for African problems, we may sow division among the Africans and undermine their ability to oppose efforts at domination by others. We will not do so.

Fourth, our policies must reflect our national values. Our deep belief in human rights--political, economic, and social--leads us to policies that support their promotion throughout Africa. This means concern for individuals whose rights are threatened--anywhere on the continent. And it means making our best effort peacefully to promote racial justice in southern Africa. In this we join the many African nations who, having won their freedom, are determined that all of Africa shall be free.

Fifth, our ties with Africa are not only political, but cultural and economic as well. It is the latter two that are most enduring.

And finally, we will seek openness in our dealings with African states. We are willing to discuss any issue, African or global; to broaden our dialogue with African nations; and to try to work with them, even when we may not agree. . . .

In the end, of course, our Africa policy will be judged by results, not intentions.

Cyrus Vance, address, Annual Convention of the National Association for the Advancement of Colored People, St. Louis, July 1, 1977; *American Foreign Policy: Basic Documents,* 1977-1980, pp. 1131-32.

4 7 1 AMERICAN GOALS AND STRATEGY FOR AFRICA IN GLOBAL PERSPECTIVE

Our first goal . . . is the building and preservation of peace in the world and thus the enhancement of American security. . . .

A second goal is the creation of a stronger world economic system which emphasizes equity as well as growth. Here, also, Africa is of increasing importance--not only because of its needs and because of its growing importance to the United States and other industrial nations as a source of raw materials, including oil, but also because African nations play a central role in the multilateral negotiations on such issues as commodities.

Closely related to economic issues are a number of other functional problems whose resolution will determine the quality of life for our children and their children; the environment, the future of the oceans, nuclear nonproliferation, energy, population growth, and the like. Each one of them affects Africa--and Africans affect them--to an increasing degree.

A fourth goal is the promotion of human rights everywhere. Southern Africa is now in the headlines, but our concern stretches to all countries. Here again our concerns and the future course of events in Africa are closely tied.

I will resist the temptation to go on at some length in this fashion. It is enough to say that on a wide variety of other American concerns--for example, limiting conventional arms sales--our global policies cut across and must be related to our policies toward Africa.

Our goals boil down to two general challenges: building peace and promoting global development.

There are six elements in our approach:

First, to engage in diplomatic activity to help resolve conflicts before outside involvement escalates. . . .

A second element in our strategy is that in our diplomatic efforts, we will strive for genuine self-determination, rather than seeking to impose made-in-America solutions. . . .

A third element in our approach to African regional conflicts is a recognition that we cannot rely on unilateral diplomacy. A unilateral American attempt to negotiate a solution to an African dispute can increase both Soviet and African suspicions that we are seeking to determine the outcome and that we are motivated primarily by concern for increasing our own influence. . . .

A fourth and major element in our strategy is closely related: support for African initiatives to mediate African disputes. . . .

Fifth, we recognize the role the United Nations can play in dealing with African problems. . . .

Finally, we seek to minimize American military involvement in African conflicts.

Director, Policy Planning Staff, Department of State, address, Johns Hopkins University School of Advanced International Studies, October 27, 1977; *American Foreign Policy: Basic Documents*, 1977-1980, pp. 1136-38.

4 7 2   IMPORTANCE OF AFRICA TO THE UNITED STATES

First, we have a significant geopolitical stake in the security of the continent and the seas surrounding it. Off its shores lie important trade routes, including those carrying most of the energy resources needed by our European allies. We are affected when Soviets, Cubans, and Libyans seek to expand their influence on the continent by force, to the detriment of both African independence and Western interests.

Second, Africa is part of the global economic system. If Africa's economies are in trouble, the reverberations are felt here. . . .

Third, Africa is important to us politically because the nations of Africa are now major players in world diplomacy. They comprise nearly one-third of the membership of the United Nations, where they form the most cohesive voting bloc in the General Assembly.

Finally, Africa is important to us, most of all, in human terms. Eleven percent of America's population traces its roots to Africa; all of us live in a society profoundly influenced by this human and cultural heritage. The revolution of Africa's independence coincided with the civil rights revolution in this country. Perhaps it was not a coincidence. Both were among the great moral events of this century; a rebirth of freedom, summoning all of us to a recognition of our common humanity.

George Shultz, address, Boston World Affairs Council, February 15, 1984; *American Foreign Policy: Current Documents*, 1984, pp. 788-89. Also see George Bush, "A New Partnership with Africa," address, Kenya Chamber of Commerce, November 19, 1982; Department of State, *Realism, Strength, Negotiation* (Washington: Department of State, 1984), pp. 16-19.

COLONIALISM, DECOLONIZATION, INDEPENDENCE, AND SELF-GOVERNMENT

4 7 3   TRANSITION FROM COLONIALISM TO ORDERLY DEVELOPMENT OF SELF-GOVERNMENT

. . . The United States has long recognized that old-fashioned,19th-century colonialism is dying--dying by mutual consent of both Africans and Europeans. We believe that the transition from current, progressively liberal colonialism to self-government and eventual self-determination should be completed in an orderly manner, with the speed of its evolution being determined by the capacity of local populations to assume and discharge the responsibilities of government. This, of course, is not the counsel of perfection. Decisions must be balanced and mutually reached. . . .

The United States role in the dynamic trend toward self-government in Africa, then, might be stated somewhat as follows: As a responsible world power and friend of European and African alike, we believe that we can assist peaceful African political evolution on the one hand by supporting liberal metropolitan measures designed to provide African self-government and eventual autonomy, and on the other by encouraging, insofar as we are able, moderate African leaders who recognize the benefit to their own people of following the evolutionary rather than the revolutionary approach to social, political, and economic progress. . . .

The African desire for speed in cutting the strings of metropolitan control is understandable in view of the "revolution of rising expectations" that now grips most of the continent. But it behooves all responsible African leaders to consider seriously the numerous pitfalls that confront a newly independent state today and to realize that premature independence can carry with it more dangers than a temporary prolongation of a dependent status.

Special Assistant to Secretary of State, address, American Assembly (Columbia University), Harriman, New York, May 1, 1958; *American Foreign Policy: Current Documents*, 1958, pp. 1077-78.

474   OBJECTIVES OF NEWLY INDEPENDENT AFRICAN NATIONS

When considering . . . what is best for Africa's development--we who are Americans might ask ourselves what our Founding Fathers wanted for this country when it, too, was first emerging as a new and independent nation. What were the feelings and attitudes, the ambitions, the aspirations, fears, and doubts of my countrymen almost 2 centuries ago? What did they and this part of North America want then, especially in relation to the rest of the world and the more powerful developed world around them?

Well, first of all--and above all--they wanted independence. On that cardinal point America was uncompromising. The young Republic of less than 3 million people was determined to exclude external interference in its internal affairs. It was equally determined to avoid what President Washington called "foreign entanglements." But it welcomed most eagerly investments from abroad. It also welcomed outside ideas and culture, not with the notion of becoming an imitation of Europe but to the end of creating a new free society which gave the best ideas of the free nations of the world completely free play. The young America was proud and did not like being patronized. It was full of plans and impatient to get on with them. It was full of the adventure of life and of fun and even of folly. Mistakes were made, but they were inevitable for a new people in a new continent bursting at the seams with vigor and with hope. . . .

Our African friends respect the great concepts of individual and of national freedom and the natural rights of human beings. They too stand for freedom, for independence, for self-determination. They too believe in the personal dignity of the individual. In support of these beliefs Africa is determined to keep itself free from any external domination, and it is to the interest of Africa as well as of the world that what is called the cold war be excluded from the African Continent.

These objectives are certainly compatible with America's hopes and interests. We seek no privileged position. We only seek to assure that people's destinies remain in their own hands. Nor is it our ambition to create an Africa in our own image but rather to help Africa create a new image of its own--a blend of the various strands woven from its history and its culture.

Adlai Stevenson, statement, committee of United Nations General Assembly, March 23, 1961; *American Foreign Policy: Current Documents,* 1961, pp. 705-6.

475   UNITED STATES SUPPORT FOR ENDING COLONIAL RULE

The fifth and most important principle of our foreign policy is support of national independence--the right of each people to govern themselves--and to shape their own institutions.

For a peaceful world order will be possible only when each country walks the way that it has chosen to walk for itself.

We follow this principle by encouraging the end of colonial rule.

We follow this principle, abroad as well as at home, by continued hostility to the rule of the many by the few--or the oppression of one race by another. . . .

The insistent urge toward national independence is the strongest force of today's world in which we live.

In Africa and Asia and Latin America it is shattering the designs of those who would subdue others to their ideas or their will. . . .

History is on the side of freedom and is on the side of societies shaped from the genius of each people. History does not favor a single system or belief--unless force is used to make it so.

Lyndon Johnson, Annual Message to Congress, January 12, 1966; *Papers of Presidents: Johnson,* 1966, p. 9.

476 UNITED STATES CONCERN WITH THE MARCH FROM COLONIALISM TO LIBERTY

One cannot dismantle a vast and highly developed power structure such as prewar colonialism in the brief period of a quarter century without creating power vacuums and power dislocations of major dimensions. Out of necessity, out of idealism, out of a mature sense of reality, the United States has acted in many of these situations to safeguard the liberty of free people from Communist aggression. We have assumed responsibility--not because we abhorred vacuums but because we abhorred tyranny.

Today, as a consequence, we find ourselves in a position unique in world history. Over the centuries a number of nations have exercised world power, and many have accepted at least some of the responsibilities that go with power. But never before in human history has a nation undertaken to play a role of world responsibility except in defense and support of a world empire. Our actions have not been motivated by pure altruism; rather we have recognized that world responsibility and American security are inseparably related. But, nevertheless, what America has done is an achievement of which the American people can be justly proud.

Under Secretary of State, address, National Foreign Policy Conference for Non-Governmental Organizations, Washington, March 16, 1965; *American Foreign Policy: Current Documents,* 1965, pp. 431-32.

NEUTRALISM AND NONALIGNMENT

477 NEUTRALITY VS. NEUTRALISM

Neutrality is a technical term of international law implying impartiality and abstention by a state in wars between other states. The United States and many other states followed the policy of neutrality in accordance with this concept during the nineteenth century.

Members of the United Nations are, however, forbidden to follow it in case the United Nations determines which side is the aggressor and which side is the defender, as it is obliged to do if hostilities occur and both belligerents fail to respond to its "cease-fire" order. . . .

In other words, "neutrality" is inconsistent with "collective security" under the United Nations Charter unless special exceptions are made, . . .

On the other hand, "neutralism" means observance of the principle that everyone should be presumed innocent until proved guilty. The "neutralist" countries have declined to assume in advance that the United States, the Soviet Union, or any other country is intending to embark upon an aggression or other violation of the Charter before an incident arises, and have therefore refused to enter alliances or collective defense arrangements directed against particular states.

They decline to assume that the ideology or the political or economic system with which a nation conducts its domestic affairs violates its international obligations. This attitude accords with the Charter provision which forbids intervention in matters essentially within the domestic jurisdiction of any state.

It would therefore seem that "neutralism" is a policy entirely in accord with the obligations of members of the United Nations but "neutrality" in the conventional sense is forbidden if the United Nations functions as it is supposed to in determining the innocent and guilty party in hostilities.

Quincy Wright, letter to New York Times, October 15, 1960, quoted in Marjorie M. Whiteman, *Digest of International Law*, XI, 162-63. For President Eisenhower's news conference statement on neutralism, June 6, 1956, see Document 381; and for White House clarification, June 7, 1956, see *American Foreign Policy: Current Documents*, 1956, pp. 32-33; also see commentary on this in Whiteman, pp. 160-62.

478 FREEDOM OF CHOICE RESPECTING NEUTRALISM

We Americans want peace, freedom, justice, prosperity, and well-being for ourselves and for all other people. We want to assure freedom of choice to all nations and societies.

No people is our enemy, although some peoples are controlled by governments which may be antagonistic to the United States for many years to come. Our ultimate aim is not only to preserve and strengthen our way of life here at home but to help all other peoples attain a way of life that is a natural reflection of their history and culture. For freedom in today's world is indivisible.

To achieve these purposes we must simultaneously pursue a variety of policies aimed at a variety of specific results. . . .

With regard to those nations that have chosen a course of neutrality, we must respect their neutrality and must help them to develop the stability and strength required for the maintenance of their own independence.

We have no desire to remake the world in the image of America. We could not do so even if we wished. Nor do we desire to dictate to our allies or to any other nation. We do not wish to establish a system of American imperialism and colonialism. The world is too big for us to run, and we would not want to run it even if we could.

Our real task is to protect and promote our own basic interests, with full realization of the fact that these interests correspond with the basic interests of other human beings in all lands.

Under Secretary of State, address, Foreign Policy Briefing Conference, Kansas City, Missouri, October 26, 1961; *American Foreign Policy: Current Documents,* 1961, pp. 51-52. For Declaration of the Heads of State or Government of Nonaligned Countries, Belgrade, September 5, 1961, see *American Foreign Policy: Current Documents,* 1961, pp. 118-24, in which they declare their rights of self-determination to pursue independent policies for the preservation of their sovereignty.

COMMUNISM AND SOVIET AND CUBAN INTERVENTION IN AFRICA

4 7 9   COMMUNISM AND NEOCOLONIALISM VS. LIBERTY AND INDEPENDENCE

To those new states whom we welcome to the ranks of the free, we pledge our word that one form of colonial control shall not have passed away merely to be replaced by a far more iron tyranny. We shall not always expect to find them supporting our view. But we shall always hope to find them strongly supporting their own freedom--and to remember that, in the past, those who foolishly sought power by riding the back of the tiger ended up inside.

John Kennedy, Inaugural Address, January 20, 1961; *Papers of Presidents: Kennedy,* 1961, p. 1.

*   *   *

Two great forces--the world of communism and the world of free choice--have, in effect, made a "bet" about the direction in which history is moving.

The Communist "bet" is that the future will be a Communist world-- that the inexorable processes of history must send all nations, some early, some late, through the Marxist wringer.

Our "bet" is that the future will be a world community of independent nations, with a diversity of economic, political and religious systems, united by a common respect for the rights of others. The history of recent years has already refuted the myth of the inevitability of Communist victory. . . .

In Asia and Africa, where the atmosphere of anticolonialism and underdevelopment was supposed to be tailor-made for Communist infiltration, their success has been slowed. . . .

But history is what men make of it--and we would be foolish to think that we can realize our own vision of a free and diverse future without unceasing vigilance, discipline and labor.

John Kennedy, magazine article "Where We Stand," January 15, 1963; *Papers of Presidents: Kennedy,* 1963, p. 20.

*   *   *

Our own response to the Communist presence in Africa is based on the premise that African nations will fundamentally seek international alignments which will further Africa's own central priorities. These priorities are:

Self-determination--an end to racial discrimination and white minority rule;

The maintenance of territorial integrity;

Progress in economic development.

A minority of the countries in Africa have felt that they have found support for these priorities in close ties with the Communist countries. . . .

But Africa is a continent of moving, not still, pictures. . . . Nationalism is a powerful force in Africa, and no African leaders or peoples wish to come under the lasting influence of any foreign power. . . .

Our African policy is on a firm footing which in the long run will serve both our own interests and those of Africa. Rather than contributing to conflict, we are attempting to foster peaceful solutions. Rather than treating the symptoms of unrest and turmoil, we are attempting to deal with the root causes. We rely on our trade, aid, and economic ties and on an open dialogue based on mutual respect. Our assistance is designed to meet the pressing needs of economic development and to help countries meet their legitimate self-defense needs.

On balance, I believe that these policies have resulted in our being in a stronger position vis-a-vis the African Continent than the Soviets and other Communist states have achieved with their MIGs and Kalashnikov-bearing troops.

Under Secretary of State, statement, Subcommittee on Africa, House Foreign Affairs Committee, October 18, 1979; *American Foreign Policy: Basic Documents,* 1977-1980, pp. 1156-57.

4 8 0   SOVIET AND CUBAN INTERVENTION IN AFRICA

A discussion of the issues and problems we face in Africa would not be complete without mention of Soviet and Cuban activities. Their increasing intervention raises serious problems. It escalates the level of conflict. It jeopardizes the independence of African states. It creates concern among moderates that Soviet weapons and Cuban troops can be used to determine the outcome of any dispute on the continent.

We are making a strenuous effort to counter Cuban and Soviet intervention in the disputes of African nations.

First, we have told the Soviets and the Cubans, publicly and privately, that we view their willingness to exacerbate armed conflict in Africa as a matter of serious concern.

Second, we have pointed out to the Soviets the dangers which their activities in Africa pose for our overall relations. . . .

Third, we will continue to take advantage of our long-term strengths in relations with Africa. These are found primarily in our substantial aid, trade, and investment ties. . . .

Fourth, our continued support for peaceful resolution of disputes and building closer diplomatic ties is in itself a barrier to Soviet and Cuban designs. African trust in the sincerity of our commitment to peaceful but meaningful change in southern Africa has been critical to minimizing Soviet and Cuban involvement. If we should abandon our efforts in support of peaceful change, the front-line states would conclude that change can only come militarily.

If we abandon our current efforts, increasing conflict will thus tend not only to radicalize southern Africa itself but to alter the policies of nations elsewhere in Africa that are now becoming increasingly friendly to us.

Cyrus Vance, statement, Subcommittee on African Affairs, Senate Foreign Relations Committee, May 12, 1978; *American Foreign Policy: Basic Documents,* 1977-1980, pp. 1144-45.

*   *   *

In Africa, we're engaged in a parallel commitment--economic development, the growth of democracies and the peaceful resolution of conflict. And here, too, our emphasis is on development and economic assistance. We maintain only a handful of military advisers on the whole African Continent. Our economic aid is four times larger than what we spend on security assistance. Contrast this with what the Soviet Union is doing. The record shows that since the Soviets began their aid program to Africa in 1954, military aid has outpaced all other Soviet aid by 7 to 1. Then add more than 40,000 Soviet and surrogate military personnel stationed in Africa, and it's no wonder that Africa is rife with conflict and tension.

Ronald Reagan, address, Annual Convention of American Legion, August 23, 1983; *American Foreign Policy: Current Documents,* 1983, p. 1125.

SOUTHERN AFRICA

4 8 1   POLICY PROPOSITIONS FOR SOUTHERN AFRICA

The problems of Southern Africa are potentially dangerous to stability in this region and in other parts of Africa. They are also subject to Communist exploitation. The U.S. is inevitably concerned with the events affecting the region because the issues at stake relate to basic tenets of our own beliefs and to our position as a responsible member of the United Nations, i.e. self-determination, majority rule, government by consent of the governed, and equal rights for all. Because of differing situations, the degree and manner in which we seek to encourage progress towards these goals have naturally varied. Throughout we have sought to make our position on these principles clear at home, in Africa and the rest of the world.

Assistant Secretary of State for African Affairs, statement, House Foreign Affairs Committee, April 20, 1967; *American Foreign Policy: Current Documents,* 1967, p. 237.

*   *   *

Our policy of promoting peaceful solutions to regional conflicts applies, as a priority, to southern Africa. Our strategy in southern Africa is to work with the parties concerned to promote fundamental and far-reaching change in three areas:

To build an overall framework for regional security;

To bring about an independent Namibia; and

To encourage positive change in the apartheid policy of South Africa itself.

Regional security is essential because our goals in the region are best served by a climate of coexistence in which the sovereignty and security of all states are respected. Economic reform and development, political pluralism, removal of outside forces, peaceful change in South Africa, and Namibian independence are more likely to be achieved in conditions of strengthened security and reduced violence. . . .

Our diplomacy has not groped for quick fixes or instant remedies to complex and deeply rooted problems. Our role is that of a catalyst, an honest broker. We have made clear we will exert ourselves where we are welcome. . . .

It is too soon to predict breakthroughs. Southern Africa today is at an early, pioneering stage on the road of peaceful change. The countries of the area must build that road; no one can do it for them. There are many bridges to be built and deep gulfs of suspicion, fear, and hatred to be overcome. But there are encouraging signs. We see a growing realism on all sides about the risks of open-ended conflict. Military solutions offer no hope. We detect a welcome glimmer of recognition that there are, indeed, common interests that bind the states of southern Africa together. After several years of tension and threats, openings for peace are being explored and developed with the active and energetic encouragement of the United States.

George Shultz, address, Boston World Affairs Council, February 15, 1984; *American Foreign Policy: Current Documents*, 1984, pp. 791-92.

4 8 2   PROBLEM OF SOUTH AFRICA

With respect to *apartheid* in South Africa, our view is clear. We are unalterably opposed to *apartheid.* Our traditions and our values permit us no other position. We believe that the continuation of *apartheid* can lead only to profound human tragedy for all races in Africa. We are firmly committed to use our best efforts to encourage South Africa to abandon these policies and to live up to its obligations under the U.N. Charter.

Deputy Assistant Secretary of State for African Affairs, address, St. Paul Social Studies Institute, St. Paul, Minnesota, July 18, 1963; *American Foreign Policy: Current Documents*, 1963, p. 618.

*   *   *

South Africa poses one of the most difficult policy problems faced by the United States Government. Essentially this is because of the nature of the problem itself. It is a problem involving one of the most sensitive aspects of human relations, the problem of getting people of different races to live together in harmony, mutual respect, and cooperation. . . .

In South Africa . . . there is no common unifying national culture, no universally spoken national language, and most of the instruments of national power are arrayed against the change desired by the majority rather than in its support. . . .

There are other difficulties. There are deep and honest differences of opinion as to how constructive change can be induced in South Africa. It is frequently said that in the last analysis the peoples of South Africa themselves must work out their own destiny. But how is this to take place with the internal forces for change so effectively repressed? It is also pointed out that in South Africa economic forces are breaking down segregationist practices and isolation patterns of thought. But how are such changes to be translated into the political and social fields? How long will it take? And what can outside forces properly do to accelerate it? There is no agreement on these important questions.

Another range of difficulties is the fact that our relations with South Africa involve mutually contradictory American national interests. In formulating our policy one must examine not only the balance sheet of our bilateral relations with South Africa but also the effect of these relations on our national goals elsewhere in the world. Bilaterally we enjoy mutually beneficial relations with South Africa in several fields. On the other hand, the racial policies of the Republic impose severe restraints on these relations. . . .

Thus in formulating our policy we must take into account the liabilities as well as the benefits from our relations.

Assistant Secretary of State for African Affairs, statement, Subcommittee on Africa, House Foreign Affairs Committee, March 1, 1966; *American Foreign Policy: Current Documents,* 1966, pp. 565-66.

*   *   *

Let us be frank at the outset by recognizing that the development of a policy that adequately reflects our moral principles, our interests as a great power, and the realities of influence and power in that distant region is one of the most thorny issues in U.S. foreign policy.

The dilemma is not that our principles and our interests are in conflict, because they are not. U.S. values and interests can only be served to the degree that there is a strengthened framework of regional security in southern Africa and a sustained process of peaceful change in South Africa. The quest for security and the imperative of change are dependent upon one another.

The challenge for U.S. policy then is to define in an operational sense how we are to pursue these goals. This means we must understand the extent of and the limits on U.S. influence, and then use that influence in a sustained and coherent manner. . . .

Recent events in South Africa serve to underscore our strong moral and political convictions about a system based on legally entrenched racism. . . .

Such actions touch a sensitive nerve in the American body politic. They threaten democratic values that we espouse as a nation and that we believe must be reflected in our foreign policy. . . .

Similarly, we are united in opposition to laws and practices in South Africa or anywhere else that offend basic concepts of due process and constitutional government. The theory of apartheid is rooted in the concept of ethnicity and ethnic separation. In practice, apartheid translates as a system based on race as the organizing principle of politics and government.

Any system that ascribes or denies political rights on this basis, including the right of citizenship itself, is bound to be termed, as President Reagan has said, "abhorrent."

Assistant Secretary of State for African Affairs, testimony, Subcommittee of Senate Foreign Relations Committee, September 26, 1984; *American Foreign Policy: Current Documents,* 1984, pp. 837-38.

28

Asia and the Pacific

We are and will remain a Pacific nation, by virtue of our geography, our history, our commerce, and our interests.

Cyrus Vance
Address, Asia Society, New York, June 29, 1977

This chapter consists of four parts: a few general policy statements concerning contemporary United States interests and policies respecting East Asia and the Western Pacific; the reversion of the Ryukyu Islands to Japan in 1972; changes in American relations with China, including rapprochement with the People's Republic of China and concomitant modification of the status of the Republic of China (Nationalist China); and negotiations to provide self-government for the Micronesian Islands, taken from Japan after World War II, leading to the termination of the Pacific Trust Agreement of 1947.

This chapter needs to be related to Chapters 7 (the Johnson, Nixon, and Ford Doctrines); 10 (the Formosa Strait Crisis and the Vietnam War); 13 (the Gulf of Tonkin, *Pueblo,* and *Mayaguez* Crises); 18 (the ANZUS and Southeast Asia Collective Defense Treaties, and the bilateral alliances with the Philippine Republic, Japan, the Republic of Korea, and Nationalist China); and 22 (East-West relations, especially Document 373, establishing basic principles to govern future relations of the United States and the People's Republic of China.

GENERAL GOALS AND OBJECTIVES

After World War II a political "Asia First" faction in the United States contended that internal American forces sabotaged the preservation of Nationalist control of continental China, evidencing primary concern with the affairs of Europe and the Cold War with the Soviet Union. During and after the Vietnam War greater emphasis was given to the future role of the United States in Asia and the Pacific, as epitomized by such pronouncements as: "Asia is now the crucial arena of man's striving for independence and order, and for life itself" (Lyndon Johnson, 1966); "We are a Pacific power" (Richard Nixon,

1970); "The center of political power in the United States has shifted west-ward" and "Our Pacific interests and concerns have increased" (Gerald Ford, 1975); "We should and will remain an Asian-Pacific power" (Walter Mondale, 1977); and "The next century will be the century of the Pacific" (Ambassador Mike Mansfield, quoted by Ronald Reagan, 1983).

General American policy pronouncements emphasize such basic goals as preserving American and Pacific security; maintaining peace, stability, and the balance of power; promoting political independence, democracy, freedom, and human rights; and restraining Communist expansion and hegemonism. Policy emphasis has shifted from combating Communist revolution in China and aggression in Korea and Indochina (see Chapter 10) and negotiating a series of mutual defense treaties (see Chapter 18) to rapprochement with the People's Republic of China, supplemented with programs supporting economic and social development as well as military and financial assistance, and eventually to espousal of the notion of "Pacific partnership." The documents selected for this section, arranged chronologically, represent a selected spectrum of general statements of these goals and objectives (Documents 483-489).

483   PACIFIC CHARTER, 1954

First, in accordance with the provisions of the United Nations Charter, they uphold the principle of equal rights and self-determination of peoples and they will earnestly strive by every peaceful means to promote self-government and to secure the independence of all countries whose peoples desire it and are able to undertake its responsibilities;

Second, they are each prepared to continue taking effective practical measures to ensure conditions favorable to the orderly achievement of the foregoing purposes in accordance with their constitutional processes;

Third, they will continue to cooperate in the economic, social and cultural fields in order to promote higher living standards, economic progress and social well-being in this region;

Fourth, as declared in the Southeast Asia Collective Defense Treaty, they are determined to prevent or counter by appropriate means any attempt in the treaty area to subvert their freedom or to destroy their sovereignty or territorial integrity.

Agreed to by Australia, France, New Zealand, Pakistan, the Philippines, Thailand, the United Kingdom, and the United States, September 8, 1954; *American Foreign Policy: Basic Documents*, 1950-1955, pp. 916-17; also TIAS 3171, 6 *U.S. Treaties* 91-92. For commentary, see report of Senate Foreign Relations Committee, January 25, 1955; *American Foreign Policy: Basic Documents*, 1950-1955, p. 943.

484   UNITED STATES GOALS IN ASIA, 1956

What is it that we seek? It is not conquest or domination. . . . Our desire is a world in which peoples who want political independence shall possess it whenever they are capable of sustaining it and discharging its responsibilities in accordance with the accepted standards of civilized nations. That condition of independence is developing throughout non-Communist Asia, and I believe that it will continue to develop as against assault from any quarter.

But we also realize that political independence is not enough. It is a means to certain ends. One of these ends is the infusing of men with reasonable hope that, if they strive, they can build a better world for their children and their children's children. That reasonable hope we can help to provide without any encroachment whatsoever on the political independence of others.

John Foster Dulles, "The State of Asia," national radio and television address, March 23, 1956; *American Foreign Policy: Current Documents*, 1956, pp. 751-52. For President Kennedy's designation of China's Communism and expansionism as America's "major problem" in Asia, see his remarks, December 3, 1962, in *Papers of Presidents: Kennedy*, 1962, pp. 850-51.

4 8 5   DECLARATION OF PEACE AND PROGRESS IN ASIA AND THE PACIFIC, 1966

I. Aggression must not succeed.

The peace and security of Asia and the Pacific and, indeed, of the entire world, are indivisible. The nations of the Asian and Pacific region shall enjoy their independence and sovereignty free from aggression, outside interference, or the domination of any nation. . . .

II. We must break the bonds of poverty, illiteracy and disease.

In the region of Asia and the Pacific, where there is a rich heritage of the intrinsic worth and dignity of every man, we recognize the responsibility of every nation to join in an expanding offensive against poverty, illiteracy and disease. For these bind men to lives of hopelessness and despair; these are the roots of violence and war. . . .

III. We must strengthen economic, social and cultural cooperation within the Asian and Pacific region.

Together with our other partners of Asia and the Pacific, we will develop the institutions and practice of regional cooperation. Through sustained effort we aim to build in this vast area, where almost two-thirds of humanity live, a region of security and order and progress, realizing its common destiny in the light of its own traditions and aspirations. The peoples of this region have the right as well as the primary responsibility to deal with their own problems and to shape their own future in terms of their own wisdom and experience. . . .

IV. We must seek reconciliation and peace throughout Asia.

We do not threaten the sovereignty or territorial integrity of our neighbors, whatever their ideological alignment. We ask only that this be reciprocated. The quarrels and ambitions of ideology and the painful frictions arising from national fears and grievances should belong to the past. Aggression rooted in them must not succeed. We shall play our full part in creating an environment in which reconciliation becomes possible, for in the modern world men and nations have no choice but to learn to live together as brothers.

Subscribed to at Manila summit meeting by Australia, the Republic of Korea, New Zealand, the Philippines, Thailand, South Vietnam, and the United States, October 24-25, 1966; *American Foreign Policy: Current Documents*, 1966, p. 871. Also see President Johnson's essentials for peace in Asia, radio and television address, July 12, 1966, pp. 626-27, and his statement on United States goals in Asia, address, East-West Center, Honolulu, October 17, 1966, pp. 634-35.

486 UNITED STATES GOALS AND PRECEPTS FOR ASIA AND THE PACIFIC, 1969-1970

"What we seek for Asia is a community of free nations able to go their own way and seek their own destiny with whatever cooperation we can provide--a community of independent Asian countries, each maintaining its own traditions and yet each developing through mutual cooperation. In such an arrangement, we stand ready to play a responsible role in accordance with our commitments and basic interests." (Statement by President Nixon, Bangkok, Thailand, July 28, 1969.)

First, we remain involved in Asia. We are a Pacific power. We have learned that peace for us is much less likely if there is no peace in Asia.

Second, behind the headlines of strife and turmoil, the fact remains that no region contains a greater diversity of vital and gifted peoples, and thus a greater potential for cooperative enterprises. . . . Thus, despite its troubled past, Asia's future is rich in promise. That promise has been nurtured in part by America's participation.

Third, while we will maintain our interests in Asia and the commitments that flow from them, the changes taking place in that region enable us to change the character of our involvement. The responsibilities once borne by the United States at such great cost can now be shared. America **can** be effective in helping the peoples of Asia harness the forces of change to peaceful progress, and in supporting them as they defend themselves from those who would subvert this process and fling Asia again into conflict.

Richard Nixon, *U.S. Foreign Policy for the 1970's: A New Strategy for Peace* (1970), pp. 53-55. Also see his statements in his reports for 1971, pp. 93-94, and 1973, pp. 109-13.

487   AMERICA'S STAKE IN ASIA AND THE PACIFIC

America, a nation of the Pacific Basin, has a very vital stake in Asia and a responsibility to take a leading part in lessening tensions, preventing hostilities, and preserving peace. World stability and our own security depend upon our Asian commitments. . . .

The center of political power in the United States has shifted westward. Our Pacific interests and concerns have increased. We have exchanged the freedom of action of an isolationist state for the responsibilities of a great global power. . . .

Asia is entering a new era. We can contribute to a new structure of stability founded on a balance among the major powers, strong ties to our allies in the region, an easing of tension between adversaries, the self-reliance and regional solidarity of smaller nations, and expanding economic ties and cultural exchanges. These components of peace are already evident. Our foreign policy in recent years and in recent days encourages their growth.

If we can remain steadfast, historians will look back and view the 1970's as the beginning of a period of peaceful cooperation and progress, a time of growing community for all the nations touched by this great ocean.

Gerald Ford, address, University of Hawaii, December 7, 1975; *Papers of Presidents: Ford,* 1975, II, 1951, 1954-55. Also see Document 122 on the Ford Doctrine.

488   ROLE OF UNITED STATES IN ASIA AND THE PACIFIC

. . . our interests in Asia are enduring, and they are substantial.

I hope to leave you with these understandings:

-- First, the United States is and will remain an Asian and Pacific power.

-- Second, the United States will continue its key role in contributing to peace and stability in Asia and the Pacific.

-- Third, the United States seeks normal and friendly relations with the countries in the area on the basis of reciprocity and mutual respect.

-- Fourth, the United States will pursue mutual expansion of trade and investment across the Pacific, recognizing the growing interdependence of the economies of the United States and the region.

-- Fifth, we will use our influence to improve the human condition of the peoples of Asia.

In all of this, there can be no doubt of the enduring vitality of our country's relationships with the peoples of Asia and the Pacific. . . .

. . . I want to close by stressing my deep hope for a new sense of community in Asia and the Pacific. We seek:

-- To build on our relationships of mutual respect;

-- To consolidate the fragile stability already achieved;

-- To bring greater freedom and greater respect for human rights; and
-- To erase the divisions that persist.

Cyrus Vance, address, Asia Society, New York, June 29, 1977; *American Foreign Policy: Basic Documents*, 1977-1980, pp. 912, 915.

4 8 9   UNITED STATES IS A TWO-OCEAN NATION

Although the United States has long been a two-ocean nation, in the past we focused most of our attention on our Atlantic coast because of our historic relationship with Europe. But during the past decade or so, the growth of democracy and the dynamic economic development of the Pacific region also have earned our admiration and our very close attention. As a result, while Europe certainly remains as vital as ever to us, a new perspective has emerged toward the Pacific. . . . Pacific Basin cooperation, in whatever form it eventually emerges, will not be successful and will not last unless it has the full support of all our Pacific neighbors, and unless there is benefit for all.

Ronald Reagan, response to question, Tokyo, December 28, 1984; *Papers of Presidents: Reagan*, 1984, II, 1908. Also see address of George Shultz, World Affairs Council, San Francisco, March 5, 1983, on United States and Asia-- partnership for the future; *American Foreign Policy: Current Documents*, 1983, pp. 922-27.

RETURN OF THE RYUKYU ISLANDS INCLUDING OKINAWA TO JAPAN, 1972

Following World War II, under the Peace Treaty with Japan (signed September 8, 1951, see TIAS 2490; 3 *U.S. Treaties* 3169-3328), the United States continued to occupy and administer the Bonin and Ryukyu (Loochoo) Islands. The latter lie in the western Pacific between the Japanese main islands and Formosa. The Bonin Islands, which lie north of the Marianna Islands (Micronesia), were returned to Japan on June 26, 1968 (see agreement signed on April 5, 1968, TIAS 6495; 19 *U.S. Treaties* 4895-4914). The Ryukyu Islands, where the United States maintained an important defense base, were not returned until 1972.

Negotiations leading to the reversion of the Ryukyu Islands commenced in 1969 and were consummated by formal agreement signed in June 1971, which entered into force on May 15, 1972. The documents contained in this section include President Nixon's 1969 commitment to return the islands subject to certain reserved defense rights and an excerpt from the reversion agreement (Documents 490-491).

490   UNITED STATES COMMITMENT TO RETURN OKINAWA TO JAPAN, 1969

The Prime Minister emphasized his view that the time had come to respond to the strong desire of the people of Japan . . . to have the administrative rights over Okinawa returned to Japan on the basis of the friendly relations between the United States and Japan and thereby to restore Okinawa to its normal status.   The President expressed appreciation of the Prime Minister's view.   The President and the Prime Minister also recognized the vital role played by United States forces in Okinawa in the present situation in the Far East.   As a result of their discussion it was agreed that the mutual security interests of the United States and Japan could be accommodated within arrangements for the return of the administrative rights over Okinawa to Japan.   They therefore agreed that the two governments would immediately enter into consultations regarding specific arrangements for accomplishing the early reversion of Okinawa without detriment to the security of the Far East including Japan.   They further agreed to expedite the consultations with a view to accomplishing the reversion during 1972 subject to the conclusion of these specific arrangements with the necessary legislative support.   In this connection, the Prime Minister made clear the intention of his government, following reversion, to assume gradually the responsibility for the immediate defense of Okinawa as part of Japan's defense efforts for her own territories.   The President and the Prime Minister agreed also that the United States would retain under the terms of the Treaty of Mutual Cooperation and Security such military facilities and areas in Okinawa as required in the mutual security of both countries.

Joint statement, President Nixon and Prime Minister Eisaku Sato of Japan, November 21, 1969; *Papers of Presidents: Nixon*, 1969, pp. 954-55.

491   AGREEMENT FOR REVERSION OF THE RYUKYU AND DAITO ISLANDS TO JAPAN, 1971

Article I

1.   With respect to the Ryukyu Islands and the Daito Islands . . . the United States of America relinquishes in favor of Japan all rights and interests under Article 3 of the Treaty of Peace with Japan signed at the city of San Francisco on September 8, 1951, effective as of the date of entry into force of this Agreement.   Japan, as of such date, assumes full responsibility and authority for the exercise of all and any powers of administration, legislation and jurisdiction over the territory and inhabitants of the said islands.

2.   For the purpose of this Agreement, the term "the Ryukyu Islands and the Daito Islands" means all the territories and their territorial waters with respect to which the right to exercise all and any powers of administration, legislation and jurisdiction was accorded to the United States of America under Article 3 of the Treaty of Peace with Japan other

than those with respect to which such right has already been returned to Japan in accordance with the Agreement concerning the Amami Islands and the Agreement concerning Nanpo Shoto and Other Islands signed between the United States of America and Japan, respectively on December 24, 1953 and April 5, 1968.

Article II

It is confirmed that treaties, conventions and other agreements concluded between the United States of America and Japan, including, but without limitation, the Treaty of Mutual Cooperation and Security between the United States of America and Japan signed at Washington on January 19, 1960 and its related arrangements and the Treaty of Friendship, Commerce and Navigation between the United States of America and Japan signed at Tokyo on April 2, 1953, become applicable to the Ryukyu Islands and the Daito Islands as of the date of entry into force of this Agreement.

Article III

1. Japan will grant the United States of America on the date of entry into force of this Agreement the use of facilities and areas in the Ryukyu Islands and the Daito Islands in accordance with the Treaty of Mutual Cooperation and Security between the United States of America and Japan.
. . .

Signed June 17, 1971 and entered into force May 15, 1972; 9 articles. TIAS 7314; 23 *U.S. Treaties* 446-570. Also see Secretary of State William P. Rogers' statement on signing the agreement, June 17, 1971, in *Papers of Presidents: Nixon,* 1971, p. 737; President Nixon's message to the Senate transmitting the agreement for its approval, September 21, 1971, pp. 962-65; and joint statement of President Nixon and Prime Minister Sato of Japan, January 7, 1972, in *Papers of Presidents: Nixon,* 1972, pp. 23-24.

REVISED RELATIONS WITH CHINA(S)

For years, beginning in 1945, one of America's primary policies in Asia was to back the Nationalist government in China and assist it to maintain its power and stability, and to continue supporting it after the Communist revolution on the mainland. For illustrations, see President Truman's statements on December 16, 1945, December 18, 1946, and January 5, 1950, in *A Decade of American Foreign Policy, 1941-49,* pp. 691-700, 727-28, and President Eisenhower's letter of reaffirmation of United States support, in *American Foreign Policy: Current Documents,* 1956, p. 800. After Communist forces took over control of China and established the People's Republic and the Nationalist forces retreated to Formosa in 1949, the Korean War, and the signing of bilateral mutual defense treaties with the Republic of Korea and Nationalist China (1953 and 1954, see Documents 312-313) and the Southeast Asia Collective Defense Treaty (1954, see Document 308), antagonism reigned in the relations of the People's Republic of China with the United States during the height of the Cold War.

Although isolated expressions of the need to formulate a new policy for China were promulgated from time to time, it was not until the Nixon administration that action was taken to establish a high-level dialogue with the Beijing government to normalize relations between the United States and the People's Republic. This involved a series of complex preliminary negotiations, elevating them to the summit at the Beijing Conference in 1972, exchanging quasi-diplomatic missions called "liaison offices" the following year, and establishing formal diplomatic missions in 1979 (Documents 492-495).

This action, which recognized a single China (including Formosa) and the need for integrating the two territories and governments by peaceful process, required legal and practical changes in United States relations with the Nationalist government in Taiwan. Among the most critical were the abrogation of the bilateral Mutual Defense Treaty, while continuing to provide military defense support for Nationalist China, and creating an unofficial means of mutual diplomatic representation with the government in Taiwan (Documents 496-497). On the matter of unseating the Nationalist government and seating the People's Republic in the United Nations, see Document 430.

Normalizing relations with the People's Republic proceeded gradually and the President engaged in seven summit conferences with Chinese leaders, 1972-1989. But progress was disrupted when popular demonstrations for freedom and democracy broke out in China during April, 1989. Students, supported by workers, marched and demonstrated in Beijing, riots occurred in provincial cities, and in June the Chinese government crushed the protest with massive military force, which was condemned by the United States and other free nations as violating human rights. The White House responded by levying executive sanctions, withdrawing American personnel from China, and suspending high-level contacts. The House of Representatives condemned the Chinese government and both houses of Congress passed unanimous resolutions instituting economic sanctions against it. Although the President refrained from severing diplomatic exchanges with Beijing, this incident retarded the normalization process.

492 DESIRE TO ESTABLISH UNITED STATES DIALOGUE WITH THE PEOPLE'S REPUBLIC OF CHINA

We recognize that China's long historical experience weighs heavily on contemporary Chinese foreign policy. China has had little experience in conducting diplomacy based on the sovereign equality of nations. For centuries China dominated its neighbors, culturally and politically. In the last 150 years it has been subjected to massive foreign interventions. Thus, China's attitude toward foreign countries retains elements of aloofness, suspicion, and hostility. Under Communism these historically shaped attitudes have been sharpened by doctrines of violence and revolution, proclaimed more often than followed as principles in foreign relations. . . .

We are prepared to establish a dialogue with Peking. We cannot accept its ideological precepts, or the notion that Communist China must exercise hegemony over Asia. But neither do we wish to impose on China an international position that denies its legitimate national interests.

The evolution of our dialogue with Peking cannot be at the expense of international order or our own commitments. Our attitude is public and clear. We will continue to honor our treaty commitments to the security of our Asian allies. An honorable relationship with Peking cannot be constructed at their expense.

Richard Nixon, *U.S. Foreign Policy for the 1970's: Building for Peace* (1971), pp. 106-7.

493 ROAD TO THE 1972 SUMMIT MEETING IN BEIJING AND RAPPROCHEMENT WITH COMMUNIST CHINA

In his appearance before the Senate Foreign Relations Committee in March 1969 the Secretary of State stated that it is in the U.S. interest to reduce longstanding tensions between the United States and the People's Republic of China, to seek to resolve our differences, and to move toward a more constructive relationship. He indicated that we would welcome a renewal of meetings to pursue such goals. He subsequently noted that the U.S. Government understood perfectly well that the existence of the Republic of China on the island of Taiwan and the People's Republic of China on the mainland were both facts of life. In a September 1969 speech to the U.N. General Assembly, President Nixon emphasized that we were ready to talk to the leaders of the People's Republic of China whenever they choose to abandon their self-imposed isolation.

*   *   *

The President explained in his July 15 [1971] announcement that the purpose of the meeting would be to seek the normalization of relations between the two countries and to undertake an exchange of views on questions of mutual concern. He pointed out that he had accepted the invitation for these talks because of his profound conviction "that all nations will gain from a reduction of tensions and a better relationship between the United States and the People's Republic of China."

Soon after the President's statement, on August 2, Secretary Rogers announced a new U.S. policy regarding Chinese representation in the United Nations--that the United States would support action to seat the People's Republic of China in the United Nations and to transfer the Chinese seat in the Security Council to it. At the same time, the United States would seek to preserve representation for the Government of the Republic of China.

United States Foreign Policy, 1969-1970: A Report of the Secretary of State, p. 42, and 1971, p. 63.

494   REPORT ON THE BEIJING SUMMIT MEETING, 1972

My trip to the People's Republic of China from February 21 to February 28, 1972 was the watershed in reestablishing Sino-American relations.

The carefully nurtured preparation held out the promise of a new direction; my meetings with Chairman Mao Tse-tung and Premier Chou En-lai firmly set our course. The Joint Communique at the end of my visit established the framework for progress; developments since then have accelerated the process of normalization.

Seldom have the leaders of two major countries met with such an opportunity to create a totally new relationship. It had taken two and a half years to cross the gulf of isolation and reach the summit. At the same time, the very factors which had made this journey so complicated offered unusual opportunities. The absence of communication, while making initial contact complex to arrange, also gave us a clean slate to write upon. Factors such as geography and China's recent concentration on internal matters meant that we had few bilateral matters of contention, though we lined up often on different sides of third country or multilateral problems.

Accordingly, the agenda for our discussions could be general and our dialogue philosophical to a much greater extent than is normally possible between nations. Indeed, it was this context and these prospects that, in our view, called for a summit meeting. With the Soviet Union a meeting at the highest levels was required to give impetus to, and conclude, a broad range of concrete negotiations. With the People's Republic of China, on the other hand, such a meeting was needed to set an entirely new course. Only through direct discussions at the highest levels could we decisively bridge the gulf that had divided us, conduct discussions on a strategic plane, and launch a new process with authority.

The primary objective, then, of my talks with the Chinese leaders was not the reaching of concrete agreements but a sharing of fundamental perspectives on the world. First, we had to establish a joint perception of the shape of our future relationship and its place in the international order. We needed a mutual assessment of what was involved in the new process we were undertaking and of one another's reliability in carrying the process forward. If we could attain this type of mutual comprehension, agreements could and would flow naturally.

Richard Nixon, *U.S. Foreign Policy for the 1970's: Shaping a Durable Peace* (1973), pp. 18-19. For additional commentary on the summit meeting, see pp. 16-25, and for commentary concerning earlier developments, see Richard Nixon, *U.S. Foreign Policy for the 1970's: The Emerging Structure of Peace* (1972), pp. 26-37. For the Shanghai Communique, see Document 373, and for commentary on it, see Richard Nixon, *U.S. Foreign Policy for the 1970's: Shaping a Durable Peace* (1973), pp. 20-21. For President Nixon's remarks on his return from Beijing, Andrews Air Force Base, February 28, 1972, see *Papers of Presidents: Nixon*, 1972, pp. 381-83.

4 9 5   NORMALIZATION OF DIPLOMATIC RELATIONS WITH THE PEOPLE'S REPUBLIC OF CHINA, 1979

The United States of America and the People's Republic of China have agreed to recognize each other and to establish diplomatic relations as of January 1, 1979.

The United States of America recognizes the Government of the People's Republic of China as the sole legal Government of China. Within this context, the people of the United States will maintain cultural, commercial, and other unofficial relations with the people of Taiwan.

The United States of America and the People's Republic of China reaffirm the principles agreed on by the two sides in the Shanghai Communique and emphasize once again that . . .

-- The Government of the United States of America acknowledges the Chinese position that there is but one China and Taiwan is part of China.

-- Both believe that normalization of Sino-American relations is not only in the interest of the Chinese and American peoples but also contributes to the cause of peace in Asia and the world.

The United States of America and the People's Republic of China will exchange Ambassadors and establish Embassies on March 1, 1979.

*   *   *

Before the estrangement of recent decades, the American and the Chinese people had a long history of friendship. We've already begun to rebuild some of those previous ties. Now our rapidly expanding relationship requires the kind of structure that only full diplomatic relations will make possible.

The change that I'm announcing tonight will be of great long-term benefit to the peoples of both our country and China--and, I believe, to all the peoples of the world. Normalization--and the expanded commercial and cultural relations that it will bring--will contribute to the well-being of our own Nation, to our own national interest, and it will also enhance the stability of Asia. . . .

As the United States asserted in the Shanghai Communique of 1972, issued on President Nixon's historic visit, we will continue to have an interest in the peaceful resolution of the Taiwan issue. I have paid special attention to ensuring that normalization of relations between our country and the People's Republic will not jeopardize the well-being of the people of Taiwan. The people of our country will maintain our current commercial, cultural, trade, and other relations with Taiwan through non-governmental means. Many other countries in the world are already successfully doing this.

Joint communique of United States and People's Republic of China, December 15, 1978; *American Foreign Relations: Basic Documents,* 1977-1980, pp. 967-68, and Jimmy Carter, Address to the Nation, December 15,1978, p. 969. For commentary on the meaning of normalization, see Cyrus Vance, statement, January 15, 1979, pp. 974-78; and for background and commentary, see *Digest of United States Practice in International Law,* 1978, pp. 70-75. For the

Shanghai Communique, see Document 373.

496 CHANGED RELATIONS WITH THE REPUBLIC OF CHINA

. . . in the future, the American people will maintain commercial, cultural and other relations with the people of Taiwan without official government representation and without diplomatic relations. I am issuing this memorandum to facilitate maintaining those relations pending the enactment of legislation on the subject.

I therefore declare and direct that:

(A) Departments and agencies currently having authority to conduct or carry out programs, transactions, or other relations with or relating to Taiwan are directed to conduct and carry out those programs, transactions, and relations beginning January 1, 1979, in accordance with such authority and, as appropriate, through the instrumentality referred to in paragraph D below.

(B) Existing international agreements and arrangements in force between the United States and Taiwan shall continue in force and shall be performed and enforced by departments and agencies beginning January 1, 1979, in accordance with their terms and, as appropriate, through that instrumentality.

(C) In order to effectuate all of the provisions of this memorandum, whenever any law, regulation, or order of the United States refers to a foreign country, nation, state, government, or similar entity, departments and agencies shall construe those terms and apply those laws, regulations, or orders to include Taiwan.

(D) In conducting and carrying out programs, transactions, and other relations with the people on Taiwan, interests of the people of the United States will be represented as appropriate by an unofficial instrumentality in corporate form, to be identified shortly.

Jimmy Carter, memorandum to all departments and agencies of the United States government, December 30, 1978; *American Foreign Policy: Basic Documents,* 1977-1980, pp. 973-74.

497 TAIWAN RELATIONS ACT, 1979

Sec. 2. (b) It is the policy of the United States--

(1   to preserve and promote extensive, close, and friendly commercial, cultural, and other relations between the people of the United States and the people on Taiwan, as well as the people on the China mainland and all other peoples of the Western Pacific area;

(2) to declare that peace and stability in the area are in the political, security, and economic interests of the United States, and are matters of international concern;

(3) to make clear that the United States decision to establish diplomatic relations with the People's Republic of China rests upon the expectation that the future of Taiwan will be determined by peaceful means;

(4) to consider any effort to determine the future of Taiwan by other than peaceful means, including by boycotts or embargoes, a threat to the peace and security of the Western Pacific area and of grave concern to the United States;

(5) to provide Taiwan with arms of a defensive character; and

(6) to maintain the capacity of the United States to resist any resort to force or other forms of coercion that would jeopardize the security, or the social or economic system, of the people on Taiwan. . . .

Sec. 6. (a) Programs, transactions, and other relations conducted or carried out by the President or any agency of the United States Government with respect to Taiwan shall, in the manner and to the extent directed by the President, be conducted and carried out by or through--

(1) the American Institute in Taiwan, a nonprofit corporation incorporated under the laws of the District of Columbia, or

(2) such comparable successor non-governmental entity as the President may designate.

Public Law 96-8, approved April 10, 1979, and effective January 1, 1979; 96th Congress, 93 *U.S. Statutes at Large* 14-21, and *American Foreign Policy: Basic Documents,* 1977-1980, pp. 989-94. This enactment also deals with the application of United States laws and international agreements to Taiwan, the functions and manning of the Institute, and other matters. For President Carter's statement concerning the significance of this act, see pp. 988-89, and for documents on trade relations and most-favored-nation treatment, see pp. 994-97, 999-1000. Termination of the Mutual Defense Treaty with Nationalist China is dealt with in Documents 79 and 313.

TRUST TERRITORY OF THE PACIFIC--SELF-GOVERNMENT FOR THE MICRO-NESIAN ISLANDS

Micronesia, in the northwest quadrant of the Pacific basin, consists of the Marianna Islands to the north and, ranging from west to east, the Palau, Caroline, and Marshall Islands lying to the south. In the nineteenth century many of these islands were possessed by Spain, which ceded Guam to the United States in 1898 following the Spanish-American War and sold the remaining archipelagoes to Germany. The latter were taken from Germany by the Versailles Treaty in 1919 and converted into a League of Nations mandate under the administration of Japan. During World War II the United States wrested them from Japan and they were converted into the Trust Territory of the Pacific, assigned by the United Nations to the United States in 1947. The Trusteeship Agreement stipulated that the United States was bound to promote the development of "self-government or independence" in accordance with the people's "freely expressed wishes."

In June 1975 residents of the Northern Mariannas voted overwhelmingly (78%) to become a commonwealth of the United States; on March 24, 1976, President Ford signed a congressionally-approved commonwealth covenant giving the Mariannas control over domestic affairs and the United States management over foreign relations and defense and the right to maintain military bases in the islands. On October 24, 1977, President Carter approved the Constitution of the Northern Mariannas, to become effective on January 1 of the following year. On the other hand, the Caroline and Marshall Islands established a commission in 1969 that recommended self-government for internal affairs in "free association" with the United States. These island groups and Palau rejected commonwealth status in 1970 and, after lengthy negotiations with the United States, signed individual compacts for free association, which were separately approved by the electorates of Palau, the Federated States of Micronesia, and the Marshall Islands in 1983.

Eventually the Commonwealth of the Northern Marianna Islands was established formally in November 1986, and the free association arrangements for the Republic of the Marshall Islands became effective in October 1986 and for the Federated States of Micronesia the following month. Termination of the Trusteeship Agreement of 1947 was delayed awaiting the resolution of certain issues in the compact between the United States and Palau.

The documents contained in this section consist of excerpts from the Trusteeship Agreement between the United States and the United Nations, 1947 (Document 498), and a number of statements concerning the application of self-determination to the islands constituting the Trust Territory (Document 499). For additional documentation on the Covenant to Establish a Commonwealth of the Northern Marianna Islands in Political Union with the United States, see P.L. 94-241, 90 *Statutes at Large* 263-79; Presidential Proclamation 4938, May 3, 1982, in *Papers of Presidents: Reagan,* 1982, 550-51; and President Reagan's statement, November 3, 1986 on the implementation of the Commonwealth, in *Papers of Presidents: Reagan,* 1986, II, 1511-12. On the free association of Palau, the Federated States of Micronesia, and the Marshall Islands, see Department of State statements in *American Foreign Policy: Current Documents,* 1983, pp. 941-42, 945-46, 949-50; and President Reagan's Message to Congress in *Papers of Presidents: Reagan,* 1984, I, 442. For a general survey of the negotiations to produce these arrangements, see Arthur J. Armstrong and Howard L. Hills, "The Negotiations for the Future Status of Micronesia (1980-1984);" 78 *American Journal of International Law* (April 1984): 484-97.

498 TRUSTEESHIP FOR MICRONESIAN ISLANDS--U.S.-UNITED NATIONS AGREEMENT, 1947

Article 1

The Territory of the Pacific Islands, consisting of the islands formerly held by Japan under mandate in accordance with Article 22 of the Covenant of the League of Nations, is hereby designated as a strategic area and placed under the trusteeship system established in the Charter of the United Nations. The Territory of the Pacific Islands is hereinafter referred to as the trust territory.

Article 2

The United States of America is designated as the administering authority of the trust territory.

Article 3

The administering authority shall have full powers of administration, legislation, and jurisdiction over the territory subject to the provisions of this agreement, and may apply to the trust territory, subject to any modifications which the administering authority may consider desirable, such of the laws of the United States as it may deem appropriate to local conditions and requirements.

Article 4

The administering authority, in discharging the obligations of trusteeship in the trust territory, shall act in accordance with the Charter of the United Nations, and the provisions of this agreement. . . .

Article 5

In discharging its obligations . . . the administering authority shall ensure that the trust territory shall play its part, in accordance with the Charter of the United Nations, in the maintenance of international peace and security. To this end the administering authority shall be entitled:

1.   to establish naval, military and air bases and to erect fortifications in the trust territory;

2.   to station and employ armed forces in the territory; and

3.   to make use of volunteer forces, facilities and assistance from the trust territory in carrying out the obligations towards the Security Council undertaken in this regard by the administering authority, as well as for the local defense and the maintenance of law and order within the trust territory.

Article 6

In discharging its obligations . . . the administering authority shall:

1.   foster the development of such political institutions as are suited to the trust territory and shall promote the development of the inhabitants of the trust territory toward self-government or independence, as may be appropriate to the particular circumstances of the trust territory and its peoples and the freely expressed wishes of the peoples concerned; and to this end shall give to the inhabitants of the trust territory a progressively increasing share in the administrative services in the territory; shall develop their participation in government; shall give due recognition to the customs of the inhabitants in providing a system of law for the territory; and shall take other appropriate measures toward these ends;

2.   promote the economic advancement and self-sufficiency of the inhabitants and to this end shall regulate the use of natural resources; encourage the development of fisheries, agriculture, and

industries; protect the inhabitants against the loss of their lands and resources; and improve the means of transportation and communication;

3.   promote the social advancement of the inhabitants, and to this end shall protect the rights and fundamental freedoms of all elements of the population without discrimination; protect the health of the inhabitants; control the traffic in arms and ammunition, opium and other dangerous drugs, and alcohol and other spirituous beverages; and institute such other regulations as may be necessary to protect the inhabitants against social abuses; and

4.   promote the educational advancement of the inhabitants, and to this end shall take steps toward the establishment of a general system of elementary education; facilitate the vocational and cultural advancement of the population; and shall encourage qualified students to pursue higher education, including training on the professional level.

Dated April 2, 1947; 16 articles.   United Nations Security Council Resolution; *A Decade of American Foreign Policy: Basic Documents, 1941-49*, pp. 1031-35. For the text of the agreement see TIAS 1665; 12 Bevans, *Treaties and Other International Agreements,* 951-55. The agreement also provides for the personal freedoms, treatment, and citizenship of the people, applicability of American treaties, and restricted security areas.   Also see President Truman's Message to Congress requesting action to approve the agreement, July 3, 1947; *Papers of Presidents: Truman,* 1947, pp. 322-23, and President Truman's statement on signing the resolution, July 19, 1947, pp 346-47.   For the text of the congressional resolution, see P.L. 204, 80th Cong., 1st sess., 61 *U.S. Statutes at Large* 397, in *A Decade of American Foreign Policy, 1941-49,* pp. 1035-36.   Also see commentary in Marjorie M. Whiteman, *Digest of International Law,* III, 592-94.

499   PROMOTING SELF-DETERMINATION FOR THE MICRONESIAN ISLANDS

The principle of government by consent of the governed is the foundation of democracy.

Today, I urge the Congress to join me in taking a further step toward self-determination for the 93,000 Micronesian people who live in the Marianna, Caroline and Marshall Islands that comprise the Trust Territory of the Pacific Islands.   The United States administers this trust territory through a 1947 agreement with the United Nations.   Under that responsibility we have encouraged the Micronesians to participate fully in determining their own future and shaping their own free institutions.

I am sure the Congress shares my deep interest in the status and well-being of Micronesia.   Congress approved the original trusteeship agreement.   It has supported an intensive program to promote the political, economic, social and educational advancement of the islands.

In 1966, the people of the territory, acting through their popularly elected legislature, called upon the President of the United States to create a Commission to consider their future status.

I am happy to honor their request. The Joint Resolution I am submitting would provide for such a Commission.

Lyndon Johnson, letter to leaders of both houses of Congress, August 21, 1967; *Papers of Presidents: Johnson*, 1967, II, 797-98. For commentary during the Nixon administration, see *United States Foreign Policy*, 1969-1970, pp. 233-34; 1971, pp. 284-86; and 1972, pp. 111-12. Also see *Digest of United States Practice in International Law*, 1977, pp. 71-76.

*   *   *

[American policy goals] include:

-- detailing a procedure for the orderly political development of the territories;
-- providing opportunity for and a stimulus to their economic growth;
-- rationalizing the existing Federal-territorial financial relationship and improving local financial management;
-- enhancing territorial treatment under Federal programs; and
-- elevating the Federal organization for dealing with territorial matters. . . .

These measures will improve the attention given the territories. They will make explicit Interior's responsibilities for the Northern Marianna Islands but will not change the Department's responsibilities for the Trust Territory of the Pacific Islands prior to the termination of the Trusteeship.

The organizational arrangements for handling United States relations with the freely associated States of Micronesia after termination of the Trusteeship, however, will not be determined until the final character of our responsibilities with regard to those island States is fully defined through the agreements now being negotiated. . . .

In keeping with our fundamental policy of self-determination, all options for political development should be open to the people of the insular territories so long as their choices are implemented when economically feasible and in a manner that does not compromise the national security of the United States.

If the people of any of the territories wish to modify their current political status, they should express their aspirations to the Secretary of the Interior through their elected leaders, as is the case now. The Secretary, along with representatives of the appropriate Federal agencies, will in turn, consult with territorial leaders on the issues raised. Following such discussions, a full report will be submitted to the Congress, along with the Secretary's proposals and recommendations.

This procedure will permit an orderly development of the Federal-territorial relationship.

Jimmy Carter, Message to Congress on federal territorial policy, February 14, 1980; *Papers of Presidents: Carter*, 1980, pp. 318-19.

*   *   *

Representatives of the United States, the Marshall Islands Government, and the Federated States of Micronesia today initialed a Compact of Free Association, a basic document which will, when finally approved, authorize self-government for the 120,000 inhabitants of hundreds of islands ranged across 3,000 miles of the mid-Pacific and will also establish the terms of a unique, continuing, close relationship with the United States. The initialing also advances President Carter's goal, announced in 1977, of terminating in 1981 the United Nations Trusteeship Agreement. . . .

Today's initialing represents the virtual completion of a negotiating process that began in 1969. The Compact provides that the United States will retain plenary authority in defense and security matters and that three Micronesian entities--the Marshall Islands, the Federated States of Micronesia, and Palau--will acquire full internal self-government and authority over all aspects of their foreign relations other than those which the United States determines to be defense- and security-related. The Compact also sets forth the financial and other types of assistance which the United States will provide over a 15-year period and covers the many other realms--including environmental regulations, trade, finance, and taxation--in which the United States and Micronesia will remain linked. The Compact's aid and defense provisions continue for 15 years and thereafter, as may be mutually agreed. It also provides each of the Micronesian entities the option of unilateral termination should any of them later decide to seek full independence or any other political status. However, such unilateral termination would be subject to continuation of U.S. defense rights and economic assistance for their full terms.

During several months following today's initialing ceremony, negotiators for all of the governments involved will conclude their work on a dozen or more detailed subsidiary agreements covering such subjects as telecommunications, extradition, and military land-use and operating rights. Once these subsidiary agreements have been completed, the Compact of Free Association will be formally signed. At that point the Compact will be presented to the voters of Micronesia for approval by plebiscite and submitted to the United States Congress as a joint resolution for enactment into law. If the Compact is approved, the United States will present the completed arrangements to the United Nations and seek termination of the Trusteeship Agreement. The United States strategic trusteeship in Micronesia is the last of the 11 U.N. trusteeships established after World War II.

White House announcement concerning agreement between the United States and the Marshall Islands, October 31, 1980; *American Foreign Policy: Basic Documents,* 1977-1980, pp. 962-63.

29

Europe

The postwar policy of the United States has been consistently direct
ed toward the rebuilding of Europe and the rebirth of Europe's historic identity. The nations of the West have worked together for
peace and progress throughout Europe. From the very start, we
have taken the initiative by stating clear goals and areas of
negotiation.

We have sought a structure of European relations, tempering
rivalry with restraint, power with moderation, building upon the
traditional bonds that link us with old friends and reaching out to
forge new ties with former and potential adversaries.

Gerald Ford
Address, Helsinki, 1975

Shortly after World War II President Truman informed Congress: "Rapid
changes are taking place in Europe which affect our foreign policy and our
national security. . . . The United States is deeply concerned with the survival of
freedom in those nations. It is of vital importance that we act now, in order to
preserve the conditions under which we can achieve lasting peace based on
freedom and justice. The achievement of such a peace has been the great goal of
this nation." A few years later President Eisenhower proclaimed: "We should
do all we can to help and encourage the move toward a strong and united Europe."
Such statements--emphasizing freedom, peace, security, and unity--epitomize
contemporary American goals for Europe.

Perusal of policy documents reveals that since World War II--in addition
to special assistance to Greece and Turkey (see Truman Doctrine, Documents
111-112), the Marshall Plan and economic recovery and assistance (see Document 397), the German and Berlin questions (see Chapter 8), containment,
Western security and the North Atlantic Alliance (see Documents 306, 314-
322), and East-West relations (see Chapter 22), as well as such general subjects as trade and commerce (see Chapter 17, especially Documents 293-294,
296-299) and peacekeeping and the pacific settlement of disputes (see Chapter
15), the United States is concerned with a host of major and minor policy

issues.

Aside from the negotiation of the World War II peace treaties with Austria, Bulgaria, Hungary, Italy, and Rumania, and various crises in which the United States was not a primary participant (such as the Cyprus problem and Soviet military interventions to suppress anti-Communist liberalization in Hungary, 1956, and Czechoslovakia, 1968), these policy issues range from stabilizing the post-World War II territorial settlements to dealing with displaced persons and refugees; from Western unity and the reunification of free Europe to international trade, industrial development, financial credits, and American investments; from curtailing international terrorism (see Chapter 19) and drug smuggling to outer space exploration; and from the proposal to denuclearize central Europe to withdrawal of American postwar occupation troops, military contributions to European defense, mutual and balanced force reductions, and defense burden sharing. United States policy and interests also involve dozens of other matters, such as civil aviation, claims, customs, extradition, pacific settlement of disputes, shipping, space science, and telecommunications, many of which were made the subjects of scores of multilateral and bilateral treaties and agreements (for lists, see *Treaties in Force*).

The documents provided in this chapter are grouped in four categories: general goals, objectives, interests, and policies (Documents 500-504); unity and interdependence (Documents 505-510); United States-European partnership (Documents 511-514); and the Helsinki peace process (Documents 515-519). For documentation on East-West relations, see Chapter 22.

GENERAL GOALS, OBJECTIVES, INTERESTS, AND POLICIES

5 0 0   AMERICAN CONCERN WITH EUROPEAN ECONOMIC AND SECURITY AFFAIRS

During these meetings, the continuing interest of the United States in European affairs was expressed to the other governments and also our genuine desire to work on the economic problems ahead in cooperation with Canada and the Western European countries. There has been some concern in Western Europe that, despite the North Atlantic Treaty, the concern of this country with European affairs would slacken after 1952.
. . .

We can no longer afford the luxury of regarding these problems as purely national in character. The additional economic strength which will flow from a cooperative approach is required to meet the cost of defense, to maintain and improve standards of living, and to provide essential assistance to other free nations of the world in their development. A new attitude is required of each of us, for we must work out solutions to these problems which will strengthen the community as a whole and advance the welfare of us all.

Success in this venture will be of the greatest practical significance, both for the economic benefits it can bring to every one of us and because the security of free institutions is directly related to their economic health and vitality.

There were many other evidences of the necessity of avoiding purely unilateral treatment of problems which affect more than one state even though one may have a primary concern in their solution.

Dean Acheson, address, to members of the Senate and the House of Representatives, May 31, 1950; *American Foreign Policy: Basic Documents, 1950-1955,* I, 1436. He also discussed the Atlantic Community, defending the North Atlantic area, and the principle of balanced collective forces. Also see President Truman's Special Message to Congress on the Threat to the Freedom of Europe, March 17, 1948; *Papers of Presidents: Truman,* 1948, pp. 182-86.

501   AMERICAN ASSISTANCE TO EUROPE AFTER WORLD WAR II

Second: If the United States had to try to stand alone against a Soviet-dominated world, it would destroy the life we know and the ideals we hold dear. Our allies are essential to us, just as we are essential to them. The more shoulders there are to bear the burden the lighter it will be.

Third: The things we believe in most deeply are under relentless attack. We have the great responsibility of saving the basic moral and spiritual values of our civilization. We have started out well, with a program for peace that is unparalleled in history. If we believe in ourselves and the faith we profess, we will stick to the job.

In Europe we must go on helping our friends and allies to build up their military forces. This means we must send weapons in large volume to our European allies. I have directed that weapons for Europe be given a very high priority. Economic aid is necessary, too, to supply the margin of difference between success and failure in making Europe a strong partner in our joint defense.

In the long run we want to see Europe freed from any dependence on our aid. Our European allies want that just as much as we do. The steps that are now being taken to build European unity should help bring that about. Five European countries are pooling their coal and steel production under the Schuman plan. Work is going forward on the merger of European national forces on the Continent into a single army. These great projects should become realities in 1952.

We should do all we can to help and encourage the move toward a strong and united Europe.

Harry Truman, Annual Message on the State of the Union, January 9, 1952; *American Foreign Policy: Basic Documents,* 1950-1955, I, 30-31. For the Marshall Plan, the European Recovery Program, 1947, and the Mutual Defense Assistance Program, 1949, see Documents 397-398.

5 0 2   UNITED STATES AND EUROPE--COMMON INTERESTS AND VENTURES

The United States has no policy *for* the people of Europe, but we do have a policy *toward* the people of Europe. And we do have common hopes and common objectives shared with most of the people of Europe. Answers to our common problems must emerge from the consent of free countries, and that consent, in turn, will be based on discussion and debate and respect for the ideas and the proposals of all. But there must be progress. A Chinese proverb says there are many paths up the mountain but the view from the top is always the same. We are always ready to look for a better or easier path, but we intend to climb to the summit.

First, we must all seek to assist in increasing the unity of Europe as a key to Western strength and a barrier to resurgent and erosive nationalism.

Second, we must all work to multiply in number and intimacy the ties between North America and Europe. For we shape an Atlantic civilization with an Atlantic destiny.

Third, we must all make sure that the Federal Republic of Germany is always treated as an honorable partner in the affairs of the West. Germany has labored to build a stable and a free society in complete loyalty to European unity and to Atlantic partnership. . . . In particular, our friends and comrades throughout Germany deserve assurance from their allies that there shall be no acceptance of the lasting threat to peace which is the forced division of Germany. No one seeks to end this grim and dangerous injustice by force. But there can be no stable peace in Europe while one part of Germany is denied the basic right to choose freely its own destiny and to choose, without threat to anyone, reunion with the Germans in the Federal Republic.

Fourth, those of us who are ready to proceed in common ventures must decide to go forward together, always with due deliberation, with due respect for the interests of others, and with an open door for those who may join later. We shall always seek agreement. We shall never insist on unanimity. This is the course which has brought fruitful results and almost every major advance in the 20 years since World War II.

Lyndon Johnson, address, Georgetown University, December 3, 1964; *American Foreign Policy: Current Documents,* 1964, pp. 499-500.

5 0 3   AMERICAN OBJECTIVES FOR EUROPE

Europe has been at peace since 1945. But it is a restless peace that's shadowed by the threat of violence.

Europe is partitioned. An unnatural line runs through the heart of a very great and a very proud nation. History warns us that until this harsh division has been resolved, peace in Europe will never be secure.

We must turn to one of the great unfinished tasks of our generation-- and that unfinished task is making Europe whole again.

Our purpose is not to overturn other governments, but to help the people of Europe to achieve together:

-- a continent in which the peoples of Eastern and Western Europe work shoulder to shoulder together for the common good;

-- a continent in which alliances do not confront each other in bitter hostility, but instead provide a framework in which West and East can act together in order to assure the security of all.

In a restored Europe, Germany can and will be united.

This remains a vital purpose of American policy. . . .

We must move ahead on three fronts:

-- First, to modernize NATO and strengthen other Atlantic alliances.

-- Second, to further the integration of the Western European community.

-- Third, to quicken progress in East-West relations.

Lyndon Johnson, remarks, National Conference of Editorial Writers, New York, October 7, 1966; *Papers of Presidents: Johnson,* 1966, II, 1126 The previous year he stressed that the United States sought reconciliation rather than revenge, unity rather than nationalism, prosperity rather than depression, firmness rather than appeasement, and partnership rather than isolation; see his address, May 7, 1965, in *Papers of Presidents: Johnson,* 1965, I, 507.

504 AMERICAN-EUROPEAN PURPOSE AND BURDEN SHARING

In the 1940's and into the 1950's, Western Europe was prostrate-- politically, economically, and militarily. The United States, preeminent in the world, had only just emerged from its isolationist tradition. In this environment, our allies shifted the responsibility for major decisions to us. In their eyes, the overriding purpose of the new arrangements--for defense, economic policy, and foreign policy--was to link us to Europe in tangible ways on a long term peacetime basis. They therefore deferred to our prescriptions and welcomed our lead--even on formulas for European integration.

Both to us and to them the advantages of European unification were unambiguous. It would help dispel the internecine hatreds of the recent past; it would maximize the effectiveness of U.S. assistance; it would hasten Western Europe's political and economic recovery and thereby enhance its security. These were common interests, and no inconsistency was seen between European unity and broader Atlantic unity. Cooperation came so easily that it was widely assumed for years in the United States that a strong and united Europe would readily take up a large part of the American burden, while still accepting American leadership.

But a self-respecting nation or group of nations will take up a burden only if it sees it as its own burden. By the 1960's Europe was in a position to do more for itself and for the Alliance. Nevertheless, old habits on both sides of the Atlantic persisted and inhibited the development of a more balanced relationship.

Richard Nixon, *U.S. Foreign Policy for the 1970's: The Emerging Structure of Peace* (1972), p. 39. Also see his report for 1971, p. 29, and for 1973, pp. 83-84.

UNITY AND INTERDEPENDENCE

The United States has been a consistent supporter of post-World War II European unity, including not only concord and cooperation within the Atlantic alliance, but also unity between West and East and the unification and confederation of Western Europe. The latter, sparked in part by the Robert Schuman, Rene Pleven, and Jean Monnet Plans of the 1950's, involved the creation and functioning of a series of integrating arrangements: the Council of Europe, the European Coal and Steel (ECSC), Economic (EEC), and Atomic Energy (EURATOM) Communities, the European Development Fund (EDF), the European Free Trade Association (EFTA), the European Payments Union (EPU), the Organization for European Economic Cooperation (OEEC) to implement the Marshall Plan, and the Western European Union (WEU) to succeed the Brussels Pact defense arrangement. On the other hand, in 1961, on American initiative, the Organization for Economic Cooperation and Development (OECD), which the United States joined as a full-fledged member, superseded the OEEC (see TIAS 4891; 12 *U.S. Treaties* 1728-59).

The documents contained in this section are devoted largely to general statements concerned with the goals and essentiality of European unity, the American role in, and commitment to, such unity, and President Kennedy's proposal for a declaration of interdependence of the United States with a united Europe.

5 0 5   GOAL OF EUROPEAN UNITY

In some areas, this has meant primarily efforts to develop the underlying conditions of the life of the people, so that there could be an orderly development toward freedom and progress. In other areas, this has meant dealing with outright aggression by force of arms. . . .

With this setting in mind, I come back to what has been happening in Europe. Here all that has been going on since 1945--the programs of relief, of economic recovery, of bold and courageous action to build stable governments free from foreign domination, and the growth toward vigorous military establishments capable of deterring attack--all these things have brought our friends in Europe to the threshold of the larger conception of the unity of all Western Europe.

European unity has been a goal for which men have striven for centuries, by diplomacy and by force. What is important about this effort we see before us now is that it will bring together, in free and voluntary association, in practical institutions growing out of the urgent necessities of the times, much of Western Europe. . . .

What has been going on in Western Europe is a totally different thing. It will have strength because it meets human needs and desires. It has been a process of practical growth, moving haltingly at times, because it has sought to accommodate real conflicts by negotiation and peaceful persuasion.

The margin between success and failure in this operation has sometimes been a narrow one. The difficulties are deep and real. Our allies have been grappling with critical economic problems. They have wrestled with ancient rivalries and painful memories of recent conflicts.

Despite all this, they have come now within sight of the goal, and the thing that is at stake at this moment is whether they and we will be able to go forward to the realization of this conception. That is the issue.

Dean Acheson, address, American Society of Newspaper Editors, Washington, April 19, 1952; *American Foreign Policy: Basic Documents, 1950-1955,* I, 35. For a more comprehensive and concrete discussion of his views on this matter, see his remarks before the North Atlantic Council, Paris, December 18, 1952, pp. 1624-29.

506   SHORT-RANGE PRESAGING LONG-RANGE UNITY FOR EUROPE

All the measures of collective security, resistance to aggression, and the building of defenses, constitute the first requirement for the survival and progress of the free world. But . . . they are interwoven with the necessity of taking steps to create and maintain economic and social progress in the free nations. There can be no military strength except where there is economic capacity to back it. There can be no freedom where there is economic chaos or social collapse. For these reasons our national policy has included a wide range of economic measures.

In Europe the grand design of the Marshall plan permitted the people of Britain and France and Italy and a half dozen other countries, with help from the United States, to lift themselves from stagnation and find again the path of rising production, rising incomes, rising standards of living. The situation was changed almost overnight by the Marshall plan; the people of Europe have a renewed hope and vitality, and they are able to carry a share of the military defense of the free world that would have been impossible a few years ago.

Now the countries of Europe are moving rapidly toward political and economic unity, changing the map of Europe in more hopeful ways than it has been changed for 500 years. Customs unions, European economic institutions like the Schuman plan, the movement toward European political integration, the European Defense Community, all are signs of practical and effective growth toward greater common strength and unity. The countries of Western Europe, including the free Republic of Germany are working together, and the whole free world is the gainer.

It sometimes happens, in the course of history, that steps taken to meet an immediate necessity serve an ultimate purpose greater than may be apparent at the time. This, I believe, is the meaning of what has been going on in Europe under the threat of aggression. The free nations there, with our help, have been drawing together in defense of their free institutions. In so doing they have laid the foundations of a unity that will endure as a major creative force beyond the exigencies of this period of history. We may, at this close range, be but dimly aware of the creative surge this movement represents, but I believe it to be of historic importance. I believe its benefits will survive long after Communist tyranny is nothing but an unhappy memory.

Harry Truman, Annual State of the Union Message to Congress, January 7, 1953; *American Foreign Policy: Basic Documents,* 1950-1955, I, 50.

507 FREE EUROPE'S UNITY ESSENTIAL TO PRESERVE ITS HERITAGE AND PROMOTE ITS PROGRESS AND SECURITY

In Europe, we ask that enlightened and inspired leaders of the Western nations strive with renewed vigor to make the unity of their peoples a reality. Only as free Europe unitedly marshals its strength can it effectively safeguard, even with our help, its spiritual and cultural heritage.

*   *   *

Fifth. Our policy will be designed to foster the advent of practical unity in Western Europe. The nations of that region have contributed notably to the effort of sustaining the security of the free world. From the jungles of Indochina and Malaya to the northern shores of Europe, they have vastly improved their defensive strength. Where called upon to do so, they have made costly and bitter sacrifices to hold the line of freedom.

But the problem of security demands closer cooperation among the nations of Europe than has been known to date. Only a more closely integrated economic and political system can provide the greatly increased economic strength needed to maintain both necessary military readiness and respectable living standards.

Europe's enlightened leaders have long been aware of these facts. All the devoted work that has gone into the Schuman plan, the European Army, and the Strasbourg Conference has testified to their vision and determination. These achievements are the more remarkable when we realize that each of them has marked a victory--for France and Germany alike--over the divisions that in the past have brought tragedy to these two great nations and to the world.

The needed unity of Western Europe manifestly cannot be manufactured from without; it can only be created from within. But it is right and necessary that we encourage Europe's leaders by informing them of the high value we place upon the earnestness of their efforts toward this goal. Real progress will be conclusive evidence to the American people that our material sacrifices in the cause of collective security are matched by essential political, economic, and military accomplishments in Western Europe.

                 *   *   *

But effective cooperation is not easily accomplished among free nations. Permit me in one illustration to point up the difficulty, among free peoples, of progress toward this type of union.

The statesmen of Western Europe have long been aware that only in broad and effective cooperation among the nations of that region can true security for all be found. They know that real unification of the separate countries there would make their combined 250 million highly civilized people a mighty pillar of free strength in the modern world. A free United States of Europe would be strong in the skills of its people, adequately endowed with material resources, and rich in their common cultural and artistic heritage. It would be a highly prosperous community.

Without such unification the history of the past half century in Europe could go on in dreary repetition, possibly to the ultimate destruction of all the values those people themselves hold most dear. With unification, a new sun of hope, security and confidence would shine for Europe, for us, and for the free world.

Another stumbling block to European unity is the failure of populations as a whole to grasp the long-term political, economic and security advantage of union. These are matters that do not make for a soul-stirring address on a national holiday. They can be approached only in thought, in wisdom--almost, I think we may say, in prayer.

Dwight Eisenhower, Inaugural Address, January 20, 1953, in *Papers of Presidents,* 1953, p. 6; Message on the State of the Union, February 2, 1953, pp. 14-15; and address, Baylor University, Waco, Texas, May 25, 1956, in *Papers of Presidents: Eisenhower,* 1956, p. 531.

508 PROPOSED DECLARATION OF INTERDEPENDENCE WITH UNITED EUROPE

The theory of independence--as old as man himself--was not invented in this hall, but it was in this hall that the theory became a practice--that the word went out to all the world that "The God who gave us life, gave us liberty at the same time."

And today this nation--conceived in revolution, nurtured in liberty, matured in independence--has no intention of abdicating its leadership in that worldwide movement for independence to any nation or society committed to systematic human suppression. . . .

That spirit is today most clearly seen across the Atlantic Ocean. The nations of Western Europe, long divided by feuds more bitter than any which existed among the Thirteen Colonies, are joining together, seeking, as our forefathers sought, to find freedom in diversity and unity in strength.

The United States looks on this vast new enterprise with hope and admiration. We do not regard a strong and united Europe as a rival but as a partner. To aid its progress has been the basic objective of our foreign policy for 17 years.   We believe that a united Europe will be capable of playing a greater role in the common defense, of responding more generously to the needs of poorer nations, of joining with the United States and others in lowering trade barriers, resolving problems of currency and commodities, and developing coordinated policies in all other economic, diplomatic, and political areas.   We see in such a Europe a partner with whom we could deal on a basis of full equality in all the great and burdensome tasks of building and defending a community of free nations.

It would be premature at this time to do more than to indicate the high regard with which we view the formation of this partnership.   The first order of business is for our European friends to go forward in forming the more perfect union which will some day make this partnership possible. . . .

But I will say here and now on this day of independence that the United States will be ready for a "Declaration of Interdependence," that we will be prepared to discuss with a United Europe the ways and means of forming a concrete Atlantic partnership, a mutually beneficial partnership between the new union now emerging in Europe and the old American Union founded here 175 years ago.

All this will not be completed in a year, but let the world know it is our goal. . . .

Acting on our own by ourselves, we cannot establish justice throughout the world.   We cannot insure its domestic tranquility, or provide for its common defense, or promote its general welfare, or secure the blessings of liberty to ourselves and our posterity.   But joined with other free nations, we can do all this and more.   We can assist the developing nations to throw off the yoke of poverty.   We can balance our worldwide trade and payments at the highest possible level of growth.   We can mount a deterrent powerful enough to deter any aggression, and ultimately we can help achieve a world of law and free choice, banishing the world of war and coercion.

For the Atlantic partnership of which I speak would not look inward only, preoccupied with its own welfare and advancement.   It must look outward to cooperate with all nations in meeting their common concern.   It would serve as a nucleus for the eventual union of all free men--those who are now free and those who are avowing that some day they will be free.

John Kennedy, address, Independence Hall, Philadelphia, July 4, 1962; *American Foreign Policy: Current Documents,* 1962, pp. 552-54.

509   ROLE OF UNITED STATES IN SUPPORTING IDEAL OF EUROPEAN UNITY

We can also say that . . . the United States has indicated its continuing support of the Alliance--the Atlantic Alliance--and that we have also indicated our support of the concept and ideal of European unity.

In addition, we have indicated that we recognize our limitations insofar as European unity is concerned. Americans cannot unify Europe. Europeans must do so. And we should not become involved in differences among Europeans in which our vital interests are not involved.

Richard Nixon, statement, news conference, March 4, 1969; *Papers of Presidents: Nixon,* 1969, p. 180. Also see his reports on *U.S. Foreign Policy for the 1970's,* 1971, pp. 25-31; 1972, pp. 39-42; and 1973, pp. 78-81.

5 1 0   AMERICAN CONTINUING COMMITMENT TO EUROPEAN UNITY

. . . I have stressed the importance of democratic political values, and the steps needed to defend them; the economic challenges we face in our relations with the developing world, and the need to cope with problems of our own. We must also open our hearts to improve the chances for peace, while always maintaining the strong right arm of our defense.

I have repeated these themes because they need repetition, because they express to the world the values my Nation most deeply holds.

I am proud today to add another--that the United States welcomes a strong, united Europe as a common force for the values our peoples share.

The United States will do its part to work with you. . . .

Finally, in stressing our commitment to European unity, I look forward to continuing a close and productive association between the United States and the European Community in the years ahead. And I can think of no more fitting tribute to what you are doing than to cite the words of Jean Monnet, the father of European unity: "You are not making a coalition of states; you are uniting peoples."

Jimmy Carter, address, Commission of the European Communities, Brussels, January 6, 1978; *American Foreign Policy: Basic Documents,* 1977-1980, pp. 513-14.

PARTNERSHIP WITH EUROPE

Whereas unity and unification were major American objectives for Europe into the 1960s, since the Kennedy administration emphasis has shifted, in part, to the concept of United States-European partnership--within the North Atlantic Alliance, in East-West relations, and in the field of economic development in Europe and in North-South relations. The documents that follow emphasize the effort to develop partnership, and its essence, value, and results.

5 1 1   EFFORT TO DEVELOP PARTNERSHIP WITH EUROPE

The second area of continuing effort is the development of Atlantic partnership with a stronger and a more unified Europe. Having begun this policy when peril was great, we will not now abandon it as success moves closer. We worked for a stronger and more prosperous Europe, and Europe is strong and prosperous today because of our work and beyond our expectation.

We have supported a close partnership with a more unified Europe and in the past 15 years more peaceful steps have been taken in this direction than have been taken at any time in our history.

The pursuit of this goal, like the pursuit of any large and worthy cause, will not be easy or will not be untroubled. But the realities of the modern world teach that increased greatness and prosperity demand increased unity and partnership.

The underlying forces of European life are eroding old barriers and they are dissolving old suspicions. Common institutions are expanding common interests. National boundaries continue to fade under the impact of travel and commerce and communication. A new generation is coming of age, unscarred by old hostilities or old ambitions, thinking of themselves as Europeans, their values shaped by a common Western culture.

These forces and the steadfast effort of all who share common goals will shape the future. And unity based on hope will ultimately prove stronger than unity based on fear.

We realize that sharing the burden of leadership requires us to share the responsibilities of power.

Lyndon Johnson, remarks, Associated Press, New York, April 20, 1964; *Papers of Presidents: Johnson,* 1963-1964, pp. 496-97. Also see President Kennedy's reference to an American-European partnership in Document 508. Concepts of both unity and partnership were expressed as early as 1952 by President Truman; see Document 501.

5 1 2   ESSENCE OF PARTNERSHIP WITH EUROPE

None of us has sought--or will seek--domination over others. We have resisted the temptation to serve only our own interests. We have been successful because we have acted in a wider interest than our own alone. Thus the European nations have found strength and prosperity in building communities that stretch beyond old frontiers. The United States has committed its resources to European reconstruction and its military strength to European defense. America has steadily sought the strength of European unity rather than to exploit the weakness of European division. Our policy has had a single aim--to restore the vitality, the safety, and the integrity of free Europe. And with our help, Europe is better able to resist domination--from within or without--than ever before.

There are some efforts today to replace partnership with suspicion, and the drive toward unity with a policy of division.

The peoples of the Atlantic will not return to that narrow nationalism which has torn and bloodied the fabric of our society for generations. Every accomplishment of the past has been built on common action and increasing unity. . . .

Of course there will be differences among us, but they can be resolved through reason founded on respect.

Of course there will be difficulties, but they can be overcome by determination founded on belief.

Of course there will be dangers, but they can be faced by unity founded on experience.

So let us therefore continue the task we have begun, attentive to counsel but unmoved by any who seek to turn us aside. We will go all together if we can, but if one of us cannot join in a common venture, it will not stand in the way of the rest of us. Each of our nations will, of course, respect and honor the achievements, and the culture, and the dignity of its neighbors. But we do this better joined in common trust than divided by suspicion. For we do have a civilization to build.

Lyndon Johnson, address, broadcast to Europe, May 7, 1965; *American Foreign Policy: Current Document*, 1965, p. 437. Also see his reference to partnership in note for Document 503.

513 ADVANTAGE AND AGENDA FOR PARTNERSHIP WITH EUROPE

The peace of Europe is crucial to the peace of the world. This truth, a lesson learned at a terrible cost twice in the Twentieth Century, is a central principle of United States foreign policy. For the foreseeable future, Europe must be the cornerstone of the structure of a durable peace.

Since 1945, the nations of Western Europe and North America have built together an alliance and a mutual respect worthy of the values and heritage we share. Our partnership is founded not merely on a common perception of common dangers but on a shared vision of a better world. . . .

*   *   *

The agenda for the future of American relations with Europe is implicit in the statement of the issues we face together:

-- The evolution of a mature partnership reflecting the vitality and the independence of Western European nations;

-- the continuation of genuine consultation with our allies on the nature of the threats to alliance security, on maintenance of a common and credible strategy, and on an appropriate and sustainable level of forces;

-- the continuation of genuine consultations with our allies on the mutual interests affected by the U.S.-Soviet talks on strategic arms limitation;

-- the development of a European-American understanding on our common purposes and respective roles in seeking a peaceful and stable order in all of Europe;

-- the expansion of allied and worldwide cooperation in facing the common social and human challenges of modern societies.

*   *   *

Throughout the postwar period, the United States has supported the concept of a unified Western Europe. We recognized that such a Europe might be more difficult to deal with, but we foresaw manifold advantages. Unity would replace the devastating nationalist rivalries of the past. It would strengthen Europe's economic recovery and expand Europe's potential contributions to the free world. We believed that ultimately a highly cohesive Western Europe would relieve the United States of many burdens. We expected that unity would not be limited to economic integration, but would include a significant political dimension. We assumed, perhaps too uncritically, that our basic interests would be assured by our long history of cooperation, by our common cultures and our political similarities.

Richard Nixon, *U.S. Foreign Policy for the 1970's: A New Strategy for Peace* (1970), pp. 27 and 40, and *U.S. Foreign Policy for the 1970's: Shaping a Durable Peace* (1973), p. 78.

5 1 4   EXPECTATIONS AND RESULTS OF PARTNERSHIP WITH EUROPE

More than three decades ago the United States and the nations of Western Europe joined together to rebuild a devastated continent and to create a military alliance to protect freedom.

On both sides of the Atlantic, those who fashioned the Marshall Plan and worked to create NATO possessed a vision of a strong America and a strong Europe bound by common interests. From this vision, they created a self-renewing partnership that derives continuing vitality from the values and hopes that we share.

We have passed through a particularly difficult period during the 1970's. But we have navigated these turbulent waters. Although the course ahead remains demanding, the progress we have made should give us great confidence in our future.

For the first time in its history, all members of the NATO alliance are democracies.

NATO is strong and growing stronger.

We have not only resisted the worst protectionist pressures in a generation; we are working together to shape a healthier and more open world trading system.

We have established a pattern of closer consultation on economic and security matters than at any point in recent history.

European integration is proceeding, confirming our belief that a strong Europe is good for a strong America.

And we are moving toward more normal relations with the nations of Eastern Europe. Progress toward this goal has reflected our support for full implementation of the Helsinki Final Act and recognition of the sovereignty and independence of the nations of this area.

Cyrus Vance, address, London, December 9, 1978; *American Foreign Policy: Basic Documents,* 1977-1980, p. 516.

HELSINKI PEACE PROCESS

After nearly two years of intensive negotiations, the Conference on Security and Cooperation in Europe (CSCE), held in Helsinki, adopted its "Final Act" on August 1, 1975. It was signed by the United States, Canada, and thirty-three European nations--including the North Atlantic powers, Warsaw Pact members, and thirteen neutral and nonaligned countries. This culminated an extended process commenced in the 1950's, during which various European security plans were proposed. Only after the status quo of Germany and Berlin was accepted by the East and West in the early 1970's, which ratified the boundaries between the two Germanys and Poland, was progress possible on an overarching agreement.

The Final Act is not a formal treaty or agreement and, therefore, is technically not a binding commitment, but it has been defined as an agreed statement of purpose and policy or a summary of consensus of the participants in the conference and it provides evidence of customary international law (see *Digest of United States Practice in International Law* (1980), p. 255). It consists of two basic instruments--a "Declaration on Principles Guiding Relations Between Participating States" and a "Document on Confidence-Building Measures and Certain Aspects of Security and Disarmament" (Document 517). Substantively, the accord consists of four segments or "baskets": questions relating to security in Europe; cooperation in economic, scientific, technical, and environmental affairs; cooperation in humanitarian matters, including human rights, culture, education, and the exchange of persons and information; and the holding of review conferences to continue the multilateral process initiated at Helsinki.

To summarize, the Declaration specifically addresses such principles as the sovereign equality of nations, the inviolability of frontiers and territorial integrity (accepting the post-World War II status quo), equal rights and self-determination, nonintervention in internal affairs, refraining from the use of force, fulfillment of obligations under international law, respect for human rights and fundamental freedoms, cooperation in a number of fields, and peaceful change and the peaceful settlement of disputes.

This section provides documents concerned with preconference plans and preparatory negotiations (Document 515); the Helsinki Conference, including its Final Act (Documents 516-518); and a subsequent review of the Helsinki peace process (Document 519). For additional commentary, see *Historic Documents,* 1975, pp. 559-70, and *Digest of United States Practice in International Law,* 1975, pp. 7-13, 190-93, 236-38, 271, 326-27, 591-94, and for the follow-up conference in Belgrade, 1977-1978, see volume for 1978, pp. 430-36, 1560-61.

515   PRE-HELSINKI CONFERENCE PLANS AND PREPARATORY NEGOTIATIONS

The Conference on Security and Cooperation in Europe. In March 1969, the Warsaw Pact revived its proposal to convene a European Security Conference. Such a conference would be largely symbolic; its purpose would be to confirm the territorial and political status quo in Europe. There was some feeling in the West that this proposal should be accepted. . . .

Preparatory talks began last November to find out whether there was sufficient common ground to justify a conference of Foreign Ministers. A provisional agenda is being developed, which the Foreign Ministers could consider. Progress thus far suggests that the conference can be convened this year and that it may be possible to move forward on several important questions.

-- The participants will address certain principles of security and co-operation. If all European countries subscribe to common principles of conduct, and carry them out in practice, there could be a further relaxation of tensions. Certain military security matters designed to improve confidence will also be considered.

-- The conference would be an appropriate forum to discuss practical cooperation in economic, cultural exchange, science, and technology, on which there has already been progress in bilateral relations.

-- The conference can consider how to facilitate contacts among the peoples of Europe and how to encourage countries to exchange ideas and information. . . .

Mutual and Balanced Force Reductions. The exchanges leading up to the conference also acted as a bridge to negotiations on a more specific and central security issue--mutual and balanced force reductions in Central Europe. The prospects for arms control in Europe are obviously linked to political improvements between East and West. Throughout the 1950's and 1960's there were proposals for arms control in Europe. But it was unrealistic to expect to negotiate a reduction of forces--for example, in Germany, where there were almost continuous crises over Berlin. Moreover, the reduction of military forces in Central Europe was related to the strategic balance between the United States and Soviet Union and to the political situation within the Warsaw Pact. . . .

Our goal must be agreement on basic security principles. We must meet individual national concerns within a common concept of security, and forthrightly address the question of how to maintain our security at reduced force levels. The issues are highly sensitive, and Alliance discussions will be painstaking and difficult.

The United States is engaged in the most serious consultations with our allies to prepare for negotiations later this year. Force reductions in Central Europe are, of course, an element of the complex of U.S.-Soviet relations. The U.S. and Soviet forces are comparable in that they are not indigenous to Central Europe and might be candidates for reduction.

Richard Nixon, *U.S. Foreign Policy for the 1970's: Shaping a Durable Peace* (1973), pp. 88-91. For his comment on the limitations of the role of the United States and the Soviet Union, see pp. 38-39.

516   AMERICAN POSITION AT HELSINKI CONFERENCE

The nations assembled here have kept the general peace in Europe for 30 years. Yet there have been too many narrow escapes from major conflict. There remains, to this day, the urgent issue of how to construct a just and lasting peace for all peoples. . . .

I have come to Helsinki as a spokesman for a nation whose vision has always been forward, whose people have always demanded that the future be brighter than the past, and whose united will and purpose at this hour is to work diligently to promote peace and progress not only for ourselves but for all mankind.

I am simply here to say to my colleagues: We owe it to our children, to the children of all continents, not to miss any opportunity, not to malinger for one minute, not to spare ourselves or allow others to shirk in the monumental task of building a better and a safer world.

The American people, like the people of Europe, know well that mere assertions of good will, passing changes in the political mood of governments, laudable declarations of principles are not enough. But if we proceed with care, with commitment to real progress, there is now an opportunity to turn our peoples' hopes into realities. . . .

Military competition must be controlled. Political competition must be restrained. Crises must not be manipulated or exploited for unilateral advantages that could lead us again to the brink of war. The process of negotiation must be sustained, not at a snail's pace, but with demonstrated enthusiasm and visible progress. . . .

The era of confrontation that has divided Europe since the end of the Second World War may now be ending. There is a new perception and a shared perception of a change for the better, away from confrontation and toward new possibilities for secure and mutually beneficial cooperation. That is what we all have been saying here. I welcome and I share these hopes for the future. . . .

The documents produced here represent compromises, like all international negotiations, but these principles we have agreed upon are more than the lowest common denominator of governmental positions.

They affirm the most fundamental human rights: liberty of thought, conscience, and faith; the exercise of civil and political rights; the rights of minorities.

They call for a freer flow of information, ideas, and people; greater scope for the press, cultural and educational exchange, family reunification, the right to travel and to marriage between nationals of different states; and for the protection of the priceless heritage of our diverse cultures.

They offer wide areas for greater cooperation: trade, industrial production, science and technology, the environment, transportation, health, space, and the oceans.

They reaffirm the basic principles of relations between states: non-intervention, sovereign equality, self-determination, territorial integrity, inviolability of frontiers, and the possibility of change by peaceful means.

The United States gladly subscribes to this document because we subscribe to every one of these principles. . . .

To our fellow participants in this Conference: My presence here symbolizes my country's vital interest in Europe's future. Our future is bound with yours. Our economic well-being, as well as our security, is linked increasingly with yours. The distance of geography is bridged by our common heritage and our common destiny. The United States, therefore, intends to participate fully in the affairs of Europe and in turning the results of this Conference into a living reality.

Gerald Ford, address, Conference on Security and Cooperation in Europe, Helsinki, August 1, 1975; *Papers of Presidents: Ford,* 1975, II, 1074-79.

5 1 7 HELSINKI CONFERENCE ON SECURITY AND COOPERATION IN EUROPE-- FINAL ACT, 1975

DECLARATION ON PRINCIPLES GUIDING RELATIONS

Between Participating States

I. Sovereign equality, respect for the rights inherent in sovereignty

The participating States will respect each other's sovereign equality and individuality as well as all the rights inherent in and encompassed by its sovereignty, including in particular the right of every State to juridical equality, to territorial integrity and to freedom and political independence. They will also respect each other's right freely to choose and develop its political, social, economic and cultural systems as well as its right to determine its laws and regulations.

Within the framework of international law, all the participating States have equal rights and duties. They will respect each other's right to define and conduct as it wishes its relations with other States in accordance with international law and in the spirit of the present Declaration. They consider that their frontiers can be changed, in accordance with international law, by peaceful means and by agreement. They also have the right to belong or not to belong to international organizations, to be or not to be a party to bilateral or multilateral treaties including the right to be or not to be a party to treaties of alliance; they also have the right to neutrality.

II. Refraining from the threat or use of force

The participating States will refrain in their mutual relations, as well as in their international relations in general, from the threat or use of force against the territorial integrity or political independence of any State, or in any other manner inconsistent with the purposes of the United Nations and with the present Declaration. No consideration may be invoked to serve to warrant resort to the threat or use of force in contravention of this principle. . . .

III. Inviolability of frontiers

The participating States regard as inviolable all one another's frontiers as well as the frontiers of all States in Europe and therefore they will refrain now and in the future from assaulting those frontiers.

Accordingly, they will also refrain from any demand for, or act of, seizure and usurpation of part or all of the territory of any participating State.

IV. Territorial integrity of States

The participating States will respect the territorial integrity of each of the participating States.

Accordingly, they will refrain from any action inconsistent with the purposes and principles of the Charter of the United Nations against the territorial integrity, political independence or the unity of any participating State, and in particular from any such action constituting a threat or use of force. . . .

V. Peaceful settlement of disputes

The participating States will settle disputes among them by peaceful means in such a manner as not to endanger international peace and security, and justice.

They will endeavour in good faith and a spirit of cooperation to reach a rapid and equitable solution on the basis of international law.

For this purpose they will use such means as negotiation, enquiry, mediation, conciliation, arbitration, judicial settlement or other peaceful means of their own choice including any settlement procedure agreed to in advance of disputes to which they are parties. . . .

VI. Non-intervention in internal affairs

The participating States will refrain from any intervention, direct or indirect, individual or collective, in the internal or external affairs falling within the domestic jurisdiction of another participating State, regardless of their mutual relations.

They will accordingly refrain from any form of armed intervention or threat of such intervention against another participating State. . . .

VII. Respect for human rights and fundamental freedoms, including the freedom of thought, conscience, religion or belief

The participating States will respect human rights and fundamental freedoms, including the freedom of thought, conscience, religion or belief, for all without distinction as to race, sex, language or religion.

They will promote and encourage the effective exercise of civil, political, economic, social, cultural and other rights and freedoms all of which derive from the inherent dignity of the human person and are essential for his free and full development. . . .

VIII. Equal rights and self-determination of peoples

The participating States will respect the equal rights of peoples and their right to self-determination, acting at all times in conformity with the purposes and principles of the Charter of the United Nations and with the relevant norms of international law, including those relating to territorial integrity of States.

By virtue of the principle of equal rights and self-determination of peoples, all peoples always have the right, in full freedom, to determine, when and as they wish, their internal and external political status, without external interference, and to pursue as they wish their political, economic, social and cultural development. . . .

* * *

DOCUMENT ON CONFIDENCE-BUILDING MEASURES

General Considerations

Having considered the views expressed on various subjects related to the strengthening of security in Europe through joint efforts aimed at promoting detente and disarmament, the participating States, when engaged in such efforts, will, in this context, proceed, in particular, from the following essential considerations:

-- The complementary nature of the political and military aspects of security;
-- The interrelation between the security of each participating State and security in Europe as a whole and the relationship which exists, in the broader context of world security, between security in Europe and security in the Mediterranean area;
-- Respect for the security interests of all States participating in the Conference on Security and Co-operation in Europe inherent in their sovereign equality;

The importance that participants in negotiating fora see to it that information about relevant developments, progress and results is provided on an appropriate basis to other States participating in the Conference on Security and Co-operation in Europe and, in return, the justified interest of any of those States in having their views considered.

Dated August 1, 1975; consisting of "Declaration of Principles Guiding Relations Between Participating 'States'" and "Document on Confidence-Building Measures and Certain Aspects of Security and Disarmament;" subscribed to by Canada, the United States, and thirty-three European countries. "Conference on Security and Co-operation in Europe, Final Act, Helsinki, 1975," Department of State publication 8826, General Foreign Policy Series 298 (August 1975), reproduced in 73 Department of State Bulletin (September 1, 1975) 323-50, and Department of State, Documents on Germany, 1944-1985, pp. 1285-96.

For commentary, see *Digest of United States Practice in International Law,*
1975, pp. 325-27, 866-67, and *Historic Documents,* 1975, pp. 559-70.

5 1 8   ASSESSMENT OF HELSINKI CONFERENCE

. . . By representing the United States of America at the 35-nation
Conference on Security and Cooperation in Europe at Helsinki, I was able
to deliver in person a message of enormous significance to all Europeans.

That message was--America still cares. The torch in the Statue of
Liberty still burns bright. We will stand for freedom and independence in
1976 as we did in 1776. The United States of America still believes that
all men and women, everywhere, should enjoy the God-given blessings of
life, liberty, and the pursuit of happiness in a world of peace. . . .

And we will continue to encourage the full implementation of the
principles embodied in the CSCE declarations until the 1977 followup
meeting to assess how well all the signatory states have translated these
principles into concrete action for the benefit of their peoples and the
common progress in Europe.

Europeans--East and West--will also be watching. If the principles of Helsinki are lived up to, as each leader solemnly pledged, then
we can consider the Conference a success in which we have played a
significant part. . . .

I believe we are on the right course and the course that offers the
best hope for a better world. I will continue to steer that steady course,
because this experience has further convinced me that millions of hopeful
people, in all parts of Europe, still look to the United States of America as
the champion of human freedom everywhere and of a just peace among the
nations of the world.

Gerald Ford, remarks on returning from Helsinki, August 4, 1975; *Papers of
Presidents: Ford,* 1975, II, 1109-10. Also see his responses to questions
during his return trip, August 2, 1975, p. 1088, and to World Affairs Council,
San Francisco, September 22, 1975, pp. 1505-6.

5 1 9   SUBSEQUENT REVIEW OF HELSINKI PROCESS

. . . the Helsinki process was launched with great hopes 10 years
ago. It was born at what seemed to be an encouraging moment in East-
West relations: The United States and the Soviet Union had just reached
the first agreements on strategic arms limitation. Broad vistas of
economic cooperation appeared open. Progress seemed possible on human
rights. There was an awareness that lasting peace required us to look at
the totality of our relations. And so Helsinki was an attempt to deal com-
prehensively with the problems of security, economic relations, contacts
between our peoples, their basic freedoms, and standards of international
conduct.

The Helsinki Final Act is an eloquent statement of aspirations, to which the United States gladly subscribed because we subscribe to every one of its principles.

The United States has always been realistic about the Helsinki process. We did not expect it to resolve all of the difficult security issues we face in an era of ideological conflict and military competition. We knew, from the beginning, that some would distort it to reinforce the division of the continent and the domination of Eastern Europe by the Soviet Union, despite the Final Act's clear reaffirmation of freedom, political independence, sovereignty, self-determination, and noninterference.

Thus, when heads of state and government met in Helsinki in 1975 to conclude the first conference and sign the Final Act, the United States took the position that hope had to be tempered by realism and backed up by efforts. . . .

After almost 3 years of patient negotiation, we have a document that will expand and improve upon the 1975 Final Act. It adds important new commitments with respect to human rights, trade union freedoms, religious liberties, reunification of families, free flow of information, and measures against terrorism. It also provides, significantly, for followup in the human rights and security fields. . . .

As sober realists, we are--and must be--prepared for continued and often arduous competition. Yet we also believe that this competition can--and must be--conducted in a way that leaves room for practical agreements that push back the specter of major conflict. In the nuclear age, this is our mutual responsibility. It is my government's solemn commitment.

George Shultz, address, concluding session of the Madrid Conference on Security and Cooperation in Europe, September 9, 1983; *American Foreign Policy: Current Documents*, 1983, pp. 435-38. Also see statement by President Reagan, July 15, 1983, pp. 431-32, and statement of Max Kampelman, chairman of the American delegation to the Madrid Conference, July 15, 1983, pp. 432-33. For earlier documentation on this conference, also see *Papers of Presidents: Carter*, 1980-81, I, 848, and II, 1434-39, 1659, 1855-56, and *Reagan*, 1981, pp. 1066-67.

30

Middle East

the history of this century shows to my mind . . . the basic purposes and principles of the United States as they are applied to the rest of the world. We have sought sovereignty over no other country. We have not tried to make any country or any people or any nation subservient to us in any way. . . . We do believe that freedom and the principle of liberty is indivisible in the world and, therefore, when freedom of the weak . . . is threatened, the United States has a very deep responsibility.

Dwight Eisenhower
News Conference on the Middle East, August 6, 1958

The Middle East is variously defined, but usually is regarded as embracing the Arab tier of North Africa from Morocco to Egypt and the northern Sudan, the Arabian Peninsula, and Asia Minor (the peninsula in western Asia between the Mediterranean and Black seas) including Iran. Prior to World War II the United States had no special policy for this region. Its primary interests centered on navigation, shipping, commerce, petroleum development and trade, and normal diplomatic and consular relations.

By the mid-1940's only Egypt, Iran, Iraq, Saudi Arabia, Turkey, and Yemen were held to be independent states, whereas much of the rest of the area was composed of either colonies of Great Britain, France, and Spain or post-World War I mandates of Britain and France. Great Britain was dominant in Egypt, Sudan, Iraq, Jordan, Palestine, and the Persian Gulf area, whereas France dominated in North Africa, Lebanon, and Syria.

The principal catalysts that produced change and the post-World War II Middle East problem embrace decolonization and the withdrawal of Britain, France, and Spain (especially Britain's withdrawal from Palestine and the Persian Gulf and Indian Ocean areas); the creation of fifteen new states (especially the establishment of Israel in Palestinian territory); endemic territorial, economic, and ethnic ferment and strife (especially between Israel and its Arab neighbors); the possession, development, and shipping of Middle East oil resources; conflict among Moslem factions and between the Moslem and other religions; and such geopolitical factors as the strategic interests and rivalries of great powers, the Cold War, containment, and the Baghdad Pact and Central Treaty Organization (CENTO) (see Document 309).

This chapter consists of four segments. The first illustrates the general goals, policies, principles, and strategy of the United States in the Middle East. The second focuses on Israel's independence and its wars with neighboring Arab states. The third deals with the Middle East peace process and proposals for improving Arab-Israeli relations and resolving the Palestine question. The final section provides commentary and documents on the Iran-Iraq War in the 1980's. Related matters treated in other chapters include the Eisenhower and Carter Middle East Doctrines (Chapter 7); the Israeli attack on the U.S.S. *Liberty* (Chapter 13); several Middle East crises in which the United States was a principal participant (Chapter 14)--the Iranian hostage crisis (1979-1981), the crisis in Lebanon (1983), and the air strike on Libya (1986); the Middle East collective defense arrangement--the Baghdad Pact and the Central Treaty Organization (Chapter 18); and the problem of international terrorism, involving several Middle East governments (Chapter 19).

GENERAL AMERICAN GOALS, PRINCIPLES, AND STRATEGY

Many American goals and substantive policies for the Middle East are essentially global in nature. These include such traditional principles as self-determination and independence of peoples, sovereignty and national security, territorial integrity and the sanctity of boundaries, opposition to aggression by any country, the maintenance of peace and amicable settlement of disputes, and national and regional stability. Related and procedural policies espoused by the United States embrace the alignment of idealism and realism, the tempering of the rhetoric of Middle East leaders, insistence that differences and the settlement of controversies be negotiated directly by their governments, United States cooperation with the United Nations and other nations mediating differences and disputes, and the establishment and support of a continuing and viable peace process.

Due to the volatility and, in some cases, the bitterness of relations between certain states, these policies have been more crucial and more difficult to implement in the Middle East than in some other regions. In addition, the United States has sought to maintain its pledges to, and friendly relations with, both Israel and the Arab and other nations, to counter Iranian and Arab-sponsored terrorism, to preserve access to Middle East oil resources and, so far as geopolitical considerations are concerned, to thwart Soviet intervention and adventurism in the area. Many of these goals and principles are addressed in Documents 520-527, and each needs to be related to the immediate context of developing events. For the essence of, and commentary on, the Eisenhower and Carter presidential doctrines, see Documents 113-114, 123-124.

520   IMPORTANCE OF THE MIDDLE EAST TO THE UNITED STATES

The countries of the Middle East are, for the most part, less developed industrially than those of Europe. They are, nevertheless, of great importance to the security of the entire free world. This region is a vital link of land, sea, and air communications between Europe, Asia, and Africa. In the free nations of the Middle East, lie half of the oil reserves of the world. . . .

There is no simple formula for increasing stability and security in the Middle East. With the help of American military and economic assistance, Soviet pressure has already been firmly resisted in Turkey and the Soviet-inspired guerrilla war has been decisively defeated in Greece. But the pressure against the Middle East is unremitting. It can be overcome only by a continued build-up of armed defenses and the fostering of economic development. Only through such measures can these peoples advance toward stability and improved living conditions, and be assured that their aims can best be achieved through strengthening their associations in the free world.

Harry Truman, Message to Congress, May 24, 1951; *American Foreign Policy: Basic Documents, 1950-1955*, II, 2167.   Also see Secretary of State, statement, Senate Committee on Foreign Relations, February 24, 1956, on preservation of peace in the Middle East; *American Foreign Policy: Current Documents*, 1956, pp. 586-89.

521   AMERICAN COMMITMENT TO PEACE AND STABILITY IN THE MIDDLE EAST

. . . This ancient crossroads of the world was, as we all know, an area long subject to colonial rule. This rule ended after World War II, when all countries there won full independence. Out of the Palestinian mandated territory was born the new State of Israel.

These historic changes could not, however, instantly banish animosities born of the ages. Israel and her Arab neighbors soon found themselves at war with one another. And the Arab nations showed continuing anger toward their former colonial rulers, notably France and Great Britain.

The United States--through all the years since the close of World War II--has labored tirelessly to bring peace and stability to this area.

We have considered it a basic matter of United States policy to support the new State of Israel and--at the same time--to strengthen our bonds both with Israel and with the Arab countries. But, unfortunately through all these years, passion in the area threatened to prevail over peaceful purposes, and in one form or another, there has been almost continuous fighting.

*   *   *

Tonight, I want to report to you on the steps we have taken, and the prospects they can open up for a just and lasting peace in the Middle East.

. . . Our involvement in the search for Mid-East peace is not a matter of preference, it is a moral imperative. The strategic importance of the region to the United States is well known.

But our policy is motivated by more than strategic interests. We also have an irreversible commitment to the survival and territorial integrity of friendly states. Nor can we ignore the fact that the well-being of much of the world's economy is tied to stability in the strife-torn Middle East. Finally, our traditional humanitarian concerns dictate a continuing effort to peacefully resolve conflicts.

When our Administration assumed office in January 1981, I decided that the general framework for our Middle East policy should follow the broad guidelines laid down by my predecessors. There were two basic issues we had to address. First, there was the strategic threat to the region posed by the Soviet Union and its surrogates . . . and, second, the peace process between Israel and its Arab neighbors. With regard to the Soviet threat, we have strengthened our efforts to develop with our friends and allies a joint policy to deter the Soviets and their surrogates from further expansion in the region and, if necessary, to defend against it. With respect to the Arab-Israeli conflict, we have embraced the Camp David framework as the only way to proceed. We have also recognized, however, that solving the Arab-Israeli conflict, in and of itself, cannot assure peace throughout a region as vast and troubled as the Middle East.

Dwight Eisenhower, televised Address to the Nation on developments in the Middle East, October 31, 1956; in *American Foreign Policy: Current Documents,* 1956, p. 648; and Ronald Reagan, televised Address to the Nation, Burbank, September 1, 1982, in *Papers of Presidents: Reagan,* 1982, II, 1093 (this was a major address presenting an overall plan for peace in the Middle East--also see Document 544).

522   INGREDIENTS OF REALISTIC AMERICAN POLICY FOR THE MIDDLE EAST

For hundreds of years the people of this crucial area were buffeted by wars and exploitation. World War I generated high hopes for independence, prosperity, and a growing unity. However, the political vacuum created by the collapse of the Ottoman Empire was soon filled by the British and French, and new conflicts replaced the old. In the wake of World War II came the final liquidation of European colonialism in the Arab world and the establishment of Israel as an independent new nation.
. . .

In this context what are the basic ingredients for a realistic American Middle Eastern policy?

First, it seems to me, we must be prepared to help all the nations of the area maintain their independence. This requires an adequate and readily available United States deterrent to aggression from any source. Second, we must use the instruments of the U.N. for the reduction of specific tensions and to prevent the Arab-Israeli dispute from developing into an open conflict that could rapidly spread.

Third, we can encourage all Middle Eastern nations to devote less time to angry propaganda debates with their neighbors and more to the solution of their own problems of internal development. We can also give special priority assistance to those countries which are genuinely concerned with improving the lot of *all* their citizens, not just a wealthy few. Our primary objective is the development of prosperous and stable societies throughout the Middle East whose material benefits are spread throughout every level of the economy and whose energies would be increasingly devoted to the creation of an atmosphere of live and let live.

Fourth, a persistent, patient effort should be made to find some basis of cooperation between neighboring Middle Eastern nations, however tentative or restrictive the areas of cooperation may be.

There is no magic dramatic formula for stability in the Middle East or anywhere else. In spite of our vast military and industrial power, our capacity to shape events there, as elsewhere, is no more than marginal. Yet a patient diplomacy, a firm willingness to stand against threats of aggression, a sensitive understanding of what motivates others, and the wise use of our resources in assisting economic development may provide the margin between chaos on the one hand and growing political and economic stability on the other.

One thing at least is certain: Only through the creation of just societies, whose citizens have genuine independence, individual dignity, and material welfare, can world peace with dignity be established.

Chester Bowles, President's Special Adviser, address, American Jewish Congress, New York, April 12, 1962; *American Foreign Policy: Current Documents,* 1962, pp. 746, 751-52.

523 PRESERVATION OF AMERICAN VITAL INTERESTS IN THE MIDDLE EAST

Ever since the dawn of history the Near East has been a critical crossroads in world affairs. It forms the land bridge between Europe and the Far East and between Europe and Africa. It contains more than two-thirds of the world's proven resources of oil. Particularly since the creation of the State of Israel in 1948, the whole area has been in a state of constant tension. . . .

The events of the 1950's brought into focus the hard fact that what happens in the Near East is of critical interest to our strategic sea, land, and air routes; to our vast oil investments; to the security of Israel and other countries in the area. And closely related to these other interests is the prevention of expanded Communist penetration into the Arab world.

This lesson has served to shape United States policy during the past 5 years. We have sought to restore stability to the Near East. We have used all of the weapons of persuasion at our command. On some matters we have been able to make our influence felt, on others not. . . .

Faced with this situation, what should the United States Government do?

The fundamental answer, of course, is that we should not compromise with the protection of American vital interests. . . .

Meanwhile, we shall continue, as we have been doing, to work assiduously for peace and stability in the Near East through all of the diplomatic means at our command. In that process . . . our prime objective will be the protection of U.S. vital interests in a critical area of the world--an area that at once contains vast resources for peace and the elements that could lead to an explosion endangering the whole free world.

*   *   *

These events have found the American people inadequately informed of our vital interests in the area and inadequately prepared to take the necessary actions to defend them.

What are these interests? First, we need to limit and check the expansion of Soviet influence in the region.

Second, we will have to counter terrorists who aren't going to let us off because we are democratic, decent, or fair. Iran, should it be successful in the war [between Iran and Iraq], or decide to retaliate against the Gulf States, isn't going to be persuaded by sweet reason.

Third, the economic and military viability of our alliances in the world depend upon our ability to maintain Western and Japanese access to the oil resources of the Gulf. . . .

The lack of peace between Israel and its neighbors raises a number of divisive issues for Americans. In principle we are all committed to the security of both Israel and friendly moderate Arab States.

George W. Ball, Under Secretary of State, statement, Senate Appropriations Committee, February 1, 1965; *American Foreign Policy: Current Documents,* 1965, pp. 616-18; and Richard W. Murphy, Assistant Secretary of State, address, American-Arab Affairs Council, Chicago, March 23, 1984; *American Foreign Policy: Current Documents,* 1984, p. 484. Also see Document 526, which emphasizes United States national interests.

524 AMERICAN SUPPORT OF INDEPENDENCE AND TERRITORIAL INTEGRITY OF MIDDLE EAST NATIONS

To the leaders of all the nations of the Near East, I wish to say what three Presidents have said before--that the United States is firmly committed to the support of the political independence and territorial integrity of all the nations of the area. . . .

The United States has consistently sought to have good relations with all the states of the Near East. Regrettably this has not always been possible, but we are convinced that our differences with individual states of the area and their differences with each other must be worked out peacefully and in accordance with accepted international practice.

We have always opposed . . . the efforts of other nations to resolve their problems with their neighbors by aggression. We shall continue to do so. And we appeal to all other peace-loving nations to do likewise.

Lyndon Johnson, statement, White House, May 23, 1967; *Papers of Presidents: Johnson,* 1967, p. 62. Also see Document 535.

525   SEARCH FOR NEGOTIATED POLITICAL SOLUTIONS AND COEXISTENCE IN THE MIDDLE EAST

Peace in the Middle East is central to the global structure of peace. Strategically, the Middle East is a point where interests of the major powers converge. It is a reservoir of energy resources on which much of the world depends. Politically, it is a region of diversity, dynamism, and turmoil, rent by national, social, and ideological division--and of course by the Arab-Israeli conflict. Two world wars and the rising tide of nationalism have broken down the pre-1914 order, but new patterns of stability have not yet been established. Modern quarrels have compounded long-standing ones. Because of the area's strategic importance, outside powers have continued to involve themselves, often competitively. Several times since World War II, the Middle East has been an arena of major crisis.

The irony is that the Middle East also has such great potential for progress and peaceful development. Of all the regions of the developing world, the Middle East, because of its wealth, is uniquely not dependent on the heavy infusion of capital resources from outside. Its wealthier nations have been willing and able to provide the capital for their own development and have begun to assist their neighbors' development. Mechanisms of regional self-reliance and cooperation are already functioning. The yearning for unity is strong within the Arab world; it has deep historical and cultural roots and its positive thrust has found new expression in these cooperative enterprises.

The region's drive for self-reliance matches the philosophy of United States foreign policy in a new era. Technical assistance and the provision of skills, now the most relevant forms of external aid in much of the Middle East, are forms of aid which the United States is uniquely capable of providing and can sustain over a long term. The United States has long been a champion of the region's independence from colonial or other external domination. In conditions of peace, there is a natural community of interest between the United States and all the nations of the Middle East--an interest in the region's progress, stability, and independence.

The requirements of peace in the Middle East are not hard to define in principle. It requires basic decisions by the countries of the Middle East to pursue political solutions and coexist with one another. Outside powers with interests in the area must accept their responsibility for restraint and for helping to mitigate tensions rather than exploiting them for their own advantage.

These are principles which the United States has sought to engage the other great powers in observing. Coexistence, negotiated solutions, avoiding the use or threat of force, great power restraint, noninterference, respect for the sovereignty and territorial integrity of states, renunciation of hegemony or unilateral advantage--these . . . are not new principles; every member state of the United Nations has subscribed to their essential elements. . . .

A commitment to such principles by the outside powers is itself a contribution to the framework for peace in the Middle East. A similar commitment by the principal countries directly involved, concretely expressed in processes of negotiation, is essential.

Richard Nixon, *U.S. Foreign Policy for the 1970's: Shaping a Durable Peace* (1973), pp. 132-33. For a continuation of this statement, see Document 541, part 2. For annual surveys in the early 1970's, see Richard Nixon's reports on *U.S. Foreign Policy for the 1970's,* 1970, pp. 77-83; 1971, pp. 121-34; 1972, pp. 133-40; 1973, pp. 132-42.

526   COMPONENTS OF COMPREHENSIVE AND BALANCED AMERICAN POLICY FOR THE MIDDLE EAST

. . . peace, security and well-being for the nations of the Middle East are critical to a broad range of American interests. That is why we continue to place high priority on a comprehensive and balanced policy to protect these interests, which include:

Meeting responsibilities we bear, because of our role in the world and our deep ties to the Middle East, to work for the settlement of conflicts there which stand in the way of progress and endanger international security, especially the Arab-Israeli dispute and the struggle for a fully sovereign Lebanon;

Assuring the security and contributing to the welfare of friendly nations in the region;

Prevention of wider Soviet influence in this strategic region;

Supporting major U.S. economic interests, including access to oil and markets for U.S. goods and services, and assisting in meeting the economic development needs of the region; and

Cooperating with the more well-endowed states of the area to maintain a healthy international financial and economic order. . . .

The pursuit of these policies contributes to the fundamental goal of U.S. foreign policy: the promotion of U.S. national interests by working to create an international environment in which free and independent nations of the world, including those of the Middle East, can realize their rightful aspirations and the blessings of peace and progress.

Assistant Secretary of State for Near Eastern and South Asian Affairs, statement, House Foreign Affairs Subcommittee, June 2, 1983; *American Foreign Policy: Current Documents,* 1983, pp. 639-40. Also see statement on principal American policies for the Middle East, pp. 642-45, and statement of Secretary of State on the need for peace in the Middle East, pp. 672-76.

527 PRINCIPLES OF AMERICAN STRATEGY IN THE MIDDLE EAST

First, the United States believes that the objective of the peace process is a comprehensive settlement achieved through negotiations based on UN Security Council Resolutions 242 and 338. In our view, these negotiations must involve territory for peace, security and recognition for Israel and all of the states of the region, and Palestinian political rights.

Second, for negotiations to succeed, they must allow the parties to deal directly with each other, face to face. A properly structured international conference could be useful at an appropriate time, but only if it did not interfere with or in any way replace or be a substitute for direct talks between the parties.

Third, the issues involved in the negotiations are far too complex, and the emotions are far too deep, to move directly to a final settlement. Accordingly, some transitional period is needed, associated in time and sequence with negotiations on final status. Such a transition will allow the parties to take the measure of each other's performance, to encourage attitudes to change, and to demonstrate that peace and coexistence is desired.

Fourth, in advance of direct negotiations, neither the United States nor any other party, inside or outside, can or will dictate an outcome. That is why the United States does not support annexation or permanent Israeli control of the West Bank and Gaza, nor do we support the creation of an independent Palestinian state.

I would add here, that we do have an idea about the reasonable middle ground to which a settlement should be directed; that is, self-government for Palestinians in the West Bank and Gaza in a manner acceptable to Palestinians, Israel, and Jordan. Such a formula provides ample scope for Palestinians to achieve their full political rights. It also provides ample protection for Israel's security as well.

Following these principles, we face a pragmatic issue, the issue of how do we get negotiations underway. Unfortunately, the gap between the parties on key issues such as Palestinian representation and the shape of a final settlement remains very, very wide. Violence has soured the atmosphere, and so a quick move to negotiations is quite unlikely. And in the absence of either a minimum of good will or any movement to close the gap, a high-visibility American initiative, we think, has little basis on which to stand.

If we were to stop here, the situation would, I think, be gloomy, indeed. But we are not going to stop with the *status quo*. We are engaged . . . we will remain engaged; and we will work to help create an environment to launch and sustain negotiations. This will require tough but necessary decisions for peace by all of the parties. It will also require a commitment to a process of negotiations clearly tied to the search for a permanent settlement of the conflict.

James A. Baker III, address, American-Israel Public Affairs Committee, May 22, 1989; 89 *Department of State Bulletin* (July 1989):   25-26.   Also see documents in section on the Middle East peace process.

ARAB-ISRAELI WARS

Four intense though relatively short wars were fought between Israel and its Arab neighbors from the late 1940's to the mid-1970's--the War of Independence (1948), the Suez War (1956), the Six-Day War (1967), and the Yom Kippur War (1973).   All resulted in Israeli victories, but none was conclusive.   They were generated by Jewish determination to create a "national home" in the former British mandate of Palestine and Arab resolve to preserve the territory as an Arab homeland.

When the British government decided to relinquish its mandate and the United Nations adopted a resolution to partition Palestine, Israel declared itself independent on May 14, 1948, and was recognized immediately by the United States (Document 528).   Arab forces of Egypt, Lebanon, Syria, and Transjordan (later Jordan) launched an invasion.   The United Nations passed a four-week truce resolution in June, but fighting resumed and armistice agreements were not signed by Israel with the four Arab governments until 1949.   However, the Arabs refused to recognize either Israel as a sovereign state or its truce boundaries.   The United States recognized the partition boundaries (Document 529), and joined with the British and French governments in issuing a Tripartite Declaration, which denounced the use of force between any states in the area and reconfirmed the boundary lines (Document 530).

After Gamal Nasser came to power in Egypt in 1954, nationalized the Suez Canal two years later, denied the use of both the Canal and the Gulf of Aqaba to Israel-bound ships, in October 1956 Israel launched an attack upon the Sinai Peninsula and the coastal Gaza strip.   Anglo-French forces joined the assault on Egypt with air and naval power early in November.   Again the United Nations issued a cease-fire proposal (including a provision to free shipping in the Gulf of Aqaba), which was accepted by the four powers, and major fighting ended November 7.   The Eisenhower administration sent urgent messages to the British and French governments condemning the use of force, supported the United Nations cease-fire resolution, and appealed to Israel to withdraw its forces from Egypt (Documents 531-534).   Because Egypt continued to deny the Suez Canal to Israeli shipping, Israel refused to allow United Nations peace-keeping troops on its side of the border.   In 1957 President Eisenhower promulgated his Middle East Doctrine (see Documents 113-114) and then sent Congressman James P. Richards on a special mission to implement the doctrine; see *American Foreign Policy: Current Documents,* 1957, pp. 831-71.

In May 1967 Egypt, under Nasser, demanded the withdrawal of the United Nations constabulary forces, again closed the Gulf of Aqaba, and proclaimed its intention to destroy Israel. The following month Israeli forces attacked, primarily in the Sinai and Gaza strip.   As they reached the Suez Canal, Egypt capitulated and agreed to a cease-fire. In the meantime, Israel also attacked Jordan (in the West Bank territory and Jerusalem) and Syria (in the Golan

Heights), and they also rapidly acceded to a cease-fire. The Israeli government vowed to retain permanent control of Jerusalem and occupied territory in Egypt, Jordan, and Syria. The United States continued to espouse its policies of self-determination, nonaggression, peaceful settlement, negotiation of differences, and United Nations peacemaking (Documents 535-538). It was during this war that Israel attacked the U.S.S. *Liberty* in the Mediterranean Sea (see the commentary in Chapter 13, Documents 215-217).

The fourth war, in 1973, was launched by Egypt and Syria on October 6, the Jewish Yom Kippur holy day. Egypt struck across the Suez Canal in the south and Syria invaded the Israeli-held Golan Heights in the north. Again Israel forced its enemies back and cease-fires were agreed to with Egypt in late October and with Syria on November 11. But fighting continued in the north until another cease-fire was finally negotiated under the diplomatic mediation of Henry Kissinger and was signed in May 1974. For commentary on the Egyptian-Israeli truce terms, see *Historic Documents,* 1973, pp. 931-37; for the United Nations cease-fire resolution, see *Digest of United States Practice in International Law,* 1973, pp. 484-85; and for President Nixon's televised statement on the disengagement of Syrian and Israeli forces, May 29, 1974, see *Papers of Presidents: Nixon,* 1974, pp. 463-64.

Two developments during this war are worthy of special interest. When the Soviet Union became involved by providing substantial assistance to Egypt and Syria, President Nixon ordered a worldwide American military "precautionary alert." Document 539 addresses the matter of American policy on aggression and concern with limiting the hostilities to the Middle East nations. Moreover, the United States became directly involved diplomatically and assumed a major mediatory role in developing a Middle East "peace process," which is discussed in the next section.

President Nixon discussed the Middle East problem with Soviet leaders when Leonid Brezhnev met with him in Washington in June 1973, when he visited Moscow in June the following year, and by exchanges of written communications.

In addition to appointing special emissaries to serve as his personal surrogates to promote the peace process, President Nixon also undertook a sweeping Middle East summit tour in June 1974--visiting Egypt, Saudi Arabia, Syria, Israel, and Jordan--during which a number of basic agreements were consummated. These include "Principles of Relations and Cooperation Between Egypt and the United States," June 14, 1974 (for its text see *Papers of Presidents: Nixon,* 1974, pp. 503-6, and for the President's comments on signing, see pp. 499-502), and joint statements of the President and the Prime Minister of Israel and King Hussein of Jordan, June 17 and 18, 1974 (for their texts, see pp. 526-28, 534-35).

528 UNITED STATES RECOGNITION OF INDEPENDENT ISRAEL, 1948-1949

THIS GOVERNMENT has been informed that a Jewish state has been proclaimed in Palestine, and recognition has been requested by the provisional government thereof.

The United States recognizes the provisional government as the de facto authority of the new State of Israel.

*   *   *

On October 24, 1948, the President stated that when a permanent government was elected in Israel, it would promptly be given de jure recognition. Elections for such a government were held on January 25th. The votes have now been counted, and this Government has been officially informed of the results. The United States Government is therefore pleased to extend de jure recognition to the Government of Israel as of this date.

Harry Truman, statements concerning de facto and de jure recognition of the state of Israel, May 14, 1948 and January 31, 1949; *Papers of Presidents: Truman,* 1948, p. 258, and 1949, p. 121.

529   UNITED STATES BASIC POLICY ON INDEPENDENT ISRAEL, 1948

"We pledge full recognition to the State of Israel. We affirm our pride that the United States, under the leadership of President Truman, played a leading role in the adoption of the resolution of November 29, 1947, by the United Nations General Assembly for the creation of a Jewish state.

"We approve the claims of the State of Israel to the boundaries set forth in the United Nations' resolution of November 29 and consider that modifications thereof should be made only if fully acceptable to the State of Israel.

"We look forward to the admission of the State of Israel to the United Nations and its full participation in the international community of nations. We pledge appropriate aid to the State of Israel in developing its economy and resources. . . .

"We continue to support, within the framework of the United Nations, the internationalization of Jerusalem and the protection of the holy places in Palestine.". . .

This has been and is now my position.

Proceedings are now taking place in the United Nations looking toward an amicable settlement of the conflicting positions of the parties in Palestine. In the interests of peace this work must go forward.

A plan has been submitted which provides a basis for a renewed effort to bring about a peaceful adjustment of differences. It is hoped that by using this plan as a basis of negotiation, the conflicting claims of the parties can be settled.

Harry Truman, statement, including provisions of the Democratic Party platform, with commentary; *Papers of Presidents: Truman,* 1948, pp. 843-44. A summary of the United Nations resolution, November 29, 1947, providing for the partition of Palestine into independent Arab and Jewish states is provided in 17, *Department of State Bulletin,* p. 1163. For comprehensive collections of documents on the Palestine and Israel problems, see *A Decade of American Foreign Policy: Basic Documents, 1941-49,* pp. 810-60, and *American Foreign Policy: Basic Documents, 1950-1955,* II, 2170, 2177-78, 2254-55. Also see *Foreign Relations,* 1948, V, Part 2, *The Near East . . . ,* pp. 999-1328; 1949, VI, pp. 594-1565 (which includes materials on armistice agreements and the unsuccessful attempts to attain a final peace settlement), and 1950, V, pp. 658-1086.

530 TRIPARTITE DECLARATION REGARDING ARMISTICE BORDERS IN PALESTINE, 1950

1. The three Governments recognize that the Arab states and Israel all need to maintain a certain level of armed forces for the purposes of assuring their internal security and their legitimate self-defense and to permit them to play their part in the defense of the area as a whole. . . .

3. The three Governments take this opportunity of declaring their deep interest in and their desire to promote the establishment and maintenance of peace and stability in the area and their unalterable opposition to the use of force or threat of force between any of the states in that area. The three Governments, should they find that any of these states was preparing to violate frontiers or armistice lines, would, consistently with their obligations as members of the United Nations, immediately take action, both within and outside the United Nations, to prevent such violation.

Declaration of governments of France, the United Kingdom, and the United States, May 25, 1950; *American Foreign Policy: Basic Documents,* 1950-1955, II, 2237. For President Eisenhower's reaffirmation of this declaration, in which he stated that true security must be based upon "a just and reasonable settlement" in the Middle East, November 9, 1955, see p. 2238.

531 HOSTILITIES BETWEEN ISRAEL AND EGYPT IN VIOLATION OF ARMISTICE AGREEMENT, 1955

ALL AMERICANS have been following with deep concern the latest developments in the Near East. The recent outbreak of hostilities has led to a sharp increase in tensions. These events inevitably retard our search for world peace. Insecurity in one region is bound to affect the world as a whole.

While we continue willing to consider request for arms needed for legitimate self-defense, we do not intend to contribute to an arms competition in the Near East because we do not think such a race would be in the true interest of any of the participants. The policy which we believed would best promote the interests and the security of the peoples of the area was expressed in the Tripartite Declaration of May 25, 1950. This still remains our policy.

I stated last year that our goal in the Near East as elsewhere is a just peace. Nothing has taken place since which invalidates our fundamental policies, policies based on friendship for all of the peoples of the area.

We believe that true security must be based upon a just and reasonable settlement. . . . I authorized Mr. [Secretary of State John Foster] Dulles to state that, given a solution of the other related problems, I would recommend that the United States join in formal treaty engagements to prevent or thwart any effort by either side to alter by force the boundaries between Israel and its Arab neighbors.

Recent developments have made it all the more imperative that a settlement be found. The United States will continue to play its full part and will support firmly the United Nations which has already contributed so markedly to minimize violence in the area. I hope that other nations of the world will cooperate in this endeavor, thereby contributing significantly to world peace.

Dwight Eisenhower, statement, November 9, 1955; *Papers of Presidents: Eisenhower,* 1955, pp. 839-40.

5 3 2   UNITED STATES REACTION TO ANGLO-FRENCH ULTIMATUM TO EGYPT AND ISRAEL, 1956

As soon as the President received his first knowledge, obtained through press reports, of the ultimatum delivered by the French and United Kingdom Governments to Egypt and Israel, planning temporary occupation within 12 hours of the Suez Canal Zone, he sent an urgent personal message to the Prime Minister of Great Britain and the Prime Minister of the Republic of France.

The President expressed his earnest hope that the United Nations Organization would be given full opportunity to settle the items in the controversy by peaceful means instead of by forceful ones.

This Government continues to believe that it is possible by such peaceful means to secure a solution which would restore the armistice conditions between Egypt and Israel, as well as bring about a just settlement of the Suez Canal controversy.

White House, Press Secretary, statement, October 30, 1956; *American Foreign Policy: Current Documents,* 1956, pp. 646-47. Also see Press Secretary's statement on American policy concerning intervention in Egypt, October 29, 1956, p. 646, and text of the United Nations Security Council cease-fire resolution, October 30, 1956, p. 647.

5 3 3   REPORT ON OUTBREAK OF HOSTILITIES IN THE MIDDLE EAST, 1956

The United States--through all the years since the close of World War II--has labored tirelessly to bring peace and stability to this area.

We have considered it a basic matter of United States policy to support the new State of Israel and--at the same time--to strengthen our bonds both with Israel and with the Arab countries. But, unfortunately through all these years, passion in the area threatened to prevail over peaceful purposes, and in one form or another, there has been almost continuous fighting. . . .

These matters came to a crisis on July 26th of this year, when the Egyptian Government seized the Universal Suez Canal Company. For 90 years--ever since the inauguration of the canal--that company has operated the canal, largely under British and French technical supervision.

Now there were some among our allies who urged an immediate reaction to this event by use of force. We insistently urged otherwise, and our wish prevailed--through a long succession of conferences and negotiations for weeks--even months--with participation by the United Nations. And there, in the United Nations, only a short while ago, on the basis of agreed principles, it seemed that an acceptable accord was within our reach.

But the direct relations of Egypt with both Israel and France kept worsening to a point at which first Israel--then France--and Great Britain also--determined that, in their judgment, there could be no protection of their vital interests without resort to force.

Upon this decision, events followed swiftly. On Sunday the Israeli Government ordered total mobilization. On Monday, their armed forces penetrated deeply into Egypt and to the vicinity of the Suez Canal, nearly 100 miles away. And on Tuesday, the British and French Governments delivered a 12-hour ultimatum to Israel and Egypt--now followed up by armed attack against Egypt.

The United States was not consulted in any way about any phase of these actions. Nor were we informed of them in advance.

As it is the manifest right of any of these nations to take such decisions and actions, it is likewise our right--if our judgment so dictates--to dissent. We believe these actions to have been taken in error. For we do not accept the use of force as a wise or proper instrument for the settlement of international disputes. . . .

At the same time it is--and it will remain--the dedicated purpose of your government to do all in its power to localize the fighting and to end the conflict.

Dwight Eisenhower, television Address to the Nation, October 31, 1956; *American Foreign Policy: Current Documents,* 1956, pp. 040-50. Also see the President's letter appealing to Israel to withdraw from Egypt, November 7, 1956, pp. 676-77. Note the difference on the matter of consultation with the United States, as explained in Document 534.

534 UNITED STATES POSITION ON BRITISH AND FRENCH ARMED INTER-VENTION IN EGYPT, 1956

. . . It is assumed that our complaint about the British and the French is primarily because they failed to consult with us, or with the NATO Council. That is not the case. . . . our complaint is not that there was not a discussion of these matters; not that we had not had an opportunity to make our views known--the point was that we considered that such an attack under the circumstances would violate the charter of the United Nations, and would violate article 1 of the North Atlantic Treaty itself, which requires all the parties to that treaty to renounce the use of force, and to settle their disputes by peaceful means. That is our complaint: that the treaty was violated; not that there was not consultation.

John Foster Dulles, response to question at news conference, December 18, 1956; *American Foreign Policy: Current Documents*, 1956, p. 701. For a comprehensive collection of documents on the Suez War, see pp. 561-703; also see *Foreign Relations*, 1955-1957, XIV-XV, *The Near East* . . . (on the Arab-Israeli dispute).

535 UNITED STATES OPPOSITION TO AGGRESSION BY ANY NATION IN THE MIDDLE EAST, 1967

The Near East links three continents. The birthplace of civilization and of three of the world's great religions, it is the home of some 60 million people and the crossroads between East and West.

The world community has a vital interest in peace and stability in the Near East, one that has been expressed primarily through continuing United Nations action and assistance over the past 20 years. . . .

To the leaders of all the nations of the Near East, I wish to say what three American Presidents have said before me--that the United States is firmly committed to the support of the political independence and ter-ritorial integrity of all the nations of that area. The United States strongly opposes aggression by anyone in the area, in any form, overt or clandestine. This has been the policy of the United States led by four Presidents--President Truman, President Eisenhower, President John F. Kennedy, and myself. . . . The record of the actions of the United States over the past 20 years, within and outside the United Nations, is abundant-ly clear on this point.

Lyndon Johnson, Address to the Nation, May 23, 1967; *American Foreign Policy: Current Documents*, 1967, pp. 494-95. For a comprehensive collection on the Six-Day War, see pp. 480-626. Also see Document 524.

536 CONTINUING BASIC AMERICAN POLICY FOR THE MIDDLE EAST, 1967

Our most urgent present concern is to find a way to bring the fighting in the Middle East to an end. . . .

So we continue to believe that a cease-fire is the urgent first step required to bring about peace in that troubled part of the world. At the same time we know, of course, that a cease-fire will be only a beginning and that many more fundamental questions must be tackled promptly if the area is to enjoy genuine stability. . . .

Let me emphasize that the U.S. continues to be guided by the same basic policies which have been followed by this Administration and three previous Administrations. These policies have always included a consistent effort on our part to maintain good relations with all the peoples of the area in spite of the difficulties caused by some of their leaders. . . .

We hope that the individual states in the Middle East will now find new ways to work out their differences with each other by the means of peace, and in accordance with the Charter of the United Nations. We look beyond the current conflict to a new era of greater stability which will permit all the peoples of the area to enjoy the fruits of lasting peace. Our full efforts will be directed to this end.

Lyndon Johnson, letter to Senator Mike Mansfield, June 8, 1967; *Papers of Presidents: Johnson,* 1967, I, 602. For the joint statement of the President and the Israeli Prime Minister concerning their dedication to the establishment of a just and lasting peace in the Middle East, January 8, 1969, see volume for 1968-1969, I, 20-21. For statement of White House Press Secretary on the outbreak of fighting in the Middle East, June 5, 1967, see *American Foreign Policy: Current Documents,* 1967, pp. 505-6.

537 FIVE PRINCIPLES FOR PEACE IN THE MIDDLE EAST, 1967

. . . Let me turn to the Middle East--and to the tumultuous events of the past months. Those events have proved the wisdom of five great principles of peace in the region.

The first and greatest principle is that every nation in the area has a fundamental right to live and to have this right respected by its neighbors.

For the people of the Middle East the path to hope does not lie in threats to end the life of any nation. Such threats have become a burden to the peace, not only of that region but a burden to the peace of the entire world.

In the same way, no nation would be true to the United Nations Charter or to its own true interests if it should permit military success to blind it to the fact that its neighbors have rights and its neighbors have interests of their own. Each nation, therefore, must accept the right of others to live.

This last month, I think, shows us another basic requirement for settlement. It is a human requirement: justice for the refugees. . . .

. . . There will be no peace for any party in the Middle East unless this problem is attacked with new energy by all and, certainly, primarily by those who are immediately concerned.

A third lesson from this last month is that maritime rights must be respected. Our nation has long been committed to free maritime passage through international waterways; and we, along with other nations, were taking the necessary steps to implement this principle when hostilities exploded. . . .

Fourth, this last conflict has demonstrated the danger of the Middle Eastern arms race of the last 12 years. Here the responsibility must rest not only on those in the area but upon the larger states outside the area. We believe that scarce resources could be used much better for technical and economic development. We have always opposed this arms race, and our own military shipments to the area have consequently been severely limited. . . .

Fifth, the crisis underlines the importance of respect for political independence and territorial integrity of all the states of the area. We reaffirmed that principle at the height of this crisis. We affirm it again today on behalf of all. This principle can be effective in the Middle East only on the basis of peace between the parties. The nations of the region have had only fragile and violated truce lines for 20 years. What they now need are recognized boundaries and other arrangements that will give them security against terror, destruction, and war. Further, there just must be adequate recognition of the special interest of three great religions in the holy places of Jerusalem.

These five principles are not new, but we do think they are fundamental. Taken together, they point the way from uncertain armistice to durable peace. We believe there must be progress toward all of them if there is to be progress toward any.

Lyndon Johnson, address, Department of State Foreign Policy Conference, June 19, 1967; *American Foreign Policy: Current Documents,* 1967, pp. 532-33. For reiteration and explanation of these precepts of American policy, see statement of the United States Representative to the United Nations, General Assembly, September 21, 1967, pp. 597-98, and for the text of the United Nations resolution to restore peace, see p. 616. For comparison of fundamental American policy, also see Documents 543 and 544.

538   NEED FOR COEXISTENCE IN THE MIDDLE EAST, 1967

Our own position [on the Near East] remains that stated by President Johnson on June 19, and the five principles which we have announced.

We do believe that those who live in the area have the primary responsibility for finding answers to the question. We do not believe that a state of belligerency or a state of war is consistent with peace in the Near East. And we know that those who have to face the prospect of living there for generations to come certainly for the next decades have got to find some basis on which coexistence is tolerable, and that applies to both sides. We would hope that now . . . the voices of moderation would make it possible to stabilize a peace in an area where peace has been long delayed and where it is desperately needed.

Dean Rusk, reply to question at news conference, September 8, 1967; *American Foreign Policy: Current Documents,* 1967, p. 591. For commentary on coexistence, also see Documents 525 and 527; it also is implied in many other policy statements.

539 UNITED STATES-SOVIET UNION RELATIONS DURING THE YOM KIPPUR WAR, 1973

The parties [Richard Nixon and Leonid Brezhnev] expressed their deep concern with the situation in the Middle East and exchanged opinions regarding ways of reaching a Middle East settlement.

Each of the parties set forth its position on this problem.

Both parties agreed to continue to exert their efforts to promote the quickest possible settlement in the Middle East. This settlement should be in accordance with the interests of all states in the area, be consistent with their independence and sovereignty and should take into due account the legitimate interests of the Palestinian people.

*   *   *

With regard to the peacekeeping force, I think it is important for all . . . to know why the United States has insisted that major powers not be part of the peacekeeping force and that major powers not introduce military forces into the Mideast. A very significant and potentially explosive crisis developed on Wednesday of this week. We obtained information which led us to believe that the Soviet Union was planning to send a very substantial force into the Mideast, a military force.

When I received that information, I ordered, shortly after midnight on Thursday morning, an alert for all American forces around the world. This was a precautionary alert. The purpose of that was to indicate to the Soviet Union that we could not accept any unilateral move on their part to move military forces into the Mideast. At the same time, in the early morning hours, I also proceeded on the diplomatic front. In a message to Mr. Brezhnev--an urgent message--I indicated to him our reasoning, and I urged that we not proceed along that course and that, instead, we join in the United Nations in supporting a resolution which would exclude any major powers from participating in a peacekeeping force.

As a result of that communication and the return that I received from Mr. Brezhnev--we had several exchanges, I should say--we reached the conclusion that we would jointly support the resolution which was adopted in the United Nations.

We now come, of course, to the critical time in terms of the future of the Mideast. And here, the outlook is far more hopeful than what we have been through this past week. I think I could safely say that the chances for not just a cease-fire--which we presently have and which, of course, we have had in the Mideast for some time--but the outlook for a permanent peace is the best that it has been in 20 years. . . .

What the developments of this week should indicate to all of us is that the United States and the Soviet Union, who admittedly have very different objectives in the Mideast, have now agreed that it is not in their interest to have a confrontation there, a confrontation which might lead to a nuclear confrontation, and neither of the two major powers wants that.

We have agreed, also, that if we are to avoid that, it is necessary for us to use our influence more than we have in the past, to get the negotiating track moving again, but this time, moving to a conclusion-- not simply a temporary truce but a permanent peace.

*   *   *

We will pursue our relations with the Soviet Union in the climate of detente established two years ago in Moscow and reaffirmed by General Secretary Brezhnev's visit to Washington last year. During the fateful weeks of the Middle East war last October, the strength of our detente was severely tested. Since then, American diplomatic leadership and initiative have played a central role in the search for a final settlement in the long-troubled Middle East. This began with the ceasefire of October 22, worked out with the Soviet Union's assistance, and was later strengthened by the Six-Point Agreement in November to consolidate the ceasefire, then by the Geneva Peace Conference--under the co-sponsorship of the United States and the Soviet Union--and most recently by the agreement on the disengagement of Egyptian and Israeli military forces, which is being implemented in cooperation with the United Nations Emergency Force. These steps are but the beginning of broadened efforts to find a lasting settlement of the area's problems.

Richard Nixon and Leonid Brezhnev, joint communique, June 25, 1973; Richard Nixon, statement, news conference, October 26, 1973; in *Papers of Presidents: Nixon, 1973*, pp. 615, 896-97; and Richard Nixon, State of the Union Message, January 30, 1974, in *Papers of Presidents: Nixon, 1974*, p. 97. For President Nixon's statements and news conference comments on the war of 1973, also see *Papers of Presidents: Nixon, 1973*, pp. 848-49, 901-2.

5 4 0   BASIC AMERICAN POLICY IN THE MIDDLE EAST DURING THE YOM KIPPUR WAR, 1973

. . . The policy of the United States in the Mideast, very simply stated, is this: We stand for the right of every nation in the Mideast to maintain its independence and security. We want this fighting to end. We want the fighting to end on a basis where we can build a lasting peace.

But the policy of the United States is that of peacemaker in the area.
. . .

Richard Nixon, remarks, Congressional Medal of Honor ceremony, October 15, 1973; *Papers of Presidents: Nixon,* 1973, p. 871.   Also see President Nixon's statements in Documents 525 and 541.   For commentary on Egyptian-Israeli truce terms, see *Historic Documents,* 1973, pp. 931-37.

MIDDLE EAST PEACE PROCESS

The United States has become directly, sometimes centrally, involved in the Middle East peace process since the early 1970's, seeking to achieve agreement on a basic "framework" for peace and eventually a negotiated settlement on Arab-Israeli relations.   This is a complicated, often frustrating, and difficult undertaking--resulting from unrealistic demands, preconditions, and obstinacy respecting what the Middle East nations regard as their vital interests, especially Israel's right to exist and be recognized as an independent nation, the Palestinian right to self-determination and a homeland, the status of Israeli-occupied territories and Jerusalem, and the settlement of national boundaries.

The peace process, grounded on the principles established in United Nations resolutions, has been under way for many years.   It was contributed to by the Nixon and Ford administrations (Documents 541-542); it achieved major progress during the Carter administration, producing the Camp David Accords and the Egyptian-Israeli Peace Treaty in 1979 (Document 543); and it was augmented by President Reagan's comprehensive Middle East plan, promulgated in 1982 (Document 544).   The problem, the challenge, and the task continue and, given the stated goals and objectives of the United States, summarized earlier, accomplishment, at best, is likely to be slow and piecemeal.

5 4 1   LAUNCHING THE MIDDLE EAST PEACE PROCESS, 1974

. . . In the past generation there have been, as we know, four wars in the Mideast, followed by uneasy truces.   This, I would say, is the first significant step toward a permanent peace in the Mideast.   I do not understate . . . the difficulties that lie ahead in settling the differences that must be settled before a permanent peace is reached, not only here but between the other countries involved.   But this is a very significant step reached directly as a result of negotiations between the two parties [Egypt and Israel] and, therefore, has, it seems to me, a great deal of meaning to all of us here in this country and around the world who recognize the importance of having peace in this part of the world.

. . . Our role has been one of being of assistance to both parties to bring them together, to help to narrow differences, working toward a fair and just settlement for all parties concerned, where every nation in that area will be able to live in peace and also to be secure insofar as its defense is concerned. . . .

Now, the announcement we have made today is only a first step, but it is a very significant step. It paves the way for more steps which can lead to a permanent peace.

*   *   *

The focus of attention in the Middle East has been the prolonged crisis of the Arab-Israeli conflict and the persistent efforts to resolve it.

. . . It was a dispute in which each side saw vital interests at stake that could not be compromised. To Israel, the issue was survival. The physical security provided by the territories it occupied in 1967 seemed a better safeguard than Arab commitments to live in peace in exchange for return of all those territories--commitments whose reliability could be fully tested only after Israel had withdrawn. To the Arabs, negotiating new borders directly with Israel, as the latter wished, while Israel occupied Arab lands and while Palestinian aspirations went unfulfilled, seemed incompatible with justice and with the sovereignty of Arab nations. A powerful legacy of mutual fear and mistrust had to be overcome. Until that was done no compromise formula for settlement was acceptable to either side. To the major powers outside, important interests and relationships were at stake which drew them into positions of confrontation.

The problem remains. For this very reason, I have said that no other crisis area of the world has greater importance or higher priority for the United States. . . .

The United States has no illusions. Instant peace in the Middle East is a dream--yet the absence of progress toward a settlement means an ever-present risk of wider war, and a steady deterioration of the prospects for regional stability and for constructive relations between the countries of the area and the world outside. Arab-Israeli reconciliation may seem impossible--but in many areas of the world, accommodations not fully satisfactory to either side have eased the intensity of conflict and provided an additional measure of security to both sides. Peace cannot be imposed from outside--but I am convinced that a settlement in the Middle East is in the national interest of the United States and that for us to abandon the quest for a settlement would be inconsistent with our responsibility as a great power.

The issue for the United States, therefore, is not the desirability of an Arab-Israeli settlement, but how it can be achieved. The issue is not whether the United States will be involved in the effort to achieve it, but how the United States can be involved usefully and effectively.

Richard Nixon, remarks about Egyptian-Israeli agreement on disengagement of military forces, January 17, 1974; *Papers of Presidents: Nixon,* 1974, pp. 11-12; and *U.S. Foreign Policy for the 1970's: Shaping a Durable Peace* (1973), pp. 133-34. The latter is a continuation of Document 525.

5 4 2   GUIDELINES FOR THE MIDDLE EAST PEACE PROCESS, 1976

The Middle East policy is aimed at following the U.N. Resolutions 242 and 338 which were agreed to by . . . almost a unanimous vote in the United Nations a few years ago. Those two resolutions are the guidelines for the settlement of a long and controversial problem in the most volatile area of the world. It means that we have to have a permanent peace, we have to have readjustments in territory, we have to have the disavowal of military action.

It will follow, of course, the two successive steps that this government, our government, has been involved in--first, the settlement of the Yom Kippur war and then the very major step of a few months ago when we were able to get an agreement between Egypt and Israel for the Sinai agreement. This was a very important step, but it is not the final answer. We have to follow the guidelines, as I indicated, of Resolutions 242 and 338 in the United Nations.

Gerald Ford, response to question, Economic Club of Detroit, May 12, 1976; *Papers of Presidents: Ford*, 1976, p. 1543.

5 4 3   MAJOR THRUST IN THE PEACE PROCESS, 1977-1978

We believe strongly that progress toward a negotiated peace in the Middle East is essential this year if future disaster is to be avoided. We also believe that the only true security for any country in that troubled area is a true peace negotiated between the parties.

Fortunately, we do not begin our efforts in a vacuum. A starting point exists in U.N. Security Council Resolution 242 of November 1967, which all the governments involved have accepted.

The United States policy since 1967 has consistently sought to apply the principles agreed in that resolution through the process of negotiations called for in Security Council Resolution 338 of October 1973, which, I might add, all the parties involved also accepted.

The peace foreseen in these resolutions will require both sides in the dispute to make difficult compromises. We are not asking for one-sided concessions from anyone. The Arab States will have to agree to implement a kind of peace which produces confidence in its durability.

In our view, that means security arrangements on all fronts satisfactory to all parties to guarantee established borders. It also involves steps toward the normalization of relations with Israel.

The peace, to be durable, must also deal with the Palestinian issue.

In this connection, the President has spoken of the need for a homeland for the Palestinians whose exact nature should be negotiated between the parties.

Clearly, whatever arrangements were made would have to take into account the security requirements of all parties involved.

Within the terms of Resolution 242, in return for this kind of peace Israel clearly should withdraw from occupied territories. We consider that this resolution means withdrawal on all three fronts in the Middle East dispute--that is, Sinai, Golan, West Bank-Gaza--with the exact borders and security arrangements being agreed in the negotiations.

Further, these negotiations must start without any preconditions from any side. This means no territories, including the West Bank, are automatically excluded from the items to be negotiated.

To automatically exclude any territories under dispute would be contradictory to the principle of negotiating without precondition. Nor does it conform to the spirit of Resolution 242, which forms a framework for these negotiations.

Every administration since 1967 has consistently supported Resolution 242, and it has the widest international support as well.

*   *   *

Through the long years of conflict, four main issues have divided the parties involved. One is the nature of peace--whether peace will simply mean that the guns are silenced, that the bombs no longer fall, that the tanks cease to roll, or whether it will mean that the nations of the Middle East can deal with each other as neighbors and as equals and as friends, with a full range of diplomatic and cultural and economic and human relations between them. That's been the basic question. The Camp David agreement has defined such relationships . . . between Israel and Egypt.

The second main issue is providing for the security of all parties involved, including, of course, our friends, the Israelis, so that none of them need fear attack or military threats from one another. When implemented, the Camp David agreement . . . will provide for such mutual security.

Third is the question of agreement on secure and recognized boundaries, the end of military occupation, and the granting of self-government or else the return to other nations of territories which have been occupied by Israel since the 1967 conflict. The Camp David agreement . . . provides for the realization of all these goals.

And finally, there is the painful human question of the fate of the Palestinians who live or who have lived in these disputed regions. The Camp David agreement guarantees that the Palestinian people may participate in the resolution of the Palestinian problem in all its aspects, a commitment that Israel has made in writing and which is supported and appreciated, I'm sure, by all the world.

Over the last 18 months, there has been, of course, some progress on these issues. Egypt and Israel came close to agreeing about the first issue, the nature of peace. They then saw that the second and third issues, that is, withdrawal and security, were intimately connected, closely entwined. But fundamental divisions still remained in other areas--about the fate of the Palestinians, the future of the West Bank and Gaza, and the future of Israeli settlements in occupied Arab territories. . . .

But President Sadat and Prime Minister Begin have overcome these barriers, exceeded our fondest expectations, and have signed two agreements that hold out the possibility of resolving issues that history had taught us could not be resolved.

The first of these documents is entitled, "A Framework for Peace in the Middle East Agreed at Camp David." It deals with a comprehensive settlement, comprehensive agreement, between Israel and all her neighbors, as well as the difficult question of the Palestinian people and the future of the West Bank and the Gaza area. . . .

The second agreement is entitled, "A Framework for the Conclusion of a Peace Treaty Between Egypt and Israel." It returns to Egypt its full exercise of sovereignty over the Sinai Peninsula and establishes several security zones, recognizing carefully that sovereignty right for the protection of all parties. It also provides that Egypt will extend full diplomatic recognition to Israel at the time the Israelis complete an interim withdrawal from most of the Sinai, which will take place between 3 months and 9 months after the conclusion of the peace treaty. And the peace treaty is to be fully negotiated and signed no later than 3 months from last night. . . .

Finally, let me say that for many years the Middle East has been a textbook for pessimism, a demonstration that diplomatic ingenuity was no match for intractable human conflicts. Today we are privileged to see the chance for one of the sometimes rare, bright moments in human history-- a chance that may offer the way to peace.

Department of State spokesman, news conference, June 27, 1977, and President Carter, address, joint session of Congress, September 18, 1978; *American Foreign Policy: Basic Documents,* 1977-1980, pp. 617-18, 657-60. For comprehensive compilation of documents on the Arab-Israeli dispute, the Camp David accords, and the Egyptian-Israeli peace treaty, see pp. 609-719, with the texts of the Camp David accords (1978), pp. 653-57, and of the peace treaty and the United States guarantee of the treaty (1979), pp. 669-85. Also compare with President Johnson's earlier five principles in Document 537, and President Reagan's later proposal in Document 544.

For additional materials on the peace process, Camp David Accords (1978), and Egyptian-Israeli Peace Treaty (1979), see *American Foreign Policy: Basic Documents,* 1977-1980, pp. 617-97; *Digest of United States Practice in International Law,* 1978, pp. 1541-60, and 1979, pp. 1686-1724; and *Historic Documents,* 1978, pp. 605-32; 1982, pp. 337-44.

544 UNITED STATES PROPOSAL FOR PEACE IN THE MIDDLE EAST, 1982

The question now is how to reconcile Israel's legitimate security concerns with the legitimate rights of the Palestinians. And that answer can only come at the negotiating table. Each party must recognize that the outcome must be acceptable to all and that true peace will require compromises by all. . . .

. . . The Camp David agreement remains the foundation of our policy. Its language provides all parties with the leeway they need for successful negotiations.

• I call on Israel to make clear that the security for which she yearns can only be achieved through genuine peace, a peace requiring magnanimity, vision, and courage.

• I call on the Palestinian people to recognize that their own political aspirations are inextricably bound to recognition of Israel's right to a secure future.

• And I call on the Arab states to accept the reality of Israel and the reality that peace and justice are to be gained only through hard, fair, direct negotiation.

In making these calls upon others, I recognize that the United States has a special responsibility. No other nation is in a position to deal with the key parties to the conflict on the basis of trust and reliability. . . .

The United States has thus far sought to play the role of mediator; we have avoided public comment on the key issues. We have always recognized--and continue to recognize--that only the voluntary agreement of those parties most directly involved in the conflict can provide an enduring solution. But it has become evident to me that some clearer sense of America's position on the key issues is necessary to encourage wider support for the peace process.

First, as outlined in the Camp David accords, there must be a period of time during which the Palestinian inhabitants of the West Bank and Gaza will have full autonomy over their own affairs. Due consideration must be given to the principle of self-government by the inhabitants of the territories and to the legitimate security concerns of the parties involved.

The purpose of the 5-year period of transition, which would begin after free elections for a self-governing Palestinian authority, is to prove to the Palestinians that they can run their own affairs and that such Palestinian autonomy poses no threat to Israel's security.

The United States will not support the use of any additional land for the purpose of settlements during the transition period. Indeed, the immediate adoption of a settlement freeze by Israel, more than any other action, could create the confidence needed for wider participation in these talks. Further settlement activity is in no way necessary for the security of Israel and only diminishes the confidence of the Arabs that a final outcome can be freely and fairly negotiated.

I want to make the American position well understood: The purpose of this transition period is the peaceful and orderly transfer of authority from Israel to the Palestinian inhabitants of the West Bank and Gaza. . . .

Beyond the transition period, as we look to the future of the West Bank and Gaza, it is clear to me that peace cannot be achieved by the formation of an independent Palestinian state in those territories. Nor is it achievable on the basis of Israeli sovereignty or permanent control over the West Bank and Gaza.

So the United States will not support the establishment of an independent Palestinian state in the West Bank and Gaza, and we will not support annexation or permanent control by Israel.

There is, however, another way to peace. The final status of these lands must, of course, be reached through the give-and-take of negotiations. But it is the firm view of the United States that self-government by the Palestinians of the West Bank and Gaza in association with Jordan offers the best chance for a durable, just and lasting peace.

We base our approach squarely on the principle that the Arab-Israeli conflict should be resolved through negotiations involving an exchange of territory for peace. This exchange is enshrined in U.N. Security Council Resolution 242, which is, in turn, incorporated in all its parts in the Camp David agreements. U.N. Resolution 242 remains wholly valid as the foundation stone of America's Middle East peace effort.

It is the United States' position that--in return for peace--the withdrawal provision of Resolution 242 applies to all fronts, including the West Bank and Gaza.

When the border is negotiated between Jordan and Israel, our view on the extent to which Israel should be asked to give up territory will be heavily affected by the extent of true peace and normalization and the security arrangements offered in return.

Finally, we remain convinced that Jerusalem must remain undivided, but its final status should be decided through negotiations. . . .

It has often been said--and regrettably too often been true--that the story of the search for peace and justice in the Middle East is a tragedy of opportunities missed. . . . We must look beyond the difficulties and obstacles of the present and move with fairness and resolve toward a brighter future. We owe it to ourselves--and to posterity--to do no less. For if we miss this chance to make a fresh start, we may look back on this moment from some later vantage point and realize how much that failure cost us all.

These, then, are the principles upon which American policy toward the Arab-Israeli conflict will be based. I have made a personal commitment to see that they endure and, God willing, that they will come to be seen by all reasonable, compassionate people as fair, achievable, and in the interests of all who wish to see peace in the Middle East.

Ronald Reagan, televised Address to the Nation, Burbank, September 1, 1982; *Papers of Presidents: Reagan,* 1982, II, 1095-96. For commentary, see "Reagan Peace Plan for the Middle East," *Historic Documents,* 1982, pp. 753-67. For comments of Secretary of State George Shultz on negotiation and reconciliation in the Middle East, see his address, Business Council, Hot Springs, Virginia, May 13, 1983, in which he emphasized President Reagan's proposal, *American Foreign Policy: Current Documents,* 1983, pp. 665-66, and for letter of American Representative to the United Nations, commenting on the convening of an international conference on the Middle East, January 13, 1984, see volume for 1984, p. 492. Also see Document 527 on the peace process.

For additional documents and commentary on United States policy concerning the treatment and disposition of Jerusalem, see Documents 529 and 537 and *A Decade of American Foreign Policy, 1941-49*, pp. 859-60 (for United Nations General Assembly resolution, December 9, 1949) and *American Foreign Policy: Current Documents*, 1967, pp. 563-64 and 571-5, and for the United Nations resolution on the status of Jerusalem, July 14, 1967, pp. 577-79. Also see *American Foreign Policy: Basic Documents*, 1977-1980, pp. 711-72; *Current Documents*, 1984, pp. 492-93, 497-99; and *Digest of United States Practice in International Law*, 1979, p. 258.

On the matter of the occupied territories and Jewish settlements, also see *Digest of United States Practice in International Law*, 1976, pp. 700-12, and 1977, pp. 920-27; also *American Foreign Policy: Basic Documents*, 1977-1980, pp. 703-6; and *Current Documents*, 1984, p. 496; and *Historic Documents*, 1980, pp. 235-42, and 1981, pp. 899-909.

IRAN-IRAQ WAR AND ITS EXTENSION TO THE PERSIAN GULF, 1980-1988

War broke out in the Middle East in September 1980 when Iraq attacked Iran over a border dispute and waterway rights. From the outset the United States sought to maintain an uncommitted posture toward the belligerents. However, a number of related events affected American policy--especially the Iranian hostage crisis that began in November 1979 (see Chapter 14, Documents 227-233); the Soviet incursion into Afghanistan the following month, constraining the President to issue his Carter Doctrine (see Chapter 7, Documents 123-124) and to bolster American forces in the Persian Gulf and Indian Ocean; United States involvement in the pacification of conflict in Lebanon in the early 1980's (see Chapter 14, Documents 234-240); and extension of the Iran-Iraq War to the Persian Gulf area in 1984.

The war between Iran and Iraq--one of the bloodiest in recent history--lasted eight years, entailed massive destruction of property and loss of life in both countries, curtailed their oil production and export, and eventually threatened American and other neutral shipping in the Persian Gulf and Strait of Hormuz, the security of the Gulf states, and the petroleum supplies of Western and other oil-importing nations. Initially Iraq, supported by other Arab powers and supplied with arms by the Soviet Union, was successful in occupying Iranian territory and accepted a United Nations-sponsored cease-fire, but it was rejected by Iran. Hostilities escalated in the mid-1980's but reached a stalemate in 1987. The following year Iran launched a final attempt to achieve a military victory and continued to reject United Nations efforts to produce a cease-fire (for background, see "UN Resolution on Iran-Iraq War, July 20, 1987," *Historic Documents*, 1987, pp. 609-13).

The United States decided to refrain from direct involvement in continental hostilities, to press to keep the war from spreading, to prevent either belligerent from attaining a decisive victory, and to restrain the Soviet government from venturing into the area. Originally American policy consisted of neutrality for itself, noninterference by other powers, freedom of navigation and commerce in the Persian Gulf, and the signing of a truce followed by negotiations to produce a political settlement. However, when the war was extended to the Gulf in 1984 and neutral shipping came under attack by both belligerents, even in international waters, the United States joined other powers in providing naval and air protection, which involved it in a number of major and minor incidents and military actions in the shipping lanes, and in furnishing military assistance to preserve the security of the neutral Gulf states.

Lacking authoritative influence in both Tehran and Baghdad, the United States supported third-party mediation and United Nations Security Council action which, after several aborted attempts to terminate the fighting, finally produced a cease-fire agreed to by both Iran and Iraq in August 1988. The Soviet Union withdrew its troops from Afghanistan early in 1989, the Ayatollah Ruholla Khomeini died in June, and peace was finally restored.

The documents selected for this section consist of statements of initial American general goals and policies concerning the continental hostilities (Document 545); the extension of the war to the Persian Gulf area (Document 546); reaction to the Iraqi attack in 1987 on the U.S.S. *Stark,* a frigate on security patrol in the Gulf (Document 547); and official commentary on the cease-fire agreed to in 1988 to end the hostilities (Document 548).

545 INITIAL AMERICAN GOALS AND POSTURE

. . . Although the United States is in no way involved in this dispute--and charges to the contrary are obviously and patently false--it is important to make clear our position in this matter.

The fighting between Iran and Iraq is causing needless hardship and suffering among tho poople involved. It represents a danger to the peace and stability of the region. There should be absolutely no interference by any other nation in this conflict. The fighting should be promptly terminated. Any grievances between Iran and Iraq should be settled at the negotiating table and not on the battlefield. . . .

Let me repeat that we have not been and we will not become involved in the conflict between Iran and Iraq.

*   *   *

The United States Government has remained from the beginning, and will remain, neutral in the war between Iran and Iraq. We remain deeply concerned, however, about the continuation of this conflict and the attendant loss of life and destruction. The United States supports the independence and territorial integrity of both Iran and Iraq, as well as that of other states in the region. In keeping with our policy worldwide, we oppose the seizure of territory by force. We urge an immediate end to hostilities and a negotiated settlement. We support constructive international efforts for a peaceful solution to the conflict on the basis of each state's respect for the territorial integrity of its neighbors and each state's freedom from external coercion. In keeping with this policy we have joined with other members of the United Nations Security Council in 1980 and on July 12 of this year in resolutions calling for an end to the conflict.

Our support for the security of friendly states in the region which might feel threatened by the conflict is well known, and the United States is prepared to consult with these states on appropriate steps to support their security.

* * *

Another issue of war and peace in the Middle East that greatly concerns the United States is the war between Iran and Iraq. For many, this seems a remote and distant conflict, but it demands the attention of the entire international community. It has inflicted a cruel toll in lives and suffering. And it continues to threaten the security of the entire Persian Gulf region, an area of vital importance to the world economy.

Since the beginning of this war, we have called for an immediate cease-fire and a negotiated settlement to protect the independence and territorial integrity of both countries, reached without interference in their internal affairs. We deplore the continuation of this senseless war and the harm it has caused to both Iran and Iraq. There is no victor in this conflict, since both Iran and Iraq retain the capacity to do great damage to each other. Dreams of military victory or overthrow of governments are futile. Only a negotiated settlement that protects the basic interests of both countries can rescue them from this continuing disaster.

We also deplore the threats of both belligerents to escalate the war in the Gulf. Such a reckless course, by either Iran or Iraq, could be ruinous to both sides. It could also threaten the safety of other Gulf States. And it could endanger freedom of navigation and access to oil in the Gulf which is essential to the economic wellbeing of scores of nations, both industrialized and developing.

The United States welcomed the recent adoption of U.N. Security Council Resolution 540, which called for an end to hostilities in the Gulf, acknowledged the high cost of civilian casualties and damage in the war, and called for renewed efforts toward peace. We have also reaffirmed, and put all parties on notice of, our strong commitment to the right of free navigation in international waters.

Jimmy Carter, remarks, White House, September 24, 1980, in *American Foreign Policy: Basic Documents,* 1977-1980, p. 605; Deputy Press Secretary, White House, statement, July 14, 1982, in *Papers of Presidents: Reagan,* 1982, II, 923-24; and Assistant Secretary of State for Near Eastern and South Asian Affairs, statement, House Foreign Affairs Subcommittee, November 14, 1983, in *American Foreign Policy: Current Documents,* 1983, p. 712. Also see statement of United States Representative to the United Nations, September 28, 1980, with commentary, in *Digest of United States Practice in International Law,* 1980, pp. 996-998, which defines a fourfold American policy.

546 AMERICAN REACTION TO EXTENSION OF THE WAR TO THE PERSIAN GULF

As we've said on previous occasions, the United States deplores continuation and extension of the fighting between Iran and Iraq and urges the parties to agree to a cease-fire and negotiate their differences. We would view with grave concern attempts by any party to interfere with the right of passage of nonbelligerent ships through international waters.

The principle of freedom of navigation in the Gulf is, we believe, an important interest of the international community. If this principle should be challenged, apart from whatever action we may deem it in the United States interest to take, we would consult urgently with those states most directly concerned--both in the region and in the wider international community.

*   *   *

. . . While avoiding direct American involvement in the gulf war, we have worked successfully with other countries to prevent that war from ocoalating to threaten the overall stability of the region and to harm the free world's oil lifeline.

*   *   *

The war not only continues but it expands, posing an increasing threat to the stability of the region and even to the global economic system. The acceleration of attacks against shipping in the gulf, particularly attacks against shipping going into or out of the ports of nonbelligerent states, threatens not only those states but indirectly poses a potential threat to world price levels and inflation. . . .

The [United Nations Security] Council's specific concern today is the request of the six members of the Gulf Cooperative Council to consider attacks against nonbelligerent merchant vessels in international waters of the gulf and in the territorial waters of nonbelligerent states. It is completely appropriate that we should directly address this problem.

It is well known that rights of free passage of innocent shipping in international waters has long been enshrined in international law as a fundamental right, representing common interests of all states. Roman lawyers characterized the sea as *res communis*--by which they meant it is beyond appropriation. Their characterization has influenced the concept of freedom of the seas as we know it today. It is too important a right, too important a concept to an increasingly interdependent world, to permit it to be trampled upon.

We recognize that many of the issues which have been raised concerning this ongoing war are complicated. We wish they all could be resolved. We earnestly desire an overall settlement. We welcomed the fact that one of the parties to the war accepted in principle the cease-fire called for in Security Council Resolution 540, and we hope that . . . the time will come when both parties can agree to a cease-fire and mediation leading to a resolution of their differences.

However, we believe this is no reason not to straightforwardly address the issue of attacks on shipping as requested by the representatives of six states which asked for this meeting. . . .

We, therefore, agree with the members of the Gulf Cooperative Council that this Council should take a clear and unambiguous stand against the extremely dangerous expansion of the war by attacks on innocent vessels in international waters or in the territorial waters of noncombatants.

*   *   *

Our Middle East policy has long been based on our recognition that the region is a strategic crossroads between East and West and a source of energy for much of the free world, that Soviet dominance there would gravely disturb the worldwide strategic balance, and that we have close and historic ties with Israel and moderate Arab states in the area. Because of these basic interests, we have worked for over three decades to resolve regional conflicts and to seek a real peace between Israel and its Arab neighbors.

The war between Iran and Iraq, now in its fourth year, directly affects those interests. The continuing escalation in the Gulf threatens to widen the conflict, to curtail the Gulf's supply of oil to the West, and to endanger the security of our moderate Arab friends and the stability of the entire Middle East.

With that recognition, our policy consists of four crucial elements:

--The first is ensure the free flow of oil to the West;

--Second, to contain the expansion of Soviet and other radical influence;

--Third, to maintain the security of the Arab States of the Gulf. . . .

--Finally, and equally important, whatever steps we take must complement our efforts to achieve peace between the Arab States and Israel. . . .

Our objective is to bring the Gulf war to a negotiated end, in which neither belligerent is dominant, and in which the sovereignty and territorial integrity of both are preserved. It is our basic position that a victory by either side is neither militarily achievable nor strategically desirable because of its destabilizing effect on the region. Further, it is our objective to avoid direct U.S. military involvement in the war. We believe that a crucial factor in achieving that objective is to enable the Gulf states to defend themselves, rather than having to call for U.S. intervention for their protection.

Our policy in the Gulf, during more than 10 years and four administrations, has been to strengthen our friends' abilities to defend themselves while avoiding direct U.S. military involvement. We have been successful. Our security assistance program with Saudi Arabia, our cooperation with other states in the region, our military presence in the Arabian Sea, have all enhanced the confidence and capabilities of our friends. The tragic war in the Gulf has raged for almost 4 years. Not only has the oil continued to flow from the Gulf, but also our friends have been able to defend themselves without the presence of U.S. combat forces. These facts prove the validity of the objectives we established 10 years ago and are witness to our effectiveness at meeting them.

*   *   *

For more than 6 years, the war between Iran and Iraq has gone on, resulting in tremendous suffering and cost to Iran and Iraq as well as bringing instability to the Gulf region. As I have said many times, the United States is deeply concerned over the war's continuation. We are strongly interested in seeing it brought to a speedy conclusion through negotiations which will preserve the sovereignty and territorial integrity of both Iran and Iraq. Through our campaign to slow down and shut off the military supply pipelines to Iran, through our support of mediation efforts by the appropriate international organizations, we are working with many other governments in seeking to create a situation where the parties will sit down and negotiate.

At the same time, we also have a well-known policy regarding the Gulf. We are firmly committed to assisting our friends there with their collective and individual self defense efforts. We are also strongly committed to ensuring the free flow of oil through the Strait of Hormuz and hold as a very important tenet the principle of freedom of navigation in international waters. In brief, we want to see this long, costly, destabilizing, and tragic war brought to a negotiated end in the quickest time possible. . . .

The United States is neutral in the Iran-Iraq war. We do not now ship weapons to Iran or Iraq, nor do we intend to do so. This policy is firm.

Through Operation Staunch we try to persuade third countries not to supply Iran with arms, munitions, and dual-use items it needs to continue fighting. Operation Staunch is not directed towards Iraq; that country for some time has agreed to negotiate a settlement to the war. Iran remains the intransigent party and is occupying Iraqi territory and trying to take more.

The United States has taken an active role in searching for a peaceful solution to this tragic war. We want neither victor nor vanquished and continue to work for a settlement that will preserve the sovereignty and territorial integrity of both Iran and Iraq. I have urged the international community, in the appropriate fora and through the appropriate mechanisms, to work for an immediate cease-fire, negotiations, and withdrawal to borders. In line with this general policy, we have been actively consulting with other interested governments regarding efforts to bring the war to a negotiated end. . . .

We believe the U.N. Security Council has an important role to play in the effort to end the Gulf war and would strongly support effective action by the United Nations to end this conflict.

Department of State press briefing, September 18, 1983, in *American Foreign Policy: Current Documents*, 1983, p. 709; George Shultz, address, World

Affairs Council, Los Angeles, October 19, 1984, in *American Foreign Policy: Current Documents,* 1984, p. 18; Deputy Representative of the United States to the United Nations, statement, Security Council, May 30, 1984, pp. 521-22; Assistant Secretary of State for Near Eastern and South Asian Affairs, House Foreign Affairs Subcommittee, June 11, 1984, pp. 523-24; and Ronald Reagan, response to questions, University of Tennessee, Chattanooga, May 19, 1987, in 23 *Weekly Compilation of Presidential Documents* (May 25, 1987): 556. For commentary on the war in the Persian Gulf, with background, see *Historic Documents,* 1984, pp. 747-55.

5 4 7   IRAQI ATTACK ON THE U.S.S. *STARK,* MAY 1987

President Reagan met with the National Security Planning Group in the Situation Room from 2:30 until 3:45 this afternoon to discuss the status of the attack on the U.S.S. *Stark* in the Persian Gulf. The President has ordered a higher state of alert for U.S. vessels in the area. The belligerents in the war, Iran and Iraq, will be formally notified today of this change in status. Under this status, aircraft of either country flying in a pattern which indicates hostile intent will be fired upon, unless they provide adequate notification of their intentions.

The administration will consult with Congress on these changes and related issues.

We have issued a vigorous protest to the Government of Iraq. We have noted the profound regrets issued by the Iraqi Ambassador in the name of his Foreign Minister and Iraqi President Sadam Hussein. However, we are awaiting official notification of this statement. We expect an apology and compensation for the men who died in this tragic incident. We also seek compensation for the ship. The President shares the sense of concern and anger that Americans feel at this time.

*   *   *

I want to say something about yesterday's incident in the Persian Gulf. This tragedy must never be repeated. Our ships are deployed in the gulf in order to protect the United States interests and maintain freedom of navigation and access to the area's oil supplies. It's a vital mission. But our ships need to protect themselves, and they will. From now on, if aircraft approach any of our ships in a way that appears hostile, there is one order of battle: Defend yourselves, defend American lives. America's sailors are putting their lives on the line in the gulf. They have the right to protect themselves against any threat from any quarter at any time. . . .

Too often Americans are called upon to give their lives in the cause of world peace and freedom. Yet our glory as a people is that we do devote ourselves to those causes, not to conquest, not to territory, and not to supremacy, but to peace and freedom.

Assistant to the President for Press Relations, May 18, 1987, in 23 *Weekly Compilation of Presidential Documents* (May 25, 1987): 544-45; and Ronald Reagan, remarks, commencement ceremony, Chattanooga, Tennessee, p. 555.

Also see President Reagan's proclamation honoring Americans killed in the *Stark* attack, May 19, 1987, p. 561, and "Navy Reports on Attack on USS *Stark*," *Historic Documents*, 1987, pp. 791-815, which contains background, the text of the Iraqi apology, and the escalation of reprisals. Nearly forty Americans were killed in the attack.

548   ENDING HOSTILITIES--IRAN-IRAQ TRUCE, 1988

Before I begin my prepared remarks, I have a piece of very good news for you. The United Nations Secretary-General will announce later today a cease-fire in the Persian Gulf. This is news the world has waited for and the United States has pressed for--news that we may finally see an end to that long and bloody war. Although this is only a first step, it's an affirmation of a policy of strength and commitment. Our forces in the Persian Gulf and those of our allies have demonstrated that we have the resolve and the staying power in the Gulf, as well as in the Security Council when it comes to securing peace.

*   *   *

Turning now to regional conflicts, we feel again the uplift of hope. In the Gulf war between Iran and Iraq, one of the bloodiest conflicts since World War II, we have a cease-fire. The resolution and the firmness of the allied nations in keeping the Persian Gulf open to international shipping not only upheld the rule of law, it helped prevent further spread of the conflict and laid the basis for peace. So, too, the Security Council's decisive resolution in July a year ago has become the blueprint for a peaceful Gulf. Let this war--a war in which there has been no victor or vanquished, only victims--let this war end now. Let both Iran and Iraq cooperate with the Secretary-General and the Security Council in implementing Resolution 598. Let peace come.

Ronald Reagan, remarks, annual meeting of National Governors' Association, August 8, 1988, in 24 *Weekly Compilation of Presidential Documents* (August 15, 1988):   1020; and Ronald Reagan, address, United Nations General Assembly, September 26, 1988, p. 1208.   Also see statement of Assistant to the President for Press Relations, on continuing protection of United States shipping in the Persian Gulf, September 26, 1988, p. 1212.   For commentary on the origins of the Iran-Iraq War, the development of hostilities, and the truce of 1988, see *Historic Documents*, 1988, pp. 529-32.

31

Western Hemisphere

I have always believed that this hemisphere was a special place with a special destiny. I believe that we are destined to be the beacon of hope for all mankind. With God's help we can make it so. We can create a peaceful, free, and prospering hemisphere based on our shared ideals and reaching from pole to pole of what we proudly call the New World.

Ronald Reagan
Address,
Permanent Council of the Organization of American States, 1982

This chapter consists of two sections, providing general policy statements that propound United States policy themes for the Western Hemisphere and documentation concerning selected issues and problems in inter-American relations. The materials contained in this chapter need to be correlated with those presented in Chapters 6 (general policy propositions), 7 (Monroe, Johnson, and Reagan presidential doctrines), 11 and 12 (Bay of Pigs, Cuban missile, Panamanian, Dominican, and Grenada crises), 18 (alliances), and especially 26 (inter-American system).

POLICY THEMES

United States policy statements pertaining to the Western Hemisphere frequently reiterate themes of three types (Documents 549-556). The first consists of those generic precepts--often stated as goals--that are universal, namely, peace and the avoidance or prevention of war, national security, and the establishment of democracy and enhancement of human rights.

The second category overlaps those themes that focus on broad-scale Latin American relations, which parallel those applied to the inter-American system as noted in Chapter 26. They range from basic United States precepts, such as unity in forestalling and opposing outside intervention or aggression, independence of both the Western Hemisphere and individual national states, and the peaceful settlement of disputes, to those that emphasize common historical roots and aspirations, cooperation, and mutuality, including partnership, mutual confidence and respect, interdependence, multilateralism, collective consultation, and commitment to the functioning of the inter-American system--while recognizing national diversity and respecting individual national identity.

The third type, less general but often equally important, embraces such matters as action to comport with changes since World War II (characterized as the forces or tides of change), the qualities of realism and restraint, political and social stability, socioeconomic equity, the quality of life, energizing Latin American initiatives and the sharing of responsibility, and, in recent decades, increasing concern with economic matters. The latter include trade, development, capital flow, indebtedness, and multilateral and bilateral assistance.

5 4 9   COOPERATION, UNDERSTANDING, AND RESOLVE

The Western Hemisphere cannot alone assure world peace, but without the Western Hemisphere no peace is possible. The Western Hemisphere cannot alone provide world prosperity, but without the Western Hemisphere no world prosperity is possible.

Insofar as the economic problems common to the nations of North and South America are concerned, we have long been aware that much remains to be done. . . .

If acceptable solutions to these economic problems can be found, and if we can continue to work with mutual confidence and courage at the building of the great edifice of political security, . . . then I believe that we can look with high hopes on the further development of our community life in this hemisphere.

I have no desire to overlook the difficulties that have been encountered in the past and will continue to be encountered in the future. All of us are young and vigorous nations. At times we have been impetuous in our relations with one another. There has been a natural tendency for us to exhibit the same exuberance in our differences and our criticisms as in our friendships. Wide differences of background and tradition have had to be overcome.

But I believe that we may view with sober satisfaction the general history of our hemisphere. There has been steady progress in the development of mutual respect and of understanding among us. As the United States acquires greater maturity, as its experience becomes deeper and richer, our people gain in appreciation of the distinguished cultural traditions which flourish among our neighbors in the Western Hemisphere. I hope that as your acquaintance with us broadens, you will appreciate our fundamental good will and will understand that we are trying to bear with dignity and decency the responsibility of an economic power unique in human history.

There are many concrete problems ahead of us on the path to inter-American relations. They will not be solved with generalities or with sentimentality. They will call for the utmost we can give in practical ingenuity, in patience, and good will. But their solution will be easier if we are able to set our sights above the troubles of the moment and to bear in mind the great truths upon which our common prosperity and our common destiny must rest. . . .

The United States seeks world peace--a peace of free men. I know that you stand with us. United, we can constitute the greatest single force in the world for the good of humanity.

Harry Truman, address, Rio de Janeiro Inter-American Conference for the Maintenance of Peace and Security, September 2, 1947; *Papers of Presidents: Truman,* 1947, pp. 431-32.

5 5 0 ESSENCE OF THE NEW WORLD

Out of the crucible of our common past, the Americas have emerged as more equal and more understanding partners. . . . We are the New World, a world of sovereign and independent states that today stands shoulder to shoulder with a common respect for one another and a greater tolerance of one another's shortcomings.

Ronald Reagan, Caribbean Basin Initiative address, Permanent Council of the Organization of American States, February 24, 1982; Department of State, *Realism, Strength, Negotiation* (Washington: Department of State, 1984), p. 114. Also see Document 565.

5 5 1 BASIC POLICY PRECEPTS

In October 1969, I said that our policy toward Latin American would be based on five principles:
--firm commitment to the inter-American system;
--respect for national identity and national dignity;
--continued U.S. assistance to economic development;
--belief that this assistance should take the form of support for Latin American initiatives and should be extended primarily on a multilateral basis;
--dedication to improving the quality of life in the New World.

Those principles remain as valid today as when I first stated them. In candor, however, we must admit that our performance has not always been fully what we and our friends may have wished. . . .

Richard Nixon, *U.S. Foreign Policy for the 1970's: Shaping a Decade of Peace* (1973), p. 126.

* * *

The principles of our policies in this hemisphere have been clear and constant. . . . We support democracy and respect for human rights. We have struggled with many to help free the region of both repression and terrorism. We have respected ideological diversity and opposed outside intervention in purely internal affairs. We will act, though, in response to a request for assistance by a country threatened by external aggression. We support social and economic development within a democratic framework. We support the peaceful settlement of disputes. We strongly encourage regional cooperation and shared responsibilities within the hemisphere to all these ends, . . .

Jimmy Carter, State of the Union Message, January 16, 1981; *Papers of Presidents: Carter, 1980-1981*, p. 2988, and *Historic Documents, 1981*, p. 97.

552 SHARING IDEAS, INITIATIVES, AND RESPONSIBILITY

The nations of Latin America are our partners, not our dependents.

A tutelary style of United States leadership is unsuited to today's political conditions. The most effective form of hemispheric collaboration . . . is based on a wider sharing of ideas and a wider devolution of initiative. . . .

This is one function of consultation--to foster a sense of shared objectives and help achieve them. Hemispheric enterprises are most effective--and best help Latin America realize its great promise--when Latin Americans themselves play the major part in designing them. This strengthens the hemisphere-wide community.

However, it has long been obvious to our Latin American neighbors that within the wider community they share certain major interests and viewpoints as a group vis-a-vis the United States. The United States gains nothing by ignoring this or trying to deny it. The differences between us are apparent. What will preserve the hemisphere-wide community is practical cooperation among nations which have much to offer one another.

Richard Nixon, *U.S. Foreign Policy for the 1970's: The Emerging Structure of Peace*, 1972, pp. 92-93.

553 HEMISPHERIC INDEPENDENCE, DIVERSITY, AND INTERDEPENDENCE

Within the broad commonality of our relationship, there is great diversity. In a period of such profound social and cultural change, emerging domestic structures will differ by country, reflecting various historical roots, particular contexts, and national priorities. We can anticipate different interpretations of reality, different conceptions of self-interest and different conclusions on how to resolve problems.

The United States must comprehend these phenomena. We must recognize national interests may indeed diverge from ours rather than merge. Our joint task is to construct a community of institutions and interests broad and resilient enough to accommodate our national divergencies. . . .

Richard Nixon, *U.S. Foreign Policy for the 1970's: A New Strategy for Peace,* 1970, p. 52.

*   *   *

For more than a century and a half, our most consistent peacetime foreign relations were hemispheric relations. We have shared with our sister republics the experience of gaining and preserving our independence from the Old World. It was only natural that the nations of the New World should see their destinies as intertwined and continue to pay special attention to their ties with each other. Geography and history have bound us together and nurtured a sense of community, now formalized in the treaties and institutions of the inter-American system.

The purposes and practices of our association have changed over time, but its benefits have endured. It has helped to maintain the independence of the hemisphere from outside domination, to facilitate political and economic progress, and to enhance the region's influence in the world community.

Richard Nixon, *U.S. Foreign Policy for the 1970's: Building for Peace,* 1971, pp. 45-46.

5 5 4   DEMOCRACY AND HUMAN RIGHTS

A second dimension of the changes now taking place in the region is the gradual, uneven, but nonetheless distinct, movement toward greater democracy and respect for human rights. . . .

But the competition between democracy and authoritarianism is far from over. Injustice, frustration, and fear can breed cycles of violent extremes, producing polarization within countries and in the region. Repression, terrorism, or their scars persist, even in nations with once proud democratic traditions.

Thus, the prospects for democracy and human rights are far from uniform. But the currents are moving in favorable directions. The transition to more stable and open systems is underway and gaining momentum.

These moves toward more democratic and open societies in Latin America are distinctly in our interest. The great strength of democracy is its flexibility and resilience. It opens opportunities for broadly based political and economic participation. By encouraging compromise and accommodation, it fosters evolutionary change. In short, the evolution toward democracy serves our interests in a dynamic community of nations in this hemisphere.

Cyrus Vance, address, Foreign Policy Association, New York, September 27, 1979; *American Foreign Policy: Basic Documents,* 1977-1980, pp. 1295-96. Vance also discusses international engagement, economic development, and social change.

555   PEACE, MANAGEMENT OF ECONOMIES, INTERDEPENDENCE, AND DE-MOCRACY

Geography makes us neighbors. History, religion, and the shared experience of the frontier make us friends. There is far more that unites us in this hemishpere than can ever divide us. . . .

The striking thing to me, thinking over what has occurred in our lifetimes, is the success the American states have had in preventing war. . . .

Once actually confronted with crisis, I have no doubt that we will all react with good intentions, urging negotiations, offering good offices. But recent experience suggests that could be too late. Good intentions matter, but they are not enough. . . .

Clearly, no strategy for peace can succeed if those who take up arms against their fellow citizens and neighbors go unopposed. . . . Peace is impossible without security. . . . Neither democracy, nor human rights, nor socioeconomic equity are possible in a climate of insecurity, where hostile neighbors or violent internal minorities make war on society. . . .

My second group of reflections concerns the management of our economies. We are all members of the world economy and not dependent on the inter-American system for the management of our economies in the same way we are for the preservation of peace. Yet what each of us does-- in the management or mismanagement of our domestic economies--can greatly affect others in the hemisphere positively or negatively.

For the developing countries of the hemisphere, this last generation has been a period of soaring growth. The motors of that growth--savings and investment--have been largely fueled from within. . . .

That brings me to my third set of reflections, on what you might call the balance of our interdependence. No one doubts that we depend vitally on each other, for our prosperity, for our security, for peace. We can celebrate it--or we can deplore it--but it is a fact. . . .

But it is also natural that we should each be concerned about the balance of mutual accommodation. Some of the most difficult and important questions in international relations revolve around relations among neighbors. If we have to adjust our economies, who should adjust more or most? If we must compromise to keep the peace, who should go the longest way? And how do you measure it?

I think we all agree that matters such as these must not be decided simply by might or size but by principle and concept. I do not mean by that that we should attempt to write a book of codes anticipating every situation and dictating pre-agreed rules of the game. But we should always be prepared to examine together the justice and consistency of our actions, so that a balance acceptable to all can emerge. . . .

Finally, let me conclude with a word about democracy in the hemisphere. Our record is uneven. For some countries . . . democratic institutions have functioned without interruption for a generation and more. Other countries have faced instability despite long democratic periods. A few have experienced only interludes of democratic governance.

But what is most striking is that democracy is everywhere the hemisphere's recurring ideal and practical standard. In fact, our collective commitment is so strong that sometimes I think even the criticism of our failings is intensified by it. . . .

George Shultz, address, General Assembly of the Organization of American States, November 17, 1982; 82 *Department of State Bulletin* (December 1982), 64-67.

556   DEMOCRACY AND FREEDOM IN THE AMERICAS

The resurgence of democratic government in this hemisphere is a natural foundation for mutual understanding and improved cooperation. And I believe our common strength will increase the more consistently we apply our democratic principles--the more we provide good government as well as free elections and economic opportunity as well as political competition.

The challenges are awesome. But great ideas can be turned into great achievements. . . . And democracy can help us to turn our greatest visions into achievements.

We can, I believe, show that freedom, social justice, and economic development are mutually reinforcing and not mutually contradictory as our communist adversaries claim. We can show that democracies can combat antisocial violence such as terrorism and narcotics trafficking more successfully than dictatorships or regimes that rely on force. And we can show that the strength of democracy is the path to peace, at home and abroad. . . .

Freedom is the ingredient that makes participation meaningful and competition genuine--freedom from coercion and fear; freedom of speech and of the press; freedom of assembly; freedom to choose.

Because it fully expresses their interests and idiosyncracies, democracy protects the distinctiveness of our peoples and nations. It is a means of managing differences without depending on force. It is a means of enhancing individuality through freedom, and, therefore, democracy also creates powerful bonds among nations. Relations among democracies are more complex but more peaceful. Democratic governments listen to their peoples' voices, and agreements, once reached, have the strength that comes from popular support.

For much of the past generation, there has been a tendency to focus on what divides the peoples and nations of the Americas. We all know the refrains of division and doubt: north or south; poor or rich; Anglo or Latin; debtor or creditor; black or Indian; oil exporter or oil importer. Differences there are, but these litanies ignore more powerful realities: we are united by geography; we are united by the course of history; and we are united by choice--by the respect for individual decisions that are at the core of democracy and the secret of its success.

In short, democracy is a means of building strength out of diversity. The United States finds it easier to cooperate with nations that are democratic. And today, more OAS members are practicing democracies than ever before.

George Shultz, address, General Assembly of the Organization of American States, November 12, 1984; *American Foreign Policy: Current Documents,* 1984, pp. 983-84.

SELECTED ISSUES AND DEVELOPMENTS

Recent issues and developments selected for this section are of major and/or continuing significance. The documents provided pertain to the following five subjects. The first concerns the Alliance for Progress, initiated by John Kennedy and supported by subsequent presidents and Congress, which was launched in the 1960's to promote economic progress in the Americas (Documents 557-558).

In 1967 the Latin American nations signed a multilateral treaty to restrict their use of nuclear material and facilities solely to peaceful purposes and to prohibit the testing, manufacture, production, acquisition, or use by any means of nuclear weapons within their jurisdiction. Although the United States is not a party to this treaty, it signed its two protocols which, respectively, create obligations for the states that possess dependent territories within the area and for the principal nuclear powers (Document 559).

The United States and Panama negotiated new treaties in 1977 pre-scribing revised arrangements respecting the Panama Canal and the admin-istration of the Canal Zone through the year 1999 and for the permanent neutralization of the canal. The first of these treaties applies to the United States-Panamanian rights and responsibilities, whereas the second, open to accession by other nations as well, applies to the permanent international status of the canal when United States proprietary rights terminate (Documents 560-563). On the Panamanian crises of 1964 and 1989, also see Documents 191-197 and 208-210, especially Document 197 on the canal.

When Argentina invaded the Falkland Islands in April 1982 and the United Kingdom immediately responded militarily, the United States found itself in the unenviable position of having two allies at war with each other--one a member of the North Atlantic Alliance (see Documents 306, 319-320) and the other a member of the Organization of American States and a signatory of the Rio Pact (see Document 304). Although the United States, treading a diplomatic tight-rope, maintained a posture of neutrality on the crucial matter of sovereignty but played a key role in seeking to ameliorate and later to end the war by means of direct mediation and participation in the deliberations of both the Organ-ization of American States and the United Nations, hostilities were not termi-nated until Argentine forces surrendered in June (Document 564).

The final set of documents concerns the Caribbean and Central America. These deal with the Caribbean Basin Initiative of 1982, the struggle for democracy and the preservation of United States vital interests in Central

America, and United States objectives toward the Sandinista regime in Nicaragua (Documents 565-567).

On occasion the President commissions special envoys as his ambassador at large or his personal surrogates to undertake ceremonial, information-gathering, good-will, policy coordination, mediatory, or negotiating missions. In recent decades such appointments to Latin America have been made by President Eisenhower (Vice President Richard Nixon, 1955 and 1958, and Milton Eisenhower, 1953, 1957, and 1958), Kennedy (Adlai Stevenson, 1961, and Robert Kennedy, 1962), Johnson (Ellsworth Bunker, Dominican crisis, 1965), Nixon (Nelson Rockefeller, 1969), and Reagan (Henry Kissinger, 1983). In addition, for unofficial commentary on Western Hemisphere relations, see the report of the "Inter-American Dialogue Commission," which was prepared by forty-eight leading private citizens of the United States, Latin America, and Canada, and issued in April 1983 (see *Historic Documents,* 1983, pp. 375-91).

Other bilateral matters of interest include the problem of Soviet troops in Cuba (1979, see *American Foreign Policy: Basic Documents,* 1977-1980, pp 1342-56) and United States special relations with Canada and Mexico. Those pertaining to Canada--aside from bilateral defense cooperation (see Chapter 18)--embrace the agreement concerning the St. Lawrence Seaway project (1954, dedicated in 1959; see exchange of notes, June 8, 1959, and October 17, 1961, TIAS 4883; 12 *U.S. Treaties* 1669-73), the Columbia River Treaty providing for cooperation on water resources in the Northwest (1961, dedicated in 1964), navigation on the Great Lakes, maritime boundaries, fisheries, the Alaskan Highway and natural gas pipeline, acid rain, and the free trade treaty (1900). Those relating to Mexico include the construction of the Falcon Dam (dedicated in 1953) and the Armistad Dam (dedicated in 1969), the transfer of the El Chamizal territory to Mexico (1967), petroleum imports and other trade matters, Mexico's international indebtedness, drug traffic, and the control of illegal immigration.

557 KENNEDY'S ALLIANCE FOR PROGRESS PROPOSAL, 1961

We meet together as firm and ancient friends, united by history and experience and by our determination to advance the values of American civilization. For this New World of ours is not a mere accident of geography. Our continents are bound together by a common history, the endless exploration of new frontiers. Our nations are the product of a common struggle, the revolt from colonial rule. And our people share a common heritage, the quest for the dignity and the freedom of man.

The revolutions which gave us birth ignited, in the words of Thomas Paine, "a spark never to be extinguished." And across vast, turbulent continents these American ideals still stir man's struggle for national independence and individual freedom. But as we welcome the spread of the American revolution to other lands, we must also remember that our own struggle--the revolution which began in Philadelphia in 1776, and in Caracas in 1811--is not yet finished. Our hemishpere's mission is not yet completed. For our unfulfilled task is to demonstrate to the entire world that man's unsatisfied aspiration for economic progress and social justice can best be achieved by free men working within a framework of democratic institutions. . . .

Throughout Latin America, a continent rich in resources and in the spiritual and cultural achievements of its people, millions of men and women suffer the daily degradations of poverty and hunger. They lack decent shelter or protection from disease. Their children are deprived of the education or the jobs which are the gateway to a better life. And each day the problems grow more urgent. Population growth is outpacing economic growth--low living standards are further endangered--and discontent--the discontent of a people who know that abundance and the tools of progress are at last within their reach--that discontent is growing. . . .

If we are to meet a problem so staggering in its dimensions, our approach must itself be equally bold--an approach consistent with the majestic concept of Operation Pan America. Therefore I have called on all people of the hemisphere to join in a new Alliance for Progress--*Alianza para Progreso*--a vast cooperative effort, unparalleled in magnitude and nobility of purpose, to satisfy the basic needs of the American people for homes, work and land, health and schools. . . .

First, I propose that the American Republics begin on a vast new Ten Year Plan for the Americas, a plan to transform the 1960's into a historic decade of democratic progress.

These 10 years will be the years of maximum progress--maximum effort, the years when the greatest obstacles must be overcome, the years when the need for assistance will be the greatest.

And if we are successful, if our effort is bold enough and determined enough, then the close of this decade will mark the beginning of a new era in the American experience. . . .

Let me stress that only the most determined efforts of the American nations themselves can bring success to this effort. They, and they alone, can mobilize their resources, enlist the energies of their people, and modify their social patterns so that all, and not just a privileged few, share in the fruits of growth. If this effort is made, then outside assistance will give vital impetus to progress; without it, no amount of help will advance the welfare of the people.

Thus if the countries of Latin America are ready to do their part, and I am sure they are, then I believe the United States, for its part, should help provide resources of a scope and magnitude sufficient to make this bold development plan a success. . . .

Secondly, I will shortly request a ministerial meeting of the Inter-American Economic and Social Council, a meeting at which we can begin the massive planning effort which will be at the heart of the Alliance for Progress. . . .

Third, I have this evening signed a request to the Congress for $500 million as a first step in fulfilling the Act of Bogota. This is the first large-scale Inter-American effort, instituted by my predecessor President Eisenhower, to attack the social barriers which block economic progress. . . .

Fourth, we must support all economic integration which is a genuine step toward larger markets and greater competitive opportunity. The fragmentation of Latin American economies is a serious barrier to industrial growth. . . .

Fifth, the United States is ready to cooperate in serious, case-by-case examinations of commodity market problems. . . .

Sixth, we will immediately step up our Food for Peace emergency program, help establish food reserves in areas of recurrent drought, help provide school lunches for children, and offer feed grains for use in rural developments. . . .

Seventh, all the people of the hemisphere must be allowed to share in the expanding wonders of science--wonders which have captured man's imagination, challenged the powers of his mind, and given him the tools for rapid progress. . . .

Eighth, we must rapidly expand the training of those needed to man the economies of rapidly developing countries. This means expanded technical training programs, . . . It also means assistance to Latin American universities, graduate schools, and research institutes. . . .

Ninth, we reaffirm our pledge to come to the defense of any American nation whose independence is endangered. As its confidence in the collective security system of the OAS spreads, it will be possible to devote to constructive use a major share of those resources now spent on the instruments of war. . . .

Tenth, we invite our friends in Latin America to contribute to the enrichment of life and culture in the United States. . . .

With steps such as these, we propose to complete the revolution of the Americas, to build a hemisphere where all men can hope for a suitable standard of living, and all can live out their lives in dignity and in freedom.

To achieve this goal political freedom must accompany material progress. Our Alliance for Progress is an alliance of free governments, and it must work to eliminate tyranny from a hemisphere in which it has no rightful place. . . .

The completion of our task will, of course, require the efforts of all governments of our hemisphere. But the efforts of governments alone will never be enough. In the end, the people must choose and the people must help themselves.

John Kennedy, address, White House reception for members of Congress and diplomatic corps of Latin American republics, March 13, 1961; *Papers of Presidents: Kennedy*, 1961, pp. 170-75. For the Act of Bogota, adopted by the Council of the Organization of American States, October 11, 1960, which provided for social improvement and economic development of the Americas, see *American Foreign Policy: Current Documents*, 1960, pp. 293-99; and for President Kennedy's statement concerning Adlai Stevenson's special diplomatic mission to South America, May 29, 1961, see *Papers of Presidents: Kennedy*, 1961, pp. 414-15.

558   DECLARATION TO PEOPLES OF AMERICA, PUNTA DEL ESTE, 1961

Assembled in Punta del Este, inspired by the principles consecrated in the Charter of the Organization of American States, in Operation Pan America and in the Act of Bogota, the representatives of the American Republics hereby agree to establish an Alliance for Progress: a vast effort to bring a better life to all the people of the Continent.

This Alliance is established on the basic principle that free men working through the institution of representative democracy can best satisfy man's aspirations, including those for work, home and land, health and schools. No system can guarantee true progress unless it affirms the dignity of the individual which is the foundation of our civilization.

Therefore the countries signing this declaration in the exercise of their sovereignty have agreed to work toward the following goals during the coming years:

To improve and strengthen democratic institutions through application of the principle of self-determination by the people.

To accelerate economic and social development, thus rapidly bringing about a substantial and steady increase in the average income in order to narrow the gap between the standard of living in Latin American countries and that enjoyed in the industrialized countries.

To carry out urban and rural housing programs to provide decent homes for all our people.

To encourage, in accordance with the characteristics of each country, programs of comprehensive agrarian reform, leading to the effective transformation, where required, of unjust structures and systems of land tenure and use; . . .

To assure fair wages and satisfactory working conditions to all our workers; to establish effective systems of labor-management relations and procedures for consultation and cooperation among government authorities, employers' associations, and trade unions in the interests of social and economic development.

To wipe out illiteracy; to extend, as quickly as possible, the benefits of primary education to all Latin Americans; and to provide broader facilities, on a vast scale, for secondary and technical training and for higher education.

To press forward with programs of health and sanitation in order to prevent sickness, combat contagious disease, and strengthen our human potential.

To reform tax laws, demanding more from those who have most, to punish tax evasion severely, and to redistribute the national income in order to benefit those who are most in need, while, at the same time, promoting savings and investment and reinvestment of capital.

To maintain monetary and fiscal policies which, while avoiding the disastrous effects of inflation or deflation, will protect the purchasing power of the many, guarantee the greatest possible price stability, and form an adequate basis for economic development.

To stimulate private enterprise in order to encourage the development of Latin American countries at a rate which will help them to provide jobs for their growing populations, to eliminate unemployment, and to take their place among the modern industrialized nations of the world.

To find a quick and lasting solution to the grave problem created by excessive price fluctuations in the basic exports of Latin American countries on which their prosperity so heavily depends.

To accelerate the integration of Latin America so as to stimulate the economic and social development of the Continent. . . .

This declaration expresses the conviction of the nations of Latin America that these profound economic, social, and cultural changes can come about only through the self-help efforts of each country. Nonetheless, in order to achieve the goals which have been established with the necessary speed, domestic efforts must be reinforced by essential contributions of external assistance.

The United States, for its part, pledges its efforts to supply financial and technical cooperation in order to achieve the aims of the Alliance for Progress. . . .

For their part, the countries of Latin America agree to devote a steadily increasing share of their own resources to economic and social development, and to make the reforms necessary to assure that all share fully in the fruits of the Alliance for Progress.

Further, as a contribution to the Alliance for Progress, each of the countries of Latin America will formulate a comprehensive and well-conceived national program for the development of its own economy. . . .

Conscious of the overriding importance of this declaration, the signatory countries declare that the inter-American community is now beginning a new era when it will supplement its institutional, legal, natural and social accomplishments with immediate and concrete actions to secure a better life, under freedom and democracy, for the present and future generations.

Signed August 17, 1961, by all American republics except Cuba; *The Record of Punta del Este* (Washington: Pan American Union and the Agency for International Development, 1962), pp. 1-2, and *American Foreign Policy: Current Documents,* 1961, pp. 393-95.   For the text of the accompanying Charter of Punta del Este, establishing the multipartite Alliance for Progress, signed at Punta del Este, August 17, 1961, see *American Foreign Policy: Current Documents,* 1961, pp. 395-409.   It consists of four "titles" concerned with objectives, economic and social development, economic integration, and basic export commodities.   At Rio de Janeiro, November 1965, the original 10-year program was extended indefinitely.   Also see Declaration of Presidents of America, signed at Punta del Este, April 14, 1967; *American Foreign Policy: Current Documents,* 1967, pp. 673-85.

559   NUCLEAR FREE ZONE--LATIN AMERICA (TREATY OF TLATELOLCO), 1967

PROTOCOL I

The undersigned Plenipotentiaries, furnished with full powers by their respective Governments,

Convinced that the Treaty for the Prohibition of Nuclear Weapons in Latin America, negotiated and signed in accordance with the recommendations of the General Assembly of the United Nations in Resolution 1911 (XVIII) of 27 November 1963, represents an important step towards ensuring the non-proliferation of nuclear weapons,

Aware that the non-proliferation of nuclear weapons is not an end in itself but, rather, a means of achieving general and complete disarmament at a later stage, and

Desiring to contribute, so far as lies in their power, towards ending the armaments race, especially in the field of nuclear weapons, and towards strengthening a world at peace, based on mutual respect and sovereign equality of States,

Have agreed as follows:

ARTICLE 1.   To undertake to apply the status of denuclearization in respect of warlike purposes as defined in articles 1, 3, 5 and 13 of the Treaty for the Prohibition of Nuclear Weapons in Latin America in territories for which, *de jure* or *de facto,* they are internationally responsible and which lie within the limits of the geographical zone established in that Treaty.

ARTICLE 2.   The duration of this Protocol shall be the same as that of the Treaty for the Prohibition of Nuclear Weapons in Latin America of which this Protocol is an annex, and the provisions regarding ratification and denunciation contained in the Treaty shall be applicable to it.

ARTICLE 3.   This Protocol shall enter into force, for the States which have ratified it, on the date of the deposit of their respective instruments of ratification.

*   *   *

PROTOCOL II

The undersigned Plenipotentiaries, furnished with full powers by their respective Governments, . . .

Have agreed as follows:

Article 1.   The statute of denuclearization of Latin America in respect of warlike purposes, as defined, delimited and set forth in the Treaty for the Prohibition of Nuclear Weapons in Latin America of which this instrument is an annex, shall be fully respected by the Parties to this Protocol in all its express aims and provisions.

Article 2.   The Governments represented by the undersigned Plenipotentiaries undertake, therefore, not to contribute in any way to the performance of acts involving a violation of the obligations of article 1 of the Treaty in the territories to which the Treaty applies in accordance with article 4 thereof.

Article 3.   The Governments represented by the undersigned Plenipotentiaries also undertake not to use or threaten to use nuclear weapons against the Contracting Parties of the Treaty for the Prohibition of Nuclear Weapons in Latin America.

Article 4.   The duration of this Protocol shall be the same as that of the Treaty for the Prohibition of Nuclear Weapons in Latin America of which this Protocol is an annex, and the definitions of territory and nuclear weapons set forth in articles 3 and 5 of the Treaty shall be applicable to this Protocol, as well as the provisions regarding ratification, reservations, denunciation, authentic texts and registration contained in articles 26, 27, 30 and 31 of the Treaty.

Article 5.   This Protocol shall enter into force, for the States which have ratified it, on the date of the deposit of their respective instruments of ratification.

For the text of the Treaty of Tlatelolco, providing for the Prohibition of Nuclear Weapons in Latin America, negotiated and signed on February 14, 1967--to which the United States is not a party see TIAS 7137; 22 *U.S. Treaties* 762-86.   Protocols I and II were also negotiated in 1967.   Protocol I was ratified by the United States in 1981; see TIAS 10147; 33 *U.S. Treaties* 1792-99. Protocol II was ratified in 1971; see TIAS 7137; 22 *U.S. Treaties* 754-56.   Signatories of Protocol I include the Netherlands, the United Kingdom, and the United States, and signatories of Protocol II include China, France, the Soviet Union, the United Kingdom, and the United States.   Also see the Antarctic Treaty (Document 573) which, in Article 1, prohibits arms (including nuclear) in the Antarctic area.

560 PANAMA CANAL TREATY NEGOTIATIONS

Immediately after its formation as a nation in 1903, Panama signed a treaty with the United States which granted the United States--in perpetuity--the use of a 10-mile wide strip of Panamanian territory for the "construction, maintenance, operation, and protection" of an interoceanic canal as well as all the rights, power, and authority which the United States would possess "if it were the sovereign."   The very favorable terms of the treaty were a major factor in the decision by the United States to build the canal in Panama rather than in Nicaragua, which was widely favored at the time.

Despite some revisions in 1936 and 1955, the 1903 treaty has been and remains a source of friction and conflict between the United States and Panama. . . .

Historically, the canal has made a significant contribution to our country's military security.   It remains an important defense asset, the use of which enhances U.S. capability for timely reinforcement and resupply of U.S. forces.   Its strategic military advantage lies in the economy and flexibility it provides to accelerate the shift of military forces and logistic support by sea between the Atlantic and Pacific Oceans to overseas areas.

For the foreseeable future the canal will continue to have economic and military value for the United States; therefore, we believe it must continue to function efficiently. The principal objective of the United States in the current treaty negotiations is to assure that the Panama Canal is operational, secure, efficient, and open on a non-discriminatory basis to world shipping. . . .

Panamanian discontent, however, is primarily political. It is focused on the treaty's terms which granted to the United States "in perpetuity" sweeping jurisdictional powers as "if it were the sovereign," over 550 square miles of Panamanian territory. The problem, Panama asserts, is that the United States operates a full-fledged foreign government on Panamanian territory. To back up its contention Panama states that the United States exercises almost total jurisdictional rights, maintaining a police force, courts, and jails to enforce U.S. laws which are applicable equally to Panamanian as well as U.S. citizens in the Canal Zone. . . .

Over the years the United States has attempted to respond to some of Panama's most pressing concerns. The 1903 treaty was revised in 1936 and again in 1955. As a result Panama now receives a greater share of the economic benefits related to the canal. Also, certain outdated powers have been eliminated, such as our right to interfere in Panama's internal affairs.

Despite these modifications, however, the most objectionable feature in the present treaty, from Panama's viewpoint--the U.S. exercise of rights over the Canal Zone as if it were sovereign forever-- has remained unchanged.

In recent years the other Latin American nations have strongly supported Panama's quest for a more modern treaty. They have made the negotiation of a new treaty a major hemispheric issue as well as a general test of U.S. intentions regarding all of Latin America. . . .

During 1964, the status of the canal was debated in the United Nations, the Organization of American States (OAS), and other international bodies. On April 3, 1964, following discussions in the OAS, the United States and Panama agreed to appoint special ambassadors to work out existing differences between the two countries. . . . On December 18, 1964, President Johnson, after consulting with Presidents Truman and Eisenhower, and with bipartisan support, made a public commitment to negotiate a wholly new, fixed-term canal treaty. . . . President Nixon and President Ford subsequently reaffirmed that commitment.

In 1967 three draft agreements were prepared but neither government moved to ratify them. Later the Government of Panama, under General Omar Torrijos, formally rejected these draft treaties. The United States and Panama renewed negotiations in 1971 but progress was limited. . . .

On February 7, 1974, Secretary of State Kissinger and Panamanian Foreign Minister Juan Antonio Tack met in Panama City and signed a Joint Statement of Principles . . . which has served as the framework for the present negotiations. . . .

In summary, the mutual goal of Panama and the United States is to negotiate a treaty which will satisfy the basic concerns of both nations, gain the appropriate constitutional acceptance in both nations, and evoke the full support of both the American and Panamanian people.

Policy statement issued by Department of State, January 1977; *American Foreign Policy: Basic Documents,* 1977-1980, pp. 1379-83. For additional documentation concerning the Panama Canal treaties, with treaty texts and ratification instruments, see pp. 1383-1424. For President John Kennedy's letter to the President of Panama, November 2, 1961, concerning United States reexamination of current and future needs respecting isthmian canal facilities, see *American Foreign Policy: Current Documents,* 1961, pp. 339-40. For President Lyndon Johnson's statement concerning his decision to plan a new sea-level canal and to negotiate a new treaty on the existing Panama Canal, December 18, 1964, see *American Foreign Policy: Current Documents,* 1964, pp. 370-72. For President Johnson's statement concerning "agreement in principle" with the Panamanian government respecting revision of existing Panama Canal treaties, September 24, 1965, see *American Foreign Policy: Current Documents,* 1965, pp. 1013-14. For the United States-Panamanian joint declaration of principles for a new Canal treaty, signed by Henry Kissinger on February 7, 1974, see *Digest of United States Practice in International Law,* 1974, pp. 355-56.

561   PANAMA CANAL TREATY, 1977

ARTICLE I
ABROGATION OF PRIOR TREATIES AND
ESTABLISHMENT OF A NEW RELATIONSHIP

1. Upon its entry into force, this Treaty terminates and supersedes:

(a) The Isthmian Canal Convention between the United States of America and the Republic of Panama, signed at Washington, November 18, 1903;

(b) The Treaty of Friendship and Cooperation signed at Washington, March 2, 1936, and the Treaty of Mutual Understanding and Cooperation and the related Memorandum of Understandings Reached, signed at Panama, January 25, 1955, between the United States of America and the Republic of Panama;

(c) All other treaties, conventions, agreements and exchanges of notes between the United States of America and the Republic of Panama, concerning the Panama Canal which were in force prior to the entry into force of this Treaty; and

(d) Provisions concerning the Panama Canal which appear in other treaties, conventions, agreements and exchanges of notes between the United States of America and the Republic of Panama which were in force prior to the entry into force of this Treaty.

2. In accordance with the terms of this Treaty and related agreements, the Republic of Panama, as territorial sovereign, grants to the

United States of America, for the duration of this Treaty, the rights necessary to regulate the transit of ships through the Panama Canal, and to manage, operate, maintain, improve, protect and defend the Canal. The Republic of Panama guarantees to the United States of America the peaceful use of the land and water areas which it has been granted the rights to use for such purposes pursuant to this Treaty and related agreements.

3. The Republic of Panama shall participate increasingly in the management and protection and defense of the Canal, as provided in this Treaty.

4. In view of the special relationship established by this Treaty, the United States of America and the Republic of Panama shall cooperate to assure the uninterrupted and efficient operation of the Panama Canal.

ARTICLE II
RATIFICATION, ENTRY INTO FORCE, AND TERMINATION

1. This Treaty shall be subject to ratification in accordance with the constitutional procedures of the two Parties. The instruments of ratification of this Treaty shall be exchanged at Panama at the same time as the instruments of ratification of the Treaty Concerning the Permanent Neutrality and Operation of the Panama Canal, signed this date, are exchanged. This Treaty shall enter into force, simultaneously with the Treaty Concerning the Permanent Neutrality and Operation of the Panama Canal, six calendar months from the date of the exchange of the instruments of ratification.

2. This Treaty shall terminate at noon, Panama time, December 31, 1999.

ARTICLE III
CANAL OPERATION AND MANAGEMENT

1. The Republic of Panama, as territorial sovereign, grants to the United States of America the rights to manage, operate, and maintain the Panama Canal, its complementary works, installations and equipment and to provide for the orderly transit of vessels through the Panama Canal. The United States of America accepts the grant of such rights and undertakes to exercise them in accordance with this Treaty and related agreements. . . .

3. Pursuant to the foregoing grant of rights, the United States of America shall, in accordance with the terms of this Treaty and the provisions of United States law, carry out its responsibilities by means of a United States Government agency called the Panama Canal Commission, which shall be constituted by and in conformity with the laws of the United States of America.

(a) The Panama Canal Commission shall be supervised by a Board composed of nine members, five of whom shall be nationals of the United States of America, and four of whom shall be Panamanian nationals proposed by the Republic of Panama for appointment to such positions by the United States of America in a timely manner. . . .

(c) The United States of America shall employ a national of the United States of America as Administrator of the Panama Canal Commission, and a Panamanian national as Deputy Administrator, through December 31, 1989. Beginning January 1, 1990, a Panamanian national shall be employed as the Administrator and a national of the United States of America shall occupy the position of Deputy Administrator. . . .

10. Upon entry into force of this Treaty, the United States Government agencies known as the Panama Canal Company and the Canal Zone Government shall cease to operate within the territory of the Republic of Panama that formerly constituted the Canal Zone.

ARTICLE IV
PROTECTION AND DEFENSE

1. The United States of America and the Republic of Panama commit themselves to protect and defend the Panama Canal. Each Party shall act, in accordance with its constitutional processes, to meet the danger resulting from an armed attack or other actions which threaten the security of the Panama Canal or of ships transiting it.

2. For the duration of this Treaty, the United States of America shall have primary responsibility to protect and defend the Canal. The rights of the United States of America to station, train, and move military forces within the Republic of Panama are described in the Agreement in Implementation of this Article, signed this date. The use of areas and installations and the legal status of the armed forces of the United States of America in the Republic of Panama shall be governed by the aforesaid Agreement.

3. In order to facilitate the participation and cooperation of the armed forces of both Parties in the protection and defense of the Canal, the United States of America and the Republic of Panama shall establish a Combined Board comprised of an equal number of senior military representatives of each Party. These representatives shall be charged by their respective governments with consulting and cooperating on all matters pertaining to the protection and defense of the Canal, and with planning for actions to be taken in concert for that purpose. Such combined protection and defense arrangements shall not inhibit the identity or lines of authority of the armed forces of the United States of America or the Republic of Panama. The Combined Board shall provide for coordination and cooperation concerning such matters as:

(a) The preparation of contingency plans for the protection and defense of the Canal based upon the cooperative efforts of the armed forces of both Parties;

(b) The planning and conduct of combined military exercises; and

(c) The conduct of United States and Panamanian military operations with respect to the protection and defense of the Canal.

4. The Combined Board shall, at five-year intervals throughout the duration of this Treaty, review the resources being made available by the two Parties for the protection and defense of the Canal. Also, the Combined Board shall make appropriate recommendations to the two Governments respecting projected requirements, the efficient utilization of available resources of the two Parties, and other matters of mutual

interest with respect to the protection and defense of the Canal.

5. To the extent possible consistent with its primary responsibility for the protection and defense of the Panama Canal, the United States of America will endeavor to maintain its armed forces in the Republic of Panama in normal times at a level not in excess of that of the armed forces of the United States of America in the territory of the former Canal Zone immediately prior to the entry into force of this Treaty.

ARTICLE V
PRINCIPLE OF NON-INTERVENTION

Employees of the Panama Canal Commission, their dependents and designated contractors of the Panama Canal Commission, who are nationals of the United States of America, shall respect the laws of the Republic of Panama and shall abstain from any activity incompatible with the spirit of this Treaty. Accordingly, they shall abstain from any political activity in the Republic of Panama as well as from any intervention in the internal affairs of the Republic of Panama. The United States of America shall take all measures within its authority to ensure that the provisions of this Article are fulfilled. . . .

ARTICLE XII
A SEA-LEVEL CANAL OR A THIRD LANE OF LOCKS

1. The United States of America and the Republic of Panama recognize that a sea-level canal may be important for international navigation in the future. Consequently, during the duration of this Treaty, both Parties commit themselves to study jointly the feasibility of a sea-level canal in the Republic of Panama, and in the event they determine that such a waterway is necessary, they shall negotiate terms, agreeable to both Parties, for its construction.

2. The United States of America and the Republic of Panama agree on the following:

(a) No new interoceanic canal shall be constructed in the territory of the Republic of Panama during the duration of this Treaty, except in accordance with the provisions of this Treaty, or as the two Parties may otherwise agree; and

(b) During the duration of this Treaty, the United States of America shall not negotiate with third States for the right to construct an interoceanic canal on any other route in the Western Hemisphere, except as the two Parties may otherwise agree. . . .

ARTICLE XIII
PROPERTY TRANSFER AND ECONOMIC
PARTICIPATION BY THE REPUBLIC OF PANAMA

1. Upon termination of this Treaty, the Republic of Panama shall assume total responsibility for the management, operation, and maintenance of the Panama Canal, which shall be turned over in operating condition and free of liens and debts, except as the two Parties may otherwise agree.

2. The United States of America transfers, without charge, to the Republic of Panama all right, title and interest the United States of

America may have with respect to all real property, including non-removable improvements thereon, as set forth below. . . .

Treaty consists of 14 articles, an "annex," and an "agreed minute," signed by President Jimmy Carter and the President of Panama on September 7, 1977. It also provides for protection of the environment, the use of national flags, privileges and immunities of canal agencies and instrumentalities, law enforcement, employment arrangements, and principles governing the transition period and the settlement of disputes. TIAS 10030; and *American Foreign Policy: Basic Documents,* 1977-1980, pp. 1386-1400. The treaty was supplemented with a series of agreements to implement specific treaty articles; for citations see *Treaties in Force.* For commentary on, summary of terms, relation to other treaties, and implementing legislation, see *Digest of United States Practice in International Law,* 1977, pp. 575-96; 1978, pp. 1027-70; and 1979, pp. 1070-82. For comprehensive documentation, including the texts of this and the neutrality treaty (Document 562), and the ratification resolutions and instruments, see *American Foreign Policy: Basic Documents,* 1977-1980, pp. 1379-1424. Also see *Historic Documents,* 1977, pp. 591-623, and on ratification, see 1978, pp. 177-222. For Panama Canal Act, see Public Law 96-70; 93 *Statutes at Large,* 452.

562 TREATY CONCERNING THE PERMANENT NEUTRALITY OF THE PANAMA CANAL, 1977

Article I
The Republic of Panama declares that the Canal, as an international transit waterway, shall be permanently neutral in accordance with the regime established in this Treaty. The same regime of neutrality shall apply to any other international waterway that may be built either partially or wholly in the territory of the Republic of Panama.

Article II
The Republic of Panama declares the neutrality of the Canal in order that both in time of peace and in time of war it shall remain secure and open to peaceful transit by the vessels of all nations on terms of entire equality, so that there will be no discrimination against any nation, or its citizens or subjects, concerning the conditions or charges of transit, or for any other reason, and so that the Canal, and therefore the Isthmus of Panama, shall not be the target of reprisals in any armed conflict between other nations of the world. . . .

Article IV
The United States of America and the Republic of Panama agree to maintain the regime of neutrality established in this Treaty, which shall be maintained in order that the Canal shall remain permanently neutral, notwithstanding the termination of any other treaties entered into by the two Contracting Parties.

Article V

After the termination of the Panama Canal Treaty, only the Republic of Panama shall operate the Canal and maintain military forces, defense sites and military installations within its national territory.

Article VI

1. In recognition of the important contributions of the United States of America and of the Republic of Panama to the construction, operation, maintenance, and protection and defense of the Canal, vessels of war and auxiliary vessels of those nations shall, notwithstanding any other provisions of this Treaty, be entitled to transit the Canal irrespective of their internal operation, means of propulsion, origin, destination, armament or cargo carried. Such vessels of war and auxiliary vessels will be entitled to transit the Canal expeditiously. . . .

Article VII

1. The United States of America and the Republic of Panama shall jointly sponsor a resolution in the Organization of American States opening to accession by all States of the world the Protocol to this Treaty whereby all the signatories will adhere to the objectives of this Treaty, agreeing to respect the regime of neutrality set forth herein. . . .

Treaty consists of 8 articles and "annexes," signed by President Jimmy Carter and the President of Panama, September 7, 1977. TIAS 10029; and *American Foreign Policy: Basic Documents,* 1977-1980, pp. 1400-2. A protocol was added, open for signature by additional states to honor the neutrality of the Canal, which has been signed by some two dozen governments; see *Treaties in Force.*

563 PANAMA CANAL NEUTRALITY--CARTER-TORRIJOS STATEMENT, 1977

Under the Treaty Concerning the Permanent Neutrality and Operation of the Panama Canal (the Neutrality Treaty), Panama and the United States have the responsibility to assure that the Panama Canal will remain open and secure to ships of all nations. The correct interpretation of this principle is that each of the two countries shall, in accordance with their respective constitutional processes, defend the Canal against any threat to the regime of neutrality, and consequently shall have the right to act against any aggression or threat directed against the Canal or against the peaceful transit of vessels through the Canal.

This does not mean, nor shall it be interpreted as a right of intervention of the United States in the internal affairs of Panama. Any United States action will be directed at insuring that the Canal will remain open, secure and accessible, and it shall never be directed against the territorial integrity or political independence of Panama.

The Neutrality Treaty provides that the vessels of war and auxiliary vessels of the United States and Panama will be entitled to transit the Canal expeditiously. This is intended, and it shall so be interpreted, to assure the transit of such vessels through the Canal as quickly as possible, without any impediment, with expedited treatment, and in case of need or emergency, to go to the head of the line of vessels in order to transit the Canal rapidly.

This addendum to the Panama Canal neutrality treaty constituted a joint statement of interpretation, signed October 14, 1977. *Papers of Presidents: Carter,* 1977, p. 1793; and *American Foreign Policy: Basic Documents,* 1977-1980, p. 1403. For President Carter's address to the nation, February 1, 1978, presenting "the facts" about the canal treaties, see *American Foreign Policy: Basic Documents,* 1977-1980, pp. 1408-12. For commentary on the approval and ratification of the canal treaties, see *Digest of United States Practice in International Law,* 1977-1979, cited in note for Document 561.

564 FALKLAND ISLANDS WAR, 1982

BACKGROUND SUMMARY

The Falkland Islands dispute dates to the era of early European exploration. Spain and England nearly went to war over control of the area in the 18th century, and the question of sovereignty has been a matter of keen significance to Argentina from its moment of independence in 1816. The United States was involved in events of the early 1830s. In 1833 the British established an enduring British presence. For the next 150 years, the British developed the islands as a colony supporting a whaling and a sheep industry protected by the Royal Navy. Argentina never allowed its sense of grievance to cool and in the post 1945 era raised the claim repeatedly. Sporadic U.K.-Argentina negotiations have occurred since 1966. The U.S. position has been to accept the fact of British presence without prejudice to the question of ultimate sovereignty and to avoid taking sides on the issue. . . .

Since the Second World War, successive U.S. Administrations have hewed to a course of strict neutrality on the Falklands issue despite repeated Argentine requests for support. At inter-American conferences of the 1945-55 period, the United States reiterated its neutral position and called for a peaceful settlement. With the Falklands in mind it abstained or voted against resolutions calling for a definitive end to colonialism in the Americas, self-determination for the colonies of extracontinental powers, and the monitoring of dependent territories by the Organization of American States.

In 1964 Argentina began a concerted international campaign for the "return of the Malvinas," taking its case to the United Nations and the Committee of 24 as a colonial issue. The United States declined formal and informal Argentine requests for support and abstained on a resolution calling for bilaterial U.K.-Argentine negotiations and an end to "colonialism" in the Falklands. In 1965 the United States again abstained on an Argentine-initiated resolution at the U.N. General Assembly. The United Kingdom and Argentina did begin negotiations in January 1966, but a hijacking and symbolic "invasion" of the islands by a handful of Argentine nationalists occurred in October, followed by anti-British demonstrations in Argentina.

In November 1967 Prime Minister Harold Wilson's Labor government appeared to accept the principle of eventual Argentine control of the islands, dependent on the will of the inhabitants. A visit to the Falklands by Lord Chalfont, Minister of State, in November 1968 raised the islanders' fears of abandonment. An uproar in the London press and Conservative Party opposition in Parliament fueled sentiment to retain the islands. Rumors in 1969 of possible oil deposits added another dimension to the controversy.

In July 1971 the two sides announced a series of agreements increasing commercial, communications, social, and cultural links between the Falklands and Argentina. However, following the return of Juan Peron, the negotiations collapsed in November 1973. The Argentine Government again asked for U.S. support but was rebuffed by the familiar stance of impartiality. A British economic survey of the Falklands in 1976 met with a vigorous protest from Argentina, and there occurred an incident at sea involving the Argentine Navy and a British research vessel. Probable oil deposits seemed to be a cause for heightened tension. British and Argentine negotiators resumed discussions in 1977 and by December 1978 had agreed on scientific cooperation in research on the Falkland dependencies. A new round of negotiations commenced in March 1981. In October the United Kingdom conducted elections for a local legislative council.

Early in 1982, Argentina insisted upon monthly bilateral negotiations with a preestablished agenda and escalated the level of its rhetoric on the issue. Disagreement over the presence of Argentines on the South Georgia Islands to dismantle an abandoned whaling factory led to sharply rising tensions. There followed the Argentine invasion of the Falklands on April 2 and on South Georgia on April 4.

Throughout the postwar period the United States had not deviated from its refusal to take a position on the issue of sovereignty.

Statement prepared by Neal H. Petersen, Office of the Historian, Department of State, in 82 *Department of State Bulletin* (June 1982): 88-89. For a later background survey, also see statement by Thomas O. Enders, Assistant Secretary of State for Inter-American Affairs, submitted to the House Foreign Affairs Committee, August 5, 1982, in 82 *Department of State Bulletin* (October 1982): 78-80. For comprehensive collection of documents, including the texts of United Nations and Organization of American States resolutions and presidential and other statements, see 82 *Department of State Bulletin* (June 1982); 81-89 and (July 1982): 86-91. For general background, see *Historic Documents,* 1982, pp. 283-304, and 1983, pp. 3-23.

*   *   *

WHITE HOUSE STATEMENT

The President and this administration have been intensely involved in the search for peace since the beginning of the dispute in the South Atlantic. Our deep concern over the threat of conflict has been evident to the international community. We have made bilateral and multilateral efforts in support of that effort. . . .

Let me emphasize, there will be no involvement whatsoever of U.S. military personnel in the conflict in the South Atlantic. As the President and Secretary Haig have said, we will meet our commitments to Great Britain. Any responses made to requests for assistance will be carefully evaluated on a case-by-case basis. We will, however, not address reports of specific requests for assistance or how we respond.

Our position throughout this dispute has been to do whatever we can to advance the chances for a peaceful resolution, and that remains our stance. Every step, every action of the President and the United States Government shall be taken with one thought in mind--a peaceful solution. We stand ready to assist in any way we can.

Deputy White House Press Secretary, statement, press briefing, May 21, 1982; *Papers of Presidents: Reagan,* 1982, p. 662.

*   *   *

ANALYSIS OF THE CONFLICT

It is from Great Britain that the United States drew the inspiration for many of its most cherished institutions. Most of us stood at the side of Great Britain in two world wars in this century. Great Britain is a vital partner in the alliance with Europe which is the first line of defense for Western civilization against the dangers of Soviet aggression.

Argentina is an American republic, one of us. It is a nation, like the United States, founded on the republican ideal that all men are created equal. Like my country it is a nation of immigrants and settlers whose own culture and civilization have long had the respect of my countrymen and the world. President Reagan moved early in his Administration to make clear the high value we place on our relations with the Government of Argentina and the high esteem in which we hold the Argentine people.

It is not only our friendship and our ties with the two countries that are at stake. This festering dispute has suddenly become a violent conflict that poses dangers to the very institutions and principles . . . that have made this hemisphere, in many ways, the envy of the world.

The war puts the inter-American system under stress. Some say that this is an "anticolonial war" because the islands were formally administered as a British colony. Some say that since this is a war that pits an American republic against an outside power, the Rio treaty requires that all its members come to the assistance of the American republic.

Others say that it is impossible to speak of colonialism when a people is not subjugated to another. . . . Others say there is no way in which the inter-American system--which protects regional order based on law and the peaceful settlement of dispute--can be interpreted as sanctioning the first use of armed force to settle a dispute.

With full respect for the views of others, the U.S. position is clear: Since the first use of force did not come from outside the hemisphere, this is not a case of extracontinental aggression against which we are all committed to rally. . . .

We face a conflict that involves us all, but to which the Rio treaty does not well apply. It is a dispute over competing claims of sovereignty, each with profound historical and emotional sources.

We know how deep is the Argentine commitment to recover islands Argentines believe were taken from them by illegal force. This is not some sudden passion but a longstanding national concern that reaches back 150 years and is heightened by the sense of frustration over what Argentina feels were nearly 20 years of fruitless negotiation.

We know, too, how deeply Britain, in peaceful possession of the disputed territory for 150 years, has been devoted to the proposition that the rights and views of the inhabitants should be considered in any future disposition of the islands. No one can say that Britain's attitude is simply a colonial reflex to retain possession of distant islands. In the last 20 years no less than nine of the members of the Organization of American States received their independence in peace and goodwill from Great Britain.

For its part, the United States has not taken--and will not take-- any position on the substance of the dispute. We are completely neutral on the question of who has sovereignty. Indeed, 35 years ago, at the 1947 signing of the final act of the Rio conference which created the Rio treaty, the U.S. delegation made this clear at the same time it set forth our position that the treaty is without effect upon outstanding territorial disputes between American and European states. . . .

What has been the approach of the international community as a whole must remain the policy of this body. We must strive to resolve the conflict, not seek to widen it. We must work to use the rule of law and the principle of non-use of force to settle the conflict, not seek to challenge these vital principles. We must search for ways in which we can all join to help bring about peace, not ask the Rio treaty mechanism to adjucate a conflict for which it was not conceived. . . .

Now the time has come for older heads to accept the risks of compromise and the hazards of conciliation to bring the suffering and dying to an end. Wisdom as well as struggle is a test of valor. The dignity of a nation is honored not only with sacrifices but with peace. The South Atlantic has reverberated with the fury of war. It must now be calmed by the wisdom and courage of peace.

Alexander Haig, statement, meeting of Consultation of Ministers of Foreign Affairs, Organization of American States, May 27, 1982; 82 *Department of*

State Bulletin (July 1982): 87-90.   Argentine forces surrendered in June 1982.

565   CARIBBEAN BASIN INITIATIVE, 1982

The principles which the Organization of American States embodies--democracy, self-determination, economic development, and collective security--are at the heart of U.S. foreign policy. The United States of America is a proud member of this organization. What happens anywhere in the Americas affects us in this country. In that very real sense, we share a common destiny. We, the peoples of the Americas, have much more in common than geographical proximity. For over 400 years our peoples have shared the dangers and dreams of building a new world. From colonialism to nationhood, our common quest has been for freedom. . . .

Our hemisphere has an unlimited potential for economic development and human fulfillment. We have a combined population of more than 600 million people; our continents and our Islands boast vast reservoirs of food and raw materials; and the markets of the Americas have already produced the highest standard of living among the advanced as well as the developing countries of the world. The example that we could offer to the world would not only discourage foes, it would project like a beacon of hope to all of the oppressed and impoverished nations of the world. . . .

Today I would like to talk about our other neighbors--neighbors by the sea--some two dozen countries of the Caribbean and Central America. . . .

Economic health is one of the keys to a secure future for our Caribbean Basin and to the neighbors there. I'm happy to say that Mexico, Canada, and Venezuela have joined in this search for ways to help these countries realize their economic potential. Each of our four nations has its own unique position and approach. Mexico and Venezuela are helping to offset energy costs to Caribbean Basin countries by means of an oil facility that is already in operation. Canada is doubling its already significant economic assistance.

We all seek to insure that the peoples of this area have the right to preserve their own national identities, to improve their economic lot, and to develop their political institutions to suit their own unique social and historical needs. The Central American and Caribbean countries differ widely in culture, personality, and needs. . . .

We've taken the time to consult closely with other governments in the region, both sponsors and beneficiaries, to ask them what they need and what they think will work. And we've labored long to develop an economic program that integrates trade, aid, and investment--a program that represents a long-term commitment to the countries of the Caribbean and Central America to make use of the magic of the marketplace, the market of the Americas, and to earn their own way toward self-sustaining growth.

At the Cancun summit last October, I presented a fresh view of a development which stressed more than aid and government intervention. As I pointed out then, nearly all of the countries that have succeeded in their development over the past 30 years have done so on the strength of market-oriented policies and vigorous participation in the international economy. Aid must be complemented by trade and investment.

The program I'm proposing today puts these principles into practice. It is an integrated program that helps our neighbors help themselves, a program that will create conditions under which creativity and private entrepreneurship and self-help can flourish. Aid is an important part of this program because many of our neighbors need it to put themselves in a starting position from which they can begin to earn their own way. But this aid will encourage private sector activities but not displace them.

First.   The centerpiece of the program that I am sending to the Congress is free trade for Caribbean Basin products exported to the United States. . . .

Second.   To further attract investment, I will ask the Congress to provide significant tax incentives for investment in the Caribbean Basin. We also stand ready to negotiate bilateral investment treaties with interested basin countries.

Third. I'm asking for a supplemental fiscal year 1982 appropriation of $350 million to assist those countries which are particularly hard hit economically.   Much of this aid will be concentrated on the private sector.   These steps will help foster the spirit of enterprise necessary to take advantage of the trade and investment portions of the program.

Fourth.   We will offer technical assistance and training to assist the private sector in the basin countries to benefit from the opportunities of this program.   This will include investment promotion, export marketing, and technology transfer efforts, as well as programs to facilitate adjustments to greater competition and production in agriculture and industry. . . .

Fifth.   We will work closely with Mexico, Canada, and Venezuela, all of whom have already begun substantial and innovative programs of their own to encourage stronger international efforts to coordinate our own development measures with their vital contributions, and with those of other potential donors. . . .

This program has been carefully prepared.   It represents a farsighted act by our own people at a time of considerable economic difficulty at home. I wouldn't propose it if I were not convinced that it is vital to the security interests of this nation and of this hemisphere. The energy, the time, and the treasure we dedicate to assisting the development of our neighbors now can help to prevent the much larger expenditures of treasure as well as human lives which would flow from their collapse. . . .

Ronald Reagan, address, Permanent Council of the Organization of American States, February 24, 1982; *Department of State, Realism, Strength, Negotiation* (Washington: Department of State, 1984), pp. 114-18. The President also spoke at length concerning threats to security in Central America and the Caribbean. Also see Documents 125 and 550.

In 1946 the United States had also signed an agreement with France, the Netherlands, and the United Kingdom to establish a Caribbean Commission to promote economic and social development in their Caribbean territories; see *A Decade of American Foreign Policy, 1941-49,* pp. 1039-45. This was succeeded by the Caribbean Organization, consisting of the same members, in 1961; see *American Foreign Policy: Current Documents,* 1961, pp. 265-67. In 1963 the governments of Central America, Panama, and the United States proclaimed the Declaration of Central America, San Jose, signed March 19, 1963; see *American Foreign Policy: Current Documents,* 1963, pp. 234-38.

566   STRUGGLE FOR DEMOCRACY IN CENTRAL AMERICA

I think that any discussion of Central America must address three questions.
- First of all, why should we care about Central America?
- Second, what's going on there now?
- And, third, what should we do about it?

. . . I think, first of all, that Central America's importance to the United States cannot be denied. Central America is so close that its troubles automatically spill over onto us; so close that the strategic posture of its countries affect ours; so close that its people's suffering brings pain to us as well. . . .

In the great debate about how best to protect our interests in the Panama Canal, the only thing all sides agreed on was that the canal is critical and must be kept open and defended. Yet the security of the Panama Canal is directly affected by the stability and security of Central America. . . .

Most Americans have assumed that, because the Soviet Union knows that we will not accept the emplacement of strategic weapons in Cuba, we had nothing more to fear. It's true that there are no nuclear weapons in Cuba, and it is true that Cuba's communist utopia has proved such an economic disaster that it is entirely dependent on massive Soviet aid. . . . Yet this has not kept Cuba from portraying itself as the vanguard of a better future and mounting a campaign to establish new communist dictatorships in Central America. . . .

Our analysis, our strategy, our predictions for the future of Central America are rooted in two perceptions. One is that democracy cannot flourish in the presence of extreme inequalities in access to land, opportunity, or justice. The second perception is that Mr. Carpio and his allies are exploiting such inequities for antidemocratic ends.

I quoted a terrorist leader because it is beliefs like his, backed by armed violence, that so concern our friends in Central America. . . .

. . . We cannot in good conscience look the other way when democracy and human rights are challenged in countries very near to us, countries that look to us for help. President Reagan put it well last month: "Human rights," he said, "means working at problems, not walking away from them."

So the key question is: What should we do? A primary element of our strategy must be to support democracy, reform, and the protection of human rights. Democracies are far less likely to threaten their neighbors or abuse their citizens than dictatorships. . . .

The forces of dictatorship are of two kinds. One is old, the other new. The old variety is that of economic oligarchy, political despotism, and military repression. Except for Costa Rica, this has been the traditional method of social organization for most of Central America's history. The new form of dictatorship is that of a command economy, a self-appointed elitist vanguard, and guerrilla war. Nicaragua has become its base, all of Central America its target.

Before the Sandinistas came to power in Nicaragua in 1979, they promised free elections, political pluralism, and nonalignment. Today every one of these promises is being betrayed. First the Sandinistas moved to squeeze the democrats out of the governing junta; then to restrict all political opposition, all press freedom, and the independence of the church; then to build what is now the largest armed force in the history of Central America; then to align themselves with the Soviet Union and Cuba in subverting their neighbors.

El Salvador became the first target. In 1980, at Cuban direction, several Salvadoran extremist groups were unified in Managua, where their operational headquarters remains to this day. Cuba and its Soviet-bloc allies then provided training and supplies which began to flow clandestinely through Nicaragua to El Salvador to fuel an armed assault. . . .

The struggle for democracy is made even more difficult by the heavy legacy of decades of social and economic inequities. . . .

We must also, therefore, support economic development. . . . Three-quarters of the funds that we are spending in support of our Central American policy go to economic assistance. And our economic program goes beyond traditional aid: The President's Caribbean Basin Initiative is meant to provide powerful trade and investment incentives to help these countries achieve self-sustaining economic growth. . . .

In summation, let me say again that there are many reasons for us to care about what happens in Central America. One is strategic, and we better remember it. What is happening in Central America could endanger our own security and that of our friends throughout the Caribbean Basin, from Mexico to the Panama Canal.

But an equal reason is moral. How can we, in the name of human rights, abandon our neighbors to a brutal, military takeover by a totalitarian minority? If our concern is freedom, will a communist victory provide it? If our concern is judicial fairness, will a communist regime provide it? If our concern is poverty, will a communist economic system provide prosperity?

The American people and their elected representatives have difficult choices to make. It is easy to play the demagogue, and it is tempting to avoid hard decisions. But if we walk away from this challenge, we will have let down not only all those in Central America who yearn for democracy, but we will have let ourselves down. We cannot be for freedom and human rights only in the abstract. If our ideals are to have meaning, we must defend them when they are threatened. Let us meet our responsibility.

George Shultz, address, World Affairs Council and Chamber of Commerce, Dallas, April 15, 1983; Department of State, *Realism, Strength, and Negotiation* (Washington: Department of State, 1984), pp. 124-27. Secretary Shultz also discussed United States commitment to peace and specifically the problems of El Salvador and Nicaragua.

567 UNITED STATES VITAL INTERESTS AND OBJECTIVES IN CENTRAL AMERICA

. . . Central America's problems do directly affect the security and the well-being of our own people. And Central America is much closer to the United States than many of the world trouble spots that concern us. . . .

If the Nazis during World War II and the Soviets today could recognize the Caribbean and Central America as vital to our interests, shouldn't we also? . . .

. . . In 1979, when the new government took over in Nicaragua, after a revolution which overthrew the authoritarian rule of Somoza, everyone hoped for the growth of democracy. We in the United States did too. By January of 1981, our emergency relief and recovery aid to Nicaragua totaled $118 million--more than provided by any other developed country. In fact, in the first 2 years of Sandinista rule, the United States directly or indirectly sent five times more aid to Nicaragua than it had in the 2 years prior to the revolution. Can anyone doubt the generosity and good faith of the American people?

These were hardly the actions of a nation implacably hostile to Nicaragua. Yet, the Government of Nicaragua has treated us as an enemy. It has rejected our repeated peace efforts. It has broken its promises to us, to the Organization of American States, and, most important of all, to the people of Nicaragua.

No sooner was victory achieved than a small clique ousted others who had been part of the revolution from having any voice in government. Humberto Ortega, the Minister of Defense, declared Marxism-Leninism would be their guide, and so it is. The Government of Nicaragua has imposed a new dictatorship; it has refused to hold the elections it promised; it has seized control of most media and subjects all media to heavy prior censorship; it denied the bishops and priests of the Roman Catholic Church the right to say mass on radio during holy week; it insulted and mocked the Pope; it has driven the Miskito Indians from their homelands--burning their villages, destroying their crops, and forcing them into involuntary internment camps far from home; it has moved against the private sector and free labor unions; it condoned mob action against Nicaragua's independent human rights commission and drove the director of that commission into exile.

In short, after all these acts of repression by the government, is it any wonder that opposition has formed? Contrary to propaganda, the opponents of the Sandinistas are not die-hard supporters of the previous Somoza regime. In fact, many are anti-Somoza heroes who fought beside the Sandinistas to bring down the Somoza government. Now they've been denied any part in the new government because they truly wanted democracy for Nicaragua, and they still do. Others are Miskito Indians fighting for their homes, their lands, and their lives.

The Sandinista revolution in Nicaragua turned out to be just an exchange of one set of autocratic rulers for another, and the people still have no freedom, no democratic rights, and more poverty. Even worse than its predecessor, it is helping Cuba and the Soviets to destabilize our hemisphere. . . .

But let us be clear as to the American attitude toward the Government of Nicaragua. We do not seek its overthrow. Our interest is to ensure that it does not infect its neighbors through the export of subversion and violence. Our purpose, in conformity with American and international law, is to prevent the flow of arms to El Salvador, Honduras, Guatemala, and Costa Rica. We have attempted to have a dialogue with the Government of Nicaragua, but it persists in its efforts to spread violence.

We should not--and we will not--protect the Nicaragua Government from the anger of its own people. But we should, through diplomacy, offer an alternative. And, as Nicaragua ponders its options, we can and will-- with all the resources of diplomacy--protect each country of Central America from the danger of war. Even Costa Rica, Central America's oldest and strongest democracy, a government so peaceful it doesn't even have an army, is the object of bullying and threats from Nicaragua's dictators. . . .

We will pursue four basic goals in Central America.

First. In response to decades of inequity and indifference, we will support democracy, reform, and human freedom. This means using our assistance, our powers of persuasion, and our legitimate "leverage" to bolster humane democratic systems where they already exist and to help countries on their way to that goal complete the process as quickly as human institutions can be changed. . . .

Second. In response to the challenge of world recession and, in the case of El Salvador, to the unrelenting campaign of economic sabotage by the guerillas, we will support economic development. By a margin of two-to-one, our aid is economic now, not military. . . . And our economic program goes beyond traditional aid: The Caribbean initiative . . . will provide powerful trade and investment incentives to help these countries achieve self-sustaining economic growth without exporting U.S. jobs. . . .

Third. In response to the military challenge from Cuba and Nicaragua--to their deliberate use of force to spread tyranny--we will support the security of the region's threatened nations. We do not view security assistance as an end in itself but as a shield for democratization, economic development, and diplomacy. No amount of reform will bring peace so long as guerrillas believe they will win by force. No amount of economic help will suffice if guerrilla units can destroy roads and bridges and power stations and crops again and again with impunity. But, with better training and material help, our neighbors can hold off the guerrillas and give democratic reform time to take root.

Fourth. We will support dialogue and negotiations--both among the countries of the region and within each country. . . . The United States will work toward a political solution in Central America which will serve the interests of the democratic process.

To support these diplomatic goals, I offer these assurances:

- The United States will support any agreement among Central American countries for the withdrawal--under fully verifiable and reciprocal conditions--of all foreign military and security advisers and troops.

- We want to help opposition groups join the political process in all countries and compete by ballots instead of bullets.

- We will support any verifiable, reciprocal agreement among Central American countries on the renunciation of support for insurgencies on neighbors' territory.

- And, finally, we desire to help Central America end its costly arms race and will support any verifiable, reciprocal agreements on the non-importation of offensive weapons. . . .

In summation, I say to you that tonight there can be no question: The national security of all the Americas is at stake in Central America. If we cannot defend ourselves there, we cannot expect to prevail elsewhere. Our credibility would collapse, our alliances would crumble, and the safety of our homeland would be put at jeopardy.

We have a vital interest, a moral duty, and a solemn responsibility. This is not a partisan issue. It is a question of our meeting our moral responsibility to ourselves, our friends, and our posterity. It is a duty that falls on all of us--the President, the Congress, and the people. We must perform it together. Who among us would wish to bear responsibility for failing to meet our shared obligation?

Ronald Reagan, address on national security in Central America, joint session of Congress, April 27, 1983, Department of State, *Realism, Strength, Negotiation* (Washington: Department of State, 1984), pp. 128-31, and *American Foreign Relations: Basic Documents*, 1983, pp. 1314-20. For additional documentation on United States policy toward the Sandinista regime in Nicaragua, see the volumes of *American Foreign Policy: Current Documents, Papers of Presidents,* and the *Department of State Bulletin.* The Sandinistas were defeated in a national election early in 1990, and Violeta Barrios de Chamorro became President in April.

32

Polar Regions

... President Reagan has affirmed that the United States has unique
and critical interests in the Arctic region related directly to
national defense, resource and energy development, scientific
inquiry, and environmental protection.

Department of State, May 9, 1983

The United States has significant political, security, economic,
environmental, and scientific interests in Antarctica.

White House Press Secretary, March 29, 1982

The polar regions are unique in that foreign policy primarily concerns matters
of possession and jurisdiction, maritime and aerial usage, and resource
extraction and preservation. The Arctic, consisting of an ocean area with
various polar islands and archipelagoes, surrounded by circumjacent Western
Hemisphere (Alaska and Canada), European, and Soviet subpolar land masses,
whereas the Antarctic consists of a polar continent, some peripheral islands,
and in the surrounding temperate zone the continent of Australia, New Zealand,
and the southerly extensions of South America and Africa. As a consequence, the
geographic, jurisdictional, maritime, economic, and other features of these two
areas differ substantially.

Historically, the legal principles by which states acquired valid title to
"unoccupied territory" (*terra nullius*) progressed from allegations based on
discovery, exploration, and symbolical appropriation or annexation to the
nineteenth-century principles of "effective occupation" (the actual administration of territory) and prescription (the continuous and unchallenged possession of territory for such an extended length of time that possession becomes
an accepted fact in the international order). Because effective occupation is
difficult to implement in the polar regions, in the early twentieth century the
polar "sector principle" was introduced as an alternative means of gaining
possessory rights. A polar sector is a triangular slice of space with its apex at
the pole, bounded by two meridians of longitude, and usually having a
territorial coastline or a parallel of latitude as its base, with Arctic sectors

converging at the North Pole and Antarctic sectors meeting at the South Pole.

In the Arctic, surrounded by great subpolar land masses, the base of the sector is formed by the northern boundary of the subjacent continental or island territory, and the sides of the triangle are extensions of the westernmost and easternmost extremities of the territory. Practical application of the sector principle to Arctic landed territory was restricted entirely to islands and archipelagoes. As a consequence, by the time of World War II, because sovereignty over Greenland (Danish), Iceland (which became an independent state in 1941), and Spitzbergen (recognized as belonging to Norway by . multipartite treaty in 1920--see TS 686; 2 Bevans, *Treaties and Other International Agreements* 269-77) was generally acknowledged, and because titles to the islands to the north of Canada and the Soviet Union were largely uncontested, polar sectorism was discounted in favor of possession by virtue of effective occupation.

In the Antarctic, on the other hand, where there are no prominent sub-polar land masses, more or less arbitrary parallels of latitude have been established as the northern bases of the sectors, while the sides are extended to the widest extent possible, in some cases based on subpolar possessions (such as the Bouvet, Falkland, South Georgia, South Orkney, South Shetland, and other islands) or on exploration in Antarctica. Sweeping and in some cases overlapping sectors have been claimed by Argentina, Australia, Chile, France, Great Britain, and New Zealand.

Aside from sovereign possession of landed territory and marginal maritime and aerial jurisdiction, and legal treatment of continental shelf ice (differentiated from floating ice), the principal subjects of policy interest in the polar regions embrace such subjects as: scientific exploration, research, and the dissemination of information resulting from them; the use and conservation of marine, mineral, animal, and flora resources (including multipartite treaties concerning fishing, sealing, and whaling); resource and energy development; pollution and environmental protection; the application of civil and criminal law, jurisdiction over nationals, and liability; various other aspects of international cooperation and settlement of disputes; and defense, including the issue of transpolar aerial and missile warfare in the Arctic and the prohibition of all military activity and the testing and emplacement of nuclear weaponry in the Antarctic. For illustrative documents on defense against surprise attack over the Arctic, see *Papers of Presidents: Eisenhower,* 1958, pp. 350, 361, 530; also see lists of bilateral treaties and agreements with Canada and the Soviet Union in *Treaties in Force,* which deal with transpolar aerial and missile security, boundaries and boundary waters, fisheries, pipelines, oceanography, and other matters. For stipulations concerning the prohibition of military activity in, and the limited denuclearization of, Antarctica, see Document 573, Articles I and V.

The documents selected for this chapter are grouped in three categories. They deal with polar jurisdiction and the sector principle (Document 568); the Arctic, including commentary on United States interest in Wrangell Island and on contemporary American policy for the Arctic area (Documents 569-570); and the Antarctic, including American interests and policy, and the text and consequences of the Antarctic Treaty of 1959 (Documents 571-576).

POLAR SECTOR PRINCIPLE

568 POLAR JURISDICTION AND THE SECTOR PRINCIPLE

The so-called "sector principle" first was given impetus by a Canadian senator, P. Poirier, who, in 1907, recommended to the Canadian Senate that Canada lay claim to all lands lying between its northernmost borders and the North Pole, the extent of said area to be determined by drawing lines directly to the North Pole from their eastern and westernmost borders lying within the Arctic Circle; that is, all land lying to the north of sixty degrees west longitude, and one hundred and forty-one degrees west longitude, Greenland excepted. Since the time of this proposal both Canada and Russia, either by official proclamation or by various acts of state, have adopted this principle as a basis for laying claim to vast areas of the Arctic. . . . The nations adopting the "sector principle" no longer give the same validity to the principle of occupation in polar areas. Claims to their respective sectors have been declared to include not only lands which already have been discovered, but in addition lands which still remain undiscovered and unoccupied. . . .

The adherents to the "sector principle" lay special emphasis upon the alleged impracticability of application of the well recognized principle of occupation to the Arctic regions, where actual occupation as known in the temperate regions is not presently possible. Primarily upon this ground they have attempted to justify the development of this entirely new concept. Although there appears on the surface some justification for this new approach, it is interesting to note that, while laying claim to vast Polar areas within their so-called sectors, both Canada and Russia consistently have attempted to bolster their sector claims by increased activities in exploration, establishment of weather stations and outposts, and by showing as great a semblance to *actual* occupation and control as the land in these areas will permit. . . .

The 20th century "sector principle" is merely a variation of the 19th century geographical doctrines based upon the idea of contiguity or proximity of islands to mainland. . . .

. . . The United States, a potential claimant in both the Arctic and Antarctic, has consistently denied that sector claims have any legal force. . . .

The sector theory as applied to Antarctica bears relation in name only to the doctrine as originally developed in reference to the Arctic. Because the national territory of none of the claimant states extends into the Antarctic Circle, a line cannot be drawn merely marking the continuation of their continental territory into the polar region; hence two variations of the sector theory have been proposed for this area: (1) the European adaption, and (2) the South American view.

(1) The European Adaption of the Sector Theory. Under the European interpretation of the sector theory an "arc is produced extending from the South Pole, embracing between its longitudinal lines

the full areas within which discoveries or explorations or takings of possession have been made in behalf of the claimant state." . . . This arc or sector is then assigned to a particular political subdivision of the claimant state, located within the temperate zone, and which faces the explored area on its southerly side. This theory has formed the basis of: Great Britain's claim to the New Zealand sector, the Australian sector, and the Falkland Islands sector; and France's claim to Adelie Land. On the other hand, Norway has expressly denounced the sector theory both in regard to the Arctic and the Antarctic. . . .

(2) The South American Adaption of the Sector Theory. While Europeans and North Americans, on the whole, regard "effective occupation" as the criterion of sovereignty, no Latin American government or jurist will admit that mere physical occupation of a territory can constitute valid title to sovereignty. . . .

On winning independence from Spain, Argentina automatically became heir to all Spanish dominions within the area which had been the vice royalty of Rio de la Plata. As the southern limits of this vice royalty have never been specified, Argentina claims her dominion toward the south is unlimited. . . .

Chile bases her claim on licenses and concessions made by the Spanish Crown. In 1539, when the *conquistadores* were receiving from their governments extensive territories in the new Continent, including zones then unexplored (which at that date was the greater part of South America), the King gave Sancho de la Hoz the government of all the territories situated to the south of the Strait of Magellan. This territory, known as Tierra Australia, allegedly extended from the Strait of Magellan southwards. (At that time, it was believed that Tierra del Fuego was not an island, but was united to and was an integral part of the Antarctic continent). . . .

Other bases Chile and Argentina advance for these historical claims are "geographical propinquity" . . . and "the conclusions of the geologists that the highlands of Antarctica must be regarded as a continuation of the Andes which are partly submerged, as shown by such features of the ocean floor as Burwood Bank.". . .

Further, Chile and Argentina invoke the Monroe Doctrine as one among many pronouncements made between 1810 and 1826 which proscribe all conquest or colonization of the western hemisphere. . . . Carried to its logical extreme this theory would lead to the conclusion that no nation other than an American State could claim any territory in that half of the Antarctic continent lying within the Western hemisphere. It should be noted that the United States has not invoked the Monroe Doctrine in reference to this land.

Marjorie M. Whiteman, *Digest of International Law,* II, 1051-61. For earlier commentary, see Green H. Hackworth, *Digest of International Law* (Washington: Government Printing Office, 1940), I, 461-65.

ARCTIC

569   UNITED STATES INTEREST IN AND CLAIM TO WRANGELL ISLAND

We have found little evidence that the United States has ever actively asserted a claim to Wrangell Island. We are unaware of American actions subsequent to 1881 which evidence the actual, effective, and continuous functions of a state required to preserve and perfect a claim of sovereignty. While it is true that Wrangell Island was indicated shortly after the turn of the century as part of Alaska on Interior Department maps and in their geographical publications, this would not constitute by itself an exercise of such functions. Mere discovery, unsupported by effective occupation over time, is insufficient to acquire sovereignty over a "terra nullius," according to the legal authorities. The most recent official United States statement on Wrangell contained in our files dates from the period when the Soviets were establishing their control of it, in the early twenties. At the time, it was merely noted that the United States had not relinquished its claim. Notwithstanding considerable in-house study of the issue in the early twenties, we are unaware of diplomatic activity at any time to advance such a claim against the British, or after 1924, the Soviets.

The United States has never had occasion formally to recognize Soviet ownership of Wrangell Island, although it did reject Soviet claims based on a sector principle in the Arctic. The United States, however, has long since adopted the practice of dealing with authorities in *de facto* control of territory, and we do not consider that recent scientific cooperative activities with the Soviet Union with respect to Wrangell Island necessarily import any recognition of legal status.

Digest of United States Practice in International Law, 1978, pp. 816-17. Discovery, exploration, and settlement interests involved American, British, Canadian, and Russian expeditions, and the Soviet government has alleged sovereign claims since the 1920's.

570   UNITED STATES ARCTIC POLICY

After review of a report by the Inter-Agency Arctic Policy Group (IAPG), President Reagan has affirmed that the United States has unique and critical interests in the arctic region related directly to national defense, resource and energy development, scientific inquiry, and environmental protection.

In light of the region's growing importance, it warrants priority attention by the United States. U.S. arctic policy will continue to be based on the following major elements:

--protection of essential security interests in the arctic region, including preservation of the principle of freedom of the seas and superjacent airspace;

--support for sound and rational development in the arctic region, while minimizing adverse effects on the environment;

--promotion of scientific research in fields contributing to knowledge of the arctic environment or of aspects of science which are most advantageously studied in the Arctic; and

--promotion of mutually beneficial international cooperation in the Arctic to achieve the above objectives. . . .

The IAPG will give priority attention to the following reviews:

--How should U.S. activities in the arctic region be coordinated with those of other countries bordering on the Arctic Ocean to serve best U.S. arctic interests? This will include consideration of possible actions for increased cooperation.

--What federal services may be necessary for the United States to provide in the arctic region over the next decade and what are their relative priorities? This will take into account projected developments in the Arctic that could have an important impact upon federal agencies with statutory responsibility for areas such as search and rescue; protecting life, property, resources and wildlife; enforcing U.S. laws and international treaties; and promoting commerce. This review will also recognize that resource development is primarily a private sector activity.

Statement, issued by Department of State, May 9, 1983; *American Foreign Policy: Current Documents,* 1983, p. 294. The report of the Inter-Agency Arctic Policy Group, entitled "American Evaluation of Future Federal Levels of Effort in the Arctic in Relation to Foreign and Domestic Energy Development Programs," was transmitted to the Assistant to the President for National Security Affairs on October 25, 1982. The 60-page report deals with the impact of oil and gas exploration and development in the Arctic on American foreign relations.

ANTARCTIC

571 STATUS OF THE ANTARCTIC REGION, 1956

1) The Governments of the United Kingdom, Argentina, Chile, France, Norway, New Zealand and Australia have already advanced formal claims to portions of the Antarctic. In fact, official claims advanced by other countries cover all of Antarctica except for that area lying between 90 degrees E and 150 degrees E. Those of the United Kingdom, Argentina and Chile overlap and have been the source of considerable controversy among those countries since the end of World War II.

2) The advancing of formal claims at some point is usually considered a prerequisite to establishing sovereignty over *terra nullia.* However, the significance of such a formal act with respect to virtually

unoccupied and uninhabitable territory such as the Antarctic is not clear. It is also true that the customary rule that claims depend to a great extent on effective occupation may not apply in the same measure as in more temperate zones.

3)   Claims alone do not convey title to territory, particularly in an area where another country may hold equal or superior rights. It will thus be seen that protection of United States interests involves more than the assertion of claims.

4)   Over a long period of time the Antarctic has been . . . the scene of extensive American exploration.   At the present time United States participation in the International Geophysical Year encompasses an extensive program of American exploration and scientific study.   The United States Government has consistently and on all appropriate occasions reserved American rights derived from official and unofficial activity of this kind and we have made clear that we do not recognize any of the claims of other Governments.

5)   As yet knowledge of the Antarctic Continent is insufficient to permit an informal decision as to what value United States sovereignty over parts of the continent would have.   Traditionally the United States does not take lightly the obligation to protect areas under its sovereignty. Until more is known it may be questioned whether it is advisable to advance claims which would conflict with those of other friendly governments and which would involve very large appropriations to establish and maintain.   It is hoped, however, that information collected during the International Geophysical Year will perhaps assist in deciding on the present and potential value of various parts of the continent.

6)   In view of all the considerations discussed above it is not considered advisable for the United States to advance an official claim at the present time. The various Government agencies concerned with the subject will, however, continue to take steps to insure that United States activities in the area support American interests.   The United States will continue its past policy of reserving American rights and does not plan to recognize the claims of other Governments. It is believed that these courses of action will protect the national interest.   We shall, however, follow developments carefully and take or recommend such steps, including the advancing of official claims, as are required to protect the national interest.

Memorandum, Department of State, March 30, 1956; *American Foreign Policy: Basic Documents*, 1950-1955, I, 1430-31.

572   AMERICAN INTERESTS AND RIGHTS IN ANTARCTICA, 1958

The United States for many years has had, and at the present time continues to have, direct and substantial rights and interests in Antarctica. Throughout a period of many years, commencing in the early eighteen-hundreds, many areas of the Antarctic region have been discovered, sighted, explored and claimed on behalf of the United States by nationals of the United States and by expeditions carrying the flag of the United States. During this period, the Government of the United States and its nationals have engaged in well-known and extensive activities in Antarctica.

In view of the activities of the United States and its nationals referred to above, my Government reserves all of the rights of the United States with respect to the Antarctic region, including the right to assert a territorial claim or claims.

*   *   *

. . . There [in Antarctica], for many, many years, the United States has been engaged in activities which under established principles of international law, without any question whatsoever, created rights upon which the United States would be justified in asserting territorial claims. I mean by that, claims to sovereignty over one or more areas of the Antarctic.

Notwithstanding this fact, the United States has not asserted any claim of sovereignty over any portion of Antarctica, although the United States has, at the same time, made it perfectly plain that it did not recognize any such claims made by other States.

Nonetheless, the United States has been consistent in asserting that under international law and practice, its activities in the Antarctic Continent have entitled it to rights in that area which it has at all times expressly reserved.

It is the position of the United States Government, and one well founded in international law, that the fact that the United States has not based a claim of sovereignty over one or more areas of Antarctica, upon the basis of the activities it has engaged in there, in no way derogates from the rights that were established by its activities.

United States note, proposing a conference on Antarctica, addressed to eleven nations with interests in Antarctica, May 2, 1958, and statement by Legal Adviser, Department of State, May 14, 1958; Marjorie M. Whiteman, *Digest of International Law,* II, 1250. Also see statement of President Eisenhower, May 3, 1958, in *Papers of Presidents: Eisenhower,* 1958, pp. 367-68.

573 ANTARCTIC TREATY, 1959

Article I

1.   Antarctica shall be used for peaceful purposes only. There shall be prohibited, *inter alia,* any measures of a military nature, such as the establishment of military bases and fortifications, the carrying out of military maneuvers, as well as the testing of any type of weapons. . . .

Article III

1.   In order to promote international cooperation in scientific investigation in Antarctica, . . . the Contracting Parties agree that, to the

greatest extent feasible and practicable:

(a) information regarding plans for scientific programs in Antarctica shall be exchanged to permit maximum economy and efficiency of operations;

(b) scientific personnel shall be exchanged in Antarctica between expeditions and stations;

(c) scientific observations and results from Antarctica shall be exchanged and made freely available. . . .

Article IV

1.   Nothing contained in the present Treaty shall be interpreted as:

(a) a renunciation by any Contracting Party of previously asserted rights of or claims to territorial sovereignty in Antarctica;

(b) a renunciation or diminution by any Contracting Party of any basis of claim to territorial sovereignty in Antarctica which it may have whether as a result of its activities or those of its nationals in Antarctica, or otherwise;

(c) prejudicing the position of any Contracting Party as regards its recognition or non-recognition of any other State's right of or claim or basis of claim to territorial sovereignty in Antarctica.

2.   No acts or activities taking place while the present Treaty is in force shall constitute a basis for asserting, supporting or denying a claim to territorial sovereignty in Antarctica or create any rights of sovereignty in Antarctica. No new claim, or enlargement of an existing claim, to territorial sovereignty in Antarctica shall be asserted while the present Treaty is in force.

Article V

1.   Any nuclear explosions in Antarctica and the disposal there of radioactive waste material shall be prohibited. . . .

Article VI

The provisions of the present Treaty shall apply to the area south of 60 degrees South Latitude, including all ice shelves, but nothing in the present Treaty shall prejudice or in any way affect the rights, or the exercise of the rights, of any State under international law with regard to the high seas within that area. . . .

Article IX

1.   Representatives of the Contracting Parties named in the preamble to the present Treaty shall meet at the City of Canberra within two months after the date of entry into force of the Treaty, and thereafter at suitable intervals and places, for the purpose of exchanging information, consulting together on matters of common interest pertaining to Antarctica, and formulating and considering, and recommending to their Governments, measures in furtherance of the principles and objectives of the Treaty, including measures regarding:

(a) use of Antarctica for peaceful purposes only;

(b) facilitation of scientific research in Antarctica;

(c) facilitation of international scientific cooperation in Antarctica;

(d) facilitation of the exercise of the rights of inspection . . .

(e) questions relating to the exercise of jurisdiction in Antarctica;

(f) preservation and conservation of living resources in Antarctica. . . .

Article XI

1.   If any dispute arises between two or more of the Contracting Parties concerning the interpretation or application of the present Treaty, those Contracting Parties shall consult among themselves with a view to having the dispute resolved by negotiation, inquiry, mediation, conciliation, arbitration, judicial settlement or other peaceful means of their own choice.

2.   Any dispute of this character not so resolved shall, with the consent, in each case, of all parties to the dispute, be referred to the International Court of Justice for settlement; but failure to reach agreement on reference to the International Court shall not absolve parties to the dispute from the responsibility of continuing to seek to resolve it by any of the various peaceful means referred to in paragraph 1 of this Article.

Signed December 1, 1959, by Argentina, Australia, Belgium, Chile, France, Japan, New Zealand, Norway, South Africa, the Soviet Union, the United Kingdom, and the United States; 14 articles. TIAS 4780; 12 *U.S. Treaties* 794-829. This treaty was subsequently acceded to by more than a dozen additional states.   Articles VII and VIII deal with the functions and rights of national observers.   It should be noted that Article IV straddles the jurisdiction issue and Antarctic sector principle, and Article IX provides for periodic future consultative meetings of signatories.

Also, so far as defense and security are concerned, it is important to remember that the Inter-American Treaty of Reciprocal Assistance (Rio Pact, 1947), Article 4, applies to the Western Hemisphere from pole to pole (see Document 304) and that the Treaty of Tlatelolco, providing for a nuclear free zone in Latin America (to which the United States is not a signatory but has become a party to Protocols I and II (see Document 559).   Its area of applicability extends south of the United States, covering much of the South Atlantic basin and encompasses all of South America and several sub-Antarctic archipelagoes, but excludes Antarctica.

For the supplementary agreement dealing with Measures in Furtherance of Principles and Objectives of the Antarctic Treaty, July 24, 1961, see TIAS 5094; 13 *U.S. Treaties* 1349-57. For the second implementing agreement, July 28, 1962, see TIAS 5274; 14 *U.S. Treaties* 99-103.

574 COMMENTARY ON ANTARCTIC TREATY

The Treaty provides for freedom of scientific investigation in Antarctica and for carrying on undiminished the cooperation started during the International Geophysical Year. It prohibits nuclear explosions in Antarctica and the disposal there of radioactive waste.

To see that the Treaty is complied with, national Observers may be sent at any time to any part of Antarctica to inspect various national installations.   In late 1963, the United States sent two such inspection teams to examine facilities of six other countries.   In January 1964 they reported that no Treaty violations were observed in any of the installations visited.

Since the Treaty came into force in 1961, the parties have held periodic meetings in a rare spirit of frankness and cooperation to find acceptable ways to carry out various provisions of the Treaty.

On Antarctica's icy wastes, scientists visit freely between their various national installations, sometimes spending an entire year working with their counterparts from other countries.   Many important expeditions have been completed and lives saved in time of danger because of timely assistance from other national stations.

*   *   *

I have been deeply Impressed by the sensible way in which the 12 nations active in Antarctica work together.   In that frozen continent we have, through international cooperation, shown how nations of many different outlooks can cooperate for peaceful purposes and mutual benefit. National differences are no barrier to a common effort in which everyone gains and no one loses.   The scientific findings of all countries are pooled for the benefit of all.   Men in danger or in need can call for help knowing that it will be given unstintingly by any country that can provide it. . . .

The United States today pursues a vigorous program in Antarctica. We have begun to explore the southern ocean and the last great unknown reaches of the Polar Plateau.   We have established new research stations in West Antarctica and on the Antarctic Peninsula.   We have completed geologic surveys of most of the ice-free areas of West Antarctica.   We have photographed hundreds of thousands of square miles for mapping purposes.   We are conducting scientific programs to study the unique physical and biological features of the area. . . .

The kind of international cooperation that has become accepted practice in Antarctica is both practical and mutually beneficial. . . .

The peaceful framework on which these widespread activities depend is the Antarctic Treaty.   The countries adhering to the treaty have pledged that Antarctica shall be used for peaceful purposes only.   No activities of a military nature are permitted. Nuclear explosions or dumping atomic waste is prohibited. But scientific research is open to all, and international cooperation in that research is encouraged.

Any signatory country may satisfy itself that the treaty is being observed by inspecting any station or expedition anywhere in Antarctica. In short, the United States and other signatories have agreed that it is in the interest of all mankind that Antarctica shall continue forever to be used exclusively for peaceful purposes and shall not become the scene or object of international discord.

Lyndon Johnson, Special Message to Congress, September 2, 1964; *Papers of Presidents: Johnson,* 1963-1964, II, 1031-32, and statement, May 1, 1965; *American Foreign Policy: Current Documents,* 1965, pp. 1047-48. Also see President Kennedy's statement on entry into force of the Antarctic Treaty, June 23, 1961, in *Papers of Presidents: Kennedy,* 1961, pp. 471-72. For additional commentary, see *Digest of United States Practice in International Law,* 1975, pp. 106-11; 1978, pp. 1485-91, on the Antarctic Conservation Act of 1978; and 1980, pp. 628-31, on the marine environment in the Antarctic area.

575 AMERICAN ANTARCTIC POLICY, 1982

The United States has significant political, security, economic, environmental, and scientific interests in Antarctica. These are reflected in the Antarctic Treaty of 1959. The system established by that treaty has permitted its parties, who maintain different positions concerning claims to territorial sovereignty in Antarctica, to work together to further scientific research and to ensure that Antarctica does not become the scene or object of international discord.

President Reagan has affirmed the United States commitment to a leadership role in Antarctica, both in the conduct of scientific research on and around the continent and in the system of international cooperation established pursuant to the Antarctic Treaty. Following review of a study of U.S. interests in Antarctica prepared by the interagency Antarctic Policy Group, the President has decided that:

-- The United States Antarctic Program shall be maintained at a level providing an active and influential presence in Antarctica, designed to support the range of U.S. Antarctic interests.

-- This presence shall include the conduct of scientific activities in major disciplines, year-round occupation of the South Pole and two coastal stations, and availability of related necessary logistics support.

-- Every effort shall be made to manage the program in a manner that maximizes cost-effectiveness and return on investment.

Statement, White House Press Secretary, March 29, 1982; *Papers of Presidents: Reagan,* 1982, I, 392. This statement also comments on the Convention on the Conservation of Antarctic Marine Living Resources, signed by the United States and twelve other nations. For the text of this convention, signed on May 20, 1980, see TIAS 10240; 33 *U.S. Treaties* 3476-3558.

576 MESSAGE ON TWENTY-FIFTH ANNIVERSARY OF ANTARCTIC TREATY

On December 1, 1959, in Washington, DC, the twelve nations then active in Antarctica pledged themselves to an imaginative experiment in international cooperation and understanding. The Antarctic Treaty, signed that day, reserves a major region of our planet exclusively for scientific research and other peaceful endeavors. The Treaty bans all military activities, including the testing of weapons in Antarctica, and prohibits nuclear explosions and the disposal of radioactive wastes there. It guarantees the freedom of scientific research and establishes a consultative mechanism to allow the Treaty system to meet new challenges and adapt to new circumstances. To achieve these objectives, it embodies unique conflict-avoidance provisions permitting countries which disagree over the legal status of Antarctica to work together harmoniously.

Now a quarter century later, we can all take pride in the accomplishments and vitality of this important treaty system. It has fully realized its objectives of maintaining Antarctica as an area free of conflict and devoted to peaceful international cooperation. Membership in the Treaty system has continued to expand and, within this system, effective steps are being taken to ensure that new activities in Antarctica are managed in a responsible fashion and do not threaten Antarctica's environment. The Antarctic Treaty represents an outstanding example of how countries with diverse political perspectives and interests--East and West, North and South--can work together for the benefit of all.

Ronald Reagan, message, November 26, 1984; *Papers of Presidents: Reagan, 1984,* II, 1839-40. Also see statement, United States Representative to Committee of United Nations General Assembly, November 29, 1984; *American Foreign Policy: Current Documents,* 1984, pp. 276-78.

Index

tries, 39, 49, 727; non-aligned nations, 557-58, 621, 677; self-
determination and, 160, 466; UN as
instrument for, 170 (*see also* Colonialism; Decolonization; Freedom;
Non-intervention; Self-determination; Territorial integrity)

India, 15, 610

Indian Ocean, 666, 725, 752

Indochina, 257-59, 261, 268, 269,
273, 684 (*see also* Cambodia, Laos,
Vietnam, Vietnam War)

Indonesia, 273, 610

Information Agency, U.S. (USIA), 237

Inquiry (peaceful settlement). *See*
Commissions of inquiry

Insurgency, 465 (*see also* Guerilla action; Subversion)

Integration, international, 21 (*see also*
Cooperation; OAS; UN)

Intelligence/information, 2, 30, 66, 71,
72, 73, 121-31, 162, 163, 464;
and policy-making, 121-25; community, 121; documents, 17; limits
on, 125-26; national estimates, 17,
123, 126; nature of, 123; need for,
122-23; reforming system, 126-
31; secrecy and, 122, 126-31 (*see
also* Documentation)

Intelligence, Director of, 128-29

Intelligence Oversight Board, 128-29

Inter-Agency Antarctic Policy Group,
806

Inter-Agency Arctic Policy Group
(IAPG), 799-800

Inter-American Commission of Women,
632

Inter-American Commission on Human
Rights, 386, 632, 633, 637, 656

Inter-American Committee on Dependent
Territories, 374

Inter-American Court of Human Rights,
656, 658n

Inter-American Defense Board, 419,
424-26, 643, 644

Inter-American Dialogue Commission,
769

Inter-American Institute of Agricultural
Sciences, 632

Inter-American Juridical Committee,
632, 633, 637

Inter-American Neutrality Committee,
632

Inter-American Peace Commission,
302, 632

Inter-American Peace Committee, 298,
300, 632

Inter-American Statistical Institute,
632

Inter-American system, 21, 30, 362,
589, 631-60, 765, 766; Bay of Pigs
crisis, 277-79, 282; commitment to,
762, 763; Cuban missile crisis, 277,
285; development of, 633-45; Dominican crisis, 193; Falkland Islands
War, 783-87; Panama crisis, 295-
301, 312-15; Western Hemisphere
alliances, 423-31 (*see also* OAS;
Western Hemisphere)

Inter-American Treaty of Reciprocal Assistance (Rio Pact), 427-31 (*see also*
Treaties and agreements)

Inter-Americanism, 159

Interdependence, 49, 51, 67, 167, 173,
396, 456, 544, 568, 569, 579,
602, 650, 651, 687, 708-13, 762,
764-65, 766-67 (*see also* Cooperation; Partnership)

Interdiction, 284, 287-94, 329

Interests, national: and UN, 626, 628;
as analytical tool, 40-41; as political
rhetoric, 40; as superordinate criterion, 40; common/mutual interests,
38-39, 47, 48, 50, 53, 55, 97,
196, 421, 431, 435, 462, 531,
536, 540, 541, 544, 550, 557,
564, 680, 706, 707, 712, 714,
715, 716, 803; concerns, national,
2, 34, 196, 199, 335; defined, 33-
34, 39; factor in foreign relations,
27, 33-41, 52, 53, 93, 97, 159,
168, 172, 180, 411, 602; factor in
policy making, 57-63 passim; foreign relations documentation and, 17;
in Africa, 665-66, 669, 673, 680-
81; in Asia and Pacific, 190, 196,
256-57, 258, 683, 686, 687, 692,
694, 695; in East-West relations,
534-35, 540, 542; in Europe, 704-
8; in Middle East, 199-202, 333,
335, 341, 342, 731, 732, 741,
743, 744, 755, 756; in North-South
relations, 553, 559-60; in polar regions, 795-807 passim; in seas,

About the Editor

ELMER PLISCHKE is Professor Emeritus at the University of Maryland. He is author of *Foreign Relations: Analysis of its Anatomy* (Greenwood Press, 1988) and *Diplomat in Chief: The President at the Summit* (Praeger, 1985). He has written dozens of articles for scholarly journals, including *World Affairs, Review of Politics,* and *Presidential Studies Quarterly.*